Test Item File

PRECALCULUS

FIFTH EDITION

Larson / Hostetler

Cynthia M. Barb

Kent State University Stark Campus

HOUGHTON MIFFLIN COMPANY Boston New York

Editor-in-Chief, Mathematics: Jack Shira
Managing Editor: Cathy Cantin
Development Manager: Maureen Ross
Associate Editor: Laura Wheel
Assistant Editor: Carolyn Johnson
Supervising Editor: Karen Carter
Project Editor: Patty Bergin
Editorial Assistant: Lindsey Gulden
Production Technology Supervisor: Gary Crespo
Marketing Manager: Michael Busnach
Senior Manufacturing Coordinator: Sally Culler
Composition and Art: Engineering Software Associates; Meridian Creative Group

Printed in the U.S.A.

ISBN: 0-618-07272-1

123456789–B+B-04-03-02 01 00

PREFACE

The *Test Item File for Precalculus,* Fifth Edition, is a supplement to the text by Ron Larson and Robert P. Hostetler.

Part 1 of the test item file is a bank of questions arranged by text section. To assist you in selecting questions and administering examinations, each question is followed by a code line. The first item of the code indicates the level of difficulty of the question: routine (1) or challenging (2). (Challenging questions require three or more steps to obtain the solution.) If the solution to the problem requires the use of a graphing utility, the next code is (T) for technology-required. The last item in the code is the answer.

Part 2 of the test item file is a bank of chapter tests. For each chapter, there are three tests with multiple choice questions and two tests with open-ended questions. The tests are geared to 50-minute class periods. The two final exams (one with multiple-choice questions and one with open-ended questions) are primarily intended as samples to give instructors ideas for questions.

Finally, Part 3 of this test item file includes the answers to the chapter tests and final exams. I have made every effort to see that the answers are correct. However, I would appreciate very much hearing about any errors or other suggestions for improvement.

Computerized versions of this test item file are available for Windows and Macintosh users.

Cynthia M. Barb
Kent State University Stark Campus

CONTENTS

Chapter 0P1: Real Numbers

MULTIPLE CHOICE

1. Determine how many natural numbers there are in the set:

   $\left\{-3, -\frac{1}{2}, 2, 0.\overline{35}\right\}.$

   a) 1 b) 2 c) 3 d) 4
   e) None of the numbers are natural numbers.

   Answer: a Difficulty: 1

2. Determine how many integers there are in the set:

   $\left\{-3, -\frac{1}{2}, 2, 0.\overline{35}\right\}.$

   a) 1 b) 2 c) 3 d) 4
   e) None of the numbers are integers.

   Answer: b Difficulty: 1

3. Determine how many integers there are in the set:

   $\left\{5, -16, \frac{2}{3}, 0\right\}.$

   a) 4 b) 3 c) 2 d) 1
   e) None of the numbers are integers.

   Answer: b Difficulty: 1

4. Determine how many rational numbers there are in the set:

   $\left\{-3, -\frac{1}{2}, 2, 0.\overline{35}\right\}.$

   a) 4 b) 3 c) 2 d) 1
   e) None of the numbers are rational.

   Answer: a Difficulty: 1

5. Determine how many irrational numbers there are in the set:

   $\left\{-3, -\frac{1}{2}, 2, 0.\overline{35}\right\}.$

   a) 4 b) 3 c) 2 d) 1
   e) None of the numbers are irrational.

   Answer: e Difficulty: 1

SHORT ANSWER

6. Which numbers in the following set are integers?

$\left\{-3, \frac{1}{2}, 0, 0.\overline{35}, \frac{1}{2}, 2\right\}.$

Answer: -3, 0, 2 Difficulty: 1

MULTIPLE CHOICE

7. Use a calculator to find the decimal form of the rational number: $\frac{4}{9}$.

a) 0.4 b) 0.44 c) 0.43 d) $0.\overline{4}$ e) None of these

Answer: d Difficulty: 1

8. Use a calculator to find the decimal form of the rational number: $\frac{62}{495}$.

a) 0.125 b) $0.\overline{125}$ c) 0.13 d) 0.1 e) None of these

Answer: b Difficulty: 1 Key 1: T

SHORT ANSWER

9. Use a calculator to find the decimal form of the rational number: $\frac{10}{11}$.

Answer:

$0.\overline{90}$

Difficulty: 1 Key 1: T

10. Use a calculator to find the decimal form of the rational number: $\frac{173}{330}$.

Answer:

$0.5\overline{24}$

Difficulty: 1 Key 1: T

11. Plot the real numbers on the number line: $\left\{\frac{2}{3}, -4, 1 -\frac{3}{2}, 2\right\}$.

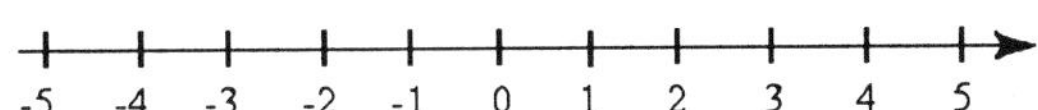

Answer: See graph below.

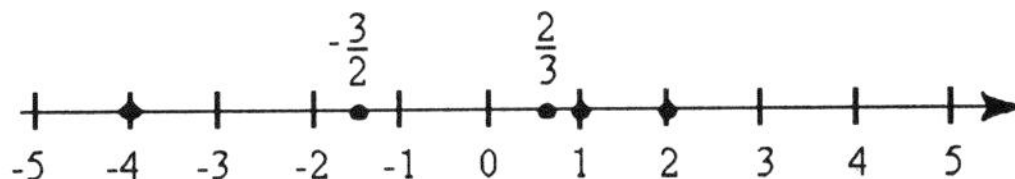

Difficulty: 1

12. Plot the real numbers on the number line: $\left\{-\frac{5}{3}, 3, -1, 4, -\frac{1}{4}\right\}$.

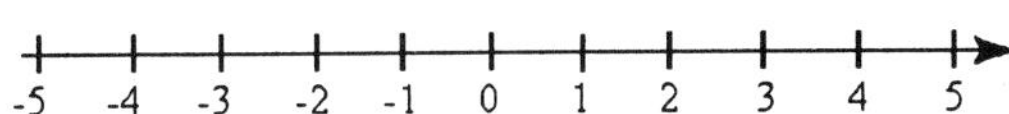

Answer: See graph below.

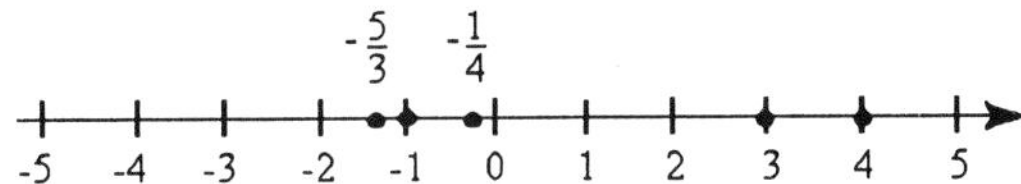

Difficulty: 1

MULTIPLE CHOICE

13. Use inequality notation to describe: b is at least 5.
a) $b > 5$ b) $b \geq 5$ c) $b < 5$ d) $b \leq 5$ e) None of these

Answer: b Difficulty: 1

SHORT ANSWER

14. Use inequality notation to describe: x is positive.

Answer: $x > 0$ Difficulty: 1

MULTIPLE CHOICE

15. Use inequality notation to describe: x is nonnegative.
a) $x > 0$ b) $x < 0$ c) $x \geq 0$ d) $x \leq 0$ e) None of these

Answer: c Difficulty: 1

16. Use inequality notation to describe: y is no larger than 10.
a) $y \leq 10$ b) $y < 10$ c) $y \geq 10$ d) $y > 10$ e) None of these

Answer: a Difficulty: 1

17. Use inequality notation to describe: y is at most 5.
a) $y \leq 5$ b) $y < 5$ c) $y \geq 5$ d) $y > 5$ e) None of these

Answer: a Difficulty: 1

SHORT ANSWER

18. Describe the subset of real numbers represented by the inequality: $x < 3$.

Answer: The set of real numbers that are less than 3. Difficulty: 1

19. Describe the subset of real numbers represented by the inequality: $y \geq 5$.

Answer: The set of real numbers that are at least 5. Difficulty: 1

MULTIPLE CHOICE

20. Use inequality notation to describe the set of real numbers that are less than 4 and at least -2.
a) $-2 < x < 4$ b) $-2 < x \leq 4$ c) $-2 \leq x < 4$
d) $-2 \leq x \leq 4$ e) None of these

Answer: c Difficulty: 1

21. Use inequality notation to describe the set of real numbers that are more than 5 and at most 10.
a) $5 \leq x \leq 10$ b) $5 \leq x < 10$ c) $5 < x < 10$
d) $5 < x \leq 10$ e) None of these

Answer: d Difficulty: 1

22. Use inequality notation to describe the set of real numbers that are at least -1 and at most 3.
a) $-1 \leq x \leq 3$ b) $-1 < x < 3$ c) $-1 \leq x < 3$
d) $-1 < x \leq 3$ e) None of these

Answer: a Difficulty: 1

SHORT ANSWER

23. Verbally describe the subset of real numbers represented by $-4 < x \leq 1$ and sketch the subset on the real number line.

Answer: $-4 < x \leq 1$ is the set of all real numbers greater than -4 and less than or equal to 1.

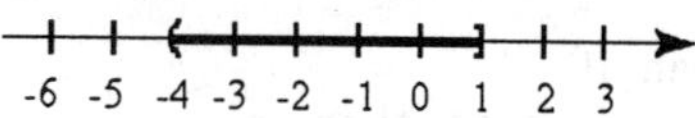

Difficulty: 2

24. Use a calculator to order the number from smallest to largest:
$\left\{\frac{13}{2}, \frac{28}{5}, \frac{650}{99}, 6.56, 6.065\right\}$.

Answer:
$\frac{28}{5}$, 6.065, $\frac{13}{2}$, 6.56, $\frac{650}{99}$

Difficulty: 2 Key 1: T

MULTIPLE CHOICE

25. Which of the following is the best response?
a) $|-3| + |6 - 5| \leq -(-4)$ is true.
b) $|14 + (-2)| - |-16| = 28$ is true.
c) $|16 - (-4)| - |3 - 5| \geq 12$ is true.
d) Both $|-3| + |6 - 5| \leq -(-4)$ and $|14 + (-2)| - |-16| = 28$ are true.
e) Both $|-3| + |6 - 5| \leq -(-4)$ and $|16 - (-4)| - |3 - 5| \geq 12$ are true.

Answer: e Difficulty: 1

26. Which of the following is the best response?
a) $|-3| - |4 - 6| = 1$ is true.
b) $|-5| + |-13| = -|-18|$ is true.
c) $|-6 - (-3)| \geq |-4|$ is true.
d) Both $|-3| - |4 - 6| = 1$ and $|-5| + |-13| = -|-18|$ are true.
e) Both $|-5| + |-13| = -|-18|$ and $|-6 - (-3)| \geq |-4|$ are true.

Answer: a Difficulty: 1

27. Which of the following is the best response?
a) $\frac{-5}{|-5|} = 1$ is true.
b) $-|-5| + |-3 - 2| \geq -1$ is true.
c) $|-6 + 4| < |-3 - 8|$ is true.
d) Both $\frac{-5}{|-5|} = 1$ and $|-6 + 4| < |-3 - 8|$ are true.
e) Both $-|-5| + |-3 - 2| \geq -1$ and $|-6 + 4| < |-3 - 8|$ are true.

Answer: e Difficulty: 1

28. Which of the following is the best response?

a) $-3|-3| < |-3(-3)|$ is true.　　b) $\frac{4}{|-12|} \le \frac{|-12|}{-4}$ is true.

c) $|16| - |12| \ge |16 - 12|$ is true.

d) Both $-3|-3| < |-3(-3)|$ and $|16| - |12| \ge |16 - 12|$ are true.

e) Both $\frac{4}{|-12|} \le \frac{|-12|}{-4}$ and $|16| - |12| \ge |16 - 12|$ are true.

Answer: d Difficulty: 1

29. Which of the following is the best response?

a) $4|-3| - 6 = -18$ is true.　　b) $\frac{|-3|}{-3} \le 0$ is true.

c) $|-5 - (-7)| = |-5| - |-7|$ is true.

d) Both $4|-3| - 6 = -18$ and $\frac{|-3|}{-3} \le 0$ are true.

e) Both $\frac{|-3|}{-3} \le 0$ and $|-5 - (-7)| = |-5| - |-7|$ are true.

Answer: b Difficulty: 1

30. Evaluate: $|-3 + 2|$.
a) 1　b) -1　c) 5　d) -5　e) None of these

Answer: a Difficulty: 1

31. Evaluate: $|-4| - |-2|$.
a) -2　b) 2　c) -6　d) 6　e) None of these

Answer: b Difficulty: 1

32. Evaluate: $-3|-6| + |-1|$.
a) -19　b) 19　c) 17　d) -17　e) None of these

Answer: d Difficulty: 1

33. Evaluate: $-|-5| - 5$.
a) 0　b) -10　c) 10　d) 25　e) None of these

Answer: b Difficulty: 1

34. Use absolute value notation to describe: The distance between x and 5 is at least 6.
a) $|x + 5| > 6$ b) $|x - 5| > 6$ c) $|x - 5| \geq 6$
d) $|6 - x| \geq 5$ e) None of these

Answer: c Difficulty: 2

35. Use absolute value notation to describe: 6 is at most 3 units from x.
a) $|x - 3| < 6$ b) $|x - 6| \leq 3$ c) $|x - 6| \geq 3$
d) $|x - 3| \geq 6$ e) None of these

Answer: b Difficulty: 2

36. Use absolute value notation to describe: The distance between x and 7 is greater than 2.
a) $|x - 7| \geq 2$ b) $|x - 2| < 7$ c) $|x - 7| > 2$
d) $|x - 2| > 7$ e) None of these

Answer: c Difficulty: 2

SHORT ANSWER

37. Use absolute value notation to describe: y is closer to 5 than y is to -6.

Answer: $|y - 5| < |y + 6|$ Difficulty: 2

MULTIPLE CHOICE

38. Use absolute value notation to describe: The distance between x and 16 is no more than 5.
a) $|x - 5| \leq 16$ b) $|x - 5| > 16$ c) $|x - 16| \leq 5$
d) $|x - 16| > 5$ e) None of these

Answer: c Difficulty: 2

39. Find the distance between -43 and 16.
a) 27 b) -27 c) -59 d) 59 e) None of these

Answer: d Difficulty: 1

40. Find the distance between x and -42.
a) $x - 42$ b) $x + 42$ c) $|x - 42|$
d) $|x + 42|$ e) None of these

Answer: d Difficulty: 1

41. Find the distance between $-\frac{2}{3}$ and $-\frac{1}{2}$.

a) $-\frac{1}{3}$ b) $\frac{1}{6}$ c) $\frac{1}{2}$ d) $\frac{7}{6}$ e) None of these

Answer: b Difficulty: 1

42. Determine the distance between a and b given $a > b$.

a) $a - b$ b) $b - a$ c) $a + b$ d) ab e) None of these

Answer: a Difficulty: 1

43. The sales at a local store were projected to be $13,750 per week. The accuracy of this projection is considered good if the actual sales differ from the projected sales by no more than $1375. Determine from weekly sales listed below any weeks when the projection was not considered good.

a) $12,370 b) $14,980 c) $15,025
d) $12,475 e) The projection was good in each of these cases.

Answer: a Difficulty: 2

44. The sales at a local store were projected to be $15,970 per week. The accuracy of this projection is considered good if the actual sales differ from the projected sales by no more than $1597. Determine from the weekly sales listed below any weeks when the projection was not considered good.

a) $17,470 b) $14,520 c) $15,370
d) $16,570 e) The projection was good in each of these cases.

Answer: e Difficulty: 2

45. While traveling you enter the interstate near the 234 mile marker, then exit near the 130 mile marker. Determine the number of miles traveled on the interstate.

a) 364 b) 104 c) 234 d) 130 e) None of these

Answer: b Difficulty: 1

46. While traveling you enter the interstate near the 125 mile marker, then exit near the 81 mile marker. Determine the number of miles traveled on the interstate.

a) 125 b) 81 c) 44 d) 206 e) None of these

Answer: c Difficulty: 1

47. The temperature was 38° F at noon and dropped to a low of -5° F at midnight. What was the change in temperature over the 12-hr. period?

a) 33° F b) 43° F c) 5° F d) -5° F e) None of these

Answer: b Difficulty: 1

48. While traveling you enter the interstate near the 26 mile marker, then exit near the 180 mile marker. Determine the number of miles traveled on the interstate.

a) 154 b) 206 c) 180 d) 26 e) None of these

Answer: a Difficulty: 1

49. Identify the terms of the expression: $3x^2 - 6x + 1$.
   a) 3, -6, 1
   b) x^2, x
   c) $3x^2$, $6x$, 1
   d) $3x^2$, $-6x$, 1
   e) None of these

   Answer: d Difficulty: 1

50. Identify the terms of the expression: $6x^4 - 3x^2 + 16$.
   a) 6, -3, 16
   b) x^4, x^2
   c) $6x^4$, $-3x^2$, 16
   d) $6x^4$, $-3x^2$
   e) None of these

   Answer: c Difficulty: 1

SHORT ANSWER

51. Identify the terms of the expression: $2x^4 - 3x^3 + 2x + 1$.

   Answer:

   $2x^4$, $-3x^3$, $2x$, 1

   Difficulty: 1

52. Identify the terms of the expression: $6x^3 - 2x^2 + 4x - 3$.

   Answer:

   $6x^3$, $-2x^2$, $4x$, -3

   Difficulty: 1

MULTIPLE CHOICE

53. Evaluate $3x - 7$ for $x = 4$.
   a) 4
   b) 5
   c) 0
   d) -5
   e) none of these

   Answer: b Difficulty: 1

54. Evaluate $3x^2 - 4x$ for $x = 2$.
   a) -2
   b) 4
   c) 28
   d) 2
   e) None of these

   Answer: b Difficulty: 1

55. Evaluate $2x^2 - 4x$ for $x = 3$.
   a) 0
   b) -6
   c) 24
   d) 6
   e) None of these

   Answer: d Difficulty: 1

56. Evaluate $4x^2 - 5x + 1$ for $x = -3$.
   a) 52
   b) 20
   c) 22
   d) -50
   e) None of these

   Answer: a Difficulty: 1

SHORT ANSWER

57. Evaluate: $6x^2 - 2x$ for $x = 3$.

Answer: 48 Difficulty: 1

58. Evaluate: $5x^2 - 2x - 1$ for $x = -1$.

Answer: 6 Difficulty: 1

MULTIPLE CHOICE

59. Identify the property illustrated by $5 + (\frac{1}{5} + x) = (5 + \frac{1}{5}) + x$.

a) Commutative
b) Distributive
c) Associative
d) Inverse
e) None of these

Answer: c Difficulty: 1

60. Identify the property illustrated by $(x - 8) + (-x + 8) = 0$.

a) Inverse
b) Identity
c) Associative
d) Commutative
e) None of these

Answer: a Difficulty: 1

61. Identify the property illustrated by $3[x + (-1)] = 3x + 3(-1)$.

a) Commutative
b) Associative
c) Distributive
d) Identity
e) Inverse

Answer: c Difficulty: 1

SHORT ANSWER

62. Identify the property illustrated by $3 + (2 + 7) = (2 + 7) + 3$.

Answer: Commutative Difficulty: 1

63. Identify the property illustrated by $7\left[\frac{1}{7}\right] = 1$.

Answer: Inverse Difficulty: 1

64. Identify the property illustrated by $1 \cdot (x + 7) = x + 7$.

Answer: Identity Difficulty: 1

MULTIPLE CHOICE

65. Perform the operations. Write fractional answers in reduced form.
$\frac{1}{2} - \frac{1}{6} + \frac{3}{4}$
a) $\frac{17}{12}$ b) $\frac{13}{12}$ c) $\frac{1}{4}$ d) Undefined e) None of these

Answer: b Difficulty: 1

66. Perform the operations. Write fractional answers in reduced form.
$\frac{3}{8} - \frac{2}{3} + \frac{1}{4}$
a) $\frac{2}{9}$ b) $\frac{31}{24}$ c) $\frac{19}{24}$ d) $-\frac{1}{24}$ e) None of these

Answer: d Difficulty: 1

67. Perform the operations. Write fractional answers in reduced form.
$\frac{2}{5} - \frac{1}{3} + \frac{7}{10}$
a) $\frac{43}{30}$ b) $\frac{2}{15}$ c) $\frac{23}{30}$ d) $\frac{2}{3}$ e) None of these

Answer: c Difficulty: 1

SHORT ANSWER

68. Perform the operations. Write fractional answers in reduced form.
$\frac{3}{5} - \frac{1}{2} + \frac{3}{10}$

Answer:
$\frac{2}{5}$

Difficulty: 1

69. Perform the operations. Write fractional answers in reduced form.
$\frac{2}{5} - \frac{1}{3} + \frac{3}{10}$

Answer:
$\frac{11}{30}$

Difficulty: 1

70. Use a calculator to evaluate the expression. Round your answer to two decimal places.

$$\frac{1.25 - 3.89}{4.2}$$

Answer: -0.63 Difficulty: 1 Key 1: T

71. Use a calculator to evaluate the expression. Round your answer to two decimal places.

$$\frac{3.84 - 2.51}{3.6}$$

Answer: 0.37 Difficulty: 1 Key 1: T

72. Use a calculator to evaluate the expression. Round your answer to two decimal places.

$$\frac{2.41(3.86 - 10.25)}{2.42}$$

Answer: -6.36 Difficulty: 1 Key 1: T

73. Use a calculator to evaluate the expression. Round your answer to two decimal places.

$$\frac{3.21(6.14 + 2.56)}{-2.5}$$

Answer: -11.17 Difficulty: 1 Key 1: T

Chapter 0P2: Exponents and Radicals

SHORT ANSWER

1. Write the expression as a repeated multiplication: $(2x)^3$.

   Answer: $(2x)(2x)(2x)$ Difficulty: 1

2. Write the expression as a repeated multiplication: -3^4.

   Answer: $-(3 \cdot 3 \cdot 3 \cdot 3)$ or -81 Difficulty: 1

3. Write the expression as a repeated multiplication: $(-3a)^2$.

   Answer: $(-3a)(-3a)$ Difficulty: 1

MULTIPLE CHOICE

4. Write the expression using exponential notation: $(2a)(2a)(2a)(2a)$.
   a) $2a^4$ b) $8a^4$ c) $(2a)^4$
   d) All of these e) None of these

   Answer: c Difficulty: 2

5. Write the expression using exponential notation: $(-3x)(-3x)$.
   a) $-3x^2$ b) $-(3x)^2$ c) $(-3x)^2$ d) $6x^2$ e) None of these

   Answer: c Difficulty: 2

6. Write the expression using exponential notation: $(5x)(5x)(5x)$.
   a) $5x^3$ b) $15x^3$ c) $125x^3$ d) $15x$ e) None of these

   Answer: c Difficulty: 2

7. Write the expression using exponential notation: $-(8y \cdot 8y \cdot 8y \cdot 8y)$.
   a) $-(8y)^4$ b) $(-8y)^4$ c) $8y^4$ d) $(8y)^4$ e) None of these

   Answer: a Difficulty: 1

8. Evaluate: $(2^3 \cdot 3^2)^{-1}$.
   a) -72 b) $\frac{1}{46,656}$ c) $-\frac{1}{36}$ d) $\frac{1}{72}$ e) None of these

   Answer: d Difficulty: 1

9. Evaluate: $(6^{-2})(3^0)(2^3)$.
   a) $\frac{2}{9}$ b) -288 c) -216 d) $\frac{1}{6}$ e) None of these

   Answer: a Difficulty: 1

10. Evaluate: $(4)^{-2}(3)^0(-1)^2$.
a) 0 b) -8 c) -16 d) $\frac{1}{16}$ e) None of these

Answer: d Difficulty: 1

11. Evaluate: $(2)^3(2)^{-3}$.
a) 1 b) 0 c) -36 d) -64 e) None of these

Answer: a Difficulty: 1

12. Evaluate: $\frac{4(2)^{-1}}{(3)^{-2}(2)}$.
a) $\frac{2}{3}$ b) 0 c) 9 d) $\frac{4}{9}$ e) None of these

Answer: c Difficulty: 2

SHORT ANSWER

13. Evaluate $3^{-1} + 4^{-1}$.

Answer:
$\frac{7}{12}$

Difficulty: 2

14. Use a calculator to evaluate the expression. Round to three decimal places.
$\frac{2^6}{3^4}$

Answer: 0.790 Difficulty: 2 Key 1: T

15. Use a calculator to evaluate the expression. Round to three decimal places.
$\frac{2^{-5}}{3^{-4}}$

Answer: 2.531 Difficulty: 2 Key 1: T

16. Use a calculator to evaluate the expression. Round to three decimal places.
$(8^{-2})(3^3)$

Answer: 0.422 Difficulty: 2 Key 1: T

17. Use a calculator to evaluate the expression. Round to three decimal places.
$(-4)^5(3^{-2})$

Answer: -113.778 Difficulty: 2 Key 1: T

18. Evaluate $3x^2y^{-4}$ when $x = -1$ and $y = -2$.

Answer:
$\frac{3}{16}$

Difficulty: 1

MULTIPLE CHOICE

19. Evaluate $2x^4 + 3x$ when $x = -3$.
a) 1287 b) 153 c) -15 d) 1215 e) None of these

Answer: b Difficulty: 1

20. Evaluate $7(-x)^3$ for $x = 2$.
a) -1 b) -42 c) -56 d) 2744 e) None of these

Answer: c Difficulty: 1

21. Evaluate $4x^{-2}$ for $x = 3$.
a) 36 b) -24 c) $\frac{1}{144}$ d) $\frac{4}{9}$ e) None of these

Answer: d Difficulty: 1

22. Evaluate $3x^2$ for $x = \frac{1}{4}$.
a) $\frac{3}{8}$ b) 48 c) $\frac{3}{2}$ d) $\frac{3}{16}$ e) None of these

Answer: d Difficulty: 1

23. Evaluate $3x^0 - x^{-2}$ for $x = 4$.
a) -16 b) $\frac{47}{16}$ c) $\frac{15}{16}$ d) -5 e) None of these

Answer: b Difficulty: 1

24. Simplify: $\left[\frac{x^{-3}y^2}{z}\right]^{-4}$.
a) $\frac{z^4}{x^7y^6}$ b) $\frac{y^2z^4}{x^7}$ c) $\frac{x^{12}z^4}{y^8}$ d) $\frac{z^4}{x^{12}y^8}$ e) None of these

Answer: c Difficulty: 1

25. Simplify: $\left[\frac{3x^2y^3}{xw^{-2}}\right]^3$.

a) $9w^6x^3y^9$ b) $9w^{-8}x^8y^{27}$ c) $27w^6x^3y^9$
d) $3w^6x^3y^9$ e) None of these

Answer: c Difficulty: 1

26. Simplify: $3x^2(2x)^3(5x^{-1})$.

a) $30x^{-6}$ b) $\frac{6}{5}x^6$ c) $\frac{24}{5}x^4$ d) $120x^4$ e) None of these

Answer: d Difficulty: 1

SHORT ANSWER

27. Simplify: $(3x^2y^3z)^{-2}(xy^4)$.

Answer:

$\frac{1}{9x^3y^2z^2}$

Difficulty: 1

28. Simplify: $(-2x^2)^5(5x^3)^{-2}$.

Answer:

$-\frac{32x^4}{25}$.

Difficulty: 1

29. Simplify: $\frac{2x^{-5}y^2}{z^2}$.

Answer:

$\frac{2y^2}{x^5z^2}$

Difficulty: 1

MULTIPLE CHOICE

30. Simplify: $x^2 \cdot x^3 \cdot x^4$.

a) x^{24} b) x^9 c) $3x^{24}$ d) x^{10} e) None of these

Answer: b Difficulty: 1

31. Simplify: $[(A^2)^3]^2$.
a) A^{12} b) A^7 c) A^{10} d) A^8 e) None of these

Answer: a Difficulty: 1

32. Simplify: $(-x^2)^3(-x^3)^2$.
a) x^{10} b) $-x^{10}$ c) $-x^{12}$ d) x^{12} e) None of these

Answer: c Difficulty: 1

SHORT ANSWER

33. Simplify:
$(-3x^2)^3 \cdot (-3x^2)^{-3}$.

Answer: 1 Difficulty: 1

MULTIPLE CHOICE

34. Simplify: $(-x^2)(-x)^3(-x)^4$.
a) $-x^{24}$ b) x^{24} c) $-x^9$ d) x^9 e) None of these

Answer: d Difficulty: 1

SHORT ANSWER

35. Simplify: $(-3x^2)^2(-3x)^3$.

Answer:

$-243x^7$

Difficulty: 1

36. Simplify: $(-3x^2)^3(-3x)^2$.

Answer:

$-243x^8$

Difficulty: 1

37. Simplify and write the answer without negative exponents.
$(-2a^2b^3)(-3ab)^3$

Answer:

$54a^5b^6$

Difficulty: 1

38. Simplify and write the answer without negative exponents.

$$\frac{-3y^{-2}}{(2y)^{-3}}$$

Answer: $-24y$ Difficulty: 1

39. Simplify and write the answer without negative exponents.
$(-2a^0b^{-2})(3b^{-1}a^{-2})^{-2}$

Answer:
$-\frac{2}{9}a^4$

Difficulty: 1

40. Simplify: $-(3x^2)^2(-3x^2)^3$.

Answer:

$243x^{10}$

Difficulty: 1

41. Simplify: $(-3x^2)^3(3x^2)^2$.

Answer:

$-243x^{10}$

Difficulty: 1

42. Use the rules of exponents to write without negative exponents.
$2x^{-2}(2x^2y)^0$

Answer:

$$\frac{2}{x^2}$$

Difficulty: 1

43. Use the rules of exponents to write without negative exponents.

$$\left[\frac{3x^2}{y^{-2}}\right]^{-1}$$

Answer:

$$\frac{1}{3x^2y^2}$$

Difficulty: 1

44. Use the rules of exponents to write without negative exponents.
$\left(\frac{b^2}{3a}\right)^{-2}$

Answer:
$\frac{9a^2}{b^4}$

Difficulty: 1

45. Use the rules of exponents to write without negative exponents.
$\left(\frac{x^{-2}y^3}{4}\right)^{-2}$

Answer:
$\frac{16x^4}{y^6}$

Difficulty: 1

46. Convert to rational exponent form: $\sqrt[3]{125} = 5$.

Answer:
$125^{1/3} = 5$

Difficulty: 1

47. Convert to radical form: $(8xy^2z^4)^{3/2}$.

Answer:
$\sqrt{(8xy^2z^4)^3}$

Difficulty: 1

MULTIPLE CHOICE

48. Evaluate: $\frac{1}{81^{-1/2}}$.

a) $\frac{1}{9}$ b) 9 c) $-\frac{1}{9}$ d) -9 e) None of these

Answer: b Difficulty: 1

SHORT ANSWER

49. Evaluate: $\left(\frac{8}{27}\right)^{-2/3}$.

Answer:
$\frac{9}{4}$

Difficulty: 1

MULTIPLE CHOICE

50. Evaluate: $\left(\frac{1}{64}\right)^{-2/3}$.

a) -16 b) $\frac{1}{16}$ c) $\frac{1}{512}$ d) -512 e) None of these

Answer: e Difficulty: 1

51. Evaluate: $\left(\frac{1}{64}\right)^{3/2}$.

a) $\frac{1}{512}$ b) -512 c) $\frac{1}{16}$ d) -16 e) None of these

Answer: a Difficulty: 1

52. Evaluate: $\frac{1}{27^{-1/3}}$.

a) $\frac{1}{3}$ b) 3 c) $-\frac{1}{3}$ d) $-\frac{1}{9}$ e) None of these

Answer: b Difficulty: 1

SHORT ANSWER

53. Use a calculator to approximate the number. Round to three decimal places.
$\sqrt[3]{51}$

Answer: 3.708 Difficulty: 1 Key 1: T

54. Use a calculator to approximate the number. Round to three decimal places.
$\frac{3 + \sqrt{21}}{5}$

Answer: 1.517 Difficulty: 2 Key 1: T

55. Use a calculator to approximate the number. Round to three decimal places. $(2.4)^{3/5}$

Answer: 1.691 Difficulty: 2 Key 1: T

56. Use a calculator to approximate the number. Round to three decimal places. $(15.25)^{-1.2}$

Answer: 0.380 Difficulty: 2 Key 1: T

MULTIPLE CHOICE

57. Simplify: $\sqrt[3]{-625x^7y^5}$.
a) $5xy\sqrt[3]{-5x^4y^2}$ b) $-5xy\sqrt[3]{5x^4y^2}$ c) $-125x^2y\sqrt[3]{5xy^2}$
d) $-5x^2y\sqrt[3]{5xy^2}$ e) Does not simplify

Answer: d Difficulty: 1

58. Simplify: $\sqrt{75x^2y^{-4}}$.
a) $\frac{5\sqrt{3}x}{y^2}$ b) $\frac{3\sqrt{5}|x|}{y^2}$ c) $5\sqrt{3}|x|y^2$ d) $\frac{5\sqrt{3}|x|}{y^2}$
e) None of these

Answer: d Difficulty: 1

59. Simplify: $\sqrt{x^2y^2}$.
a) $\pm|xy|$ b) $|xy|$ c) xy d) $-xy$ e) None of these

Answer: b Difficulty: 1

60. Simplify $\sqrt{a^4b^2}$ if a and b are both negative.
a) a^2 b) $\pm|a^2b|$ c) $-a^2b$ d) $\pm a^2b$ e) None of these

Answer: c Difficulty: 2

61. Simplify: $\sqrt[3]{24x^4y^5}$.
a) $3x^2y^2\sqrt[3]{6x^2y^3}$ b) $8xy\sqrt[3]{3xy}$ c) $2xy\sqrt[3]{6xy^2}$
d) $2xy\sqrt[3]{3xy^2}$ e) None of these

Answer: d Difficulty: 1

62. Simplify $\sqrt{x^2 + y^2}$.
a) $x + y$ b) $|x| + |y|$ c) $\pm(x + y)$
d) Does not simplify e) None of these

Answer: d Difficulty: 1

SHORT ANSWER

63. Perform the operation and simplify: $2^{3/2} \cdot 2^{5/2}$.

Answer: 16 Difficulty: 2

64. Perform the operation and simplify: $\dfrac{5^{5/3}}{5^{2/3}}$.

Answer: 5 Difficulty: 2

65. Perform the operation and simplify: $\dfrac{x^{4/3}y^{1/3}}{(xy)^{2/3}}$.

Answer:

$\dfrac{x^{2/3}}{y^{1/3}}$

Difficulty: 2

66. Perform the operation and simplify: $\dfrac{x^{-1/2} \cdot x^{1/3}}{x^2 \cdot x^{-3}}$.

Answer:

$x^{5/6}$

Difficulty: 2

MULTIPLE CHOICE

67. Rationalize the denominator: $\dfrac{3}{\sqrt{7} + 2}$.

a) $\sqrt{7} - 2$ b) $\dfrac{3\sqrt{7} - 6}{5}$ c) $\dfrac{3\sqrt{7} - 2}{3}$ d) $\dfrac{3\sqrt{7} - 2}{5}$

e) None of these

Answer: a Difficulty: 1

68. Rationalize the denominator: $\dfrac{5}{7 - \sqrt{2}}$.

a) $\dfrac{35 + 5\sqrt{2}}{47}$ b) $\dfrac{35 + \sqrt{2}}{47}$ c) $7 + \sqrt{2}$

d) $\dfrac{35 + \sqrt{2}}{3}$ e) None of these

Answer: a Difficulty: 1

69. Rationalize the denominator: $\frac{2}{\sqrt[3]{2x}}$.

a) $\frac{\sqrt[3]{2x}}{x}$ b) $\frac{\sqrt[3]{4x^2}}{x}$ c) $\frac{2\sqrt[3]{2x}}{2x}$ d) $\sqrt[3]{4x}$ e) None of these

Answer: b Difficulty: 2

70. Simplify by rationalizing the denominator: $\frac{6x}{5 - \sqrt{2}}$.

a) $\frac{6x(5 + \sqrt{2})}{23}$ b) $2x(5 + \sqrt{2})$ c) $\frac{30x - \sqrt{2}}{23}$

d) $\frac{6x(5 - \sqrt{2})}{21}$ e) None of these

Answer: a Difficulty: 1

71. Simplify by rationalizing the denominator: $\frac{4}{\sqrt[3]{x}}$.

a) $\frac{4\sqrt[3]{x}}{x}$ b) $\frac{4\sqrt[3]{x^2}}{x}$ c) 4 d) $4\sqrt[3]{x}$ e) None of these

Answer: b Difficulty: 1

72. Simplify by rationalizing the numerator: $\frac{6 - \sqrt{2}}{5}$.

a) $\frac{34}{5(6 + \sqrt{2})}$ b) $\frac{4}{30 + \sqrt{2}}$ c) $\frac{34}{5(6 - \sqrt{2})}$

d) $\frac{32}{5(6 - \sqrt{2})}$ e) None of these

Answer: a Difficulty: 1

73. Simplify by rationalizing the numerator: $\frac{\sqrt[3]{3}}{12}$.

a) $\frac{1}{\sqrt[3]{4}}$ b) $\frac{3}{4\sqrt[3]{3}}$ c) $\frac{1}{4\sqrt[3]{3}}$ d) $\frac{1}{4\sqrt[3]{9}}$ e) None of these

Answer: d Difficulty: 1

74.
Simplify by rationalizing the numerator: $\frac{\sqrt{2} - \sqrt{5}}{12}$.

a) $\frac{1}{4(\sqrt{2} - \sqrt{5})}$ b) $\frac{-1}{4(\sqrt{2} + \sqrt{5})}$ c) $\frac{-7}{4(\sqrt{2} + \sqrt{5})}$

d) $\frac{1}{4\sqrt{2} + \sqrt{5}}$ e) None of these

Answer: b Difficulty: 1

75.
Simplify by rationalizing the numerator: $\frac{5 + 2\sqrt{5}}{15}$.

a) $\frac{-4}{5(1 - \sqrt{5})}$ b) $\frac{2}{3(5 + 2\sqrt{5})}$ c) $\frac{1}{5 - 2\sqrt{5}}$

d) $\frac{1}{3(5 - 2\sqrt{5})}$ e) None of these

Answer: d Difficulty: 1

76.
Simplify by rationalizing the numerator: $\frac{\sqrt[3]{16}}{7}$.

a) $\frac{16}{7\sqrt[3]{16}}$ b) $\frac{1}{7\sqrt[3]{256}}$ c) $\frac{4}{7\sqrt[3]{4}}$

d) $\frac{2}{7\sqrt[3]{16}}$ e) None of these

Answer: c Difficulty: 1

SHORT ANSWER

77.
Rationalize the numerator: $\frac{3 - \sqrt{2}}{5}$.

Answer:
$\frac{7}{5(3 + \sqrt{2})}$
Difficulty: 1

MULTIPLE CHOICE

78.
Write as a single radical: $\sqrt[3]{\sqrt{2x}}$.

a) $\sqrt[6]{2x}$ b) $\sqrt[5]{2x}$ c) $\sqrt[3]{2x}$ d) $\sqrt[3]{4x^2}$ e) None of these

Answer: a Difficulty: 1 Key 1: M

SHORT ANSWER

79. Simplify: $\sqrt[3]{\sqrt{3x+1}}$.

Answer:

$\sqrt[6]{3x+1}$

Difficulty: 1

MULTIPLE CHOICE

80. Simplify: $\sqrt[3]{2}\sqrt[3]{4}$.

a) $6\sqrt[6]{2}$ b) $3\sqrt[6]{8}$ c) $6\sqrt{2}$ d) $3\sqrt[6]{32}$ e) None of these

Answer: a Difficulty: 2 Key 1: M

SHORT ANSWER

81. Simplify: $(\sqrt[3]{81x^4y^9})(\sqrt[3]{2xy^2})$.

Answer:

$3xy^3\sqrt[3]{6x^2y^2}$

Difficulty: 2

82. Simplify: $\sqrt{3x^2}\sqrt[3]{3x^2}$.

Answer:

$\sqrt[6]{(3x^2)^5}$

Difficulty: 2

MULTIPLE CHOICE

83. Simplify: $\sqrt[6]{8x^3y^3}$.

a) $\sqrt{8xy}$ b) $\sqrt[3]{2xy}$ c) $\sqrt{2xy}$ d) $\sqrt[3]{8xy}$ e) None of these

Answer: c Difficulty: 1

84. Simplify: $\sqrt[6]{9x^2y^2}$.

a) $\sqrt{3xy}$ b) $\sqrt[3]{3xy}$ c) $\sqrt{9xy}$ d) $\sqrt[3]{9xy}$ e) None of these

Answer: b Difficulty: 1

SHORT ANSWER

85. Simplify: $3\sqrt[3]{4x^5y^3} + 7x\sqrt[3]{32x^2y^6}$.

Answer:

$(3 + 14y)xy\sqrt[3]{4x^2}$

Difficulty: 2

MULTIPLE CHOICE

86. Simplify: $4\sqrt{9x} - 2\sqrt{4x} + 7$.

a) $8x + 7$ b) $8\sqrt{x} + 7$ c) $2\sqrt{5x} + 7$

d) Does not simplify e) None of these

Answer: b Difficulty: 1

87. Simplify: $7\sqrt{25xy^2} - 4\sqrt{75xy^2} + 2\sqrt{12xy^2}$.

a) $35|y|\sqrt{x} - 16|y|\sqrt{3x}$ b) $19|y|\sqrt{2x}$ c) $35|y|\sqrt{x} - 6|y|\sqrt{2x}$

d) $5|y|\sqrt{38x}$ e) None of these

Answer: a Difficulty: 1

88. Simplify: $2x^2y\sqrt[3]{2x} + 7x^2\sqrt[3]{2xy^3} - 4\sqrt[3]{16x^7y^3}$.

a) $x^6y^3\sqrt[3]{2x}$ b) $x^2y\sqrt[3]{2x}$ c) $9x^2y\sqrt[3]{2x} - 8y\sqrt[3]{2x^7y}$

d) $2x^3y$ e) None of these

Answer: b Difficulty: 2

89. Write $\sqrt[3]{2x^2}$ in exponential form.

a) $2x^{3/2}$ b) $2x^{2/3}$ c) $(2x)^{2/3}$

d) $(2x^2)^{1/3}$ e) None of these

Answer: d Difficulty: 1

90. The period T, in seconds, of a pendulum is $T = 2\pi\sqrt{\frac{L}{32}}$ where L is the length of the pendulum in feet. Find the period of a pendulum whose length is $\frac{1}{2}$ foot.

a) π b) $\frac{\pi}{2}$ c) $\frac{\pi}{4}$ d) $\frac{\pi}{8}$ e) None of these

Answer: c Difficulty: 2

91. The period T, in seconds, of a pendulum is $T = 2\pi\sqrt{\frac{L}{32}}$ where L is the length of the pendulum in feet. Find the period of a pendulum whose length is 8 feet.

a) π b) $\frac{\pi}{2}$ c) $\frac{\pi}{4}$ d) $\frac{\pi}{8}$ e) None of these

Answer: a Difficulty: 2

92. Rewrite in scientific notation: 0.000004792.

a) 0.4792×10^5 b) 4.792×10^{-6} c) 4.792×10^{-5}

d) 4.792×10^6 e) None of these

Answer: b Difficulty: 1

SHORT ANSWER

93. Rewrite in decimal form: 3.75×10^{-7}.

Answer: 0.000000375 Difficulty: 1

MULTIPLE CHOICE

94. Multiply: $(0.00000526)(72{,}000{,}000{,}000)^2$.

a) 3.7872×10^4 b) 2.726784×10^{-20} c) 2.726784×10^{16}

d) 2.726784×10^{-14} e) None of these

Answer: c Difficulty: 2

SHORT ANSWER

95. Simplify and write in decimal form: $\dfrac{(5.1 \times 10^{-5})(3 \times 10^6)}{1.7 \times 10^{-2}}$.

Answer: 9000 Difficulty: 2

96. Simplify and write in scientific notation:

$$\frac{(32{,}700{,}000{,}000{,}000)(72{,}000{,}000{,}000)^2}{0.0000000041}.$$

Answer:

4.13×10^{43}

Difficulty: 2

MULTIPLE CHOICE

97. Represent the number 0.0021367 in scientific notation.
    a) 0.21367×10^{-2} b) 21367×10^{-7} c) 2.1367×10^{-2}
    d) 2.1367×10^{-3} e) None of these

    Answer: d Difficulty: 1

98. The highest peak in the Western hemisphere, located in Argentina, has an elevation of 22,831 feet. Represent this in scientific notation.
    a) 22.831×10^4 b) 2.2831×10^4 c) 0.22831×10^5
    d) 2.2831×10^3 e) None of these

    Answer: b Difficulty: 1

99. The total area of Chile is approximately 2.9×10^5 square miles. Write this in decimal form.
    a) 2900 b) 29,000 c) 290,000
    d) 2,900,000 e) None of these

    Answer: c Difficulty: 1

Chapter 0P3: Polynomials and Factoring

MULTIPLE CHOICE

1. Find the degree of the polynomial: $5x^4 - 2x^3 - 7x + 1$.
   a) 4 b) 5 c) 8 d) 12 e) None of these

   Answer: a Difficulty: 1

2. Find the degree of the polynomial: $5x^4 - 2x^2 + x$.
   a) 7 b) 6 c) 5 d) 4 e) None of these

   Answer: d Difficulty: 1

3. Find the degree of the polynomial: $4x^3 - 2x + 1$.
   a) 2 b) 3 c) 4 d) 5 e) This is not a polynomial.

   Answer: b Difficulty: 1

4. Find the degree of the polynomial: $5x^2 - 3x + 1$.
   a) 2 b) 3 c) 4 d) 5 e) This is not a polynomial.

   Answer: a Difficulty: 1

5. Identify any polynomials.
   a) $4x^3 - 7\sqrt{x} + 3$ b) $\dfrac{x^2 + 2x + 1}{x - 3}$ c) $x^{-3} + 2x^{-2} + x$
   d) None of these are polynomials. e) All of these are polynomials.

   Answer: d Difficulty: 1

6. Identify any polynomials.
   a) $3x^2 - 2x + 1$ b) $\dfrac{x + 1}{x - 1}$ c) $x + \dfrac{1}{x}$
   d) None of these are polynomials. e) All of these are polynomials.

   Answer: a Difficulty: 1

7. Identify any polynomials.
   a) $\dfrac{3x + 1}{2x - 2}$ b) $x + 2x^{-1} + 1$ c) $\dfrac{1}{4}x^3 - \dfrac{2}{3}x - 2$
   d) None of these are polynomials. e) All of these are polynomials.

   Answer: c Difficulty: 1

8. Identify any polynomials.
   a) $\dfrac{1}{2}x^3 + x - \dfrac{1}{3}$ b) $7 + 4x^3 - 6x^7$ c) $x + 1$
   d) None of these are polynomials. e) All of these are polynomials.

   Answer: e Difficulty: 1

9. Simplify: $(6x^3 + 2x - 7) + (4x^2 + x + 1) - (x^3 + 3x^2 - 2)$.
   a) $5x^3 + 7x^2 + 3x - 8$ b) $5x^3 + x^2 + 3x - 4$ c) $5x^6 - x^4 + x - 8$
   d) $7x^6 - 8$ e) Nonc of these

   Answer: b Difficulty: 1

10. Simplify: $(7x^4 - 2x^3 + 5x^2) + (7x^3 - 2x^2 + 5) - (6x^3 + 2x^2 - 12x)$.
   a) $7x^4 - x^3 + x^2 + 12x + 5$ b) $7x^4 - x^3 + 5x^2 - 12x + 5$ c) $-x^{10} + 5$
   d) $-x^9 + x^6 + 7x^4 - 12x + 5$ e) None of these

   Answer: a Difficulty: 1

11. Simplify: $(-4x^2 + 2x) - (5x^3 + 2x^2 - 1) + (x^2 + 1)$.
   a) $-9x^3 + 5x^2$ b) $5x^3 - x^2 + 2x + 1$ c) $6x^6$
   d) $-5x^3 - 5x^2 + 2x + 2$ e) None of these

   Answer: d Difficulty: 1

12. Simplify: $(2x^2 + 3x - 1) + (x^3 + x^2 + 5) - (2x^2 - 5x + 7)$.
   a) $x^3 - 2x + x^2 + 4$ b) $x^3 + x^2 + 8x - 3$ c) $8x^5 + 4$
   d) $63x^3 + 5x^6$ e) None of these

   Answer: b Difficulty: 1

13. Simplify: $(3x^2 - 2x) + (7x^3 - 2x^2 + 1) - (16x^2 - 7)$.
   a) $7x^3 - 15x^2 - 2x + 8$ b) $7x^3 + 15x^2 - 6$ c) $7x^3 - 15x^2 - 2x - 6$
   d) $15x^5 + 7x^3 - 2x - 6$ e) None of these

   Answer: a Difficulty: 1

14. Simplify: $(-2x^2 + 3x - 9) - (4x^2 - x + 2) + (x^3 - 2x^2 + 1)$.
   a) $x^3 - 8x^2 + 3x - 6$ b) $x^3 - 8x^2 + 4x - 10$ c) $x^3 - 2x^2 + 2x - 6$
   d) $x^3 - 4x^2 + 2x - 6$ e) None of these

   Answer: b Difficulty: 1

15. Simplify: $3x(5x + 2) - 14(2x^2 - x + 1)$.
   a) $28x^2 - 3x - 14$ b) $13x^2 - 8x + 14$ c) $-13x^2 + 20x - 14$
   d) $13x^2 - 20x + 14$ e) None of these

   Answer: c Difficulty: 1

16. Simplify: $3x(7x - 6) - 4x(x - 2)$.
   a) $17x^2 - 10x$ b) $-84x^4 + 240x^3 - 144x^2$ c) $21x^2 - 14x$
   d) $72x^3 - 96x^2$ e) None of these

   Answer: a Difficulty: 1

17. Simplify: $(3x^4 - 7x^2) + 2x(x^2 - 1)(3x)$.
   a) $9x^4 - 13x^2$ b) $9x^4 - 19x^3 - 2x$ c) $3x^4 + 2x^3 - 7x^2 - 3x$
   d) $15x^7 - 50x^5 + 35x^3$ e) None of these

   Answer: a Difficulty: 1

18. Simplify: $(5 - 2x)(3) - (3x + 2)(-2)$.
    a) $-6x^2 + 11x + 10$ b) $-9x + 1$ c) $-10x + 20$
    d) 19 e) None of these

    Answer: d Difficulty: 1

SHORT ANSWER

19. Write in standard form: $(3x^2 + 2x) + x(1 - 7x) + (2x + 5)$.

    Answer:

    $-4x^2 + 5x + 5$

    Difficulty: 1

20. Write in standard form: $3x^2 - 2x(1 + 3x - x^2)$.

    Answer:

    $2x^3 - 3x^2 - 2x$

    Difficulty: 1

MULTIPLE CHOICE

21. Multiply: $(2x^2 - 5)^2$.
    a) $4x^2 - 25$ b) $4x^4 - 25$ c) $4x^4 - 20x^2 + 25$
    d) $4x^4 - 10x^2 - 25$ e) None of these

    Answer: c Difficulty: 1

22. Multiply: $(x - 2)(x^2 + 2x + 4)$.
    a) $x^3 - 8$ b) $x^3 - 6x^2 + 12x - 8$ c) $x^3 + 4x^2 - 8$
    d) $x^3 + 4x^2 + 8x - 8$ e) None of these

    Answer: a Difficulty: 1

23. Multiply: $(x + 4y)^2$.
    a) $x^2 + 4xy + y^2$ b) $x^2 + 16y^2$ c) $x^2 + 8xy + 16y^2$
    d) $x^2 + 4y^2$ e) None of these

    Answer: c Difficulty: 1

24. Multiply: $(x - 2\sqrt{3})(x + 2\sqrt{3})$.
    a) $x^2 - 12$ b) $x^2 - 36$ c) $x^2 - 6$ d) $x^2 - 4\sqrt{3}$ e) None of these

    Answer: a Difficulty: 1

25. Multiply: $(3x + 8)(3x - 8)$.
a) $3x^2 - 64$ b) $9x^2 + 48x - 64$ c) $9x^2 - 64$
d) $6x^2 - 16$ e) None of these

Answer: c Difficulty: 1

SHORT ANSWER

26. Multiply: $(x^2 + 5)(x^2 - 5)$.

Answer:

$x^4 - 25$

Difficulty: 1

MULTIPLE CHOICE

27. Multiply: $(3x - 7)(2x + 9)$.
a) $6x^2 + 13x - 63$ b) $6x^2 - 63$ c) $6x^2 - 13x - 63$
d) $6x^2 + 63$ e) None of these

Answer: a Difficulty: 1

SHORT ANSWER

28. Expand: $(2x - 1)^3$.

Answer:

$8x^3 - 12x^2 + 6x - 1$

Difficulty: 2

29. Expand: $[(x - 1) + y]^2$.

Answer:

$x^2 - 2x + 1 + 2xy - 2y + y^2$

Difficulty: 2

30. Multiply: $(x - 2)(x + 2)(x^2 + 4)$.

Answer:

$x^4 - 16$

Difficulty: 2

MULTIPLE CHOICE

31. Multiply: $(2x - y)(x + y)$.

   a) $2x^2 - y^2$ b) $2x^2 + xy - y^2$ c) $-2x^2y^2$

   d) $x^2y^2 - xy$ e) None of these

   Answer: b Difficulty: 1

32. Multiply: $[(x + 1) - y][(x + 1) + y]$.

   a) $x^2 + 2x + 1 - y^2$ b) $x^2 + 1 - y^2$ c) $x^2y^2 + y^2$

   d) $-x^2y^2 + 2xy^2 + y^2$ e) None of these

   Answer: a Difficulty: 1

33. Expand: $(3 + 2y)^3$.

   a) $9 + 6y^3$ b) $27 + 8y^3$ c) $27 + 54y + 36y^2 + 8y^3$

   d) $27 + 18y + 12y^2 + 8y^3$ e) None of these

   Answer: d Difficulty: 2

34. Represent the area of the region as a polynomial in standard form.

   a) $-x^2 - 8x + 96$ b) $-3x^2 + 72$ c) 40

   d) $3x^2 - 24x + 96$ e) None of these

   Answer: d Difficulty: 2

35. Represent the area of the region as a polynomial in standard form.

   a) $84x$ b) $-10x^2 + 18x + 90$ c) $-6x^2 + 90x$

   d) $10x + 36$ e) None of these

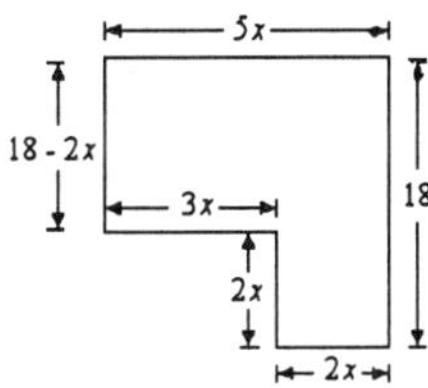

   Answer: c Difficulty: 2

36. Represent the area of the shaded region as a polynomial in standard form.
a) $6x^2 - 72x$ b) $48x - 18$ c) $90x - 6x^2$
d) $90x$ e) None of these

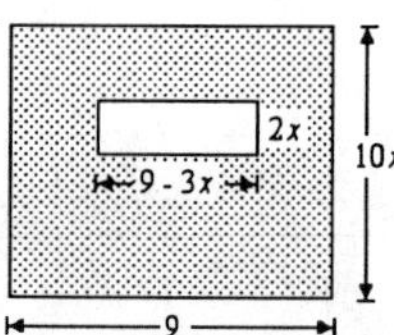

Answer: a Difficulty: 2

37. Represent the area of the shaded region as a polynomial in standard form.
a) $140x$ b) $144x - 4x^2$ c) $55x$
d) $120x^2$ e) None of these

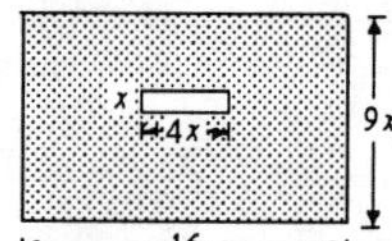

Answer: b Difficulty: 2

38. Represent the area of the shaded region as a polynomial in standard form.
a) $-2x + 18$ b) $12x + 14$ c) 14
d) $11x + 14$ e) None of these

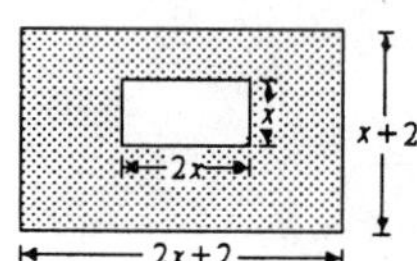

Answer: d Difficulty: 2

39. The height, in feet, of a free-falling object after t seconds is given by the polynomial:

$$\text{Height} = -16t^2 + 60t + 25.$$

Determine the height of the object when $t = 2.5$ seconds.
a) 215 feet b) 165 feet c) 39 feet
d) 75 feet e) None of these

Answer: d Difficulty: 1

40. The height, in feet, of a free-falling object after t seconds is given by the polynomial:

    Height $= -16t^2 + 60t + 25$.

    Determine the height of the object when $t = 3.5$ seconds.

    a) 61 feet b) 79 feet c) 39 feet
    d) 75 feet e) None of these

    Answer: c Difficulty: 1

41. The height, in feet, of a free-falling object after t seconds is given by the polynomial:

    Height $= -16t^2 + 60t + 25$.

    Determine the height of the object when $t = 1.5$ seconds.

    a) 61 feet b) 79 feet c) 39 feet
    d) 75 feet e) None of these

    Answer: b Difficulty: 1

42. The height, in feet, of a free-falling object after t seconds is given by the polynomial:

    Height $= -16t^2 + 60t + 25$.

    Determine the height of the object when $t = 3.0$ seconds.

    a) 61 feet b) 79 feet c) 39 feet
    d) 75 feet e) None of these

    Answer: a Difficulty: 1

SHORT ANSWER

43. After t seconds, the height in feet of an object dropped from a hot air balloon is given by:

    Height $= 300 - 16t^2$.

    Find the height after 1.5 seconds.

    Answer: 264 feet Difficulty: 1

44. After t seconds, the height in feet of an object dropped from a hot air balloon is given by:

    Height $= 300 - 16t^2$.

    Find the height after 2.5 seconds.

    Answer: 200 feet Difficulty: 1

45. After t seconds, the height in feet of an object dropped from a hot air balloon is given by:

$$\text{Height} = 300 - 16t^2.$$

Find the height after 3.5 seconds.

Answer: 104 feet Difficulty: 1

46. After t seconds, the height in feet of an object dropped from a hot air balloon is given by:

$$\text{Height} = 300 - 16t^2.$$

Find the height after 4.0 seconds.

Answer: 44 feet Difficulty: 1

47. Find the area of the shaded region.

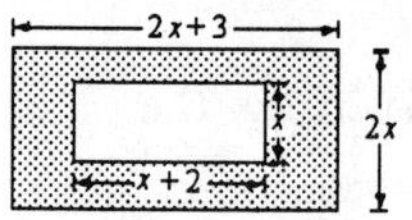

Answer:

$3x^2 + 4x$ square units

Difficulty: 2

48. Find the area of the shaded region.

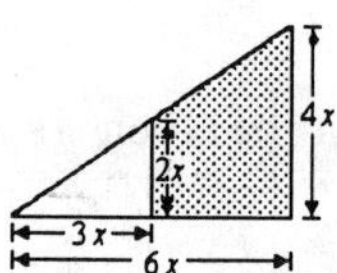

Answer:

$9x^2$ square units

Difficulty: 2

MULTIPLE CHOICE

49. Factor: $3x^2 - 15x$.
   a) $45x^3$
   b) $3(x^2 - 5)$
   c) $3x(x - 5)$
   d) $3x(x - 5x)$
   e) None of these

Answer: c Difficulty: 1

SHORT ANSWER

50. Factor: $(2x - 1)(x + 3) + (2x - 1)(2x + 1)$.

    Answer: $(2x - 1)(3x + 4)$ Difficulty: 2

51. Factor: $(3x + 2)(x - 7) + (4x - 1)(x - 7)$.

    Answer: $(x - 7)(7x + 1)$ Difficulty: 2

MULTIPLE CHOICE

52. Factor: $8x^3 - 27$.
    a) $(2x - 3)^3$
    b) $(2x - 3)(4x^2 - 12x + 9)$
    c) $(2x - 3)(4x^2 + 6x + 9)$
    d) $(2x + 3)(4x^2 - 6x + 9)$
    e) None of these

    Answer: c Difficulty: 1

53. Factor: $x^3 + 216$.
    a) $(x + 6)^3$
    b) $(x + 6)(x^2 - 6x + 36)$
    c) $(x - 6)(x^2 + 6x - 36)$
    d) $(x + 6)(x^2 + 36)$
    e) None of these

    Answer: b Difficulty: 1

54. Factor: $y^3 - (x + 1)^3$.
    a) $(y - x - 1)(y^2 + xy + y + x^2 + 2x + 1)$
    b) $(y - x + 1)(y^2 + xy + y + x^2 + 1)$
    c) $(y + x - 1)(y^2 - xy - y + x^2 - 2x - 1)$
    d) $(y - x - 1)^3$
    e) None of these

    Answer: a Difficulty: 2

55. Factor: $(a - b)^2 - x^2$.
    a) $(a - b - x)^2$
    b) $(a - b - x)(a + b + x)$
    c) $(a - b - x)(a - b + x)$
    d) $a^2 - 2ab + b^2 - x^2$
    e) None of these

    Answer: c Difficulty: 1

56. Factor: $81 - 4x^2$.
    a) $(9 - 2x)^2$
    b) $(9 - 2x)(9 + 2x)$
    c) $(81 - 4x)^2$
    d) $(3 - 2x)^2(3 + 2x)^2$
    e) None of these

    Answer: b Difficulty: 1

SHORT ANSWER

57. Factor: $(x + 3)^2 - a^2$.

    Answer: $(x + 3 - a)(x + 3 + a)$ Difficulty: 2

MULTIPLE CHOICE

58. Factor: $9x^2 + 24xy + 16y^2$.
   a) $(9x + 4y)(x + 4y)$ b) $(9x + 16y)(x + y)$ c) $(3x - 4y)^2$
   d) $(3x + 4y)^2$ e) None of these

   Answer: d Difficulty: 1

SHORT ANSWER

59. Factor: $9x^2 - 24x + 16$.

   Answer:

   $(3x - 4)^2$

   Difficulty: 1

MULTIPLE CHOICE

60. Factor: $9x^2 - 42x + 49$.
   a) $(3x - 7)^2$ b) $(9x - 7)^2$ c) $(3x + 7)^2$
   d) $x(9x - 42 + 49)$ e) None of these

   Answer: a Difficulty: 1

61. Factor: $x^2 + 13x - 14$.
   a) $(x - 7)(x + 2)$ b) $(x + 7)(x - 2)$ c) $(x - 14)(x - 1)$
   d) $(x - 14)(x + 1)$ e) None of these

   Answer: e Difficulty: 1

62. Factor: $x^2 + x - 12$.
   a) $(x - 4)(x - 3)$ b) $(x + 4)(x - 3)$ c) $(x + 6)(x - 2)$
   d) $(x - 12)(x - 1)$ e) None of these

   Answer: b Difficulty: 1

63. Factor: $x^2 - 2x - 15$.
   a) $(x - 3)(x + 5)$ b) $(x - 15)(x + 1)$ c) $(x + 3)(x - 5)$
   d) $(x + 3)(x + 5)$ e) None of these

   Answer: c Difficulty: 1

64. Factor: $3x^2 - 13x - 16$.
   a) $(3x - 16)(x - 1)$ b) $(3x + 16)(x - 1)$ c) $(x + 16)(3x - 1)$
   d) $(x - 16)(3x + 1)$ e) None of these

   Answer: e Difficulty: 1

65. Factor: $3x^2 - 19x - 14$.
    a) $(3x + 2)(x - 7)$ b) $(3x - 7)(x + 2)$ c) $(3x - 2)(x + 7)$
    d) $(3x + 7)(x - 2)$ e) None of these

    Answer: a Difficulty: 1

SHORT ANSWER

66. Factor: $14x^2 - 19x - 3$.

    Answer: $(2x - 3)(7x + 1)$ Difficulty: 1

67. Factor: $35x^2 + 9x - 2$.

    Answer: $(5x + 2)(7x - 1)$ Difficulty: 1

MULTIPLE CHOICE

68. Factor: $2rs + 3rst - 8r - 12rt$.
    a) $r(2s + 3st - 8 - 12t)$ b) $(rs - 4r)(2 + 3t)$ c) $r(s - 4)(2 - 3t)$
    d) $r(s - 4)(2 + 3t)$ e) None of these

    Answer: d Difficulty: 2

SHORT ANSWER

69. Factor: $3rv - 2vt - 6rs + 4st$.

    Answer: $(v - 2s)(3r - 2t)$ Difficulty: 2

MULTIPLE CHOICE

70. Factor: $3xz + 2yz - 6xw - 4yw$.
    a) $(3x + 2y)(z + 2w)$ b) $(3x + 2y)(z - 2w)$ c) $(3x - 2y)(z - 2w)$
    d) $(3xz + 2yz)(6xw + 4yw)$ e) None of these

    Answer: b Difficulty: 2

SHORT ANSWER

71. Factor: $4x^3 + 6x^2 - 10x$.

    Answer: $2x(2x + 5)(x - 1)$ Difficulty: 1

MULTIPLE CHOICE

72. Factor into linear factors: $6x^3 + 33x^2y - 63xy^2$.
    a) $3x(2x - 3y)(x + 7y)$ b) $(6x^2 - 9xy)(x + 7y)$
    c) $3x(2x + 3y)(x + 7y)$ d) $(6x^2 + 9xy)(x + 7y)$
    e) None of these

    Answer: a Difficulty: 1

73. Factor completely: $3x^4 - 48$.
a) $3(x - 2)^2(x + 2)^2$ b) $3(x - 2)^4$ c) $3x^2(x - 4)^2$
d) $3(x^2 + 4)(x + 2)(x - 2)$ e) None of these

Answer: d Difficulty: 2

SHORT ANSWER

74. Factor: $3x - 24x^4$.

Answer:

$3x(1 - 2x)(1 + 2x + 4x^2)$

Difficulty: 2

MULTIPLE CHOICE

75. Factor completely: $x^2(2x + 1)^3 - 4(2x + 1)^2$.
a) $(2x + 1)^2(2x^3 - 3)$ b) $(2x + 1)^2(2x^3 + x^2 - 4)$
c) $(2x + 1)^3(x^2 - 4)$ d) $(2x + 1)^3(x^2 - 8x - 4)$
e) None of these

Answer: b Difficulty: 2

76. Factor: $4(x + 2)^2 - 3x(x + 2)^3$.
a) $-(x + 2)^2(3x - 2)(x + 2)$ b) $-(x + 2)^2(3x^2 + 6x - 4)$
c) $(x + 2)^2(-3x^2 + 6)$ d) $(x + 2)^2(-3x^2 + 6x + 4)$
e) None of these

Answer: b Difficulty: 1

77. Factor: $9x(3x - 5)^2 + (3x - 5)^3$.
a) $(3x - 5)^3(9x + 1)$ b) $(3x - 5)^2(6x - 5)$ c) $(3x - 5)^2(12x - 5)$
d) $(3x - 5)(30x^2 - 70)$ e) None of these

Answer: c Difficulty: 1

78. Factor: $6x(2x + 3)^{-4} - 24x^2(2x + 3)^{-5}$.
a) $-6x(2x - 3)(2x + 3)^{-5}$ b) $-6x(8x^2 + 12x - 1)(2x + 3)^{-4}$
c) $6x(2x + 3)^{-5}[(2x + 3)^{-1} + 4x]$ d) $6x(2x + 3)^{-4}(-8x^2 - 12x)$
e) None of these

Answer: a Difficulty: 2

79. Factor: $(3x + 2)^{-3} - 9x(3x + 2)^{-4}$.
a) $(3x + 2)^{-4}[(3x + 2)^{-1} - 9x]$ b) $(-27x^2 - 18x)(3x + 2)^{-3}$
c) $-2(3x - 1)(3x + 2)^{-4}$ d) $-(27x^2 + 18x - 1)(3x + 2)^{-3}$
e) None of these

Answer: c Difficulty: 2

80. Factor: $2x(4x - 1)^{-2} + (4x - 1)^{-1}$.
   a) $(8x^2 - 1)(4x - 1)^{-1}$
   b) $(4x - 1)^{-1}(8x^2 - 2x + 1)$
   c) $(2x + 1)(4x - 1)^{-2}$
   d) $(6x - 1)(4x - 1)^{-2}$
   e) None of these

   Answer: d Difficulty: 1

81. The trinomial $x^2 - 4x + c$ will factor for which of the following values of c?
   a) 3 b) -5 c) -12 d) All of these e) None of these

   Answer: d Difficulty: 2

82. The trinomial $4x^2 + 3x + c$ will factor for which of the following values of c?
   a) 6 b) 0 c) -1 d) Both 6 and 0 e) Both 0 and -1

   Answer: e Difficulty: 1

SHORT ANSWER

83. The total surface area of a right circular cylinder is found by using the formula $S = 2\pi r^2 + 2\pi rh$. Write the formula in factored form.

   Answer: $S = 2\pi r(r + h)$ Difficulty: 1

84. The volume of the frustum of a cone can be found by using the formula $V = \frac{1}{3}(a^2\pi h + ab\pi h + b^2\pi h)$. Write the formula in factored form.

   Answer:
   $V = \frac{1}{3}\pi h(a^2 + ab + b^2)$
   Difficulty: 1

MULTIPLE CHOICE

85. Find the perimeter, P, of the rectangle where the lengths of the sides can be obtained by factoring the expression for the area,

   Area = $x^2 - 64$.

   a) $P = 2x$
   b) $P = 4x$
   c) $P = 4x + 32$
   d) $P = 4x + 16$
   e) None of these

   Answer: b Difficulty: 2

86. Find the perimeter, P, of the rectangle where the lengths of the sides can be obtained by factoring the expression for the area,

Area = $2x^2 - 6x$.

a) $P = 3x$
b) $P = 3x - 3$
c) $P = 4x - 3$
d) $P = 6x - 6$
e) None of these

Answer: d Difficulty: 2

SHORT ANSWER

87. The selling price, S, of a product is equal to the cost, C, plus the markup. The markup may be expressed as a percent, R, of the cost. Write an equation for the selling price in terms of the cost and markup, then factor that expression.

Answer: $S = C + RC \Rightarrow S = C(1 + R)$ Difficulty: 1

88. The sale price, S, of a product is equal to the list price, L, minus the discount. The discount may be expressed as a percent, R, of the list price. Write an equation for the sale price in terms of the list price and discount, then factor that expression.

Answer: $S = L - RL \Rightarrow S = L(1 - R)$ Difficulty: 1

89. Find the surface area of a compact disc with outside radius, R, and inside radius, r, then factor that expression.

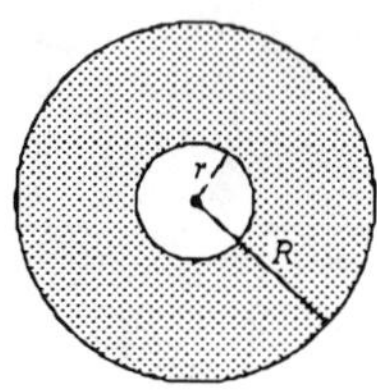

Answer:

$A = \pi R^2 - \pi r^2 \Rightarrow$
$A = \pi(R^2 - r^2)$

Difficulty: 1

90. Write a polynomial and the correct factorization for the geometric factoring model.

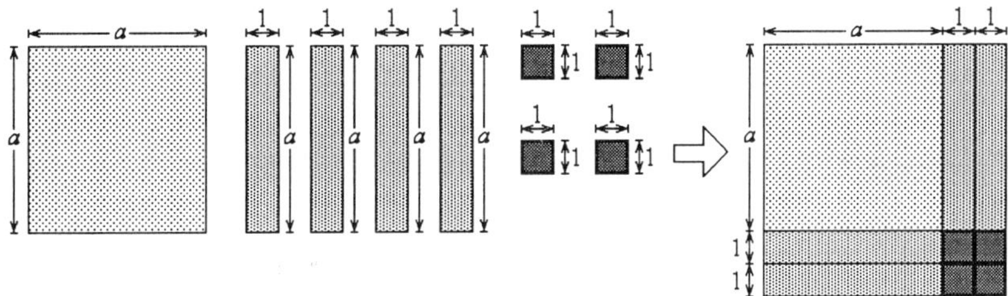

Answer:

$a^2 + 4a + 4 = (a + 2)^2$

Difficulty: 2

91. Write a polynomial and the correct factorization for the geometric factoring model.

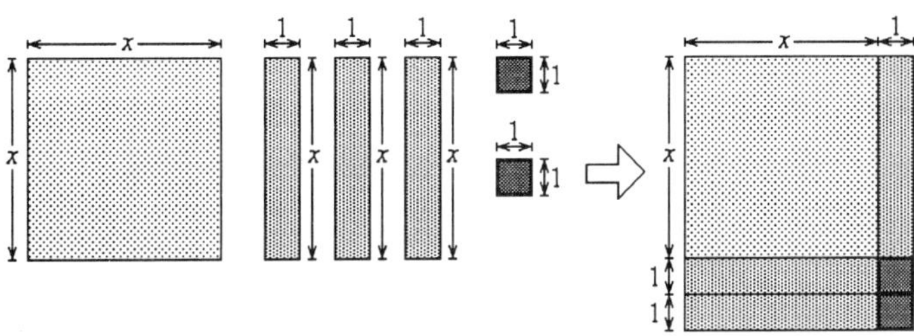

Answer:

$x^2 + 3x + 2 = (x + 1)(x + 2)$

Difficulty: 2

92. Write a polynomial and the correct factorization for the geometric factoring model.

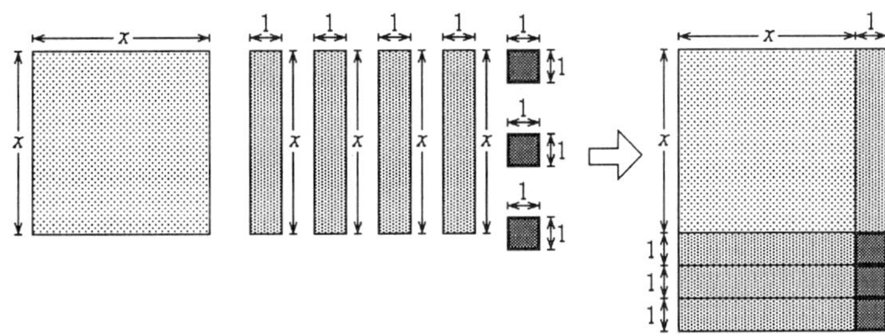

Answer:

$x^2 + 4x + 3 = (x + 3)(x + 1)$

Difficulty: 2

93. Write a polynomial and the correct factorization for the geometric factoring model.

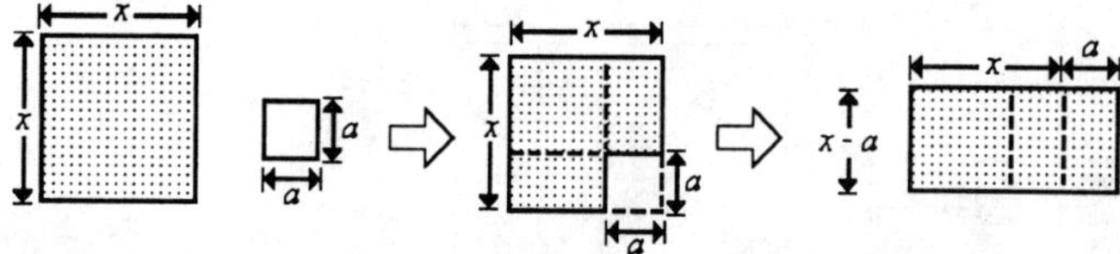

Answer:

$x^2 - a^2 = (x + a)(x - a)$

Difficulty: 2

Chapter 0P4: Rational Expressions

MULTIPLE CHOICE

1. Find the domain: $\frac{1}{2}x^2 + 2x + 1$.

a) $(-\infty, \infty)$ b) $[0, \infty)$ c) $\left[-\infty, \frac{1}{2}\right]\left[\frac{1}{2}, \infty\right]$

d) $\left[\frac{1}{2}, \infty\right]$ e) None of these

Answer: a Difficulty: 1

2. Find the domain: $\frac{3x + 1}{x^2 - 2x}$.

a) $(-\infty, 0)(0, \infty)$ b) $(-\infty, -2)(0, \infty)$

c) $(-\infty, 0)(0, 2)(2, \infty)$ d) $\left[-\infty, \frac{1}{3}\right]\left[\frac{1}{3}, 0\right](0, 2)(2, \infty)$

e) None of these

Answer: c Difficulty: 1

3. Find the domain: $\frac{x + 1}{4 - x^2}$.

a) $(-\infty, \infty)$ b) $(-\infty, -1)(-1, 2)(2, \infty)$

c) $(-\infty, -2)(2, \infty)$ d) $(-\infty, -2)(-2, -1)(-1, 2)(2, \infty)$

e) None of these

Answer: e Difficulty: 1

4. Find the domain: $\sqrt{x + 2}$.

a) $(-\infty, \infty)$ b) $[0, \infty)$ c) $[-2, \infty)$

d) $(-\infty, -2)$ e) None of these

Answer: c Difficulty: 1

5. Find the domain: $\sqrt{3 - x}$.

a) $(-\infty, 3]$ b) $[3, \infty)$ c) $(-\infty, 0]$

d) $(-3, 3)$ e) None of these

Answer: a Difficulty: 1

6. Write: $\frac{x^2 - 8x + 12}{5x - 30}$ in simplest form.

a) $\frac{x - 2}{5}$ b) $\frac{2 + x}{-5}$ c) $\frac{x + 2}{5}$

d) $\frac{-x - 2}{5}$ e) None of these

Answer: a Difficulty: 1

SHORT ANSWER

7. Write in lowest terms: $\dfrac{2x^2 + 5x - 3}{6x - 3}$.

Answer:
$\dfrac{x + 3}{3}$

Difficulty: 1

8. Write in lowest terms: $\dfrac{4x - 2x^2}{x^2 + x - 6}$.

Answer:
$\dfrac{-2x}{x + 3}$

Difficulty: 1

MULTIPLE CHOICE

9. Simplify: $\dfrac{x^2 - 7x + 10}{x^2 - 8x + 15}$.

a) $\dfrac{x + 2}{x + 3}$
b) $\dfrac{x - 2}{x - 3}$
c) $\dfrac{x + 3}{x + 2}$
d) $\dfrac{x - 2}{x + 3}$
e) None of these

Answer: b Difficulty: 1

10. Simplify: $\dfrac{x^2 + 3x - 10}{x^2 + 2x - 15}$.

a) $\dfrac{x - 2}{x - 3}$
b) $\dfrac{x - 3}{x - 2}$
c) $\dfrac{x + 2}{x - 3}$
d) $\dfrac{x + 2}{x + 3}$
e) None of these

Answer: a Difficulty: 1

11. Multiply: $\dfrac{1}{x + y}\left[\dfrac{x}{y} + \dfrac{y}{x}\right]$.

a) $\dfrac{1}{y} + \dfrac{1}{x}$
b) 1
c) $\dfrac{x + y}{xy}$
d) $\dfrac{x^2 + y^2}{xy(x + y)}$
e) None of these

Answer: d Difficulty: 1

12. Multiply, then simplify: $\dfrac{2 - x}{x^2 + 4} \cdot \dfrac{x + 2}{x^2 + 5x - 14}$.

a) $-\dfrac{x + 2}{(x^2 + 4)(x + 7)}$ b) $\dfrac{1}{(x + 2)(x + 7)}$ c) $\dfrac{x + 2}{(x^2 + 4)(x + 7)}$

d) $\dfrac{-1}{(x + 2)(x + 7)}$ e) None of these

Answer: a Difficulty: 1

SHORT ANSWER

13. Multiply, then simplify: $\dfrac{x^2 - 5x + 4}{x^2 + 4} \cdot \dfrac{x + 2}{x^2 + 3x - 4}$.

Answer:

$\dfrac{x^2 - 2x - 8}{(x^2 + 4)(x + 4)}$

Difficulty: 1

MULTIPLE CHOICE

14. Multiply, then simplify: $\dfrac{x^2 + 4x + 4}{x - 2} \cdot \dfrac{2 - x}{3x + 6}$.

a) $\dfrac{x - 2}{3}$ b) $\dfrac{x + 2}{3}$ c) $-\dfrac{x - 2}{3}$

d) $-\dfrac{x + 2}{3}$ e) None of these

Answer: d Difficulty: 1

SHORT ANSWER

15. Divide, then simplify: $\dfrac{x + 1}{x^2 - 1} \div \dfrac{x^2 + 1}{x - 1}$.

Answer:

$\dfrac{1}{x^2 + 1}$

Difficulty: 1

MULTIPLE CHOICE

16. Divide, then simplify: $\frac{x + y}{x^3 - x^2} \div \frac{x^2 + y^2}{x^2 - x}$.

a) $\frac{1}{x(x + y)}$ b) $\frac{x + y}{x(x^2 + y^2)}$ c) $\frac{x(x^2 + y^2)}{x + y}$
d) $-x$ e) None of these

Answer: b Difficulty: 1

17. Divide, then simplify: $\frac{4x - 16}{5x + 15} \div \frac{4 - x}{2x + 6}$.

a) 0 b) $-\frac{4(x - 4)}{5(x + 3)^2}$ c) $-\frac{8}{5}$ d) $-\frac{3}{10}$ e) None of these

Answer: c Difficulty: 1

18. Divide, then simplify: $\frac{x^2 - 2x - 63}{x + 1} \div \frac{9 - x}{x^2 + x}$.

a) 585 b) $-x(x + 7)$ c) $x^2 + 7x$
d) $\frac{x^2 - 2x - 63}{9 - x}$ e) None of these

Answer: b Difficulty: 1

19. Subtract, then simplify: $\frac{1}{x} - \frac{x}{2y}$.

a) $\frac{2y - x}{2xy}$ b) $\frac{1 - x}{2xy}$ c) $\frac{1 - x}{x - 2y}$
d) $\frac{2y - x^2}{2xy}$ e) None of these

Answer: d Difficulty: 1

20. Subtract, then simplify: $\frac{2}{x - 3} - \frac{1}{x + 2}$.

a) $\frac{1}{(x - 3)(x + 2)}$ b) $\frac{x - 1}{(x - 3)(x + 2)}$ c) $\frac{x + 7}{(x - 3)(x + 2)}$
d) $\frac{x + 1}{(x - 3)(x + 2)}$ e) None of these

Answer: c Difficulty: 1

SHORT ANSWER

21. Subtract, then simplify: $\frac{3}{x} - \frac{9}{x + 1}$.

Answer:
$\frac{3(1 - 2x)}{x(x + 1)}$ or $\frac{3 - 6x}{x(x + 1)}$
Difficulty: 1

MULTIPLE CHOICE

22. Add, then simplify: $\frac{4}{x+2} + \frac{7}{x-3}$.

a) $\frac{11}{x-1}$ b) $\frac{11}{2x-1}$ c) $\frac{11x+2}{(x+2)(x-3)}$

d) $\frac{11x+2}{x^2-6}$ e) None of these

Answer: c Difficulty: 1

23. Add, then simplify: $\frac{2}{x^2-9} + \frac{5}{x^2-x-12}$.

a) $\frac{7}{(x^2-9)(x^2-x-12)}$ b) $\frac{7x^2-x-21}{(x^2-9)(x^2-x-12)}$

c) $\frac{7x-7}{(x-3)(x-4)(x+3)}$ d) $\frac{7x-23}{(x-3)(x+3)(x-4)}$

e) None of these

Answer: d Difficulty: 2

24. Subtract, then simplify: $\frac{3}{x^2+2x+1} - \frac{1}{x+1}$.

a) $\frac{4-x}{x^2+2x+1}$ b) $\frac{-x^2+5x+2}{(x+1)(x^2+2x+1)}$

c) $\frac{-x^2+x+2}{(x^2+2x+1)(x+1)}$ d) $\frac{2-x}{x^2+2x+1}$

e) None of these

Answer: d Difficulty: 2

25. Add, then simplify: $\frac{3}{x^2+x-2} + \frac{x}{x^2-x-6}$.

a) $\frac{x^2+2x-9}{(x-3)(x+2)(x-1)}$ b) $\frac{x^3+3x^2-5x-6}{(x^2+x-2)(x^2-x-6)}$

c) $\frac{4x-10}{(x-3)(x+2)(x-1)}$ d) $\frac{3+x}{2x^2-8}$

e) None of these

Answer: a Difficulty: 2

26. Add, then simplify: $\frac{x+1}{x^2+x-2} + \frac{x+3}{x^2-4x+3}$.

a) $\frac{2x^2+3}{(x-1)(x-3)(x+2)}$ b) $\frac{2x^3+x^2-3}{(x^2+x-2)(x^2-4x+3)}$

c) $\frac{2x+4}{-3x+1}$ d) $\frac{2x^2+3x+3}{(x-1)(x-3)(x+2)}$

e) None of these

Answer: d Difficulty: 2

27.

Simplify the complex fraction: $\dfrac{\dfrac{2}{x+1} - \dfrac{x}{x+2}}{\dfrac{1}{x+1}}$.

a) $\dfrac{-x^2 + 3x + 4}{x + 2}$ b) $\dfrac{-x^2 + x + 4}{x + 2}$ c) $\dfrac{2 - x}{x + 2}$

d) $\dfrac{-x^2 + 3x + 3}{(x + 1)(x + 2)}$ e) None of these

Answer: b Difficulty: 1

28.

Simplify the complex fraction: $\dfrac{\dfrac{1}{x} - \dfrac{1}{x+1}}{\dfrac{1}{x^2 + 2x + 1}}$.

a) $x + 1$ b) $\dfrac{x}{x + 1}$ c) $\dfrac{x + 1}{x}$

d) $\dfrac{1}{x(x + 1)(x^2 + 2x + 1)}$ e) None of these

Answer: c Difficulty: 2

29.

Simplify the complex fraction: $\dfrac{\dfrac{1}{x} + \dfrac{7}{x+1}}{\dfrac{1}{x^2 - 1}}$.

a) $\dfrac{8x^2 - 7x - 1}{x}$ b) $\dfrac{8x^2 - 1}{x}$ c) $\dfrac{7x^2 - 6x + 1}{x}$

d) $\dfrac{8x + 1}{x(x + 1)(x^2 - 1)}$ e) None of these

Answer: a Difficulty: 2

30.

Simplify: $\dfrac{\dfrac{1}{x} - \dfrac{1}{y}}{xy}$.

a) $\dfrac{1}{x^2y^2}$ b) $\dfrac{y - x}{x^2y^2}$ c) $\dfrac{x - y}{x^2y^2}$ d) $y - x$ e) None of these

Answer: b Difficulty: 1

31. Simplify: $\dfrac{(3x+5)^{1/3} - \dfrac{x}{(3x+5)^{2/3}}}{(3x+5)^{2/3}}$.

a) $\dfrac{x-1}{(3x+5)^{4/3}}$ b) $\dfrac{9x^2+29x+25}{(3x+5)^{2/3}}$ c) $\dfrac{2x+5}{(3x+5)^{2/3}}$

d) $\dfrac{2x+5}{(3x+5)^{4/3}}$ e) None of these

Answer: d Difficulty: 2

32. Simplify: $\dfrac{(7x+2)^{1/3} - x(7x+2)^{-2/3}}{(7x+2)^{2/3}}$.

a) $\dfrac{6x+2}{(7x+2)^{4/3}}$ b) $\dfrac{6x+2}{(7x+2)^{2/3}}$ c) $\dfrac{49x^2+13x+4}{(7x+2)^{4/3}}$

d) $\dfrac{x+4}{(7x+2)^{4/3}}$ e) None of these

Answer: a Difficulty: 2

SHORT ANSWER

33. Simplify: $\dfrac{(x+2)^{1/2}}{(x+2)^{1/2} - 4(x+2)^{3/2}}$.

Answer:
$-\dfrac{1}{4x+7}$

Difficulty: 2

MULTIPLE CHOICE

34. Simplify: $\dfrac{\sqrt{x} + (6/\sqrt{x})}{\sqrt{x}}$.

a) $\dfrac{6}{x}$ b) $1 + 6\sqrt{x}$ c) $\dfrac{x + 6\sqrt{x}}{x}$

d) $\dfrac{x+6}{x}$ e) None of these

Answer: d Difficulty: 2

35. Simplify: $\frac{\sqrt{1 + x} - (x/\sqrt{1 + x})}{1 + x}$.

a) $\frac{1 + 2\sqrt{1 + x}}{1 + x}$
b) $\frac{-x + \sqrt{1 + x}}{(1 + x)\sqrt{1 + x}}$
c) $\frac{1}{1 + x}$
d) $\frac{\sqrt{1 + x}}{(1 + x)^2}$
e) None of these

Answer: d Difficulty: 2

SHORT ANSWER

36. Simplify: $\frac{(3/\sqrt{x + 2}) - \sqrt{x + 2}}{5\sqrt{x + 2}}$.

Answer:
$\frac{1 - x}{5(x + 2)}$
Difficulty: 2

37. Rationalize the denominator: $\frac{x}{3 - \sqrt{x + 9}}$.

Answer:
$-(3 + \sqrt{x + 9})$
Difficulty: 2

MULTIPLE CHOICE

38. The efficiency of a Carnot engine can be determined by using the formula Eff $= 1 - \frac{T_2}{T_1}$. Write this as a single fraction.

a) $\frac{T_1}{1 - T_2}$
b) $\frac{1 - T_2}{T_1}$
c) $\frac{T_1 - T_2}{T_1}$
d) $\frac{T_1 - T_2}{T_1 T_2}$
e) None of these

Answer: c Difficulty: 1

39. After working for t hours on a common task, the fractional part of the job done by three workers is $t/2$, $t/3$, and $t/12$. What fractional part of the task has been completed?

a) $\frac{3t}{17}$ b) $\frac{11t}{12}$ c) $\frac{t^3}{72}$ d) $\frac{t}{4}$ e) None of these

Answer: b Difficulty: 1

40. After working for t hours on a common task, the fractional part of the job done by three workers is $t/5$, $t/3$, and $2t/5$. What fractional part of the task has been completed?

a) $\frac{4t}{13}$ b) $\frac{4t}{15}$ c) $\frac{9t}{15}$ d) $\frac{14t}{15}$ e) None of these

Answer: d Difficulty: 1

41. After working for t hours on a common task, the fractional part of the job done by two workers is $t/3$, and $t/2$. What fractional part of the task has *not* been completed?

a) $\frac{5t}{6}$ b) $\frac{3t}{5}$ c) $\frac{t}{6}$ d) $\frac{6 - t^2}{6}$ e) None of these

Answer: c Difficulty: 1

42. After working for t hours on a common task, the fractional part of the job done by two workers is $t/5$, and $t/2$. What fractional part of the task has *not* been completed?

a) $\frac{7t}{10}$ b) $\frac{3t}{10}$ c) $\frac{4t}{5}$ d) $\frac{10 - t^2}{10}$ e) None of these

Answer: b Difficulty: 1

SHORT ANSWER

43. Determine the average of the two real numbers $\frac{x}{10}$ and $\frac{x}{2}$.

Answer:
$\frac{3x}{10}$

Difficulty: 1

44. Determine the average of the three real numbers $\frac{x}{5}$, $\frac{x}{3}$, and $\frac{x}{6}$.

Answer:
$\frac{7x}{30}$

Difficulty: 1

45. Find two real numbers that divide the real number line between $\frac{x}{9}$ and $\frac{x}{2}$ into three equal parts.

Answer:
$x_1 = \frac{13x}{54}$, $x_2 = \frac{10x}{27}$

Difficulty: 2

46. Find three real numbers that divide the real number line between $\frac{x}{10}$ and $\frac{x}{5}$ into four equal parts.

Answer:
$x_1 = \frac{x}{8}$, $x_2 = \frac{3x}{20}$, and $x_3 = \frac{7x}{40}$

Difficulty: 2

47. A marble is tossed into a box whose base is shown. Find the probability that the marble will come to rest in the shaded portion of the box.

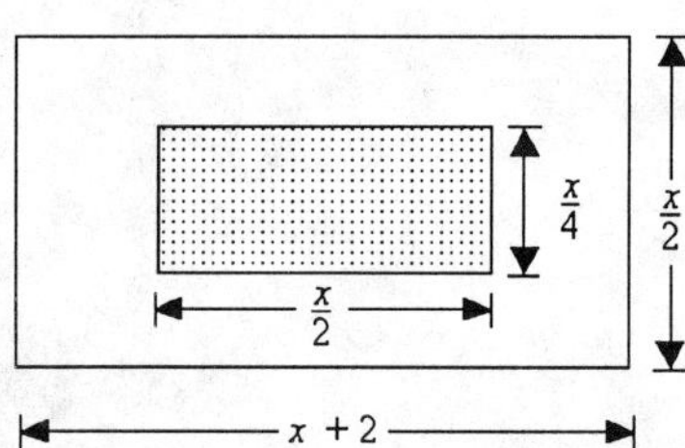

Answer:
$\frac{x}{4(x + 2)}$

Difficulty: 2

48. A marble is tossed into a triangle whose base is shown. Find the probability that the marble will come to rest in the shaded portion of the triangle.

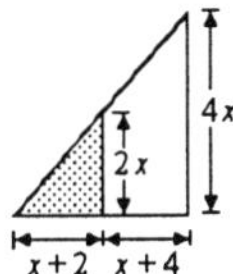

Answer:
$$\frac{x + 2}{4(x + 3)}$$

Difficulty: 2

Chapter 0P5: Solving Equations

MULTIPLE CHOICE

1. Is $3x + 4(x - 2) = 10x$ a conditional equation or an identity?
a) Conditional b) Identity c) Neither d) Both

Answer: a Difficulty: 1

2. Is $3(x^2 + 2) = 5x^2 - 9$ a conditional equation or an identity?
a) Conditional b) Identity c) Neither d) Both

Answer: a Difficulty: 1

SHORT ANSWER

3. Is $3x + 2 = 9x^2 - 1$ a conditional equation or an identity?

Answer: Conditional Difficulty: 1

MULTIPLE CHOICE

4. Is $3(x^2 + 2x) = 7 + 3x^2$ a conditional equation or an identity?
a) Conditional b) Identity c) Neither d) Both

Answer: a Difficulty: 1

5. Is $2x + (3 - x)(3 + x) + 1 = 2 - (x - 4)(x + 2)$ a conditional equation or an identity?
a) Conditional b) Identity c) Neither d) Both

Answer: b Difficulty: 1

6. Is $3 + \frac{3}{x - 1} = \frac{3x}{x - 1}$ a conditional equation or an identity?
a) Conditional b) Identity c) Neither d) Both

Answer: b Difficulty: 1

7. Solve for x: $8x - 2 = 13 - 2x$.
a) $\frac{2}{3}$ b) $\frac{3}{2}$ c) $\frac{11}{6}$ d) $-\frac{2}{3}$ e) None of these

Answer: b Difficulty: 1

8. Solve for x: $7 - 3x + 3 = 4 + 2x - 6$.
a) $x = 2$ b) $x = \frac{1}{2}$ c) $x = \frac{12}{5}$
d) There is no solution. e) None of these

Answer: c Difficulty: 1

9. Solve for x: $2 - 3x + 3 = 1 + 2x + 2$.
   a) $x = -\frac{2}{5}$ b) $x = \frac{5}{2}$ c) $x = 0$
   d) There is no solution. e) None of these

   Answer: e Difficulty: 1

10. Solve for x: $13x - 9 = 3x + 10$.
   a) $\frac{19}{10}$ b) $\frac{10}{19}$ c) $\frac{1}{10}$ d) $\frac{19}{16}$ e) None of these

   Answer: a Difficulty: 1

11. Solve for x: $7 - 3x + 2 = 4x - 1$.
   a) 5 b) 10 c) $\frac{7}{10}$ d) $\frac{10}{7}$ e) None of these

   Answer: d Difficulty: 1

12. Solve for x: $4 + 7x - 3x + 2 = 8x + 6$.
   a) There is no solution. b) 0 c) 1 d) 2 e) None of these

   Answer: b Difficulty: 1

13. Solve for x: $2 - 6 + 3x = 3x + 7$.
   a) $x = -\frac{11}{6}$ b) $x = \frac{11}{6}$ c) $x = \frac{1}{6}$
   d) There is no solution. e) None of these

   Answer: d Difficulty: 1

14. Solve for x: $0.3x - 4 = 2$.
   a) 2 b) $\frac{9}{5}$ c) 20 d) $-\frac{20}{3}$ e) None of these

   Answer: c Difficulty: 1

15. Solve for x: $4x - 7(3x + 6) = 4x - 9$.
   a) $\frac{7}{11}$ b) $-\frac{11}{7}$ c) $-\frac{33}{13}$ d) $-\frac{17}{7}$ e) None of these

   Answer: b Difficulty: 1

SHORT ANSWER

16. Solve for x: $5(3x - 2) + 5x - 7 = 16 + 2x$.

   Answer:
   $\frac{11}{6}$

   Difficulty: 1

MULTIPLE CHOICE

17. Solve for x: $2[x - (3x + 1)] = 4 - 2x$.
    a) -1 b) -3 c) 1 d) $-\frac{1}{3}$ e) None of these

    Answer: b Difficulty: 2

SHORT ANSWER

18. Solve the equation $4(x + 3) + (6 - x) = 0$.

    Answer: $x = -6$ Difficulty: 1

19. Solve the equation $2(2 - x) = 3(x + 8)$.

    Answer: $x = -4$ Difficulty: 1

20. Solve the equation $3(x + 3) = 2 - (1 - 2x)$.

    Answer: $x = -8$ Difficulty: 1

21. Solve the equation $3(x - 6) = 2 + 2(x - 5)$.

    Answer: $x = 10$ Difficulty: 1

MULTIPLE CHOICE

22. The solution to the linear equation $2 - 3[7 - 2(4 - x)] = 2x - 1$ is:
    a) $x = -\frac{3}{4}$. b) $x = \frac{4}{3}$. c) $x = \frac{3}{4}$. d) $x = -\frac{4}{3}$. e) None of these

    Answer: c Difficulty: 1

23. The solution to the linear equation $3x - [x - 2(3 - 2x)] = -5$ is:
    a) $x = \frac{2}{11}$. b) $x = \frac{11}{2}$. c) $x = -\frac{2}{11}$. d) $x = -\frac{11}{2}$. e) None of these

    Answer: b Difficulty: 1

24. The solution to the linear equation $3x - [2(3 - 2x) - x] = 4$ is:
    a) $x = \frac{5}{4}$. b) $x = -\frac{4}{5}$. c) $x = -\frac{5}{4}$. d) $x = \frac{4}{5}$. e) None of these

    Answer: a Difficulty: 1

SHORT ANSWER

25. Solve the equation $3x - [5 - 2(1 - 2x)] = 7x - 5$.

Answer:
$x = \frac{1}{4}$

Difficulty: 1

26. Solve the equation $3x + [2(1 - 2x) + 5] = 5 - 7x$.

Answer:
$x = -\frac{1}{3}$

Difficulty: 1

27. Solve the equation $3x - [5 - 2(1 - 2x)] = 5 - 7x$.

Answer:
$x = \frac{4}{3}$

Difficulty: 1

28. Solve the equation $3x - [2(1 - 2x) - 5] = 5 - 7x$.

Answer:
$x = \frac{1}{7}$

Difficulty: 1

MULTIPLE CHOICE

29. Determine which of the following is a solution of the equation $2(1 - x) - (4x + 3) = 11$.
a) 2 b) -2 c) 1 d) -3 e) None of these

Answer: b Difficulty: 1

30. Determine which of the following is a solution of the equation $2(3x - 6) - 3(5 - x) = 9$.
a) -2 b) 5 c) 2 d) 4 e) None of these

Answer: d Difficulty: 1

31. Solve for x: $0.15x + 0.10(30 - x) = 20$.
a) -56 b) 340 c) 1695 d) $\frac{850}{7}$ e) None of these

Answer: b Difficulty: 2

32. Solve for r: $6390 = 6000(1 + r)$.
a) 0.07 b) 0.065 c) 0.06 d) 0.09 e) None of these

Answer: b Difficulty: 1

33. Solve for x: $3[2x - (7x - 1)] = 5x + 13$.
a) $\frac{4}{5}$ b) -2 c) $\frac{7}{13}$ d) $-\frac{1}{2}$ e) None of these

Answer: d Difficulty: 2

SHORT ANSWER

34. Solve for x: $\frac{3x}{5} + x = \frac{2}{3}$.

Answer:
$\frac{5}{12}$
Difficulty: 2

MULTIPLE CHOICE

35. Solve for x: $\frac{4x + 1}{4} - \frac{2x + 3}{3} = \frac{7}{12}$.
a) 4 b) $\frac{9}{2}$ c) -2 d) $\frac{3}{2}$ e) None of these

Answer: a Difficulty: 2

36. Solve for x: $\frac{3x}{2} - \frac{x + 1}{4} = 6$.
a) 5 b) $\frac{23}{5}$ c) $\frac{35}{8}$ d) $\frac{1}{2}$ e) None of these

Answer: a Difficulty: 1

37. Solve for x: $\frac{3}{4}x - \frac{1}{2}(x + 5) = 2$.
a) -2 b) 18 c) 26 d) 28 e) None of these

Answer: b Difficulty: 1

38. Solve for x: $\frac{3x + 2}{5} - \frac{6x + 4}{3} = \frac{14}{3}$.

a) $-\frac{44}{21}$ b) 5 c) $\frac{37}{12}$ d) -4 e) None of these

Answer: d Difficulty: 1

SHORT ANSWER

39. Solve for x: $\frac{2x - 5}{x - 3} = \frac{4x + 1}{2x}$.

Answer: -3 Difficulty: 2

MULTIPLE CHOICE

40. Solve for x: $3 - \frac{4x + 5}{x - 2} = \frac{7x - 9}{x - 2}$.

a) $-\frac{1}{4}$ b) -1 c) 1 d) No solution e) None of these

Answer: a Difficulty: 2

41. Solve for x: $\frac{7x}{x - 2} + \frac{2x}{x + 2} = 9$.

a) $-\frac{18}{5}$ b) $\frac{2}{3}$ c) $-\frac{2}{5}$ d) $\frac{5}{18}$ e) None of these

Answer: a Difficulty: 2

42. Solve for x: $\frac{4}{x} = \frac{7}{3}$.

a) $\frac{7}{12}$ b) $\frac{3}{28}$ c) $\frac{28}{3}$ d) $\frac{12}{7}$ e) None of these

Answer: d Difficulty: 1

43. Solve for x: $8 = 3 + \frac{2}{x}$.

a) $\frac{2}{5}$ b) $\frac{5}{2}$ c) $\frac{8}{5}$ d) $\frac{4}{3}$ e) None of these

Answer: a Difficulty: 1

44. Solve for x: $\frac{1}{x - 2} + \frac{3}{x + 3} = \frac{4}{x^2 + x - 6}$.

a) $\frac{4}{7}$ b) 3 c) $\frac{7}{4}$ d) 1 e) None of these

Answer: c Difficulty: 1

45. Solve for x: $\frac{1}{x - 3} - \frac{2}{x + 3} = \frac{2x}{x^2 - 9}$.
a) $-\frac{1}{2}$ b) 3 c) -3 d) -3 and 3 e) None of these

Answer: e Difficulty: 1

46. Solve $0.134x + 0.12(250 - x) = 50$ for x. Round your result to two decimal places.
a) 1428.57 b) 5624.30 c) 3562.86 d) -23.09 e) None of these

Answer: a Difficulty: 1

47. Solve $1.93(x - 1) + 0.911x = 65.3$ for x. Round your result to two decimal places.
a) 23.34 b) 0.04 c) 22.31 d) 23.66 e) None of these

Answer: d Difficulty: 1

48. Solve $2.25(x - 2) + 0.365x = 52.2$ for x. Round your result to two decimal places.
a) 20.73 b) 19.20 c) 18.24 d) 21.68 e) None of these

Answer: d Difficulty: 2

SHORT ANSWER

49. Solve $0.55 + 13.9(2.1 - x) = 14$ for x. Round your result to two decimal places.

Answer: 1.13 Difficulty: 2

50. Solve $0.68 + 12.5(3.2 - x) = 16$ for x. Round your result to two decimal places.

Answer: 1.97 Difficulty: 2

51. Solve the equation and round your answer to two decimal places:

$$1.576x + 4 = 5.5.$$

Answer: $x = 0.95$ Difficulty: 1

52. Solve the equation and round your answer to two decimal places:

$$315x - 267 = 25x + 765.$$

Answer: $x = 3.56$ Difficulty: 1

53. Solve the equation and round your answer to two decimal places:

$$\frac{x}{5.25} = 3x + 10.25.$$

Answer: $x = -3.65$ Difficulty: 2

54. Solve the equation and round your answer to two decimal places:

$$5x + \frac{5.2}{6} = \frac{3}{2}.$$

Answer: $x = 0.13$ Difficulty: 2

MULTIPLE CHOICE

55. The handicap, H, for the bowler with an average score, A, of less than 200 is determined using the formula $H = 0.8(200 - A)$. Find a bowler's average score if his handicap is 64.
a) 110 b) 120 c) 130 d) 140 e) None of these

Answer: b Difficulty: 1

56. The handicap, H, for the bowler with an average score, A, of less than 200 is determined using the formula $H = 0.8(200 - A)$. Find a bowler's average score if his handicap is 8.
a) 160 b) 170 c) 180 d) 190 e) None of these

Answer: d Difficulty: 1

57. The handicap, H, for the bowler with an average score, A, of less than 200 is determined using the formula $H = 0.8(200 - A)$. Find a bowler's average score if his handicap is 32.
a) 160 b) 170 c) 180 d) 190 e) None of these

Answer: a Difficulty: 1

SHORT ANSWER

58. The cost of x hundred pounds of fertilizer produced is given by $C = 0.55x + 210$. How many pounds of fertilizer cost $328.25?

Answer: 215 pounds Difficulty: 1

59. The formula that converts Celsius temperature to Fahrenheit temperature is $F = \frac{9}{5}C + 32$. Find the Celsius temperature that corresponds to 98.6 °F.

Answer: 37° C Difficulty: 2

60. A new coffee shop has determined that its profit is growing according to the equation $P = 180t - 200$ where t is time in months with $t = 1$ corresponding to January. Determine the month its profit will reach $1780.

Answer: $t = 11$; November Difficulty: 2

MULTIPLE CHOICE

61. Write the quadratic equation in standard form: $x^2 - 4x = x + 2$.
    a) $x^2 - 3x = 2$ b) $x^2 - 5x = 2$ c) $x^2 - 5x - 2 = 0$
    d) $x^2 = 3x - 2$ e) None of these

    Answer: c Difficulty: 1

62. Write the quadratic equation in standard form: $\frac{3}{x + 7} - \frac{4}{x + 2} = 6$.
    a) $6x^2 - 55x + 106 = 0$ b) $6x^2 + 55x + 72 = 0$ c) $6x^2 - x + 106 = 0$
    d) $6x^2 - x = 72$ e) None of these

    Answer: a Difficulty: 2

63. Write the quadratic equation in standard form: $x^2 = 64x$.
    a) $x^2 = 64x$ b) $x^2 - 64x = 0$ c) $x - 64 = 0$
    d) $64 - x^2 = 0$ e) None of these

    Answer: b Difficulty: 1

64. Write the quadratic equation in standard form: $\frac{1}{x + 1} - \frac{3}{x - 2} = 5$.
    a) $x = -5$ b) $2x - 6 = 0$ c) $5x^2 + 2x - 5 = 0$
    d) $5x^2 - 3x - 5 = 0$ e) None of these

    Answer: d Difficulty: 1

65. Write the quadratic equation in standard form: $x^2 + 1 = \frac{3x - 2}{5}$.
    a) $x^2 - \frac{3}{5}x + 3 = 0$ b) $5x^2 - 3x + 15 = 0$ c) $5x^2 - 3x + 7 = 0$
    d) $5x^2 - 3x + 3 = 0$ e) None of these

    Answer: c Difficulty: 1

66. Solve for x: $5x^2 - 2 = 3x$.
    a) $\frac{2}{5}, -1$ b) $-\frac{1}{5}, 2$ c) $-\frac{2}{5}, 1$ d) $\frac{1}{5}, -2$ e) None of these

    Answer: c Difficulty: 2

67. Solve for x: $2x^2 + 4x = 9x + 18$.
    a) $-2, \frac{9}{2}$ b) $2, -\frac{9}{2}$ c) $\frac{9}{2}$ d) $-\frac{9}{2}$ e) None of these

    Answer: a Difficulty: 1

SHORT ANSWER

68. Solve for x: $4x^2 + 12x + 9 = 0$.

Answer:
$-\frac{3}{2}$

Difficulty: 1

69. Solve for x: $3x^2 + 19x - 14 = 0$.

Answer:
$-7, \frac{2}{3}$

Difficulty: 1

70. Solve for x: $2x^2 + x = 3$.

Answer:
$-\frac{3}{2}, 1$

Difficulty: 1

MULTIPLE CHOICE

71. Solve for x: $2x^2 = 162$.
a) 9 b) -9 c) -9, 9 d) 81 e) None of these

Answer: c Difficulty: 1

SHORT ANSWER

72. Solve for x: $7(x + 2)^2 = 12$.

Answer:
$\frac{1}{7}(-14 \pm 2\sqrt{21})$

Difficulty: 1

73. Solve for x: $(x + 7)^2 = 5$.

Answer:
$-7 \pm \sqrt{5}$

Difficulty: 1

MULTIPLE CHOICE

74. Solve for x: $3x^2 = 192$.
a) ± 8 b) 8 c) -1 d) 64 e) None of these

Answer: a Difficulty: 1

75. Solve for x: $(2x + 3)^2 = 4$.
a) $\frac{1}{2}, \frac{5}{2}$ b) $-\frac{1}{2}$ c) $-\frac{5}{2}, -\frac{1}{2}$ d) ± 2 e) None of these

Answer: c Difficulty: 1

SHORT ANSWER

76. Solve by completing the square: $x^2 - 8x + 2 = 0$.

Answer:

$4 \pm \sqrt{14}$

Difficulty: 1

MULTIPLE CHOICE

77. Solve by completing the square: $x^2 + 4x - 2 = 0$.
a) $2 \pm \sqrt{6}$ b) $2 \pm \sqrt{2}$ c) $-2 \pm \sqrt{2}$ d) $-2 \pm \sqrt{6}$ e) None of these

Answer: d Difficulty: 1

78. Solve by completing the square: $x^2 - 6x + 1 = 0$.
a) $3 \pm \sqrt{26}$ b) $3 \pm \sqrt{10}$ c) $3 \pm \sqrt{17}$
d) $3 \pm 2\sqrt{2}$ e) None of these

Answer: d Difficulty: 1

79. Solve by completing the square: $1 - x = x(x + 3)$.
a) $x = -\frac{3}{2} \pm \frac{\sqrt{13}}{2}$ b) $-2 \pm \sqrt{5}$ c) $-1 \pm \sqrt{2}$
d) $\frac{3}{2} \pm \frac{\sqrt{11}}{2}$ e) None of these

Answer: b Difficulty: 1

80. Solve by completing the square: $6x - x^2 = 3$.
a) $-3 \pm 2\sqrt{3}$ b) $3 \pm \sqrt{6}$ c) $3 \pm 2\sqrt{3}$ d) 3, 9 e) None of these

Answer: b Difficulty: 1

81. Solve by completing the square: $2x^2 - 8x + 5 = 0$.
a) $2 \pm \frac{\sqrt{6}}{2}$
b) $-2 \pm \frac{\sqrt{3}}{2}$
c) $4 \pm \frac{\sqrt{19}}{2}$
d) $8 \pm \frac{\sqrt{5}}{2}$
e) None of these

Answer: a Difficulty: 2

82. Solve by completing the square: $3x^2 + 18x - 22 = 0$.
a) $-18 \pm \frac{\sqrt{22}}{3}$
b) $-3 \pm \frac{\sqrt{15}}{3}$
c) $-3 \pm \frac{4\sqrt{2}}{3}$
d) $6 \pm \frac{3\sqrt{3}}{5}$
e) None of these

Answer: e Difficulty: 2

83. Solve by completing the square: $7x^2 - 14x + 6 = 0$.
a) $1 \pm \frac{\sqrt{-5}}{7}$
b) $14 \pm \frac{\sqrt{6}}{7}$
c) $1 \pm \frac{5\sqrt{2}}{7}$
d) $1 \pm \frac{\sqrt{7}}{7}$
e) None of these

Answer: d Difficulty: 2

84. Solve by completing the square: $4x^2 - 16x - 13 = 0$.
a) $2 \pm \frac{\sqrt{17}}{2}$
b) $4 \pm \frac{\sqrt{17}}{4}$
c) $2 \pm \frac{\sqrt{3}}{2}$
d) $-2 \pm \frac{\sqrt{-9}}{2}$
e) None of these

Answer: e Difficulty: 2

85. Solve by completing the square: $2x^2 + 12x + 13 = 0$.
a) $-6 \pm \frac{\sqrt{13}}{2}$
b) $-3 \pm \frac{\sqrt{10}}{2}$
c) $\frac{3 \pm \sqrt{5}}{2}$
d) $\pm \frac{\sqrt{23}}{2}$
e) None of these

Answer: b Difficulty: 2

SHORT ANSWER

86. Solve by completing the square: $2x^2 - 7x - 12 = 0$.

Answer:
$\frac{1}{4}(7 \pm \sqrt{145})$

Difficulty: 2

MULTIPLE CHOICE

87. Solve for x: $\frac{3x + 25}{x + 7} - 5 = \frac{3}{x}$.

a) $\frac{3}{2}, 7$ b) $\frac{7}{2}, 3$ c) $-\frac{3}{2}, -7$ d) $-\frac{7}{2}, -3$ e) None of these

Answer: d Difficulty: 1

88. Complete the square: $2x^2 + 9x - 4$.

a) $2\left(x + \frac{9}{4}\right)^2 - \frac{113}{8}$ b) $2\left(x + \frac{9}{4}\right)^2 - \frac{145}{16}$ c) $2\left(x + \frac{9}{4}\right)^2 + \frac{49}{8}$

d) $2\left(x + \frac{9}{4}\right)^2 + \frac{17}{16}$ e) None of these

Answer: a Difficulty: 2

89. Complete the square: $3x^2 - 2x + 1$.

a) $(3x - 1)^2$ b) $3(x - 1)^2 + 1$ c) $3\left(x - \frac{1}{3}\right)^2 + \frac{1}{9}$

d) $3\left(x - \frac{1}{3}\right)^2 + \frac{2}{3}$ e) None of these

Answer: d Difficulty: 2

SHORT ANSWER

90. Complete the square: $2x^2 - 6x + 9$.

Answer:

$2\left(x - \frac{3}{2}\right)^2 + \frac{9}{2}$

Difficulty: 2

MULTIPLE CHOICE

91. Complete the square in the denominator: $\frac{3}{4x^2 + 10x - 7}$.

a) $\frac{3}{4\left(x + \frac{5}{4}\right)^2 - \frac{53}{4}}$ b) $\frac{3}{4\left(x + \frac{5}{2}\right)^2 - 32}$ c) $\frac{3}{4\left(x + \frac{5}{4}\right)^2 - \frac{3}{4}}$

d) $\frac{3}{4\left(x + \frac{5}{2}\right)^2 + 18}$ e) None of these

Answer: a Difficulty: 2

92. Complete the square in the denominator: $\dfrac{5}{2x^2 - 3x + 1}$.

a) $\dfrac{5}{2\left[x - \frac{3}{2}\right]^2 + \frac{13}{4}}$
b) $\dfrac{5}{2\left[x - \frac{3}{2}\right]^2 + 1}$
c) $\dfrac{5}{2\left[x - \frac{3}{4}\right]^2 + \frac{11}{2}}$
d) $\dfrac{5}{2\left[x - \frac{3}{2}\right] - \frac{5}{4}}$
e) None of these

Answer: e Difficulty: 2

93. Identify the Quadratic Formula.

a) $x = -b \pm \dfrac{\sqrt{b^2 - 4ac}}{2a}$
b) $x = \dfrac{-b \pm \sqrt{b^2 - 4a}}{2c}$
c) $x = \dfrac{-b \pm \sqrt{b^2 - 4ac}}{2a}$
d) $x = \dfrac{-b \pm \sqrt{b^2 - 4ac}}{2}$
e) None of these

Answer: c Difficulty: 1

SHORT ANSWER

94. Solve for x: $x^2 - 3x + \dfrac{3}{2} = 0$.

Answer:

$\dfrac{3 \pm \sqrt{3}}{2}$

Difficulty: 1

95. Solve for x: $-3x^2 + 4x + 6 = 0$.

Answer:

$\dfrac{2 \pm \sqrt{22}}{3}$

Difficulty: 1

MULTIPLE CHOICE

96. Solve for x: $(x + 2)^2 = -16x$.

a) $-8 \pm 2\sqrt{15}$
b) $-10 \pm 4\sqrt{6}$
c) $-10 \pm 2\sqrt{26}$
d) $-8 \pm 4\sqrt{15}$
e) None of these

Answer: b Difficulty: 1

SHORT ANSWER

97. Solve for x: $\frac{1}{x - 1} + \frac{x}{x + 2} = 2$.

Answer:

$-1 \pm \sqrt{7}$

Difficulty: 1

MULTIPLE CHOICE

98. Solve for x: $3x^2 - 6x + 2 = 0$.
a) $\frac{3 \pm \sqrt{3}}{3}$ b) $1 \pm \sqrt{3}$ c) $\frac{3 \pm \sqrt{15}}{3}$ d) $\frac{1}{3}, 2$ e) None of these

Answer: a Difficulty: 1

99. Solve for x: $(x - 1)^2 = 3x + 5$.
a) 1, 4 b) $\frac{5 \pm \sqrt{39}}{2}$ c) $\frac{5 \pm \sqrt{41}}{2}$ d) -1, 6 e) None of these

Answer: c Difficulty: 2

100. Solve for x: $4x^2 + 12x = 135$.
a) $-\frac{9}{2}, \frac{15}{2}$ b) $-\frac{5}{2}, \frac{3}{2}$ c) $-\frac{15}{2}, \frac{9}{2}$ d) $\frac{-3 \pm \sqrt{6}}{2}$ e) None of these

Answer: c Difficulty: 2

101. Use a calculator to solve: $2.5x^2 + 3.267x - 8.97 = 0$. Round your answers to three decimal places.
a) -6.643, 3.376 b) -5.271, -1.263 c) -8.276, 1.742
d) -2.657, 1.350 e) None of these

Answer: d Difficulty: 2 Key 1: T

102. Use a calculator to solve: $1.37x^2 - 2.4x - 5.41 = 0$. Round your answers to three decimal places.
a) 0.228, 4.572 b) -1.296, 3.048 c) -1.775, 4.175
d) -5.720, 2.432 e) None of these

Answer: b Difficulty: 2 Key 1: T

103. Use a calculator to solve: $3x^2 - 0.24x - 0.57 = 0$. Round your answers to three decimal places.
a) 0.478, -0.398 b) 0.474, -0.394 c) 1.434, -1.194
d) 1.422, -1.182 e) None of these

Answer: a Difficulty: 1 Key 1: T

104. Use a calculator to solve: $27x^2 - 3.2x - 71 = 0$. Round your answers to three decimal places.
a) 1.680, -1.561 b) 1.682, -1.563 c) -1.678, 1.623
d) -1.680, 1.569 e) None of these

Answer: b Difficulty: 2 Key 1: T

105. Use a calculator to solve: $3x^2 - 0.482x - 1.2 = 0$. Round your answers to three decimal places.
a) -0.557, 0.718 b) -0.718, 0.557 c) -1.671, 2.154
d) -0.547, 0.708 e) None of these

Answer: a Difficulty: 2 Key 1: T

106. Use a calculator to solve: $62x^2 - 78.2x + 5.1 = 0$. Round your answers to three decimal places.
a) -0.062, 1.323 b) -3.244, 1.983 c) 0.069, 1.192
d) 4.277, 73.903 e) None of these

Answer: c Difficulty: 2 Key 1: T

107. Use a calculator to solve: $3.2x^2 + 0.61x - 7.4 = 0$. Round your answers to three decimal places.
a) -1.619, 1.428 b) -0.842, 2.748 c) -5.181, 4.570
d) -0.617, 1.529 e) None of these

Answer: a Difficulty: 2 Key 1: T

108. Solve for x: $2x^2 - 5(x - 1) = 3(x + 5)$.
a) $\frac{1 \pm \sqrt{39}}{2}$ b) $\pm\frac{\sqrt{15}}{3}$ c) 0, 1, -5 d) -1, 5 e) None of these

Answer: d Difficulty: 2

109. Solve for x: $(2x + 5)^2 = 9$.
a) -4, -1 b) -1 c) 38 d) 14, 8 e) None of these

Answer: a Difficulty: 1

110. Solve for x: $\frac{2}{5}x^2 - \frac{1}{2} = 0$.
a) $\pm\frac{\sqrt{2}}{5}$ b) $\pm\frac{\sqrt{5}}{5}$ c) $\pm\frac{5\sqrt{2}}{4}$ d) $\pm\frac{1}{2}\sqrt{5}$ e) None of these

Answer: d Difficulty: 1

111. Solve for x: $4x + 3(x^2 - 1) = 2 + 3x^2$.
a) $\pm\frac{\sqrt{5}}{2}$ b) $\frac{5}{4}$ c) $\frac{2 \pm \sqrt{34}}{12}$ d) $\frac{-2 \pm \sqrt{10}}{6}$ e) None of these

Answer: b Difficulty: 1

112. Solve for x: $(x - 2)(x + 1) = (x - 3)^2$.
a) $\frac{11}{5}$ b) 2, 9 c) 11 d) 7, -2 e) None of these

Answer: a Difficulty: 1

113. Solve for x: $2x^2 - 5x = x^2 + 1$.
a) 0, 5 b) $\frac{4}{11}$ c) $\frac{5 \pm \sqrt{29}}{2}$ d) $\frac{-5 \pm \sqrt{21}}{2}$ e) None of these

Answer: c Difficulty: 1

114. Solve for x: $(x + 1)^2 + x^2 = 9$.
a) 8 b) ± 2 c) $\frac{1 \pm \sqrt{15}}{2}$ d) $\frac{-1 \pm \sqrt{17}}{2}$ e) None of these

Answer: d Difficulty: 1

115. Solve for x: $(x - 1)^2 + (x + 1)^2 = 100$.
a) $\pm 5\sqrt{2}$ b) $\pm 2\sqrt{5}$ c) ± 7 d) -4, 6 e) None of these

Answer: c Difficulty: 1

116. Two airplanes leave simultaneously from the same airport, one flying due east, and the other flying due north. The eastbound plane is flying 50 miles per hour slower than the northbound one. If after 4 hours they are 1000 miles apart, how fast is the northbound plane traveling?
a) 150 mph b) 200 mph c) 100 mph
d) 300 mph e) None of these

Answer: b Difficulty: 2

117. An open box is to be constructed from a square piece of material by cutting a 3-inch square from each corner. Find the dimensions of the square piece of material if the box is to have a volume of 363 cubic inches.
a) 14" by 14" b) 17" by 17" c) 20" by 20"
d) 23" by 23" e) None of these

Answer: b Difficulty: 2

SHORT ANSWER

118. Find two consecutive positive integers m and n such that $n^2 - m^2 = 27$.

Answer: 13, 14 Difficulty: 2

119. The Curriers have decided to fence in part of their back yard to form a rectangular region with an area of 1248 square feet. The fence will extend 2 feet on each side of their 48-foot wide house. How many feet of fencing will they need to enclose the play area? (There is no fence along the house wall.)

Answer: 104 feet Difficulty: 2

MULTIPLE CHOICE

120. Use the cost equation, $C = 0.5x^2 + 15x + 6000$, to find the number of units, x, that a manufacturer can produce with a total cost, C, of $13,700.
a) 140 b) 110 c) 94,056,500 d) 47,134,000 e) None of these

Answer: b Difficulty: 2

121. The daily cost in dollars, C, of producing x chairs is given by the quadratic equation $C = x^2 - 120x + 4200$. How many chairs are produced each day if the daily cost is $600?
a) 60 b) 600 c) 90 d) 40 e) None of these

Answer: a Difficulty: 2

122. You plan to stabilize a T.V. antenna with two guy wires. The guy wires are attached to the antenna 30 feet from the base. How much wire will you need if each of the wires is secured 20 feet from the base of the antenna?
a) $10\sqrt{13}$ ft b) $20\sqrt{5}$ ft c) $20\sqrt{13}$ ft
d) $10\sqrt{5}$ ft e) None of these

Answer: c Difficulty: 2

123. Find the smaller of two consecutive positive integers such that the one number times twice the other equals 612.
a) -18 b) 12 c) 18 d) 17 e) None of these

Answer: d Difficulty: 2

SHORT ANSWER

124. Find two consecutive *odd* numbers whose product is 483.

Answer: 21 and 23 Difficulty: 1

125. Find two consecutive *even* numbers whose product is 288.

Answer: 16 and 18 Difficulty: 1

126. Find two consecutive *odd* numbers, the sum of whose squares is 394.

Answer: 13 and 15 Difficulty: 1

127. Find two consecutive *even* numbers, the sum of whose squares is 724.

Answer: 18 and 20 Difficulty: 1

128. The area of a rectangle is 56 square yards. Its length is 2 yards more than three times its width. Find its dimensions.

Answer: 4 yards by 14 yards Difficulty: 1

129. The area of a rectangle is 221 square feet. Its perimeter is 60 feet. Find its dimensions.

Answer: 17 feet by 13 feet Difficulty: 1

130. The area of a rectangle is 270 square feet. Its perimeter is 66 feet. Find its dimensions.

Answer: 18 feet by 15 feet Difficulty: 1

131. The area of a rectangle is 434 square yards. Its length is 3 yards more than twice its width. Find its dimensions.

Answer: 14 yards by 31 yards Difficulty: 1

132. The area of a triangle is given by $A = \frac{1}{2}bh$ where A is in square inches when b and h are in inches. The height of a triangle is 4 inches longer than the base and its area is 336 square inches. Find the base and height.

Answer: b = 24 inches and h = 28 inches Difficulty: 1

133. The area of a triangle is given by $A = \frac{1}{2}bh$ where A is in square inches when b and h are in inches. The height of a triangle is 4 inches shorter than the base and its area is 198 square inches. Find the base and height.

Answer: b = 22 inches and h = 18 inches Difficulty: 1

134. The area of a triangle is given by $A = \frac{1}{2}bh$ where A is in square inches when b and h are in inches. The height of a triangle is 2 inches longer than the base and its area is 18 square inches. Find the base (round to two decimal places).

Answer: $b \approx 5.08$ inches Difficulty: 1

135. The height of an object dropped from an initial height of 350 feet is given by $h = 350 - 16t^2$, where t is in seconds and h is in feet. How many seconds (to two decimal places) has the object been falling when it strikes the ground?

Answer: 4.68 seconds Difficulty: 1

136. The height of an object dropped from an initial height of 450 feet is given by $h = 450 - 16t^2$, where t is in seconds and h is in feet. How many seconds (to two decimal places) has the object been falling when it strikes the ground?

Answer: 5.30 seconds Difficulty: 1

137. A train makes a round trip between cities 300 miles apart. On the return half, the average speed is 25 mph faster than the average speed on the trip out and takes 1 hour less time. Find the time required on the trip out.

Answer: 4 hours Difficulty: 1

138. A train makes a round trip between cities 300 miles apart. On the return half, the average speed is 25 mph faster than the average speed on the trip out and takes 1 hour less time. Find the time required on the return trip.

Answer: 3 hours Difficulty: 1

139. A group of people could rent a social hall for \$600. When 5 more people join the venture the cost per person is decreased by \$10. How many people are in the larger group?

Answer: 20 Difficulty: 1

140. A group of people could rent a social hall for \$500. When 15 more people join the venture the cost per person is decreased by \$7.50. How many people are in the larger group?

Answer: 40 Difficulty: 1

MULTIPLE CHOICE

141. Solve for x: $3x^3 = 27x$.
a) 3 b) -3, 3 c) -3, 0, 3 d) 0, $3i$, $-3i$ e) None of these

Answer: c Difficulty: 1

142. Solve for x: $3x^3 - 24x^2 + 21x = 0$.
a) 7, 1 b) -7, -1 c) 0, 1, 7 d) 0, -1, -7 e) None of these

Answer: c Difficulty: 1

SHORT ANSWER

143. Solve for x: $20x^3 - 500x = 0$.

Answer: 0, ± 5 Difficulty: 1

144. Solve for x: $7x^3 = 252x$.

Answer: ± 6, 0 Difficulty: 1

MULTIPLE CHOICE

145. Solve for x: $x^3 + x^2 - 2x = 2$.
a) $-1, \pm\sqrt{2}$ b) $1, \pm\sqrt{3}$ c) $0, 1 \pm\sqrt{3}$ d) $-2, 1$ e) None of these

Answer: a Difficulty: 2

146. Solve for x: $x^3 - 5x - 2x^2 + 10 = 0$.
a) $-2, \pm\sqrt{5}$ b) $\pm\sqrt{5}$ c) $2, \sqrt{5}$ d) $2, \pm\sqrt{5}$ e) None of these

Answer: d Difficulty: 2

147. Solve for x: $x^4 + 5x^2 - 36 = 0$.
a) $\pm 3, \pm 2$ b) $9, 4$ c) $\pm 2, \pm 3i$ d) $-9, 4$ e) None of these

Answer: c Difficulty: 1

SHORT ANSWER

148. Solve for x: $2x^4 - 7x^2 + 5 = 0$.

Answer:

$\pm 1, \pm\frac{\sqrt{10}}{2}$

Difficulty: 1

MULTIPLE CHOICE

149. Solve for x: $9x^4 - 24x^2 + 16 = 0$.
a) $\pm\frac{2}{\sqrt{3}}$ b) $\frac{2}{\sqrt{3}}$ c) $0, \pm\frac{2}{\sqrt{3}}$ d) $\frac{4}{3}$ e) None of these

Answer: a Difficulty: 1

150. Solve for x: $3x - 2\sqrt{x} - 5 = 0$.
a) $\frac{5}{3}$ b) $-1, \frac{5}{3}$ c) $1, \frac{25}{9}$ d) $\frac{25}{9}$ e) None of these

Answer: d Difficulty: 1

SHORT ANSWER

151. Solve for x: $x^{2/3} - 6x^{1/3} = 7$.

Answer: 343, -1 Difficulty: 2

MULTIPLE CHOICE

152. Solve for x: $\sqrt{2 - 5x} = 5x$.
a) $\frac{1}{5}$ b) $-\frac{2}{5}$ c) $\frac{1}{5}, -\frac{2}{5}$ d) $\frac{1}{10}$ e) None of these

Answer: a Difficulty: 1

SHORT ANSWER

153. Solve for x: $3x + 5 = \sqrt{2 - 2x}$.

Answer: -1 Difficulty: 1

154. Solve for x: $\sqrt[3]{4x - 1} = 3$.

Answer: 7 Difficulty: 1

MULTIPLE CHOICE

155. Solve for x: $\sqrt{15x + 4} = 4 - \sqrt{2x + 3}$.
a) 3 b) $\frac{11}{169}$ c) $3, \frac{11}{169}$ d) $-3, -\frac{11}{169}$ e) None of these

Answer: b Difficulty: 2

156. Solve for x: $\sqrt{x + 16} = 3 + \sqrt{x - 2}$.
a) 3 b) $\frac{17}{4}$ c) $\frac{1}{2}$ d) No solution e) None of these

Answer: b Difficulty: 2

SHORT ANSWER

157. Solve for x: $\sqrt{x + 1} = 9 - \sqrt{x}$.

Answer:
$\frac{1600}{81}$

Difficulty: 2

MULTIPLE CHOICE

158. Solve for x: $(x^2 + 4)^{2/3} = 25$.
a) -5.8, 5.8 b) -4.6, 4.6 c) 21
d) -11, 11 e) None of these

Answer: d Difficulty: 1

159. Solve for x: $(x^2 - 9x + 2)^{3/2} = 216$.
a) $9, -\frac{1}{2}$ b) $\frac{9}{2} \pm 3i$ c) $\frac{9}{2} \pm \frac{\sqrt{217}}{2}$ d) $9 \pm \frac{\sqrt{217}}{2}$ e) None of these

Answer: c Difficulty: 2

160. Solve for x: $(x^2 - 2x + 5)^{2/3} = 4$.
a) -3, 1 b) $-1 \pm \sqrt{13}$ c) -1, 3 d) 1 e) None of these

Answer: c Difficulty: 2

161. Solve for x: $\frac{1}{x} - \frac{1}{x + 1} = 1$.
a) -1, 0 b) $\frac{-1 - \sqrt{5}}{2}, \frac{-1 + \sqrt{5}}{2}$ c) $-1 - \frac{\sqrt{5}}{2}, -1 + \frac{\sqrt{5}}{2}$
d) -1, 1 e) None of these

Answer: b Difficulty: 2

162. Solve for x: $\frac{1}{x - 1} + \frac{x}{x + 2} = 2$.
a) -2, 1 b) -2, 0, 1 c) $-1 \pm \sqrt{7}$ d) $-1 \pm \sqrt{3}$ e) None of these

Answer: c Difficulty: 2

163. Solve for x: $\frac{2}{x^2 - 1} + \frac{1}{x + 1} = 5$.
a) $\frac{6}{5}$ b) $-1, \frac{6}{5}$ c) $\frac{1 \pm \sqrt{41}}{10}$ d) $\pm\frac{\sqrt{2}}{2}$ e) None of these

Answer: a Difficulty: 1

164. Solve for x: $\frac{4}{x} - \frac{3}{x + 1} = 7$.
a) -1, 5 b) 3 c) $\frac{-3 \pm \sqrt{37}}{7}$ d) $\frac{-7 \pm \sqrt{77}}{14}$ e) None of these

Answer: c Difficulty: 1

165. Solve for x: $\frac{x}{x^2 - 9} + \frac{2}{x + 3} = 3$.
a) $\frac{3}{7}, -\frac{1}{5}$ b) $\frac{-1 \pm \sqrt{17}}{2}$ c) -3, 7 d) $\frac{1 \pm \sqrt{5}}{2}$ e) None of these

Answer: e Difficulty: 1

166. Solve for x: $|3x + 10| = 13$.
a) 1 b) 1, -1 c) $1, -\frac{23}{3}$ d) $1, \frac{23}{3}$ e) None of these

Answer: c Difficulty: 1

167. Solve for x: $|2 - 4x| = 12$.
a) $-\frac{5}{2}, \frac{7}{2}$ b) $-\frac{5}{2}, -\frac{7}{2}$ c) $\frac{5}{2}, -\frac{5}{2}$ d) $-\frac{5}{2}$ e) None of these

Answer: a Difficulty: 1

168. Solve for x: $|x^2 - 2x| = 2x - 3$.
a) $1, 3, \pm\sqrt{3}$ b) $\sqrt{3}, 3$ c) 1, 3 d) 3 e) None of these

Answer: b Difficulty: 2

169. Solve for x: $|x^2 - 2x| = x$.
a) 0 b) $0, \pm 1$ c) $0, \pm 3$ d) 0, 1, 3 e) None of these

Answer: d Difficulty: 1

170. Solve for x: $|x^2 - 2x| = 3x - 6$.
a) 2 b) $2, \pm 3$ c) 2, 3 d) ± 3 e) None of these

Answer: c Difficulty: 2

171. Use a calculator to approximate the solutions of $x^3 + 3x^2 = 5x$. (Round to two decimal places.)
a) -4.19, 1.19 b) $0, \pm 4.19$ c) $0, \pm 1.19$
d) 0, -4.19, 1.19 e) None of these

Answer: d Difficulty: 1 Key 1: T

172. Use a calculator to approximate the solutions of $9x^4 - 24x^2 + 16 = 0$. (Round to two decimal places.)
a) ± 1.15 b) 1.15 c) $0, \pm 1.15$ d) 1.33 e) None of these

Answer: a Difficulty: 1 Key 1: T

173. Use a graphing utility to approximate the solution of $\sqrt{x + 16} = 3 + \sqrt{x - 2}$. (Round to two decimal places.)
a) 3 b) 4.25 c) 0.5 d) No solution e) None of these

Answer: b Difficulty: 2 Key 1: T

174. Use a calculator to approximate the solution(s) of $(x^2 - 9x + 2)^{3/2} = 216$. (Round to two decimal places.)
a) -0.5 b) ±3, 4.5 c) -2.87, 11.87
d) 1.63, 16.37 e) None of these

Answer: c Difficulty: 2 Key 1: T

175. Use a graphing utility to approximate the solutions of $\frac{1}{x} - \frac{1}{x + 1} = 1$. (Round to two decimal places.)
a) -1, 0 b) -1.62, 0.62 c) -2.12, 0.12
d) -1, 1 e) None of these

Answer: b Difficulty: 2 Key 1: T

176. Use a graphing utility to approximate the solutions of $\frac{x}{x^2 - 9} + \frac{2}{x + 3} = 3$. (Round to two decimal places.)
a) -0.20, 0.43 b) -2.56, 1.56 c) -3, 7
d) -0.62, 1.62 e) None of these

Answer: e Difficulty: 2 Key 1: T

177. Use a calculator to approximate the solution(s) of $|3x + 10| = 13$. (Round to two decimal places.)
a) 1 b) -1, 1 c) -7.67, 1 d) -1, 7.67 e) None of these

Answer: c Difficulty: 2 Key 1: T

178. A church youth group decides to go bowling. They can rent three lanes for two hours for a total of \$60. The cost per person will drop by \$.60 if they can get 5 visitors to attend also. How many people are in the youth group?
a) 18 b) 20 c) 22 d) 24 e) None of these

Answer: b Difficulty: 2

179. During a one week leave, three military personnel decide to rent a car and share equally in the cost. By adding a fourth person to the group, each person could save \$12.25. How much is the weekly rental for the car?
a) \$49 b) \$163 c) \$189 d) \$147 e) None of these

Answer: d Difficulty: 2

180. The demand equation for a certain product is $p = 25(20 - \sqrt{x})$ where x is the number of units demanded per day and p is the price per unit. Find the demand if the price is set at \$250.

a) 100 b) 10 c) 19 d) 14 e) None of these

Answer: a Difficulty: 2

181. The demand equation for a certain product is $p = 40 - \sqrt{0.0001x + 1}$ where x is the number of units demanded per day and p is the price per unit. Find the demand if the price is set at \$10.50.

a) 92,316,410 b) 4,765,180 c) 8,692,500
d) 576,910 e) None of these

Answer: c Difficulty: 2

182. Find the height of the rectangular solid if the volume is $80x$ cubic units.

a) 5 b) 10 c) 3 d) 6 e) None of these

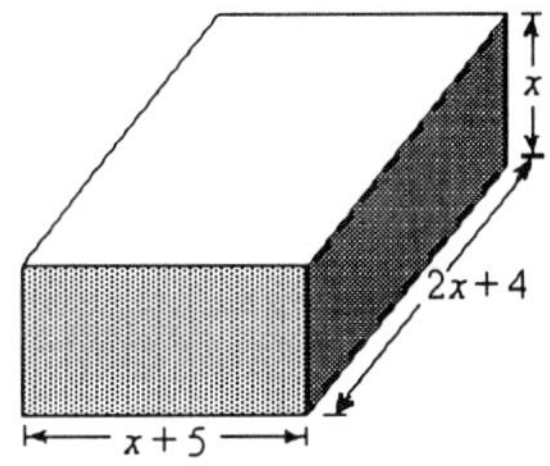

Answer: c Difficulty: 1

Chapter 0P6: Solving Inequalities

MULTIPLE CHOICE

1. Write an inequality to represent the interval.
   a) $-3 \le x < 5$ b) $-3 \ge x < 5$ c) $-3 < x \le 5$
   d) $5 > x \le -3$ e) None of these

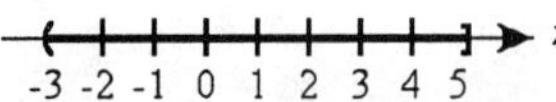

Answer: c Difficulty: 1

2. Write an inequality to represent the interval.
   a) $x < -7$ or $x \ge -3$ b) $-7 \le x > -3$ c) $-7 < x < -3$
   d) $x \le -7$ or $x > -3$ e) None of these

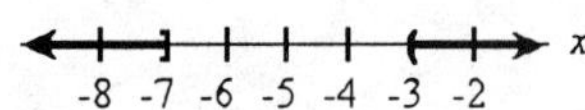

Answer: d Difficulty: 1

3. Graph the solution: $3 - 2x < 15$.
   a) I b) II c) III d) IV e) None of these

(I) 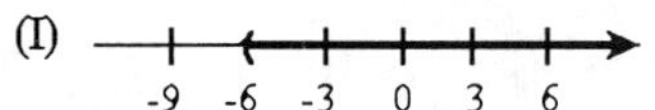

(II) 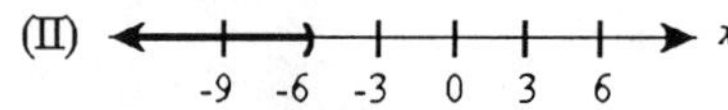

(III) 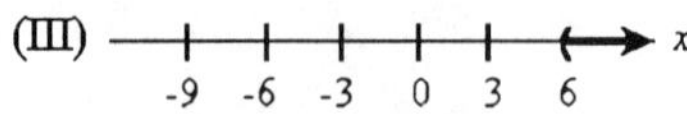

(IV) 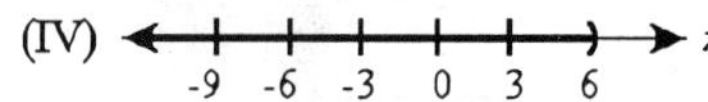

Answer: a Difficulty: 1

4. Graph the solution: $2x - 4 < 8$.
   a) I b) II c) III d) IV e) None of these

(I) 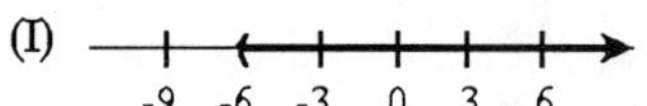

(II) 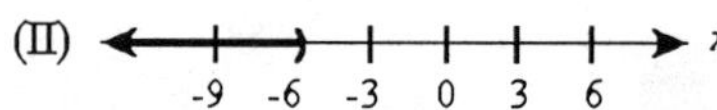

(III) 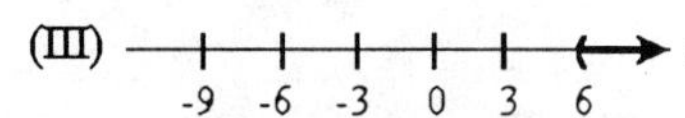

(IV) 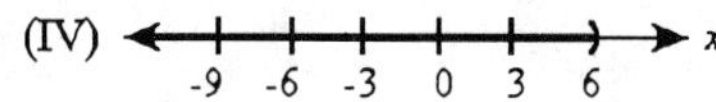

Answer: d Difficulty: 1

5. Graph the solution: $-3 \le 2x + 1 \le 5$.
   a) I b) II c) III d) IV e) None of these

(I) x
-4 -2 0 2 4

(II) 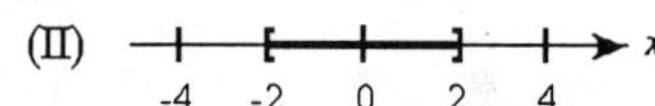

(III) x
-4 -2 0 2 4

(IV) 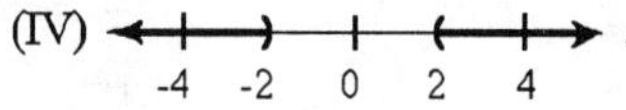

Answer: b Difficulty: 1

6. Graph the solution: $-6 < 7x + 2 \leq 5$.
   a) I b) II c) III d) IV e) None of these

(I) 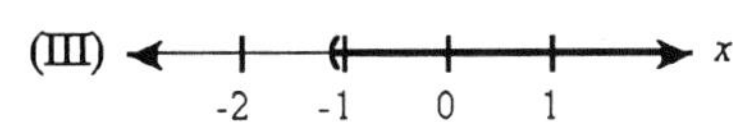

(II) 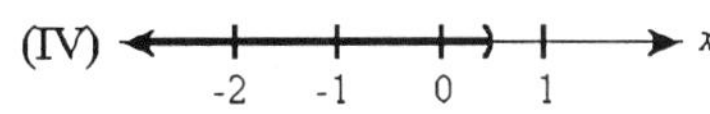

(III) x; -2 -1 0 1

(IV) x; -2 -1 0 1

Answer: b Difficulty: 1

SHORT ANSWER

7. Graph the solution: $\frac{1}{2} < 3 - x < 5$.

Answer: See graph below.

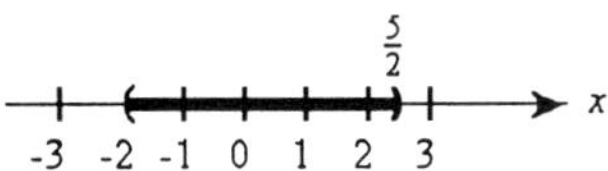

Difficulty: 1

8. Graph the solution: $-16 \leq 7 - 2x < 5$.

Answer: See graph below.

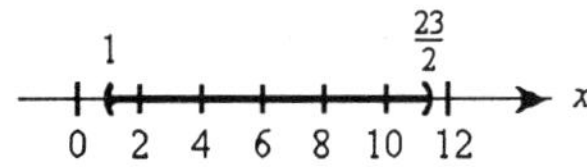

Difficulty: 1

MULTIPLE CHOICE

9. Solve the inequality: $14 - 2x \leq 5$.
   a) $\left(-\infty, \frac{9}{2}\right)$ b) $\left(-\infty, \frac{9}{2}\right]$ c) $\left(\frac{9}{2}, \infty\right)$ d) $\left[\frac{9}{2}, \infty\right)$ e) None of these

Answer: d Difficulty: 1

10. Solve the inequality: $3 - 2x \leq 9$.
    a) $(-\infty, -3]$ b) $(-\infty, 3]$ c) $[-3, \infty)$ d) $[3, \infty)$ e) None of these

Answer: c Difficulty: 1

11. Solve the inequality: $5x + 6 > 7x + 9$.
a) $\left(-\frac{3}{2}, \infty\right)$ b) $\left[\frac{6}{5}, \frac{9}{7}\right]$ c) $\left(-\infty, -\frac{3}{2}\right]$ d) $\left[\frac{3}{2}, \infty\right)$ e) None of these

Answer: c Difficulty: 1

12. Solve the inequality: $4 - 3x \geq 5x + 12$.
a) $(-\infty, -1]$ b) $(-\infty, 8]$ c) $[-1, \infty)$ d) $(-\infty, -2)$ e) None of these

Answer: a Difficulty: 1

13. Solve the inequality: $6 - 5x \leq x - 6$.
a) $[0, \infty)$ b) $[2, \infty)$ c) $(-\infty, 2]$ d) $(-\infty, 0)$ e) None of these

Answer: b Difficulty: 1

14. Solve the inequality: $-2 < 3x + 1 < 7$.
a) $-1 \leq x \leq 2$ b) $-\frac{1}{3} < x < \frac{8}{3}$ c) $x > 2$
d) $-1 < x < 2$ e) None of these

Answer: d Difficulty: 1

15. Solve the inequality: $-6 < 7x + 2 \leq 5$.
a) $\left(-\infty, -\frac{8}{7}\right]$ or $\left[\frac{3}{7}, \infty\right)$ b) $\left(-\frac{8}{7}, \frac{3}{7}\right]$ c) $\left(-\frac{8}{7}, \infty\right)$
d) $\left(-\infty, \frac{3}{7}\right]$ e) None of these

Answer: b Difficulty: 1

16. Solve the inequality: $-16 \leq 7 - 2x \leq 5$.
a) $x \leq 1$ or $x \geq \frac{23}{2}$ b) $-1 \leq x \leq \frac{23}{2}$ c) $1 \leq x \leq \frac{23}{2}$
d) $-\frac{23}{2} \leq x \leq 1$ e) None of these

Answer: c Difficulty: 1

17. Solve the inequality: $-2 < 3x + 1 < 7$.
a) $-1 \leq x \leq 2$ b) $-\frac{1}{3} < x < \frac{8}{3}$ c) $x > 2$
d) $-1 < x < 2$ e) None of these

Answer: d Difficulty: 1

18. Solve the inequality: $12 - 2x \leq 5$.
a) $\left(-\infty, \frac{7}{2}\right]$ b) $\left(-\infty, \frac{7}{2}\right]$ c) $\left[\frac{7}{2}, \infty\right)$ d) $\left[\frac{7}{2}, \infty\right)$ e) None of these

Answer: d Difficulty: 1

19. Solve the inequality: $8 - 2x - 5 \le 9$.
a) $(-\infty, -3]$ b) $(-\infty, 3]$ c) $[-3, \infty)$ d) $[3, \infty)$ e) None of these

Answer: c Difficulty: 1

20. Solve the inequality: $6 - 2x \ge 5x + 9$.
a) $\left[-\frac{15}{7}, \infty\right]$ b) $\left[-\frac{2}{6}, \frac{9}{5}\right]$ c) $\left[-\infty, -\frac{3}{7}\right]$ d) $\left[\frac{15}{7}, \infty\right]$ e) None of these

Answer: c Difficulty: 1

21. Solve the inequality: $3x - 8 \ge 8x + 3$.
a) $(-\infty, -1]$ b) $[4, \infty)$ c) $[-1, \infty)$ d) $\left[-\infty, -\frac{11}{5}\right]$ e) None of these

Answer: a Difficulty: 1

22. Solve the inequality: $-18 \le 6 - 2x \le 7$.
a) $x \le -\frac{1}{2}$ or $x \ge 12$ b) $-\frac{1}{2} \le x \le 12$ c) $\frac{1}{2} \le x < 12$
d) $x \le \frac{1}{2}$ or $x > 12$ e) None of these

Answer: c Difficulty: 1

23. Solve the inequality: $-3 < 2x + 1 < 7$.
a) $1 < x < 3$ b) $1 < x < 4$ c) $x > 3$
d) $-2 < x < 3$ e) None of these

Answer: d Difficulty: 1

24. Solve the inequality: $5 + 2x > 4x + 7$.
a) $x < 1$ b) $x > 1$ c) $x > -1$
d) $x < -1$ e) None of these

Answer: d Difficulty: 1

25. Find the interval for which the radicand is nonnegative: $\sqrt{5 - 4x}$.
a) $\left[-\infty, -\frac{4}{5}\right]$ b) $\left[\frac{5}{4}, \infty\right]$ c) $\left[-\infty, \frac{4}{5}\right]$ d) $\left[-\infty, \frac{5}{4}\right]$ e) None of these

Answer: d Difficulty: 1

26. Find the interval for which the radicand is nonnegative: $\sqrt{2 - 3x}$.
a) $\left[-\infty, -\frac{3}{2}\right]$ b) $\left[-\infty, \frac{2}{3}\right]$ c) $\left[\frac{2}{3}, \infty\right]$ d) $\left[\frac{3}{2}, \infty\right]$ e) None of these

Answer: b Difficulty: 1

27. Find the interval for which the radicand is nonnegative: $\sqrt{7 + 5x}$.

a) $\left(-\infty, \frac{5}{7}\right]$ b) $\left(-\infty, -\frac{7}{5}\right]$ c) $\left[-\frac{5}{7}, \infty\right)$ d) $\left[\frac{7}{5}, \infty\right)$ e) None of these

Answer: e Difficulty: 1

28. Find the interval for which the radicand is positive: $\frac{1}{\sqrt{2 + 5x}}$.

a) $\left(-\infty, -\frac{2}{5}\right)$ b) $\left(-\infty, -\frac{5}{2}\right)$ c) $\left(-\frac{5}{2}, \infty\right)$ d) $\left(-\frac{2}{5}, \infty\right)$ e) None of these

Answer: d Difficulty: 1

29. Find the interval for which the radicand is positive: $\frac{1}{\sqrt[4]{3 - 4x}}$.

a) $\left(\frac{4}{3}, \infty\right)$ b) $\left(-\frac{3}{4}, \infty\right)$ c) $\left(-\infty, \frac{3}{4}\right)$ d) $\left(-\infty, -\frac{4}{3}\right)$ e) None of these

Answer: c Difficulty: 1

30. Match graph with the correct inequality.

a) $|x - 7| < 4$ b) $|x - 1| < 3$ c) $|x + 3| < 7$

d) $|x + 3| < 4$ e) None of these

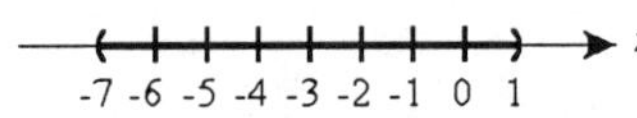

Answer: d Difficulty: 1

31. Match graph with the correct inequality.

a) $|x + 4| < -2$ b) $|x - 2| > 4$ c) $|x - 2| < 4$

d) $|x - 6| > 2$ e) None of these

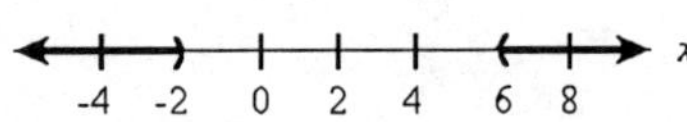

Answer: b Difficulty: 1

32. Match graph with the correct inequality.

a) $|x + 2| > 5$ b) $|x + 3| \geq 2$ c) $|x - 1| \leq 5$

d) $|x - 5| \geq 2$ e) None of these

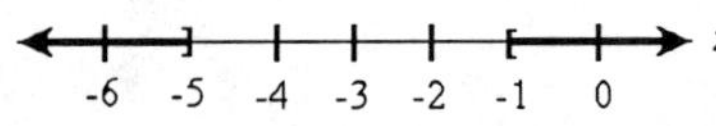

Answer: b Difficulty: 1

33. Graph the solution: $|3x - 1| \geq 5$.
a) I b) II c) III d) IV e) None of these

(I) -2 -1 0 1 2 3 x (II) -2 -1 0 1 2 3 x

(III) -3 -2 -1 0 1 2 x (IV) -3 -2 -1 0 1 2 x

Answer: b Difficulty: 1

34. Graph the solution: $|x + 2| < 9$.
a) I b) II c) III d) IV e) None of these

(I) -15 -5 5 x (II) -15 -5 5 x

(III) -10 0 10 x (IV) -10 0 10 x

Answer: a Difficulty: 1

SHORT ANSWER

35. Graph the solution: $|3x - 1| > 9$.

Answer: See graph below.

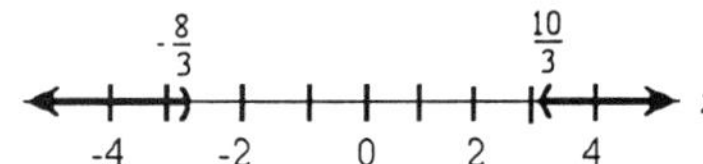

Difficulty: 1

MULTIPLE CHOICE

36. Solve the inequality: $|3x - 1| > 2$.
a) $\left[-\frac{1}{3}, 1\right]$ b) $\left[-\frac{1}{3}, 1\right]$ c) $\left[-\infty, -\frac{1}{3}\right], (1, \infty)$
d) $\left[-\infty, -\frac{1}{3}\right], [1, \infty)$ e) None of these

Answer: c Difficulty: 1

SHORT ANSWER

37. Solve the inequality: $|x + 5| \leq 2$.

Answer: $-7 \leq x \leq -3$ Difficulty: 1

MULTIPLE CHOICE

38. Solve the inequality: $|2x + 5| > 3$.
    a) $x < -4$ or $x > -1$ b) $-4 < x < -1$ c) $x < 1$ or $x > 4$
    d) $x < -1$ or $x > 4$ e) None of these

    Answer: a Difficulty: 1

39. Use absolute value notation to define all real numbers on the real number line within 6 units of 10.
    a) $|x - 6| \geq 10$ b) $|x - 10| \geq 6$ c) $|x - 6| \leq 10$
    d) $|x - 10| \leq 6$ e) None of these

    Answer: d Difficulty: 1

40. Use absolute value notation to denote all real numbers x that are at least 3 units from the number 5.
    a) $|x - 3| < 5$ b) $|x - 3| \geq 5$ c) $|x - 5| < 3$
    d) $|x - 5| \geq 3$ e) None of these

    Answer: d Difficulty: 1

SHORT ANSWER

41. Use absolute value notation to define the interval: $-7 \leq x \leq 7$.

    Answer: $|x| \leq 7$ Difficulty: 1

42. Use absolute value notation to define the interval: $x < -3$ or $x > 3$.

    Answer: $|x| > 3$ Difficulty: 1

43. Use absolute value notation to define the interval: $-7 < x < 3$.

    Answer: $|x + 2| < 5$ Difficulty: 2

44. Use absolute value notation to define the interval on the real number line.

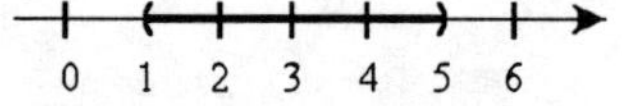

    Answer: $|x - 3| < 2$ Difficulty: 1

45. Use absolute value notation to define the interval on the real number line.

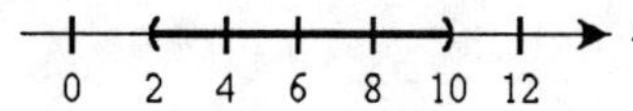

    Answer: $|x - 6| < 4$ Difficulty: 1

46. Use absolute value notation to define the interval on the real number line.

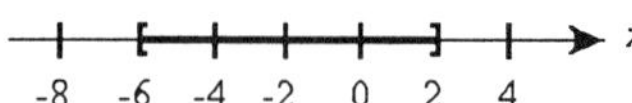

Answer: $|x + 2| \leq 4$ Difficulty: 1

47. Use absolute value notation to define the interval on the real number line.

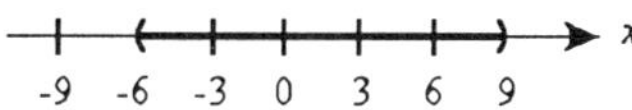

Answer:
$$\left|x - \frac{3}{2}\right| < \frac{15}{2}$$
Difficulty: 1

MULTIPLE CHOICE

48. The revenue for selling x units of a product is $R = 35.95x$. The cost of producing x units is $C = 14.75x + 848$. In order to obtain a profit, the revenue must be greater than the cost. For what values of x will this product return a profit?
a) $x > 123$ b) $x > 117$ c) $x > 52$ d) $x > 40$ e) None of these

Answer: d Difficulty: 2

49. The revenue for selling x units of a product is $R = 257x$. The cost of producing x units is $C = 193x + 5248$. In order to obtain a profit, the revenue must be greater than the cost. For what values of x will this product return a profit?
a) $x > 103$ b) $x > 82$ c) $x > 77$ d) $x > 12$ e) None of these

Answer: b Difficulty: 2

50. The revenue for selling x units of a product is $R = 4.50x$. The cost of producing x units is $C = 3x + 3717$. In order to obtain a profit, the revenue must be greater than the cost. For what values of x will this product return a profit?
a) $x > 1893$ b) $x > 1239$ c) $x > 2478$ d) $x > 496$ e) None of these

Answer: c Difficulty: 2

51. You buy a bag of candy that costs \$2.90 per pound. The weight that is listed on the bag is 1.10 pounds. If the scale that weighed the candy is only accurate to within 0.125 of a pound, how much money might you have been overcharged or undercharged?
a) $22\frac{1}{8}$¢ b) $17\frac{3}{4}$¢ c) $36\frac{1}{4}$¢ d) $31\frac{1}{2}$¢ e) None of these

Answer: c Difficulty: 2

52. You buy a bag of candy that costs \$3.15 per pound. The weight that is listed on the bag is 0.90 pounds. If the scale that weighed the candy is only accurate to within 0.125 of a pound, how much money might you have been overcharged or undercharged?
   a) $39\frac{3}{8}$¢ b) $29\frac{1}{4}$¢ c) $16\frac{2}{3}$¢ d) $51\frac{1}{2}$¢ e) None of these

   Answer: a Difficulty: 2

SHORT ANSWER

53. Solve the inequality: $(x - 2)^2 \leq 9$.

   Answer: [-1, 5] Difficulty: 1

MULTIPLE CHOICE

54. Solve the inequality: $(x + 3)^2 \geq 4$.
   a) $[1, 5]$ b) $(-\infty, 5]$ c) $(-\infty, -5] \cup [-1, \infty)$
   d) $[-5, -1]$ e) None of these

   Answer: c Difficulty: 1

55. Solve the inequality: $(x - 1)^2 \leq 25$.
   a) $[-4, 6]$ b) $(-\infty, -4] \cup [6, \infty)$ c) $(-\infty, -6] \cup [4, \infty)$
   d) $[-6, 4]$ e) None of these

   Answer: a Difficulty: 1

56. Solve the inequality: $(x + 1)^2 \geq 9$.
   a) $-4, 2$ b) $(-\infty, -4] \cup [2, \infty)$ c) $[-2, 4]$
   d) $(-\infty, -2) \cup (4, \infty)$ e) None of these

   Answer: b Difficulty: 1

SHORT ANSWER

57. Solve the inequality: $x^2 - x > 6$.

   Answer: $(-\infty, -2) \cup (3, \infty)$ Difficulty: 1

MULTIPLE CHOICE

58. Solve the inequality: $3x^3 - 6x^2 > 0$.
   a) $(-\infty, 0) \cup (2, \infty)$ b) $(0, 2)$ c) $(-\infty, 0)$
   d) $(2, \infty)$ e) None of these

   Answer: d Difficulty: 1

59. Solve the inequality: $2x^2 + 3x \geq 5$.
a) $\left[-\frac{5}{2}, 1\right]$
b) $\left[-\frac{5}{2}, \infty\right]$
c) $\left[-\infty, -\frac{5}{2}\right] \cup [1, \infty)$
d) $\left[-\infty, -\frac{3}{2}\right] \cup [5, \infty)$
e) None of these

Answer: c Difficulty: 1

60. Solve the inequality: $2x^2 + 3x < 9$.
a) $\left(-3, \frac{3}{2}\right)$
b) $(-\infty, -3) \cup \left(\frac{3}{2}, \infty\right)$
c) $\left[-3, \frac{3}{2}\right]$
d) $(-\infty, 3) \cup (9, \infty)$
e) None of these

Answer: a Difficulty: 1

61. Solve the inequality: $2x^3 \leq 4x^4$.
a) $(-\infty, \infty)$
b) $\left[0, \frac{1}{2}\right]$
c) $(-\infty, 0] \cup \left[\frac{1}{2}, \infty\right)$
d) $\left[\frac{1}{2}, \infty\right)$
e) None of these

Answer: c Difficulty: 1

62. Solve the inequality: $x^2 + 1 \geq 0$.
a) $(-\infty, \infty)$
b) $[-1, 1]$
c) $(-\infty, -1] \cup [1, \infty)$
d) $(-1, 1)$
e) None of these

Answer: a Difficulty: 2

63. Solve the inequality: $2x^2 - 5x > 3$.
a) $\left(-\frac{1}{2}, 3\right)$
b) $\left(-\infty, -\frac{1}{2}\right) \cup (3, \infty)$
c) $(-\infty, -3) \cup \left(\frac{1}{2}, \infty\right)$
d) $\left(-\frac{1}{2}, \infty\right)$
e) None of these

Answer: b Difficulty: 1

64. Solve the inequality: $x^2 + 6x + 1 \geq 0$.
a) $(-\infty, -3 - 2\sqrt{2}]$ or $[-3 + 2\sqrt{2}, \infty)$
b) $[-3 - 2\sqrt{2}, -3 + 2\sqrt{2}]$
c) $(-\infty, -3 - \sqrt{10}]$ or $[-3 + \sqrt{10}, \infty)$
d) $[-3 - \sqrt{10}, -3\sqrt{10}]$
e) None of these

Answer: a Difficulty: 2

65. Solve the inequality: $x^2 + x - 3 < 0$.
a) $(-\infty, -3)$ or $(1, \infty)$
b) $\left[-\infty, \frac{-1 - \sqrt{13}}{2}\right]$ or $\left[\frac{-1 + \sqrt{13}}{2}, \infty\right]$
c) $\left[\frac{-1 - \sqrt{13}}{2}, \frac{-1 + \sqrt{13}}{2}\right]$
d) $(-3, 1)$
e) None of these

Answer: c Difficulty: 2

66. Solve the inequality: $x^2 + 6x + 1 \geq 0$.
a) $\left[-\infty, -3 - 2\sqrt{2}\,\right] \cup \left[-3 + 2\sqrt{2}, \infty\right]$
b) $\left[-3 - 2\sqrt{2}, -3 + 2\sqrt{2}\,\right]$
c) $\left[-\infty, -3 - \sqrt{10}\,\right] \cup \left[-3 + \sqrt{10}, \infty\right]$
d) $\left[-3 - \sqrt{10}, -3 + \sqrt{10}\right]$
e) None of these

Answer: a Difficulty: 2

67. Solve the inequality: $x^2 + x - 3 < 0$.
a) $(-\infty, -3) \cup (1, \infty)$
b) $(-\infty, -2.30) \cup (1.30, \infty)$
c) $(-2.30, 1.30)$
d) $(-3, 1)$
e) None of these

Answer: c Difficulty: 2

68. Solve the inequality: $x^2 - 4x + 2 < 0$. Round your result to two decimal places.
a) $(-3.41, -0.59)$
b) $(0.59, 3.41)$
c) $(-\infty, -3.41) \cup (-0.59, \infty)$
d) $(-\infty, 0.59) \cup (3.41, \infty)$
e) None of these

Answer: b Difficulty: 2

69. Solve the inequality: $x^2 + 4x + 2 \leq 0$. Round your result to two decimal places.
a) $[-3.41, \infty)$
b) $[-3.41, -0.59]$
c) $(-\infty, -3.41] \cup [-0.59, \infty)$
d) $[-2, 2]$
e) None of these

Answer: b Difficulty: 2

70. Solve the inequality: $x^2 + 3x + 4 > 0$.
a) $(-\infty, \infty)$
b) $(-\infty, 0) \cup (0, \infty)$
c) Empty set
d) $\left[\frac{-3 - \sqrt{7}}{2}, \frac{-3 + \sqrt{7}}{2}\right]$
e) None of these

Answer: a Difficulty: 2

71. Solve the inequality: $x^2 - 3x + 4 < 0$.
a) $(-\infty, \infty)$
b) $(-\infty, 0) \cup (0, \infty)$
c) Empty set
d) $\left[\frac{3 - \sqrt{7}}{2}, \frac{3 + \sqrt{7}}{2}\right]$
e) None of these

Answer: c Difficulty: 2

72. Solve the inequality: $x^2 + 6x + 9 \leq 0$.
a) $(-\infty, -3] \cup [-3, \infty)$ b) -3 c) $(-\infty, \infty)$
d) Empty set e) None of these

Answer: b Difficulty: 2

73. Solve the inequality: $x^2 + 3x + 9 \geq 0$.
a) $(-\infty, -3] \cup [3, \infty)$ b) $[-3, 3]$ c) $(-\infty, \infty)$
d) Empty set e) None of these

Answer: c Difficulty: 2

74. Solve the inequality: $x^2 + 4 < 2x$.
a) $(-\infty, \infty)$ b) $(-\infty, -2) \cup (2, \infty)$ c) $(-2, 2)$
d) Empty set e) None of these

Answer: d Difficulty: 2

75. Solve the inequality: $\dfrac{x + 16}{3x + 2} \leq 5$.
a) $\left[-\infty, -\dfrac{2}{3}\right] \cup \left[\dfrac{3}{7}, \infty\right]$ b) $\left[-\dfrac{2}{3}, \dfrac{3}{7}\right]$ c) $\left[-\infty, -\dfrac{2}{3}\right] \cup \left[\dfrac{3}{7}, \infty\right]$
d) $\left[-\dfrac{2}{3}, \dfrac{3}{7}\right]$ e) None of these

Answer: c Difficulty: 2

76. Solve the inequality: $\dfrac{x + 7}{3x - 1} < 1$. Round your answer to two decimal places.
a) $(0.33, 4)$ b) $[0.33, 4]$ c) $(-\infty, 0.33) \cup (4, \infty)$
d) $(-\infty, 0.33] \cup [4, \infty)$ e) None of these

Answer: c Difficulty: 2

SHORT ANSWER

77. Solve the inequality: $\dfrac{3x - 7}{x + 2} < 1$.

Answer:
$\left[-2, \dfrac{9}{2}\right]$

Difficulty: 2

MULTIPLE CHOICE

78. Solve the inequality: $\frac{2}{x-1} < 5$.

a) $(-\infty, 1)$ b) $\left[\frac{7}{5}, \infty\right]$ c) $\left[-\infty, -\frac{3}{5}\right] \cup \left[\frac{7}{5}, \infty\right]$

d) $(-\infty, 1) \cup \left[\frac{7}{5}, \infty\right]$ e) None of these

Answer: d Difficulty: 2

79. Solve the inequality: $\frac{2}{x+1} \geq 5$.

a) $(-\infty, -1) \cup \left[-\frac{3}{5}, \infty\right]$ b) $\left[-\infty, -\frac{3}{5}\right]$ c) $\left[-1, -\frac{3}{5}\right]$

d) $\left[-\infty, \frac{1}{5}\right]$ e) None of these

Answer: c Difficulty: 2

80. Solve the inequality: $\frac{4}{x+1} \leq \frac{3}{x+2}$.

a) $(-\infty, -5] \cup (-2, -1)$ b) $(-5, -2) \cup [-1, \infty)$
c) $(-\infty, -5) \cup (-2, -1)$ d) $(-5, -2] \cup (-1, \infty)$
e) None of these

Answer: a Difficulty: 2

81. Solve the inequality: $\frac{3}{x-2} \leq \frac{5}{x+2}$.

a) $(-\infty, -2) \cup (2, 6)$ b) $(-2, 2) \cup [6, \infty)$ c) $[8, \infty)$
d) $(-2, 2) \cup [8, \infty)$ e) None of these

Answer: d Difficulty: 2

82. Solve the inequality: $\frac{2}{x-1} \leq \frac{3}{x+1}$.

a) $(-1, 1) \cup [5, \infty)$ b) $(-\infty, -1) \cup (1, 5]$ c) $[5, \infty)$
d) Empty set e) None of these

Answer: a Difficulty: 2

83. Solve the inequality: $\frac{3}{x-1} \leq \frac{2}{x+1}$.

a) $(-\infty, -5]$ b) $(-\infty, -5] \cup (-1, 1)$ c) $[-5, -1) \cup (1, \infty)$
d) $(-\infty, -2] \cup (1, \infty)$ e) None of these

Answer: b Difficulty: 2

84. Solve the inequality: $\frac{2}{x + 2} \geq \frac{3}{x - 1}$.

a) $[-8, \infty)$ b) $[-8, -2) \cup (1, \infty)$ c) $(-\infty, -8] \cup (-2, 1)$
d) $(-\infty, -8]$ e) None of these

Answer: c Difficulty: 2

85. Find the domain of $\sqrt{x^2 - 7x - 8}$.

a) $(-\infty, -1] \cup [8, \infty)$ b) $(-\infty, -1) \cup (8, \infty)$ c) $[-1, 8]$
d) $(-1, 8)$ e) None of these

Answer: a Difficulty: 1

86. Find the domain $\sqrt{169 - 9x^2}$.

a) $\left(-\frac{13}{3}, \frac{13}{3}\right]$ b) $\left[-\frac{13}{3}, \frac{13}{3}\right]$ c) $\left(-\infty, -\frac{13}{3}\right] \cup \left[\frac{13}{3}, \infty\right)$

d) $\left(-\infty, -\frac{13}{3}\right] \cup \left(\frac{13}{3}, \infty\right)$ e) None of these

Answer: b Difficulty: 1

SHORT ANSWER

87. Find the domain of $\sqrt{36 - x^2}$.

Answer: [-6, 6] Difficulty: 1

88. Find the domain of $\sqrt{16 - 4x^2}$.

Answer: [-2, 2] Difficulty: 1

MULTIPLE CHOICE

89. Find the domain of $\frac{1}{\sqrt{x^2 - 7x - 8}}$.

a) $[-1, 8]$ b) $(-\infty, -1] \cup [8, \infty)$ c) $(-\infty, -1) \cup (8, \infty)$
d) $(-1, 8)$ e) None of these

Answer: c Difficulty: 1

90. P dollars, invested at interest rate, r, compounded annually, increases to an amount $A = P(1 + r)^2$ in two years. If an investment of \$750 is to increase to an amount greater than \$883 in two years, then the interest rate must be greater than what percentage?
a) 8.86%   b) 8.5%   c) 17.7%   d) 5.6%   e) None of these

Answer: b Difficulty: 2

91. P dollars, invested at interest rate, r, compounded annually, increases to an amount $A = P(1 + r)^2$ in two years. If an investment of \$970 is to increase to an amount greater than \$1100 in two years, then the interest rate must be greater than what percentage?
a) 5.5% b) 6.0% c) 6.5% d) 7.0% e) None of these

Answer: c Difficulty: 2

SHORT ANSWER

92. Solve the inequality $0.2x^2 + 3.6 < 10.6$. Round each number in your solution to two decimal places.

Answer: (-5.92, 5.92) Difficulty: 2

93. Solve the inequality $-0.5x^2 + 4.26 \geq 2.56$. Round each number in your solution to two decimal places.

Answer: [-1.84, 1.84] Difficulty: 2

94. Solve the inequality $-6.26x^2 + 7.10 \leq 2.4x$. Round each number in your solution to two decimal places.

Answer: $(-\infty, -1.27] \cup [0.89, \infty)$ Difficulty: 2

95. Solve the inequality $1.4x^2 + 5.6x - 10.75 \geq 0$. Round each number in your solution to two decimal places.

Answer: $(-\infty, -5.42] \cup [1.42, \infty)$ Difficulty: 2

96. Solve the inequality $\frac{1}{3.2x - 6} > 2.4$. Round each number in your solution to two decimal places.

Answer: (1.88, 2.00) Difficulty: 2

97. A projectile is fired straight upward from ground level with an initial velocity of 64 feet per second. When will the height be less than 48 feet?

Answer: $(0, 1) \cup (3, 4)$ Difficulty: 2

98. A projectile is fired straight upward from ground level with an initial velocity of 64 feet per second. When will the height be more than 48 feet?

Answer: (1, 3) Difficulty: 2

99. A projectile is fired straight upward from ground level with an initial velocity of 96 feet per second. When will the height be less than 84 feet?

Answer: $(0, 1.06) \cup (4.94, 6)$ Difficulty: 2

100. A projectile is fired straight upward from ground level with an initial velocity of 96 feet per second. When will the height be more than 84 feet?

Answer: (1.06, 4.94) Difficulty: 2

Chapter 0P7: Errors and the Algebra of Calculus

SHORT ANSWER

1. Insert the required factor in the parentheses: $5x^3(7 - 2x^4)^5 =$ ( )$(-40x^3)(7 - 2x^4)^5$.

Answer:
$-\frac{1}{8}$

Difficulty: 1

MULTIPLE CHOICE

2. Insert the required factor in the parentheses: $-2x(3x^2 - 4)^{1/2} =$ ( )$(3x^2 - 4)^{1/2}(6x)$.

a) $3x$ b) $\left(-\frac{1}{3}\right)$ c) $\left(\frac{1}{3}\right)$ d) 3 e) None of these

Answer: b Difficulty: 1

3. Insert the required factor in the parentheses:

$$\frac{3x^2 + 2x}{(2x^3 + 2x^2 - 1)^2} = (\quad)\frac{1}{(2x^3 + 2x^2 - 1)^2}(6x^2 + 4x).$$

a) $\frac{1}{2}$ b) 2 c) 4 d) $\frac{1}{4}$ e) None of these

Answer: a Difficulty: 1

SHORT ANSWER

4. Insert the required factor in the parentheses: $3x(2x + 1)^{1/2} + 5(2x + 1)^{3/2} = (2x + 1)^{1/2}(\quad)$.

Answer: $13x + 5$ Difficulty: 2

5. Insert the required factor in the parentheses: $\frac{3}{4}(1 - x)^{2/3} + \frac{7}{8}(1 - x)^{5/3} = \frac{(1 - x)^{2/3}}{8}(\quad)$.

Answer: $13 - 7x$ Difficulty: 2

6. Insert the required factor in the parentheses: $2(3x + 5)^{-1/2} + 9x(3x + 5)^{-3/2} = 5(3x + 5)^{-3/2}(\quad)$.

Answer: $3x + 2$ Difficulty: 2

MULTIPLE CHOICE

7. Insert the required factor in the parentheses:
$$\frac{-3}{16x^2 + 1} = (\quad)\frac{4}{16x^2 + 1}.$$

a) $-\frac{3}{4}$ b) $-\frac{4}{3}$ c) $\frac{4}{3}$ d) $\frac{3}{4}$ e) None of these

Answer: a Difficulty: 1

8. Insert the required factor in the parentheses:
$$5\sqrt{x + 3} - \frac{5x}{2\sqrt{x + 3}} = \frac{1}{2\sqrt{x + 3}}(\quad).$$

a) $2\sqrt{x + 3} - 5x$ b) $5x + 30$ c) 15

d) $5 - 5x$ e) None of these

Answer: b Difficulty: 1

9. Determine b^2: $\frac{4x^2}{7} + \frac{9y^2}{4} = \frac{x^2}{a^2} + \frac{y^2}{b^2}$.

a) $\frac{9}{4}$ b) $\frac{4}{9}$ c) 4 d) $\frac{1}{4}$ e) None of these

Answer: b Difficulty: 1

10. Determine a^2: $\frac{3x^2}{2} + \frac{7y^2}{9} = \frac{x^2}{a^2} + \frac{y^2}{b^2}$.

a) $\frac{7}{9}$ b) $\frac{9}{7}$ c) $\frac{3}{2}$ d) $\frac{2}{3}$ e) None of these

Answer: d Difficulty: 1

SHORT ANSWER

11. Rewrite $\frac{9x^2}{25} + 4y^2 = 1$ in the form $\frac{x^2}{a^2} + \frac{y^2}{b^2} = 1$.

Answer:

$$\frac{x^2}{(5/3)^2} + \frac{y^2}{(1/2)^2} = 1$$

Difficulty: 1

12. Rewrite $12x^2 - 9y^2 = 16$ in the form $\frac{x^2}{a^2} - \frac{y^2}{b^2} = 1$.

Answer:

$$\frac{x^2}{(2/\sqrt{3})^2} - \frac{y^2}{(4/3)^2} = 1$$

Difficulty: 1

MULTIPLE CHOICE

13. Solve for a: $\frac{9x^2}{49} - \frac{4y^2}{25} = \frac{x^2}{a} - \frac{y^2}{b}$.

a) $\frac{9}{49}$ b) $\frac{49}{9}$ c) $\frac{3}{7}$ d) $\frac{7}{3}$ e) None of these

Answer: b Difficulty: 2

SHORT ANSWER

14. Rewrite the fraction as the sum of two terms: $\frac{4x^3 - 7x^2}{2x}$.

Answer:

$2x^2 - \frac{7}{2}x$

Difficulty: 1

15. Rewrite the fraction as the sum of three terms: $\frac{3x^2 - 2x - 6}{3\sqrt{x}}$. Leave no variable in the denominator.

Answer:

$x^{3/2} - \frac{2}{3}x^{1/2} - 2x^{-1/2}$

Difficulty: 1

16. Rewrite the fractions with no variables in the denominators: $\frac{1}{(2x)^2} - \frac{2}{\sqrt{x}} + \frac{5}{2x^3}$.

Answer:

$\frac{1}{4}x^{-2} - 2x^{-1/2} + \frac{5}{2}x^{-3}$

Difficulty: 1

MULTIPLE CHOICE

17. Write as a sum of terms: $\dfrac{x - 2x^2 + x^3}{\sqrt{x}}$.

a) $x - 2x^2 + x^3 - x^{1/2}$
b) $x^{-1/2} + 2x^{-2} - x^{-3} + x^{1/2}$
c) $x^{1/2} - 2x^{1/2} + x^{3/2}$
d) $x^{1/2} - 2x^{3/2} + x^{5/2}$
e) None of these

Answer: d Difficulty: 1

18. Write as a sum of terms: $\dfrac{4x^3 - 3x^2 + 1}{x^{3/2}}$.

a) $4x^{9/2} - 3x^3 + x^{3/2}$
b) $4x^3 - 3x^2 + 1 - x^{3/2}$
c) $4x^{1/2} - 3x^{-1/2} + x^{-3/2}$
d) $4x^{-3/2} - 3x^{-1/2} + x^{-3/2}$
e) None of these

Answer: e Difficulty: 1

19. Write as a sum of terms: $\dfrac{3x^4 - 2x^2 + 1}{\sqrt[3]{x}}$.

a) $3x^4 - 2x^2 + x^{-3}$
b) $3x^4 - 2x^2 + 1 - x^{1/3}$
c) $3x^{11/3} - 2x^{5/3} + x^{-1/3}$
d) $3x - 2^{-1} + x^{-1/3}$
e) None of these

Answer: c Difficulty: 1

20. Simplify: $\frac{5}{2}x^2 + \frac{1}{3}x$.

a) $x\left[\frac{5}{2}x - \frac{1}{3}\right]$
b) $\frac{x}{6}(15x + 2)$
c) $\frac{x}{6}(10x + 3)$
d) $\frac{1}{6}x(5x + 1)$
e) None of these

Answer: b Difficulty: 1

21. Simplify: $\frac{2}{3}x^3 + \frac{1}{8}x^2$.

a) $\frac{x}{24}(16x^2 + 3)$
b) $\dfrac{x^2(16x + 3)}{24}$
c) $\dfrac{x^2(2x + 1)}{24}$
d) $x^2\left[\frac{2}{3}x - \frac{1}{8}\right]$
e) None of these

Answer: b Difficulty: 1

22. Simplify: $\frac{8}{3}x^{5/3} + \frac{2}{3}x^{-1/3} - \frac{1}{3}x^{-4/3}$.

a) $\frac{8}{3}x^{5/3}\left[1 + \frac{1}{4}x^{2} - \frac{1}{8}x^{1/3}\right]$

b) $\frac{x^{5/3}}{3}(8 + 2x^{-2} - x^{-4})$

c) $\dfrac{8x^3 + 2x - 1}{3x^{4/3}}$

d) $\dfrac{8x^{1/3} + 2x^{-5/3} - 1}{3x^{4/3}}$

e) None of these

Answer: c Difficulty: 2

SHORT ANSWER

23. Simplify: $\frac{1}{8}(3x + 1)^{3/2} + \frac{1}{4}(3x + 1)^{1/2}$.

Answer:

$\frac{3}{8}(3x + 1)^{1/2}(x + 1)$

Difficulty: 2

MULTIPLE CHOICE

24. Simplify: $\dfrac{(5x - 2)^{1/2}(2) - 2x\left(\frac{1}{2}\right)(5x - 2)^{-1/2}(5)}{(\sqrt{5x - 2})^2}$.

a) $\dfrac{2\sqrt{5x - 2} - 5x}{5x - 2}$

b) $\dfrac{-4}{(5x - 2)}$

c) $\dfrac{25x^2 + 2x + 8}{(5x - 2)^{3/2}}$

d) $\dfrac{5x - 4}{(5x - 2)^{3/2}}$

e) None of these

Answer: d Difficulty: 2

SHORT ANSWER

25. Simplify: $\dfrac{3x\left(\frac{5}{2}\right)(2x - 1)^{3/2} - (2x - 1)^{5/2}(3)}{(3x)^2}$.

Answer:

$-\dfrac{(x + 2)(2x - 1)^{3/2}}{6x^2}$

Difficulty: 2

MULTIPLE CHOICE

26. Simplify: $\dfrac{(3x+1)^{3/2}(2) - 2x\left[\frac{3}{2}\right](3x+1)^{1/2}(3)}{[(3x+1)^{3/2}]^2}$.

a) $\dfrac{6x-7}{(3x+1)^{7/4}}$ b) $\dfrac{6x-7}{(3x+1)^{5/2}}$ c) $\dfrac{2-3x}{(3x+1)^{5/2}}$

d) $\dfrac{1-3x}{(3x+1)^2}$ e) None of these

Answer: c Difficulty: 2

27. Simplify: $7x(-5)(3-2x)^{-6}(-2) + (3-2x)^{-5}(7)$.

a) $\dfrac{70x+21}{(3-2x)^5}$ b) $\dfrac{-140x^2+210x+7}{(3-2x)^6}$ c) $\dfrac{68x+21}{(3-2x)^5}$

d) $\dfrac{56x+21}{(3-2x)^6}$ e) None of these

Answer: d Difficulty: 2

28. Simplify: $5x^2(-2)(3+2x)^{-2} + (3+2x)^{-1}(10x)$.

a) $\dfrac{10x(x+3)}{(3+2x)^2}$ b) $\dfrac{2x(15-4x)}{(3+2x)^2}$ c) $\dfrac{10x(1-x)}{(3+2x)}$

d) $\dfrac{-6}{3+2x}$ e) None of these

Answer: a Difficulty: 2

29. Simplify: $\frac{4}{3}x^3(7x+1)^{-2/3} + (7x+1)^{1/3}(12x^2)$.

a) $\dfrac{4x^3+12x^2(7x+1)^{1/3}}{3(7x+1)^{2/3}}$ b) $\dfrac{x(91x+7)}{3(7x+1)^{2/3}}$ c) $\dfrac{4x(64x+9)}{3(7x+1)^{2/3}}$

d) $\dfrac{4x^2(64x+9)}{3(7x+1)^{2/3}}$ e) None of these

Answer: c Difficulty: 2

SHORT ANSWER

30. Insert the required factor in the parentheses:
$\dfrac{30x^2+18}{(5x^3+9x+2)^3} = (\quad)\dfrac{15x^2+9}{(5x^3+9x+2)^3}$.

Answer: 2 Difficulty: 1

MULTIPLE CHOICE

31. Insert the required factor in the parentheses:

$$\frac{3}{2}x^2(3x+2)^{-3/4} + (3x+2)^{1/4}(6x^2) = \frac{9}{2}x^2(3x+2)^{-3/4}(\quad).$$

a) $4x + 3$ b) $4x + 1$ c) $12x + 8$
d) $18x + 12$ e) None of these

Answer: a Difficulty: 2

32. Insert the required factor: $\dfrac{\frac{3}{2}x^2 + \frac{1}{4}}{2} = (\quad)(6x^2+1).$

a) $\frac{1}{6}$ b) $\frac{1}{4}$ c) $\frac{1}{8}$ d) $\frac{1}{2}$ e) None of these

Answer: c Difficulty: 1

33. Factor: $5x^2(x+3)^{1/2} + \frac{3}{2}(x+3)^{3/2}$.

a) $3(x+3)^{1/2}(5x^2+2x+6)$ b) $\frac{1}{3}(x+3)^{1/2}(15x^2+2x+3)$
c) $3(x+3)^{1/2}(15x^2+2x+6)$ d) $\frac{1}{3}(x+3)^{1/2}(15x^2+2x+6)$
e) None of these

Answer: d Difficulty: 2

34. Factor: $\frac{2}{3}(x+5)^{4/3} - \frac{1}{5}(x+5)^{7/3}$.

a) $\frac{7}{15}(x+5)$ b) $\frac{(x+5)^{4/3}}{15}(-5-3x)$ c) $15(x+5)^{4/3}(5-3x)$
d) $15(x+5)^{4/3}(15-3x)$ e) None of these

Answer: b Difficulty: 2

Chapter 0P8: Graphical Representation of Data

MULTIPLE CHOICE

1. The triangle shown in the figure has vertices at the points (-1, -1), (-1, 2), and (1, 1). Shift the triangle 3 units to the right and 2 units down and find the vertices of the shifted triangle.
   a) (2, 1), (2, 4), (4, 3)
   b) (-4, 1), (-4, 4), (-2, 3)
   c) (-4, -3), (-4, 0), (-2, -1)
   d) (2, -3), (2, 0), (4, -1)
   e) None of these

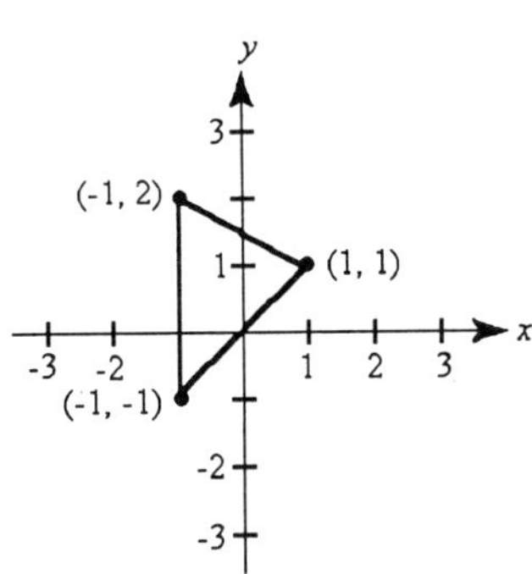

Answer: d Difficulty: 1

2. The triangle shown in the figure has vertices at the points (-1, 2), (1, 2) and (0, 0). Shift the triangle 2 units up and find the vertices of the shifted triangle.
   a) (1, 2), (3, 2), (2, 0)
   b) (-1, 4), (1, 4), (0, 2)
   c) (-1, 0), (1, 0), (0, -2)
   d) (-3, 2), (-1, 2), (-2, 2)
   e) None of these

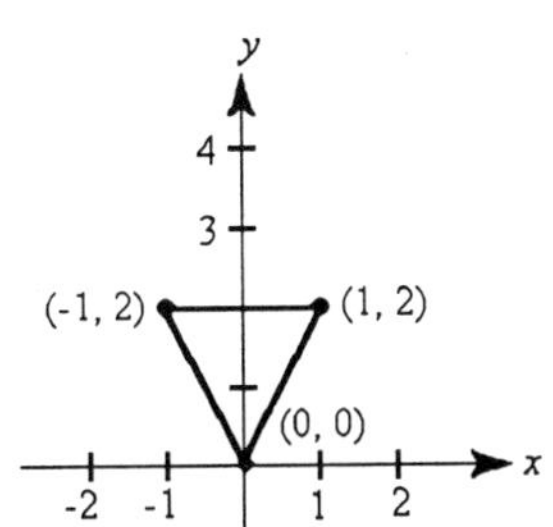

Answer: b Difficulty: 1

3. The translated triangle shown in the figure has vertices at the points (-1, 2), (1, 2) and (0, 0). It was shifted 3 units to the left. Find the vertices of the original triangle.
   a) (-1, -1), (1, -1), (0, -3) b) (-4, 2), (-2, 2), (-3, 0)
   c) (2, 2), (4, 2), (3, 0) d) (2, 2), (-2, 2), (-3, 0)
   e) None of these

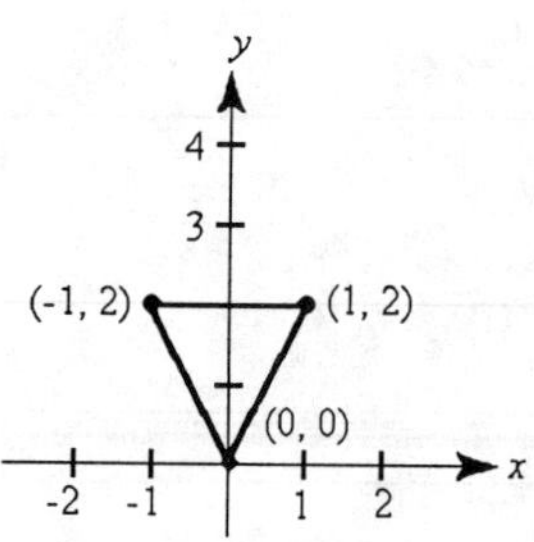

Answer: c Difficulty: 1

4. Find the distance between the points (3, 17) and (-2, 5).
   a) 13 b) $\sqrt{145}$ c) $\sqrt{485}$ d) $3\sqrt{51}$ e) None of these

Answer: a Difficulty: 1

5. Find the distance between the points (-6, 10) and (4, 2).
   a) $2\sqrt{37}$ b) $2\sqrt{41}$ c) $\sqrt{10}$ d) $2\sqrt{17}$ e) None of these

Answer: b Difficulty: 1

SHORT ANSWER

6. Find the distance between the points (3, -1) and (7, 2).

Answer: 5 Difficulty: 1

7. Find the distance between the points (3, 5) and (-2, -1).

Answer:

$\sqrt{61}$

Difficulty: 1

MULTIPLE CHOICE

8. Find the midpoint of the line segment joining (3, 7) and (-6, 1).
   a) $\left(-\frac{3}{2}, 4\right)$ b) $\left(\frac{9}{2}, 3\right)$ c) (-3, 6)
   d) (-3, 4) e) None of these

Answer: a Difficulty: 1

9. Find the midpoint of the line segment joining (-3, 1) and (-5, -7).
   a) (-4, -4) b) (1, -3) c) (-4, -3)
   d) $\left(\frac{15}{2}, \frac{-7}{2}\right)$ e) None of these

   Answer: c Difficulty: 1

10. Find the midpoint of the line segment joining (-2, 1) and (16, 3).
    a) (7, 2) b) (9, 1) c) (14, 4)
    d) (-9, -1) e) None of these

    Answer: a Difficulty: 1

SHORT ANSWER

11. Find the midpoint of the line segment joining (6, 9) and (-3, 1).

    Answer:
    $\left(\frac{3}{2}, 5\right)$
    Difficulty: 1

12. Find the midpoint of the line segment joining (-6, -2) and (5, -1).

    Answer:
    $\left(-\frac{1}{2}, -\frac{3}{2}\right)$
    Difficulty: 1

MULTIPLE CHOICE

13. The point (3, 2) is the midpoint of (x, y) and (5, 1). Find the point (x, y).
    a) (3, 1) b) (1, 3) c) (10, 2)
    d) $\left(4, \frac{3}{2}\right)$ e) None of these

    Answer: b Difficulty: 1

14. Find the distance between the origin and the midpoint of the two points (3, 3) and (3, 5).
    a) $3\sqrt{2}$ b) 7 c) $\sqrt{34}$ d) 5 e) None of these

    Answer: d Difficulty: 2

15. Find the distance between the origin and the midpoint of the two points (2, 7) and (6, 5).
   a) 10 b) $2\sqrt{13}$ c) $4\sqrt{13}$ d) $2\sqrt{5}$ e) None of these

   Answer: b Difficulty: 2

SHORT ANSWER

16. Find three points on a segment with endpoints (2, 10) and (8, -4) that are equidistant from each other.

   Answer:
   $\left(\frac{7}{2}, \frac{13}{2}\right)$, (5, 3), $\left(\frac{13}{2}, \frac{-1}{2}\right)$
   Difficulty: 2

MULTIPLE CHOICE

17. Identify the type of triangle that has (-5, -1), (2, 2), and (0, -3) as vertices.
   a) Scalene b) Right isosceles c) Equilateral
   d) Isosceles e) None of these

   Answer: b Difficulty: 2

18. Identify the type of triangle that has (1, 10), (-3, -2), and (3, 16) as vertices.
   a) Isosceles b) Right c) Scalene
   d) Equilateral e) These points do not form a triangle.

   Answer: e Difficulty: 2

19. Identify the type of triangle that has (0, 0), (4, 0), and $(2, 2\sqrt{3})$ as vertices.
   a) Scalene b) Right c) Isosceles
   d) Equilateral e) These points do not form a triangle.

   Answer: d Difficulty: 2

20. Identify the type of triangle that has (0, 0), (4, 0) and $(2, 4\sqrt{2})$ as vertices.
   a) Scalene b) Right c) Isosceles
   d) Equilateral e) These points do not form a triangle.

   Answer: c Difficulty: 2

21. Determine the quadrant in which the point (x, y) must be located if $x > 0$ and $y < 0$.
   a) I b) II c) III d) IV e) None of these

   Answer: d Difficulty: 1

22. Determine the quadrant in which the point (x, y) must be located if $x < 0$ and $y > 0$.
    a) I   b) II   c) III   d) IV   e) None of these

    Answer: b Difficulty: 1

23. Determine the quadrant(s) in which the point (x, y) must be located if $xy < 0$.
    a) II   b) II and III   c) II and IV
    d) I and III   e) None of these

    Answer: c Difficulty: 1

24. If $x < 0$ and $y > 0$, in what quadrant is $(-x, -y)$ located?
    a) I   b) II   c) III   d) IV   e) None of these

    Answer: d Difficulty: 1

SHORT ANSWER

25. Find the length of the hypotenuse of the right triangle determined by the points (1, 1), (-2, 1), and (-2, 4).

    Answer:

    $3\sqrt{2}$

    Difficulty: 2

26. Find the length of the hypotenuse of the right triangle determined by the points (-1, 1), (3, 1), and (3, -3).

    Answer:

    $4\sqrt{2}$

    Difficulty: 2

MULTIPLE CHOICE

27. In a football game, the quarterback throws a pass from the 8-yard line, 15 yards from the sideline. The pass is caught on the 43-yard line, 3 yards from the same sideline. How long was the pass? (Assume the pass and the reception are on the same side of midfield.)
    a) 40 yards   b) 36.1 yards   c) 39.4 yards
    d) 37 yards   e) None of these

    Answer: d Difficulty: 2 Key 1: T

28. In a football game, the quarterback throws a pass from the 3-yard line, 10 yards from the sideline. The pass is caught on the 43-yard line, 40 yards from the same sideline. How long was the pass? (Assume the pass and the reception are on the same side of midfield.)
    a) 60 yards b) 55 yards c) 50 yards
    d) 45 yards e) None of these

    Answer: c Difficulty: 2 Key 1: T

SHORT ANSWER

29. A homeowner needs to determine the distance y from the peak to the lower edge of the roof on the garage. He knows the distance from the ground to the peak is $14\frac{1}{2}$ feet and the distance from the lower edge of the roof to the ground is 11 feet. Find y if the garage is 20 feet wide.

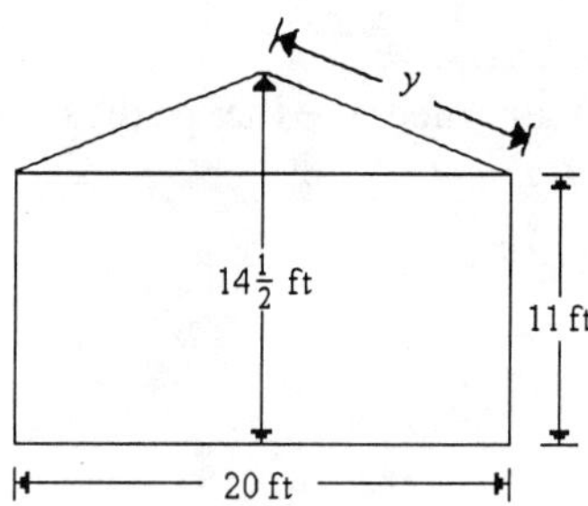

Answer: 10.6 feet Difficulty: 2 Key 1: T

MULTIPLE CHOICE

30. A homeowner needs to determine the distance y from the peak to the lower edge of the roof on his garage. He knows the distance from the ground to the peak is 13 feet and the distance from the lower edge of the roof to the ground is 10 feet. Find y if the garage is 18 feet wide. (Round to 1 decimal place.)
    a) 10.1 feet b) 9.8 feet c) 9.5 feet
    d) 9.3 feet e) None of these

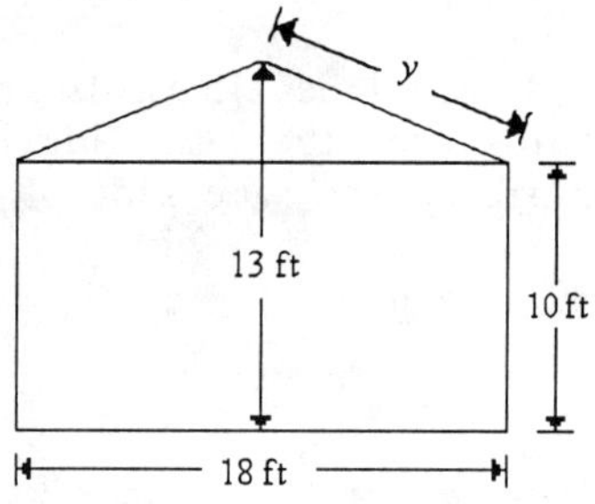

Answer: c Difficulty: 2 Key 1: T

SHORT ANSWER

31. The accompanying figure gives the speed of a car (in mph) and the approximate stopping distance in feet.

Complete the table by approximating the stopping distance.

Speed, x	30	40	50	60	70	80
Stopping distance, y						

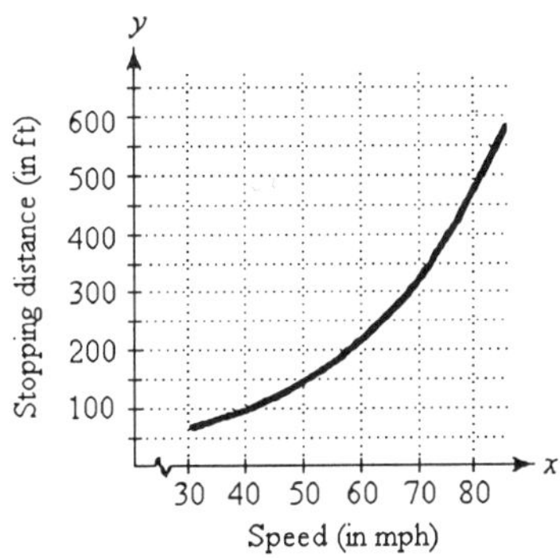

Answer:

Speed, x	30	40	50	60	70	80
Stopping distance, y	65	95	140	205	300	450

Difficulty: 2

32. The accompanying figure gives the normal Fahrenheit temperature, y, for Anchorage, Alaska, for each month, x, of the year where $x = 1$ represents January.

Complete the table by approximating the temperature.

Month, x	1	2	3	4	5	6	7	8	9	10	11	12
Temperature, y												

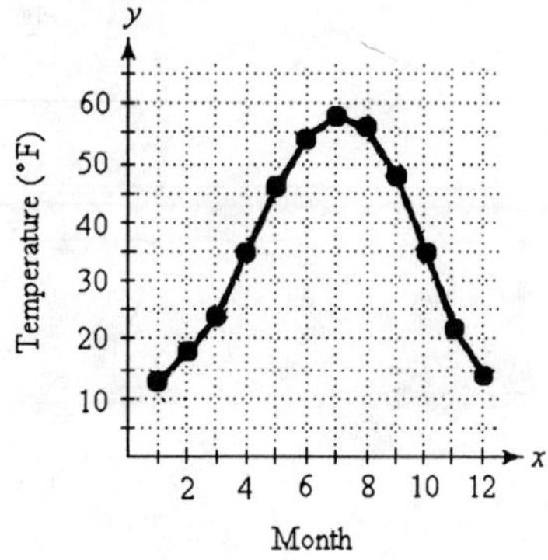

Answer:

Month, x	1	2	3	4	5	6	7	8	9	10	11	12
Temperature, y	13	18	24	35	46	54	58	56	48	35	22	14

Difficulty: 2

Chapter 011: Graphs of Equations

MULTIPLE CHOICE

1. Determine which of the following ordered pairs is not a solution of the equation $7x - 3y = 5$.
   a) (2, 3)
   b) $\left(1, \frac{2}{3}\right)$
   c) (4, 11)
   d) $\left(-\frac{1}{7}, -2\right)$
   e) All of these are solutions.

   Answer: c Difficulty: 1

2. Determine which of the following points does not lie on the graph of $y = \dfrac{1}{x^2 + 1}$.
   a) $\left(-1, \frac{1}{2}\right)$
   b) $\left(-2, -\frac{1}{3}\right)$
   c) $\left(3, \frac{1}{10}\right)$
   d) $\left(6, \frac{1}{37}\right)$
   e) All of these lie on the graph.

   Answer: b Difficulty: 1

3. Determine which of the following ordered pairs is a solution of the equation $y = x\sqrt{x + 1}$.
   a) (1, 2)
   b) (2, 6)
   c) (-1, 1)
   d) (3, 6)
   e) None of these are solutions.

   Answer: d Difficulty: 1

SHORT ANSWER

4. Complete the following table for $y = 4x^2 + 2$.

x	-2	0	2
y			

Answer:

x	-2	0	2
y	18	2	18

Difficulty: 1

5. Complete the following table for $y = 25x\left[\dfrac{4x}{x^2 + 5} + 2\right]$.

x	-2	0	2	4
y				

Answer:

x	-2	0	2	4
y	$-\dfrac{500}{9}$	0	$\dfrac{1300}{9}$	$\dfrac{5800}{21}$

Difficulty: 1

6. Complete the following table for $y = 9 - x^2$.

x	-3	-1	0	2	3
y					

Answer:

x	-3	-1	0	2	3
y	0	8	9	5	0

Difficulty: 1

7. Find the x-intercept(s) and the y-intercept(s) of the graph of the equation $y = x^2 - 5x + 6$.

Answer:
x-intercepts: (2, 0), (3, 0)
y-intercept: (0, 6)

Difficulty: 1

8. Find the x-intercept(s) and the y-intercept(s) of the graph of the equation $y = x^2 - 3x - 4$.

Answer:
x-intercepts: (-1, 0), (4, 0)
y-intercept: (0, -4)

Difficulty: 1

9. Find the x-intercept(s) and the y-intercept(s) of the graph of the equation $y^2 = x + 9$.

Answer:
x-intercept: (-9, 0)
y-intercepts: (0, 3), (0, -3)

Difficulty: 1

10. Find the x-intercept(s) and the y-intercept(s) of the graph of the equation $y = -2x + 6$.

Answer:
x-intercept: (3, 0)
y-intercept: (0, 6)

Difficulty: 1

11. Use a graphing utility to graph $y = x^2 - 2x - 3$. Use a standard setting. Approximate any intercepts.

Answer: x-intercepts: (-1, 0), (3, 0); y-intercept: (0, -3)

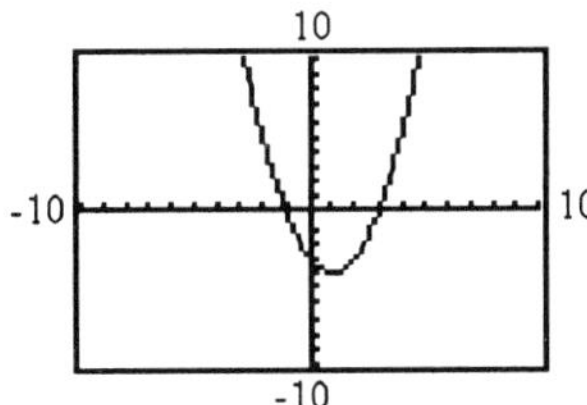

Difficulty: 2 Key 1: T

12. Use a graphing utility to graph $y = x(x + 6)$. Use a standard setting. Approximate any intercepts.

Answer: x-intercepts: (-6, 0), (0, 0); y-intercept: (0, 0)

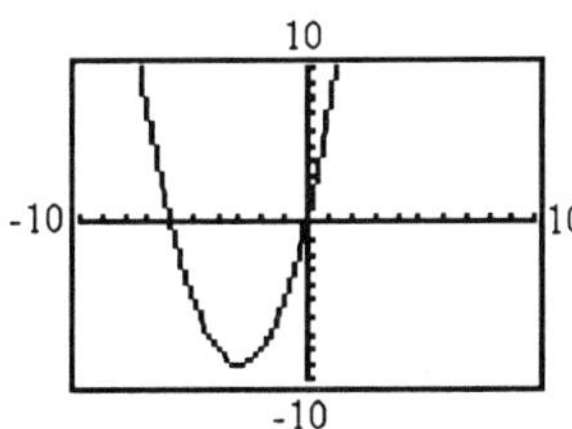

Difficulty: 2 Key 1: T

13. Use a graphing utility to graph $y = \frac{2x}{x - 2}$. Use a standard setting. Approximate any intercepts.

Answer: x-intercept: (0, 0); y-intercept: (0, 0)

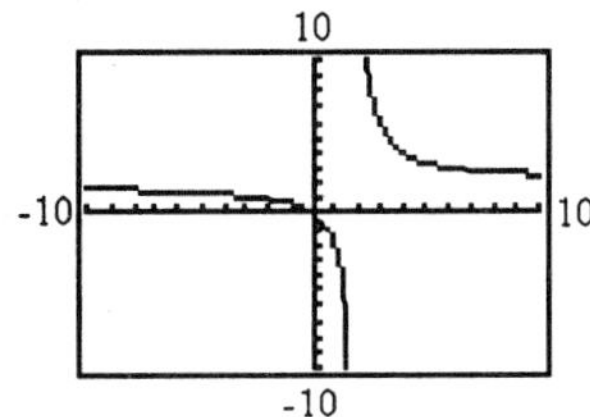

Difficulty: 2 Key 1: T

14. Sketch the complete graph of the equation if the graph has y-axis symmetry.

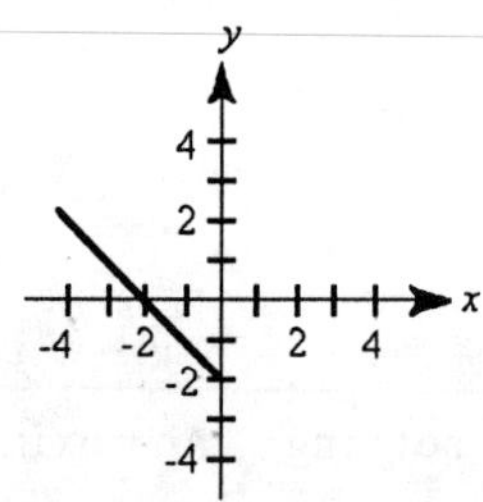

Answer: See graph below

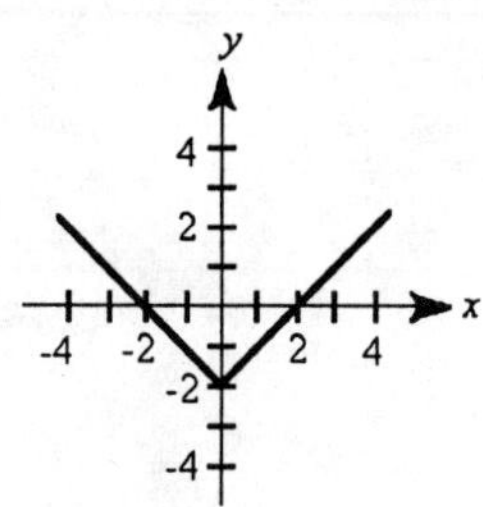

Difficulty: 1

MULTIPLE CHOICE

15. Identify the type(s) of symmetry: $x^4y^2 + 2x^2y - 1 = 0$.
    a) x-axis b) y-axis c) Origin
    d) Both x-axis and y-axis e) None of these

    Answer: b Difficulty: 1

16. Identify the type(s) of symmetry: $3x^4 + xy - 2 = 0$.
    a) x-axis b) y-axis c) Origin
    d) Both y-axis and origin e) None of these

    Answer: c Difficulty: 1

17. Identify the type(s) of symmetry: $y = x^3 + 3x$.
    a) x-axis b) y-axis c) Origin
    d) Both x-axis and y-axis e) None of these

    Answer: c Difficulty: 1

SHORT ANSWER

18. Identify the type(s) of symmetry: $y = |x| - 2$.

    Answer: Symmetric to the y-axis. Difficulty: 1

19. Identify the type(s) of symmetry: $x^2 + xy + y^2 = 0$.

    Answer: Symmetric to the origin. Difficulty: 1

MULTIPLE CHOICE

20. Identify the graph of the equation: $y = |x + 7|$.
a) I b) II c) III d) IV e) None of these

(I)

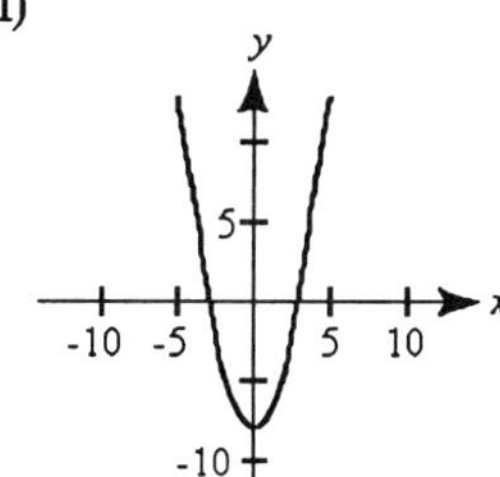

(II)

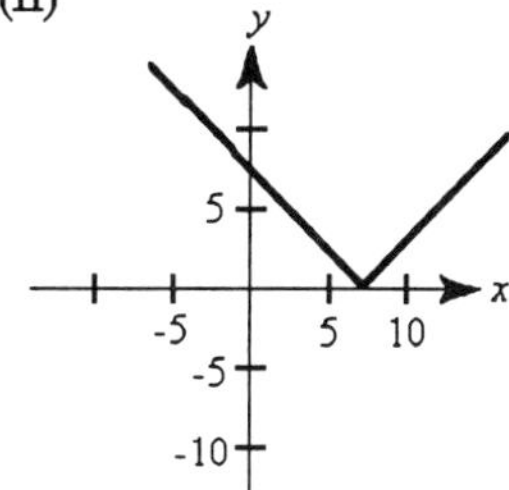

(III)

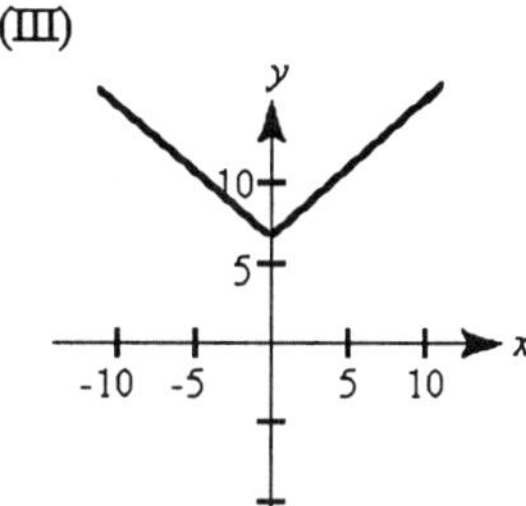

(IV)

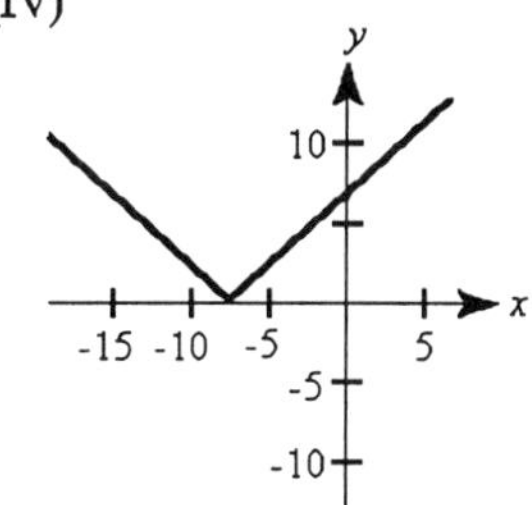

Answer: d Difficulty: 1

21. Identify the graph of the equation: $y = \sqrt{2 - x}$.
a) I b) II c) III d) IV e) None of these

(I)

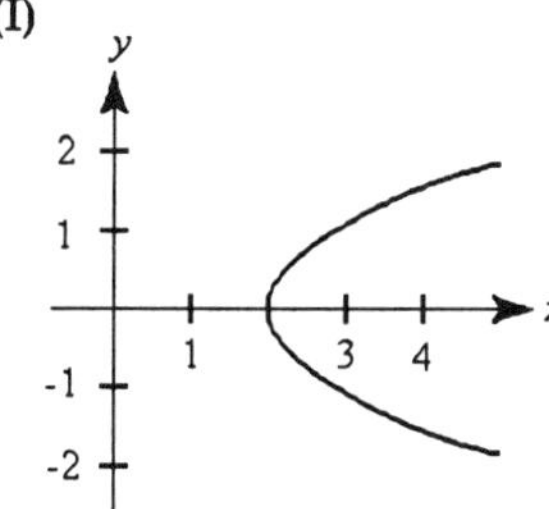

(II)

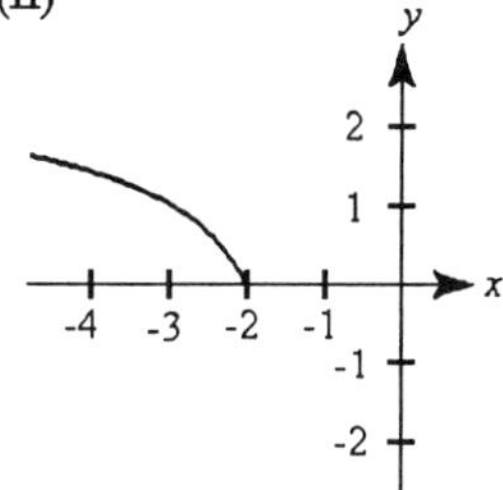

(III)

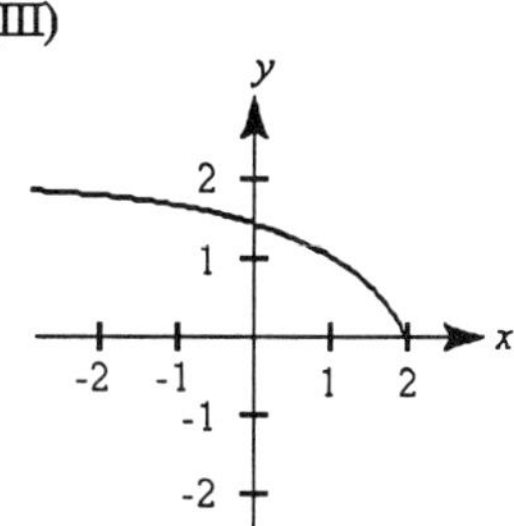

(IV)

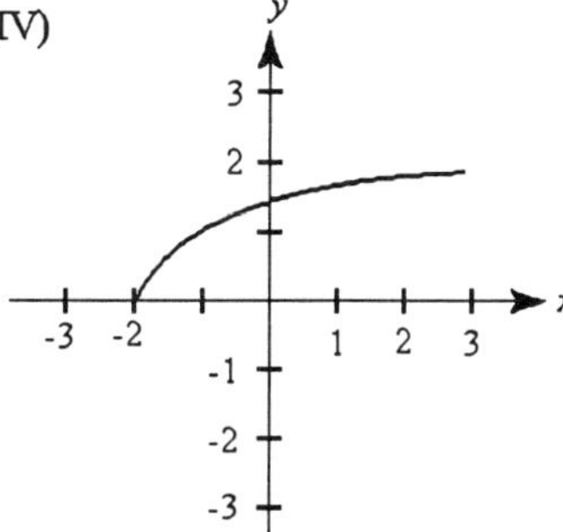

Answer: c Difficulty: 1

22. Identify the graph of the equation: $y = \sqrt{x + 3}$.

a) I b) II c) III d) IV e) None of these

(I)

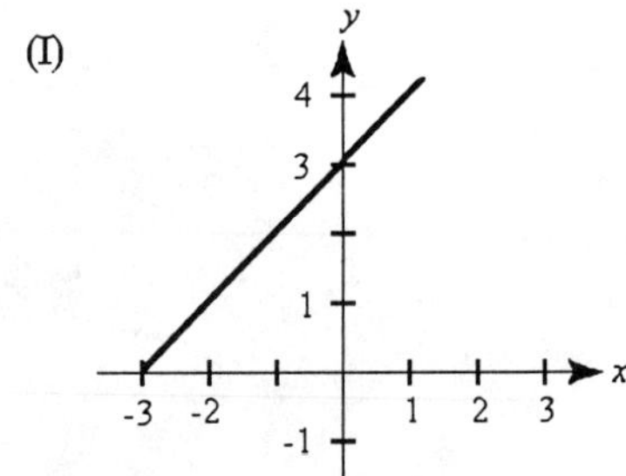

(II)

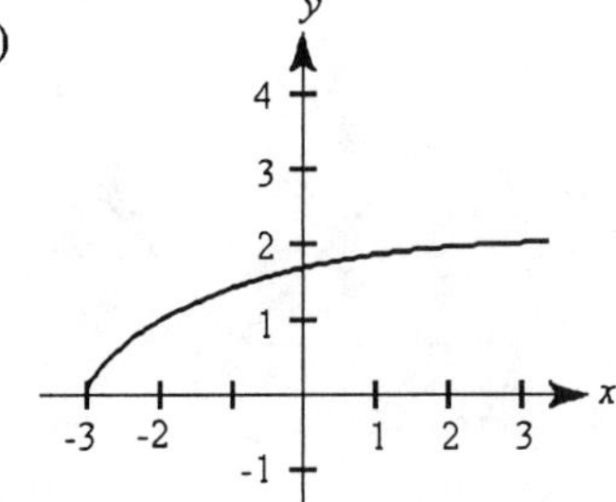

(III)

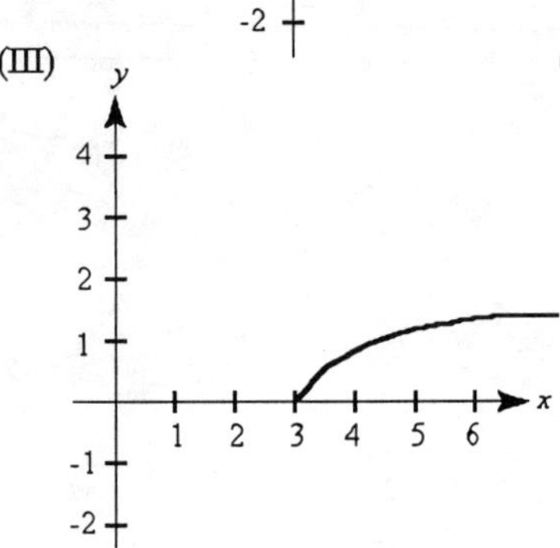

(IV)

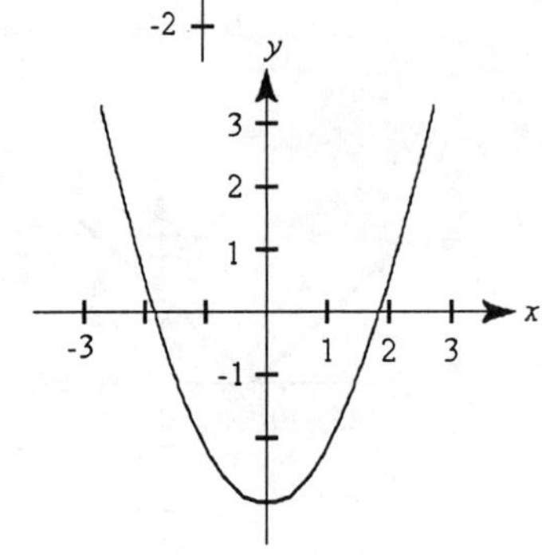

Answer: b Difficulty: 1

23. Match the equation with the graph.

a) $y = \sqrt{9 - x^2}$ b) $y = |x^2 - 9|$ c) $y = \sqrt{x^2 - 9}$

d) $y = (9 - x)^2$ e) None of these

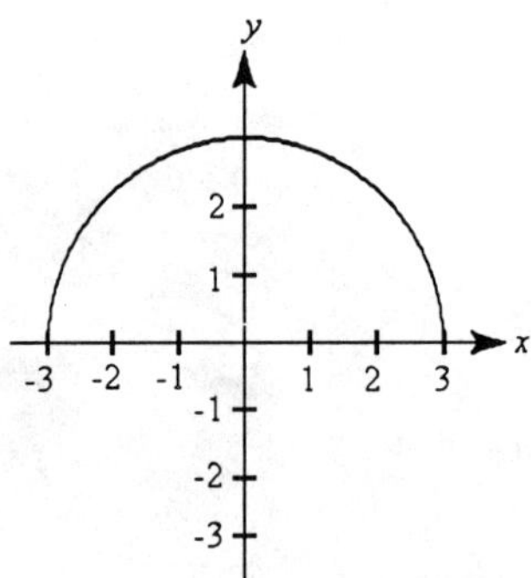

Answer: a Difficulty: 1

24. Match the equation with the graph.

a) $y = \sqrt{x - 3}$ b) $y = |x - 3|$ c) $y = (x - 3)^2$

d) $y = x - 3$ e) None of these

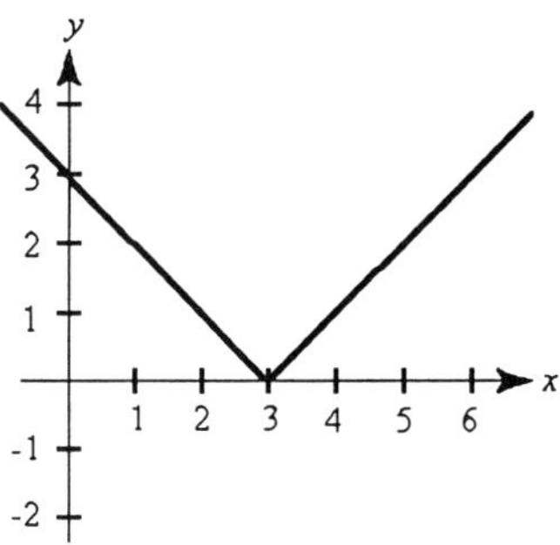

Answer: b Difficulty: 1

25. Match the equation with the graph.

a) $y = (x + 3)^2$ b) $y = x^2 - 3$ c) $y = (x - 3)^2$

d) $y = x^2 + 3$ e) None of these

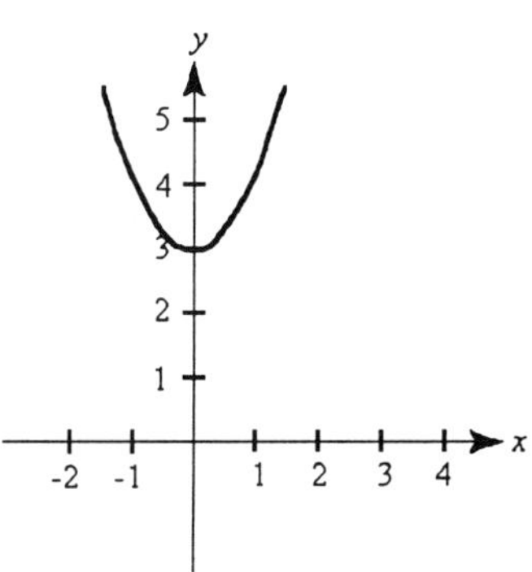

Answer: d Difficulty: 1

26. Match the equation with the graph.

a) $x^3 - 2$ b) $x^3 + 2$ c) $(x + 2)^3$

d) $(x - 2)^3$ e) None of these

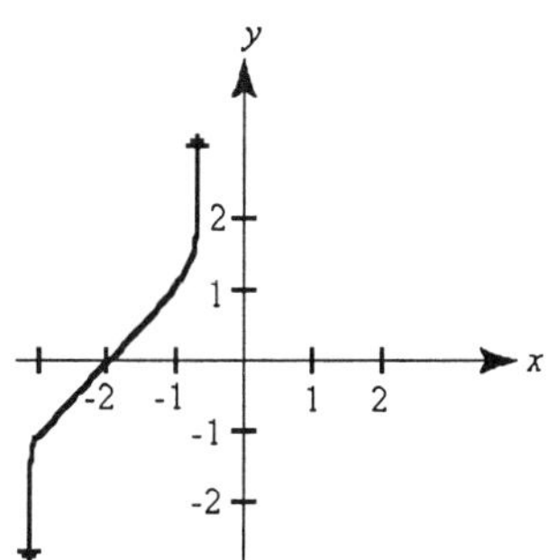

Answer: c Difficulty: 1

27. Match the equation with the graph.
    a) $y = (x - 2)^2 + 1$ b) $y = (x + 2)^2 + 1$ c) $y = (x - 2)^2 - 1$
    d) $y = (x + 2)^2 - 1$ e) None of these

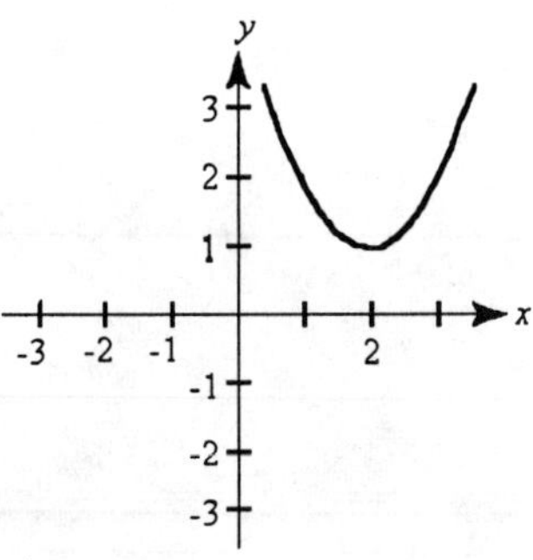

Answer: a Difficulty: 1

28. Match the equation with the graph.
    a) $y = (x - 3)^2 + 1$ b) $y = (x + 1)^2 - 3$ c) $y = (x + 3)^2 - 1$
    d) $y = x^2 - 3x + 1$ e) None of these

Answer: e Difficulty: 1

SHORT ANSWER

29. Write the equation that matches the graph.

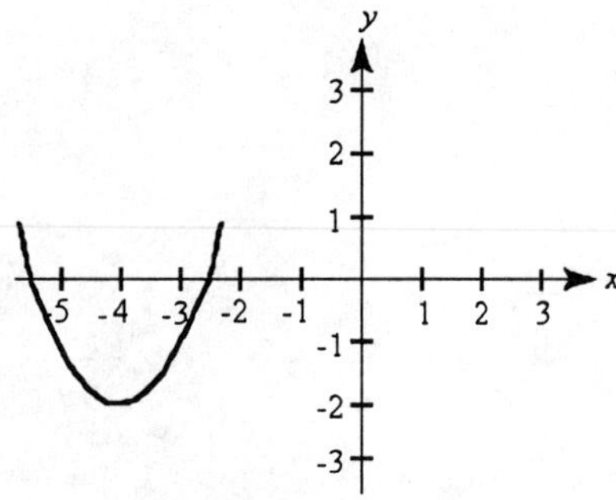

Answer:

$y = (x + 4)^2 - 2$
Difficulty: 1

MULTIPLE CHOICE

30. Determine the standard equation of the circle with radius 3 and center (3, -2).
    a) $(x - 3)^2 + (y - 2)^2 = 3$
    b) $(x - 3)(y - 2) = 9$
    c) $(x - 3)^2 + (y + 2)^2 = \sqrt{3}$
    d) $(x - 3)^2 + (y + 2)^2 = 9$
    e) None of these

    Answer: d Difficulty: 1

31. Determine the standard equation of the circle with radius 5 and center (-4, -3).
    a) $(x - 4)^2 + (y - 3)^2 = 25$
    b) $(x - 4)(x - 3) = 5$
    c) $(x + 4)^2 + (y + 3)^2 = 5$
    d) $(x + 4)^2 + (y - 3)^2 = 25$
    e) None of these

    Answer: e Difficulty: 1

32. Determine the standard equation of the circle with radius 2 and center (-1, 3).
    a) $(x - 1)^2 + (y - 3)^2 = 2$
    b) $(x - 1)^2 + (y - 3)^2 = 4$
    c) $(x + 1)^2 + (y - 3)^2 = 2$
    d) $(x + 1)^2 + (y- 3)^2 = 4$
    e) None of these

    Answer: d Difficulty: 1

SHORT ANSWER

33. Determine the standard equation of the circle with radius 7 and center (-2, -4).

    Answer:

    $(x + 2)^2 + (y + 4)^2 = 49$

    Difficulty: 1

34. Determine the standard equation of the circle with radius 16 and center $\left(0, \frac{1}{2}\right)$.

    Answer:

    $x^2 + \left(y = \frac{1}{2}\right)^2 = 256$

    Difficulty: 1

MULTIPLE CHOICE

35. Find the center and radius of the circle: $(x - 2)^2 + (y + 4)^2 = 25$.
    a) Center: (2, -4); radius: 5
    b) Center: (-2, 4); radius: 5
    c) Center: (2, -4); radius: 25
    d) Center: (-2, 4); radius: 25
    e) None of these

    Answer: a Difficulty: 1

36. Find the center and radius of the circle: $(x + 4)^2 + (y - 1)^2 = 36$.
   a) Center: (-4, 1); radius: 36
   b) Center: (4, -1); radius: 36
   c) Center: (-4, 1); radius: 6
   d) Center: (4, -1); radius: 6
   e) None of these

   Answer: c Difficulty: 1

37. Find the center and radius of the circle: $(x + 1)^2 + (y + 2)^2 = 4$.
   a) Center: (-1, -2); radius: 16
   b) Center: (-1, -2); radius: 2
   c) Center: (1, 2); radius: 16
   d) Center: (1, 2); radius: 2
   e) None of these

   Answer: b Difficulty: 1

SHORT ANSWER

38. Use a graphing utility to graph $y_1 = \sqrt{64 - x^2}$ and $y_2 = -\sqrt{64 - x^2}$. Use a square setting. Identify the graph.

   Answer: See graph below.

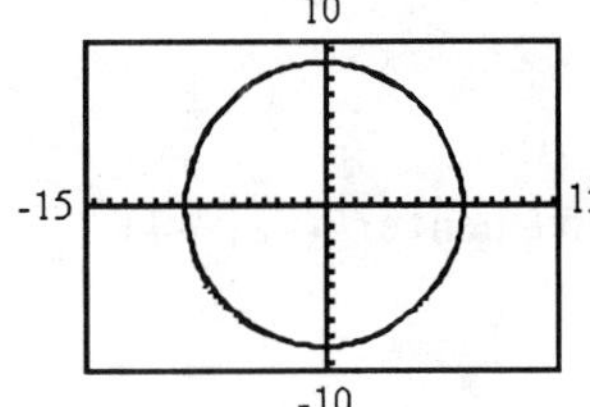

; a circle

   Difficulty: 2 Key 1: T

39. Use a graphing utility to graph $y_1 = 4 + \sqrt{25 - (x - 1)^2}$ and $y_2 = 4 - \sqrt{25 - (x - 1)^2}$. Use a square setting. Identify the graph.

   Answer: See graph below.

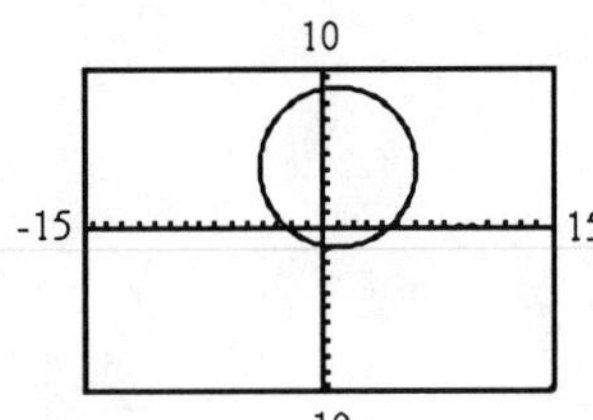

; a circle

   Difficulty: 2 Key 1: T

40. Find the center and radius of the circle: $\left(x - \frac{1}{2}\right)^2 + (y + 3)^2 = \frac{4}{9}$.

   Answer:

   Center: $\left(\frac{1}{2}, -3\right)$; radius: $\frac{2}{3}$

   Difficulty: 1

41. Find the center and radius of the circle: $(x - 5)^2 + (y + 4)^2 = 10$.

Answer:

Center: (5, -4); radius: $\sqrt{10}$

Difficulty: 1

MULTIPLE CHOICE

42. The earnings per share for a certain corporation from 1995 to 2000 can be approximated by the mathematical model $y = 1.23t + 0.25$ where y is the earnings and t represents the calendar year with $t = 0$ corresponding to the year 1995. Identify the graph of this equation.

a) I b) II c) III d) IV e) None of these

(I)

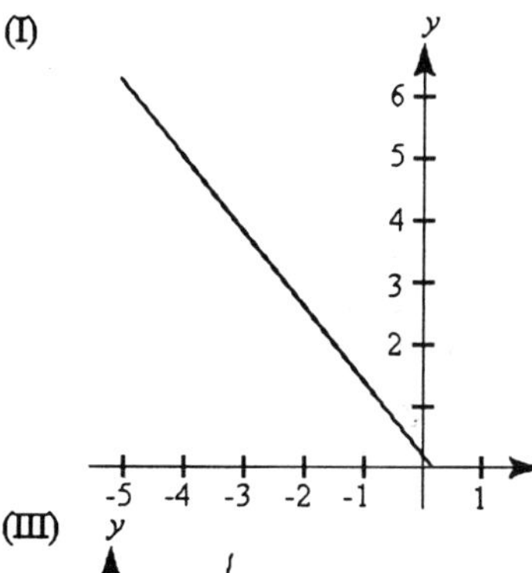

(II)

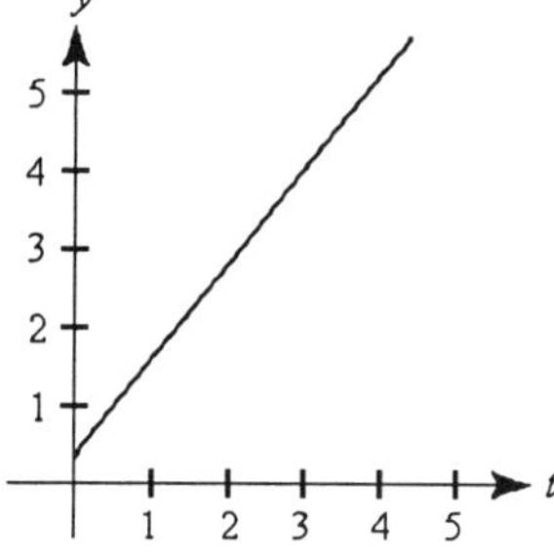

(III)

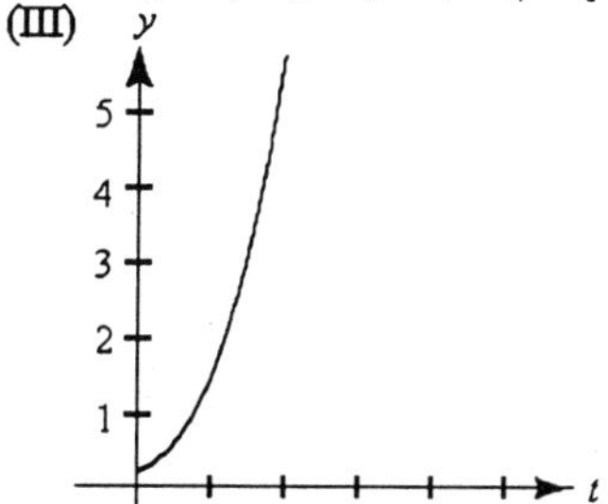

(IV)

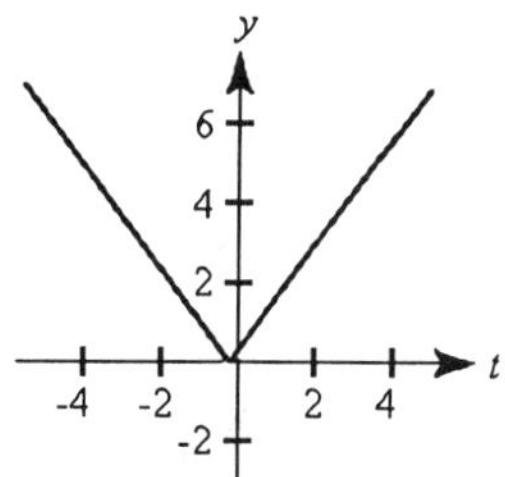

Answer: b Difficulty: 1

SHORT ANSWER

43. The depreciated value y of a certain machine after t years is determined using the model $y = 36{,}000 - 4300t$, $0 \le t \le 5$. Sketch the graph of the equation over the given interval.

Answer: See graph below.

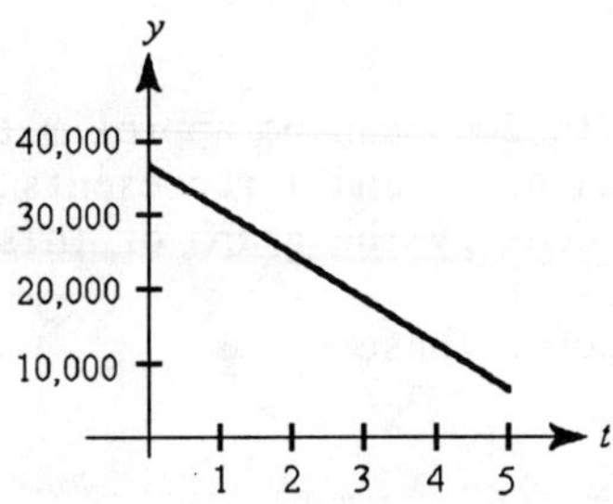

Difficulty: 1

MULTIPLE CHOICE

44. The depreciated value y of a certain machine after t years is determined using the model $y = 35{,}000 - 5000t$, $0 \le t \le 5$. Sketch the graph of the equation over the given interval.

a) I b) II c) III d) IV e) None of these

(I)

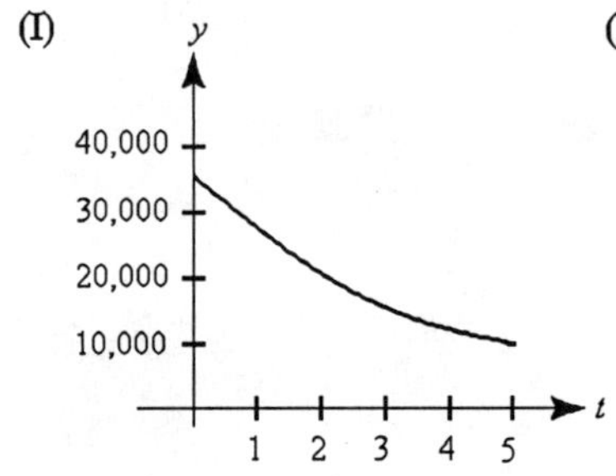

(II)

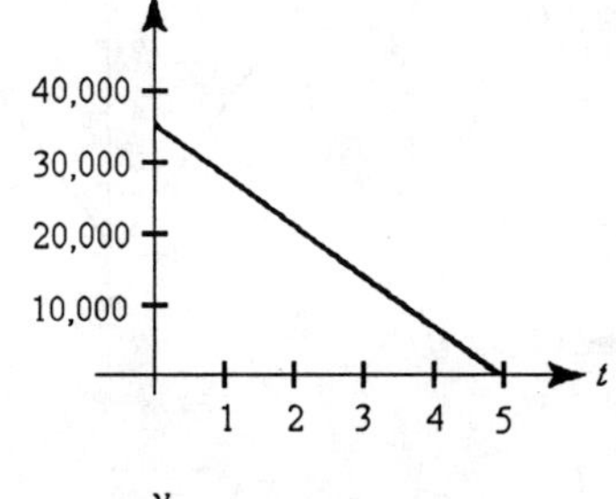

(III)

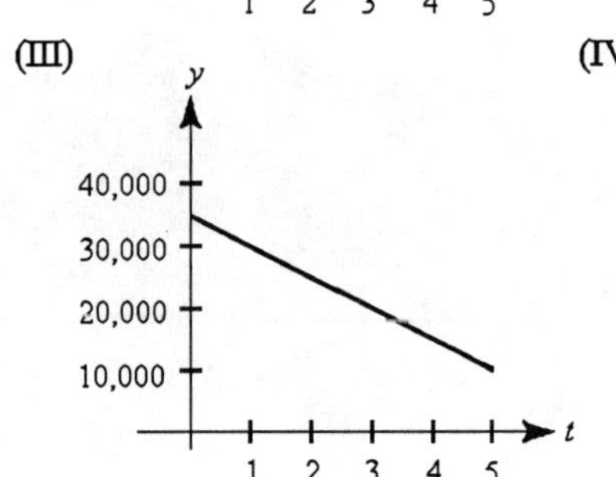

(IV)

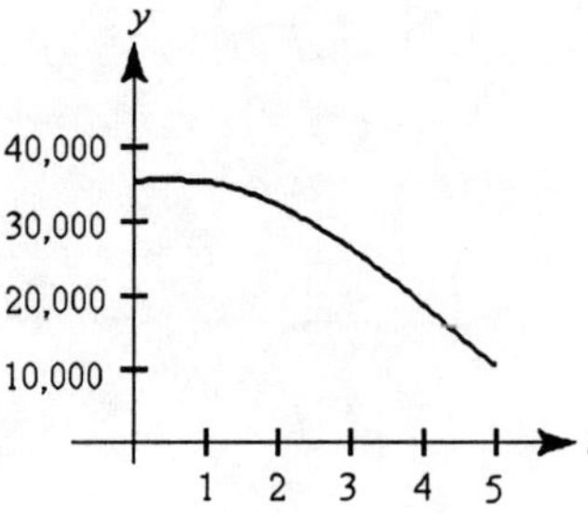

Answer: c Difficulty: 1

45. The total cost C of a taxable item, in a state that has a 7% sales tax, is $C = 0.07p + p$ where p is the price of the item. Graph this equation over the interval $0 \le p \le 100$.
a) I b) II c) III d) IV e) None of these

(I)

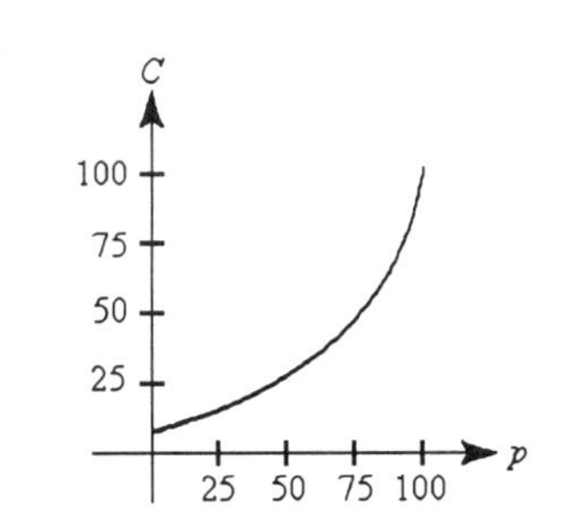

(II)

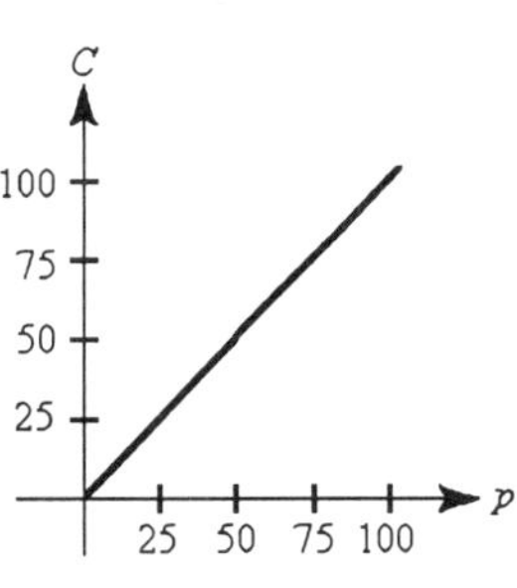

(III)

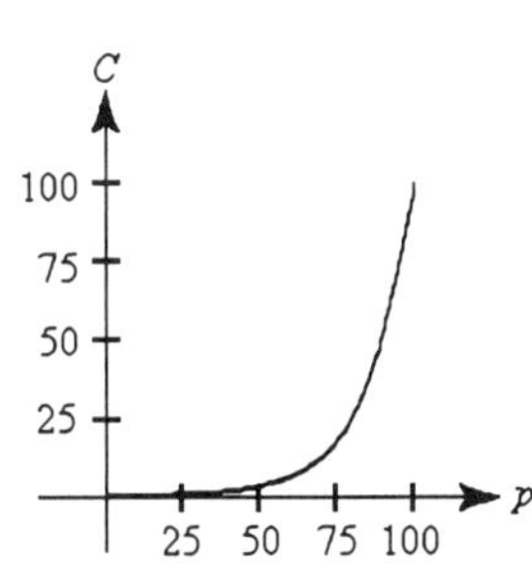

(IV)

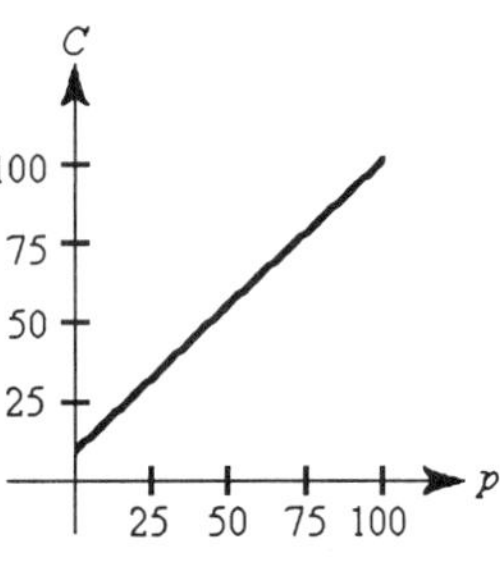

Answer: b Difficulty: 1

46. The table gives the average attendance per professional basketball game in the United States.

Year	1992	1993	1994	1995	1996	1997	1998
Attendance per game	15,689	16,060	16,246	16,727	17,252	17,077	17,135

(Source: *National Basketball Association*)

A model for the average attendance per game between 1992 and 1998 is

$y = 1.4129x^4 - 44.285x^3 + 399.75x^2 - 1006.9x + 16{,}462$

where y is the average attendance per game and x is the year with $x = 2$ corresponding to 1992. Use a graphing utility to estimate the average attendance per game in 2000 according to the model.
a) 15,499 b) 16,766 c) 16,212 d) 18,323 e) None of these

Answer: c Difficulty: 2 Key 1: T

SHORT ANSWER

47. The total amount spent on television advertising in the United States between 1990 and 1998 can be approximated by the model

$$y = -51.418x^3 + 825.46x^2 - 948.0x + 28{,}893, \quad 0 \le x \le 8$$

where y is the amount spent, in millions of dollars, and x is the year with $x = 0$ corresponding to 1990. Use a graphing utility to graph this equation. (Source: McCann-Erickson, Inc.)

Answer: See graph below.

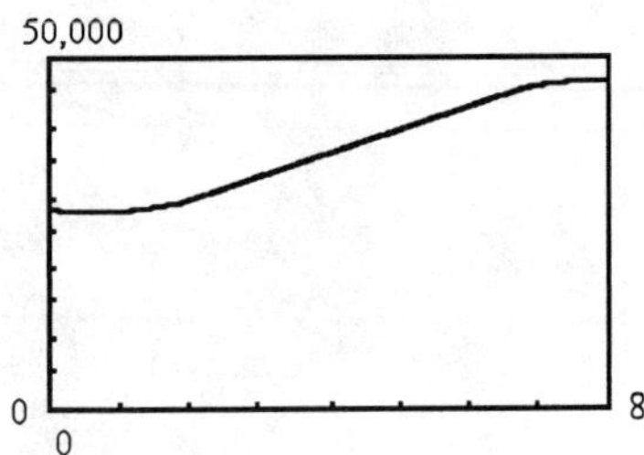

Difficulty: 2 Key 1: T

48. The formula to convert temperature in degrees Celsius to temperature in degrees Fahrenheit is $F = \frac{9}{5}C + 32$. Graph this equation for $0 \le C \le 100$.

Answer: See graph below.

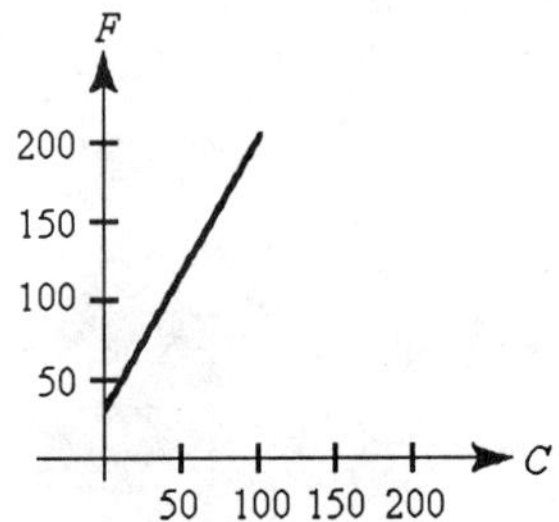

Difficulty: 1

Chapter 012: Linear Equations in Two Variables

MULTIPLE CHOICE

1. If L_1 has a slope of 1, which of the following is true?
   a) L_1 is horizontal. b) L_1 is vertical.
   c) L_1 rises from left to right. d) L_1 falls from left to right.
   e) None of these

   Answer: c Difficulty: 1

2. Determine the slope of the line.
   a) 1 b) $\frac{1}{2}$ c) -2 d) $-\frac{1}{2}$ e) None of these

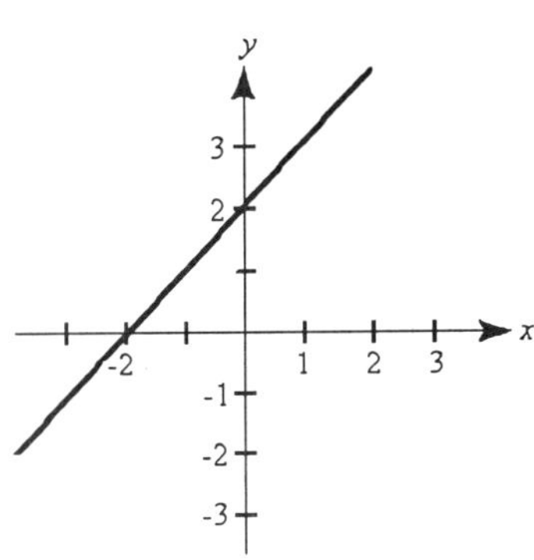

   Answer: a Difficulty: 1

3. Determine the slope of the line.
   a) $\frac{5}{2}$ b) $-\frac{5}{2}$ c) $\frac{2}{5}$ d) $-\frac{2}{5}$ e) None of these

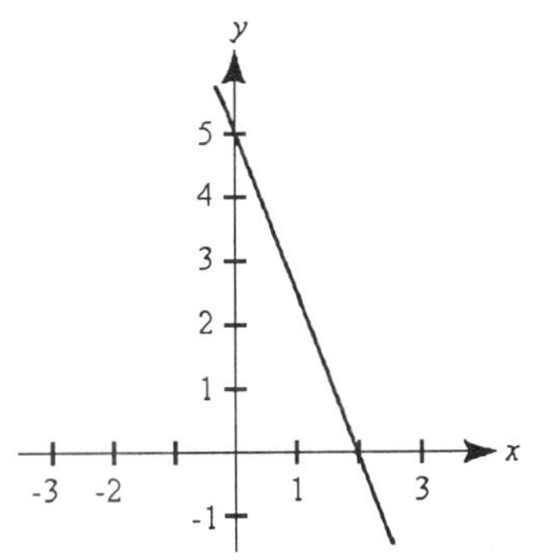

   Answer: b Difficulty: 1

4. Determine the slope of the line.
   a) $\frac{2}{3}$ b) $-\frac{2}{3}$ c) $\frac{3}{2}$ d) $-\frac{3}{2}$ e) None of these

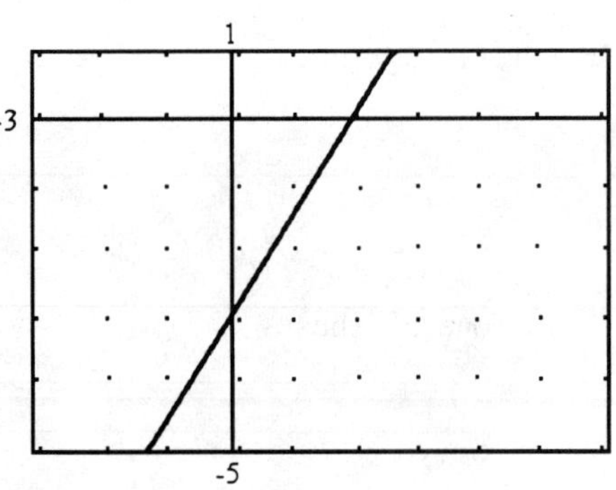

Answer: c Difficulty: 1

5. Determine the slope of the line.
   a) $-\frac{1}{2}$ b) $\frac{1}{2}$ c) 2 d) -2 e) None of these

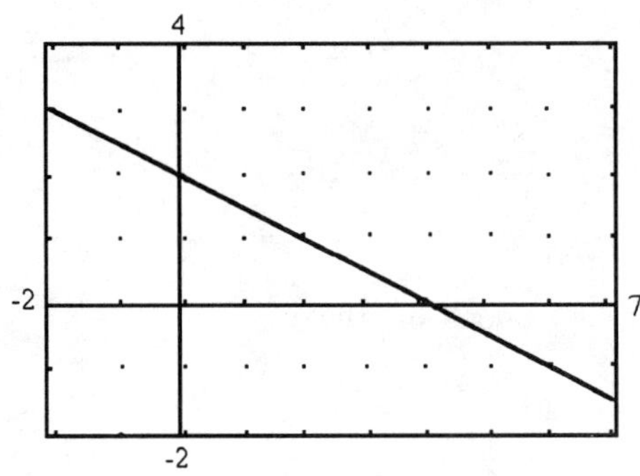

Answer: a Difficulty: 1

6. Determine the slope of the line.
   a) $\frac{1}{5}$ b) $-\frac{1}{5}$ c) 5 d) -5 e) None of these

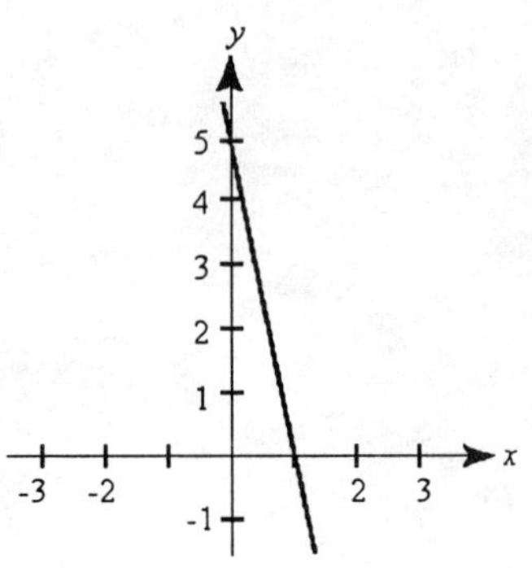

Answer: d Difficulty: 1

7. Find the slope of the line passing through (6, 10) and (-1, 4).
   a) $\frac{7}{6}$ b) $-\frac{7}{6}$ c) $\frac{6}{7}$ d) $-\frac{6}{7}$ e) None of these

   Answer: c Difficulty: 1

8. Find the slope of the line passing through (-1, 16) and (4, 2).
   a) $-\frac{5}{14}$ b) $-\frac{14}{5}$ c) $\frac{5}{14}$ d) $\frac{14}{5}$ e) None of these

   Answer: b Difficulty: 1

9. Find the slope of the line passing through (3, -2) and (5, 7).
   a) $-\frac{9}{2}$ b) $\frac{9}{2}$ c) $\frac{5}{2}$ d) $\frac{2}{9}$ e) None of these

   Answer: b Difficulty: 1

SHORT ANSWER

10. Find the slope of the line passing through (5, 9) and (-1, -3).

    Answer: 2 Difficulty: 1

11. Find the slope of the line passing through (2, 7) and (-8, 7).

    Answer: 0 Difficulty: 1

12. Find the slope of the line passing through (3, 7) and (-1, -2).

    Answer:
    $\frac{9}{4}$
    Difficulty: 1

13. Find the slope of the line passing through (-1, -3) and (-1, 4).

    Answer: slope is undefined. Difficulty: 1

MULTIPLE CHOICE

14. Find the slope of the line passing through $\left(-\frac{5}{2}, \frac{4}{3}\right)$ and $\left(-\frac{9}{2}, -\frac{14}{3}\right)$.
    a) $\frac{-1}{3}$ b) -3 c) $\frac{1}{3}$ d) 3 e) None of these

    Answer: d Difficulty: 1

SHORT ANSWER

15. Find the slope of the line passing through (-1.8, 2.7) and (4.6, 4.3).

Answer: 0.25 Difficulty: 1

MULTIPLE CHOICE

16. Which of the following points does **not** lie on the line that contains the point (7, 7) and has slope $\frac{2}{7}$?

a) $\left(4, \frac{43}{7}\right)$ b) (0, 5) c) (-7, 2)
d) (-14, 1) e) All of these lie on the line.

Answer: c Difficulty: 2

17. Determine which points lie on the line that contains the point (5, 7) with slope 0.

a) (5, 0) b) (0, 7) c) (7, 5)
d) All of these lie on the line. e) None of these lie on the line.

Answer: b Difficulty: 1

18. Determine which points lie on the vertical line that contains the point (5, 1).

a) (5, 0) b) (0, 1) c) (1, 5)
d) All of these points lie on the line.
e) None of these points lie on the line.

Answer: a Difficulty: 1

19. Determine which points lie on the line that contains the point (2, -3) and has a slope of $-\frac{7}{4}$.

a) $\left(4, -\frac{13}{2}\right)$ b) (-2, 4) c) $\left(0, \frac{1}{2}\right)$
d) All of these points lie on the line.
e) None of these points lie on the line.

Answer: d Difficulty: 2

20. Use the slope to describe the behavior of the line that passes through (3, 0) and (9, -2).

a) Rises from left to right b) Falls from left to right
c) Horizontal d) Vertical
e) None of these

Answer: b Difficulty: 2

21. Use the slope to describe the behavior of the line that passes through (5, 6) and (-1, 6).
    a) Rises from left to right
    b) Falls from left to right
    c) Horizontal
    d) Vertical
    e) None of these

    Answer: c Difficulty: 2

22. Find the slope of the line $7x - 2y = 12$.
    a) $\frac{7}{2}$ b) $-\frac{2}{7}$ c) $\frac{12}{7}$ d) -6 e) None of these

    Answer: a Difficulty: 1

23. Find the slope of the line $y = \frac{4x - 13}{7}$.
    a) 4 b) $\frac{4}{7}$ c) $-\frac{13}{7}$ d) $\frac{1}{7}$ e) None of these

    Answer: b Difficulty: 1

24. Find the slope of the line $y = 3$.
    a) 3 b) 0 c) $\frac{1}{3}$ d) Undefined e) None of these

    Answer: b Difficulty: 1

25. Find the slope of the line $x = \frac{1}{2}$.
    a) $\frac{1}{2}$ b) 0 c) -2 d) Undefined e) None of these

    Answer: d Difficulty: 1

26. What is the slope of the line perpendicular to the line given by $2x + 3y + 9 = 0$?
    a) $\frac{2}{3}$ b) $-\frac{2}{3}$ c) $\frac{3}{2}$ d) $-\frac{3}{2}$ e) None of these

    Answer: c Difficulty: 1

27. What is the slope of the line parallel to the line given by $4x - 2y = 9$?
    a) $\frac{9}{2}$ b) $\frac{9}{4}$ c) $-\frac{2}{4}$ d) 2 e) None of these

    Answer: d Difficulty: 1

28. What is the slope of the line perpendicular to the line given by $y = 7$?
    a) 0 b) Undefined c) $\frac{1}{7}$ d) $-\frac{1}{7}$ e) None of these

    Answer: b Difficulty: 1

29. Find the slope of the line perpendicular to the line given by $3x - 4y = 12$.
a) Undefined b) 0 c) $\frac{4}{3}$ d) $-\frac{3}{4}$ e) None of these

Answer: e Difficulty: 1

30. Find the equation of the line that has a slope of $-\frac{3}{4}$ and passes through (1, 2).
a) $3x - 4y - 7 = 0$ b) $3x - 4y - 11 = 0$ c) $3x + 4y - 11 = 0$
d) $3x + 4y + 11 = 0$ e) None of these

Answer: c Difficulty: 1

SHORT ANSWER

31. Find the equation of the line that passes through (-1, 5) and has a slope of 2.

Answer: $2x - y + 7 = 0$ Difficulty: 1

32. Find the equation of the line that passes through (3, -7) and has a slope of $\frac{1}{2}$.

Answer: $x - 2y - 17 = 0$ Difficulty: 1

33. Find the equation of the line that passes through $\left(\frac{-3}{4}, \frac{5}{3}\right)$ and has a slope of -8.

Answer: $24x + 3y + 13 = 0$ Difficulty: 1

MULTIPLE CHOICE

34. Find the equation of the vertical line that passes through (2, 5).
a) $y = 2$ b) $y = 5$ c) $x = 2$ d) $x = 5$ e) None of these

Answer: c Difficulty: 1

35. Find the equation of the line that passes through (0, 0) and has a slope that is undefined.
a) $y = 0$ b) $x = 0$ c) $x + y = 0$
d) $x = y$ e) None of these

Answer: b Difficulty: 1

SHORT ANSWER

36. Find the equation of the line that passes through (1.8, -7.2) and has a slope of $\frac{-1}{3}$.

Answer: $5x + 15y + 99 = 0$ Difficulty: 1

MULTIPLE CHOICE

37. Find the equation of the line that is perpendicular to $2x + 3y = 12$ but has the same y-intercept.
a) $2x + 3y = 8$
b) $2x - 3y = 12$
c) $2x + 3y = -12$
d) $3x - 2y = -8$
e) None of these

Answer: d Difficulty: 2

38. Rewrite the equation of the line $2x - 5y = 20$ in slope-intercept form.
a) $y = -\frac{5}{2}x + 4$
b) $y = \frac{5}{2}x - 4$
c) $y = \frac{2}{5}x - 4$
d) $y = -\frac{2}{5}x + 4$
e) None of these

Answer: c Difficulty: 1

39. Rewrite the equation of the line $x + 7y = 35$ in slope-intercept form.
a) $y = \frac{1}{7}x - 5$
b) $y = -\frac{1}{7}x + 5$
c) $y = 7x + 5$
d) $y = -7x + 5$
e) None of these

Answer: b Difficulty: 1

40. Describe the graph of $6x - y = 12$.
a) Rises from left to right
b) Falls from left to right
c) Horizontal
d) Vertical
e) None of these

Answer: a Difficulty: 2

41. Find an equation of the line that passes through (3, 10) and is parallel to the line $x - 3y = 1$.
a) $y = \frac{1}{3}x + 9$
b) $y = 3x + 1$
c) $y = -3x + 19$
d) $y = -\frac{1}{3}x + 11$
e) None of these

Answer: a Difficulty: 2

42. Find an equation of the line that passes through (-1, -3) and is parallel to the line $2x + y = 19$.
a) $y = -2x - 3$ b) $y = -2x - 5$ c) $y = 2x - 1$
d) $y = -\frac{1}{2}x - \frac{7}{2}$ e) None of these

Answer: b Difficulty: 2

43. Find an equation of the line that passes through (6, 2) and is perpendicular to the line $3x + 2y = 2$.
a) $y = -\frac{3}{2}x + 11$ b) $y = -\frac{2}{3}x + 6$ c) $y = \frac{3}{2}x - 7$
d) $y = \frac{2}{3}x - 2$ e) None of these

Answer: d Difficulty: 2

SHORT ANSWER

44. Find an equation of the line that passes through (8, 17) and is perpendicular to the line $x + 2y = 2$.

Answer: $y = 2x + 1$ Difficulty: 2

45. Find an equation of the line that passes through (2.4, 5.1) and is perpendicular to the line $x + 3y = 6$.

Answer: $y = 3x - 2.1$ Difficulty: 2

MULTIPLE CHOICE

46. Find the equation of the line that passes through (1, 3) and is perpendicular to the line $2x + 3y + 5 = 0$.
a) $3x - 2y + 3 = 0$ b) $2x + 3y - 11 = 0$ c) $2x + 3y - 9 = 0$
d) $3x - 2y - 7 = 0$ e) None of these

Answer: a Difficulty: 2

47. Find the equation of the line that passes through (2, -1) and is parallel to the line $2x + 7y = 5$.
a) $2x - 7y - 11 = 0$ b) $2x + 7y + 3 = 0$ c) $2x + 7y - 12 = 0$
d) $7x - 2y - 16 = 0$ e) None of these

Answer: b Difficulty: 2

SHORT ANSWER

48. Find the equation of the line that passes through (-3, -2) and is parallel to the line $3x + 2y - 5 = 0$.

Answer: $3x + 2y + 13 = 0$ Difficulty: 2

MULTIPLE CHOICE

49. Write the equation of the line that passes through the points (3, -1) and (-4, -1).
    a) $x = -1$ b) $y = -1$ c) $4x - 3y = 1$
    d) $7x + 2y = 19$ e) None of these

    Answer: b Difficulty: 1

50. Find the equation of the line that passes through the points $\left(\frac{5}{3}, -\frac{1}{2}\right)$ and $\left(-\frac{4}{3}, \frac{3}{2}\right)$.
    a) $9x + 6y - 12 = 0$ b) $12x + 18y - 11 = 0$ c) $2x + 3y - 4 = 0$
    d) $18x + 12y - 29 = 0$ e) None of these

    Answer: b Difficulty: 1

51. Find the equation of the line that passes through the points (0, -1) and (5, 9).
    a) $2x - y - 1 = 0$ b) $x - 2y + 13 = 0$ c) $x - 2y + 1 = 0$
    d) $2x - y - 13 = 0$ e) None of these

    Answer: a Difficulty: 1

52. Find the equation of the line that passes through the points (-1.4, 1.2) and (2.1, 2.6).
    a) $25x - 10y + 47 = 0$ b) $10x - 25y + 44 = 0$
    c) $10x - 25y - 47 = 0$ d) $10x - 40y + 58 = 0$
    e) None of these

    Answer: b Difficulty: 1

53. Write the equation of the line that passes through the points (2, -1) and (2, -6).
    a) $7x + 4y = 10$ b) $x + y = -7$ c) $x = 2$
    d) $y = 2$ e) None of these

    Answer: c Difficulty: 1

SHORT ANSWER

54. An employee is paid \$200 plus 8% of her net sales. Write a linear equation of her wages, W, in terms of her net sales, x.

    Answer: $W = 0.08x + 200$ Difficulty: 1

55. A new vehicle worth \$15,000 depreciates \$2500 every year after it is purchased. Write a linear equation of its value, V, in terms of the number of years, t, since it was purchased.

    Answer: $V = -2500t + 15{,}000$ Difficulty: 1

56. A lawyer charges an initial fee of $500 plus $50 per hour. Write a linear equation of the fee, F, in terms of the number of hours of service, t.

Answer: $F = 50t + 500$ Difficulty: 1

57. Morgan Sporting Goods had net sales of $150,000 in January of this past year. In March, their net sales were $300,000. Assuming that their sales are increasing linearly, write an equation of net sales, S, in terms of the month using $t = 1$ for January.

Answer: $S = 75{,}000t + 75{,}000$ Difficulty: 2

58. Curtis Area Schools had an enrollment of 2800 students in 1990 and 12,600 in 1998. Assuming the growth is linear, write an equation of the enrollment, E, in terms of the year using $t = 0$ for 1990.

Answer: $E = 1225t + 2800$ Difficulty: 2

59. A new Audi purchased in 1994 was valued at $28,000. In 2000, it was worth $16,000. Assuming the depreciation is linear, write an equation of its value, V, in terms of the number of years since its purchase using $t = 0$ for 1994.

Answer: $V = -2000t + 28{,}000$ Difficulty: 2

60. The cost for parts on your automobile repair bill was $152. The cost for labor was $30 per hour. Write a linear equation giving the total cost C, in terms of t, the number of hours.

Answer: $C = 152 + 30t$ Difficulty: 1

MULTIPLE CHOICE

61. An employee is paid $15 per hour plus $2 for each unit produced per hour. Match this with the appropriate graph.
a) I b) II c) III d) IV e) None of these

(I)
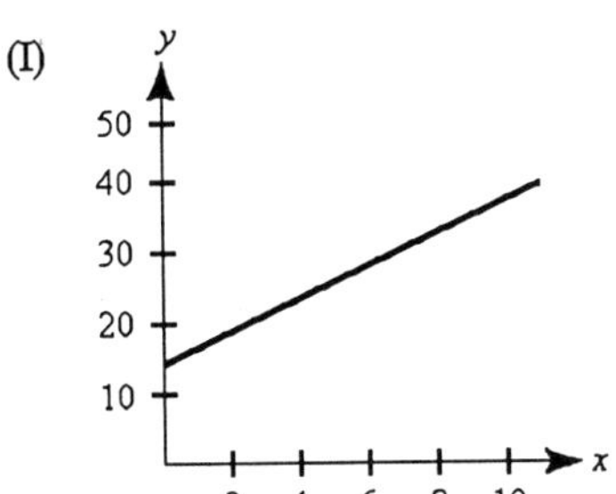

(II)
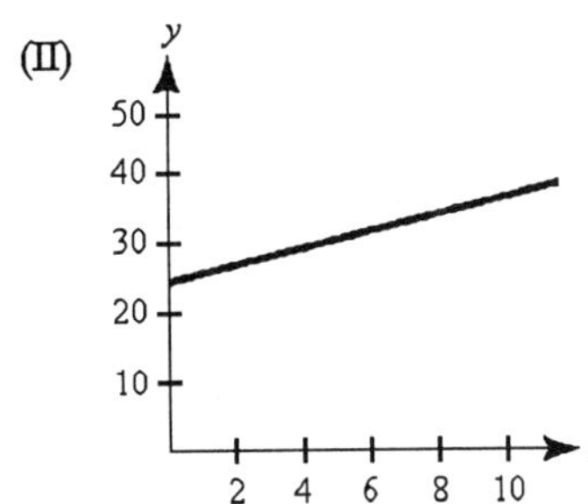

(III)
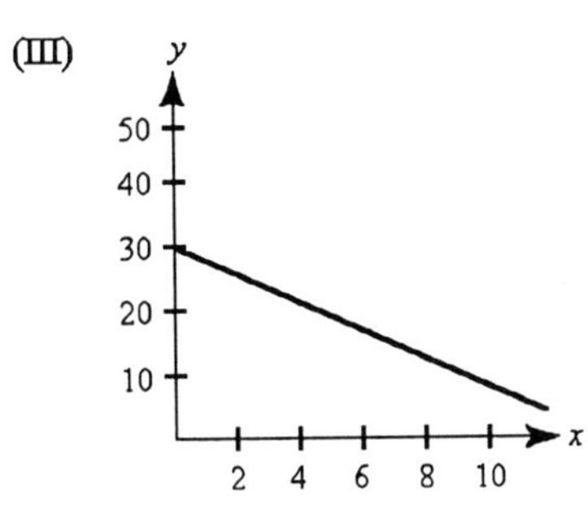

(IV)
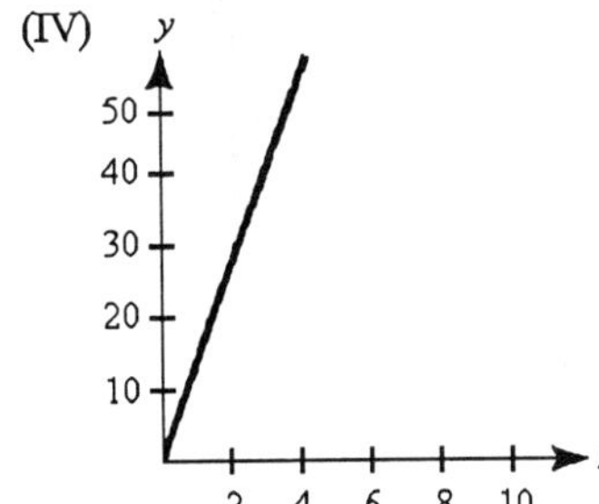

Answer: a Difficulty: 1

62. A sales representative receives $25 per day for food and $0.30 for each mile traveled. Match this with the appropriate graph.
a) I b) II c) III d) IV e) None of these

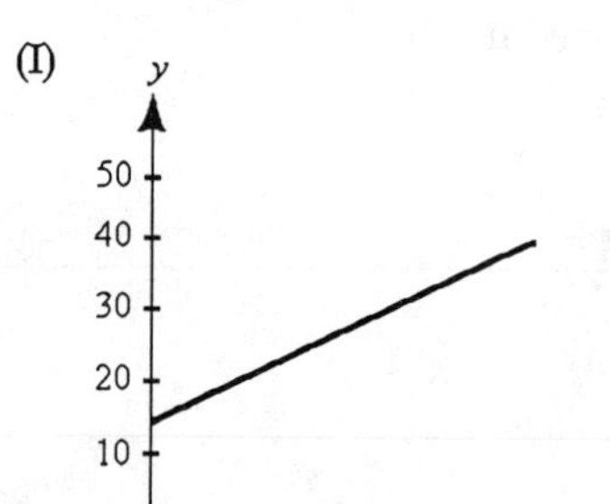
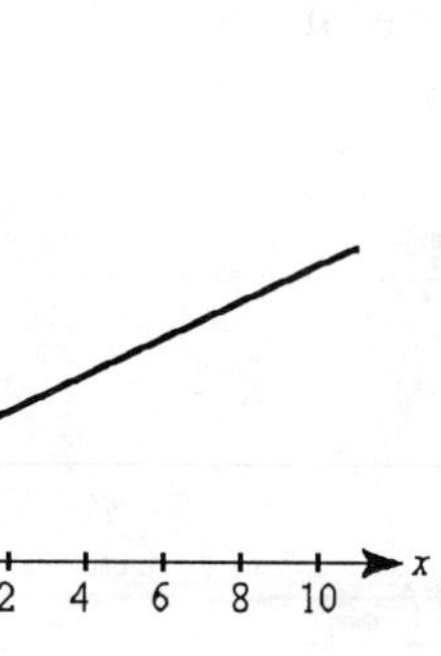

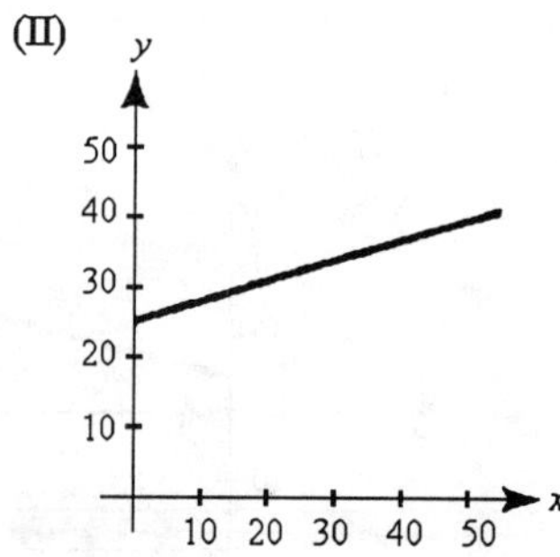

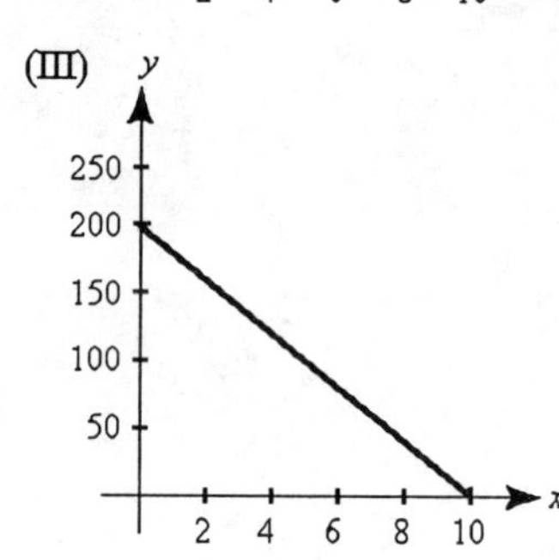

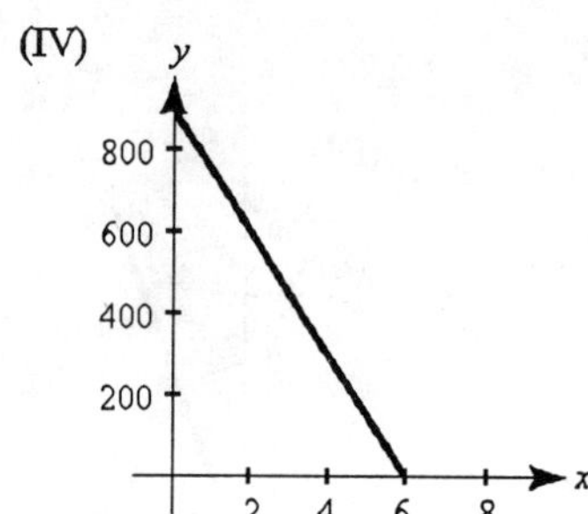

Answer: b Difficulty: 1

63. A word processor that was purchased for $900 depreciates $150 per year. Match this with the appropriate graph.
a) I b) II c) III d) IV e) None of these

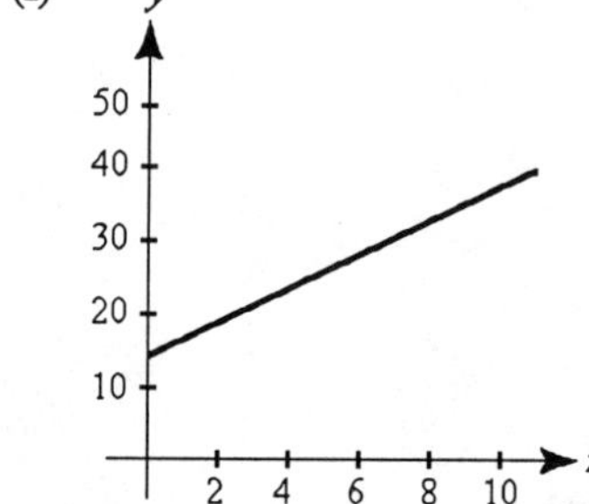

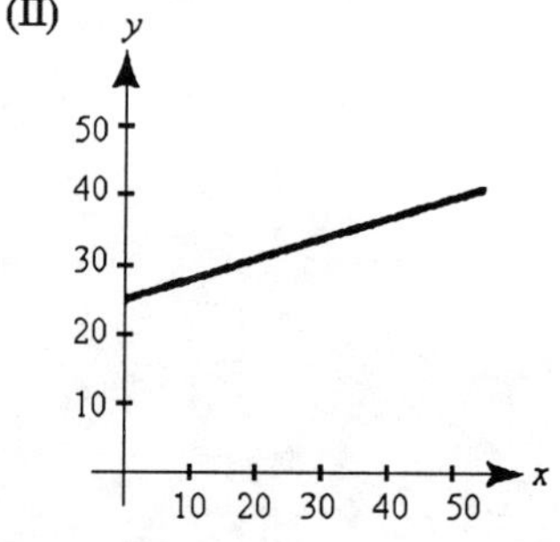

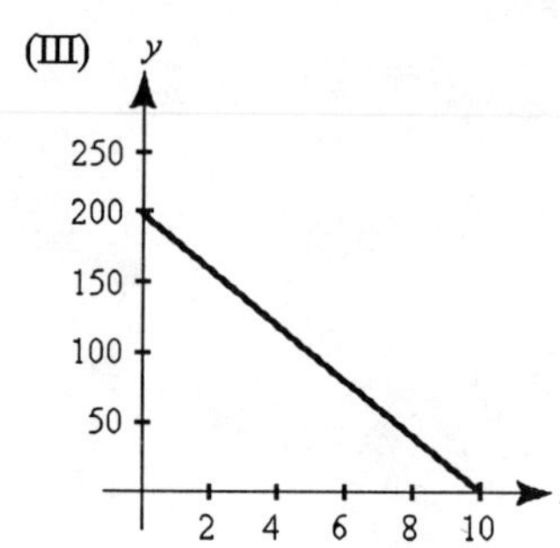

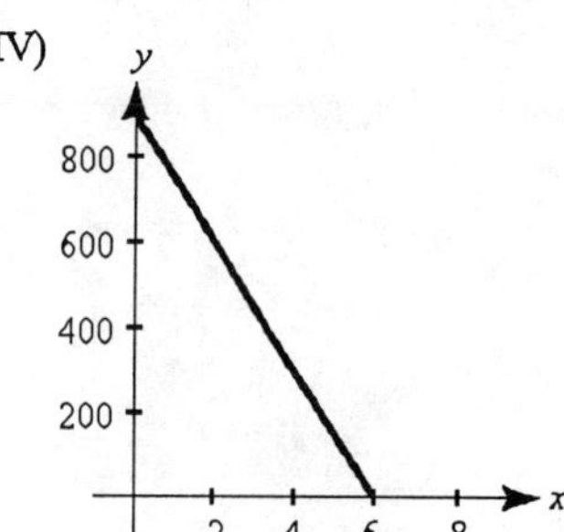

Answer: d Difficulty: 1

64. The radio advertising expenditures in the United States were about $8700 million in 1990 and $14,500 million in 1998. Predict the expenditures in 2002, assuming the expenditures follow a linear growth pattern. (Source: *McCann-Erickson, Inc.*)
a) $15,600 million b) $17,400 million c) $17,800 million
d) $16,100 million e) None of these

Answer: b Difficulty: 2

65. Your salary was $20,000 in 1990 and $29,900 in 1999. If your salary follows a linear growth pattern, what will it be in 2004?
a) $28,800 b) $29,900 c) $35,400
d) $37,200 e) None of these

Answer: c Difficulty: 2

66. The population of Morgan Falls in 1995 was 12,500 and in 2000 it was 18,750. If the population follows a linear growth pattern, what will it be in 2003?
a) 20,000 b) 25,000 c) 27,500
d) 22,500 e) None of these

Answer: d Difficulty: 1

67. A school's growth in enrollment is approximately linear. In 1980 it had 2000 students and in 2000 there were 3000. Estimate the approximate number of students in 1992.
a) 2500 b) 2600 c) 2650 d) 2550 e) None of these

Answer: b Difficulty: 1

68. A school's growth in enrollment is approximately linear. In 1980 it had 2000 students and in 2000 there were 3000. Estimate the approximate number of students in 1988.
a) 2400 b) 2350 c) 2500 d) 2450 e) None of these

Answer: a Difficulty: 1

69. A school's growth in enrollment is approximately linear. In 1980 it had 2000 students and in 2000 there were 3000. Estimate the approximate number of students in 1993.
a) 2700 b) 2550 c) 2600 d) 2650 e) None of these

Answer: d Difficulty: 1

SHORT ANSWER

70. The growth of the number of employees hired by a company has been linear for the past ten years, starting at 323 ten years ago and currently standing at 393. Estimate the number of employees that will be employed three years from now (by linear extrapolation).

Answer: 414 Difficulty: 1

71. The growth of the number of employees hired by a company has been linear for the past ten years, starting at 287 ten years ago and currently standing at 347. Estimate the number of employees that will be employed three years from now (by linear extrapolation).

    Answer: 365 Difficulty: 1

72. The growth of the number of employees hired by a company has been linear for the past ten years, starting at 415 ten years ago and currently standing at 495. Estimate the number of employees that will be employed two years from now (by linear extrapolation).

    Answer: 511 Difficulty: 1

73. The growth of the number of employees hired by a company has been linear for the past ten years, starting at 242 ten years ago and currently standing at 312. Estimate the number of employees that will be employed three years from now (by linear extrapolation).

    Answer: 333 Difficulty: 1

Chapter 013: Functions

MULTIPLE CHOICE

1. Given $A = \{-2, -1, 0, 1\}$ and $B = \{1, 2, 3\}$, determine which of the sets of ordered pairs represents a function from A to B.
   a) {(-2, 1), (-1, 1), (0, 1), (1, 1)}
   b) {(-2, 1), (-2, 2), (-2, 3)}
   c) {(-2, 1), (-1, 2), (-1, 3)}
   d) {(-2, 1), (-2, 2), (-2, 3)} and {(-2, 1), (-1, 2), (-1, 3)} only
   e) All of these

   Answer: a Difficulty: 1

2. Given $A = \{-1, 0, 1, 2\}$ and $B = \{1, 2, 3\}$, determine which of the sets of ordered pairs represents a function from A to B.
   a) {(-1, 1), (0, 2), (1, 2), (2, 3)}
   b) {(-1, 2), (0, 1), (2, 3)}
   c) {(-1, 2), (0, 2), (1, 3), (2, 3)}
   d) All of these
   e) None of these

   Answer: d Difficulty: 1

3. Given $A = \{1, 2, 3\}$ and $B = \{-2, -1, 0, 1\}$, determine which of the sets of ordered pairs represents a function from A to B.
   a) {(1, -2), (2, -2), (3, -1), (2, 0), (2, 1)}
   b) {(1, -2), (2, -1), (2, 0), (3, 1)}
   c) {(1, -2), (2, -1), (3, 0), (1, 1)}
   d) All of these
   e) None of these

   Answer: e Difficulty: 1

4. Let $A = \{0, 1, 2, 3\}$ and $B = \{-4, -2, 0, 2, 4\}$. Which set of ordered pairs represents a function from A to B?
   a) {(1, -4), (1, -2), (2, 0), (2, 4)}
   b) {(0, -3), (1, -1), (2, 1), (3, 3)}
   c) {(0, 4), (1, 0), (2, -2), (3, -4)}
   d) {(2, -2), (2, 0), (2, 2), (2, 4)}
   e) None of these

   Answer: c Difficulty: 1

5. Let $A = \{0, 1, 2, 3\}$ and $B = \{-4, -2, 0, 2, 4\}$. Which set of ordered pairs represents a function from A to B?
   a) {(1, -4), (1, -2), (2, 0), (2, 4)}
   b) {(0, 4), (1, 2), (2, 0), (3, 2)}
   c) {(0, 3), (1, 1), (2, -1), (3, -3)}
   d) Both {(0, 4), (1, 2), (2, 0), (3, 2)} and {(0, 3), (1, 1), (2, -1), (3, -3)}
   e) None of these

   Answer: b Difficulty: 1

6. Let $A = \{0, 1, 2, 3\}$ and $B = \{-4, -2, 0, 2, 4\}$. Which set of ordered pairs represents a function from A to B?
a) $\{(0, -2), (0, 0), (0, 2), (0, 4)\}$
b) $\{(1, -2), (1, 0), (1, 2), (1, 4)\}$
c) $\{(2, -2), (2, 0), (2, 2), (2, 4)\}$
d) $\{(3, -2), (3, 0), (3, 2), (3, 4)\}$
e) None of these

Answer: e Difficulty: 1

7. In which of the following equations is y a function of x?
a) $3y + 2x - 9 = 17$
b) $2x^2 + x = 4y$
c) $2x^2 + x = 4y^2$
d) Both $3y + 2x - 9 = 17$ and $2x^2 + x = 4y$
e) None of these

Answer: d Difficulty: 1

8. In which of the following equations is y a function of x?
a) $2x + 3y - 1 = 0$
b) $x^2 + 3y^2 = 7$
c) $2x^2y = 7$
d) Both $2x + 3y - 1 = 0$ and $x^2 + 3y^2 = 7$
e) Both $2x + 3y - 1 = 0$ and $2x^2y = 7$

Answer: e Difficulty: 1

9. In which of the following equations is y a function of x?
a) $3y + 2x - 7 = 0$
b) $5x^2y = 9 - 2x$
c) $3x^2 - 4y^2 = 9$
d) Both $5x^2y = 9 - 2x$ and $3x^2 - 4y^2 = 9$
e) Both $3y + 2x - 7 = 0$ and $5x^2y = 9 - 2x$

Answer: e Difficulty: 1

10. In which of the following equations is y a function of x?
a) $y = 3x^2 - 9$
b) $3x + 2y = 5$
c) $|x| = y$
d) All of these
e) None of these

Answer: d Difficulty: 1

11. Determine which equation represents y as a function of x.
a) $|x| + |y| = 1$
b) $x^2 + y^2 = 1$
c) $y^2 = 7 - x$
d) $2x - 3y = 7$
e) None of these

Answer: d Difficulty: 1

12. Determine which equation represents y as a function of x.
a) $x^2 + 2x - y + 3 = 0$
b) $y^2 + 2x + 4 = 0$
c) $|y| - x = 1$
d) $x^2 + y^2 = 25$
e) None of these

Answer: a Difficulty: 1

13. Determine which equation represents y as a function of x.
a) $x + 4y^2 - 7 = 0$ b) $x + 4y - 7 = 0$ c) $x + 4|y| - 7 = 0$
d) $|x| + 4|y| - 7 = 0$ e) None of these

Answer: b Difficulty: 1

SHORT ANSWER

14. Let $A = \{0, 2, 4\}$ and $B = \{1, 3, 5\}$. Fill in the missing number so that the set of ordered pairs represents a function from A to B.
$\{(0, 3), (\ \ , 5), (2, 1)\}$

Answer: 4 Difficulty: 1

15. Determine which of the two equations represents y as a function of x and specify why the other does not.

(a) $x^2 + 5y - x = 7$ (b) $y^2 - 5x = 7$

Answer: (a); in (b), some values of x determine more than one value of y. Difficulty: 1

16. Determine which of the two equations represents y as a function of x and specify why the other does not.

(a) $|x| + y = 4$ (b) $x + |y| = 4$

Answer: (a); in (b), some values of x determine more than one value of y. Difficulty: 1

17. Determine which of the two equations represents y as a function of x and specify why the other does not.

(a) $x^2 + y^2 = 4$ (b) $x^2 + y = 4$

Answer: (b); in (a), some values of x determine more than one value of y. Difficulty: 1

18. Determine which of the two equations represents y as a function of x and specify why the other does not.

(a) $y^2 - 4y = x$ (b) $x^2 - 4x = y$

Answer: (b); in (a), some value of x determine more than one value of y. Difficulty: 1

MULTIPLE CHOICE

19. Given $f(x) = 4x^2 - 2$, find $f(-2)$.
a) 62 b) -66 c) 14 d) -18 e) None of these

Answer: c Difficulty: 1

20. Given $g(x) = 3 - 4x^2$, find $g(-2)$.
a) -13 b) 19 c) -61 d) -3 e) None of these

Answer: a Difficulty: 1

21. Given $f(x) = 4x^2 - 8x + 9$, find $f\left(\frac{-1}{2}\right)$.
a) 17 b) 14 c) 21 d) 2 e) None of these

Answer: b Difficulty: 1

22. Given $f(x) = \sqrt{x + 4} - 2$, find $f(5)$.
a) $\sqrt{5}$ b) -1 c) 1 d) 7 e) None of these

Answer: c Difficulty: 1

23. Given $g(x) = \dfrac{6}{x^2 - \frac{1}{27}}$, find $g\left(\frac{1}{3}\right)$.
a) 81 b) $\frac{81}{4}$ c) $\frac{4}{9}$ d) $\frac{9}{4}$ e) None of these

Answer: a Difficulty: 1

24. Given $h(x) = 10x + 2x^2$, find $h(-2)$.
a) 6 b) -22 c) -28 d) -12 e) None of these

Answer: d Difficulty: 1

25. Given $f(x) = \begin{cases} 7x - 10, & x \le 2 \\ x^2 + 6, & x > 2 \end{cases}$, find $f(0)$.
a) -10 b) 0 c) -4 d) 6 e) None of these

Answer: a Difficulty: 1

26. Given $f(x) = \begin{cases} 3x + 4, & x \le 2 \\ x^2 + 1, & x > 2 \end{cases}$, find $f(3)$.
a) 13 b) 10 c) 5 d) 3 e) None of these

Answer: b Difficulty: 1

27. Given $f(x) = \begin{cases} 2x - 1, & x \le -2 \\ x + 6, & x > -2 \end{cases}$, find $f(-6)$.
a) -11 b) -13 c) 0 d) 11 e) None of these

Answer: b Difficulty: 1

28. Given $f(x) = |x - 3| - 5$, find $f(1) - f(5)$.
a) 0 b) -4 c) 14 d) -14 e) None of these

Answer: a Difficulty: 1

29. Given $f(x) = x^2 - 3x + 4$, find $f(x + 2) - f(2)$.
a) $x^2 - 3x + 4$ b) $x^2 + x$ c) $x^2 + x - 8$
d) $x^2 - 3x - 4$ e) None of these

Answer: b Difficulty: 2

30. Given $f(x) = |3x + 1| - 5$, find $f(x + 1) - f(x)$.
a) 3 b) -5 c) $|3x + 4| - |3x + 1| - 10$
d) $|3x + 4| - |3x + 1|$ e) None of these

Answer: d Difficulty: 2

SHORT ANSWER

31. Given $f(x) = 3x - 7$, find $f(x + 1) + f(1)$.

Answer: $3x - 8$ Difficulty: 2

32. Given $g(x) = \frac{x}{2x + 1}$, find $g(k - 2)$.

Answer:
$\frac{k - 2}{2k - 3}$
Difficulty: 2

33. Given $h(x) = \frac{1}{2}x^3$, find $h(t + 1) - h(1)$.

Answer:
$\frac{1}{2}(t^3 + 3t^2 + 3t)$
Difficulty: 2

MULTIPLE CHOICE

34. $F(x) = \begin{cases} 3 - x^2, & \text{if } x \geq 0 \\ 3 + 2x, & \text{if } x < 0 \end{cases}$

$F(1) - F(-1) =$
a) 0 b) 1 c) 3 d) $F(2)$ e) None of these

Answer: b Difficulty: 1

35. $F(x) = \begin{cases} 3 - x^2, & \text{if } x \geq 0 \\ 3 + 2x, & \text{if } x < 0 \end{cases}$

$F(2) - F(-1) =$
a) -6 b) 0 c) -2 d) $F(3)$ e) None of these

Answer: c Difficulty: 1

36. $F(x) = \begin{cases} 3 - x^2, & \text{if } x \geq 0 \\ 3 + 2x, & \text{if } x < 0 \end{cases}$

$F(3) - F(-3) =$
a) 0 b) 3 c) $F(6)$ d) -3 e) None of these

Answer: d Difficulty: 1

37. Given $f(x) = \begin{cases} x^2 + 1, & x < 4 \\ 6x - 7, & x \geq 4 \end{cases}$, find $f(-2)$.
a) -19 b) 5 c) 4 d) -5 e) None of these

Answer: b Difficulty: 1

38. Given $f(x) = \begin{cases} \sqrt{-x}, & x \leq 0 \\ 6x, & x > 0 \end{cases}$, find $f(4)$.
a) 2 b) -2 c) 10 d) 24 e) None of these

Answer: d Difficulty: 1

39. Given $f(x) = \begin{cases} x - 19, & x < -5 \\ |x + 3|, & x \geq -5 \end{cases}$, find $f(-4)$.
a) -15 b) 1 c) -1 d) -23 e) None of these

Answer: b Difficulty: 1

40. Given $f(x) = \begin{cases} |x - 2|, & x \leq 1 \\ |2x - 5|, & x > 1 \end{cases}$, find $f(1)$.
a) 1 b) -1 c) 3 d) -3 e) None of these

Answer: a Difficulty: 1

SHORT ANSWER

41. $F(x) = -1 + 2x - x^2$, find $F(k + 1)$ and simplify.

Answer:

$-k^2$

Difficulty: 2

42. $F(x) = 5 + 2x - x^2$, find $F(k + 1) - F(k)$ and simplify.

Answer: $1 - 2k$ Difficulty: 2

43. $F(x) = 5 + 2x - x^2$, find $F(k + 1) - F(k - 1)$ and simplify.

Answer: $4 - 4k$ Difficulty: 2

MULTIPLE CHOICE

44. Given $f(x) = 2 - x^2$, find $\frac{f(x + \Delta x) - f(x)}{\Delta x}$.

a) $\frac{x^2 - \Delta x - (\Delta x)^2}{\Delta x}$ b) $\frac{-2x^2 - \Delta x^2}{\Delta x}$ c) $-2x - \Delta x$

d) $\frac{1}{2}$ e) None of these

Answer: c Difficulty: 2

45. Given $f(x) = 1 - 2x^2$, find $\frac{f(x + \Delta x) - f(x)}{\Delta x}$.

a) $-4x - 2\Delta x$ b) $2x + \Delta x$ c) $\frac{4x^2 + 2x\Delta x + (\Delta x)^2}{\Delta x}$

d) -9 e) None of these

Answer: a Difficulty: 2

SHORT ANSWER

46. Given $f(x) = 2 - 4x^2$, find $\frac{f(x + \Delta x) - f(x)}{\Delta x}$.

Answer: $-8x - 4\Delta x$ Difficulty: 2

47. Given $f(x) = 3 - 2x^2$, find $\frac{f(x + \Delta x) - f(x)}{\Delta x}$.

Answer: $-4x - 2\Delta x$ Difficulty: 2

MULTIPLE CHOICE

48. Find all real values of x such that $f(x) = 0$: $f(x) = \frac{x - 3}{x + 4}$.

a) $\frac{-3}{4}$ b) 3 c) -4 d) 3, -4 e) None of these

Answer: b Difficulty: 1

49. Find all real values of x such that $f(x) = 0$: $f(x) = \frac{x - 6}{x + 5}$.

a) 6 b) -5 c) $-\frac{6}{5}$ d) 6, -5 e) None of these

Answer: a Difficulty: 1

50. Find all real values of x such that $f(x) = 0$: $f(x) = x^2 - 3x - 18$.

a) -6 b) -3 c) -6, 3 d) 6, -3 e) None of these

Answer: d Difficulty: 1

51. Find all real values of x such that $f(x) = 0$: $f(x) = |x + 3|$.

a) ± 3 b) -3 c) 3 d) $-\frac{1}{3}$ e) None of these

Answer: b Difficulty: 1

52. Find all real values of x such that $f(x) = 0$: $f(x) = x\sqrt{x^2 - 9}$.

a) ± 3 b) 3 c) 0, ± 3 d) 0, 3 e) None of these

Answer: c Difficulty: 1

SHORT ANSWER

53. Find all real values of x such that $f(x) = 0$: $f(x) = x^3 - 2x^2 - 5x$.

Answer:

$x = 0, 1 \pm \sqrt{6}$

Difficulty: 2

54. Find all real values of x such that $f(x) = 0$: $f(x) = x^3 - 2x^2 - 4x$.

Answer:

$x = 0, 1 \pm \sqrt{5}$

Difficulty: 2

MULTIPLE CHOICE

55. Which of the functions fits the data?

x	-4	-2	0	2	4	6
y	8	4	0	4	8	12

a) $f(x) = 2|x|$ b) $f(x) = 2x^2$ c) $f(x) = 2x$
d) $f(x) = 2\sqrt{x}$ e) None of these

Answer: a Difficulty: 1

56. Which of the functions fits the data?

x	-2	0	1	3	5	10
y	-6	0	3	9	15	30

a) $f(x) = x^3$ b) $f(x) = \sqrt[3]{x}$ c) $f(x) = |x|^3$
d) $f(x) = 3x$ e) None of these

Answer: d Difficulty: 1

57. Which of the functions fits the data?

x	-4	-2	0	2	8
y	16	4	0	4	64

a) $f(x) = 4x$ b) $f(x) = x^2$ c) $f(x) = \frac{1}{2}x^2$
d) $f(x) = 2|x|$ e) None of these

Answer: b Difficulty: 1

58. Find all real values of x for which $f(x) = g(x)$.
$f(x) = 3x + 1,\ g(x) = x^2 - 3$
a) 0 b) 4, 1 c) -4, -1 d) 4, -1 e) None of these

Answer: d Difficulty: 1

59. Find all real values of x for which $f(x) = g(x)$.
$f(x) = x^4 + 3x^2,\ g(x) = 7x^2$
a) -4, 0, 4 b) 0, 2 c) 2 d) 0, 2, -2 e) None of these

Answer: d Difficulty: 1

60. Find all real values of x for which $f(x) = g(x)$.
$f(x) = x - 2,\ g(x) = \sqrt{x}$
a) $\dfrac{1 \pm \sqrt{17}}{2}$ b) $\dfrac{-1 \pm \sqrt{15}}{2}$ c) 1, 4
d) -1, 3 e) None of these

Answer: c Difficulty: 2

61. Find all real values of x for which $f(x) = g(x)$.
$f(x) = x^2 - 2,\ g(x) = 2x + 1$
a) 1, -3 b) 1, 3 c) No real values of x
d) -1, 3 e) None of these

Answer: d Difficulty: 1

SHORT ANSWER

62. Find all real values of x for which $f(x) = g(x)$.
$f(x) = x^2 - 5$, $g(x) = x + 1$

Answer: -2, 3 Difficulty: 1

63. Find all real value of x for which $f(x) = g(x)$.
$f(x) = x^2$, $g(x) = x + 9$

Answer:

$$\frac{1 \pm \sqrt{37}}{2}$$

Difficulty: 2

MULTIPLE CHOICE

64. Find the domain of the function {(-2, 1), (-1, 0), (0, -3), (1, -8)}.
a) [-2, 1] b) $(-\infty, \infty)$ c) {-2, -1, 0, 1}
d) {1, 0, -3, -8} e) {-8, -3, -2, -1, 0, 1}

Answer: c Difficulty: 1

65. Find the domain of the function {(1, 1), (2, 4), (3, 9)}.
a) [1, 9] b) {1, 2, 3, 4, 9} c) {1, 4, 9}
d) {1, 2, 3} e) None of these

Answer: d Difficulty: 1

66. Find the domain of the function: $f(x) = \frac{9}{x}$.
a) $(9, \infty)$ b) $(-\infty, \infty)$ c) All real numbers $x \neq 0$
d) All real numbers $x \neq 9$ e) None of these

Answer: c Difficulty: 1

67. Find the domain of the function $g(x) = \frac{x}{x^2 + 1}$.
a) All real numbers $x \neq 1$ b) All real numbers $x \neq -1$
c) All real numbers $x \neq 0$ d) All real numbers x
e) None of these

Answer: d Difficulty: 1

SHORT ANSWER

68. Find the domain of the function: $h(x) = \frac{x + 4}{x(x - 5)}$.

Answer: All real numbers $x \neq 0$, $x \neq 5$ Difficulty: 1

69. Find the domain of the function: $g(x) = \dfrac{5x}{x^2 - 7x + 12}$.

Answer: All real numbers $x \neq 3$, $x \neq 4$ Difficulty: 1

70. Find the domain of the function: $f(x) = \dfrac{2x - 1}{2x + 1}$.

Answer:

All real numbers $x \neq -\dfrac{1}{2}$

Difficulty: 1

71. Find the domain of the function: $h(x) = \sqrt{x - 7}$.

Answer: $[7, \infty)$ Difficulty: 1

72. Find the domain of the function: $g(x) = \sqrt{2x + 9}$.

Answer:

$\left[-\dfrac{9}{2}, \infty\right)$

Difficulty: 1

MULTIPLE CHOICE

73. Find the domain of the function: $y = \dfrac{1}{\sqrt{x + 4}}$.

a) $(-\infty, \infty)$ b) $(-\infty, -4]$ c) $(-4, \infty)$
d) $[-4, \infty)$ e) None of these

Answer: c Difficulty: 1

74. Find the domain of the function: $y = \dfrac{1}{x}$.

a) $(-\infty, \infty)$ b) $(-\infty, 0)$, $(0, \infty)$ c) $(-\infty, 0)$
d) $(0, \infty)$ e) None of these

Answer: b Difficulty: 1

SHORT ANSWER

75. Find the domain of the function: $f(x) = \dfrac{1}{x + 2}$.

Answer: $(-\infty, -2)$, $(-2, \infty)$ Difficulty: 1

MULTIPLE CHOICE

76. Find the domain of the function: $f(x) = \sqrt{2x + 3}$.

a) $[0, \infty)$
b) $(0, \infty)$
c) $\left[-\frac{3}{2}, \infty\right)$
d) $\left[\frac{3}{2}, \infty\right)$
e) None of these

Answer: c Difficulty: 1

77. Find the domain of the function: $f(x) = \dfrac{1}{\sqrt{x^2 + 1}}$.

a) $(-\infty, -1), (-1, 1), (1, \infty)$
b) $(-\infty, 0), (0, \infty)$
c) $(-\infty, \infty)$
d) $(-\infty, -1), (-1, \infty)$
e) None of these

Answer: c Difficulty: 1

78. Find the domain of the function: $f(x) = \dfrac{1}{x^2 - 3x + 2}$.

a) $(-\infty, -2), (-2, 1), (1, \infty)$
b) $(-\infty, 1), (1, 2), (2, \infty)$
c) $(-\infty, \infty)$
d) $\left(-\infty, \frac{1}{2}\right], \left[\frac{1}{2}, \infty\right)$
e) None of these

Answer: b Difficulty: 2

79. Find the domain of the function: $f(x) = \dfrac{1}{\sqrt{x - 4}}$.

a) All real numbers $x \geq 4$
b) All real numbers x
c) All real numbers $x > 4$
d) All positive real numbers
e) None of these

Answer: c Difficulty: 1

80. Find the domain of the function: $f(x) = \dfrac{3 - x}{4 + x}$.

a) All real numbers $x \neq 4$
b) All real numbers x
c) $-4 < x \leq 3$
d) All real numbers $x \geq 3$ and $x < -4$
e) None of these

Answer: a Difficulty: 1

81. Find the domain of the function: $f(x) = \dfrac{x - 2}{(x - 5)(x + 3)}$.

a) All real numbers $x \neq 5$
b) All real numbers $x \neq -3$
c) All real numbers $x \neq 5$, $x \neq -3$
d) All real numbers $x \neq 5$, $x \neq -3$ and $x \neq 2$
e) None of these

Answer: c Difficulty: 1

82. The length of a rectangle is four times the width. Express the perimeter, P, as a function of the width, w.

a) $P(w) = 6w$
b) $P(w) = 10w$
c) $P(w) = 5w$
d) $P(w) = 8w$
e) None of these

Answer: b Difficulty: 1

83. The length of a rectangle is four times the width. Express the area, A, as a function of the length, l.

a) $A(l) = \dfrac{l}{4}$
b) $A(l) = 4l^2$
c) $A(l) = \dfrac{l^2}{4}$
d) $A(l) = \dfrac{9l}{4}$
e) None of these

Answer: c Difficulty: 1

84. The height of a rectangular solid is three times its width and the length is one-half the width. Express the volume, V, as a function of the width, w.

a) $V(w) = \dfrac{3}{2}w^3$
b) $V(w) = \dfrac{9}{2}w$
c) $V(w) = 6w^3$
d) $V(w) = \dfrac{7}{2}w$
e) None of these

Answer: a Difficulty: 1

85. The height of a rectangular solid is four inches more than the length and six times the width. Express the volume, V, as a function of the height, h.

a) $V(h) = \dfrac{1}{6}(h^2 - 4h)$
b) $V(h) = \dfrac{1}{6}(h^3 - 4h^2)$
c) $V(h) = \dfrac{1}{6}(3h - 4)$
d) $V(h) = 6h^3 - 24h^2$
e) None of these

Answer: b Difficulty: 2

SHORT ANSWER

86. Express the length of the diagonal, L, of a square as a function of the length, x, of a side.

Answer:

$L(x) = \sqrt{2}x$

Difficulty: 1

87. Express the volume, V, of a cube as a function of the length, x, of a side.

Answer:

$V(x) = x^3$

Difficulty: 1

88. Express the perimeter, P, of a square as a function of the length, x, of a side.

Answer: $P(x) = 4x$ Difficulty: 1

89. Express the area, A, of a square as a function of the length, x, of a side.

Answer:

$A(x) = x^2$

Difficulty: 1

90. The number of public elementary and secondary classroom teachers, in thousands, in the United States from 1990 to 1998 can be modeled by

$$f(t) = \begin{cases} 33.2t + 2368, & 0 \le t \le 3 \\ 48.7t + 2319, & 4 \le t \le 8 \end{cases}$$

where t is the year with $t = 0$ corresponding to 1990. Use this model to find the Number of classroom teachers in 1995. (Source: *National Education Association*)

Answer: 2563 thousand teachers Difficulty: 1

MULTIPLE CHOICE

91. You invest $12,000 to start a business. Each unit cost $3.40 and is sold for $5.60. Let x be the number of units produced and sold. Write the profit P as a function of x. (P = Revenue - Cost)

a) $P = 9.00x + 12{,}000$
b) $P = 9.00x - 12{,}000$
c) $P = 2.20x + 12{,}000$
d) $P = 2.20x - 12{,}000$
e) None of these

Answer: d Difficulty: 2

92. To produce x units of a product, there are fixed costs of $23,000 and a production cost of $4.78 per unit. Write the total cost C as a function of x.

a) $C = 4.78x + 23{,}000$
b) $C = 23{,}000 - 4.78x$
c) $C = \dfrac{4.78}{x} + 23{,}000$
d) $C = 23{,}004.78x$
e) None of these

Answer: a Difficulty: 1

93. An open box is made from a rectangular piece of material by cutting equal squares from each corner and turning up the sides. Write the volume of the box as a function of x if the material is 24 inches by 16 inches.
    a) $V = (24 - x)(16 - x)$
    b) $V = x(24 - x)(16 - x)$
    c) $V = x(24 - 2x)(16 - 2x)$
    d) $V = (24 - 2x)(16 - 2x)$
    e) None of these

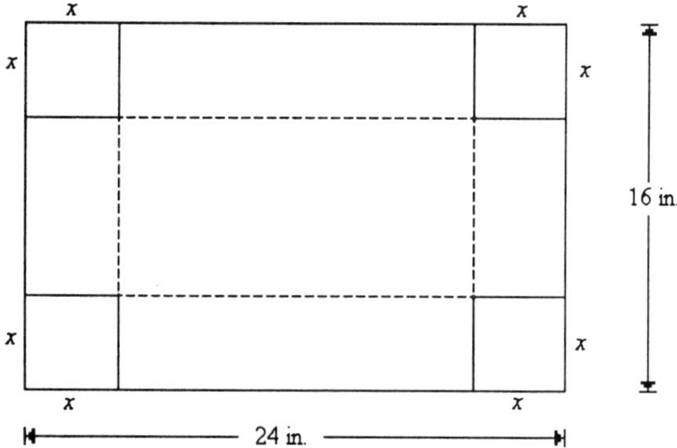

Answer: c Difficulty: 1

SHORT ANSWER

94. An open box is made from a rectangular piece of material by cutting equal squares from each corner and turning up the sides. Write the volume of the box as a function of x if the material is 18 inches by 12 inches.

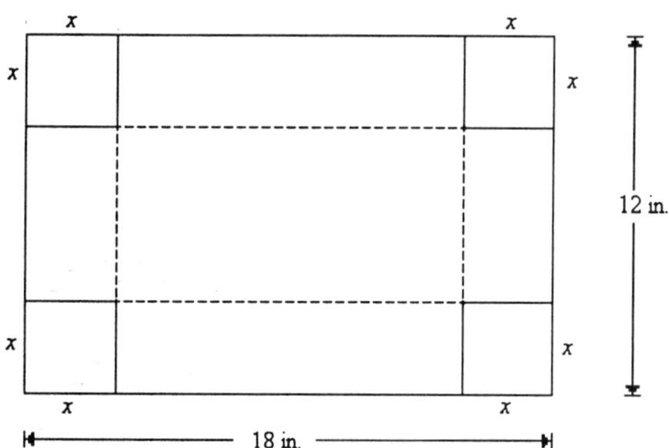

Answer: $V = x(12 - 2x)(18 - 2x)$ Difficulty: 1

95. Strips of width x are added to the four sides of a square, which are 16 inches on a side. Write the area A of the remaining figure as a function of x.

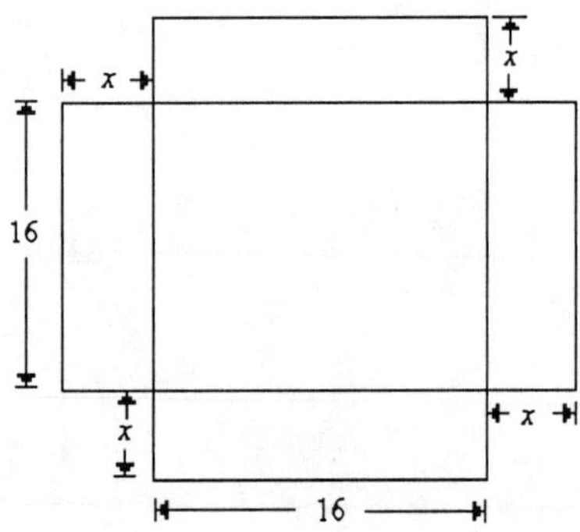

Answer: $A(x) = 64x + 256$ Difficulty: 2

96. Strips of width x are cut from two sides of a square that is 16 inches on a side. Write the area A of the remaining square as a function of x.

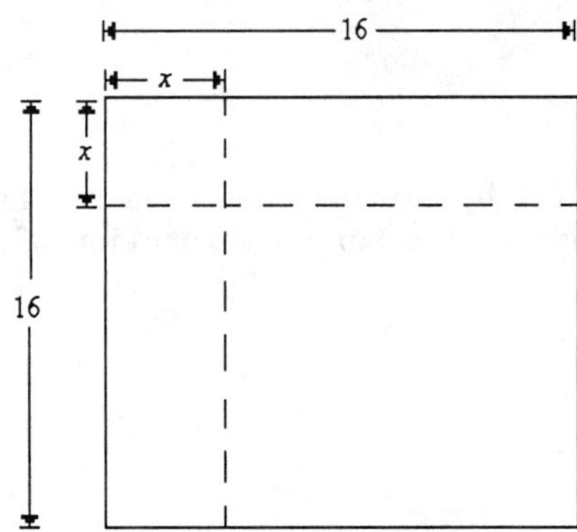

Answer:

$A(x) = (16 - x)^2$ or $A(x) = 256 - 32x + x^2$

Difficulty: 2

Chapter 014: Analyzing Graphs of Functions

MULTIPLE CHOICE

1. Find the range of the function: $y = \sqrt{9 - x^2}$.
   a) $(-\infty, -3]$, $[3, \infty)$ b) $[-3, 3]$ c) $[0, 3]$
   d) $[3, \infty)$ e) None of these

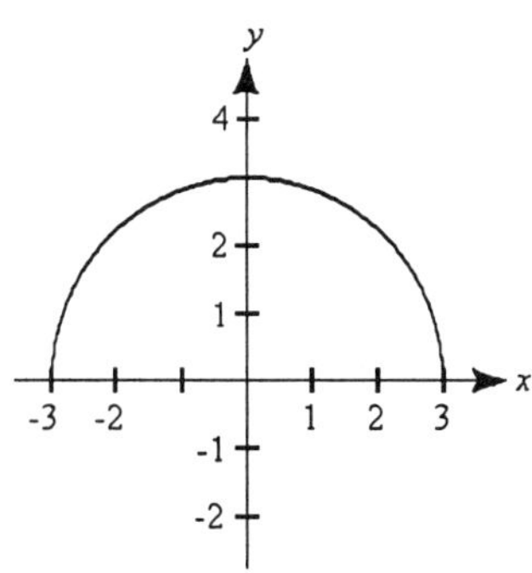

Answer: c Difficulty: 1

2. Find the range of the function: $f(x) = \sqrt{x^2 - 9}$.
   a) $[-3, 3]$ b) $(-\infty, -3]$, $[3, \infty)$ c) $[0, \infty)$
   d) $(-\infty, \infty)$ e) None of these

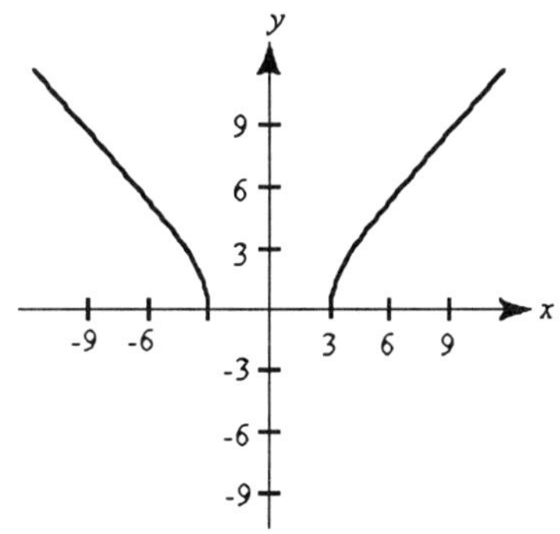

Answer: c Difficulty: 1

3. Find the range of the function: $f(x) = x\sqrt{x + 1}$.

a) $\left[-\frac{1}{2}, \infty\right]$
b) $\left[-\frac{\sqrt{2}}{4}, \infty\right]$
c) $[-1, \infty)$
d) $\left[\frac{1}{2}, -\frac{\sqrt{2}}{4}\right]$
e) None of these

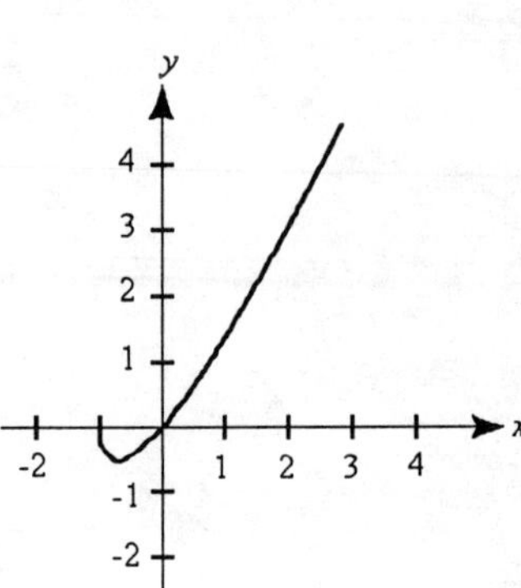

Answer: b Difficulty: 1

SHORT ANSWER

4. Find the domain and range of the function: $f(x) = |3 + x|$.

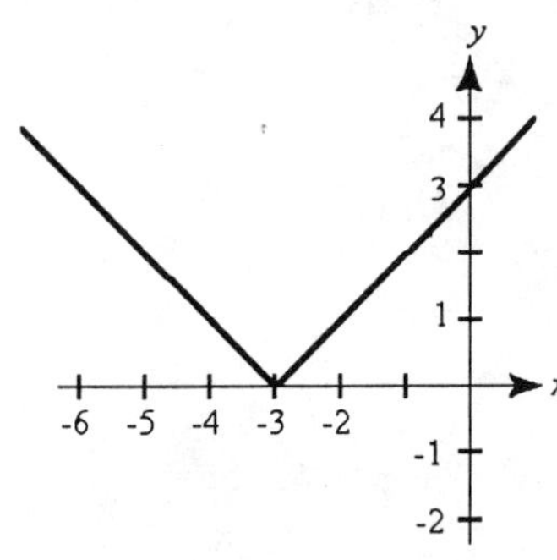

Answer: Domain: $(-\infty, \infty)$, Range: $[0, \infty)$ Difficulty: 1

5. Determine the domain and range of the function $f(x) = 3 - |x|$.

Answer: Domain $(-\infty, \infty)$, Range: $(-\infty, 3]$ Difficulty: 1

6. Determine the domain and range of the function $f(x) = 3 - x^2$.

Answer: Domain: $(-\infty, \infty)$, Range: $(-\infty, 3]$ Difficulty: 1

7. Determine the domain and range of the function $f(x) = |3 - x|$.

Answer: Domain: $(-\infty, \infty)$, Range $[0, \infty)$ Difficulty: 1

8. Determine the domain and range of the function $f(x) = x^3 + 3$.

   Answer: Domain: $(-\infty, \infty)$, Range: $(-\infty, \infty)$ Difficulty: 1

9. Use a graphing utility to graph the function $f(x) = x^2 + 2$. Then determine the domain and range.

   Answer: See graph below.

   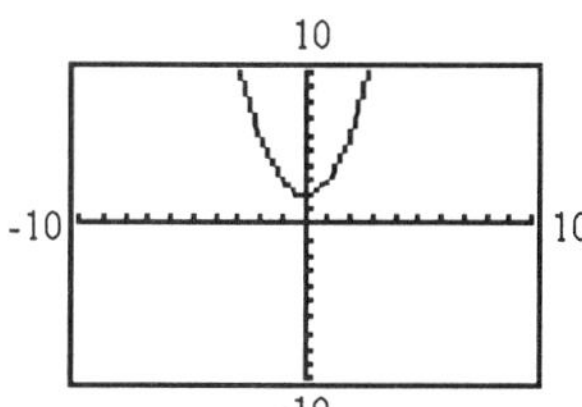

   ; Domain: $(-\infty, \infty)$, Range: $[2, \infty)$

   Difficulty: 2 Key 1: T

10. Use a graphing utility to graph the function $f(x) = |x^2 - 2|$. Then determine the domain and range.

    Answer: See graph below.

    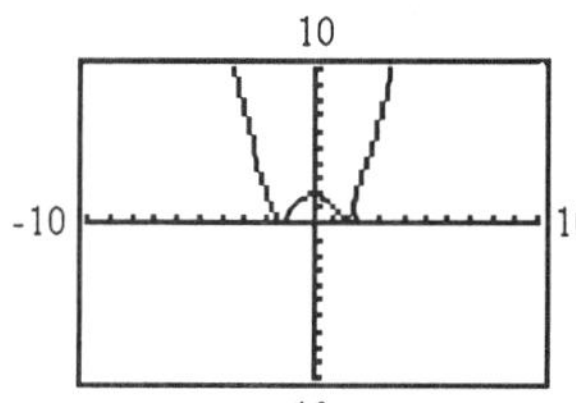

    ; Domain: $(-\infty, \infty)$, Range: $[2, \infty)$

    Difficulty: 2 Key 1: T

11. Use a graphing utility to graph the function $f(x) = -|x - 3|$. Then determine the domain and range.

    Answer: See graph below.

    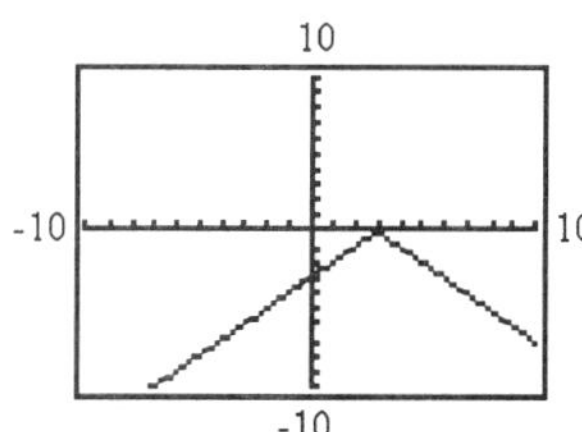

    ; Domain: $(-\infty, \infty)$, Range: $(-\infty, 0]$

    Difficulty: 2 Key 1: T

12. Use a graphing utility to graph the function $f(x) = \sqrt{x^2 - 4}$. Then determine the domain and range.

Answer: See graph below.

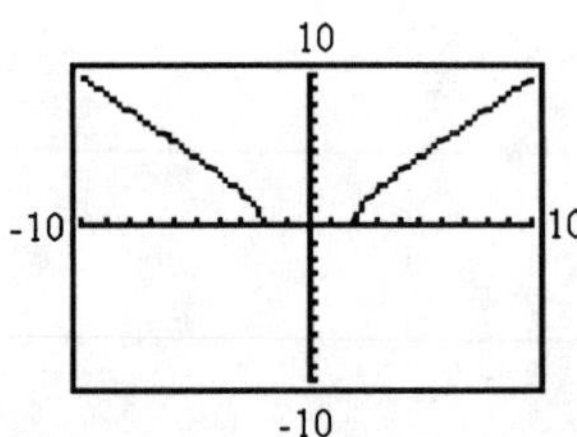

; Domain: $(-\infty, -2], [2, \infty)$, Range: $[0, \infty)$

Difficulty: 2 Key 1: T

13. Use a graphing utility to graph the function $f(x) = 1 - \sqrt{x}$. Then determine the domain and range.

Answer: See graph below.

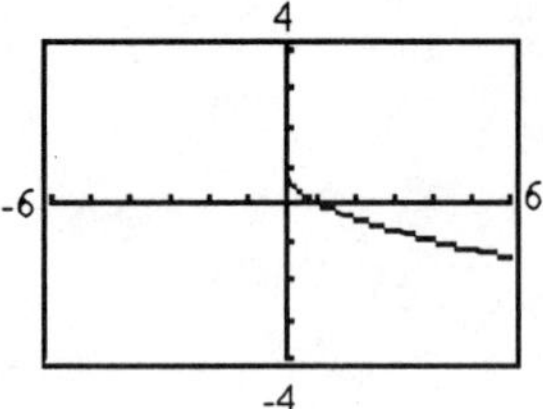

; Domain: $[0, \infty)$, Range: $(-\infty, 1]$

Difficulty: 2 Key 1: T

MULTIPLE CHOICE

14. Use the graph shown below to find $f(-1)$.
a) -1 b) 0 c) 2 d) 3 e) None of these

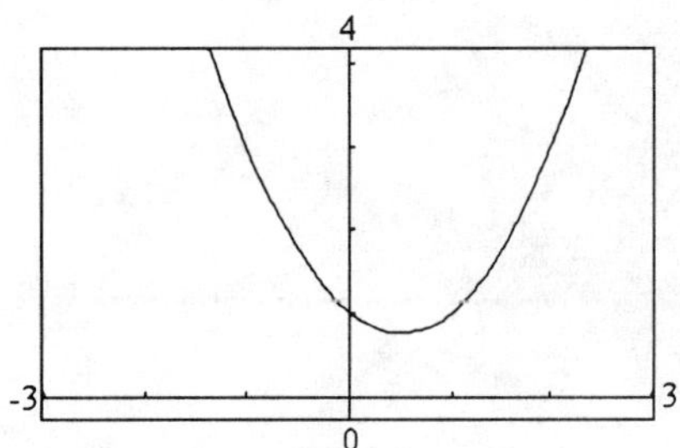

Answer: d Difficulty: 1

15. Use the graph shown below to find $f(-2)$.
a) 2 b) -2 c) 3 d) -6 e) None of these

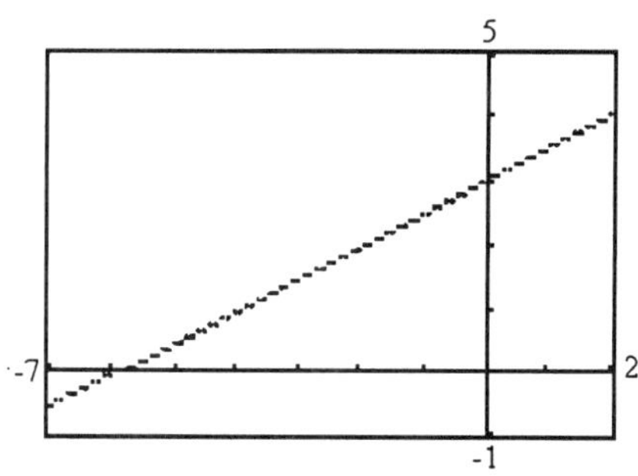

Answer: a Difficulty: 1

16. Use the graph shown below to find $f(3)$.
a) 3 b) -3 c) -3 and 3 d) 0 e) None of these

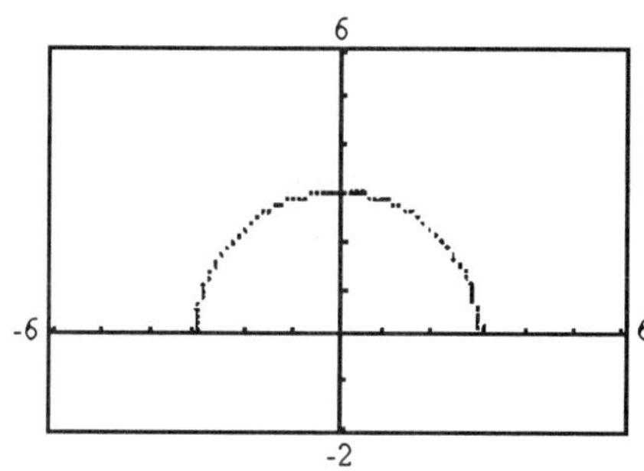

Answer: d Difficulty: 1

17. Use the vertical line test to determine in which case y is a function of x.
a) I b) II c) III d) IV e) None of these

(I)
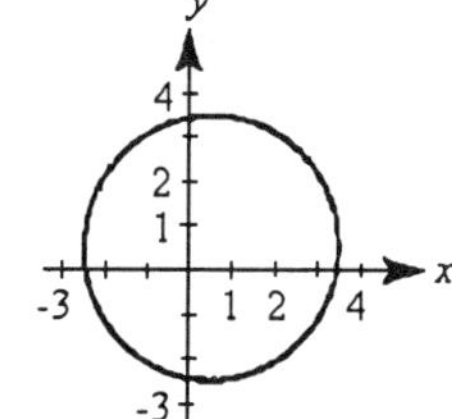

(II)
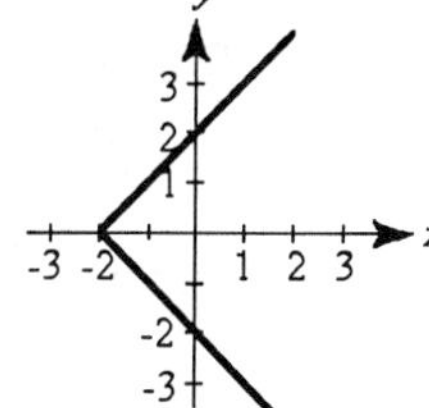

(III)
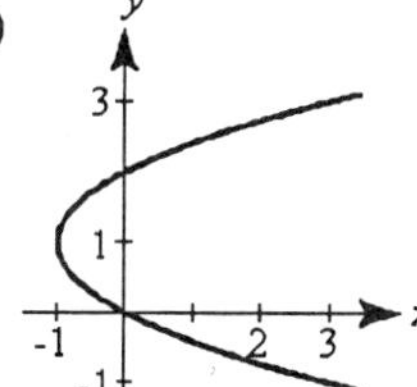

(IV)
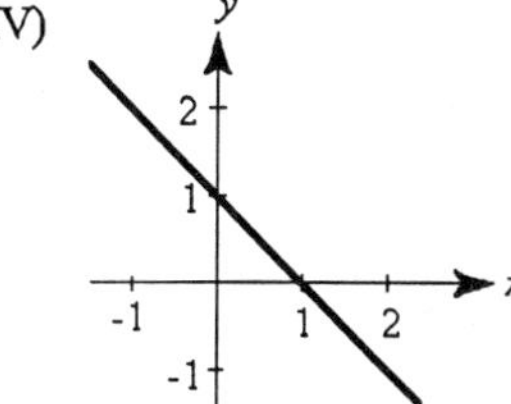

Answer: d Difficulty: 1

18. Use the vertical line test to determine in which case y is a function of x.
a) I b) II c) III d) IV e) None of these

(I)
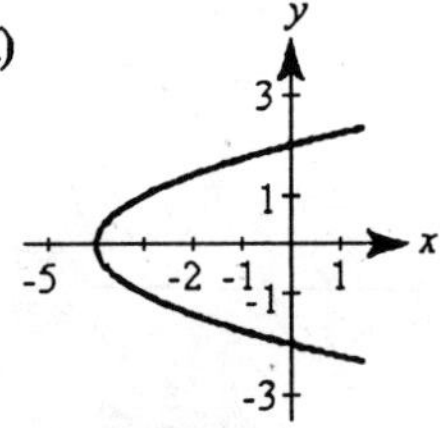

(II)
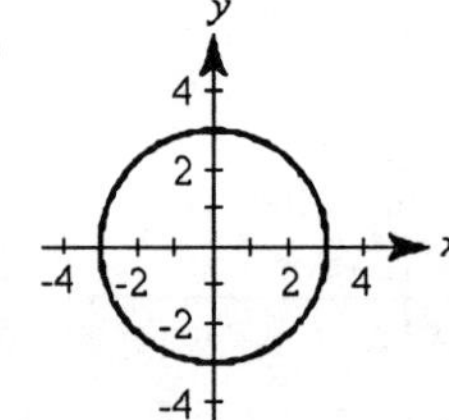

(III)
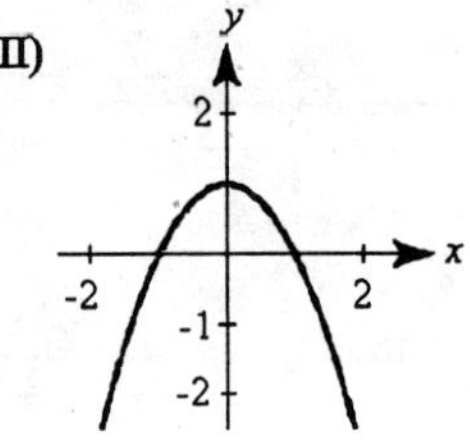

(IV)
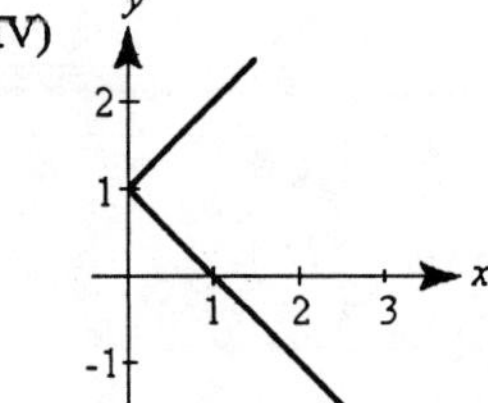

Answer: c Difficulty: 1

19. Use the vertical line test to determine in which case y is a function of x.
a) I b) II c) III d) IV e) None of these

(I)
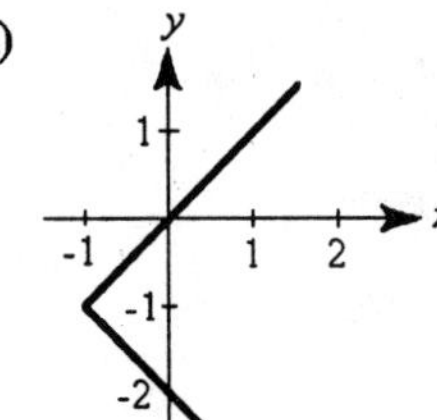

(II)
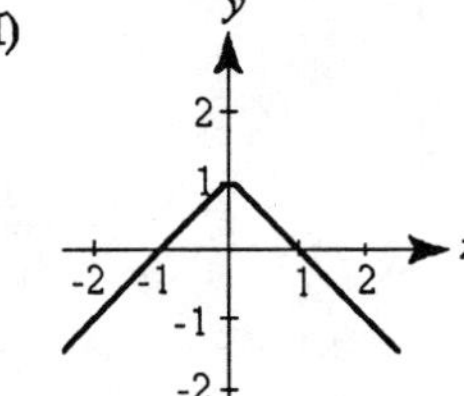

(III)
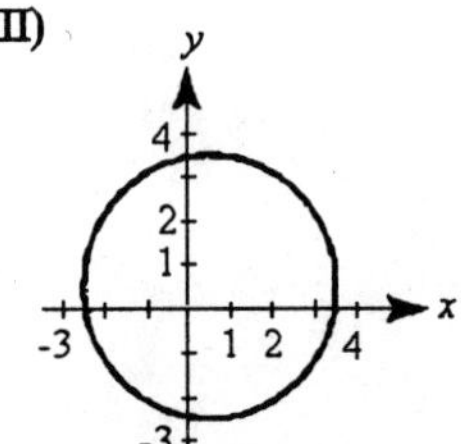

(IV)
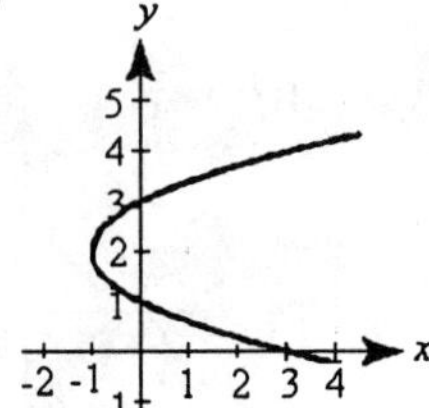

Answer: b Difficulty: 1

20. Use the vertical line test to determine in which case y is a function of x.
    a) I b) II c) III d) IV e) None of these

(I)

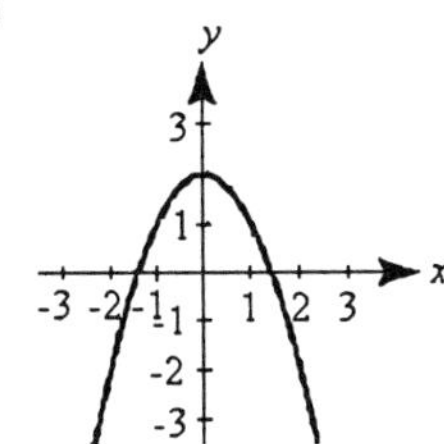

(II)

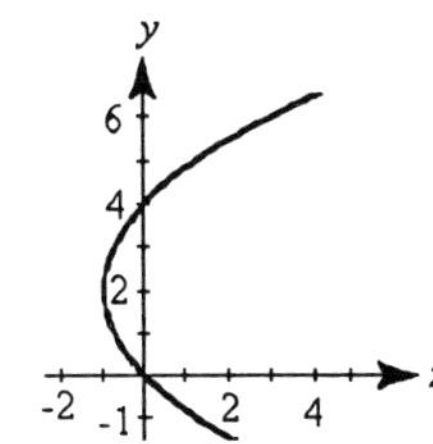

(III)

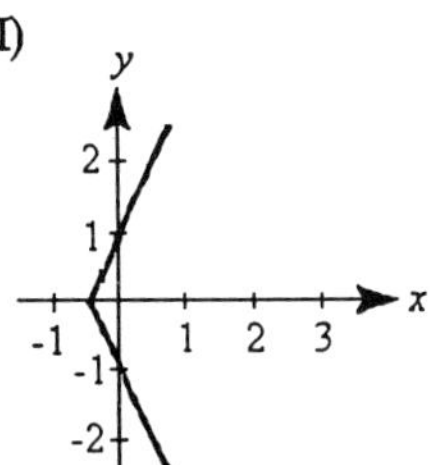

(IV)

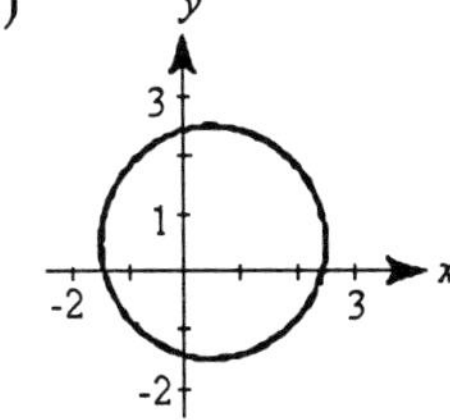

Answer: a Difficulty: 1

21. Does the graph below depict y as a function of x?
    a) y is a function of x. b) y is not a function of x.

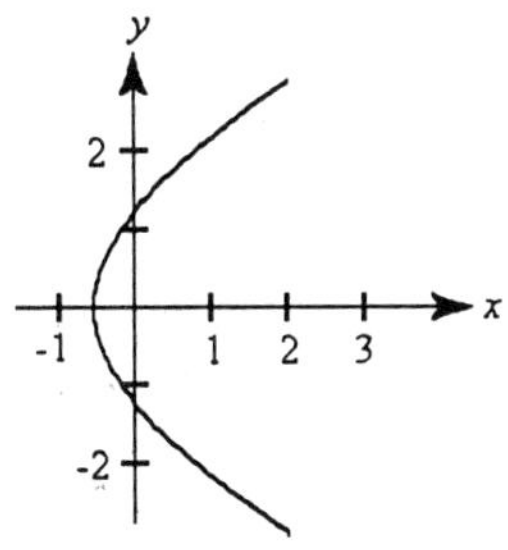

Answer: b Difficulty: 1

22. Does the graph below depict y as a function of x?
    a) y is a function of x. b) y is not a function of x.

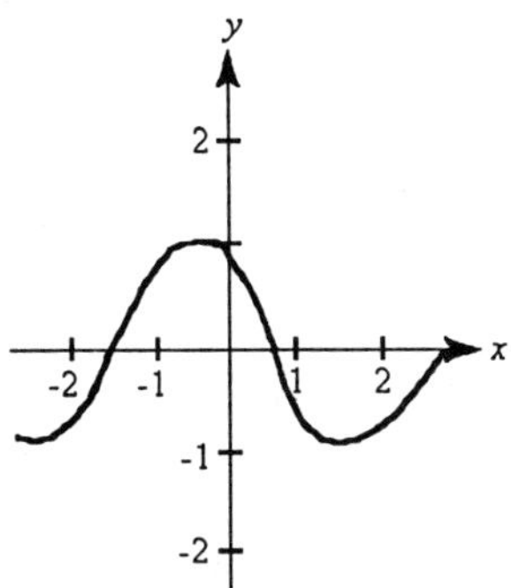

Answer: a Difficulty: 1

23. Which of the following graphs represent y as a function of x?
    a) I b) II c) III d) IV e) None of these

(I)

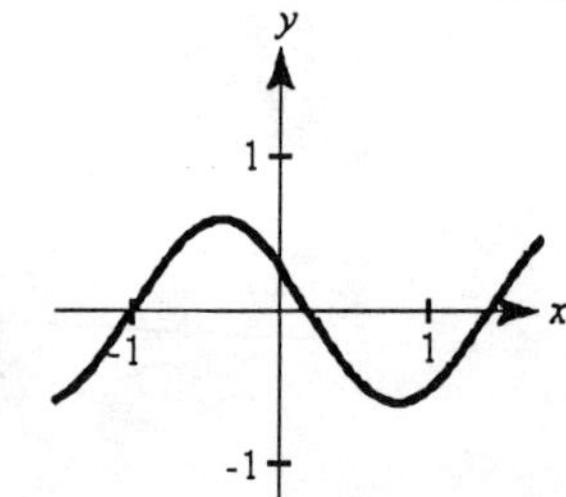

(II)

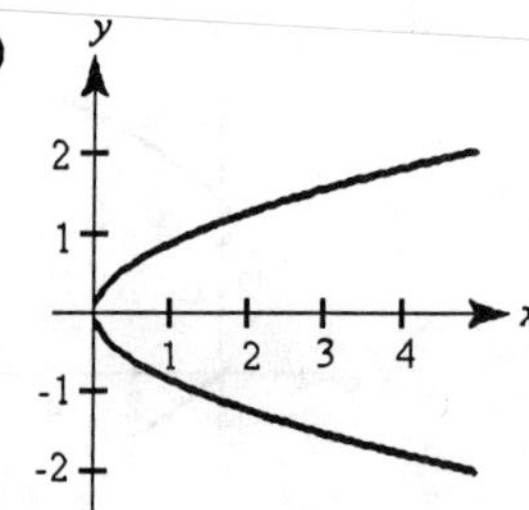

(III)

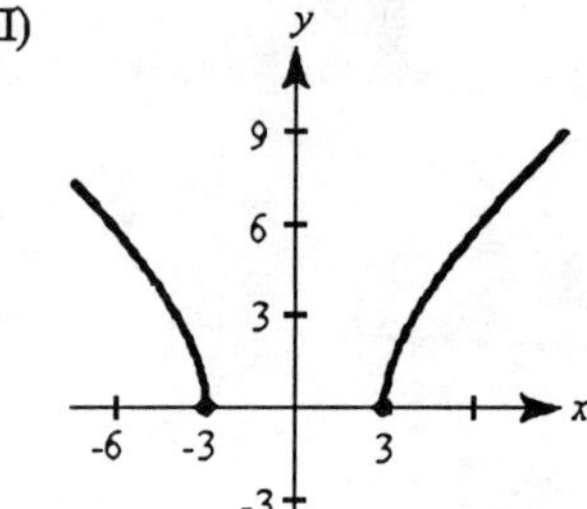

(IV)

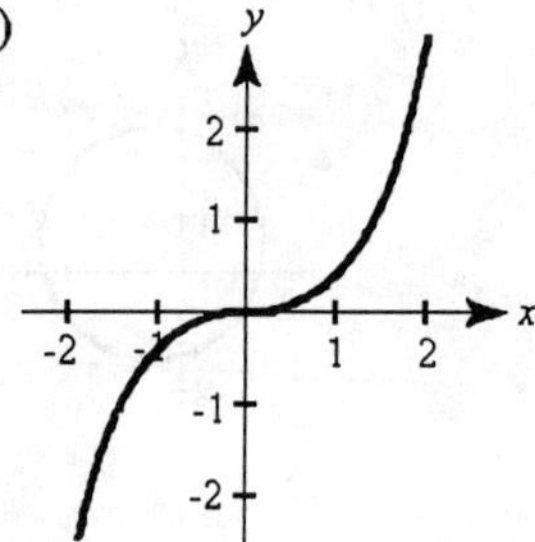

Answer: {a; c; d} Difficulty: 1

24. Which of the following graphs represent y as a function of x?
    a) I b) II c) III
    d) All of these are functions of x.
    e) None of these are functions of x.

(I)

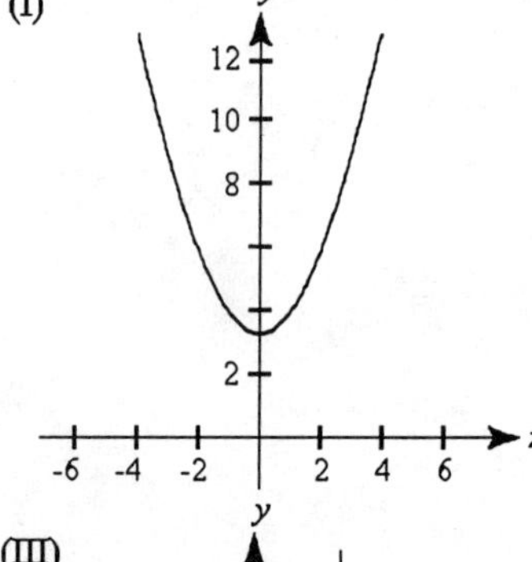

(II)

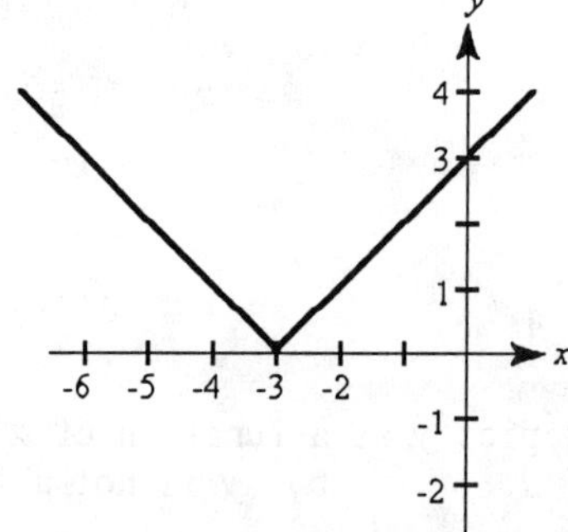

(III)

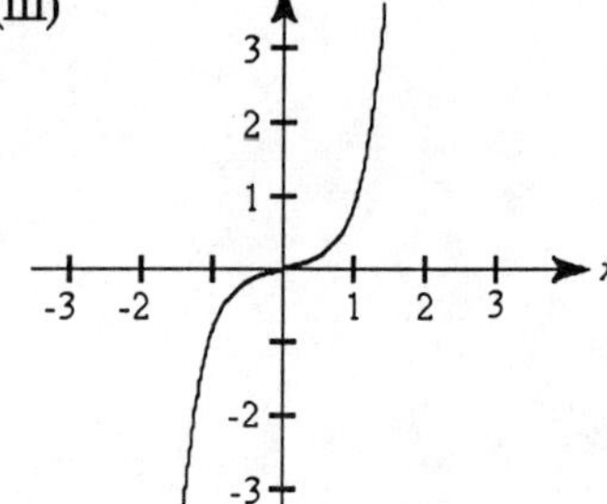

Answer: d Difficulty: 1

25. Find the zeros of the function $f(x) = 2x^2 + 7x - 15$.

a) 2, -15 b) -2, 15 c) -3/2, 5
d) -5, 3/2 e) None of these

Answer: d Difficulty: 1

26. Find the zeros of the function $f(x) = 6x^2 - 11x + 4$.

a) 4/3, 1/2 b) -2/3, -1 c) -4/3, -1/2
d) 2/3, 1 e) None of these

Answer: a Difficulty: 1

27. Find the zeros of the function $f(x) = x^3 - 7x^2 - 4x + 28$.

a) 1, 4, 7 b) -2, 2, 7 c) -7, 7, 2
d) -7, -4, 28 e) None of these

Answer: b Difficulty: 1

28. Find the zeros of the function $f(x) = \sqrt{8 - x^2}$.

a) $\pm 2\sqrt{2}$ b) ±4 c) 8 d) 0 e) None of these

Answer: a Difficulty: 1

29. Find the zeros of the function $f(x) = \frac{x}{x^2 - 4}$.

a) 0, -2, 2 b) -2, 2 c) 0 d) -4, 4 e) None of these

Answer: c Difficulty: 1

SHORT ANSWER

30. Find the zeros of the function $f(x) = 6x^2 - 19x + 10$.

Answer: $x = 5/2$, $x = 2/3$ Difficulty: 1

31. Find the zeros of the function $f(x) = 2x^3 - 10x^2 - 18x + 90$.

Answer: $x = 5$, $x = 3$, $x = -3$ Difficulty: 1

32. Find the zeros of the function $f(x) = 2x^3 - 8x$.

Answer: $x = 2$, $x = 0$, $x = -2$ Difficulty: 1

33. Find the zeros of the function $f(x) = \sqrt{12 - x^2}$.

Answer:

$x = \pm 2\sqrt{3}$

Difficulty: 1

34. Find the zeros of the function $f(x) = \frac{3x + 1}{6x - 4}$.

Answer: $x = -1/3$ Difficulty: 1

MULTIPLE CHOICE

35. Determine which of the following are graphs of odd functions.

a) I b) II c) III
d) All are odd functions. e) None of these.

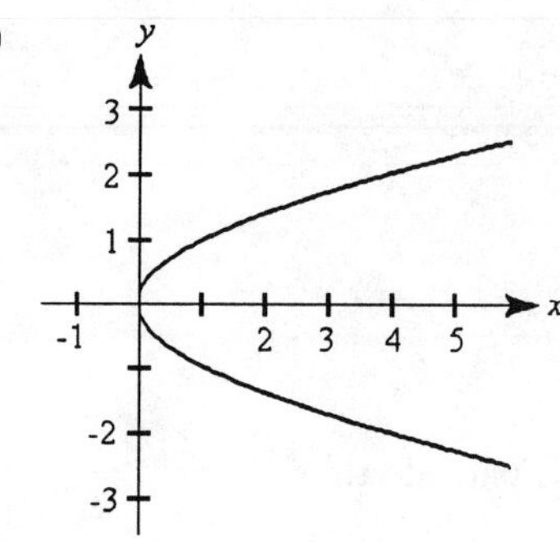

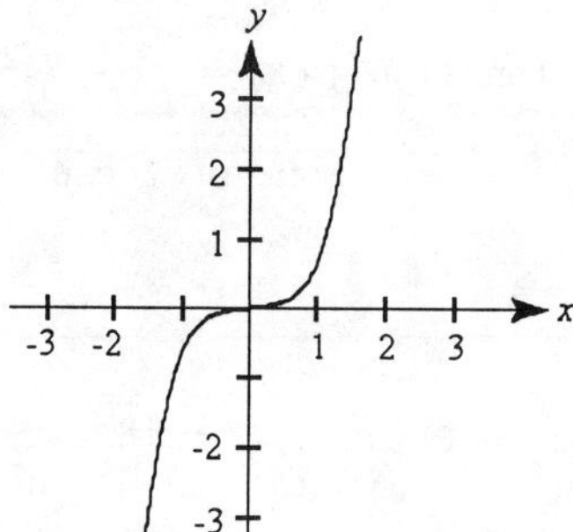

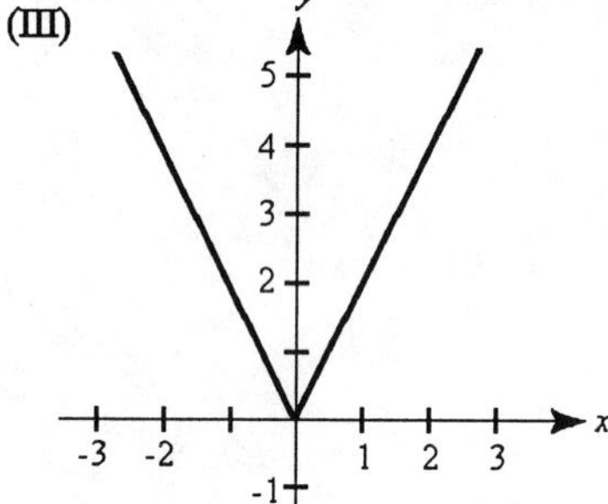

Answer: b Difficulty: 1

36. Determine which of the following are graphs of even functions.
    a) I b) II c) III
    d) All are even functions. e) None of these.

(I)
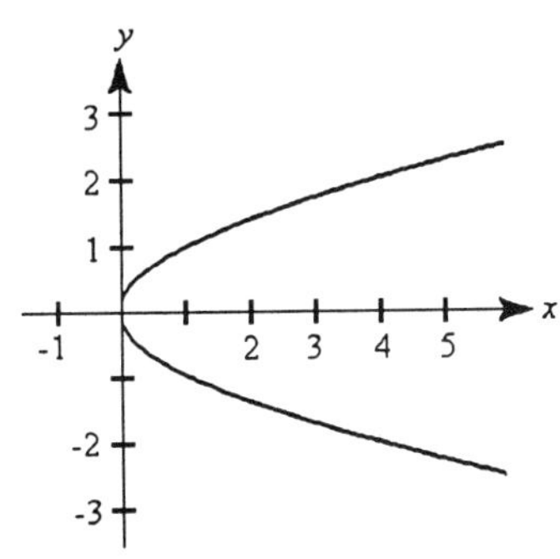

(II)
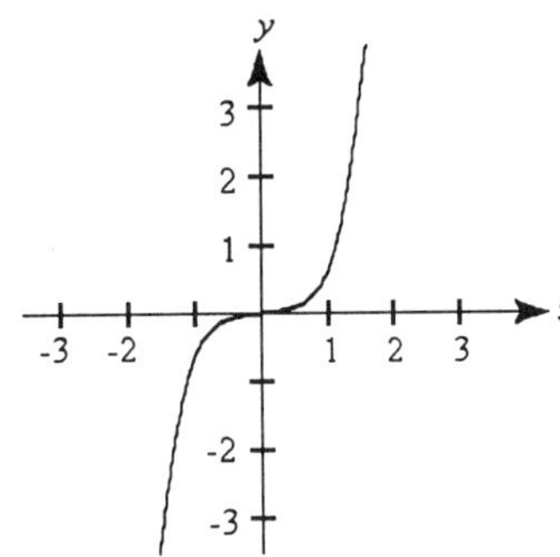

(III)
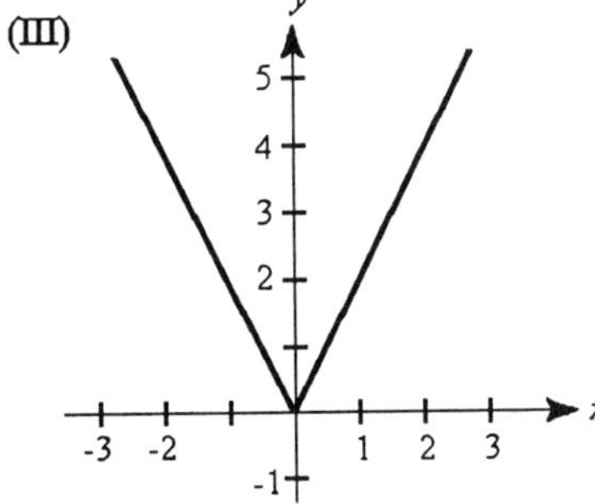

Answer: c Difficulty: 1

37. Determine which of the following are graphs of odd functions.
    a) I b) II c) III
    d) All are odd functions. e) None of these.

(I)
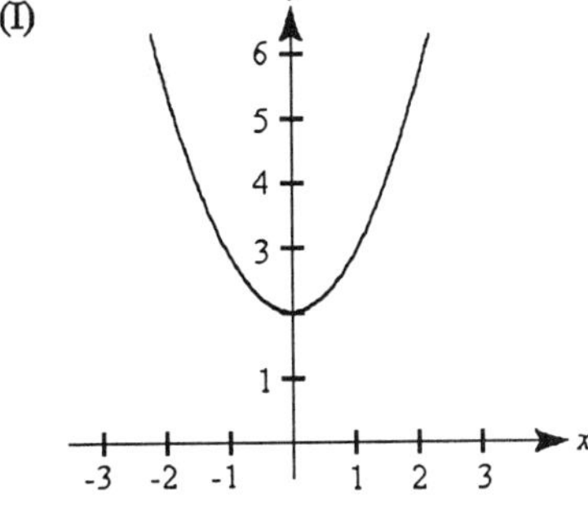

(II)
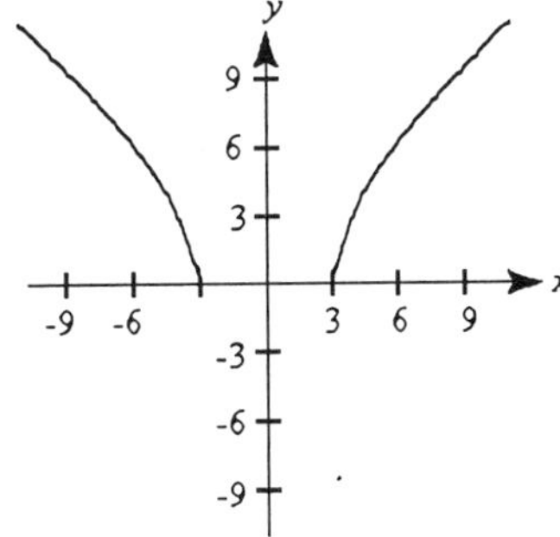

(II)
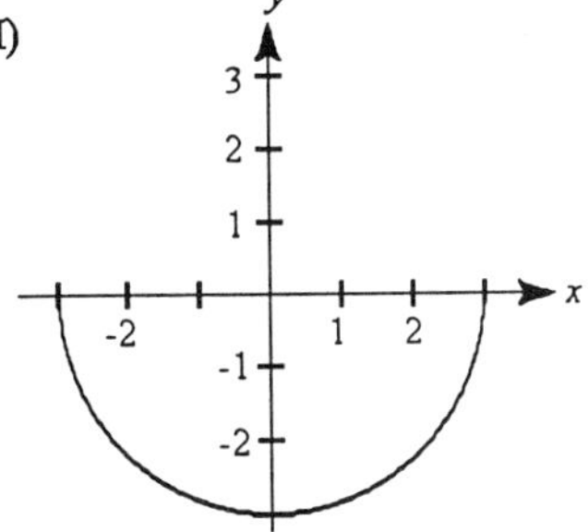

Answer: e Difficulty: 1

38. Determine which of the following are graphs of even functions.
a) I b) II c) III
d) All are even functions. e) None of these.

(I)

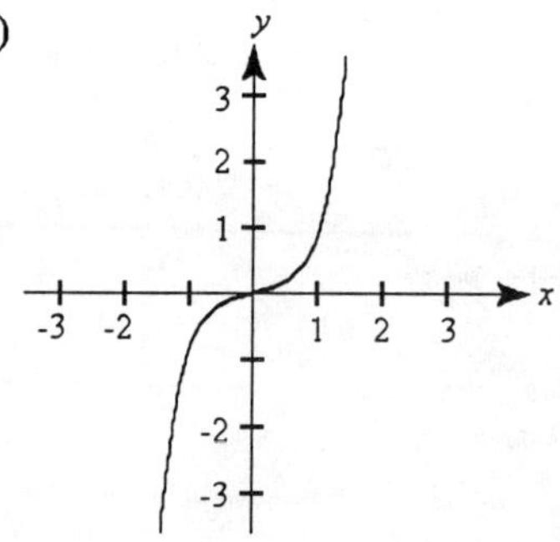

(II)

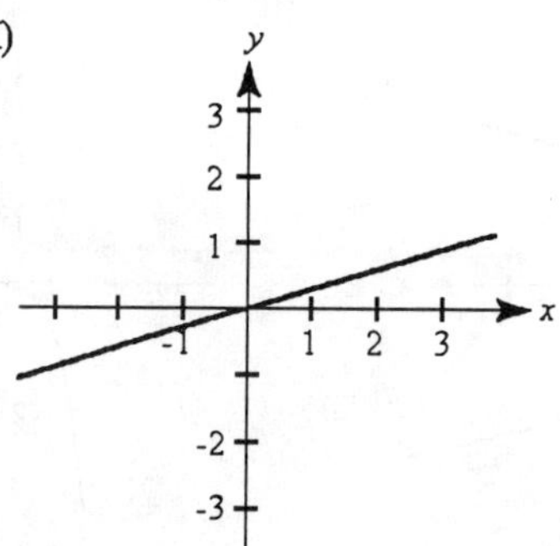

(III)

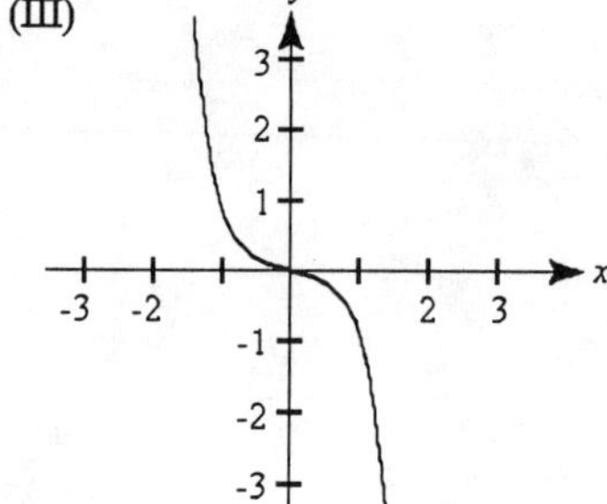

Answer: e Difficulty: 1

39. Is the following function even or odd? $f(x) = 3x^4 - x^2 + 2$
a) Odd b) Even c) Both d) Neither

Answer: b Difficulty: 1

SHORT ANSWER

40. Is the following function even or odd? $y = -x^4 + 2x^2 - 1$

Answer: Even Difficulty: 1

MULTIPLE CHOICE

41. Is the following function even or odd? $f(x) = 2x^3 + 3x^2$
a) Odd b) Even c) Both d) Neither

Answer: d Difficulty: 1

42. Is the following function even or odd? $f(x) = 4x^3 + 3x$
a) Even b) Odd c) Both d) Neither

Answer: b Difficulty: 1

43. Determine the interval(s) over which the function is increasing:
$y = 2x^3 + 3x^2 - 12x$.
a) $(-\infty, -2), (1, \infty)$ b) $(-\infty, 20), (-7, \infty)$ c) $(-2, 1)$
d) $(20, -7)$ e) None of these

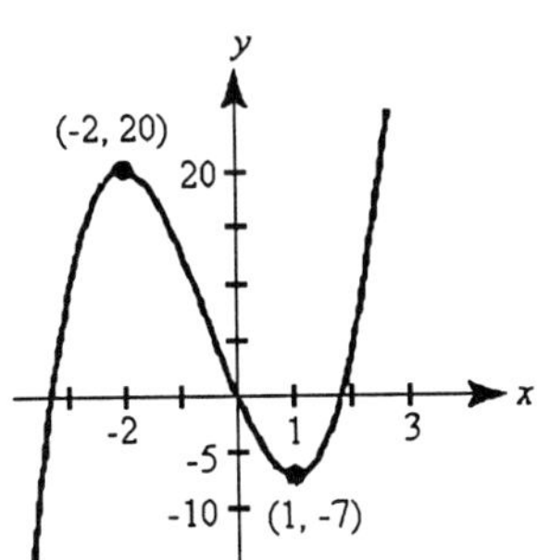

Answer: a Difficulty: 2

44. Determine the interval(s) over which the function is increasing:
$y = x^4 - 2x^2$.
a) $(-\infty, -1)$ b) $(-\infty, -1), (0, 1)$ c) $(-1, 0), (1, \infty)$
d) $(-\infty, -1), (0, -1)$ e) None of these

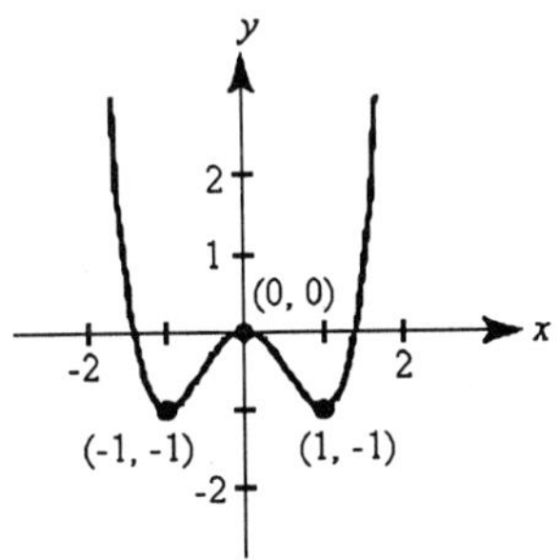

Answer: c Difficulty: 2

SHORT ANSWER

45. Determine the interval(s) over which the function is increasing:
$y = \frac{2}{3}x^3 - x^2$.

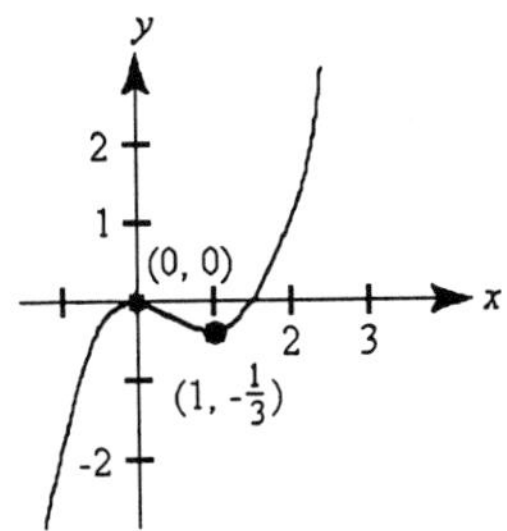

Answer: $(-\infty, 0), (1, \infty)$ Difficulty: 2

46. Determine the interval(s) over which the function is increasing: $y = \frac{1}{x^2 - 1}$.

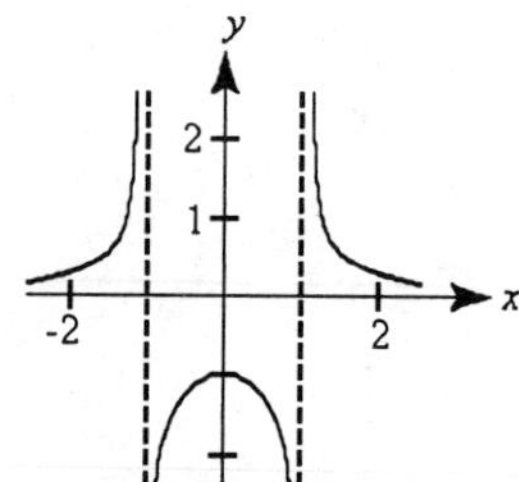

Answer: $(-\infty, -1), (-1, 0)$ Difficulty: 2

47. Use a graphing utility to determine the interval(s) over which the function is increasing: $f(x) = \frac{1}{3}x^3 - x + 1$.

Answer: $(-\infty, -1), (1, \infty)$ Difficulty: 2 Key 1: T

48. Use a graphing utility to determine the interval(s) over which the function is increasing: $f(x) = -\frac{1}{3}x^3 + \frac{1}{2}x^2 + 2x$.

Answer: $(-1, 2)$ Difficulty: 2 Key 1: T

49. Use a graphing utility to determine the interval(s) over which the function is increasing: $f(x) = \frac{1}{3}x^3 + \frac{1}{2}x^2 - 2x$.

Answer: $(-\infty, -2), (1, \infty)$ Difficulty: 2 Key 1: T

50. Use a graphing utility to determine the interval(s) over which the function is increasing: $f(x) = -\frac{1}{3}x^3 - \frac{1}{2}x^2 + 2x$.

Answer: $(-2, 1)$ Difficulty: 2 Key 1: T

MULTIPLE CHOICE

51. Determine the open intervals in which the function is increasing, decreasing, or constant.
    a) Increasing on $(-\infty, \infty)$
    b) Increasing on $(-\infty, 0)$
    Decreasing on $(0, \infty)$
    c) Increasing on $(-\infty, -2)$, $(0, \infty)$
    Decreasing on $(-2, 0)$
    d) Increasing on $(-\infty, 3)$
    Decreasing on $(3, \infty)$
    e) None of these

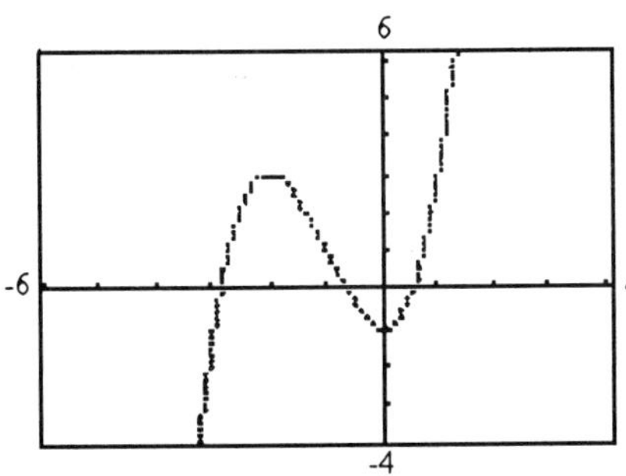

Answer: c Difficulty: 1

52. Determine the open intervals in which the function is increasing, decreasing, or constant.
    a) Increasing on $(-5, 5)$
    b) Increasing on $(-\infty, 0)$
    Decreasing on $(0, \infty)$
    c) Increasing on $(0, 6)$
    d) Increasing on $(-\infty, 6)$
    Decreasing on $(6, \infty)$
    e) None of these

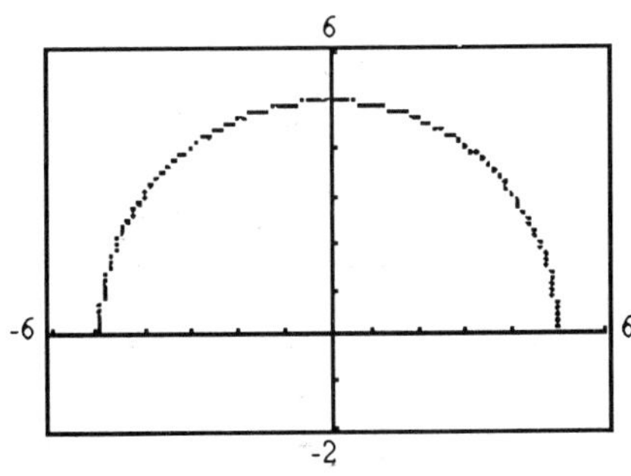

Answer: e Difficulty: 1

SHORT ANSWER

53. Use a graphing utility to approximate the relative minimum and/or relative maximum of $f(x) = x^2 - 6x + 1$.

    Answer: (3, -8) is a relative minimum. Difficulty: 2 Key 1: T

54. Use a graphing utility to approximate the relative minimum and/or relative maximum of $f(x) = x^3 - 3x^2 + 2$.

Answer: (0, 2) is a relative maximum and (2, -2) is a relative minimum. Difficulty: 2

Key 1: T

MULTIPLE CHOICE

55. Write the linear function that has the indicated function values: $f(2) = 6$ and $f(5) = -6$.
a) $f(x) = \frac{1}{4}x + \frac{11}{2}$ b) $f(x) = 6$ c) $f(x) = 4x - 14$
d) $f(x) = -4x + 14$ e) None of these

Answer: d Difficulty: 2

SHORT ANSWER

56. Write the linear function that has the indicated function values: $\left(-\frac{1}{2}, 3\right)$ and $(-1, 2)$.

Answer: $f(x) = 2x + 4$ Difficulty: 2

MULTIPLE CHOICE

57. Which of the following functions is represented by the graph shown?
a) $f(x) = 2x + 5$ b) $f(x) = 5x + 2$ c) $f(x) = \frac{-5}{2}x + 5$
d) $f(x) = \frac{-2}{5}x - 2$ e) None of these

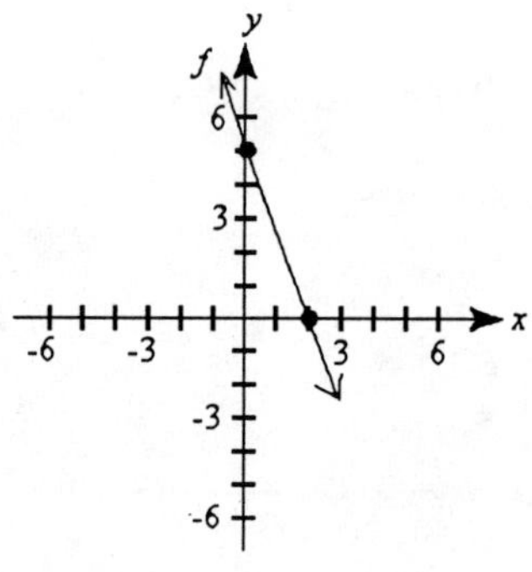

Answer: c Difficulty: 1

58. Which of the following functions is represented by the graph shown?
a) $f(x) = -6x + 2$ b) $f(x) = \frac{1}{3}x + 2$ c) $f(x) = -3x - 6$
d) $f(x) = 2x - 6$ e) None of these

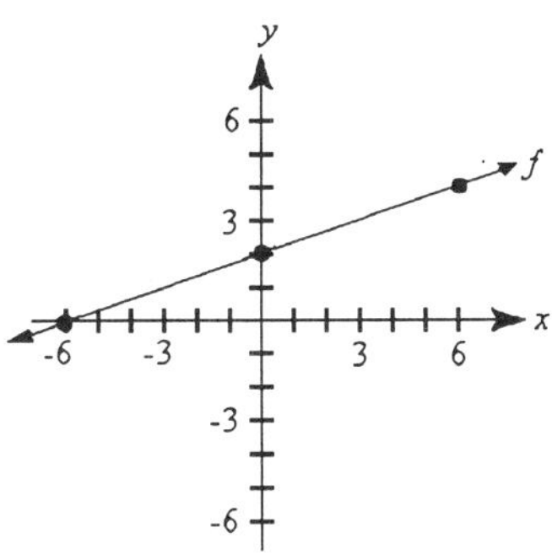

Answer: b Difficulty: 1

SHORT ANSWER

59. Sketch the graph of the function: $f(x) = \begin{cases} 3x - 1, & x < 1 \\ x^2 + 1, & x \geq 1 \end{cases}$.

Answer: See graph below.

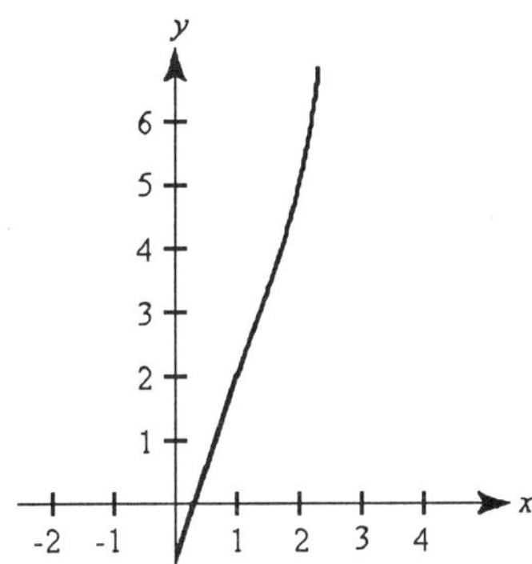

Difficulty: 2

MULTIPLE CHOICE

60. Identify the graph: $f(x) = \begin{cases} 2x + 1, & x \le 1 \\ x^2, & x > 1 \end{cases}$.

a) I b) II c) III d) IV e) None of these

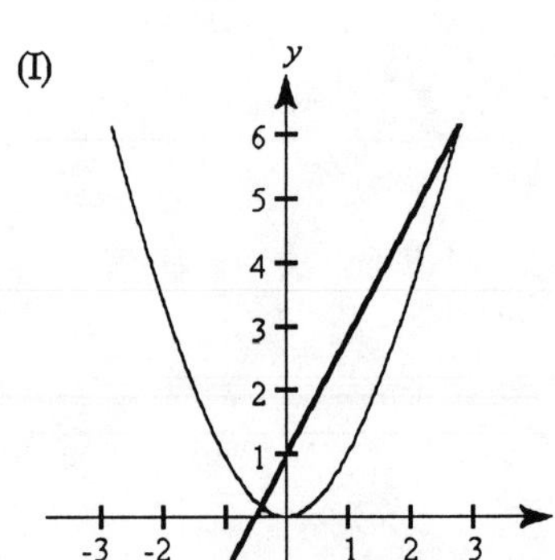

(II)

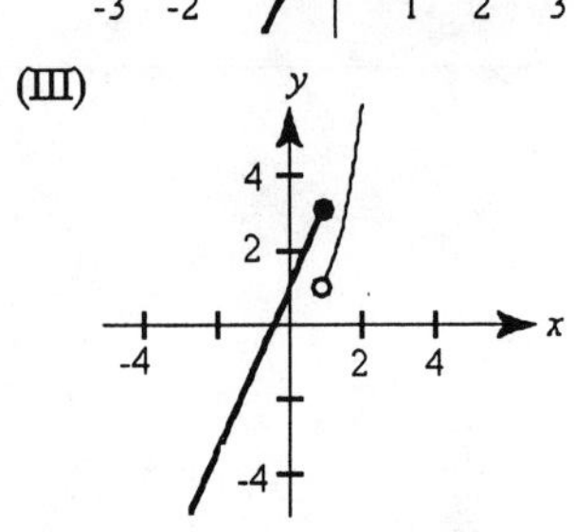

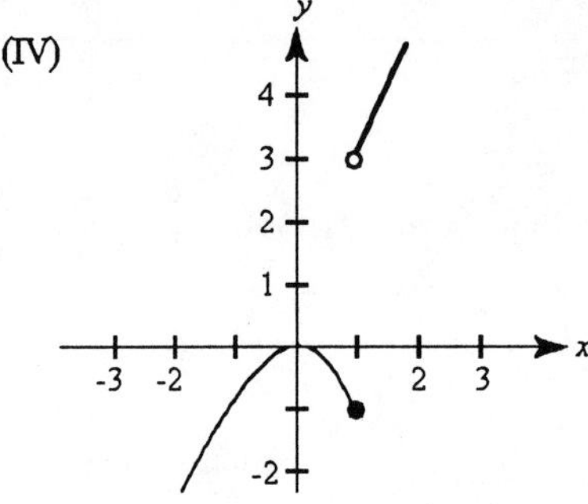

Answer: c Difficulty: 2

61. Identify the graph: $f(x) = \begin{cases} -x^2 + 2, & x \leq 0 \\ x + 2, & x > 0 \end{cases}$.

a) I b) II c) III d) IV e) None of these

(I)
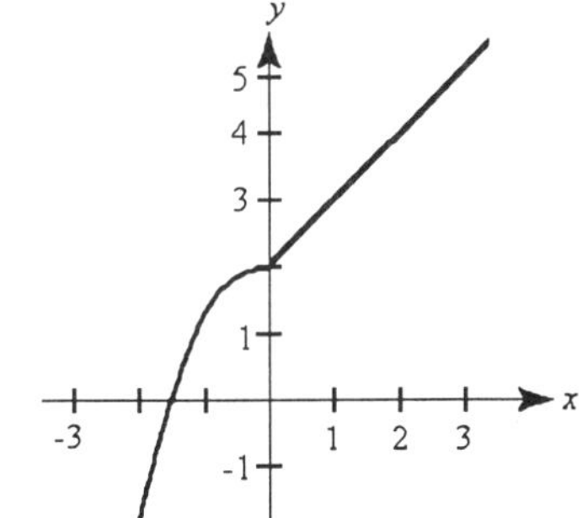

(II)
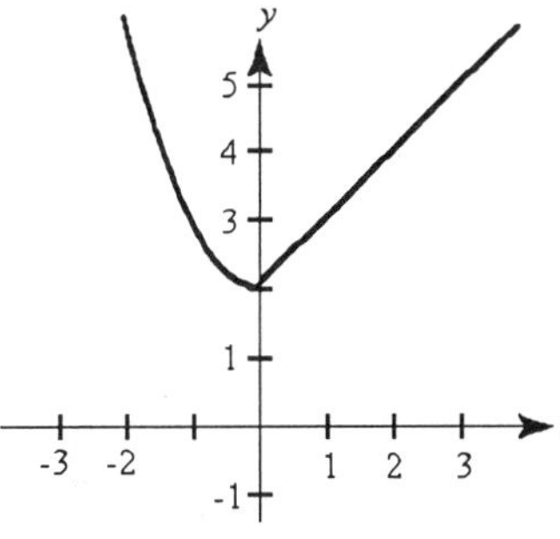

(III)
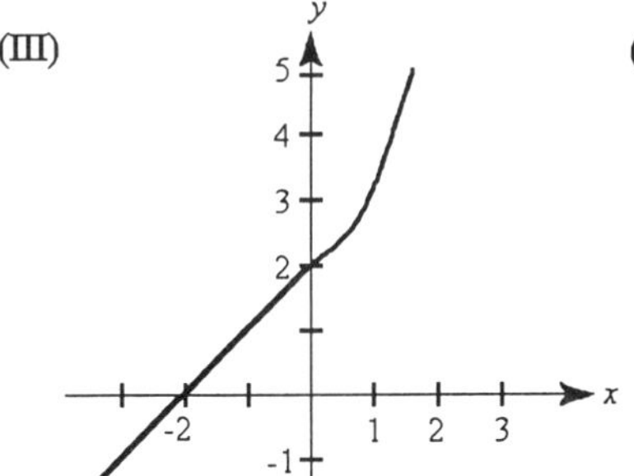

(IV)
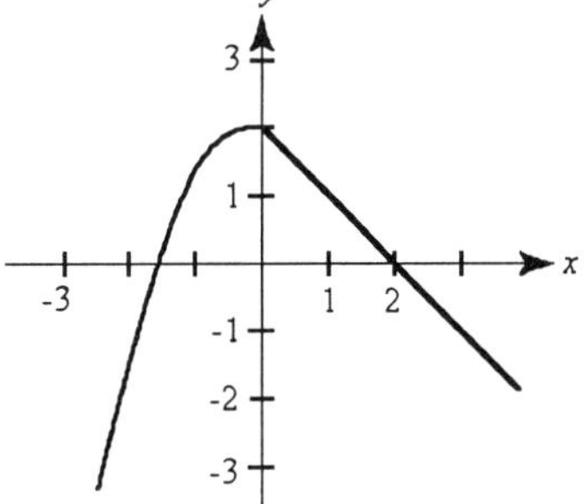

Answer: a Difficulty: 1

62. Identify the graph: $f(x) = \begin{cases} 3x - 1, & x \le 1 \\ 2 + x^2, & x > 1 \end{cases}$.

a) I   b) II   c) III   d) IV   e) None of these

(I)

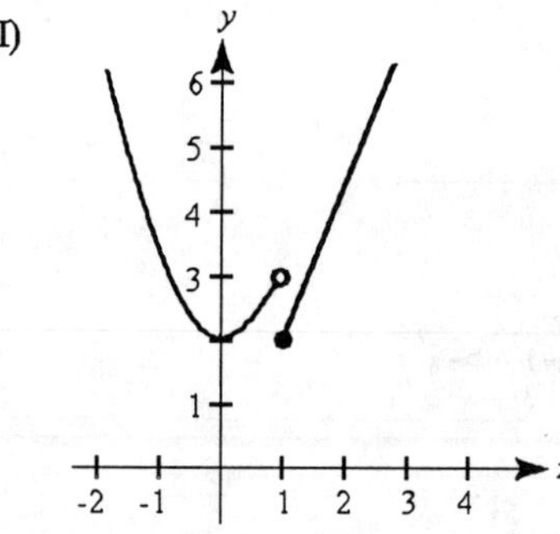

(II)

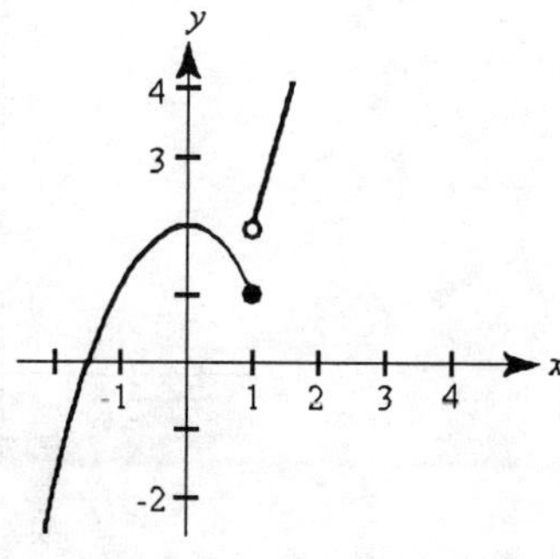

(III)

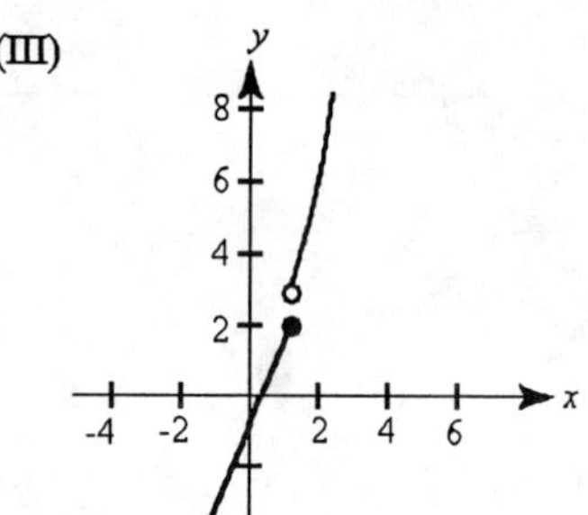

(IV)

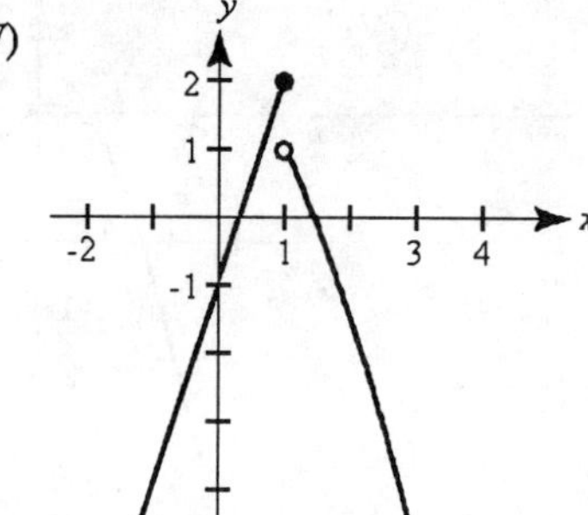

Answer: c Difficulty: 2

63. Use a graphing utility to determine the interval(s) on the real axis for which $f(x) \ge 0$ for $f(x) = 9 - x^2$.
a) $(-\infty, \infty)$ b) $[-3, 3]$ c) $[0, 3]$
d) $(-\infty, -3), (3, \infty)$ e) None of these

Answer: b Difficulty: 1 Key 1: T

64. Use a graphing utility to determine the interval(s) on the real axis for which $f(x) \ge 0$ for $f(x) = \sqrt{x - 9}$.
a) $(-\infty, \infty)$ b) $[-9, 9]$ c) $[-3, 3]$
d) $[9, \infty)$ e) None of these

Answer: d Difficulty: 1 Key 1: T

SHORT ANSWER

65. Use a graphing utility to determine the interval(s) on the real axis for which $f(x) \ge 0$ for $f(x) = \sqrt{4 - x^2}$.

Answer: $[-2, 2]$ Difficulty: 1 Key 1: T

66. Use a graphing utility to determine the interval(s) on the real axis for which $f(x) \geq 0$ for $f(x) = \sqrt{x^2 - 4}$.

Answer: $(-\infty, -2]$, $[2, \infty)$ Difficulty: 1 Key 1: T

MULTIPLE CHOICE

67. Write the height h of the rectangle as a function of x.
a) $h(x) = 2x + 3 - x^2$
b) $h(x) = x^2 - 2x + 3$
c) $h(x) = x^2 - 2x - 3$
d) $h(x) = 2x + 3 + x^2$
e) None of these

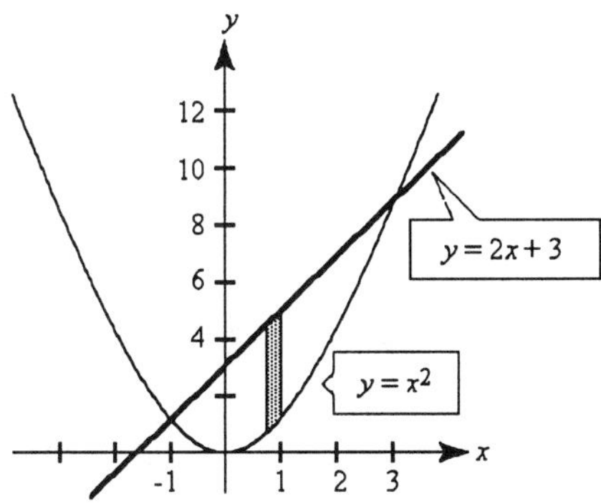

Answer: a Difficulty: 2

68. Write the height h of the rectangle as a function of x.

a) $h(x) = -x^2 + 4x + 1 - \frac{2}{3}x - \frac{2}{3}$
$= -x^2 + \frac{10}{3}x + \frac{1}{3}$

b) $h(x) = -x^2 + 4x + 1 + \frac{2}{3}x + \frac{2}{3}$
$= -x^2 + \frac{14}{3}x + \frac{5}{3}$

c) $h(x) = \frac{2}{3}x + \frac{2}{3} - x^2 - 4x - 1$
$= -x^2 - \frac{10}{3}x - \frac{1}{2}$

d) $h(x) = \frac{2}{3}x + \frac{2}{3} + x^2 - 4x + 1$
$= x^2 - \frac{10}{3} + \frac{5}{3}$

e) None of these

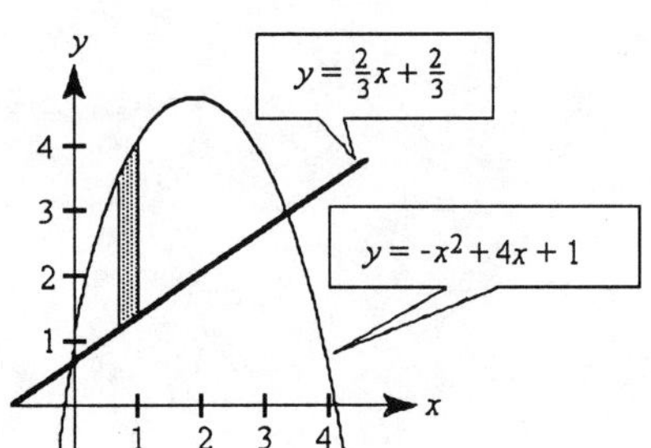

Answer: a Difficulty: 2

69. Write the height h of the rectangle as a function of x.

a) $h(x) = x^2 - 5x + 3$
b) $h(x) = -x^2 + 5x - 3$
c) $h(x) = 3 - 5x + x^2$
d) $h(x) = 5x - 3 + x^2$
e) None of these

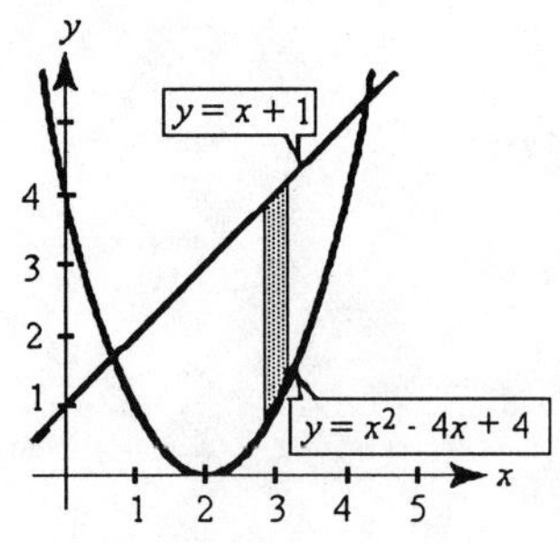

Answer: b Difficulty: 2

SHORT ANSWER

70. Write the height h of the rectangle as a function of x.

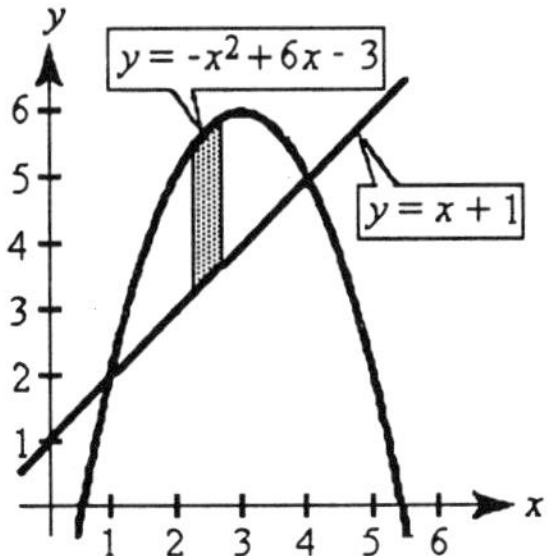

Answer:

$h(x) = -x^2 + 5x - 4$

Difficulty: 2

71. Write the height h of the rectangle as a function of x.

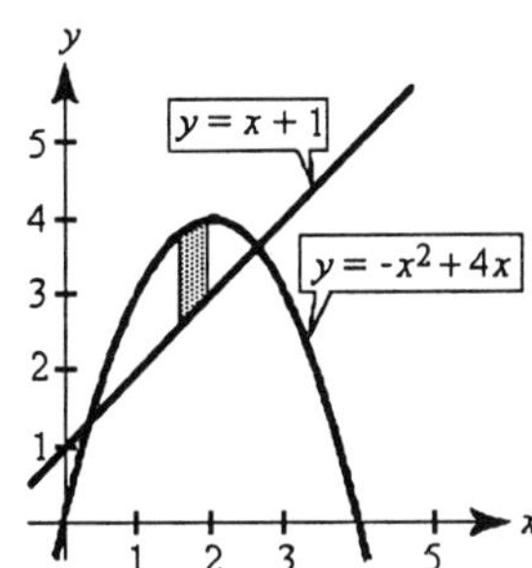

Answer:

$h(x) = -x^2 + 3x - 1$

Difficulty: 2

72. Use a graphing utility to graph the function $f(x) = [[x + 2]]$.

Answer: See graph below.

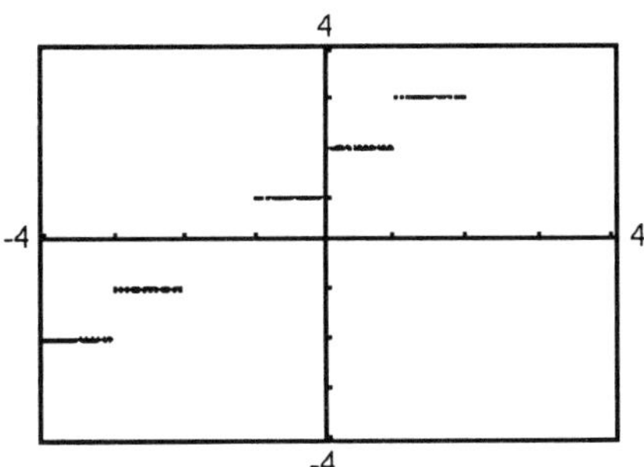

Difficulty: 1 Key 1: T

73. Use a graphing utility to graph the function $f(x) = 4 + [[x]]$.

Answer: See graph below.

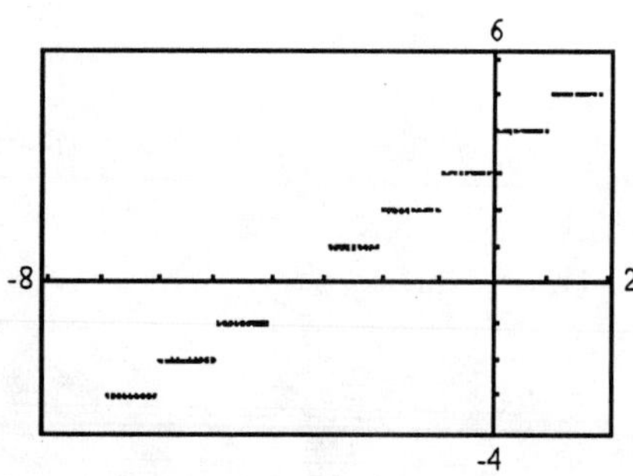

Difficulty: 1 Key 1: T

74. Sketch the graph of the function $f(x) = \begin{cases} -x, & \text{if } -2 \leq x < 0 \\ \frac{1}{4}x^2, & \text{if } 0 \leq x \leq 2 \end{cases}$.

Answer: See graph below.

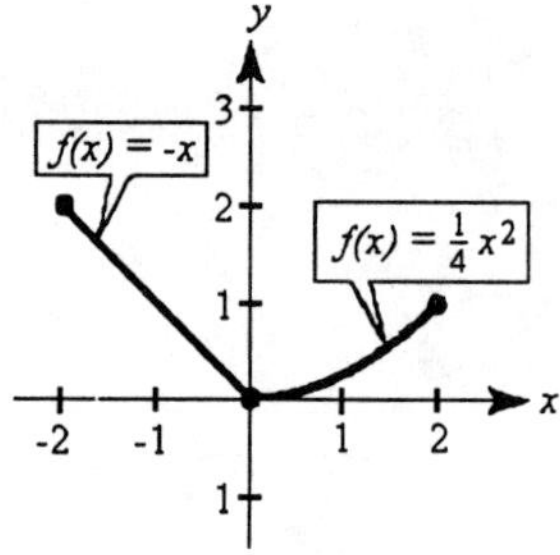

Difficulty: 2

75. Sketch the graph of the function $f(x) = \begin{cases} 3 + 2x, & \text{if } -2 \leq x \leq 0 \\ 3 - x, & \text{if } 0 < x \leq 4 \end{cases}$.

Answer: See graph below.

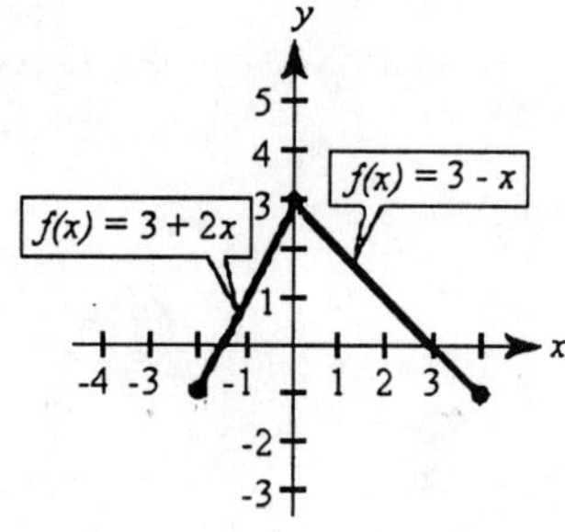

Difficulty: 2

76. The height in feet of a ball thrown by a child is

$$y = -\frac{4}{5}x^2 + 6x + 4$$

where y is the horizontal distance (in feet) when the ball is thrown. Graph the function using a graphing utility. Use the graph to estimate the maximum height the ball reaches.

Answer: The maximum height ≈ 15 feet.

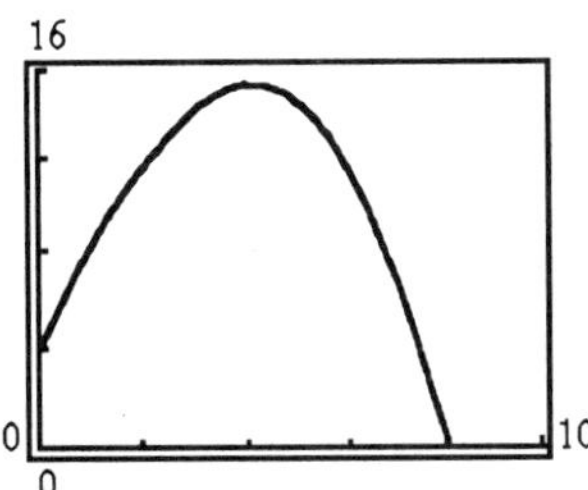

Difficulty: 2 Key 1: T

77. The height in feet of a ball thrown by a child is

$$y = -\frac{1}{4}x^2 + 4x + 5$$

where y is the horizontal distance (in feet) when the ball is thrown. Graph the function using a graphing utility. Use the graph to estimate the maximum height the ball reaches.

Answer: The maximum height ≈ 21 feet.

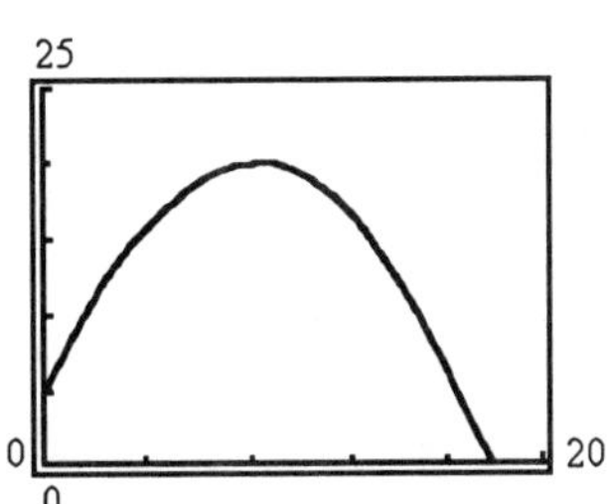

Difficulty: 2 Key 1: T

78. The height in feet of a ball thrown by a child is

$$y = -\frac{1}{2}x^2 + 2x + 3$$

where y is the horizontal distance (in feet) when the ball is thrown. Graph the function using a graphing utility. Use the graph to estimate the maximum height the ball reaches.

Answer: The maximum height ≈ 5 feet.

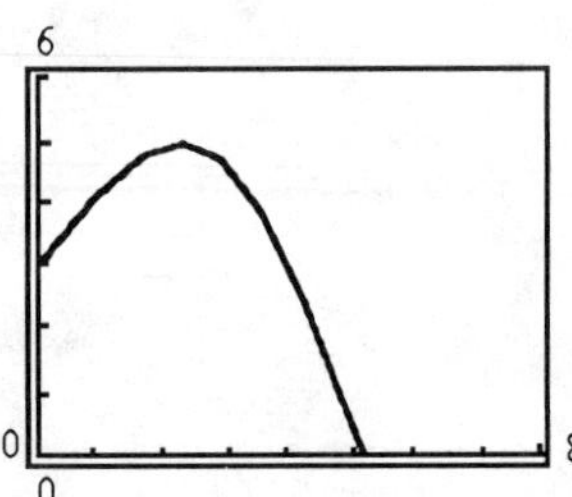

Difficulty: 2 Key 1: T

79. The height in feet of a ball thrown by a child is

$$y = -x^2 + 6x + 10$$

where y is the horizontal distance (in feet) when the ball is thrown. Graph the function using a graphing utility. Use the graph to estimate the maximum height the ball reaches.

Answer: The maximum height ≈ 19 feet.

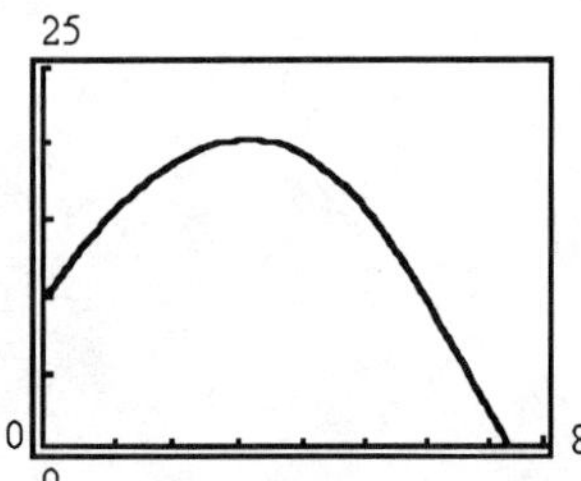

Difficulty: 2 Key 1: T

80. A ball is shot vertically upward at a speed of 64 feet per second. The equation that relates the position, s, of the ball as a function of time, t, is $s = 64t - 16t^2$, $0 \leq t$: 4. Sketch the graph over the interval.

Answer: See graph below.

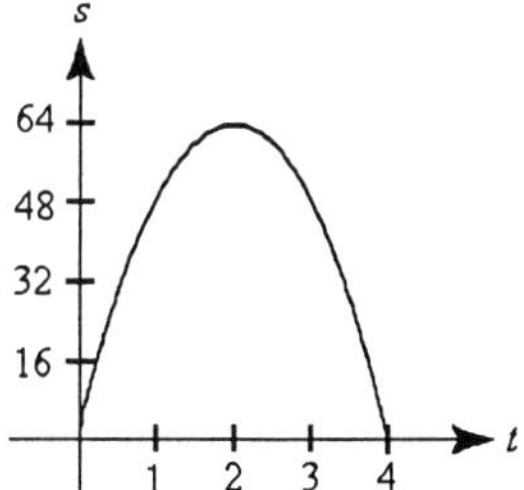

Difficulty: 1

81. A ball is shot vertically upward at a speed of 32 feet per second. The equation that relates the position, s, of the ball as a function of time, t, is $s = 32t - 16t^2$, $0 \leq t$: 2. Sketch the graph over the interval.

Answer: See graph below.

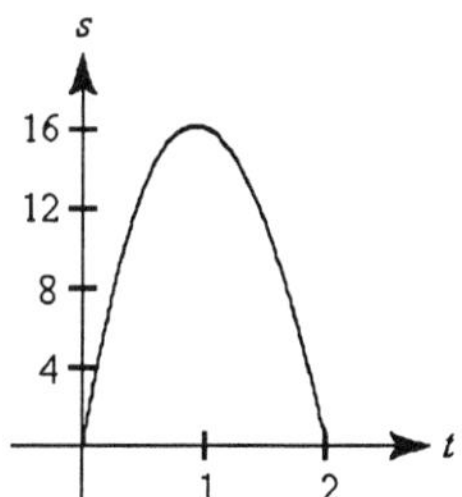

Difficulty: 1

Chapter 015: Shifting, Reflecting, and Stretching Graphs

MULTIPLE CHOICE

1. Describe the transformation of the graph of $f(x) = x^2$ for the graph of $g(x) = (x + 9)^2$.
   a) Vertical shift 9 units up
   b) Vertical shift 9 units down
   c) Horizontal shift 9 units to the right
   d) Horizontal shift 9 units to the left
   e) None of these

   Answer: d Difficulty: 1

2. Describe the transformation of the graph of $f(x) = |x|$ for the graph of $g(x) = |x|$ -20.
   a) Vertical shift 20 units up
   b) Vertical shift 20 units down
   c) Horizontal shift 20 units to the right
   d) Horizontal shift 20 units to the left
   e) None of these

   Answer: b Difficulty: 1

3. Describe the transformation of the graph of $f(x) = \sqrt{x}$ for the graph of $g(x) = \sqrt{x - 5}$.
   a) Vertical shift 5 units up
   b) Vertical shift 5 units down
   c) Horizontal shift 5 units to the right
   d) Horizontal shift 5 units to the left
   e) None of these

   Answer: c Difficulty: 1

4. Describe the transformation of the graph of $f(x) = x^3$ for the graph of $g(x) = 7 + x^3$.
   a) Vertical shift 7 units up
   b) Vertical shift 7 units down
   c) Horizontal shift 7 units to the right
   d) Horizontal shift 7 units to the left
   e) None of these

   Answer: a Difficulty: 1

5. The graph below is a transformation of the graph of $f(x) = x^2$. Find an equation for the function.
a) $g(x) = (x - 3)^2$ b) $g(x) = x^2 + 3$ c) $g(x) = (x + 3)^2$
d) $g(x) = x^2 - 3$ e) None of these

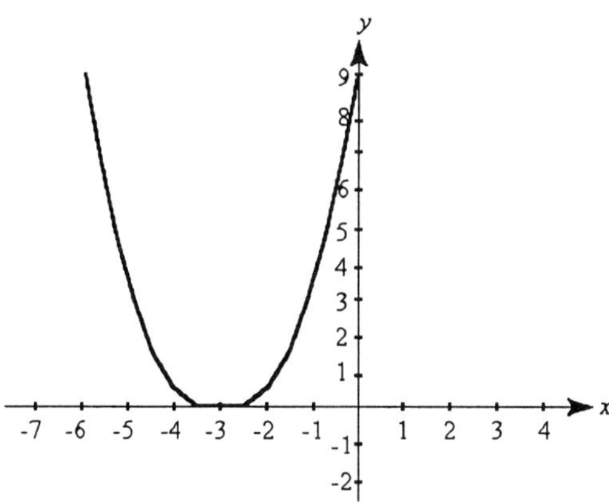

Answer: c Difficulty: 1

6. The graph below is a transformation of the graph of $f(x) = \sqrt{x}$. Find an equation for the function.
a) $g(x) = \sqrt{x} + 1$ b) $g(x) = \sqrt{x} - 1$ c) $g(x) = \sqrt{x - 1}$
d) $g(x) = \sqrt{x + 1}$ e) None of these

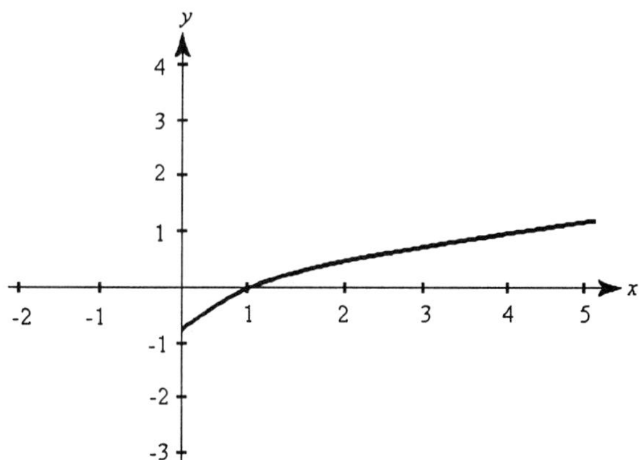

Answer: a Difficulty: 1

7. The graph below is a transformation of the graph of $f(x) = x^3$. Find an equation for the function.
   a) $g(x) = x^3 + 3$ b) $g(x) = (x + 3)^3$ c) $g(x) = x^3 - 3$
   d) $g(x) = (x - 3)^3$ e) None of these

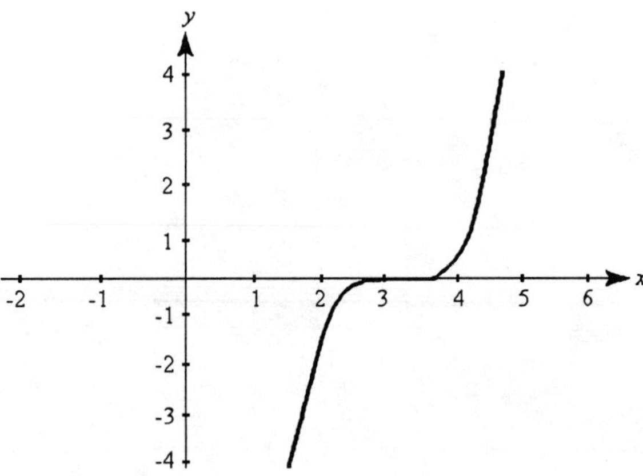

Answer: d Difficulty: 1

8. The graph below is a transformation of the graph of $f(x) = |x|$. Find an equation for the function.
   a) $g(x) = |x + 4|$ b) $g(x) = |x| + 4$ c) $g(x) = |x| - 4$
   d) $g(x) = |x - 4|$ e) None of these

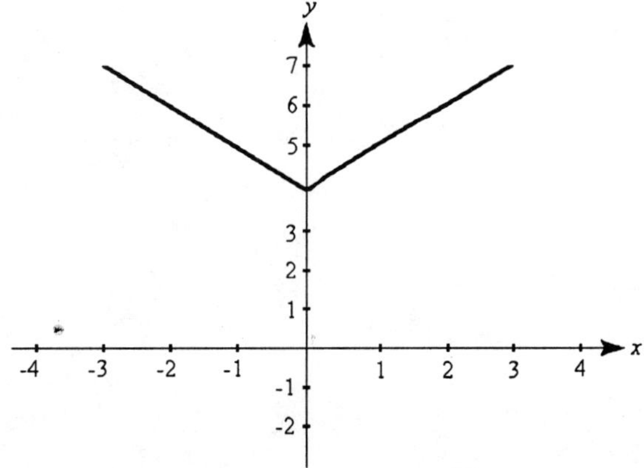

Answer: b Difficulty: 1

9. Graph $g(x) = |x + 2|$ using a transformation of the graph of $f(x) = |x|$.
   a) I b) II c) III d) IV e) None of these

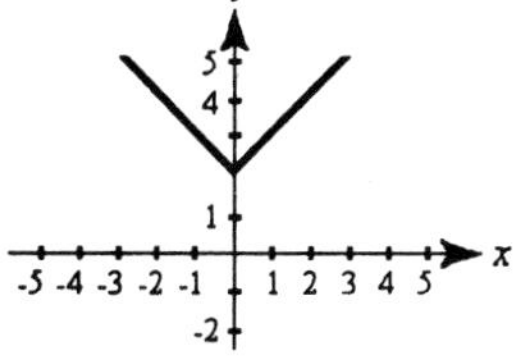

(I) (II)

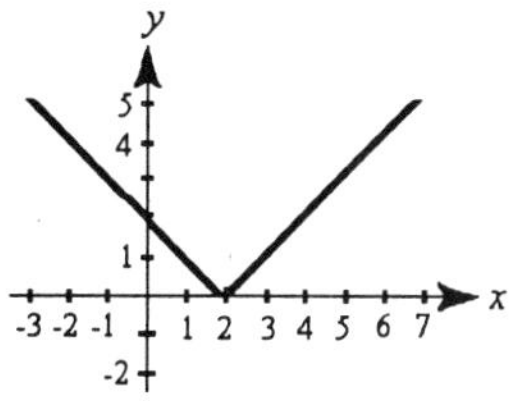

(III) 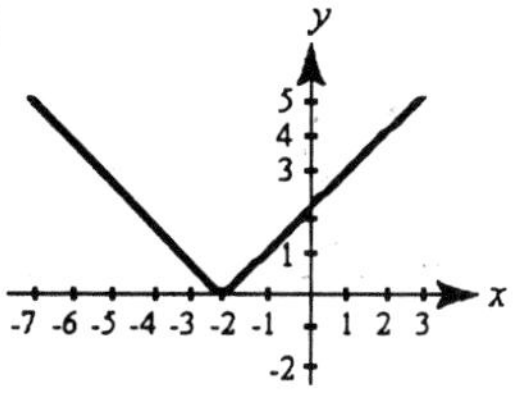 (IV)

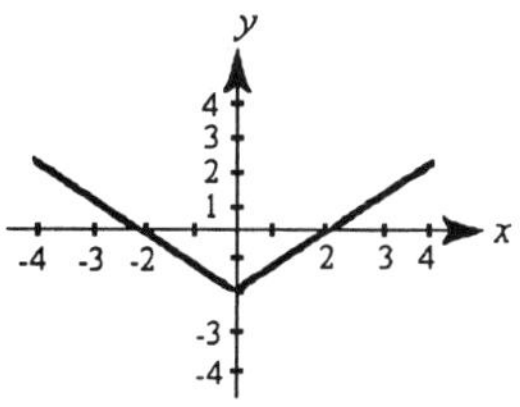

Answer: c Difficulty: 1

10. Graph $g(x) = (x - 1)^2$ using a transformation of the graph of $f(x) = x^2$.
   a) I b) II c) III d) IV e) None of these

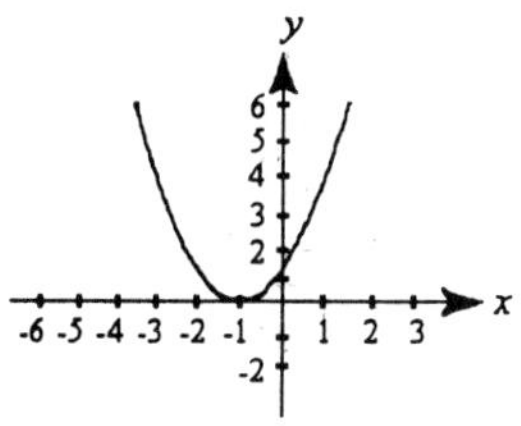

(I) (II)

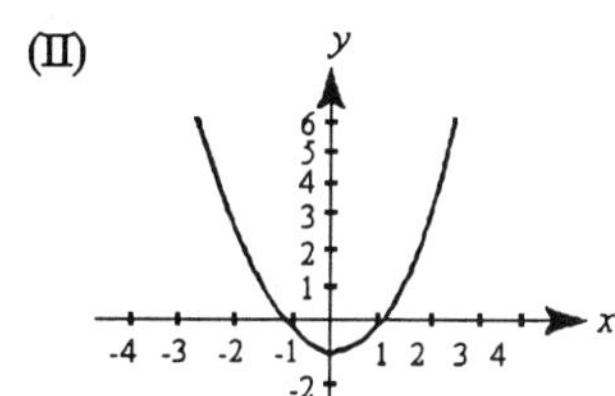

(III) 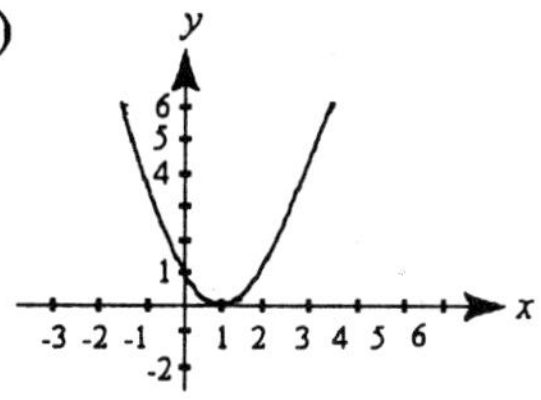 (IV)

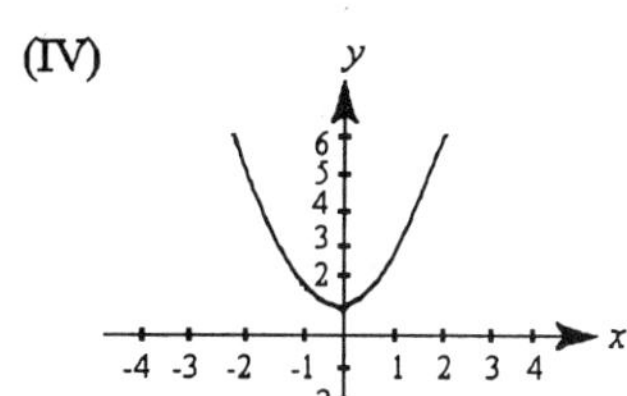

Answer: c Difficulty: 1

11. Graph $g(x) = 3 + \sqrt{x}$ using a transformation of the graph of $f(x) = \sqrt{x}$.
a) I b) II c) III d) IV e) None of these

(I)

(II)

(III)

(IV)

Answer: b Difficulty: 1

SHORT ANSWER

12. Graph $g(x) = \sqrt[3]{x + 4}$ using a transformation of the graph of $f(x) = \sqrt[3]{x}$.

Answer: See graph below.

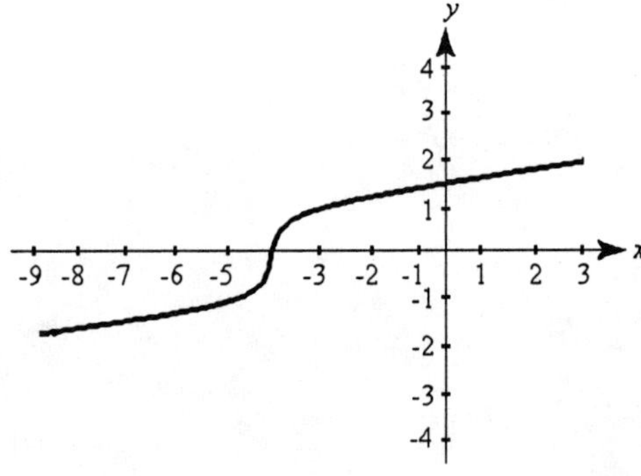

Difficulty: 1

MULTIPLE CHOICE

13. Describe the transformation of the graph of $f(x) = |x|$ for the graph of $g(x) = -|x|$.
    a) Reflection in the x-axis
    b) Reflection in the y-axis
    c) Horizontal shift 1 unit to the right
    d) Vertical shift 1 unit down
    e) None of these

    Answer: a Difficulty: 1

14. Describe the transformation of the graph of $f(x) = x^6$ for the graph of $g(x) = (-x)^6$.
    a) Reflection in the x-axis
    b) Reflection in the y-axis
    c) Horizontal shift 1 unit to the right
    d) Vertical shift 1 unit down
    e) None of these

    Answer: b Difficulty: 1

SHORT ANSWER

15. The graph is a transformation of the graph of $f(x) = x^3$. Find the equation for the function.

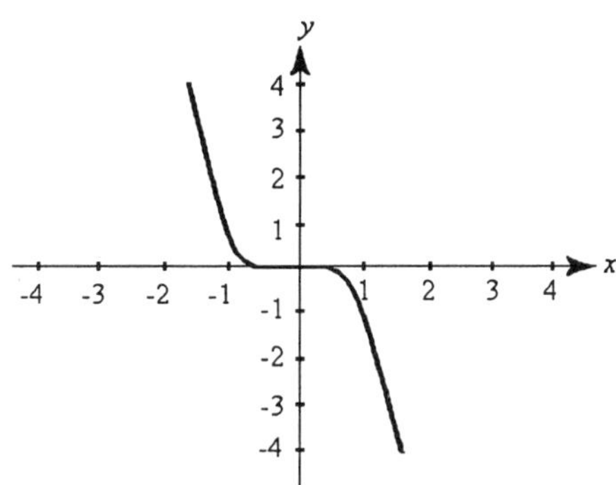

    Answer: $g(x) = -x^3$ Difficulty: 1

16. The graph is a transformation of the graph of $f(x) = x^4$. Find the equation for the function.

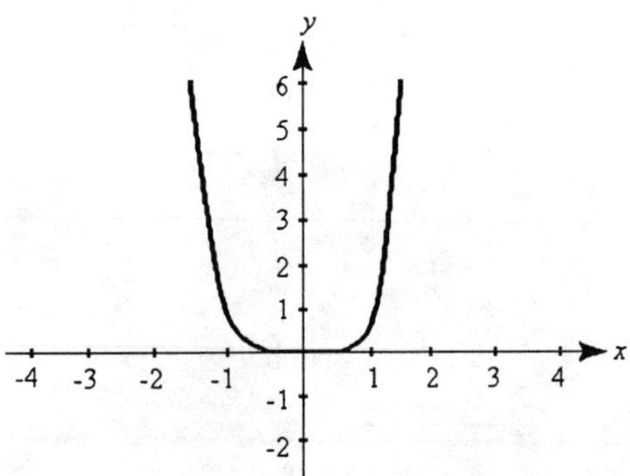

Answer:

$g(x) = (-x)^4$

Difficulty: 1

MULTIPLE CHOICE

17. Graph $g(x) = (-x)^2$ using a transformation of the graph of $f(x) = x^2$.
a) I b) II c) III d) IV e) None of these

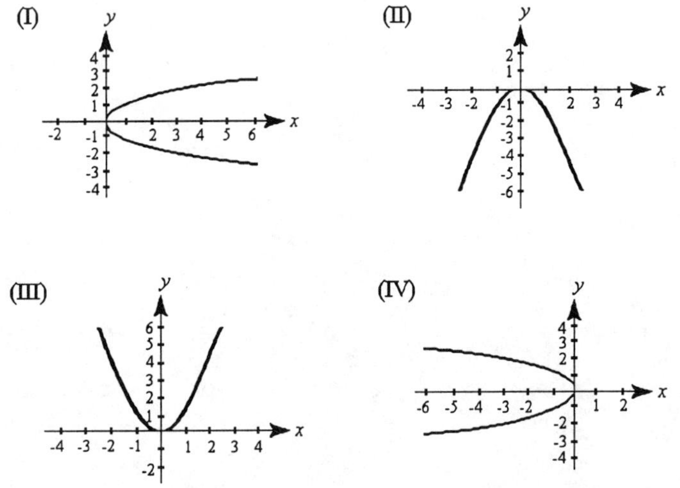

(I)

(II)

(III)

(IV)

Answer: c Difficulty: 1

18. Graph $g(x) = -\sqrt{x}$ using a transformation of the graph of $f(x) = \sqrt{x}$.
a) I b) II c) III d) IV e) None of these

(I)

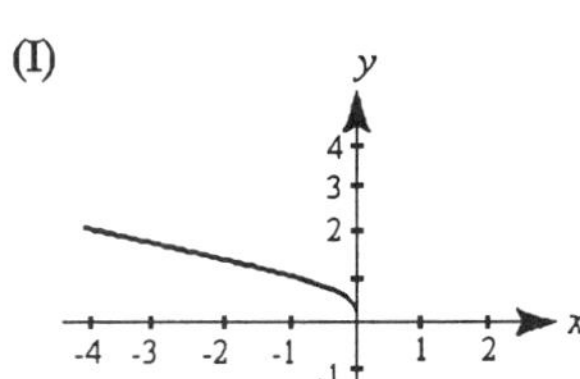

(II)

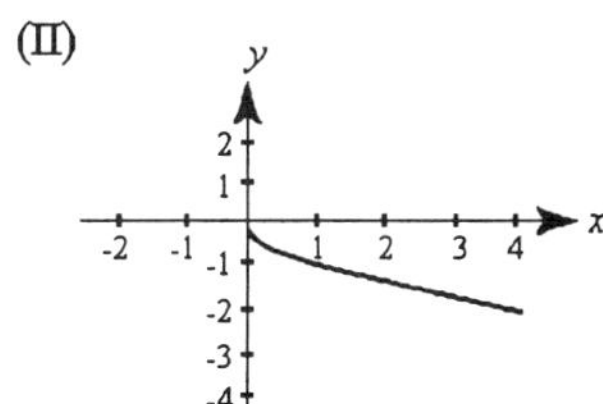

(III)

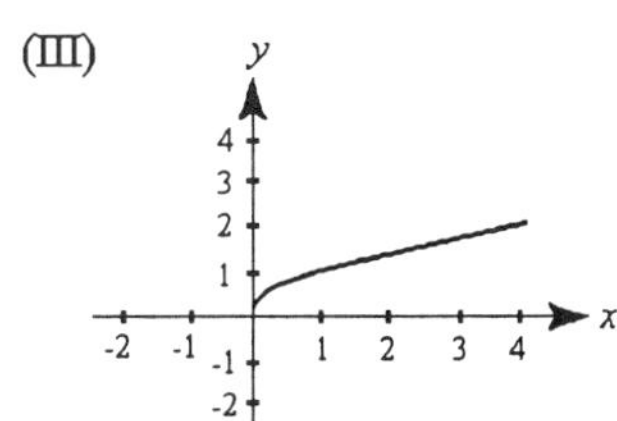

(IV)

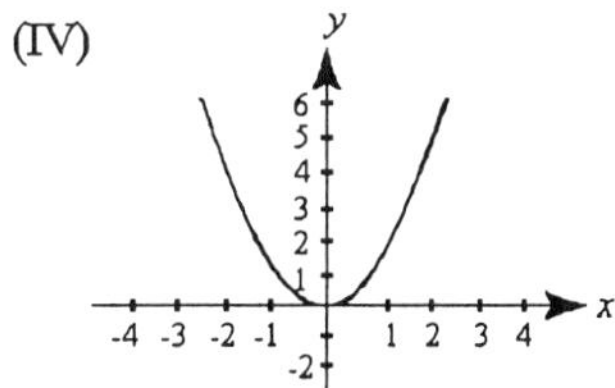

Answer: b Difficulty: 1

19. Which sequence of transformations will yield the graph of $g(x) = (x + 1)^2 + 10$ from the graph of $f(x) = x^2$?
a) Horizontal shift 10 units to the right
Vertical shift 1 unit up
b) Horizontal shift 1 unit to the left
Vertical shift 10 units up
c) Horizontal shift 1 unit to the right
Vertical shift 10 units up
d) Horizontal shift 10 units to the left
Vertical shift 1 unit up

Answer: b Difficulty: 1

20. Which sequence of transformations will yield the graph of $g(x) = -|x + 9|$ from the graph of $f(x) = |x|$?
a) Reflection in the x-axis
Horizontal shift 9 units to the left
b) Reflection in the y-axis
Horizontal shift 9 units to the left
c) Reflection in the x-axis
Horizontal shift 9 units to the right
d) Reflection in the y-axis
Horizontal shift 9 units to the right

Answer: a Difficulty: 1

SHORT ANSWER

21. What sequence of transformations will yield the graph of $g(x) = \sqrt[4]{x - 3} + 2$ from the graph of $f(x) = \sqrt[4]{x}$?

Answer:
Horizontal shift 3 units to the right
Vertical shift 2 units up

Difficulty: 1

MULTIPLE CHOICE

22. A function is a reflection in the y-axis and a vertical shift 5 units up of the graph of $f(x) = |x|$. Write an equation for the function.
a) $g(x) = |x| + 5$ b) $g(x) = -|x| + 5$ c) $g(x) = |-x| + 5$
d) $g(x) = -|x| - 5$ e) None of these

Answer: c Difficulty: 1

23. The graph below is a transformation of the graph of $f(x) = x^2$. Find an equation for the function.
a) $g(x) = (x + 3)^2 + 1$ b) $g(x) = (x + 1)^2 - 3$
c) $g(x) = (x - 3)^2 + 1$ d) $g(x) = (x + 1)^2 + 3$
e) None of these

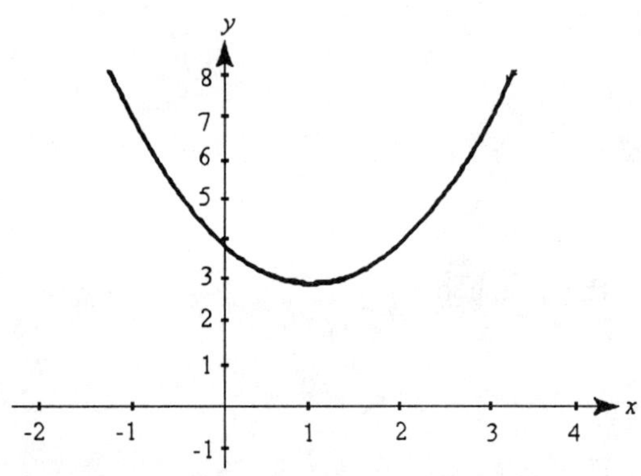

Answer: e Difficulty: 1

24. The graph below is a transformation of the graph of $f(x) = \sqrt{x}$. Find an equation for the function.

a) $g(x) = \sqrt{-x} + 2$ b) $g(x) = \sqrt{-x + 2}$ c) $g(x) = -\sqrt{x} + 2$

d) $g(x) = -\sqrt{x - 2}$ e) None of these

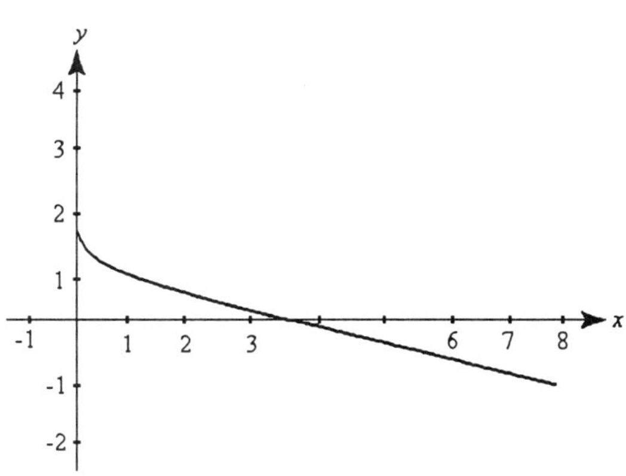

Answer: c Difficulty: 1

25. The graph below is a transformation of the graph of $f(x) = |x|$. Find an equation for the function.

a) $g(x) = |x - 1| - 4$ b) $g(x) = |x - 4| - 1$

c) $g(x) = |x - 1| + 4$ d) $g(x) = |x + 4| - 1$

e) None of these

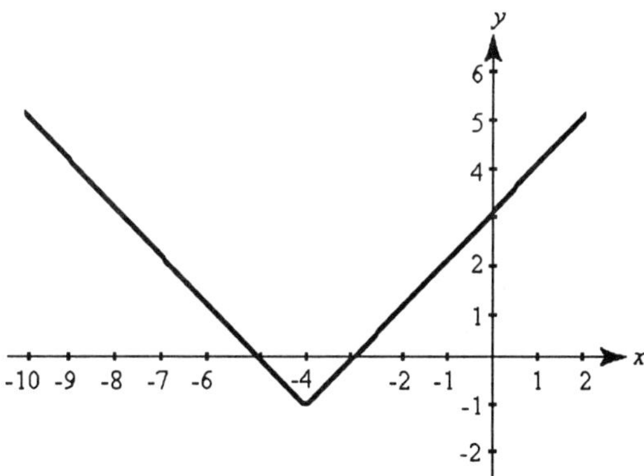

Answer: d Difficulty: 1

26. The graph below is a transformation of the graph of $f(x) = x^3$. Find an equation for the function.
a) $g(x) = -x^3 + 3$ b) $g(x) = -(x - 3)^3$ c) $g(x) = -(x + 3)^3$
d) $g(x) = -x^3 - 3$ e) None of these

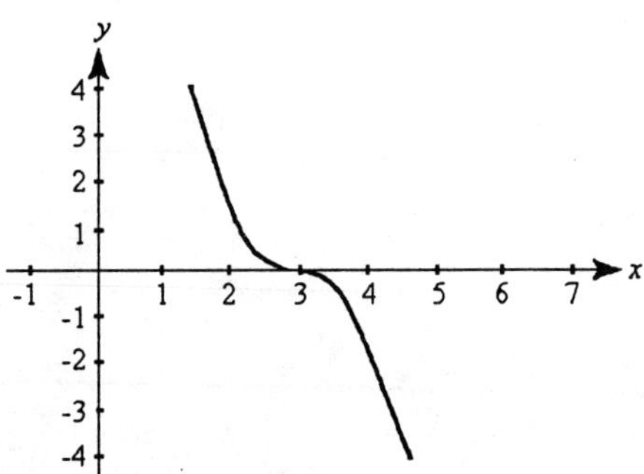

Answer: b Difficulty: 1

27. Graph $g(x) = |x + 2| - 3$ using a transformation of the graph of $f(x) = |x|$.
a) I b) II c) III d) IV e) None of these

(I)

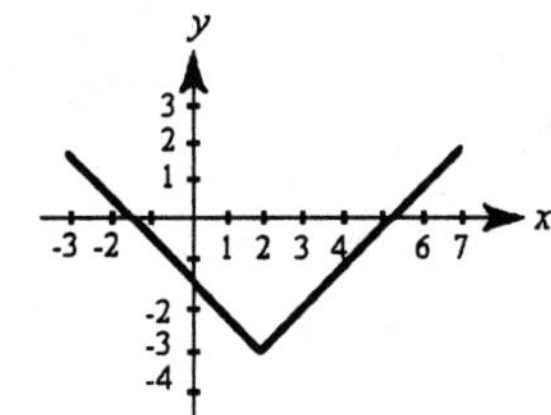

(II)

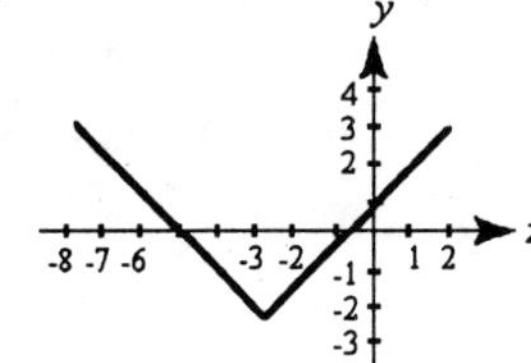

(III)

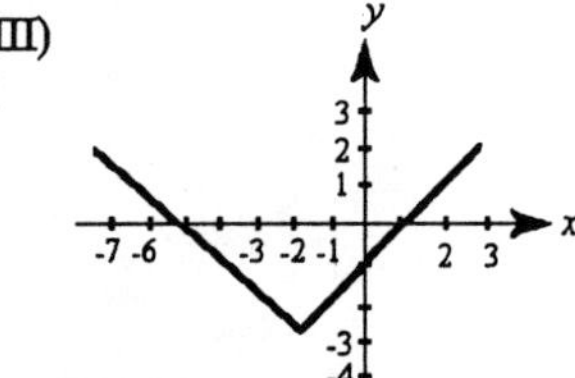

(IV)

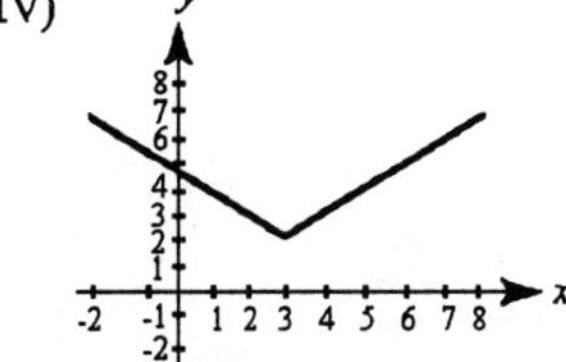

Answer: c Difficulty: 1

28. Graph $g(x) = -x^2 + 2$ using a transformation of the graph of $f(x) = x^2$.
a) I   b) II   c) III   d) IV   e) None of these

(I)   (II)

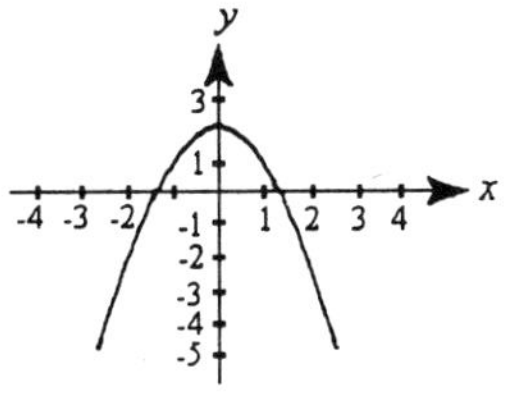

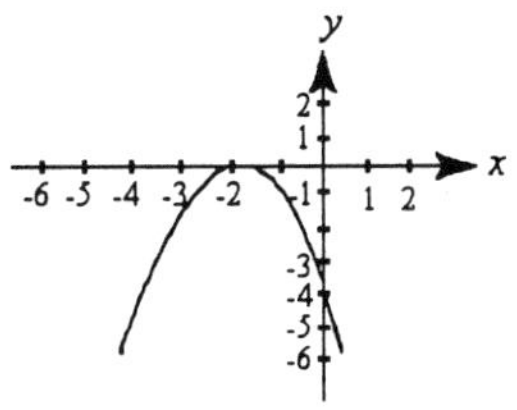

(III) 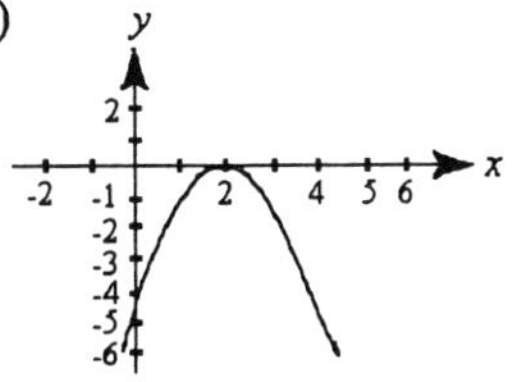   (IV)

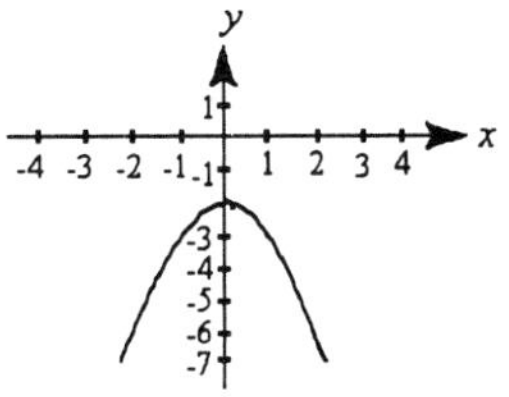

Answer: a Difficulty: 1

29. Graph $g(x) = (x - 1)^3 + 1$ using a transformation of the graph of $f(x) = x^3$.
a) I   b) II   c) III   d) IV   e) None of these

(I)
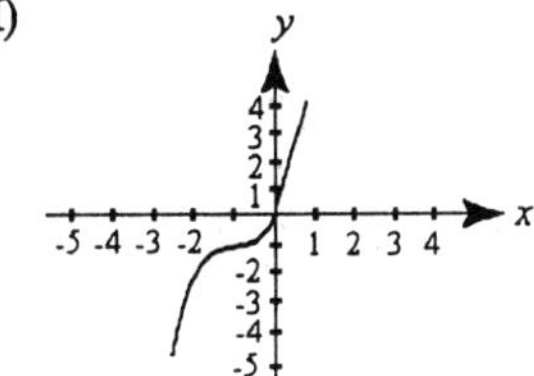

(II)
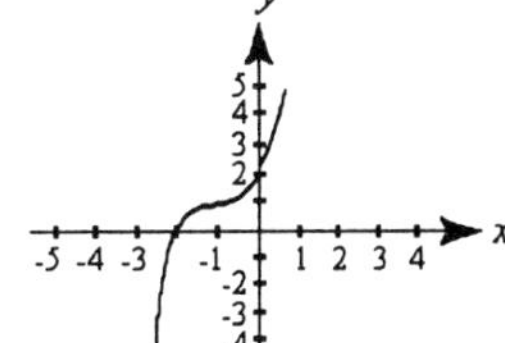

(III)
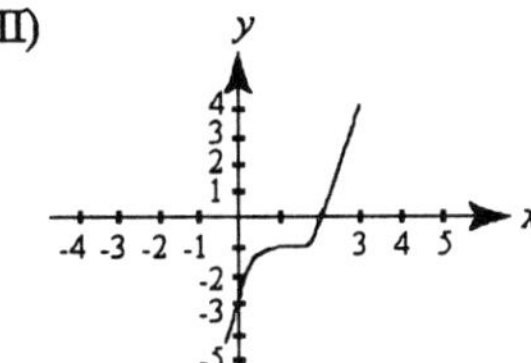

(IV)
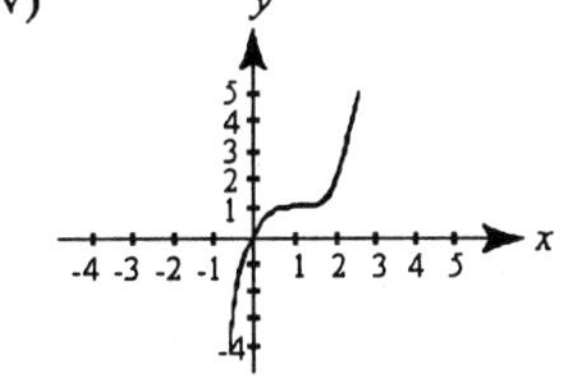

Answer: d Difficulty: 1

SHORT ANSWER

30. Graph $g(x) = \sqrt{x - 4} - 3$ using a transformation of the graph of $f(x) = \sqrt{x}$.

Answer: See graph below.

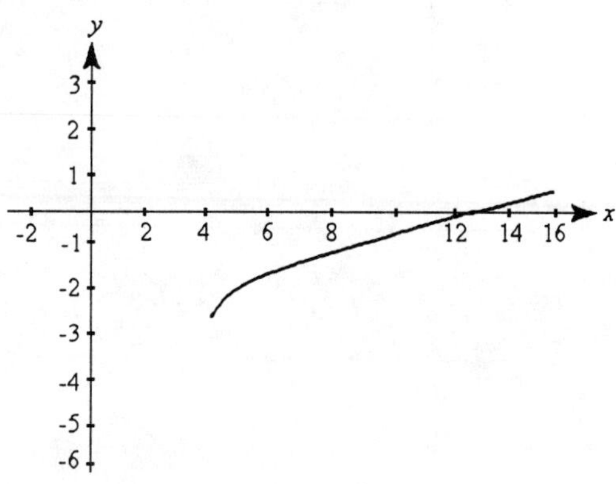

Difficulty: 1

MULTIPLE CHOICE

31. Describe the nonrigid transformation of the graph of $f(x) = x^2$ for the graph of $g(x) = 2x^2 + 1$.

a) Vertical shift 1 unit down
Vertical stretch

b) Vertical shift 1 unit up
Vertical shrink

c) Horizontal shift 2 units to the left
Vertical shrink

d) Vertical shift 1 unit up
Vertical stretch

e) None of these

Answer: d Difficulty: 2

32. Describe the nonrigid transformation of the graph of $f(x) = \sqrt{x}$ for the graph of $g(x) = \frac{1}{3}\sqrt{x + 4}$.

a) Horizontal shift 4 units to the left
Vertical shrink

b) Horizontal shift 4 units to the left
Vertical stretch

c) Horizontal shift 4 units to the right
Vertical stretch

d) Horizontal shift 4 units to the right
Vertical shrink

e) None of these

Answer: a Difficulty: 2

33. Find an equation of the function whose graph is a horizontal shift 9 units to the right and a vertical stretch (by 4) of the graph of $f(x) = \sqrt[3]{x}$.

a) $g(x) = \frac{1}{4}\sqrt[3]{x + 9}$ b) $g(x) = \frac{1}{4}\sqrt[3]{x - 9}$ c) $g(x) = 4\sqrt[3]{x - 9}$

d) $g(x) = 4\sqrt[3]{x + 9}$ e) None of these

Answer: c Difficulty: 2 Key 1: T

34. Find an equation of the function whose graph is a vertical shift 5 units down and a vertical shrink (by 6) of the graph of $f(x) = |x|$.

a) $g(x) = \frac{1}{6}|x + 5|$ b) $g(x) = \frac{1}{6}|x| - 5$ c) $g(x) = 6|x| - 5$

d) $g(x) = 6|x - 5|$ e) None of these

Answer: b Difficulty: 2

SHORT ANSWER

35. Given the graph of $y = x^4$ sketch the graph of $y = (x - 2)^4 + 6$.

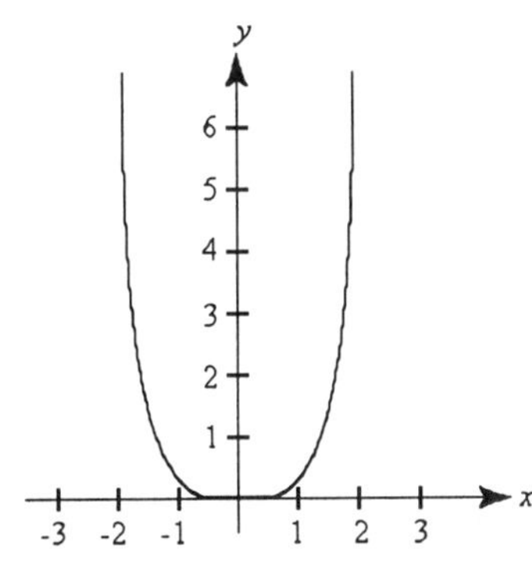

Answer: See graph below.

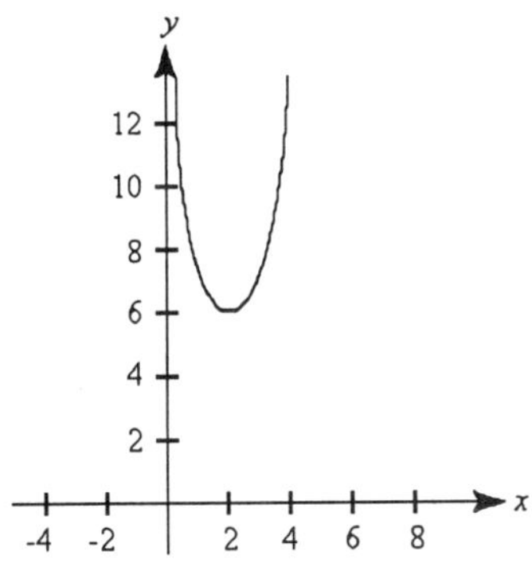

Difficulty: 2

36. Given the graph of $y = x^2$ sketch the graph of $y = (x + 3)^2 - 1$.

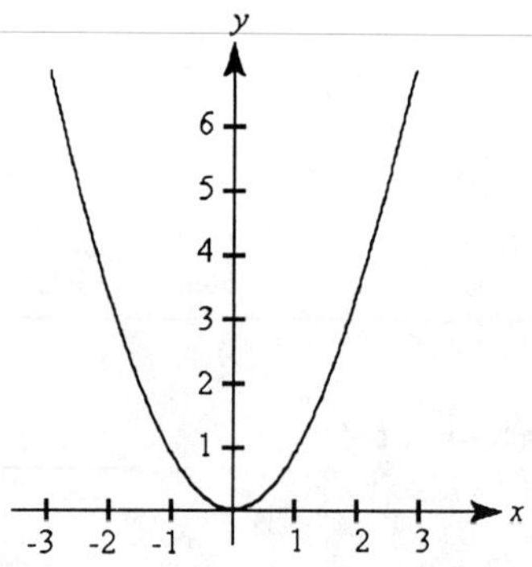

Answer: See graph below.

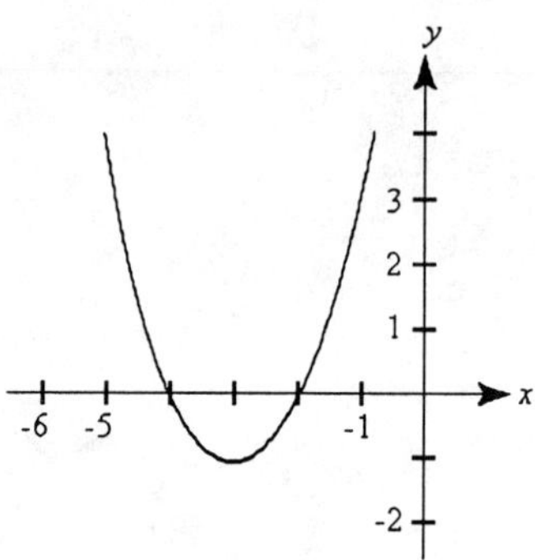

Difficulty: 2

MULTIPLE CHOICE

37. Given the graph of $y = -\sqrt{x}$, identify the graph of $y = 2 - \sqrt{x + 3}$.
a) I b) II c) III d) IV e) None of these

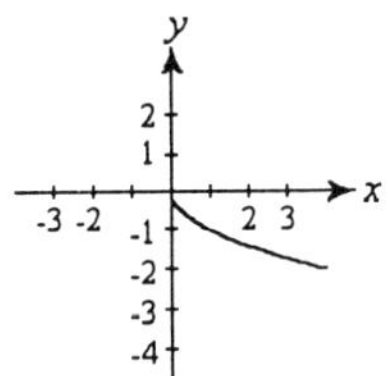

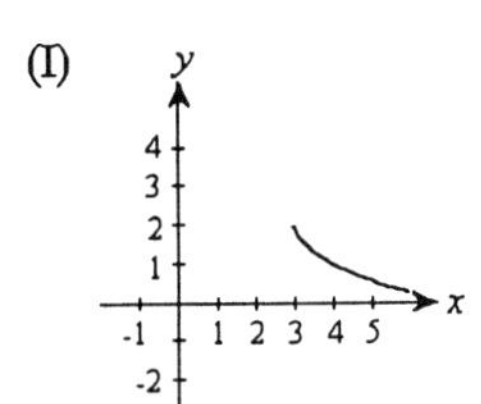

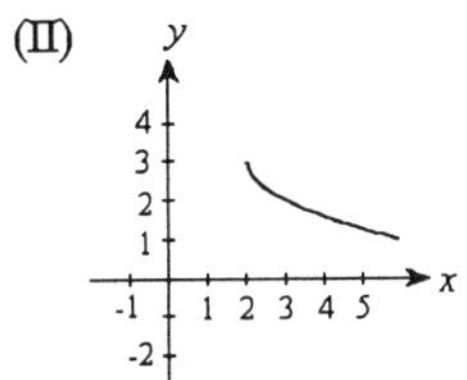

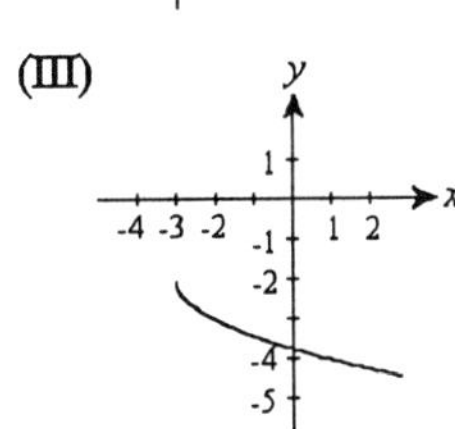

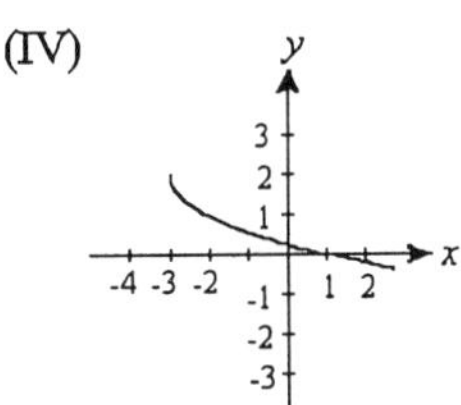

Answer: d Difficulty: 1

38. Use the graph of $y = x^2$ to find a formula for the function $y = f(x)$.
a) $f(x) = (x - 2)^2 + 1$
b) $f(x) = (x - 1)^2 + 2$
c) $f(x) = (x + 2)^2 + 1$
d) $f(x) = (x + 1)^2 - 2$
e) None of these

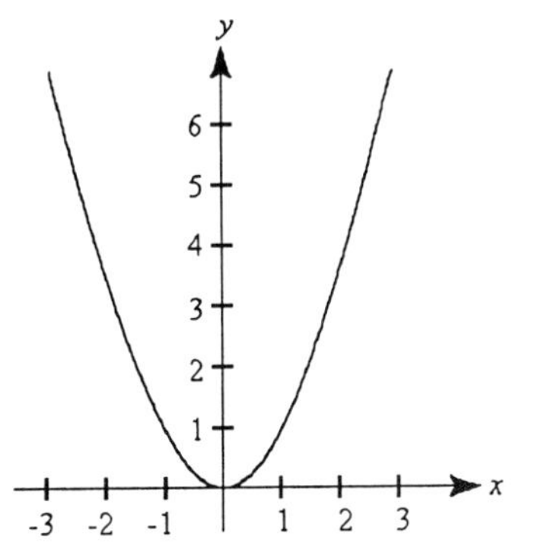

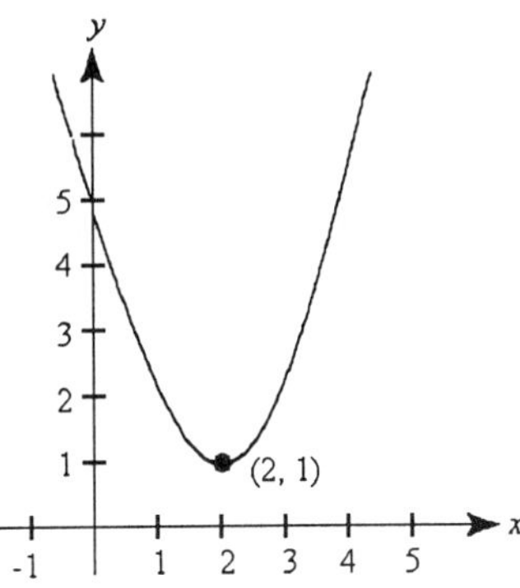

Answer: a Difficulty: 2

39. Use the graph of $y = x^4$ to find a formula for the function $y = f(x)$.
a) $y = (x + 1)^4 + 2$ b) $y = (x - 1)^4 + 2$ c) $y = (x - 2)^4 + 1$
d) $y = (x + 2)^4 + 1$ e) None of these

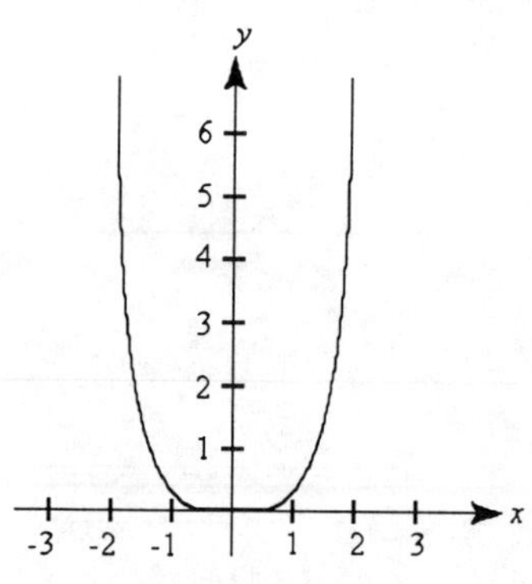

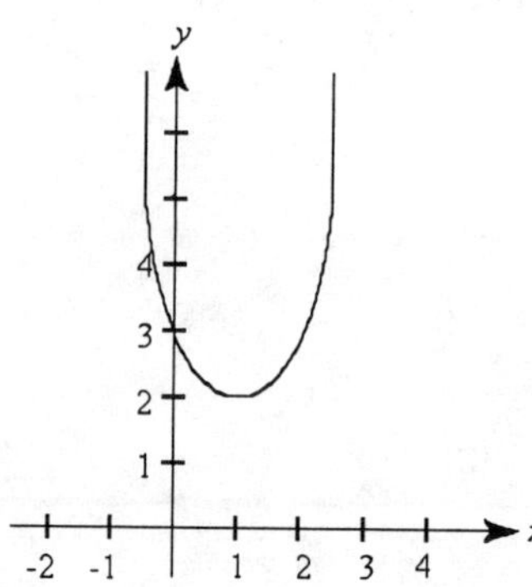

Answer: b Difficulty: 1

40. Use the graph of $y = x^3$ to find a formula for the function $y = f(x)$.
a) $y = (x + 1)^3 - 2$ b) $y = (x - 1)^3 - 2$ c) $y = (x + 2)^3 - 1$
d) $y = (x - 2)^3 - 1$
e) None of these

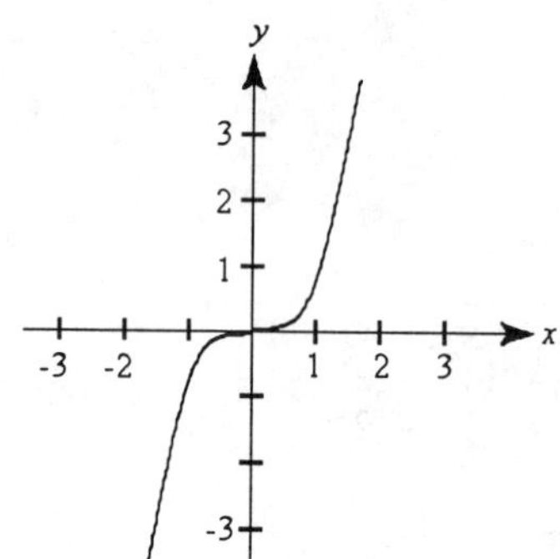

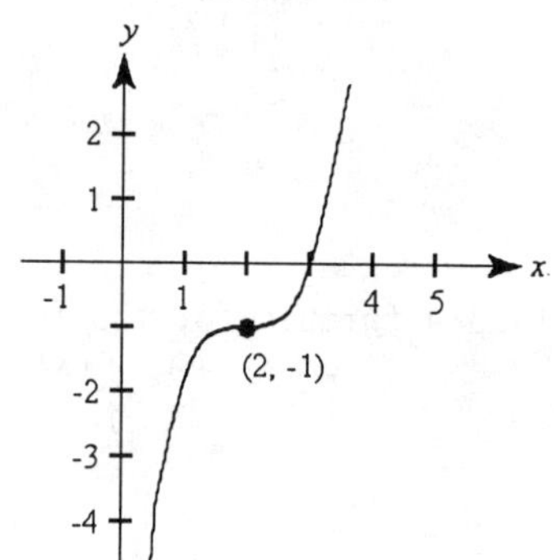

Answer: d Difficulty: 1

41. The point (3, -1) is on the graph of f. If g is a translation of f so that $g(x) = f(x + 2) + 5$, what are the coordinates of the translated point?
a) (5, 4) b) (2, 5) c) (1, 4) d) (8, 1) e) None of these

Answer: c Difficulty: 1

42. The point (-2, 7) is on the graph of f. If g is a translation of f so that $g(x) = f(x - 3) - 4$, what are the coordinates of the translated point?
a) (1, 3) b) (3, -4) c) (-5, 3) d) (-5, 11) e) None of these

Answer: a Difficulty: 1

43. The point $\left(\frac{-1}{2}, \frac{-2}{5}\right)$ is on the graph of f. If g is a translation of f so that $g(x) = f\left(x + \frac{3}{2}\right) - \frac{8}{5}$, what are the coordinates of the translated point?

a) $(1, -2)$ b) $\left(\frac{-3}{2}, \frac{8}{5}\right)$ c) $\left(-2, \frac{6}{5}\right)$

d) $\left(1, \frac{-6}{5}\right)$ e) None of these

Answer: e Difficulty: 1

Chapter 016: Combinations of Functions

MULTIPLE CHOICE

1. Given $f(x) = 2x - 4$ and $g(x) = 1 + 3x$, find $(f + g)(x)$.
   a) $5x - 3$ b) $x - 3$ c) $-(x + 3)$
   d) 0 e) None of these

   Answer: a Difficulty: 1

2. Given $f(x) = 6$ and $g(x) = 2x^2 - 1$, find $(f - g)(x)$.
   a) $2x^2 + 5$ b) $2x^2 - 7$ c) $-2x^2 + 7$
   d) $-2x^2 + 5$ e) None of these

   Answer: c Difficulty: 1

3. Given $f(x) = 2x$ and $g(x) = x - 1$, find $(fg)(x)$.
   a) $x + 1$ b) $2x^2 - 2x$ c) $3x - 1$
   d) $2x^2 - 1$ e) None of these

   Answer: b Difficulty: 1

4. Given $f(x) = \frac{1}{x}$ and $g(x) = x^2 - 5$ find $(fg)(x)$.
   a) $\frac{x}{x^2 - 5}$ b) $x(x^2 - 5)$ c) $\frac{x^2 - 5}{x}$
   d) $x - 5$ e) None of these

   Answer: c Difficulty: 1 Key 1: T

5. Given $f(x) = x$ and $g(x) = 3x - 1$, find $(f/g)(x)$.
   a) $3x^2 - x$ b) $\frac{3x - 1}{x}$ c) $\frac{x}{3x - 1}$
   d) $4x - 1$ e) None of these

   Answer: c Difficulty: 1

6. Given $f(x) = 1/x$ and $g(x) = x/4$, find $(f/g)(x)$.
   a) $\frac{x^2}{4}$ b) 4 c) $\frac{x + 4}{4x}$ d) $\frac{4}{x^2}$ e) None of these

   Answer: d Difficulty: 1

7. Given $f(x) = x - 2$ and $g(x) = 6 - 2x$, find $(f + g)(-2)$.
   a) 6 b) 2 c) -2 d) -14 e) None of these

   Answer: a Difficulty: 1

8. Given $f(x) = x$ and $g(x) = x^2 - 7$, find $(fg)(3)$.
   a) -13 b) 29 c) 5 d) 6 e) None of these

   Answer: d Difficulty: 1

9. Given $f(x) = 9x$ and $g(x) = 4 - x$, find $(f - g)(5)$.
   a) 37 b) 47 c) 55 d) -46 e) None of these

   Answer: b Difficulty: 1

10. Given $f(x) = x^2 + 3$ and $g(x) = x - 1$, find $(f/g)(-1)$.
    a) 2 b) 0 c) -2 d) Undefined e) None of these

    Answer: c Difficulty: 1

11. Given $f(x) = x^2 - 9$ and $g(x) = x + 2$, find the domain of f/g.
    a) $(-\infty, -3] \cup [-3, 3] \cup [3, \infty)$ b) $(-\infty, -2) \cup (-2, \infty)$ c) $(-3, 3)$
    d) $[-3, -2) \cup (-2, 3]$ e) None of these

    Answer: b Difficulty: 1

12. Given $f(x) = \sqrt{9 - x^2}$ and $g(x) = \sqrt{x}$, find the domain of f/g.
    a) $[-3, 0]$ b) $[3, \infty)$ c) $[0, 3)$ d) $(0, 3]$ e) None of these

    Answer: d Difficulty: 1

13. Use a graphing utility to graph $(f + g)(x)$ if $f(x) = 2x - 3$ and $g(x) = x + 5$.
    a) I b) II c) III d) IV e) None of these

(I)

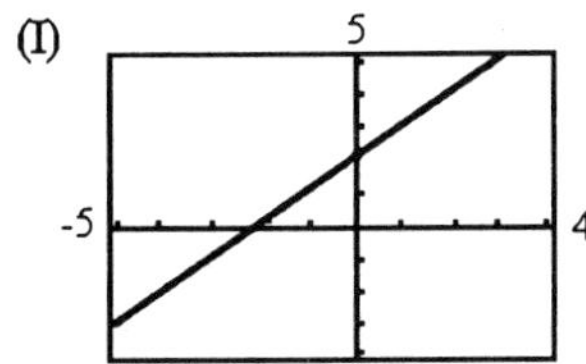

(II)

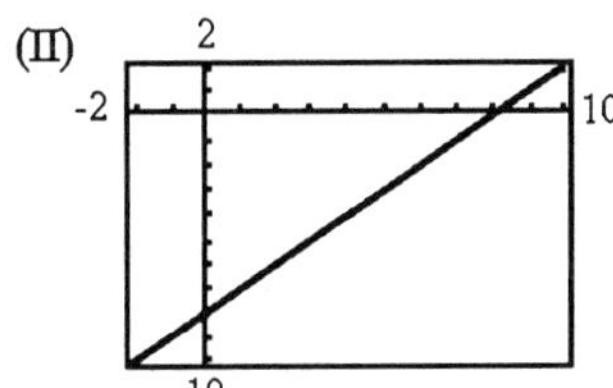

(III)

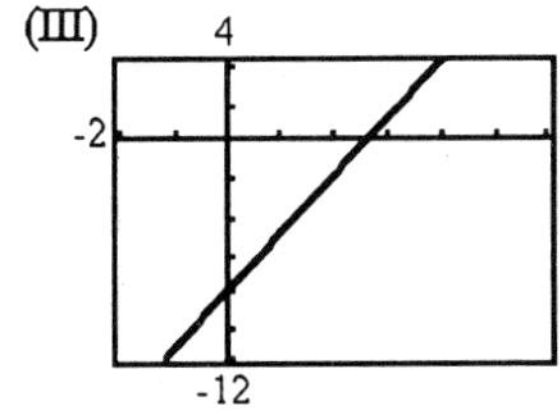

(IV)

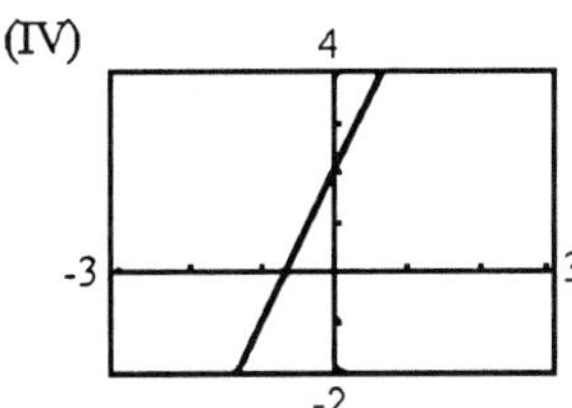

Answer: d Difficulty: 1 Key 1: T

14. Use a graphing utility to graph $(f - g)(x)$ if $f(x) = x^2$ and $g(x) = -x$.
    a) I b) II c) III d) IV e) None of these

(I)

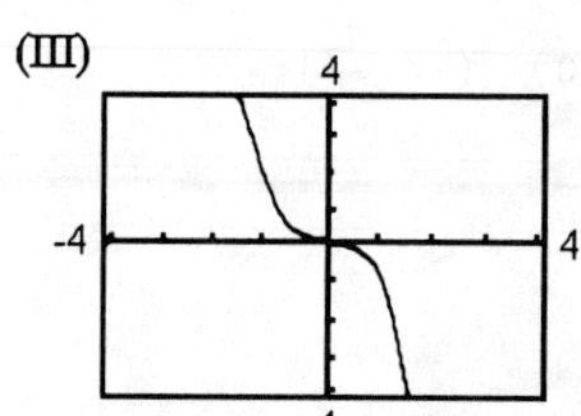

(II)

(III)

(IV)

Answer: a Difficulty: 1 Key 1: T

SHORT ANSWER

15. Use a graphing utility to graph $(f/g)(x)$ if $f(x) = 2x^2 - x$ and $g(x) = x$.

Answer: See graph below.

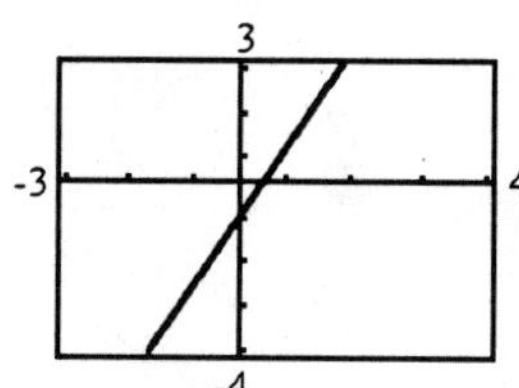

Difficulty: 1 Key 1: T

MULTIPLE CHOICE

16. Given $f(x) = x - 7$ and $g(x) = 4x$, find $(f \circ g)(x)$.
    a) $3x - 7$ b) $4x^2 - 7x$ c) $4x - 7$
    d) $4(x - 7)$ e) None of these

Answer: c Difficulty: 1

17. Given $f(x) = x^2$ and $g(x) = x + 5$, find $(g \circ f)(x)$.
    a) $(x + 5)^2$ b) $x^2 + 5$ c) $x^2 + 25$
    d) $x^2 + 5x^2$ e) None of these

Answer: b Difficulty: 1

18. Given $f(x) = x^2 + 5$ and $g(x) = 6 - x$, find $(f \circ g)(x)$.
    a) $x^4 + 10$ b) $x^4 + 25$ c) $(x^2 + 5)^2 + 5$
    d) $x^2 + 10$ e) None of these

    Answer: c Difficulty: 1

19. Given $f(x) = x^2 - 2x$ and $g(x) = 3x + 2x$, find $(f \circ g)(x)$.
    a) $4x^2 + 8x + 3$ b) $2x^2 - 4x + 3$ c) $2x^3 - x^2 - 6x$
    d) $3x^2 + x$ e) None of these

    Answer: a Difficulty: 1

20. Given $f(x) = \frac{1}{x^2}$ and $g(x) = \sqrt{x^2 + 4}$, find $(f \circ g)(x)$.
    a) $\frac{1}{x^2 + 4}$ b) $\frac{1}{\sqrt{x^2 + 4}}$ c) $x^2 + 4$
    d) $\frac{1}{x^2\sqrt{x^2 + 4}}$ e) None of these

    Answer: a Difficulty: 1

21. Given $f(x) = 4 - 2x^2$ and $g(x) = 2 - x$, find $(g \circ f)(x)$.
    a) $4x^2 - 16x + 20$ b) $2x^2 - 4$ c) $2x^2 - 2$
    d) $-2x^3 - 4x^2 - 4x + 8$ e) None of these

    Answer: c Difficulty: 1

22. Given $f(x) = x + 4$ and $g(x) = 3x$, find $(f \circ g)(2)$.
    a) 36 b) 10 c) 32 d) 18 e) None of these

    Answer: b Difficulty: 1

23. Given $f(x) = x^2$ and $g(x) = \sqrt{x - 6}$, find $(g \circ f)(-3)$.
    a) $\sqrt{3}$ b) 9 c) 81 d) Undefined e) None of these

    Answer: a Difficulty: 1

SHORT ANSWER

24. Given $f(x) = \frac{1}{x}$ and $g(x) = \frac{1}{x}$, find $(f \circ g)(9)$.

    Answer: 9 Difficulty: 1

25. Given $f(x) = x^3 + 4$ and $g(x) = \sqrt[3]{x}$, find $(f \circ g)(-3)$.

    Answer: 1 Difficulty: 1

MULTIPLE CHOICE

26. Use a graphing utility to graph $(f \circ g)(x)$ if $f(x) = x - 1$ and $g(x) = x + 9$.
   a) I b) II c) III d) IV e) None of these

(I)

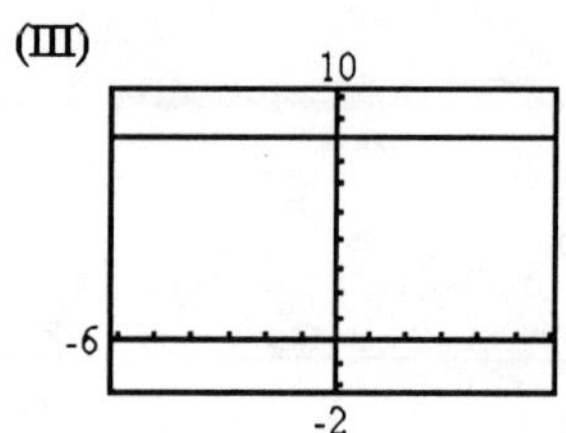

(II)

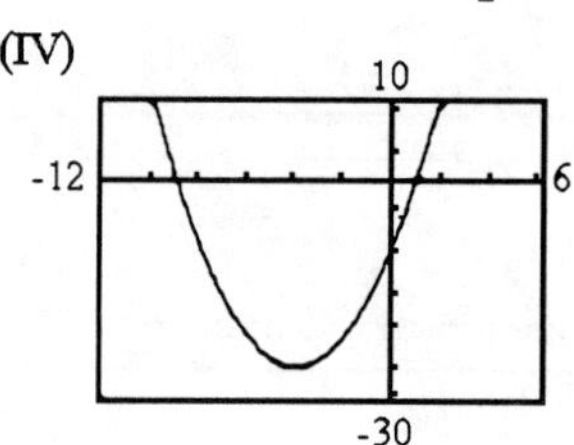

(III)
10
-6
6
-2

(IV)
10
-12
6
-30

Answer: b Difficulty: 1 Key 1: T

27. Use a graphing utility to graph $(f \circ g)(x)$ if $f(x) = x^2 - 2$ and $g(x) = \sqrt{x + 6}$.
   a) I b) II c) III d) IV e) None of these

(I)

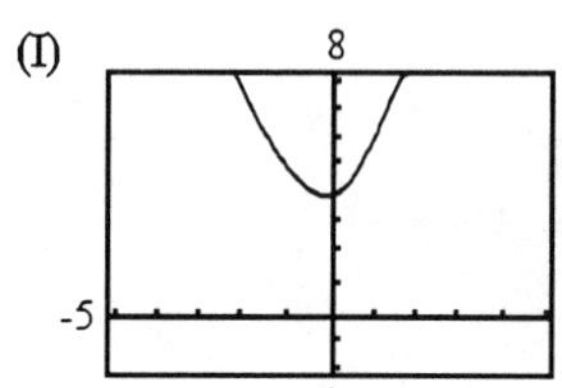

(II)

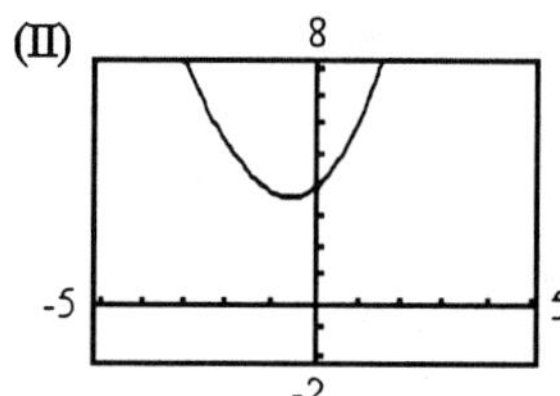

(III)

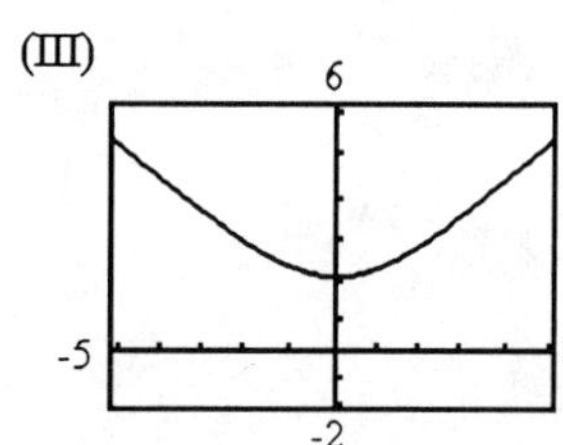

(IV)

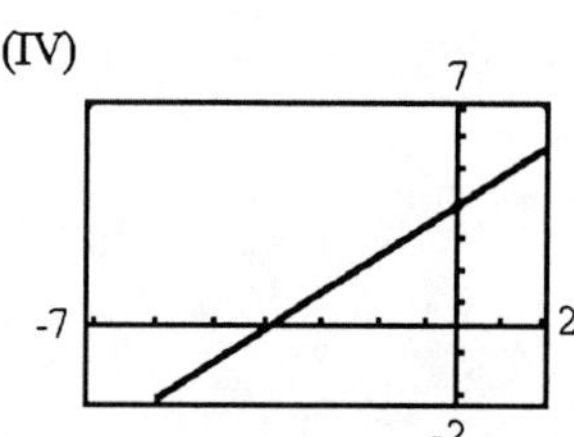

Answer: d Difficulty: 1 Key 1: T

28. Find functions f and g such that $(f \circ g)(x) = h(x)$: $h(x)\ \sqrt{(x + 1)^2 - 3}$.
   a) $f(x) = x + 1,\ g(x) = \sqrt{x - 3}$
   b) $f(x) = \sqrt{(x + 1)^2},\ g(x) = \sqrt{3}$
   c) $f(x) = (x + 1)^2,\ g(x) = -3$
   d) $f(x) = \sqrt{x^2 - 3},\ g(x) = x + 1$
   e) None of these

Answer: d Difficulty: 2

29. Find functions f and g such that $(f \circ g)(x) = h(x)$: $h(x) = (x + 2)^4 - x - 2$.
   a) $f(x) = x^4 - x - 2$, $g(x) = x + 2$ b) $f(x) = x^4 - x$, $g(x) = x + 2$
   c) $f(x) = x + 2$, $g(x) = x^4 - x - 2$ d) $f(x) = x^4$, $g(x) = x - 2$
   e) None of these

   Answer: b Difficulty: 2

30. Given $f(x) = \sqrt{x}$ and $g(x) = x^2 + 4$, find the domain of $(f \circ g)(x)$.
   a) $(-\infty, 0]$ b) $[0, \infty)$ c) $(-\infty, \infty)$
   d) $(-\infty, -2), (-2, 2)$ e) None of these

   Answer: c Difficulty: 2

31. Given $f(x) = \dfrac{1}{x^2 - 1}$ and $g(x) = x + 3$, find the domain of $(f \circ g)(x)$.
   a) $(-\infty, \infty)$ b) $(-\infty, -1), (-1, 1), (1, \infty)$
   c) $(-\infty, -4), (-4, -2), (-2, \infty)$ d) $[-3, \infty)$
   e) None of these

   Answer: c Difficulty: 2

32. Given $f(x) = \dfrac{1}{\sqrt{x}}$ and $g(x) = x + 3$, find the domain of $(f \circ g)(x)$.
   a) $(0, \infty)$ b) $(-3, \infty)$ c) $(-\infty, -3), (-3, \infty)$
   d) $(-\infty, 0), (0, \infty)$ e) None of these

   Answer: b Difficulty: 2

33. Given $f(x) = \dfrac{1}{x^2 - 1}$ and $g(x) = 1 - x$, find the domain of $(f \circ g)(x)$.
   a) $(-\infty, 0), (0, 2), (2, \infty)$ b) $(-\infty, -1), (-1, 1), (1, \infty)$
   c) $(1, \infty)$ d) $(-1, 1)$
   e) None of these

   Answer: a Difficulty: 2

SHORT ANSWER

34. The weekly cost of producing x units in a manufacturing process is given by the function $C(x) = 30x + 400$. If the number of units produced in t hours is given by $x(t) = 75t$, find $(C \circ x)(t)$.

   Answer: $(C \circ x)(t) = 2250x + 400$ Difficulty: 2

35. The cost of producing x units in a manufacturing process is given by the function $C(x) = 1.25x + 65$. The revenue obtained from selling x units is given by $R(x) = 2.75x - 0.0025x^2$. Determine the profit as a function of the number of units sold if $P = R - C$.

   Answer: $P = -0.0025x^2 + 1.50x - 65$ Difficulty: 2

36. An environmental study of a small town has shown that the average daily level of a certain pollutant in the air can be modeled by $P(n) = \sqrt{n^2 + 4}$ parts per million when the population is n hundred people. It is estimated that t years from now the population will be $n(t) = 4 + 0.25t^2$ hundred. Determine the level of pollutant as a function of time.

Answer:

$$(P \circ n)(t) = \sqrt{(4 + 0.25t^2)^2 + 4}$$
$$= \sqrt{0.0625t^4 + 2t^2 + 20}$$

Difficulty: 2

37. A company has determined that consumers will buy $L(p) = \frac{600}{p^2}$ liters of a soft drink when the price per liter is p dollars. It is also determined that the price per liter t months from now is $p(t) = 0.4t^2 + 2t + 1$. Determine the number of liters that consumers will buy as a function of time.

Answer:

$$(L \circ p)(t) = \frac{600}{(0.4t^2 + 2t + 1)^2}$$
$$= \frac{600}{0.16t^4 + 1.6t^3 + 4.8t^2 + 4t + 1}$$

Difficulty: 2

Chapter 017: Inverse Functions

MULTIPLE CHOICE

1. Given $f(x) = x - 1$, identify the graph of $f^{-1}(x)$.
   a) I b) II c) III d) IV e) None of these

(I)

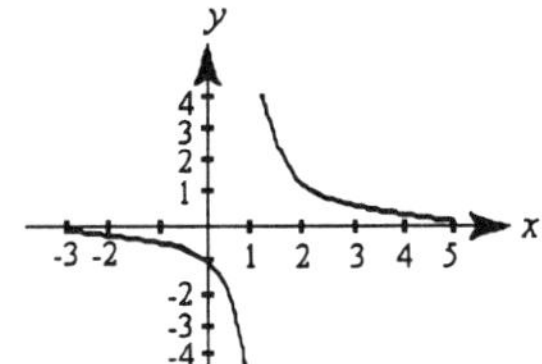

(II)

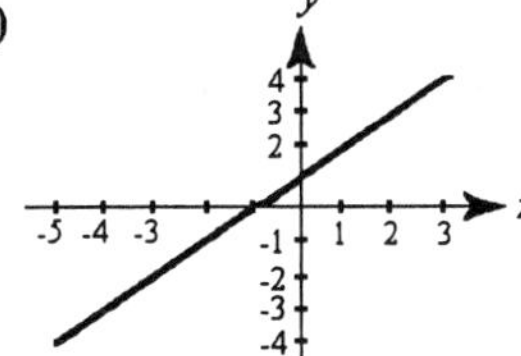

(III)

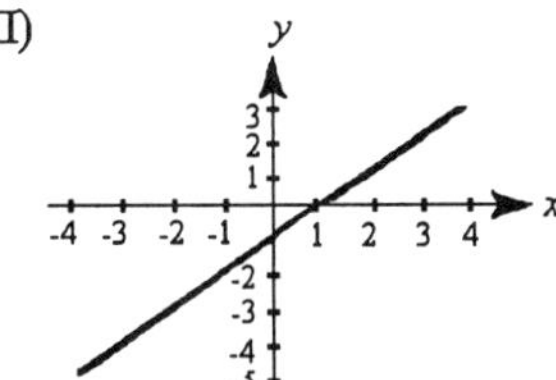

(IV)

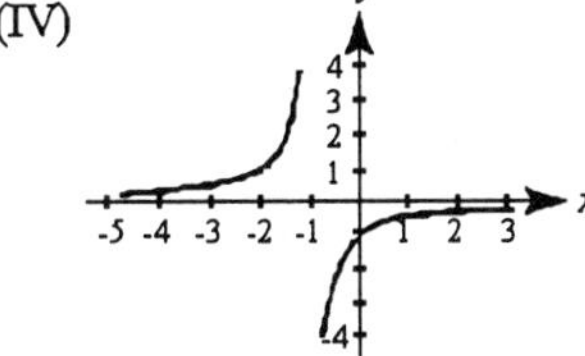

Answer: b Difficulty: 1

2. Given $f(x) = \frac{x}{3}$, identify the graph of $f^{-1}(x)$.
   a) I b) II c) III d) IV e) None of these

(I)

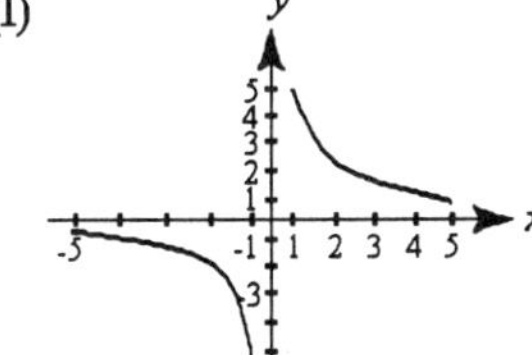

(II)

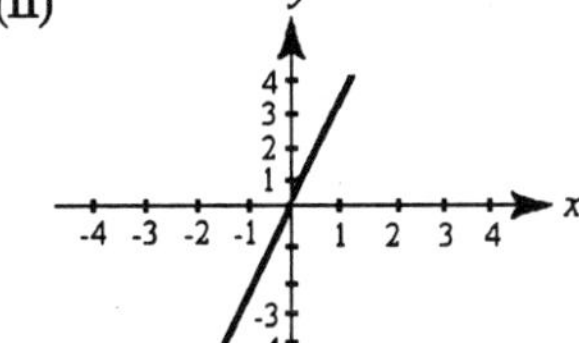

(III)

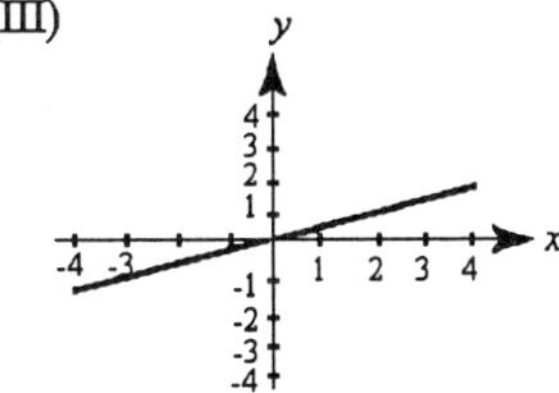

(IV)

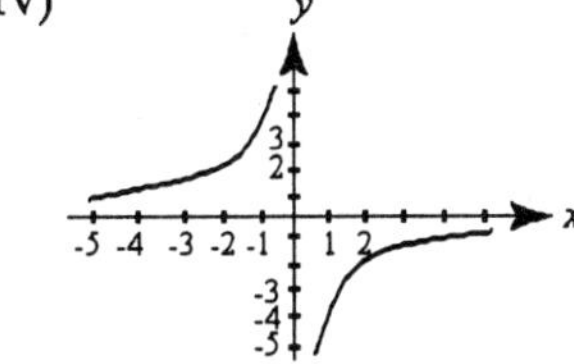

Answer: b Difficulty: 1

3. Given $f(x) = 3 + x$, identify the graph of $f^{-1}(x)$.
   a) I b) II c) III d) IV e) None of these

(I)

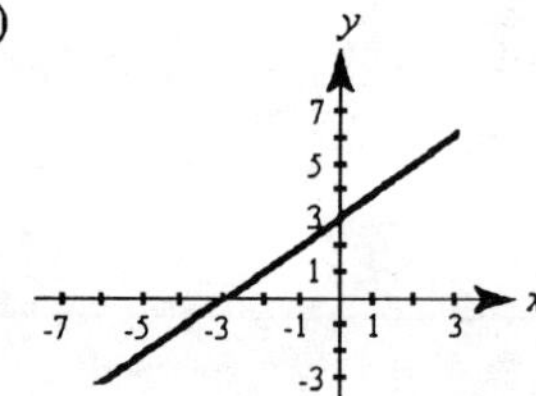

(II)

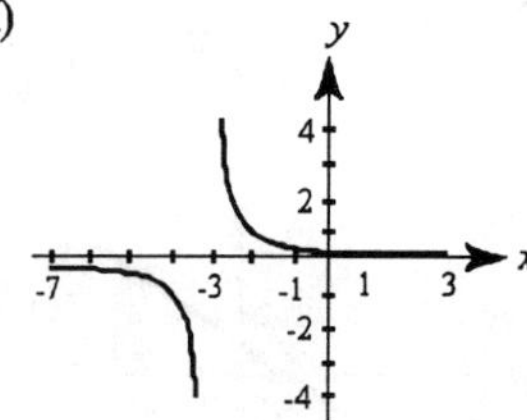

(III)

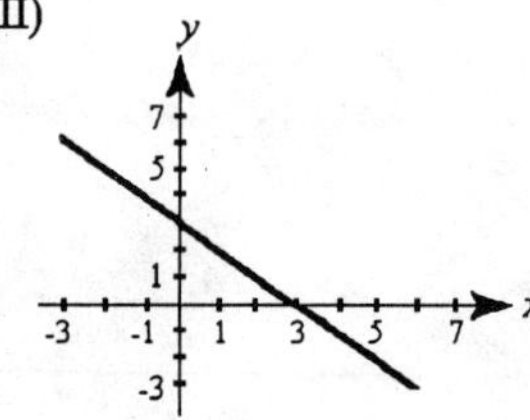

(IV)

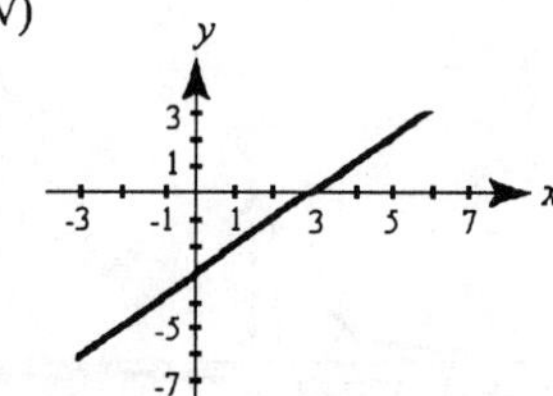

Answer: d Difficulty: 1

4. Given $f(x) = 4x$, identify the graph of $f^{-1}(x)$.
   a) I b) II c) III d) IV e) None of these

(I)

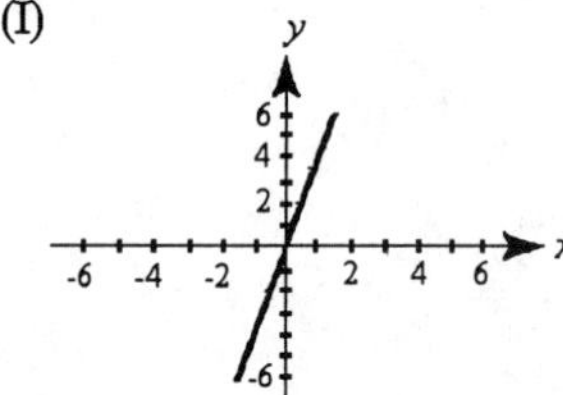

(II)

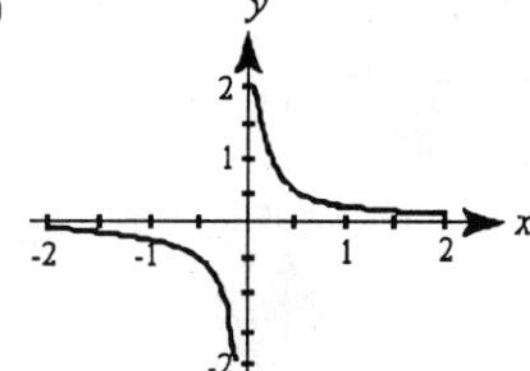

(III)

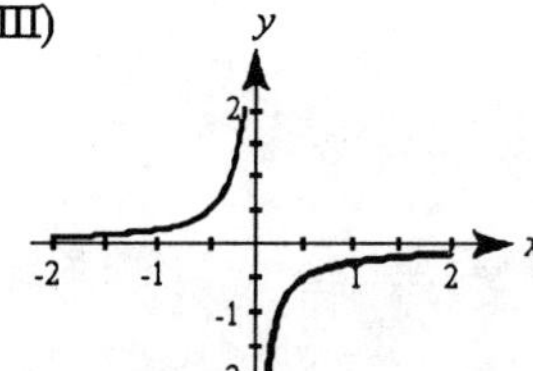

(IV)

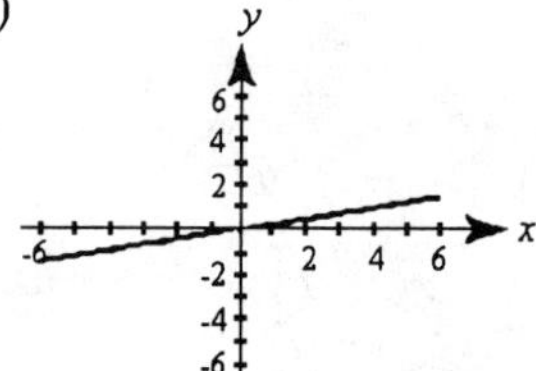

Answer: d Difficulty: 1

SHORT ANSWER

5. Find the inverse of f informally: $f(x) = 2x$.

Answer:

$f^{-1}(x) = \frac{x}{2}$

Difficulty: 1

6. Find the inverse of f informally: $f(x) = \frac{x}{3}$.

Answer:

$f^{-1}(x) = 3x$

Difficulty: 1

7. Find the inverse of f informally: $f(x) = x + 5$.

Answer:

$f^{-1}(x) = x - 5$

Difficulty: 1

8. Find the inverse of f informally: $f(x) = \sqrt[5]{x}$.

Answer:

$f^{-1}(x) = x^5$

Difficulty: 1

MULTIPLE CHOICE

9. Algebraically, determine which sets of functions are not inverses of each other.
   a) $f(x) = x^2 + 1$, $g(x) = \sqrt{x - 1}$
   b) $f(x) = x^2 - 1$, $g(x) = \sqrt{x + 1}$
   c) $f(x) = 1 - x^2$, $g(x) = \sqrt{1 + x^2}$
   d) All of these are inverses of each other.
   e) None of these are inverses of each other.

Answer: c Difficulty: 1

10. Algebraically, determine which sets of functions are not inverses of each other.
   a) $f(x) = x^3 + 2$, $g(x) = \sqrt[3]{x - 2}$
   b) $f(x) = 2 - x^3$, $g(x) = \sqrt[3]{2 - x}$
   c) $f(x) = x^3 - 2$, $g(x) = \sqrt[3]{x + 2}$
   d) All of these are inverses of each other.
   e) None of these are inverses of each other.

Answer: d Difficulty: 1

11. Algebraically, determine which sets of functions are not inverses of each other.

a) $f(x) = \dfrac{2}{x - 3}$, $g(x) = \dfrac{x - 3}{2}$

b) $f(x) = \dfrac{5}{x}$, $g(x) = \dfrac{5}{x}$

c) $f(x) = \dfrac{x}{2}$, $g(x) = 2x$

d) All of these are inverses of each other.

e) None of these are inverses of each other.

Answer: a Difficulty: 1

12. If f is a one-to-one function on its domain, the graph of $f^{-1}(x)$ is a reflection of the graph of $f(x)$ with respect to:

a) x-axis b) y-axis c) line $y = x$

d) line $y = -x$ e) origin

Answer: c Difficulty: 1

13. Graphically, determine which sets of functions are not inverses of each other.

a) $f(x) = 9 + x$, $g(x) = 9 - x$

b) $f(x) = x^2$, $g(x) = -x^2$

c) $f(x) = \dfrac{x + 3}{3}$, $g(x) = \dfrac{3}{x + 3}$

d) All of these are inverses of each other.

e) None of these are inverses of each other.

Answer: e Difficulty: 2

14. Graphically determine which sets of functions are not inverses of each other.

a) $f(x) = x + 5$, $g(x) = x - 5$

b) $f(x) = x^3$, $g(x) = \sqrt[3]{x}$

c) $f(x) = \dfrac{x + 2}{4}$, $g(x) = 4x - 2$

d) All of these are inverses of each other.

e) None of these are inverses of each other.

Answer: d Difficulty: 2

15. Graphically determine which sets of functions are not inverses of each other.

a) $f(x) = \dfrac{1}{2}x - 1$, $g(x) = 2x + 1$

b) $f(x) = \sqrt[5]{x}$, $g(x) = \dfrac{1}{\sqrt[5]{x}}$

c) $f(x) = \dfrac{x - 1}{5}$, $g(x) = x + \dfrac{1}{5}$

d) All of these are inverses of each other.

e) None of these are inverses of each other.

Answer: e Difficulty: 2

SHORT ANSWER

16. Graphically, determine whether the functions $f(x) = (x + 1)^3$ and $g(x) = \sqrt[3]{x} - 1$ are inverses of each other.

    Answer: Yes, they are inverses of each other. Difficulty: 1

17. Graphically, determine whether the functions $f(x) = \sqrt{x^2 - 5}$ and $g(x) = x^2 + 5$ are inverses of each other.

    Answer: No, they are not inverses of each other. Difficulty: 1

MULTIPLE CHOICE

18. In which graph does y not represent a one-to-one function of x?
    a) I
    b) II
    c) III
    d) All of these are one-to-one functions of x.
    e) None of these are one-to-one functions of x.

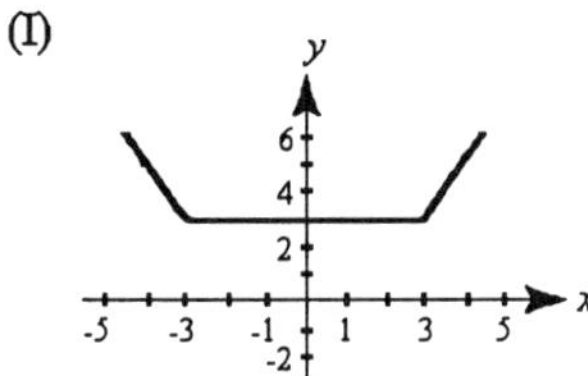

(II)

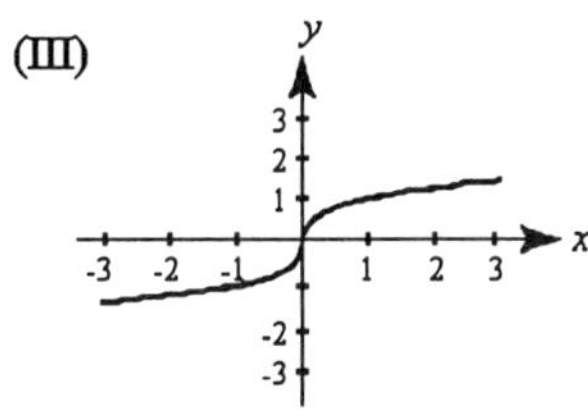

Answer: a Difficulty: 2

19. In which graph does y *not* represent a one-to-one function of x?
a) I b) II c) III d) IV e) None of these are one-to-one.

(I)
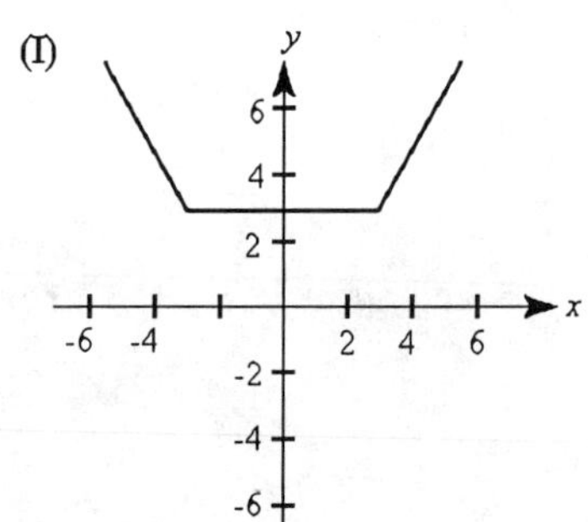

(II)
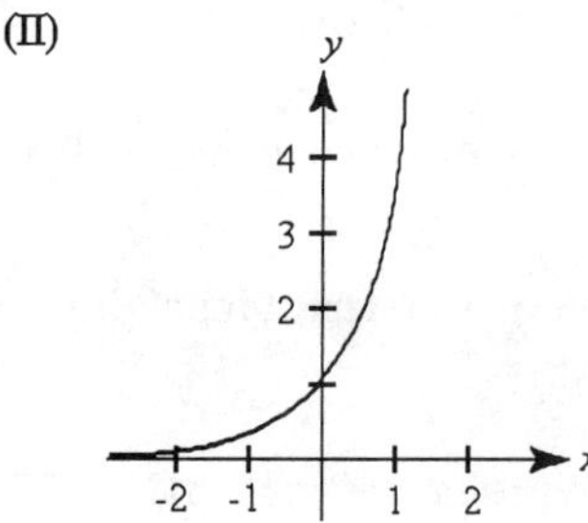

(III)
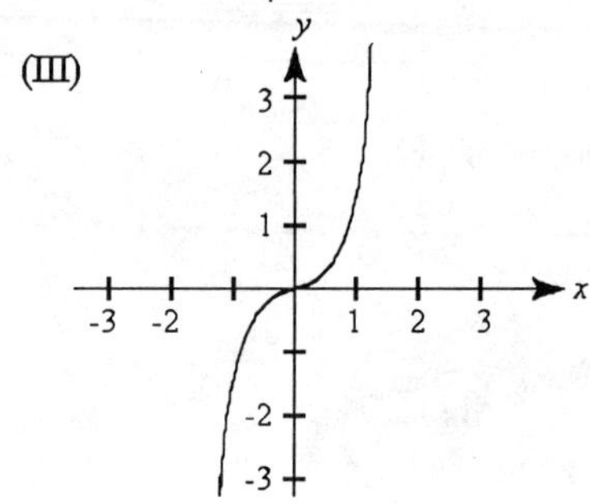

(IV)
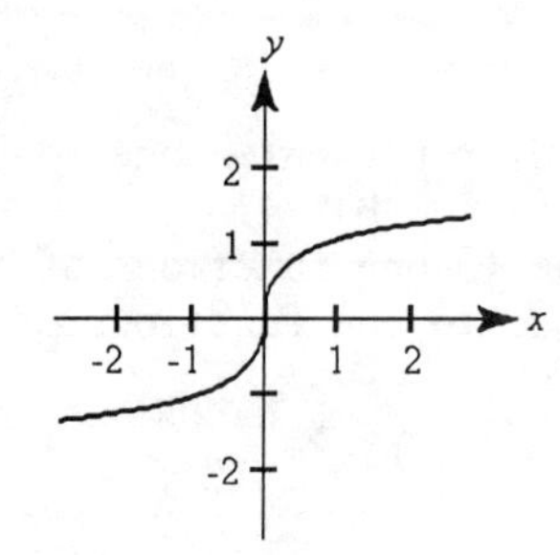

Answer: a Difficulty: 1

20. In which graph does y represent a one-to-one function of x?
a) I b) II c) III d) IV e) None of these

(I)
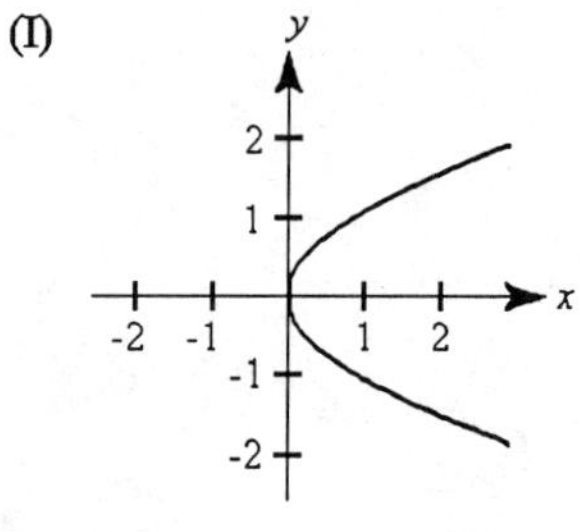

(II)
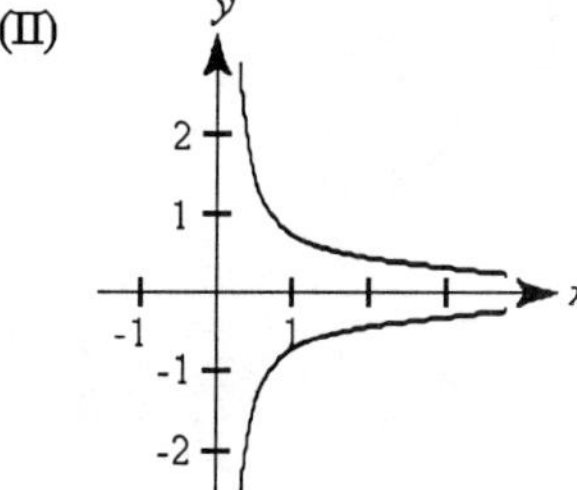

(III)
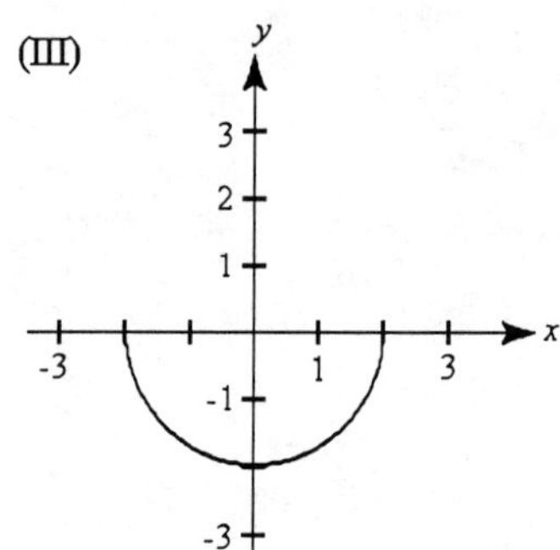

(IV)
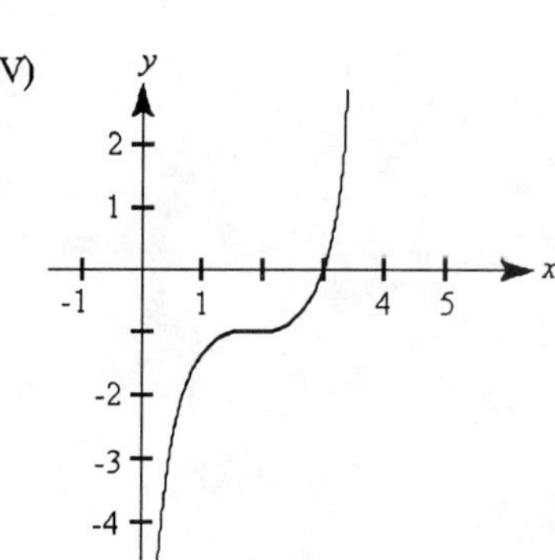

Answer: d Difficulty: 1

21. In which graph does y *not* represent a one-to-one function of x?
 a) I b) II c) III d) IV e) All of these are one-to-one.

(I)

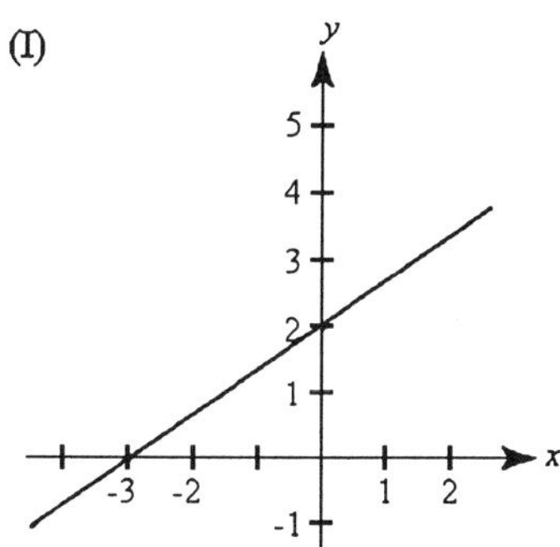

(II)

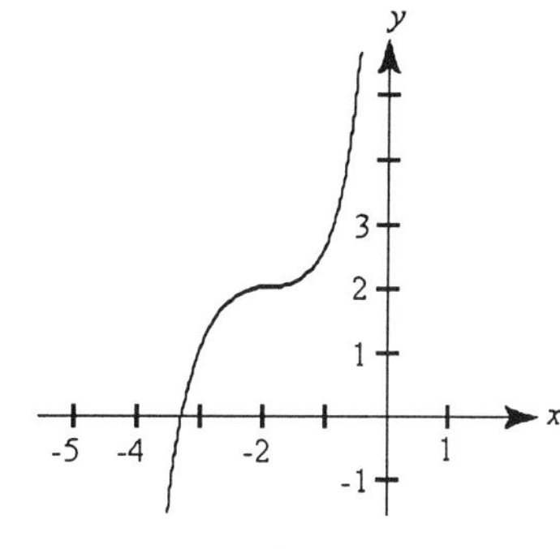

(III)

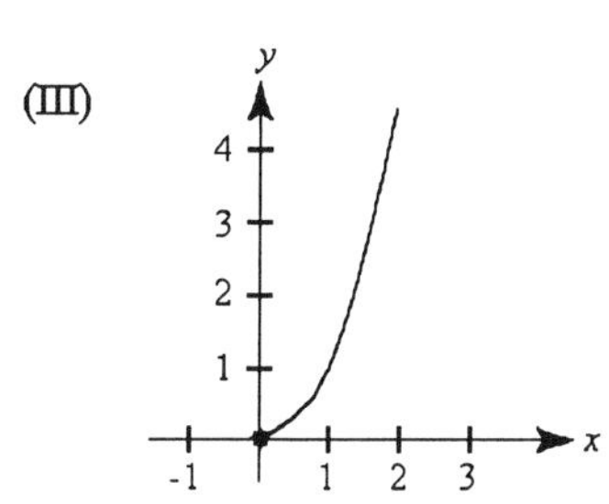

(IV)

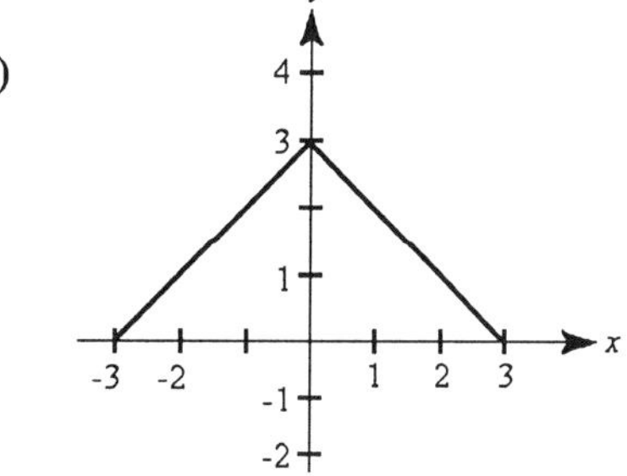

Answer: d Difficulty: 1

22. In which graph does y *not* represent a one-to-one function of x?
 a) I b) II c) III d) IV e) All of these are one-to-one.

(I)

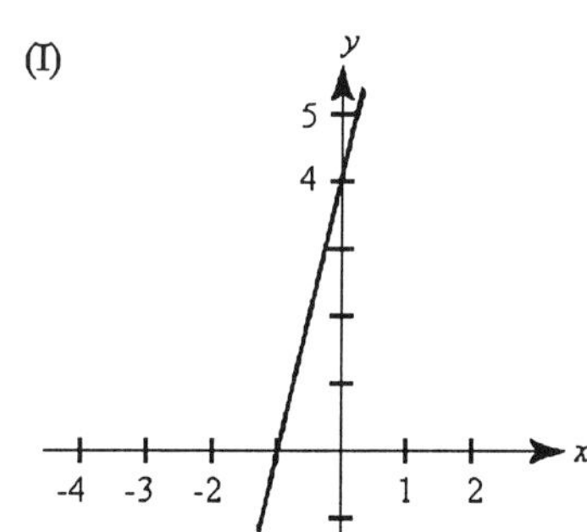

(II)

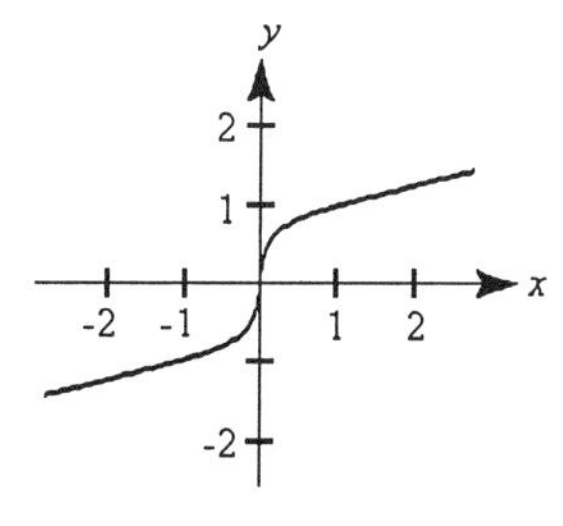

(III)

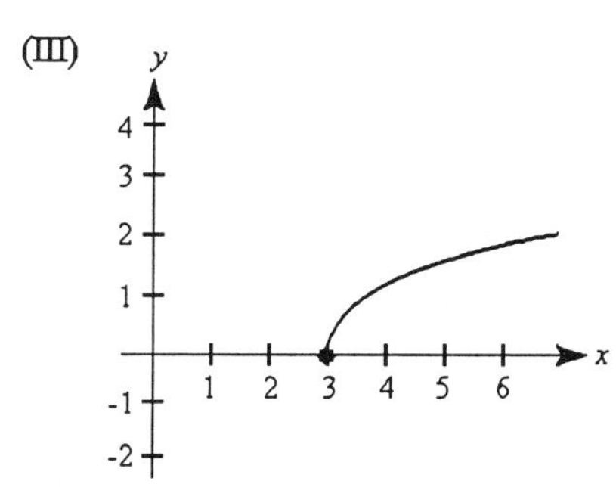

(IV)

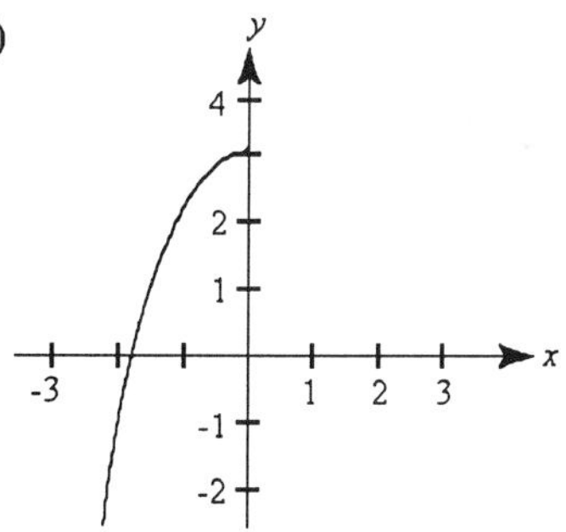

Answer: e Difficulty: 1

23. In which graph does y represent a one-to-one function of x?
   a) I b) II c) III d) IV e) None of these

(I)

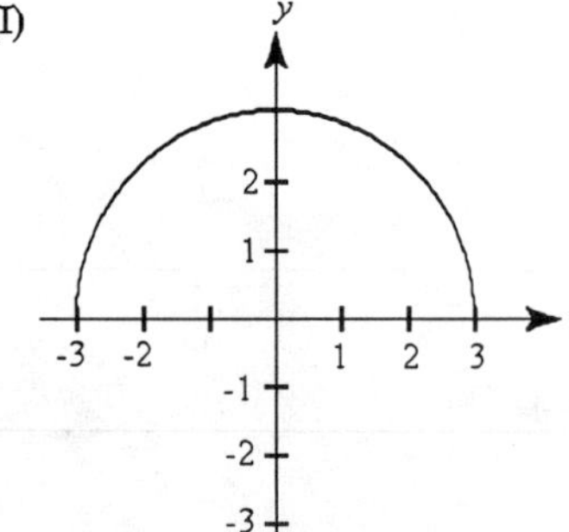

(II)

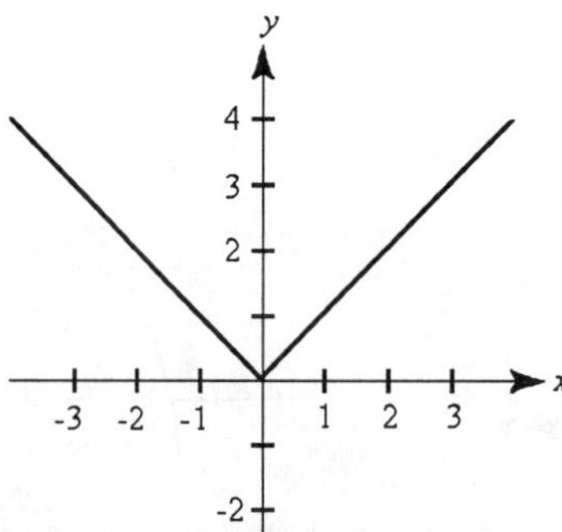

(III)

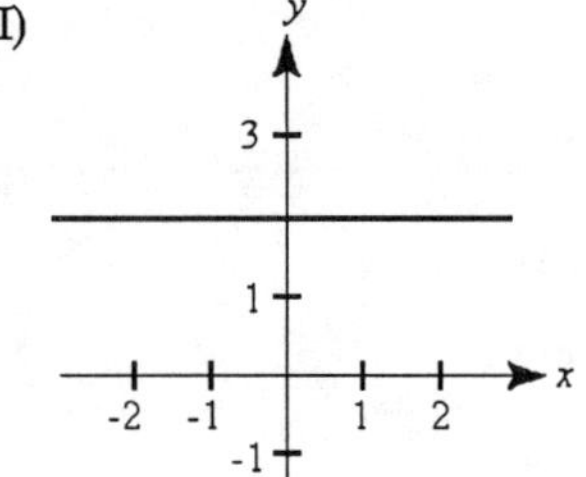

(IV)

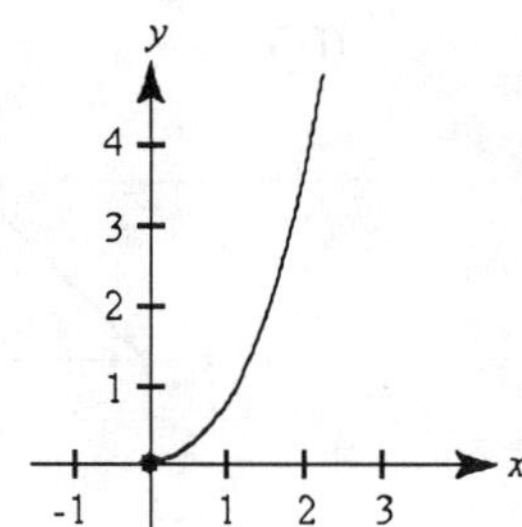

Answer: d Difficulty: 1

24. In which graph does y *not* represent a one-to-one function of x?
   a) I b) II c) III d) IV e) None of these

(I)

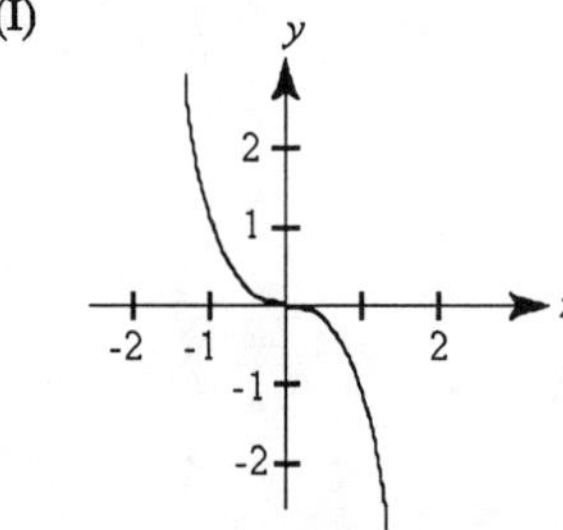

(II)

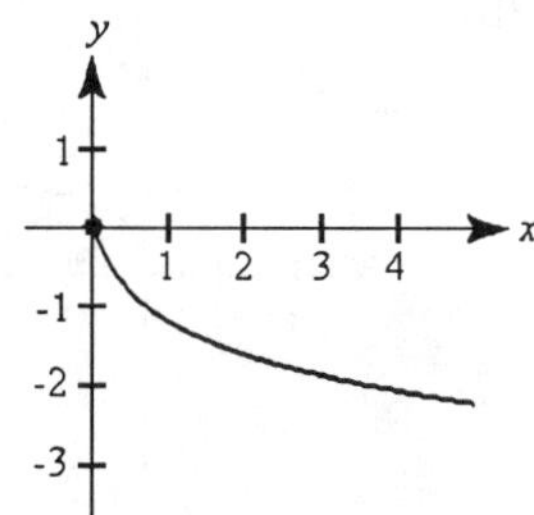

(III)

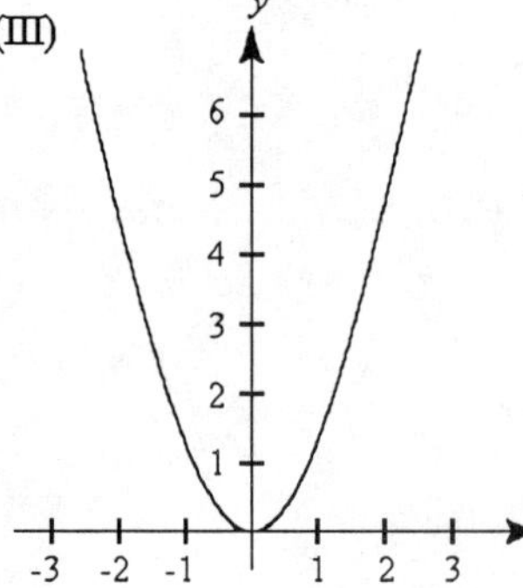

(IV)

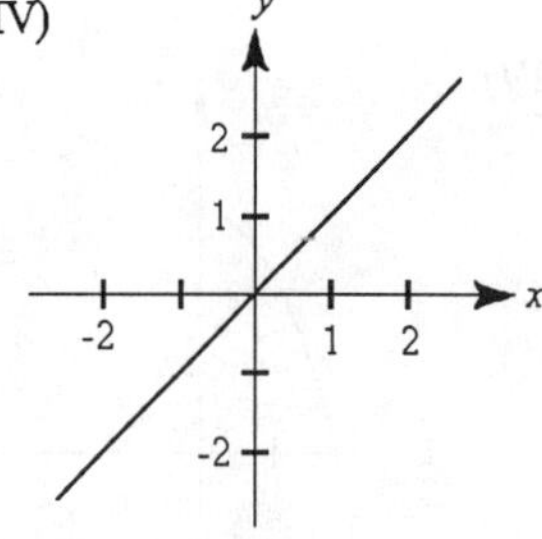

Answer: c Difficulty: 1

25. Determine which function is *not* one-to-one.
a) $y = \sqrt[3]{x^2 + 1}$ b) $y = \frac{2}{x}$ c) $y = 7x - 2$
d) $y = \sqrt{2 - x}$ e) None of these

Answer: a Difficulty: 2

26. Determine which function is one-to-one.
a) $y = |2 - x|$ b) $y = x^2 + 2$ c) $y = \sqrt{2 - x^2}$
d) $y = \frac{1}{x + 2}$ e) None of these

Answer: d Difficulty: 2

27. Determine which function is one-to-one.
a) $y = |x + 1|$ b) $y = \sqrt{5 + x}$ c) $y = \sqrt{x^2 + 1}$
d) $y = x^2 + 1$ e) None of these

Answer: b Difficulty: 1

28. Determine which function is one-to-one.
a) $y = \frac{9}{x}$ b) $y = 3 + x^2$ c) $y = |-4x|$
d) $y = x^4$ e) None of these

Answer: a Difficulty: 1

29. Find the inverse of the function: $f(x) = 2 - x$.
a) $\frac{1}{2 - x}$ b) $2 + x$ c) $-2 - x$
d) $x - 2$ e) None of these

Answer: e Difficulty: 1

30. Find the inverse of the function: $f(x) = \frac{x + 3}{2}$.
a) $2x - \frac{2}{3}$ b) $\frac{2}{x + 3}$ c) $2x - 6$
d) $2x - 3$ e) None of these

Answer: d Difficulty: 1

31. Find the inverse of the function: $f(x) = \frac{4 + 5x}{7}$.
a) $\frac{7}{5}(x - 4)$ b) $\frac{1}{5}(7x - 4)$ c) $-\frac{7}{4} - \frac{7}{5x}$
d) $\frac{7}{4 + 5x}$ e) None of these

Answer: b Difficulty: 1

32. Find the inverse of the function: $f(x) = \dfrac{2}{3x + 1}$.

a) $\dfrac{3x - 1}{2}$ b) $\dfrac{2 - x}{3x}$ c) $\dfrac{3x + 1}{2}$
d) $\dfrac{1 - x}{2}$ e) None of these

Answer: b Difficulty: 1

33. Find the inverse of the function: $f(x) = \dfrac{x}{6}$.

a) $6x$ b) $\dfrac{x}{6}$ c) $\dfrac{6}{x}$ d) $x - 6$ e) None of these

Answer: a Difficulty: 1

SHORT ANSWER

34. Determine whether the function $f(x) = \dfrac{x - 4}{x + 3}$ is one-to-one. If it is, find its inverse.

Answer:

f is one-to-one, $f^{-1}(x) = \dfrac{3x + 4}{1 - x}$.

Difficulty: 1

MULTIPLE CHOICE

35. Determine whether the function $f(x) = \dfrac{7}{x + 2}$ is one-to-one. If it is, find its inverse.

a) Not one-to-one b) $f^{-1}(x) = \dfrac{x + 2}{7}$ c) $f^{-1}(x) = \dfrac{7 - 2x}{x}$
d) $f^{-1}(x) = -\dfrac{7}{x + 2}$ e) None of these

Answer: c Difficulty: 2

SHORT ANSWER

36. Determine whether the function $f(x) = \dfrac{1}{x}$ is one-to-one. If it is, find its inverse.

Answer:

f is one-to-one, $f^{-1}(x) = \dfrac{1}{x}$.

Difficulty: 1

MULTIPLE CHOICE

37. Given $f(x) = 7x + 2$, find $f^{-1}(x)$.
a) $7x + 2$
b) $\frac{1}{7x + 2}$
c) $\frac{x - 2}{7}$
d) $\frac{x}{7} - 2$
e) None of these

Answer: c Difficulty: 1

38. Given $f(x) = \sqrt{2x - 1}$, find $f^{-1}(x)$.
a) $\sqrt{2x - 1},\ x \geq \frac{1}{2}$
b) $x^2 + 1,\ x \geq 0$
c) $\frac{1}{2}(x^2 + 1),\ x \geq 0$
d) $\frac{1}{\sqrt{2x - 1}},\ x \geq \frac{1}{2}$
e) None of these

Answer: c Difficulty: 2

39. Given $f(x) = 3x^3 - 1$, find $f^{-1}(x)$.
a) $\frac{1}{3x^3 - 1}$
b) $3x^{-1} - 1$
c) $3(x + 1)$
d) $\sqrt[3]{\frac{x + 1}{3}}$
e) None of these

Answer: d Difficulty: 1

SHORT ANSWER

40. Given $f(x) = 2x^2 + 1$ for $x \geq 0$, find $f^{-1}(x)$.

Answer:

$f^{-1}(x) = \sqrt{\frac{x - 1}{2}}$

Difficulty: 2

41. Given $f(x) = \frac{2x + 1}{3}$, find $f^{-1}(x)$.

Answer:

$f^{-1}(x) = \frac{3x - 1}{2}$

Difficulty: 1

MULTIPLE CHOICE

42. Given $f(x) = 2x^5$, find $f^{-1}(x)$.
a) $\sqrt[5]{\frac{x}{2}}$ b) $\frac{1}{2}\sqrt[5]{x}$ c) $\frac{1}{2x^5}$ d) $\frac{2}{x^5}$ e) None of these

Answer: a Difficulty: 1

SHORT ANSWER

43. Restrict the domain of the function $f(x) = (x - 1)^2$ so that it is one-to-one. Then find the inverse and give its domain.

Answer:

Possible answers: $f(x) = (x - 1)^2,\ x \geq 1$ or $f(x) = (x - 1)^2,\ x \leq 1$
$f^{-1}(x) = 1 + \sqrt{x},\ x \geq 0$ or $f^{-1}(x) = 1 - \sqrt{x},\ x \geq 0$

Difficulty: 2

44. Restrict the domain of the function $f(x) = |x + 5|$ so that it is one-to-one. Then find the inverse and give its domain.

Answer:
Possible answers: $f(x) = |x + 5|,\ x \geq -5$ or $f(x) = |x + 5|,\ x \leq -5$
$f^{-1}(x) = x - 5,\ x \geq 0$ or $f^{-1}(x) = -x - 5,\ x \geq 0$

Difficulty: 2

45. Restrict the domain of the function $f(x) = (x + 2)^2$ so that it is one-to-one. Then find the inverse and give its domain.

Answer:

Possible answers: $f(x) = (x + 2)^2,\ x \geq -2$ or $f(x) = (x + 2)^2,\ x \leq -2$
$f^{-1}(x) = \sqrt{x} - 2,\ x \geq 0$ or $f^{-1}(x) = -\sqrt{x} - 2,\ x \geq 0$

Difficulty: 2

46. Restrict the domain of the function $f(x) = |x - 1|$ so that it is one-to-one. Then find the inverse and give its domain.

Answer:
Possible answers: $f(x) = |x - 1|,\ x \geq 1$ or $f(x) = |x - 1|,\ x \leq 1$
$f^{-1}(x) = x + 1,\ x \geq 0$ or $f^{-1}(x) = -x + 1,\ x \geq 0$

Difficulty: 2

MULTIPLE CHOICE

47. Use a graphing utility to graph $f(x) = x + 1$ and its inverse on the same viewing window.
    a) I b) II c) III d) IV e) None of these

(I)
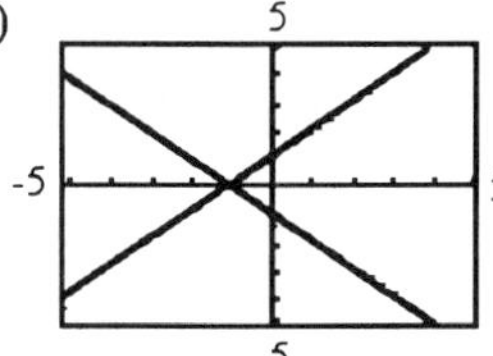

(II)
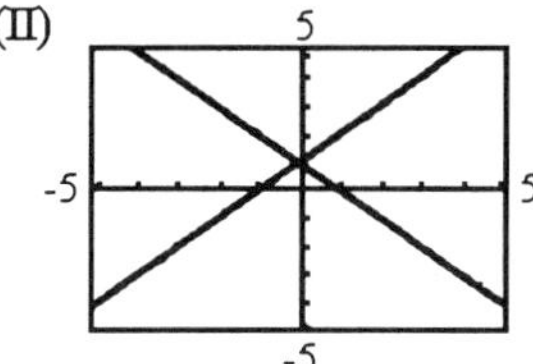

(III)
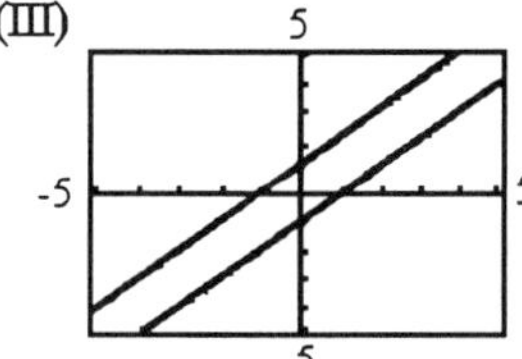

(IV)
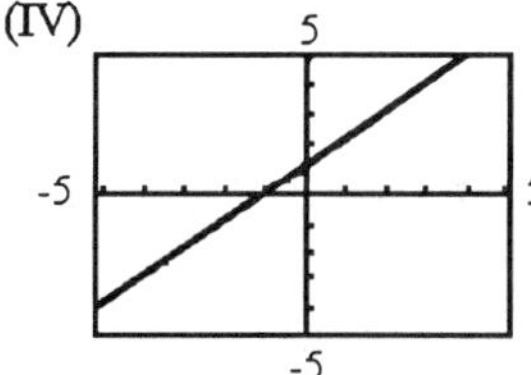

Answer: c Difficulty: 2 Key 1: T

48. Use a graphing utility to graph $f(x) = x^2 + 2$, $x \geq 0$ and its inverse on the same viewing window.
    a) I b) II c) III d) IV e) None of these

(I)
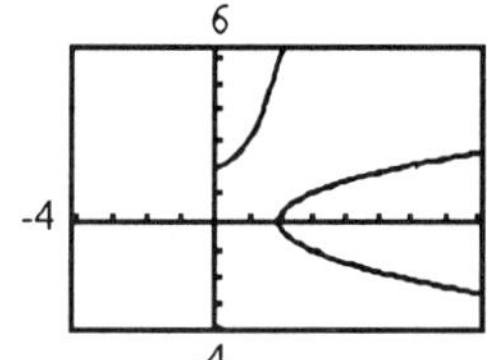

(II)
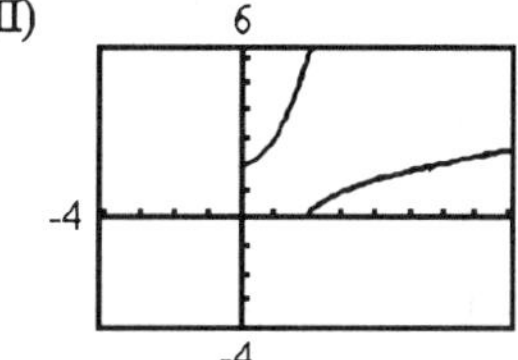

(III)
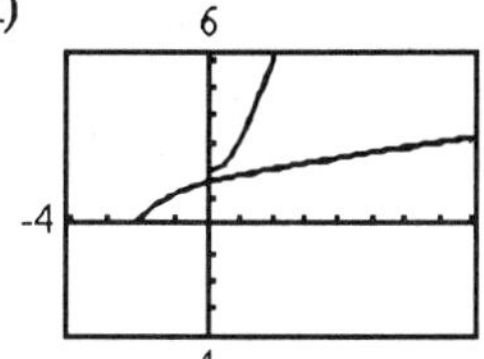

(IV)
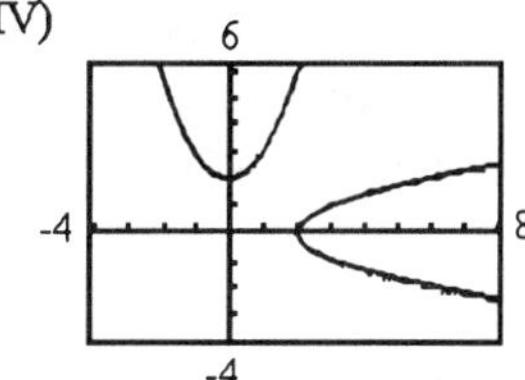

Answer: b Difficulty: 2 Key 1: T

49. Given $f(x) = 1 - 3x$ and $g(x) = x + 2$, find $(f^{-1} \circ g^{-1})(1)$.
    a) $\frac{2}{3}$ b) -6 c) -11 d) $-\frac{1}{3}$ e) None of these

Answer: a Difficulty: 2

50. Given $f(x) = x^2$ and $g(x) = 2x - 3$, find $(g^{-1} \circ f^{-1})(9)$.
a) 66 b) -6 c) -3 d) 3 e) None of these

Answer: d Difficulty: 2

51. Given $f(x) = x - 4$ and $g(x) = 3 - x$, find $(f^{-1} \circ g^{-1})(-1)$.
a) 6 b) 8 c) -6 d) -1 e) None of these

Answer: b Difficulty: 2

52. Given $f(x) = \sqrt[3]{x}$ and $g(x) = x - 5$, find $(f^{-1} \circ g^{-1})(-3)$.
a) -6 b) -4 c) 2 d) -8 e) None of these

Answer: e Difficulty: 2

53. Given $f(x) = 3 - x$ and $g(x) = x^3$, find $(g^{-1} \circ f^{-1})(-5)$.
a) $3 + \sqrt[3]{-5}$ b) $\sqrt[3]{-2}$ c) 2
d) $\dfrac{1}{\sqrt[3]{-2}}$ e) None of these

Answer: c Difficulty: 2

SHORT ANSWER

54. Given $f(x) = x + 2$ and $g(x) = \sqrt[3]{x}$, find $(f^{-1} \circ g^{-1})(2)$.

Answer: 6 Difficulty: 2

55. Given $f(x) = \sqrt[3]{x - 1}$ and $g(x) = x - 4$, find $(f^{-1} \circ g^{-1})(-2)$.

Answer: 9 Difficulty: 2

56. The function $f(x) = 0.25x^2 + 10$, $0 \le x \le 20$ approximates the population of bacteria (in thousands) in terms of the hour x since the culture was exposed to the air. Find the inverse function. What does each variable represent in the inverse function?

Answer:

$f(x) = \sqrt{4(x - 10)} = 2\sqrt{x - 10}$, $x \ge 10$

$f(x)$ is the hour since exposure where x is the population of the culture in thousands.

Difficulty: 2

57. The function $y = \sqrt{0.5x + 10}$, $0 \leq x \leq 10$ approximates the population of a small town in thousands where x is the year with $x = 0$ representing 1990. Find the inverse function. What does each variable represent in the function?

Answer:

$y = 2(x^2 - 10) = 2x^2 - 20$, $x \geq \sqrt{10}$

y is the year with $y = 0$ is representing 1990 in terms of x, and x is population in thousands of a small town.

Difficulty: 2

Chapter 018: Mathematical Modeling

MULTIPLE CHOICE

1. Find a mathematical model for the statement "y varies directly as the cube root of x."

a) $y = \dfrac{k}{\sqrt[3]{x}}$ b) $y = k\sqrt[3]{x}$ c) $y\sqrt[3]{x} = 1$

d) $\dfrac{y}{x^3} = 1$ e) None of these

Answer: b Difficulty: 1

2. Find a mathematical model for the statement "y varies directly as the cube of x."

a) $y = kx^3$ b) $y = \dfrac{k}{x^3}$ c) $x^3y = 1$

d) $\dfrac{\sqrt[3]{x}}{y} = 1$ e) None of these

Answer: a Difficulty: 1

3. Find a mathematical model for the statement "y is inversely proportional to $x + 3$."

a) $y = k(x + 3)$ b) $y = \dfrac{k}{(x + 3)}$ c) $\dfrac{y}{x + 3} = 1$

d) $xy + 3 = k$ e) None of these

Answer: b Difficulty: 1

4. Find a mathematical model for the statement "y is inversely proportional to $7 - x$."

a) $\dfrac{y}{7 - x} = 1$ b) $7y - x = k$ c) $y = k(7 - x)$

d) $y = \dfrac{k}{7 - x}$ e) None of these

Answer: d Difficulty: 1

5. Find a mathematical model for the statement "y varies jointly with the square of x and the square root of z."

a) $\dfrac{y}{x^2} = \dfrac{k}{\sqrt{z}}$ b) $y = \dfrac{k}{x^2\sqrt{z}}$ c) $y = kx^2\sqrt{z}$

d) $y = \dfrac{kx^2}{\sqrt{z}}$ e) None of these

Answer: c Difficulty: 1

SHORT ANSWER

6. Find a mathematical model for the statement "y varies jointly with x and the cube of z and inversely with w."

   Answer:

   $$y = \frac{kxz^3}{w}$$

   Difficulty: 1

MULTIPLE CHOICE

7. Which of the following sentences describes the formula to find the volume of a right circular cone, $V = \frac{\pi r^2 h}{3}$?
   a) The volume of a right circular cone is directly proportional to the height and jointly proportional to the square of the radius.
   b) The volume of a right circular cone is indirectly proportional to the height and radius.
   c) The volume of a right circular cone varies inversely with the height and the square of the radius.
   d) The volume of a right circular cone is jointly proportional to the height and the square of the radius.
   e) None of these

   Answer: d Difficulty: 2

8. Which of the following sentences describes the formula to find the lateral surface area of a right circular cylinder, $S = 2\pi rh$?
   a) The lateral surface area of a right circular cylinder is inversely proportional to the radius and the height.
   b) The lateral surface area of a right circular cylinder is jointly proportional to the radius and the height.
   c) The lateral surface area of a right circular cylinder is directly proportional to the radius and the height.
   d) The lateral surface area of a right circular cylinder varies indirectly with the radius and height.
   e) None of these

   Answer: b Difficulty: 1

SHORT ANSWER

9. Write a sentence using variation terminology to describe the formula to find the volume of a right circular cylinder, $V = \pi r^2 h$.

   Answer: The volume is jointly proportional to the height and the square of the radius.

   Difficulty: 1

MULTIPLE CHOICE

10. Write a sentence using variation terminology to describe the equation relating the distance, d, a spring is stretched to the force, F, applied, $d = kF$.
    a) The distance a spring is stretched is jointly proportional to the force applied.
    b) The distance a spring is stretched varies inversely with the force applied.
    c) The distance a spring is stretched varies directly with the force applied.
    d) The distance a spring is stretched is indirectly proportional to the force applied.
    e) None of these

    Answer: c Difficulty: 1

11. y is directly proportional to x. If $y = 35$ when $x = 5$, find the constant of proportionality.
    a) $\frac{1}{7}$ b) 7 c) 175 d) $\frac{1}{175}$ e) None of these

    Answer: b Difficulty: 1

SHORT ANSWER

12. x varies inversely with the square of y. If $x = 1$ when $y = 5$, find the constant of proportionality.

    Answer: 25 Difficulty: 1

MULTIPLE CHOICE

13. h varies jointly with the square of x and the cube root of y. If $h = \frac{1}{4}$ when $x = 2$ and $y = 8$, find the constant of proportionality.
    a) $\frac{1}{4}$ b) 4 c) $\frac{1}{32}$ d) 64 e) None of these

    Answer: c Difficulty: 1

14. W varies directly with the square of x and inversely with the cube root of y. If $W = \frac{1}{2}$ when $x = 6$ and $y = 8$, find the constant of proportionality.
    a) $\frac{1}{9}$ b) $\frac{1}{36}$ c) $\frac{1}{6}$ d) $\frac{9}{2}$ e) None of these

    Answer: b Difficulty: 1

15. V varies jointly with g and the square of t. Find the constant of proportionality if $V = -144$ when $t = 3$ and $g = -32$.
    a) 5 b) $\frac{1}{36}$ c) $\frac{1}{3}$ d) $\frac{1}{2}$ e) None of these

    Answer: d Difficulty: 1

16. T varies directly with the square root of L and inversely with the square root of g. If $T = \pi/2$ when $L = 2$ and $g = 32$, find the constant of proportionality.
a) 2π b) $\frac{\pi}{8}$ c) π d) $\frac{\pi}{2}$ e) None of these

Answer: a Difficulty: 1

17. A is jointly proportional to P and $(1 + N)$. Find the constant of proportionality if $A = 180$ when $P = 300$ and $N = 2$.
a) 1 b) $\frac{1}{2}$ c) $\frac{1}{5}$ d) 10 e) None of these

Answer: c Difficulty: 1

18. x varies directly as y and $x = 3$ when $y = 10$. Find the equation relating the variables.
a) $3x = 10y$ b) $10x = 3y$ c) $xy = 30$
d) $\frac{x}{y} = 30$ e) None of these

Answer: b Difficulty: 1

19. P varies jointly with x and y and inversely with the square of z. If $P = -17/50$ when $x = 3$, $y = 17$, and $z = 10$, find the equation relating the variables.
a) $P = \frac{-17(x + y)}{10z^2}$ b) $P = \frac{-867z^2}{5000xy}$ c) $P = \frac{-2xy}{3z^2}$
d) $P = \frac{-17z^2}{10(x + y)}$ e) None of these

Answer: c Difficulty: 2

20. z varies jointly with x and the square of y and inversely with w. If $z = 5$ when $x = 5$, $y = 3$, and $w = 6$, find the equation relating the variables.
a) $z = \frac{35w}{3(x + y^2)}$ b) $z = \frac{75w}{2xy^2}$ c) $z = \frac{15(x + y^2)}{7w}$
d) $z = \frac{2xy^2}{3w}$ e) None of these

Answer: d Difficulty: 2

21. P varies jointly with x and w and inversely with the square root of y. If $P = 30$ when $x = 2$, $w = 5$ and $y = 9$, find the mathematical model relating the variables.
a) $P = \frac{9xw}{\sqrt{y}}$ b) $P = \frac{240xw}{y^2}$ c) $P = \frac{90(x + w)}{\sqrt{y}}$
d) $P = \frac{100\sqrt{y}}{xy}$ e) None of these

Answer: a Difficulty: 2

22. x varies jointly with x and $y + 1$ and inversely with z. If $x = -\frac{1}{6}$ when $y = 2$ and $z = 3$, find the mathematical model relating the variables.

a) $x = -\frac{z}{3y(y + 1)}$ b) $x = -\frac{y(y + 1)}{12z}$ c) $x = -\frac{1}{16}\left(2y + 1 + \frac{1}{z}\right)$
d) $x = -\frac{2y + 1}{10z}$ e) None of these

Answer: b Difficulty: 2

23. V varies directly as the square of P and inversely as Q. If $V = 2$ when $P = 2$ and $Q = 4$, find a mathematical model relating the variables.

a) $V = \frac{2P^2}{Q}$ b) $V = \frac{Q}{P^2}$ c) $V = \frac{8}{17}\left(P^2 + \frac{1}{Q}\right)$
d) $V = \frac{8}{17}\left(Q + \frac{1}{P^2}\right)$ e) None of these

Answer: a Difficulty: 2

SHORT ANSWER

24. x varies jointly with y and the square of z and inversely with w. If $x = 4/3$ when $y = 1$, $z = -2$, and $w = 7$, find x when $y = 2$, $z = -1$, and $w = 6$.

Answer:
$\frac{7}{9}$

Difficulty: 2

MULTIPLE CHOICE

25. V varies directly with the cube of P and inversely with Q. If $V = 2$ when $P = 2$ and $Q = 8$, find V when $P = 1$ and $Q = 2$.

a) 4 b) 2 c) 1 d) $\frac{1}{2}$ e) None of these

Answer: c Difficulty: 2

26. V varies jointly with P and the square of Q and inversely with the cube of S. If $V = 8$ when $P = 12$, $Q = 4$ and $S = 2$, find V when $P = 6$, $Q = 1$ and $S = 1$.

a) 16 b) 8 c) 4 d) 2 e) None of these

Answer: d Difficulty: 2

27. x varies jointly with y and the cube of z and inversely with w. If $x = 64$ when $y = 2$, $z = 4$ and $w = 6$, find x when $y = 1$, $z = 3$ and $w = 15$.
a) $\frac{84}{165}$ b) $\frac{3}{7}$ c) 16 d) $\frac{27}{5}$ e) None of these

Answer: d Difficulty: 2

28. z varies directly as the square of x and inversely as y. If $z = \frac{3}{2}$ when $x = 3$ and $y = 4$, find z when $x = 12$ and $y = 6$.
a) $\frac{207}{5}$ b) 16 c) 3 d) $\frac{21}{2}$ e) None of these

Answer: d Difficulty: 2

29. x is jointly proportional to y and $w - y$. If $x = 30$ when $w = 20$ and $y = 5$, find x when $y = 10$ and $w = 30$.
a) 10 b) 20 c) 40 d) 80 e) None of these

Answer: d Difficulty: 2

30. x is jointly proportional to y and $y + 1$ and inversely proportional to w. If $x = 20$ when $y = 5$ and $w = 3$, find x when $y = 7$ and $w = 4$.
a) 16 b) 28 c) $\frac{45}{22}$ d) $\frac{9}{2}$ e) None of these

Answer: b Difficulty: 2

31. z is jointly proportional to x and the square of y. If x and y are both tripled what happens to z?
a) z is tripled.
b) z is multiplied by $3\sqrt{3}$.
c) z is multiplied by 27.
d) z is multiplied by $\frac{1}{27}$.
e) None of these

Answer: c Difficulty: 2

32. Ohms Law states that the voltage E across a given resistor is proportional to the current I. If the voltage is 12 volts when there is a current of 2 amps, what is the voltage when the current is 1.5 amps?
a) 8 volts b) 16 volts c) 9 volts
d) 15 volts e) None of these

Answer: c Difficulty: 2

33. Boyle's Law states that for a fixed amount of gas, the volume of the gas at a constant temperature is inversely proportional to the pressure. If a certain gas occupies 9.84 liters at a pressure of 50 cm.Hg., what is the pressure when the volume is increased to 10 liters?
a) 0.02 cm.Hg. b) 4920 cm.Hg. c) 49.2 cm.Hg.
d) 50.8 cm.Hg. e) None of these

Answer: c Difficulty: 2

34. Ohms Law states that the voltage E across a given resistor is proportional to the current I. If the voltage is 12 volts when there is a current of $\frac{3}{2}$ amps, what is the voltage when the current is 1 amp?
a) 8 volts
b) 9 volts
c) 11 volts
d) 6 volts
e) None of these

Answer: a Difficulty: 2 Key 1: T

35. Boyle's Law states that for a fixed amount of gas, the volume of the gas at a constant temperature is inversely proportional to the pressure. If a certain gas occupies 9.84 liters at a pressure of 50 cm.Hg., what is the pressure when the volume is increased to 12 liters?
a) 43.2 cm.Hg.
b) 45.1 cm.Hg.
c) 39.8 cm.Hg.
d) 41.0 cm.Hg.
e) None of these

Answer: d Difficulty: 2 Key 1: T

SHORT ANSWER

36. The table shows the per capita consumption of cheese, y (in pounds), for the years 1988 through 1997.

Year, t	1988	1989	1990	1991	1992	1993	1994	1995	1996	1997
Pounds, y	23.7	23.8	24.6	25.0	26.0	26.2	26.8	27.3	27.7	28.0

Construct a scatter plot for the data, let $t = 0$ represent 1988. Find the least squares regression line that fits this data, and graph the linear model on the same set of axes as the scatter plot.
(Source: U.S. Department of Agriculture)

Answer: See graph below.

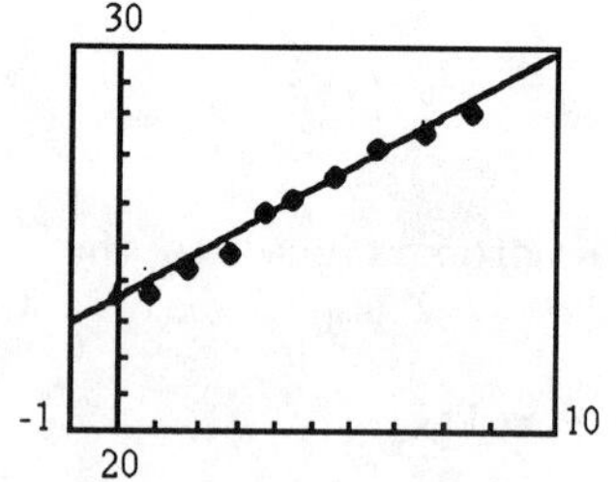

$;y = 0.52t + 23.6$

Difficulty: 2 Key 1: T

37. The table shows the total amount, y in millions of dollars, spent by the federal government on mathematics computer science research and development from 1988 through 1998.

Year, t	1988	1989	1990	1991	1992	1993	1994	1995	1996	1997	1998
Amount, y	643	735	841	904	1160	1225	1292	1531	1554	1672	1831

Construct a scatter plot for the date, let $t = 1$ represent 1988. Find the least squares regression line that fits the data and graph the model on the same set of axes as the scatter plot. (Source: U.S. National Science Foundation)

Answer: See graph below.

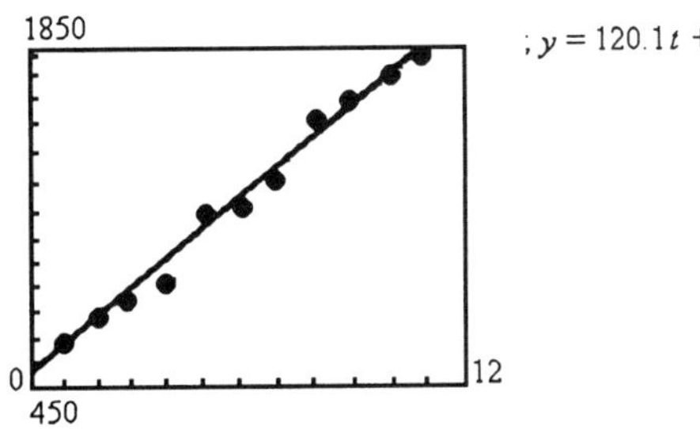

Difficulty: 2 Key 1: T

38. The table shows the number of households, y in millions, in the U.S. that owned VCRs between 1992 and 1997.

Year, t	1992	1993	1994	1995	1996	1997
Households, y	69	72	74	77	79	82

Construct a scatter plot for the date. Let $t = 2$ represent 1992. Find the least squares regression line that fits the data and graph the model on the same set of axes as the scatter plot.

Answer: See graph below.

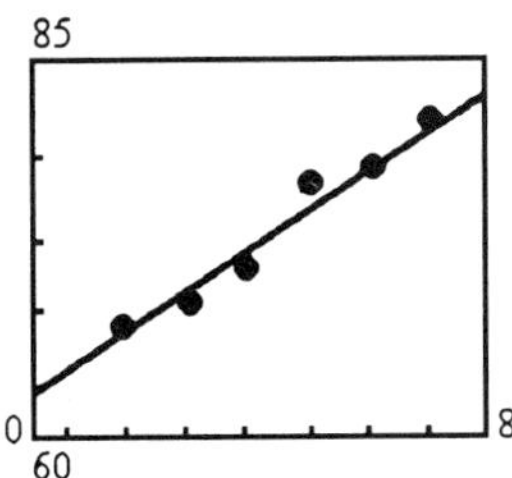

Difficulty: 2

Chapter 021: Quadratic Functions

MULTIPLE CHOICE

1. Match the correct graph with the function: $f(x) = 2(x - 3)^2 - 1$.
   a) I b) II c) III d) IV e) None of these

(I)

(-3, -1)

(II)

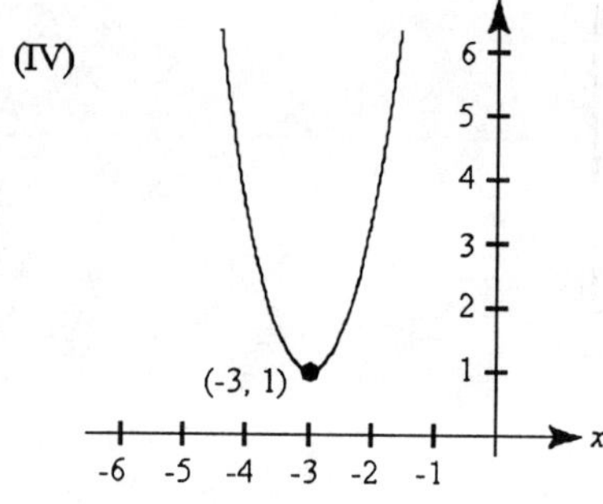

(III)

(3, 1)

(IV)

(-3, 1)

Answer: b Difficulty: 1

2. Match the correct graph with the function: $f(x) = -\frac{1}{2}(x - 2)^2 + 1$.

a) I b) II c) III d) IV e) None of these

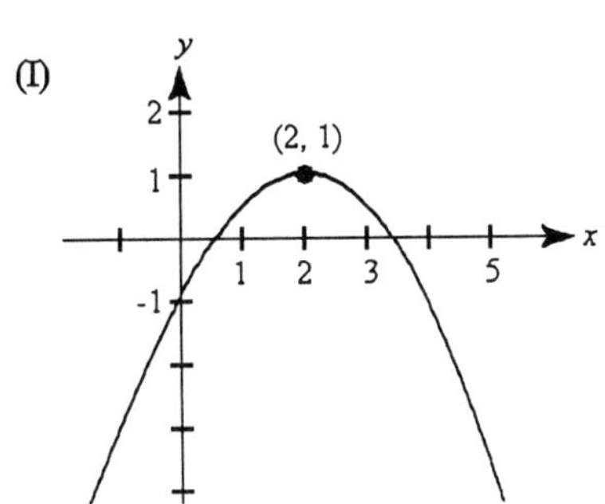

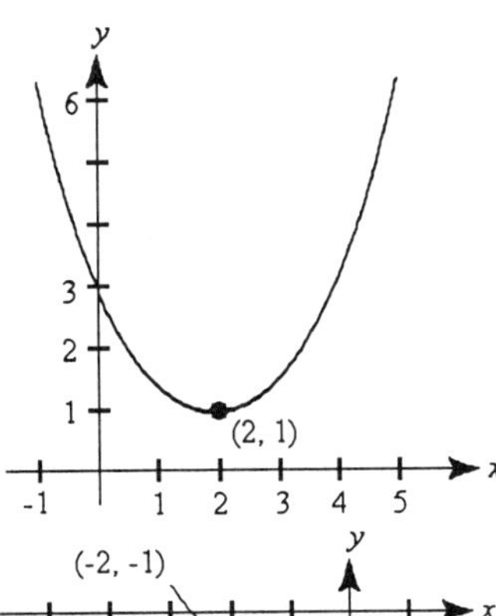

(III)

(-2, 1)

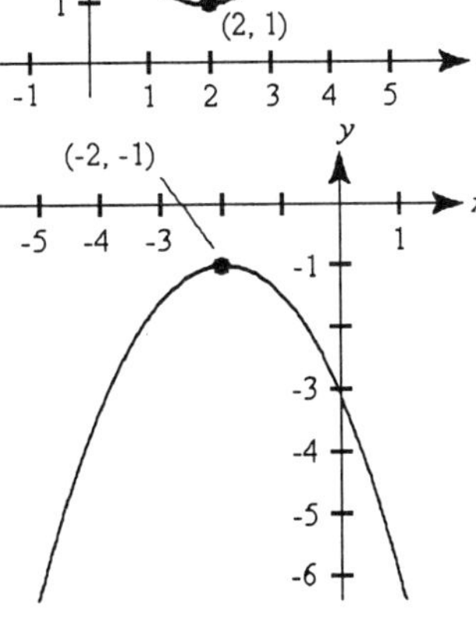

Answer: a Difficulty: 1

3. Match the correct graph with the function: $f(x) = 3(x + 2)^2 - 1$.

a) I b) II c) III d) IV e) None of these

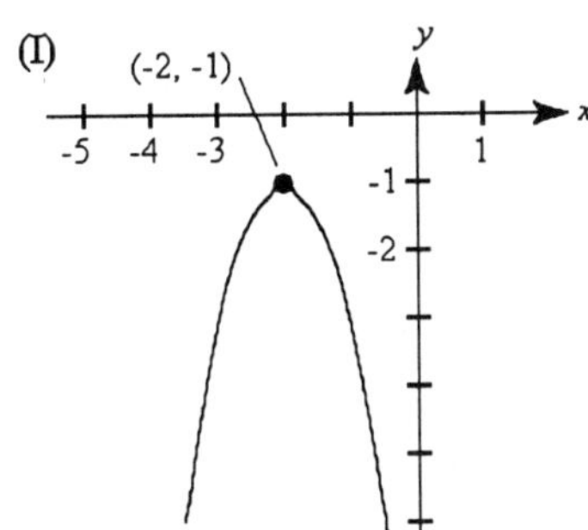

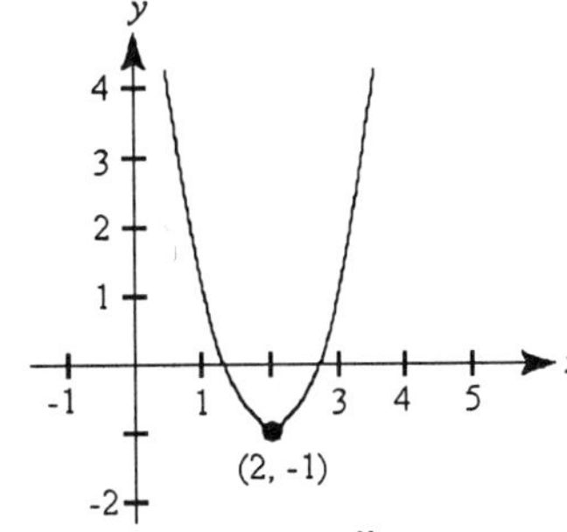

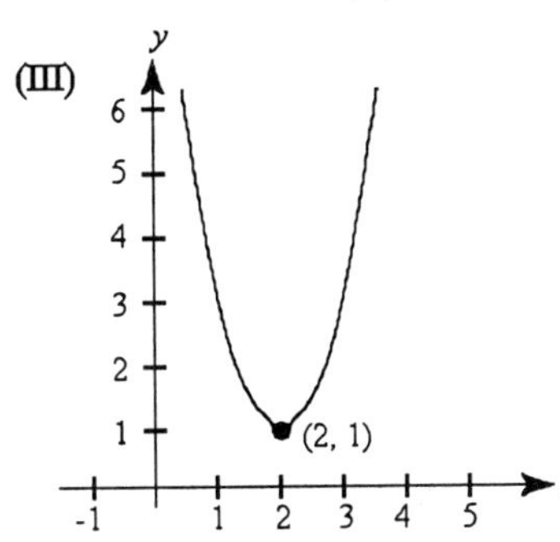

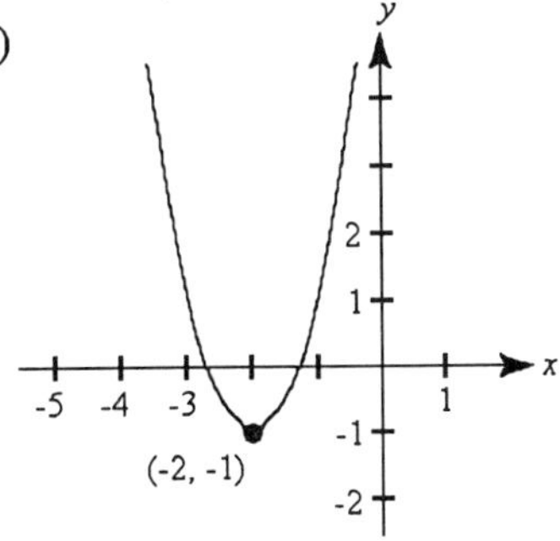

Answer: d Difficulty: 1

4. Match the correct graph with the function: $f(x) = \frac{1}{3}(x + 3)^2 + 1$.

a) I b) II c) III d) IV e) None of these

(I)

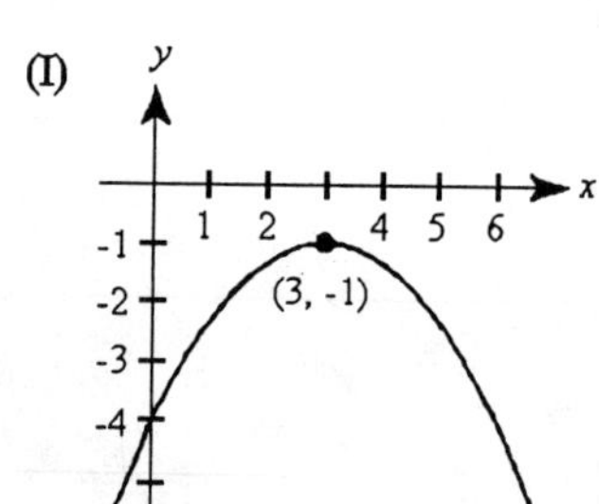

(II)

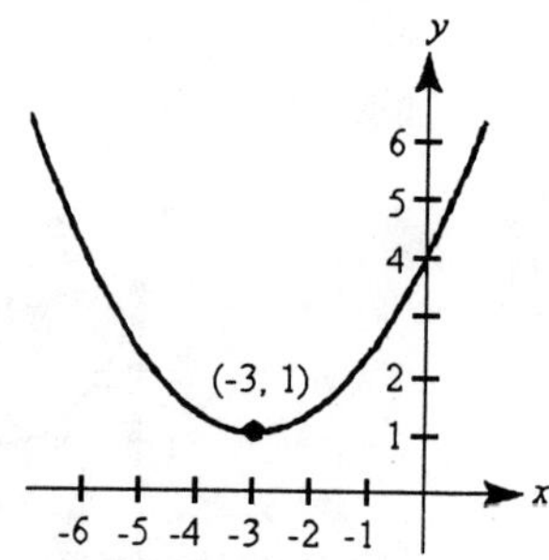

(III)

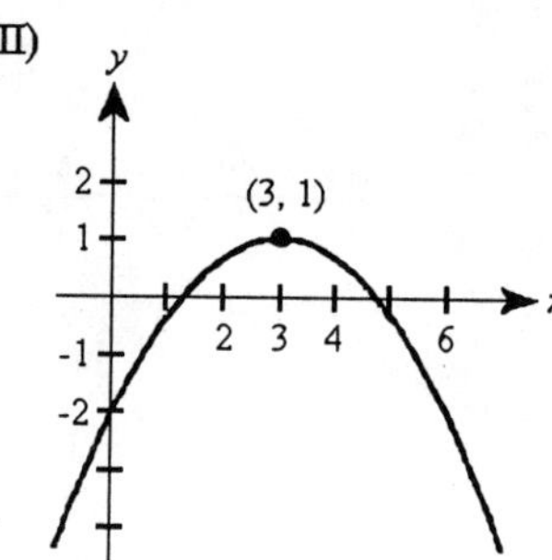

(IV)

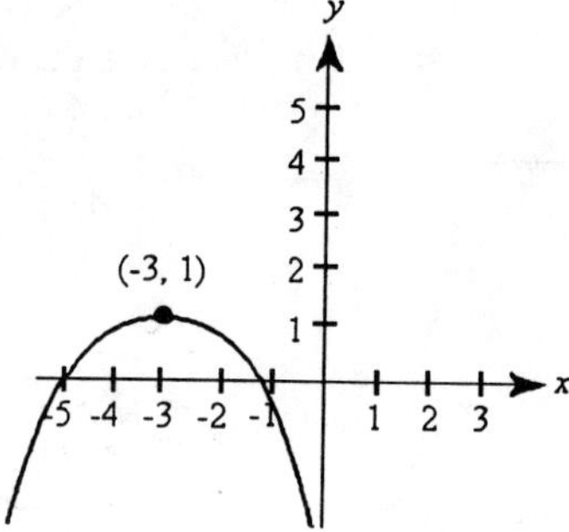

Answer: b Difficulty: 1

5. Write the standard form of the equation of the parabola.

a) $y = (x - 2)^2 + 3$ b) $y = (x + 2)^2 - 3$ c) $y = (x - 2)^2 - 3$
d) $y = (x + 2)^2 + 3$ e) None of these

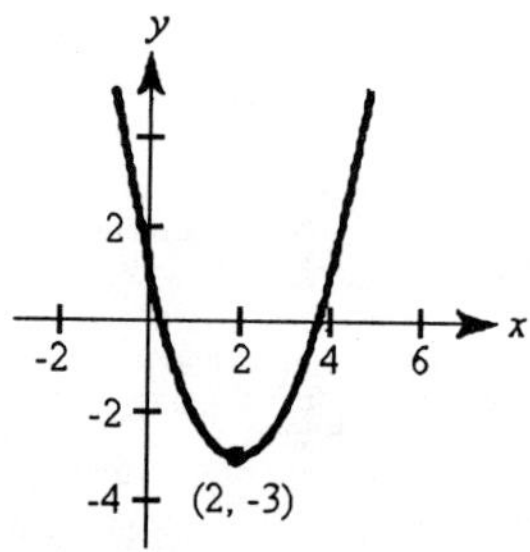

Answer: c Difficulty: 1

6. Write the standard form of the equation of the parabola.
a) $y = -(x - 3)^2 - 1$ b) $y = -(x + 3)^2 - 1$ c) $y = -(x + 1)^2 + 3$
d) $y = -(x - 1)^2 - 3$ e) None of these

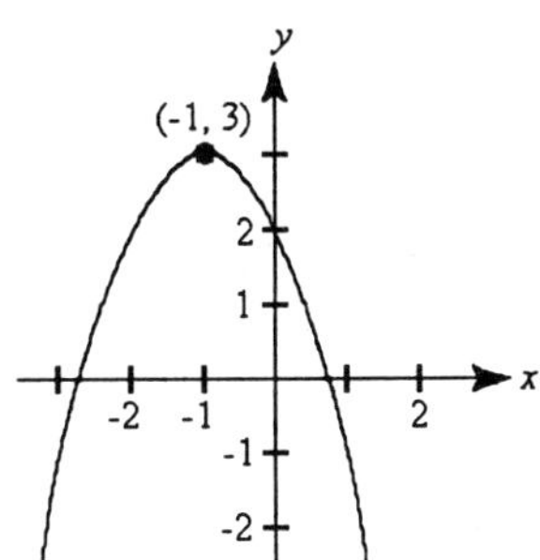

Answer: c Difficulty: 1

SHORT ANSWER

7. Write the standard form of the equation of the parabola.

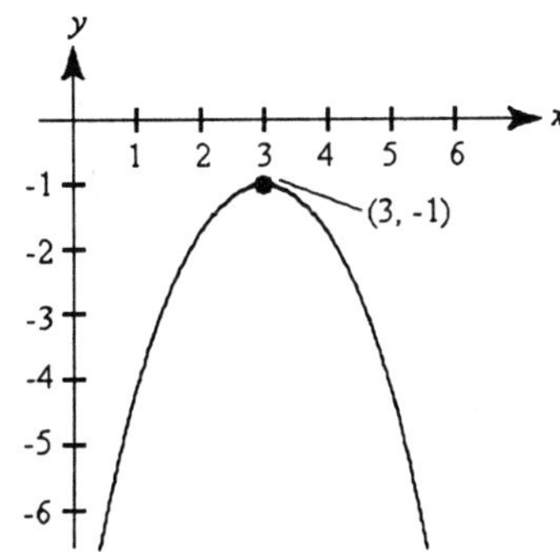

Answer:

$f(x) = -(x - 3)^2 - 1$

Difficulty: 1

MULTIPLE CHOICE

8. Match the correct equation with the parabola.
   a) $y = 5(x - 1)^2 - 2$ b) $y = (x + 2)^2 - 1$ c) $y = (x - 2)^2 - 1$
   d) $y = (x - 1)^2 + 2$ e) None of these

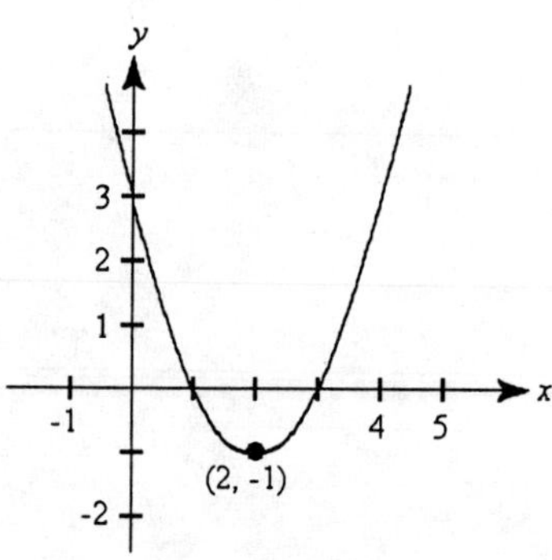

Answer: c Difficulty: 1

9. Match the correct equation with the parabola.
   a) $y = -\frac{1}{4}(x - 4)^2 - 1$ b) $y = -\frac{1}{4}(x + 4)^2 - 1$
   c) $y = -(x - 1) + 4$ d) $y = -(x - 1)^2 - 4$
   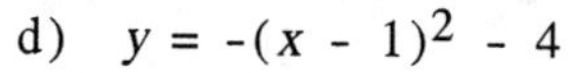
   e) None of these

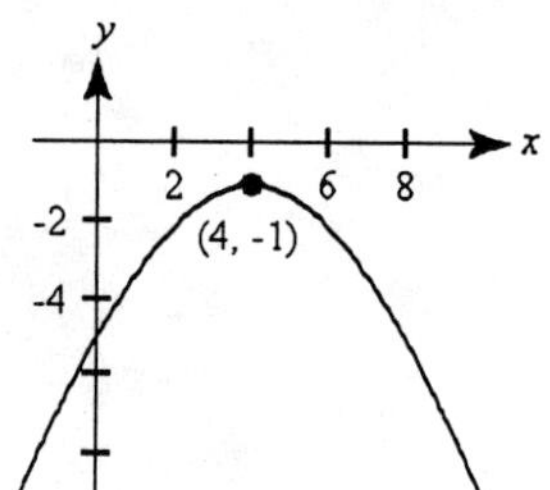

Answer: a Difficulty: 1

10. Write in the form $y = a(x - h)^2 + k$: $y = 2x^2 + 16x + 9$.
   a) $y = 2(x + 4)^2 - 7$ b) $y = 2(x + 2)^2 + 5$
   c) $y = 2(x + 4)^2 - 23$ d) $y = 2(x + 8)^2 + 73$
   e) None of these

Answer: c Difficulty: 1

11. Write in the form $y = a(x - h)^2 + k$: $y = x^2 - 8x + 2$.
   a) $y = (x - 4)^2 - 18$ b) $y = (x - 4)^2 - 14$
   c) $y = (x - 8)^2 + 66$ d) $y = (x - 4)^2 + 18$
   e) None of these

Answer: b Difficulty: 1

SHORT ANSWER

12. Write in the form $y = a(x - h)^2 + k$: $y = -x^2 + 3x - 2$.

Answer:

$$y = -\left(x - \frac{3}{2}\right)^2 + \frac{1}{4}$$

Difficulty: 1

MULTIPLE CHOICE

13. Write in the form $y = a(x - h)^2 + k$: $y = -2x^2 - 4x - 5$.
    a) $y = -2(x - 1)^2 - 2$
    b) $y = (2x - 2)^2 - 1$
    c) $y = -2(x + 2)^2 - 1$
    d) $y = -2(x + 1)^2 - 3$
    e) None of these

Answer: d Difficulty: 2

14. Write in the form $y = a(x - h)^2 + k$: $y = 3x^2 + 12x + 17$.
    a) $y = (x + 2)^2 + \frac{13}{3}$
    b) $y = 3(x + 2)^2 + 21$
    c) $y = 3(x + 2)^2 + 5$
    d) $y = (x + 2)^2 + \frac{29}{3}$
    e) None of these

Answer: c Difficulty: 2

SHORT ANSWER

15. Sketch the graph and label the vertex of the function: $f(x) = (x - 2)^2 + 6$.

Answer: See graph below.

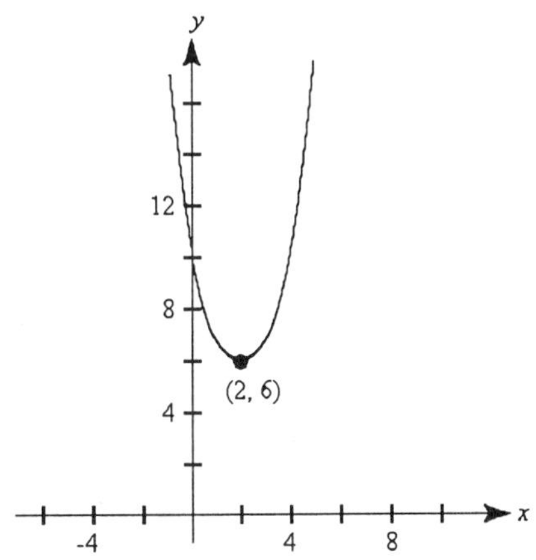

Difficulty: 1

16. Sketch the graph and label the vertex of the function: $f(x) = (x + 5)^2 - 4$.

Answer: See graph below.

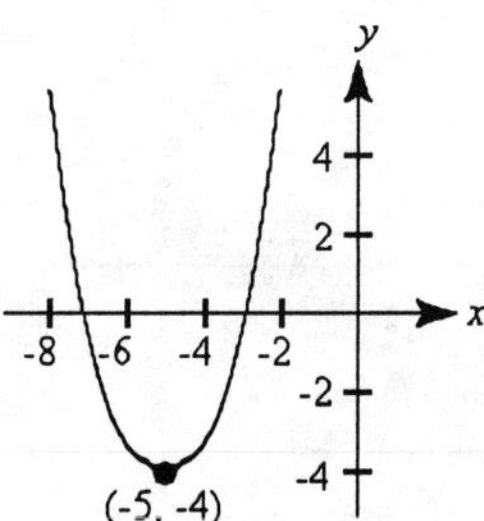

Difficulty: 1

17. Sketch the graph and label the vertex of the function: $f(x) = -x^2 - 4x$.

Answer: See graph below.

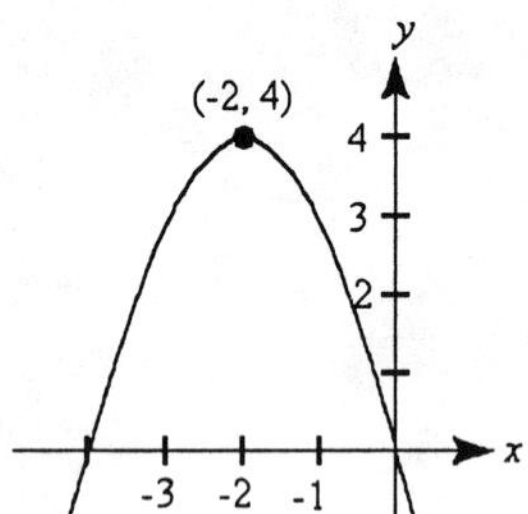

Difficulty: 2

MULTIPLE CHOICE

18. Sketch the graph of the function: $f(x) = x^2 + 4x + 3$. Label the vertex.
a) I b) II c) III d) IV e) None of these

(I) (2, -1)

(II)

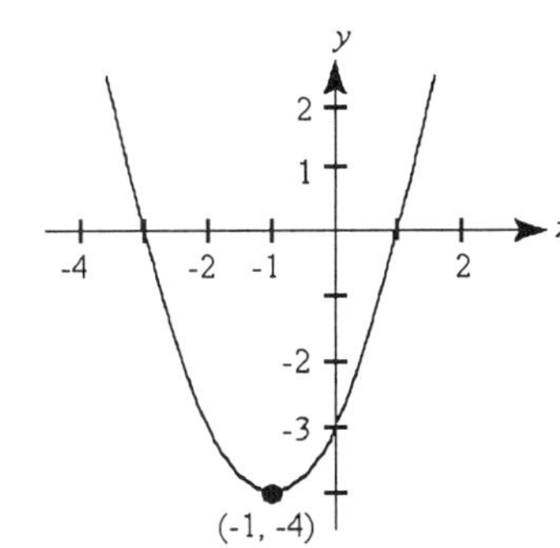

(III) (-2, -1)

(IV)

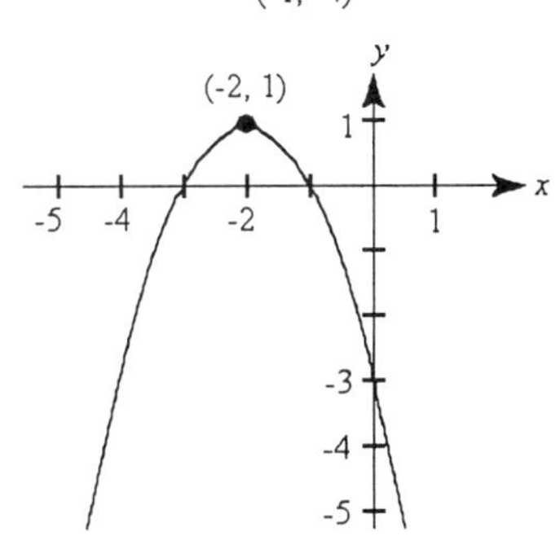

Answer: c Difficulty: 2

19. Sketch the graph of the function: $f(x) = 4x^2 - 8x + 4$. Label the vertex.
a) I b) II c) III d) IV e) None of these

(I) (2, -1)

(II)

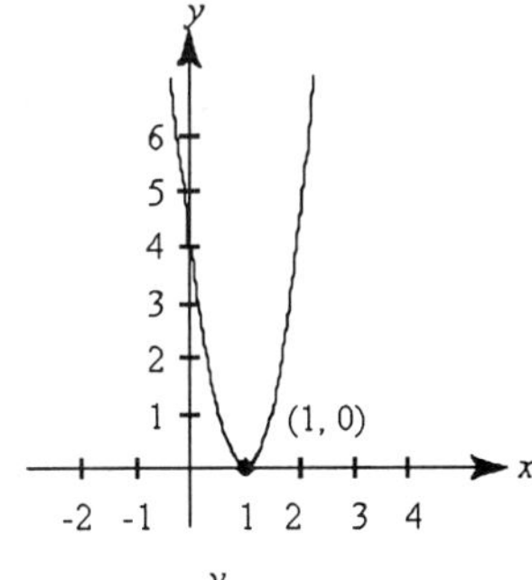

(III) (0, 4)

(IV)

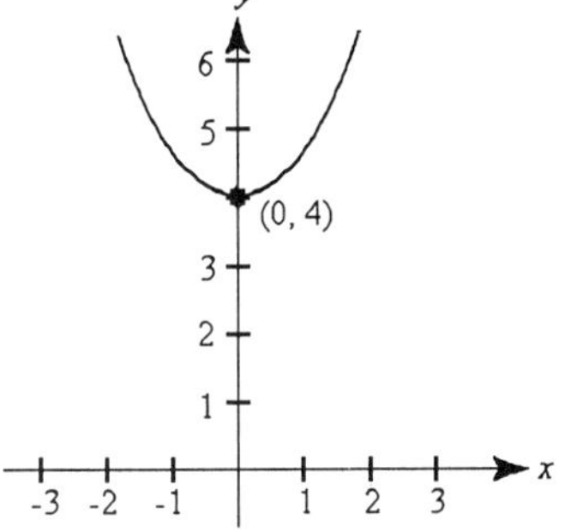

Answer: b Difficulty: 2

SHORT ANSWER

20. Use a graphing utility to graph the quadratic function and identify the vertex and x-intercepts: $f(x) = x^2 - 6x + 8$.

 Answer: See graph below.

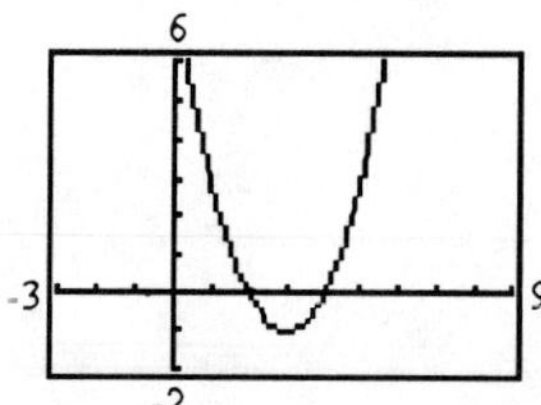

; (3, -1); (2, 0), (4, 0)

 Difficulty: 2 Key 1: T

21. Use a graphing utility to graph the quadratic function and identify the vertex and x-intercepts: $f(x) = x^2 - 2x + 3$.

 Answer: See graph below.

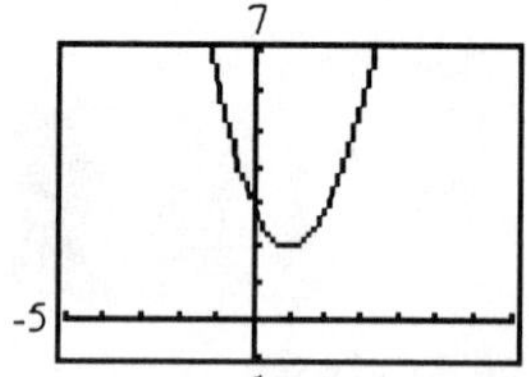

; (1, 2); no x-intercepts

 Difficulty: 2 Key 1: T

22. Use a graphing utility to graph the quadratic function and identify the vertex and x-intercepts: $f(x) = -x^2 + 4x - 3$.

 Answer: See graph below.

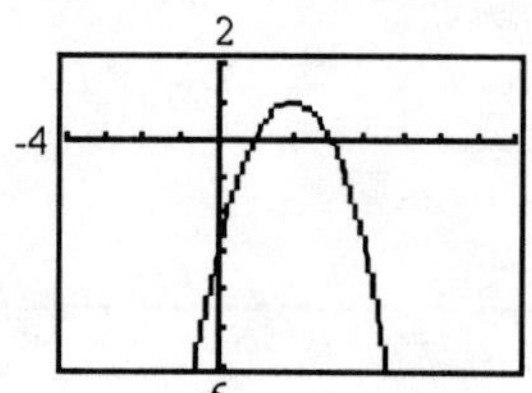

; (2, 1); (1, 0), (3, 0)

 Difficulty: 2 Key 1: T

23. Use a graphing utility to graph the quadratic function and identify the vertex and x-intercepts: $f(x) = -2x^2 - 4x - 3$.

Answer: See graph below.

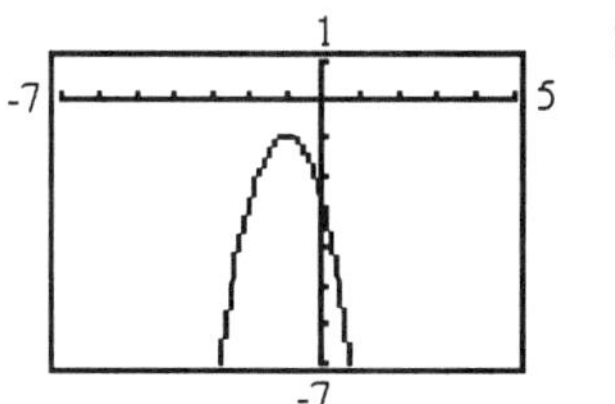

; (-1, 1); no x-intercepts

Difficulty: 2 Key 1: T

24. Use a graphing utility to graph the quadratic function and identify the vertex and x-intercepts: $f(x) = -x^2 - 4x + 5$.

Answer: See graph below.

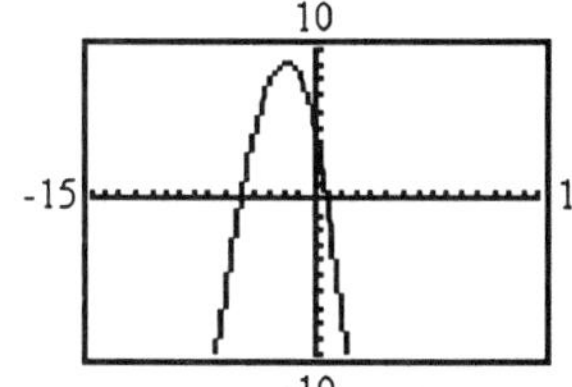

; (-2, 9); (-5, 0), (1, 0)

Difficulty: 2 Key 1: T

25. Use a graphing utility to graph the quadratic function and identify the vertex and x-intercepts: $f(x) = -x^2 + 8x - 12$.

Answer: See graph below.

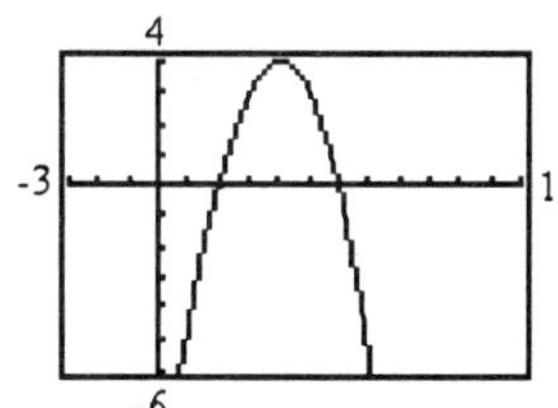

; (4, 4); (2, 0), (6, 0)

Difficulty: 2 Key 1: T

MULTIPLE CHOICE

26. Find the vertex and the x-intercepts of the quadratic function: $f(x) = -x^2 - 6x$.
a) (-3, -9); (0, 0), (-6, 0)
b) (-3, 9); (0, 0), (-6, 0)
c) (-3, -9); (6, 0), (0, 0)
d) (3, -9); (6, 0), (0, 0)
e) None of these

Answer: b Difficulty: 2

27. Find the vertex of the parabola: $y = 4x^2 + 8x + 1$.
   a) (-2, 1)
   b) (1, 13)
   c) (0, 1)
   d) (-1, -3)
   e) None of these

   Answer: d Difficulty: 2

28. Find the vertex of the parabola: $y = 2x^2 + 8x + 9$.
   a) (-2, 1)
   b) (2, 33)
   c) (2, 17)
   d) (-2, -17)
   e) None of these

   Answer: a Difficulty: 2

29. Find the minimum point on the graph of $f(x) = x^2 - 4x + 14$.
   a) (2, 18)
   b) (-2, 18)
   c) (-2, 26)
   d) (2, 10)
   e) None of these

   Answer: d Difficulty: 2

30. Find the maximum point on the graph of $f(x) = -3x^2 + 12x + 1$.
   a) (6, -5)
   b) (-2, -19)
   c) (2, 13)
   d) (1, 14)
   e) None of these

   Answer: c Difficulty: 2

31. Find the x- and y-intercepts: $y = x^2 - 5x + 4$.
   a) (0, -4), (0, 1), (4, 0)
   b) (0, 4), (4, 0), (1, 0)
   c) (0, -4), (-4, 0), (-1, 0)
   d) (0, 4), (-4, 0), (-1, 0)
   e) None of these

   Answer: b Difficulty: 1

32. Find the x- and y- intercepts: $y = x^2 + 3x - 4$.
   a) (0, -4), (-4, 0), (1, 0)
   b) (0, -4), (4, 0), (-1, 0)
   c) (0, 4), (-4, 0), (0, 1)
   d) (4, 0), (0, 4), (-1, 0)
   e) None of these

   Answer: a Difficulty: 1

33. Find the quadratic function that has a maximum point at (-1, 17) and passes through (7, 1).
   a) $y = \frac{1}{4}(-x^2 - 2x + 16)$
   b) $y = -\frac{1}{4}(x + 1)^2 + 17$
   c) $y = (x - 7)^2 + 1$
   d) $y = (x - 1)^2 + 17$
   e) None of these

   Answer: b Difficulty: 2

34. Find the quadratic function that has a minimum at (1, -2) and passes through (0, 0).
   a) $y = 2(x - 1)^2 - 2$
   b) $y = 2(x + 1)^2 - 2$
   c) $y = -2(x - 1)^2 + 2$
   d) $y = -2(x + 1)^2 + 2$
   e) None of these

   Answer: a Difficulty: 2

SHORT ANSWER

35. Find the quadratic function that has a maximum at (-1, 2) and passes through (0, 1).

Answer:

$f(x) = -(x + 1)^2 + 2$

Difficulty: 2

36. Find the quadratic function that has a minimum at $\left(\frac{1}{2}, \frac{3}{4}\right)$ and passes through (2, 6).

Answer:

$f(x) = \frac{7}{3}\left(x - \frac{1}{2}\right) + \frac{3}{4}$

Difficulty: 2

37. Find the quadratic function whose graph opens upward and has x-intercepts at (0, 0) and (6, 0).

Answer:

$f(x) = x^2 - 6x$

Difficulty: 2

MULTIPLE CHOICE

38. Find the quadratic function whose graph opens upward and has x-intercepts at (0, 0) and (-6, 0).

a) $y = x^2 - 6x + 9$ b) $y = x^2 + 12x + 36$ c) $y = x^2 + 6x$
d) $y = x^3 + 12x^2 + 36x$ e) None of these

Answer: c Difficulty: 1

39. Find the quadratic function whose graph opens downward and has x-intercepts at (0, 0) and (-6, 0).

a) $y = -x^2 - 6x + 9$ b) $y = -x^2 - 6x$ c) $y = -x^2 + 6x$
d) $y = x^2 - 6x$ e) None of these

Answer: b Difficulty: 1

40. Find the quadratic function whose graph opens downward and has x-intercepts at (2, 0) and (-3, 0).

a) $y = 6 - x^2$ b) $y = 6 + x - x^2$ c) $y = 6 - x - x^2$
d) $y = 3x^2 - 2x$ e) None of these

Answer: c Difficulty: 1

41. Find the quadratic function whose graph opens upward and has x-intercepts at (-4, 0) and (1, 0).
a) $y = x^2 + 3x - 4$ b) $y = 4 - 3x - x^2$ c) $y = x^2 + 5x + 4$
d) $y = x^2 - 3x - 4$ e) None of these

Answer: a Difficulty: 1

42. Find the number of units that produce a maximum revenue, $R = 95x - 0.1x^2$, where R is the total revenue in dollars and x is the number of units sold.
a) 716 b) 475 c) 371 d) 550 e) None of these

Answer: b Difficulty: 1

43. Find the number of units that produce a maximum revenue, $R = 400x - 0.01x^2$, where R is the total revenue in dollars and x is the number of units sold.
a) 15,000 b) 32,000 c) 4500 d) 20,000 e) None of these

Answer: d Difficulty: 1

44. The profit for a company is given by the equation

$$P = -0.0002x^2 + 140x - 250{,}000$$

where x is the number of units produced. What production level will yield a maximum profit?
a) 700,000 b) 350,000 c) 893 d) 350 e) None of these

Answer: b Difficulty: 2

45. The revenue R for a symphony concert is given by the equation

$$R = -\frac{1}{400}(x^2 - 4800x)$$

where x is the number of tickets sold. Determine the number of tickets that will yield a maximum revenue.
a) 4800 b) 14,400 c) 48,000 d) 2400 e) None of these

Answer: d Difficulty: 2

46. The perimeter of a rectangle is 300 feet. What is the width of the rectangle of maximum area?
a) 100 feet b) 50 feet c) 75 feet
d) 60 feet e) None of these

Answer: c Difficulty: 2

SHORT ANSWER

47. A rancher wishes to enclose a rectangular corral with 320 feet of fencing. The fencing is only required on three sides because of an existing stone wall. What are the dimensions of the corral of maximum area?

Answer: 80 feet by 160 feet Difficulty: 2

48. A rancher wishes to enclose a rectangular corral with 360 feet of fencing. The fencing is only required on three sides because of an existing stone wall. What are the dimensions of the corral of maximum area?

    Answer: 90 feet by 180 feet Difficulty: 2

49. An object is thrown upward from a height of 48 feet with a velocity 32 feet per second. Its height is given by $h(t) = -16t^2 + 32t + 48$ when t is time in seconds. Use a graphing utility to graph the function. Use an appropriate window, estimate its maximum height and the time it strikes the ground. Then algebraically, identify its vertex and x-intercepts.

    Answer: (1, 64); (3, 0); vertex: (1, 64); x-intercepts: (3, 0), (-1, 0)

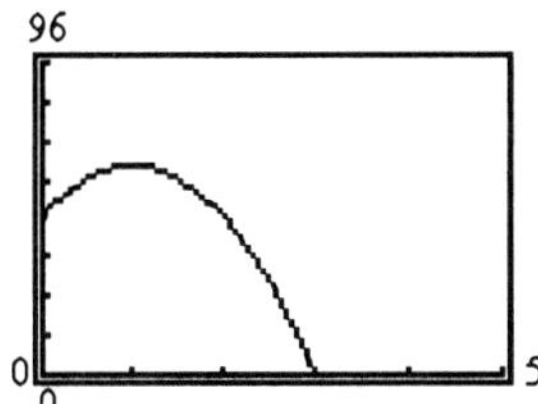

    Difficulty: 2 Key 1: T

Chapter 022: Polynomial Functions of Higher Degree

MULTIPLE CHOICE

1. Determine the left-hand and right-hand behavior of the graph: $y = 4x^2 - 2x + 1$.
   a) Up to the left, down to the right
   b) Down to the left, up to the right
   c) Up to the left, up to the right
   d) Down to the left, down to the right
   e) None of these

   Answer: c Difficulty: 1

2. Determine the left-hand and right-hand behavior of the graph:
   $f(x) = -x^5 + 2x^2 - 1$.
   a) Up to the left, down to the right
   b) Down to the left, up to the right
   c) Up to the left, up to the right
   d) Down to the left, down to the right
   e) None of these

   Answer: a Difficulty: 1

3. Determine the left-hand and right-hand behavior of the graph:
   $f(x) = 3x^5 - 7x^2 + 2$.
   a) Down to the left, up to the right
   b) Up to the right, down to the left
   c) Up to the left, up to the right
   d) Down to the left, down to the right
   e) None of these

   Answer: a Difficulty: 1

SHORT ANSWER

4. Determine the left-hand and right-hand behavior of the graph:
   $f(x) = -4x^3 + 3x^2 - 1$.

   Answer: Up to the left, down to the right Difficulty: 1

5. Determine the left-hand and right-hand behavior of the graph:
   $f(x) = 3x^4 + 2x^3 + 7x^2 + x - 1$.

   Answer: Up to the left and right Difficulty: 1

MULTIPLE CHOICE

6. Determine the left-hand and right-hand behavior of the graph:
   $f(x) = -2x^4 + 3x^3 + 5x^2$.
   a) Up to the left, down to the right
   b) Down to the left, up to the right
   c) Up to the left, up to the right
   d) Down to the left, down to the right
   e) None of these

   Answer: d Difficulty: 1

7. Find all the real zeros of the polynomial function:
$f(x) = x^3 - 3x^2 - 4x$.
a) -1, 4 b) -4, 1 c) -1, 0, 4 d) 0, 4 e) None of these

Answer: c Difficulty: 1

8. Find all the real zeros of the polynomial function: $f(x) = x^6 - x^2$.
a) 0 b) 0, 1 c) 1 d) 0, 1, -1 e) None of these

Answer: d Difficulty: 1

9. Find all the real zeros of the polynomial function: $f(x) = x^3 + x$.
a) 0 b) 0, 1 c) 0, 1, -1 d) 1, -1 e) None of these

Answer: a Difficulty: 1

10. Find all the real zeros of the polynomial function: $f(x) = x^4 - 5x^2 - 36$.
a) 3, 2 b) ± 3 c) $\pm 3, \pm 2$ d) ± 2 e) None of these

Answer: b Difficulty: 2

11. Find all the real zeros of the polynomial function: $g(t) = t^3 + 3t^2 - 16t - 48$.
a) -3 b) 3 c) -4, -3, 4 d) -3, 4 e) None of these

Answer: c Difficulty: 2

SHORT ANSWER

12. Find all the real zeros of the polynomial function: $f(x) = 9x^4 - 37x^2 + 4$.

Answer:
$\pm 2, \pm\frac{1}{3}$
Difficulty: 2

13. Find all the real zeros of the polynomial function:
$f(x) = \frac{1}{4}x^2 + \frac{1}{2}x - \frac{3}{4}$.

Answer: 1, -3 Difficulty: 2

14. Find all the real zeros of the polynomial function: $f(x) = x^3 - 4x$.

Answer: -2, 0, 2 Difficulty: 2

MULTIPLE CHOICE

15. Find a polynomial function with the given zeros: 0, -1, 2.
   a) $f(x) = x(x - 1)(x + 2)$
   b) $f(x) = x(x + 1)(x - 2)$
   c) $f(x) = (x + 1)(x - 2)$
   d) $f(x) = (x + 1)^2(x - 2)$
   e) None of these

   Answer: b Difficulty: 1

16. Find a polynomial function with the given zeros: -2, -2, 1, 3.
   a) $f(x) = (x + 1)(x + 3)(x - 2)$
   b) $f(x) = (x - 2)^2(x - 1)(x - 3)$
   c) $f(x) = (x + 2)(x - 1)(x - 3)$
   d) $f(x) = (x + 2)^2(x - 1)(x - 3)$
   e) None of these

   Answer: d Difficulty: 1

17. Find a polynomial function with the given zeros: 1, 0, -3.
   a) $f(x) = x(x - 3)^3(x + 1)^2$
   b) $f(x) = x^2(x - 1)(x + 3)$
   c) $f(x) = x(x - 3)(x - 1)$
   d) $f(x) = (x - 1)(x + 3)^2$
   e) None of these

   Answer: b Difficulty: 1

18. Find a polynomial function with zeros: 0, 1, -2.
   a) $f(x) = x(x - 1)(x - 2)$
   b) $f(x) = x(x + 1)(x + 2)$
   c) $f(x) = (x - 1)(x + 2)$
   d) $f(x) = x^2(x - 1)(x + 2)$
   e) None of these

   Answer: d Difficulty: 1

19. Find a polynomial function of degree 3 that has zeros: -5, $-\sqrt{2}$, $\sqrt{2}$.
   a) $f(x) = x^3 + 5x^2 - 2x - 10$
   b) $f(x) = x^3 - 5x^2 - 2x + 10$
   c) $f(x) = x^3 + 5x^2 + 2x + 10$
   d) $f(x) = -x^3 + 5x^2 - 2x + 10$
   e) None of these

   Answer: a Difficulty: 2

20. Find a polynomial function of degree 4 that has zeros: 0, -6.
   a) $f(x) = x^2(x - 6)^2$
   b) $f(x) = x^3(x + 6)$
   c) $f(x) = x^2(x + 6)(x - 6)$
   d) $f(x) = (x + 6)^2(x - 6)^2$
   e) None of these

   Answer: b Difficulty: 2

21. Determine the correct function for the given graph.
    a) $f(x) = x^5 + 2$
    b) $f(x) = -x^5 - 2$
    c) $f(x) = x^4 + 2$
    d) $f(x) = x^4 + 2x^2$
    e) None of these

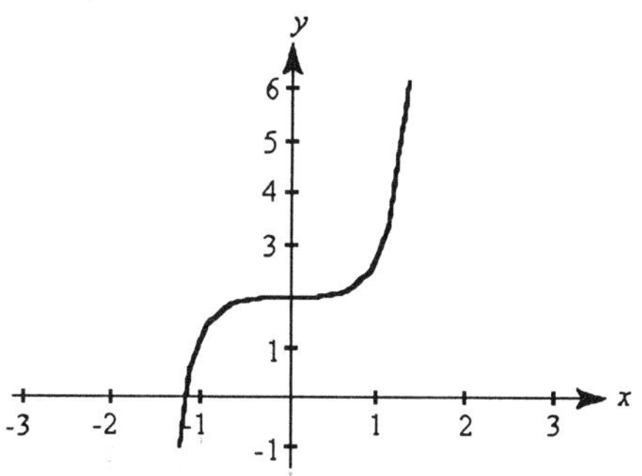

Answer: a Difficulty: 2

22. Determine the correct function for the given graph.
    a) $f(x) = x^3 + x^2 - 6$
    b) $f(x) = -x^3 - x^2 + 6x$
    c) $f(x) = x^3 + x^2 - 6x$
    d) $f(x) = x^4 + x^2 - 6x$
    e) None of these

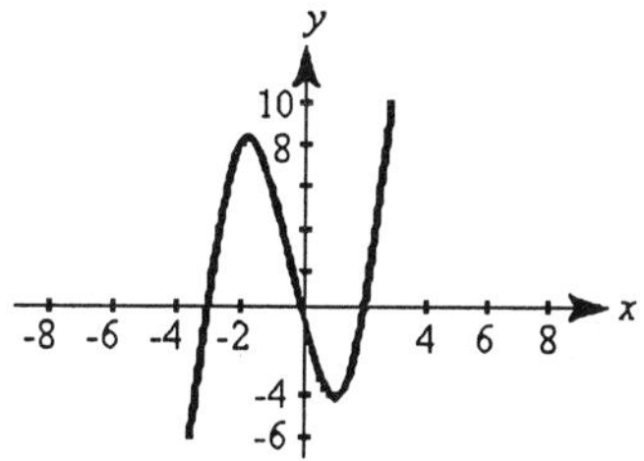

Answer: c Difficulty: 2

23. Determine the correct function for the given graph.
    a) $f(x) = 2x^3 - 3x^2$
    b) $f(x) = 3x^4 - 2x^3$
    c) $f(x) = 2x^3 + 3x^2$
    d) $f(x) = 3x^2 - 2x^3$
    e) None of these

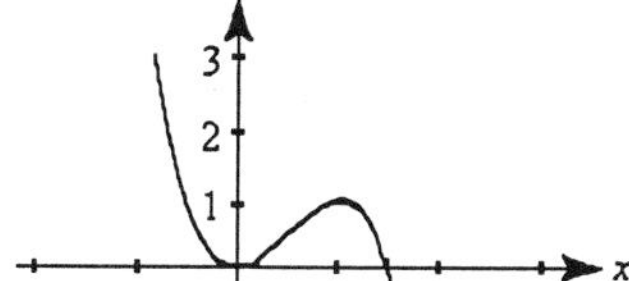

Answer: d Difficulty: 2

24. Determine the correct function for the given graph.
   a) $f(x) = 2x^4 + 8x^2$
   b) $f(x) = -2x^4 - 8x^2$
   c) $f(x) = 8x^2 - 2x^4$
   d) $f(x) = 2x^4 - 8x^2$
   e) None of these

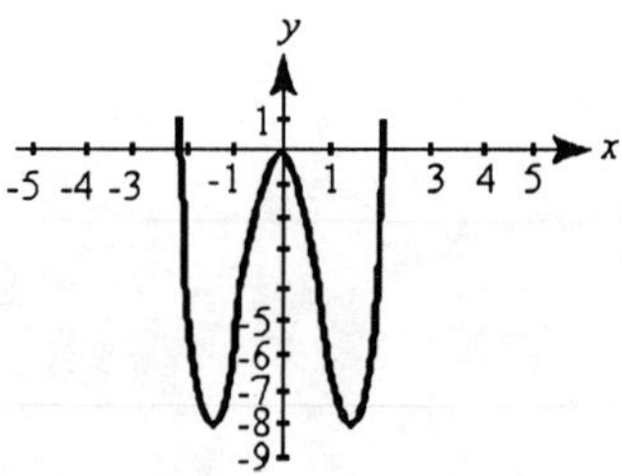

Answer: d Difficulty: 2

SHORT ANSWER

25. Use a graph utility to graph the function: $f(x) = 2x^3 - 3x^2$.

Answer: See graph below.

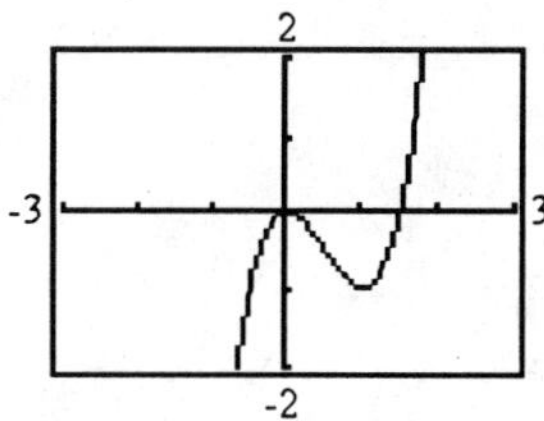

Difficulty: 1 Key 1: T

26. Use a graph utility to graph the function: $f(x) = -2x^4 + x$.

Answer: See graph below.

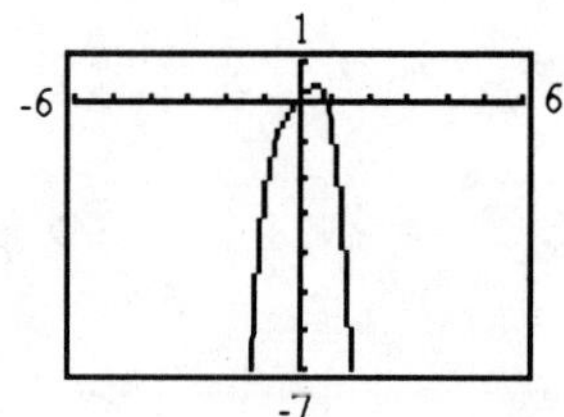

Difficulty: 1 Key 1: T

27. Use a graph utility to graph the function: $f(x) = -x^5 + 4$.

    Answer: See graph below.

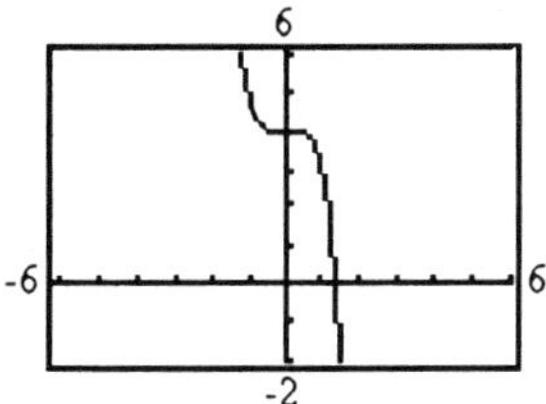

    Difficulty: 1 Key 1: T

28. Use a graph utility to graph the function: $f(x) = x^4 + 2x^3 + 1$.

    Answer: See graph below.

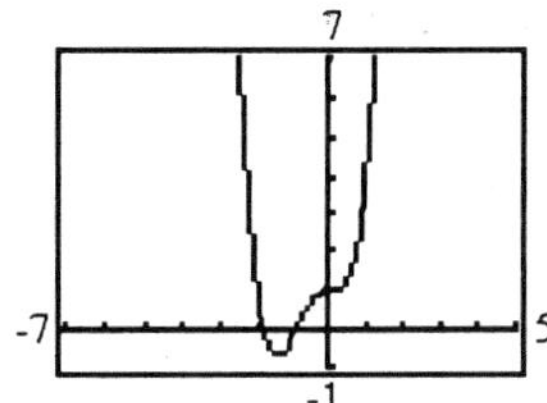

    Difficulty: 1 Key 1: T

MULTIPLE CHOICE

29. Use the Intermediate Value Theorem to estimate the real zero in the interval [0, 1]: $f(x) = 3x^3 + 7x - 9$.

    a) Between 0.2 and 0.3
    b) Between 0.5 and 0.7
    c) Between 0.7 and 0.8
    d) Between 0.9 and 1.0
    e) None of these

    Answer: d Difficulty: 2 Key 1: T

30. Use the Intermediate Value Theorem to estimate the real zero in the interval [1, 2]: $f(x) = 3x^3 - 2x^2 - 2$.

    a) Between 1.0 and 1.1
    b) Between 1.1 and 1.2
    c) Between 1.3 and 1.4
    d) Between 0.7 and 0.8
    e) None of these

    Answer: b Difficulty: 2 Key 1: T

31. Use the Intermediate Value Theorem to estimate the real zero in the interval [0, 1]: $f(x) = 2x^3 + 7x^2 - 1$.

a) Between 0.1 and 0.2
b) Between 0.2 and 0.3
c) Between 0.3 and 0.4
d) Between 0.4 and 0.5
e) None of these

Answer: c Difficulty: 2 Key 1: T

32. Use the Intermediate Value Theorem to estimate the real zero in the interval [1, 2]: $f(x) = x^4 - 4x - 1$.

a) Between 1.5 and 1.6
b) Between 1.6 and 1.7
c) Between 1.7 and 1.8
d) Between 1.8 and 1.9
e) None of these

Answer: b Difficulty: 2 Key 1: T

33. The function $f(x)$ has a zero of 2 with multiplicity 3. We know
a) since 3 is an odd number, the graph touches but does not cross the x-axis.
b) since 3 is an odd number, the graph crosses the x-axis.
c) since 2 is an even number, the graph touches but does not cross the x-axis.
d) since 2 is an even number, the graph crosses the x-axis.
e) None of these

Answer: b Difficulty: 1

34. The function $f(x)$ has a zero of -1 with multiplicity 1. We know
a) since the multiplicity is 1, the graph crosses the x-axis.
b) since the multiplicity is 1, the graph touches but does not cross the x-axis.
c) since the zero is -1, the graph crosses the y-axis at -1.
d) since the zero is -1, the graph goes down to the left.
e) None of these

Answer: a Difficulty: 1

35. The function $f(x)$ has a zero of 3 with multiplicity 2. We know
a) since the zero is 3, the graph crosses the y-axis at 3.
b) since the zero is 3, the graph goes up to the right.
c) since the multiplicity is 2, the graph crosses the x-axis.
d) since the multiplicity is 2, the graph touches but does not cross the x-axis.
e) None of these

Answer: d Difficulty: 1

36. An open box is made from a 16-inch square piece of material by cutting equal squares with sides of length, x, from all corners and turning up the sides. The volume of the box is $V(x) = 4x(8 - x)^2$. Estimate the value of x for which the volume is maximum.
a) 2.7 inches
b) 3.0 inches
c) 1.9 inches
d) 8 inches
e) None of these

Answer: a Difficulty: 2

37. An open box is made from a 24-inch square piece of material by cutting equal squares with sides of length, x, from all corners and turning up the sides. The volume of the box is $V(x) = 4x(12 - x)^2$. Estimate the value of x for which the volume is maximum.

a) 12 inches b) 3 inches c) 6 inches
d) 4 inches e) None of these

Answer: d Difficulty: 2

38. An open box is made from a 10-inch square piece of material by cutting equal squares with sides of length, x, from all corners and turning up the sides. The volume of the box is $V(x) = 4x(5 - x)^2$. Estimate the value of x for which the volume is maximum.

a) 2.0 inches b) 1.7 inches c) 3.4 inches
d) 2.5 inches e) None of these

Answer: b Difficulty: 2

SHORT ANSWER

39. An open box is to be made from a 16-inch square piece of material by cutting equal squares from each corner and turning up the sides. Verify the volume of the box is $V(x) = 4x(8 - x)^2$. Graph the function using a graphing utility and use the graph to estimate the value of x for which $V(x)$ is maximum.

Answer:

$$\begin{aligned} V(x) &= x \cdot (16 - 2x) \cdot (16 - 2x) \\ &= x \cdot 2(8 - x) \cdot 2(8 - x) \\ &= 4x(8 - x)^2 \end{aligned}$$

When $x \approx 2.67$ inches, $V(x)$ is a maximum ≈ 303.4 inches^3.

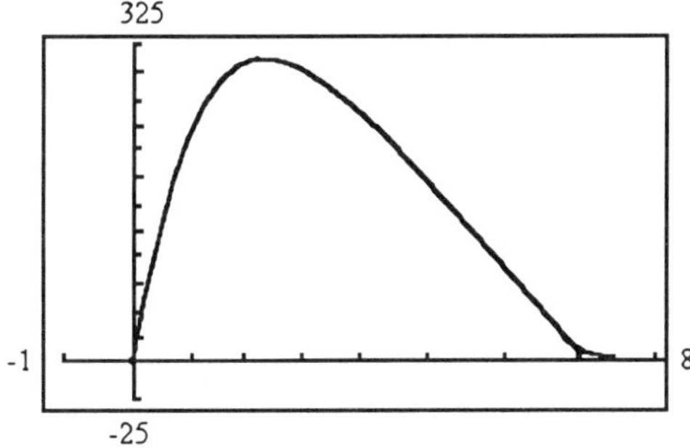

Difficulty: 2 Key 1: T

40. An open box is to be made from a 20-inch square piece of material by cutting equal squares from each corner and turning up the sides. Verify the volume of the box is $V(x) = 4x(10 - x)^2$. Graph the function using a graphing utility and use the graph to estimate the value of x for which $V(x)$ is maximum.

Answer:
$V(x) = x \cdot (20 - 2x) \cdot (20 - 2x)$
$= x \cdot 2(10 - x) \cdot 2(10 - x)$
$= 4x(10 - x)^2$
When $x \approx 3.33$ inches, $V(x)$ is a maximum ≈ 592.6 inches^3.

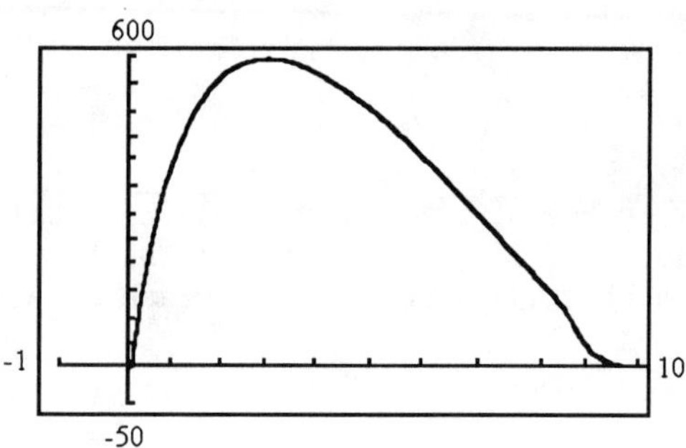

Difficulty: 2 Key 1: T

41. An open box is to be made from a 14-inch square piece of material by cutting equal squares from each corner and turning up the sides. Verify the volume of the box is $V(x) = 4x(7 - x)^2$. Graph the function using a graphing utility and use the graph to estimate the value of x for which $V(x)$ is maximum.

Answer:
$V(x) = x \cdot (14 - 2x) \cdot (14 - 2x)$
$= x \cdot 2(7 - x) \cdot 2(7 - x)$
$= 4x(7 - x)^2$
When $x \approx 2.33$ inches, $V(x)$ is a maximum ≈ 203.3 inches^3.

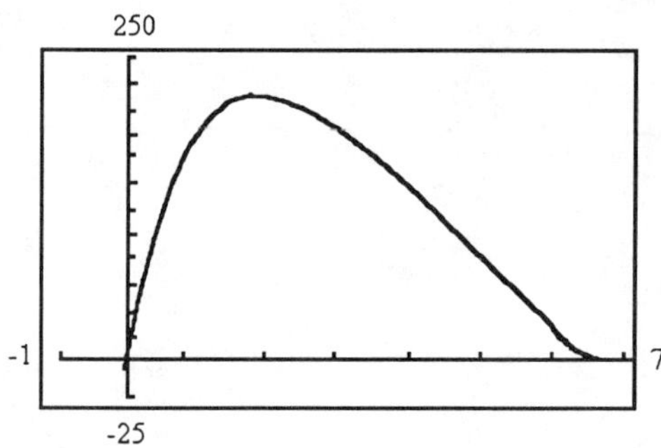

Difficulty: 2 Key 1: T

42. An open box is to be made from an 8-inch square piece of material by cutting equal squares from each corner and turning up the sides. Verify the volume of the box is $V(x) = 4x(4 - x)^2$. Graph the function using a graphing utility and use the graph to estimate the value of x for which $V(x)$ is maximum.

Answer:

$$V(x) = x \cdot (8 - 2x) \cdot (8 - 2x)$$
$$= x \cdot 2(4 - x) \cdot 2(4 - x)$$
$$= 4x(4 - x)^2$$

When $x \approx 1.33$ inches, $V(x)$ is a maximum ≈ 37.9 inches^3.

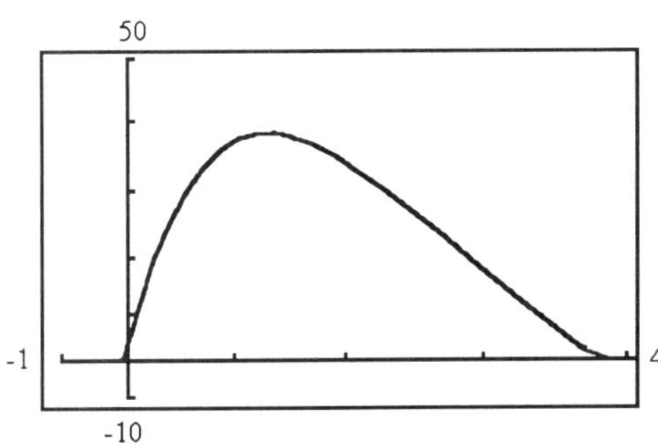

Difficulty: 2 Key 1: T

Chapter 023: Polynomial and Synthetic Division

MULTIPLE CHOICE

1. Divide: $(9x^3 - 6x^2 - 8x - 3) \div (3x + 2)$.

a) $3x^2 - \frac{8}{3}x - \frac{7/3}{3x + 2}$

b) $3x^2 - 4x - 2 + \frac{7}{3x + 2}$

c) $3x^2 - 4x - \frac{3}{3x + 2}$

d) $3x^2 - 4x - \frac{16}{3} + \frac{23/3}{3x + 2}$

e) None of these

Answer: c Difficulty: 1

2. Divide: $(6x^3 + 7x^2 - 15x + 6) \div (2x - 1)$.

a) $3x^2 + 2x - \frac{17}{2} - \frac{5}{2(2x - 1)}$

b) $3x^2 + 5x - 5 + \frac{1}{2x - 1}$

c) $3x^2 + 5x + 5 + \frac{11}{2x - 1}$

d) $3x^2 + 4x - 17 + \frac{29/2}{2x - 1}$

e) None of these

Answer: b Difficulty: 1

3. Divide: $(3x^4 + 2x^3 - 3x + 1) \div (x^2 + 1)$.

a) $3x^2 + 2x + 3 - \frac{5x + 2}{x^2 + 1}$

b) $3x^2 + 2x - 3 + \frac{-5x + 4}{x^2 + 1}$

c) $3x^2 - x^2 - 4 + \frac{5}{x^2 + 1}$

d) $3x^2 - x + 1 + \frac{-4x + 5}{x^2 + 1}$

e) None of these

Answer: b Difficulty: 1

SHORT ANSWER

4. Divide: $(6x^4 - 4x^3 + x^2 + 10x - 1) \div (3x + 1)$.

Answer:

$2x^3 - 2x^2 + x + 3 - \frac{4}{3x + 1}$

Difficulty: 1

5. Divide: $(2x^4 + 7x - 2) \div (x^2 + 3)$.

Answer:

$2x^2 - 6 + \frac{7x + 16}{x^2 + 3}$

Difficulty: 2

MULTIPLE CHOICE

6. Divide by long division: $(2x^3 - x^2 - 3x + 4) \div (2x + 1)$.
   a) $x^2 - x - 1 + \dfrac{5}{2x + 1}$
   b) $x^2 - \dfrac{3}{2} + \dfrac{5}{2(2x + 1)}$
   c) $x^2 - x - 1 + \dfrac{3}{2x + 1}$
   d) $x^2 - x - 2 + \dfrac{6}{2x + 1}$
   e) None of these

   Answer: a Difficulty: 1

7. Divide by long division: $(x^4 + 3x^3 - 3x^2 - 12x - 4) \div (x^2 + 3x + 1)$.
   a) $x^2 - 2 - \dfrac{6x + 2}{x^2 + 3x + 1}$
   b) $x^2 - 4$
   c) $x^2 + 2 - \dfrac{18x - 6}{x^2 + 3x + 1}$
   d) $x^2 - 4x$
   e) None of these

   Answer: b Difficulty: 1

8. Use synthetic division to divide: $(5x^4 - 2x^2 + 1) \div (x + 1)$.
   a) $5x^3 - 5x^2 + 3x - 3 + \dfrac{4}{x + 1}$
   b) $5x^2 - 7x + 8$
   c) $5x^2 + 3x + 4$
   d) $5x^3 + 5x^2 + 3x + 3 + \dfrac{4}{x + 1}$
   e) None of these

   Answer: a Difficulty: 1

9. Use synthetic division to divide: $(3x^4 + 4x^3 - 2x^2 + 1) \div (x + 2)$.
   a) $3x^3 + 10x^2 + 18x + 37$
   b) $3x^3 - 2x^2 + 2x - 3$
   c) $3x^3 - 2x^2 + 2x - 4 + \dfrac{9}{x + 2}$
   d) $3x^3 + 10x^2 + 18x + 36 + \dfrac{73}{x + 2}$
   e) None of these

   Answer: c Difficulty: 1

SHORT ANSWER

10. Use synthetic division to divide: $(x^4 + 2x^2 - x + 1) \div (x - 2)$.

    Answer:

    $x^3 + 2x^2 + 6x + 11 + \dfrac{23}{x - 2}$

    Difficulty: 1

MULTIPLE CHOICE

11. Divide: $(x^3 + 4x^2 + 4x + 3) \div (x + 3)$.
 a) $x^2 + 7x - 17 + \dfrac{54}{x + 3}$
 b) $x^2 - x + 7 - \dfrac{21}{x + 3}$
 c) $x^2 + x + 1$
 d) $x^2 + x + 1 + \dfrac{6}{x + 3}$
 e) None of these

Answer: c Difficulty: 1

12. Divide: $(x^3 + 8) \div (x + 2)$.
 a) $x^2 - 2x + 4$
 b) $x^2 + 4$
 c) $x^2 + 2x + 4$
 d) $x^2 + 2x - 4$
 e) None of these

Answer: a Difficulty: 1

13. Divide by synthetic division: $(x^3 - 6x^2 - 3x + 1) \div (x + 2)$.
 a) $x^2 - 4x - 11 - \dfrac{21}{x + 2}$
 b) $x^2 - 8x + 13 - \dfrac{25}{x + 2}$
 c) $x^2 - 4x + 5 - \dfrac{9}{x + 2}$
 d) $x^2 - 8x + 13 - \dfrac{27}{x + 2}$
 e) None of these

Answer: b Difficulty: 1

14. Divide by synthetic division: $(2x^3 + 3x^2 - 19x - 1) \div (x + 4)$.
 a) $2x^2 - 5x + 1 - \dfrac{3}{x + 4}$
 b) $2x^2 - x - 15 + \dfrac{54}{x + 4}$
 c) $2x^2 - 5x + 1 - \dfrac{5}{x + 4}$
 d) $2x^2 + 11x + 25 + \dfrac{99}{x + 4}$
 e) None of these

Answer: c Difficulty: 1

15. Divide using synthetic division: $(x^3 - x - 6) \div (x - 2)$.
 a) $x^2 - x - 3$
 b) $x^2 + 2x + 3$
 c) $x^2 + x + 2 + \dfrac{2}{x - 2}$
 d) $x^2 + 2x + 5$
 e) None of these

Answer: b Difficulty: 1

16. Use synthetic division to determine which of the following is a solution of the equation: $3x^4 - 2x^3 + 26x^2 - 18x - 9 = 0$.
 a) 3
 b) 1
 c) -3
 d) $\dfrac{1}{3}$
 e) None of these

Answer: b Difficulty: 2

17. Use synthetic division to determine which of the following is a solution of the equation: $3x^3 - 11x^2 - 6x + 8 = 0$.
a) $\frac{2}{3}$ b) -1 c) 4 d) All of these e) None of these

Answer: d Difficulty: 1

18. Use synthetic division to determine which of the following is a solution of the equation: $6x^4 - 11x^3 - 10x^2 + 19x - 6 = 0$.
a) 2 b) 3 c) -2 d) -3 e) None of these

Answer: a Difficulty: 1

19. Use synthetic division to factor the polynomial $x^3 - x^2 - 10x - 8$ completely if -2 is a zero.
a) $(x - 2)(x - 4)(x + 1)$ b) -2, 4, -1 c) $(x + 2)(x + 1)(x - 4)$
d) $(x + 2)(x + 4)(x - 1)$ e) Does not factor

Answer: c Difficulty: 1

20. Use synthetic division to factor the polynomial $x^3 - 4x^2 - 7x + 10$ completely if -2 is a zero.
a) $(x + 2)(x + 1)(x + 5)$ b) -2, 1, 5 c) $(x + 2)(x - 1)(x - 5)$
d) $(x - 2)(x - 1)(x + 5)$ e) Does not factor

Answer: c Difficulty: 1

21. Use synthetic division to factor the polynomial $x^3 + 4x^2 + x - 6$ completely if 1 is a zero.
a) $(x + 1)(x + 2)(x + 3)$ b) $(x - 1)(x - 2)(x - 3)$
c) 1, -2, -3 d) $(x - 1)(x + 2)(x + 3)$
e) Does not factor

Answer: d Difficulty: 1

22. Use synthetic division to factor the polynomial $2x^3 - 7x^2 + 7x - 2$ completely if $\frac{1}{2}$ is a zero.
a) $2(x + \frac{1}{2})(x - 1)(x - 2)$ b) $2(x - \frac{1}{2})(x + 1)(x + 2)$
c) $2(x - \frac{1}{2})(x - 1)(x - 2)$ d) $2(x + \frac{1}{2})(x + 1)(x + 2)$
e) Does not factor

Answer: c Difficulty: 2

23. Factor the polynomial $x^3 + 3x^2 - 10x - 24$ completely knowing that $x - 3$ is a factor.
a) $(x - 3)(x + 2)(x + 4)$ b) $(x - 3)(x - 2)(x - 4)$
c) $(x - 3)(x + 1)(x + 7)$ d) $(x - 3)(x - 1)(x + 7)$
e) None of these

Answer: a Difficulty: 1

SHORT ANSWER

24. Factor the polynomial $x^3 + 2x^2 - 7x - 14$ completely if $(x + 2)$ is a factor.

Answer:

$(x + 2)(x + \sqrt{7})(x - \sqrt{7})$

Difficulty: 2

25. Factor the polynomial $3x^3 - 2x^2 - 15x + 10$ completely if $\frac{2}{3}$ is a zero.

Answer:

$(3x - 2)(x + \sqrt{5})(x - \sqrt{5})$

Difficulty: 2

MULTIPLE CHOICE

26. Express $f(x) = 3x^4 - 2x^2 + x - 1$ in the form $f(x) = (x - k)q(x) + r$ for $k = -1$.
a) $f(x) = (x - 1)(3x^3 + 3x^2 + x + 2) + 1$
b) $f(x) = (x + 1)(3x^3 - 3x^2 + x) - 1$
c) $f(x) = (x - 1)(3x^3 + x^2 + 2x) + 1$
d) $f(x) = (x + 1)(3x^3 - 5x^2 + 6x) - 7$
e) None of these

Answer: b Difficulty: 1

27. Express $f(x) = 2x^3 - 3x + 2$ in the form $f(x) = (x - k)q(x) + r$ for $k = -2$.
a) $f(x) = (x - 2)(2x^2 - x) + 4$ b) $f(x) = (x + 2)(2x^2 - 7x) + 16$
c) $f(x) = (x - 2)(2x^2 + 4x + 5)$ d) $f(x) = (x + 2)(2x^2 - 4x + 5) - 8$
e) None of these

Answer: d Difficulty: 1

28. Express $f(x) = 3x^4 - 7x^3 + x - 1$ in the form $f(x) = (x - k)q(x) + r$ for $k = 2$.
a) $f(x) = (x + 2)(3x^3 - 13x^2 + 26x - 51) + 101$
b) $f(x) = (x - 2)(3x^3 - x^2 - 2x - 3) - 7$
c) $f(x) = (x + 2)(3x^3 - 13x^2 - 25x) + 49$
d) $f(x) = (x - 2)(3x^3 - x^2 - x) - 3$
e) None of these

Answer: b Difficulty: 1

29. Express $f(x) = 2x^3 - 5x^2 + 3$ in the form $f(x) = (x - k)q(x) + r$ for $k = -2$.
a) $f(x) = (x + 2)(2x^2 - 9x + 18) - 33$
b) $f(x) = (x - 2)(2x^2 - x - 2) - 1$
c) $f(x) = (x + 2)(2x^2 - 9x) + 21$
d) $f(x) = (x - 2)(2x^2 - x) + 1$
e) None of these

Answer: a Difficulty: 1

30. Use synthetic division to find $f(-2)$: $f(x) = 4x^3 + 3x + 10$.
a) 20 b) -20 c) 36 d) -28 e) None of these

Answer: d Difficulty: 2

31. Use synthetic division to find $f(-3)$: $f(x) = 3x^3 + 2x^2 - 1$.
a) 98 b) $3x^2 - 7x + 21 - \dfrac{64}{x + 3}$ c) -64
d) 20 e) None of these

Answer: c Difficulty: 1

32. Use synthetic division to find $f(3)$: $f(x) = x^4 + 2x^2 - x - 1$.
a) $x^3 + 3x^2 + 11x + 32 + \dfrac{95}{x - 3}$ b) 95 c) 101
d) 122 e) None of these

Answer: b Difficulty: 1

33. Use synthetic division to find $f(-2)$: $f(x) = 3x^4 - 2x^2 + 1$.
a) 23 b) -16 c) 17 d) 21 e) None of these

Answer: e Difficulty: 1

34. Simplify the rational function: $f(x) = \dfrac{x^3 + 4x^2 - 3x + 10}{x + 5}$.
a) $f(x) = 0$
b) $f(x) = x^2 - x + 2$
c) $f(x) = 5x^2 - 3x + 2$
d) $f(x) = x^2 + 9x + 42$
e) None of these

Answer: b Difficulty: 1

35. Simplify the rational function: $f(x) = \dfrac{x^5 - 1}{x - 1}$.
a) $f(x) = x^4$
b) $f(x) = x^4 + x^3 + x^2 + x$
c) $f(x) = x^4 + x^3 + x^2 + x + 1$
d) $f(x) = x^4 - x^3 + x^2 - x + 1$
e) None of these

Answer: c Difficulty: 1

36. Simplify the rational expression: $\dfrac{2x^4 - x^3 - 4x^2 + x - 3}{2x + 3}$.

a) $x^3 + x^2 - x + 1$
b) $x^3 - 2x^2 - 5x - 1$
c) $x^3 + x^2 - 5x - 1$
d) $(x^3 - 2x^2 + x - 1)$
e) None of these

Answer: d Difficulty: 1

37. Simplify the rational expression: $\dfrac{4x^5 - 3x^4 + 8x^3 - 3x^2 + 6}{x^2 + 2}$.

a) $4x^3 - 3x^2 + 6x + 3 + \dfrac{12x}{x^2 + 2}$
b) $4x^3 - 3x^2 + 3$
c) $4x^3 - 3x^2 - 9 + \dfrac{24}{x^2 + 2}$
d) $4x^3 + 5x^2 + 6$
e) None of these

Answer: b Difficulty: 2

38. A rectangular room has a volume of $3x^3 - 2x^2 - 11x + 10$ cubic feet. The height of the room is $x - 1$. Find the algebraic expression for the number of square feet of floor space in the room.

a) 20
b) $3x^3 - 2x^2 - 10x + 9$
c) $3x^2 + x - 10$
d) $3x^2 - 5x - 5 + \dfrac{15}{x - 1}$
e) None of these

Answer: c Difficulty: 2

39. A rectangular room has a volume of $3x^3 + 20x^2 + 10$ cubic feet. The height of the room is $x + 1$. Find the algebraic expression for the number of square feet of floor space in the room.

a) 126
b) $3x^3 + 20x^2 + 26x + 9$
c) $3x^2 + 23x + 50 + \dfrac{60}{x + 1}$
d) $3x^2 + 17x + 10$
e) None of these

Answer: d Difficulty: 2

40. A rectangular room has a volume of $3x^3 + 8x^2 + 5x + 2$ cubic feet. The height of the room is $x + 2$. Find the algebraic expression for the number of square feet of floor space in the room.

a) 86
b) $3x^3 + 8x^2 + 4x$
c) $3x^2 + 2x + 1$
d) $3x^2 + 14x + 33 + \dfrac{68}{x + 2}$
e) None of these

Answer: c Difficulty: 2

SHORT ANSWER

41. A rectangular room has a volume of $4x^3 - 7x^2 - 16x + 3$ cubic feet. The height of the room is $x - 3$. Find the algebraic expression for the number of square feet of floor space in the room.

Answer:

$4x^2 + 5x - 1$

Difficulty: 2

42. A rectangular room has a volume of $2x^3 - 17x + 3$ cubic feet. The height of the room is $x + 3$. Find the algebraic expression for the number of square feet of floor space in the room.

Answer:

$2x^2 - 6x + 1$

Difficulty: 2

43. Use the root-finding capabilities of a graphing utility to approximate the indicated zero. Use synthetic division to verify your result and then factor the polynomial completely: $f(x) = 6x^3 + 17x^2 - 4x - 3$.

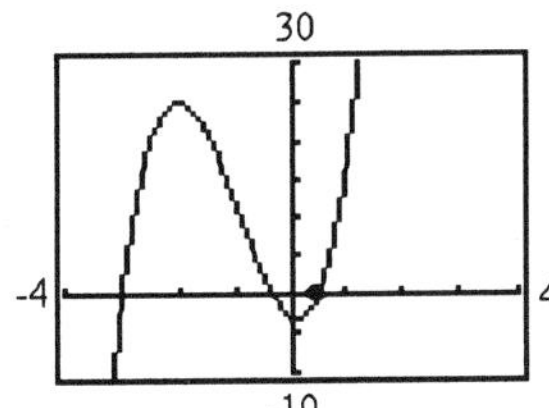

Answer:

$x = \frac{1}{2}$, $f(x) = (2x - 1)(x + 3)(3x + 1)$

Difficulty: 2 Key 1: T

44. Use the root-finding capabilities of a graphing utility to approximate the indicated zero. Use synthetic division to verify your result and then factor the polynomial completely: $f(x) = 10x^3 + 3x^2 - 16x + 3$.

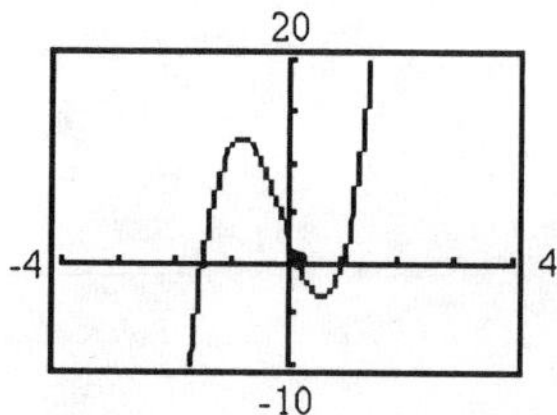

Answer:
$x = \frac{1}{5}$; $f(x) = (5x - 1)(2x + 3)(x - 1)$

Difficulty: 2 Key 1: T

45. Use the root-finding capabilities of a graphing utility to approximate the indicated zero. Use synthetic division to verify your result and then factor the polynomial completely: $f(x) = 3x^3 + 2x^2 - 7x + 2$.

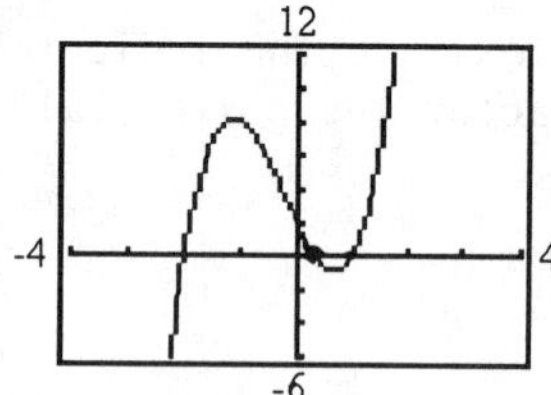

Answer:
$x = \frac{1}{3}$; $f(x) = (3x - 1)(x + 2)(x - 1)$

Difficulty: 2 Key 1: T

46. Use the root-finding capabilities of a graphing utility to approximate the indicated zero. Use synthetic division to verify your result and then factor the polynomial completely: $f(x) = 6x^3 - 13x^2 + 4$.

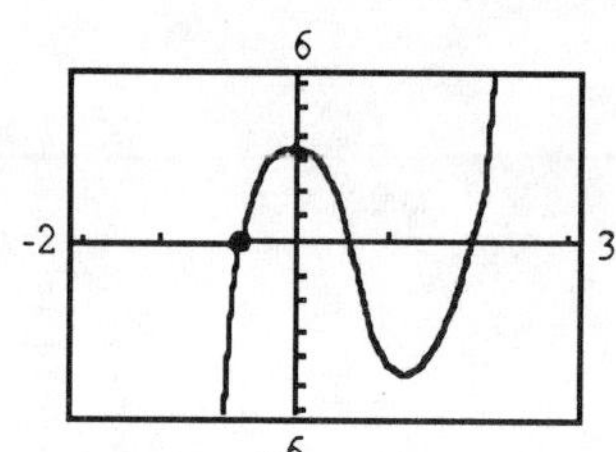

Answer:
$x = -\frac{1}{2}$; $f(x) = (2x + 1)(x - 2)(3x - 2)$

Difficulty: 2 Key 1: T

Chapter 024: Complex Numbers

MULTIPLE CHOICE

1. Find b so that the equation is true: $(a + 3) + (2b - 1)i = 5 + 9i$.
   a) 2 b) 4 c) 5 d) 8 e) None of these

   Answer: c Difficulty: 1

2. Find a so that the equation is true: $(a + 6) + (3b + 1)i = 4 + 3i$.
   a) -2 b) $\frac{2}{3}$ c) 10 d) $\frac{3}{2}$ e) None of these

   Answer: a Difficulty: 1

3. Find b so that the equation is true: $(2a + 1) + (b - 2)i = 3 + 7i$.
   a) -1 b) 1 c) 5 d) 9 e) None of these

   Answer: d Difficulty: 1

4. Find b so that the equation is true: $(3a + 1) + (b - 6)i = 4 - 5i$.
   a) -1 b) 1 c) 7 d) 5 e) None of these

   Answer: b Difficulty: 1

5. Find b so that the equation is true: $(2a + 1) + (2b + 3)i = 4 - 7i$.
   a) $\frac{2}{3}$ b) 5 c) -5 d) -2 e) None of these

   Answer: c Difficulty: 1

6. Write in standard form: $3 + \sqrt{-9} - 16 + 2i^2$.
   a) $-15 - 3i$ b) $-15 + 3i$ c) -18
   d) $-17 + 3i$ e) None of these

   Answer: b Difficulty: 1

7. Write in standard form: $2i^3 - 3\sqrt{-16} + 2$.
   a) $2 - 14i$ b) $14 - 2i$ c) $2 + 10i$
   d) $2 - 4i$ e) None of these

   Answer: a Difficulty: 1

8. Write in standard form: $4 - \sqrt{-8}$.
   a) $4 - 2i$ b) $4 + 2\sqrt{2}i$ c) $4 - 2\sqrt{2}i$
   d) $4 + 2\sqrt{2}$ e) None of these

   Answer: c Difficulty: 1

9. Write in standard form: $2i^4 + 7i^3$.
a) $2 - 7i$ b) $-2 + 7i$ c) $7 - 2i$
d) $-7 + 2i$ e) None of these

Answer: a Difficulty: 1

10. Write in standard form: $(16 + 2i) - (3 + 4i^2)$.
a) $9 + 2i$ b) $13 - 2i$ c) $15 + 2i$
d) $17 + 2i$ e) None of these

Answer: d Difficulty: 1

11. Simplify, then write your result in standard form: $(3 + 6i) - 2(i + 7) - \sqrt{-4}$.
a) $1 + 4i$ b) $-11 + 6i$ c) $-11 + 2i$
d) $3 + 4i$ e) None of these

Answer: c Difficulty: 1

12. Simplify, then write your result in standard form: $(6 + \sqrt{-9}) - 2i + 10 - \sqrt{16}$.
a) $16 - 3i$ b) $13 - 6i$ c) $9 - 2i$
d) $12 + i$ e) None of these

Answer: d Difficulty: 1

13. Simplify, then write your result in standard form:
$(4 - \sqrt{-1}) - 2(3 + 2i)$.
a) $-2 - 3i$ b) $-2 + 5i$ c) $-2 - 5i$
d) $-2 + i$ e) None of these

Answer: c Difficulty: 1

SHORT ANSWER

14. Simplify, then write your result in standard form:
$\left(\frac{4}{5} + \frac{2}{3}i\right) - \left(\frac{3}{4} - \frac{1}{2}i\right)$

Answer:
$\frac{1}{20} + \frac{7}{6}i$
Difficulty: 1

15. Simplify, then write your result in standard form:
$3(2 - \sqrt{-9}) + 2i(4i - 7)$.

Answer: $-2 - 23i$ Difficulty: 1

MULTIPLE CHOICE

16. Write the conjugate: $4 - \sqrt{-3}$.

a) $-4 + \sqrt{3}i$ b) $16 - 3i$ c) $4 + \sqrt{3}i$
d) $4 - \sqrt{3}i$ e) None of these

Answer: c Difficulty: 1

17. Write the conjugate: $6 + \sqrt{-16}$.

a) $6 - 4i$ b) $6 + 4i$ c) $-6 - 4i$
d) $-6 + 4i$ e) None of these

Answer: a Difficulty: 1

18. Write the conjugate: $3 - \sqrt{-1}$.

a) $-3 - i$ b) $-3 + i$ c) 4
d) $3 + i$ e) None of these

Answer: d Difficulty: 1

19. Write the conjugate: $\frac{1}{2} + 4i$.

a) $\frac{1}{2} - 4i$ b) $2 - \frac{1}{4}i$ c) $-\frac{1}{2} + 4i$
d) $-2 - 4i$ e) None of these

Answer: a Difficulty: 1

20. Write the conjugate: $\frac{3 + 4i}{16}$.

a) $\frac{3}{16} + \frac{1}{4}i$ b) $\frac{16}{3 + 4i}$ c) $\frac{3}{16} - \frac{1}{4}i$
d) $-\frac{3 + 4i}{16}$ e) None of these

Answer: c Difficulty: 1

21. Multiply: $(3 + 7i)(6 - 2i)$.

a) $18 - 14i^2$ b) $4 + 48i$ c) $4 + 36i$
d) $32 + 36i$ e) None of these

Answer: d Difficulty: 1

22. Multiply: $(3 - \sqrt{-4})(7 + \sqrt{-9})$.

a) $15 + 23i$ b) $27 - 5i$ c) $27 + 5i$
d) $15 + 5i$ e) None of these

Answer: b Difficulty: 1

23. Multiply: $(4 - \sqrt{-9})^2$.
a) 7
b) $7 - 24i$
c) $25 - 24i$
d) $7 - 12i$
e) None of these

Answer: b Difficulty: 1

24. Simplify, then write your result in standard form: $\frac{6 + 10i}{2i}$.
a) $\frac{3}{i} + 5$
b) $5 - 3i$
c) $5 + 3i$
d) $3 + 5i$
e) None of these

Answer: b Difficulty: 1

25. Simplify, then write your answer in standard form: $\frac{-4 + i}{1 + 4i}$.
a) $-\frac{8}{17} + i$
b) $-i$
c) i
d) $\frac{8}{17} - i$
e) None of these

Answer: c Difficulty: 2

26. $\frac{3 - 2i}{2 + 4i}$ written in standard form is:
a) $\frac{1}{10} - \frac{4}{5}i$
b) $-\frac{1}{10} + \frac{4}{5}i$
c) $-\frac{1}{10} - \frac{4}{5}i$
d) $\frac{1}{10} + \frac{4}{5}i$
e) None of these

Answer: c Difficulty: 2

27. $\frac{2 + 4i}{3 - 2i}$ written in standard form is:
a) $-\frac{2}{13} - \frac{16}{13}i$
b) $\frac{2}{13} - \frac{16}{13}i$
c) $\frac{2}{13} + \frac{16}{13}i$
d) $-\frac{2}{13} + \frac{16}{13}i$
e) None of these

Answer: d Difficulty: 2

SHORT ANSWER

28. Simplify, then write your result in standard form: $\frac{3 + 7i}{3 - 7i}$.

Answer:
$-\frac{20}{29} + \frac{21}{29}i$
Difficulty: 2

29. Simplify, then write your result in standard form: $\frac{3 - 7i}{3 + 7i}$.

Answer:
$-\frac{20}{29} - \frac{21}{29}i$

Difficulty: 2

30. Simplify, then write your result in standard form: $\frac{1 + 4i}{4 - i}$.

Answer: i Difficulty: 2

31. Simplify, then write your result in standard form: $\frac{4 - i}{1 + 4i}$.

Answer: $-i$ Difficulty: 2

32. Simplify, then write your result in standard form: $\frac{2 + 3i}{1 - i}$.

Answer:
$\frac{-1}{2} + \frac{5}{2}i$

Difficulty: 2

MULTIPLE CHOICE

33. Solve for x: $3x^2 = 4x - 2$.

a) $\frac{2 \pm 2\sqrt{2}i}{3}$
b) $\frac{2 \pm 2\sqrt{10}}{3}$
c) $\frac{2 \pm \sqrt{2}i}{3}$
d) $\frac{2 \pm \sqrt{10}}{3}$
e) None of these

Answer: c Difficulty: 1

34. Solve for x: $3x^2 = x + 14$.

a) $-7, \frac{2}{3}$
b) $\frac{7}{3}, -2$
c) $\frac{x + 14}{3x}$
d) $-\frac{1}{6} \pm \frac{\sqrt{167}}{6}i$
e) None of these

Answer: b Difficulty: 1

35. Solve for x: $8x^2 = 2x - 3$.
a) $\frac{2x - 3}{8}$
b) $\frac{1}{16} \pm \frac{\sqrt{23}}{16}i$
c) $\frac{2 \pm \sqrt{23}i}{16}$
d) $\frac{1 \pm \sqrt{23}i}{8}$
e) None of these

Answer: d Difficulty: 1

36. Solve for x: $x^2 - 2x + 10 = 0$.
a) 7, -1
b) $1 + 3i$, $-1 + 3i$
c) $1 + 3i$, $1 - 3i$
d) 4, -2
e) None of these

Answer: c Difficulty: 1

SHORT ANSWER

37. Use the Quadratic Formula to solve for x: $5x^2 - 2x + 6 = 0$.

Answer:

$$x = \frac{1 + \sqrt{29}i}{5}$$

Difficulty: 1

38. Use the Quadratic Formula to solve for x: $2x^2 - 4x + 3 = 0$.

Answer:

$$x = \frac{2 \pm \sqrt{2}i}{2}$$

Difficulty: 1

39. Use the Quadratic Formula to solve for x: $3x^2 - 2x + 1 = 0$, and write your answer in standard form.

Answer:

$$x = \frac{1}{3} \pm \frac{\sqrt{2}}{3}i$$

Difficulty: 1

40. Use the Quadratic Formula to solve for x: $4x^2 - 4x + 3 = 0$, and write your answer in standard form.

Answer:

$$x = \frac{1}{2} \pm \frac{\sqrt{2}}{2}i$$

Difficulty: 1

41. Use the Quadratic Formula to solve for x: $2x^2 - 5x + 6 = 0$, and write your answer in standard form.

Answer:

$$x = \frac{5}{4} \pm \frac{\sqrt{23}}{4}i$$

Difficulty: 1

42. Use the Quadratic Formula to solve for x: $1.5x^2 - x - 2.5 = 0$, and write your answer in standard form.

Answer:

$$x = \frac{1}{3} \pm \frac{\sqrt{14}}{3}i$$

Difficulty: 1

MULTIPLE CHOICE

43. Solve for x: $x^2 + 36 = 0$.
a) 6, -6 b) $\sqrt{6}, -\sqrt{6}$ c) $6i, -6i$
d) $\sqrt{6}i, -\sqrt{6}i$ e) None of these

Answer: c Difficulty: 1

44. $(i)^{26} =$
a) 1 b) i c) -1 d) $-i$ e) None of these

Answer: c Difficulty: 1

45. $(i)^{448} =$
a) 1 b) i c) -1 d) $-i$ e) None of these

Answer: a Difficulty: 1

46. $(i)^{337} =$
a) 1 b) i c) -1 d) $-i$ e) None of these

Answer: b Difficulty: 1

47. Simplify: $(\sqrt{-25})^3$.
a) -125 b) $125i$ c) $-125i$ d) 125 e) None of these

Answer: c Difficulty: 1

48. Simplify: $4i^{16} + 3i^{12}$.
a) 7 b) $4 - 3i$ c) $7i$ d) $-3 + 4i$ e) None of these

Answer: a Difficulty: 1

49. Simplify: $6i^{17} + 4i^{20}$.
a) $6 - 4i$ b) $4 - 6i$ c) $-6 + 4i$ d) $4 + 6i$ e) None of these

Answer: d Difficulty: 1

SHORT ANSWER

50. Use a graphing utility to graph $y = x^2 - 2x + 5$. Use the graph to approximate the x-intercepts. Then set $y = 0$ and solve the equation. Compare the result with the x-intercepts of the graph.

Answer: See graph below.

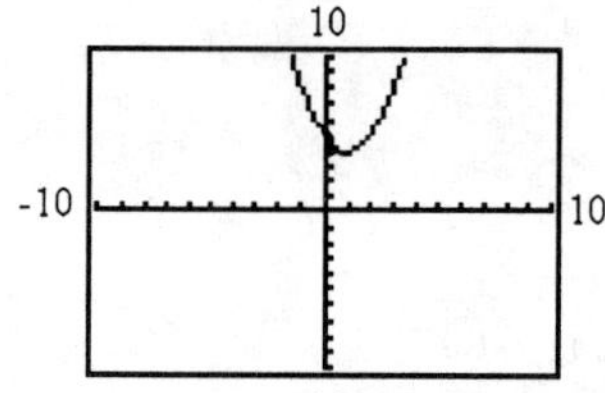

; $x = 1 \pm 2i$; no x-intercepts

Difficulty: 2 Key 1: T

Chapter 025: Zeros of Polynomial Functions

MULTIPLE CHOICE

1. List the possible rational zeros of the function: $f(x) = 3x^5 + 2x^2 - 3x + 2$.
   a) $\pm 3, \pm 2, \pm\frac{3}{2}, \pm 1, \pm\frac{2}{3}$
   b) $\pm 3, \pm\frac{1}{3}, \pm 2, \pm\frac{1}{2}, \pm 1$
   c) $\pm 2, \pm 1, \pm\frac{2}{3}, \pm\frac{1}{3}$
   d) $\pm 3, \pm 1, \pm\frac{3}{2}, \pm\frac{1}{2}$
   e) None of these

   Answer: c Difficulty: 1

2. List the possible rational zeros of the function: $f(x) = 3x^5 - 2x^3 + 3x - 5$.
   a) $\pm\frac{5}{3}, \pm 3, \pm\frac{1}{3}, \pm 5, \pm 1, \pm\frac{1}{5}, \pm\frac{3}{5}$
   b) $\pm\frac{3}{5}, \pm 1, \pm\frac{1}{5}, \pm 3$
   c) $\pm\frac{1}{3}, \pm 1, \pm\frac{5}{3}, \pm 5$
   d) $\pm 1, \pm 3, \pm\frac{3}{5}, \pm\frac{5}{3}$
   e) None of these

   Answer: c Difficulty: 1

3. List the possible rational zeros of the function: $f(x) = 3x^5 + 7x^3 - 3x^2 + 2$.
   a) $\pm\frac{2}{3}, \pm\frac{3}{2}, \pm 2, \pm 3$
   b) $\pm\frac{1}{3}, \pm\frac{2}{3}, \pm 1, \pm 2$
   c) $\pm\frac{3}{2}, \pm\frac{1}{2}, \pm 3, \pm 1$
   d) $\pm\frac{3}{2}, \pm\frac{2}{3}, \pm\frac{1}{2}, \pm\frac{1}{3}$
   e) None of these

   Answer: b Difficulty: 1

4. Which of the following is *not* a possible rational zero of: $f(x) = 2x^3 + 5x^2 + 3$?
   a) $\frac{1}{2}$ b) $-\frac{3}{2}$ c) $\frac{2}{3}$ d) 3 e) All of these

   Answer: c Difficulty: 1

5. Which of the following is *not* a possible rational zero of: $f(x) = 5x^3 + 3x^2 + 2$?
   a) $-\frac{5}{2}$ b) 2 c) $\frac{2}{5}$ d) $\frac{1}{5}$ e) All of these

   Answer: a Difficulty: 1

6. List the possible rational zeros of the function: $f(x) = 3x^5 + 2x^2 - 3x + 2$.
   a) $\pm\frac{2}{3}, \pm 1, \pm\frac{3}{2}, \pm 2, \pm 3$
   b) $\pm\frac{1}{3}, \pm\frac{1}{2}, \pm 1, \pm 2, \pm 3$
   c) $\pm\frac{1}{3}, \pm\frac{2}{3}, \pm 1, \pm 2$
   d) $\pm\frac{1}{2}, \pm 1, \pm\frac{3}{2}, \pm 3$
   e) None of these

   Answer: c Difficulty: 1

SHORT ANSWER

7. List the possible rational zeros of the function: $f(x) = 2x^4 - 3x^2 + 15$.

Answer:
$\pm\frac{1}{2}$, ± 1, $\pm\frac{3}{2}$, $\pm\frac{5}{2}$, ± 3, ± 5, $\pm\frac{15}{2}$, ± 15

Difficulty: 1

MULTIPLE CHOICE

8. Find all of the real zeros of the function: $f(x) = 2x^3 + 14x^2 + 24x$.
   a) 0, 3, 4
   b) 3, 4
   c) -4, -3, 0
   d) 0, 1, 6
   e) None of these

   Answer: c Difficulty: 1

9. Find all of the real zeros of the function: $f(x) = 3x^4 - 27x^3 + 54x^2$.
   a) 0, 3, 9, 2
   b) 0, 6, 3
   c) 0, 9, 2
   d) 0, 6
   e) None of these

   Answer: b Difficulty: 1

10. Find all of the real zeros of the function: $f(x) = 6x^4 + 32x^3 - 70x^2$.
   a) 0, -1, 5
   b) $0, -7, \frac{5}{3}$
   c) $\frac{7}{3}, 5$
   d) $0, -1, -7, \frac{5}{3}$
   e) None of these

   Answer: b Difficulty: 1

11. Find all of the real zeros of the function: $f(x) = x^3 + 6x^2 + 12x + 7$.
   a) $\frac{-5 \pm \sqrt{3}}{2}$
   b) $-1, \frac{-5 \pm \sqrt{3}}{2}$
   c) -1
   d) -1, 7
   e) None of these

   Answer: c Difficulty: 2

12. Find all of the real zeros of the function: $f(x) = 4x^3 - 3x - 1$.
   a) $1, -\frac{1}{2}$
   b) $1, \frac{1}{2}, -\frac{1}{2}$
   c) $\frac{1}{2}, 1$
   d) 1
   e) None of these

   Answer: a Difficulty: 2

SHORT ANSWER

13. Find all of the real roots: $x^3 - 7x + 6 = 0$.

   Answer: $x = -3, 1, 2$ Difficulty: 2

14. Find all of the real roots: $2x^3 + 5x^2 - x - 6 = 0$.

Answer:

$x = -2, \frac{-3}{2}, 1$

Difficulty: 1

MULTIPLE CHOICE

15. Find all of the real roots: $x^3 - 5x^2 + 5x - 1 = 0$.
a) $1, 2 \pm 2\sqrt{3}$
b) $1, 2 \pm \sqrt{3}$
c) 1
d) $-1, 2 \pm 2\sqrt{3}$
e) None of these

Answer: b Difficulty: 2

16. Find all of the real roots: $3x^4 - 4x^3 + 4x^2 - 4x + 1 = 0$.
a) $-1, \frac{1}{3}, 1$
b) $-1, -\frac{1}{3}, 1$
c) $\frac{1}{3}, 1$
d) 1
e) None of these

Answer: c Difficulty: 1

17. Find all of the real roots: $x^3 + 8x^2 + 17x + 6 = 0$.
a) -3
b) $-3, \frac{-5 \pm \sqrt{17}}{2}$
c) -3, -1, 2
d) $-3, \frac{-5 \pm \sqrt{33}}{2}$
e) None of these

Answer: b Difficulty: 2

18. Find all of the real zeros of the function: $f(x) = x^3 - \frac{4}{3}x^2 - \frac{5}{3}x + \frac{2}{3}$.
a) $-1, \frac{1}{3}, 2$
b) $1, \frac{2}{3}, -2$
c) $-2, -\frac{1}{3}, 1$
d) $-1, \frac{2}{3}, 1$
e) None of these

Answer: a Difficulty: 2

19. Find all of the real zeros of the function: $f(x) = x^3 - \frac{9}{2}x^2 + \frac{11}{2}x - \frac{3}{2}$.
a) $1, 4 \pm \sqrt{13}$
b) $\frac{3}{2}, \frac{3 \pm \sqrt{13}}{2}$
c) $\frac{3}{2}, \frac{3 \pm \sqrt{5}}{2}$
d) $1, 4 \pm \sqrt{19}$
e) None of these

Answer: c Difficulty: 2

SHORT ANSWER

20. Find all of the real zeros of the function: $f(x) = x^3 - \frac{11}{3}x^2 + \frac{5}{3}x + 1$.

Answer:

$-\frac{1}{3}$, 1, 3

Difficulty: 2

21. List the possible rational zeros of the function. Then use a graphing utility to graph the function to eliminate some of the possible zeros. Finally determine all real zeros of the function: $f(x) = 3x^3 - x^2 - 12x + 4$.

Answer:

See graph below. $\pm\frac{1}{3}$, $\pm\frac{2}{3}$, ±1, $\pm\frac{4}{3}$, ±2, ±4;

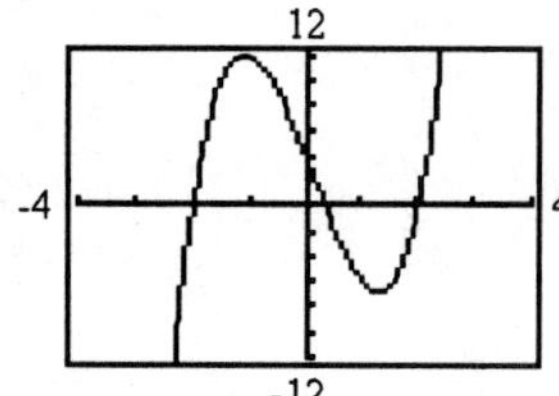

; $\frac{1}{3}$, ±2

Difficulty: 2 Key 1: T

22. List the possible rational zeros of the function. Then use a graphing utility to graph the function to eliminate some of the possible zeros. Finally determine all real zeros of the function: $f(x) = 2x^3 - x^2 - 18x + 9$.

Answer:

See graph below. $\pm\frac{1}{2}$, ±1, $\pm\frac{3}{2}$, ±3, $\pm\frac{9}{2}$, ±9;

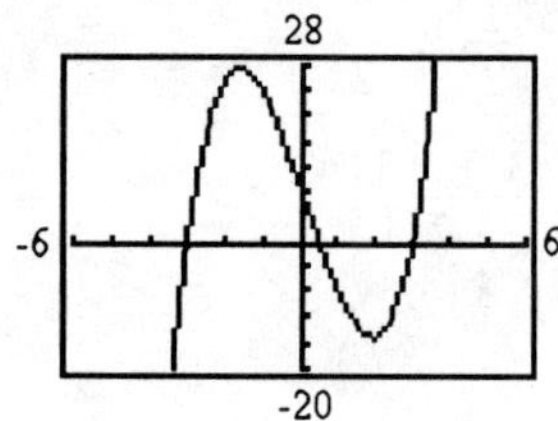

; $\frac{1}{2}$, ±3

Difficulty: 2 Key 1: T

23. List the possible rational zeros of the function. Then use a graphing utility to graph the function to eliminate some of the possible zeros. Finally determine all real zeros of the function: $f(x) = 2x^3 - 7x^2 + x + 10$.

Answer:

See graph below. $\pm\frac{1}{2}$, ± 1, $\pm\frac{5}{2}$, ± 5, ± 10;

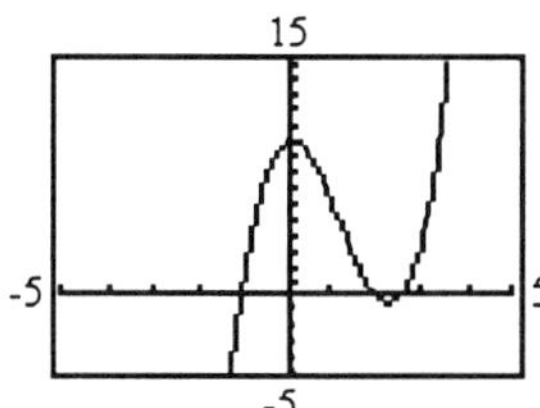

; $-1, 2, \frac{5}{2}$

Difficulty: 2 Key 1: T

24. List the possible rational zeros of the function. Then use a graphing utility to graph the function to eliminate some of the possible zeros. Finally determine all real zeros of the function: $f(x) = 5x^3 - 12x^2 - 11x + 6$.

Answer:

See graph below. $\pm\frac{1}{5}$, $\pm\frac{2}{5}$, $\pm\frac{3}{5}$, ± 1, $\pm\frac{6}{5}$, ± 2, ± 3, ± 6;

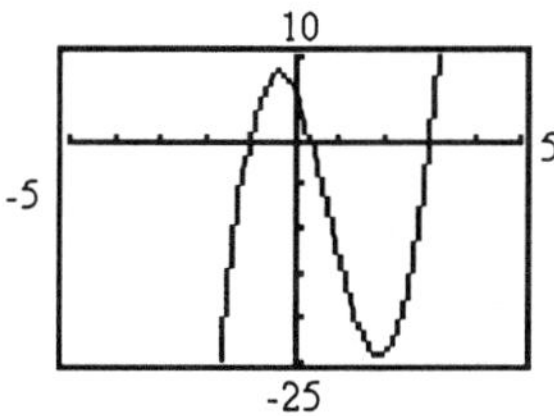

; $-1, \frac{2}{5}, 3$

Difficulty: 2 Key 1: T

MULTIPLE CHOICE

25. Find a polynomial with real coefficients that has zeros: 0, 3, -3, i, and $-i$.

a) $f(x) = x^5 - 8x^3 - 9x$
b) $f(x) = x^5 - 10x^3 + 9x$
c) $f(x) = x^3 - 4x^2 + 3$
d) $f(x) = x^5 - 9x$
e) None of these

Answer: a Difficulty: 1

SHORT ANSWER

26. Find a fourth degree polynomial function with real coefficients that has zeros: 1, -1, 0, and 2.

Answer:

$f(x) = x^4 - 2x^3 - x^2 + 2x$

Difficulty: 1

MULTIPLE CHOICE

27. Find a fourth degree polynomial with real coefficients that has zeros: 1, -1, i, $-i$.
a) $x^4 + 1$ b) $x^4 - 1$ c) $x^4 + 2x^2 + 1$
d) $x^4 - 2x^2 + 1$ e) None of these

Answer: b Difficulty: 1

28. Find a third degree polynomial with real coefficients that has zeros: 0, 2, $-i$, $2 + i$.
a) $x^3 - 5x^2 + 4x$ b) $x^3 + 4x^2 - 5x$ c) $x^3 - 4x^2 + 5x$
d) $x^3 + 5x$ e) None of these

Answer: c Difficulty: 1

29. Find a fourth degree polynomial with real coefficients that has zeros:
2, 3, $\sqrt{2}i$.
a) $x^4 - 5x^3 + 8x^2 - 10x + 12$ b) $x^4 - 5x^2 + 6$
c) $x^4 - 5x^3 + 6x^2$ d) $x^4 - 5x^3 + 8x^2 - 10x - 12$
e) None of these

Answer: a Difficulty: 2

30. Find a fourth degree polynomial with real coefficients that has zeros: 1, -3, $2i$.
a) $x^4 - 2x^3 + x^2 - 8x - 12$ b) $x^4 + 2x^3 - 7x^2 - 8x + 12$
c) $x^4 + 2x^3 + x^2 + 8x - 12$ d) $x^4 - 2x^3 - 7x^2 + 8x - 12$
e) None of these

Answer: c Difficulty: 1

31. Find a fourth degree polynomial with real coefficients that has zeros: 3, -2, i.
a) $x^4 - x^3 - 5x^2 - x - 6$ b) $x^4 + x^3 + 5x^2 - x - 6$
c) $x^4 - x^3 + 5x^2 + x - 6$ d) $x^4 + x^3 - 5x^2 + x - 6$
e) None of these

Answer: a Difficulty: 1

32. Find a third degree polynomial with real coefficients that has zeros: -2, $-4i$.
a) $x^3 - 4x^2 + 4x - 32$ b) $x^3 + 4x^2 - 4x + 16$
c) $x^3 - 2x^2 - 14x + 32$ d) $x^3 + 2x^2 + 16x + 32$
e) None of these

Answer: d Difficulty: 1

33. Find a third degree polynomial with real coefficients that has zeros: 6 and $-2i$.
    a) $x^3 + 6x^2 + 2x + 12$
    b) $x^3 - 6x^2 + 4x - 24$
    c) $x^3 - 6x^2 + 2x - 12$
    d) $x^3 + 6x^2 + 4x + 24$
    e) None of these

    Answer: b Difficulty: 1

34. Use the fact that $3i$ is a zero of f to find the remaining zeros: $f(x) = x^4 - 6x^3 + 14x^2 - 54x + 45$.
    a) $0, \pm 3i$
    b) $-1, -5, \pm 3i$
    c) $2, 3, \pm 3i$
    d) $1, 5, \pm 3i$
    e) None of these

    Answer: d Difficulty: 1

SHORT ANSWER

35. Use the fact that i is a zero of f to find the remaining zeros: $f(x) = x^4 - 5x^3 + 7x^2 - 5x + 6$.

    Answer: $2, 3, \pm i$ Difficulty: 2

36. Use the fact that $1 - 2i$ is a zero of f to find the remaining zeros: $f(x) = x^3 - 3x^2 + 7x - 5$.

    Answer: $1, 1 \pm 2i$ Difficulty: 1

37. Use the fact that $2 + \sqrt{3}i$ is a zero of f to find the remaining zeros: $f(x) = x^4 - 6x^3 + 12x^2 - 2x - 21$.

    Answer:

    $-1, 3, 2 \pm \sqrt{3}i$

    Difficulty: 2

MULTIPLE CHOICE

38. Write as a product of linear factors: $f(x) = x^4 + 25x^2 + 144$.
    a) $(x^2 + 9)(x^2 + 16)$
    b) $(x + 3i)(x + 3i)(x + 4i)(x + 4i)$
    c) $(x + 3i)(x - 3i)(x + 4i)(x - 4i)$
    d) $(x - 3i)(x - 3i)(x - 4i)(x - 4i)$
    e) None of these

    Answer: c Difficulty: 1

39. Write as a product of linear factors: $f(x) = x^4 - 3x^2 - 28$.
   a) $(x^2 + 4)(x^2 - 7)$
   b) $(x - 2i)(x + 2i)(x - \sqrt{7})(x + \sqrt{7})$
   c) $(x + 2i)(x + 2i)(x + \sqrt{7})(x - \sqrt{7})$
   d) $(x - 2i)(x - 2i)(x - \sqrt{7})(x + \sqrt{7})$
   e) None of these

   Answer: b Difficulty: 1

40. Write as a product of linear factors: $f(x) = x^4 - 5x^3 + 8x^2 - 20x + 16$.
   a) $(x + 2)(x - 2)(x - 4)(x - 1)$ b) $(x + 4)(x + 1)(x - 2i)(x + 2i)$
   c) $(x - 4)(x - 1)(x + 2i)(x - 2i)$ d) $(x + 4)(x + 1)(x + 2i)(x + 2i)$
   e) None of these

   Answer: c Difficulty: 2

SHORT ANSWER

41. Write as a product of linear factors: $f(x) = x^2 - 16$.

   Answer: $(x + 2)(x - 2)(x + 2i)(x - 2i)$ Difficulty: 1

42. Write as a product of linear factors: $f(x) = x^4 - 100$.

   Answer:
   $f(x) = (x + \sqrt{10})(x - \sqrt{10})(x + \sqrt{10i})(x - \sqrt{10i})$
   Difficulty: 1

MULTIPLE CHOICE

43. Write as a product of linear factors: $f(x) = x^4 - 6x^3 - 4x^2 + 40x + 32$.
   a) $(x - 4)(x + 2)(x + 2 + \sqrt{8})(x + 2 - \sqrt{8})$
   b) $(x + 4)(x - 2)(x - 2 + \sqrt{8})(x - 2 - \sqrt{8})$
   c) $(x - 4)(x - 2)(x - 2 + \sqrt{8})(x - 2 - \sqrt{8})$
   d) $(x + 4)(x + 2)(x + 2 + \sqrt{8})(x + 2 - \sqrt{8})$
   e) None of these

   Answer: a Difficulty: 2

44. Write as a product of linear factors: $f(x) = x^4 + 2x^3 - 5x^2 - 18x - 36$.
   a) $(x + 3)(x + 3)(x + 1 + \sqrt{3})(x + 1 - \sqrt{3})$
   b) $(x - 3)(x - 3)(x - 1 + \sqrt{6})(x - 1 - \sqrt{6})$
   c) $(x - 3)(x + 3)(x + 1 + \sqrt{3}i)(x + 1 - \sqrt{3}i)$
   d) $(x - 3)(x + 3)(x - 1 + \sqrt{3}i)(x - 1 - \sqrt{3}i)$
   e) None of these

   Answer: c Difficulty: 2

45. Write as a product of linear factors: $f(x) = x^4 - 49$.
   a) $(x - \sqrt{7i})(x + \sqrt{7i})$
   b) $(x - 7i)^2(x + 7)^2$
   c) $(x - \sqrt{7})^2(x + \sqrt{7})^2$
   d) $(x - \sqrt{7})(x + \sqrt{7})(x - \sqrt{7}i)(x + \sqrt{7}i)$
   e) None of these

   Answer: d Difficulty: 1

46. Write as a product of linear factors: $f(x) = x^4 + 13x^2 + 36$.
   a) $(x - 2i)^2(x - 3i)^2$
   b) $(x - 2i)(x + 2i)(x - 3i)(x - 3i)$
   c) $(x - \sqrt{2}i)(x + \sqrt{2}i)(x - \sqrt{3}i)(x + \sqrt{3}i)$
   d) $(x - \sqrt{2}i)^2(x - \sqrt{3}i)^2$
   e) None of these

   Answer: b Difficulty: 1

47. Write the polynomial as a product of factors irreducible over the rational numbers: $f(x) = x^4 - 3x^2 - 28$.
   a) $(x^2 + 4)(x^2 - 7)$
   b) $(x - 2i)(x + 2i)(x - \sqrt{7})(x + \sqrt{7})$
   c) $(x^2 + 4)(x - \sqrt{7})(x + \sqrt{7})$
   d) $(x - 2i)(x + 2i)(x^2 - 7)$
   e) None of these

   Answer: a Difficulty: 1

48. Write the polynomial as a product of factors irreducible over the rational numbers: $f(x) = x^4 + 4x^2 - 45$.
   a) $(x^2 - 5)(x - 3i)(x + 3i)$
   b) $(x^2 - 5)(x^2 + 9)$
   c) $(x - \sqrt{5})(x + \sqrt{5})(x - 3i)(x + 3i)$
   d) $(x - \sqrt{5})(x + \sqrt{5})(x^2 + 9)$
   e) None of these

   Answer: b Difficulty: 1

49. Write the polynomial as a product of factors irreducible over the rational numbers: $f(x) = x^4 - 1$.
   a) $(x^2 - 1)(x^2 + 1)$
   b) $(x^2 - 1)(x - i)(x + i)$
   c) $(x - 1)(x + 1)(x - i)(x + i)$
   d) $(x - 1)(x + 1)(x^2 + 1)$
   e) None of these

   Answer: d Difficulty: 1

50. Write the polynomial as a product of factors irreducible over the real numbers: $f(x) = x^4 - 3x^2 - 28$.
   a) $(x^2 + 4)(x^2 - 7)$
   b) $(x - 2i)(x + 2i)(x - \sqrt{7})(x + \sqrt{7})$
   c) $(x^2 + 4)(x - \sqrt{7})(x + \sqrt{7})$
   d) $(x - 2i)(x + 2i)(x^2 - 7)$
   e) None of these

   Answer: c Difficulty: 1

51. Write the polynomial as a product of factors irreducible over the real numbers: $f(x) = x^4 + 4x^2 - 45$.
   a) $(x^2 - 5)(x - 3i)(x + 3i)$
   b) $(x^2 - 5)(x^2 + 9)$
   c) $(x - \sqrt{5})(x + \sqrt{5})(x - 3i)(x + 3i)$
   d) $(x - \sqrt{5})(x + \sqrt{5})(x^2 + 9)$
   e) None of these

   Answer: d Difficulty: 1

52. Write the polynomial as a product of factors irreducible over the real numbers: $f(x) = x^4 + 23x^2 - 50$.
   a) $(x^2 + 25)(x^2 - 2)$
   b) $(x^2 - 2)(x - 5i)(x + 5i)$
   c) $(x - \sqrt{2})(x + \sqrt{2})(x^2 + 25)$
   d) $(x - \sqrt{2})(x + \sqrt{2})(x - 5i)(x + 5i)$
   e) None of these

   Answer: c Difficulty: 1

53. Write the polynomial in completely factored form: $f(x) = x^4 - 16$.
   a) $(x^2 - 4)(x^2 + 4)$
   b) $(x - 2)(x + 2)(x^2 + 4)$
   c) $(x - 2)(x + 2)(x - 2i)(x + 2i)$
   d) $(x^2 - 4)(x - 2i)(x + 2i)$
   e) None of these

   Answer: c Difficulty: 1

SHORT ANSWER

54. Write the polynomial function in completely factored form: $f(x) = 3x^4 - 4x^3 + 4x^2 - 4x + 1$.

   Answer: $f(x) = (x - 1)(3x - 1)(x + i)(x - i)$ Difficulty: 2

55. Write the polynomial function in completely factored form: $f(x) = x^4 - 2x^3 - x^2 + 2x$.

   Answer: $f(x) = x(x - 1)(x + 1)(x - 2)$ Difficulty: 1

MULTIPLE CHOICE

56. Write the polynomial function in completely factored form: $f(x) = x^3 - x + 6$.
   a) $(x + 2)(x^2 - 2x + 3)$
   b) $(x + 2)(x - 1 + \sqrt{2}i)(x + 1 - \sqrt{2}i)$
   c) $(x + 2)(x - 1 - \sqrt{2}i)(x - 1 + \sqrt{2}i)$
   d) $(x + 2)(x + 1 - \sqrt{2}i)(x + 1 + \sqrt{2}i)$
   e) None of these

   Answer: c Difficulty: 2

57. Find all of the zeros of the function: $f(x) = x^4 + 25x^2 + 144$.
   a) $\pm 2\sqrt{3}$, ± 5 b) $-3i$, $-3i$, $-4i$, $-4i$ c) $\pm 3i$, $\pm 4i$
   d) $3i$, $3i$, $4i$, $4i$ e) None of these

   Answer: c Difficulty: 1

58. Find all of the zeros of the function: $f(x) = x^3 - \frac{1}{2}x^2 + \frac{3}{4}x - \frac{5}{4}$.
   a) $1, \frac{1 \pm \sqrt{19}i}{4}$ b) 1, -2, 3 c) $1, \frac{3 \pm \sqrt{5}i}{4}$
   d) $1, 1 \pm i$ e) None of these

   Answer: a Difficulty: 1

59. Find all of the zeros of the function: $f(x) = x^3 + 5x^2 + 10x + 6$.
   a) -1, 6 b) $-1, -2 \pm \sqrt{2}$ c) -1
   d) $-1, -2 \pm \sqrt{2}i$ e) None of these

   Answer: d Difficulty: 1

60. Find all of the zeros of the function: $f(x) = x^4 - 5x^3 + 8x^2 - 20x + 16$.
   a) 1, 4, ± 2 b) -4, -1, $\pm 2i$ c) 1, 4, $\pm 2i$
   d) -4, -1, $-2i$, $-2i$ e) None of these

   Answer: c Difficulty: 2

SHORT ANSWER

61. Find all of the zeros of the function: $f(x) = 3x^4 - 7x^3 + 21x^2 - 63x - 54$.

   Answer:
   $-\frac{2}{3}$, 3, $\pm 3i$

   Difficulty: 2

62. Find all the zeros of the function: $f(x) = x^4 + 2x^3 + 3x^2 - 2x - 4$. Use a graphing utility to graph the function to discard any rational zeros that are obviously not zeros of the function.

Answer: See graph below.

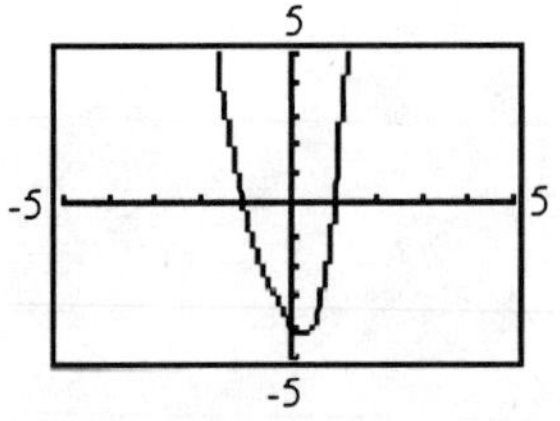

; ± 1; $-1 \pm \sqrt{3}i$

Difficulty: 2 Key 1: T

63. Find all the zeros of the function: $f(x) = x^4 + 2x^3 + x^2 - 8x - 20$. Use a graphing utility to graph the function to discard any rational zeros that are obviously not zeros of the function.

Answer: See graph below.

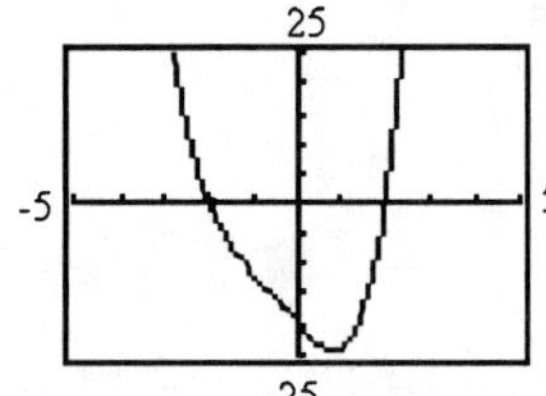

; ± 2, $-1 \pm 2i$

Difficulty: 2 Key 1: T

64. Find all the zeros of the function: $f(x) = x^4 + 2x^3 + 2x^2 - 8x - 24$. Use a graphing utility to graph the function to discard any rational zeros that are obviously not zeros of the function.

Answer: See graph below.

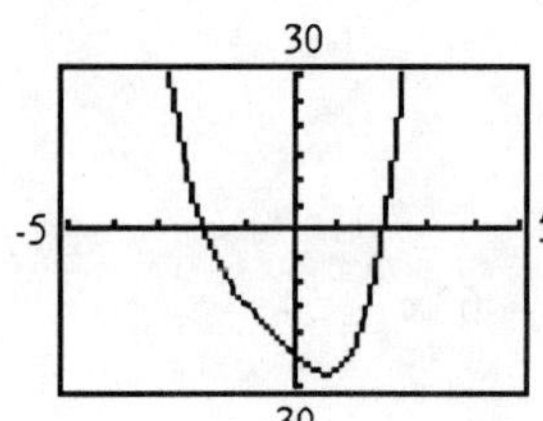

; ± 2, $-1 \pm \sqrt{5}i$

Difficulty: 2 Key 1: T

65. Find all the zeros of the function: $f(x) = x^4 - 2x^3 + 5x^2 - 8x + 4$. Use a graphing utility to graph the function to discard any rational zeros that are obviously not zeros of the function.

Answer: See graph below.

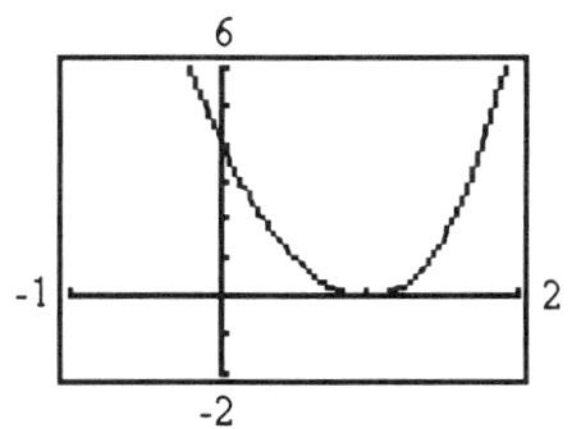

; $1 \pm 2i$

Difficulty: 2 Key 1: T

MULTIPLE CHOICE

66. Use Descartes's Rule of Signs to determine the possible number of positive and negative zeros: $f(x) = 5x^4 - 3x^3 - 4x + 2$.
   a) 2 positive, 2 negative
   b) 2 or 0 positive, 0 negative
   c) 4 positive, 0 negative
   d) 0 positive, 4 negative
   e) None of these

   Answer: b Difficulty: 1

67. Use Descartes's Rule of Signs to determine the possible number of positive and negative zeros: $f(x) = x^3 + 2x - 1$.
   a) 1 positive, 0 negative
   b) 0 positive, 1 negative
   c) 3 or 1 positive, 0 or 2 negative
   d) 1 positive, 2 negative
   e) None of these

   Answer: a Difficulty: 1

68. Use Descartes's Rule of Signs to determine the possible number of positive and negative zeros: $f(x) = 6x^5 - 6x^3 + 10x + 5$.
   a) 4 or 2 or 0 positive, 1 negative
   b) 3 or 1 positive, 2 or 4 negative
   c) 2 or 0 positive, 3 or 1 negative
   d) 1 positive, 0 negative
   e) None of these

   Answer: c Difficulty: 1

69. Use Descartes's Rule of Signs to determine the possible number of positive and negative zeros: $f(x) = x^3 + 1$.
   a) 3 positive, 0 negative
   b) 0 positive, 1 negative
   c) 1 positive, 2 negative
   d) 1 positive, 0 negative
   e) None of these

   Answer: b Difficulty: 1

70. Use Descartes's Rule of Signs to determine which of the polynomial functions has the following possible zeros: 0 or 2 positive and 0 negative.
    a) $f(x) = 5x^4 - 3x^3 - 4x + 2$
    b) $f(x) = 4x^4 - 3x^3 - x^2 + 1$
    c) $f(x) = 3x^4 - 4x^2 - 4x + 2$
    d) Both $f(x) = 5x^4 - 3x^3 - 4x + 2$ and $f(x) = 4x^4 - 3x^3 - x^2 + 1$
    e) Both $f(x) = 4x^4 - 3x^3 - x^2 + 1$ and $f(x) = 3x^4 - 4x^2 - 4x + 2$

    Answer: a Difficulty: 1

71. Use Descartes's Rule of Signs to determine which of the polynomial functions has the following possible zeros: 0 or 2 negative and 0 positive.
    a) $f(x) = 3x^4 + x^3 + 4x^2 + x$
    b) $f(x) = 5x^4 + 3x^3 + x^2 + 1$
    c) $f(x) = 2x^4 - 4x^2 + x$
    d) Both $f(x) = 3x^4 + x^3 + 4x^2 + x$ and $f(x) = 5x^4 + 3x^3 + x^2 + 1$
    e) Both $f(x) = 5x^4 + 3x^3 + x^2 + 1$ and $f(x) = 2x^4 - 4x^2 + x$

    Answer: b Difficulty: 1

72. Given $f(x) = x^4 - 2x^3 + x^2 - x - 5$, determine the possible number of negative zeros.
    a) None b) Either 3 or 1 c) Exactly one
    d) Either 2 or 0 e) None of these

    Answer: c Difficulty: 1

73. Given $f(x) = x^4 - 3x^3 + x^2 - 6x - 5$, determine the possible number of negative zeros.
    a) None b) Either 3 or 1 c) Exactly one
    d) Either 2 or 0 e) None of these

    Answer: c Difficulty: 1

SHORT ANSWER

74. Given $f(x) = 3x^3 + 4x - 1$, determine whether $x = -2$ is an upper bound for the zeros of f, a lower bound for the zeros of f, or neither.

    Answer: Lower bound Difficulty: 2

MULTIPLE CHOICE

75. Which of the following are upper bounds for the zeros of f: $f(x) = x^5 + 2x^4 - x^3 - 2x^2 - 30x - 60$?
    a) 1 b) 2 c) 3 d) Both 2 and 3 e) None of these

    Answer: c Difficulty: 2

76. Which of the following are lower bounds for the zeros of f: $f(x) = 6x^4 + 3x^3 + 5x - 10$?
    a) 0 b) -1 c) -2 d) Both -1 and -2 e) None of these

    Answer: c Difficulty: 2

77. Which of the following are upper bounds for the zeros of f: $f(x) = 3x^3 + x^2 - 7x + 2$?
a) 1 b) 2 c) 3 d) Both 2 and 3 e) None of these

Answer: d Difficulty: 2

78. Which of the following are lower bounds for the zeros of f: $f(x) = 3x^3 + x^2 - 11x - 5$?
a) -3 b) -2 c) -1 d) All of these e) None of these

Answer: a Difficulty: 2

79. Which of the following are lower bounds for the zeros of f: $f(x) = 3x^4 + x^2 + 3x - 1$?
a) -3 b) -2 c) -1 d) All of these e) None of these

Answer: d Difficulty: 2

Chapter 026: Rational Functions

MULTIPLE CHOICE

1. Determine the horizontal asymptote of the graph of $f(x) = \frac{x}{x + 1}$ by using its graph below.

a) $y = -1$ b) $y = 1$ c) $x = -1$
d) $x = 1$ e) None of these

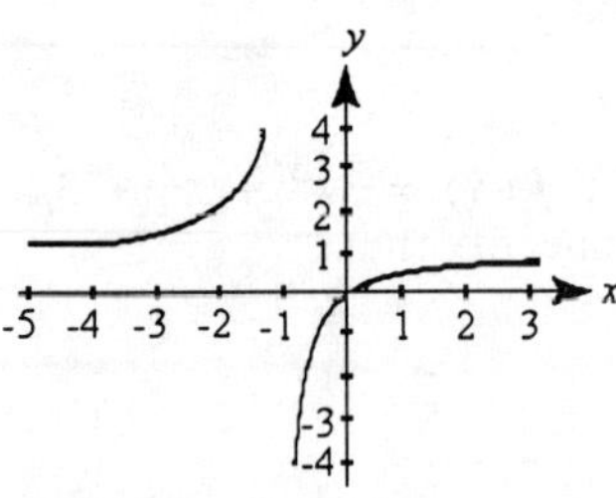

Answer: b Difficulty: 1

2. Determine the horizontal asymptote of the graph of $f(x) = \frac{2x^2 - 1}{x^2 + 3}$ by using its graph below.

a) $x = 2$ b) $y = -\frac{1}{2}$ c) $y = 2$ d) $x = -\frac{1}{2}$ e) None of these

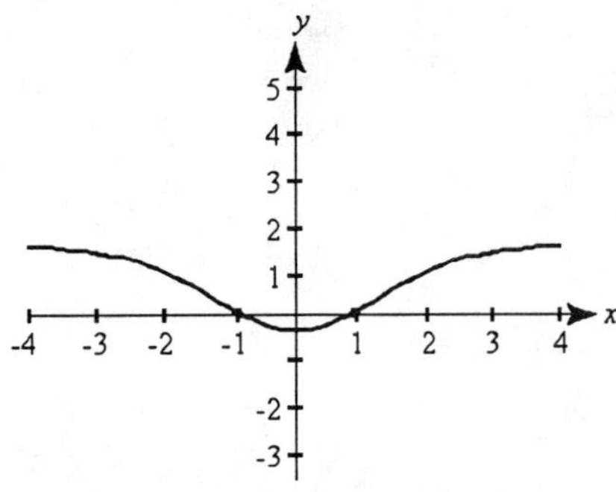

Answer: c Difficulty: 1

3. Find the vertical asymptote: $f(x) = \frac{7}{x + 2}$.

a) $x = -2$ b) $y = -2$ c) $(0, -2)$ d) $y = 0$ e) None of these

Answer: a Difficulty: 1

4. Find the vertical asymptote(s): $f(x) = \frac{1}{(x + 2)(x - 5)}$.

a) $x = -2$, $x = 5$ b) $y = 1$ c) $y = 0$
d) $y = 1$, $y = 0$ e) None of these

Answer: a Difficulty: 1

5. Find the vertical asymptote(s): $f(x) = \frac{x + 3}{(x - 2)(x + 5)}$.

a) $y = 2$, $y = -5$, $y = -3$
b) $x = 2$, $x = -5$, $x = -3$, $x = 1$
c) $x = 1$
d) $x = 2$, $x = -5$
e) None of these

Answer: d Difficulty: 1

6. Find the vertical asymptote(s): $f(x) = \frac{x + 5}{x^2 + 4}$.

a) $x = -2$, $x = 2$
b) $x = -5$
c) $x = 0$
d) $y = -2$, $y = 2$
e) None of these

Answer: e Difficulty: 1

7. Find the vertical asymptote(s): $f(x) = x + 2 - \frac{3}{x}$.

a) $x = -2$, $x = 0$
b) $y = 0$
c) $y = -2$
d) $x = 0$
e) None of these

Answer: d Difficulty: 1

8. Find the vertical asymptote(s): $f(x) = \frac{x + 2}{x^2 - 9}$.

a) $x = 3$
b) $x = -2$, $x = -3$, $x = 3$
c) $y = 0$, $x = -2$
d) $x = -3$, $x = 3$
e) None of these

Answer: d Difficulty: 1

9. Find the horizontal asymptote(s): $f(x) = \frac{x^2 - 1}{x^2 + 9}$.

a) $y = 1$ b) $y = 0$ c) $x = 1$ d) $x = \pm 1$ e) None of these

Answer: a Difficulty: 1

10. Find the horizontal asymptote: $f(x) = \frac{3x - 2}{x + 2}$.

a) $y = 0$ b) $x = -2$ c) $x = \frac{1}{3}$ d) $y = 3$ e) None of these

Answer: d Difficulty: 1

11. Find the horizontal asymptote(s): $f(x) = \frac{x^2 - 4}{x^2 - 9}$.

a) $y = \pm 3$ b) $x = \pm 3$ c) $y = 1$ d) $y = 0$ e) None of these

Answer: c Difficulty: 1

12. Find the horizontal asymptote: $f(x) = \frac{7}{x - 4}$.

a) $x = 4$ b) $y = 0$ c) $y = 7$ d) $x = 0$ e) None of these

Answer: b Difficulty: 1

SHORT ANSWER

13. Find the horizontal asymptote(s): $f(x) = \frac{3x^2 + 2x - 16}{x^2 - 7}$.

Answer: $y = 3$ Difficulty: 1

14. Find the horizontal asymptote(s): $f(x) = \frac{x^2 - 3}{(x - 2)(x + 1)}$.

Answer: $y = 1$ Difficulty: 1

MULTIPLE CHOICE

15. Find the domain: $f(x) = \frac{x + 2}{x^2 - 3x + 2}$.

a) All reals except $x = -2, 1, 2$
b) All reals except $x = -2$
c) All reals except $x = 1, 2$
d) All reals
e) None of these

Answer: c Difficulty: 1

16. Find the domain: $f(x) = \frac{3x - 2}{x^2 + 9}$.

a) All reals
b) All reals except $x = \pm 3$
c) All reals except $x = \frac{1}{3}$
d) All reals except $x = \frac{1}{3}, \pm 3$
e) None of these

Answer: a Difficulty: 1

17. Find the domain: $f(x) = \frac{x^2}{x + 1}$.

a) All reals
b) All reals except $x = -1$
c) All reals except $x = 0$
d) All reals except $x = -1, 0$
e) None of these

Answer: b Difficulty: 1

18. Find the domain: $f(x) = \frac{x^3 - 1}{x^2 - 4}$.

a) All reals
b) All reals except $x = 2$
c) All reals except $x = 1$
d) All reals except $x = 1, 2$
e) None of these

Answer: e Difficulty: 1

19. Find the domain: $f(x) = \frac{x^3 + 1}{x^2 + 4}$.

a) All reals
b) All reals except $x = -2$
c) All reals except $x = -1$
d) All reals except $x = -2, -1$
e) None of these

Answer: a Difficulty: 1

20. Find the domain: $f(x) = \frac{3x^2 - 4x + 1}{x + 2}$.

a) All reals
b) All reals except $x = \frac{1}{3}, 1$
c) All reals except $x = -2, \frac{1}{3}, 1$
d) All reals except $x = -2$
e) None of these

Answer: d Difficulty: 1

SHORT ANSWER

21. Find the domain: $f(x) = \frac{x}{x^2 + 3x - 4}$.

Answer: All reals except $x = -4, 1$ Difficulty: 1

22. Find the domain: $f(x) = \frac{4 + x}{x^2 - 10}$.

Answer:

All reals except $x = \pm\sqrt{10}$

Difficulty: 1

23. Use a graphing utility with the given window setting to graph $f(x) = \frac{x + 1}{x - 3}$ and its horizontal asymptote(s).

Xmin = -3
Xmax = 7
Xscl = 1
Ymin = -5
Ymax = 5
Yscl = 1

Answer: See graph below.

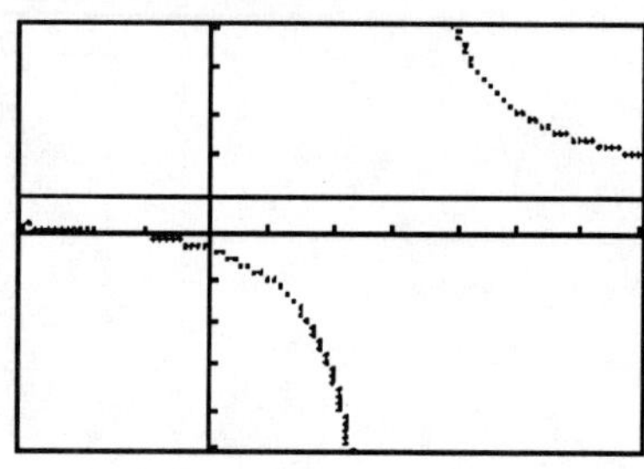

Difficulty: 2 Key 1: T

24. Use a graphing utility with the given window setting to graph $f(x) = \frac{x^2}{x^2 - 6x + 9}$ and its horizontal asymptote(s).

Xmin = -12
Xmax = 16
Xscl = 2
Ymin = -2
Ymax = 6
Yscl = 1

Answer: See graph below.

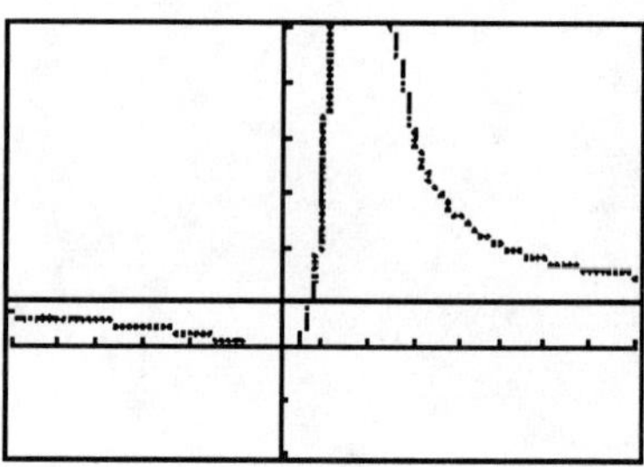

Difficulty: 2 Key 1: T

MULTIPLE CHOICE

25. Find the real zeros of f: $f(x) = \frac{2x - 1}{x^2 + 2}$.

a) $\left(-\sqrt{2}, 0\right)$ b) $\left(\frac{1}{2}, 0\right)$ c) $\left(-\sqrt{2}, 0\right), \left(\frac{1}{2}, 0\right)$
d) $\left(\sqrt{2}, 0\right)$ e) None of these

Answer: b Difficulty: 1

26. Find the real zeros of f: $f(x) = \frac{x + 2}{x - 1}$.

a) (1, 0) b) (-2, 0), (1, 0) c) (1, -2)
d) (-2, 0) e) None of these

Answer: d Difficulty: 1

27. Use a graphing utility to find the horizontal asymptote(s) of $f(x) = \frac{x - 3}{|x| - 2}$.

a) $y = -1$, $y = 1$ b) $y = 2$ c) $x = 2$
d) $x = -2$, $x = 2$ e) None of these

Answer: a Difficulty: 2 Key 1: T

28. Use a graphing utility to find the horizontal asymptote(s) of $f(x) = \frac{3x + 1}{2 + |x|}$.

a) $y = -\frac{3}{2}$, $y = \frac{3}{2}$ b) $y = -3$, $y = 3$ c) $x = -2$, $x = 2$
d) $x = -3$, $x = 3$ e) None of these

Answer: b Difficulty: 2 Key 1: T

29. Find the real zeros of f: $f(x) = \frac{6x + 3}{x^2 - 1}$.

a) $-\frac{1}{2}$ b) $\frac{1}{2}$ c) ± 1 d) $-\frac{1}{2}$, ± 1 e) None of these

Answer: a Difficulty: 1

30. Find the real zeros of f: $f(x) = \frac{x^2 - 9}{2x - 1}$.

a) $\frac{1}{2}$ b) $-\frac{1}{2}$ c) ± 3 d) $\frac{1}{2}$, ± 3 e) None of these

Answer: c Difficulty: 1

31. Suppose the cost C of removing p% of pollutants is

$$C = \frac{25{,}000p}{100 - p}, \quad 0 \le p < 100.$$

Find the cost of removing 60%.
a) \$167 b) \$25,000 c) \$37,500 d) \$375 e) None of these

Answer: c Difficulty: 1

32. Suppose the cost C of removing p% of pollutants is

$$C = \frac{25{,}000p}{100 - p}, \quad 0 \le p < 100.$$

Find the cost of removing 90%.
a) \$225,000 b) \$2778 c) \$2 d) \$2250 e) None of these

Answer: a Difficulty: 1

SHORT ANSWER

33. A herd of 40 elk is introduced into state game lands. The population of the herd is expected to follow the model

$$P(t) = \frac{40(1 + 2t)}{1 + 0.2t}, \quad t \ge 0.$$

Determine the limiting size of the herd.

Answer: 400 elk Difficulty: 2

34. A herd of 40 elk is introduced into state game lands. The population of the herd is expected to follow the model

$$P(t) = \frac{40(1 + 3t)}{1 + 0.2t}, \quad t \ge 0.$$

Determine the limiting size of the herd.

Answer: 600 elk Difficulty: 2

35. Find the vertical asymptote(s): $f(x) = \dfrac{x^2 - 9}{x^2 - 6x + 8}$.

Answer: $x = 2$, $x = 4$ Difficulty: 1

36. Find the vertical asymptote(s): $f(x) = \dfrac{x^2 - 4}{x^2 - 6x + 5}$.

Answer: $x = 1$, $x = 5$ Difficulty: 1

MULTIPLE CHOICE

37. Find the intercepts: $f(x) = \frac{x^2 - 16}{x^2 - 9}$.

a) (-4, 0), (4, 0), (0, -3), (0, 3)
b) (-4, 0), (4, 0)
c) (0, 1), (-4, 0), (4, 0)
d) $\left(0, \frac{16}{9}\right)$, (-4, 0), (4, 0)
e) None of these

Answer: d Difficulty: 1

38. Find the intercepts: $f(x) = \frac{x - 14}{2x + 7}$.

a) (0, -2), (14, 0)
b) (-14, 0), $\left(\frac{1}{2}, 0\right)$
c) (14, 0), $\left(0, \frac{1}{2}\right)$
d) (14, 0), $\left(0, -\frac{7}{2}\right)$
e) None of these

Answer: a Difficulty: 1

SHORT ANSWER

39. Find any horizontal and vertical asymptotes: $f(x) = \frac{x^2}{x^2 + 9}$.

Answer: $y = 1$ Difficulty: 1

40. Find any horizontal and vertical asymptotes: $f(x) = \frac{x}{x^3 - 1}$.

Answer: $y = 0$, $x = 1$ Difficulty: 1

MULTIPLE CHOICE

41. Match the rational function with the correct graph: $f(x) = \frac{3 + x}{x - 1}$.

a) I b) II c) III d) IV e) None of these

(I)

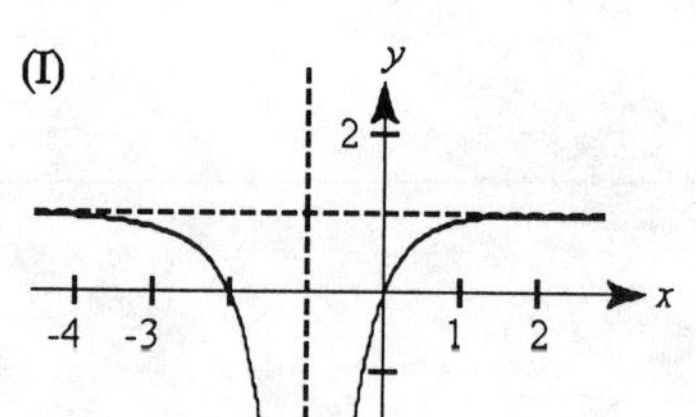

(II)

(III)

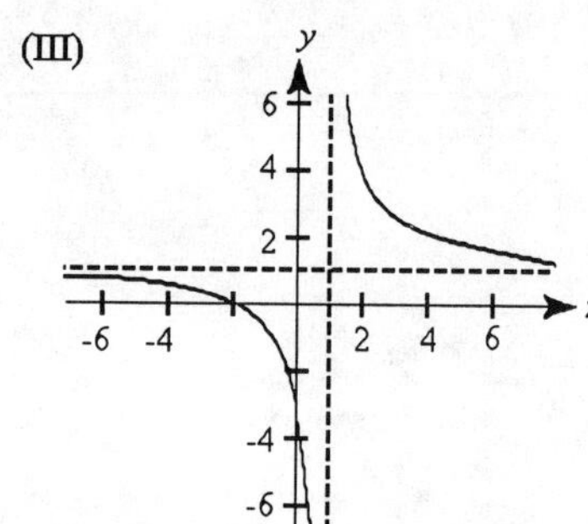

(IV)

Answer: c Difficulty: 1

42. Match the rational function with the correct graph: $f(x) = \frac{6}{x + 2}$.

a) I b) II c) III d) IV e) None of these

(I)
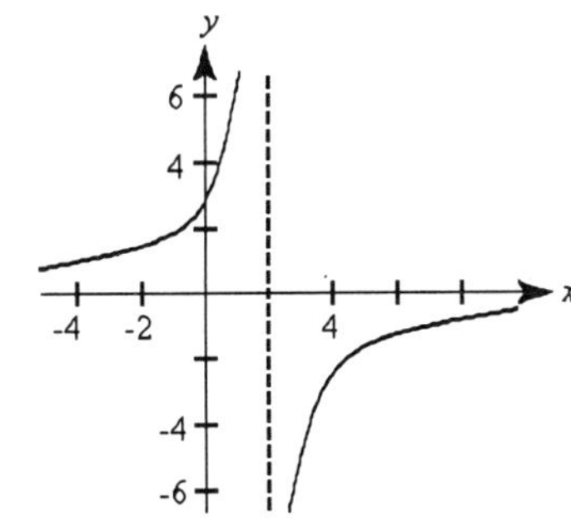

(II)
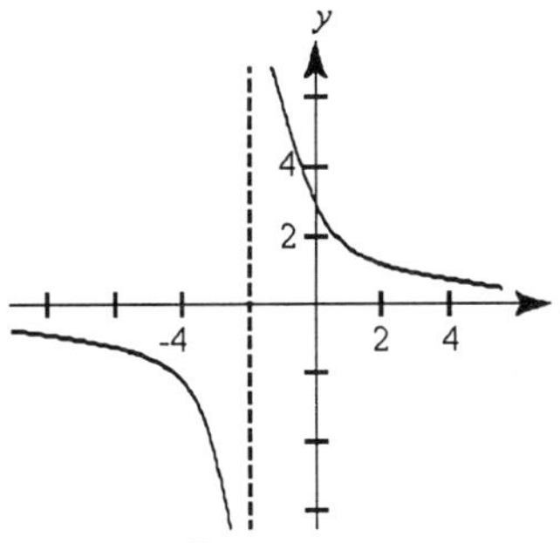

(III)
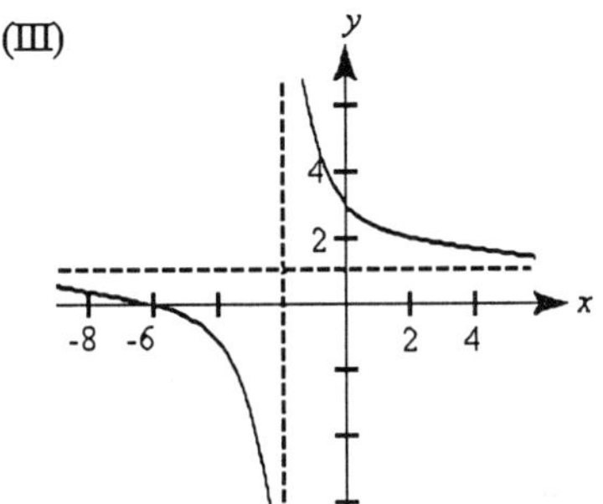

(IV)
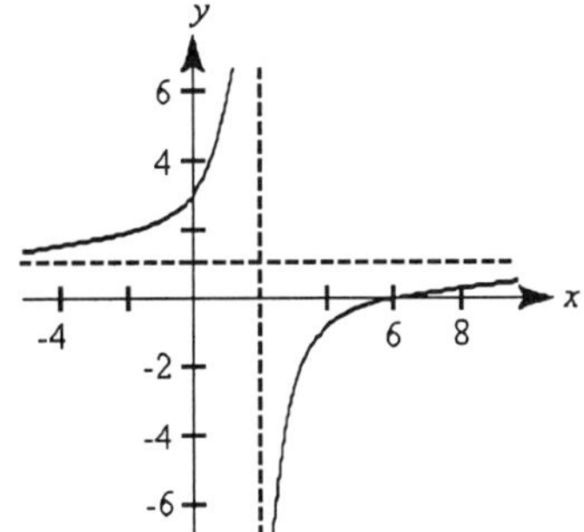

Answer: b Difficulty: 1

43. Match the rational function with the correct graph: $f(x) = \frac{x^2}{x + 2}$.

a) I b) II c) III d) IV e) None of these

(I)
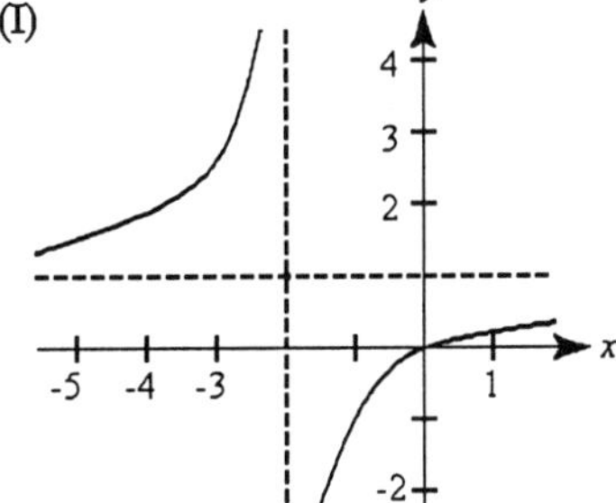

(II)
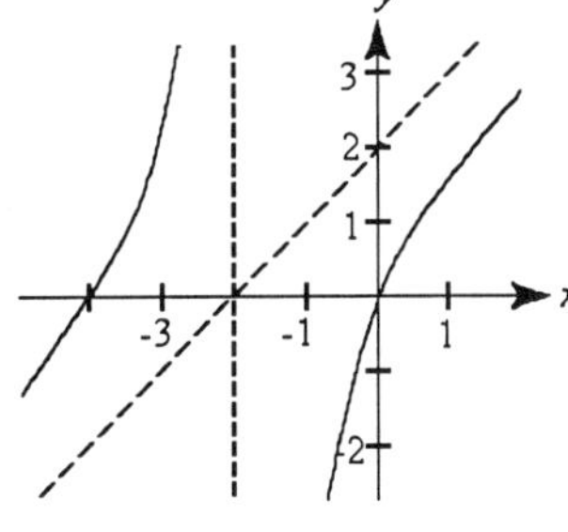

(III)
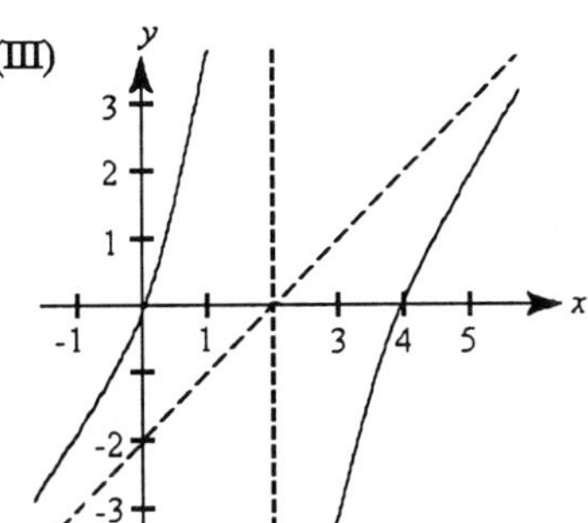

(IV)
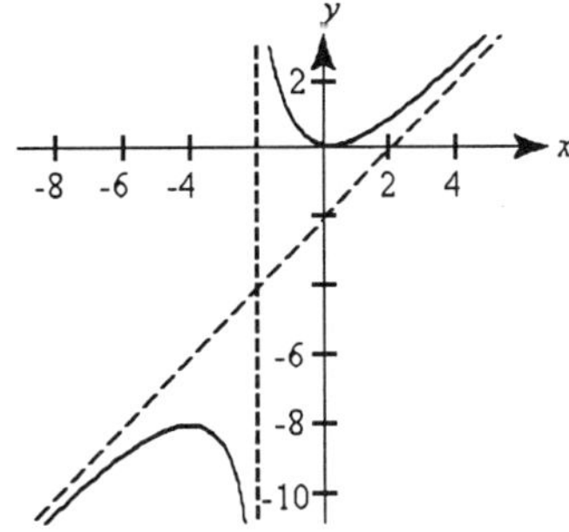

Answer: d Difficulty: 2

44. Match the graph with the correct function.

a) $f(x) = \dfrac{1}{2x + 1}$ b) $f(x) = \dfrac{x - 1}{2x + 1}$ c) $f(x) = \dfrac{x^2 + 2x + 2}{2x - 1}$

d) $f(x) = \dfrac{x^3 + 2x^2 + x - 2}{2x + 1}$ e) None of these

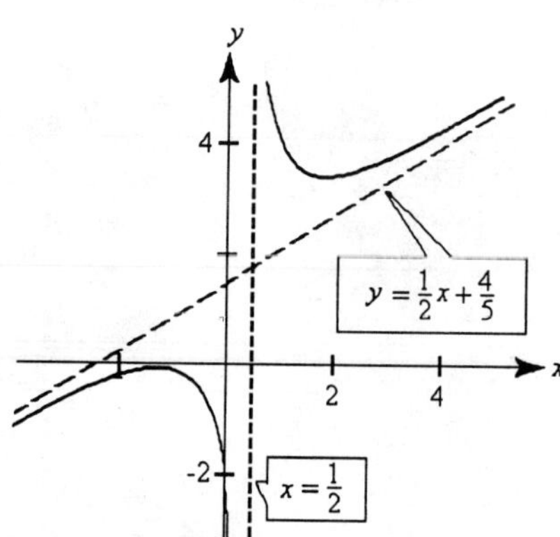

Answer: c Difficulty: 1

45. Match the graph with the correct function.

a) $f(x) = \dfrac{x + 3}{x - 1}$ b) $f(x) = x + 3$ c) $f(x) = \dfrac{x - 1}{x^2 + 2x - 3}$

d) $f(x) = \dfrac{x^2 + 2x - 3}{x - 1}$ e) None of these

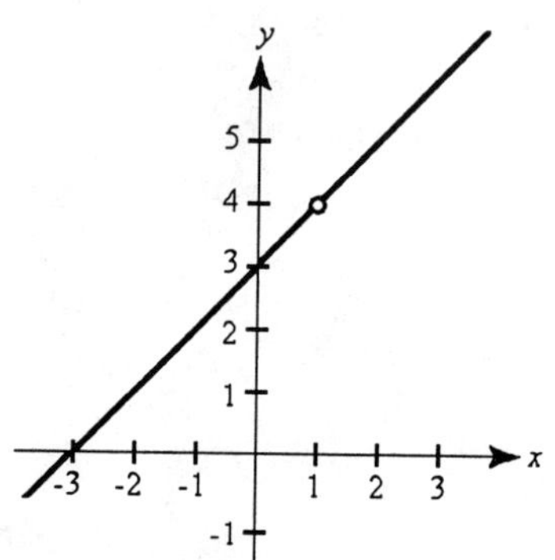

Answer: d Difficulty: 1

46. Match the graph with the correct function.

a) $f(x) = \dfrac{x - 5}{x + 3}$ b) $f(x) = \dfrac{5 - x}{x + 3}$ c) $f(x) = -\dfrac{x + 5}{x + 3}$

d) $f(x) = \dfrac{x + 5}{x + 3}$ e) None of these

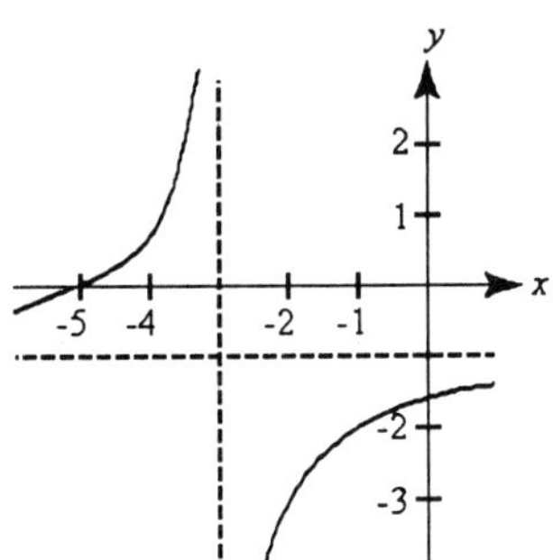

Answer: c Difficulty: 1

47. Use a graphing utility to graph $f(x) = \dfrac{x - 2}{x + 2}$.

a) I b) II c) III d) IV e) None of these

(I)

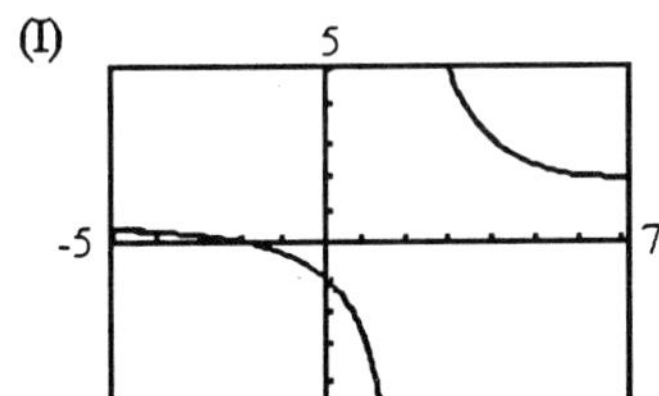

(II)

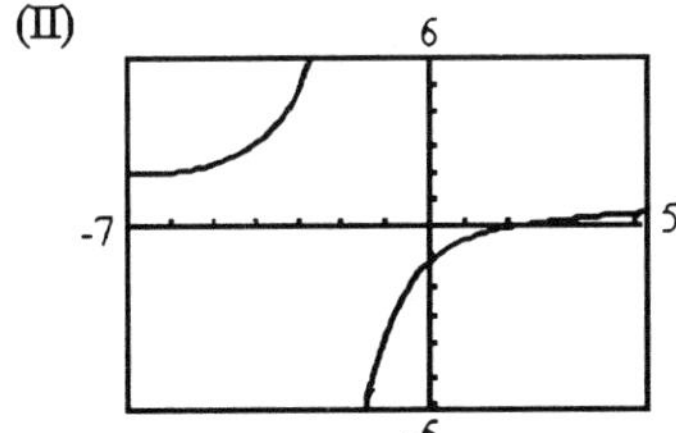

(III)

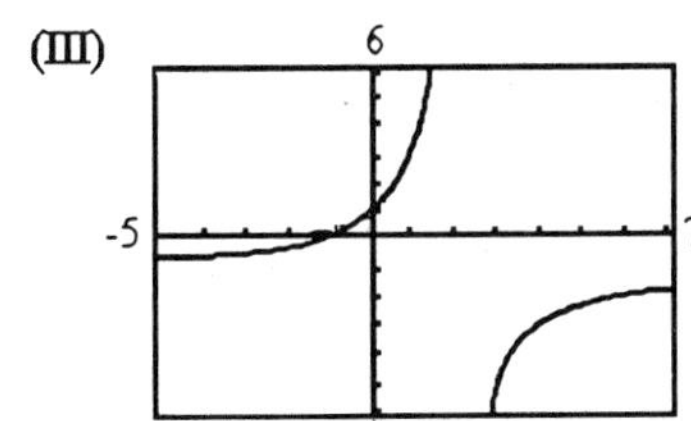

(IV)

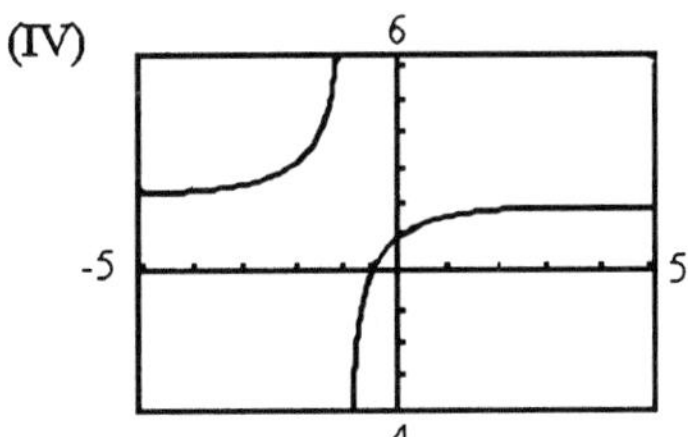

Answer: b Difficulty: 1 Key 1: T

48. Use a graphing utility to graph $f(x) = \frac{3x + 1}{x}$.

a) I b) II c) III d) IV e) None of these

(I)

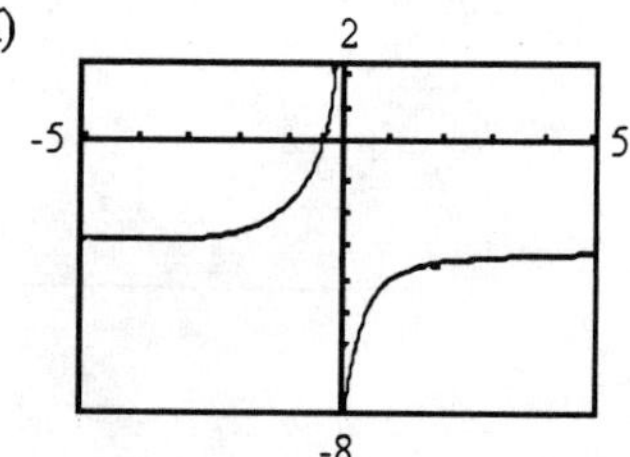

(II)

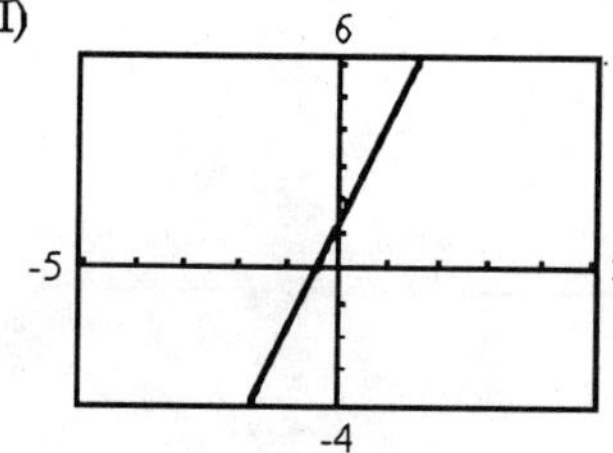

(III)

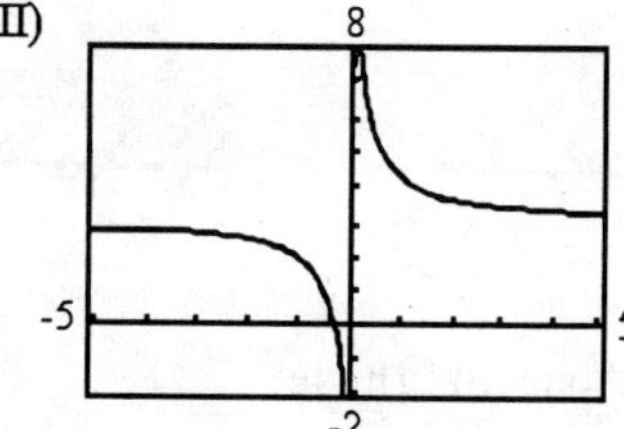

(IV)

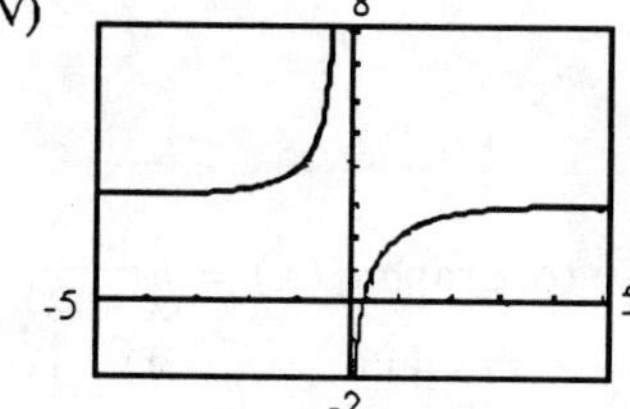

Answer: c Difficulty: 1 Key 1: T

SHORT ANSWER

49. Use a graphing utility to graph

$$f(x) = \frac{2}{x - 1}.$$

Answer: See graph below.

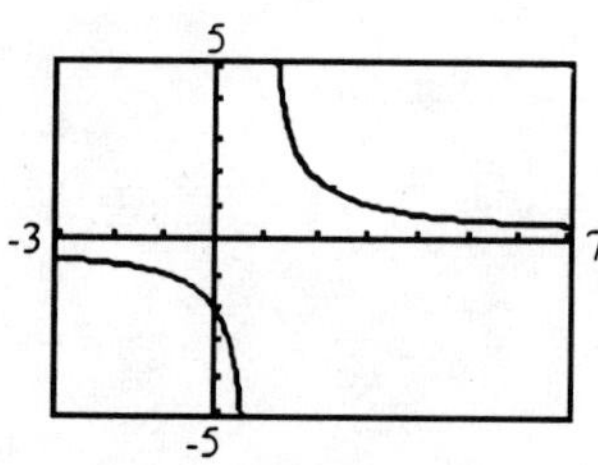

Difficulty: 1 Key 1: T

50. Use a graphing utility to graph

$$f(x) = \frac{x}{x^2 - 1}.$$

Answer: See graph below.

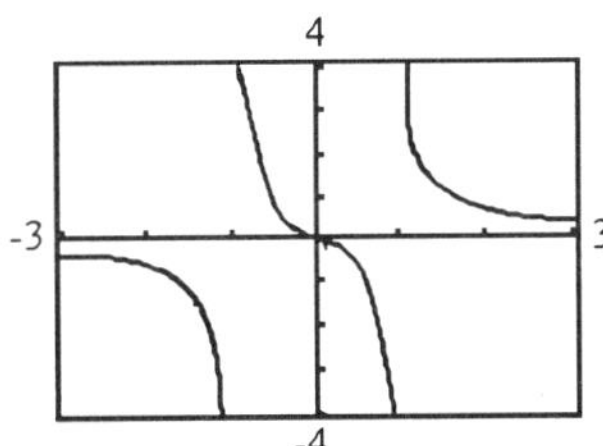

Difficulty: 1 Key 1: T

MULTIPLE CHOICE

51. Match the graph with the correct function.

a) $f(x) = \frac{3}{x - 2}$ b) $f(x) = \frac{3x}{x^2 - 4}$ c) $f(x) = \frac{3}{x^2 - 4}$

d) $f(x) = \frac{3}{x + 2}$ e) None of these

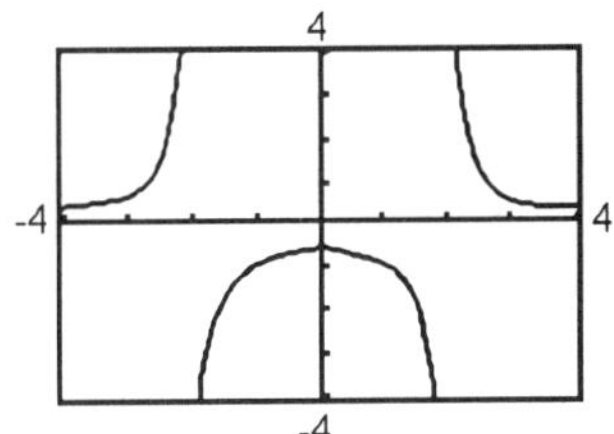

Answer: c Difficulty: 1

52. Match the graph with the correct function.

a) $f(x) = \frac{1}{x - 3}$ b) $f(x) = \frac{1}{x + 3}$ c) 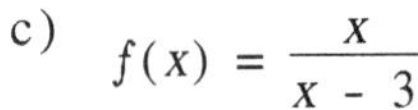 $f(x) = \frac{x}{x - 3}$

d) $f(x) = \frac{x}{x + 3}$ e) None of these

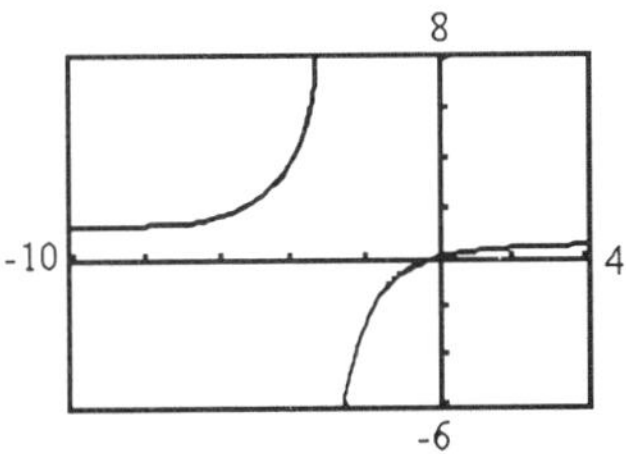

Answer: d Difficulty: 1

53. Find the slant asymptote: $f(x) = \frac{3x^2 + 2x - 1}{x - 1}$.

a) $y = -3x + 5$ b) $y = 3x + 5$ c) $y = 3x - 5$
d) $y = -3x - 5$ e) None of these

Answer: b Difficulty: 1

54. Find the slant asymptote: $f(x) = x - 2 + \frac{3}{x + 4}$.

a) $y = 0$ b) $y = x + 4$ c) $y = x - 2$
d) $y = x + 3$ e) None of these

Answer: c Difficulty: 1

55. Find the slant asymptote: $f(x) = \frac{x^3 + 7x^2 - 1}{x^2 + 1}$.

a) $y = 1$ b) $y = x + 7$ c) $y = x - 8$
d) $y = x + 1$ e) None of these

Answer: b Difficulty: 1

56. Find the slant asymptote: $f(x) = \frac{x^2 + 2x - 1}{x - 1}$.

a) $y = 1$ b) $y = x - 1$ c) $y = x + 1$
d) $y = x + 3$ e) None of these

Answer: d Difficulty: 1

57. Find the slant asymptote: $f(x) = \frac{x^3 + 2x^2 - 3}{x + 1}$.

a) $y = -1$ b) $y = x^2 + x - 1$ c) $y = 0$
d) $y = x^2 + 2x$ e) None of these

Answer: e Difficulty: 1

58. Find the horizontal or slant asymptote: $f(x) = \frac{x^2 + 3x + 1}{x + 1}$.

a) $x = -1$ b) $y = x + 3$ c) $y = x + 2$
d) $y = 0$ e) None of these

Answer: c Difficulty: 2

SHORT ANSWER

59. Find the vertical, horizontal, or slant asymptotes:

$f(x) = \frac{x^3 - 2x^2 + 5}{x^2}$.

Answer: $x = 0$, $y = x - 2$ Difficulty: 1

60. Find the vertical, horizontal, or slant asymptotes:
$f(x) = \dfrac{x - 2}{x^2 - 2x - 3}$.

Answer: $x = -1$, $y = 3$, $y = 0$ Difficulty: 1

61. Find the vertical, horizontal, or slant asymptotes:
$f(x) = \dfrac{3x^2 - 2x + 4}{x - 3}$.

Answer: $x = 3$, $y = 3x + 7$ Difficulty: 1

62. Label all intercepts and asymptotes, and sketch the graph:
$f(x) = \dfrac{x + 2}{x + 1}$.

Answer: See graph below.

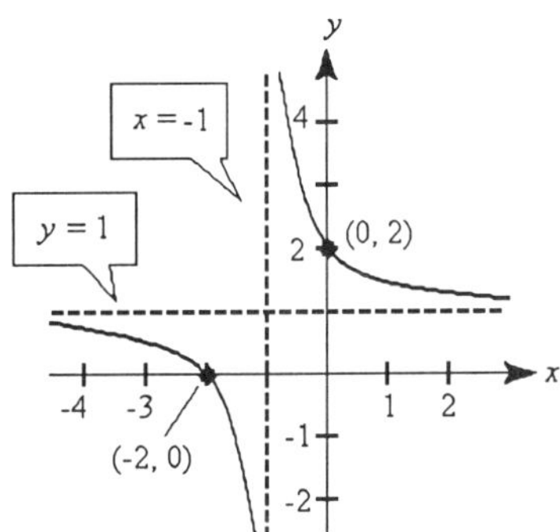

Difficulty: 2

63. Label all intercepts and asymptotes, and sketch the graph:
$f(x) = \dfrac{3x + 2}{x - 5}$.

Answer: See graph below.

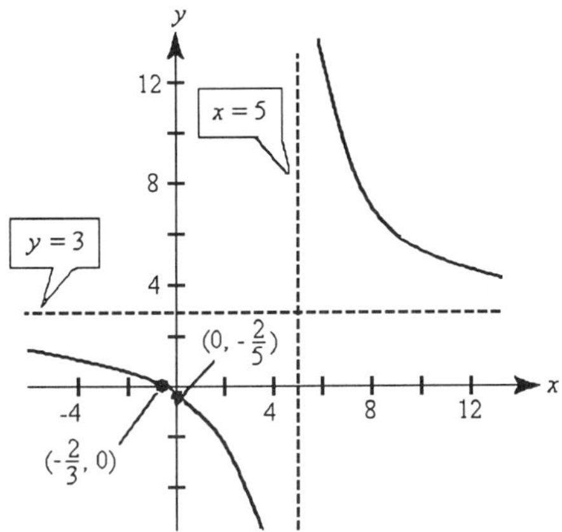

Difficulty: 2

64. Label all intercepts and asymptotes, and sketch the graph:
$f(x) = \frac{x^2 + x - 2}{x - 3}$

Answer: See graph below.

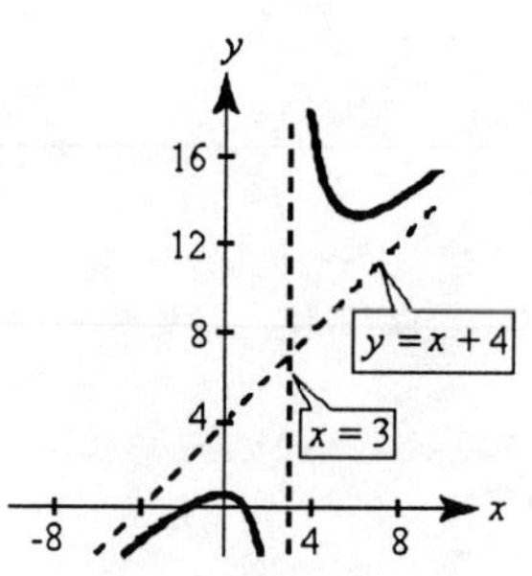

Difficulty: 2

MULTIPLE CHOICE

65. The concentration of a mixture is given by

$$C = \frac{2x + 9}{3(x + 12)}.$$

Use a graphing utility with the indicated window setting to determine what the concentration approaches.

Xmin = 0
Xmax = 280
Xscl = 50
Ymin = 0
Ymax = 1
Yscl = .1

a) 33% b) 67% c) 50% d) 75% e) None of these

Answer: b Difficulty: 2

66. The concentration of a mixture is given by

$$C = \frac{3x + 8}{4(x + 8)}.$$

Use a graphing utility with the indicated window setting to determine what the concentration approaches.

Xmin = 0
Xmax = 200
Xscl = 50
Ymin = 0
Ymax = 1
Yscl = .1

a) 75% b) 25% c) 50% d) 33% e) None of these

Answer: a Difficulty: 2

SHORT ANSWER

67. The population of a bacteria culture is given by

$$P = \frac{20t + 2}{5 + 0.2t}, \quad t \geq 0$$

where t is the time in hours. Use a graphing utility, with the indicated window setting, to graph the function and determine the value which the population approaches.

Xmin = 0
Xmax = 200
Xscl = 25
Ymin = 0
Ymax = 125
Yscl = 25

Answer: See graph below.

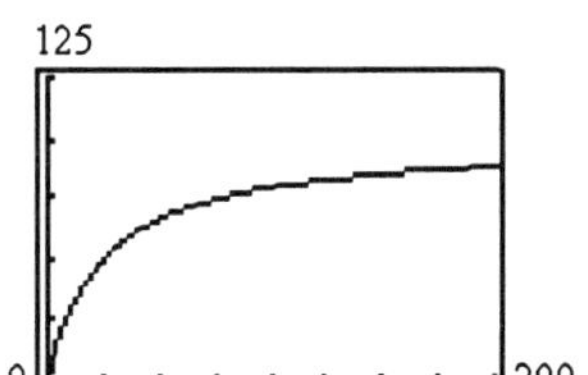

;100

Difficulty: 2 Key 1: T

68. The population of a bacteria culture is given by

$$P = \frac{20t + 2}{10 + 0.02t}, \quad t \geq 0$$

where t is the time in hours. Use a graphing utility, with the indicated window setting, to graph the function and determine the value which the population approaches.

Xmin = 0
Xmax = 15000
Xscl = 1000
Ymin = 0
Ymax = 1250
Yscl = 250

Answer: See graph below.

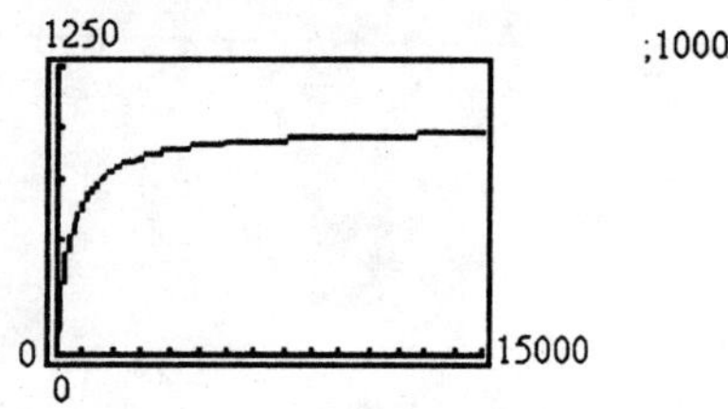

Difficulty: 2 Key 1: T

Chapter 027: Partial Fractions

SHORT ANSWER

1. Find the partial fraction decomposition: $\dfrac{1 - x}{2x^2 + x}$.

Answer:
$\dfrac{1}{x} - \dfrac{3}{2x + 1}$

Difficulty: 1

2. Find the partial fraction decomposition: $\dfrac{7x - 2}{3x^2 - x}$.

Answer:
$\dfrac{2}{x} - \dfrac{3}{3x + 1}$

Difficulty: 1

MULTIPLE CHOICE

3. Find the partial fraction decomposition: $\dfrac{4x + 23}{x^2 - x - 6}$.

a) $\dfrac{4x}{x + 2} + \dfrac{23}{x - 3}$ b) $\dfrac{2}{x + 2} - \dfrac{13}{x - 3}$ c) $\dfrac{5}{x - 3} - \dfrac{2}{x + 2}$
d) $\dfrac{7}{x - 3} - \dfrac{3}{x + 2}$ e) None of these

Answer:
d

Difficulty: 1

4. Find the partial fraction decomposition: $\dfrac{5x + 3}{x^2 - 3x - 10}$.

a) $\dfrac{2}{x + 5} - \dfrac{7}{x - 2}$ b) $\dfrac{7}{x - 5} - \dfrac{2}{x + 2}$ c) $\dfrac{2}{x - 5} + \dfrac{3}{x + 2}$
d) $\dfrac{4}{x - 5} + \dfrac{1}{x + 2}$ e) None of these

Answer: d Difficulty: 1

5. Find the partial fraction decomposition: $\dfrac{7}{3x^2 + 5x - 2}$.

a) $\dfrac{6}{(3x - 2)} + \dfrac{1}{x - 1}$ b) $\dfrac{3}{3x - 1} - \dfrac{1}{x + 2}$ c) $\dfrac{6}{x + 2} - \dfrac{18}{3x - 1}$
d) $\dfrac{4}{3x - 1} + \dfrac{2}{x + 2}$ e) None of these

Answer: b Difficulty: 1

SHORT ANSWER

6. Find the partial fraction decomposition: $\dfrac{7x + 4}{4x^2 + 7x - 15}$.

Answer:
$\dfrac{3}{4x - 5} + \dfrac{1}{x + 3}$
Difficulty: 2

MULTIPLE CHOICE

7. Find the partial fraction decomposition: $\dfrac{-5x - 3}{x^2 - 9}$

a) $\dfrac{-7}{x - 3} + \dfrac{2x - 3}{(x - 3)^2}$ b) $\dfrac{-3}{x - 3} - \dfrac{2}{x + 3}$ c) $\dfrac{1}{x + 3} - \dfrac{6}{x - 3}$
d) $\dfrac{4}{x - 3} - \dfrac{9}{x + 3}$ e) None of these

Answer: b Difficulty: 1

8. Find the partial fraction decomposition: $\dfrac{x - 7}{x^2 - 1}$.

a) $\dfrac{3}{x + 1} - \dfrac{4}{x - 1}$ b) $-\dfrac{2}{x + 1} + \dfrac{1}{x - 1}$ c) $\dfrac{3}{x + 1} - \dfrac{2}{x - 1}$
d) $\dfrac{4}{x + 1} - \dfrac{3}{x - 1}$ e) None of these

Answer: d Difficulty: 1

SHORT ANSWER

9. Find the partial decomposition: $\dfrac{2x^2 + 12x - 24}{x^3 - 4x}$.

Answer:
$\dfrac{6}{x} + \dfrac{1}{x - 2} - \dfrac{5}{x + 2}$
Difficulty: 2

MULTIPLE CHOICE

10. Find the partial fraction decomposition: $\frac{-3}{2x^2 + 3x}$.

a) $-\frac{1}{x} + \frac{2}{2x + 3}$　　b) $\frac{3}{x} - \frac{9}{2x + 3}$　　c) $\frac{-1}{x} - \frac{2}{2x + 3}$

d) $\frac{6}{2x + 3} - \frac{9}{x}$　　e) None of these

Answer: a　Difficulty: 1

SHORT ANSWER

11. Find the partial fraction decomposition: $\frac{3x^2 - 7x + 1}{(x - 1)^3}$.

Answer:
$\frac{3}{x - 1} - \frac{1}{(x - 1)^2} - \frac{3}{(x - 1)^3}$

Difficulty: 2

MULTIPLE CHOICE

12. Find the partial fraction decomposition: $-\frac{2x + 1}{(x + 1)^2}$.

a) $\frac{-2}{x + 1} + \frac{1}{(x + 1)^2}$　　b) $\frac{1}{x + 1} - \frac{2x}{(x + 1)^2}$　　c) $\frac{-6}{x + 1} - \frac{1}{(x + 1)^2}$

d) $\frac{-2}{x + 1} + \frac{-2x + 3}{(x + 1)^2}$　　e) None of these

Answer: a　Difficulty: 1

13. Find the partial fraction decomposition: $\frac{5x - 2}{(x - 1)^2}$.

a) $\frac{5}{x - 1} + \frac{-2}{(x - 1)^2}$　　b) $\frac{-2}{x - 1} + \frac{5x}{(x - 1)^2}$

c) $\frac{5}{x - 1} + \frac{3}{(x - 1)^2}$　　d) $\frac{3}{(x - 1)} + \frac{-2x + 1}{(x - 1)^2}$

e) None of these

Answer: c　Difficulty: 1

14. Find the partial fraction decomposition: $\dfrac{6x - 13}{x^2 - 2x + 1}$.

a) $\dfrac{6x}{(x-1)} + \dfrac{13}{(x-1)^2}$
b) $\dfrac{6}{x-1} - \dfrac{7}{(x-1)^2}$
c) $\dfrac{6}{x-1} - \dfrac{6x+7}{(x-1)^2}$
d) $\dfrac{4}{x-1} + \dfrac{2}{(x-1)^2}$
e) None of these

Answer: b Difficulty: 1

15. Find the partial fraction decomposition: $\dfrac{2x^2 - 9x + 11}{(x-2)^3}$.

a) $\dfrac{3}{x-2} + \dfrac{4}{(x-2)^2} - \dfrac{1}{(x-2)^3}$
b) $\dfrac{2}{x-2} + \dfrac{4x+1}{(x-2)^2} + \dfrac{x^2-3x}{(x-2)^3}$
c) $\dfrac{2}{x-2} + \dfrac{-1}{(x-2)^2} + \dfrac{1}{(x-2)^3}$
d) $\dfrac{2x^2}{(x-2)^3} - \dfrac{9x}{(x-2)^2} - \dfrac{11}{(x-2)}$
e) None of these

Answer: c Difficulty: 2

SHORT ANSWER

16. Find the partial fraction decomposition: $\dfrac{5x^2 + 12x + 10}{(x+1)^3}$.

Answer:
$\dfrac{5}{x+1} + \dfrac{2}{(x+1)^2} + \dfrac{3}{(x+1)^3}$
Difficulty: 2

MULTIPLE CHOICE

17. Find the partial fraction decomposition: $\dfrac{9x^2 + x - 1}{x^2(x+1)}$

a) $\dfrac{2}{x} - \dfrac{1}{x^2} + \dfrac{7}{x+1}$
b) $\dfrac{20}{x} - \dfrac{1}{x^2} - \dfrac{11}{x+1}$
c) $\dfrac{9}{x} + \dfrac{1}{x^2} - \dfrac{1}{x+1}$
d) $\dfrac{-1}{x^2} + \dfrac{9}{x+1}$
e) None of these

Answer: a Difficulty: 2

18. Find the partial fraction decomposition: $\dfrac{-9}{(x+1)^2(x-2)}$.

a) $\dfrac{1}{x+1} + \dfrac{3}{(x+1)^2} - \dfrac{1}{x-2}$

b) $\dfrac{10}{x+1} - \dfrac{4}{(x+1)^2} - \dfrac{15}{x-2}$

c) $\dfrac{2}{x+1} - \dfrac{1}{(x+1)^2} - \dfrac{1}{x-2}$

d) $\dfrac{1}{x+1} - \dfrac{3}{(x+1)^2} + \dfrac{5}{x-2}$

e) None of these

Answer: a Difficulty: 2

19. Find the partial fraction decomposition: $\dfrac{-5x^2 - 19x - 28}{x^3 + 4x^2 + 4x}$.

a) $-\dfrac{5x^2}{x^3} - \dfrac{19x}{4x^2} - \dfrac{28}{4x}$

b) $-\dfrac{5x^2}{x} - \dfrac{19x}{x+2} - \dfrac{28}{(x+2)^2}$

c) $\dfrac{2}{x} - \dfrac{5}{x+2} + \dfrac{16}{(x+2)^2}$

d) $-\dfrac{7}{x} + \dfrac{2}{x+2} + \dfrac{5}{(x+2)^2}$

e) None of these

Answer: d Difficulty: 2

SHORT ANSWER

20. Find the partial fraction decomposition: $\dfrac{12x^2 - 13x - 3}{(x-1)^2(x+3)}$.

Answer:
$\dfrac{3}{x-1} - \dfrac{1}{(x-1)^2} + \dfrac{9}{x+3}$

Difficulty: 2

21. Find the partial fraction decomposition $\dfrac{-16x^3 + 2x^2 - 28x + 8}{x^4 + 4x^2}$.

Answer:
$\dfrac{-7}{x} + \dfrac{2}{x^2} - \dfrac{9x}{x^2+4}$

Difficulty: 2

MULTIPLE CHOICE

22. Find the partial fraction decomposition: $\dfrac{2x^2 + 6x - 11}{(x - 3)(x + 2)^2}$.

a) $\dfrac{6}{x + 2} + \dfrac{1}{(x + 2)^2} - \dfrac{1}{x - 3}$
b) $\dfrac{-3}{x + 2} + \dfrac{5}{(x + 2)^2} - \dfrac{2}{x - 3}$
c) $\dfrac{2}{x + 2} + \dfrac{7}{(x + 2)^2} - \dfrac{11}{x - 3}$
d) $\dfrac{1}{x + 2} + \dfrac{3}{(x + 2)^2} + \dfrac{1}{x - 3}$
e) None of these

Answer: d Difficulty: 2

23. Find the partial fraction decomposition: $\dfrac{17x^2 - 14x + 3}{x^3 - x^2}$.

a) $\dfrac{5}{x} + \dfrac{2}{x^2} + \dfrac{5}{x - 1}$
b) $\dfrac{1}{x} + \dfrac{1}{x^2} + \dfrac{1}{x - 1}$
c) $\dfrac{11}{x} - \dfrac{3}{x^2} + \dfrac{6}{x - 1}$
d) $\dfrac{7}{x} + \dfrac{2}{x^2} - \dfrac{8}{x - 1}$
e) None of these

Answer: c Difficulty: 2

SHORT ANSWER

24. Find the partial fraction decomposition: $\dfrac{3x^2 - 31x - 25}{(x + 1)(x^2 - 7x - 8)}$.

Answer:
$\dfrac{4}{x + 1} - \dfrac{1}{(x + 1)^2} - \dfrac{1}{x - 8}$
Difficulty: 2

MULTIPLE CHOICE

25. Find the partial fraction decomposition: $\dfrac{-x^2 - 7x + 27}{x(x^2 + 9)}$.

a) $\dfrac{3}{x} + \dfrac{4}{x + 3} - \dfrac{7}{x^2 + 9}$
b) $\dfrac{3}{x} - \dfrac{4x + 7}{x^2 + 9}$
c) $\dfrac{2}{x} + \dfrac{3x + 5}{x^2 + 9}$
d) $\dfrac{2}{x} + \dfrac{3}{x + 3} - \dfrac{5}{x^2 + 9}$
e) None of these

Answer: b Difficulty: 2

26. Find the partial fraction decomposition: $\dfrac{5x^2 - 9x + 12}{(x - 2)(x^2 + x + 1)}$.

a) $\dfrac{5x^2}{x - 2} - \dfrac{9x + 12}{x^2 + x + 1}$

b) $-\dfrac{4/9}{x - 2} + \dfrac{22/9}{x + 1} - \dfrac{26/3}{(x + 1)^2}$

c) $\dfrac{2}{x - 2} + \dfrac{3x - 5}{x^2 + x + 1}$

d) $\dfrac{5}{x - 2} + \dfrac{2x - 7}{x^2 + x + 1}$

e) None of these

Answer: c Difficulty: 2

SHORT ANSWER

27. Find the partial fraction decomposition: $\dfrac{x^2 - x - 4}{x(x^2 + 2)}$.

Answer:
$-\dfrac{2}{x} + \dfrac{3x - 1}{x^2 + 2}$

Difficulty: 2

28. Find the partial fraction decomposition: $\dfrac{4 - x}{x(x^2 + 4)}$.

Answer:
$\dfrac{1}{x} - \dfrac{x + 1}{x^2 + 4}$

Difficulty: 2

MULTIPLE CHOICE

29. Find the partial fraction decomposition: $\dfrac{x^2 - 4x + 1}{(x - 3)(x^2 + 1)}$.

a) $\dfrac{-1/5}{x - 3} + \dfrac{2}{x + 1} + \dfrac{4/5}{x + 1}$

b) $\dfrac{1}{x - 3} + \dfrac{-4x + 1}{x^2 + 1}$

c) $\dfrac{1}{x - 3} - \dfrac{4}{x + 1} + \dfrac{1}{x + 1}$

d) $\dfrac{-1/5}{x - 3} + \dfrac{(6/5)x - (2/5)}{x^2 + 1}$

e) None of these

Answer: d Difficulty: 2

30. Find the partial fraction decomposition: $\dfrac{7x^2 + 24x - 1}{(x^2 + 2)(x + 5)}$.

a) $\dfrac{2}{x + 5} + \dfrac{5x - 1}{x^2 + 2}$

b) $\dfrac{3}{x + 5} + \dfrac{5x + 2}{x^2 + 2}$

c) $\dfrac{3}{x + 5} - \dfrac{1}{x^2 + 2}$

d) $\dfrac{1}{x + 5} - \dfrac{3x}{x^2 + 2}$

e) None of these

Answer: a Difficulty: 2

31. Find the partial fraction decomposition: $\dfrac{x^2 + 11x + 2}{(x - 3)(x^2 + 2)}$.

a) $\dfrac{x - 6}{x^2 + 2} + \dfrac{4}{x - 3}$

b) $\dfrac{7x - 5}{x^2 + 2} - \dfrac{1}{x - 3}$

c) $\dfrac{-3x + 2}{x^2 + 2} + \dfrac{4}{x - 3}$

d) $\dfrac{2x + 1}{x^2 + 2} + \dfrac{3}{x - 3}$

e) None of these

Answer: c Difficulty: 2

SHORT ANSWER

32. Find the partial fraction decomposition: $\dfrac{x^2 - x + 2}{(x^2 + 2)^2}$.

Answer:

$\dfrac{1}{x^2 + 2} - \dfrac{x}{(x^2 + 2)^2}$

Difficulty: 2

MULTIPLE CHOICE

33. Find the partial fraction decomposition: $\dfrac{2x^3 - x^2 + 2x + 2}{(x^2 + 1)^2}$.

a) $\dfrac{x + 1}{x^2 + 1} + \dfrac{x - 1}{(x^2 + 1)^2}$

b) $\dfrac{2x - 1}{x^2 + 1} + \dfrac{3}{(x^2 + 1)^2}$

c) $\dfrac{x - 3}{x^2 + 1} + \dfrac{2x + 5}{(x^2 + 1)^2}$

d) $\dfrac{7}{x^2 + 1} + \dfrac{-3x + 2}{(x^2 + 1)^2}$

e) None of these

Answer: b Difficulty: 2

34. Find the partial fraction decomposition: $\frac{2x^2 - 6x + 4}{(x^2 + 1)^2}$.

a) $\frac{3x + 1}{x^2 + 1} - \frac{x + 1}{(x^2 + 1)^2}$

b) $\frac{4}{x^2 + 1} - \frac{6x}{(x^2 + 1)^2}$

c) $\frac{2x - 6}{x^2 + 1} + \frac{4}{(x^2 + 1)^2}$

d) $\frac{2}{x^2 + 1} - \frac{6x - 2}{(x^2 + 1)^2}$

e) None of these

Answer: d Difficulty: 1

35. Find the partial fraction decomposition: $\frac{3x^2 + 9x + 4}{(x^2 + x + 1)^2}$.

a) $\frac{3}{x^2 + x + 1} + \frac{6x + 1}{(x^2 + x + 1)^2}$

b) $\frac{2x - 1}{x^2 + x + 1} + \frac{4x + 7}{(x^2 + x + 1)}$

c) $\frac{9x - 1}{x^2 + x + 1} + \frac{4x}{(x^2 + x + 1)^2}$

d) $\frac{3x + 6}{x^2 + x + 1} + \frac{3x - 6}{(x^2 + x + 1)^2}$

e) None of these

Answer: a Difficulty: 2

36. Find the partial fraction decomposition: $\frac{6x^3 + 24x - 7}{(x^2 + 4)^2}$.

a) $\frac{-2x + 1}{x^2 + 4} + \frac{16x - 5}{(x^2 + 4)^2}$

b) $\frac{-4x + 3}{x^2 + 4} + \frac{x + 1}{(x^2 + 4)^2}$

c) $\frac{6x}{x^2 + 4} - \frac{7}{(x^2 + 4)^2}$

d) $\frac{2 - 3x}{x^2 + 4} + \frac{4x - 1}{(x^2 + 4)^2}$

e) None of these

Answer: c Difficulty: 1

37. Find the partial fraction decomposition: $\frac{x^3 + x}{(x^2 + x + 1)^2}$.

a) $\frac{x + 1}{x^2 + x + 1} - \frac{x + 1}{(x^2 + x + 1)^2}$

b) $\frac{x - 1}{x^2 + x + 1} + \frac{x + 1}{(x^2 + x + 1)^2}$

c) $\frac{x + 1}{x^2 + x + 1} + \frac{x - 1}{(x^2 + x + 1)^2}$

d) $\frac{x - 1}{x^2 + x + 1} + \frac{x - 1}{(x^2 + x + 1)^2}$

e) None of these

Answer: b Difficulty: 2

SHORT ANSWER

38. Find the partial fraction decomposition: $\dfrac{5x^3 + 4x^2 + 7x + 3}{(x^2 + 2)(x^2 + 1)}$.

Answer:
$\dfrac{2x - 1}{x^2 + 1} + \dfrac{3x + 5}{x^2 + 2}$
Difficulty: 2

39. Find the partial fraction decomposition: $\dfrac{5x + 5}{(x^2 + 1)(x^2 + 5)}$.

Answer:
$\dfrac{x + 1}{x^2 + 1} - \dfrac{x}{x^2 + 5}$
Difficulty: 2

40. Find the partial fraction decomposition: $\dfrac{x^3 + x^2 + 2x - 2}{x^2 - 1}$.

Answer:
$x + 1 + \dfrac{1}{x - 1} + \dfrac{2}{x + 1}$
Difficulty: 2

MULTIPLE CHOICE

41. Find the partial fraction decomposition: $\dfrac{x^3 - x^2 + 4}{x^2 - 1}$.

a) $x - 1 + \dfrac{x}{x - 1} + \dfrac{1}{x + 1}$
b) $x + 1 + \dfrac{4}{x + 1} + \dfrac{-2}{x - 1}$
c) $x - 1 + \dfrac{2}{x - 1} - \dfrac{1}{x + 1}$
d) $x + 1 - \dfrac{3}{x + 1} + \dfrac{1}{x - 1}$
e) None of these

Answer: c Difficulty: 2

42. Find the partial fraction decomposition: $\dfrac{3x^4 + x^2 - 2}{x^2 - 1}$.

a) $3x^2 - 2 - \dfrac{2}{x - 1} + \dfrac{1}{x + 1}$

b) $3x^2 - 2$

c) $3x^2 - 4 + \dfrac{2}{x + 1} - \dfrac{1}{x - 1}$

d) $3x^2 + 4 + \dfrac{1}{x - 1} - \dfrac{1}{x + 1}$

e) None of these

Answer: d Difficulty: 2

Chapter 031: Exponential Functions and Their Graphs

MULTIPLE CHOICE

1. Evaluate: $5.1(1.32)^{\sqrt{2}}$. Round your answer to 3 decimal places.
a) 14.831 b) 27.693 c) 9.520
d) 7.552 e) None of these

Answer: d Difficulty: 1

2. Evaluate: $4.7e^{\sqrt{3}}$. Round your answer to 3 decimal places.
a) 82.476 b) 74.108 c) 26.565
d) 22.128 e) None of these

Answer: c Difficulty: 1

3. Evaluate: $\sqrt[3]{e}$. Round your answer to 3 decimal places.
a) 0.910 b) 1.396 c) 0.050
d) 20.086 e) None of these

Answer: b Difficulty: 1

4. Evaluate: $(2)(4^{2e})$. Round your answer to 3 decimal places.
a) 86.985 b) 81,228.082 c) 12,343.031
d) 3751.176 e) None of these

Answer: d Difficulty: 1

5. Evaluate $300e^{-0.076t}$ when $t = 15$. Round your answer to 2 decimal places.
a) 95.95 b) 39.31 c) 0.000479718
d) -1906.12 e) None of these

Answer: a Difficulty: 1

6. Evaluate: $\dfrac{3e^{52t}}{1 - t}$ when $t = 0.0721$. Round your answer to 4 decimal places.
a) 4.2727 b) 180.6908 c) 137.3653
d) -410.3055 e) None of these

Answer: c Difficulty: 1

7. Evaluate $y = \dfrac{300}{1 + e^{-2t}}$ when $t = 3$. Round your answer to 4 decimal places.
a) 299.2582 b) 213.3704 c) 300.0025
d) 107.4591 e) None of these

Answer: a Difficulty: 1

SHORT ANSWER

8. Evaluate $200 - 5e^{0.002x}$ when $x = 65$. Round your answer to 4 decimal places.

   Answer: 194.3059 Difficulty: 1

9. Evaluate $16e^{-0.015x}$ when $x = -20$. Round your answer to 4 decimal places.

   Answer: 21.5977 Difficulty: 1 Key 1: T

MULTIPLE CHOICE

10. If $g(x) = 2^{x+3} - 1$ is a transformation of $f(x) = 2^x$, then $g(x)$ is:
    a) shifted right 3 units and down 1 unit.
    b) shifted up 3 units and left 1 unit.
    c) shifted left 3 units and down 1 unit.
    d) shifted up 3 units and right 1 unit.

    Answer: c Difficulty: 1

11. If $g(x) = -2^x + 5$ is a transformation of $f(x) = 2^x$, then $g(x)$ is:
    a) shifted left 5 units and down 1 unit.
    b) reflected over the x-axis and shifted up 5 units.
    c) shifted right 5 units and down 1 unit.
    d) reflected over the y-axis and shifted up 5 units.

    Answer: b Difficulty: 1

12. If $g(x) = 2^{-x} - 7$ is a transformation of $f(x) = 2^x$, then $g(x)$ is:
    a) shifted left 1 unit and down 7 units.
    b) shifted right 1 unit and down 7 units.
    c) reflected over the x-axis and shifted down 7 units.
    d) reflected over the y-axis and shifted down 7 units.

    Answer: d Difficulty: 1

13. If $g(x) = -2^{4-x}$ is a transformation of $f(x) = 2^x$, then $g(x)$ is:
    a) reflected over the x-axis and shifted to the left 4 units.
    b) reflected over both the x- and y-axis and shifted to the right 4 units.
    c) reflected over both the x- and y-axis and shifted to the left 4 units.
    d) reflected over the y-axis and shifted to the left 4 units.

    Answer: b Difficulty: 1

14. Match the graph with the correct function.

a) $f(x) = 4^x - 5$ b) $f(x) = 4^x + 5$ c) $f(x) = 4^{-x} + 5$

d) $f(x) = 4^{-x} - 5$ e) None of these

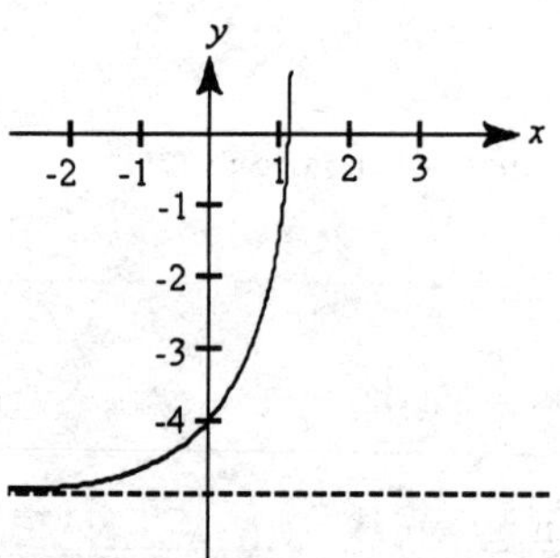

Answer: a Difficulty: 1

15. Match the graph with the correct function.

a) $y = 3^{x-1}$ b) $y = 3^x - 1$ c) $y = 3^{1-x}$

d) $y = 3^{-x} - 1$ e) None of these

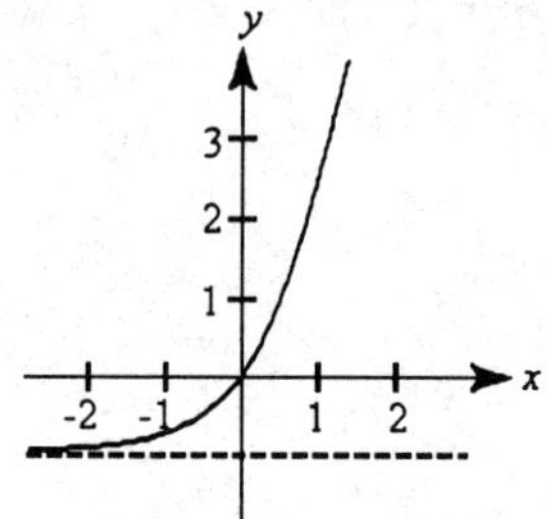

Answer: b Difficulty: 1

16. Match the graph with the correct function.

a) $f(x) = \left(\frac{1}{2}\right)^x - 1$ b) 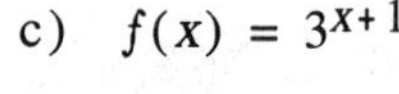 $f(x) = 3^{-x^2} - 1$ c) $f(x) = 3^{x+1}$

d) $f(x) = 4^{-x}$ e) None of these

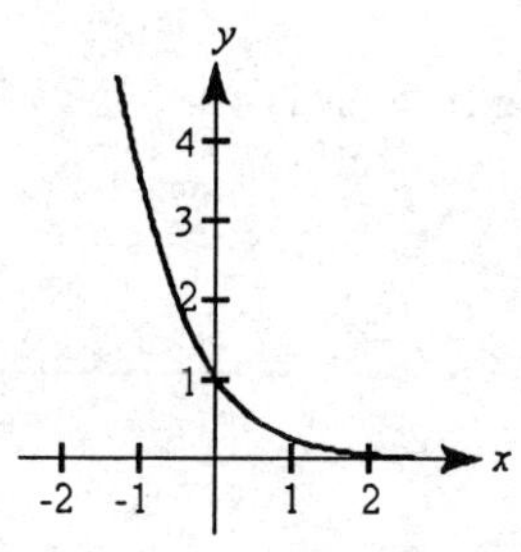

Answer: d Difficulty: 2

17. Match the graph with the correct function.

a) $f(x) = 5^{x+3}$ b) $f(x) = 5^{x} + 3$
c) $f(x) = 5^{x-3}$ d) $f(x) = 5^{x} - 3$

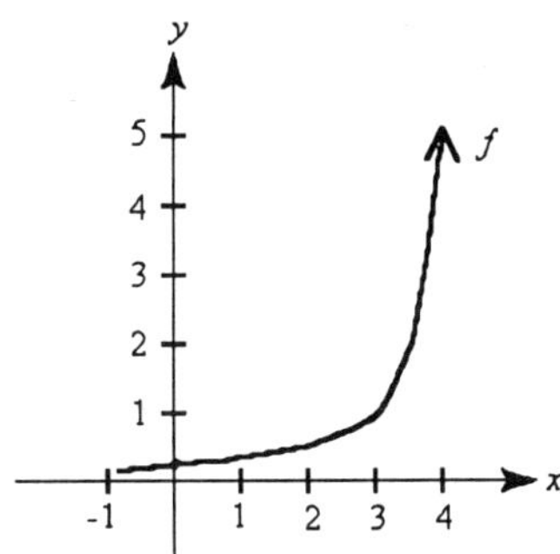

Answer: c Difficulty: 1

18. Match the graph with the correct function.

a) $f(x) = 5^{x+3}$ b) $f(x) = 5^{x} + 3$
c) $f(x) = 5^{x-3}$ d) $f(x) = 5^{x} - 3$

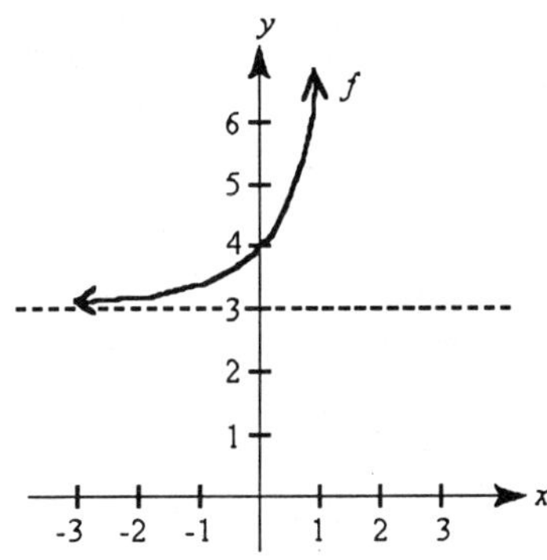

Answer: b Difficulty: 1

19. Match the graph with the correct function.

a) $f(x) = 5^{x+1} - 2$ b) $f(x) = 5^{x+2} - 1$
c) $f(x) = 5^{x-1} + 2$ d) $f(x) = 5^{x-2} + 1$

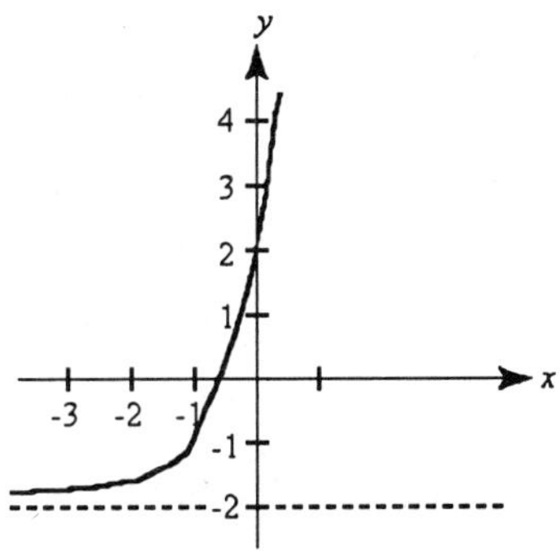

Answer: a Difficulty: 1

SHORT ANSWER

20. Without using a graphing utility, sketch the graph of $f(x) = 3^x - 5$.

Answer: See graph below.

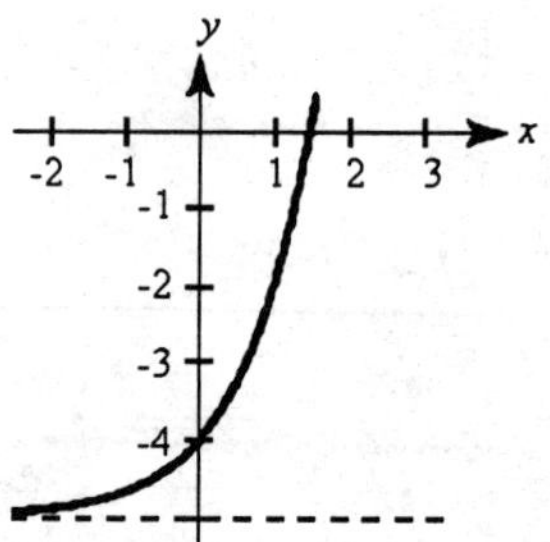

Difficulty: 1

21. Without using a graphing utility, sketch the graph of $f(x) = 3^x - 2$.

Answer: See graph below.

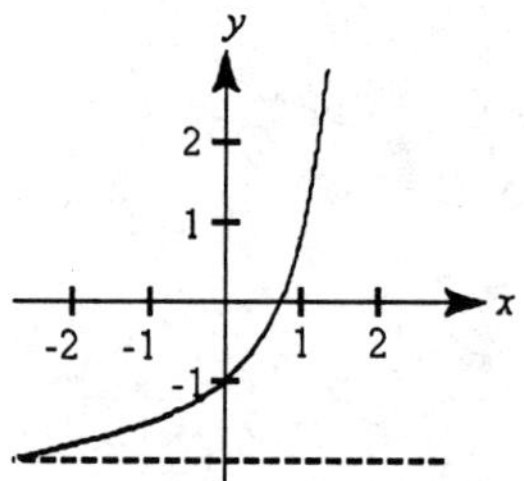

Difficulty: 1

MULTIPLE CHOICE

22. Match the exponential function with the correct graph of $f(x) = e^x$.
a) I b) II c) III d) IV e) None of these

(I)
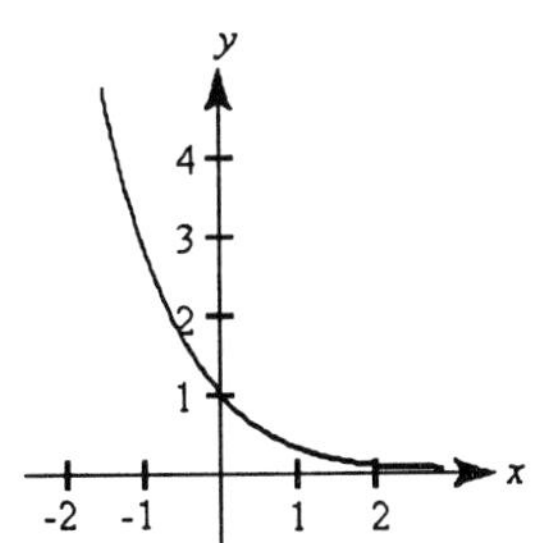

(II)
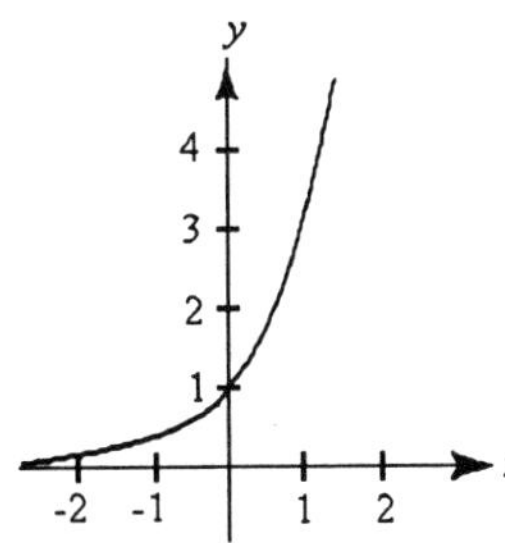

(III)
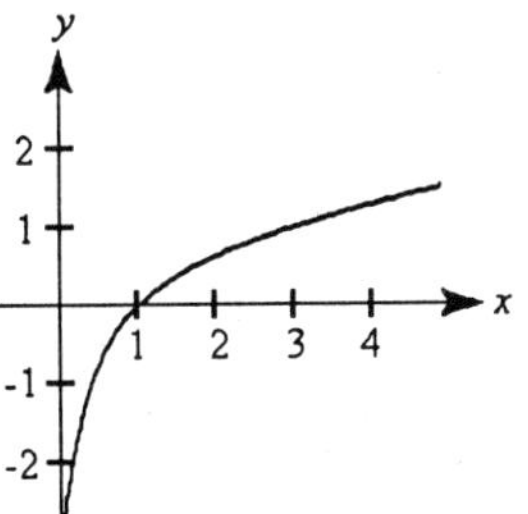

(IV)
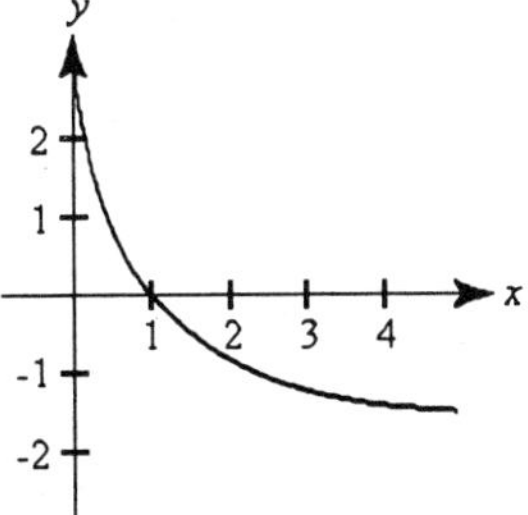

Answer: b Difficulty: 1

23. Match the exponential function with the correct graph of: $f(x) = 2 - e^x$.
a) I b) II c) III d) IV e) None of these

(I)
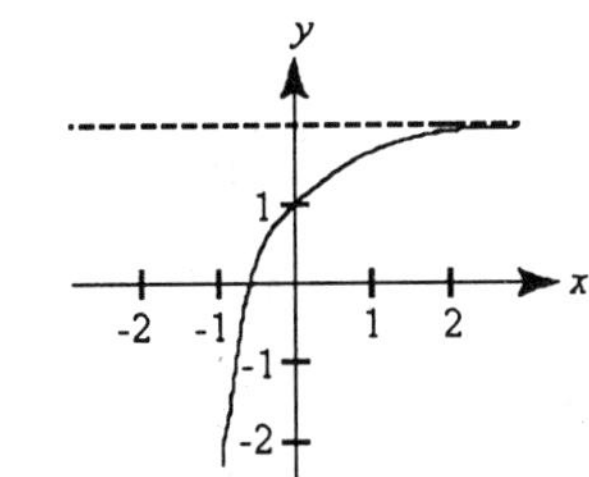

(II)
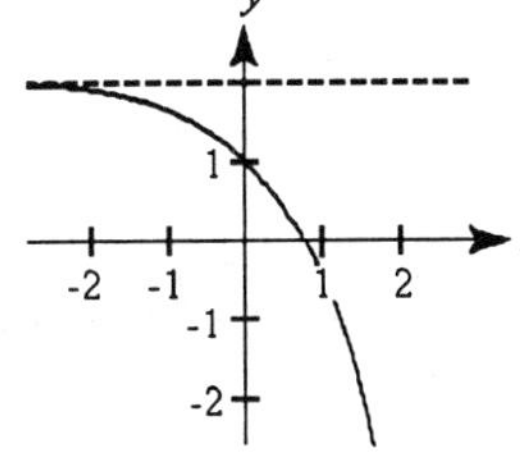

(III)
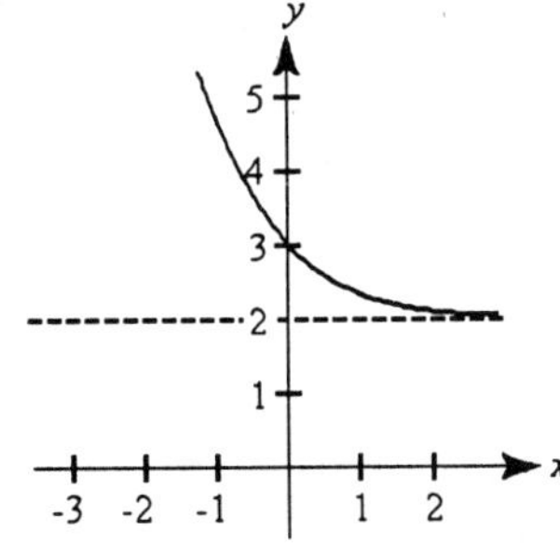

(IV)
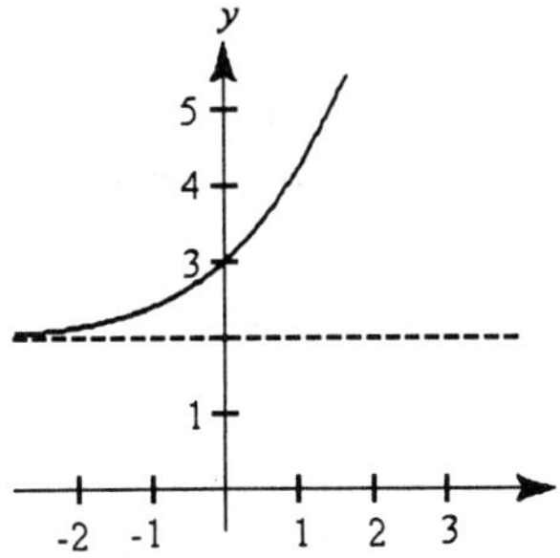

Answer: b Difficulty: 1

24. Match the exponential function with the correct graph of:

$f(x) = \left(\frac{1}{5}\right)^x + 1$

a) I b) II c) III d) IV e) None of these

(I)

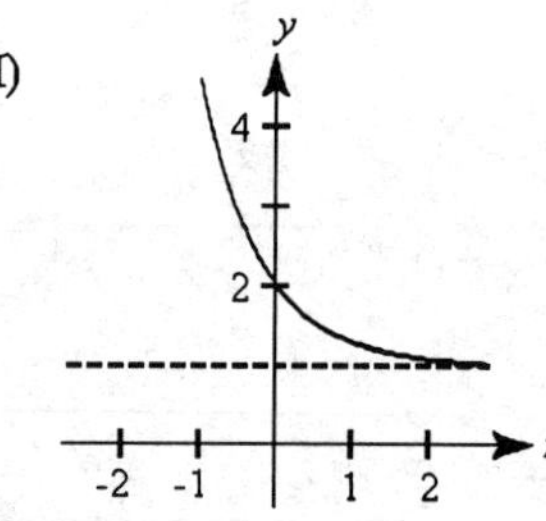

(II)

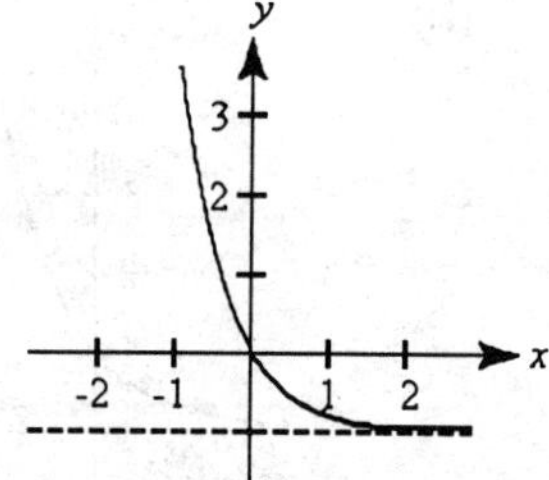

(III)

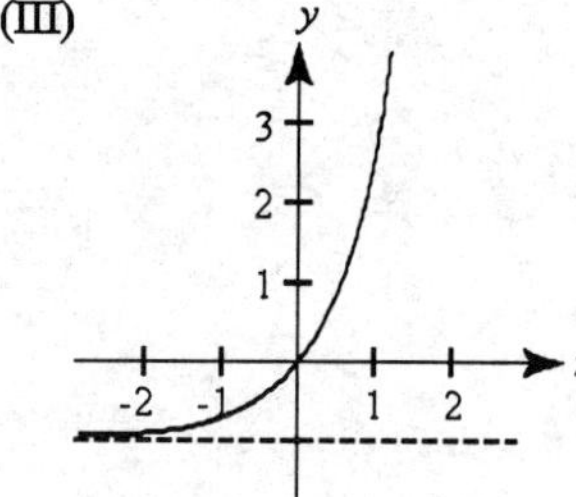

(IV)

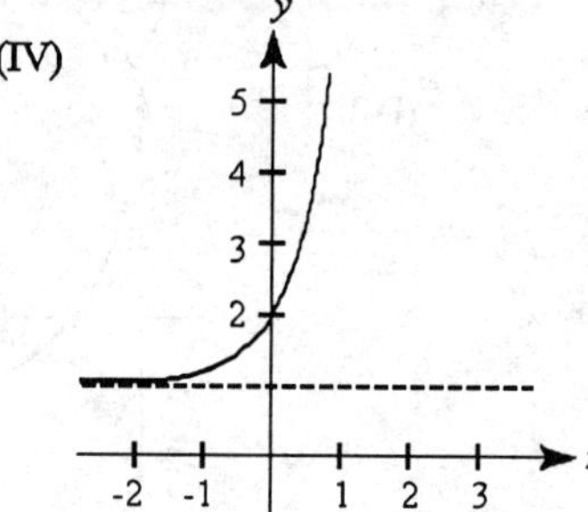

Answer: a Difficulty: 1

25. The domain of $f(x) = 1 + e^{-x}$ is:

a) $(-\infty, \infty)$ b) $(0, \infty)$ c) $(-1, \infty)$
d) $(1, \infty)$ e) None of these

Answer: a Difficulty: 1

26. The domain of $f(x) = 3 - e^x$ is:

a) $(3, \infty)$ b) $(0, \infty)$ c) $(-\infty, \infty)$
d) $(-\infty, 3)$ e) None of these

Answer: c Difficulty: 1

27. The range of $f(x) = 1 + e^{-x}$ is:

a) $(-\infty, \infty)$ b) $(0, \infty)$ c) $(-1, \infty)$
d) $(1, \infty)$ e) None of these

Answer: d Difficulty: 2

28. The range of $f(x) = 3 - e^x$ is

a) $(3, \infty)$ b) $(0, \infty)$ c) $(-\infty, \infty)$
d) $(-\infty, 3)$ e) None of these

Answer: d Difficulty: 2

SHORT ANSWER

29. Use a graphing utility to graph $f(x) = 2^{x-1}$.

Answer: See graph below.

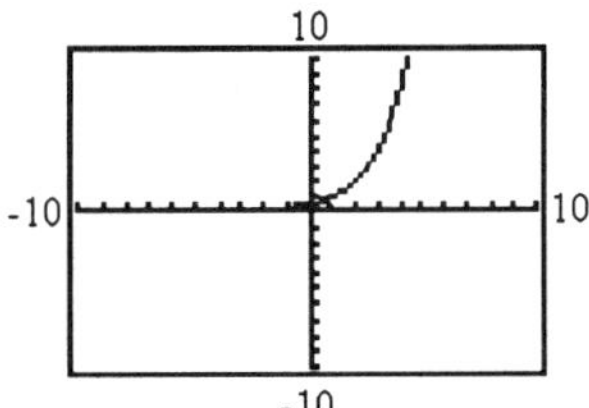

Difficulty: 1 Key 1: T

30. Use a graphing utility to graph $y = 3^{x+1} - 1$.

Answer: See graph below.

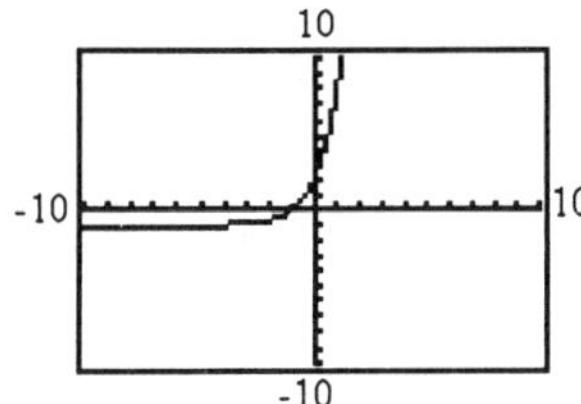

Difficulty: 1 Key 1: T

31. Use a graphing utility to graph $y = \left(\frac{2}{5}\right)^x$.

Answer: See graph below.

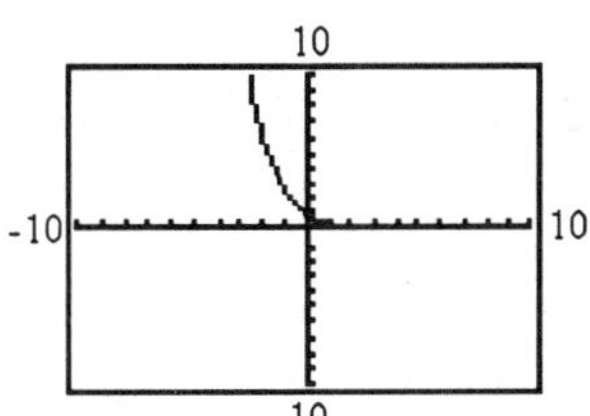

Difficulty: 1 Key 1: T

32. Use a graphing utility to graph $s(t) = 2e^{0.5t}$

Answer: See graph below.

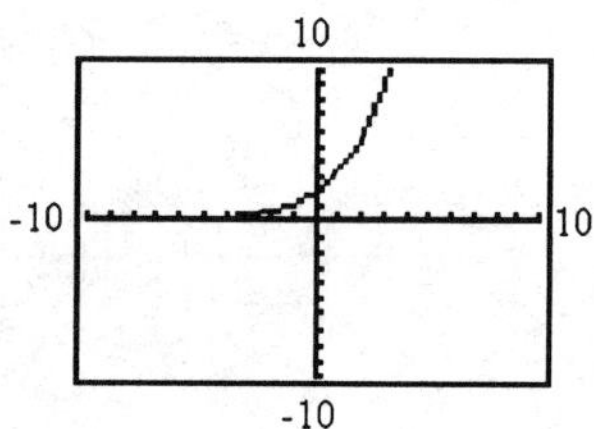

Difficulty: 1 Key 1: T

33. Use a graphing utility to graph the function $f(x) = \dfrac{2}{1 + e^{-0.2/x}}$. Use the graph to find any asymptotes of the function.

Answer: See graph below.

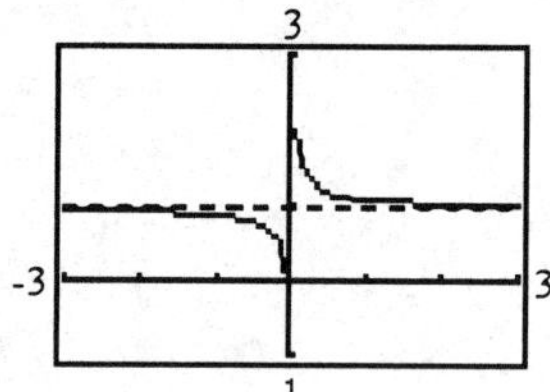

; Vertical asymptote: $x = 0$
Horizontal asymptote: $y = 1$

Difficulty: 2 Key 1: T

34. Use a graphing utility to graph the function $f(x) = \dfrac{4}{2 + e^{-0.2/x}}$. Use the graph to find any asymptotes of the function.

Answer: See graph below.

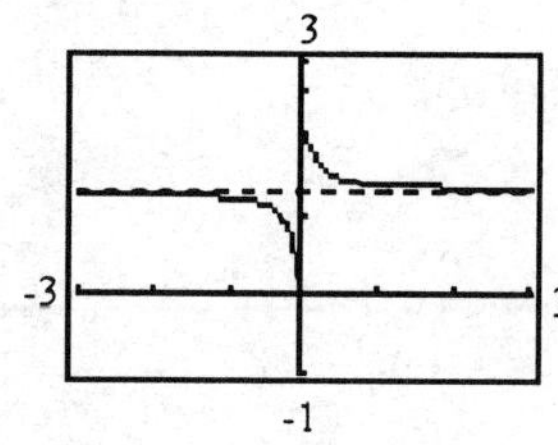

; Vertical asymptote: $x = 0$
Horizontal asymptote: $y = \frac{4}{3}$

Difficulty: 2 Key 1: T

35. Use a graphing utility to graph the function $f(x) = x^2e^x$. Use the graph to determine the intervals for which the function is increasing and decreasing and any relative extrema.

Answer: See graph below.

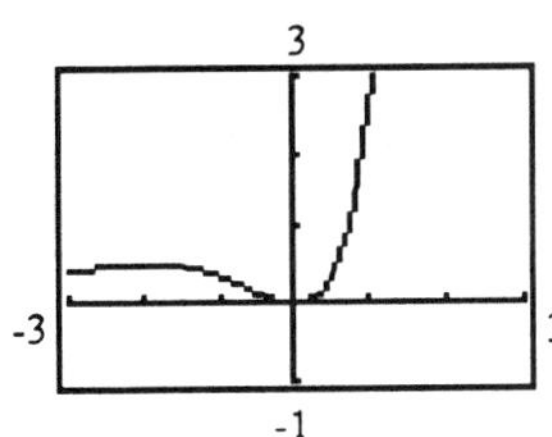

; Increasing on $(-\infty, -2)$ and $(0, \infty)$
Decreasing on $(-2, 0)$

Relative maximum: $(-2, 0.541)$ or $\left(-2, \frac{4}{e^2}\right)$
Relative minimum: $(0, 0)$

Difficulty: 2 Key 1: T

36. Use a graphing utility to graph the function $f(x) = xe^{-x}$. Use the graph to determine the intervals for which the function is increasing and decreasing and any relative extrema.

Answer: See graph below.

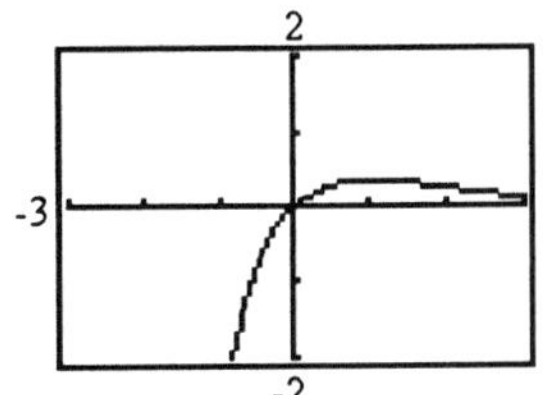

; Increasing on $(-\infty, -1)$
Decreasing on $(1, \infty)$

Relative maximum: $(1, 0.368)$ or $\left(1, \frac{1}{e}\right)$

Difficulty: 2 Key 1: T

MULTIPLE CHOICE

37. \$1500 is invested at a rate of 8% compounded quarterly. What is the balance at the end of 5 years?

a) \$1624.67　b) \$2237.74　c) \$2228.92
d) \$2226.04　e) None of these

Answer: c Difficulty: 1

38. \$1500 is invested at a rate of 10% compounded quarterly. What is the balance at the end of 12 years?

a) \$1657.70　b) \$3512.55　c) \$4955.47
d) \$4980.18　e) None of these

Answer: c Difficulty: 1

SHORT ANSWER

39. $2100 is invested at a rate of 7% compounded monthly. What is the balance at the end of 10 years?

Answer: $4220.29 Difficulty: 1

40. $3500 is invested at a rate of 9% compounded continuously. What is the balance at the end of 18 months?

Answer: $4005.88 Difficulty: 1

MULTIPLE CHOICE

41. $3500 is invested at a rate of $4\frac{1}{2}\%$ compounded continuously. What is the balance at the end of 10 years?
a) $315,059.96 b) $5472.45 c) $5221.39
d) $5489.09 e) None of these

Answer: d Difficulty: 1

SHORT ANSWER

42. $2000 is invested at a rate of $7\frac{1}{2}\%$ compounded continuously. What is the balance at the end of 20 years?

Answer: $8963.38 Difficulty: 1

MULTIPLE CHOICE

43. Determine the amount of money that should be invested at a rate of 8% compounded quarterly to produce a final balance of $20,000 in 10 years.
a) $16,406.97 b) $9057.81 c) $18,463.80
d) $9081.26 e) None of these

Answer: b Difficulty: 2

44. Determine the amount of money that should be invested at a rate of $6\frac{1}{2}\%$ compounded monthly to produce a final balance of $15,000 in 20 years.
a) $4102.34 b) $5216.07 c) $2458.83
d) $14,056.14 e) None of these

Answer: a Difficulty: 2

SHORT ANSWER

45. Determine the amount of money that should be invested at a rate of 7% compounded continuously to produce a final balance of $15,000 in 20 years.

Answer: $3698.95 Difficulty: 2

46. A certain population decreases according to the equation $y = 300 - 5e^{0.2t}$. Find the initial population and the population (to the nearest integer) when $t = 10$.

Answer: 295, 263 Difficulty: 2

47. A certain population grows according to the equation $y = 40e^{0.025t}$. Find the initial population and the population (to the nearest integer) when $t = 50$.

Answer: 40, 140 Difficulty: 2

MULTIPLE CHOICE

48. A certain population increases according to the model $P(t) = 250e^{0.47t}$. Use the model to determine $P(5)$. Round your answer to the nearest integer.
a) 40 b) 1597 c) 1998 d) 2621 e) None of these

Answer: d Difficulty: 1

49. A certain population increases according to the model $P(t) = 250e^{0.47t}$ with $t = 0$ corresponding to 1990. Use the model to determine the population in the year 2000. Round your answer to the nearest integer.
a) 400 b) 4091 c) 27,487 d) 23,716 e) None of these

Answer: c Difficulty: 1

50. A certain population increases according to the model $P(t) = 250e^{0.47t}$ with $t = 0$ corresponding to 1995. Use the model to determine the population in the year 2003. Round your answer to the nearest integer.
a) 400 b) 2621 c) 10,737 d) 27,487 e) None of these

Answer: c Difficulty: 1

Chapter 032: Logarithmic Functions and Their Graphs

MULTIPLE CHOICE

1. Evaluate: $\log_7 7$.
   a) 1 b) 0 c) 2 d) 49 e) None of these

   Answer: a Difficulty: 1

2. Evaluate: $\log_a a^3$.
   a) a^3 b) a c) 3 d) $3a$ e) None of these

   Answer: c Difficulty: 1

3. Evaluate: $\log_a 1$.
   a) 1 b) a c) $\frac{1}{a}$ d) 0 e) None of these

   Answer: d Difficulty: 1

4. Evaluate: $\log_a \frac{1}{a}$.
   a) 1 b) -1 c) a d) $\frac{1}{a}$ e) None of these

   Answer: b Difficulty: 1

5. Evaluate: $\ln e^{1-x}$.
   a) e^{1-x} b) e c) $1 - x$ d) $\ln(1 - x)$ e) None of these

   Answer: c Difficulty: 1

6. Evaluate: ln 3.76. Round your answer to 4 decimal places.
   a) 1.3244 b) 0.5752 c) 42.9484
   d) 5754.3994 e) None of these

   Answer: a Difficulty: 1

7. Evaluate: $\log\sqrt{18}$. Round your answer to 4 decimal places.
   a) $\sqrt{18}$ b) 4.2426 c) 1.4452
   d) 0.6276 e) None of these

   Answer: d Difficulty: 1

8. Evaluate: $\ln(1 + \sqrt{2})$. Round your answer to 4 decimal places.
   a) 0.3828 b) 0.8814 c) 0.3466
   d) 0.1505 e) None of these

   Answer: b Difficulty: 1

9. Evaluate: $\log(1 + \sqrt{2})$. Round your answer to 4 decimal places.
a) 0.3828 b) 0.8814 c) 0.3466
d) 0.1505 e) None of these

Answer: a Difficulty: 1

10. Evaluate 3 ln*e*.
a) 3 b) -3 c) 0 d) $\frac{1}{3}$ e) None of these

Answer: a Difficulty: 1

11. Write the logarithmic form: $4^3 = 64$.
a) $4 \log 3 = 64$ b) $\log_4 64 = 3$ c) $\log_3 4 = 64$
d) $\log_3 64 = 4$ e) None of these

Answer: b Difficulty: 1

12. Write in logarithmic form: $64^{1/6} = 2$.
a) $\log_{1/6} 2 = 64$ b) $\log_2 \frac{1}{6} = 64$ c) $\log_{64} \frac{1}{6} = 2$
d) $\log_{64} 2 = \frac{1}{6}$ e) None of these

Answer: d Difficulty: 1

SHORT ANSWER

13. Write the logarithmic form: $5^2 = 25$.

Answer: $\log_5 25 = 2$ Difficulty: 1

14. Write the logarithmic form: $3^5 = 243$.

Answer: $\log_3 243 = 5$ Difficulty: 1

MULTIPLE CHOICE

15. Write the exponential form: $\log_b 37 = 2$.
a) $37^2 = b$ b) $2^b = 37$ c) $b = 10$
d) $b^2 = 37$ e) None of these

Answer: d Difficulty: 1

16. Write the exponential form: $\log_b 7 = 13$.
a) $7^{13} = b$ b) $b^{13} = 7$ c) $b^7 = 13$
d) $7^b = 13$ e) None of these

Answer: b Difficulty: 1

17. Write the exponential form: $\log_7 b = 12$.
a) $7^{12} = b$
b) $b^7 = 12$
c) $7^b = 12$
d) $b^{12} = 7$
e) None of these

Answer: a Difficulty: 1

SHORT ANSWER

18. Write the exponential form: $\log_b 2 = 8$.

Answer:

$b^8 = 2$

Difficulty: 1

MULTIPLE CHOICE

19. Evaluate: $\dfrac{15 \ln 23}{\ln 7 - \ln 2}$. Round your answer to 4 decimal places.
a) 37.5429
b) 23.4767
c) 34.8698
d) 22,218,828.2613
e) None of these

Answer: a Difficulty: 1

20. Evaluate: $\dfrac{3 \ln 5}{7 \ln 6 - 2 \ln 7}$. Round your answer to 4 decimal places.
a) -3.8222
b) -2.6559
c) 0.5582
d) -11.6058
e) None of these

Answer: c Difficulty: 1

21. Evaluate: $\dfrac{16 \ln 5}{1 + 2 \ln 3}$. Round your answer to 4 decimal places.
a) 918.3228
b) 27.9482
c) 8.0542
d) 22.5538
e) None of these

Answer: c Difficulty: 1

SHORT ANSWER

22. Evaluate: $\dfrac{16 \ln(1/2)}{3 \ln 10}$. Round your answer to 4 decimal places.

Answer: -1.6055 Difficulty: 1

MULTIPLE CHOICE

23. Find the domain of the function: $f(x) = \ln(3x + 1)$.
    a) $(-\infty, \infty)$ b) $\left(-\frac{1}{3}, \infty\right)$ c) $(0, \infty)$
    d) $\left(\frac{1}{3}, \infty\right)$ e) None of these

    Answer: b Difficulty: 1

24. Find the domain of the function: $f(x) = 3\log(5x - 2)$.
    a) $(-\infty, \infty)$ b) $(0, \infty)$ c) $\left(\frac{2}{5}, \infty\right)$
    d) $\left(\frac{2}{15}, \infty\right)$ e) None of these

    Answer: c Difficulty: 1

25. Find the domain of the function: $f(x) = 3 + \ln(x - 1)$.
    a) $(-\infty, \infty)$ b) $(0, \infty)$ c) $(1, \infty)$
    d) $(3, \infty)$ e) None of these

    Answer: c Difficulty: 1

SHORT ANSWER

26. Find the domain of the function: $f(x) = 3 - \log(x^2 - 1)$.

    Answer: $(-\infty, -1)$, $(1, \infty)$ Difficulty: 2

27. Find the domain of the function: $f(x) = \log_3(x^2 - 4)$.

    Answer: $(-\infty, -2)$, $(2, \infty)$ Difficulty: 2

28. Find the domain of the function: $f(x) = -\log_2 x + 5$.

    Answer: $(0, \infty)$ Difficulty: 1

MULTIPLE CHOICE

29. Find the vertical asymptote: $f(x) = \ln(x + 2)$.
    a) $x = 2$ b) $x = 0$ c) $y = 2$
    d) $x = -2$ e) None of these

    Answer: d Difficulty: 2

30. Find the vertical asymptote: $f(x) = 2 + \ln x$.
    a) $x = 2$ b) $y = 2$ c) $x = 0$
    d) $x = -2$ e) None of these

    Answer: c Difficulty: 2

SHORT ANSWER

31. Find the vertical asymptote: $f(x) = \log_{10}\left(\frac{x}{2}\right) + 6$.

Answer: $x = 0$ Difficulty: 2

MULTIPLE CHOICE

32. Match the graph with the correct function.
a) $f(x) = -3 + \ln x$
b) $f(x) = 3 + \ln x$
c) $f(x) = \ln(x - 3)$
d) $f(x) = \ln(x + 3)$

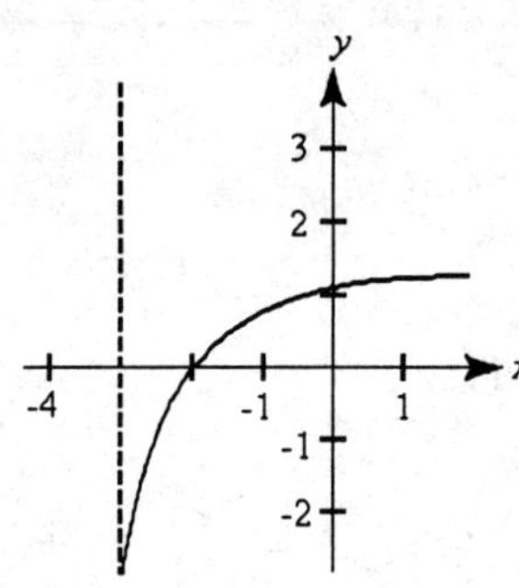

Answer: d Difficulty: 1

33. Match the graph with the correct function.
a) $f(x) = 3 + \log x$
b) $f(x) = \log(x + 3)$
c) $f(x) = \frac{1}{3} \log x$
d) $f(x) = 3 \log x$

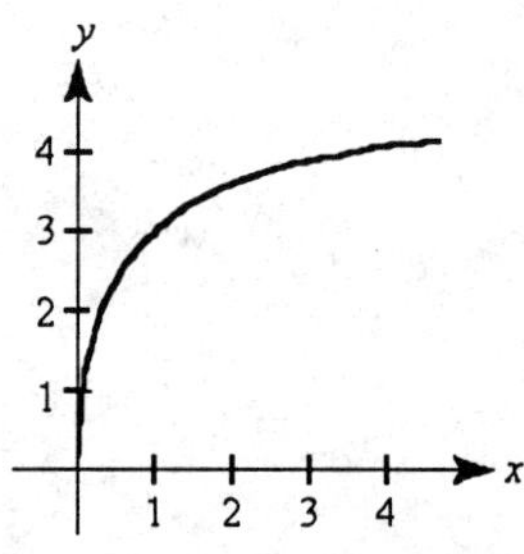

Answer: a Difficulty: 1

34. Match the graph with the correct function.

a) $f(x) = e^x$

b) $f(x) = e^{x-1}$

c) $f(x) = \ln x$

d) $f(x) = \ln(x - 1)$

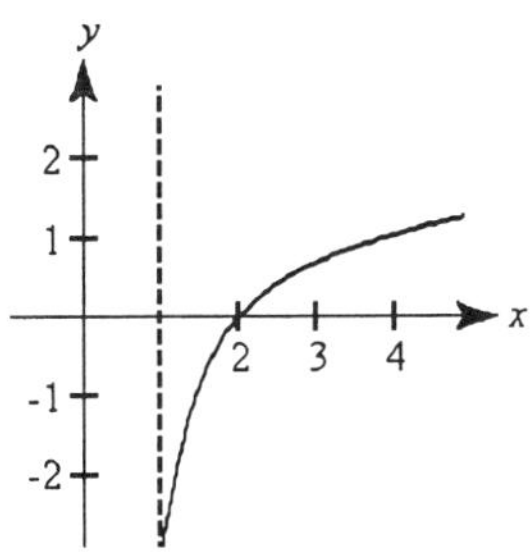

Answer: d Difficulty: 1

SHORT ANSWER

35. Sketch the graph: $f(x) = 1 + \log_5 x$.

Answer: See graph below.

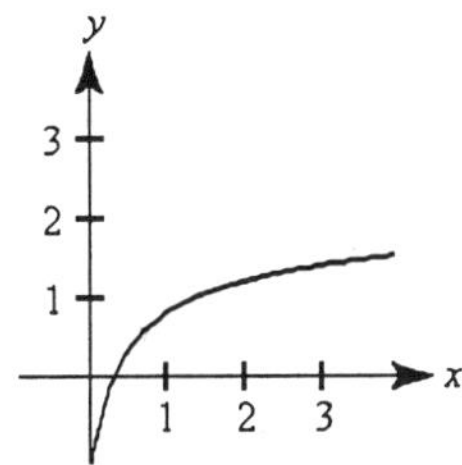

Difficulty: 1

36. Sketch the graph: $y = \ln(1 - x)$.

Answer: See graph below.

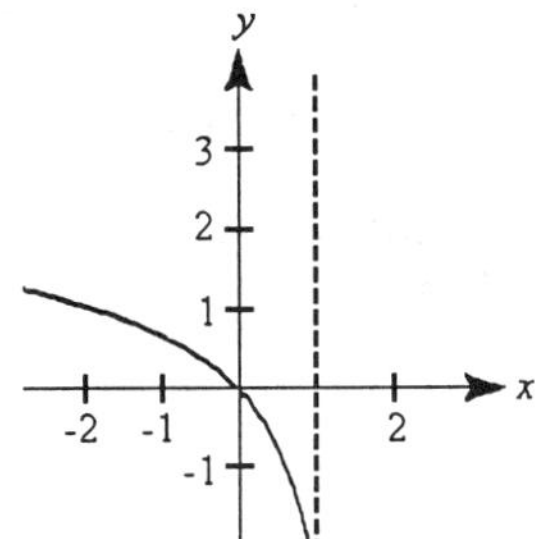

Difficulty: 2

37. Use a graphing utility to graph $f(x) = \ln(x + 1)$. Determine the domain, x-intercept, and vertical asymptote of the function.

Answer:
See graph below.
Domain: $(-1, \infty)$
x-intercept: $(0, 0)$
Vertical asymptote: $x = -1$

Difficulty: 2 Key 1: T

38. Use a graphing utility to graph $f(x) = \ln(2 - x)$. Determine the domain, x-intercept, and vertical asymptote of the function.

Answer:
See graph below.
Domain: $(-\infty, 2)$
x-intercept: $(0, 0)$
Vertical asymptote: $x = 2$

Difficulty: 2 Key 1: T

MULTIPLE CHOICE

39. Students in an algebra class were given an exam and then tested monthly with an equivalent exam. The average score for the class was given by the human memory model

$$f(t) = 85 - 16 \log_{10}(t + 1), \ 0 \le t \le 12$$

where t is the time in months. What is the average score after 3 months?
a) 77 b) 67 c) 75 d) 63 e) None of these

Answer: c Difficulty: 2

40. Students in an algebra class were given an exam and then tested monthly with an equivalent exam. The average score for the class was given by the human memory model

$$f(t) = 85 - 16 \log_{10}(t + 1), \ 0 \le t \le 12$$

where t is the time in months. What is the average score after 5 months?
a) 73 b) 74 c) 59 d) 56 e) None of these

Answer: a Difficulty: 2

41. Students in an algebra class were given an exam and then tested monthly with an equivalent exam. The average score for the class was given by the human memory model

$$f(t) = 85 - 16 \log_{10}(t + 1), \ 0 \le t \le 12$$

where t is the time in months. What is the average score after 10 months?
a) 69 b) 48 c) 47 d) 68 e) None of these

Answer: d Difficulty: 2

42. A principal P invested at $7\frac{1}{2}\%$ interest compounded continuously increases to an amount K times the original principal after t years, where t is given by $t = \frac{\ln K}{0.075}$. Determine the number of years necessary to triple the investment (Hint: $K = 3$).
a) 6.4 b) 14.6 c) 12.8 d) 8.2 e) None of these

Answer: b Difficulty: 2

43. A principal P invested at $6\frac{1}{2}\%$ interest compounded continuously increases to an amount K times the original principal after t years, where t is given by $t = \frac{\ln K}{0.065}$. Determine the number of years necessary to triple the investment (Hint: $K = 3$).
a) 7.3 b) 9.2 c) 14.8 d) 16.9 e) None of these

Answer: d Difficulty: 2

44. A principal P invested at $8\frac{1}{2}\%$ interest compounded continuously increases to an amount K times the original principal after t years, where t is given by $t = \frac{\ln K}{0.085}$. Determine the number of years necessary to triple the investment (Hint: $K = 3$).
a) 5.6 b) 8.2 c) 12.9 d) 15.1 e) None of these

Answer: c Difficulty: 2

Chapter 033: Properties of Logarithms

MULTIPLE CHOICE

1. Use the change of base formula to identify the expression that is equivalent to $\log_2 7$.
   a) $\frac{\log 2}{\log 7}$ b) $\frac{\ln 2}{\ln 7}$ c) $\frac{\ln 7}{\ln 2}$
   d) $2 \log 7$ e) None of these

   Answer: c Difficulty: 1

2. Use the change of base formula to identify the expression that is equivalent to $\log_3 5$.
   a) $\frac{\log 5}{\log 3}$ b) $\frac{\ln 3}{\ln 5}$ c) $5 \ln 3$
   d) $\log \frac{5}{3}$ e) None of these

   Answer: a Difficulty: 1

3. Use the change of base formula to identify the expression that is equivalent to $\log_3 10$.
   a) $\frac{\ln 3}{\ln 10}$ b) $10 \log 3$ c) $\ln \frac{10}{3}$
   d) $\frac{1}{\log 3}$ e) None of these

   Answer: d Difficulty: 2

4. Use the change of base formula to identify the expression that is equivalent to $\log_t u$.
   a) $\frac{\log t}{\log u}$ b) $u \log t$ c) $\frac{\log u}{\log t}$
   d) $t \log u$ e) None of these

   Answer: c Difficulty: 1

5. Evaluate $\log_4 7$ using the change of base formula. Round your answer to 4 decimal places.
   a) 0.2430 b) 0.5596 c) 0.7124
   d) 1.4037 e) None of these

   Answer: d Difficulty: 2

6. Evaluate $\log_{1/2} 13$ using the change of base formula. Round your answer to 4 decimal places.
   a) 2.5649 b) 1.1139 c) -0.2702
   d) -3.7004 e) None of these

   Answer: d Difficulty: 2

7. Evaluate $\log_7 15$ using the change of base formula. Round your answer to 4 decimal places.
   a) 1.3917 b) 12.6765 c) 2.1429
   d) 0.7186 e) None of these

   Answer: a Difficulty: 2

SHORT ANSWER

8. Evaluate $\log_5 22$ using the change of base formula. Round your answer to 4 decimal places.

   Answer: 1.9206 Difficulty: 2

9. Evaluate $\log_5 17$ using the change of base formula. Round your answer to 4 decimal places.

   Answer: 1.7604 Difficulty: 2

10. Evaluate $\log_{1/2} 6.8$ using the change of base formula. Round your answer to 4 decimal places.

    Answer: -2.7655 Difficulty: 2

11. Evaluate $\log_{3.2} \frac{1}{10}$ using the change of base formula. Round your answer to 4 decimal places.

    Answer: -1.9796 Difficulty: 2

MULTIPLE CHOICE

12. Write as a sum, difference, or multiple of logarithms: $\log \sqrt[3]{\frac{a^2 b}{c}}$.
    a) $\sqrt[3]{\frac{2 \log a + \log b}{\log c}}$ b) $\frac{1}{3}\left[\frac{2 \log a + \log b}{\log c}\right]$
    c) $\frac{1}{3}(2 \log a + \log b - \log c)$ d) $\sqrt[3]{2 \log a^2 + \log b - \log c}$
    e) None of these

    Answer: c Difficulty: 1

13. Write as a sum, difference, or multiple of logarithms: $\log_b\left[\frac{x^3 y^2}{\sqrt{w}}\right]$.
    a) $x^3 + y^3 - \sqrt{w}$ b) $\frac{1}{3} \log_b x + \frac{1}{2} \log_b y - 2 \log_b w$
    c) $3 \log_b x + 2 \log_b y - \frac{1}{2} \log_b w$ d) $\frac{3 \log x + 2 \log y}{(1/2) \log w}$
    e) None of these

    Answer: c Difficulty: 1

SHORT ANSWER

14. Write as a sum, difference, or multiple of logarithms: $\ln \dfrac{5x}{\sqrt[3]{x^2 + 1}}$.

Answer:

$\ln 5 + \ln x - \frac{1}{3}\ln(x^2 + 1)$

Difficulty: 1

15. Write as a sum, difference, or multiple of logarithms:

$\ln \left[\dfrac{x^3\sqrt{y}}{(x^2 + 4)^5}\right]$.

Answer:

$3\ln x + \frac{1}{2}\ln y - 5\ln(x^2 + 4)$

Difficulty: 2

MULTIPLE CHOICE

16. The expression $\log_2 \sqrt{\dfrac{x^2}{y}}$ is equivalent to:

a) $\frac{1}{2}[\log_2 x - \log_2 y]$
b) $\log_2 x - \frac{1}{2}\log_2 y$
c) $\frac{1}{2}[\log_2 x + \log_2 y]$
d) $\log_2 x + \frac{1}{2}\log_2 y$
e) None of these

Answer: b Difficulty: 1

17. Write as the logarithm of a single quantity:
$\frac{1}{4}\log_b 16 - 2\log_b 5 + \log_b 7$.

a) $\frac{14}{25}$
b) $\log_b \frac{2}{175}$
c) 1
d) $\log_b \frac{14}{25}$
e) None of these

Answer: d Difficulty: 1

SHORT ANSWER

18. Write as the logarithm of a single quantity:
$\frac{1}{5}$ [3 log(x + 1) + 2 log(x - 1) - log 7].

Answer:
$\log \sqrt[5]{\frac{(x+1)^3(x-1)^2}{7}}$

Difficulty: 2

MULTIPLE CHOICE

19. Write as the logarithm of a single quantity:
$\frac{1}{2}$ [ln(x + 1) + 2 ln(x - 1)] + $\frac{1}{3}$ ln x.
a) $\ln \sqrt[3]{x}\sqrt{(x+1)(x^2-1)}$
b) $\ln \sqrt[3]{x}\sqrt{x^2-1}$
c) $\ln \sqrt{x(x^2-1)}$
d) $\ln \sqrt[3]{x(x+1)(x-1)^2}$
e) None of these

Answer: e Difficulty: 2

20. Write as the logarithm of a single quantity: $\log_2(x - 2) + \log_2(x + 2)$.
a) $-2 + 2\log_2 x$
b) $\log_2(x^2 - 4)$
c) $2\log_2 x$
d) $\log_2 2x$
e) None of these

Answer: b Difficulty: 1

21. Evaluate $\log_a 24$, given that $\log_a 2 = 0.4307$ and $\log_a 3 = 0.6826$.
a) 0.8820
b) 1.9747
c) 0.2940
d) 1.1133
e) None of these

Answer: b Difficulty: 2

SHORT ANSWER

22. Evaluate $\log_b \left(\frac{14}{3b}\right)$, given that $\log_b 2 = 0.2789$, $\log_b 3 = 0.4421$, and $\log_b 7 = 0.7831$.

Answer: -0.3801 Difficulty: 2

23. Evaluate $\log_b \sqrt{10b}$, given that $\log_b 2 = 0.3562$ and $\log_b 5 = 0.8271$.

Answer: 1.09165 Difficulty: 2

MULTIPLE CHOICE

24. Evaluate Log_a 16, given that $\log_a 2 = 0.4307$.
    a) 0.0344 b) 1.7228 c) 4.4307
    d) 1.8168 e) None of these

    Answer: b Difficulty: 1

25. Evaluate: $\log_a 18$, given that $\log_a 2 = 0.2789$ and $\log_a 3 = 0.4421$.
    a) 1.1631 b) 0.2466 c) 0.0349
    d) 1.4420 e) None of these

    Answer: a Difficulty: 1

26. Evaluate: $\log_a \frac{9}{2}$, given that $\log_a 2 = 0.2789$ and $\log_a 3 = 0.4421$.
    a) -0.0834 b) 1.1631 c) -0.3264
    d) 0.6053 e) None of these

    Answer: d Difficulty: 1

27. Simplify: $\ln 5e^3$.
    a) $3 + \ln 5$ b) $3 \ln 5$ c) $3 + 3 \ln 5$
    d) $5e^3$ e) None of these

    Answer: a Difficulty: 2

28. Simplify: $\log_a \sqrt[3]{a}$.
    a) 1 b) -3 c) 0 d) $\frac{1}{3}$ e) None of these

    Answer: d Difficulty: 1

SHORT ANSWER

29. Simplify: $\log_3 405 - \log_3 5$.

    Answer: 4 Difficulty: 1

MULTIPLE CHOICE

30. Simplify: $\log_6 \sqrt{6}$.
    a) 2.4495 b) -2 c) 1 d) $\frac{1}{2}$ e) None of these

    Answer: d Difficulty: 1

31. Simplify: $\log_2 \frac{1}{16}$.

a) 4 b) -4 c) 8 d) $\frac{1}{2}$ e) None of these

Answer: b Difficulty: 1

32. Simplify: $\ln \sqrt{e^3}$.

a) $\ln \frac{3}{2}$ b) $\ln \frac{2}{3}$ c) $\frac{3}{2}$ d) $\frac{2}{3}$ e) None of these

Answer: c Difficulty: 1

33. Simplify: $\log_b 3b^4$.

a) $4 \log_b 3 + 1$ b) $4 + 4 \log_b 3$ c) $4 + \log_b 3$
d) 12 e) None of these

Answer: c Difficulty: 1

34. Simplify: $\ln \sqrt[3]{e^2 x}$.

a) $\frac{2e}{3} + \frac{1}{3} \ln x$ b) $\frac{2}{3} + \ln \frac{x}{3}$ c) $\frac{2}{3} + \frac{1}{3} \ln x$
d) $\frac{2e}{3} + \ln \frac{x}{3}$ e) None of these

Answer: c Difficulty: 2

35. Simplify: $\ln \sqrt[4]{e^3 x}$.

a) $\frac{3}{4} + \frac{1}{4} \ln x$ b) $\frac{3}{4} + \ln \frac{x}{4}$ c) $\frac{3e}{4} + \frac{1}{4} \ln x$
d) $\frac{3e}{4} + \ln \frac{x}{4}$ e) None of these

Answer: a Difficulty: 2

36. Simplify: $\ln \sqrt[5]{e^3 x}$.

a) $\frac{3e}{5} + \frac{1}{5} \ln x$ b) $\frac{3e}{5} + \ln \frac{x}{5}$ c) $\frac{3}{5} + \ln \frac{x}{5}$
d) $\frac{3}{5} + \frac{1}{5} \ln x$ e) None of these

Answer: d Difficulty: 2

37. Simplify: $\log_b \sqrt{4b^3}$.

a) $\log_b 2 + \sqrt{b^3}$ b) $\frac{3}{2} + \frac{3}{2} \log_b 4$ c) $\frac{3}{2} + 3 \log_b 2$
d) $\frac{3}{2} + \log_b 2$ e) None of these

Answer: d Difficulty: 1

38. Which of the following is equivalent to $\log_b 9$?
    a) $\frac{1}{2}\log_b 3$ b) $\log_b 63 + \log_b 7$ c) $\frac{\log_b 27}{\log_b 3}$
    d) $\log_b 54 - \log_b 6$ e) None of these

    Answer: d Difficulty: 1

Chapter 034: Exponential and Logarithmic Equations

MULTIPLE CHOICE

1. Solve for x: $3^{2x} = 81$.
   a) $\frac{27}{2}$ b) $\frac{1}{4}$ c) 4 d) 2 e) None of these

   Answer: d Difficulty: 1

2. Solve for x: $16 = 2^{7x-5}$.
   a) 3 b) $\frac{11}{7}$ c) $\frac{13}{7}$ d) $\frac{9}{7}$ e) None of these

   Answer: d Difficulty: 1

3. Solve for x: $27^x = 81$.
   a) $\frac{3}{4}$ b) $-\frac{1}{3}$ c) $\frac{4}{3}$ d) $\frac{2}{3}$ e) None of these

   Answer: c Difficulty: 1

4. Solve for x: $\left(\frac{1}{2}\right)^x = 16$.
   a) $\frac{1}{8}$ b) -4 c) $\frac{-1}{4}$ d) 8 e) None of these

   Answer: b Difficulty: 1

SHORT ANSWER

5. Solve for x: $2^{x-1} = 16$.

   Answer: 5 Difficulty: 1

MULTIPLE CHOICE

6. Solve for x: $\ln x = -3$.
   a) $\frac{1}{3}$ b) 3 c) $\frac{1}{e^3}$ d) e^3 e) None of these

   Answer: c Difficulty: 1

7. Solve for x: $\log_{10}(x + 4) = 0$.
   a) -3 b) 6 c) -4 d) -14 e) None of these

   Answer: a Difficulty: 1

8. Solve for x: $e^x = 9$.
   a) e^9 b) -9 c) ln 9 d) 3^2 e) None of these

   Answer: c Difficulty: 1

9. Which of the following equations is false?
   a) $b^{\log_b c} = c$ b) $\log_1 b = b$ c) $\log_b b = 1$
   d) All of these equations are false.
   e) All of these equations are true.

   Answer: b Difficulty: 1

10. Simplify: $e^{3 \ln 2}$.
   a) 6 b) 8 c) 9 d) 5 e) None of these

   Answer: b Difficulty: 1

11. Simplify: $e^{2\ln(x+1)}$.
   a) $(x + 1)^2$ b) $2(x + 1)$ c) $e^2 \ln(x + 1)$
   d) $x + 1$ e) None of these

   Answer: a Difficulty: 1

12. Simplify: $3e^{2 \ln x}$.
   a) $3x$ b) $3xe^2$ c) $3x^2$ d) $\ln x^3$ e) None of these

   Answer: c Difficulty: 1

13. Simplify: $2e^{3 \ln(x+1)}$.
   a) $2(x + 1)e^3$ b) $6(x + 1)$ c) $3(x + 1)\ln 2$
   d) $2(x + 1)^3$ e) None of these

   Answer: d Difficulty: 1

14. Simplify: $3 + \ln e^{5x}$.
   a) $\frac{\ln 3}{5x}$ b) $\ln 3 + 5x$ c) $3 + 5x$
   d) $5x \ln 3$ e) None of these

   Answer: c Difficulty: 1

15. Simplify: $7 + 2 \ln e^{5x}$.
   a) $7 + 10x$ b) $7 + 2^{5x}$ c) $45x$
   d) $7 + 2e^{5x}$ e) None of these

   Answer: a Difficulty: 1

16. Simplify: $7 + \ln e^{5x}$.
   a) $5x + \ln 7$ b) $7 + 5x$ c) $\frac{\ln 7}{5x}$
   d) $35x$ e) None of these

   Answer: b Difficulty: 1

17. Solve for x: $\log_x 8 = -3$.
    a) 2 b) 512 c) $\frac{1}{2}$ d) -2 e) None of these

    Answer: c Difficulty: 1

18. Solve for x: $\ln e^{4x} = 60$.
    a) 2.7832 b) 15 c) 1.0236 d) 2.7081 e) None of these

    Answer: b Difficulty: 1

19. Solve for x: $\ln e^{2x+1} = 9$.
    a) $\frac{-1 + \ln 9}{2}$ b) $\frac{9}{2 \ln e} - \frac{1}{2}$ c) 23
    d) 4 e) None of these

    Answer: d Difficulty: 1

SHORT ANSWER

20. Solve for x: $25^{x-2} = 5^{3x}$.

    Answer: -4 Difficulty: 1

21. Solve for x: $2x + \ln e^{4x} = 12$

    Answer: 2 Difficulty: 1

MULTIPLE CHOICE

22. Solve for x: $3^{5x+1} = 5$. Round your answer to 4 decimal places.
    a) 0.1022 b) 0.0930 c) 0.1333
    d) 0.2218 e) None of these

    Answer: b Difficulty: 1

23. Solve for t: $e^{-0.0097t} = 12$. Round your answer to 4 decimal places.
    a) -256.1759 b) -1237.1134 c) 16,778,844.47
    d) -2.5886 e) None of these

    Answer: a Difficulty: 1

24. Solve for x: $3^{2x} = 5^{x-1}$. Round your answer to 4 decimal places.
    a) -0.5563 b) -1 c) -2.7381
    d) 15.2755 e) None of these

    Answer: c Difficulty: 2

SHORT ANSWER

25. Solve for x: $2^{x-1} = 5^{2x+6}$. Round your answer to 4 decimal places.

Answer: -4.0977 Difficulty: 2

26. Solve for x: $16^x = 8^{2x-1}$.

Answer:
$\frac{3}{2}$

Difficulty: 2

MULTIPLE CHOICE

27. Solve for x: $3^{1-x} = 5^x$.
a) $\ln \frac{1}{5}$ b) $\ln \frac{3}{5}$ c) $\frac{\ln 3}{\ln 15}$
d) $(\ln 3)\ln(15)$ e) None of these

Answer: c Difficulty: 2

28. Solve for x: $2^{1-x} = 3^x$.
a) $\frac{\ln 2}{\ln 6}$ b) $\ln \frac{1}{3}$ c) $\ln \frac{2}{3}$
d) $\ln 3 + \ln 2$ e) None of these

Answer: a Difficulty: 2

SHORT ANSWER

29. Solve for x: $\ln x = 5.3670$. Round your answer to 4 decimal places.

Answer: 214.2192 Difficulty: 1

30. Solve for x: $\log_x 16 = 5$. Round your answer to 4 decimal places.

Answer: 1.7411 Difficulty: 2

31. Solve for x: $e^{2x} - 5e^x + 6 = 0$.

Answer: ln 2, ln 3 Difficulty: 2

MULTIPLE CHOICE

32. Solve for x: $\log(3x + 7) + \log(x - 2) = 1$.
a) $\frac{8}{3}$ b) $3, -\frac{8}{3}$ c) 2 d) $2, -\frac{5}{3}$ e) None of these

Answer: a Difficulty: 2

33. Solve for x: $\ln(7 - x) + \ln(3x + 5) = \ln(24x)$.
a) $\frac{6}{11}$ b) $\frac{7}{3}$ c) $\frac{7}{3}, -5$ d) $\frac{6}{11}, 5$ e) None of these

Answer: b Difficulty: 2

34. Solve for x: $\log(7 - x) - \log(3x + 2) = 1$.
a) $\frac{19}{31}$ b) $-\frac{13}{31}$ c) $-\frac{27}{29}$ d) $\frac{9}{4}$ e) None of these

Answer: b Difficulty: 2

SHORT ANSWER

35. Solve for x: $\log x + \log(x + 3) = 1$.

Answer: 2 Difficulty: 2

36. Solve for x: $x^2 - 4x = \log_2 32$.

Answer: -1, 5 Difficulty: 2

37. Solve for x: $\log_3(x^2 + 5) = \log_3(4x^2 - 2x)$.

Answer:
$-1, \frac{5}{3}$

Difficulty: 1

MULTIPLE CHOICE

38. Use a graphing utility to graph $f(x) = 5e^{x+1} - 10$ and approximate its zero accurate to three decimal places.
a) 1.693 b) -0.307 c) 0.588
d) -1.693 e) None of these

Answer: b Difficulty: 2 Key 1: T

SHORT ANSWER

39. Use a graphing utility to graph $f(x) = 4e^{x-5/2} - 2$ and approximate its zero accurate to three decimal places.

Answer: 3.614 Difficulty: 2 Key 1: T

40. Use a graphing utility to approximate the point of intersection of the graphs of $y_1 = 10$ and $y_2 = e^{x+1}$. Round the result to three decimal places.

Answer: (1.303, 10) Difficulty: 2 Key 1: T

41. Use a graphing utility to approximate the point of intersection of the graphs of $y_1 = 5$ and $y_2 = 2 \ln(x + 1)$. Round the result to three decimal places.

Answer: (11.064, 5) Difficulty: 2 Key 1: T

42. Find the number of years required for a \$3000 investment to double at a 7% interest rate compounded continuously.

Answer: 9.9 years Difficulty: 2 Key 1: T

MULTIPLE CHOICE

43. Find the number of years required for a \$2000 investment to triple at an 8% interest rate compounded continuously.
a) 12.6 b) 13.7 c) 11.2 d) 15.1 e) None of these

Answer: b Difficulty: 2 Key 1: T

44. Find the number of years required for a \$2000 investment to triple at a $9\frac{1}{2}\%$ interest rate compounded continuously.
a) 12.6 b) 13.7 c) 11.6 d) 15.1 e) None of these

Answer: c Difficulty: 2 Key 1: T

SHORT ANSWER

45. The yield V (in millions of cubic feet per acre) for the forest at age t years is given by $V = 6.7e^{-48.1/t}$. Find the time necessary to have a yield of 1.7 million cubic feet.

Answer: 35 years Difficulty: 2 Key 1: T

MULTIPLE CHOICE

46. The yield V (in millions of cubic feet per acre) for the forest at age t years is given by $V = 6.7e^{-48.1/t}$. Find the time necessary to have a yield of 2.1 million cubic feet.
a) 22.1 b) 25.2 c) 39.8 d) 41.5 e) None of these

Answer: d Difficulty: 2 Key 1: T

Chapter 035: Exponential and Logarithmic Models

MULTIPLE CHOICE

1. Match the graph with its function.
   a) $y = \dfrac{3}{1 + e^{-x}}$ b) $y = 3e^{-x}$ c) $y = 3e^{-x^2}$
   d) $y = 3 + \log_{10}x$ e) None of these

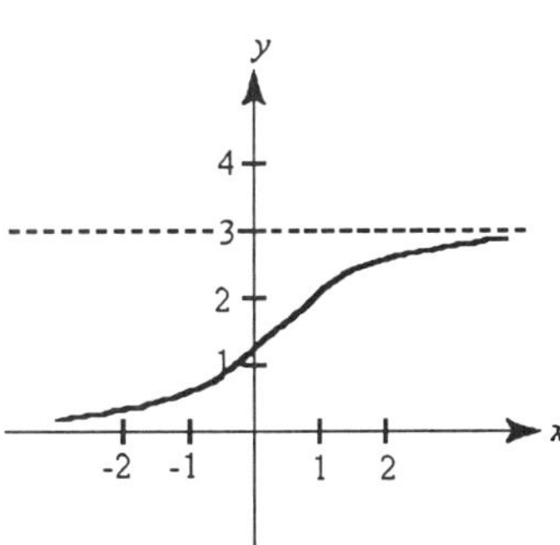

Answer: a Difficulty: 1

2. Match the graph with its function.
   a) $y = \dfrac{3}{1 + e^{-x}}$ b) $y = 3e^{-x}$ c) $y = 3e^{-x^2}$
   d) $y = 3 + \log_{10}x$ e) None of these

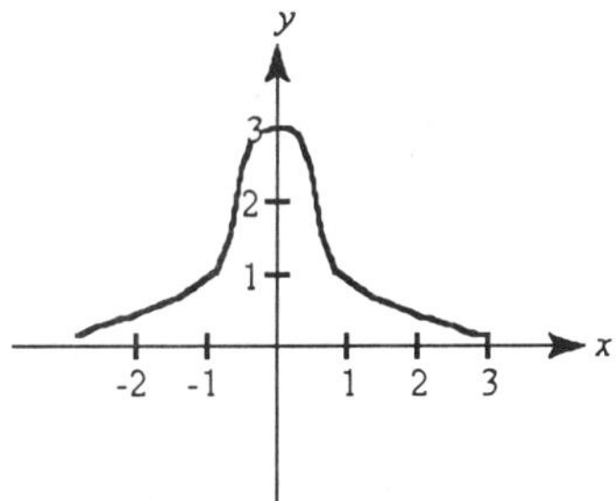

Answer: c Difficulty: 1

3. If \$3700 is invested at $11\frac{1}{2}\%$ interest compounded continuously, find the balance, B, in the account after 5 years.
   a) \$3918.99 b) \$20,754.65 c) \$6575.38
   d) \$7376.75 e) None of these

Answer: c Difficulty: 1

4. If \$9200 is invested at $9\frac{1}{2}\%$ interest compounded continuously, find the balance, B, in the account after 10 years.
   a) \$22,628.35 b) \$25,040.56 c) \$17,940.00
   d) \$23,788.53 e) None of these

Answer: d Difficulty: 1

5. Find the balance after 15 years if $1500 is invested in an account that pays $8\frac{1}{2}\%$ compounded quarterly.

a) $5273.72 b) $5296.82 c) $1978.13
d) $1632.98 e) None of these

Answer: b Difficulty: 1

6. Find the balance after 10 years if $1500 is invested in an account that pays $7\frac{1}{2}\%$ compounded quarterly.

a) $3153.52 b) $4151.16 c) $2625.00
d) $2997.10 e) None of these

Answer: a Difficulty: 1

7. Determine the principal P that must be invested at a rate of 8% compounded quarterly so that the balance B in 40 years will be $200,000. $\left[B = P\left(1 + \frac{r}{n}\right)^{nt}\right]$

a) $90,578.10 b) $47,539.00 c) $12,416.00
d) $8414.00 e) None of these

Answer: d Difficulty: 1

8. Determine the principal that must be invested at a rate of $7\frac{1}{2}\%$ compounded quarterly so that the balance in 20 years will be $35,000.

a) $2333.33 b) $14,000.00 c) $9635.17
d) $7918.78 e) None of these

Answer: d Difficulty: 1

9. Determine the principal that must be invested at a rate of 9% compounded monthly so that the balance in 20 years will be $35,000.

a) $12,500.00 b) $9470.02 c) $6914.23
d) $5824.45 e) None of these

Answer: d Difficulty: 1

SHORT ANSWER

10. Determine the principal that must be invested at a rate of $9\frac{1}{2}\%$ compounded quarterly so that the balance in 15 years will be $40,000.

Answer: $9781.94 Difficulty: 1

MULTIPLE CHOICE

11. An initial deposit of $2000 is compounded continuously at an annual percentage rate of 9%. Find the effective yield.
    a) 9.4% b) 9.2% c) $188.00
    d) $180.00 e) None of these

    Answer: a Difficulty: 2

SHORT ANSWER

12. An initial deposit of $2500 is compounded continuously at 7%. Find the effective yield.

    Answer: 7.25% Difficulty: 2

MULTIPLE CHOICE

13. An initial deposit of $3000 is made in a savings account for which the interest is compounded continuously. The balance will double in seven years. What is the annual rate of interest for this account?
    a) 4.3% b) 6.2% c) 8.1%
    d) 9.9% e) None of these

    Answer: d Difficulty: 2

14. An initial deposit of $4000 is made in a savings account for which the interest is compounded continuously. The balance will triple in 15 years. What is the annual rate of interest for this account?
    a) 6.2% b) 7.3% c) 7.9%
    d) 8.2% e) None of these

    Answer: b Difficulty: 2

15. Determine the annual rate of interest compounded continuously for the sum of money in an account to double in 10 years.
    a) 6.9% b) 7.4% c) 8.2%
    d) 9.9% e) None of these

    Answer: a Difficulty: 2

SHORT ANSWER

16. Determine the annual rate of interest compounded continuously for the sum of money in an account to become four times the original amount in 15 years.

    Answer: 9.2% Difficulty: 2

MULTIPLE CHOICE

17. The ice trays in a freezer are filled with water at 68° F. The freezer maintains a temperature of 20° F. According to Newton's Law of Cooling, the water temperature T is related to the time t (in hours) by the equation

$$kt = \ln \frac{T - 20}{68 - 20}.$$

After 1 hour, the water temperature in the ice trays is 49° F. Use the fact that $T = 49$ when $t = 1$ to find how long it takes the water to freeze (water freezes at 32° F).
a) 3.27 hours b) 2.75 hours c) 5.10 hours
d) 1.17 hours e) None of these

Answer: b Difficulty: 2

18. The ice trays in a freezer are filled with water at 60° F. The freezer maintains a temperature of 20° F. According to Newton's Law of Cooling, the water temperature T is related to the time t (in hours) by the equation

$$kt = \ln \frac{T - 20}{60 - 20}.$$

After 1 hour, the water temperature in the ice trays is 44° F. Use the fact that $T = 44$ when $t = 1$ to find how long it takes the water to freeze (water freezes at 32° F).
a) 2.4 hours b) 3.2 hours c) 1.7 hours
d) 5.1 hours e) None of these

Answer: a Difficulty: 2

19. The ice trays in a freezer are filled with water at 50° F. The freezer maintains a temperature of 0° F. According to Newton's Law of Cooling, the water temperature T is related to the time t (in hours) by the equation

$$kt = \ln \frac{T}{50}.$$

After 1 hour, the water temperature in the ice trays is 43° F. Use the fact that $T = 43$ when $t = 1$ to find how long it takes the water to freeze (water freezes at 32° F).
a) 2.4 hours b) 3.0 hours c) 3.6 hours
d) 2.1 hours e) None of these

Answer: b Difficulty: 2

SHORT ANSWER

20. The ice trays in a freezer are filled with water at 60° F. The freezer maintains a temperature of 0° F. According to Newton's Law of Cooling, the water temperature T is related to the time t (in hours) by the equation

$$kt = \ln \frac{T}{60}.$$

After 1 hour, the water temperature in the ice trays is 51° F. Use the fact that $T = 51$ when $t = 1$ to find how long it takes the water to freeze (water freezes at 32° F).

Answer: 3.9 hours Difficulty: 2

MULTIPLE CHOICE

21. The spread of a flu virus through a certain population is modeled by

$$y = \frac{1000}{1 + 990e^{-0.7t}},$$

where y is the total number infected after t days. In how many days will 820 people be infected with the virus?

a) 10 days b) 11 days c) 12 days
d) 13 days e) None of these

Answer: c Difficulty: 2

22. The spread of a flu virus through a certain population is modeled by

$$y = \frac{1000}{1 + 990e^{-0.7t}},$$

where y is the total number infected after t days. In how many days will 690 people be infected with the virus?

a) 10 days b) 11 days c) 12 days
d) 13 days e) None of these

Answer: b Difficulty: 2

23. The spread of a flu virus through a certain population is modeled by

$$y = \frac{1000}{1 + 990e^{-0.7t}},$$

where y is the total number infected after t days. In how many days will 900 people be infected with the virus?

a) 11 days b) 13 days c) 15 days
d) 17 days e) None of these

Answer: b Difficulty: 2

24. The spread of a flu virus through a certain population is modeled by

$$y = \frac{1000}{1 + 990e^{-0.7t}},$$

where y is the total number infected after t days. In how many days will 530 people be infected with the virus?

a) 13 days b) 12 days c) 11 days
d) 10 days e) None of these

Answer: d Difficulty: 2

25. The relationship between the level of sound β, in decibels, and the intensity of sound, I, in watts per centimeter squared is given by

$$\beta = 10 \log_{10}\left[\frac{I}{10^{-16}}\right].$$

Determine the level of sound when $I = 10^{-12}$.

a) 93 b) 74 c) 56 d) 40 e) None of these

Answer: d Difficulty: 1

26. The relationship between the level of sound β, in decibels, and the intensity of sound, I, in watts per centimeter squared is given by

$$\beta = 10 \log_{10}\left[\frac{I}{10^{-16}}\right].$$

Determine the level of sound when $I = 10^{-10}$.

a) 92 b) 60 c) 51 d) 100 e) None of these

Answer: b Difficulty: 1

27. The relationship between the level of sound β, in decibels, and the intensity of sound, I, in watts per centimeter squared is given by

$$\beta = 10 \log_{10}\left[\frac{I}{10^{-16}}\right].$$

Determine the level of sound when $I = 10^{-8}$.

a) 50 b) 60 c) 70 d) 80 e) None of these

Answer: d Difficulty: 1

28. The relationship between the level of sound β, in decibels, and the intensity of sound, I, in watts per centimeter squared is given by

$$\beta = 10 \log_{10}\left[\frac{I}{10^{-16}}\right].$$

Determine the level of sound when $I = 10^{-6}$.

a) 100 b) 90 c) 80 d) 70 e) None of these

Answer: a Difficulty: 1

29. The relationship between the level of sound β, in decibels, and the intensity of sound, I, in watts per centimeter squared is given by

$$\beta = 10 \log_{10}\left[\frac{I}{10^{-16}}\right].$$

Determine the level of sound when $I = 10^{-5}$.
a) 100 b) 110 c) 120 d) 125 e) None of these

Answer: b Difficulty: 1

30. The pH of a solution is determined by pH = $-\log_{10}$ [H^+] where pH is a measure of the hydrogen ion concentration [H^+], measured in moles per liter. Find the pH of a solution for which [H^+] = 7.61×10^{-6}.
a) -5.12 b) 5.12 c) -11.79 d) 11.79 e) None of these

Answer: b Difficulty: 2

SHORT ANSWER

31. The pH of a solution is determined by pH = $-\log_{10}$[H^+] where pH is a measure of the hydrogen ion concentration [H^+], measured in moles per liter.
Find the pH of a solution for which [H^+] = 5.93×10^{-7}.

Answer: 6.23 Difficulty: 2

32. The demand equation for a certain product is given by $p = 450 - 0.4e^{0.007x}$. Find the demand x if the price charged is $300.

Answer: 847 Difficulty: 1

33. The demand equation for a certain product is given by $p = 450 - 0.4e^{0.007x}$. Find the demand x if the price charged is $250.

Answer: 888 Difficulty: 1

34. The number N of bacteria in a culture is given by

$$N = 200e^{kt}.$$

If $N = 300$ when $t = 4$ hours, find k (to the nearest tenth) and then determine approximately how long it will take for the number of bacteria to triple in size.

Answer: $k = 0.1$, $t \approx 11$ hours Difficulty: 2

35. Write an equation for the amount Q of a radioactive substance with a half-life of 30 days, if 10 grams are present when $t = 0$.

Answer:

$$Q(t) = 10e^{-0.0231t}$$

Difficulty: 2

36. A state game commission releases 200 deer into state game lands. The commission believes that the growth of the herd will be modeled by

$$p(t) = \frac{400}{1 + 2e^{-0.025t}}$$

where t is measured in years. Use a graphing utility to graph the function, using an appropriate window. Determine the following.

a) The population after 10 years, 50 years, and 100 years

b) The limiting size of the herd

Answer:
a) $\approx$ 156 deer, $\approx$ 254 deer, $\approx$ 343 deer
b) 400 deer

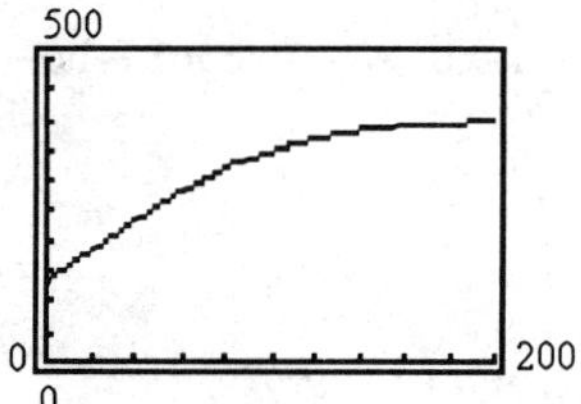

Difficulty: 2 Key 1: T

37. A state game commission releases 200 deer into state game lands. The commission believes that the growth of the herd will be modeled by

$$p(t) = \frac{600}{1 + 3e^{-0.025t}}$$

where t is measured in years. Use a graphing utility to graph the function, using an appropriate window. Determine the following.

a) The population after 10 years, 50 years, and 100 years

b) The limiting size of the herd

Answer:
a) $\approx$ 180 deer, $\approx$ 323 deer, $\approx$ 481 deer
b) 600 deer

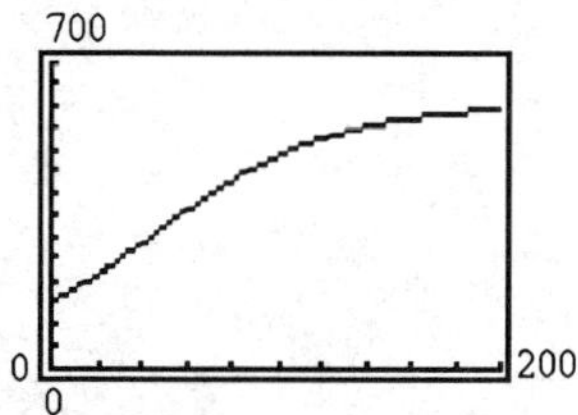

Difficulty: 2 Key 1: T

MULTIPLE CHOICE

38. The population of the world was 5.7 billion in 1995 and the growth rate is assumed to be 2%, exponentially. What will be the population in the year 2005?
    a) 5.93 billion　　b) 6.96 billion　　c) 7.70 billion
    d) 11.45 billion　　e) None of these

    Answer: b Difficulty: 2

SHORT ANSWER

39. The population of the world was 5.7 billion in 1995 and the growth rate is assumed to be 2%, exponentially. When will the population double?

    Answer: The year 2029. Difficulty: 2

Chapter 041: Radian and Degree Measure

MULTIPLE CHOICE

1. Determine the quadrant in which the terminal side of an angle of $\frac{6\pi}{5}$ lies.
a) I b) II c) III d) IV
e) The terminal side lies on one of the axes.

Answer: c Difficulty: 1

2. Determine the quadrant in which the terminal side of an angle of $395°$ lies.
a) I b) II c) III d) IV
e) The terminal side lies on one of the axes.

Answer: a Difficulty: 1

3. Deterine the quadrant in which the terminal side of an angle of $\frac{17\pi}{2}$ lies.
a) I b) II c) III d) IV
e) The terminal side lies on one of the axes.

Answer: e Difficulty: 1

4. Determine the quadrant in which the terminal side of an angle of $215°$ lies.
a) I b) II c) III d) IV
e) The terminal side lies on one of the axes.

Answer: c Difficulty: 1

5. Which of the following angles is coterminal to $\theta = -\frac{7\pi}{12}$?
a) $\frac{5\pi}{12}$ b) $\frac{17\pi}{12}$ c) $-\frac{19\pi}{12}$ d) Both $\frac{5\pi}{12}$ and $-\frac{19\pi}{12}$ e) None of these

Answer: b Difficulty: 1

SHORT ANSWER

6. Find an angle θ that is coterminal to $\frac{11\pi}{4}$ such that $0 \le \theta < 2\pi$.

Answer:
$\frac{3\pi}{4}$

Difficulty: 1

MULTIPLE CHOICE

7. Determine which angle is coterminal to $\theta = -\frac{5\pi}{6}$.

a) $\frac{5\pi}{6}$ b) $\frac{7\pi}{6}$ c) $\frac{\pi}{6}$ d) $\frac{11\pi}{6}$ e) None of these

Answer: b Difficulty: 1

8. Which of the following angles is coterminal to $\theta = -73°$?
a) 107° b) 287° c) -253° d) 17° e) None of these

Answer: b Difficulty: 1

SHORT ANSWER

9. Find an angle θ that is coterminal to -423° such that $0 \le \theta < 360°$.

Answer: 297° Difficulty: 1

10. Find an angle θ that is coterminal to -495° such that $0 \le \theta < 360°$.

Answer: 225° Difficulty: 1

MULTIPLE CHOICE

11. Determine which of the following angles is complementary to $\theta = \frac{\pi}{6}$.

a) $\frac{5\pi}{6}$ b) $\frac{13\pi}{6}$ c) $\frac{\pi}{3}$ d) $-\frac{11\pi}{6}$ e) None of these

Answer: c Difficulty: 1

12. Determine which of the following angles is complementary to $\theta = \frac{\pi}{12}$.

a) $\frac{5\pi}{12}$ b) $\frac{11\pi}{12}$ c) $\frac{13\pi}{12}$ d) $\frac{25\pi}{12}$ e) None of these

Answer: a Difficulty: 1

13. Determine which of the following angles is complementary to $\theta = \frac{2\pi}{7}$.

a) $\frac{5\pi}{7}$ b) $\frac{16\pi}{7}$ c) $-\frac{10\pi}{7}$ d) $\frac{3\pi}{14}$ e) None of these

Answer: d Difficulty: 1

14. Determine which of the following angles is supplementary to $\theta = \frac{2\pi}{5}$.

a) $\frac{3\pi}{5}$ b) $\frac{3\pi}{10}$ c) $\frac{7\pi}{5}$ d) $-\frac{8\pi}{5}$ e) None of these

Answer: a Difficulty: 1

15. Determine which of the following angles is supplementary to $\theta = \frac{\pi}{15}$.

a) $\frac{16\pi}{15}$ b) $\frac{14\pi}{15}$ c) $\frac{13\pi}{30}$ d) $\frac{29\pi}{15}$ e) None of these

Answer: b Difficulty: 1

16. Determine which of the following angles is supplementary to $\theta = \frac{\pi}{4}$.

a) $\frac{3\pi}{4}$ b) $\frac{\pi}{4}$ c) $\frac{5\pi}{4}$ d) $\frac{9\pi}{4}$ e) None of these

Answer: a Difficulty: 1

17. Convert to degrees: $\frac{5\pi}{12}$.

a) 82° b) 150° c) 36° d) 75° e) None of these

Answer: d Difficulty: 1

18. Convert to degrees: 2.5 radians.

a) 143.24° b) 0.04° c) 286.48° d) 450.00° e) None of these

Answer: a Difficulty: 1

19. Convert to degrees: $\frac{3\pi}{5}$ radians.

a) 0.0329° b) 108° c) 216° d) 54° e) None of these

Answer: b Difficulty: 1

20. Convert to radians: 240° .

a) $\frac{3\pi}{4}$ b) $\frac{43{,}200}{\pi}$ c) $\frac{3\pi}{2}$ d) $\frac{4\pi}{3}$ e) None of these

Answer: d Difficulty: 1

21. Convert to radians: 25° .

a) $\frac{5\pi}{36}$ b) $\frac{36}{5\pi}$ c) $\frac{4500}{\pi}$ d) $\frac{5\pi}{18}$ e) None of these

Answer: a Difficulty: 1

SHORT ANSWER

22. Convert to radians: 330° . (Write your answer as a multiple of π .)

    Answer:
    $\frac{11\pi}{6}$

    Difficulty: 1

MULTIPLE CHOICE

23. Convert to radians: 42° 15'.
    a) 0.7374 b) 0.7346 c) 2420.7467
    d) 0.7357 e) None of these

    Answer: a Difficulty: 1

24. Convert to (degree) decimal form: -13° 42' 15".
    a) -13.95° b) -12.05° c) -13.7042°
    d) -12.2958° e) None of these

    Answer: c Difficulty: 1

25. Convert to (degree) decimal form 72° 15".
    a) 72.25° b) 72.0042° c) 72.09°
    d) 72.00054° e) None of these

    Answer: b Difficulty: 1

SHORT ANSWER

26. Convert to (degree) decimal form: 128° 35' 18".

    Answer: 128.5883° Difficulty: 1

MULTIPLE CHOICE

27. Convert to degrees, minutes, and seconds: 178.463° .
    a) 178° 77' 50" b) 178° 46' 30" c) 178° 7' 12"
    d) 178° 27' 47" e) None of these

    Answer: d Difficulty: 1

SHORT ANSWER

28. Convert to degrees, minutes, and seconds: 12.4762° .

    Answer: 12° 28' 34" Difficulty: 1

MULTIPLE CHOICE

29. Convert to degrees, minutes, and seconds: 17.3872° .

a) 17° 23' 14" b) 17° 29' 17" c) 17° 42' 06"
d) 17° 38' 72" e) None of these

Answer: a Difficulty: 1

30. A central angle θ of a circle with radius 16 inches intercepts an arc of 19.36 inches. Find θ .

a) 47.3519° b) 1.21° c) 69.3279° d) 0.8264° e) None of these

Answer: c Difficulty: 1

31. The central angle θ of a circle with radius 9 inches intercepts an arc of 20 inches. Find θ .

a) 2.22° b) 127.32° c) 0.45° d) 25.78° e) None of these

Answer: b Difficulty: 1

32. The central angle θ of a circle with radius 5 inches intercepts an arc of 15 inches. Find θ .

a) 168.2° b) 171.9° c) 166.1° d) 177.9° e) None of these

Answer: b Difficulty: 2

SHORT ANSWER

33. Find the arc length s shown in the figure.

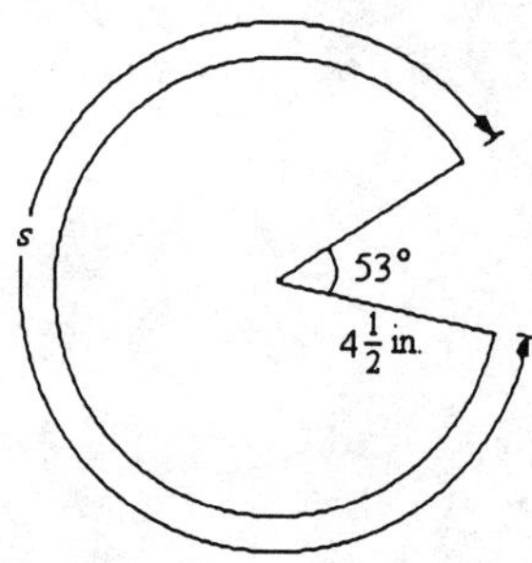

Answer: 24.1 inches Difficulty: 1

34. A bicycle wheel with an 18 inch diameter rotates 120° . What distance has the bicycle traveled?

Answer: $6\pi \approx 18.85$ inches Difficulty: 1

MULTIPLE CHOICE

35. Find the arc length s shown in the figure.
   a) 3.49"   b) 37.22"   c) 27.93"   d) 17.41"   e) None of these

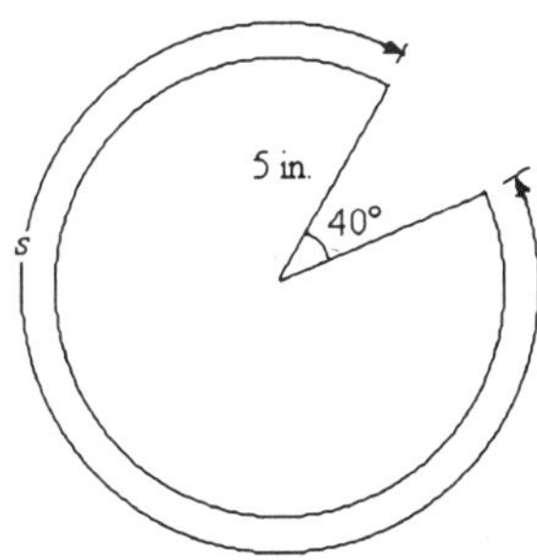

Answer: c Difficulty: 1

36. A circle of radius r has a central angle of 15° which intercepts an arc of 23 inches. Find r.
   a) 105.27 in.   b) 41.16 in.   c) 94.98 in.
   d) 87.85 in.   e) None of these

Answer: d Difficulty: 1

37. A circle of radius r has a central angle of $\theta = 45°$ which intercepts an arc of 16 inches. Find r.
   a) 0.3556 inch   b) 12.5664 inches   c) 2.8125 inches
   d) 20.3718 inches   e) None of these

Answer: d Difficulty: 1

38. Assuming that the earth is a sphere of radius 4000 miles, what is the difference in latitude of 2 cities, one of which is 500 miles due north of the other?
   a) 7° 9' 43"   b) 4° 10' 51"   c) 6° 49' 44"
   d) 5° 7' 48"   e) None of these

Answer: a Difficulty: 1

39. Assuming that the earth is a sphere of radius 4000 miles, what is the difference in latitude of 2 cities, one of which is 1500 miles due north of the other?
   a) 10° 17' 6"   b) 21° 29' 9"   c) 12° 15' 42"
   d) 19° 44' 7"   e) None of these

Answer: b Difficulty: 1

SHORT ANSWER

40. A car is moving at a rate of 55 mph and the diamter of its wheels is 2 feet. Find the number of revolutions per minute the wheels are rotating and the angular speed of the wheels in radians per minute.

Answer: 385.2 revolutions per minute; 2420 radians per minute Difficulty: 2

Chapter 042: Trigonometric Functions: The Unit Circle

MULTIPLE CHOICE

1. Find the point (x, y) on the unit circle that corresponds to the real number $t = -\frac{\pi}{4}$.

a) $\left(\frac{\sqrt{2}}{2}, \frac{\sqrt{2}}{2}\right)$ b) $\left(\frac{1}{2}, -\frac{1}{2}\right)$ c) $(1, -1)$

d) $\left(\frac{\sqrt{2}}{2}, -\frac{\sqrt{2}}{2}\right)$ e) None of these

Answer: d Difficulty: 1

2. Find the point (x, y) on the unit circle that corresponds to the real number $t = \frac{3\pi}{2}$.

a) $(1, -1)$ b) $(0, -1)$ c) $(-1, 0)$ d) $(-1, 1)$ e) None of these

Answer: b Difficulty: 1

3. Find the point (x, y) on the unit circle that corresponds to the real number $t = \frac{17\pi}{6}$.

a) $\left(\frac{\sqrt{3}}{2}, \frac{1}{2}\right)$ b) $\left(-\frac{1}{2}, \frac{\sqrt{3}}{2}\right)$ c) $\left(-\frac{\sqrt{3}}{2}, \frac{1}{2}\right)$

d) $\left(\frac{\sqrt{3}}{2}, -\frac{1}{2}\right)$ e) None of these

Answer: c Difficulty: 1

SHORT ANSWER

4. Find the point (x, y) on the unit circle that corresponds to the real number $t = \frac{4\pi}{3}$.

Answer:
$\left(-\frac{1}{2}, -\frac{\sqrt{3}}{2}\right)$
Difficulty: 1

5. Find the point (x, y) on the unit circle that corresponds to the real number $t = -\frac{7\pi}{4}$.

Answer:
$\left(\frac{\sqrt{2}}{2}, \frac{\sqrt{2}}{2}\right)$
Difficulty: 1

6. Find the point (x, y) on the unit circle that corresponds to the real number $t = 3\pi$.

Answer: (-1, 0) Difficulty: 1

MULTIPLE CHOICE

7. Give the exact value of $\tan \frac{4\pi}{3}$.

a) $-\sqrt{3}$ b) $\frac{1}{\sqrt{3}}$ c) $-\frac{1}{\sqrt{2}}$ d) $\sqrt{2}$ e) None of these

Answer: e Difficulty: 1

8. Give the exact value of $\cos\left(-\frac{3\pi}{4}\right)$.

a) $-\frac{\sqrt{2}}{2}$ b) $-\frac{1}{2}$ c) $\frac{\sqrt{3}}{2}$ d) $\frac{\sqrt{2}}{2}$ e) None of these

Answer: a Difficulty: 1

SHORT ANSWER

9. Give the exact value of $\cos\left(-\frac{\pi}{6}\right)$.

Answer:
$\frac{\sqrt{3}}{2}$
Difficulty: 1

10. Give the exact value of $\sin -\frac{7\pi}{6}$.

Answer:
$-\frac{1}{2}$
Difficulty: 1

11. Give the exact value of $\tan\left(-\frac{3\pi}{4}\right)$.

Answer: 1 Difficulty: 1

12. Give the exact value of the six trigonometric functions of $t = -\frac{5\pi}{6}$.

Answer:

$\sin\left(-\frac{5\pi}{6}\right) = -\frac{1}{2},$ $\csc\left(-\frac{5\pi}{6}\right) = -2$

$\cos\left(-\frac{5\pi}{6}\right) = -\frac{\sqrt{3}}{2},$ $\sec\left(-\frac{5\pi}{6}\right) = -\frac{2\sqrt{3}}{3}$

$\tan\left(-\frac{5\pi}{6}\right) = \frac{\sqrt{3}}{32}$ $\cot\left(-\frac{5\pi}{6}\right) = \sqrt{3}$

Difficulty: 1

MULTIPLE CHOICE

13. Give the exact value of $\tan\left(-\frac{\pi}{3}\right)$.

a) $-\frac{1}{\sqrt{2}}$ b) $-\frac{1}{\sqrt{3}}$ c) -2 d) $-\sqrt{3}$ e) None of these

Answer: d Difficulty: 1

14. Give the exact value of $\sec \pi$.

a) Undefined b) -1 c) 1 d) $\frac{1}{2}$ e) None of these

Answer: b Difficulty: 1

15. Give the exact value of $\csc \frac{3\pi}{2}$.

a) 2 b) Undefined c) -1 d) 1 e) None of these

Answer: c Difficulty: 1

16. Give the exact value of $\tan \frac{15\pi}{6}$.

a) $\frac{1}{\sqrt{3}}$ b) $\frac{1}{\sqrt{2}}$ c) $\sqrt{3}$ d) 1 e) None of these

Answer: e Difficulty: 1

17. Give the exact value of $\sin \frac{7\pi}{2}$.

a) 0 b) 1 c) 7 d) -1 e) None of these

Answer: d Difficulty: 1

SHORT ANSWER

18. Give the exact value (if defined) of $\tan \frac{5\pi}{2}$.

Answer: Not defined Difficulty: 1

MULTIPLE CHOICE

19. Give the exact value of $\cos \frac{13\pi}{4}$.

a) $\frac{\sqrt{2}}{2}$ b) $-\sqrt{2}$ c) $-\frac{\sqrt{2}}{2}$ d) $\frac{\sqrt{3}}{2}$ e) None of these

Answer: c Difficulty: 1

20. Give the exact value of $\sin \frac{11\pi}{3}$.

a) $\frac{1}{2}$ b) $-\frac{1}{2}$ c) $\frac{2}{\sqrt{3}}$ d) $-\frac{2}{\sqrt{3}}$ e) None of these

Answer: e Difficulty: 1

SHORT ANSWER

21. Give the exact value of the six trigonometric functions of $t = 5\pi$.

Answer:
$\sin(5\pi) = 0$, $\csc(5\pi)$ = not defined
$\cos(5\pi) = -1$, $\sec(5\pi) = -1$
$\tan(5\pi) = 0$, $\cot(5\pi)$ = not defined

Difficulty: 1

22. Use the function value, $\sin t = \frac{2}{5}$, to find the values of (a) $\sin(-t)$ and (b) $\csc t$.

Answer:
(a) $-\frac{2}{5}$ **(b)** $\frac{5}{2}$

Difficulty: 1

23. Use the function value, $\sin t = -\frac{1}{4}$, to find the values of (a) $\cos(-t)$ and (b) $\sec(-t)$.

Answer:
(a) $-\frac{1}{4}$ **(b)** -4

Difficulty: 1

24. Use the function value, $\tan t = 3$, to find the values of (a) $\tan(-t)$ and (b) $\cot t$.

Answer:

(a) -3 **(b)** $\frac{1}{3}$

Difficulty: 1

MULTIPLE CHOICE

25. Evaluate: sin(-4.1). Round your answer to four decimal places.
a) 0.8183 b) -0.0715 c) 0.9974 d) -0.5748 e) None of these

Answer: a Difficulty: 1

26. Evaluate: cos 2.3. Round your answer to four decimal places.
a) -0.0401 b) 0.9992 c) 0.9070 d) -0.6663 e) None of these

Answer: d Difficulty: 1

27. Evaluate: csc(-7.1). Round your answer to four decimal places.
a) -0.1404 b) -1.3718 c) -0.0025 d) -8.0905 e) None of these

Answer: b Difficulty: 1

28. Evaluate: sec 4.6. Round your answer to four decimal places.
a) 1.0000 b) 0.9765 c) -8.9164 d) 1.0032 e) None of these

Answer: c Difficulty: 1

29. Evaluate: csc 5.23. Round your answer to four decimal places.
a) 10.9704 b) 0.0033 c) -1.1507 d) 0.1900 e) None of these

Answer: c Difficulty: 1

30. Evaluate: sec(-1.42). Round your answer to four decimal places.
a) 6.6567 b) 0.7621 c) 0.9997 d) 40.3533 e) None of these

Answer: a Difficulty: 1

31. The displacement from equilibrium of an oscillating weight suspended by a spring is given by $y(t) = \frac{1}{4}\sin 6t$ where y is the displacement in feet and t is the time in seconds. Find the displacement when $t = \frac{1}{4}$. Round your answer to four decimal places.
a) 0.2494 ft b) 3.9900 ft c) 0.0065 ft
d) 0.1047 ft e) None of these

Answer: a Difficulty: 1

32. The displacement from equilibrium of an oscillating weight suspended by a spring is given by $y(t) = \frac{1}{2}\cos 6t$ where y is the displacement in feet and t is the time in seconds. Find the displacement when $t = \frac{1}{2}$. Round your answer to four decimal places.

a) 0.4993 ft b) 1.9973 ft c) -0.4950 ft
d) -0.2081 ft e) None of these

Answer: c Difficulty: 1

33. The displacement from equilibrium of an oscillating weight suspended by a spring is given by $y(t) = \frac{1}{2}\cos 6t$ where y is the displacement in feet and t is the time in seconds. Find the displacement when $t = \frac{1}{4}$. Round your answer to four decimal places.

a) 0.0354 ft b) 0.1415 ft c) 0.4998 ft
d) 1.9993 ft e) None of these

Answer: a Difficulty: 1

34. The displacement from equilibrium of an oscillating weight suspended by a spring and subject to the damping effect of friction is given by $y(t) = \frac{1}{4}e^{-t}\sin 6t$ where y is the displacement in feet and t is the time in seconds. Find the displacement when $t = \frac{1}{4}$. Round your answer to four decimal places.

a) 0.1963 ft b) 0.0051 ft c) 0.3202 ft
d) 0.1942 ft e) None of these

Answer: d Difficulty: 1

Chapter 043: Right Triangle Trigonometry

SHORT ANSWER

1. Use the triangle shown below to find $\tan\theta$.

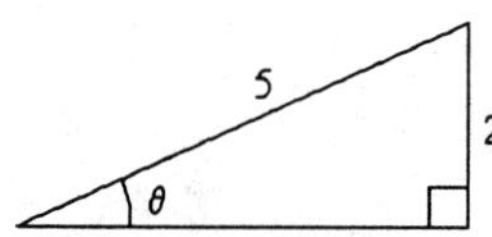

Answer:

$\frac{2\sqrt{21}}{4}$

Difficulty: 1

2. Use the triangle shown below to find $\cot\theta$.

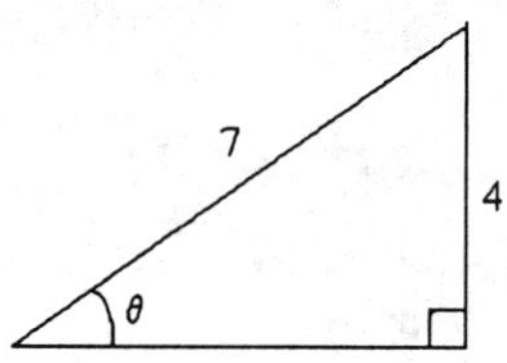

Answer:

$\frac{\sqrt{33}}{4}$

Difficulty: 1

MULTIPLE CHOICE

3. Use the triangle shown below to find $\sec\theta$.
   a) $\frac{9}{5}$ b) $\frac{9\sqrt{14}}{28}$ c) $\frac{\sqrt{106}}{5}$ d) $\frac{\sqrt{106}}{9}$ e) None of these

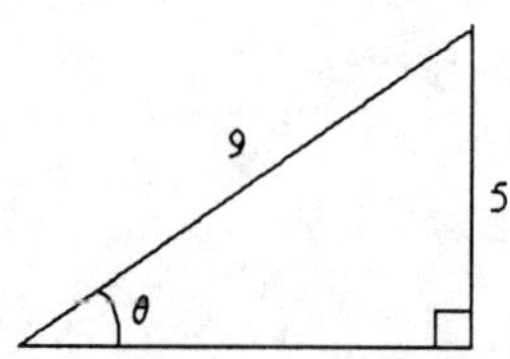

Answer: b Difficulty: 1

4. A right triangle has an acute angle θ such that $\cot\theta = 15$. Find $\cos\theta$.
   a) $\sqrt{226}$ b) $\frac{\sqrt{226}}{226}$ c) $\frac{15\sqrt{226}}{226}$ d) $\frac{\sqrt{226}}{15}$ e) None of these

Answer: c Difficulty: 1

5. A right triangle has an acute angle θ such that $\csc\theta = \frac{7}{3}$. Find $\tan\theta$.

a) $\frac{2\sqrt{10}}{7}$ b) $\frac{3\sqrt{10}}{20}$ c) $\frac{2\sqrt{10}}{3}$ d) $\frac{3}{7}$ e) None of these

Answer: b Difficulty: 1

6. A right triangle has an acute angle θ such that $\sin\theta = \frac{7}{9}$. Find $\tan\theta$.

a) $\frac{7\sqrt{2}}{8}$ b) $\frac{4\sqrt{2}}{7}$ c) $\frac{\sqrt{130}}{7}$ d) $\frac{9\sqrt{130}}{130}$ e) None of these

Answer: a Difficulty: 1

7. Given $\sec\theta = 3$, find $\csc(90° - \theta)$.

a) $\frac{1}{3}$ b) $\frac{3\sqrt{2}}{4}$ c) 3 d) $\frac{2\sqrt{2}}{3}$ e) None of these

Answer: c Difficulty: 1

8. Given $\sec\theta = 5$, find $\csc(90° - \theta)$.

a) $\frac{5\sqrt{6}}{12}$ b) 5 c) $\frac{1}{5}$ d) $\frac{2\sqrt{6}}{5}$ e) None of these

Answer: b Difficulty: 1

9. Given $\cos\theta = \frac{1}{2}$, find $\csc(90° - \theta)$.

a) 2 b) $\frac{1}{2}$ c) $\sqrt{3}$ d) $\frac{2}{\sqrt{3}}$ e) None of these

Answer: a Difficulty: 1

10. Evaluate: $\sec\frac{\pi}{3}$.

a) $\frac{\sqrt{2}}{2}$ b) $\frac{\sqrt{3}}{2}$ c) $\frac{\sqrt{3}}{3}$ d) 2 e) None of these

Answer: d Difficulty: 1

SHORT ANSWER

11. Evaluate: $\cot\frac{\pi}{3}$.

Answer:

$\frac{\sqrt{3}}{3}$

Difficulty: 1

MULTIPLE CHOICE

12. Evaluate: $\cot \frac{\pi}{6}$.
a) $\sqrt{3}$ b) $\frac{1}{2}$ c) $\frac{\sqrt{3}}{2}$ d) $\frac{\sqrt{3}}{3}$ e) None of these

Answer: a Difficulty: 1

13. Evaluate: $\csc 45°$.
a) $\frac{1}{2}$ b) $\sqrt{2}$ c) $\frac{\sqrt{2}}{2}$ d) 1 e) None of these

Answer: b Difficulty: 1

14. Evaluate: $\tan 60°$.
a) $\frac{1}{2}$ b) $\frac{1}{3}$ c) $\frac{\sqrt{3}}{3}$ d) $\sqrt{3}$ e) None of these

Answer: d Difficulty: 1

15. Evaluate: $\cos 60°$.
a) $\sqrt{3}$ b) $\frac{1}{2}$ c) 2 d) $\frac{\sqrt{3}}{2}$ e) None of these

Answer: b Difficulty: 1

16. Evaluate: $\csc 14°$.
a) 4.0960 b) 4.1336 c) 1.0306 d) 0.9999 e) None of these

Answer: b Difficulty: 1

17. Evaluate: $\cot 15°$.
a) 3.7321 b) 0.0012 c) 86.1859 d) 1.0353 e) None of these

Answer: a Difficulty: 1

18. Evaluate: sec(4° 15' 42").
a) 13.4569 b) 0.9999 c) 1.0028 d) 13.8043 e) None of these

Answer: c Difficulty: 1

SHORT ANSWER

19. Evaluate: $\cot 49°$.

Answer: 0.8693 Difficulty: 1

MULTIPLE CHOICE

20. Evaluate: sec 1.2.
a) 0.6724 b) 1.0002 c) 2.7597 d) 0.9999 e) None of these

Answer: c Difficulty: 1

21. Evaluate: csc 1.32.
a) 2.0132 b) 1.0323 c) 0.0230 d) 0.6872 e) None of these

Answer: b Difficulty: 1

22. Evaluate: cot 1.14.
a) 0.4596 b) 1.2028 c) 50.2528 d) 0.0153 e) None of these

Answer: a Difficulty: 1

23. Find the acute angle θ, if $\tan \theta = 1$.
a) $\frac{\pi}{3}$ b) $\frac{\pi}{4}$ c) $\frac{\pi}{5}$ d) $\frac{\pi}{6}$ e) None of these

Answer: b Difficulty: 1

24. Find the acute angle θ, if $\sin \theta = \frac{1}{2}$.
a) $\frac{\pi}{3}$ b) $\frac{\pi}{4}$ c) $\frac{\pi}{5}$ d) $\frac{\pi}{6}$ e) None of these

Answer: d Difficulty: 1

25. Find the acute angle θ, if $\sin \theta = \frac{\sqrt{3}}{2}$.
a) $\frac{\pi}{2}$ b) $\frac{\pi}{3}$ c) $\frac{\pi}{4}$ d) $\frac{\pi}{6}$ e) None of these

Answer: b Difficulty: 1

SHORT ANSWER

26. Find θ such that $0 \le \theta < \frac{\pi}{2}$ and $\csc \theta = 1.4736$.

Answer: 0.7459 Difficulty: 1

MULTIPLE CHOICE

27. Given $\tan \theta = 1.2617$, find θ.
a) 0.0220 b) 0.9006 c) 1.0145 d) 0.3193 e) None of these

Answer: b Difficulty: 1

28. Given $\cos\theta = 0.9872$, find θ.
    a) 80.8229° b) 0.9998° c) 9.1771° d) 1.0001° e) None of these

    Answer: c Difficulty: 1

29. Find x for the triangle shown below.
    a) $7\sqrt{3}$ b) $\frac{7}{\sqrt{3}}$ c) 14 d) $\frac{7}{2}$ e) None of these

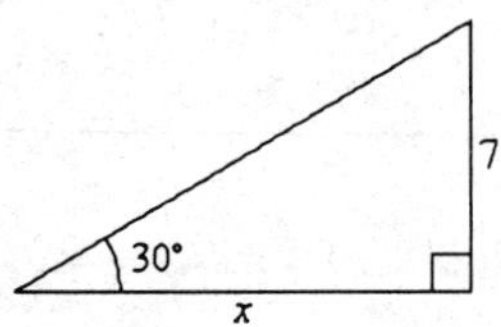

Answer: a Difficulty: 1

SHORT ANSWER

30. Find x for the triangle shown below.

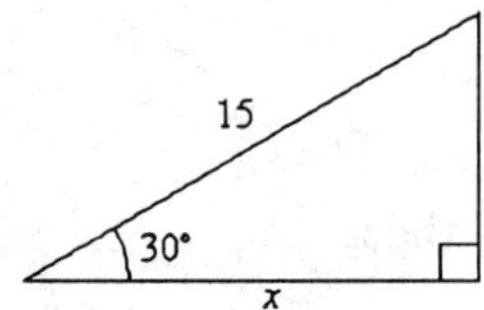

Answer:

$\frac{15\sqrt{3}}{2}$

Difficulty: 1

MULTIPLE CHOICE

31. Find x for the triangle shown below.
    a) $15\sqrt{2}$ b) $15\sqrt{3}$ c) 30 d) $\frac{15}{2}$ e) None of these

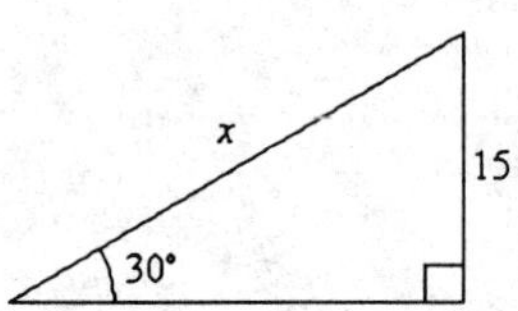

Answer: c Difficulty: 1

32. Find x for the triangle shown below.
    a) 0.1047 b) 11.9638 c) 5.4256 d) 9.5547 e) None of these

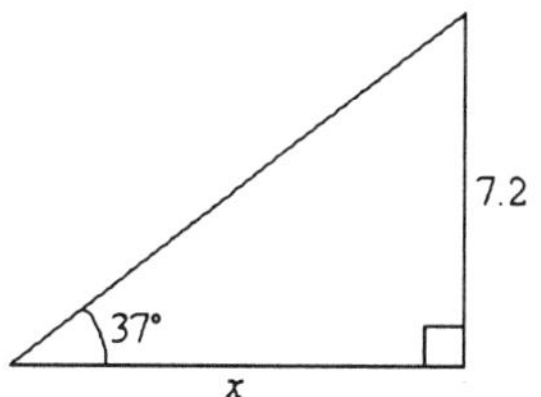

Answer: d Difficulty: 1

SHORT ANSWER

33. Find x for the triangle shown below.

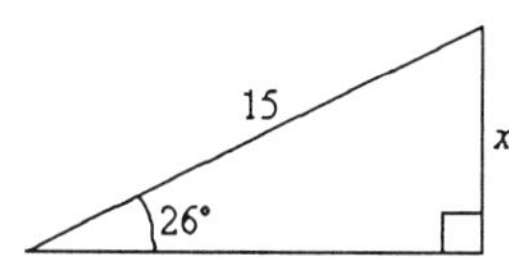

Answer: 6.5756 Difficulty: 1

MULTIPLE CHOICE

34. Find x for the triangle shown below.
    a) 9.7174 b) 15.4411 c) 14.8188 d) 7.5518 e) None of these

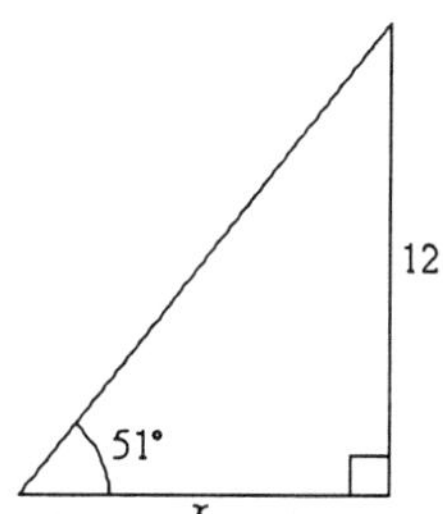

Answer: a Difficulty: 1

35. A man that is 6 feet tall casts a shadow 14 feet long. Find the angle of elevation of the sun.
    a) 23.2° b) 66.8° c) 25.4° d) 64.6° e) None of these

Answer: a Difficulty: 1

36. The pilot of an airplane flying 12,000 feet sights a water tower. The angle of depression to the base of the tower is 25° . What is the length of the line of sight from the plant to the tower?
    a) 28,394 feet b) 27,962 feet c) 23,662 feet
    d) 13,241 feet e) None of these

Answer: a Difficulty: 2

37. A 16-foot ladder leaning against the side of a house reaches 12 feet up the side of the house. What angle does the ladder make with the ground?
a) 57.7° b) 63.1° c) 42.9° d) 48.6° e) None of these

Answer: d Difficulty: 2

SHORT ANSWER

38. An airplane leaves the runway climbing at 18° with a speed of 275 feet per second. Find the altitude of the plane after 1 minute.

Answer: 5098.8 feet Difficulty: 2

39. The angle of elevation from a point 100 feet from the base of a school to the top of a flagpole on the school is 39°. The angle of elevation from the same point to the base of the flagpole is 28°. Find the height of the flagpole. (See figure.)

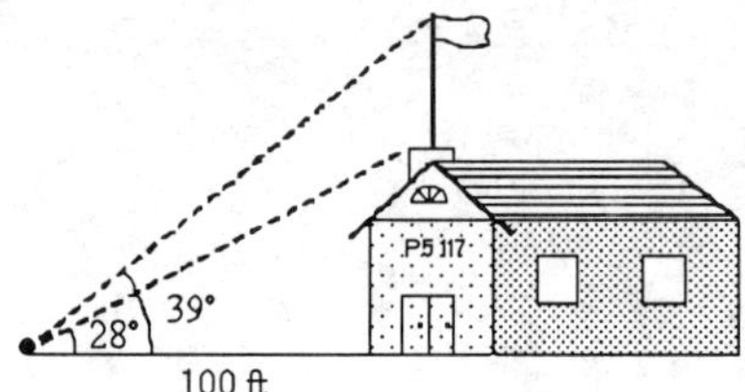

Answer: 27.8 feet Difficulty: 2

40. The angle of depression from the top of a building to the base of a statue 40 feet from the base of the building is 72°. Determine the height of the building.

Answer: 123.1 feet Difficulty: 2

41. In traveling across a flatland, you notice a mountain directly in front of you. The angle of elevation to the peak is 3.5°. After you drive 13 miles closer to the mountain, the angle of elevation is 9°. Approximate the height of the mountain.

(Hint: Construct two equations and solve the system by substitution.)

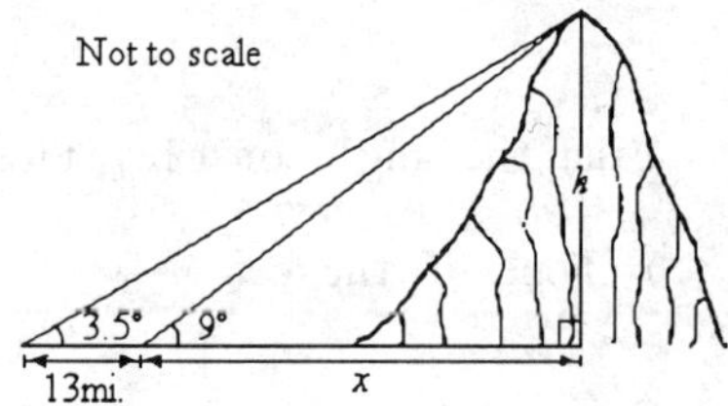

Answer: 1.3 miles Difficulty: 2

MULTIPLE CHOICE

42. Complete the following Pythagorean identity: $\tan^2 \theta$ = _________.
    a) $1 - \sec^2 \theta$ b) $1 - \csc^2 \theta$ c) $\csc^2 \theta + 1$
    d) $\sec^2 \theta - 1$ e) None of these

    Answer: d Difficulty: 1

43. Complete the following Pythagorean identity: $\sec^2 \theta$ = _________.
    a) $1 - \tan^2 \theta$ b) $1 + \tan^2 \theta$ c) $1 + \csc^2 \theta$
    d) $\csc^2 \theta - 1$ e) None of these

    Answer: b Difficulty: 1

44. Complete the following Pythagorean identity: $\cos^2 \theta$ = _________.
    a) $\sec^2 \theta + 1$ b) $1 - \sin^2 \theta$ c) $\sin^2 \theta + 1$
    d) $1 - \sec^2 \theta$ e) None of these

    Answer: b Difficulty: 1

45. The ramp approaching a loading platform that is 6 feet off the ground is to have an angle of 20° with the ground (see figure). Find the length l of the ramp. (Round your answer to two decimal places.)
    a) 31.02 feet b) 19.37 feet c) 16.48 feet
    d) 17.54 feet e) None of these

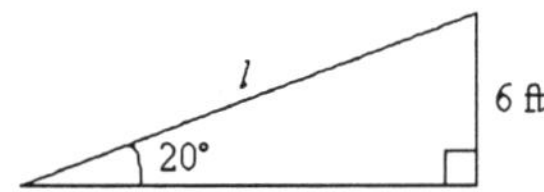

    Answer: d Difficulty: 1

46. The height of a tree can be determined by measuring the length of the shadow of the tree and the angle of elevation of the sun from the tip of the shadow. Find the height of a tree that casts a 20 foot shadow when the angle of elevation is 60° . (See figure.)
    a) $10\sqrt{3}$ feet b) $20\sqrt{3}$ feet c) 30 feet
    d) $20\sqrt{2}$ feet e) None of these

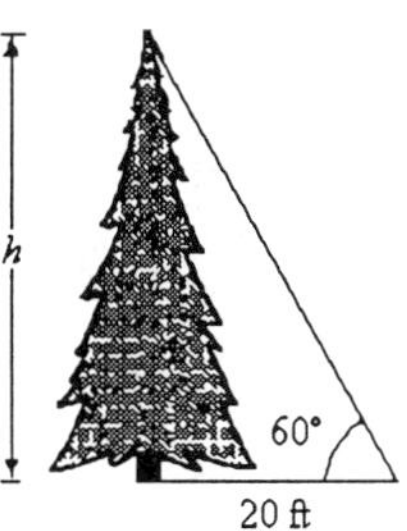

    Answer: b Difficulty: 1

SHORT ANSWER

47. Use trigonometric identities to simplify the expression: $\cos\theta \tan\theta$.

    Answer: $\sin\theta$ Difficulty: 1

48. Use trigonometric identities to simplify the expression: $(\sin\theta - 1)(\sin\theta + 1)$.

    Answer:

    $-\cos^2\theta$

    Difficulty: 2

49. Use trigonometric identities to simplify the expression: $(\csc\theta - \cot\theta)(\csc\theta + \cot\theta)$.

    Answer: 1 Difficulty: 1

50. Use trigonometric identities to simplify the expression: $\tan\theta \csc\theta$.

    Answer: $\sec\theta$ Difficulty: 1

51. Use trigonometric identities to simplify the expression: $\sin\theta \sec\theta$.

    Answer: $\tan\theta$ Difficulty: 1

Chapter 044: Trigonometric Functions of Any Angle

MULTIPLE CHOICE

1. Find tan θ, for the angle θ shown below.
   a) $-\frac{9\sqrt{130}}{7}$ b) $\frac{\sqrt{130}}{7}$ c) $-\frac{7}{9}$ d) $-\frac{9}{7}$ e) None of these

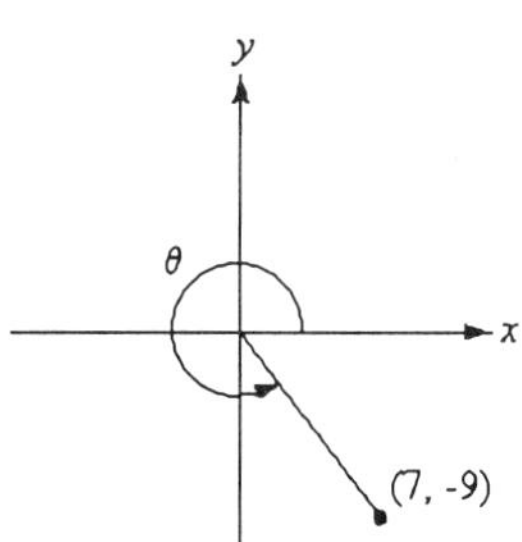

Answer: d Difficulty: 1

SHORT ANSWER

2. Find csc θ for the angle θ shown below.

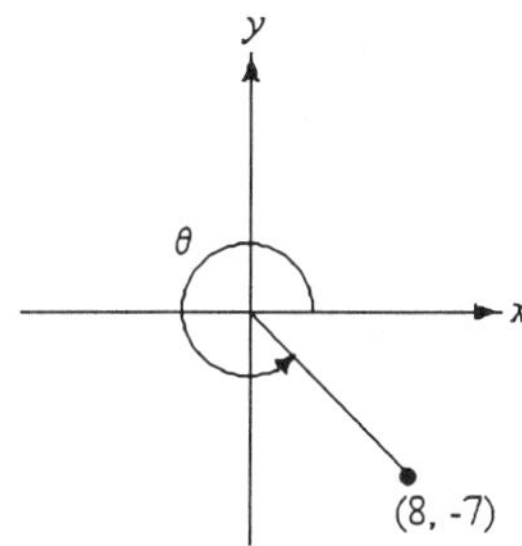

Answer:
$-\frac{\sqrt{113}}{7}$
Difficulty: 1

3. Determine the exact value of cos θ, if θ is in standard position and its terminal side passes through the point (-3, 3).

Answer:
$-\frac{\sqrt{2}}{2}$
Difficulty: 1

MULTIPLE CHOICE

4. Determine the quadrant in which θ lies: $\sin \theta < 0$ and $\cos \theta < 0$.
   a) I b) II c) III d) IV e) None of these

   Answer: c Difficulty: 1

5. Determine the quadrant in which θ lies: $\tan \theta < 0$ and $\cos \theta > 0$.
   a) I b) II c) III d) IV e) None of these

   Answer: d Difficulty: 1

6. Determine the quadrant in which θ lies: $\tan \theta < 0$ and $\sin \theta > 0$.
   a) I b) II c) III d) IV e) None of these

   Answer: b Difficulty: 1

7. Given $\sin \theta = -\frac{1}{5}$ and $\tan \theta < 0$, find $\cos \theta$.
   a) $-\frac{\sqrt{26}}{5}$ b) $\frac{\sqrt{26}}{5}$ c) $-\frac{2\sqrt{6}}{5}$ d) $\frac{2\sqrt{6}}{5}$ e) None of these

   Answer: d Difficulty: 1

8. Given $\sin \theta = \frac{7}{13}$, and $\tan \theta < 0$, find $\tan \theta$.
   a) $-\frac{7\sqrt{3}}{2}$ b) $-\frac{2\sqrt{3}}{7}$ c) $-\frac{2\sqrt{3}}{13}$ d) $-\frac{7\sqrt{3}}{60}$ e) None of these

   Answer: d Difficulty: 1

SHORT ANSWER

9. Given $\tan \theta = -\frac{7}{8}$ and $\cos \theta > 0$, find $\csc \theta$.

   Answer:
   $-\frac{\sqrt{113}}{7}$
   Difficulty: 1

10. Given $\sin \theta = -\frac{2}{9}$, and $\tan \theta > 0$, find $\cos \theta$.

    Answer:
    $-\frac{\sqrt{77}}{9}$
    Difficulty: 1

MULTIPLE CHOICE

11. Find the reference angle for $\theta = 305°$.
    a) $35°$ b) $-55°$ c) $55°$ d) $125°$ e) None of these

    Answer: c Difficulty: 1

SHORT ANSWER

12. Find the reference angle for $\theta = -155°$.

    Answer: $25°$ Difficulty: 1

MULTIPLE CHOICE

13. Find the reference angle for $\theta = \frac{19\pi}{15}$.
    a) $\frac{4\pi}{15}$ b) $\frac{7\pi}{30}$ c) $\frac{11\pi}{30}$ d) $\frac{49\pi}{15}$ e) None of these

    Answer: a Difficulty: 1

14. Find the reference angle for $\theta = \frac{7\pi}{3}$.
    a) $\frac{\pi}{3}$ b) $\frac{2\pi}{3}$ c) $\frac{\pi}{6}$ d) $\frac{\pi}{2}$ e) None of these

    Answer: a Difficulty: 1

15. Find the reference angle for $\theta = \frac{17\pi}{15}$.
    a) $\frac{32\pi}{15}$ b) $\frac{13\pi}{15}$ c) $\frac{2\pi}{15}$ d) $\frac{11\pi}{30}$ e) None of these

    Answer: c Difficulty: 1

16. Find the exact value of $\cot(-150°)$.
    a) $\sqrt{3}$ b) $-\frac{1}{2}$ c) $-\frac{1}{\sqrt{3}}$ d) 1 e) None of these

    Answer: a Difficulty: 1

17. Find the exact value of $\csc 225°$.
    a) 2 b) $\frac{\sqrt{3}}{2}$ c) $-\sqrt{2}$ d) $-\frac{\sqrt{3}}{2}$ e) None of these

    Answer: c Difficulty: 1

18. Find the exact value of $\tan(-210°)$.
a) 1 b) $-\frac{\sqrt{3}}{3}$ c) $-\sqrt{3}$ d) $\frac{1}{2}$ e) None of these

Answer: b Difficulty: 1

19. Find the exact value of $\tan 870°$.
a) $\sqrt{3}$ b) $\frac{\sqrt{3}}{3}$ c) $-\frac{\sqrt{3}}{3}$ d) $-\sqrt{3}$ e) None of these

Answer: c Difficulty: 1

20. Find the exact value of $\sin\left(-\frac{8\pi}{3}\right)$.
a) $\frac{\sqrt{3}}{2}$ b) $\frac{1}{2}$ c) $-\frac{1}{2}$ d) $-\frac{\sqrt{3}}{2}$ e) None of these

Answer: d Difficulty: 1

21. Find the exact value of $\sec \frac{7\pi}{4}$.
a) $\sqrt{2}$ b) $\frac{\sqrt{3}}{2}$ c) $\frac{1}{\sqrt{3}}$ d) 1 e) None of these

Answer: a Difficulty: 1

22. Find the exact value of $\tan \frac{5\pi}{6}$.
a) $\frac{\sqrt{3}}{2}$ b) $\sqrt{3}$ c) -1 d) $-\frac{\sqrt{3}}{3}$ e) None of these

Answer: d Difficulty: 1

23. Find the exact value of $\sin \frac{7\pi}{6}$.
a) $-\frac{1}{2}$ b) $-\frac{\sqrt{3}}{2}$ c) $\frac{\sqrt{3}}{3}$ d) $\frac{\sqrt{2}}{2}$ e) None of these

Answer: a Difficulty: 1

SHORT ANSWER

24. Find two radian value of θ $(0 \le \theta < 2\pi)$ that satisfy $\cos \theta = 0.7833$. (Round your answers to 4 decimal places.)

Answer: 0.6708 and 5.6123 Difficulty: 2

MULTIPLE CHOICE

25. Find two values of θ $(0 \le \theta < 2\pi)$ that satisfy $\cot\theta = -1$. (Round your answers to 4 decimal places.)
    a) 2.3562 and 5.4977 b) -0.7854 and 3.9270 c) -0.7854 and 5.4977
    d) 0.7854 and 2.3562 e) None of these

    Answer: a Difficulty: 2

26. Find two values of θ $(0 \le \theta < 2\pi)$ that satisfy $\sec\theta = 5.1258$. (Round your answers to 4 decimal places.)
    a) 1.7672 and 4.5160 b) 1.3744 and 4.9087 c) 1.1344 and 1.7672
    d) 1.7672 and 4.9088 e) None of these

    Answer: b Difficulty: 2

27. Find two values of θ $(0 \le \theta < 360°)$ that satisfy $\csc\theta = 2.5593$.
    a) 23° and 157° b) 67° and 293° c) 157° and 293°
    d) 23° and 203° e) None of these

    Answer: a Difficulty: 2

28. Find two values of θ $(0 \le \theta < 360°)$ that satisfy $\cot\theta = -0.2679$.
    a) 165° and 345° b) 75° and 285° c) 15° and 165°
    d) 105° and 285° e) None of these

    Answer: d Difficulty: 2

29. Given $\cos\theta = -\frac{7}{8}$, $\frac{\pi}{2} \le \theta \le \pi$, find $\tan\theta$.
    a) $-\frac{7\sqrt{15}}{15}$ b) $-\frac{7\sqrt{113}}{113}$ c) $-\frac{\sqrt{15}}{7}$ d) $-\frac{1}{7}$ e) None of these

    Answer: c Difficulty: 1

30. Given $\csc\theta = -\frac{16}{5}$, $\pi \le \theta \le \frac{3\pi}{2}$, find $\tan\theta$.
    a) $-\frac{16\sqrt{281}}{281}$ b) $\frac{5\sqrt{231}}{231}$ c) $\frac{\sqrt{231}}{5}$ d) $-\frac{16\sqrt{231}}{231}$ e) None of these

    Answer: b Difficulty: 1

31. Given $\sin\theta = -\frac{4}{7}$, $\frac{3\pi}{2} \le \theta \le 2\pi$, find $\sec\theta$.
    a) $\frac{\sqrt{33}}{7}$ b) $\frac{7\sqrt{33}}{33}$ c) $-\frac{\sqrt{65}}{4}$ d) $\frac{7\sqrt{65}}{65}$ e) None of these

    Answer: b Difficulty: 1

Chapter 045: Graphs of Sine and Cosine Functions

MULTIPLE CHOICE

1. Determine the amplitude: $f(x) = \sin\left[\frac{x}{4} - \pi\right]$.

a) 1 b) π c) π^2 d) 0 e) None of these

Answer: a Difficulty: 1

2. Determine the amplitude: $f(x) = -3\cos\left[\frac{x}{2} + \pi\right]$.

a) 0 b) -2π c) 3π d) 3 e) None of these

Answer: d Difficulty: 1

3. Determine the amplitude: $f(x) = -\frac{2}{3}\sin(4x)$.

a) $\frac{2}{3}$ b) $\frac{3}{2}$ c) 4 d) $\frac{\pi}{2}$ e) None of these

Answer: a Difficulty: 1

4. Determine the amplitude: $f(x) = 4\cos(3x)$.

a) 3 b) $\frac{1}{3}$ c) 4 d) -4 e) None of these

Answer: c Difficulty: 1

5. Determine the amplitude: $f(x) = \frac{2}{3}\sin\left[4x - \frac{\pi}{2}\right]$.

a) $\frac{\pi}{2}$ b) 4 c) $\frac{2}{3}$ d) 2π e) None of these

Answer: c Difficulty: 1

6. Determine the period: $f(x) = 3\sin(4x - \pi)$.

a) 3π b) $\frac{\pi}{2}$ c) 2π d) $\frac{3\pi}{2}$ e) None of these

Answer: b Difficulty: 1

7. Determine the period: $f(x) = -\frac{2}{3}\cos\left[\frac{x}{3} - \frac{1}{2}\right]$.

a) 6π b) $\frac{2\pi}{3}$ c) $\frac{2}{3}$ d) $\frac{1}{2}$ e) None of these

Answer: a Difficulty: 1

8. Determine the period: $f(x) = -\frac{1}{2}\sin\left(\frac{3x}{2} - \frac{1}{2}\right)$.

a) $\frac{1}{2}$ b) $\frac{1}{2^{\pi}}$ c) $\frac{3\pi}{4}$ d) $\frac{4\pi}{3}$ e) None of these

Answer: d Difficulty: 1

9. Determine the period of the function: $y = \frac{1}{2}\sin\left(\frac{x}{3} - \pi\right)$.

a) $\frac{1}{2}$ b) $\frac{2\pi}{3}$ c) 6π d) 3π e) None of these

Answer: c Difficulty: 1

SHORT ANSWER

10. Determine the period and amplitude of the function: $f(x) = -7\cos 3x$.

Answer:

Period: $\frac{2\pi}{3}$, Amplitude: 7

Difficulty: 1

11. Determine the period and amplitude of the function: $f(x) = 5\cos\frac{x}{2}$.

Answer: Period: 4π, Amplitude: 5 Difficulty: 1

MULTIPLE CHOICE

12. Describe the horizontal shift to the graph of g with respect of the graph of f:
$g(x) = 4\sin\left(2x - \frac{\pi}{3}\right)$ and $f(x) = 4\sin(2x)$.

a) $\frac{\pi}{6}$ units to the left
b) $\frac{\pi}{6}$ units to the right
c) $\frac{2\pi}{3}$ units to the left
d) $\frac{2\pi}{3}$ units to the right
e) None of these

Answer: b Difficulty: 1

13. Describe the horizontal shift of the graph of g with respect to the graph of f:
$g(x) = 3\sin\left(2x - \frac{\pi}{3}\right)$ and $f(x) = 3\sin(2x)$.

a) $\frac{\pi}{4}$ units to the left
b) $\frac{\pi}{8}$ units to the right
c) $\frac{\pi}{4}$ units to the right
d) $\frac{\pi}{8}$ units to the left
e) None of these

Answer: b Difficulty: 1

14. Describe the horizontal shift of the graph of g with respect to the graph of f:
$g(x) = 4\cos\left(3x + \frac{\pi}{4}\right)$ and $f(x) = 4\cos(3x)$.

a) $\frac{\pi}{4}$ units to the right
b) $\frac{\pi}{4}$ units to the left
c) $\frac{\pi}{12}$ units to the right
d) $\frac{\pi}{12}$ units to the left
e) None of these

Answer: d Difficulty: 1

15. Describe the horizontal shift of the graph of g with respect to the graph of f:
$g(x) = 3\cos(\pi x + 3)$ and $f(x) = 3\cos(\pi x)$.

a) $\frac{3}{\pi}$ units to thc left
b) $\frac{\pi}{3}$ units to the left
c) $\frac{2\pi}{3}$ units to the right
d) $\frac{3}{2\pi}$ units to the right
e) None of these

Answer: a Difficulty: 1

16. Describe the horizontal shift of the graph of g with respect to the graph of f:
$g(x) = \frac{1}{2}\cos\left(\pi x - \frac{\pi}{2}\right)$ and $f(x) = \frac{1}{2}\cos(\pi x)$.

a) $\frac{\pi}{2}$ units to the right
b) $\frac{\pi}{2}$ units to the left
c) $\frac{1}{2}$ units to the right
d) $\frac{1}{2}$ units to the left
e) None of these

Answer: c Difficulty: 1

17. Describe the horizontal shift of the graph of g with respect to the graph of f:
$g(x) = 4\sin\left[3x - \frac{3}{2}\pi\right]$ and $f(x) = 4\sin(3x)$.

a) $\frac{3\pi}{2}$ units to the left
b) $\frac{3\pi}{2}$ units to the right
c) $\frac{\pi}{2}$ units to the left
d) $\frac{\pi}{2}$ units to the right
e) None of these

Answer: d Difficulty: 1

18. Describe the shifts in the graph of g with respect to the graph of f:
$g(x) = 1 + \cos\left[2x + \frac{\pi}{2}\right]$ and $f(x) = \cos 2x$.

a) $\frac{\pi}{2}$ right, down 1
b) $\frac{\pi}{4}$ right, up 1
c) $\frac{\pi}{4}$ left, up 1
d) $\frac{\pi}{2}$ left, up 1
e) None of these

Answer: c Difficulty: 1

19. Describe the shifts in the graph of g with respect to the graph of f:
$g(x) = -3 + \sin\left[4x + \frac{\pi}{2}\right]$ and $f(x) = \sin(4x)$.

a) $\frac{\pi}{8}$ left, 3 down
b) $\frac{\pi}{8}$ right, 3 down
c) $\frac{\pi}{2}$ left, 3 down
d) $\frac{\pi}{2}$ right, 3 up
e) None of these

Answer: a Difficulty: 1

20. Describe the shifts in the graph of g with respect to the graph of f:
$g(x) = 2 - \sin\left[3x - \frac{\pi}{4}\right]$ and $f(x) = -\sin(3x)$.

a) $\frac{\pi}{4}$ right, 2 down
b) $\frac{\pi}{12}$ left, 2 down
c) $\frac{\pi}{12}$ right, 2 up
d) $\frac{\pi}{4}$ left, 2 up
e) None of these

Answer: c Difficulty: 1

21. Describe the shifts in the graph of g with respect to the graph of f:
$g(x) = 1 - \cos\left[\frac{2x}{\pi} - \pi\right]$ and $f(x) = -\cos\frac{2x}{\pi}$

a) π right, 1 up
b) $\frac{1}{2}$ right, 1 up
c) $\frac{2}{\pi}$ left, 1 down
d) $\frac{\pi^2}{2}$ right, 1 up
e) None of these

Answer: d Difficulty: 1

22. Match the graph with the correct function.

a) $f(x) = 2\sin\frac{3x}{2}$ b) $f(x) = 2\cos\frac{3x}{2}$ c) $f(x) = 2\sin\frac{2x}{3}$

d) $f(x) = 2\cos\frac{2x}{3}$ e) None of these

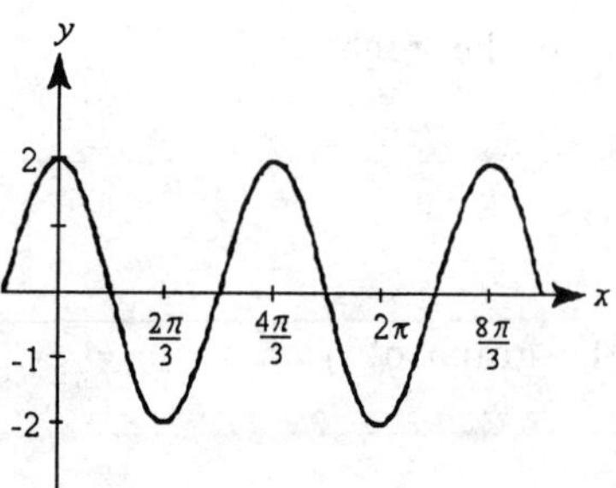

Answer: b Difficulty: 1

23. Match the graph with the correct function.

a) $f(x) = 4\sin 2x$ b) $f(x) = 2\sin 4x$ c) $f(x) = 4\cos 4x$

d) $f(x) = 2\cos 2x$ e) None of these

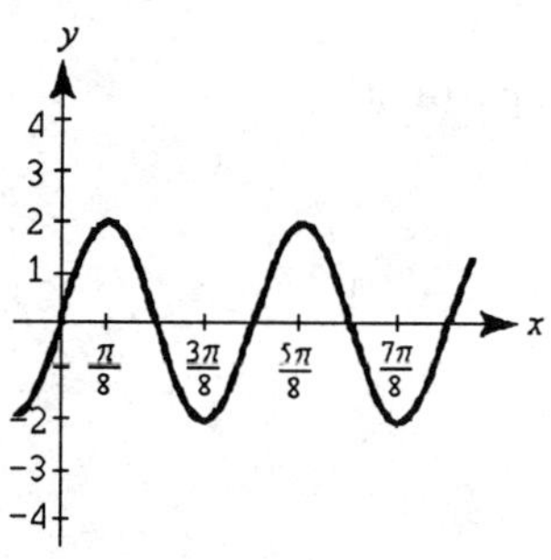

Answer: b Difficulty: 1

24. Match the graph with the correct function.

a) $f(x) = 3\cos\left[\frac{x}{2}\right]$ b) $f(x) = 3\sin\left[\frac{x}{2}\right]$ c) $f(x) = 3\cos 2x$

d) $f(x) = 3\sin 2x$ e) None of these

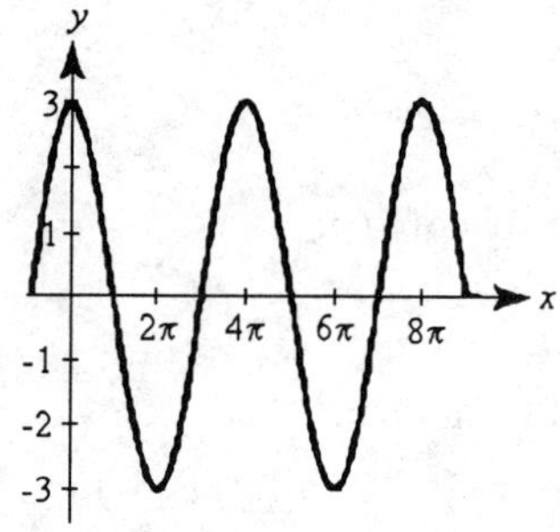

Answer: a Difficulty: 1

25. Match the graph with the correct function.

a) $f(x) = 4\cos\left[2x - \frac{\pi}{3}\right]$

b) $f(x) = 4\sin\left[2x - \frac{\pi}{3}\right]$

c) $f(x) = -4\sin\left[3x - \frac{\pi}{2}\right]$

d) $f(x) = 4\cos\left[3x + \frac{\pi}{2}\right]$

e) None of these

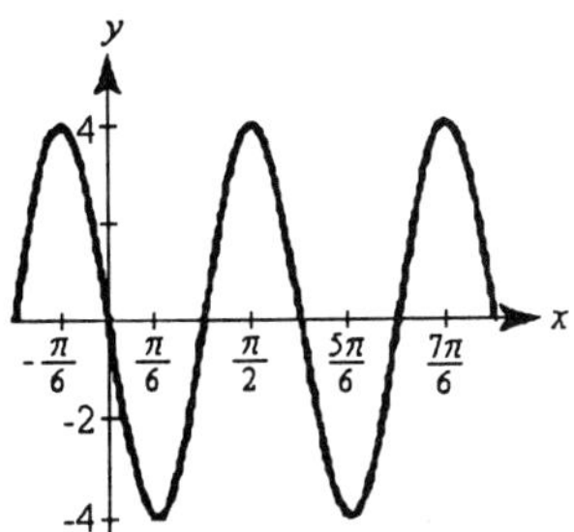

Answer: d Difficulty: 2

26. Match the graph with the correct function.

a) $f(x) = \frac{1}{2}\cos\left[\frac{2x}{3}\right]$

b) $f(x) = \frac{1}{2}\sin\left[\frac{2x}{3}\right]$

c) $f(x) = \frac{1}{2}\cos\left[\frac{3x}{2}\right]$

d) $f(x) = \frac{1}{2}\sin\left[\frac{3x}{2}\right]$

e) None of these

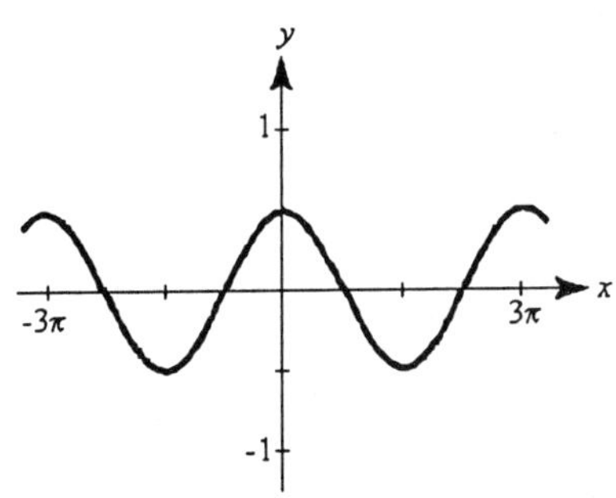

Answer: a Difficulty: 1

27. Match the graph with the correct function.
a) $f(x) = 3 \sin 4x$ b) $f(x) = 3 \sin\left(\frac{x}{4}\right)$ c) $f(x) = 3 \cos 4x$
d) $f(x) = 3 \cos\left(\frac{x}{4}\right)$ e) None of these

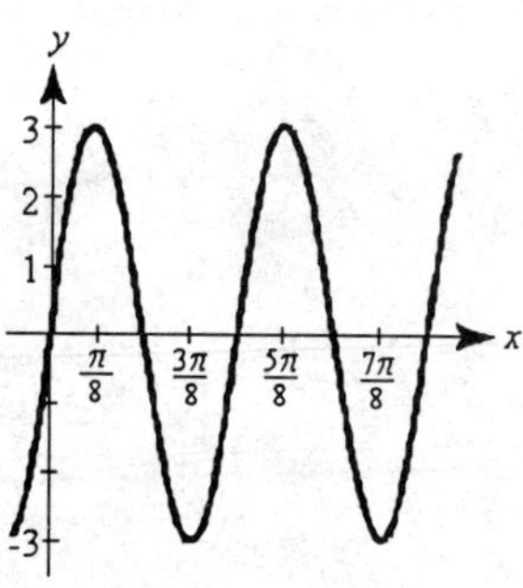

Answer: a Difficulty: 1

28. Match the graph with the correct function.
a) $f(x) = 4 \cos\left(3x - \frac{\pi}{2}\right)$ b) $f(x) = 4 \cos\left(x + \frac{\pi}{6}\right)$
c) $f(x) = 4 \sin\left(2x - \frac{\pi}{3}\right)$ d) $f(x) = 4 \cos\left(2x + \frac{\pi}{3}\right)$
e) None of these

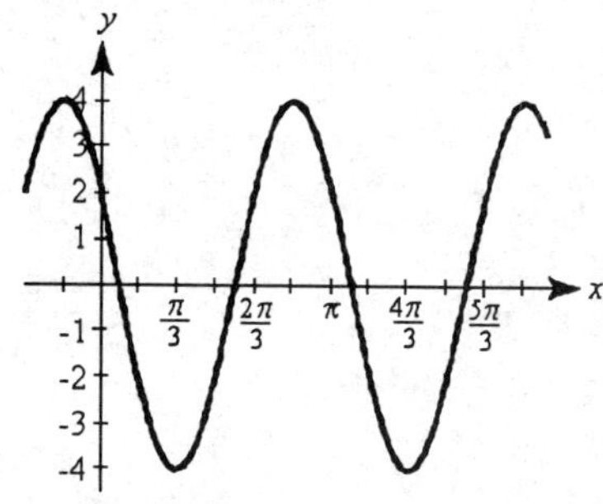

Answer: d Difficulty: 1

29. Match the function with the correct graph: $f(x) = 2 \sin 3x$.
a) I b) II c) III d) IV e) None of these

(I)

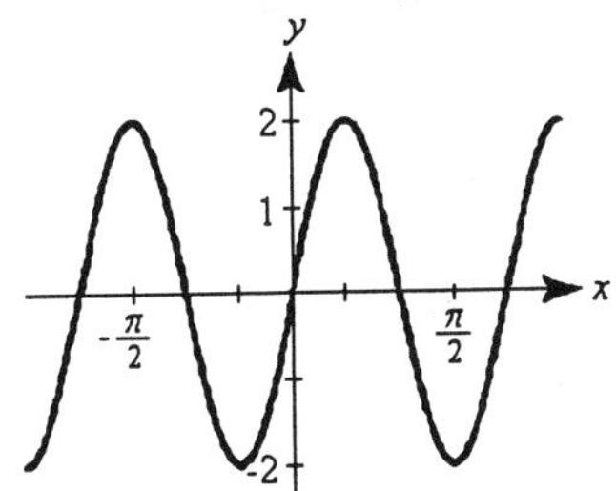

(II)

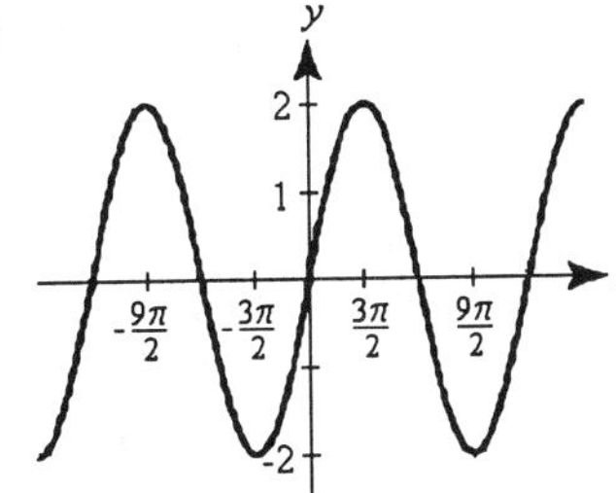

(III)

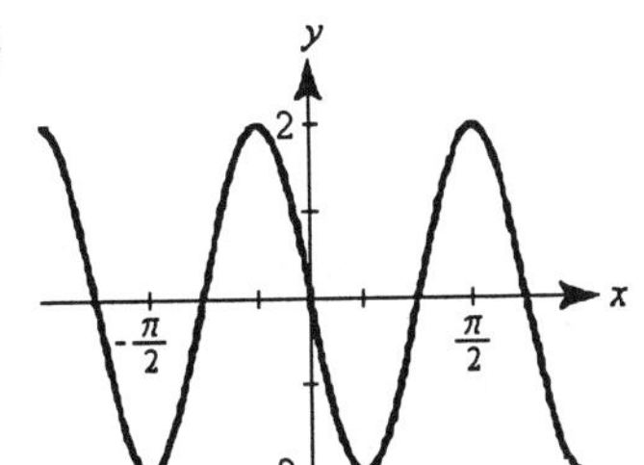

(IV)

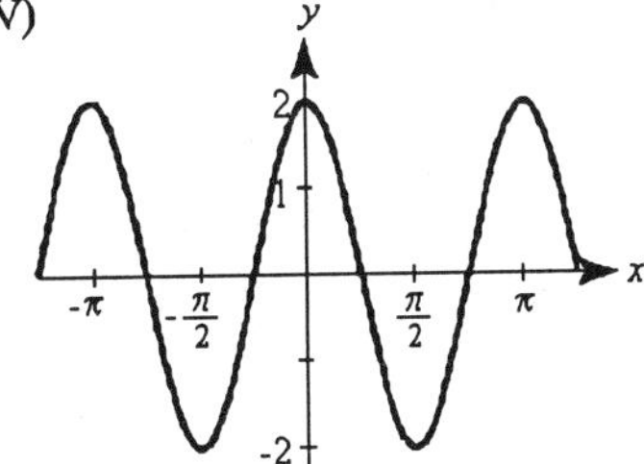

Answer: a Difficulty: 1

30. Match the function with the correct graph: $f(x) = -4 \cos \frac{1}{2}x$.
a) I b) II c) III d) IV e) None of these

(I)

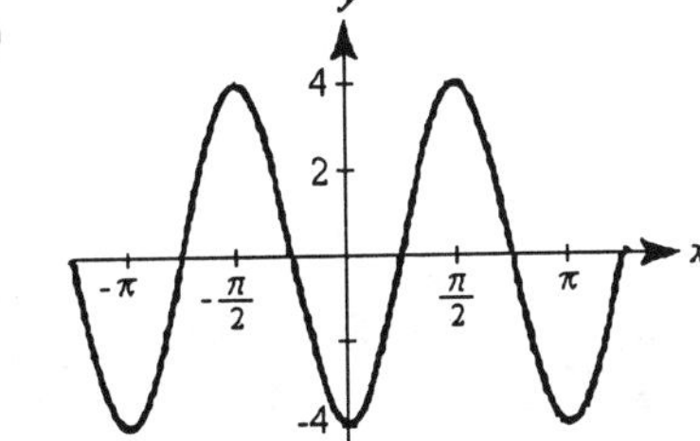

(II)

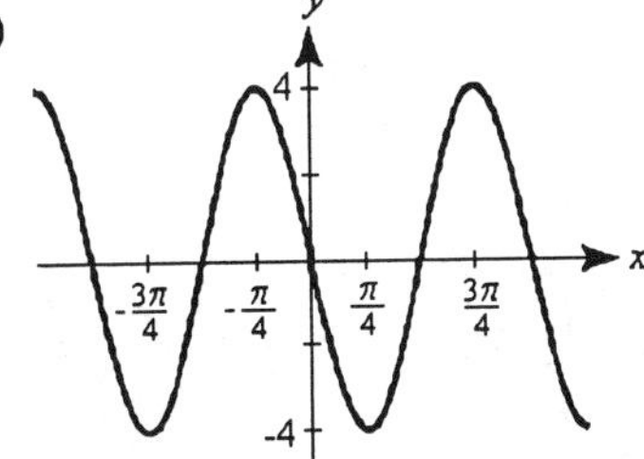

(III)

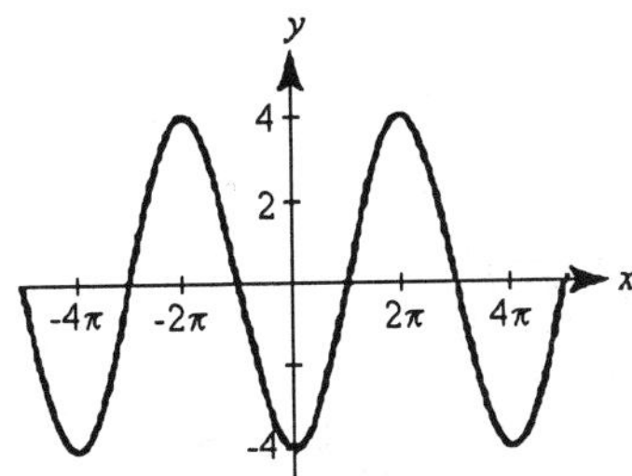

(IV)

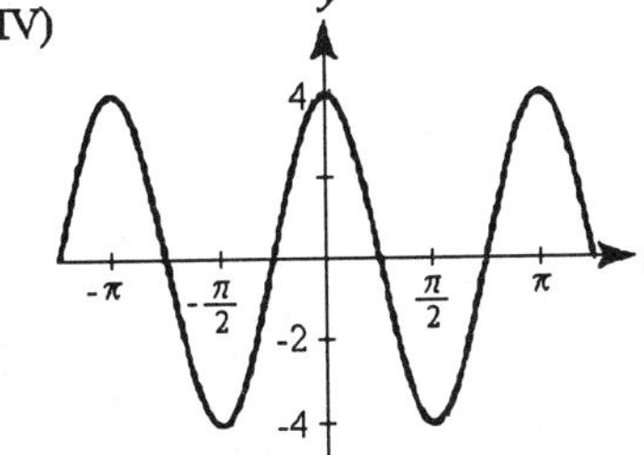

Answer: c Difficulty: 1

31. Match the function with the correct graph: $f(x) = \cos\left[2x - \frac{\pi}{3}\right]$.

a) I b) II c) III d) IV e) None of these

(I)

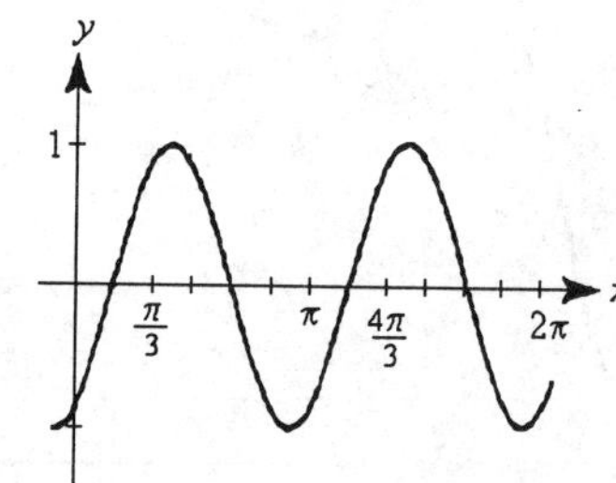

(II)

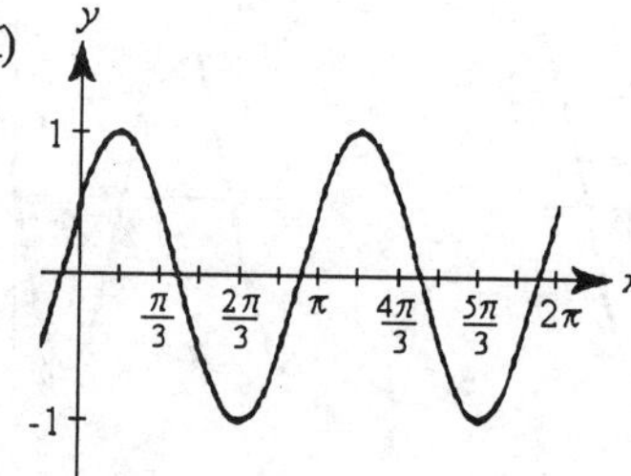

(III)

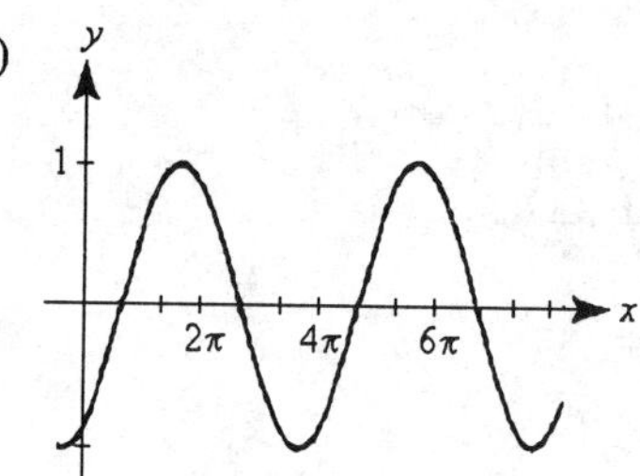

(IV)

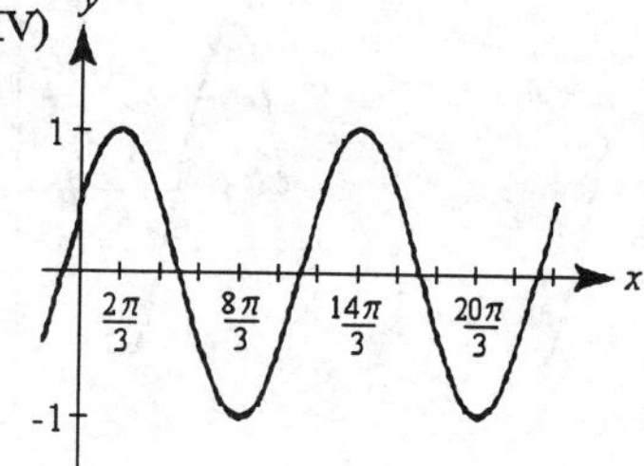

Answer: b Difficulty: 1

32. Match the function with the correct graph: $f(x) = \sin\left[3x - \frac{\pi}{4}\right]$.

a) I b) II c) III d) IV e) None of these

(I)

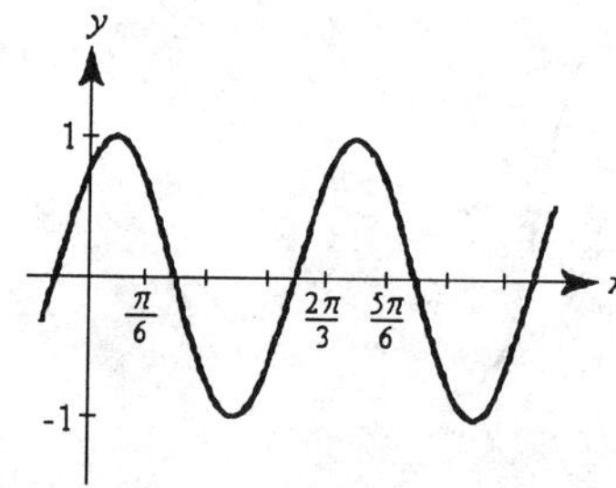

(II)

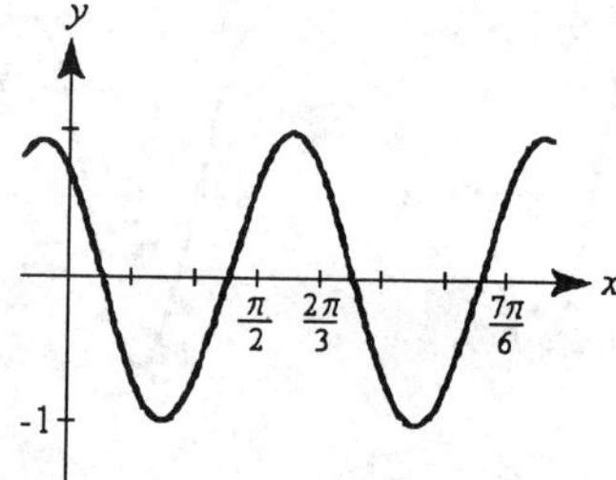

(III)

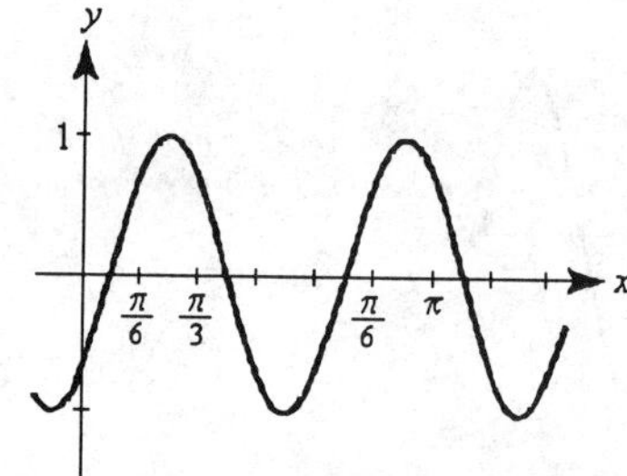

(IV)

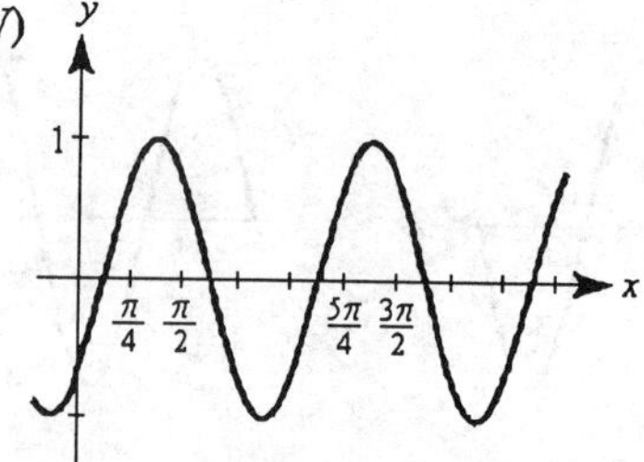

Answer: c Difficulty: 1

33. A buoy oscillates in simple harmonic motion as waves move past. An equation that describes this motion is $d = \frac{7}{4} \cos \frac{\pi t}{5}$. Find the period of the function.

a) 5 b) 10 c) $\frac{2\pi^2}{5}$ d) $\frac{2}{5}$ e) None of these

Answer: b Difficulty: 1

34. A buoy oscillates in simple harmonic motion as waves move past. An equation that describes this motion is $d = 2 \cos \frac{\pi t}{6}$. Find the period of the function.

a) 12 b) $\frac{\pi^2}{3}$ c) $\frac{1}{3}$ d) 3 e) None of these

Answer: a Difficulty: 1

SHORT ANSWER

35. Sketch by hand the graph of the function: $f(x) = 4 \sin(2x - \pi)$.

Answer: See graph below.

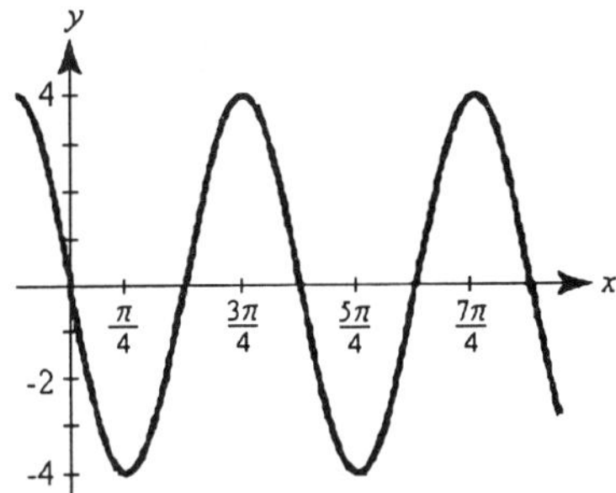

Difficulty: 1

36. Sketch by hand the graph of the function: $f(x) = 2 \cos(4x - \pi)$.

Answer: See graph below.

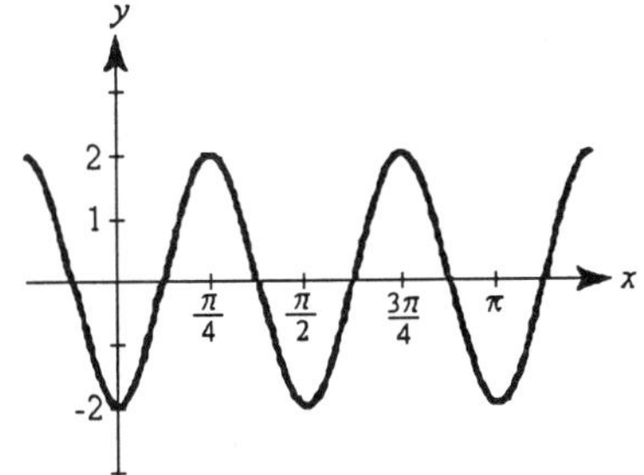

Difficulty: 1

37. Sketch by hand the graph of the function: $f(x) = -2 \sin(2x + \pi)$.

Answer: See graph below.

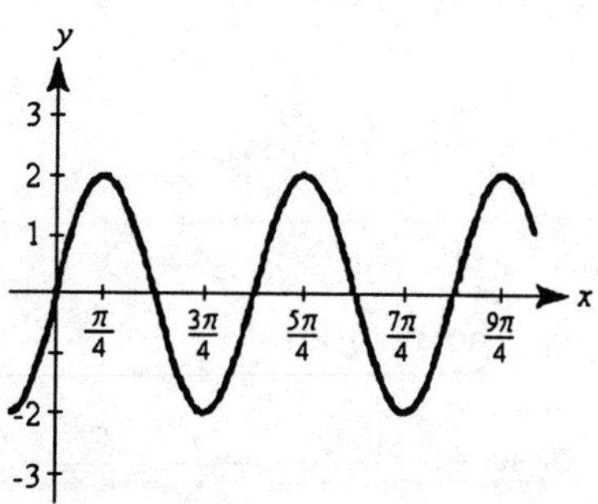

Difficulty: 1

38. Sketch by hand the graph of the function: $f(x) = -4 \cos(2x + \pi)$.

Answer: See graph below.

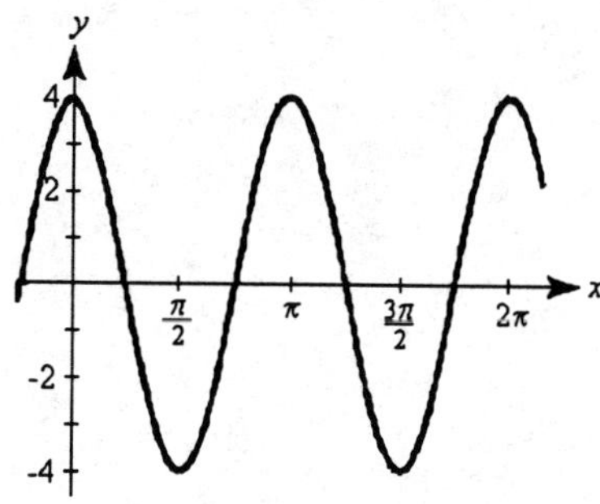

Difficulty: 1

39. Use a graphing utility to graph the function: $f(x) = \cos\left[2x - \frac{\pi}{2}\right] + 1$.

Answer: See graph below.

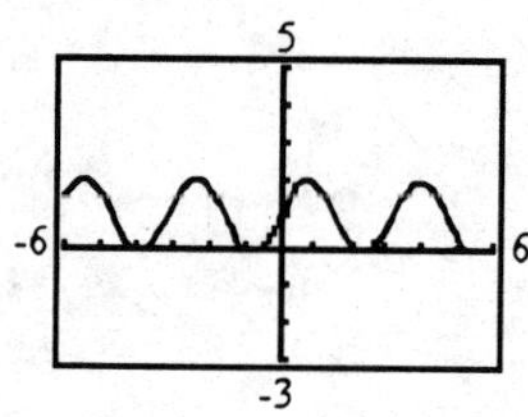

Difficulty: 1

40. Use a graphing utility to graph the function: $f(x) = \sin\left(\frac{x}{2} + \frac{\pi}{8}\right)$.

Answer: See graph below.

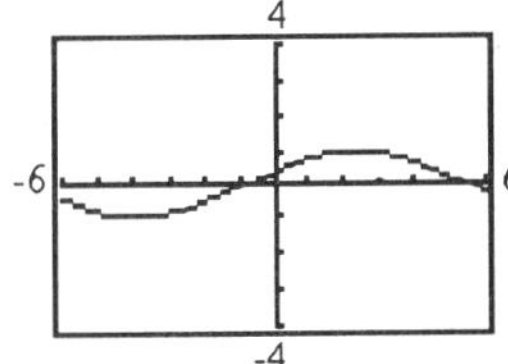

Difficulty: 1

41. Use a graphing utility to graph the function: $f(x) = \frac{1}{2}\sin\left(2x + \frac{\pi}{4}\right)$.

Answer: See graph below.

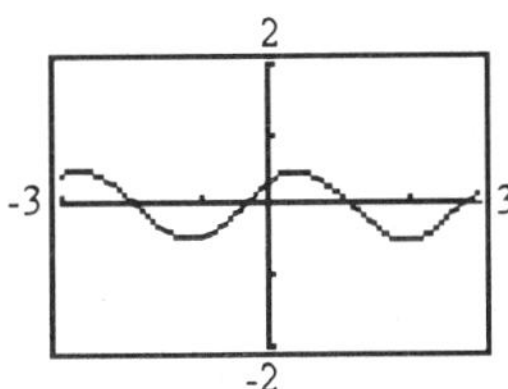

Difficulty: 1

42. Use a graphing utility to graph the function: $f(x) = 3\cos(4x - \pi)$.

Answer: See graph below.

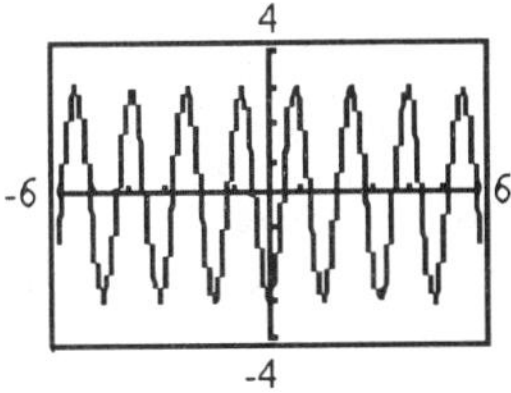

Difficulty: 1

MULTIPLE CHOICE

43. Match the graph with the correct function.

a) $f(x) = 3 + \sin\left(x + \frac{\pi}{2}\right)$

b) $f(x) = 3 + \sin\left(x - \frac{\pi}{2}\right)$

c) $f(x) = 3 + \cos\left(x + \frac{\pi}{2}\right)$

d) $f(x) = 3 + \cos\left(x - \frac{\pi}{2}\right)$

e) None of these

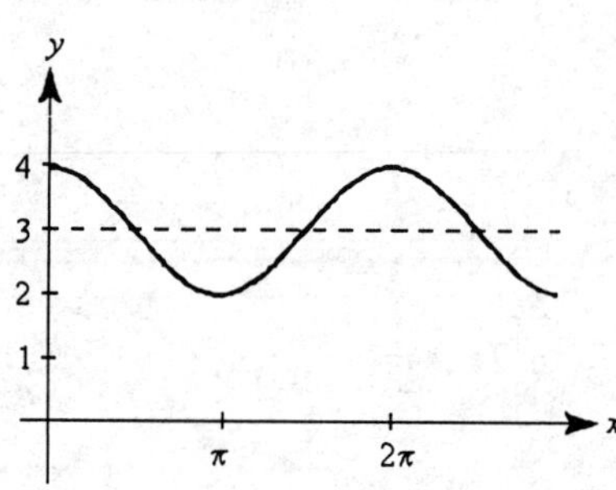

Answer: a Difficulty: 1

44. Match the graph with the correct function.

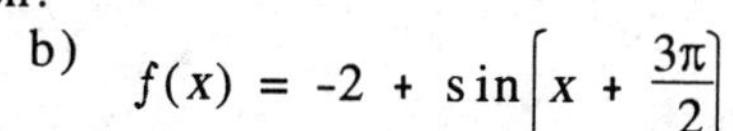

a) $f(x) = -2 + \cos\left(x - \frac{\pi}{2}\right)$

b) $f(x) = -2 + \sin\left(x + \frac{3\pi}{2}\right)$

c) $f(x) = -2 + \cos\left(x + \frac{\pi}{2}\right)$

d) $f(x) = -2 + \sin\left(x - \frac{3\pi}{2}\right)$

e) None of these

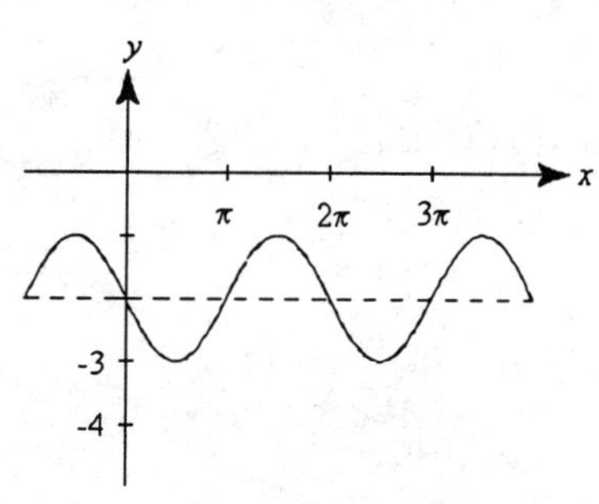

Answer: c Difficulty: 1

45. Match the graph with the correct function.

a) $f(x) = -2 + \cos\left(x - \dfrac{\pi}{2}\right)$

b) $f(x) = -2 + \sin\left(x + \dfrac{3\pi}{2}\right)$

c) $f(x) = -2 + \cos\left(x + \dfrac{\pi}{2}\right)$

d) $f(x) = -2 + \sin\left(x - \dfrac{3\pi}{2}\right)$

e) None of these

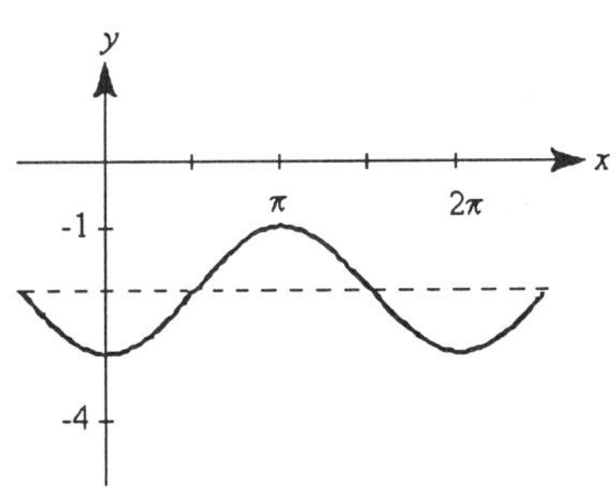

Answer: b Difficulty: 1

46. Match the graph with the correct function.

a) $f(x) = 2 + \cos\left(x + \dfrac{\pi}{4}\right)$

b) 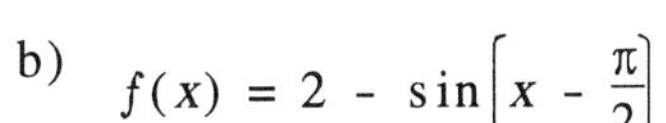 $f(x) = 2 - \sin\left(x - \dfrac{\pi}{2}\right)$

c) $f(x) = 2 + \sin\left(x + \dfrac{\pi}{4}\right)$

d) $f(x) = 2 - \cos(x + \pi)$

e) None of these

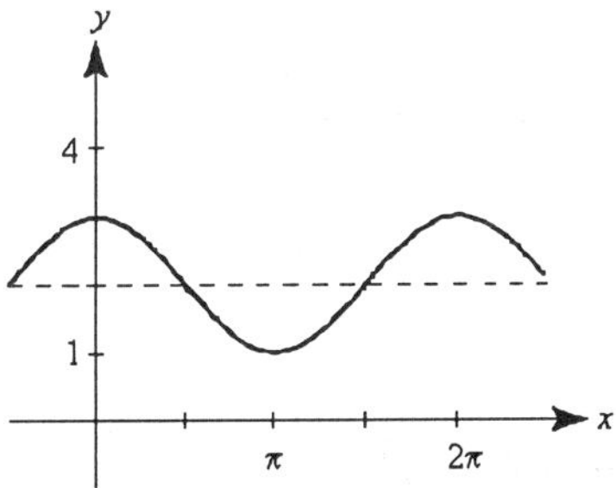

Answer: d Difficulty: 1

Chapter 046: Graphs of Other Trigonometric Functions

MULTIPLE CHOICE

1. Match the correct graph with the function: $f(x) = \csc 3x$.
   a) I b) II c) III d) IV e) None of these

(I)
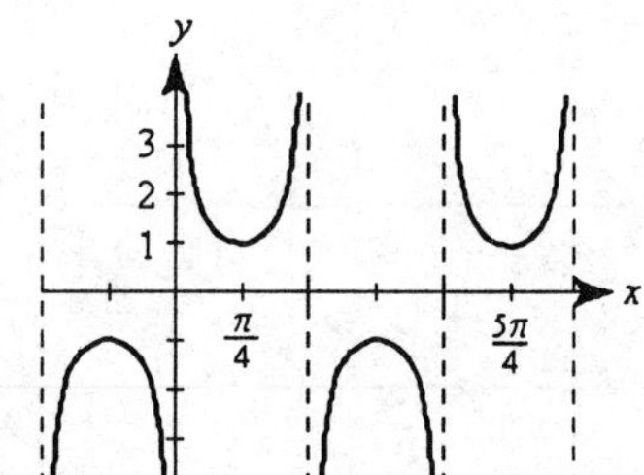

(II)
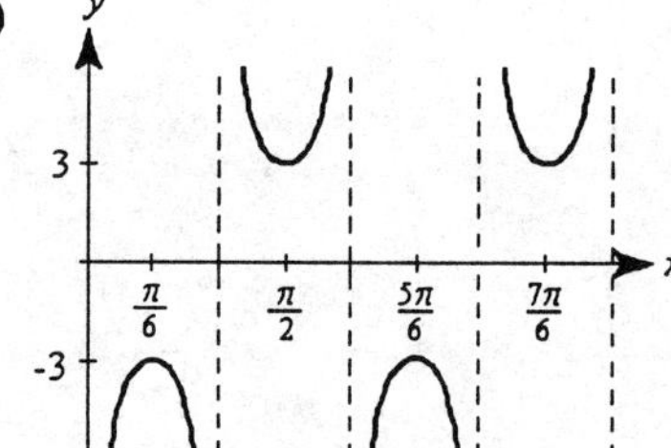

(III)
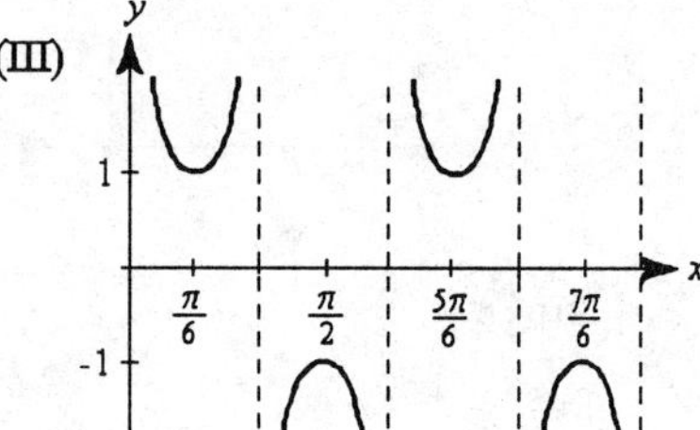

(IV)
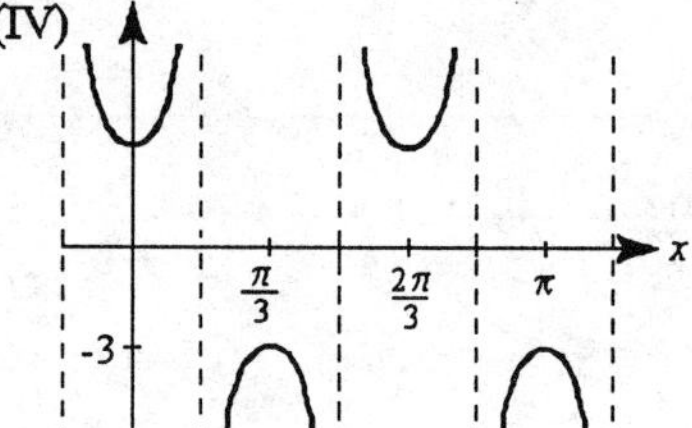

Answer: c Difficulty: 1

2. Match the correct graph with the function: $f(x) = \sec 2x$.
   a) I b) II c) III d) IV e) None of these

(I)
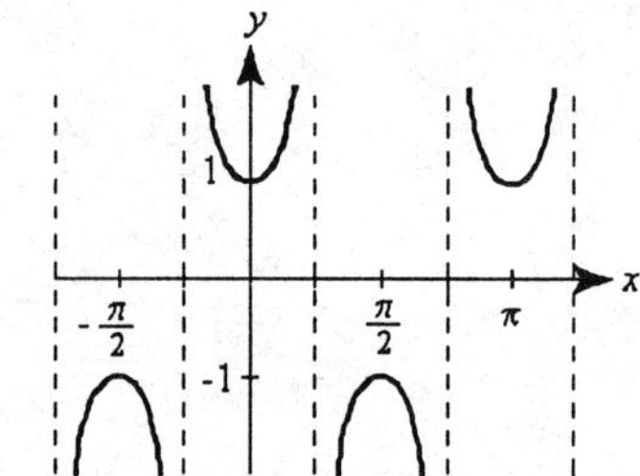

(II)
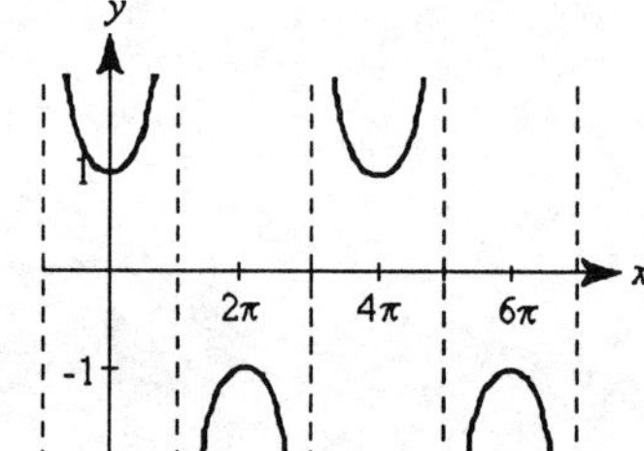

(III)
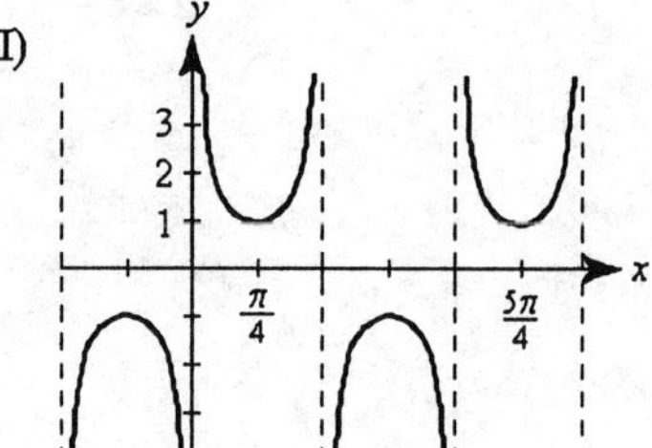

(IV)
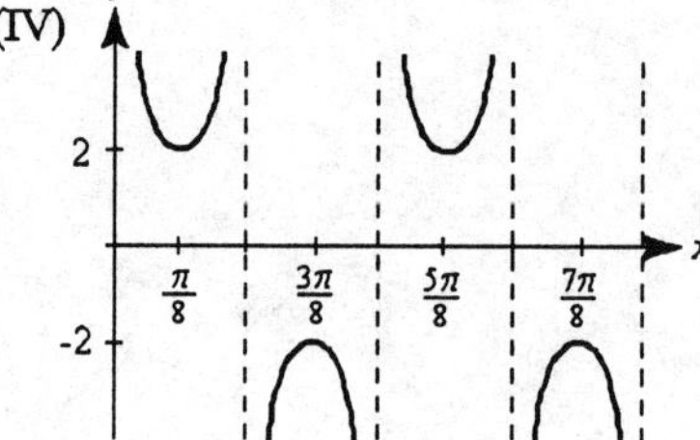

Answer: a Difficulty: 1

3. Match the correct graph with the function: $f(x) = -\tan 3x$.
a) I b) II c) III d) IV e) None of these

(I)
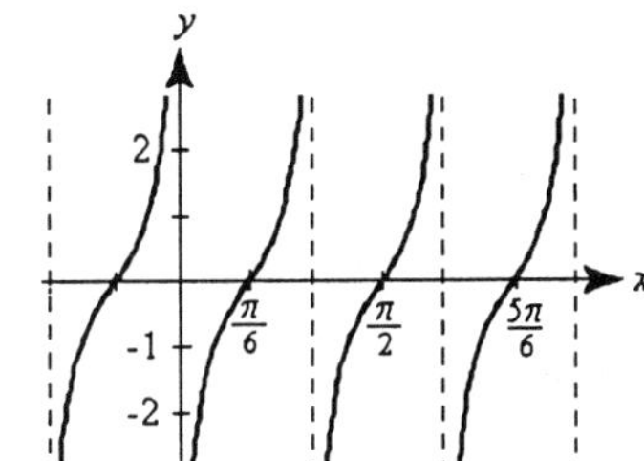

(II)
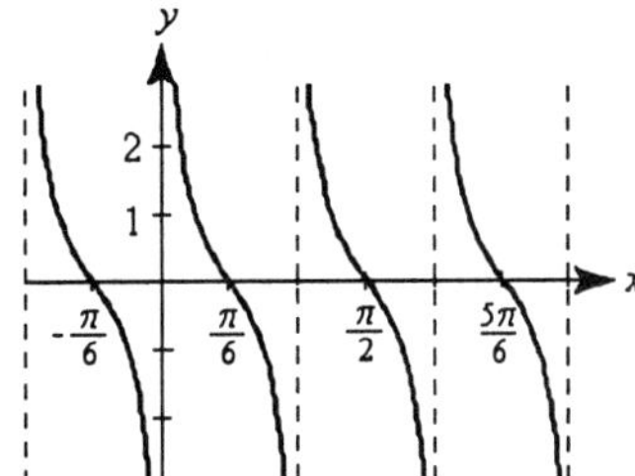

(III)
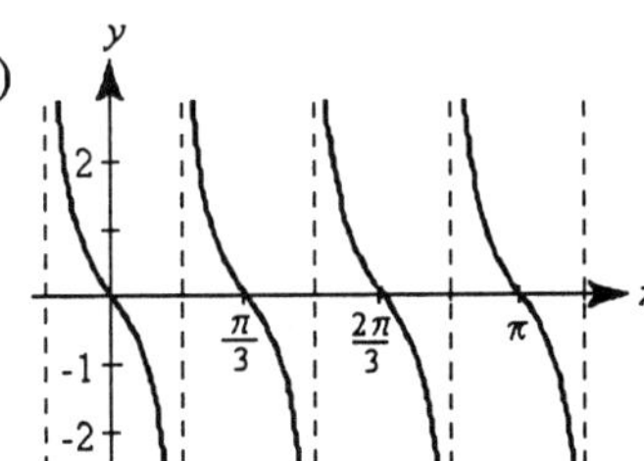

(IV)
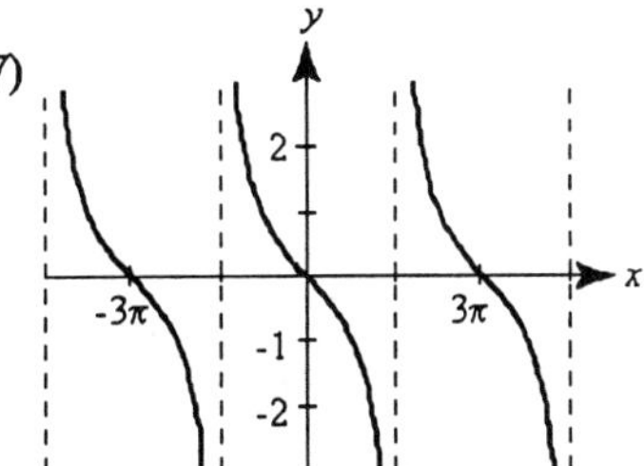

Answer: c Difficulty: 1

4. Match the correct graph with the function: $f(x) = 1 + \sec 2x$.
a) I b) II c) III d) IV e) None of these

(I)
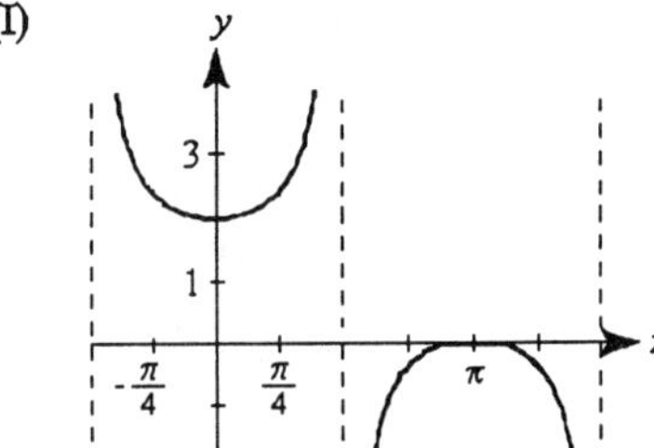

(II)
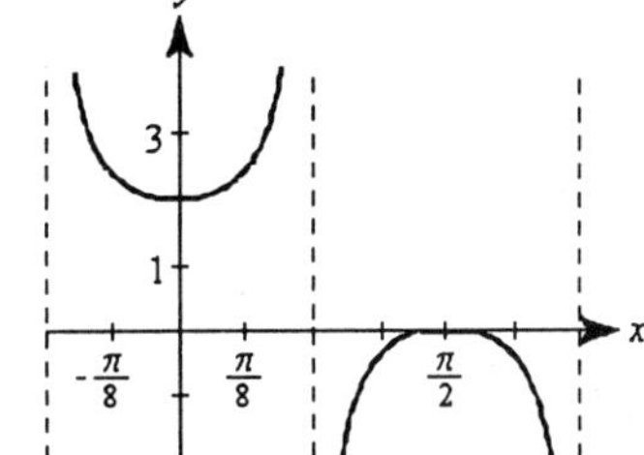

(III)
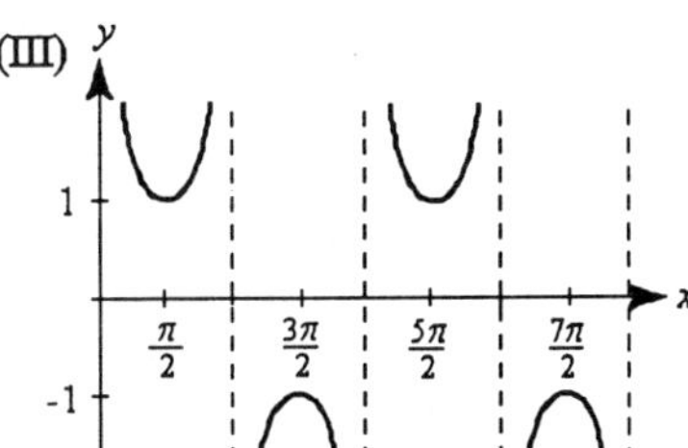

(IV)
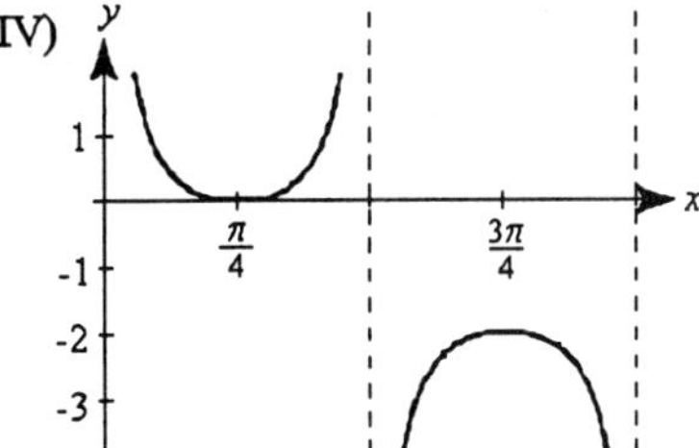

Answer: b Difficulty: 1

5. Match the correct graph with the function: $f(x) = \cot\left(x - \frac{\pi}{4}\right)$.

a) I b) II c) III d) IV e) None of these

(I)

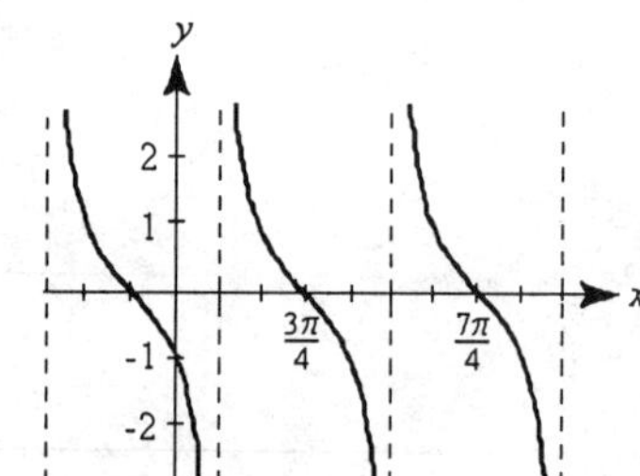

(II)

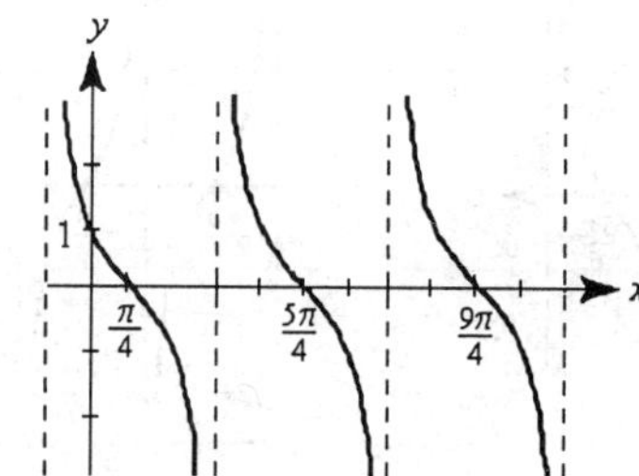

(III)

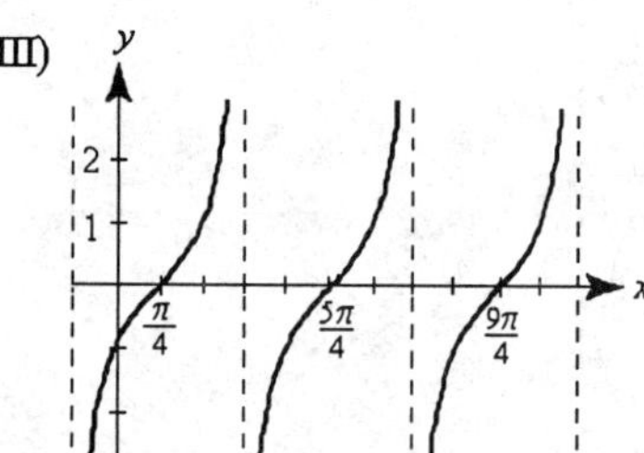

(IV)

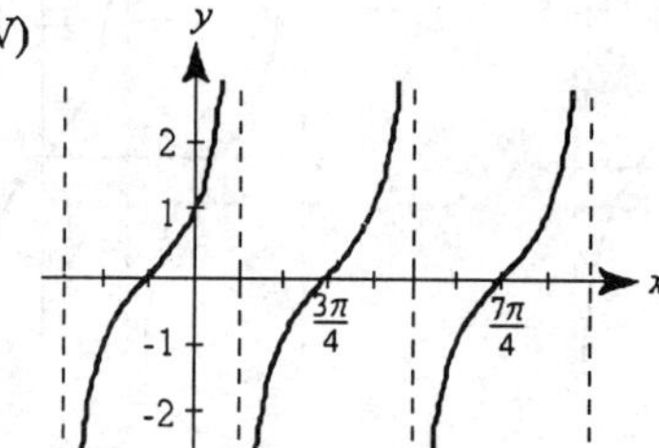

Answer: a Difficulty: 1

6. Match the correct graph with the function: $f(x) = 2 \csc \pi x$.

a) I b) II c) III d) IV e) None of these

(I)

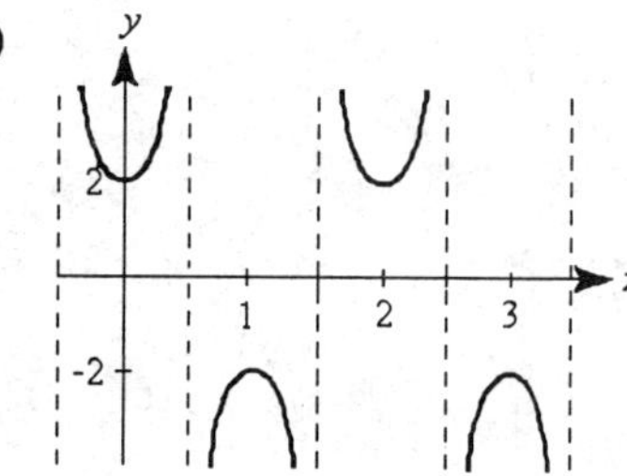

(II)

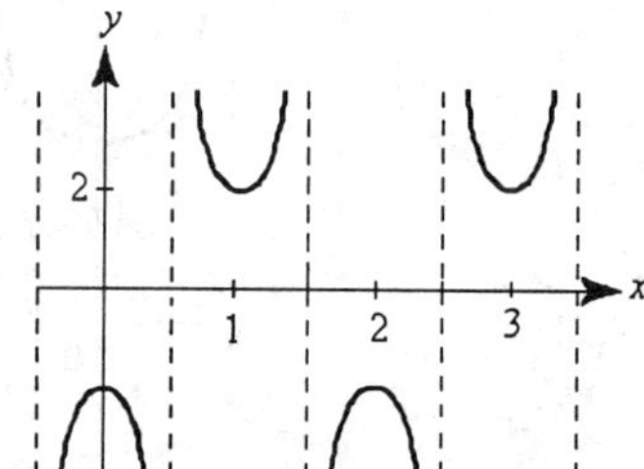

(III)

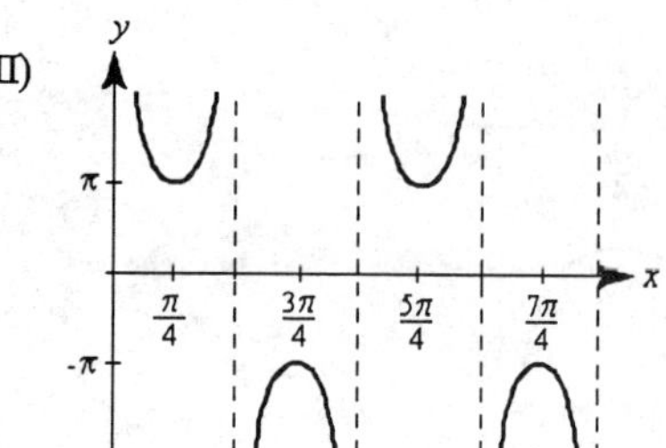

(IV)

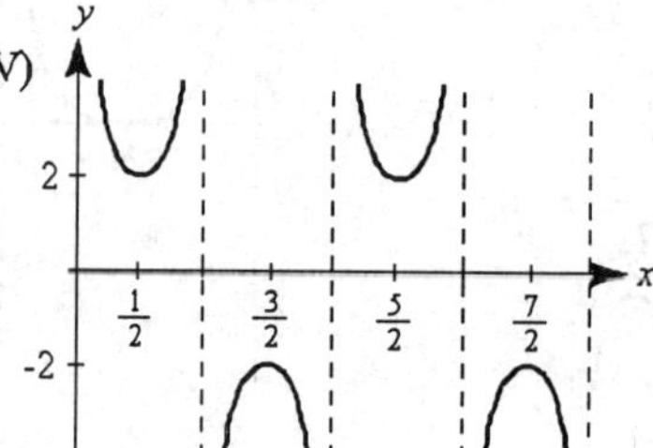

Answer: d Difficulty: 1

7. Match the graph with the correct function.
   a) $f(x) = \cot\left[x - \frac{\pi}{4}\right]$ b) $f(x) = \tan\left[x - \frac{\pi}{4}\right]$ c) $f(x) = -\cot(4x)$
   d) $f(x) = \tan 4x$ e) None of these

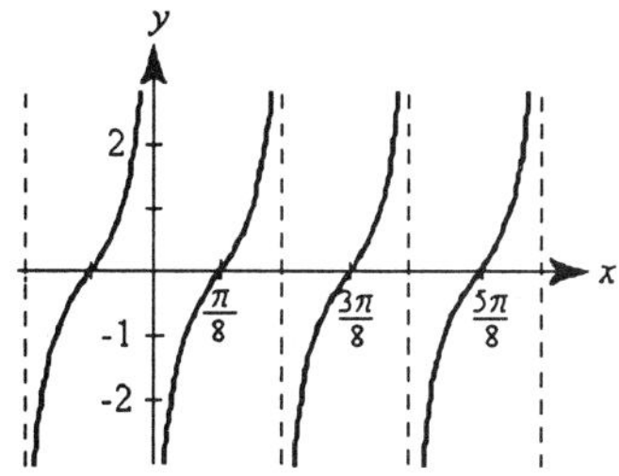

Answer: c Difficulty: 1

8. Match the graph with the correct function.
   a) $f(x) = 3 \csc 2x$ b) $f(x) = 3 \sec 2x$ c) $f(x) = -3 \sec 2x$
   d) $f(x) = -3 \csc 2x$ e) None of these

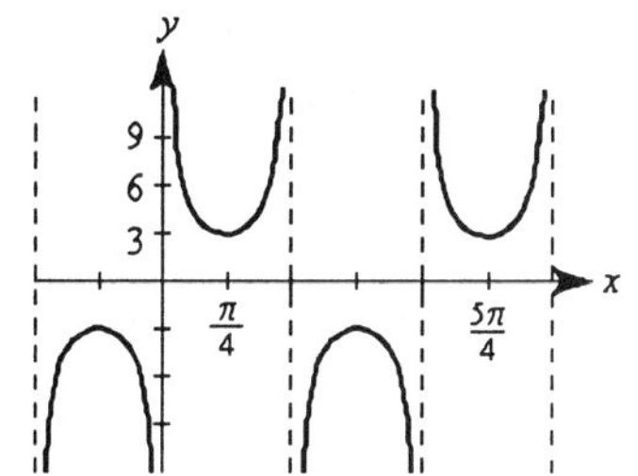

Answer: a Difficulty: 1

9. Match the graph with the correct function.
   a) $f(x) = 2 \cot 3\pi x$ b) $f(x) = -2 \tan \frac{\pi x}{3}$ c) $f(x) = 2 \cot \frac{\pi x}{3}$
   d) $f(x) = -2 \tan 3\pi x$ e) None of these

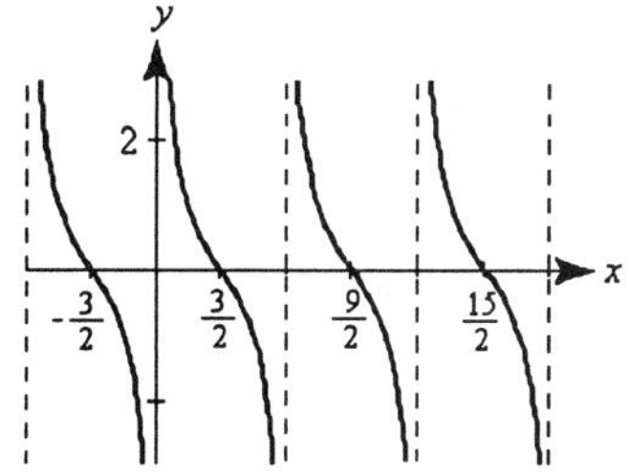

Answer: c Difficulty: 1

10. Match the graph with the correct function.
    a) $f(x) = -\sec \pi x$ b) $f(x) = -\csc \pi x$ c) $f(x) = \sec\left[x - \frac{\pi}{2}\right]$
    d) $f(x) = -\csc\left[x + \frac{1}{2}\right]$ e) None of these

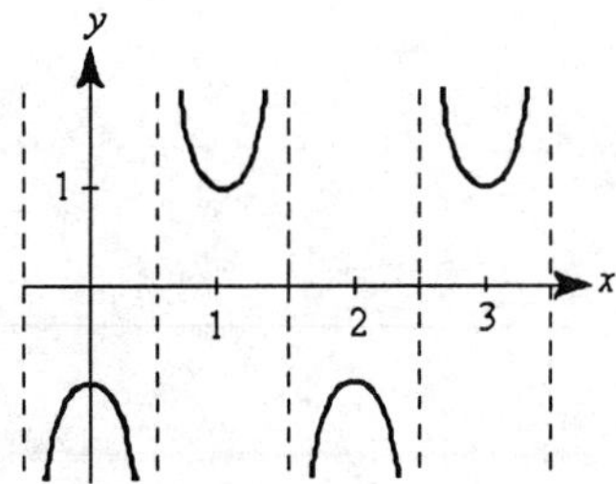

Answer: a Difficulty: 1

11. Match the graph with the correct function.
    a) $f(x) = -\csc 3x$ b) $f(x) = \sec 3x$ c) $f(x) = -\sec\frac{x}{3}$
    d) $f(x) = -\csc\frac{x}{3}$ e) None of these

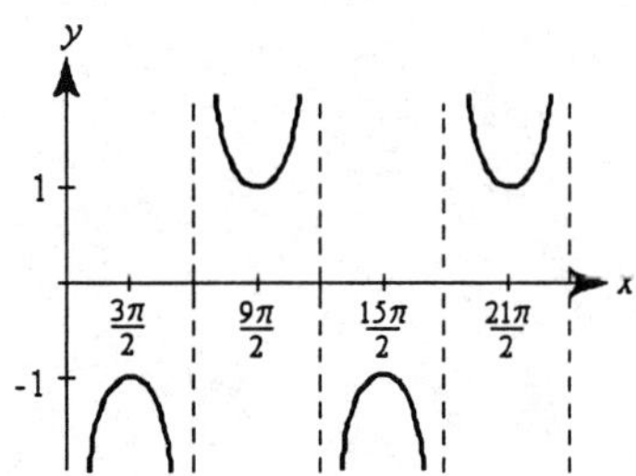

Answer: d Difficulty: 1

12. Match the graph with the correct function.
    a) $f(x) = 3 - \sec x$ b) $f(x) = x + \csc x$ c) $f(x) = x + \sec x$
    d) $f(x) = 3 + \csc x$ e) None of these

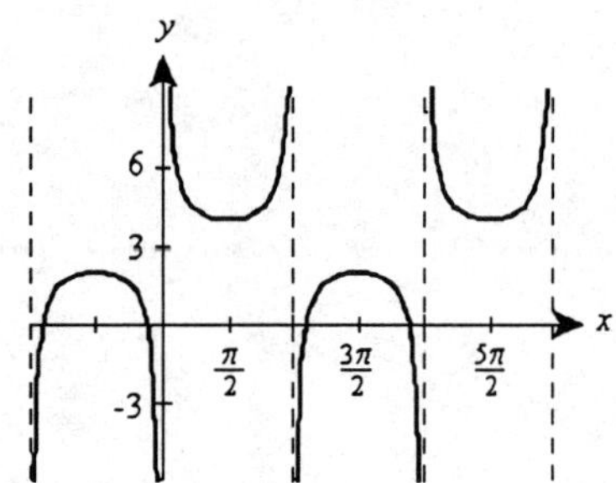

Answer: d Difficulty: 1

13. Match the graph with the correct function.
a) $f(x) = 2 \sec 2\pi x$ b) $f(x) = -2 \csc\left(\frac{\pi x}{2}\right)$ c) $f(x) = -2 \cot\left(\frac{\pi x}{4}\right)$
d) $f(x) = -\sin\left(\frac{\pi}{2}\right)$ e) None of these

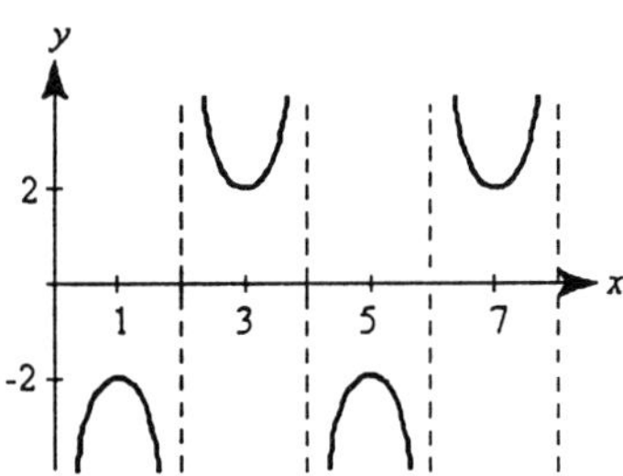

Answer: b Difficulty: 1

SHORT ANSWER

14. Sketch by hand the graph of the function: $f(x) = \frac{1}{2} \sec\left(x - \frac{\pi}{2}\right)$.

Answer: See graph below.

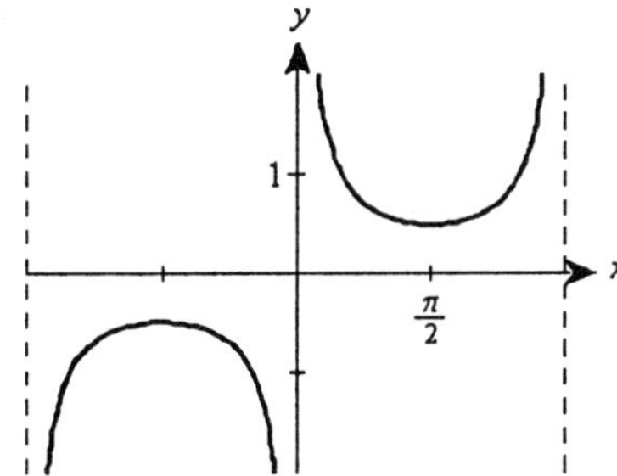

Difficulty: 2

15. Sketch by hand the graph of the function: $f(x) = -\csc\left(x + \frac{\pi}{3}\right)$.

Answer: See graph below.

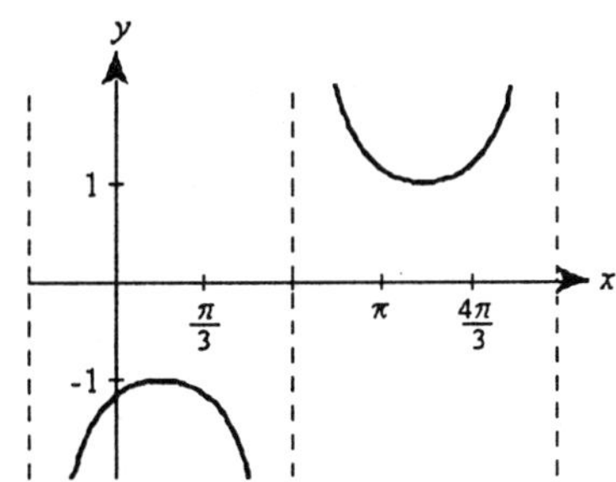

Difficulty: 2

16. Sketch by hand the graph of the function: $f(x) = \cot\left(x - \frac{\pi}{6}\right)$.

Answer: See graph below.

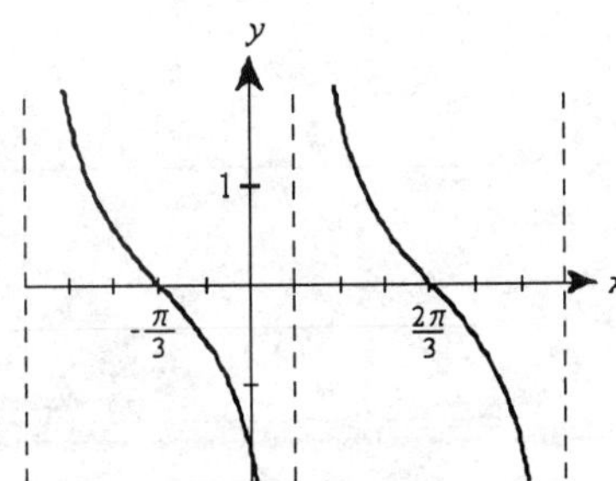

Difficulty: 2

17. Sketch by hand the graph of the function: $f(x) = -\csc(2x - \pi)$.

Answer: See graph below.

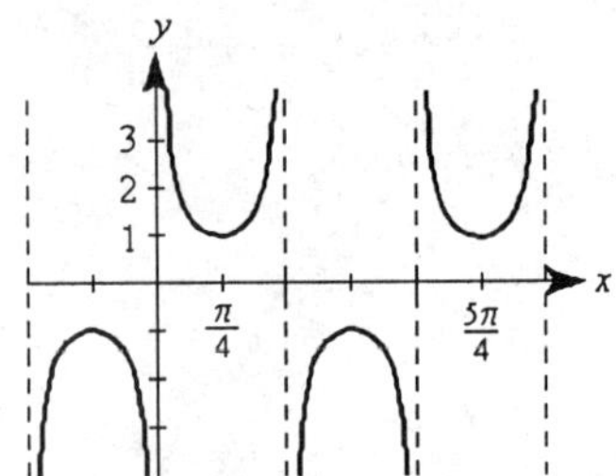

Difficulty: 2

18. Sketch by hand the graph of the function: $f(x) = -\sec\left(3x - \frac{\pi}{2}\right)$.

Answer: See graph below.

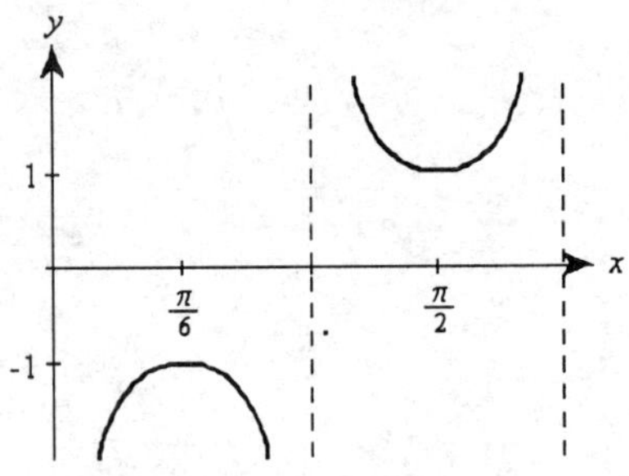

Difficulty: 2

19. Determine the period of the function: $f(x) = 3 \tan 7x$.

Answer:
$\frac{\pi}{7}$

Difficulty: 1

20. Determine the period of the function: $f(x) = \frac{1}{5} \tan\left(3x + \frac{\pi}{2}\right)$.

Answer:
$\frac{\pi}{3}$

Difficulty: 1

MULTIPLE CHOICE

21. Determine the period of the function: $f(x) = 3 \cot 4x$.
a) $\frac{\pi}{2}$ b) $\frac{\pi}{4}$ c) 2π d) 4π e) None of these

Answer: b Difficulty: 1

22. Determine the period of the function: $f(x) = 2 \tan(3x - \pi)$.
a) $\frac{\pi}{3}$ b) $\frac{2\pi}{3}$ c) 6π d) 3π e) None of these

Answer: a Difficulty: 1

23. Determine the period of the function: $f(x) = -\sec\left(\frac{x}{2} - \frac{\pi}{3}\right)$.
a) $\frac{\pi}{2}$ b) π c) 2π d) 4π e) None of these

Answer: d Difficulty: 1

24. Determine the period of the function: $f(x) = \csc\left(\frac{x}{3} - \frac{\pi}{2}\right)$.
a) 3π b) $\frac{\pi}{2}$ c) $\frac{2\pi}{3}$ d) 6π e) None of these

Answer: d Difficulty: 1

25. Determine the period of the function: $f(x) = \tan\left(\frac{x}{2}\right)$.
a) π b) 2π c) $\frac{\pi}{2}$ d) 4π e) None of these

Answer: b Difficulty: 1

26. To sketch the graph of the cosecant function, it is convenient to first sketch the graph of the _________ function.
a) sine b) cosine c) tangent
d) cotangent e) secant

Answer: a Difficulty: 1

27. To sketch the graph of the secant function, it is convenient to first sketch the graph of the _________ function.
a) sine b) cosine c) tangent
d) cotangent e) secant

Answer: b Difficulty: 1

28. Which of the following is a vertical asymptote to the graph of $y = \csc 3x$?
a) $x = \frac{\pi}{2}$ b) $x = \frac{3\pi}{2}$ c) $x = \frac{\pi}{3}$ d) $x = \frac{\pi}{4}$ e) None of these

Answer: c Difficulty: 1

29. Which of the following is a vertical asymptote to the graph of
$y = -\tan\left(x - \frac{\pi}{3}\right)$?
a) $x = \frac{\pi}{3}$ b) $x = \frac{\pi}{2}$ c) $x = \frac{3\pi}{2}$ d) $x = \frac{5\pi}{6}$ e) None of these

Answer: d Difficulty: 1

30. Which of the following is a vertical asymptote to the graph of
$y = \tan\left(2x - \frac{\pi}{3}\right)$?
a) $x = \frac{5\pi}{6}$ b) $x = \frac{5\pi}{12}$ c) $x = \frac{6\pi}{5}$ d) $x = \frac{\pi}{2}$ e) None of these

Answer: b Difficulty: 1

31. Which of the following is a vertical asymptote to the graph of
$y = -2\csc\left(3x - \frac{\pi}{3}\right)$?
a) $x = \frac{2\pi}{3}$ b) $x = \frac{5\pi}{12}$ c) $x = \frac{7\pi}{9}$ d) $x = \frac{8\pi}{15}$ e) None of these

Answer: c Difficulty: 1

32. Which of the following is a vertical asymptote to the graph of
$y = \frac{1}{2}\sec\left(2x - \frac{\pi}{4}\right)$?
a) $x = \frac{\pi}{8}$ b) $x = \frac{9\pi}{8}$ c) $x = \frac{7\pi}{8}$ d) $x = \frac{\pi}{4}$ e) None of these

Answer: c Difficulty: 1

33. Which of the following is a vertical asymptote to the graph of $y = -\cot\left[\frac{x}{2}\right]$?

a) $x = \pi$ b) $x = 2\pi$ c) $x = \frac{\pi}{2}$ d) $x = \frac{\pi}{4}$ e) None of these

Answer: b Difficulty: 1

34. Match the graph with the correct function.

a) $f(x) = 2x \cos x$ b) $f(x) = 2x \sin x$ c) $f(x) = 2x + \cos x$
d) $f(x) = 2x + \sin x$ e) None of these

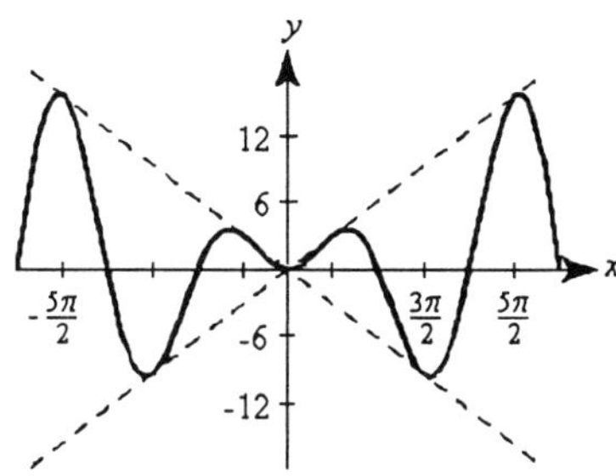

Answer: b Difficulty: 1

35. Match the graph with the correct function.

a) $f(x) = |x| \cos x$ b) $f(x) = 2^x \sin x$ c) $f(x) = |x| \sin 2x$
d) $f(x) = x \sin x$ e) None of these

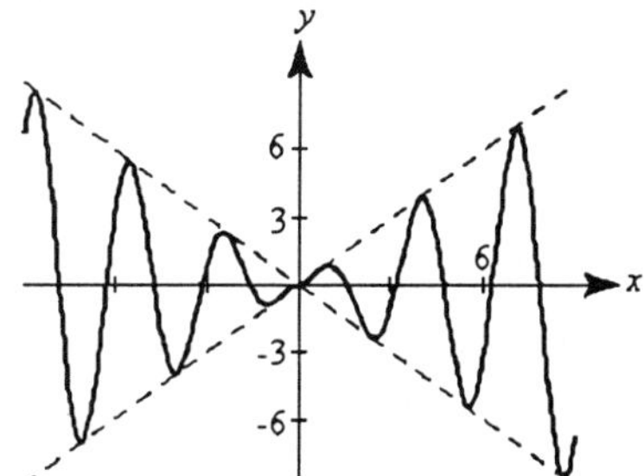

Answer: c Difficulty: 1

36. Match the graph with the correct function.
    a) $f(x) = |x| \sin 2x$ b) $f(x) = x \sin x$ c) $f(x) = |x| \cos 2x$
    d) $f(x) = x \cos x$ e) None of these

Answer: c Difficulty: 1

37. Match the graph with the correct function.
    a) $f(x) = e^x \cos x$ b) $f(x) = x \cos x$ c) $f(x) = x \sin x$
    d) $f(x) = e^x \sin x$ e) None of these

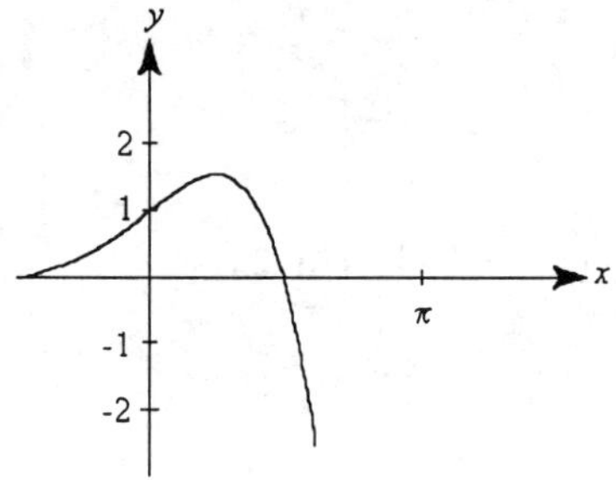

Answer: a Difficulty: 1

38. Match the graph with the correct function.
    a) $f(x) = e^x \cos x$ b) $f(x) = x \cos x$ c) $f(x) = x \sin x$
    d) $f(x) = e^x \sin x$ e) None of these

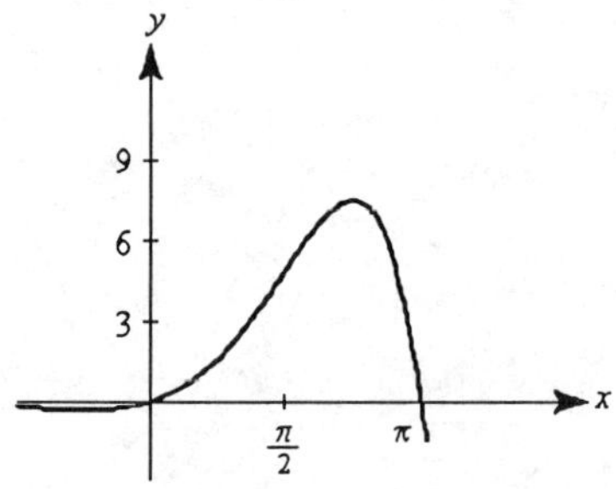

Answer: d Difficulty: 1

SHORT ANSWER

39. Sketch by hand the graph of the function: $f(x) = e^{-x} \sin x$.

Answer: See graph below.

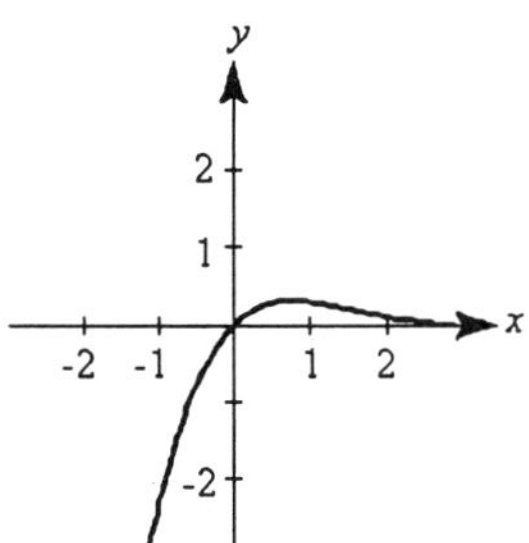

Difficulty: 2

40. Sketch by hand the graph of the function: $f(x) = x \sin 2x$.

Answer: See graph below.

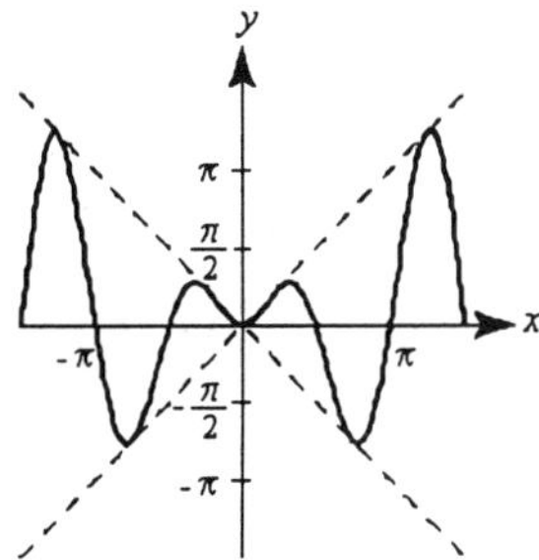

Difficulty: 2

41. Use a graphing utility to graph the function: $f(x) = x^2 \sin x$.

Answer: See graph below.

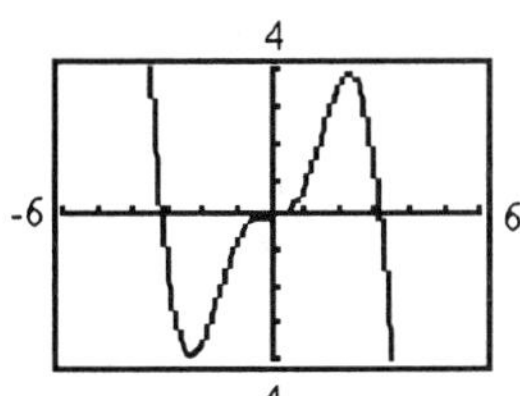

Difficulty: 1 Key 1: T

42. Use a graphing utility to graph the function: $f(x) = x^2 \cos x$.

Answer: See graph below.

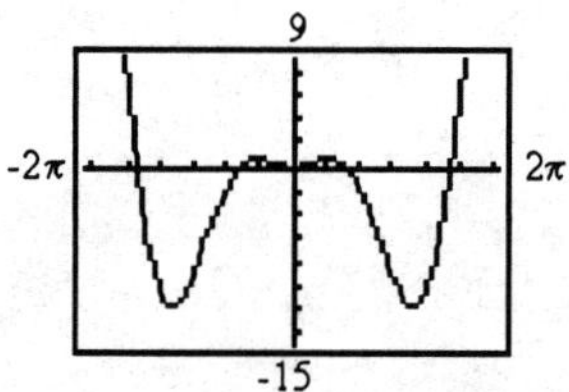

Difficulty: 1 Key 1: T

Chapter 047: Inverse Trigonometric Functions

MULTIPLE CHOICE

1. Evaluate: $\arccos\left(-\frac{1}{2}\right)$.

   a) $\frac{\pi}{6}$ b) $\frac{\pi}{3}$ c) $-\frac{\pi}{3}$ d) $\frac{2\pi}{3}$ e) None of these

   Answer: d Difficulty: 1

2. Evaluate: arcsin 0.

   a) $\frac{\pi}{2}$ b) π c) 0 d) $-\frac{\pi}{2}$ e) None of these

   Answer: c Difficulty: 1

3. Evaluate: arctan(-1).

   a) $\frac{\pi}{4}$ b) $-\frac{\pi}{4}$ c) $\frac{3\pi}{4}$ d) $\frac{7\pi}{4}$ e) None of these

   Answer: b Difficulty: 1

4. Evaluate: $\arcsin\left(-\frac{1}{2}\right)$.

   a) $-\frac{\pi}{6}$ b) $\frac{11\pi}{6}$ c) $\frac{5\pi}{6}$ d) $\frac{\pi}{6}$ e) None of these

   Answer: a Difficulty: 1

5. Evaluate: $\arccos\left(-\frac{1}{2}\right)$.

   a) $-\frac{\pi}{6}$ b) $\frac{11\pi}{6}$ c) $\frac{5\pi}{6}$ d) $\frac{\pi}{6}$ e) None of these

   Answer: e Difficulty: 1

SHORT ANSWER

6. Evaluate: $\arcsin\left(-\frac{\sqrt{2}}{2}\right)$.

   Answer:
   $-\frac{\pi}{4}$

   Difficulty: 1

7. Evaluate: $\arcsin\left(-\frac{\sqrt{3}}{2}\right)$.

Answer:
$-\frac{\pi}{3}$

Difficulty: 1

8. Evaluate: $\arccos\left(-\frac{\sqrt{2}}{2}\right)$.

Answer:
$\frac{3\pi}{4}$

Difficulty: 1

9. Evaluate: $\arccos\left(-\frac{\sqrt{3}}{2}\right)$.

Answer:
$\frac{5\pi}{6}$

Difficulty: 1

10. Evaluate: $\arctan\left(-\sqrt{3}\right)$.

Answer:
$-\frac{\pi}{3}$

Difficulty: 1

11. Evaluate: $\arctan\left(-\frac{\sqrt{3}}{3}\right)$.

Answer:
$-\frac{\pi}{6}$

Difficulty: 1

12. Evaluate: $\arccos -\frac{\sqrt{2}}{2}$.

Answer:
$\frac{\pi}{4}$

Difficulty: 1

13. Evaluate: $\arctan \frac{\sqrt{3}}{3}$.

Answer:
$\frac{\pi}{6}$

Difficulty: 1

14. Evaluate: arcsin(-1).

Answer:
$-\frac{\pi}{2}$

Difficulty: 1

15. Evaluate: arccos(-1).

Answer: π Difficulty: 1

MULTIPLE CHOICE

16. Evaluate: arctan(2.41).
a) 1.1775 b) -0.8978 c) 0.4149
d) 0.9732 e) None of these

Answer: a Difficulty: 1

17. Evaluate: arccos(-0.4777).
a) -1.0049 b) 1.0728 c) 2.0934
d) 2.0688 e) None of these

Answer: d Difficulty: 1

18. Evaluate: arcsin(-0.7182).
a) -0.5771 b) 1.3924 c) -0.8012
d) 4.2318 e) None of these

Answer: c Difficulty: 1

19. Evaluate: arccos(-0.923).
    a) -1.1758 b) -0.3950 c) 2.7466
    d) 1.1758 e) None of these

    Answer: c Difficulty: 1

20. Evaluate: arctan 5.572.
    a) 1.3932 b) 1.7484 c) 0.1795
    d) -0.8616 e) None of these

    Answer: a Difficulty: 1

SHORT ANSWER

21. Evaluate: arccos(-0.8923).

    Answer: 2.6732 radians Difficulty: 1

22. Evaluate: arctan(-3).

    Answer: -1.2490 radians Difficulty: 1

MULTIPLE CHOICE

23. Evaluate: sec(arctan 3).
    a) $\sqrt{10}$ b) $\frac{\sqrt{2}}{4}$ c) $2\sqrt{2}$ d) $\frac{\sqrt{10}}{3}$ e) None of these

    Answer: a Difficulty: 1

24. Evaluate: $\cos\left[\arctan\left[-\frac{2}{3}\right]\right]$.
    a) $-\frac{3\sqrt{3}}{13}$ b) $\frac{3\sqrt{13}}{13}$ c) $-\frac{2\sqrt{13}}{13}$ d) $\frac{2\sqrt{13}}{13}$ e) None of these

    Answer: b Difficulty: 1

25. Evaluate: $\sin\left[\arccos\left[-\frac{2}{7}\right]\right]$.
    a) $\frac{\sqrt{53}}{7}$ b) $-\frac{\sqrt{53}}{7}$ c) $\frac{3\sqrt{5}}{7}$ d) $-\frac{3\sqrt{5}}{7}$ e) None of these

    Answer: c Difficulty: 1

SHORT ANSWER

26. Find the exact value: $\cos\left[\arctan\left(-\frac{3}{10}\right)\right]$.

Answer:

$\frac{10\sqrt{109}}{109}$

Difficulty: 1

27. Find the exact value: sin(arctan 3).

Answer:

$\frac{3\sqrt{10}}{10}$

Difficulty: 1

MULTIPLE CHOICE

28. Evaluate: $\sin\left(\arctan\frac{3}{8}\right)$.

a) $\frac{8}{3}$ b) $\frac{\sqrt{73}}{8}$ c) $\frac{3\sqrt{55}}{55}$ d) $\frac{3\sqrt{73}}{73}$ e) None of these

Answer: d Difficulty: 1

29. Evaluate: $\cos\left(\arctan\frac{2}{3}\right)$.

a) $\frac{2\sqrt{5}}{5}$ b) $\frac{3\sqrt{13}}{13}$ c) $\frac{2\sqrt{13}}{13}$ d) $\frac{3\sqrt{5}}{3}$ e) None of these

Answer: b Difficulty: 1

30. Evaluate: $\tan\left(\arccos\frac{3}{7}\right)$.

a) $\frac{3\sqrt{10}}{20}$ b) $\frac{2\sqrt{10}}{3}$ c) $\frac{\sqrt{58}}{7}$ d) $\frac{\sqrt{58}}{3}$ e) None of these

Answer: b Difficulty: 1

31. Evaluate: $\sec\left[\arctan\left(-\frac{2}{5}\right)\right]$.

a) $-\frac{5\sqrt{21}}{21}$ b) $-\frac{\sqrt{21}}{2}$ c) $\frac{\sqrt{21}}{5}$ d) $\frac{\sqrt{29}}{2}$ e) None of these

Answer: e Difficulty: 1

32. Evaluate: $\tan\left[\arcsin\left(-\frac{\sqrt{7}}{7}\right)\right]$.

a) $\sqrt{8}$ b) $\sqrt{6}$ c) $-\frac{\sqrt{6}}{6}$ d) $-\frac{\sqrt{8}}{8}$ e) None of these

Answer: c Difficulty: 1

33. Evaluate: $\sin\left[\arccos\left(-\frac{4}{9}\right)\right]$.

a) $\frac{\sqrt{65}}{9}$ b) $-\frac{\sqrt{65}}{9}$ c) $-\frac{9\sqrt{97}}{97}$ d) $\frac{4\sqrt{97}}{97}$ e) None of these

Answer: a Difficulty: 1

34. Evaluate: $\sin\left(\arctan\frac{x}{5}\right)$.

a) $\frac{x}{x + 5}$ b) $\frac{x}{\sqrt{x^2 + 25}}$ c) $\frac{5}{\sqrt{x^2 + 25}}$

d) $\frac{\sqrt{25 - x^2}}{5}$ e) None of these

Answer: b Difficulty: 1

35. Evaluate: $\csc\left(\arccos\frac{x}{5}\right)$.

a) $\frac{\sqrt{25 - x^2}}{5}$ b) $\frac{\sqrt{25 + x^2}}{x}$ c) $\frac{5}{\sqrt{25 - x^2}}$

d) $\frac{x}{x + 5}$ e) None of these

Answer: c Difficulty: 1

36. Evaluate: $\cot\left[\arcsin\frac{1}{x-1}\right]$.

a) $2x - x^2$ b) $x - 1$ c) $\frac{1}{\sqrt{x^2 + 2x + 2}}$

d) $\sqrt{x^2 - 2x}$ e) None of these

Answer: d Difficulty: 1

37. Write an algebraic expression for tan(arcsin x).

a) $\frac{x\sqrt{1 + x^2}}{1 + x^2}$ b) $\frac{1}{x}$ c) $\frac{\sqrt{1 - x^2}}{x}$

d) $\frac{x\sqrt{1 - x^2}}{1 - x^2}$ e) None of these

Answer: d Difficulty: 2

SHORT ANSWER

38. Use an inverse trigonometric function to write θ as a function of x (see figure).

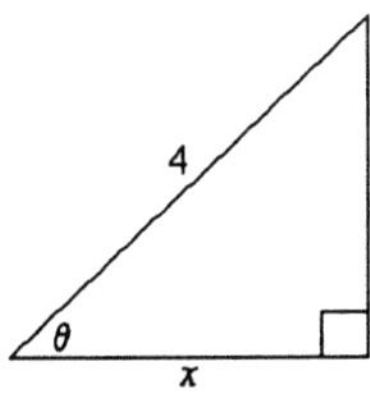

Answer:

$\theta = \arccos\left[\frac{x}{4}\right]$

Difficulty: 1

39. Use an inverse trigonometric function to write θ as a function of x (see figure).

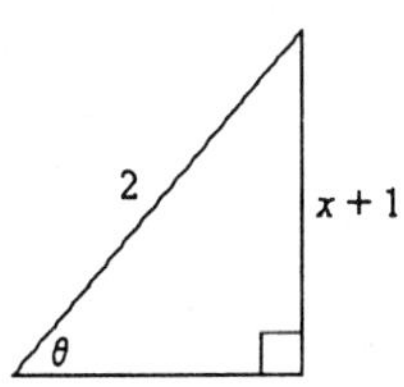

Answer:

$\theta = \arcsin\left[\frac{x + 1}{2}\right]$

Difficulty: 1

40. Use an inverse trigonometric function to write θ as a function of x (see figure).

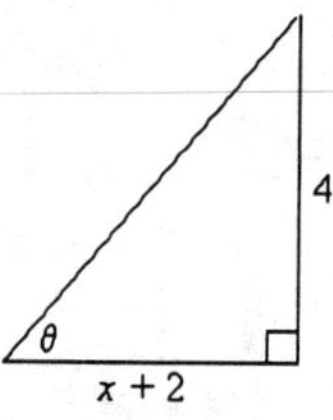

Answer:

$$\theta = \arctan\left[\frac{4}{x + 2}\right]$$

Difficulty: 1

MULTIPLE CHOICE

41. Match the graph with the correct function.
a) $f(x) = \arctan(x - 1)$
b) $f(x) = \text{arccot}(x + 1)$
c) $f(x) = \arcsin x$
d) $f(x) = \arcsin(x + 1)$
e) None of these

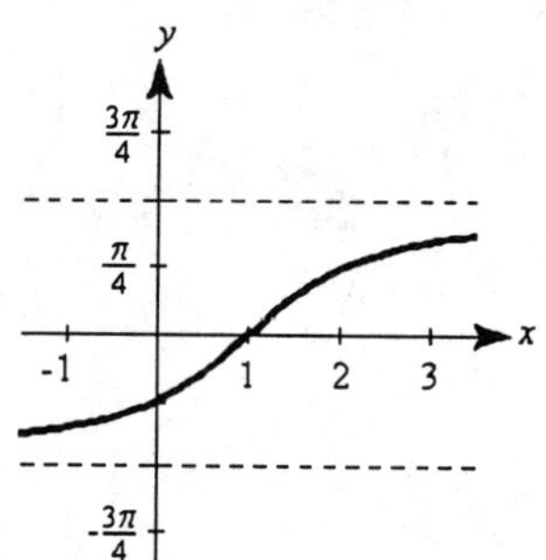

Answer: a Difficulty: 1

42. Match the graph with the correct function.
a) $f(x) = \arctan(x - 1)$
b) $f(x) = \arcsin(x - 1)$
c) $f(x) = \arcsin x$
d) $f(x) = \arctan x$
e) None of these

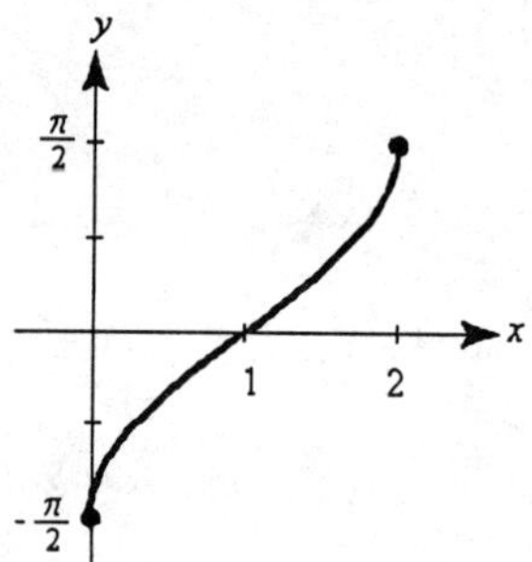

Answer: b Difficulty: 1

43. Match the graph with the correct function.
a) $f(x) = \arccos(x - 2)$
b) $f(x) = \arcsin(x + 2)$
c) $f(x) = \arccos\left(\frac{x}{2}\right)$
d) $f(x) = \arccos(2x)$
e) None of these

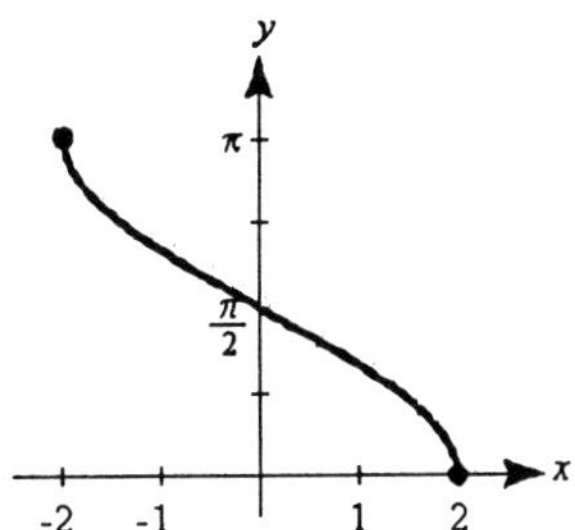

Answer: c Difficulty: 1

44. Match the graph with the correct function.
a) $f(x) = \arctan(x - 1)$
b) $f(x) = \arctan 2x$
c) $f(x) = \arccos\frac{x}{2}$
d) $f(x) = \arcsin\frac{x}{2}$
e) None of these

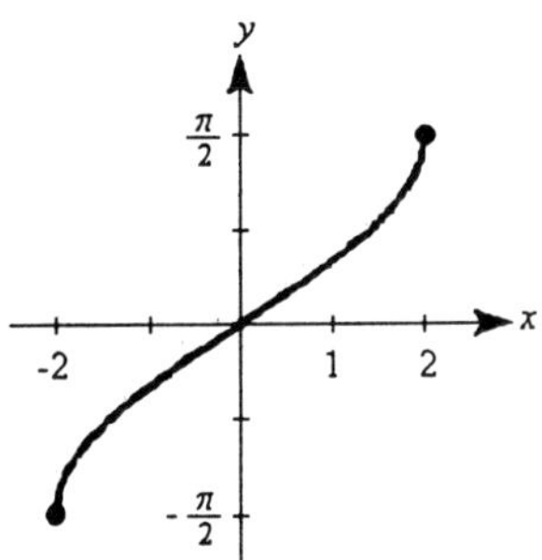

Answer: d Difficulty: 1

45. Match the graph with the correct function.

a) $f(x) = \arcsin\frac{x}{2}$

b) $f(x) = \arcsin 2x$

c) $f(x) = \arccos\frac{x}{2}$

d) $f(x) = \arccos 2x$

e) None of these

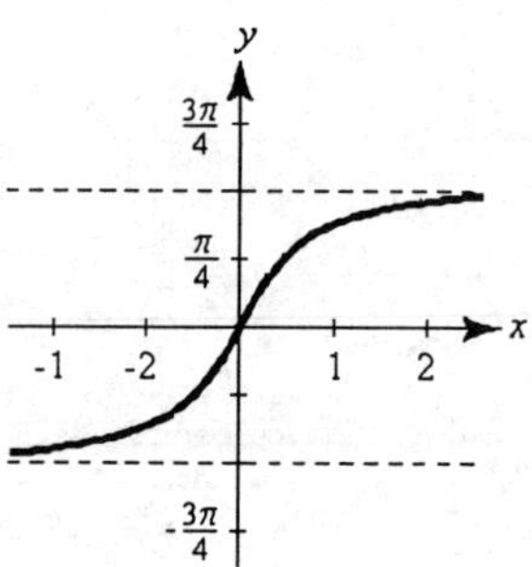

Answer: e Difficulty: 1

46. Match the graph with the correct function.

a) $f(x) = 2 + \arctan 4x$

b) $f(x) = 2 + \arcsin\frac{x}{4}$

c) $f(x) = 2 + \arccos\frac{x}{4}$

d) $f(x) = 2 + \arcsin 4x$

e) None of these

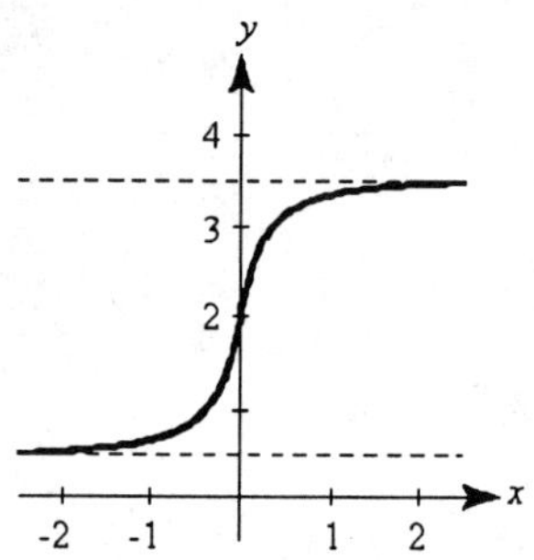

Answer: a Difficulty: 1

SHORT ANSWER

47. Use a graphing utility to graph the function: $f(x) = \arcsin \frac{x}{2}$.

Answer: See graph below.

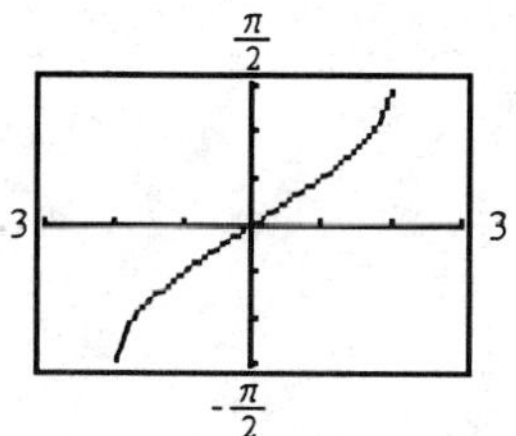

Difficulty: 1 Key 1: T

48. Use a graphing utility to graph of function: $f(x) = \arccos(x - 2)$.

Answer: See graph below.

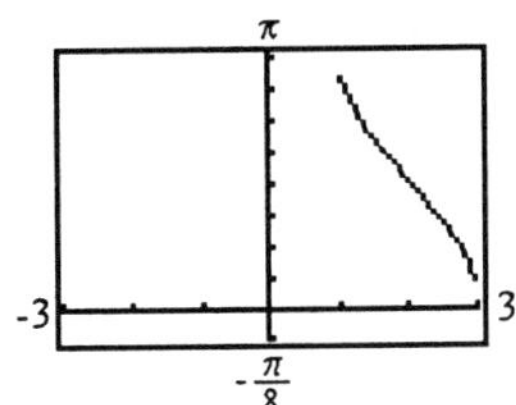

Difficulty: 1 Key 1: T

49. Use a graphing utility to graph the function: $f(x) = \arctan \frac{x}{2}$.

Answer: See graph below.

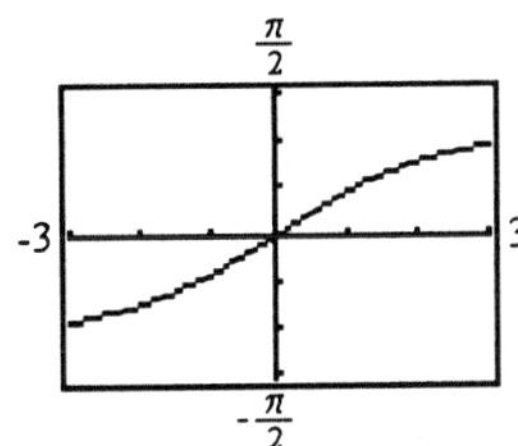

Difficulty: 1 Key 1: T

MULTIPLE CHOICE

50. A boat is d feet from shore. A person standing on the dock is 25 feet above water level. The angle of depression to the boat from the dock is θ. Write θ as a function of d.

a) $\theta = \arcsin 25d$ b) $\theta = \arctan \frac{25}{d}$ c) $\theta = \arcsin \frac{d}{25}$

d) $\theta = \arctan 25d$ e) None of these

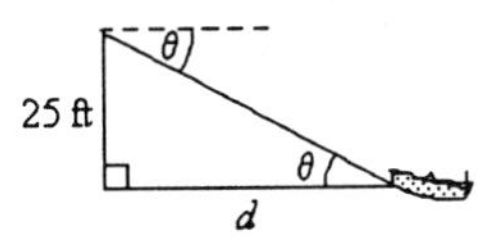

Answer: b Difficulty: 1

51. A boat is d feet from shore. A person standing on the dock is 60 feet above water level. The angle of depression from the dock to the boat is θ. Write θ as a function of d.

a) $\theta = 60 \arcsin d$
b) $\theta = \frac{\arctan d}{60}$
c) $\theta = \arcsin \frac{d}{60}$
d) $\theta = \arctan \frac{60}{d}$
e) None of these

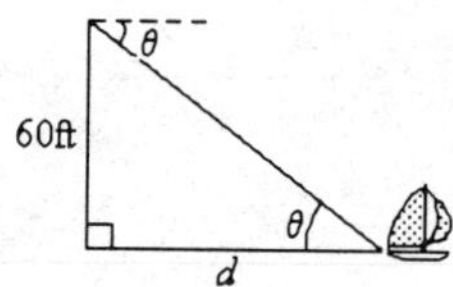

Answer: d Difficulty: 1

52. A boat is d feet from shore. A person standing on the dock is 40 feet above water level. The angle of depression from the dock to the boat is θ. Write θ as a function of d.

a) $\theta = 40 \arctan d$
b) $\theta = \arctan \frac{40}{d}$
c) $\theta = \arcsin \frac{d}{60}$
d) $\theta = \frac{\arctan d}{40}$
e) None of these

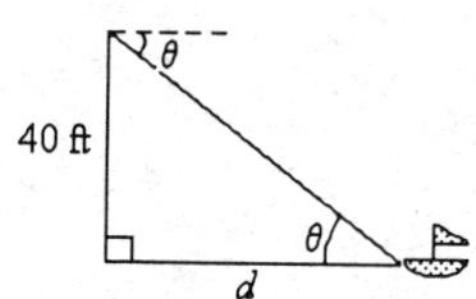

Answer: b Difficulty: 1

SHORT ANSWER

53. A boat is d feet from shore. A person standing on the dock is 35 feet above water level. The angle of depression from the dock to the boat is θ. Write θ as a function of d.

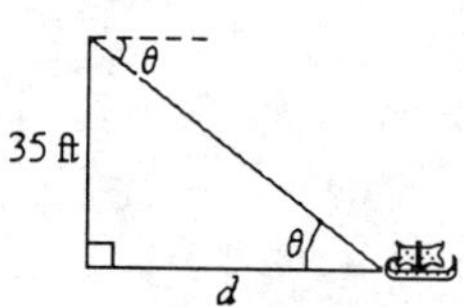

Answer:

$$\theta = \arctan \frac{35}{d}$$

Difficulty: 1

54. A boat is d feet from shore. A person standing on the dock is 45 feet above water level. The angle of depression from the dock to the boat is θ. Write θ as a function of d.

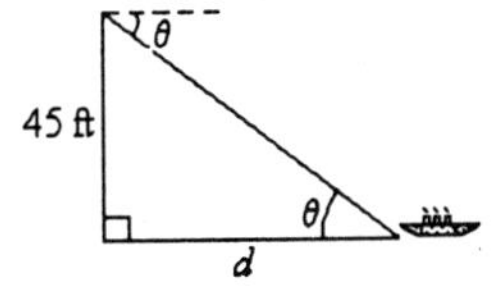

Answer:

$$\theta = \arctan \frac{45}{d}$$

Difficulty: 1

Chapter 048: Applications and Models

MULTIPLE CHOICE

1. A 40-foot extension ladder leans against the side of a building. Find the distance, h, up the side of the building if the angle of elevation of the ladder is 68° .
   a) 35 feet b) 36 feet c) 37 feet
   d) 38 feet e) None of these

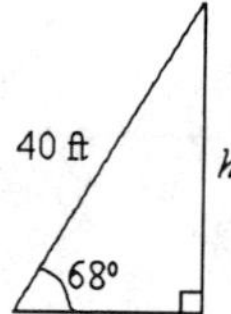

Answer: c Difficulty: 1

2. A 40-foot extension ladder leans against the side of a building. Find the distance, h, up the side of the building if the angle of elevation of the ladder is 52° .
   a) 19.6 feet b) 51.2 feet c) 29.7 feet
   d) 31.5 feet e) None of these

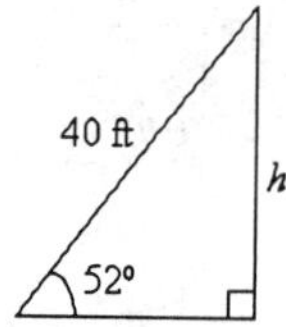

Answer: d Difficulty: 1

3. A ladder is leaning against the side of a house. The base of the ladder is 5 feet from the wall and makes an angle of 39° with the ground. Find the length of the ladder.
   a) 3.89 feet b) 6.43 feet c) 4.05 feet
   d) 7.95 feet e). None of these

Answer: b Difficulty: 1

4. A boy and his father are walking on a street with their backs to the sun. The father is 5'8" tall and casts a shadow 9 feet long. The boy is 4'9" tall. How long is his shadow?
   a) 6.7 feet b) 7.5 feet c) 5.9 feet
   d) 8.2 feet e) None of these

Answer: b Difficulty: 1

5. A lamp post that is 8 feet high casts a shadow 5 feet long. How tall is the person standing beside the lamp post if his shadow is $3\frac{1}{2}$ feet long?
   a) 5'7" b) 5'5" c) 5'3" d) 5'1" e) None of these

Answer: a Difficulty: 1

SHORT ANSWER

6. The angle of depression from the top of one building to the foot of a building across the street is 63°. The angle of depression to the top of the same building is 33°. The two buildings are 40 feet apart. What is the height of the shorter building?

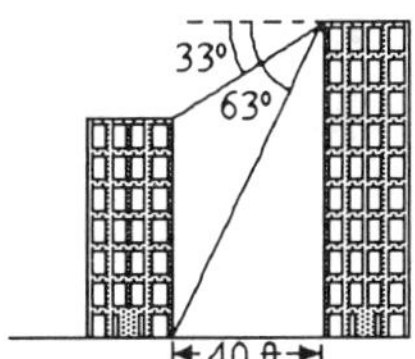

Answer: 52.5 feet Difficulty: 2

MULTIPLE CHOICE

7. From a point 300 feet from a building, the angle of elevation to the base of an antenna on the roof is 26.6° and the angle of elevation to the top of the antenna is 31.5°. Determine the height, *h*, of the antenna.

a) 42.0 feet b) 29.4 feet c) 33.6 feet
d) 45.1 feet e) None of these

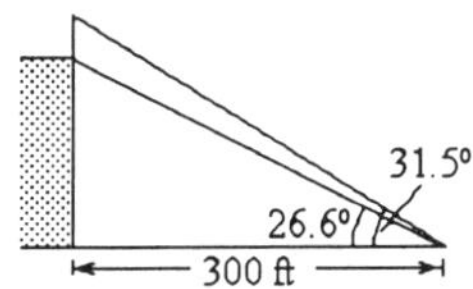

Answer: c Difficulty: 1

SHORT ANSWER

8. From a point on a cliff 75 feet above water level an observer can see a ship. The angle of depression to the ship is 4°. How far is the ship from the base of the cliff?

Answer: 1072.5 feet Difficulty: 1

MULTIPLE CHOICE

9. A pilot of an airplane flying at an altitude of 3000 feet sights two ships traveling in the same direction as the plane. The angle of depression of the farther ship is 20° and the angle of depression of the other ship is 35°. Find the distance between the two ships.

a) 470 feet b) 3541 feet c) 3958 feet
d) 1009 feet e) None of these

Answer: c Difficulty: 2

10. The sun is 30° above the horizon. Find the length of a shadow cast by a person 6 feet tall.
 a) 7.9 feet b) 8 feet c) 9.6 feet
 d) 10.4 feet e) None of these

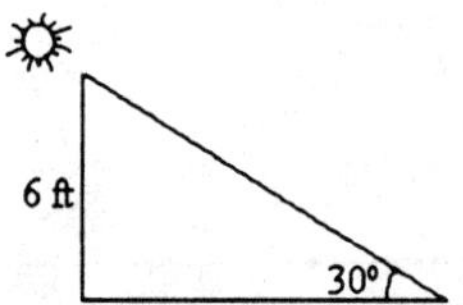

Answer: d Difficulty: 1

11. A silo is 40 feet high and 16 feet across. Find the angle of depression from the top edge of the silo to the floor on the opposite side.
 a) 68.2° b) 55.1° c) 62.5° d) 58.8° e) None of these

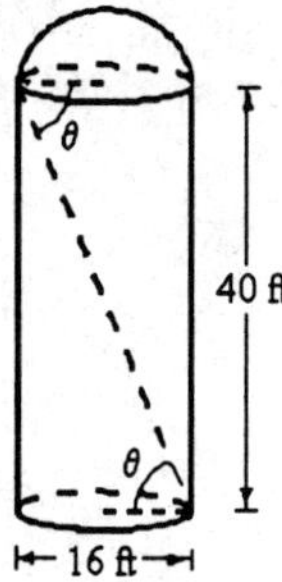

Answer: a Difficulty: 1

12. A surveyor wishes to find the distance across a river. The bearings from 2 points 70 feet apart on the same bank of the river to a tree on the opposite bank are N and N 34° W. Find the width of the river.
 a) 93.4 feet b) 100.9 feet c) 103.8 feet
 d) 111.4 feet e) None of these

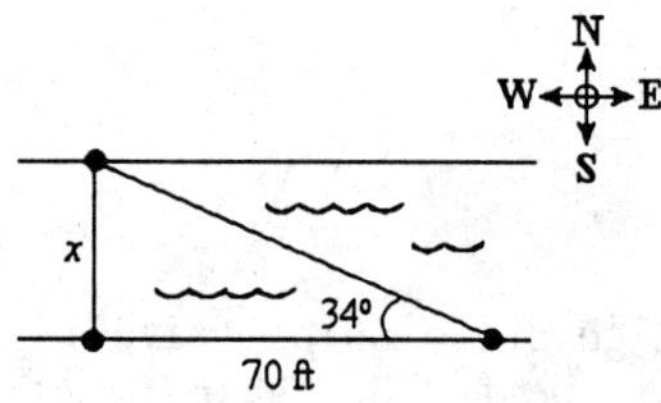

Answer: c Difficulty: 2

13. A ship is 90 miles south and 20 miles east of port. If the captain wants to travel directly to port, what bearing should be taken?
 a) S 77.5° E b) N 12.5° W c) N 77.5° E
 d) S 12.5° W e) None of these

Answer: b Difficulty: 1

14. A ship leaves port and travels due west for 30 nautical miles, then changes course to S 30° W and travels 50 more nautical miles. Find the bearing to the port of departure.
a) N 74° E b) N 38.2° E c) N 51.8° E
d) N 16° E e) None of these

Answer: c Difficulty: 2

15. A ship leaves port and travels due east 15 nautical miles, then changes course to N 20° W and travels 40 more nautical miles. Find the bearing to the port of departure.
a) S 21.8° W b) S 43.7° W c) N 15.2° E
d) S 68.3° W e) None of these

Answer: e Difficulty: 2

16. A ship leaves port and travels 30 nautical miles due north, then changes course to N 15° E and travels 10 more nautical miles. Find the ship's bearing from the port of departure.
a) N 18.2° E b) N 86.3° E c) S 21.2° W
d) N 3.7° E e) None of these

Answer: d Difficulty: 2

SHORT ANSWER

17. A guy wire attached to the top of a 90 foot antenna is fastened to the ground 40 feet from the base of the antenna. Find the angle of elevation of the wire with the ground.

Answer: 66° Difficulty: 1

18. The length of the shadow of a 200 foot tower is 70 feet. Find the angle of elevation of the sun.

Answer: 70.7° Difficulty: 1

MULTIPLE CHOICE

19. The pilot of an airplane flying at an elevation of 5000 feet sights two towers that are 300 feet apart. If the angle of depression to the tower closer to him is 30°, determine the angle of depression to the second tower.
a) 29.2° b) 28.9° c) 28.7° d) 27.6° e) None of these

Answer: a Difficulty: 2

SHORT ANSWER

20. An airplane flying at 600 miles per hour has a bearing of S 34° E. After flying 3 hours, how far south has the plane traveled from its point of departure? (Round your answer to the nearest mile.)

Answer: 1492 miles Difficulty: 1

21. An airplane flying 550 miles per hour has a bearing of S 15° W. After flying 2 hours, how far south has the plane traveled from its point of departure? (Round your answer to the nearest mile.)

Answer: 1063 miles Difficulty: 1

MULTIPLE CHOICE

22. A regular pentagon is inscribed in a circle of radius 36 inches. Find the length of the sides of the pentagon. (Round your answer to three decimal places.)
a) 38.892 in. b) 39.431 in. c) 42.321 in.
d) 44.472 in. e) None of these

Answer: c Difficulty: 1

23. A regular pentagon is inscribed in a circle of radius 10 inches. Find the length of the sides of the pentagon. (Round your answer to three decimal places.)
a) 9.771 b) 10.235 c) 11.222
d) 11.756 e) None of these

Answer: d Difficulty: 1

24. A regular octagon is inscribed in a circle of radius 36 inches. Find the length of the sides of the octagon. (Round your answer to three decimal places.)
a) 27.553 in. b) 27.731 in. c) 28.448 in.
d) 29.432 in. e) None of these

Answer: a Difficulty: 1

25. A regular octagon is inscribed in a circle of radius 10 inches. Find the length of the sides of the octagon. (Round your answer to three decimal places.)
a) 7.239 in. b) 7.654 in. c) 9.447 in.
d) 9.571 in. e) None of these

Answer: b Difficulty: 1

26. Find the frequency of a simple harmonic motion described by $d = 7 \cos 16\pi t$.
a) $3\frac{1}{2}$ b) 7 c) 16 d) 8 e) None of these

Answer: d Difficulty: 1

27. Find the frequency of a simple harmonic motion described by $d = 4 \sin 8\pi t$.
a) 2 b) 4 c) 8π d) 8 e) None of these

Answer: b Difficulty: 1

28. Find the frequency of a simple harmonic motion described by $d = 4 \cos \pi t$.
a) 4 b) π c) 2 d) 4 e) None of these

Answer: e Difficulty: 1

29. Find the frequency of a simple harmonic motion described by $d = 5 \cos 16\pi t$.
    a) 16 b) 8 c) 4 d) 2 e) None of these

    Answer: b Difficulty: 1

SHORT ANSWER

30. Find the maximum displacement for the simple harmonic motion described by $d = 2 \cos 40\pi t$.

    Answer: 2 Difficulty: 1

MULTIPLE CHOICE

31. Find the maximum displacement for the simple harmonic motion described by $d = 4 \cos \pi t$.
    a) 4 b) 8 c) $\frac{1}{2}$ d) 2 e) None of these

    Answer: a Difficulty: 1

32. Find the maximum displacement for the simple harmonic motion described by $d = 5 \cos 16\pi t$.
    a) 8 b) 10 c) 5 d) $2\frac{1}{2}$ e) None of these

    Answer: c Difficulty: 1

33. Find the maximum displacement for the simple harmonic motion described by $d = 7 \cos 8\pi t$.
    a) $3\frac{1}{2}$ b) 14 c) 4 d) 7 e) None of these

    Answer: d Difficulty: 1

34. Find the least possible value of t for which $d = 0$: $d = 7 \cos 8\pi t$.
    a) $\frac{1}{2}$ b) $\frac{1}{4}$ c) $\frac{1}{8}$ d) $\frac{1}{16}$ e) None of these

    Answer: d Difficulty: 1

35. Find the least possible value of t for which $d = 0$: $d = 5 \cos 4\pi t$.
    a) $\frac{1}{2}$ b) $\frac{1}{4}$ c) $\frac{1}{8}$ d) $\frac{1}{16}$ e) None of these

    Answer: c Difficulty: 1

36. Find the least possible value of t for which $d = 0$: $d = 7 \cos 16\pi t$.
    a) $\frac{1}{32}$ b) $\frac{1}{16}$ c) $\frac{1}{8}$ d) $\frac{1}{4}$ e) None of these

    Answer: a Difficulty: 1

Chapter 051: Using Fundamental Identities

SHORT ANSWER

1. Given $\sin x = \frac{4}{7}$ and $\cos x = \frac{-\sqrt{33}}{7}$, find $\cot x$.

Answer:

$\frac{-\sqrt{33}}{4}$

Difficulty: 1

MULTIPLE CHOICE

2. Given $\cos\left[\frac{\pi}{2} - x\right] = \frac{2}{7}$, find $\sin x$.

a) $\frac{3\sqrt{5}}{7}$ b) $\frac{7}{2}$ c) $\frac{3\sqrt{5}}{2}$ d) $\frac{2}{7}$ e) None of these

Answer: d Difficulty: 1

3. Given $\csc x = -3$ and $\tan x > 0$, find $\cos x$.

a) $\frac{2\sqrt{2}}{3}$ b) $\frac{-3\sqrt{2}}{2}$ c) $\frac{-2\sqrt{2}}{3}$ d) $\frac{3\sqrt{2}}{2}$ e) None of these

Answer: c Difficulty: 1

4. Given $\cot x$ is undefined and $\cos x > 0$, find $\csc x$.

a) 0 b) 1 c) -1 d) Undefined e) None of these

Answer: d Difficulty: 1

SHORT ANSWER

5. Given $\cos(-x) = \frac{3}{4}$ and $\tan x = \frac{\sqrt{7}}{3}$, find $\sin(-x)$.

Answer:

$-\frac{\sqrt{7}}{4}$

Difficulty: 1

MULTIPLE CHOICE

6. Simplify: $\sec x \cos\left[\frac{\pi}{2} - x\right]$.
   a) 1 b) $\frac{1}{\cos^2 x}$ c) $\tan x$ d) $\cot x$ e) None of these

   Answer: c Difficulty: 1

7. Simplify: $\frac{\csc x}{\tan x + \cot x}$.
   a) $\cos x + \tan x$ b) $\sin^2 + \cos x$ c) $\csc^2 x$ sec
   d) $\cos x$ e) None of these

   Answer: d Difficulty: 1

SHORT ANSWER

8. Simplify: $\sin\left[\frac{\pi}{2} - x\right] \cos(-x)$.

   Answer: $\cos^2 x$ Difficulty: 1

MULTIPLE CHOICE

9. Simplify: $\frac{\cos^4 x - \sin^4 x}{\cos^2 x - \sin^2 x}$.
   a) $1 - 2\sin^2 x$ b) $2\cos^2 x - 1$ c) 1
   d) -1 e) None of these

   Answer: c Difficulty: 1

10. Simplify: $\frac{\csc x \cos^2 x}{1 + \csc x}$.
    a) $\csc x + 1$ b) $1 - \sin x$ c) $\sin x - 1$
    d) $1 + \sin x$ e) None of these

    Answer: b Difficulty: 2

11. Simplify: $\frac{\sin^2 x}{\sec^2 x - 1}$.
    a) $\sin^2 x \tan^2 x$ b) $\sec^2 x$ c) $\cos^2 x$
    d) 1 e) None of these

    Answer: c Difficulty: 1

12. Simplify: $\frac{\cos(-x)}{\sin(-x)}$.
    a) $\tan x$ b) $-\tan x$ c) $\cot x$
    d) $-\cot x$ e) None of these

    Answer: d Difficulty: 1

13. Factor and simplify: $\cos^2 x - \sin^2 x \cos^2 x$.
a) $\cos^4 x$
b) $-\cos^4 x$
c) $1 - \sin^2 x$
d) $2 \cos x$
e) None of these

Answer: a Difficulty: 1

14. Factor and simplify: $\cot^4 x + 2 \cot^2 x + 1$.
a) $\tan^4 x$
b) $\csc^2 x$
c) $\sec^4 x$
d) $\csc^4 x$
e) None of these

Answer: d Difficulty: 1

15. Factor and simplify: $2 \sin^2 x - 2 \sin^4 x$.
a) $2 \tan^2 x$
b) 0
c) $2 \sin^2 x \cos^2 x$
d) $2 \cos^4 x$
e) None of these

Answer: c Difficulty: 1

16. Factor and simplify: $\sec^2 x \csc^2 x - \sec^2 x - \csc^2 x + 1$.
a) 1
b) $\cot^4 x$
c) $\cot^2 x(\sec^2 x + 1)$
d) $\tan^4 x$
e) None of these

Answer: a Difficulty: 2

17. Perform the addition and simplify: $\dfrac{\tan x}{\csc x} + \dfrac{\sin x}{\tan x}$.
a) $\cos x$
b) $\csc^2 x$
c) $\sec^2 x$
d) $\sec x$
e) None of these

Answer: d Difficulty: 2

18. Perform the subtraction and simplify: $\dfrac{\sec x}{\sin x} - \dfrac{\sin x}{\cos x}$
a) $\csc x$ b) $\tan x$ c) $\cot x$ d) $\cos^2 x$ e) None of these

Answer: c Difficulty: 1

19. Perform the addition and simplify: $\dfrac{1}{1 + \sin x} + \dfrac{1}{1 - \sin x}$.
a) 2 b) $2 \sec^2 x$ c) $2 \cos^2 x$ d) 0 e) None of these

Answer: b Difficulty: 1

20. Perform the subtraction and simplify: $\csc x - \dfrac{\cos^2 x}{\sin x}$.
a) 1 b) $\sin x$ c) $\sin^2 x$ d) $-\sin x$ e) None of these

Answer: b Difficulty: 1

21. Rewrite the expression so that it is not in fractional form: $\dfrac{\sin x}{\cos x - 1}$.

a) $-\cot x + 1$ b) $-\cot x - \csc x$ c) $\sin x \cos x + \sin x$
d) $-\tan x + 1$ e) None of these

Answer: b Difficulty: 2

22. Rewrite the expression so that it is not in fractional form: $\dfrac{1}{\csc x + 1}$.

a) $\sin x + 1$ b) $\tan x \sec x - \tan^2 x$ c) $\cot x \cos x - \cot^2 x$
d) $\csc x - 1$ e) None of these

Answer: b Difficulty: 2

23. Rewrite the expression so that it is not in fractional form: $\dfrac{\cos x}{\sec x - 1}$.

a) $\cot^2 x + \cot^2 x \cos x$ b) $2 \sin^2 x$ c) $1 - \cos x$
d) $\csc^2 x + \cos^4 x$ e) None of these

Answer: a Difficulty: 2

24. Use the substitution $x = 3 \cos \theta$ to write the algebraic expression $\sqrt{9 - x^2}$ as a trigonometric expression involving θ, where $0 < \theta < \frac{\pi}{2}$.

a) $3 \cos \theta$ b) $-3 \sin \theta$ c) $3(1 - \sin \theta)$
d) $3 \sin \theta$ e) None of these

Answer: d Difficulty: 1

25. Use the substitution $x = 2 \csc \theta$ to write the algebraic expression $\sqrt{x^2 - 4}$ as a trigonometric expression involving θ, where $0 < \theta < \frac{\pi}{2}$.

a) $2(\csc x - 1)$ b) $2 \cot \theta$ c) $2 \tan \theta$
d) $-2 \cot \theta$ e) None of these

Answer: b Difficulty: 1

SHORT ANSWER

26. Use the substitution $x = \frac{1}{2}(\sin \theta + 1)$ to write the algebraic expression $\sqrt{1 - (2x - 1)^2}$ as a trigonometric expression involving θ, where $0 < \theta < \frac{\pi}{2}$.

Answer: $\cos \theta$ Difficulty: 2

MULTIPLE CHOICE

27. For what values of θ, $0 \le \theta < 2\pi$ is it true that $\sin\theta = -\sqrt{1 - \cos^2\theta}$?

a) $\frac{\pi}{2} \le \theta \le \pi,\ \frac{3\pi}{2} < \theta < 2\pi$ b) $0 \le \theta \le \pi$ c) $\frac{\pi}{2} \le \theta \le 3\frac{\pi}{2}$
d) $\pi \le \theta \le 2\pi$ e) None of these

Answer: d Difficulty: 1

28. For what values of x, $0 \le x < 2\pi$ is it true that $\csc x = \sqrt{\cot^2 x + 1}$?

a) $0 < x < \pi$ b) $\pi < x < 2\pi$ c) $\frac{\pi}{2} \le x \le 3\frac{\pi}{2}$
d) $0 \le x < \frac{\pi}{2},\ \pi < x \le \frac{3\pi}{2}$ e) None of these

Answer: a Difficulty: 1

SHORT ANSWER

29. For what value of θ, $0 \le \theta < 2\pi$ is it true that $\cos\theta = -\sqrt{1 - \sin^2\theta}$?

Answer:
$\frac{\pi}{2} \le \theta \le \frac{3\pi}{2}$
Difficulty: 1

30. For what values of θ, $0 \le \theta < 2\pi$ is it true that $2\sec\theta = \sqrt{4 + 4\tan^2\theta}$?

Answer:
$0 \le \theta < \frac{\pi}{2},\ \frac{3\pi}{2} < \theta < 2\pi$
Difficulty: 1

MULTIPLE CHOICE

31. Simplify: $\frac{1 + \tan x}{\sin x} - \sec x$.

a) $\csc x$ b) $\tan x \csc x$ c) $\tan x$
d) 1 e) None of these

Answer: a Difficulty: 1

32. Simplify: $\frac{1 - \cos^4 x}{1 + \cos^2 x}$.

a) $1 + \cos^2 x$ b) $\sin^2 x$ c) $\sin^2 x + \tan^2 x$
d) $\sin^4 x$ e) None of these

Answer: b Difficulty: 1

33. Simplify: $\frac{1}{\cot \theta} + \frac{1}{\tan \theta}$.

a) 1 b) $\sec x \csc x$ c) 0 d) $\sin x \cos x$ e) None of these

Answer: b Difficulty: 2

SHORT ANSWER

34. In determining the path of a radiated particle moving through a charged field it is necessary to determine a constant, K, which equals the expression $2 \sec^2 x - 2 \sec^2 x \sin^2 x - \sin^2 x - \cos^2 x$. Find this constant, K.

Answer:

$K = 2 \sec^2 - 2 \sec^2 x \sin^2 x - \sin^2 x - \cos^2 x$

$= 2 \sec^2 x(1 - \sin^2 x) - (\sin^2 x + \cos^2 x)$

$= 2 \sec^2 x(\cos^2 x) - 1$

$= 2 \sec^2 x\frac{1}{\sec^2 x} - 1$

$= 2 - 1$

$K = 1$

Difficulty: 2

35. The intensity of a bright spotlight at a certain point on a stage is given by $I = \frac{k \tan \theta}{d^2 \sec \theta}$. In the formula, k, is a constant, and d is the distance from the spotlight to that point on the stage at which I is measured. Simplify the formula for I.

Answer:

$$\frac{k \tan \theta}{d^2 \sec \theta} = \frac{\frac{k\frac{\sin \theta}{\cos \theta}}{d^2}}{\cos \theta} = k\frac{\sin \theta}{\cos \theta} \frac{\cos \theta}{d^2} = \frac{k \sin \theta}{d^2}$$

Difficulty: 2

36. Use a graphing utility to graph the functions. Make a conjecture about y_1 and y_2.
$y_1 = \cot x \sec x,\ y_2 = \csc x$

Answer: See graph below.

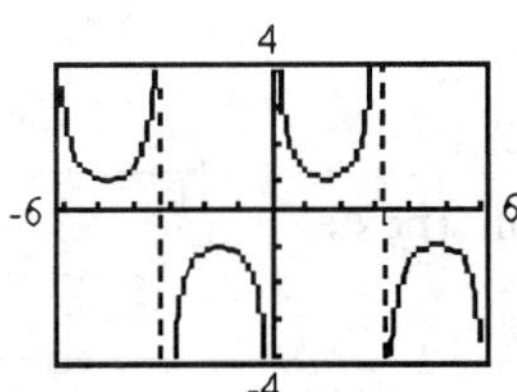

; The expressions are equivalent.

Difficulty: 1 Key 1: T

37. Use a graphing utility to graph the functions. Make a conjecture about y_1 and $_2$.
$y_1 = \cos x \tan x,\ y_2 = \sin x$

Answer: See graph below.

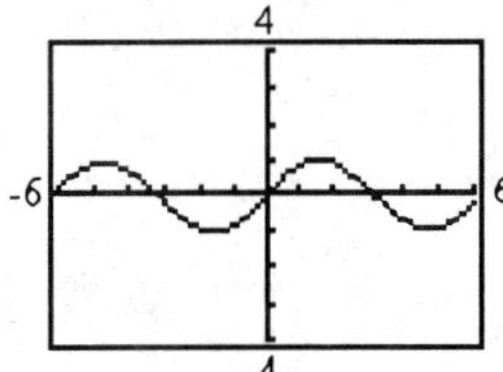

; The expressions are equivalent.

Difficulty: 1 Key 1: T

38. Use a graphing utility to graph the functions. Make a conjecture about y_1 and y_2.
$y_1 = \tan x - \tan x \sin^2 x,\ y_2 = \sin x \cos x$

Answer: See graph below.

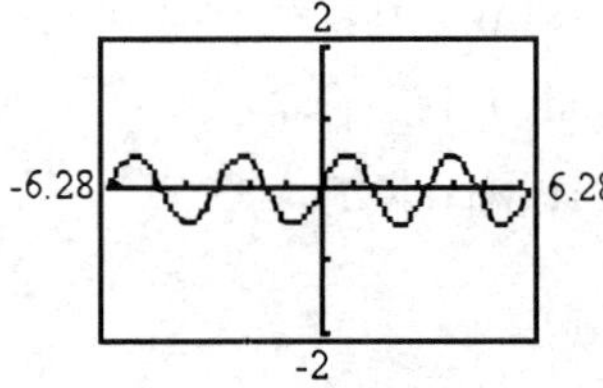

; The expressions are equivalent.

Difficulty: 1 Key 1: T

39. Rewrite the expression as a single logarithm and simplify.
$\ln|\sin\theta| - \ln|\cos\theta|$

Answer: $\ln|\tan\theta|$ Difficulty: 1

40. Rewrite the expression as a single logarithm and simplify.
$\ln|\sin\theta| - \ln|1 - \cos^2\theta|$

Answer: $\ln|\csc\theta|$ or $-\ln|\sin\theta|$ Difficulty: 1

41. Rewrite the expression as a single logarithm and simplify.

    $\ln|\csc\theta| + \ln|1 + \cot^2\theta|$

    Answer:

    $\ln|\csc^3\theta|$ or $3\ln|\csc\theta|$

    Difficulty: 1

Chapter 052: Verifying Trigonometric Identities

MULTIPLE CHOICE

1. Simplify: $\dfrac{\tan x}{\csc x + \cot x}$.

a) $\sec x - 1$ b) $\sec x + 1$ c) $\tan x \csc x + \tan x \cot x$
d) $1 - \dfrac{1}{\cos x}$ e) None of these

Answer: a Difficulty: 1

2. Simplify: $\dfrac{1}{\sec x + 1} + \dfrac{1}{\sec x - 1}$.

a) $\dfrac{2 \sin^2 x}{\cos^4 x}$ b) $2 \cot x \csc x$ c) $2 \csc x$
d) $\dfrac{\cos x}{2 \sin^2 x}$ e) None of these

Answer: b Difficulty: 2

3. Simplify: $\dfrac{\cot^2 \theta + 1}{\cos^2 \theta - 1}$.

a) $-\dfrac{1}{\sin^4 \theta}$ b) -1 c) $\csc^4 \theta$ d) $\cot^2 \theta$ e) None of these

Answer: a Difficulty: 1

4. Simplify: $\dfrac{\cos x}{1 + \sin x}$.

a) $\cos x + \cot x$ b) $\sec x - \tan x$ c) $\sec x - \cot x$
d) $\cos x + \tan x$ e) None of these

Answer: b Difficulty: 1

5. Simplify: $\dfrac{\tan^2 x}{\csc^2 x - 1}$.

a) -1 b) 1 c) $\tan^4 x$ d) $-\cot^4 x$ e) None of these

Answer: c Difficulty: 1

6. Simplify: $\dfrac{\tan x}{1 - \sec x}$.

a) $-\cot x(1 + \sec x)$ b) $\dfrac{1 + \sec x}{\tan x}$ c) $\cot x$
d) $1 - \sin x \sec^2 x$ e) None of these

Answer: a Difficulty: 2

7. Add and then simplify: $\frac{1 + \cos\theta}{\sin\theta} + \frac{\sin\theta}{1 + \cos\theta}$.

a) $\frac{1 + \cos\theta + \sin\theta}{\sin\theta + \sin\theta\cos\theta}$ b) $1 + 2\cos\theta + \cos^2\theta$ c) $\frac{2}{\sin\theta}$

d) $\cos^2\theta$ e) None of these

Answer: c Difficulty: 1

8. Add and then simplify: $\frac{1}{1 + \cos x} + \frac{1}{1 - \cos x}$.

a) $\frac{2}{1 - \cos x}$ b) 0 c) $2 \cot x \csc x$

d) $2\csc^2 x$ e) None of these

Answer: d Difficulty: 1

9. Simplify: $1 + \frac{1}{\csc^2 x - 1}$.

a) $\sin^2 x$ b) $1 - \cot^2 x$ c) $\sec^2 x$

d) $\cos^2 x$ e) None of these

Answer: c Difficulty: 1

10. Simplify: $\sin\left(\frac{\pi}{2} - x\right)[\tan(-x) + \cot(-x)]$.

a) $\sin x - \cot^2 x \csc x$ b) $-\csc x$ c) $\sin^2 x - \cos^2 x$

d) $\frac{1}{\sin x}$ e) None of these

Answer: b Difficulty: 2

11. Simplify: $\cos\left(\frac{\pi}{2} - x\right) \sec x + \frac{1}{\cos x \cdot \sec\left(\frac{\pi}{2} - x\right)}$.

a) 0 b) $\sec^2 x$ c) $2\tan x$ d) 2 e) None of these

Answer: c Difficulty: 2

12. Simplify: $1 - 2\csc x + \csc^4 x$.

a) $\tan^2 x$ b) $-\cot^2$ c) $-\cot^4 x$ d) $\cot^4 x$ e) None of these

Answer: d Difficulty: 2

13. Simplify: $\sin x - \sin x \cos^2 x$.

a) $\sin^2 x$ b) $\csc x$ c) $\sin^3 x$ d) $-\sin^3 x$ e) None of these

Answer: c Difficulty: 1

14. Verify the identity: $\dfrac{\sec^2 x}{\cot x} - \tan^3 x = \tan x$.

a) $$\frac{\sec^2 x}{\cot x} - \tan^3 x = \sec^2 x \tan x - \tan^3 x$$
$$= \tan x(\sec^2 x - \tan^2 x)$$
$$= \tan x(1)$$
$$= \tan x$$

b) $$\frac{\sec^2 x}{\cot x} - \tan^3 x = \frac{\sec^2 x - \tan^3 x(\cot x)}{\cot x}$$
$$= \frac{\sec^2 x - \tan^3 x\left(\frac{1}{\tan x}\right)}{\cot x}$$
$$= \frac{\sec^2 x - \tan^2 x}{\cot x}$$
$$= \frac{1}{\cot x}$$
$$= \tan x$$

c) $$\frac{\sec^2 x}{\cot x} - \tan^3 x = \frac{1 + \tan^2 x}{\cot x} - \tan^3 x$$
$$= \frac{1}{\cot x} + \frac{\tan^2 x}{\cot x} - \tan^3 x$$
$$= \tan x + \tan^3 x - \tan^3 x$$
$$= \tan x$$

d) All of these are correct verifications.
e) None of these

Answer: d Difficulty: 2

15. Verify the identity: $\dfrac{\cos x \csc x}{\cot^2 x} = \tan x$.

a) $\dfrac{\cos x \csc x}{\cot^2 x} = \cos x\left(\dfrac{1}{\sin x}\right)\tan^2 x$

$= \dfrac{\cos x}{\sin x}\dfrac{\sin^2 x}{\cos^2 x}$

$= \dfrac{\sin x}{\cos x}$

$= \tan x$

b) $\dfrac{\cos x \csc x}{\cot^2 x} = \dfrac{\cos x \csc x}{1 - \csc^2 x}$

$= \dfrac{\cos x}{1} - \dfrac{\csc x}{\csc^2 x}$

$= \cos x - \dfrac{1}{\csc x}$

$= \dfrac{\cos x}{\sin x}$

$= \tan x$

c) $\dfrac{\cos x \csc x}{\cot^2 x} = \dfrac{\cos x \csc x}{1 - \tan^2 x}$

$= \cos x - \dfrac{\csc x}{\tan^2 x}$

$= \cos x - \dfrac{\left(\dfrac{1}{\sin x}\right)}{\left(\dfrac{\sin x}{\cos x}\right)}$

$= \cos x - \dfrac{1}{\sin x} \cdot \dfrac{\cos x}{\sin x}$

$= \dfrac{\cos x}{\sin x}$

$= \tan x$

d) All of these are correct verifications.
e) None of these

Answer: a Difficulty: 2

16. Verify the identity: $\tan^2 x \cos^2 x + \cot^2 x \sin^2 = 1$.

a) $$\tan^2 x \cos^2 x + \cot^2 x \sin^2 x = \frac{\cos^2 x}{\sin^2 x} \cdot \cos^2 x + \frac{\sin^2 x}{\cos^2 x} \cdot \sin^2 x$$

$$= \frac{\cos^4 x + \sin^4 x}{\sin^2 x + \cos^2 x}$$

$$= \frac{(\cos^2 x + \sin^2 x)^2}{(\sin^2 x + \cos^2 x)}$$

$$= \frac{(1)^2}{(1)} = 1$$

b) $$\tan^2 x \cos^2 x + \cot^2 x \sin^2 x = (1 - \sec^2 x) \cos^2 x + (1 - \csc^2 x) \sin^2 x$$

$$= \cos^2 x - \cos^2 x \sec^2 + \sin^2 x - \sin^2 x \csc^2 x$$

$$= \cos^2 x - \cos^2 x\left[\frac{1}{\cos^2 x}\right] + \sin^2 x - \sin^2 x\left[\frac{1}{\sin^2 x}\right]$$

$$= \cos^2 x + \sin^2 x = 1$$

c) $$\tan^2 x \cos^2 x + \cot^2 x \sin^2 x = \frac{\sin^2 x}{\cos^2 x} \cdot \cos^2 x + \frac{\cos^2 x}{\sin^2 x} \cdot \sin^2 x$$

$$= \sin^2 x + \cos^2 x = 1$$

d) All of these are correct verifications.
e) None of these

Answer: c Difficulty: 1

17. Verify the identity: $\dfrac{\sec x - \cos x}{\tan x} = \sin x$.

a) $\dfrac{\sec x - \cos x}{\tan x} = \dfrac{\sec x - \cos x}{\dfrac{\sin x}{\cos x}}$

$= (\sec x - \cos x)\left(\dfrac{\cos x}{\sin x}\right)$

$= \sec x \sin x - \cos^2 x$

$= 1 - \cos^2 x$

$= \sin x$

b) $\dfrac{\sec x - \cos x}{\tan x} = \dfrac{\sec x - \cos x}{\dfrac{1}{\cot x}}$

$= (\sec x - \cos x)(\cot x)$

$= \sec x \cot x - \cos x \cot x$

$= \dfrac{1}{\cos x}\left(\dfrac{\sin x}{\cos x}\right) - \cos x\left(\dfrac{\sin x}{\cos x}\right)$

$= \dfrac{\sin x}{\cos x} - \sin x$

$= \sin x - \sin x \cos x$

$= \sin x(1 - \cos x)$

$= \sin x(1) = \sin x$

c) $\dfrac{\sec x - \cos x}{\tan x} = \dfrac{\sec x - \cos x}{\dfrac{1}{\cot x}}$

$= (\sec x - \cos x)(\cot x)$

$= \dfrac{1}{\cos x}\left(\dfrac{\cos x}{\sin x}\right) - \cos x\left(\dfrac{\cos x}{\sin x}\right)$

$= \dfrac{1}{\sin x} - \dfrac{\cos^2 x}{\sin x}$

$= \dfrac{1 - \cos^2 x}{\sin x}$

$= \dfrac{\sin^2 x}{\sin x} = \sin x$

d) All of these are correct verifications.
e) None of these

Answer: c Difficulty: 2

18. Verify the identity: $\frac{\csc x}{\sin x} - \frac{\cot x}{\tan x} = 1$.

a) $$\frac{\csc x}{\sin x} - \frac{\cot x}{\tan x} = \csc x \tan x - \sin x \cot x$$

$$= \frac{1}{\sin x} \cdot \frac{\sin x}{\cos x} - \sin x \cdot \frac{\cos x}{\sin x}$$

$$= \frac{1 - \cos x}{\cos x}$$

$$= 1 - \frac{\cos x}{\cos x} = 1$$

b) $$\frac{\csc x}{\sin x} - \frac{\cot x}{\tan x} = \frac{\csc x}{\left(\frac{1}{\csc x}\right)} - \frac{\cot x}{\left(\frac{1}{\cot x}\right)}$$

$$= \csc^2 x - \cot^2 x = 1$$

c) $$\frac{\csc x}{\sin x} - \frac{\cot x}{\tan x} = \frac{\left(\frac{1}{\sin x}\right)}{\sin x} - \frac{\left(\frac{1}{\tan x}\right)}{\tan x}$$

$$= \frac{1}{\sin^2 x} - \frac{1}{\tan^2 x}$$

$$= \frac{\tan^2 x - \sin^2 x}{\sin^2 x \tan^2 x}$$

$$= \frac{\frac{\sin^2 x}{\cos^2 x} - \sin^2 x}{\sin^2 x\left(\frac{\sin^2 x}{\cos^2 x}\right)}$$

$$= \frac{\sin^2 x - \sin^2 x \cos^2 x}{\cos^2 x} \cdot \frac{\cos^2 x}{\sin^4 x}$$

$$= \frac{\sin^2 x(1 - \cos^2 x)}{\sin^4 x}$$

$$= \frac{\sin^2 x \cdot \sin^2 x}{\sin^4 x}$$

$$= \frac{\sin^4 x}{\sin^4 x} = 1$$

d) Both b and c are correct verifications.
e) None of these

Answer: d Difficulty: 2

19. Verify the identity: $\dfrac{1 + \tan x}{\sin x} - \sec x = \csc x$.

a) $\dfrac{1 + \tan x}{\sin x} - \sec x = 1 + \tan x - \sin x \sec x$

$$= 1 + \frac{\sin x}{\cos x} - \frac{\sin x}{\cos x}$$

$$= 1 \neq \csc x$$

Therefore, this is not an identity.

b) $\dfrac{1 + \tan x}{\sin x} - \sec x = \dfrac{1 + \tan x - \sin x \sec x}{\sin x}$

$$= \frac{1 + \tan x - \sin x\left(\frac{1}{\cos x}\right)}{\sin x}$$

$$= \frac{1 + \tan x - \tan x}{\sin x}$$

$$= \frac{1}{\sin x} = \csc x$$

c) $\dfrac{1 + \tan x}{\sin x} - \sec x = 1 + \tan x - \sin x \sec x$

$$= 1 + \tan x - \sin x\left(\frac{1}{\sin x}\right)$$

$$= 1 + \tan x$$

$$= \csc x$$

d) Both b and c are correct verifications.
e) None of these

Answer: b Difficulty: 1

SHORT ANSWER

20. Verify the identity: $\dfrac{1 + \sin x}{\cos x \sin x} = \sec x(\csc x + 1)$.

Answer:
$$\frac{1 + \sin x}{\cos x \sin x} = \frac{1}{\cos x \sin x} + \frac{\sin x}{\cos x \sin x}$$

$$= \sec x \csc x + \sec x$$

$$= \sec x(\csc x + 1)$$

Difficulty: 1

MULTIPLE CHOICE

21. Simplify: $\sin x + \sin x \cot^2 x$.
    a) $\sin x \tan x$ b) $\csc x$ c) $\sin x \tan^2 x$
    d) $\csc^3 x$ e) None of these

    Answer: b Difficulty: 1

SHORT ANSWER

22. Verify the identity: $\sin x\left[\dfrac{\sin x}{1 - \cos x} + \dfrac{1 - \cos x}{\sin x}\right] = 2.$

    Answer:

$$\sin x\left[\frac{\sin x}{1 - \cos x} + \frac{1 - \cos x}{\sin x}\right] = \frac{\sin^2 x}{1 - \cos x} + 1 - \cos x$$

$$= \frac{1 - \cos^2 x}{1 - \cos x} + 1 - \cos x$$

$$= \frac{(1 + \cos x)(1 - \cos x)}{1 - \cos x} + 1 - \cos x$$

$$= (1 + \cos x) + 1 - \cos x = 2$$

    Difficulty: 2

MULTIPLE CHOICE

23. Simplify: $\sec^4 x + \sec^2 x - 2$.
    a) $2 \tan^4 x$ b) $(\sec^2 x + 2)(\tan^2 x)$ c) $2 \tan^2 x$
    d) $\tan^2 x + 2$ e) None of these

    Answer: b Difficulty: 1

24. Simplify: $\dfrac{\tan x}{\cot x} - \dfrac{\sin x}{\csc x}$.
    a) $\sec x - \cos x$ b) $\tan^2 x \sin^2 x$ c) $\tan^2 x - \sin^2 x$
    d) $\tan^2 x \sin^2 x$ and $\tan^2 x - \sin^2 x$ e) None of these

    Answer: d Difficulty: 2

25. Simplify: $\csc^4 x + 2 \csc^2 x - 3$.
    a) $4 \cot^2 x$ b) $\tan^2 x(\csc^2 x + 3)$ c) $(\cot^2 x)(\csc^2 x + 3)$
    d) $2 \csc^2 x - 2$ e) None of these

    Answer: c Difficulty: 2

26. Find the missing factors to complete the verification.

$$\sin x \cos x(\tan x + \csc x) = \sin^2 x + \cos x$$

$$\sin x \cos x \tan x + \sin x \cos x \csc x = \sin^2 x + \cos x$$

$$\sin x \cos x(\quad) + \sin x \cos x(\quad) = \sin^2 x + \cos x$$

$$\sin^2 x + \cos x = \sin^2 x + \cos^2 x$$

a) $\frac{\cos x}{\sin x}, \frac{1}{\sin x}$ b) $\frac{\sin x}{\cos x}, \frac{1}{\cos x}$ c) $\frac{\cos x}{\sin x}, \frac{1}{\cos x}$
d) $\frac{\sin x}{\cos x}, \frac{1}{\sin x}$ e) None of these

Answer: d Difficulty: 1

27. Simplify: $\sec x + \tan(-x) \sin x$.
a) $\cos^2 x$ b) $\cos x$ c) $-\cos x$ d) $-\tan x$ e) None of these

Answer: b Difficulty: 2

SHORT ANSWER

28. Verify the identity: $\sec\left[\frac{\pi}{2} - x\right] - \tan\left[\frac{\pi}{2} - x\right] \sin\left[\frac{\pi}{2} - x\right] = \sin x$.

Answer:

$$\sec\left[\frac{\pi}{2} - x\right] - \tan\left[\frac{\pi}{2} - x\right] \sin\left[\frac{\pi}{2} - x\right] = \csc x - \cot x \cos x$$

$$= \frac{1}{\sin x} - \frac{\cos x}{\sin x} \cdot \cos x$$

$$= \frac{1 - \cos^2 x}{\sin x}$$

$$= \frac{\sin^2 x}{\sin x}$$

$$= \sin x$$

Difficulty: 2

MULTIPLE CHOICE

29. Find the missing factor to rewrite the expression with a monomial denominator.

$$\frac{1}{\csc x - \cos x} \cdot (\quad)$$

a) $\dfrac{\csc x - \cot x}{\csc x - \cot x}$ b) $\dfrac{\csc x + \cot x}{\csc x + \cot x}$ c) $\sin x + \tan x$

d) $\dfrac{1}{\sin x} - \dfrac{1}{\tan x}$ e) None of these

Answer: b Difficulty: 1

30. Verify the identity: $\dfrac{\sqrt{\sec x - 1}}{\sqrt{\sec x + 1}} = \dfrac{\sec x - 1}{|\tan x|}$.

a) $\dfrac{\sqrt{\sec - 1}}{\sqrt{\sec x + 1}} \cdot \dfrac{\sqrt{\sec + 1}}{\sqrt{\sec x + 1}} = \dfrac{\sqrt{\sec^2 x - 1}}{\sqrt{(\sec^2 x + 1)^2}} = \dfrac{\sec x - 1}{\sec^2 x + 1} = \dfrac{|\tan x|}{\sec x - 1}$

b) $\dfrac{\sqrt{\sec x - 1}}{\sqrt{\sec x + 1}} \cdot \dfrac{\sqrt{\sec x - 1}}{\sqrt{\sec x - 1}} = \dfrac{\sqrt{(\sec x - 1)^2}}{\sqrt{\sec^2 x - 1}} = \dfrac{\sec x - 1}{\sqrt{\tan^2 x}} = \dfrac{\sec x - 1}{|\tan x|}$

c) Both a and b are correct verifications.
d) Neither a nor b is a correct verification.

e) The identity is not true. $\dfrac{\sqrt{\sec x - 1}}{\sqrt{\sec x + 1}} \neq \dfrac{\sec x - 1}{|\tan x|}$

Answer: b Difficulty: 2

31. Simplify: $\dfrac{\sin^3 x + \cos^3 x}{\sin x + \cos x}$.

a) $\sin^2 x + 2 \sin x \cos x + \cos^2 x$
b) $1 + 2 \sin x \cos x$
c) $1 - \sin x \cos x$
d) Both $\sin^2 x + 2 \sin x \cos x + \cos^2 x$ and $1 + 2 \sin x \cos x$
e) None of these

Answer: c Difficulty: 1

SHORT ANSWER

32. Verify the identity: $\dfrac{\tan^2 x + 1}{\tan^2 x} = \csc^2 x$.

Answer:

$$\frac{\tan^2 x + 1}{\tan^2 x} = 1 + \frac{1}{\tan^2 x} = 1 + \cot^2 x = \csc^2 x$$

Difficulty: 1

33. Verify the identity: $\sec x \csc^2 x - \csc^2 x = \dfrac{\sec x}{1 + \cos x}$.

Answer:

$$\sec x \csc^2 x - \csc^2 x = \csc^2 x(\sec x - 1) = \frac{1}{\sin^2 x}\left(\frac{1}{\cos x} - 1\right)$$

$$= \frac{1}{\sin^2 x}\left(\frac{1 - \cos x}{\cos x}\right)$$

$$= \frac{1}{1 - \cos^2 x}\left(\frac{1 - \cos x}{\cos x}\right)$$

$$= \frac{1}{(1 + \cos x)\cos x}$$

$$= \frac{\sec x}{1 + \cos x}$$

Difficulty: 2

34. While drawing the plans for the plumbing of your new home, the contractor finds it necessary for two water pipes of radius, R, and r, to be joined at right angles. The expression $(r \cos x)^2 + (R - r)(R + r)$ is used. Show that this expression can be written as $R^2 - r^2 \sin^2 x$.

Answer:

$$(r \cos x)^2 + (R - r)(R + r) = r^2 \cos^2 x + R^2 - r^2$$

$$= R^2 + r^2 \cos^2 x - r^2$$

$$= R^2 + r^2(\cos^2 x - 1)$$

$$= R^2 + r^2[-(1 - \cos^2 x)]$$

$$= R^2 + r^2(-\sin^2 x)$$

$$= R^2 - r^2 \sin^2 x$$

Difficulty: 2

35. In the study of the motion of a projectile, the expression $\sqrt{0.36 \cos^2 \beta t - 0.36 + 2.0 \sin^2 \beta t}$ arises. Simplify the expression.

Answer:

$$\sqrt{0.36 \cos^2 \beta t - 0.36 + 2.0 \sin^2 \beta t} =$$

$$\sqrt{-0.36(1 - \cos^2 \beta t) + 2.0 \sin^2 \beta t}$$

$$= \sqrt{-0.36 \sin^2 \beta t + 2.0 \sin^2 \beta t}$$

$$= \sqrt{1.44 \sin^2 \beta t}$$

$$= 1.2 \sin \beta t$$

Difficulty: 2

36. Verify the identity algebraically, and use a graphing utility to confirm it graphically.

$$\frac{1 + \cos x}{\sin x} + \frac{\sin x}{1 + \cos x} = 2 \csc x$$

Answer:

$$\frac{1 + \cos x}{\sin x} + \frac{\sin x}{1 + \cos x} = \frac{(1 + \cos x)^2 + \sin^2 x}{\sin x(1 + \cos x)}$$

$$= \frac{1 + 2 \cos x + \cos^2 x + \sin^2 x}{\sin x(1 + \cos x)}$$

$$= \frac{2 + 2 \cos x}{\sin x(1 + \cos x)}$$

$$= \frac{2(1 + \cos x)}{\sin x(1 + \cos x)}$$

$$= 2 \csc x$$

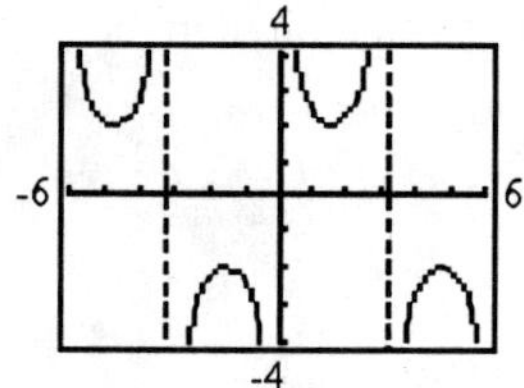

Difficulty: 1 Key 1: T

37. Verify the identity algebraically, and use a graphing utility to confirm it graphically.

$$\frac{\cos x + \tan x}{\sin x} = \cot x + \sec x$$

Answer:

$$\frac{\cos x + \tan x}{\sin x} = \frac{\cos x}{\sin x} + \frac{\tan x}{\sin x}$$

$$= \cot x + \frac{\left(\frac{\sin x}{\cos x}\right)}{\sin x}$$

$$= \cot x + \frac{\sin x}{\cos x} \cdot \frac{1}{\sin x}$$

$$= \cot x + \frac{1}{\cos x}$$

$$= \cot x + \sec x$$

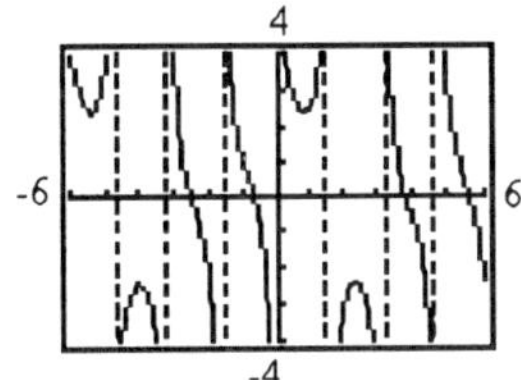

Difficulty: 1 Key 1: T

38. Verify the identity algebraically, and use a graphing utility to confirm it graphically.

$$\frac{\csc^4 x - 1}{\cot^2 x} = 2 + \cot^2 x$$

Answer:

$$\frac{\csc^4 x - 1}{\cot^2 x} = \frac{(\csc^2 x + 1)(\csc^2 x - 1)}{\cot^2 x}$$

$$= \frac{(\csc^2 x + 1)\cot^2 x}{\cot^2 x}$$

$$= \csc^2 x + 1$$

$$= 1 + \cos^2 x + 1$$

$$= 2 + \cot^2 x$$

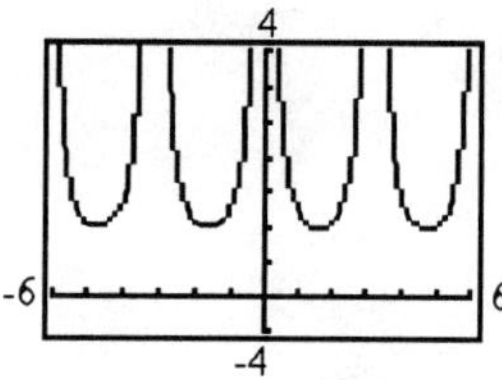

Difficulty: 1 Key 1: T

Chapter 053: Solving Trigonometric Equations

MULTIPLE CHOICE

1. Find all solutions in the interval $[0, 2\pi)$: $2 \cos x - \sqrt{3} = 0$.
   a) $\frac{\pi}{6}, \frac{11\pi}{6}$ b) $\frac{5\pi}{6}, \frac{7\pi}{6}$ c) $\frac{\pi}{3}, \frac{5\pi}{3}$
   d) $\frac{2\pi}{3}, \frac{4\pi}{3}$ e) None of these

   Answer: a Difficulty: 1

2. Find all solutions in the interval $[0, 2\pi)$: $\cos x - 1 = 0$.
   a) $\frac{\pi}{4}, \frac{7\pi}{4}$ b) $\frac{\pi}{2}, \frac{3\pi}{2}$ c) 0 d) π e) None of these

   Answer: c Difficulty: 1

3. Find all solutions in the interval $[0, 2\pi)$: $\csc x + 2 = 0$.
   a) $\frac{\pi}{3}, \frac{2\pi}{3}$ b) $\frac{\pi}{6}, \frac{5\pi}{6}$ c) $\frac{4\pi}{3}, \frac{5\pi}{3}$ d) $\frac{7\pi}{6}, \frac{11\pi}{6}$ e) None of these

   Answer: d Difficulty: 1

4. Find all solutions in the interval $[0, 2\pi)$: $\sin 2x = 0$.
   a) $0, \pi$ b) $0, \frac{\pi}{2}, \pi, \frac{3\pi}{2}$ c) $\frac{\pi}{2}, \frac{3\pi}{2}$
   d) $\frac{\pi}{4}, \frac{3\pi}{4}, \frac{5\pi}{4}, \frac{7\pi}{4}$ e) None of these

   Answer: b Difficulty: 1

5. Find all solutions in the interval $[0, 2\pi)$: $3 \tan x - 3 = 0$.
   a) $0, \pi$ b) $\frac{\pi}{2}, \frac{3\pi}{2}$ c) $\frac{\pi}{4}, \frac{5\pi}{4}$
   d) $\frac{3\pi}{4}, \frac{7\pi}{4}$ e) None of these

   Answer: c Difficulty: 1

6. Find all solutions in the interval $[0, 2\pi)$: $\cos^2 x + \sin x = 1$.
   a) $0, \pi$ b) $\frac{\pi}{2}$ c) $\frac{\pi}{2}, \frac{3\pi}{2}$ d) $0, \frac{\pi}{2}, \pi$ e) None of these

   Answer: d Difficulty: 1

7. Find all solutions in the interval $[0, 2\pi)$: $\sec^2 x = \sec x + 2$.
   a) $\frac{\pi}{2}, \frac{2\pi}{3}, \frac{4\pi}{3}, \frac{3\pi}{2}$ b) $\frac{\pi}{3}, \pi, \frac{5\pi}{3}$ c) $\frac{2\pi}{3}, \frac{4\pi}{3}$
   d) $\frac{\pi}{6}, \pi, \frac{11\pi}{6}$ e) None of these

   Answer: b Difficulty: 1

8. Find all solutions in the interval $[0, 2\pi)$: $\sin x = \frac{1}{4 \sin x}$.

a) $\frac{\pi}{6}, \frac{5\pi}{6}$ b) $\frac{7\pi}{6}, \frac{11\pi}{6}$ c) $\frac{\pi}{3}, \frac{2\pi}{3}, \frac{4\pi}{3}, \frac{5\pi}{3}$

d) $\frac{\pi}{6}, \frac{5\pi}{6}, \frac{7\pi}{6}, \frac{11\pi}{6}$ e) None of these

Answer: d Difficulty: 1

9. Find all solutions in the interval $[0, 2\pi)$: $\sec^2 x - 3 \tan x = 5$.

a) $1.1578, 4.299, \frac{3\pi}{4}, \frac{7\pi}{4}$ b) $1.3258, 4.4674, \frac{3\pi}{4}, \frac{7\pi}{4}$

c) $0.0699, \frac{3\pi}{4}, \frac{7\pi}{4}$ d) $\frac{3\pi}{4}, \frac{7\pi}{4}$

e) None of these

Answer: b Difficulty: 2

10. Find all solutions in the interval $[0, 2\pi)$: $6 \sin^2 x - \sin x - 2 = 0$.

a) 0.6667, 0.5 b) $0.7297, 2.4119, \frac{7\pi}{6}, \frac{11\pi}{6}$

c) $\frac{\pi}{6}, \frac{11\pi}{6}$ d) 0.7297, 3.871

e) None of these

Answer: b Difficulty: 2

11. Find all solutions in the interval $[0, 2\pi)$: $\tan 3t = \sqrt{3}$.

a) $\frac{\pi}{9}, \frac{4\pi}{9}$ b) $\frac{\pi}{9}, \frac{4\pi}{9}, \frac{7\pi}{9}, \frac{10\pi}{9}, \frac{13\pi}{9}, \frac{16\pi}{9}$ c) $\frac{\pi}{3}, \frac{4\pi}{3}$

d) $\frac{\pi}{6}, \frac{7\pi}{6}$ e) None of these

Answer: b Difficulty: 1

12. Find all solutions in the interval $[0, 2\pi)$: $2 \cos x \csc x - 4 \cos x - \csc x + 2 = 0$.

a) $\frac{\pi}{3}, \frac{5\pi}{3}$ b) $\frac{\pi}{6}, \frac{\pi}{3}, \frac{5\pi}{3}, \frac{11\pi}{6}$ c) $\frac{\pi}{6}, \frac{\pi}{3}, \frac{5\pi}{6}, \frac{5\pi}{3}$

d) $\frac{\pi}{6}, \frac{2\pi}{3}, \frac{5\pi}{6}, \frac{5\pi}{3}$ e) None of these

Answer: c Difficulty: 1

13. Find all solutions in the interval $[0, 2\pi)$: $5 \sin^2 x + 8 \sin x - 4 = 0$.

a) 0.4115, 2.7301 b) $\frac{\pi}{6}, \frac{5\pi}{6}$ c) 0.4, 2.7416

d) 3.5531, 5.8717 e) None of these

Answer: a Difficulty: 2

14. Find all solutions in the interval $[0, 2\pi)$: $6\cos^2 x - 5\sin x - 2 = 0$.

a) $-1.3333, -4.4749, \frac{\pi}{6}, \frac{5\pi}{6}$ b) $\frac{\pi}{6}, \frac{5\pi}{6}$ c) 2.0000, 5.1416

d) $\frac{7\pi}{6}, \frac{11\pi}{6}$ e) None of these

Answer: b Difficulty: 1

15. Find all solutions in the interval $[0, 2\pi)$: $\cot^2 x - \tan^2 x = 0$.

a) $0, \pi$ b) $0, \frac{\pi}{4}, \frac{3\pi}{4}, \pi, \frac{5\pi}{4}, \frac{7\pi}{4}$ c) $\frac{\pi}{4}, \frac{3\pi}{4}, \frac{5\pi}{4}, \frac{7\pi}{4}$

d) $\frac{\pi}{4}, \frac{3\pi}{4}, \frac{5\pi}{4}, \frac{7\pi}{4}$ e) None of these

Answer: c Difficulty: 1

16. Find all solutions in the interval $[0, 2\pi)$: $2\cos^2 x + \left(1 + 2\sqrt{3}\right)\cos x + \sqrt{3} = 0$.

a) $\frac{2\pi}{3}, \frac{5\pi}{6}, \frac{7\pi}{6}, \frac{4\pi}{3}$ b) $\frac{2\pi}{3}, \frac{4\pi}{3}$ c) $\frac{\pi}{3}, \frac{5\pi}{3}$

d) -1.7321, -4.8736 e) None of these

Answer: b Difficulty: 1

17. Find all solutions in the interval $[0, 2\pi)$: $8\sin\left(\frac{x}{2}\right) - 8 = 0$.

a) $\frac{\pi}{2}, \frac{3\pi}{2}$ b) $\frac{\pi}{4}, \frac{3\pi}{4}, \frac{5\pi}{4}, \frac{7\pi}{4}$ c) π

d) 0 e) None of these

Answer: c Difficulty: 1

18. Find all solutions in the interval $[0, 2\pi)$: $2\sin^2 \frac{x}{4} - 3\cos \frac{x}{4} = 0$.

a) $\frac{\pi}{3}, \frac{5\pi}{3}$ b) $\frac{4\pi}{3}$ c) $\frac{4\pi}{3}, \frac{2\pi}{3}$ d) $\frac{\pi}{6}, \frac{\pi}{3}$ e) None of these

Answer: b Difficulty: 2

19. Find all solutions in the interval $[0, 2\pi)$: $1 + \tan^2 \theta + \tan^4 \theta = 1$.

a) $0, \frac{\pi}{2}, \pi, \frac{3\pi}{2}$ b) $0, \pi$ c) $0, \frac{\pi}{4}, \frac{3\pi}{4}, \pi, \frac{5\pi}{4}, \frac{3\pi}{2}, \frac{7\pi}{4}$

d) $\frac{\pi}{2}, \frac{3\pi}{2}$ e) None of these

Answer: b Difficulty: 1

20. Find all solutions in the interval $[0, 2\pi)$: $2 \sin^2 x - 5 \sin x = -3$.

a) $0.7297, 2.4119, \frac{3\pi}{2}$ b) $\frac{\pi}{2}, \frac{3\pi}{2}$ c) $\frac{3}{2}, 1$

d) $\frac{\pi}{2}$ e) None of these

Answer: d Difficulty: 1

21. Find all solutions in the interval $[0, 2\pi)$: $\sec^4 x - 2 \sec^2 x \tan^2 x + \tan^4 x = \tan^2 x$.

a) $\frac{\pi}{2}, \frac{3\pi}{2}$ b) $0, \pi$ c) $\frac{\pi}{4}, \frac{3\pi}{4}, \frac{5\pi}{4}, \frac{7\pi}{4}$

d) $\frac{\pi}{4}, \frac{5\pi}{4}$ e) None of these

Answer: c Difficulty: 1

22. Find all solutions in the interval $[0, 2\pi)$: $\csc^2 x - (\cos^4 x + 2 \cos^2 x \sin^2 x + \sin^4 x) = 0$.

a) $\frac{\pi}{2}, \frac{3\pi}{2}$ b) $0, \pi$ c) $\frac{\pi}{4}, \frac{3\pi}{4}, \frac{5\pi}{4}, \frac{7\pi}{4}$

d) $\frac{\pi}{2}$ e) None of these

Answer: a Difficulty: 1

23. Find all solutions in the interval $[0, 2\pi)$: $\sec 3x = \sqrt{2}$.

a) $\frac{\pi}{4}, \frac{7\pi}{4}$

b) $\frac{\pi}{12}, \frac{7\pi}{12}, \frac{9\pi}{12}, \frac{15\pi}{12}, \frac{17\pi}{12}, \frac{23\pi}{12}$

c) $\frac{\pi}{12}, \frac{5\pi}{12}, \frac{7\pi}{12}, \frac{9\pi}{12}, \frac{11\pi}{12}, \frac{13\pi}{12}, \frac{15\pi}{12}, \frac{17\pi}{12}, \frac{19\pi}{12}, \frac{23\pi}{12}$

d) $\frac{\pi}{12}, \frac{7\pi}{12}$

e) None of these

Answer: b Difficulty: 1

24. Find all solutions in the interval $[0, 2\pi)$: $\tan \frac{x}{4} = \frac{\sqrt{3}}{3}$.

a) $\frac{2\pi}{3}$ b) $\frac{10\pi}{3}$ c) $\frac{\pi}{4}$ d) $\frac{\pi}{4}, \frac{5\pi}{4}$ e) None of these

Answer: a Difficulty: 1

25. Find all solutions in the interval $[0, 2\pi)$: $2 \sin x \cos x + \cos x = 0$.
a) $\frac{\pi}{6}, \frac{\pi}{2}, \frac{5\pi}{6}, \frac{3\pi}{2}$
b) $\frac{\pi}{2}, \frac{7\pi}{6}, \frac{3\pi}{2}, \frac{11\pi}{6}$
c) $\frac{5\pi}{6}, \frac{11\pi}{6}$
d) $0, \pi$
e) None of these

Answer: b Difficulty: 1

26. Find all solutions in the interval $[0, 2\pi)$: $2 \sin^3 x + \sin^2 x = 0$.
a) $\frac{5\pi}{6}, \frac{11\pi}{6}$
b) $\frac{4\pi}{3}, \frac{5\pi}{3}$
c) $0, \frac{7\pi}{6}, \pi, \frac{11\pi}{6}$
d) $0, \frac{\pi}{2}, \pi, \frac{4\pi}{3}, \frac{3\pi}{2}, \frac{5\pi}{3}$
e) None of these

Answer: c Difficulty: 1

27. Find all solutions in the interval $[0, 2\pi)$: $2 \cos^2(2\theta) - 1 = 0$.
a) $\frac{\pi}{4}, \frac{3\pi}{4}, \frac{5\pi}{5}, \frac{7\pi}{4}$
b) $\frac{\pi}{8}, \frac{3\pi}{8}, \frac{5\pi}{8}, \frac{7\pi}{8}, \frac{9\pi}{8}, \frac{11\pi}{8}, \frac{13\pi}{8}, \frac{15\pi}{8}$
c) $\frac{\pi}{8}, \frac{\pi}{4}, \frac{3\pi}{8}, \frac{3\pi}{4}$
d) $\frac{\pi}{2}, \frac{\pi}{4}, \frac{3\pi}{2}, \frac{3\pi}{4}, \frac{5\pi}{2}, \frac{5\pi}{4}, \frac{7\pi}{2}, \frac{7\pi}{4}$
e) None of these

Answer: b Difficulty: 1

SHORT ANSWER

28. Find all solutions in the interval $[0, 2\pi)$: $3 \tan^2 2x - 1 = 0$.

Answer:
$\frac{\pi}{12}, \frac{5\pi}{12}, \frac{7\pi}{12}, \frac{11\pi}{12}, \frac{13\pi}{12}, \frac{17\pi}{12}, \frac{19\pi}{12}, \frac{23\pi}{12}$

Difficulty: 1

29. Find all solutions in the interval $[0, 2\pi)$: $2 \sin^2 x = \sin x$.

Answer:
$0, \frac{\pi}{6}, \frac{5\pi}{6}, \pi$

Difficulty: 1

30. Find all solutions in the interval $[0, 2\pi)$: $\tan^2 \theta \csc \theta = \tan^2 \theta$.

Answer:
$0, \frac{\pi}{2}, \pi$

Difficulty: 1

31. Find all solutions in the interval $[0, 2\pi)$: $2\sin^2 2x + 5\sin 2x - 3 = 0$.

Answer:
$\frac{\pi}{12}, \frac{5\pi}{12}, \frac{13\pi}{12}, \frac{17\pi}{12}$

Difficulty: 1

32. Find all solutions in the interval $[0, 2\pi)$: $2\cos\frac{x}{2} - \sqrt{3} = 0$.

Answer:
$\frac{\pi}{3}$

Difficulty: 1

MULTIPLE CHOICE

33. Find all solutions in the interval $[0, 2\pi)$: $4\sin^2 x + 2\left(1 - \sqrt{3}\right)\sin x - \sqrt{3} = 0$.

a) $\frac{\pi}{3}, \frac{2\pi}{3}, \frac{7\pi}{6}, \frac{11\pi}{6}$
b) $\frac{\pi}{6}, \frac{5\pi}{6}, \frac{4\pi}{3}, \frac{5\pi}{3}$
c) $\frac{\pi}{6}, \frac{\pi}{3}, \frac{2\pi}{3}, \frac{5\pi}{6}$
d) $\frac{7\pi}{6}, \frac{4\pi}{3}, \frac{5\pi}{3}, \frac{11\pi}{6}$
e) None of these

Answer: a Difficulty: 2

SHORT ANSWER

34. A professional quarterback completes a pass to a receiver 75 yards away. The football was thrown with a velocity of 88 feet per second. Find the angle θ that the ball was thrown, if the range is given by $r = \frac{1}{32}V_0^2 \sin 2\theta$.

Answer:

$$r = \frac{1}{32}V_0^2 \sin 2\theta$$

$$\sin 2\theta = \frac{32r}{V_0^2} \Rightarrow \theta \; \frac{\sin^{-1}\left[\frac{32r}{V_0^2}\right]}{2}$$

$$\theta = \frac{\sin^{-1}\left[\frac{32(75 \cdot 3)}{(88)^2}\right]}{2}$$

$$\theta = 34.20° \text{ or } 55.80°$$

Difficulty: 2

35. You just received a new water gun for your birthday, and directly drench your little brother standing 100 feet away. You had pumped the gun to maximum pressure, which the manufacturer states is 60 feet per second. Find the angle θ which you must have directed the stream of water, if the range is given by

$$r = \frac{1}{32}V_0^2 \sin 2\theta.$$

Answer:

$$\sin 2\theta = \frac{32r}{V_0^2}$$

$$\theta = \frac{\sin^{-1}\left[\frac{32r}{V_0^2}\right]}{2}$$

$$\theta = \frac{\sin^{-1}\left[\frac{32(100)}{(60)^2}\right]}{2}$$

$$\theta = 31.37° \text{ or } 58.63°$$

Difficulty: 2

36. An archer intends to hit a target d at a distance of 300 feet. If the arrow travels with a velocity of 120 feet per second and at an angle of θ, determine the minimum angle of elevation of the arrow if the range is given by

$$r = \frac{1}{32}V_0^2 \sin 2\theta.$$

Answer:

$$\sin 2\theta = \frac{32r}{V_0^2}$$

$$\theta = \frac{\sin^{-1}\left[\frac{32r}{V_0^2}\right]}{2}$$

$$\theta = \frac{\sin^{-1}\left[\frac{32(300)}{120^2}\right]}{2}$$

$$\theta = 20.9°$$

Difficulty: 2

37. Find the x-intercepts of the graph: $y = \cos \frac{\pi x}{2} + 1$.

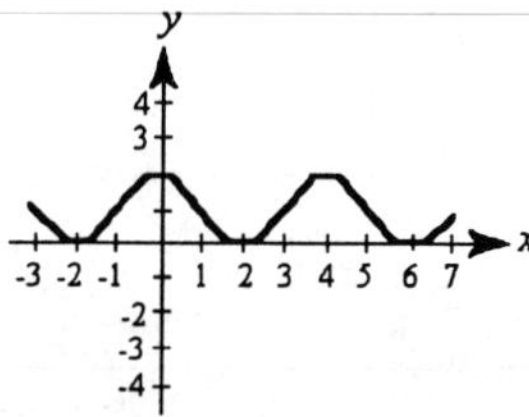

Answer: $x = -2, 2, 6$ Difficulty: 1

38. Find the x-intercepts of the graph: $y = \sin x + \cos x$.

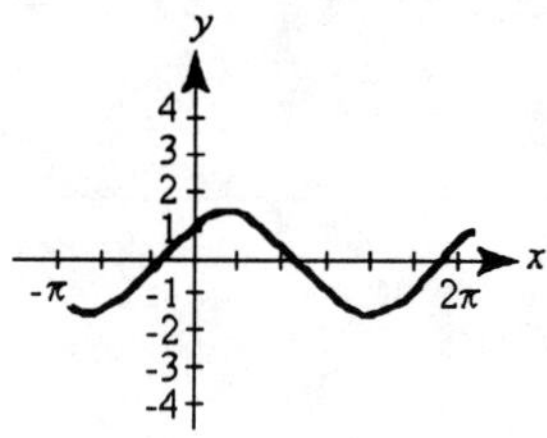

Answer:

$x = -\frac{\pi}{4}, \frac{3\pi}{4}, \frac{5\pi}{4}$

Difficulty: 1

39. Find the x-intercepts of the graph: $y = \tan^2\left(\frac{\pi x}{3}\right) - 1$.

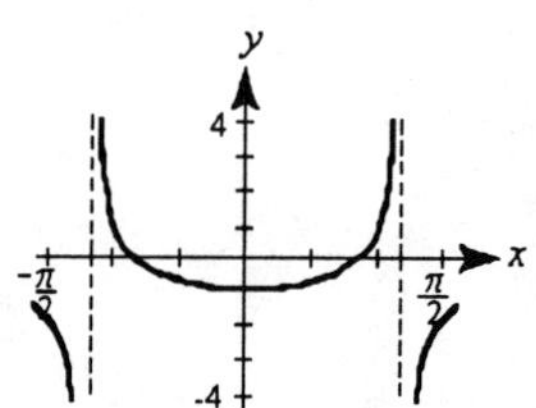

Answer:

$x = -\frac{3}{4}, \frac{3}{4}$

Difficulty: 1

40. Find the x-intercepts of the graph: $y = \csc^2\left(\frac{\pi x}{2}\right) - 4$.

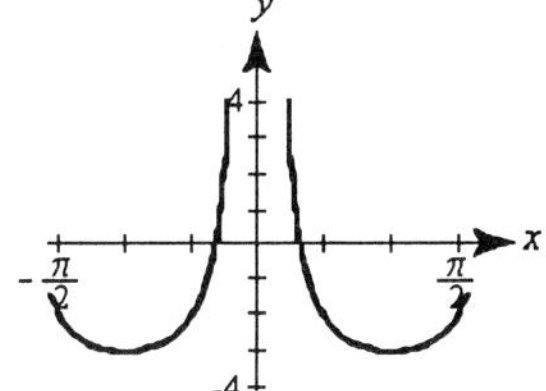

Answer:

$x = -\frac{1}{3}, \frac{1}{3}$

Difficulty: 1

Chapter 054: Sum and Difference Formulas

MULTIPLE CHOICE

1. Evaluate: sin 105°. (Use the fact that 105° = 60° + 45°.)
   a) $\frac{\sqrt{6}+\sqrt{2}}{4}$ b) $\frac{\sqrt{6}-\sqrt{2}}{4}$ c) $\frac{\sqrt{2}+\sqrt{6}}{4}$
   d) $\frac{1+\sqrt{3}}{2}$ e) None of these

Answer: a Difficulty: 1

2. Evaluate: sin 255°. (Use the fact that 255° = 210° + 45°.)
   a) $\frac{\sqrt{6}-\sqrt{2}}{4}$ b) $\frac{\sqrt{2}+\sqrt{6}}{4}$ c) $-\frac{\sqrt{2}+\sqrt{6}}{4}$
   d) $\frac{\sqrt{2}-\sqrt{6}}{4}$ e) None of these

Answer: c Difficulty: 1

3. Evaluate: $\tan \frac{13\pi}{12}$. $\left[\text{Use the fact that } \frac{13\pi}{12} = \frac{4\pi}{3} - \frac{\pi}{4}.\right]$
   a) 1 b) $1+\sqrt{3}$ c) $\sqrt{3}-1$
   d) $2-\sqrt{3}$ e) None of these

Answer: d Difficulty: 1

4. Evaluate: tan 165°. (Use the fact that 165° = 210° - 45°.)
   a) $3+2\sqrt{3}$ b) $-2+\sqrt{3}$ c) $2-\sqrt{3}$
   d) $-3-2\sqrt{3}$ e) None of these

Answer: b Difficulty: 1

5. Evaluate: $\sin \frac{\pi}{12}$. $\left[\text{Use that fact that } \frac{\pi}{12} = \frac{\pi}{4} - \frac{\pi}{6}.\right]$
   a) $\frac{\sqrt{2}-1}{2}$ b) $\frac{\sqrt{6}-\sqrt{2}}{2}$ c) $\frac{1}{2}$
   d) $\frac{\sqrt{6}-\sqrt{2}}{4}$ e) None of these

Answer: d Difficulty: 1

6. Evaluate: cos 285°. (Use the fact that 285° = 330° - 45°.)
   a) $\frac{\sqrt{6}+\sqrt{2}}{4}$ b) $\frac{\sqrt{6}-\sqrt{2}}{4}$ c) $\frac{\sqrt{3}-\sqrt{2}}{2}$
   d) $-\frac{\sqrt{3}+\sqrt{2}}{2}$ e) None of these

Answer: b Difficulty: 1

7. Evaluate: $\tan 240°$. (Use the fact that $240° = 180 + 60°$.)
   a) $-\sqrt{3}$ b) $\dfrac{\sqrt{3}}{1-\sqrt{3}}$ c) 0 d) $\sqrt{3}$ e) None of these

   Answer: d Difficulty: 1

8. Simplify: $\dfrac{\tan 37° - \tan 13°}{1 + (\tan 37°)(\tan 13°)}$.
   a) $\tan 50°$ b) $\tan 24°$ c) $\cot 50°$ d) $\cot 24°$ e) None of these

   Answer: b Difficulty: 1

9. Simplify: $\sin 8x \cos 2x + \cos 8x \sin 2x$.
   a) $\sin 10x$ b) $\sin 6x$ c) $\cos 10x$
   d) $\cos 6x$ e) None of these

   Answer: a Difficulty: 1

SHORT ANSWER

10. Find the exact value: $\dfrac{\tan 325° - \tan 25°}{1 + \tan 325° \tan 25°}$.

    Answer:
    $-\sqrt{3}$
    Difficulty: 1

11. Simplify: $\dfrac{\tan 7x + \tan 5x}{1 - \tan 7x \tan 5x}$.

    Answer: $\tan 12x$ Difficulty: 1

MULTIPLE CHOICE

12. Simplify: $\sin 8x \cos 3x + \cos 8x \sin 3x$.
    a) $\sin 5x$ b) $\sin 11x$ c) $\cos 5x$
    d) $\cos 11x$ e) None of these

    Answer: b Difficulty: 1

13. Find the exact value: $\cos 146° \cos 11° + \sin 146° \sin 11°$.
    a) $-\dfrac{\sqrt{2}}{2}$ b) -0.9205 c) $\dfrac{\sqrt{2}}{2}$ d) 0.3907 e) None of these

    Answer: a Difficulty: 1

14. Simplify: $\frac{\tan(2x - 1) + \tan(1 - x)}{1 - \tan(2x - 1)\tan(1 - x)}$.

a) $-\tan x$ b) $\tan(3x - 3)$ c) $\tan(-2x^2 + 5x - 2)$
d) $\tan x$ e) None of these

Answer: d Difficulty: 1

15. Given $\tan u = \frac{3}{4}$, $0 < u < \frac{\pi}{2}$ and $\sec v = \frac{25}{24}$, $\frac{3\pi}{2} < v < 2\pi$, find $\sin(u + v)$.

a) $\frac{8}{25}$ b) $\frac{44}{125}$ c) $\frac{22}{25}$ d) $\frac{4}{5}$ e) None of these

Answer: b Difficulty: 1

16. Given $\sin u = -\frac{5}{13}$, $\pi < u < \frac{3\pi}{2}$ and $\csc v = \frac{\sqrt{10}}{3}$, $\frac{\pi}{2} < v < \pi$, find $\cos(u - v)$.

a) $\frac{-3\sqrt{10}}{130}$ b) $\frac{-27\sqrt{10}}{130}$ c) $\frac{27\sqrt{10}}{130}$
d) $\frac{-120 + 13\sqrt{10}}{130}$ e) None of these

Answer: a Difficulty: 1

17. Given $\cot u = \frac{2}{5}$, $0 < u < \frac{\pi}{2}$ and $\cos v = -\frac{3}{5}$, $\pi < v < \frac{3\pi}{2}$, find $\tan(u + v)$.

a) $\frac{7}{26}$ b) $\frac{23}{26}$ c) $-\frac{1}{2}$ d) $-\frac{23}{14}$ e) None of these

Answer: d Difficulty: 1

18. Simplify: $\sin\left(\frac{3\pi}{2} + x\right)$.

a) $-\sin x$ b) $-\cos x$ c) $\sin \frac{3\pi}{2} + \sin x$
d) $-\cos x - \sin x$ e) None of these

Answer: b Difficulty: 1

19. Simplify: $\sin\left(x - \frac{\pi}{6}\right)$.

a) $\frac{1}{2}\sin x + \frac{\sqrt{3}}{2}\cos x$ b) $\frac{\sqrt{3}}{2}\sin x \frac{1}{2}\cos x$ c) $\sin x - \frac{1}{2}$
d) $\frac{\sqrt{3}}{2}\sin x - \frac{1}{2}\cos x$ e) None of these

Answer: d Difficulty: 1

20. Simplify: $2\sin(x+\theta) - \sin(x-\theta)$.
 a) $3\cos x\sin\theta + \sin x\cos\theta$
 b) $\sin x\cos\theta + \cos x\sin\theta$
 c) $2\cos x\sin\theta + \sin x\cos\theta$
 d) $\sin x + 3\sin\theta$
 e) None of these

 Answer: a Difficulty: 1

21. Simplify: $\tan\left(\frac{\pi}{4}+\theta\right)$.
 a) $\dfrac{\sqrt{2}+2\tan\theta}{2-\sqrt{2}\tan\theta}$
 b) $\dfrac{1-\tan\theta}{1+\tan\theta}$
 c) 1
 d) $\dfrac{1+\tan\theta}{1-\tan\theta}$
 e) None of these

 Answer: d Difficulty: 1

22. Write the trigonometric expression as an algebraic expression: $\sin(\arctan x - \arccos 2x)$.
 a) $\dfrac{x}{\sqrt{1+x^2}} - \sqrt{1-4x^2}$
 b) $\dfrac{2x^2-\sqrt{1-4x^2}}{\sqrt{1+x^2}}$
 c) $\dfrac{-2x^2-1}{\sqrt{1+x^2}}$
 d) $\dfrac{2x - x\sqrt{1-4x^2}}{\sqrt{1+x^2}}$
 e) None of these

 Answer: a Difficulty: 2

23. Simplify: $\dfrac{\sin\left(\frac{\pi}{2}+h\right) - \sin\left(\frac{\pi}{2}\right)}{h}$.
 a) $\dfrac{\sin h}{h}$
 b) $\dfrac{\sin h - 1}{h}$
 c) 1
 d) $\dfrac{\cos h - 1}{h}$
 e) None of these

 Answer: d Difficulty: 2

24. Find all solutions in the interval $[0, 2\pi)$: $2\sin^2\left(x+\frac{\pi}{2}\right) = 1$.
 a) $\frac{\pi}{6}, \frac{5\pi}{6}$
 b) $\frac{\pi}{6}, \frac{\pi}{4}, \frac{3\pi}{4}, \frac{5\pi}{6}$
 c) $\frac{\pi}{4}, \frac{3\pi}{4}, \frac{5\pi}{4}, \frac{7\pi}{4}$
 d) $0, \pi$
 e) None of these

 Answer: c Difficulty: 2

SHORT ANSWER

25. Use the formula $a \sin B\theta + b \cos B\theta = \sqrt{a^2 + b^2} \sin(B\theta + c)$ where $c = \arctan \frac{b}{a}$, to write the expression $\sin 2\theta + \sqrt{3} \cos 2\theta$ in the form $\sqrt{a^2 + b^2} \sin(B\theta + c)$.

Answer:

$$\sin 2\theta + \sqrt{3} \cos 2\theta \Rightarrow a = 1,\ b = \sqrt{3} \Rightarrow \sqrt{a^2 + b^2} = 2$$

$$B = 2$$

$$c = \arctan \frac{\sqrt{3}}{1} \Rightarrow c = \frac{\pi}{3}$$

So, $\sin 2\theta + \sqrt{3} \cos 2\theta = 2 \sin\left(2\theta + \frac{\pi}{3}\right)$.

Difficulty: 2

26. Use the formula $a \sin B\theta + b \cos B\theta = \sqrt{a^2 + b^2}\sin(B\theta + c)$ where $c = \arctan \frac{b}{a}$, to write the expression $3 \sin\left(\theta + \frac{\pi}{6}\right)$ in the form $a \sin B\theta + b \cos B\theta$.

Answer:

$$3 \sin\left(\theta + \frac{\pi}{6}\right) = 3 \sin \theta \cos \frac{\pi}{6} + 3 \cos \theta \sin \frac{\pi}{6}$$

$$= 3 \sin \theta\left(\frac{\sqrt{3}}{2}\right) + 3 \cos \theta\left(\frac{1}{2}\right)$$

$$= \frac{3\sqrt{3}}{2} \sin \theta + \frac{3}{2} \cos \theta$$

Difficulty: 1

MULTIPLE CHOICE

27. Simplify: $\cos(2x - y) \cos y - \sin(2x - y) \sin y$.
a) $\sin 2x$
b) $\sin(2x - 2y)$
c) $\cos(2x - 2y)$
d) $\cos 2x$
e) None of these

Answer: d Difficulty: 1

28. Simplify: $\sin\left(\frac{4\pi}{3} - x\right) + \cos\left(x + \frac{5\pi}{6}\right)$.

a) $\cos x - \sin x$ b) $-\sqrt{3}\cos x$ c) $\sin x - \sqrt{3}\cos x$
d) $\sin x$ e) None of these

Answer: b Difficulty: 1

SHORT ANSWER

29. Simplify: $\tan\left(\theta + \frac{\pi}{3}\right) + \tan\left(\theta - \frac{\pi}{3}\right)$.

Answer:

$$\tan\left(\theta + \frac{\pi}{3}\right) + \tan\left(\theta - \frac{\pi}{3}\right) = \frac{\tan\theta + \tan\frac{\pi}{3}}{1 - \tan\theta\tan\frac{\pi}{3}} + \frac{\tan\theta - \tan\frac{\pi}{3}}{1 + \tan\theta\tan\frac{\pi}{3}}$$

$$= \frac{\tan\theta + \sqrt{3}}{1 - \sqrt{3}\tan\theta} + \frac{\tan\theta - \sqrt{3}}{1 + \sqrt{3}\tan\theta}$$

$$= \frac{\left(\tan\theta + \sqrt{3}\right)\left(1 + \sqrt{3}\tan\theta\right) + \left(\tan\theta - \sqrt{3}\right)\left(1 - \sqrt{3}\tan\theta\right)}{\left(1 - \sqrt{3}\tan\theta\right)\left(1 + \sqrt{3}\tan\theta\right)}$$

$$= \frac{8\tan\theta}{1 - 3\tan^2\theta}$$

Difficulty: 2

MULTIPLE CHOICE

30. Simplify: $\cos(x + y)\cos y + \sin(x + y)\sin y$.

a) $\cos x + \sin x$ b) $\cos x\cos^2 y + \sin x\sin^2 y$
c) $\cos x$ d) $\cos x\ 2\sin x\sin y\cos y$
e) None of these

Answer: c Difficulty: 1

31. Find all solutions in the interval $[0, 2\pi)$: $\sin\left(x + \frac{\pi}{4}\right) + \sin\left(x - \frac{\pi}{4}\right) = 1$.

a) $\frac{\pi}{4}, \frac{3\pi}{4}$ b) $\frac{\pi}{4}, \frac{\pi}{2}$ c) $\frac{\pi}{6}, \frac{5\pi}{6}$ d) $\frac{\pi}{4}$ e) None of these

Answer: a Difficulty: 1

32. Simplify, then find all solutions in the interval $0 \le x < 2\pi$: $\cos(x - y)\cos y - \sin(x - y)\sin y = 0$.
a) No solutions
b) $\frac{\pi}{2}, \frac{3\pi}{2}$
c) $0, \pi$
d) $0, \frac{\pi}{2}, \pi, \frac{3\pi}{2}$
e) None of these

Answer: b Difficulty: 2

SHORT ANSWER

33. Find all solutions in the interval $[0, 2\pi)$: $3\sin(2t - \pi) = 3$.

Answer:

$$3\sin(2t - \pi) = 3$$

$$\sin(2t - \pi) = 1$$

$$\sin 2t \cos\pi - \cos 2t \sin \pi = 1$$

$$\sin 2t(-1) - \cos 2t(0) = 1$$

$$-\sin 2t = 1$$

$$\sin 2t = -1$$

$$2t = \frac{3\pi}{2} + 2n\pi$$

$$t = \frac{3\pi}{4} + n\pi \Rightarrow t = \frac{3\pi}{4}, \frac{7\pi}{4}$$

Difficulty: 1

34. Verify the following identity used in calculus: $\frac{\sin(x+h) - \sin x}{h} = \frac{\sin x(\cos h - 1)}{h} + \frac{\cos x \sin h}{h}$.

Answer:

$$\frac{\sin(x + h) - \sin x}{h} = \frac{\sin x \cos h + \cos x \sin h - \sin x}{h}$$

$$= \frac{\sin x \cos h - \sin x + \cos x \sin h}{h}$$

$$= \frac{\sin x(\cos h - 1) + \cos x \sin h}{h}$$

$$= \frac{\sin x(\cos h - 1)}{h} + \frac{\cos x \sin h}{h}$$

Difficulty: 1

35. The drive system of a compact disc player uses an equation $\tan x = \frac{\sin y}{r + \cos y}$, where r is the ratio of two gears. Show that $r = \frac{\sin(y - x)}{\sin x}$.

Answer:

$$\tan x = \frac{\sin y}{r + \cos y}$$

$$\tan x(r + \cos y) = \sin y$$

$$r + \cos y = \frac{\sin y}{\tan x}$$

$$r = \frac{\sin y}{\tan x} - \cos y$$

$$= \frac{\sin y}{\frac{\sin x}{\cos x}} - \cos y$$

$$= \sin y \frac{\cos x}{\sin x} - \cos y$$

$$= \frac{\sin y \cos x - \cos y \sin x}{\sin x}$$

$$= \frac{\sin(y - x)}{\sin x}$$

Difficulty: 1

36. For picking up heavy machinery, a type of jack called a screw jack can be used. The formula $aF = Wr \tan(x - \theta)$ is used, where F is the effort necessary to obtain equilibrium with pitch angle x and load W. If the pitch angle, x, is $\pi/4$, express F in terms of $\tan \theta$.

Answer:

$$aF = Wr \tan\left[\frac{\pi}{4} - \theta\right]$$

$$aF = Wr \frac{\left[\tan \frac{\pi}{4} - \tan \theta\right]}{\left[1 + \tan \frac{\pi}{4} \tan \theta\right]}$$

$$aF = Wr \frac{1 - \tan \theta}{1 + \tan \theta}$$

$$F = \frac{Wr}{a} \cdot \frac{1 - \tan \theta}{1 + \tan \theta}$$

Difficulty: 1

37. Verify the identity algebraically and use a graphing utility to confirm it graphically.
$\sin(\pi - x) = \sin x$

Answer:

$$\sin(\pi - x) = \sin \pi \cos x - \cos \pi \sin x$$
$$= (0) \cos x - (-1) \sin x$$
$$= \sin x$$

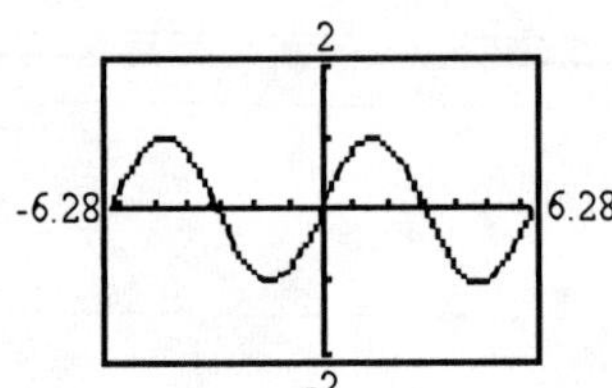

Difficulty: 1 Key 1: T

38. Verify the identity algebraically and use a graphing utility to confirm it graphically.
$\cos\left(\frac{\pi}{2} + x\right) = -\sin x$

Answer:

$$\cos\left(\frac{\pi}{2} + x\right) = \cos \frac{\pi}{2} \cos x - \sin \frac{\pi}{2} \sin x$$
$$= (0) \cos x - (1) \sin x$$
$$= -\sin x$$

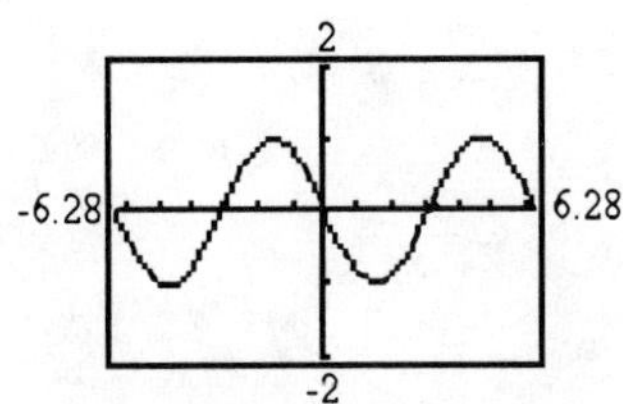

Difficulty: 1 Key 1: T

39. Use a graphing utility to approximate the solutions in the interval $[0, 2\pi)$.
$\sin\left(x + \frac{\pi}{2}\right) - \sin\left(x - \frac{\pi}{2}\right) = 1$

Answer:

1.047, 5.236; Exact: $\frac{\pi}{3}, \frac{5\pi}{3}$

Difficulty: 1 Key 1: T

40. Use a graphing utility to approximate the solutions in the interval $[0, 2\pi)$.

$$\cos\left(x - \frac{\pi}{4}\right) + \sin\left(x + \frac{\pi}{4}\right) = 1$$

Answer:

1.0833, 6.021; Exact: $\frac{7\pi}{12}, \frac{23\pi}{12}$

Difficulty: 1 Key 1: T

41. Simplify: $\sin\left(x + \frac{3\pi}{2}\right)\cos x$.

Answer:

$-\cos^2 x$

Difficulty: 1

42. Simplify: $\cos\left(x + \frac{3\pi}{2}\right)\sin x$.

Answer:

$\sin^2 x$

Difficulty: 1

Chapter 055: Multiple-Angle and Product-to-Sum Formulas

MULTIPLE CHOICE

1. Find all solutions in the interval $[0, 2\pi)$: $\cos 2x + \sin x = 0$.
   a) $0, \frac{\pi}{4}, \frac{3\pi}{4}$ b) $\frac{\pi}{2}, \frac{7\pi}{6}, \frac{11\pi}{6}$ c) $\frac{\pi}{6}, \frac{5\pi}{6}, \frac{3\pi}{2}$
   d) $0, \frac{\pi}{4}, \frac{3\pi}{4}, \frac{5\pi}{4}, \frac{7\pi}{4}$ e) None of these

   Answer: b Difficulty: 1

2. Find all solutions in the interval $[0, 2\pi)$: $\sin 2x + \sin x = 0$.
   a) $\frac{\pi}{2}, \frac{3\pi}{2}, \frac{2\pi}{3}, \frac{4\pi}{3}$ b) $0, \frac{\pi}{3}, \pi, \frac{5\pi}{3}$ c) $0, \frac{\pi}{3}$
   d) $0, \pi, \frac{2\pi}{3}, \frac{4\pi}{3}$ e) None of these

   Answer: d Difficulty: 1

3. Find all solutions in the interval $[0, 2\pi)$: $\cos^2 x - \cos 2x = 0$.
   a) $0, \frac{\pi}{2}, \frac{3\pi}{2}$ b) $0, \pi$ c) ± 1
   d) $\frac{\pi}{6}, \frac{5\pi}{6}, \frac{7\pi}{6}, \frac{11\pi}{6}$ e) None of these

   Answer: b Difficulty: 1

4. Find all solutions in the interval $[0, 2\pi)$: $2 \sin 3x \cos 3x = 1$.
   a) $\frac{\pi}{18}, \frac{\pi}{9}$ b) $\frac{\pi}{12}$ c) $\frac{\pi}{12}, \frac{5\pi}{12}, \frac{3\pi}{4}, \frac{13\pi}{12}, \frac{17\pi}{12}, \frac{7\pi}{4}$
   d) $\frac{\pi}{18}, \frac{\pi}{9}, \frac{5\pi}{18}, \frac{5\pi}{9}$ e) None of these

   Answer: c Difficulty: 1

SHORT ANSWER

5. Rewrite the function and sketch its graph:
   $f(x) = 6 \cos^2 x - 3$.

   Answer:

   $f(x) = 3(2 \cos^2 x - 1)$

   $= 3 \cos 2x$

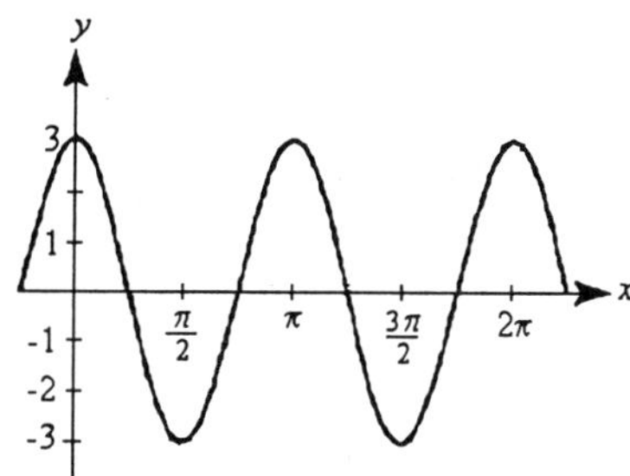

Difficulty: 1

6. Rewrite the function and sketch its graph:
$g(x) = \left(1 - \sqrt{2}\sin x\right)\left(1 + \sqrt{2}\sin x\right).$

Answer:

$$\begin{aligned} g(x) &= \left(1 - \sqrt{2}\sin x\right)\left(1 + \sqrt{2}\sin x\right) \\ &= 1 - 2\sin^2 x \\ &= \cos 2x \end{aligned}$$

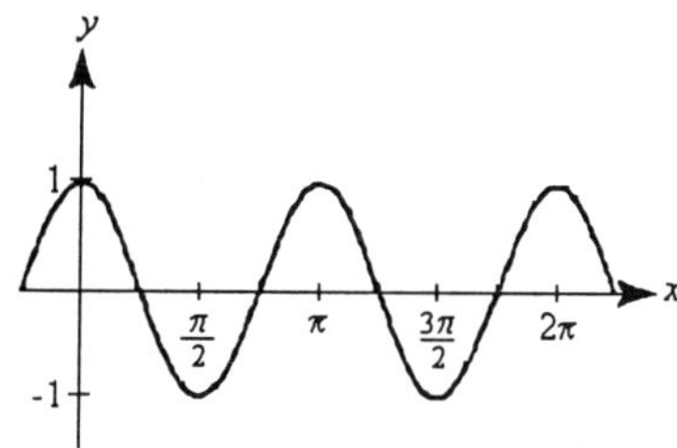

Difficulty: 1

MULTIPLE CHOICE

7. Given $\cos u = -\frac{4}{7}$, find $\cos 2u$. $\left[\text{Assume } \pi < u < \frac{3\pi}{2}.\right]$

a) $\frac{\sqrt{33}}{7}$ b) $-\frac{17}{49}$ c) $-\frac{4\sqrt{33}}{14}$ d) $-\frac{33}{49}$ e) None of these

Answer: b Difficulty: 1

8. Given $\cos \theta = -\frac{7}{9}$ and $\tan \theta < 0$, find $\sin 2\theta$.

a) $-\frac{14}{9}$ b) $-\frac{56\sqrt{2}}{81}$ c) $-\frac{32}{81}$ d) $\frac{49}{18}$ e) None of these

Answer: b Difficulty: 1

9. Given $\tan\theta = \frac{3}{4}$ and $\sin\theta < 0$, find $\tan 2\theta$.

a) $\frac{1}{3}$ b) $\frac{\sqrt{5}}{3}$ c) $\frac{5}{9}$ d) $\frac{24}{7}$ e) None of these

Answer: d Difficulty: 1

10. Given $\sin x = -\frac{1}{8}$ an $\tan x < 0$, find $\sin 2x$.

a) $-\frac{3\sqrt{7}}{32}$ b) $-\frac{\sqrt{65}}{32}$ c) $\frac{3\sqrt{7}}{32}$ d) $-\frac{1}{4}$ e) None of these

Answer: a Difficulty: 1

11. Rewrite in terms of the first power of the cosine: $\sin^4 2x$.

a) $\frac{1}{2}(1 - \cos 4x)$
b) $\frac{1}{4}(1 - 2\cos 4x + \cos 16x)$
c) $\frac{1}{4}(1 - \cos 4x)$
d) $\frac{1}{8}(3 - 4\cos 4x + \cos 8x)$
e) None of these

Answer: d Difficulty: 1

12. Rewrite in terms of the fist power of the cosine: $\sin^2 x \cos^2 2x$.

a) $\frac{1}{4}(1 - \cos 2x + \cos 4x - \cos 2x \cos 4x)$
b) $\frac{1}{4}(1 - \cos 2x + \cos 4x - \cos 8x)$
c) $\frac{1}{4}(1 + \cos 2x - \cos 8x)$
d) $\frac{1}{4}(1 + \cos 2x - \cos 4x - \cos 2x \cos 4x)$
e) None of these

Answer: a Difficulty: 1

SHORT ANSWER

13. Rewrite in terms of the first power of the cosine: $\cos^2 2x \sin^2 2x$.

Answer:
$\frac{1 - \cos 8x}{8}$

Difficulty: 1

14. Rewrite in terms of the first power of the cosine: $\tan^4 2x$.

Answer:
$\frac{3 - 4\cos 4x + \cos 8x}{3 + 4\cos 4x + \cos 8x}$

Difficulty: 1

MULTIPLE CHOICE

15. Find the exact value of $\sin \frac{7\pi}{12}$. $\left[\text{Use the fact that } \frac{1}{2}\left(\frac{7\pi}{6}\right) = \frac{7\pi}{12}.\right]$

a) $\frac{\sqrt{2 - \sqrt{3}}}{2}$　　b) $\frac{\sqrt{2 + \sqrt{3}}}{2}$　　c) $-\frac{\sqrt{2 + \sqrt{3}}}{2}$

d) $-\frac{\sqrt{2 - \sqrt{3}}}{2}$　　e) None of these

Answer: b Difficulty: 1

16. Find the exact value of cos 157° 30'. $\left[\text{Use the fact that } \frac{1}{2}(315°) = 157° 30'.\right]$

a) $\frac{\sqrt{2 + \sqrt{2}}}{2}$　　b) $-\frac{\sqrt{1 + \sqrt{2}}}{2}$　　c) $-\frac{\sqrt{2 - \sqrt{2}}}{2}$

d) $-\frac{\sqrt{2 + \sqrt{2}}}{2}$　　e) None of these

Answer: d Difficulty: 1

17. Given $\sin u = -\frac{8}{13}$, find $\cos \frac{u}{2}$. $\left[\text{Assume } \frac{3\pi}{2} < u < 2\pi.\right]$

a) $-\sqrt{\frac{13 - \sqrt{105}}{26}}$　　b) $-\sqrt{\frac{13 + \sqrt{105}}{26}}$　　c) $-\sqrt{\frac{13 - \sqrt{233}}{26}}$

d) $\sqrt{\frac{13 + \sqrt{105}}{26}}$　　e) None of these

Answer: b Difficulty: 2

18. Given $\tan u = -\frac{1}{3}$, and $\sin u < 0$, find $\sin \frac{u}{2}$. (Assume $0 \leq u < 2\pi$.)

a) $-\sqrt{\frac{10 + 3\sqrt{10}}{20}}$　　b) $\sqrt{\frac{10 - 3\sqrt{10}}{20}}$　　c) $\sqrt{\frac{10 + 3\sqrt{10}}{20}}$

d) $-\sqrt{\frac{10 - 3\sqrt{10}}{20}}$　　e) None of these

Answer: b Difficulty: 2

SHORT ANSWER

19. Given $\cos x = -\frac{3}{7}$ and $\frac{\pi}{2} < x < \pi$, find $\cos \frac{x}{2}$.

Answer:

$\frac{\sqrt{14}}{7}$

Difficulty: 1

20. Given $\cos x = \frac{2}{3}$ and $\frac{3\pi}{2} < x < 2\pi$, find $\cos \frac{x}{2}$.

Answer:

$-\frac{\sqrt{30}}{6}$

Difficulty: 1

MULTIPLE CHOICE

21. Simplify: $y^2 = \sqrt{\frac{1 - \cos 16x}{2}}$.

a) $y^2 = \sin 32x$ b) $y^2 = \cos 32x$ c) $y^2 = \sin 8x$
d) $y^2 = \cos 8x$ e) None of these

Answer: c Difficulty: 1

22. Simplify: $\sqrt{\frac{4 + 4 \cos 2x}{2}}$.

a) $2 \cos x$ b) $\cos 4x$ c) $2 \sin x$
d) $\sqrt{2} \cos x$ e) None of these

Answer: a Difficulty: 1

23. Rewrite as a sum: $9 \sin 3x \cos 7x$.

a) $\frac{9}{2}(\cos 4x + \cos 10x)$ b) $\frac{9}{2}(\sin 10x + \sin 4x)$
c) $\frac{9}{2}(\cos 4x - \cos 10x)$ d) $\frac{9}{2}(\sin 10x - \sin 4x)$
e) None of these

Answer: d Difficulty: 1

24. Rewrite as a sum: $\sin 3x \cos 4y$.
   a) $\frac{1}{2}[\sin(3x + 4y) + \sin(3x - 4y)]$ b) $\frac{1}{2}[\sin(3x + 4y) - \sin(3x - 4y)]$
   c) $2[\cos(3x + 4y) + \cos(3x - 4y)]$ d) $2[\sin(3x - 4y) + \cos(3x - 4y)]$

   Answer: a Difficulty: 1

25. Rewrite as a sum: $\sin 7x \sin 3x$.
   a) $\frac{1}{2}(\sin 4x + \cos 10x)$ b) $\frac{1}{2}(\sin 10x + \sin 4x)$
   c) $\frac{1}{2}(\cos 4x - \cos 10x)$ d) $\sin 2x + \cos 5x$
   e) None of these

   Answer: c Difficulty: 1

SHORT ANSWER

26. Rewrite as a sum: $\frac{1}{4} \cos 12x \cos 4x$.

   Answer:
   $\frac{\cos 8x + \cos 16x}{8}$

   Difficulty: 1

27. Rewrite as a sum: $3 \cos 5x \sin(-2x)$.

   Answer:
   $\frac{3(\sin 3x - \sin 7x)}{2}$

   Difficulty: 1

MULTIPLE CHOICE

28. Rewrite as a product: $\sin x + \sin 3x$.
   a) $2 \sin 2x \cos x$ b) $-2 \sin x \cos 2x$ c) $-2 \cos 2x \cos x$
   d) $2 \sin 2x \sin x$ e) None of these

   Answer: a Difficulty: 1

29. Rewrite as a product: $\sin 7\theta - \sin 3\theta$.
   a) $2 \sin 5\theta \cos 2\theta$ b) $2 \cos 5\theta \sin 2\theta$ c) $2 \cos 5\theta \cos 2\theta$
   d) $-2 \sin 5\theta \cos 2\theta$ e) None of these

   Answer: b Difficulty: 1

SHORT ANSWER

30. Rewrite as a product: $\cos(x + 2y) - \cos(x - 2y)$.

Answer: $-2\sin x \sin 2y$ Difficulty: 1

MULTIPLE CHOICE

31. Rewrite as a sum: $\sin\left[\frac{5x + 3y}{2}\right] \cos\left[\frac{5x - 3y}{2}\right]$.

a) $\frac{1}{2}(\cos 5x - \cos 3y)$

b) $\frac{1}{2}(\sin 5x - \sin 3y)$

c) $\frac{1}{2}(\cos 5x + \cos 3y)$

d) $\frac{1}{2}(\sin 5x + \sin 3y)$

e) None of these

Answer: d Difficulty: 1

SHORT ANSWER

32. Find all solutions in the interval $[0, 2\pi)$: $\sin 5x + \sin x = \sin 3x$.

Answer:

$$\sin 5x - \sin 3x + \sin x = 0$$

$$2 \cos\left[\frac{5x + 3x}{2}\right] \sin\left[\frac{5x - 3x}{2}\right] + \sin x = 0$$

$$2 \cos 4x \sin x + \sin x = 0$$

$$\sin x(2 \cos 4x + 1) = 0$$

$$\sin x = 0 \quad \text{or} \quad 2 \cos 4x = -1$$

$$x = 0, \pi \qquad \cos 4x = -\frac{1}{2}$$

$$4x = \frac{2\pi}{3}, \frac{4\pi}{3}$$

$$x = \frac{\pi}{6}, \frac{\pi}{3}, \frac{2\pi}{3}, \frac{5\pi}{6}, \frac{7\pi}{6}, \frac{4\pi}{3}, \frac{5\pi}{3}, \frac{11\pi}{6}$$

$$x = 0, \frac{\pi}{6}, \frac{\pi}{3}, \frac{2\pi}{3}, \frac{5\pi}{6}, \pi, \frac{7\pi}{6}, \frac{4\pi}{3}, \frac{5\pi}{3}, \frac{11\pi}{6}$$

Difficulty: 2

33. Find all solutions in the interval $[0, 2\pi)$: $\cos 4x + \cos 2x = 0$.

Answer:

$$\cos 4x + \cos 2x = 0$$

$$2\cos\left(\frac{4x + 2x}{2}\right)\cos\left(\frac{4x - 2x}{2}\right) = 0$$

$$2\cos 3x \cos x = 0$$

$$\cos 3x \cos x = 0$$

$\cos 3x = 0$ or $\cos x = 0$

$3x = \frac{\pi}{2}, \frac{3\pi}{2}, \frac{5\pi}{2}, \frac{7\pi}{2}, \frac{11\pi}{2}$ $\quad x = \frac{\pi}{2}, \frac{3\pi}{2}$

$x = \frac{\pi}{6}, \frac{\pi}{2}, \frac{5\pi}{6}, \frac{7\pi}{6}, \frac{3\pi}{2}, \frac{11\pi}{6}$

Difficulty: 1

34. The expression $\sqrt{\sin^2 x + (1 - \cos x)^2}$ is used in the study of gases. Simplify this expression using a half-angle formula.

Answer:

$$\sqrt{\sin^2 x + (1 - \cos x)^2} = \sqrt{\sin^2 x + 1 - 2\cos x + \cos^2 x}$$

$$= \sqrt{\sin^2 x + \cos^2 x + 1 - 2\cos x}$$

$$= \sqrt{1 + 1 - 2\cos x}$$

$$= \sqrt{2 - 2\cos x}$$

$$= \sqrt{2(1 - \cos x)}$$

$$= \sqrt{\frac{2}{2} 2(1 - \cos x)}$$

$$= \sqrt{\frac{4(1 - \cos x)}{2}}$$

$$= 2\sqrt{\frac{1 - \cos x}{2}}$$

$$= 2\sin\left(\frac{x}{2}\right)$$

Difficulty: 1

35. In the study of electronics the function $f(t) = \sin(200t + \pi) + \sin(200t + \pi)$ is used. First simplify the function using a sum-to-product formula, then graph the simplified function.

Answer:

$$f(x) = \sin(200t + \pi) + \sin(200t - \pi)$$

$$= 2\sin\left[\frac{(200t + \pi) + (200t - \pi)}{2}\right]\cos\left[\frac{(200t + \pi) - (200t - \pi)}{2}\right]$$

$$= 2(\sin 200t)(\cos \pi)$$

$$= 2(\sin 200t)(-1)$$

$$= -2\sin 200t$$

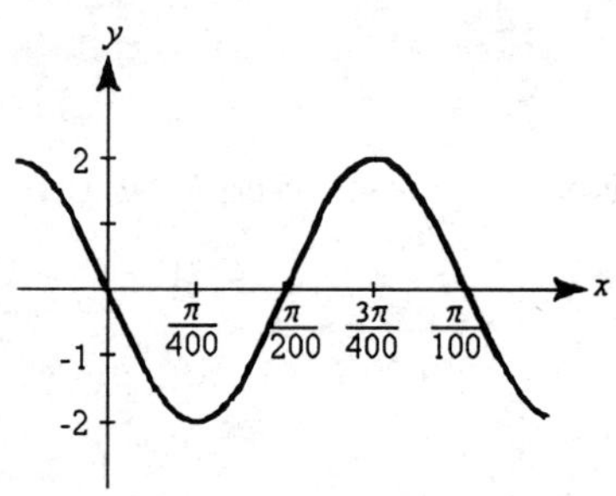

Difficulty: 1

36. Find the exact zeros of the function in the interval $[0, 2\pi)$. Use a graphing utility to graph the function and verify the zeros.
$f(x) = \sin 4x + \sin 2x$

Answer:

$x = 0, \frac{\pi}{3}, \frac{\pi}{2}, \frac{2\pi}{3}, \pi, \frac{4\pi}{3}, \frac{3\pi}{2}, \frac{5\pi}{3}$

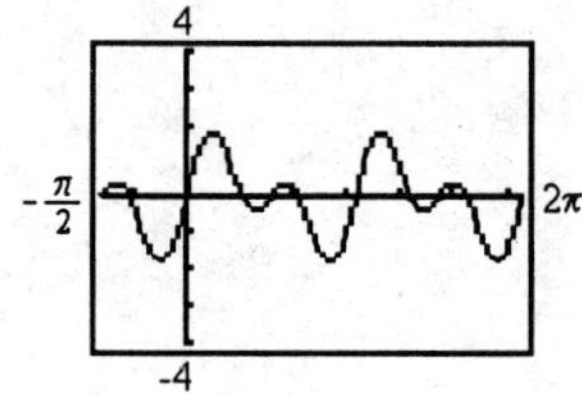

Difficulty: 2 Key 1: T

37. Find the exact zeros of the function in the interval $[0, 2\pi)$. Use a graphing utility to graph the function and verify the zeros.
    $f(x) = \cos 2x + \cos 4x$

Answer:
$x = \frac{\pi}{6}, \frac{\pi}{2}, \frac{5\pi}{6}, \frac{7\pi}{6}, \frac{3\pi}{2}, \frac{11\pi}{6}$

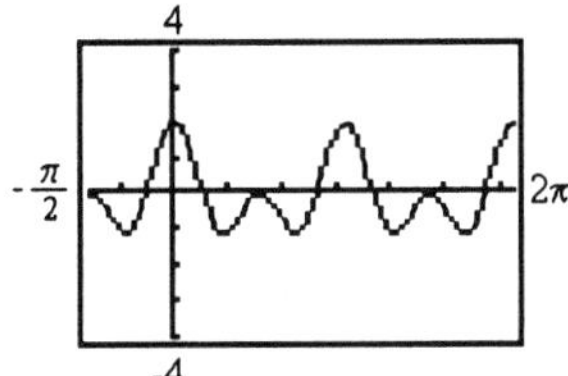

Difficulty: 2 Key 1: T

38. Use a graphing utility to graph the function and approximate the maximum and minimum points on the graph in the interval $[0, 2\pi)$. Then solve the trigonometric equation and verify that its solutions are the x-coordinates of the maximum and minimum points of f.

Function	Trigonometric Equation
$f(x) = 2 \sin 2x + \cos x$	$4 \cos 2x - \sin x = 0$

Answer:

Maximum points: (0.70, 2.74)(4.02, 1.33)

Minimum points: (2.44, -2.74), (5.40, -1.33)

Solutions to equation: $\sin x = \frac{-1 \pm \sqrt{129}}{16}$

$x \approx 0.70, 2.44, 5.40, 4.02$

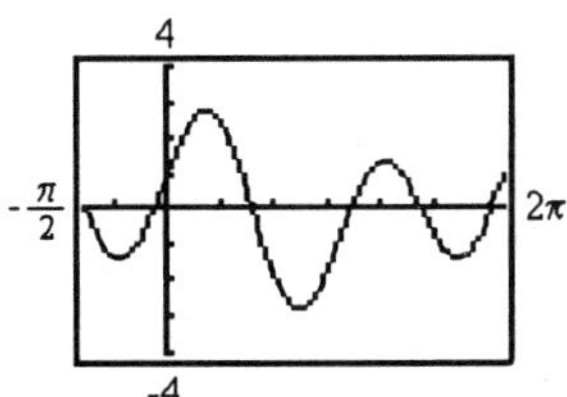

Difficulty: 2 Key 1: T

39. Use a graphing utility to graph the function and approximate the maximum and minimum points on the graph in the interval $[0, 2\pi)$. Then solve the trigonometric equation and verify that its solutions are the x-coordinates of the maximum and minimum points of f.

Function	Trigonometric Equation
$f(x) = \cos 2x + \cos x$	$-2 \sin 2x - \sin x = 0$

Answer:

Maximum points: (0, 2), (3.14, 0)

Minimum points: (1.82, -1.33), (4.48, -1.13)

Solutions to equation: $\sin x = 0$, $\cos x = -\frac{1}{4}$

$x \approx 0, 1.82, 3.14, 4.46$

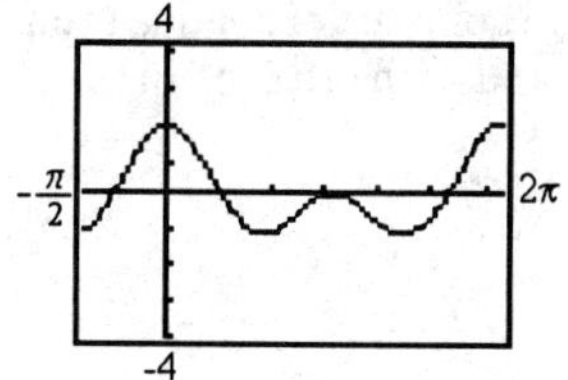

Difficulty: 2 Key 1: T

Chapter 061: Law of Sines

MULTIPLE CHOICE

1. Given a triangle with $A = 41°$, $B = 72°$, and $a = 15$, find c.
a) 19.6 b) 10.7 c) 21.0 d) 7.8 e) None of these

Answer: c Difficulty: 1

2. Given a triangle with $B = 87°$, $C = 24°$, and $a = 113$, find b.
a) 120.9 b) 142.7 c) 49.2 d) 94.4 e) None of these

Answer: a Difficulty: 1

3. Given a triangle with $A = 20°$, $C = 110°$, and $a = 5$, find b.
a) 2.2 b) 50.0 c) 11.2 d) 13.7 e) None of these

Answer: c Difficulty: 1

4. Given a triangle with $A = 10°$, $B = 30°$, and $b = 14$, find c.
a) 27.4 b) 18.0 c) 65.3 d) 34.1 e) None of these

Answer: b Difficulty: 1

5. Given a triangle with $A = 42°$, $C = 88°$, and $a = 71$, find b.
a) 87.6 b) 50.0 c) 20.3 d) 81.3 e) None of these

Answer: d Difficulty: 1

6. Given a triangle with $C = 72°$, $A = 15°$, and $b = 342.6$, find a.
a) 1258.92 b) 88.79 c) 6323.1 d) 326.28 e) None of these

Answer: b Difficulty: 1

SHORT ANSWER

7. Given a triangle with $A = 39°$, $B = 106°$, and $c = 78$, find a.

Answer: 85.6 Difficulty: 1

8. Given a triangle with $A = 102°$, $B = 23°$, and $c = 576.1$, find a.

Answer: 678.9 Difficulty: 1

9. Given a triangle with $A = 60°$, $B = 49°$, and $c = 5396$, find a, b, and C.

Answer: $C = 70°$, $a = 5022.3$, $b = 4333.8$ Difficulty: 1

MULTIPLE CHOICE

10. Given a triangle with $A = 47°$, $B = 63°$, and $c = 123$, find a.
a) 88.6 b) 95.7 c) 82.6 d) 112.1 e) None of these

Answer: b Difficulty: 1

11. Given a triangle with $a = 12$, $b = 19$, and $A = 82°$, find c.
a) 16.2, 1.4 b) 4.3 c) No solution
d) 7.6 e) None of these

Answer: c Difficulty: 1

12. Given a triangle with $a = 123$, $c = 86$, and $C = 52°$, find b.
a) No solution b) 96.9 c) 71.2, 8.4
d) 74.4 e) None of these

Answer: a Difficulty: 1

13. Given a triangle with $b = 120$, $c = 142$, and $B = 78°$, find a.
a) 138.9 b) 71.6, 113.4 c) 157.8
d) No solution e) None of these

Answer: d Difficulty: 1

14. Given a triangle with $a = 27$, $b = 46$, and $A = 71°$, find B.
a) No solution b) 1.6° c) 100.0°
d) 87.2°, 102.1° e) None of these

Answer: a Difficulty: 1

15. Given a triangle with $a = 83$, $b = 98$, and $A = 110°$, find C.
a) 57° b) 41° c) No solution
d) 62°, 28° e) None of these

Answer: c Difficulty: 1

16. Given a triangle with $C = 80.3°$, $c = 52.7$, and $b = 41.6$, find B.
a) 77.7° b) 82.4° c) 51.1° d) 0.8° e) None of these

Answer: c Difficulty: 1

17. Given a triangle with $a = 18$, $b = 23$, and $B = 97°$, find C.
a) 51.0° b) 32.0° c) 39.2° d) 13.8° e) None of these

Answer: b Difficulty: 1

18. Given a triangle with $a = 56$, $b = 71$, and $B = 100°$, find c.
a) 35.0 b) 44.2 c) 47.9 d) 51.1 e) None of these

Answer: a Difficulty: 1

19. Given a triangle with $b = 71$, $c = 63$, and $B = 110°$, find a.
a) 38.7 b) 21.2 c) 15.4 d) 17.6 e) None of these

Answer: d Difficulty: 1

20. Given a triangle with $a = 17$, $c = 51$, and $C = 100°$, find b.
a) 47.9 b) 45.2 c) 41.7 d) 35.2 e) None of these

Answer: b Difficulty: 1

21. Given a triangle with $a = 146$, $b = 148$, and $A = 78°$, find B. If there are two solutions, find both B_1 and B_2.
a) 82.5°, 97.5° b) 4.5°, 19.5° c) 82.5°
d) No solution e) None of these

Answer: a Difficulty: 1

22. Given a triangle with $a = 112$, $b = 130$, and $A = 56°$, find c. If there are two solutions, find both c_1 and c_2.
a) 61.2 b) 42.2, 103.2 c) 98.1, 103.2
d) No solution e) None of these

Answer: b Difficulty: 2

23. Given a triangle with $B = 61°$, $c = 18$, and $b = 17$, find A. If there are two solutions, find both A_1 and A_2.
a) 6.8°, 173.2° b) 51.2° c) 112.2°
d) 6.8°, 51.2° e) None of these

Answer: d Difficulty: 1

24. Given a triangle with $A = 74°$, $a = 59.2$, and $c = 60.3$, find the two possible values of B.
a) 78.3°, 101.7° b) 4.3°, 27.7° c) 73.7°, 106.3°
d) 32.3°, 0.3° e) None of these

Answer: b Difficulty: 1

SHORT ANSWER

25. Given a triangle with $B = 56°$, $a = 98$ and $b = 85$, find the two possible values of C

Answer: $C = 51.1°$ or 16.9° Difficulty: 1

MULTIPLE CHOICE

26. Given a triangle with $A = 12°$, $a = 12$, and $c = 37$, find the two possible values of b.
a) 3.04, 14.95 b) 44.30, 45.40 c) 7.57, 10.85
d) 26.98, 45.40 e) None of these

Answer: d Difficulty: 2

27. Given a triangle with $c = 24.19$, $a = 91.6$, and $B = 37°$, find the area.
a) 1769.6 square units b) 666.8 square units
c) 1107.9 square units d) 1333.5 square units
e) None of these

Answer: b Difficulty: 1

28. Given a triangle with $a = 72$, $b = 51$, and $A = 27°$, find the area.
   a) 833.5 square units
   b) 1315.3 square units
   c) 1635.9 square units
   d) 2630.6 square units
   e) None of these

   Answer: b Difficulty: 1

29. Given a triangle with $A = 98°$, $a = 27$, and $b = 16$, find the area.
   a) 155.56 square units
   b) 149.86 square units
   c) 311.11 square units
   d) 213.90 square units
   e) None of these

   Answer: a Difficulty: 1

SHORT ANSWER

30. Given a triangle with $A = 37°$, $B = 78°$, and $c = 250$, find the area.

   Answer: 20,297.5 square units Difficulty: 2

31. Given a triangle with $A = 71°$, $b = 10$, and $c = 19$, find the area.

   Answer: 89.8 square units Difficulty: 1

MULTIPLE CHOICE

32. Given a triangle with $c = 634$, $b = 600$, and $B = 78°$, find the number of solutions for a.
   a) 0
   b) 1
   c) 2
   d) 3
   e) 6

   Answer: a Difficulty: 1

SHORT ANSWER

33. Determine the number of solutions for each of the following triangles.
   a) $C = 58°$, $c = 50$, $a = 67$
   b) $A = 107°$, $b = 17$, $a = 25$
   c) $B = 27°$, $a = 78$, $b = 28$

   Answer:
   a) 0 solutions
   b) 1 solution
   c) 0 solutions
   Difficulty: 1

MULTIPLE CHOICE

34. A television antenna sits on the roof. Two 78-foot guy wires are positioned on opposite sides of the antenna. The angle of elevation each makes with the ground is 23°. How far apart are the ends of the two guy wires?
a) 71.8 feet b) 76.3 feet c) 143.6 feet
d) 152.6 feet e) None of these

Answer: c Difficulty: 1

SHORT ANSWER

35. From fire tower A a fire with a bearing N 78° E is sighted. The same fire is sighted from tower B at N 51° W. Tower B is 70 miles east of tower A. How far is it from tower A to the fire?

Answer: 56.7 miles Difficulty: 2

36. A surveyor wishes to find the distance from a rock on the east side of a river to a tree on the opposite bank. On the east side of the river he locates a second rock 135 feet from the first one. From each rock he measures the angle between the line connecting the two rocks and the tree. The angle from the first rock is 87° and from the second rock is 82°. Find the desired distance.

Answer: 700.6 feet Difficulty: 2

37. Two game wardens are known to be 1.5 miles apart and both observe a grizzly bear. The bear is N 22.5° E of Warden Wain and N 28.8° W of Warden Ryan. How far is each commissioner from the bear?

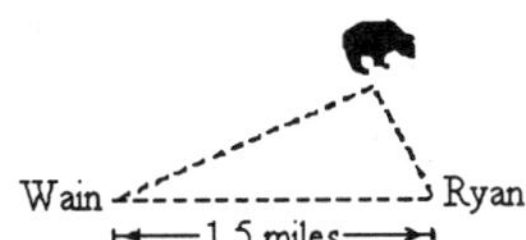

Answer:
1.68 miles from Warden Ryan and
1.78 miles from Warden Wain

Difficulty: 2

38. A room 16 feet on a side is to be added onto the side of a house. The angle of elevation of the present roof is 26.5°, and the angle of elevation of the new roof is to be 18.0°. How far along the old roof will the new roof reach?

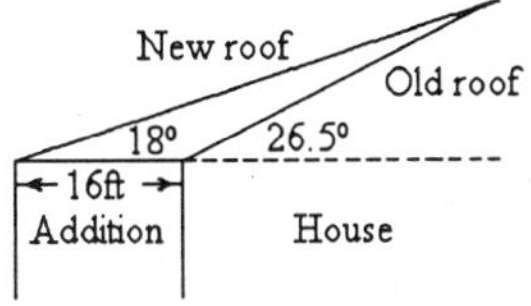

Answer: 33.5 feet Difficulty: 2

39. A used car lot has a large balloon tied down to stakes 1500 feet apart. The angle of elevation from the stake at the west end of the lot to the balloon is 50° , and the angle of elevation from the stake at the east end of the lot to the balloon is 72° . What is the altitude of the balloon?

Answer: 1288.6 feet Difficulty: 2

40. An A-frame tool shed is 12 feet wide. If the roof of the shed makes a 55° angle with the base of the shed, what is the length of the roof from ground level to the peak of the roof?

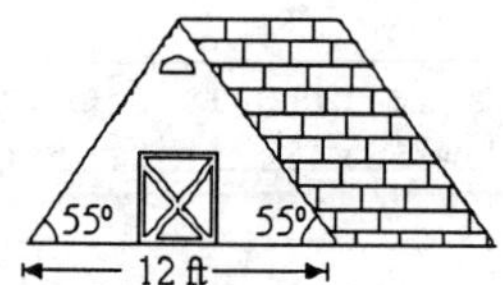

Answer: 10.5 feet Difficulty: 2

MULTIPLE CHOICE

41. A television antenna sits on a roof. Two 76-foot guy wires are positioned on opposite sides of the antenna. The angle of elevation each makes with the ground is 24° . How far apart are the ends of the two guy wires?
a) 41.6 feet b) 138.9 feet c) 251.4 feet
d) 18.4 feet e) None of these

Answer: b Difficulty: 1

42. A television antenna sits on a roof. Two 72-foot guy wires are positioned on opposite sides of the antenna. The angle of elevation each makes with the ground is 26° . How far apart are the ends of the two guy wires?
a) 24.9 feet b) 21.5 feet c) 112.1 feet
d) 129.4 feet e) None of these

Answer: d Difficulty: 1

Chapter 062: Law of Cosines

MULTIPLE CHOICE

1. Given a triangle with $a = 80$, $b = 51$, and $c = 113$, find C.
   a) 117.5° b) 27.5° c) 157.4° d) 62.5° e) None of these

   Answer: a Difficulty: 1

2. Given a triangle with $a = 17$, $b = 39$, and $c = 50$, find A.
   a) 16.88° b) 73.12° c) 163.12° d) 106.88° e) None of these

   Answer: a Difficulty: 1

3. Given a triangle with $a = 117$, $b = 230$, and $c = 185$, find B.
   a) 96.6° b) 6.6° c) 53.0° d) 37.0° e) None of these

   Answer: a Difficulty: 1

SHORT ANSWER

4. Given a triangle with $a = 78$, $b = 15$, and $c = 91$, find A, B, and C.

   Answer: $A = 27.5°$, $B = 5.1°$, $C = 147.4°$. Difficulty: 1

5. Given a triangle with $a = 135$, $b = 71.6$, and $c = 69$, find B.

   Answer: 16.5° Difficulty: 1

MULTIPLE CHOICE

6. Given a triangle with $a = 32$, $b = 47$, and $c = 25$, find C.
   a) 110.5° b) 39.6° c) 60.1° d) 29.9° e) None of these

   Answer: d Difficulty: 1

7. Given a triangle with $a = 11$, $b = 12$, and $c = 13$, find A.
   a) 38.0° b) 52.0° c) 68.7° d) 59.3° e) None of these

   Answer: b Difficulty: 1

8. Given a triangle with $a = 7$, $b = 9$, and $c = 15$, find B.
   a) 23.2° b) 66.8° c) 113.2° d) 138.9° e) None of these

   Answer: a Difficulty: 1

9. Given a triangle with $a = 19$, $b = 4$, and $c = 22$, find C.
   a) 117.4° b) 132.1° c) 87.2° d) 99.7° e) None of these

   Answer: e Difficulty: 1

10. Given a triangle with $a = 53$, $b = 94$, and $c = 87$, find A.
    a) 80.3° b) 65.9° c) 33.8° d) 48.6° e) None of these

    Answer: c Difficulty: 1

11. Given a triangle with $a = 2178$, $B = 23°$, and $c = 1719$, find b.
    a) 2184.9 b) 805,937.8 c) 2062.1
    d) 897.7 e) None of these

    Answer: d Difficulty: 1

12. Given a triangle with $B = 81°$, $a = 15$, and $c = 72$, find b.
    a) 57.2 b) 3275.6 c) 5071 d) 71.2 e) None of these

    Answer: d Difficulty: 1

13. Given a triangle with $A = 58° 20'$, $b = 23$, and $c = 18$, find a.
    a) 20.41 b) 20.45 c) 25.21 d) 35.88 e) None of these

    Answer: b Difficulty: 1

SHORT ANSWER

14. Given a triangle with $A = 38°$, $b = 22$, and $c = 98$, find a.

    Answer: $a = 81.8$ Difficulty: 1

15. Given the triangle below, find B.

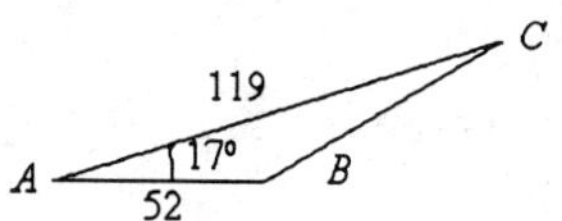

    Answer: $B = 150.6°$ Difficulty: 1

MULTIPLE CHOICE

16. Given a triangle with $a = 12$, $c = 21$, and $B = 72°$, find C.
    a) 69.2° b) 74.6° c) 81.0° d) 33.4° e) None of these

    Answer: b Difficulty: 1

17. Given a triangle with $b = 37$, $c = 96$, $A = 23°$, find C.
    a) 127.4° b) 13.1° c) 143.9° d) 36.1° e) None of these

    Answer: c Difficulty: 1

18. Given a triangle with $a = 32$, $c = 41$, and $B = 22°$, find C.
    a) 98.2° b) 111.4° c) 46.6° d) 68.6° e) None of these

    Answer: b Difficulty: 1

19. Given a triangle with $a = 15$, $b = 24$, and $C = 45°$, find B.
    a) 38.4° b) 83.4° c) 79.2° d) 96.6° e) None of these

    Answer: d Difficulty: 1

20. Given a triangle with $a = 16$, $b = 19$, and $C = 63°$, find A.
    a) 66.5° b) 50.5° c) 23.5° d) 94° e) None of these

    Answer: b Difficulty: 1

21. Given a triangle with $a = 80$, $b = 90$, and $c = 110$, find the area.
    a) 12,600,000 b) 69,135.8 c) 262.9 d) 3549.6 e) None of these

    Answer: d Difficulty: 1

22. Given a triangle with $a = 121$, $b = 82$, and $c = 90$, find the area.
    a) 9922.0 b) 4961.0 c) 523.2 d) 3689.6 e) None of these

    Answer: d Difficulty: 1

SHORT ANSWER

23. Given a triangle with $a = 78$, $b = 15$, and $c = 91$, find the area.

    Answer: 314.9 square units Difficulty: 1

24. Given a triangle with $a = 78$, $b = 91$, and $c = 72$, find the area.

    Answer: 2706.89 square units Difficulty: 1

MULTIPLE CHOICE

25. Use Heron's Formula to find the area of the triangle with $a = 23$, $b = 17$, and $c = 28$.
    a) 195.3 b) 15.1 c) 104.7 d) 195.5 e) None of these

    Answer: a Difficulty: 1

26. Use Heron's Formula to find the area of the triangle with $a = 16$, $b = 37$, and $c = 32$.
    a) 255.0 b) 256.0 c) 252.7 d) 258.0 e) None of these

    Answer: a Difficulty: 1

27. Use Heron's Formula to find the area of the triangle with $a = 21$, $b = 22$, and $c = 23$.
    a) 208.7 b) 231.0 c) 193.6 d) 205.2 e) None of these

    Answer: a Difficulty: 1

28. Use Heron's Formula to find the area of the triangle with $a = 42$, $b = 51$, and $c = 57$.
    a) 1860 b) 3136 c) 1034 d) 1071 e) None of these

    Answer: c Difficulty: 1

29. Use Heron's Formula to find the area of the triangle with $a = 11$, $b = 27$, and $c = 19$.
a) 7107.2 b) 84.3 c) 1728.9 d) 4722.3 e) None of these

Answer: b Difficulty: 1

30. Use Heron's Formula to find the area of the triangle with $a = 41.6$, $b = 54.2$, and $c = 47.1$.
a) 946.5 b) 1276.4 c) 1006.5 d) 1127.1 e) None of these

Answer: a Difficulty: 1

31. Ship A is 72 miles from a lighthouse on the shore. Its bearing from the lighthouse is N 15° E. Ship B is 81 miles from the same lighthouse. Its bearing from the lighthouse is N 52° E. Find the number of miles between the two ships.
a) 84.57 b) 44.44 c) 49.29 d) 90.75 e) None of these

Answer: c Difficulty: 1

32. Determine the number of acres in a triangular parcel of land if the lengths of the sides measure 1507 feet, 1750 feet, and 970 feet. There are 43,560 square feet in 1 acre.
a) 15.9 acres b) 21.7 acres c) 19.2 acres
d) 16.8 acres e) None of these

Answer: d Difficulty: 1

33. Determine the number of acres in a triangular parcel of land if the lengths of the sides measure 1702 feet, 4021 feet, and 4000 feet. There are 43,560 square feet in 1 acre.
a) 90.2 acres b) 76.6 acres c) 89.5 acres
d) 46.2 acres e) None of these

Answer: b Difficulty: 1

SHORT ANSWER

34. In order to determine the distance between two aircraft, a tracking station continuously determines the distance to each aircraft and the angle α between them. Determine the distance between the planes when $\alpha = 28°$, $b = 71$ miles and $c = 36$ miles.

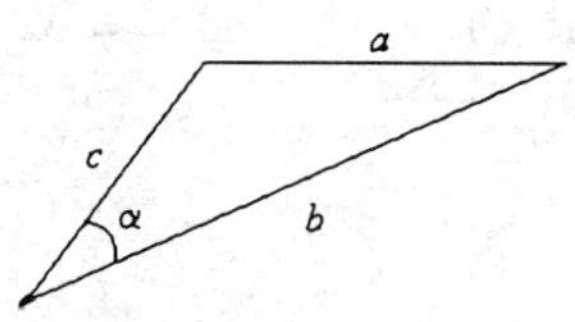

Answer: 42.7 miles Difficulty: 1

MULTIPLE CHOICE

35. A trigonometry class wants to determine the length of a pond near the school. From a point, *A*, they measure the distance to each end of the pond and the angle between these two sides. What is the approximate length *l* of the pond?

a) 352 feet b) 298 feet c) 407 feet
d) 331 feet e) None of these

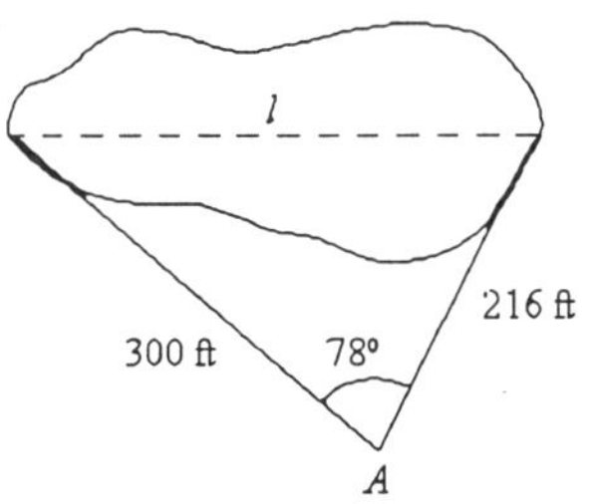

Answer: d Difficulty: 1

SHORT ANSWER

36. A boat leaves a port and sails 16 miles at a bearing of S 20° E. Another boat leaves the same port and sails 12 miles at a bearing of S 60° W. How far apart are the two boats at this point?

Answer: 18.3 miles Difficulty: 2

37. A golfer drivers a ball 21° from a line between the tee and the hole that is 320 yards away. How far is the ball from the hole if the ball landed 190 yards from the tee?

Answer: 158.0 yards Difficulty: 2

38. On a map the town of Morgan Run is due south of Davidson and is south east of Vicksburg. The distance from Morgan Run to Davidson and Vicksburg are 32 and 52 miles respectively. The distance between Davidson and Vicksburg is 42 miles. If a plane leaves Morgan Run to fly to Vicksburg, on what bearing should it travel?

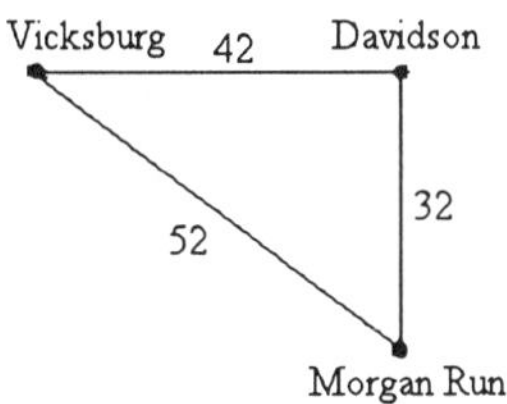

Answer: N 53.8° W Difficulty: 2

39. A 120 foot tower is leaning. A 160 foot guy wire has been anchored 82 feet from the base of the tower. How far from vertical is the tower leaning?

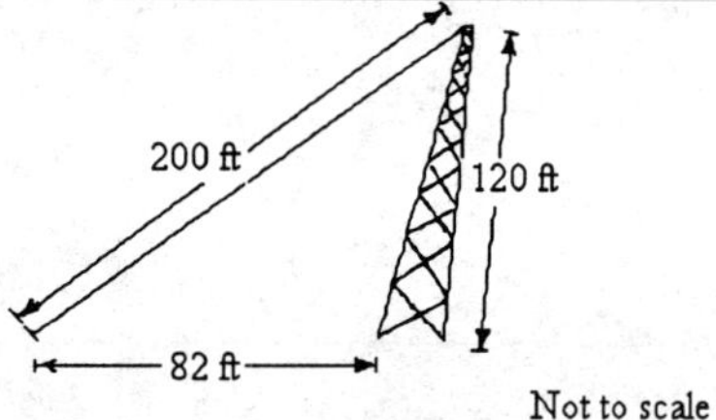

Answer: 13.15° Difficulty: 2

Chapter 063: Vectors in the Plane

MULTIPLE CHOICE

1. A vector **v** has initial point (3, 7) and terminal point (3, -2). Find its component form.
   a) $\langle 0, 9\rangle$ b) $\langle 9, 0\rangle$ c) $\langle 0, -9\rangle$
   d) $\langle -9, 0\rangle$ e) None of these

   Answer: c Difficulty: 1

2. Find the component form of the vector below.
   a) $\langle -2, 4\rangle$ b) $\langle 2, -4\rangle$ c) $\langle -6, -6\rangle$
   d) $\langle 6, 6\rangle$ e) None of these

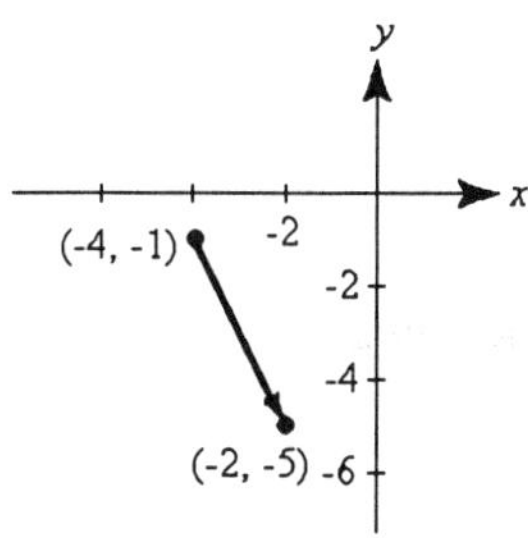

   Answer: b Difficulty: 1

3. A vector **v** has initial point (-2, 1) and terminal point (7, 6). Find the component form of vector **v**.
   a) $\langle 9, 5\rangle$ b) $\langle -9, -5\rangle$ c) $\langle 5, 7\rangle$
   d) $\langle -5, -7\rangle$ e) None of these

   Answer: a Difficulty: 1

4. Determine the magnitude of the vector with initial point (4, 6) and terminal point (7, 2).
   a) $\sqrt{73}$ b) 19 c) $\sqrt{185}$ d) 5 e) None of these

   Answer: d Difficulty: 1

5. Determine the magnitude of **v**: $\mathbf{v} = 4\mathbf{i} - 7\mathbf{j}$.
   a) 65 b) $\sqrt{65}$ c) 11 d) $\sqrt{11}$ e) None of these

   Answer: b Difficulty: 1

6. Determine the magnitude of **v**: $\mathbf{v} = \langle 5, -6\rangle$.
   a) 11 b) $\sqrt{11}$ c) 61 d) $\sqrt{61}$ e) None of these

   Answer: d Difficulty: 1

7. A vector **v** has initial point (1, 8) and terminal point (3, -7). Find its magnitude.
   a) $\sqrt{229}$ b) $\sqrt{5}$ c) $4\sqrt{14}$ d) $\sqrt{15}$ e) None of these

   Answer: a Difficulty: 1

8. Find the direction of **v**: **v** = 7**i** - 2**j**.
   a) 344° b) 16° c) 164° d) 196° e) None of these

   Answer: a Difficulty: 1

9. Find the direction of **v**: **v** = $\langle -1, -4 \rangle$.
   a) 76° b) 14° c) 256° d) 194° e) None of these

   Answer: c Difficulty: 1

10. Find the direction of **v**: **v** = $\langle -2, 5 \rangle$.
   a) 112° b) 68° c) 167° d) 193° e) None of these

   Answer: a Difficulty: 1

SHORT ANSWER

11. A vector **v** has initial point (2, 5) and terminal point (-1, 9). Find its magnitude and direction.

   Answer: $\|\mathbf{v}\| = 5$, $\theta = 126.9°$ Difficulty: 1

MULTIPLE CHOICE

12. Given **u** = 3**i** + 2**j**, **w** = **i** - **j**, and **v** = 3**u** - 2**w**, find the component form of **v**.
   a) $\langle 11, 4 \rangle$ b) $\langle 7, 8 \rangle$ c) $\langle \sqrt{77}, 4\sqrt{2} \rangle$
   d) $\langle \sqrt{85}, 2\sqrt{10} \rangle$ e) None of these

   Answer: b Difficulty: 1

13. Given **w** = **i** and **u** = 4**i** - 2**j**, find $\mathbf{v} = \frac{2}{3}\mathbf{w} + \frac{1}{2}\mathbf{u}$.
   a) $\frac{8}{3}\mathbf{i} - \mathbf{j}$ b) $\frac{8}{3}\mathbf{i} + 2\mathbf{j}$ c) $\frac{8}{3}\mathbf{i} + \mathbf{j}$
   d) $\frac{8}{3}\mathbf{i} - 2\mathbf{j}$ e) None of these

   Answer: a Difficulty: 1

SHORT ANSWER

14. Given $\mathbf{u} = 3\mathbf{i} - 2\mathbf{j}$ and $\mathbf{w} = 9\mathbf{i} + 5\mathbf{j}$, find $\mathbf{v} = \frac{1}{2}\mathbf{u} + 4\mathbf{w}$.

Answer:
$\frac{75}{2}\mathbf{i} + 19\mathbf{j}$

Difficulty: 1

MULTIPLE CHOICE

15. Given $\mathbf{u} = 4\mathbf{i} - 3\mathbf{j}$, $\mathbf{w} = \mathbf{i} - \mathbf{j}$, and $\mathbf{v} = 2\mathbf{u} + 3\mathbf{w}$, find $\mathbf{v}$.
    a) $\langle 7, -4\rangle$ b) $\langle 7, -9\rangle$ c) $\langle 11, -9\rangle$
    d) $\langle 11, -4\rangle$ e) None of these

Answer: c Difficulty: 1

16. A vector $\mathbf{v}$ has magnitude 8 and direction $\theta = 120°$. Find its component form.
    a) $\langle \frac{8\sqrt{3}}{3}, -8\sqrt{3}\rangle$ b) $\langle 8\sqrt{3}, \frac{8\sqrt{3}}{3}\rangle$ c) $\langle 4\sqrt{3}, -4\rangle$
    d) $\langle -4, 4\sqrt{3}\rangle$ e) None of these

Answer: d Difficulty: 1

SHORT ANSWER

17. A unit vector has direction $\theta = 120°$. Find its component form.

Answer:
$\langle -\frac{1}{2}, \frac{\sqrt{3}}{2}\rangle$

Difficulty: 1

18. A vector $\mathbf{v}$ has magnitude 27 and direction $\theta = 216°$. Find its component form.

Answer: $\langle -21.84, -15.87\rangle$ Difficulty: 1

MULTIPLE CHOICE

19. A vector **v** has magnitude 6 and direction $\theta = 210°$. Find its component form.
a) $\langle -3, \sqrt{3} \rangle$
b) $\langle -3\sqrt{3}, 12 \rangle$
c) $\langle 3, -\frac{\sqrt{3}}{2} \rangle$
d) $\langle -3\sqrt{3}, -3 \rangle$
e) None of these

Answer: d Difficulty: 1

20. Given **v** of magnitude 200 and direction 215°, and **w** of magnitude 150 and direction 162°, find **v** + **w**.
a) -21.2**i** - 161.1**j**
b) 350**i** + 350**j**
c) 50**i** - 50**j**
d) -306.5**i** - 68.4**j**
e) None of these

Answer: d Difficulty: 1

21. Given **v** of magnitude 150 and direction 30°, and **w** of magnitude 75 and direction 206°, find **v** + **w**.
a) 97.0**i** - 7.6**j**
b) 62.5**i** + 42.1**j**
c) 225**i** + 225**j**
d) -7.4**i** + 13.9**j**
e) None of these

Answer: b Difficulty: 1

22. Given **v** of magnitude 50 and direction 315°, and **w** of magnitude 20 and direction 210°, find **v** + **w**.
a) 18.0**i** - 45.4**j**
b) 52.7**i** - 25.4**j**
c) 18.0**i** - 25.4**j**
d) 52.7**i** - 45.4**j**
e) None of these

Answer: a Difficulty: 1

SHORT ANSWER

23. Given **v** of magnitude 100 and direction 172°, and **w** of magnitude 300 and direction 310°, find **v** + **w**.

Answer: 93.8**i** - 215.9**j** Difficulty: 1

24. Given **v** of magnitude 300 and direction 90° and **w** of magnitude 250 and direction 253°, find **v** + **w**.

Answer: -73.1**i** + 60.9**j** Difficulty: 1

MULTIPLE CHOICE

25. Find a unit vector in the direction of **v**: **v** = 3**i** - 2**j**.
a) $\langle 3\sqrt{13}, -2\sqrt{13} \rangle$
b) $\langle \frac{3\sqrt{13}}{13}, -\frac{2\sqrt{13}}{13} \rangle$
c) $\langle \sqrt{13}, -\sqrt{13} \rangle$
d) $\langle 1, -1 \rangle$
e) None of these

Answer: b Difficulty: 1

26. Find a unit vector in the direction of **v**: **v** = 4**i** + 2**j**.
a) $\frac{2\sqrt{5}}{5}\mathbf{i} + \frac{\sqrt{5}}{5}\mathbf{j}$
b) **i** + **j**
c) $\frac{4\sqrt{5}}{5}\mathbf{i} + \frac{2\sqrt{5}}{5}\mathbf{j}$
d) $8\sqrt{5}\mathbf{i} + 4\sqrt{5}\mathbf{j}$
e) None of these

Answer: a Difficulty: 1

27. Find a unit vector in the direction of **v**: **v** = 4**i** - 3**j**.
a) $\frac{4\sqrt{5}}{5}\mathbf{i} - \frac{3\sqrt{5}}{5}\mathbf{j}$
b) $\frac{4\sqrt{27}}{27}\mathbf{i} + \frac{3\sqrt{27}}{27}\mathbf{j}$
c) $\frac{4}{5}\mathbf{i} - \frac{3}{5}\mathbf{j}$
d) $\frac{\sqrt{2}}{2}\mathbf{i} - \frac{\sqrt{2}}{2}\mathbf{j}$
e) None of these

Answer: c Difficulty: 1

28. Find a unit vector in the direction of **v**: **v** = 3**i** - 3**j**.
a) 3**i** - 3**j**
b) **i** - **j**
c) $\frac{\sqrt{2}}{2}\mathbf{i} - \frac{\sqrt{2}}{2}\mathbf{j}$
d) $\frac{3\sqrt{2}}{2}\mathbf{i} - \frac{3\sqrt{2}}{2}\mathbf{j}$
e) None of these

Answer: c Difficulty: 1

29. Find a unit vector in the direction of **v**: **v** = -5**i** + 2**j**.
a) $\frac{-5\sqrt{21}}{21}\mathbf{i} + \frac{2\sqrt{21}}{21}\mathbf{j}$
b) -**i** + **j**
c) $-\sqrt{5}\mathbf{i} + \frac{\sqrt{5}}{5}\mathbf{j}$
d) $\frac{-5\sqrt{29}}{29}\mathbf{i} + \frac{2\sqrt{29}}{29}\mathbf{j}$
e) None of these

Answer: d Difficulty: 1

SHORT ANSWER

30. Given **v** = 3**i** - 2**j** and **w** = 6**i** + **j**, find the angle between **v** and **w**.

Answer: 43.15° Difficulty: 1

MULTIPLE CHOICE

31. Given **v** = 3**i** + 2**j** and **w** = 7**i** + 5**j**, find the angle between **v** and **w**.
a) 16.7° b) 110.8° c) 50.4° d) 69.2° e) None of these

Answer: d Difficulty: 1

32. Given **v** = $\langle 5, -2\rangle$ and **w** = $\langle 6, 1\rangle$, find the angle between **v** and **w**.
a) 58.7° b) 148.7° c) 31.3° d) 121.3° e) None of these

Answer: c Difficulty: 1

33. Given **v** = ⟨4, 1⟩ and **w** = ⟨-2, -3⟩ , find the angle between **v** and **w**.
   a) 47.7° b) 227.7° c) 42.3° d) 137.7° e) None of these

   Answer: d Difficulty: 1

34. Two forces, one of 120 pounds and the other of 200 pounds, act on the same objects at angles of 30° and -30° respectively, with the positive *x*-axis. Find the direction of the resultant of these two forces.
   a) 14° b) -8.2° c) 0° d) -18° e) None of these

   Answer: b Difficulty: 2

SHORT ANSWER

35. Two forces, one of 45 pounds and the other 52 pounds, act upon the same object. The angle between these forces is 25° . Find the magnitude of the resultant force.

   Answer: 94.71 pounds Difficulty: 2

36. What force is required to keep a 2000 pound vehicle from rolling down a ramp inclined at 30° from the horizontal?

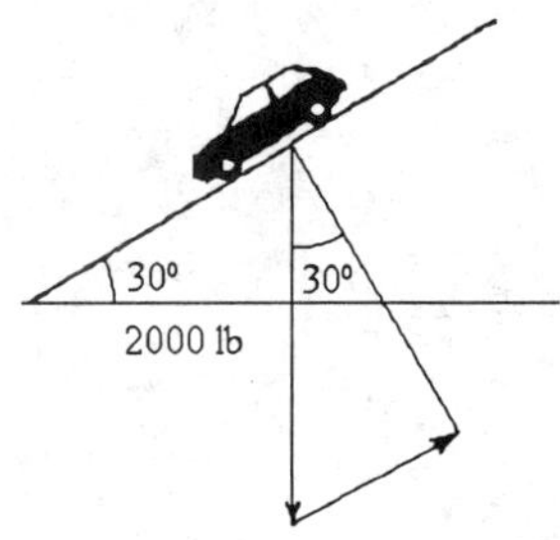

   Answer: 1000 pounds Difficulty: 1

37. A storm front is moving east at 30.0 mph and north at 18.5 mph. Find the resultant velocity of the front.

   Answer: 35.2 mph at 31.7° north of east Difficulty: 2

38. An airline's navigator determines that the jet is flying 475 mph with a heading of 42.5° north of west, but the jet is actually moving at 465 mph in a direction of 37.7° north of west. What is the velocity of the wind?

   Answer: 40.6 mph at 64.1° south of east Difficulty: 2

39. Find the component form of **u**: $\|\mathbf{u}\| = 10$ and $\theta_u = 30°$.

   Answer:

   $\langle 5\sqrt{3}, 5\rangle$

   Difficulty: 1

40. Find the component form of **u**: $\|\mathbf{u}\| = 5$ and $\theta_u = 135°$.

Answer:

$\langle \frac{-5\sqrt{2}}{2}, \frac{5\sqrt{2}}{2} \rangle$

Difficulty: 1

MULTIPLE CHOICE

41. Find the component form of **u**: $\|\mathbf{u}\| = 20$ and $\theta_u = 210°$.

a) $\langle -10\sqrt{2}, -10\sqrt{2} \rangle$
b) $\langle -10\sqrt{3}, -10 \rangle$
c) $\langle -10, -10\sqrt{3} \rangle$
d) $\langle -10\sqrt{2}, -10\sqrt{3} \rangle$
e) None of these

Answer: b Difficulty: 1

42. Find the component form of **u**: $\|\mathbf{u}\| = 35$ and $\theta_u = 180°$.

a) $\langle \frac{-35\sqrt{3}}{2}, \frac{-35}{2} \rangle$
b) $\langle 35, 0 \rangle$
c) $\langle 0, -35 \rangle$
d) $\langle -35, 0 \rangle$
e) None of these

Answer: d Difficulty: 1

43. Find the component form of **u**: $\|\mathbf{u}\| = 50$ and $\theta_u = 330°$.

a) $\langle -6\sqrt{2}, -6\sqrt{2} \rangle$
b) $\langle 6\sqrt{2}, -6\sqrt{2} \rangle$
c) $\langle 12, -12 \rangle$
d) $\langle 6\sqrt{3}, -6 \rangle$
e) None of these

Answer: e Difficulty: 1

44. Find the component form of $\|\mathbf{u}\| = 12$ and $\theta_u = 315°$.

a) $\langle -6\sqrt{2}, -6\sqrt{2} \rangle$
b) $\langle 6\sqrt{2}, -6\sqrt{2} \rangle$
c) $\langle 12, -12 \rangle$
d) $\langle 6\sqrt{3}, -6 \rangle$
e) None of these

Answer: b Difficulty: 1

Chapter 064: Vectors and Dot Products

MULTIPLE CHOICE

1. Given $\mathbf{u} = 3\mathbf{i} + 2\mathbf{j}$ and $\mathbf{v} = \mathbf{i} - \mathbf{j}$, find $\mathbf{u} \cdot \mathbf{v}$.
   a) $3\mathbf{i}^2 - \mathbf{ij} - 2\mathbf{j}^2$ b) $3\mathbf{i}^2 - 2\mathbf{j}^2$ c) 5
   d) 1 e) None of these

   Answer: d Difficulty: 1

2. Given $\mathbf{v} = \mathbf{i}$ and $\mathbf{w} = 2\mathbf{i} - 3\mathbf{j}$, find $\mathbf{v} \cdot \mathbf{w}$.
   a) -1 b) $2\mathbf{i} - 3\mathbf{j}$ c) 2
   d) $\sqrt{13}$ e) None of these

   Answer: c Difficulty: 1

3. Given $\mathbf{u} = 3\mathbf{j}$ and $\mathbf{v} = 7\mathbf{i} + \mathbf{j}$, find $\mathbf{u} \cdot \mathbf{v}$.
   a) 10 b) $7\mathbf{i} + 3\mathbf{j}$ c) $3\mathbf{j}$
   d) 3 e) None of these

   Answer: d Difficulty: 1

SHORT ANSWER

4. Given $\mathbf{v} = 5\mathbf{i} - 2\mathbf{j}$ and $\mathbf{w} = -3\mathbf{i} + \mathbf{j}$, find $\mathbf{v} \cdot \mathbf{w}$.

   Answer: -17 Difficulty: 1

5. Given $\mathbf{v} = 3\mathbf{i} - 9\mathbf{j}$ and $\mathbf{w} = 2\mathbf{i} + \mathbf{j}$, find $\mathbf{v} \cdot \mathbf{w}$.

   Answer: -3 Difficulty: 1

MULTIPLE CHOICE

6. Given $\mathbf{u} = 2\mathbf{i} - 3\mathbf{j}$ and $\mathbf{v} = -2\mathbf{i} + 5\mathbf{j}$, find $\mathbf{u} \cdot \mathbf{v}$.
   a) $2\mathbf{j}$ b) -19 c) $-4\mathbf{i} - 15\mathbf{j}$ d) $\sqrt{241}$ e) None of these

   Answer: b Difficulty: 1

7. Given $\mathbf{w} = 3\mathbf{i} + 3\mathbf{j}$ and $\mathbf{v} = -2\mathbf{i} + 5\mathbf{j}$, find $\mathbf{w} \cdot \mathbf{v}$.
   a) $-6\mathbf{i} + 15\mathbf{j}$ b) $\mathbf{i} + 8\mathbf{j}$ c) $\sqrt{261}$ d) 9 e) None of these

   Answer: d Difficulty: 1

8. Given $\mathbf{u} = 2\mathbf{i} - 2\mathbf{j}$ and $\mathbf{v} = \frac{1}{2}\mathbf{i} + \frac{1}{2}\mathbf{j}$, find $\mathbf{u} \cdot \mathbf{v}$.
   a) $\mathbf{i} - \mathbf{j}$ b) 0 c) $\frac{5}{2}\mathbf{i} - \frac{3}{2}\mathbf{j}$ d) $\sqrt{2}$ e) None of these

   Answer: b Difficulty: 1

9. Find the angle between the vectors $\mathbf{v} = 3\mathbf{i} + 2\mathbf{j}$ and $\mathbf{w} = 7\mathbf{i} - 5\mathbf{j}$.
   a) 16.7° b) 110.8° c) 50.4° d) 69.2° e) None of these

   Answer: d Difficulty: 1

10. Find the angle between the vectors $\mathbf{u} = 2\mathbf{i} + 3\mathbf{j}$ and $\mathbf{v} = 7\mathbf{i} - \mathbf{j}$.
   a) 0.43 radian b) 1.12 radians c) 6.44 radians
   d) 0.22 radian e) None of these

   Answer: b Difficulty: 1

11. Find the angle between the vectors $\mathbf{v} = 2\mathbf{i} - 3\mathbf{j}$ and $\mathbf{u} = \mathbf{i} + \mathbf{j}$.
   a) 1.8 radians b) 0.2 radian c) 1.4 radians
   d) 0.8 radian e) None of these

   Answer: a Difficulty: 1

SHORT ANSWER

12. Find the cosine of the angle θ between the vectors $\mathbf{v} = 3\mathbf{i} - 9\mathbf{j}$ and $\mathbf{w} = 2\mathbf{i} + \mathbf{j}$.

   Answer:

   $$\cos\theta = -\frac{\sqrt{2}}{10}$$

   Difficulty: 1

MULTIPLE CHOICE

13. Find the angle between the vectors $\mathbf{v} = 3\mathbf{i} - 2\mathbf{j}$ and $\mathbf{u} = 4\mathbf{i} + 3\mathbf{j}$.
   a) 0.33 radian b) 70.6° c) 109.4° d) 31.9° e) None of these

   Answer: b Difficulty: 1

14. Find the angle between the vectors $\mathbf{v} = -2\mathbf{i} - 5\mathbf{j}$ and $\mathbf{u} = 5\mathbf{i} + 2\mathbf{j}$.
   a) 180° b) 0.69 radian c) 46.4° d) 133.6° e) None of these

   Answer: d Difficulty: 1

15. Find the angle between the vectors $\mathbf{w} = \sqrt{3}\mathbf{i}$ and $\mathbf{v} = \sqrt{3}\mathbf{i} + 2\mathbf{j}$.
   a) 112.2° b) 130.9° c) 0.65 radian d) 49.1° e) None of these

   Answer: d Difficulty: 1

SHORT ANSWER

16. Find the angle between the vectors $\mathbf{w} = 5\mathbf{i} + 2\mathbf{j}$ and $\mathbf{v} = -10 - 2\mathbf{j}$.

   Answer: 169.5° or 2.96 radians Difficulty: 1

17. Find the angle between the vectors $\mathbf{w} = 3\mathbf{i} + 4\mathbf{j}$ and $\mathbf{v} = 10\mathbf{i} + 4\mathbf{j}$.

Answer: 31.3° or 0.55 radian Difficulty: 1

18. Find $\mathbf{u} \cdot \mathbf{v}$ if $\|\mathbf{u}\| = 8$ and $\|\mathbf{v}\| = 12$, and the angle between $\mathbf{u}$ and $\mathbf{v}$ is $\frac{\pi}{3}$.

Answer: 48 Difficulty: 1

19. Find $\mathbf{u} \cdot \mathbf{v}$ if $\|\mathbf{u}\| = 7$ and $\|\mathbf{v}\| = 12$, and the angle between $\mathbf{u}$ and $\mathbf{v}$ is $\frac{\pi}{4}$.

Answer:

$42\sqrt{2}$

Difficulty: 1

MULTIPLE CHOICE

20. Find $\mathbf{u} \cdot \mathbf{v}$ if $\|\mathbf{u}\| = 40$, $\|\mathbf{v}\| = 15$, and the angle between $\mathbf{u}$ and $\mathbf{v}$ is $\frac{2\pi}{3}$.

a) $-300\sqrt{3}$ b) $\frac{900}{\pi}$ c) 300 d) -300 e) None of these

Answer: d Difficulty: 1

21. Find $\mathbf{u} \cdot \mathbf{v}$ if $\|\mathbf{u}\| = 32$, and $\|\mathbf{v}\| = 15$, and the angle between $\mathbf{u}$ and $\mathbf{v}$ is $\frac{5\pi}{6}$.

a) -240 b) $240\sqrt{3}$ c) 320π d) $-240\sqrt{3}$ e) None of these

Answer: d Difficulty: 1

22. Find $\mathbf{u} \cdot \mathbf{v}$ if $\|\mathbf{u}\| = 4$, and $\|\mathbf{v}\| = 5$, and the angle between $\mathbf{u}$ and $\mathbf{v}$ is $\frac{3\pi}{4}$.

a) $-10\sqrt{2}$ b) $10\sqrt{2}$ c) 15π d) 10 e) None of these

Answer: a Difficulty: 1

23. Which of the following pairs of vectors are orthogonal?

a) $\mathbf{v} = 3\mathbf{i} - 2\mathbf{j}$, $\mathbf{w} = -\mathbf{i} + 2\mathbf{j}$
b) $\mathbf{v} = -2\mathbf{i}$, $\mathbf{w} = 5\mathbf{j}$
c) $\mathbf{v} = -\mathbf{i} + 2\mathbf{j}$, $\mathbf{w} = -\frac{1}{2}\mathbf{j}$
d) $\mathbf{v} = 2\mathbf{i} - 3\mathbf{j}$, $\mathbf{w} = -2\mathbf{i} + 3\mathbf{j}$
e) None of these

Answer: b Difficulty: 1

24. Which of the following pairs of vectors are orthogonal?
    a) $\mathbf{v} = 4\mathbf{i} - 2\mathbf{j}$, $\mathbf{w} = 2\mathbf{i} - 4\mathbf{j}$
    b) $\mathbf{v} = 3\mathbf{i} + \mathbf{j}$, $\mathbf{w} = 9\mathbf{i} + 3\mathbf{j}$
    c) $\mathbf{v} = \mathbf{i} - \mathbf{j}$, $\mathbf{w} = \mathbf{i}$
    d) $\mathbf{v} = -2\mathbf{i} + \mathbf{j}$, $\mathbf{w} = \mathbf{i} + 2\mathbf{j}$
    e) None of these

    Answer: d Difficulty: 1

25. Which of the following pairs of vectors are orthogonal?
    a) $\mathbf{v} = \mathbf{i} + 2\mathbf{j}$, $\mathbf{w} = 2\mathbf{i} - \mathbf{j}$
    b) $\mathbf{v} = 2\mathbf{i}$, $\mathbf{w} = -4$
    c) $\mathbf{v} = 3\mathbf{i} - 2\mathbf{j}$, $\mathbf{w} = 2\mathbf{i} - 3\mathbf{j}$
    d) $\mathbf{v} = \mathbf{i} + \mathbf{j}$, $\mathbf{w} = \frac{1}{2}\mathbf{i} + \frac{1}{2}\mathbf{j}$
    e) None of these

    Answer: a Difficulty: 1

SHORT ANSWER

26. Determine if the vectors $\mathbf{v} = 2\mathbf{i} - 3\mathbf{j}$ and $\mathbf{w} = \mathbf{i} + \mathbf{j}$ are orthogonal, parallel, or neither.

    Answer: Neither Difficulty: 1

27. Determine if the vectors $\mathbf{v} = 3\mathbf{i} - 7\mathbf{j}$ and $\mathbf{w} = -2\mathbf{i} + \frac{14}{3}\mathbf{j}$ are orthogonal, parallel, or neither.

    Answer: Parallel Difficulty: 1

MULTIPLE CHOICE

28. Given $\mathbf{v} = 3\mathbf{i} + 2\mathbf{j}$ and $\mathbf{w} = \mathbf{i} - 3\mathbf{j}$, find the projections of $\mathbf{v}$ onto $\mathbf{w}$.
    a) $\frac{\sqrt{10}}{10}\mathbf{i} - \frac{3\sqrt{10}}{10}\mathbf{j}$
    b) $\frac{3\sqrt{13}}{13}\mathbf{i} + \frac{2\sqrt{13}}{13}\mathbf{j}$
    c) $-\frac{3}{10}\mathbf{i} + \frac{9}{10}\mathbf{j}$
    d) $-\frac{9}{13}\mathbf{i} - \frac{6}{13}\mathbf{j}$
    e) None of these

    Answer: c Difficulty: 1

29. Given $\mathbf{v} = 2\mathbf{i} + 3\mathbf{j}$ and $\mathbf{w} = 5\mathbf{i} + 2\mathbf{j}$, find the projection of $\mathbf{v}$ onto $\mathbf{w}$.
    a) $\frac{80}{29}\mathbf{i} + \frac{32}{29}\mathbf{j}$
    b) $\frac{32}{13}\mathbf{i} + \frac{48}{13}\mathbf{j}$
    c) $7\mathbf{i} + 5\mathbf{j}$
    d) $\frac{2}{\sqrt{13}}\mathbf{i} + \frac{2}{\sqrt{13}}\mathbf{j}$
    e) None of these

    Answer: a Difficulty: 1

30. Given **v** = 2**i** - 3**j** and **w** = **i** - 7**j**, find the projection of **v** onto **w**.
   a) $\frac{1}{\sqrt{50}}\mathbf{i} - \frac{7}{\sqrt{50}}\mathbf{j}$ b) $\frac{46}{\sqrt{13}}\mathbf{i} - \frac{69}{\sqrt{13}}\mathbf{j}$ c) $\frac{2}{\sqrt{13}}\mathbf{i} - \frac{69}{\sqrt{13}}\mathbf{j}$
   d) $\frac{23}{50}\mathbf{i} - \frac{161}{50}\mathbf{j}$ e) None of these

   Answer: d Difficulty: 1

SHORT ANSWER

31. Given **v** = 5**i** - 2**j** and **w** = 3**i** + 4**j**, find the projection of **v** onto **w**.

   Answer:
   $\frac{7}{25}(3\mathbf{i} + 4\mathbf{j}) = \frac{21}{25}\mathbf{i} + \frac{28}{25}\mathbf{j}$
   Difficulty: 1

32. Given **v** = **i** - 3**j** and **w** = 2**i** + **j**, find the projection of **v** onto **w**.

   Answer:
   $-\frac{2}{5}\mathbf{i} - \frac{1}{5}\mathbf{j}$
   Difficulty: 1

33. Find the projection of **u** onto **v**. Then find the vector component of **u** orthogonal to **v**: **u** = ⟨5, 2⟩ and **v** = ⟨6, 4⟩.

   Answer:
   $\mathbf{w}_1 = \left\langle \frac{57}{13}, \frac{38}{13} \right\rangle, \mathbf{w}_2 = \left\langle \frac{8}{13}, \frac{-12}{13} \right\rangle$
   Difficulty: 2

34. Find the projection of **u** onto **v**. Then find the vector component of **u** orthogonal to **v**: **u** = ⟨-1, 2⟩ and **v** = ⟨2, -3⟩.

   Answer:
   $\mathbf{w}_1 = \left\langle \frac{-16}{13}, \frac{24}{13} \right\rangle, \mathbf{w}_2 = \left\langle \frac{3}{13}, \frac{2}{13} \right\rangle$
   Difficulty: 2

35. A truck with a gross weight of 25,000 pounds is parked on an 8° slope. Assume the only force to overcome is that due to gravity. Find the force required to keep the truck from rolling down the hill.

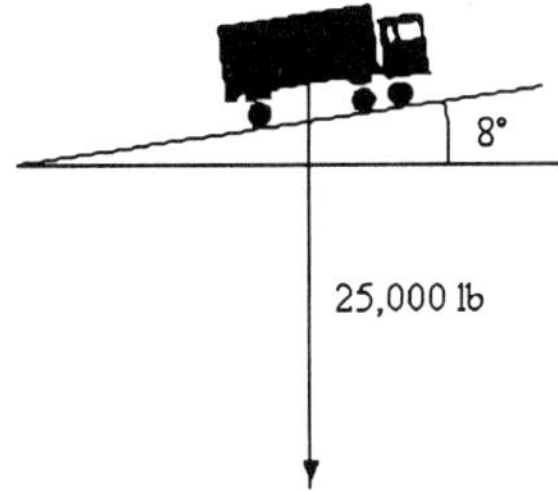

Answer: 3479.3 lbs Difficulty: 2

36. A truck with a gross weight of 22,500 pounds is parked on a 10° slope. Assume the only force to overcome is that due to gravity. Find the force required to keep the truck from rolling down the hill.

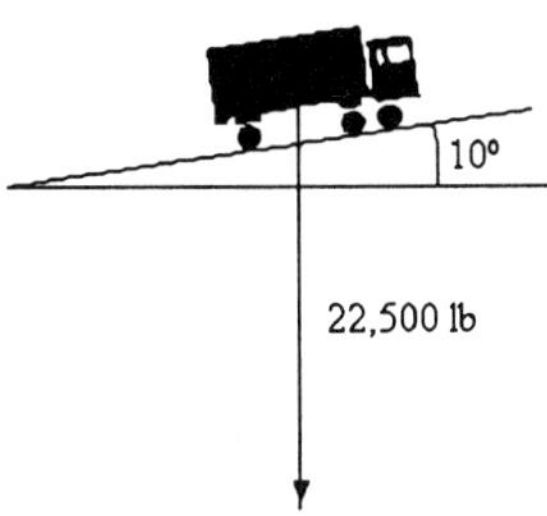

Answer: ≈ 3907.1 lbs Difficulty: 2

37. A tractor pulls a log 2000 feet and the tension in the cable connecting the tractor and the log is approximately 3200 pounds. Approximate the work done if the direction of the force is 30° above the horizontal.

Answer:

$\approx 5.54 \times 10^6$ ft-lbs (5,542,562.6 ft-lbs)

Difficulty: 2

38. A tractor pulls a log 2700 feet and the tension in the cable connecting the tractor and the log is approximately 3600 pounds. Approximate the work done if the direction of the force is 25° above the horizontal.

Answer:

$\approx 8.81 \times 10^6$ ft-lbs (8,809,311.7 ft-lbs)

Difficulty: 2

Chapter 065: Trigonometric Form of a Complex Number

MULTIPLE CHOICE

1. Represent the complex number graphically: $7 - 2i$.
   a) I b) II c) III d) IV e) None of these

(I)

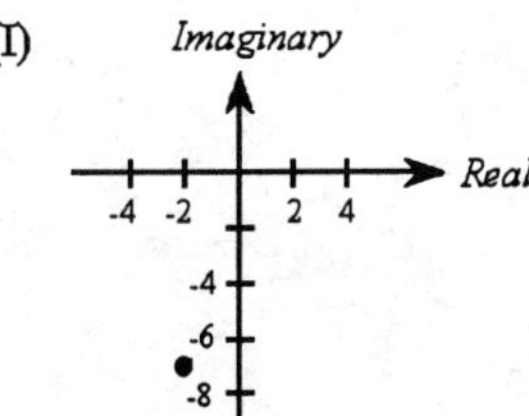

(II)

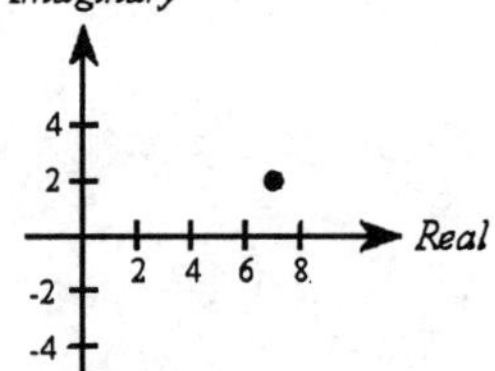

(III)

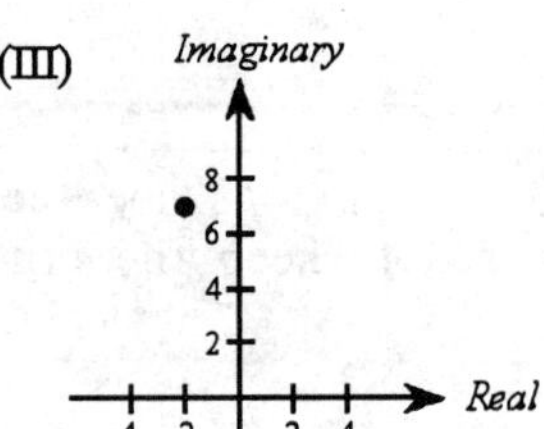

(IV)

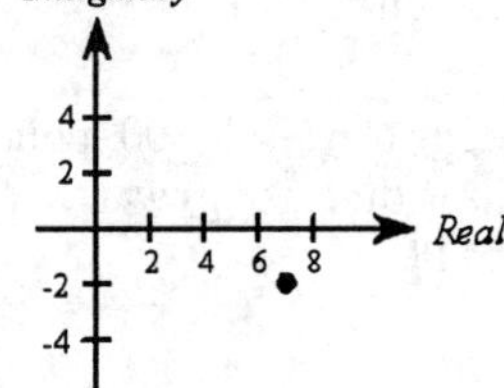

Answer: d Difficulty: 1

SHORT ANSWER

2. Represent the complex number graphically: $6 - 2i$.

Answer: See graph below.

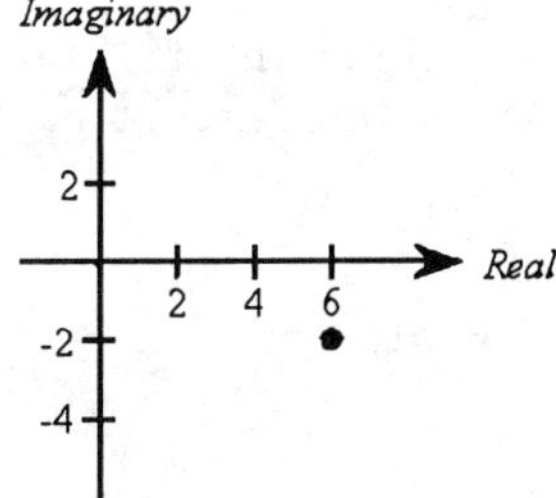

Difficulty: 1

MULTIPLE CHOICE

3. Represent the complex number graphically: $-5\left(3 - \sqrt{2}i\right)$.
a) I b) II c) III d) IV e) None of these

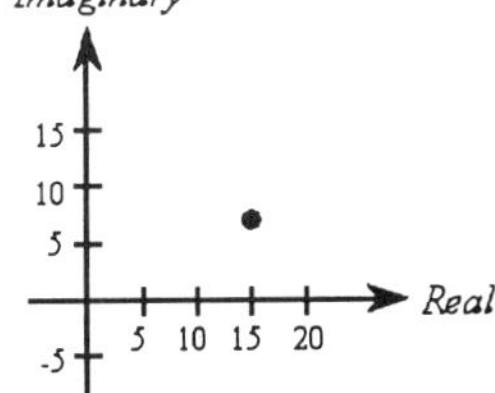

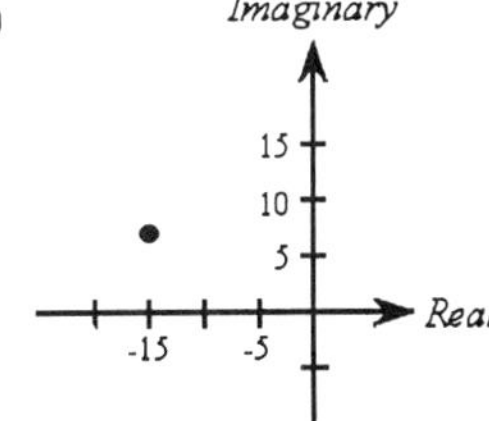

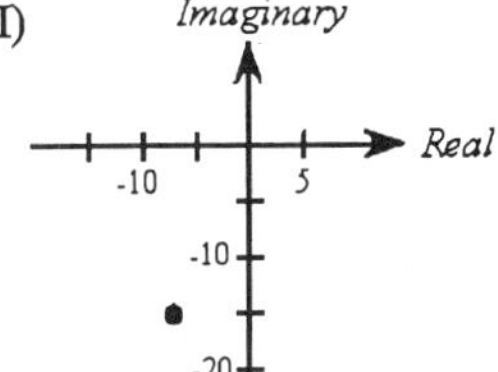

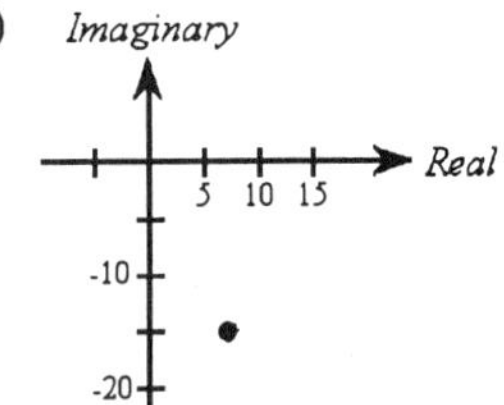

Answer: b Difficulty: 1

SHORT ANSWER

4. Rewrite in standard form and represent graphically: $3(\cos 150° + i \sin 150°)$.

Answer:

$-\frac{3\sqrt{3}}{2} + \frac{3}{2}i$

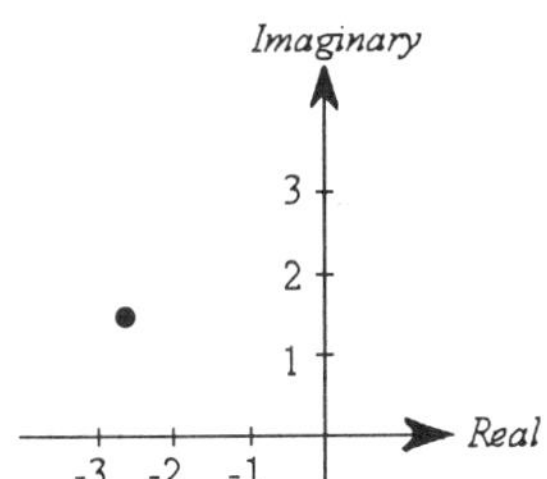

Difficulty: 1

MULTIPLE CHOICE

5. Represent the complex number graphically: $5(\cos 210° + i \sin 210°)$.
   a) I b) II c) III d) IV e) None of these

(I) Imaginary, Real; -3 -2 1 2 3; 1 -2 -3 -4 -5

(II) Imaginary, Real; -4 -2 1; 3 2 1 -2 -3

(III) Imaginary, Real; -3 -2 1 2 3; 5 4 3 2 1

(IV) Imaginary, Real; 1 2 3 4 5; 3 2 1 -2 -3

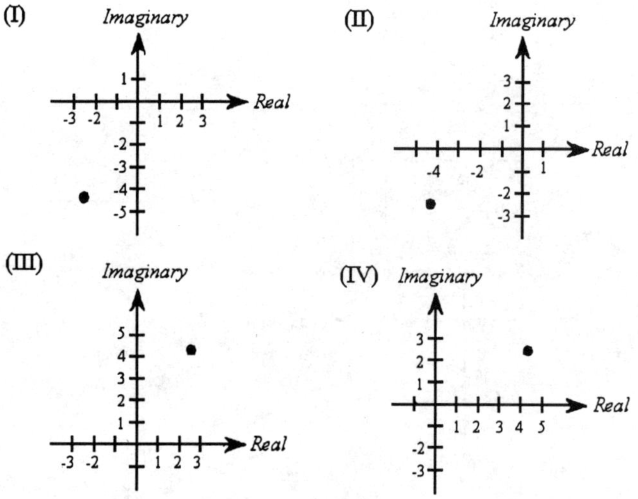

Answer: b Difficulty: 1

6. Represent the complex number graphically: $-4(1 - 2i)$.
   a) I b) II c) III d) IV e) None of these

(I) Imaginary, Real; -8 -6 -4 -2; 2 -4 -6

(II) Imaginary, Real; -3 -2 -1 1 2 3; 3 2 1 -2 -3

(III) Imaginary, Real; -6 -4 -2 2; -4 -6 -8

(IV) Imaginary, Real; -6 -4 -2 2; 8 6 4 2

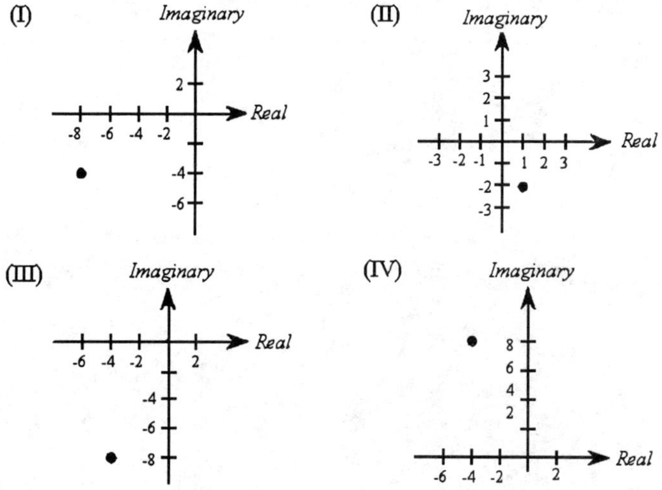

Answer: d Difficulty: 1

7. Evaluate: $|3 - 2i|$.
   a) 1 b) $\sqrt{5}$ c) $\sqrt{13}$ d) 5 e) None of these

Answer: c Difficulty: 1

8. Evaluate: $|5 + 4i|$.
a) 9 b) -9 c) 41 d) $\sqrt{41}$ e) None of these

Answer: d Difficulty: 1

9. Evaluate: $|7 - 3i|$.
a) $\sqrt{58}$ b) 4 c) 2 d) -58 e) None of these

Answer: a Difficulty: 1

10. Evaluate: $|3 - 4i|$.
a) 1 b) -1 c) 7 d) 5 e) None of these

Answer: d Difficulty: 1

11. Evaluate: $\left|2 - \frac{\sqrt{3}}{2}i\right|$.
a) $\frac{19}{4}$ b) $\frac{4 - \sqrt{3}}{2}$ c) $\frac{\sqrt{19}}{2}$ d) $\frac{1}{2}$ e) None of these

Answer: c Difficulty: 1

12. Evaluate: $|5 - 7i|$.
a) $\sqrt{74}$ b) 2 c) $\sqrt{10}$ d) $2\sqrt{3}$ e) None of these

Answer: a Difficulty: 1

13. Rewrite in trigonometric form: $16 - 4i$.
a) $4\sqrt{15}(\cos 14° + i \sin 14°)$
b) $4\sqrt{15}(\cos 346° + i \sin 346°)$
c) $4\sqrt{17}(\cos 346° + i \sin 346°)$
d) $4\sqrt{17}(\cos 194° + i \sin 194°)$
e) None of these

Answer: c Difficulty: 1

14. Rewrite in trigonometric form: $-4i$.
a) $4\left(\cos \frac{3\pi}{2} + i \sin \frac{3\pi}{2}\right)$
b) $4(\cos \pi + i \sin \pi)$
c) $4\left(\cos \frac{\pi}{2} + i \sin \frac{\pi}{2}\right)$
d) $4(\cos 0 + i \sin 0)$
e) None of these

Answer: a Difficulty: 1

15. Rewrite in trigonometric form: $-2 + 3i$.
a) $\sqrt{13}(\cos 56.3° + i \sin 56.3°)$
b) $\sqrt{13}(\cos 123.7° + i \sin 123.7°)$
c) $\sqrt{13}(\cos 236.3° + i \sin 236.3°)$
d) $\sqrt{13}(\cos 303.7° + i \sin 303.7°)$
e) None of these

Answer: b Difficulty: 1

16. Rewrite in trigonometric form: $7 - 2i$.
a) $\sqrt{53}(\cos 344.1° + i \sin 344.1°)$
b) $3\sqrt{5}(\cos 344.1° + i \sin 344.1°)$
c) $3\sqrt{5}(\cos 15.9° + i \sin 15.9°)$
d) $\sqrt{53}(\cos 15.9° + i \sin 15.9°)$
e) None of these

Answer: a Difficulty: 1

SHORT ANSWER

17. Rewrite in trigonometric form: $-2 + \sqrt{3}\, i$.

Answer:
$\sqrt{7}(\cos 139.1° + i \sin 139.1°)$
Difficulty: 1

18. Rewrite in trigonometric form: $-17 + 32i$.

Answer: $36.235(\cos 117.98° + i \sin 117.98°)$ Difficulty: 1

19. Use a graphing utility to rewrite in trigonometric form: $-3 + 4i$.

Answer: $5(\cos 126.9° + i \sin 126.9°)$ Difficulty: 1 Key 1: T

20. Use a graphing utility to rewrite in trigonometric form: $2 - 5i$.

Answer: $5.39(\cos 291.8° + i \sin 291.8°)$ Difficulty: 1 Key 1: T

MULTIPLE CHOICE

21. Rewrite in standard form: $10\left[\cos \frac{2\pi}{3} + i \sin \frac{2\pi}{3}\right]$.
a) $5\sqrt{3} + 5i$
b) $10\sqrt{3}i$
c) $5 + 5\sqrt{3}i$
d) $-5 + 5\sqrt{3}i$
e) None of these

Answer: d Difficulty: 1

22. Rewrite in standard form: $4\left[\cos \frac{7\pi}{6} + i \sin \frac{7\pi}{6}\right]$.

a) $\frac{\sqrt{3}}{2} - i$ b) $-2\sqrt{3} - 2i$ c) $-1 - 2\sqrt{3}i$

d) $-2 + 2\sqrt{2}i$ e) None of these

Answer: b Difficulty: 1

23. Rewrite in standard form: $2(\cos 240° + i \sin 240°)$.

a) $-1 - \sqrt{3}i$ b) $1 + \sqrt{3}i$ c) $-\sqrt{3} - i$

d) $-\sqrt{3} + i$ e) None of these

Answer: a Difficulty: 1

SHORT ANSWER

24. Use a graphing utility to rewrite in standard form: $3(\cos 125° + i \sin 125°)$.

Answer: $-1.72 + 2.46\ i$ Difficulty: 1 Key 1: T

25. Use a graphing utility to rewrite in standard form: $12(\cos 330° + i \sin 330°)$.

Answer: $10.39 - 6i$ Difficulty: 1 Key 1: T

MULTIPLE CHOICE

26. Rewrite in standard form: $3(\cos 300° + i \sin 300°)$.

a) $\frac{3}{2} + \frac{3\sqrt{3}}{2} i$ b) $\frac{3}{2} - \frac{3\sqrt{3}}{2} i$ c) $-\frac{3}{2} - \frac{3\sqrt{3}}{2} i$

d) $\frac{3\sqrt{3}}{2} - \frac{3}{2} i$ e) None of these

Answer: b Difficulty: 1

27. Rewrite in standard form: $5(\cos 120° + i \sin 120°)$.

a) $\frac{5}{2} + \frac{5\sqrt{3}}{2} i$ b) $-\frac{5\sqrt{3}}{2} - \frac{5}{2} i$ c) $-\frac{5}{2} + \frac{5\sqrt{3}}{2} i$

d) $\frac{5\sqrt{3}}{2} - \frac{5}{2} i$ e) None of these

Answer: c Difficulty: 1

28. Rewrite in standard form: $6\left[\cos \frac{11\pi}{6} + i \sin \frac{11\pi}{6}\right]$.

a) $-3 + 3\sqrt{3}\, i$
b) $3\sqrt{3} - 3i$
c) $3 - 3\sqrt{3}i$
d) $3\sqrt{3} + 3i$
e) None of these

Answer: b Difficulty: 1

29. Rewrite each number in standard form, then perform the addition.

$$\left[5\left[\cos \frac{7\pi}{6} + i \sin \frac{7\pi}{6}\right]\right] + \left[3\left[\cos \frac{5\pi}{6} + i \sin \frac{5\pi}{6}\right]\right]$$

a) $-1 - 4\sqrt{3}i$
b) $4\sqrt{3} - 4i$
c) $-4\sqrt{3}i - 4$
d) $-4\sqrt{3} - i$
e) None of these

Answer: d Difficulty: 1

30. Rewrite each number in standard form, then perform the subtraction.

$$\left[6\left[\cos \frac{4\pi}{3} + i \sin \frac{4\pi}{3}\right]\right] - \left[2\left[\cos \frac{5\pi}{3} + i \sin \frac{5\pi}{3}\right]\right]$$

a) $-4 - 4\sqrt{3}i$
b) $-2 - 2\sqrt{3}i$
c) $-4 - 2\sqrt{3}i$
d) $4\left[\cos\left[-\frac{\pi}{3}\right] + i \sin\left[-\frac{\pi}{3}\right]\right]$
e) None of these

Answer: c Difficulty: 1

SHORT ANSWER

31. Rewrite each number in standard form, then perform the addition.

$$\left[\frac{2}{5}\left[\cos \frac{7\pi}{4} + i \sin \frac{7\pi}{4}\right]\right] + \left[8\left[\cos \frac{\pi}{4} + i \sin \frac{\pi}{4}\right]\right]$$

Answer:

$$\frac{21\sqrt{2}}{5} + \frac{19\sqrt{2}}{5} i$$

Difficulty: 2

MULTIPLE CHOICE

32. Rewrite each number in standard form, then perform the subtraction.
$[10(\cos 180° + i \sin 180°)] - [16(\cos 270° + i \sin 270°)]$

a) $-10 + 16i$
b) $10 - 16i$
c) $-10 - 16i$
d) $10 + 16i$
e) None of these

Answer: a Difficulty: 1

33. Multiply: $[5(\cos 15° + i \sin 15°)][12(\cos 23° + i \sin 23°)]$.
   a) $60(\cos 345° + i \sin 345°)$
   b) $60(\cos 38° + i \sin 38°)$
   c) $17(\cos 38° + i \sin 38°)$
   d) $17(\cos 345° + i \sin 345°)$
   e) None of these

   Answer: b Difficulty: 1

34. Multiply: $[5(\cos 30° + i \sin 30°)][7(\cos 23° + i \sin 30°)]$.
   a) $35(\cos 60° + i \sin 60°)$
   b) $35(\cos 30° + i \sin 30°)$
   c) $35(\cos 900° + i \sin 900°)$
   d) $12(\cos 30° + i \sin 30°)$
   e) None of these

   Answer: a Difficulty: 1

SHORT ANSWER

35. Multiply: $[16(\cos 33° + i \sin 33°)][8(\cos 17° + i \sin 17°)]$.

   Answer: $128(\cos 50° + i \sin 50°)$ Difficulty: 1

MULTIPLE CHOICE

36. Multiply: $[3(\cos 85° + i \sin 85°)][12(\cos 10° + i \sin 10°)]$.
   a) $4(\cos 75° + i \sin 75°)$
   b) $36(\cos 850° + i \sin 850°)$
   c) $36(\cos 95° + i \sin 95°)$
   d) $4(\cos 95° + i \sin 95°)$
   e) None of these

   Answer: c Difficulty: 1

37. Multiply: $[6(\cos 52° + i \sin 52°)][15(\cos 8° + i \sin 8°)]$.
   a) $45 + 45\sqrt{3}i$
   b) $45\sqrt{2} + 45\sqrt{2}i$
   c) $\dfrac{21}{2} + \dfrac{21\sqrt{3}}{2}i$
   d) $21(\cos 56° + i \sin 56°)$
   e) None of these

   Answer: a Difficulty: 1

38. Multiply: $[12(\cos 15° + i \sin 15)]^2$.
   a) $134.4 + 9.6i$
   b) $124.7 + 72i$
   c) $101.8 + 101.8i$
   d) $11.6 + 3.1i$
   e) None of these

   Answer: b Difficulty: 1

39. Divide: $\dfrac{7(\cos 75° + i \sin 75°)}{2(\cos 25° + i \sin 25°)}$.
   a) $\dfrac{7}{2}(\cos 50° - i \sin 50°)$
   b) $\dfrac{7}{2}(\cos 3° + i \sin 3°)$
   c) $\dfrac{7}{2}(\cos 50° + i \sin 50°)$
   d) $\dfrac{7}{2}(\cos 3 - i \sin 3°)$
   e) None of these

   Answer: c Difficulty: 1

SHORT ANSWER

40. Divide: $\dfrac{16[\cos(3\pi/4) + i\sin(3\pi/4)]}{2[\cos(\pi/2) + i\sin(\pi/2)]}$

Answer:
$8\left[\cos\dfrac{\pi}{4} + i\sin\dfrac{\pi}{4}\right] = 4\sqrt{2} + 4\sqrt{2}i$

Difficulty: 1

MULTIPLE CHOICE

41. Divide: $\dfrac{5(\cos 200° + i\sin 200°)}{10(\cos 20° + i\sin 20°)}$.

a) $\frac{1}{2}(\cos 10° + i\sin 10°)$ b) $-\frac{1}{2}$ c) $\frac{1}{2}$
d) $\frac{7}{2}(\cos 10° - i\sin 10°)$ e) None of these

Answer: b Difficulty: 1

42. Divide: $\dfrac{12(\cos 20° + i\sin 20°)}{4(\cos 50° + i\sin 50°)}$.

a) $\frac{3\sqrt{3}}{2} + \frac{3}{2}i$ b) $-\frac{3\sqrt{3}}{2} - \frac{3}{2}i$ c) $\frac{3\sqrt{3}}{2} - \frac{3}{2}i$
d) $3(\cos 0.4° + i\sin 0.4°)$ e) None of these

Answer: c Difficulty: 1

43. Divide: $\dfrac{60(\cos 300° + i\sin 300°)}{20(\cos 30° + i\sin 30°)}$.

a) $-3i$ b) $3 + 3i$ c) $-3 - 3i$ d) -3 e) None of these

Answer: a Difficulty: 1

44. Divide: $\dfrac{12(\cos 50° + i\sin 50°)}{6(\cos 20° + i\sin 20°)}$.

a) $2 - \sqrt{3}i$ b) $1 + \sqrt{3}i$ c) $\sqrt{3} + i$
d) $2(\cos 2.5° + \sin 2.5°)$ e) None of these

Answer: c Difficulty: 1

45. Evaluate $(3 + 3i)^8$.
a) 104,976 b) 6561 c) 16 d) $6561 + 6561i$ e) None of these

Answer: a Difficulty: 1

46. Evaluate: $(-2 + 2i)^8$.

a) $-2896.3 + 2896.3i$ b) $-16i$ c) $4096i$
d) 4096 e) None of these

Answer: d Difficulty: 1

SHORT ANSWER

47. Evaluate: $\left(\sqrt{3} - i\right)^7$.

Answer:

$-64\sqrt{3} + 64i$

Difficulty: 1

MULTIPLE CHOICE

48. Evaluate: $\left[\frac{5}{2} - \frac{5\sqrt{3}}{2}i\right]^6$.

a) $15{,}625i$ b) $15{,}625$ c) $15{,}625(1 + i)$
d) $\frac{15{,}625}{64} - \frac{421{,}875}{64}i$ e) None of these

Answer: b Difficulty: 1

49. Evaluate: $\left[4\left(-\frac{\sqrt{3}}{2} + \frac{1}{2}i\right)\right]^6$.

a) $1728 + \frac{1}{64}i$ b) $4096i$ c) $4096(-1 + i)$
d) -4096 e) None of these

Answer: d Difficulty: 1

50. Evaluate: $\left[3\left(\sqrt{2} - \sqrt{2}i\right)\right]^4$.

a) -1296 b) $1296 - 1296i$ c) -81
d) $12 + 12i$ e) None of these

Answer: a Difficulty: 1

51. Evaluate: $\left[3\left(-\sqrt{2} - \sqrt{2}i\right)\right]^3$.

a) $-54\sqrt{2} - 54\sqrt{2}i$ b) $\frac{216\sqrt{3}}{3} + 216i$ c) $108\sqrt{2} - 108\sqrt{2}i$
d) $-108\sqrt{2} - 108\sqrt{2}i$ e) None of these

Answer: c Difficulty: 1

52. Evaluate: $[3(\cos 120° + i \sin 120°)]^5$.

a) $\dfrac{-243}{2} - \dfrac{243\sqrt{3}}{2}i$ b) $\dfrac{-243}{2} + \dfrac{243\sqrt{3}}{2}i$ c) $\dfrac{243}{2} + \dfrac{243\sqrt{3}}{2}i$

d) $\dfrac{243}{2} - \dfrac{243\sqrt{3}}{2}i$ e) None of these

Answer: a Difficulty: 1

53. Evaluate: $[2(\cos 15° + i \sin 15°)]^{12}$.

a) 4096 b) $4096i$ c) -4096 d) $-4096i$ e) None of these

Answer: c Difficulty: 1

SHORT ANSWER

54. Evaluate: $\left[2\left(\cos \dfrac{\pi}{4} + i \sin \dfrac{\pi}{4}\right)\right]^{12}$.

Answer: -4096 Difficulty: 1

MULTIPLE CHOICE

55. Evaluate: $\left[3\left(\cos \dfrac{\pi}{6} + i \sin \dfrac{\pi}{6}\right)\right]^{12}$.

a) 531,441 b) 22,436,771.7 c) $531{,}441 - 531{,}441i$

d) $3^{12}\left(\dfrac{729}{4096} + \dfrac{1}{4096}i\right)$ e) None of these

Answer: a Difficulty: 1

56. Evaluate: $\left[4\left(\cos \dfrac{2\pi}{3} + i \sin \dfrac{2\pi}{3}\right)\right]^{3}$.

a) $-8 + 3.5i$ b) $64\left(\cos \dfrac{2\pi}{3} + i \sin \dfrac{2\pi}{3}\right)$ c) 64

d) $64 - 64i$ e) None of these

Answer: c Difficulty: 1

57. Evaluate: $\left[4\left(\cos \dfrac{\pi}{3} + i \sin \dfrac{\pi}{3}\right)\right]^{3}$.

a) $64(1 - i)$ b) $64i$ c) $-64(1 + i)$

d) -64 e) None of these

Answer: d Difficulty: 1

58. Evaluate: $\left[4\left(\cos\frac{\pi}{3} + i\sin\frac{\pi}{3}\right)\right]^5$.

a) $512 - 512\sqrt{3}i$
b) 1024
c) $32 + 32\sqrt{3}i$
d) $-32 + 32\sqrt{3}i$
e) None of these

Answer: a Difficulty: 1

59. Find the square roots: $64\left(\cos\frac{\pi}{3} + i\sin\frac{\pi}{3}\right)$.

a) $8\left(\cos\frac{\pi}{3} + i\sin\frac{\pi}{3}\right),\ 8\left(\cos\frac{2\pi}{3} + i\sin\frac{2\pi}{3}\right)$
b) $8\left(\cos\frac{\pi}{6} + i\sin\frac{\pi}{6}\right),\ 8\left(\cos\frac{7\pi}{6} + i\sin\frac{7\pi}{6}\right)$
c) $8\left(\cos\frac{\pi}{3} + i\sin\frac{\pi}{3}\right),\ 8\left(\cos\frac{\pi}{6} + i\sin\frac{\pi}{6}\right)$
d) $4\sqrt{2} + 4\sqrt{3}i,\ 4\sqrt{2} - 4\sqrt{3}i$
e) None of these

Answer: b Difficulty: 1

SHORT ANSWER

60. Find the cube roots: $8\left(\cos\frac{\pi}{3} + i\sin\frac{\pi}{3}\right)$.

Answer:
$2\left(\cos\frac{\pi}{9} + i\sin\frac{\pi}{9}\right),\ 2\left(\cos\frac{7\pi}{9} + i\sin\frac{7\pi}{9}\right),\ 2\left(\cos\frac{13\pi}{9} + i\sin\frac{13\pi}{9}\right)$

Difficulty: 1

MULTIPLE CHOICE

61. Find the square roots: $49\left(\cos\frac{\pi}{3} + i\sin\frac{\pi}{3}\right)$.

a) $-\frac{7}{2} + \frac{7\sqrt{3}}{2}i,\ \frac{7}{2} - \frac{7\sqrt{3}}{2}i$
b) $4.9 + 6.5i,\ 4.9 - 6.5i$
c) $\frac{7\sqrt{3}}{2} + \frac{7}{2}i,\ -\frac{7\sqrt{3}}{2} - \frac{7}{2}i$
d) $-\frac{7}{2} - \frac{7\sqrt{3}}{2}i,\ \frac{7}{2} + \frac{7\sqrt{3}}{2}i$
e) None of these

Answer: c Difficulty: 1

62. Find the sqaure roots: $81\left[\cos \frac{5\pi}{3} + i \sin \frac{5\pi}{3}\right]$.

a) $6.4 + 8.4i, -6.4 - 8.4i$

b) $\frac{9}{2} - \frac{9\sqrt{3}}{2} i, -\frac{9}{2} + \frac{9\sqrt{3}}{2} i$

c) $-\frac{9}{2} - \frac{9\sqrt{3}}{2} i, \frac{9}{2} + \frac{9\sqrt{32}}{i}$

d) $-\frac{9}{2}\sqrt{3} + \frac{9}{2} i, -\frac{9}{2}\sqrt{3} - \frac{9}{2} i$

e) None of these

Answer: d Difficulty: 1

SHORT ANSWER

63. Find the cube roots: $8\left[\cos \frac{5\pi}{3} + i \sin \frac{5\pi}{3}\right]$.

Answer:

$2\left[\cos \frac{5\pi}{9} + i \sin \frac{5\pi}{9}\right], 2\left[\cos \frac{11\pi}{9} + i \sin \frac{11\pi}{9}\right], 2\left[\cos \frac{17\pi}{9} + i \sin \frac{17\pi}{9}\right]$

Difficulty: 1

MULTIPLE CHOICE

64. Find the cube roots: $-64i$.

a) $-4i$, $4(\cos 330° + i \sin 330°)$, $4(\cos 330° - i \sin 330°)$

b) $4i$ $4(\cos 90° + i \sin 90°)$, $4(\cos 270° - i \sin 270°)$

c) $-4i$, $4(\cos 210° + i \sin 210°)$, $4(\cos 70° - i \sin 70°)$

d) $4i$, $4(\cos 210° + i \sin 210°)$, $4(\cos 330° - i \sin 330°)$

e) None of these

Answer: d Difficulty: 1

65. Find the cube roots: $8\left[\cos \frac{4\pi}{3} + i \sin \frac{4\pi}{3}\right]$.

a) $2\left[\cos \frac{4\pi}{9} + i \sin \frac{4\pi}{9}\right], 2\left[\cos \frac{10\pi}{9} + i \sin \frac{10\pi}{9}\right],$
$2\left[\cos \frac{16\pi}{9} + i \sin \frac{16\pi}{9}\right]$

b) $2\left[\cos \frac{4\pi}{9} + i \sin \frac{4\pi}{9}\right], 2\left[\cos \frac{13\pi}{9} + i \sin \frac{13\pi}{9}\right],$
$2\left[\cos \frac{21\pi}{9} + i \sin \frac{21\pi}{9}\right]$

c) $2(\cos 4\pi + i \sin 4\pi), 2(\cos 6\pi + i \sin 6\pi),$
$2(\cos 18\pi + i \sin 18\pi)$

d) $2\left[\cos \frac{4\pi}{9} + i \sin \frac{4\pi}{9}\right], 2\left[\cos \frac{4\pi}{27} + i \sin \frac{4\pi}{27}\right], 2\left[\cos \frac{4\pi}{81} + i \sin \frac{4\pi}{81}\right]$

e) None of these

Answer: a Difficulty: 1

66. Find the square roots: $-4i$.
   a) $2(\cos 135° - i \sin 135°)$, $2(-\cos 135° - i \sin 135°)$
   b) $2(\cos 135° + i \sin 135°)$, $2(\cos 67.5° + i \sin 67.5°)$
   c) $2(\cos 135° + i \sin 135°)$, $2(\cos 315° + i \sin 315°)$
   d) $2i$, $-2i$
   e) None of these

   Answer: c Difficulty: 1

67. Find the square roots: $81i$.
   a) $9(\cos 90° + i \sin 90°)$, $9(-\cos 90° - i \sin 90°)$
   b) $9(\cos 45° + i \sin 45°)$, $9(\cos 225° + i \sin 225°)$
   c) $9(\cos 45° - i \sin 45°)$, $9(-\cos 45° - i \sin 45°)$
   d) $9(\cos 90° + i \sin 90°)$, $9(\cos 45° + i \sin 45°)$
   e) None of these

   Answer: b Difficulty: 1

68. Find the cube roots: $-27i$.
   a) $3(\cos 90° + i \sin 90°)$, $-3(\cos 90° + i \sin 90°)$, $3(\cos 30° + i \sin 30°)$
   b) $3(\cos 90° - i \sin 90°)$, $3(\cos 210° - i \sin 210°)$, $3(\cos 330° - i \sin 330°)$
   c) $3(\cos 45° + i \sin 45°)$, $3(\cos 135° + i \sin 135°)$, $3(\cos 180° + i \sin 180°)$
   d) $3(\cos 90° + i \sin 90°)$, $3(\cos 210° + i \sin 210°)$, $3(\cos 330° + i \sin 330°)$
   e) None of these

   Answer: d Difficulty: 1

69. Find the fourth roots: $81i$.
   a) ± 3, $\pm 3i$
   b) $3\left[\cos \frac{\pi}{8} + i \sin \frac{\pi}{8}\right]$, $3\left[\cos \frac{17\pi}{8} + i \sin \frac{\pi}{8}\right]$,
   $3\left[\cos \frac{33\pi}{8} + i \sin \frac{33\pi}{8}\right]$, $3\left[\cos \frac{49\pi}{8} + i \sin \frac{49\pi}{8}\right]$
   c) $3\left[\cos \frac{\pi}{2} + i \sin \frac{\pi}{2}\right]$, $-3\left[\cos \frac{\pi}{2} + i \sin \frac{\pi}{2}\right]$,
   $-3\left[\cos \frac{3\pi}{2} + i \sin \frac{3\pi}{2}\right]$, $-3\left[\cos \frac{3\pi}{2} + i \sin \frac{3\pi}{2}\right]$
   d) $3\left[\cos \frac{\pi}{8} + i \sin \frac{\pi}{8}\right]$, $3\left[\cos \frac{5\pi}{8} + i \sin \frac{5\pi}{8}\right]$,
   $3\left[\cos \frac{9\pi}{8} + i \sin \frac{9\pi}{8}\right]$, $3\left[\cos \frac{13\pi}{8} + i \sin \frac{13\pi}{8}\right]$
   e) None of these

   Answer: d Difficulty: 1

SHORT ANSWER

70. Find the cube roots: -64.

   Answer:

   $2 - 2\sqrt{3}i$, -4, $2 + 2\sqrt{3}i$

   Difficulty: 1

71. Find the square roots of $-64i$. Represent each of the roots in standard form graphically.

Answer: See graph below.

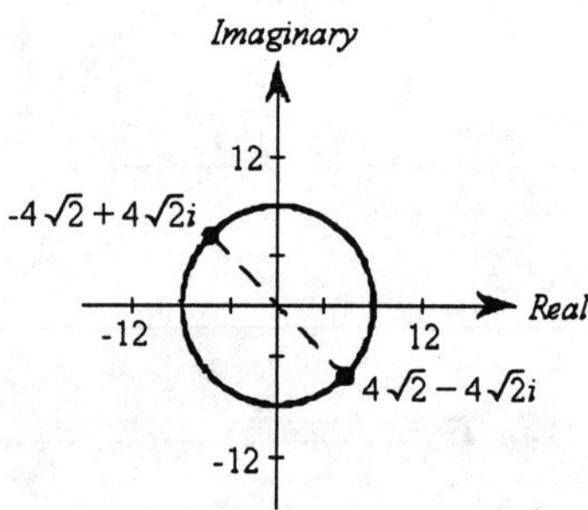

Difficulty: 2

72. Find the cube roots of 27. Represent each of the roots in standard form graphically.

Answer: See graph below.

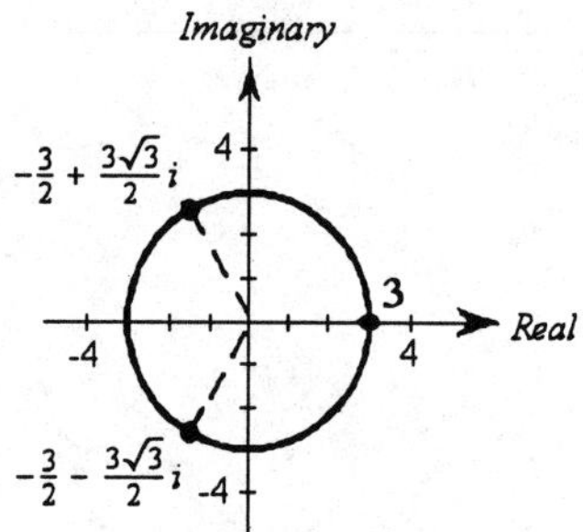

Difficulty: 2

MULTIPLE CHOICE

73. Find all solutions: $x^2 - 4i = 0$.
a) $\sqrt{2} - \sqrt{2}i$, $-\sqrt{2} + \sqrt{2}i$ b) $2 + i$, $-2 + i$ c) $2 - i$, $2 + i$
d) $\sqrt{2} + \sqrt{2}i$, $-\sqrt{2} - \sqrt{2}i$ e) None of these

Answer: d Difficulty: 1

SHORT ANSWER

74. Find all solutions: $x^2 + 4i = 0$.

Answer:

$-\sqrt{2} + \sqrt{2}i$, $\sqrt{2} - \sqrt{2}i$

Difficulty: 1

MULTIPLE CHOICE

75. Which of the following is *not* a solution to $x^3 - 1 = 0$?
   a) 1
   b) $\frac{1}{2} + \frac{\sqrt{3}}{2}i$
   c) $-\frac{1}{2} + \frac{\sqrt{3}}{2}i$
   d) $-\frac{1}{2} - \frac{\sqrt{3}}{2}i$
   e) All are solutions.

   Answer: b Difficulty: 1

76. Find all solutions: $x^2 - 16i = 0$.
   a) $2\sqrt{2} + 2\sqrt{2}i, -2\sqrt{2} - 2\sqrt{2}i$
   b) $2\sqrt{2} - 2\sqrt{2}i, -2\sqrt{2} - 2\sqrt{2}i$
   c) $-2\sqrt{2} + 2\sqrt{2}i, -2\sqrt{2} - 2\sqrt{2}i$
   d) $2\sqrt{2} + 2\sqrt{2}i, -2\sqrt{2} + 2\sqrt{2}i$
   e) None of these

   Answer: a Difficulty: 1

77. Which of the following is *not* a solution to $x^3 + 27i = 0$?
   a) $3i$
   b) $-\frac{3\sqrt{2}}{2} - \frac{3}{2}i$
   c) $-\frac{3\sqrt{3}}{2} - \frac{3}{2}i$
   d) $\frac{3\sqrt{3}}{2} - \frac{3}{2}i$
   e) Neither $-\frac{3\sqrt{2}}{2} - \frac{3}{2}$ nor $-\frac{3\sqrt{3}}{2} - \frac{3}{2}i$ is a solution.

   Answer: b Difficulty: 1

78. Which of the following is *not* a solution to $x^3 - 64 = 0$?
   a) 4
   b) $2 - 2\sqrt{3}i$
   c) $-2 + 2\sqrt{3}i$
   d) $-2 - 2\sqrt{3}i$
   e) Neither 4 nor $-2 + 2\sqrt{3}i$ is a solution.

   Answer: b Difficulty: 1

79. Which of the following is *not* a solution to $x^4 + 16i = 0$?
   a) $2(\cos 45° + i \sin 45°)$
   b) $2(\cos 157.5° + i \sin 157.5°)$
   c) $2(\cos 67.5° + i \sin 67.5°)$
   d) $2(\cos 247.5° + i \sin 247.5°)$
   e) All of these are solutions.

   Answer: a Difficulty: 1

Chapter 071: Solving Systems of Equations

MULTIPLE CHOICE

1. Determine which ordered pair(s) are solutions to the system

$$\begin{cases} x^2 - y = 2 \\ 2x - y = -1 \end{cases}.$$

a) (1, -1) b) (3, 7) c) (-1, -1)
d) Both (3, 7) and (-1, -1) e) All of these

Answer: d Difficulty: 1

2. Solve the system by the method of substitution:

$$\begin{cases} x + y = 1 \\ x^2 + 3y^2 = 21 \end{cases}.$$

a) $\left(\frac{3}{2}, -3\right)$ b) $\left(3, -\frac{3}{2}\right)$ c) $\left(-\frac{3}{2}, \frac{5}{2}\right)$, (3, -2)
d) $\left(\frac{3}{2}, -\frac{1}{2}\right)$, (-3, 4) e) No solution

Answer: c Difficulty: 1

3. Solve the system by the method of substitution:

$$\begin{cases} 2x^2 + 2y^2 = 7 \\ x + y^2 = 7 \end{cases}.$$

a) (2.8, 2.0), (-0.5, 7.3) b) (4.6, 1.5), (-2.6, 3.1)
c) (2.8, -0.5) d) (4.6), (-2.6)
e) No solution

Answer: e Difficulty: 2

SHORT ANSWER

4. Solve the system graphically:

$$\begin{cases} x^2 + y^2 = 25 \\ x - y = 1 \end{cases}.$$

Answer: See graph below.

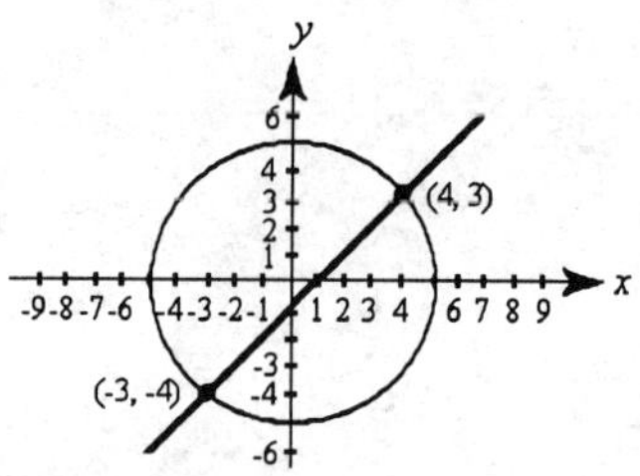

Difficulty: 1

5. Solve the system graphically:

$$\begin{cases} x^2 + 2y - 5 = 0 \\ 3x^2 - y - 1 = 0 \end{cases}$$

Answer: See graph below.

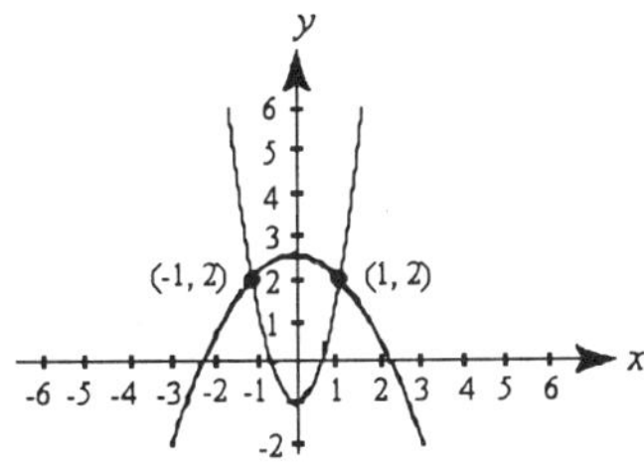

Difficulty: 1

6. Solve the system by the method of substitution:

$$\begin{cases} y = \dfrac{1}{x}. \\ x + 5y = 6 \end{cases}$$

Answer:

$(1, 1)$, $\left(5, \dfrac{1}{5}\right)$

Difficulty: 1

7. Solve the system graphically:

$$\begin{cases} x^2 - 4y = 17 \\ x - 2y = 1 \end{cases}.$$

Answer: See graph below.

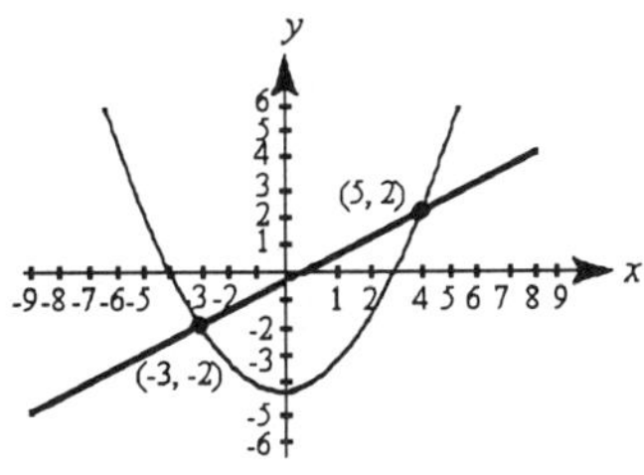

Difficulty: 1

8. Solve the system graphically:

$$\begin{cases} 2x + y = 1 \\ -x + 2y = 7 \end{cases}.$$

Answer: See graph below.

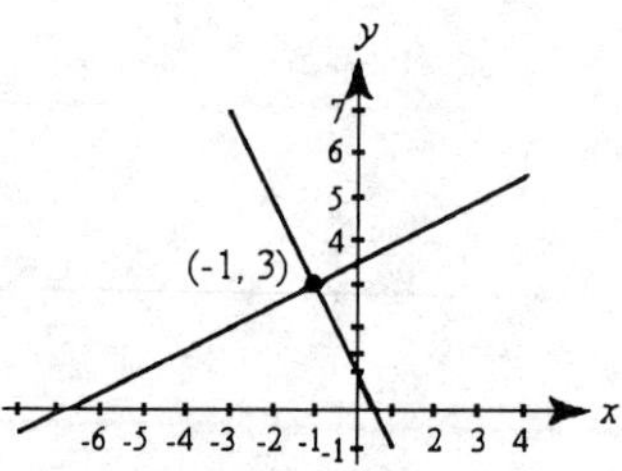

Difficulty: 1

MULTIPLE CHOICE

9. Solve the system by the method of substitution:

$$\begin{cases} 5x + y = 11 \\ 3x - 2y = 4 \end{cases}.$$

a) $\left(\frac{15}{13}, \frac{68}{13}\right)$ b) (2, 21) c) (2, 1)
d) $\left(\frac{15}{8}, -15\right)$ e) None of these

Answer: c Difficulty: 1

10. Solve the system by the method of substitution:

$$\begin{cases} 0.1x - 0.3y = 1.2 \\ 3x - 2y = 71 \end{cases}.$$

a) (5, 27) b) (1, 5) c) (27, 5)
d) $\left(\frac{61}{3}, 5\right)$ e) None of these

Answer: c Difficulty: 1

11. Solve the system by the method of substitution:

$$\begin{cases} \frac{1}{3}x - \frac{3}{5}y = -2 \\ 2x - y = 14 \end{cases}.$$

a) $\left(\frac{136}{23}, \frac{50}{23}\right)$ b) (12, 10) c) (12, -38)
d) No solution e) None of these

Answer: b Difficulty: 1

12. Solve the system by the method of substitution:

$$\begin{cases} x^2 + 2y = 6 \\ 2x + \quad y = 3 \end{cases}.$$

a) (4, -5) b) (2, 1) c) (0, 3)
d) (0, 3) and (4, -5) e) None of these

Answer: d Difficulty: 1

SHORT ANSWER

13. Solve the system graphically:

$$\begin{cases} x^2 + 2y = -6 \\ \;x - \quad y = \;\;3 \end{cases}.$$

Answer: See graph below.

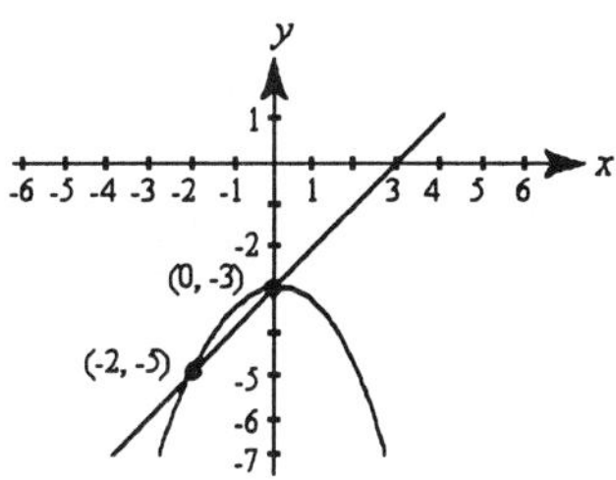

Difficulty: 1

14. Solve the system by the method of substitution:

$$\begin{cases} 2x^2 - y = -2 \\ \;\;x - y = -2 \end{cases}.$$

Answer:

(0, 2) and $\left(\frac{1}{2}, \frac{5}{2}\right)$

Difficulty: 1

MULTIPLE CHOICE

15. Solve the system by the method of substitution:

$$\begin{cases} 3x + 2y = 12 \\ 5x - \quad y = 23 \end{cases}.$$

a) $\left(-\frac{14}{13}, -\frac{344}{13}\right)$ b) $\left(\frac{58}{13}, -\frac{9}{13}\right)$ c) $\left(\frac{35}{13}, -\frac{124}{13}\right)$
d) (-17, 108) e) None of these

Answer: b Difficulty: 1

16. Solve the system by the method of substitution:

$$\begin{cases} 6x + 2y = 7 \\ 4x - 7y = -37 \end{cases}.$$

a) $\left(4, -\frac{53}{7}\right)$ b) $\left(6, \frac{61}{7}\right)$ c) $\left(6, -\frac{29}{2}\right)$
d) $\left(-\frac{1}{2}, 5\right)$ e) None of these

Answer: d Difficulty: 1

17. Solve the system by the method of substitution:

$$\begin{cases} x - 2y = 0 \\ 4y - 3x = 10 \end{cases}.$$

a) (-10, -5) b) (6, 3) c) $\left(\frac{1}{2}, \frac{1}{4}\right)$
d) $\left(1, \frac{1}{2}\right)$ e) None of these

Answer: a Difficulty: 1

SHORT ANSWER

18. Solve the system graphically:

$$\begin{cases} x - y = 4 \\ 3x - 2y = 14 \end{cases}.$$

Answer: See graph below.

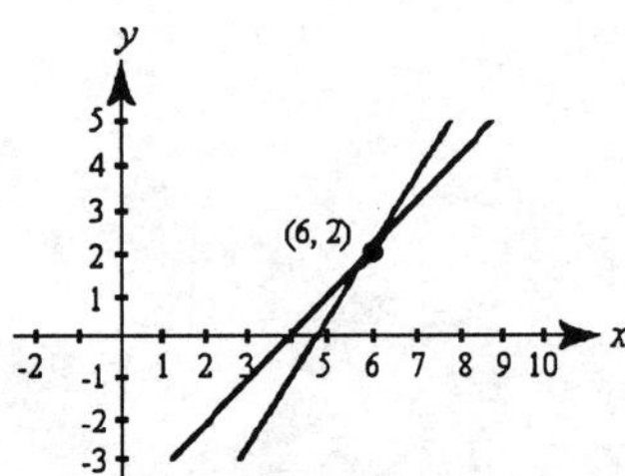

Difficulty: 1

MULTIPLE CHOICE

19. Solve the system:

$$\begin{cases} x + y = 16 \\ \frac{1}{2}x + \frac{1}{6}y = 2 \end{cases}.$$

a) (4, 12) b) (-2, 18) c) (-4, 20)
d) (2, 14) e) None of these

Answer: b Difficulty: 1

SHORT ANSWER

20. Solve the system: $\begin{cases} 0.1x - 0.1y = -0.9 \\ -0.3x + 0.5y = 3.3 \end{cases}$.

Answer: (-6, 3) Difficulty: 1

MULTIPLE CHOICE

21. Find all points of intersection of the graphs:

$\begin{cases} x^2 + y^2 = 3 \\ 2x^2 - y = 0 \end{cases}$.

a) $\left(\frac{3}{2}, -2\right)$ b) $\left(\pm\frac{\sqrt{3}}{2}, \frac{3}{2}\right)$ c) $\left(\pm\frac{\sqrt{3}}{2}, \frac{3}{2}\right)$, $(\pm 1, -2)$

d) (2, 14) e) None of these

Answer: b Difficulty: 1

SHORT ANSWER

22. Use a graphing utility to find all points of intersection of the graphs:

$\begin{cases} (x - 3)^2 + y^2 = 4 \\ -2x + y^2 = 0 \end{cases}$.

Answer: See graph below.

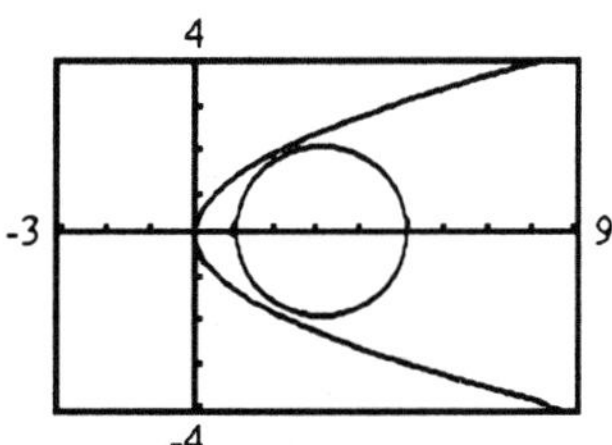

No points of intersection

Difficulty: 2 Key 1: T

23. Use a graphing utility to find all points of intersection of the graphs:

$$\begin{cases} x^2 - 4x + y = 0 \\ x - y = 0 \end{cases}.$$

Answer: See graph below.

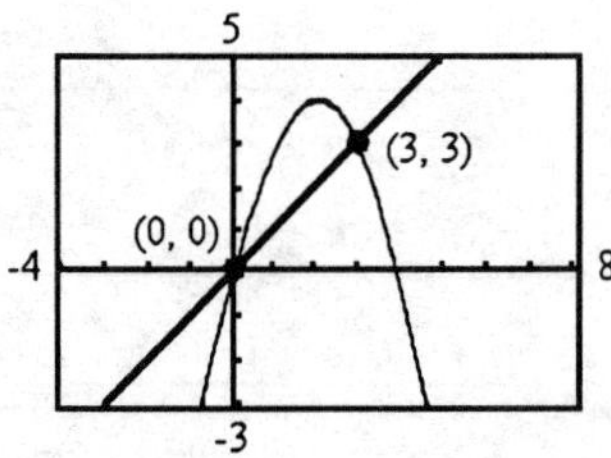

Difficulty: 1 Key 1: T

24. Use a graphing utility to find all points of intersection of the graphs:

$$\begin{cases} 2x^2 - y - 1 = 0 \\ 2x^2 + y - 3 = 0 \end{cases}.$$

Answer: See graph below.

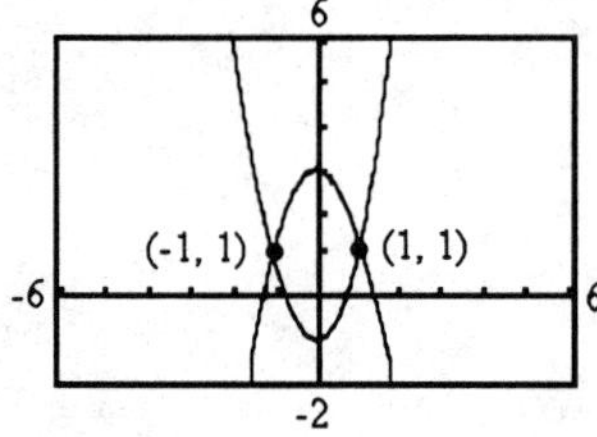

Difficulty: 1 Key 1: T

MULTIPLE CHOICE

25. Find all points of intersection of the graphs:

$$\begin{cases} 3x - y = -2 \\ x^3 - y = 0 \end{cases}.$$

a) (2, 8),(1, 1) b) (-2, -8),(-1, -1) c) (-2, -8),(1, 1)
d) (2, 8),(-1, -1) e) None of these

Answer: d Difficulty: 1

26. Find the number of points of intersection of the graphs:

$$\begin{cases} x^2 + y = 3 \\ x^2 + y^2 = 1 \end{cases}.$$

a) 4 b) 3 c) 2 d) 1 e) 0

Answer: e Difficulty: 1

27. Find the number of points of intersection of the graphs:

$$\begin{cases} x^2 + y = 1 \\ x^2 - y = 3 \end{cases}$$

a) 4 b) 3 c) 2 d) 1 e) 0

Answer: c Difficulty: 1

28. Find the number of points of intersection of the graphs:

$$\begin{cases} x^2 + y^2 = 5 \\ x + 2y - 5 = 0 \end{cases}$$

a) 4 b) 3 c) 2 d) 1 e) 0

Answer: d Difficulty: 1

29. A total of \$11,000 is invested in two funds paying 7% and 8% simple interest. If the yearly interest for both funds totals \$865, determine the amount invested at 8%.
a) \$9500 b) \$6500 c) \$1500 d) \$4500 e) None of these

Answer: a Difficulty: 1

30. A total of \$50,000 is invested in two funds paying 8% and 10% simple interest. If the yearly interest for both funds totals \$4660, determine the amount invested at 8%.
a) \$33,000 b) \$24,000 c) \$26,000
d) \$17,000 e) None of these

Answer: d Difficulty: 1

31. A total of \$12,000 is invested in two funds paying 7% and $9\frac{1}{2}$% simple interest. If the annual interest totals \$913.75, determine the amount invested at 7%.
a) \$7325 b) \$840 c) \$9050 d) \$10,000 e) None of these

Answer: c Difficulty: 1

32. A total of \$6000 is invested in two funds paying $5\frac{1}{4}$% and 6% simple interest. If the annual interest totals \$327, determine the amount invested at 6%.
a) \$1600 b) \$3750 c) \$6000 d) \$270 e) None of these

Answer: a Difficulty: 1

33. If the total cost of running a business is given by the equation $C = 450x + 1000$ and the revenue is given by the equation $R = 500x$, find the sales necessary to break even.
a) 220 b) 11 c) 20 d) 2000 e) None of these

Answer: c Difficulty: 1

34. If the total cost of running a business is given by the equation $C = 4.16x + 75{,}000$ and the revenue is given by the equation $R = 7.91x$, find the sales necessary to break even.
    a) 6214 b) 20,000 c) 200 d) 9482 e) None of these

    Answer: b Difficulty: 1

35. Suppose you are setting up for a small business and have invested $5000 to produce an item that will sell for $9. If each unit can be produced for $7, how many units must you sell to break even?
    a) 25 b) 2500 c) 556 d) 714 e) None of these

    Answer: b Difficulty: 1

36. Suppose you are setting up for a small business and have invested $18,000 to produce an item that will sell for $20.65. If each unit can be produced for $13.45, determine the number of units that you must sell in order to break even.
    a) 2500 b) 872 c) 1338 d) 250 e) None of these

    Answer: a Difficulty: 1

Chapter 072: Two-Variable Linear Systems

MULTIPLE CHOICE

1. Solve the linear system by the method of elimination:

$$\begin{cases} 7x - 3y = 26 \\ 2x + 5y = 25 \end{cases}.$$

a) $\left(-5, -\dfrac{61}{3}\right)$ b) (5, 3) c) Infinitely many solutions
d) No solution e) None of these

Answer: b Difficulty: 1

2. Solve the linear system by the method of elimination:

$$\begin{cases} 2x + 4y = 7 \\ 3x + 6y = 5 \end{cases}.$$

a) $\left(1, \dfrac{5}{4}\right)$ b) (0, 0) c) Infinitely many solutions
d) No solution e) None of these

Answer: d Difficulty: 1

3. Solve the linear system by the method of elimination:

$$\begin{cases} 6x - 5y = 4 \\ 3x + 2y = 1 \end{cases}.$$

a) $\left(\dfrac{13}{27}, -\dfrac{2}{9}\right)$ b) $\left(-\dfrac{2}{9}, -\dfrac{8}{5}\right)$ c) $\left(-\dfrac{8}{5}, -\dfrac{68}{25}\right)$
d) $\left(2, \dfrac{8}{5}\right)$ e) None of these

Answer: a Difficulty: 1

SHORT ANSWER

4. Solve the linear system by the method of elimination:

$$\begin{cases} 7x + y = 3 \\ 21x + 5y = 11 \end{cases}.$$

Answer:
$\left(\dfrac{2}{7}, 1\right)$
Difficulty: 1

MULTIPLE CHOICE

5. Use the method of elimination to find the value of y in the solution of the system of equations:

$$\begin{cases} 2x - 3y = 5 \\ 2x + 3y = -3 \end{cases}.$$

a) $\frac{1}{2}$ b) $-\frac{3}{4}$ c) $-\frac{4}{3}$ d) $\frac{4}{3}$ e) None of these

Answer: c Difficulty: 1

6. Use the method of elimination to find the value of x in the solution of the system of equations:

$$\begin{cases} 2x - y = 5 \\ 2x + 2y = -9 \end{cases}.$$

a) 2 b) $\frac{1}{2}$ c) -5 d) $\frac{21}{2}$ e) None of these

Answer: b Difficulty: 1

7. Use the method of elimination to solve the system of equations:

$$\begin{cases} 5x + 2y = -1 \\ -15x + 8y = 10 \end{cases}.$$

a) (-2/5, 1/2) b) $\left(\frac{-14}{25}, \frac{9}{10}\right)$ c) $\left(\frac{-16}{35}, \frac{9}{14}\right)$

d) $\left(\frac{-1}{5}, 0\right)$ e) None of these

Answer: a Difficulty: 1

SHORT ANSWER

8. Solve the system of equations:

$$\begin{cases} -2x + 3y = 5 \\ 3x - 2y = 0 \end{cases}.$$

Answer: (2, 3) Difficulty: 1

MULTIPLE CHOICE

9. Solve the system of equations:

$$\begin{cases} 3x + 7y = 15 \\ -5x + 2y = 16 \end{cases}.$$

a) $(-2, 3)$ b) $\left(\frac{29}{3}, -2\right)$ c) $\left(\frac{1}{3}, 2\right)$

d) $\left(3, \frac{6}{7}\right)$ e) None of these

Answer: a Difficulty: 1

SHORT ANSWER

10. Solve the system by the method of elimination and verify the solution with a graphing utility:

$$\begin{cases} 2x - 5y = -4 \\ 4x + 3y = 5 \end{cases}.$$

Answer:
$\left(\frac{1}{2}, 1\right)$

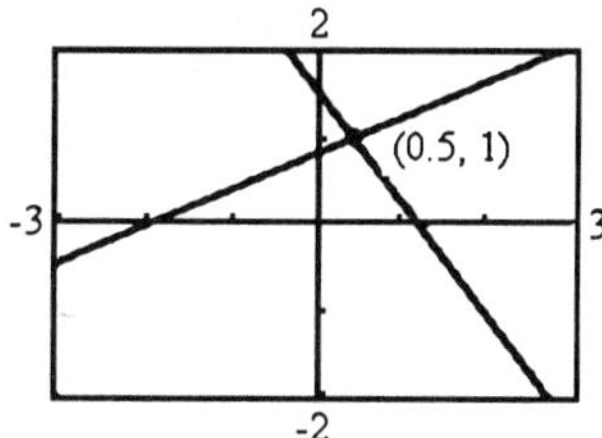

Difficulty: 2 Key 1: T

11. Solve the system by the method of elimination and verify the solution with a graphing utility:

$$\begin{cases} 6x + \ \ y = -2 \\ 4x - 3y = 17 \end{cases}.$$

Answer:
$\left(\frac{1}{2}, -5\right)$

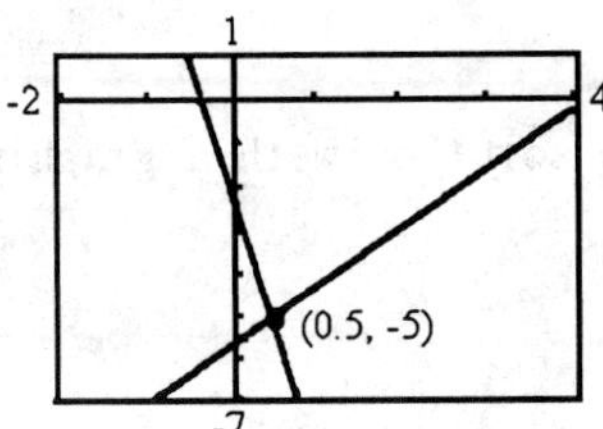

Difficulty: 2 Key 1: T

12. Solve the system by the method of elimination and verify the solution with a graphing utility:

$$\begin{cases} \frac{6}{x} - \frac{8}{y} = 2 \\ \frac{9}{2x} - \frac{6}{y} = \frac{3}{2} \end{cases}.$$

Answer: Infinitely many solutions

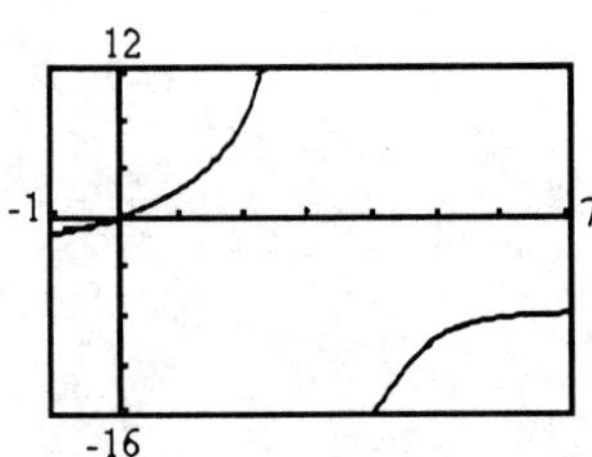

Difficulty: 2 Key 1: T

MULTIPLE CHOICE

13. Solve the system by the method of elimination:

$$\begin{cases} \frac{2}{x} - \frac{3}{y} = 8 \\ \frac{3}{x} + \frac{3}{y} = 2 \end{cases}.$$

a) $\left(2, -\frac{4}{3}\right)$ b) $\left(\frac{1}{2}, -\frac{3}{4}\right)$ c) Infinitely many solutions
d) No solution e) None of these

Answer: b Difficulty: 1

14. Solve the system by the method of elimination:

$$\begin{cases} \frac{6}{x} + \frac{3}{y} = 8 \\ \frac{9}{x} + \frac{5}{y} = 16 \end{cases}.$$

a) $\left(\frac{2}{3}, 2\right)$ b) $\left(\frac{3}{2}, \frac{1}{2}\right)$ c) $\left(2, \frac{3}{2}\right)$
d) $\left(\frac{1}{2}, \frac{2}{3}\right)$ e) None of these

Answer: b Difficulty: 2

SHORT ANSWER

15. Solve the system of equations:

$$\begin{cases} \frac{6}{x} + \frac{1}{y} = -2 \\ \frac{4}{x} - \frac{3}{y} = 17 \end{cases}.$$

Answer:
$\left(2, -\frac{1}{5}\right)$
Difficulty: 1

16. Solve the system of equations:

$$\begin{cases} 3x - 6y = 12 \\ 4x - 8y = 16 \end{cases}.$$

Answer: Infinitely many solutions. Difficulty: 1

17. Solve the system of equations:

$$\begin{cases} \dfrac{2x-5}{3} + \dfrac{y-1}{6} = \dfrac{1}{2} \\ \dfrac{x}{5} + \dfrac{y-2}{-4} = 1 \end{cases}.$$

Answer:
$\left(\dfrac{5}{2}, 4\right)$

Difficulty: 2

18. Solve the system of linear equations graphically:

$$\begin{cases} \dfrac{1}{3}x - \dfrac{3}{5}y = -2 \\ 2x - y = 14 \end{cases}$$

Answer: See graph below.

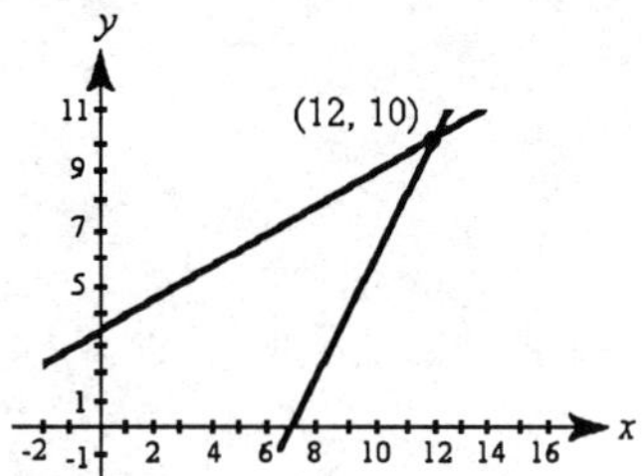

Difficulty: 2

19. Solve the system of linear equations graphically:

$$\begin{cases} 3x + 2y = 8 \\ 6x + 4y = 10 \end{cases}$$

Answer: No solutions

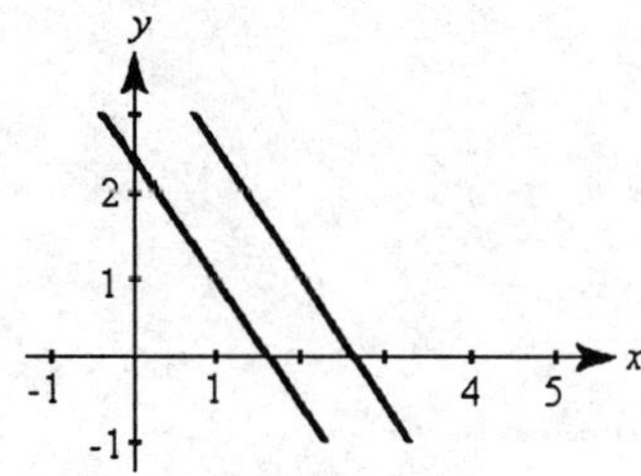

Difficulty: 2

MULTIPLE CHOICE

20. Solve the system of linear equations:

$$\begin{cases} 6x - 8y = 2 \\ \frac{9}{2}x - 6y = \frac{3}{2} \end{cases}.$$

a) $\left(\frac{3}{2}, 4\right)$ b) $\left(\frac{2}{3}, \frac{1}{4}\right)$ c) Infinitely many solutions
d) No solutions e) None of these

Answer: c Difficulty: 2

21. Solve the system of linear equations:

$$\begin{cases} 0.06x + 0.02y = 0.08 \\ 0.09x + 0.05y = 0.16 \end{cases}.$$

a) $\left(\frac{3}{2}, \frac{1}{2}\right)$ b) $\left(\frac{3}{2}, 2\right)$ c) $\left(\frac{1}{2}, \frac{2}{3}\right)$
d) $\left(2, \frac{3}{2}\right)$ e) None of these

Answer: b Difficulty: 2

22. Solve the following system of linear equations for x:

$$\begin{cases} x + y = 1000 \\ 0.03x + 0.04y = 31.50 \end{cases}.$$

a) 325 b) 540 c) 675 d) 850 e) None of these

Answer: d Difficulty: 1

23. Solve the following system of linear equations for x:

$$\begin{cases} x + 2.5y = 900 \\ 5x - 2y = 150 \end{cases}.$$

a) 300 b) 150 c) 900 d) 0 e) None of these

Answer: b Difficulty: 1

24. Solve the following system of linear equations for y:

$$\begin{cases} 3x + 4.5y = 825 \\ 0.2x + 0.5y = 89 \end{cases}.$$

a) 100 b) 150 c) 170 d) 190 e) None of these

Answer: c Difficulty: 1

25. A twenty-pound mixture of two kinds of candy sells for \$30.52. One kind of candy in the mixture sells for \$1.35 per pound. The other kind sells for \$1.79 per pound. How much of the cheaper-priced candy is in the mixture?
a) 8 pounds b) 10 pounds c) 12 pounds
d) 14 pounds e) None of these

Answer: c Difficulty: 2

SHORT ANSWER

26. How many liters of a 40% solution of acid must be combined with a 15% solution to obtain 30 liters of a 20% solution?

Answer: 6 Difficulty: 2

27. The perimeter of a rectangle is 91 feet and the length is 8 feet more than twice the width. Find the dimensions of the rectangle.

Answer: $L = 33$ feet, $W = 12.5$ feet Difficulty: 2

MULTIPLE CHOICE

28. A total of \$15,000 is invested in two corporate bonds that pay $7\frac{1}{4}\%$ and 9% simple interest. The annual income from both bonds is \$1280. Determine how much is invested at 9%.
a) \$9000 b) \$4000 c) \$11,000
d) \$6000 e) None of these

Answer: c Difficulty: 1

SHORT ANSWER

29. Suppose the demand and supply equations for a certain product are given by

$p = 220 - 0.0002x$ Demand equation

$p = 90 + 0.0003x$ Supply equation

where p is the price in dollars and x represents the number of units. Find the point of equilibrium.

Answer: $x = 260{,}000$ and $p = \$168$ Difficulty: 1

MULTIPLE CHOICE

30. Suppose the demand and supply equations for a certain product are given by

$p = 860 - 0.05x$ Demand equation

$p = 420 + 0.15x$ Supply equation

Find the point (x, p) of equilibrium.
a) (12,800,220) b) (1700,775) c) (420,839)
d) (2200,750) e) None of these

Answer: d Difficulty: 1

SHORT ANSWER

31. Find the least squares regression line $y = ax + b$ for the points (0.6, 9.3),(1.2, 12.0) and (1.8, 15.2) if

$$nb + \left[\sum_{i=1}^{n} x_i\right] a = \sum_{i=1}^{n} y_i \text{ and } \left[\sum_{i=1}^{n} x_i\right] b + \left[\sum_{i=1}^{n} x_i^2\right] a = \sum_{i=1}^{n} x_i y_i.$$

Use the linear regression capabilities of a graphing utility to confirm the result.

Answer: $y = 4.92x + 6.27$ Difficulty: 2 Key 1: T

32. Find the least squares regression line $y = ax + b$ for the points (1, 2), (2, 4), (3, 5) and (4, 7) if

$$nb + \left[\sum_{i=1}^{n} x_i\right] a = \sum_{i=1}^{n} y_i \text{ and } \left[\sum_{i=1}^{n} x_i\right] b + \left[\sum_{i=1}^{n} x_i^2\right] a = \sum_{i=1}^{n} x_i y_i.$$

Use the linear regression capabilities of a graphing utility to confirm the result.

Answer: $y = 1.6x + 0.5$ Difficulty: 2 Key 1: T

MULTIPLE CHOICE

33. Find the least squares regression line $y = ax + b$ by solving the following system for a and b.

$$\begin{cases} 5b + 10a = 12.3 \\ 10b + 30a = 29.1 \end{cases}$$

a) $y = 0.45x + 1.56$ b) $y = 0.26x + 1.94$ c) $y = 0.6x + 1.26$
d) $y = 3.2x - 3.94$ e) None of these

Answer: a Difficulty: 1

SHORT ANSWER

34. Find the least squares regression line $y = ax + b$ by solving the following system for a and b.

$$\begin{cases} 5b + 10a = 9.2 \\ 10b + 30a = 21.1 \end{cases}$$

Answer: $y = 0.27x + 1.3$ Difficulty: 1

Chapter 073: Multivariable Linear Systems

MULTIPLE CHOICE

1. Use the method of back-substitution to find the value of x for the solution of the system of equations.

$$\begin{cases} x + 2y + z = 15 \\ 5y - 2z = -16 \\ z = 3 \end{cases}$$

a) 22 b) 16 c) $\frac{15}{7}$ d) 8 e) None of these

Answer: b Difficulty: 1

2. Use the method of back-substitution to find the value of x for the solution of the system of equations.

$$\begin{cases} x + 2y - z = 26 \\ y + 3z = 5 \\ z = -2 \end{cases}$$

a) 4 b) 26 c) 6 d) 2 e) None of these

Answer: d Difficulty: 1

SHORT ANSWER

3. Use the method of back-substitution to find the solution of the system of equations.

$$\begin{cases} x + y + z = 2 \\ y - z = 5 \\ z = -2 \end{cases}$$

Answer: (1, 3, -2) Difficulty: 1

MULTIPLE CHOICE

4. Use Gaussian elimination to solve the system of equations.

$$\begin{cases} x - 6y + z = 1 \\ -x + 2y - 4z = 3 \\ 7x - 10y + 3z = -25 \end{cases}$$

a) (5, 1, 2) b) (-5, -1, 0) c) (-1, 3, 1)
d) No solution e) None of these

Answer: b Difficulty: 1

SHORT ANSWER

5. Use Gaussian elimination to solve the system of equations.

$$\begin{cases} x + 2y + z = 6 \\ 2x - y + 3z = -2 \\ x + y - 2z = 0 \end{cases}$$

Answer: (-1, 3, 1) Difficulty: 1

MULTIPLE CHOICE

6. Solve the system of linear equations:

$$\begin{cases} x - y + z = 5 \\ 3x + 2y - z = -2. \\ 2x + y + 3z = 10 \end{cases}$$

a) (1, -1, 3) b) (2, -5, -2) c) (-1, 7, 13)
d) (3, -9, -7) e) No solution

Answer: a Difficulty: 1

7. Solve the system of linear equations:

$$\begin{cases} x + y + 3z = 0 \\ 2x - y - 3z = -9. \\ x + 2y + 3z = 1 \end{cases}$$

a) $\left(-3a, a, \frac{2a}{3}\right)$ b) $\left(-1, 2, -\frac{1}{3}\right)$ c) $\left(-3, 1, \frac{2}{3}\right)$
d) No solution e) None of these

Answer: c Difficulty: 1

8. Solve the system of linear equations:

$$\begin{cases} 6x - 9y + 4z = -7 \\ 2x + 6y - z = 6. \\ 4x - 3y + 2z = -2 \end{cases}$$

a) $\left(\frac{1}{2}, \frac{2}{3}, -1\right)$ b) $\left(\frac{11}{21}, 1, -\frac{2}{7}\right)$ c) $\left(a, \frac{31a}{15}, \frac{44a}{5}\right)$
d) No solution e) None of these

Answer: a Difficulty: 2

SHORT ANSWER

9. Solve the system of linear equations:

$$\begin{cases} x + y - z = -1 \\ 2x + 3y - z = -2. \\ -3x - 2y + 2z = -3 \end{cases}$$

Answer: (5, -3, 3) Difficulty: 1

10. Solve the system of linear equations.

$$\begin{cases} x - 3y + 2z = -11 \\ x + 4y - 5z = 17. \\ -2x + y - z = 6 \end{cases}$$

Answer: (-1, 2, -2) Difficulty: 1

MULTIPLE CHOICE

11. Solve the system of linear equations:

$$\begin{cases} 2x + y - z = 3 \\ x - 3y + z = 7. \\ 3x + 5y - 3z = 0 \end{cases}$$

a) $\left(a, \frac{3a - 10}{2}, \frac{7a - 16}{2}\right)$
b) $\left(\frac{3a + 10}{3}, a, 6a - 21\right)$
c) (2, -2, -1)
d) No solution
e) None of these

Answer: d Difficulty: 2

SHORT ANSWER

12. Solve the system of linear equations:

$$\begin{cases} x + y - 2z = 1 \\ 3x + y + z = 4. \\ -x - 3y + 9z = 10 \end{cases}$$

Answer: No solution Difficulty: 1

13. Solve the system of linear equations:

$$\begin{cases} 2x - 4y + z = 7 \\ x + 3y - z = 2. \\ -5x + 15y - 4z = 10 \end{cases}$$

Answer: No solution Difficulty: 2

MULTIPLE CHOICE

14. Solve the system of linear equations:

$$\begin{cases} x - y + z = 2 \\ 2x + 3y + z = 7. \\ 3x + 2y + 2z = -8 \end{cases}$$

a) (1, 0, 1) b) (6, 4, 4) c) (1, 2, 3)
d) No solution e) None of these

Answer: d Difficulty: 1

15. Solve the system of linear equations:

$$\begin{cases} x + y + z = 4 \\ x - 3y - z = 1. \\ 2x - 2y = 9 \end{cases}$$

a) $\left(-1, \frac{4}{7}, \frac{31}{7}\right)$ b) $\left(a, \frac{2a - 9}{2}, 17 - 4a\right)$
c) $\left(\frac{9 + 2a}{2}, a, -\frac{4a + 1}{2}\right)$ d) No solution
e) None of these

Answer: d Difficulty: 1

16. Solve the system of linear equations:

$$\begin{cases} 2x - 4y + z = 5 \\ x + y + z = 3. \\ 6x + 5z = 17 \end{cases}$$

a) $\left(\frac{5}{6}, \frac{1}{6}, 0\right)$ b) $\left(a, \frac{a - 2}{5}, \frac{17 - 6a}{5}\right)$ c) $\left(a, \frac{2a - 3}{5}, \frac{a + 7}{5}\right)$
d) No solution e) None of these

Answer: b Difficulty: 1

17. Solve the system of linear equations:

$$\begin{cases} 3x + 4y - 2z = 6 \\ x + y + z = 2. \\ x + 2y - 4z = 2 \end{cases}$$

a) (20, -15, -3) b) $\left(\frac{a}{2}, \frac{5a}{4}, \frac{a}{4}\right)$ c) $(2 - 6a, 5a, a)$
d) No solution e) None of these

Answer: c Difficulty: 2

18. Solve the system of linear equations:

$$\begin{cases} x + y + z = 2 \\ 3x - 2y + z = 7. \\ 5y + 2z = -1 \end{cases}$$

a) $\left(\frac{2}{5}, -\frac{7}{5}, 3\right)$ b) $\left(a, \frac{2a}{3}, \frac{a}{3}\right)$ c) $\left(\frac{11 - 3a}{5}, \frac{-1 - 2a}{5}, a\right)$
d) No solution e) None of these

Answer: c Difficulty: 2

SHORT ANSWER

19. Solve the system of linear equations:

$$\begin{cases} 2x + y - z = 1 \\ x + 4y + 2z = 7. \\ -5x + y + 5z = 4 \end{cases}$$

Answer:
$\left(\frac{-3 + 6a}{7}, \frac{13 - 5a}{7}, a\right)$
Difficulty: 2

20. Solve the system of linear equations:

$$\begin{cases} x - y - z = 0 \\ 2x + 4y + z = 0. \\ 3x + y - z = 0 \end{cases}$$

Answer: $(a, -a, 2a)$ where a is any real number. Difficulty: 1

MULTIPLE CHOICE

21. Solve the system of linear equations:

$$\begin{cases} 2x + 3y + 3z = 6 \\ -x + y + z = 2 \end{cases}.$$

a) $(2a - 4, 2 - a, a)$ b) $(0, 2 - a, a)$ c) $(2a, 2 + a, a)$
d) No solution e) None of these

Answer: b Difficulty: 2

22. Solve the system of linear equations:

$$\begin{cases} x - 2y - z = 7 \\ -3x + 6y + 3z = 0 \end{cases}.$$

a) $(7 + 5a, 2a, a)$ b) $(1, 1, -8)$ c) $(1, 0, 1)$
d) No solution e) None of these

Answer: d Difficulty: 2

23. Solve the system of linear equations:

$$\begin{cases} 2x + 3y - z = 6 \\ x - y + 2z = 1 \end{cases}.$$

a) $\left(a, \frac{13 - 5a}{5}, \frac{9 - 5a}{5}\right)$

b) $\left(\frac{10 - 2a}{3}, a, \frac{5 - 2a}{3}\right)$

c) $\left(3, -\frac{2}{5}, -\frac{6}{5}\right)$

d) No solution

e) None of these

Answer: a Difficulty: 1

SHORT ANSWER

24. Solve the system of linear equations:

$$\begin{cases} 2x + 3y - 3z = 7 \\ -3x + y + z = 2 \end{cases}.$$

Answer:
$\left(\frac{1 + 6a}{11}, \frac{25 + 7a}{11}, a\right)$
Difficulty: 1

25. Solve the system of linear equations:

$$\begin{cases} x + 3y + z = 0 \\ 5x - y + z + w = 0 \\ 2x + 2z + w = 2 \\ 3x + 2z - w = 10 \end{cases}.$$

Answer: $x = 0$, $y = -1$, $z = 3$, $w = -4$ Difficulty: 2

MULTIPLE CHOICE

26. Find the value of b that makes the system inconsistent:

$$\begin{cases} 6x + by = 14 \\ -2x + 3y = 2 \end{cases}.$$

a) -9 b) -3 c) $\frac{1}{7}$ d) $\frac{1}{3}$ e) None of these

Answer: a Difficulty: 2

27. Find the value of a that makes the system inconsistent:

$$\begin{cases} -3x + 5y = 2 \\ ax - 10y = 0 \end{cases}.$$

a) 3 b) 6 c) 2 d) -6 e) None of these

Answer: b Difficulty: 2

28. Find an equation of the parabola, $y = ax^2 + bx + c$, that passes through (1, 4), (-1, 0), and (2, -3). Verify your result with a graphing utility.
   a) $y = 4x^2 + 2x - 2$
   b) $y = 3x^2 + 2x - 7$
   c) $y = -3x^2 + 2x + 5$
   d) $y = 4x^2$
   e) None of these

   Answer: c

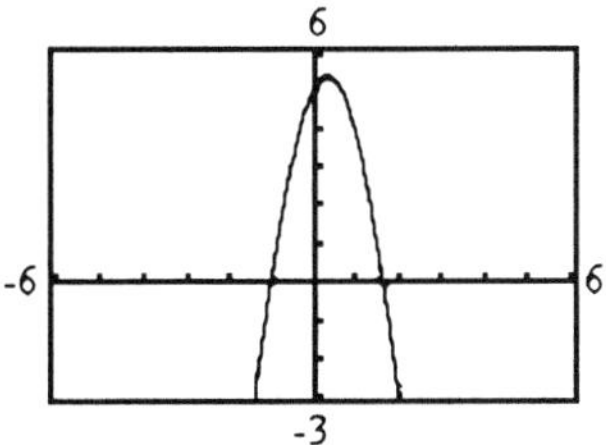

   Difficulty: 2 Key 1: T

29. Find an equation of the parabola, $y = ax^2 + bx + c$, that passes through (0, 5), (2, -5), and (-3, -40).
   a) $y = 3x^2 - 2x - 7$
   b) $y = -4x^2 + 3x + 5$
   c) $y = 4x^2 + 3x + 5$
   d) $y = 9x^2 - 121$
   e) None of these

   Answer: b Difficulty: 2

SHORT ANSWER

30. Find an equation of the parabola, $y = ax^2 + bx + c$, that passes through (0, -5), (2, 1), and (-1, -14). Verify your result with a graphing utility.

   Answer:

   $y = -2x^2 + 7x - 5$

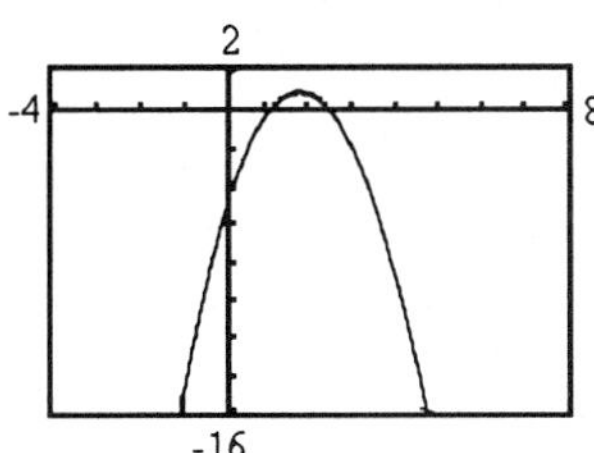

   Difficulty: 2 Key 1: T

31. Find an equation of the parabola, $y = ax^2 + bx + c$, that passes through (1, 1), (-1, 11), and (3, 23). Verify your result with a graphing utility.

Answer:

$y = 4x^2 - 5x + 2$

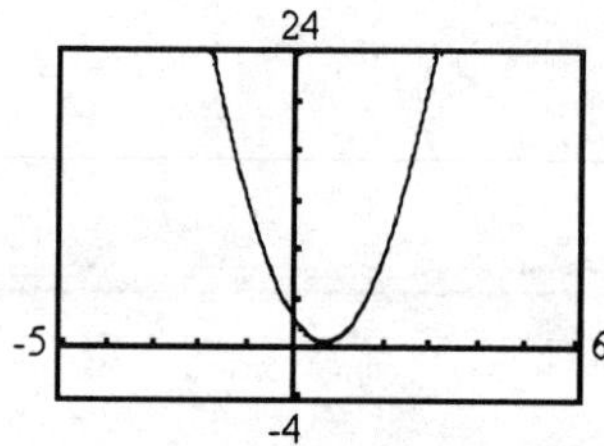

Difficulty: 2 Key 1: T

MULTIPLE CHOICE

32. Find the value of c in the quadratic equation, $y = ax^2 + bx + c$, if its graph passes through the points (1, 0), (-1, -6), and (2, 9).
a) -5 b) -4 c) 3 d) 11 e) None of these

Answer: a Difficulty: 2

33. Find the value of b in the quadratic equation, $y = ax^2 + bx + c$, if its graph passes through the points (-1, 4), (1, -2), and (2, -2).
a) -3 b) 2 c) -2 d) -1 e) None of these

Answer: a Difficulty: 2

SHORT ANSWER

34. Find an equation of the parabola, $y = ax^2 + bx + c$, that passes through the points (1, -2), (-2, 19), and (3, 4).

Answer:

$y = 2x^2 - 5x + 1$

Difficulty: 2

MULTIPLE CHOICE

35. Find an equation of the circle, $x^2 + y^2 + Dx + Ey + F = 0$, that passes through the points (9, -3), (2, 4), and (-5, -3).
a) $x^2 + y^2 + 3x - 2y + 10 = 0$
b) $x^2 + y^2 - 4x + 6y - 36 = 0$
c) $x^2 + y^2 - 8x + 2y - 12 = 0$
d) $x^2 + y^2 + 2x - 7y + 1 = 0$
e) None of these

Answer: b Difficulty: 2

36. The sum of three positive numbers is 19. Find the second number if the third is three times the first and the second is one more than twice the first.
a) 7 b) 13 c) 1 d) 9 e) None of these

Answer: a Difficulty: 1

37. The sum of three positive numbers is 180. Find the first number if the third is four times the first and the second is thirty-six less than twice the third.
a) 12 b) 36 c) 24 d) 60 e) None of these

Answer: c Difficulty: 2

SHORT ANSWER

38. A total of $7000 is invested in three separate accounts. Some of the money was invested at 6%, some at 8%, and the remaining at 9%. Find the amount invested at each rate if the total interest for one year was $555 and the amount invested at 8% was three times the amount invested at 9%. (Assume simple interest.)

Answer: $1000 at 6%, $4500 at 8%, and $1500 at 9% Difficulty: 2

MULTIPLE CHOICE

39. Write the partial fraction decomposition: $\dfrac{8x + 6}{x(x + 1)(x + 2)}$.
a) $\dfrac{2}{x + 1} - \dfrac{5}{x + 2} + \dfrac{3}{x}$
b) $\dfrac{7}{x + 1} + \dfrac{1}{x + 2} - \dfrac{6}{x}$
c) $\dfrac{1}{x + 1} + \dfrac{3}{x + 2} - \dfrac{1}{x}$
d) $\dfrac{6}{x + 1} - \dfrac{1}{x + 2} - \dfrac{1}{x}$
e) None of these

Answer: a Difficulty: 1

SHORT ANSWER

40. Write the partial fraction decomposition: $\dfrac{5}{x^2 - 7x + 12}$.

Answer:
$\dfrac{5}{x - 4} - \dfrac{5}{x - 3}$
Difficulty: 1

41. Find the position equation $s = \frac{1}{2}at^2 + v_0 t + s_0$ for an object at the given heights moving vertically at the specified times. Use a graphing utility to plot the points and graph the parabola.

At $t = 1$ second, $s = 64$.
At $t = 2$ seconds, $s = 96$.
At $t = 3$ seconds, $s = 96$.

Answer: $a = -32$, $b = 80$, $c = 0$; $s = -16t^2 + 80t$

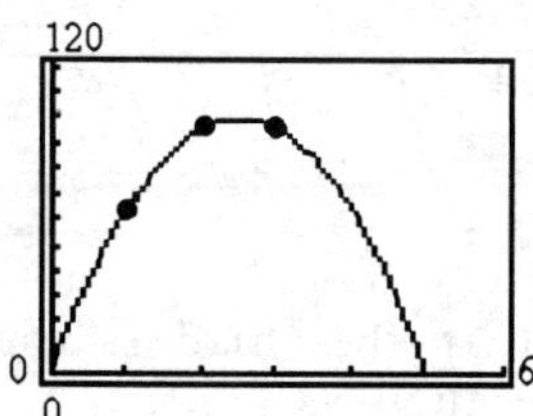

Difficulty: 2 Key 1: T

42. Find the position equation $s = \frac{1}{2}at^2 + v_0 t + s_0$ for an object at the given heights moving vertically at the specified times. Use a graphing utility to plot the points and graph the parabola.

At $t = 1$ second, $s = 36$.
At $t = 2$ seconds, $s = 36$.
At $t = 3$ seconds, $s = 4$.

Answer:

$a = -32$, $b = 48$, $c = 4$, $s = -16t^2 + 48t + 4$

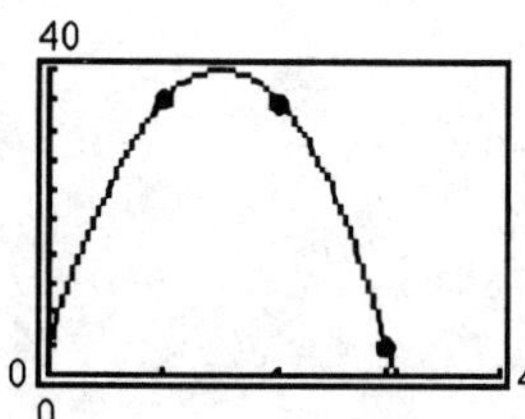

Difficulty: 2 Key 1: T

43. Find the least squares regression parabola $y = ax^2 + bx + c$ by solving the following system of linear equations for a, b, and c. Then use the least squares regression capabilities of a graphing utility to confirm the result. Then graph the data points and the parabola on a graphing utility.

$$nc + \left[\sum_{i=1}^{n} x_i\right] b + \left[\sum_{i=1}^{n} x_i^2\right] a = \sum_{i=1}^{n} y_i$$

$$\left[\sum_{i=1}^{n} x_i\right] c + \left[\sum_{i=1}^{n} x_i^2\right] b + \left[\sum_{i=1}^{n} x_i^3\right] a = \sum_{i=1}^{n} x_i y_i$$

$$\left[\sum_{i=1}^{n} x_i^2\right] c + \left[\sum_{i=1}^{n} x_i^3\right] b + \left[\sum_{i=1}^{n} x_i^4\right] a = \sum_{i=1}^{n} x_i^2 y_i$$

Points: (-2, -4), (0, 4); (2, 4), (4, -4)

Answer:

$a = -1$, $b = 2$, $c = 4$, $y = -x^2 + 2x + 4$

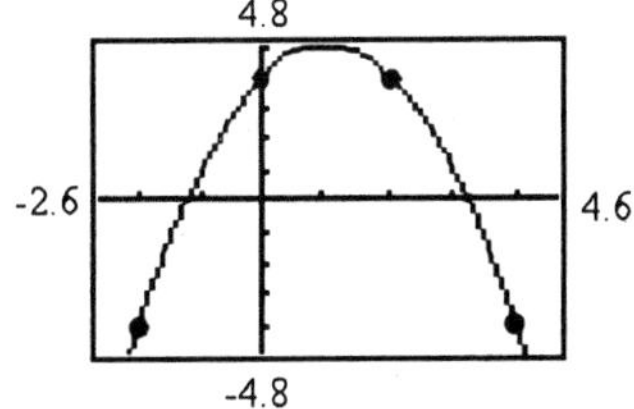

Difficulty: 2 Key 1: T

44. Find the least squares regression parabola $y = ax^2 + bx + c$ by solving the following system of linear equations for a, b, and c. Then use the least squares regression capabilities of a graphing utility to confirm the result. Then graph the data points and the parabola on a graphing utility.

$$nc + \left[\sum_{i=1}^{n} x_i\right] b + \left[\sum_{i=1}^{n} x_i^2\right] a = \sum_{i=1}^{n} y_i$$

$$\left[\sum_{i=1}^{n} x_i\right] c + \left[\sum_{i=1}^{n} x_i^2\right] b + \left[\sum_{i=1}^{n} x_i^3\right] a = \sum_{i=1}^{n} x_i y_i$$

$$\left[\sum_{i=1}^{n} x_i^2\right] c + \left[\sum_{i=1}^{n} x_i^3\right] b + \left[\sum_{i=1}^{n} x_i^4\right] a = \sum_{i=1}^{n} x_i^2 y_i$$

Points: (-1, 11), (0, 1), (2, -7), (4, 1)

Answer:

$a = 2$, $b = -8$, $c = 1$; $y = 2x^2 - 8x + 1$

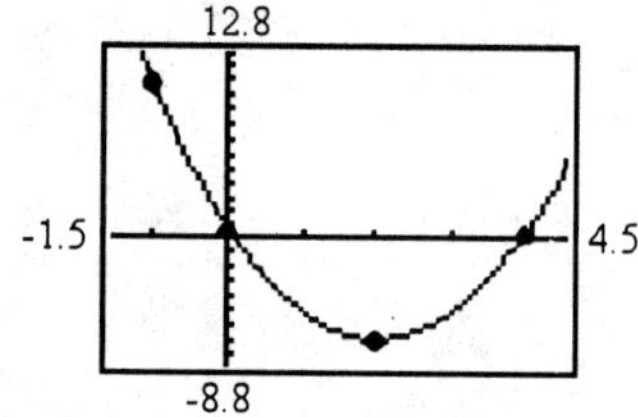

Difficulty: 2 Key 1: T

Chapter 074: Systems of Inequalities

MULTIPLE CHOICE

1. Match the graph with the correct inequality.
   a) $y < x^2 + 3x - 1$ b) $y > x^2 + 3x - 1$
   c) $y \leq x^2 + 3x - 1$ d) $y \geq x^2 + 3x - 1$

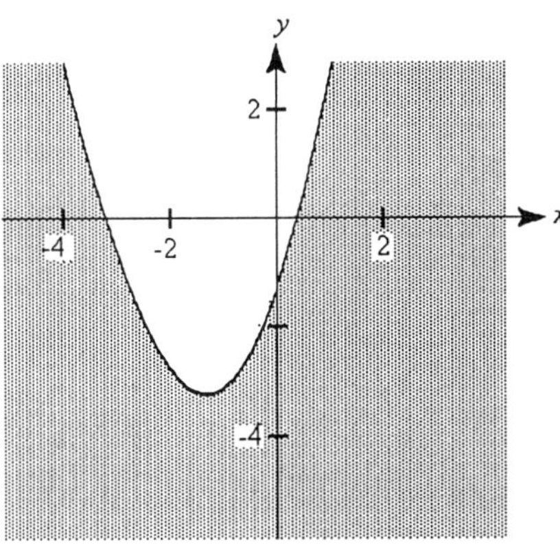

Answer: c Difficulty: 1

2. Match the graph with the correct inequality.
   a) $y > -2$ b) $y < -2$ c) $x > -2$ d) $x \geq -2$

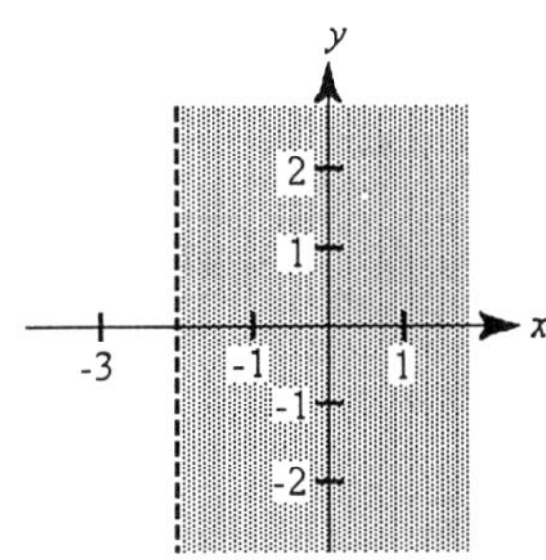

Answer: c Difficulty: 1

3. Match the graph with the correct inequality.
   a) $3x - 4y < 12$ b) $3x - 4y \leq 12$
   c) $3x - 4y > 12$ d) $3x - 4y \geq 12$

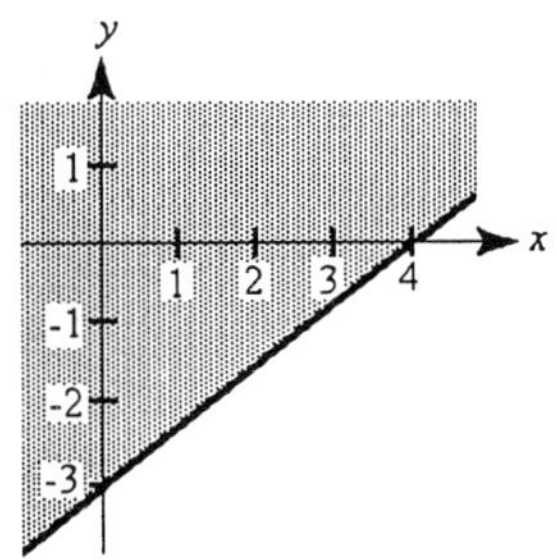

Answer: b Difficulty: 1

4. Match the graph with the correct inequality.
   a) $4x^2 - y \le 0$ b) $4x^2 - y > 0$
   c) $4x^2 - y < 0$ d) $4x^2 - y^2 \ge 0$

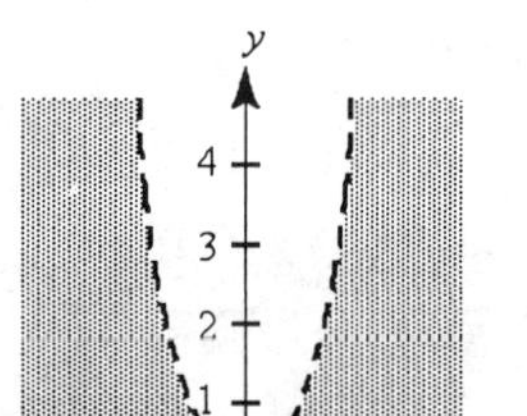

Answer: b Difficulty: 1

SHORT ANSWER

5. Use a graphing utility to graph the inequality

   $$x^2 + (y - 1)^2 \le 25.$$

   Answer: See graph below.

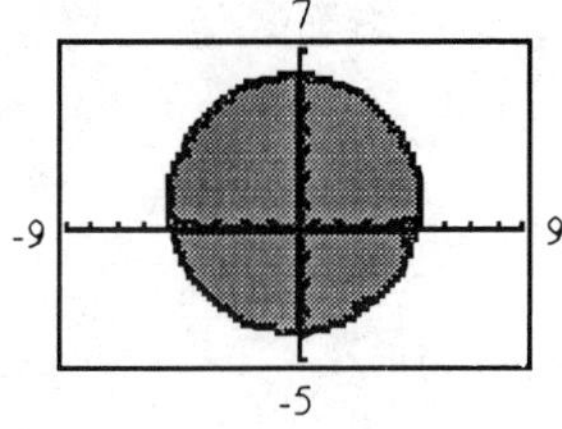

Difficulty: 1 Key 1: T

6. Use a graphing utility to graph the inequality

   $$3x^2 + y \ge 6.$$

   Answer: See graph below.

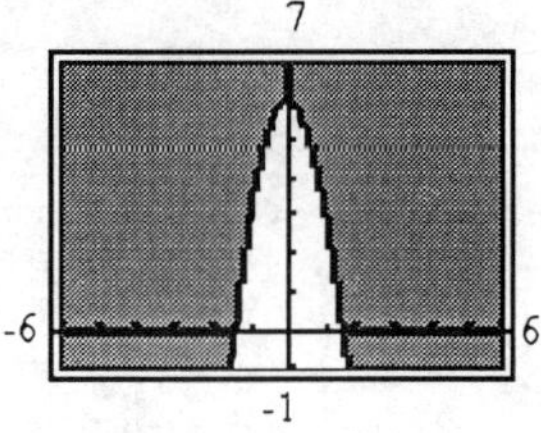

Difficulty: 1 Key 1: T

7. Use a graphing utility to graph the inequality

$y > e^x$.

Answer: See graph below.

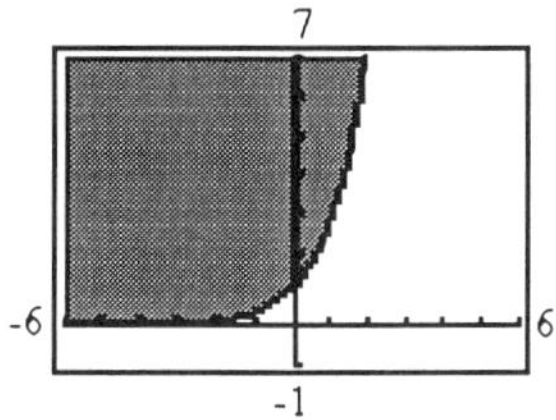

Difficulty: 1 Key 1: T

MULTIPLE CHOICE

8. Identify the graph of the inequality $x + y \leq 2$.
a) I b) II c) III d) IV e) None of these

(I)

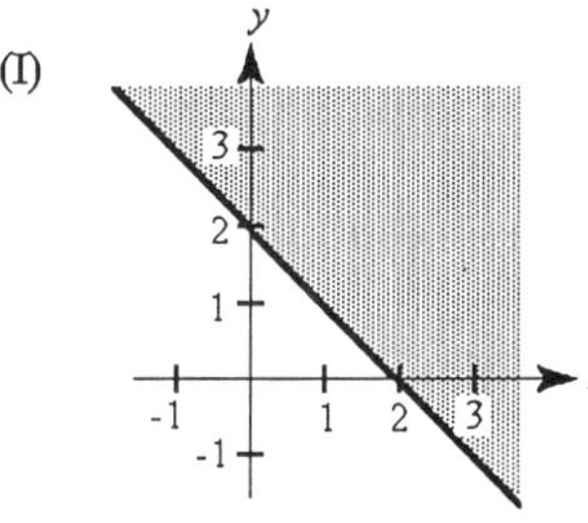

(II)

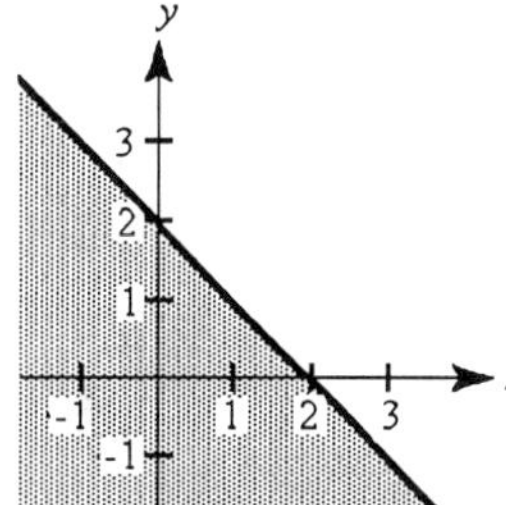

(III)

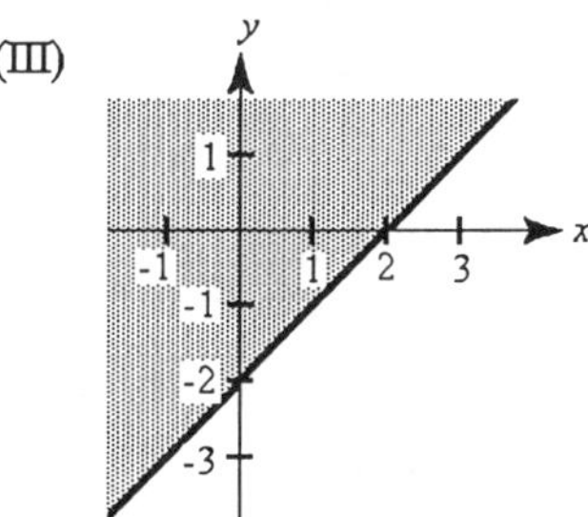

(IV)

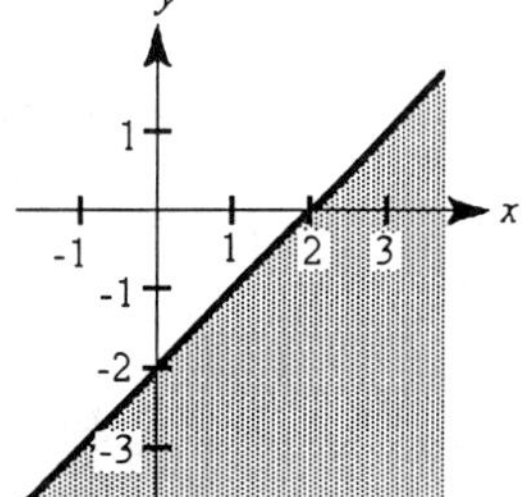

Answer: b Difficulty: 1

9. Identify the graph of the inequality $x - y > 1$.
a) I b) II c) III d) IV e) None of these

(I)
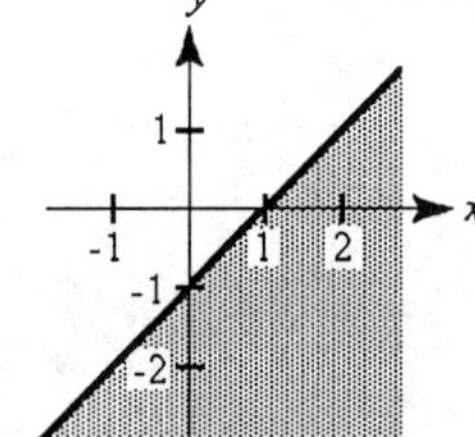
(II)
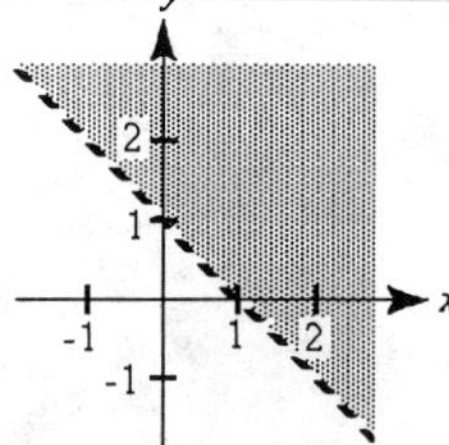
(III)
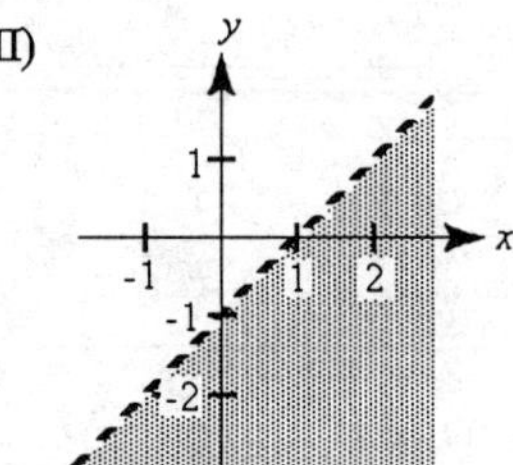
(IV)
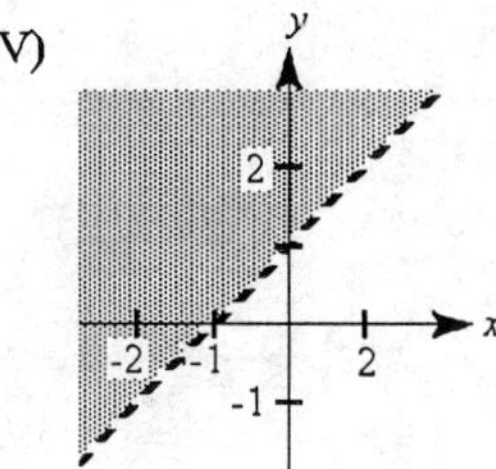

Answer: c Difficulty: 1

10. Identify the graph of the inequality $y \leq \ln(x + 2)$.
a) I b) II c) III d) IV e) None of these

(I)
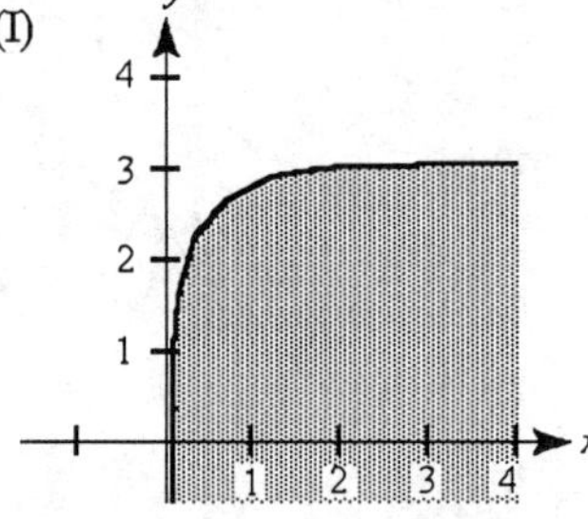
(II)
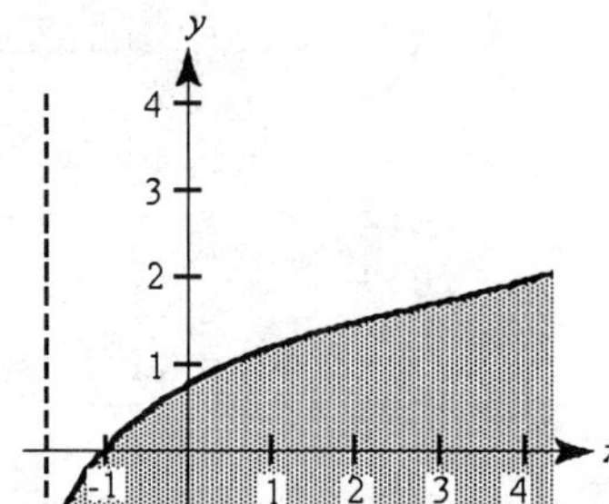
(III)
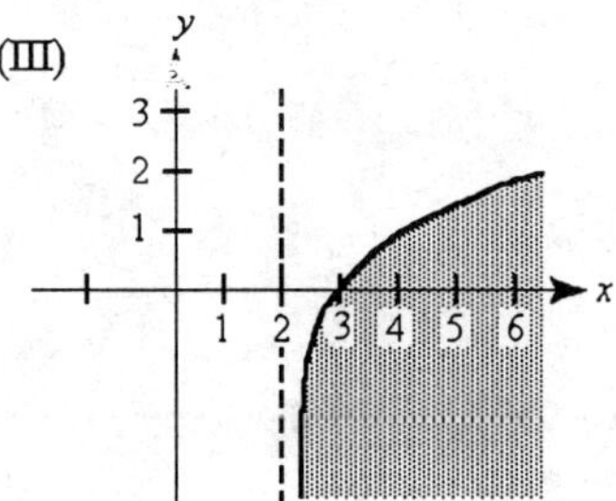
(IV)
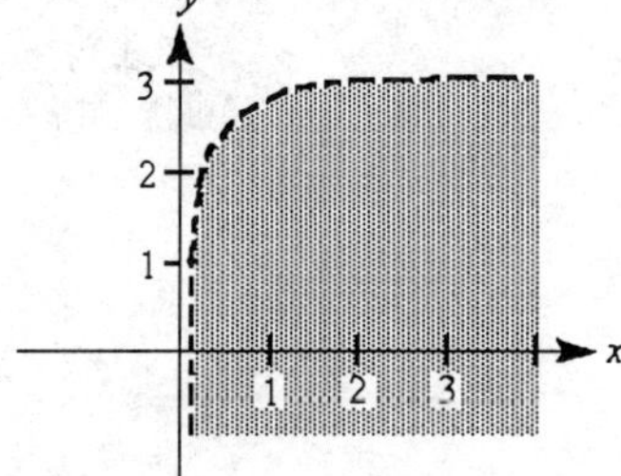

Answer: b Difficulty: 1

11. Identify the graph of the inequality $(x - 1)^2 + (y + 2)^2 > 4$.
    a) I b) II c) III d) IV e) None of these

(I)

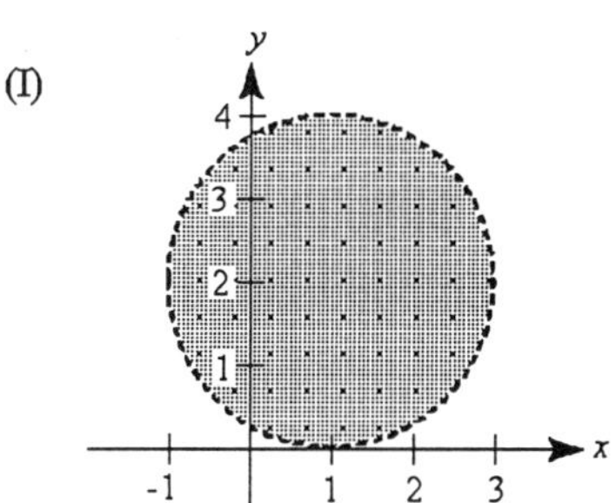

(II)

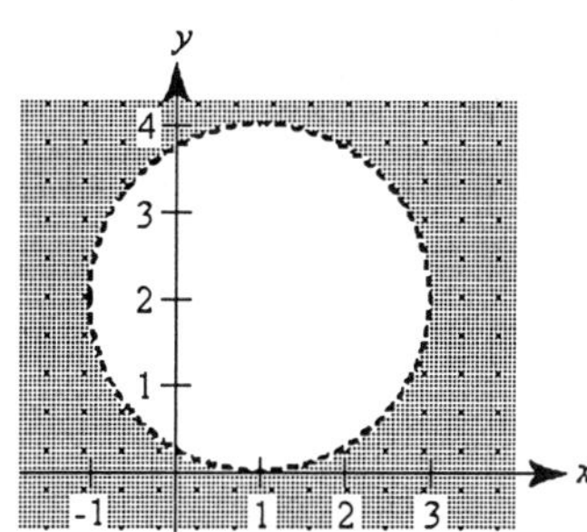

(III)

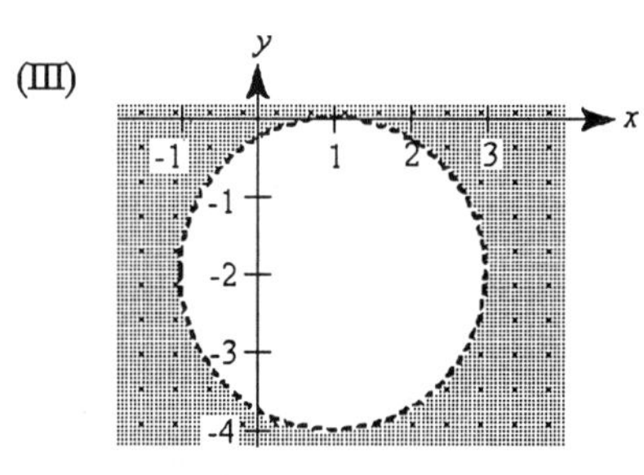

(IV)

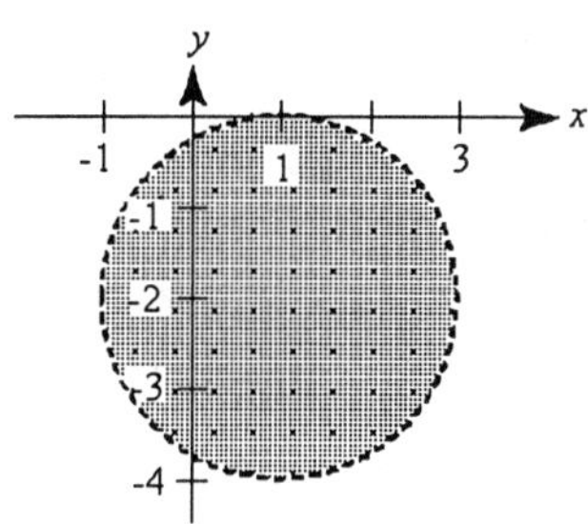

Answer: c Difficulty: 1

SHORT ANSWER

12. Sketch the graph of the system of inequalities.

$$\begin{cases} y \geq -|x + 2| \\ x \leq 0 \\ y \leq 0 \end{cases}$$

Answer: See graph below.

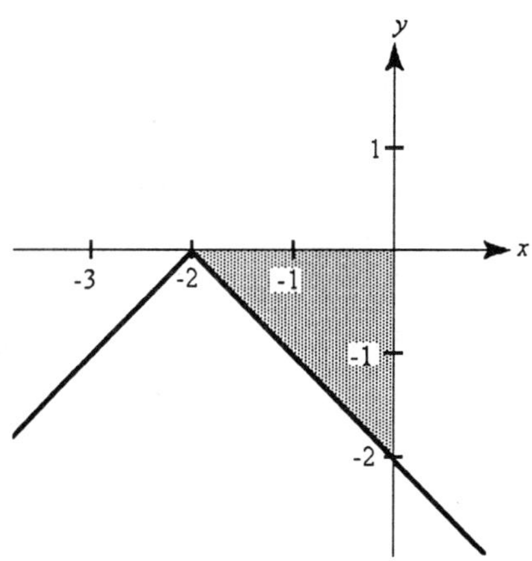

Difficulty: 2

13. Sketch the graph of the system of inequalities.

$$\begin{cases} x + y \geq 2 \\ y \leq x \\ y > 0 \end{cases}$$

Answer: See graph below.

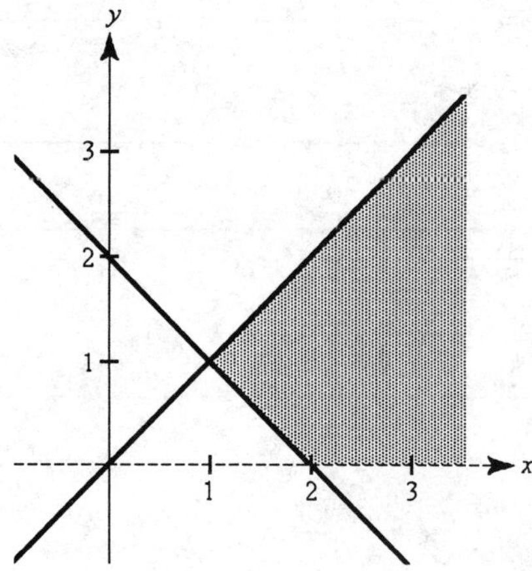

Difficulty: 1

14. Sketch the graph of the system of inequalities.

$$\begin{cases} 2x + 3y \leq 6 \\ x - 2y \geq -2 \end{cases}$$

Answer: See graph below.

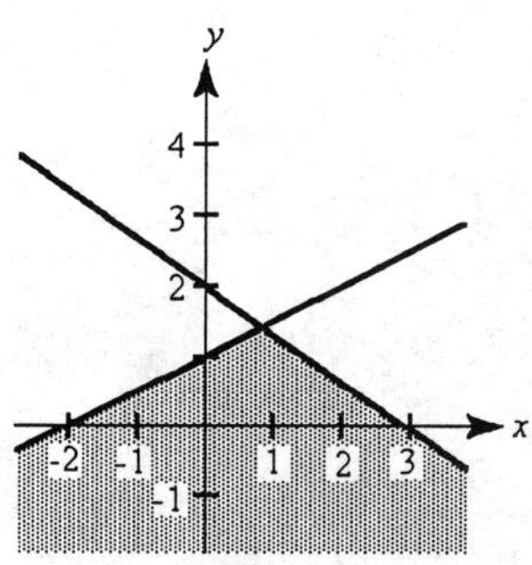

Difficulty: 1

15. Sketch the graph of the system of inequalities.

$$\begin{cases} 2y - 3x \le 10 \\ 2y \ge x^2 \end{cases}$$

Answer: See graph below.

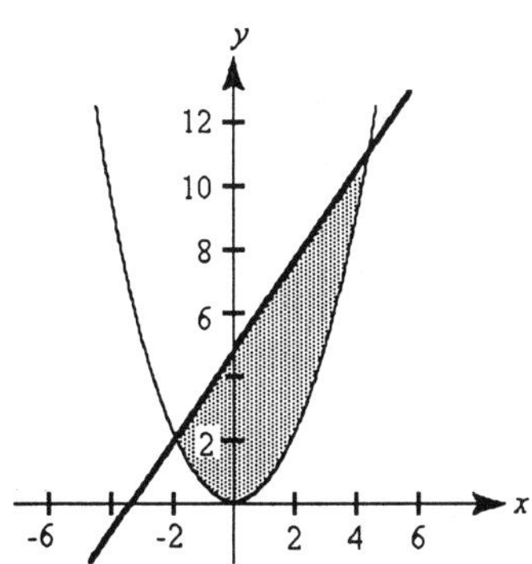

Difficulty: 2

MULTIPLE CHOICE

16. Identify the sketch of the graph of the solution for the system:

$$\begin{cases} x + y \ge 2 \\ y \le 2. \\ x \le 2 \end{cases}$$

a) I b) II c) III d) IV e) None of these

(I)

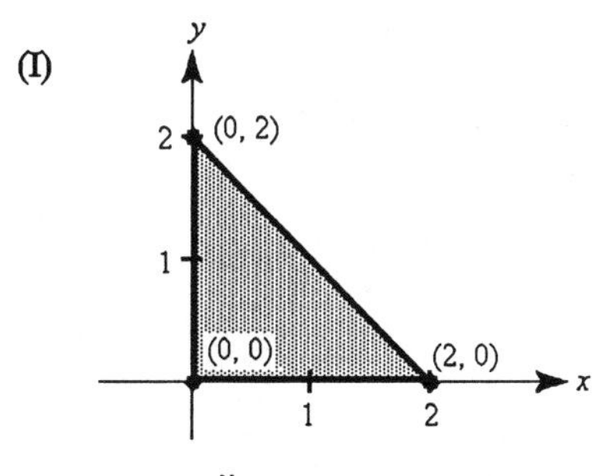

(II)

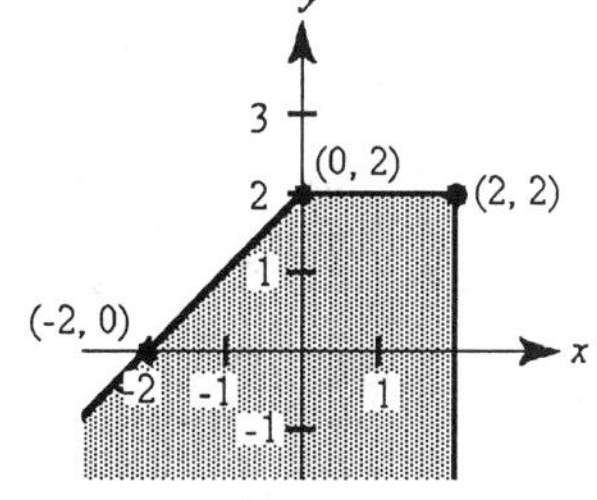

(III)

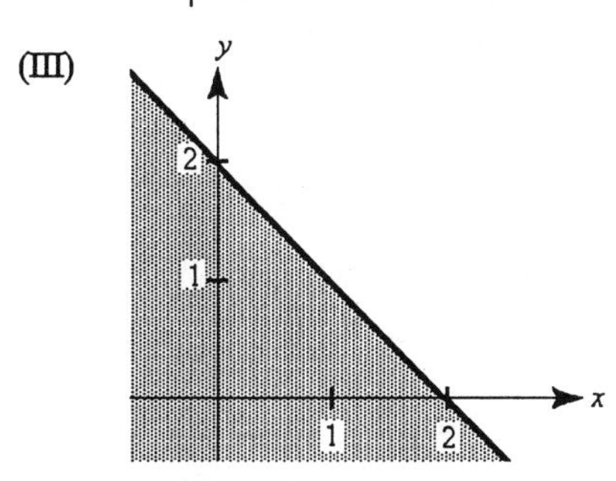

(IV)

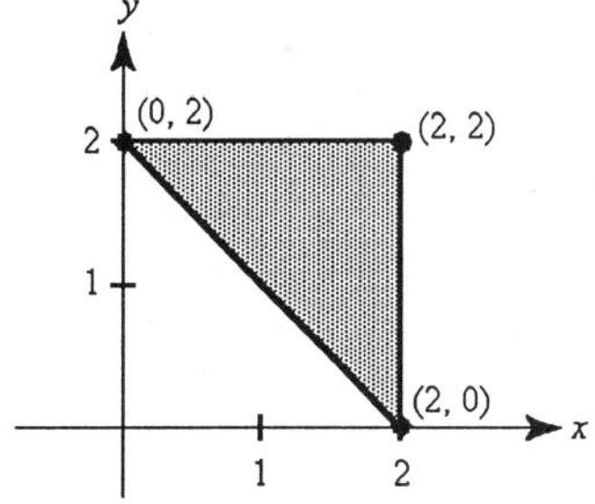

Answer: d Difficulty: 1

17. Identify the sketch of the graph of the solution for the system:

$$\begin{cases} y > x - 1 \\ x < 2. \\ y \geq 0 \end{cases}$$

a) I   b) II   c) III   d) IV   e) None of these

(I) y; 2; 1; (2, 1); (1, 0); 2; x

(II) y; 3; 2; 1; (2, 1); (2, 0); 1; 2; 3; x

(III) y; 2; 1; (2, 1); (1, 0); (2, 0); 1; 2; x

(IV) y; (0, 0); (1, 0); x; -1; (0, -1)

Answer: a Difficulty: 1

18. Match the graph with the correct system of inequalities.

a) $\begin{cases} 3x + y \leq 5 \\ y \geq 1 \\ x \geq 1 \end{cases}$ b) $\begin{cases} 3x + y \leq 5 \\ y \leq 1 \\ x \geq 1 \end{cases}$ c) $\begin{cases} y \geq 5 + 3x \\ y \leq 1 \\ x \leq 1 \end{cases}$

d) $\begin{cases} 3x + y \leq 5 \\ y \geq 1 \\ x \leq 1 \end{cases}$ e) None of these

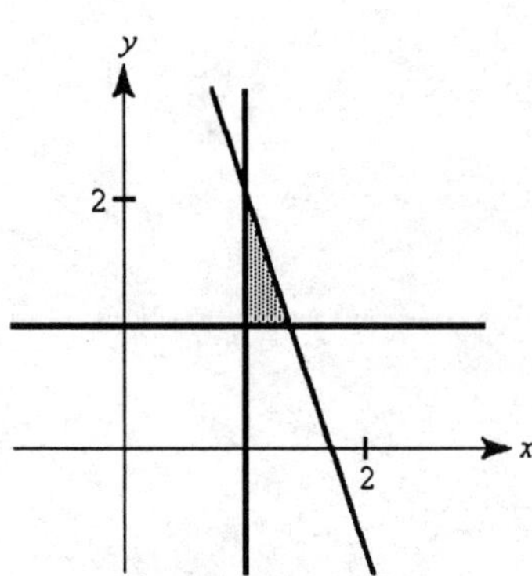

Answer: a Difficulty: 2

19. Match the graph with the correct system of inequalities.

a) $\begin{cases} x + 2y \le 6 \\ x - y \le 2 \\ y \ge 0 \end{cases}$ b) $\begin{cases} x + 2y \ge 6 \\ x - y \ge 2 \\ x \ge 0 \end{cases}$ c) $\begin{cases} x + 2y \le 6 \\ x - y \ge 2 \\ x \ge 0 \end{cases}$

d) $\begin{cases} x + 2y \ge 6 \\ x - y \ge 2 \\ y \ge 0 \end{cases}$ e) None of these

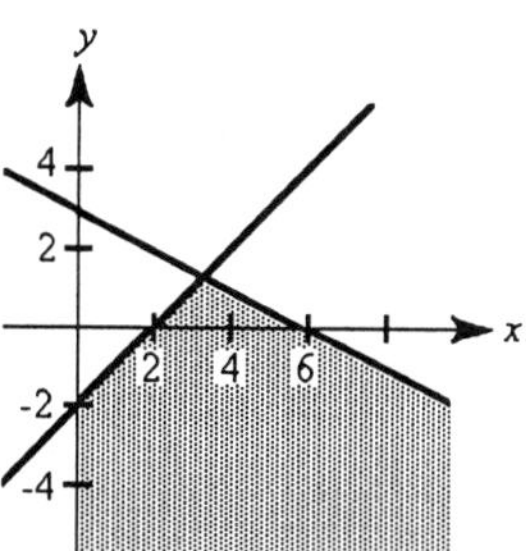

Answer: c Difficulty: 1

20. Match the graph with the correct system of inequalities.

a) $\begin{cases} x - y \le 7 \\ y \le 0 \\ x \ge 0 \\ x \le 4 \end{cases}$ b) $\begin{cases} x + y \le 7 \\ y \ge 0 \\ x \ge 0 \\ x \le 4 \end{cases}$ c) $\begin{cases} x - y \le 7 \\ y \ge 0 \\ x \ge 0 \\ x \le 4 \end{cases}$

d) $\begin{cases} x + y \ge 7 \\ y \le 0 \\ x \ge 0 \\ x \le 4 \end{cases}$ e) None of these

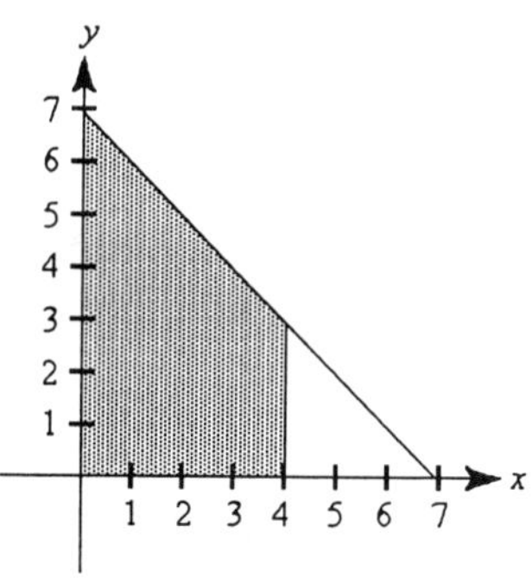

Answer: b Difficulty: 2

21. Match the graph with the correct system of inequalities.

a) $\begin{cases} x + 2y \le 4 \\ x \le y \\ x \ge 0 \end{cases}$ b) $\begin{cases} x + 2y \ge 4 \\ x \le y \\ y \ge 0 \end{cases}$ c) $\begin{cases} x + 2y \le 4 \\ x \le y \\ y \ge 0 \end{cases}$

d) $\begin{cases} x + 2y \le 4 \\ y \le x \\ y \ge 0 \end{cases}$ e) None of these

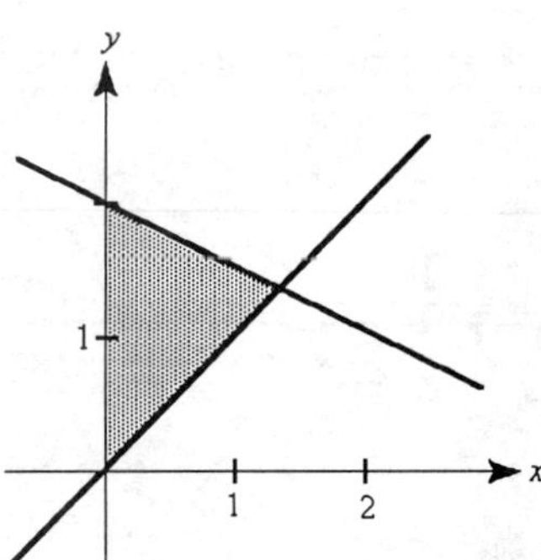

Answer: a Difficulty: 1

22. Match the graph with the correct system of inequalities.

a) $\begin{cases} x + 2y \le 4 \\ x \le y \\ x \ge 0 \end{cases}$ b) $\begin{cases} x + 2y \le 4 \\ y \le x \\ y \ge 0 \end{cases}$ c) $\begin{cases} x + 2y \ge 4 \\ y \le x \\ y \ge 0 \end{cases}$

d) $\begin{cases} x + 2y \ge 4 \\ x \le y \\ y \ge 0 \end{cases}$ e) None of these

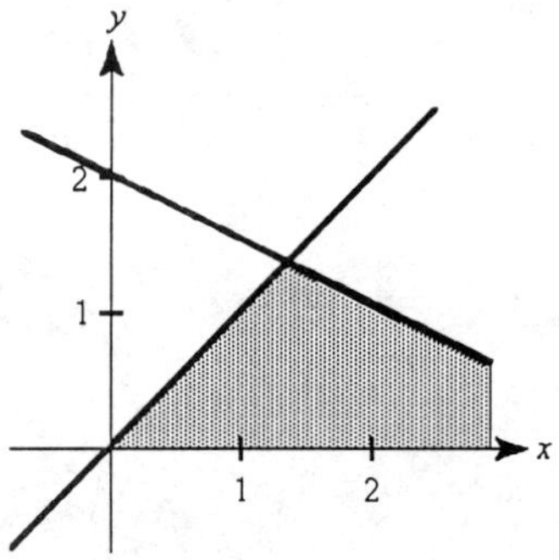

Answer: b Difficulty: 2

23. Match the graph with the correct system of inequalities.

a) $\begin{cases} x^2 + y^2 \geq 16 \\ 3x + 2y \leq 6 \end{cases}$ b) $\begin{cases} x^2 + y^2 \leq 16 \\ 3x + 2y \leq 6 \end{cases}$ c) $\begin{cases} x^2 + y^2 \geq 16 \\ 3x + 2y \geq 6 \end{cases}$

d) $\begin{cases} x^2 + y^2 \leq 16 \\ 3x + 2y \geq 6 \end{cases}$ e) None of these

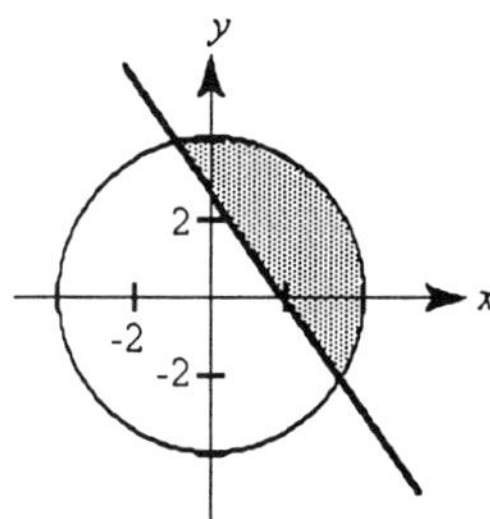

Answer: d Difficulty: 2

24. Match the graph with the correct system of inequalities.

a) $\begin{cases} x^2 + y^2 \geq 9 \\ y \geq x^2 \end{cases}$ b) $\begin{cases} x^2 + y^2 \geq 9 \\ y \leq x^2 \end{cases}$ c) $\begin{cases} x^2 + y^2 \leq 9 \\ y \leq x^2 \end{cases}$

d) $\begin{cases} x^2 + y^2 \leq 9 \\ y \geq x^2 \end{cases}$ e) None of these

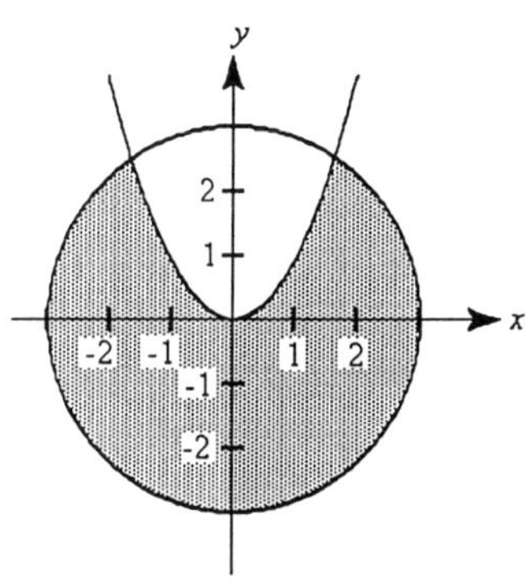

Answer: c Difficulty: 2

SHORT ANSWER

25. Find a set of inequalities that describes the triangular region with vertices at (0, 0), (3, 3), and (5, 0).

Answer: $y \geq 0$, $y \leq x$, and $3x + 2y \leq 15$ Difficulty: 2

MULTIPLE CHOICE

26. Find the vertices of the region described by the system of inequalities.

$$\begin{cases} 2x - y \le 5 \\ 3x + y \ge 0 \\ y \le 0 \end{cases}$$

a) (1, -3), (0, 0), (0, -5)
b) (2, -1), (0, 0), $\left(\frac{5}{2}, 0\right)$
c) (1, -3), (0, 0), $\left(\frac{5}{2}, 0\right)$
d) (2, -1), (0, 0), (0, -5)
e) None of these

Answer: c Difficulty: 2

SHORT ANSWER

27. Find the vertices of the region described by the system of inequalities.

$$\begin{cases} 3x + y \le 4 \\ 2x - y \ge 1 \\ x + 2y \ge -2 \end{cases}$$

Answer: (0, -1), (1, 1), and (2, -2) Difficulty: 1

MULTIPLE CHOICE

28. Find a set of inequalities that describe the triangular region with vertices (0, 0), (5, 5), and (3, 0).

a) $\begin{cases} 5x - 2y \ge 15 \\ y \le x \\ y \ge 0 \end{cases}$
b) $\begin{cases} 5x - 2y \ge 15 \\ y \ge x \\ y \ge 0 \end{cases}$
c) $\begin{cases} 5x - 2y \le 15 \\ y \le x \\ y \ge 0 \end{cases}$
d) $\begin{cases} 5x - 2y \le 15 \\ y \ge x \\ y \ge 0 \end{cases}$
e) None of these

Answer: c Difficulty: 2

29. Find a set of inequalities that describe the triangular region with vertices (0, 0), (8, 8), and (10, 0).

a) $\begin{cases} 4x + y \le 40 \\ y \le x \\ y \ge 0 \end{cases}$
b) $\begin{cases} 4x + y \le 40 \\ y \ge x \\ y \ge 0 \end{cases}$
c) $\begin{cases} 4x + y \ge 40 \\ y \le x \\ y \ge 0 \end{cases}$
d) $\begin{cases} 4x + y \ge 40 \\ y \ge x \\ y \ge 0 \end{cases}$
e) None of these

Answer: a Difficulty: 2

30. Find the consumer surplus if the demand equation is $p = 110 - 20x$ and the supply equation is $p = 50 + 10x$.
a) \$20 b) \$70 c) \$40 d) \$50 e) None of these

Answer: c Difficulty: 2

31. Find the producer surplus if the demand equation is $p = 110 - 20x$ and the supply equation is $p = 50 + 10x$.
a) \$20 b) \$70 c) \$40 d) \$50 e) None of these

Answer: a Difficulty: 2

32. Find the producer surplus if the demand equation is $p = 90 - 10x$ and the supply equation is $p = 30 + 20x$.
a) \$20 b) \$70 c) \$40 d) \$50 e) None of these

Answer: c Difficulty: 2

33. Find the consumer surplus if the demand equation is $p = 100 - 0.1x$ and the supply equation is $p = 10 + 0.4x$.
a) \$1250 b) \$1590 c) \$1620 d) \$6480 e) None of these

Answer: c Difficulty: 2

34. Find the producer surplus if the demand equation is $p = 50 - 0.1x$ and the supply equation is $p = 10 + 0.4x$.
a) \$1280 b) \$1200 c) \$560 d) \$320 e) None of these

Answer: a Difficulty: 2

35. Find the consumer surplus if the demand equation is $p = 80 - \frac{1}{2}x$ and the supply equation is $p = 20 + \frac{5}{2}x$.
a) \$500 b) \$300 c) \$100 d) \$60 e) None of these

Answer: c Difficulty: 2

SHORT ANSWER

36. A small electronics company produces two types of CD players, standard and deluxe. The standard model requires 2 hours to manufacture and 2 hours to assemble, while the deluxe model requires 2 hours to manufacture and 3 hours to assemble. If the company has 40 hours per week of manufacturing time and 42 hours per week of assembly time, find a system of inequalities describing the different numbers of standard and deluxe models that can be produced.

Answer:

$2x + 2y \le 40$

$2x + 3y \le 42$

$x \ge 0$

$y \ge 0$

where x represents the number of standard models produced and y represents the number of deluxe models produced.

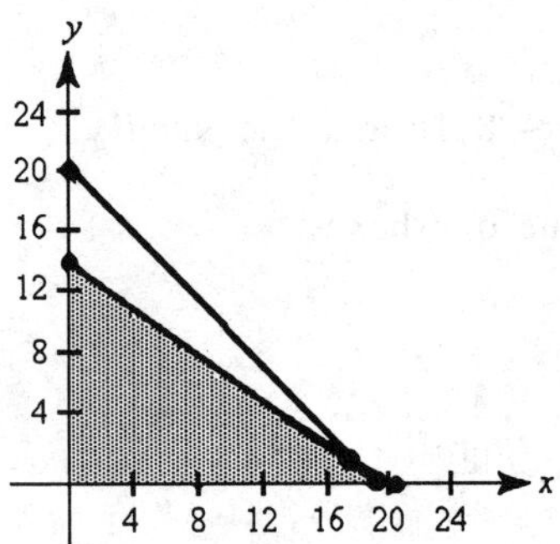

Difficulty: 2

37. A company produces two types of four-pound gift boxes of candy, regular and chewy. The regular box has 2 pounds of chocolates and 2 pounds of caramels. The chewy box has 1 pound of chocolates and 3 pounds of caramels. The company has at most 60 pounds of chocolate available and at most 96 pounds of caramels available. Find a system of inequalities describing the number of regular boxes and chewy boxes that the company can produce.

Answer:

$2x + y \leq 60$

$2x + 3y \leq 96$

$x \geq 0$

$y \geq 0$

where x represents the number of regular boxes produced and y represents the number of chewy boxes produced.

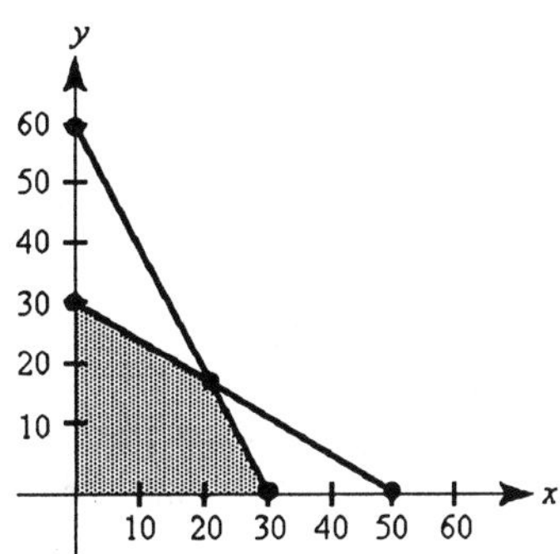

Difficulty: 2

Chapter 075: Linear Programming

MULTIPLE CHOICE

1. Find the maximum value of the objective function $z = 5x + 6y$ subject to the following constraints.

$$\begin{cases} x \geq 0 \\ y \geq 0 \\ x + 2y \leq 8 \\ 3x + 3y \leq 15 \end{cases}$$

a) 30 b) 28 c) 25 d) 24 e) None of these

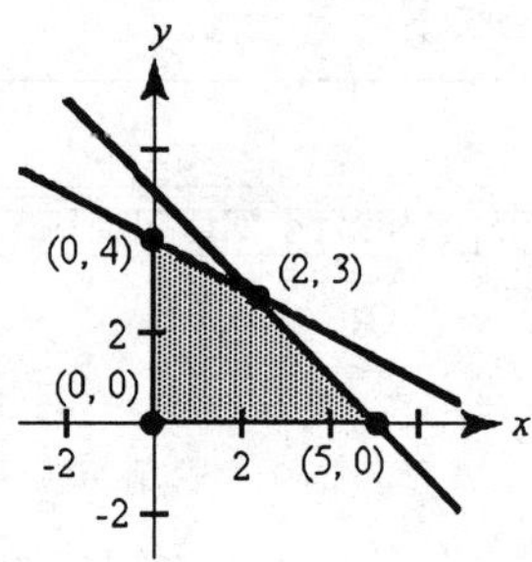

Answer: b Difficulty: 1

2. Find the maximum value of the objective function $z = 10x + 8y$ subject to the following constraints.

$$\begin{cases} x \geq 0 \\ y \geq 0 \\ x + y \leq 5 \\ 3x + y \leq 12 \\ -2x + y \leq 2 \end{cases}$$

a) 40 b) 50 c) 42 d) 47 e) None of these

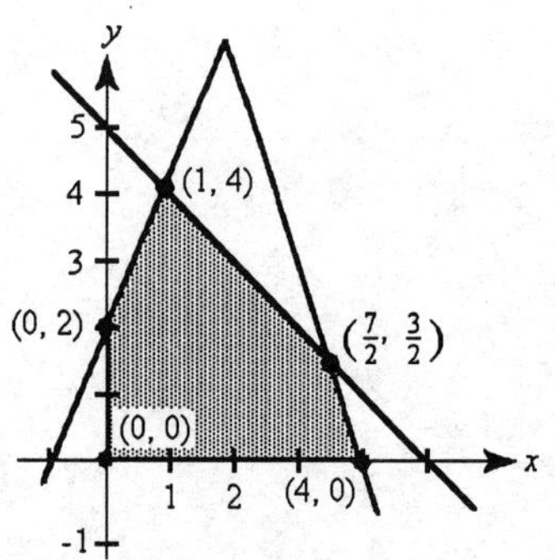

Answer: d Difficulty: 1

3. Find the maximum value of the objective function $z = 3x + 2y$ subject to the following constraints.

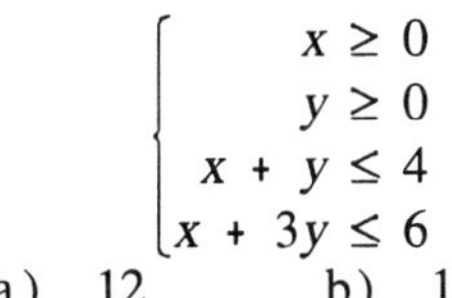

$$\begin{cases} x \geq 0 \\ y \geq 0 \\ x + y \leq 4 \\ x + 3y \leq 6 \end{cases}$$

a) 12 b) 11 c) 10 d) 13 e) None of these

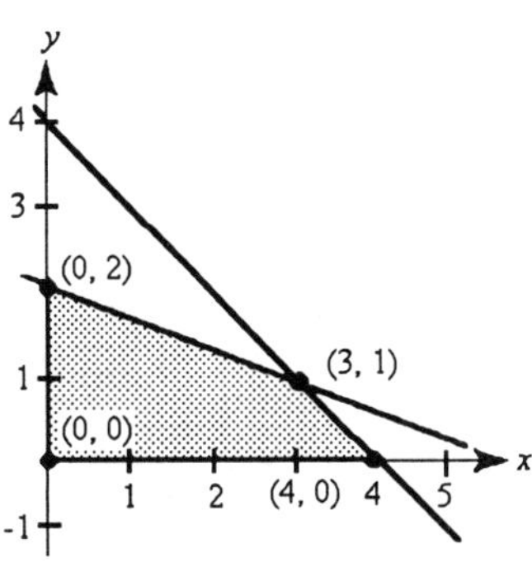

Answer: a Difficulty: 1

4. Find the maximum value of the objective function $z = 9x + 6y$ subject to the following constraints.

$$\begin{cases} x \geq 0 \\ y \geq 0 \\ x + y \leq 3 \\ 2x + 5y \leq 10 \\ x - y \leq 1 \end{cases}$$

a) 9 b) 12 c) 24 d) 36 e) None of these

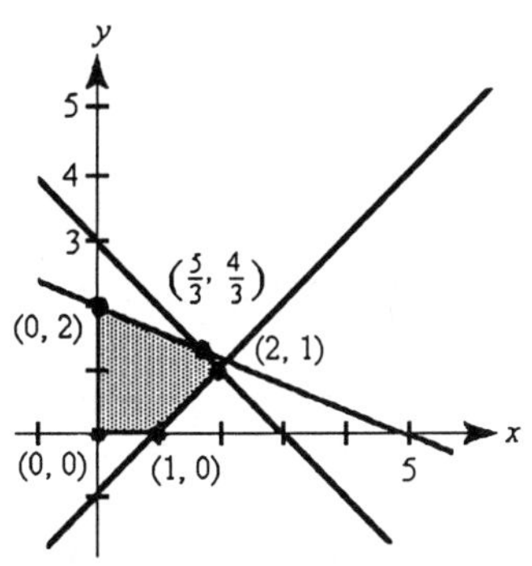

Answer: c Difficulty: 1

5. Find the maximum value of the objective function $z = 5x + 4y$ subject to the following constraints.

$$\begin{cases} 3x + 2y \le 6 \\ 2x - y \ge 2 \\ x \ge 0 \end{cases}$$

a) 11 b) 4 c) 12 d) 19 e) None of these

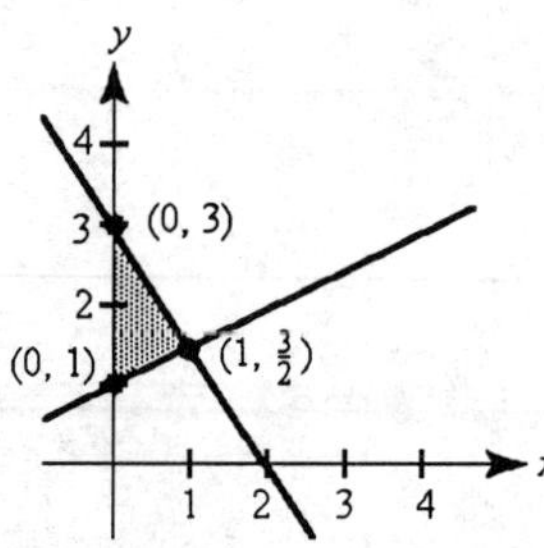

Answer: c Difficulty: 1

6. Find the minimum value of the objective function $z = 5x + 4y$ subject to the following constraints.

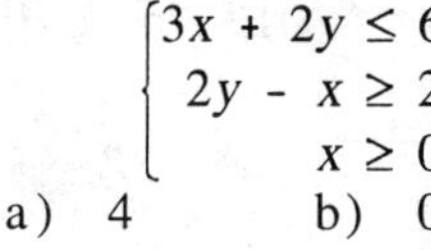

$$\begin{cases} 3x + 2y \le 6 \\ 2y - x \ge 2 \\ x \ge 0 \end{cases}$$

a) 4 b) 0 c) 12 d) 3 e) None of these

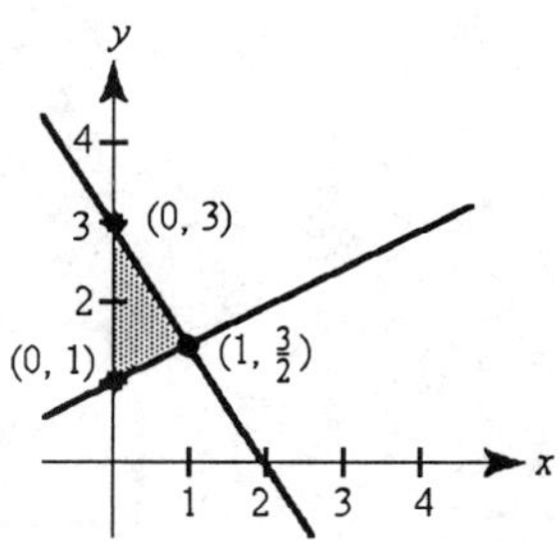

Answer: a Difficulty: 1

7. Find the minimum value of the objective function $z = 4x + 2y$ subject to the following constraints.

$$\begin{cases} x \geq 0 \\ y \geq 2 \\ y \leq 3 - x \end{cases}$$

a) 2 b) 4 c) 6 d) 8 e) None of these

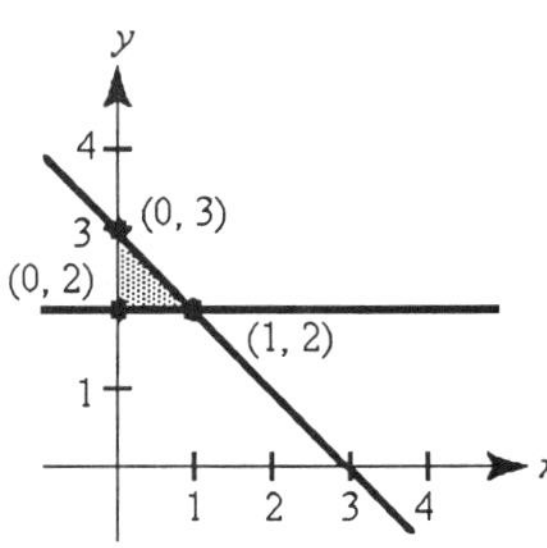

Answer: b Difficulty: 1

8. Find the maximum value of the objective function $z = 40x + 35y$ subject to the following constraints.

$$\begin{cases} x \geq 0 \\ y \geq 0 \\ 5x + 4y \leq 300 \\ x + y \leq 70 \end{cases}$$

a) 2400 b) 2625 c) 2800 d) 2550 e) None of these

Answer: d Difficulty: 1

9. Find the maximum value of the objective function $z = 40x + 35y$ subject to the following constraints.

$$\begin{cases} x \geq 0 \\ y \geq 0 \\ 4x + 6y \leq 300 \\ x + y \leq 70 \end{cases}$$

a) 2450 b) 2750 c) 2800 d) 3000 e) None of these

Answer: c Difficulty: 1

10. Find the maximum value of the objective function $z = 40x + 60y$ subject to the following constraints.

$$\begin{cases} x \geq 0 \\ y \geq 0 \\ 3x + 7y \leq 298 \\ x + y \leq 50 \end{cases}$$

a) 2000 b) 3000 c) 3973 d) 2740 e) None of these

Answer: d Difficulty: 1

11. Find the maximum value of the objective function $z = 30x + 10y$ subject to the following constraints.

$$\begin{cases} x \geq 0 \\ y \geq 0 \\ 2x + 4y \leq 60 \\ x + y \leq 25 \end{cases}$$

a) 750 b) 150 c) 900 d) 650 e) None of these

Answer: a Difficulty: 1

12. Find the maximum value of the objective function $z = 8x + 10y$ subject to the following constraints.

$$\begin{cases} x \geq 0 \\ y \geq 0 \\ x + y \leq 160 \\ x - 3y \geq 0 \end{cases}$$

a) 1280 b) 1360 c) 1500 d) 0 e) None of these

Answer: b Difficulty: 2

13. Find the maximum value of the objective function $z = 6x + 5y$ subject to the following constraints.

$$\begin{cases} x \geq 0 \\ y \geq 0 \\ x + y \leq 76 \\ x - 3y \geq 0 \end{cases}$$

a) 380 b) 437 c) 456 d) 519 e) None of these

Answer: c Difficulty: 1

SHORT ANSWER

14. Find the maximum value of the objective function $z = 3x + 2y$ subject to the following constraints:

$$\begin{cases} x \geq 0 \\ y \geq 0 \\ 3x + 4y \leq 25 \\ 3x - y \leq 5 \end{cases}$$

Answer: 17 Difficulty: 2

MULTIPLE CHOICE

15. Find the maximum value of the objective function $z = 2x + 5y$ subject to the following constraints.

$$\begin{cases} x \geq 0 \\ y \geq 0 \\ 2x + y \leq 12 \\ x - 4y \leq -3 \end{cases}$$

a) 7 b) 28 c) 20 d) 60 e) None of these

Answer: d Difficulty: 1

16. Find the maximum value of the objective function $z = 6x - 2y$ subject to the following constraints.

$$\begin{cases} x \geq 0 \\ y \geq 0 \\ x + y \leq 10 \\ 4x + y \geq 12 \end{cases}$$

a) 60 b) 84 c) 18 d) 44 e) None of these

Answer: a Difficulty: 1

SHORT ANSWER

17. Find the minimum and maximum values of the objective function $z = 4x + 16y$ subject to the following constraints.

$$\begin{cases} x \geq 0 \\ y \geq 0 \\ 3x + y \leq 23 \\ x + 2y \leq 16 \\ 3x \geq 2y \end{cases}$$

Answer: $z = 0$, minimum; $z = 112$, maximum Difficulty: 2

MULTIPLE CHOICE

18. Find the maximum value of the objective function $C = 10x + 12y$ subject to the following constraints.

$$\begin{cases} x \geq 0 \\ y \geq 0 \\ x + y \leq 36 \\ x - 2y \geq 0 \end{cases}$$

a) 0 b) 360 c) 384 d) 432 e) None of these

Answer: a Difficulty: 2

SHORT ANSWER

19. Find the minimum value of the objective function $C = 2x + y$ subject to the following constraints.

$$\begin{cases} x \geq 0 \\ y \geq 0 \\ 3x + 2y \geq 90 \\ 2x + 3y \leq 105 \end{cases}$$

Answer: 51 Difficulty: 2

MULTIPLE CHOICE

20. Find the minimum value of the objective function $z = 6x - 2y$ subject to the following constraints.

$$\begin{cases} x \geq 0 \\ y \geq 0 \\ x + y \leq 10 \\ 4x + y \geq 13 \end{cases}$$

a) 60 b) -12 c) -4 d) -18 e) None of these

Answer: b Difficulty: 1

21. Find the minimum value of the objective function $z = 3x + 2y$ subject to the following constraints.

$$\begin{cases} x \geq 0 \\ y \geq 0 \\ x + y \geq 4 \\ 3x + y \geq 6 \end{cases}$$

a) 0 b) 8 c) 9 d) 12 e) None of these

Answer: c Difficulty: 1

22. Find the minimum value of the objective function $z = 7x + 6y$ subject to the following constraints.

$$\begin{cases} x \geq 0 \\ y \geq 0 \\ 5x + 2y \geq 16 \\ 3x + 7y \geq 27 \end{cases}$$

a) $23\frac{1}{7}$ b) 32 c) $22\frac{2}{5}$ d) 0 e) None of these

Answer: b Difficulty: 1

23. Find the minimum value of the objective function $z = 3x + 4y$ subject to the following constraints.

$$\begin{cases} x \geq 0 \\ y \geq 0 \\ x + y \geq 6 \\ x + 2y \geq 8 \end{cases}$$

a) 0 b) 20 c) 16 d) 18 e) None of these

Answer: b Difficulty: 1

24. Find the minimum value of the objective function $z = 4x + y$ subject to the following constraints.

$$\begin{cases} x \geq 0 \\ y \geq 0 \\ 5x + 3y \geq 15 \\ 3x + 6y \geq 18 \end{cases}$$

a) 0 b) 3 c) 5 d) 9 e) None of these

Answer: c Difficulty: 1

SHORT ANSWER

25. A merchant plans to sell two models of an item at costs of \$350 and \$400. The \$350 model yields a profit of \$85 and the \$400 model yields a profit of \$90. The total demand per month for the two models will not exceed 150. Find the number of units of each model that should be stocked each month in order to maximize the profit. Assume the merchant can invest no more than \$56,000 for inventory of these items.

Answer: 80 of the \$350 model; 70 of the \$400 model Difficulty: 2

26. A merchant plans to sell two models of an item at costs of \$350 and \$500. The \$350 model yields a profit of \$45 and the \$500 model yields a profit of \$60. The total demand per month for the two models will not exceed 145. Find the number of units of each model that should be stocked each month in order to maximize the profit. Assume the merchant can invest no more than \$56,000 for inventory of these items.

Answer: 110 of the \$350 model; 35 of the \$500 model Difficulty: 2

MULTIPLE CHOICE

27. A merchant plans to sell two models of an item at costs of \$350 and \$500. The \$350 model yields a profit of \$80 and the \$500 model yields a profit of \$100. The total demand per month for the two models will not exceed 150. Find the maximum monthly profit. Assume the merchant can invest no more than \$63,000.

a) $P = \$33,600$ b) $P = \$13,400$ c) $P = \$12,600$
d) $P = \$12,000$ e) None of these

Answer: b Difficulty: 2

28. A merchant plans to sell two models of an item at costs of $350 and $500. The $350 model yields a profit of $60 and the $500 model yields a profit of $75. The total demand per month for the two models will not exceed 100. Find the maximum monthly profit. Assume the merchant can invest no more than $41,000.
a) $P = \$6600$ b) $P = \$6150$ c) $P = \$7020$
d) $P = \$7500$ e) None of these

Answer: a Difficulty: 2

29. A company produces two models of calculators at two different plants. In one day Plant A can produce 140 of Model I and 35 of Model II. In one day Plant B can produce 60 of Model I and 90 of Model II. The company needs to produce at least 460 of Model I and 340 of Model II. Find the minimum cost. Assume it costs $1200 per day to operate Plant A and $900 per day for Plant B.
a) $C = \$11,640$ b) $C = \$8730$ c) $C = \$5100$
d) $C = \$3948$ e) None of these

Answer: c Difficulty: 2

30. A company produces two models of calculators at two different plants. In one day Plant A can produce 60 of Model I and 70 of Model II. In one day Plant B can produce 80 of Model I and 40 of Model II. The company needs to produce at least 460 of Model I and 430 of Model II. Find the minimum cost. Assume it costs $1200 per day to operate Plant A and $900 per day for Plant B.
a) $C = \$7800$ b) $C = \$9200$ c) $C = \$7371$
d) $C = \$5175$ e) None of these

Answer: a Difficulty: 2

31. A company produces two models of calculators at two different plants. In one day Plant A can produce 70 of Model I and 40 of Model II. In one day Plant B can produce 80 of Model I and 90 of Model II. The company needs to produce at least 1370 of Model I and 1270 of Model II. Find the minimum cost. Assume it costs $900 per day to operate Plant A and $1200 per day for Plant B.
a) $C = \$32,570$ b) $C = \$28,575$ c) $C = \$20,550$
d) $C = \$19,500$ e) None of these

Answer: d Difficulty: 2

32. A company produces two models of calculators at two different plants. In one day Plant A can produce 150 of Model I and 250 of Model II. In one day Plant B can produce 175 of Model I and 140 of Model II. The company needs to produce at least 3075 of Model I and 3760 of Model II. Find the minimum cost. Assume it costs $3500 per day to operate Plant A and $3100 per day for Plant B.
a) $C = \$83,266$ b) $C = \$62,900$ c) $C = \$71,750$
d) $C = \$59,200$ e) None of these

Answer: b Difficulty: 2

SHORT ANSWER

33. A manufacturer wants to maximize the profit on two products. The first product yields a profit of \$2.30 per unit, and the second product yields a profit of \$1.50 per unit. Market tests and available resources have indicated the following constraints:

    1. The combined production level should not exceed 900 units per month.

    2. The demand for the first product is less than or equal to half the demand for the second product.

    Find the maximum profit.

    Answer: \$1590 Difficulty: 2

34. Use a graphing utility to graph the region determined by the constraints. Then find the minimum and maximum values of the objective function, subject to the constraints.

    Objective function: $z = 3x + 4y$

    Constraints:
    $$\begin{aligned} x &\geq 0 \\ y &\geq 0 \\ 2x + 3y &\geq 18 \\ 8x + 2y &\leq 32 \end{aligned}$$

    Answer: $z = 24$, minimum; $z = 64$, maximum

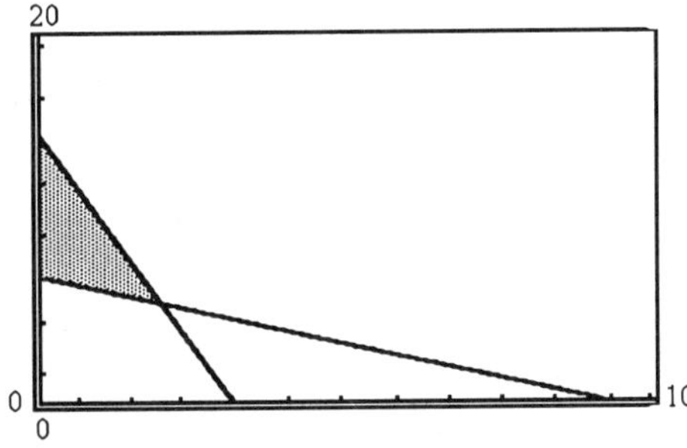

Difficulty: 2 Key 1: T

35. Use a graphing utility to graph the region determined by the constraints. Then find the minimum and maximum values of the objective function, subject to the constraints.

Objective function: $z = 5x + 3y$

Constraints:

$$\begin{aligned} x &\geq 0 \\ y &\geq 0 \\ 5x + y &\geq 14 \\ -5x + 6y &\leq 49 \\ 7x + 2y &\leq 77 \\ 4x + 9y &\geq 44 \end{aligned}$$

Answer: $z = 22$ minimum; $z = 77$ maximum

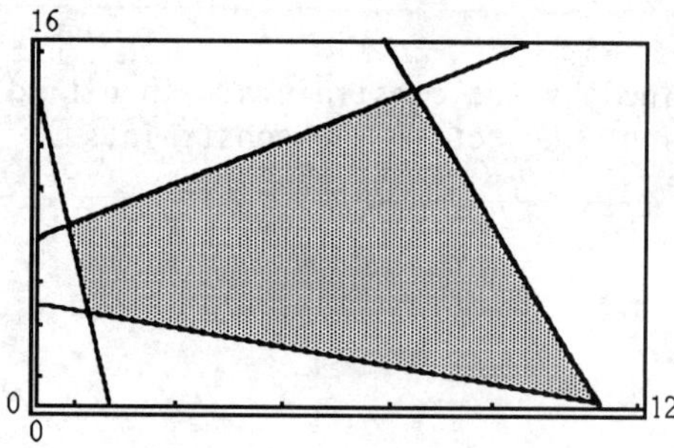

Difficulty: 2 Key 1: T

Chapter 081: Matrices and Systems of Equations

MULTIPLE CHOICE

1. Determine the order of the matrix: $\begin{bmatrix} 2 & 7 & 9 \\ 3 & 5 & -1 \end{bmatrix}$.

   a) 2 × 3 b) 3 × 2 c) 3 d) 2 e) None of these

   Answer: a Difficulty: 1

2. Determine the order of the matrix: $\begin{bmatrix} 1 & 3 \\ 0 & 6 \\ 2 & 1 \\ 4 & 7 \end{bmatrix}$.

   a) 2 × 4 b) 4 × 2 c) 4 d) 2 e) None of these

   Answer: b Difficulty: 1

3. Determine the order of the matrix: $\begin{bmatrix} 2 & 1 \\ -1 & 5 \\ 4 & -3 \end{bmatrix}$.

   a) 6 b) 2 × 3 c) 5 d) 3 × 2 e) None of these

   Answer: d Difficulty: 1

SHORT ANSWER

4. Write the augmented matrix for the given system of linear equations.

$$\begin{cases} 2x - 3y = 12 \\ x + y = 16 \end{cases}$$

Answer:

$$\left[\begin{array}{cc:c} 2 & -3 & 12 \\ 1 & 1 & 16 \end{array}\right]$$

Difficulty: 1

5. Write the augmented matrix for the given system of linear equations.

$$\begin{cases} 3x - 5y + z = -4 \\ -x + y \quad\ = 1 \end{cases}$$

Answer:

$$\left[\begin{array}{ccc:c} 3 & -5 & 1 & -4 \\ -1 & 1 & 0 & 1 \end{array}\right]$$

Difficulty: 1

MULTIPLE CHOICE

6. Write the augmented matrix for the given system of linear equations.

$$\begin{cases} 3x - y = 2 \\ x + 2y = 7 \end{cases}$$

a) $\begin{bmatrix} 3 & 1 & \vdots & -2 \\ 1 & 2 & \vdots & -7 \end{bmatrix}$

b) $\begin{bmatrix} 3 & 1 & \vdots & 2 \\ -1 & 2 & \vdots & 7 \end{bmatrix}$

c) $\begin{bmatrix} 3 & -1 & \vdots & 2 \\ 1 & 2 & \vdots & 7 \end{bmatrix}$

d) $\begin{bmatrix} -3 & 1 & \vdots & -2 \\ 1 & 2 & \vdots & -7 \end{bmatrix}$

e) None of these

Answer: c Difficulty: 1

7. Write the augmented matrix for the given system of linear equations.

$$\begin{cases} 7x + 2y = 12 \\ x - y = 16 \end{cases}$$

a) $\begin{bmatrix} 7 & 2 & \vdots & 12 \\ 1 & 1 & \vdots & 16 \end{bmatrix}$

b) $\begin{bmatrix} 7 & 2 & \vdots & -12 \\ 1 & 1 & \vdots & -16 \end{bmatrix}$

c) $\begin{bmatrix} 7 & 2 & \vdots & 12 \\ 1 & -1 & \vdots & 16 \end{bmatrix}$

d) $\begin{bmatrix} 7 & 1 & \vdots & 12 \\ 2 & -1 & \vdots & 16 \end{bmatrix}$

e) None of these

Answer: c Difficulty: 1

8. Write the augmented matrix for the given system of linear equations.

$$\begin{cases} 3x + 2y = 5 \\ 7x - 6y = 12 \end{cases}$$

a) $\begin{bmatrix} 3 & 2 & \vdots & 5 \\ 7 & -6 & \vdots & 12 \end{bmatrix}$

b) $\begin{bmatrix} 3 & 2 & \vdots & -5 \\ 7 & 6 & \vdots & -12 \end{bmatrix}$

c) $\begin{bmatrix} 3 & 2 & \vdots & 5 \\ 7 & 6 & \vdots & 12 \end{bmatrix}$

d) $\begin{bmatrix} 3 & 7 & \vdots & 5 \\ 2 & -6 & \vdots & 12 \end{bmatrix}$

e) None of these

Answer: a Difficulty: 1

9. Write the augmented matrix for the given system of linear equations.

$$\begin{cases} y - 3z = 5 \\ 2x + z = -1 \\ 4x - y = 0 \end{cases}$$

a) $\begin{bmatrix} 1 & -3 \\ 2 & 1 \\ 4 & -1 \end{bmatrix}$

b) $\begin{bmatrix} 1 & -3 & \vdots & 5 \\ 2 & 1 & \vdots & -1 \\ 4 & -1 & \vdots & 0 \end{bmatrix}$

c) $\begin{bmatrix} 0 & 1 & -3 \\ 2 & 0 & 1 \\ 4 & -1 & 0 \end{bmatrix}$

d) $\begin{bmatrix} 0 & 1 & -3 & \vdots & 5 \\ 2 & 0 & 1 & \vdots & -1 \\ 4 & -1 & 0 & \vdots & 0 \end{bmatrix}$

e) None of these

Answer: d Difficulty: 1

10. Write the system of linear equations represented by the augmented matrix.

$$\begin{bmatrix} 1 & -3 & \vdots & 4 \\ -2 & 9 & \vdots & 10 \end{bmatrix}$$

a) $\begin{cases} x + 3y = 4 \\ -2x + 9y = 10 \end{cases}$

b) $\begin{cases} x - 3y = 4 \\ -2x + 9y = 10 \end{cases}$

c) $\begin{cases} x - 3y = -4 \\ -2x + 9y = -10 \end{cases}$

d) $\begin{cases} x + 3y = 4 \\ 2x + 9y = 10 \end{cases}$

e) None of these

Answer: b Difficulty: 1

11. Write the system of linear equations represented by the augmented matrix.

$$\begin{bmatrix} 3 & 5 & 0 & \vdots & -7 \\ 4 & 1 & -2 & \vdots & 6 \\ -1 & 0 & 0 & \vdots & 4 \end{bmatrix}$$

a) $\begin{cases} 3x + 5y = -7 \\ 4x + y - 2z = 6 \\ -x = 4 \end{cases}$

b) $\begin{cases} 3x + 5y + 7z = 0 \\ 4x + y + 2z = 6 \\ -x + 4y + 0z = 0 \end{cases}$

c) $\begin{cases} -3x - 5y = -7 \\ -4x + y + 2z = 6 \\ x = 4 \end{cases}$

d) $\begin{cases} 2x = -7 \\ 3x = 6 \\ -x = 4 \end{cases}$

e) None of these

Answer: a Difficulty: 1

SHORT ANSWER

12. Use variables x, y, and z to write the system of linear equations represented by the augmented matrix:

$$\left[\begin{array}{ccc|c} 2 & -1 & 0 & 4 \\ 0 & 3 & 1 & -2 \\ 1 & -3 & 1 & 1 \end{array}\right].$$

Answer:

$$\begin{cases} 2x - y = 4 \\ 3y + z = -2 \\ x - 3y + z = 1 \end{cases}$$

Difficulty: 1

MULTIPLE CHOICE

13. Determine which of the following matrices is in row-echelon form.

a) $\begin{bmatrix} 1 & 3 & -1 & 4 \\ 0 & 2 & 1 & 1 \\ 0 & 0 & 1 & 4 \end{bmatrix}$ b) $\begin{bmatrix} 1 & 2 & 3 & 4 \\ 0 & 1 & 4 & 5 \\ 0 & 0 & 0 & 0 \end{bmatrix}$ c) $\begin{bmatrix} 2 & -1 & 6 & 3 \\ 4 & 1 & 2 & 0 \\ 0 & 1 & 2 & 0 \end{bmatrix}$

d) All of these e) None of these

Answer: b Difficulty: 1

14. Determine which of the following matrices is in row-echelon form.

a) $\begin{bmatrix} 0 & 3 & 2 & -1 \\ 4 & 0 & 1 & 0 \\ 0 & 0 & 2 & 5 \end{bmatrix}$ b) $\begin{bmatrix} 3 & 1 & 2 & 5 \\ 0 & 2 & 0 & 4 \\ 0 & 0 & 3 & 7 \end{bmatrix}$ c) $\begin{bmatrix} 1 & 2 & 3 & 4 \\ 0 & 2 & 4 & 7 \\ 0 & 0 & 1 & 0 \end{bmatrix}$

d) All of these e) None of these

Answer: e Difficulty: 1

15. Determine which of the following matrices is in row-echelon form.

a) $\begin{bmatrix} 1 & 2 & 4 & 6 \\ 0 & 1 & 3 & 2 \\ 0 & 0 & 1 & 0 \end{bmatrix}$ b) $\begin{bmatrix} 3 & 4 & 7 & 0 \\ 6 & 2 & 1 & 4 \\ 3 & 2 & 1 & 3 \end{bmatrix}$ c) $\begin{bmatrix} 1 & 6 & 4 & 2 \\ 0 & 2 & 3 & 1 \\ 0 & 0 & 1 & 0 \end{bmatrix}$

d) All of these e) None of these

Answer: a Difficulty: 1

16. Determine which of the following matrices is in row-echelon form.

a) $\begin{bmatrix} 1 & 2 & 3 & 4 \\ 0 & 1 & 7 & 2 \\ 0 & 0 & 1 & 5 \end{bmatrix}$

b) $\begin{bmatrix} 1 & 0 & 0 & 3 \\ 0 & 1 & 0 & 2 \\ 0 & 0 & 1 & 5 \end{bmatrix}$

c) $\begin{bmatrix} 1 & 0 & 4 & 7 \\ 0 & 1 & 0 & 2 \\ 0 & 0 & 1 & 2 \end{bmatrix}$

d) All of these

e) None of these

Answer: d Difficulty: 1

17. Determine which of the following matrices is in row-echelon form.

a) $\begin{bmatrix} 1 & 5 \\ 0 & 1 \\ 0 & 0 \end{bmatrix}$

b) $\begin{bmatrix} 0 & 0 & 0 \\ 0 & 1 & 2 \end{bmatrix}$

c) $\begin{bmatrix} 1 & -4 & 3 & 7 \\ 0 & 1 & 2 & -1 \\ 0 & 0 & 3 & 5 \end{bmatrix}$

d) [3]

e) None of these

Answer: a Difficulty: 1

18. Determine which of the following matrices is in reduced row-echelon form.

a) $\begin{bmatrix} 1 & -2 \\ 0 & 1 \\ 0 & 0 \end{bmatrix}$

b) $\begin{bmatrix} 1 & 0 & 4 & -2 \\ 0 & 1 & 7 & 5 \\ 0 & 0 & 0 & 0 \end{bmatrix}$

c) $\begin{bmatrix} 0 & 0 & 0 \\ 0 & 1 & 2 \end{bmatrix}$

d) $\begin{bmatrix} 1 & 1 \\ 0 & 1 \end{bmatrix}$

e) None of these

Answer: b Difficulty: 1

19. Write the matrix in reduced row-echelon form: $\begin{bmatrix} 3 & 1 & 1 & 7 \\ 1 & -2 & 0 & 5 \\ 1 & 1 & 2 & 6 \end{bmatrix}$.

a) $\begin{bmatrix} 1 & 1 & 2 & 6 \\ 0 & 3 & 2 & 1 \\ 0 & 0 & 11 & 31 \end{bmatrix}$

b) $\begin{bmatrix} 1 & 0 & 0 & \frac{21}{11} \\ 0 & 1 & 0 & -\frac{17}{11} \\ 0 & 0 & 1 & \frac{31}{11} \end{bmatrix}$

c) $\begin{bmatrix} 1 & -2 & 0 & 5 \\ 0 & 1 & \frac{1}{7} & -\frac{8}{7} \\ 0 & 0 & 11 & 31 \end{bmatrix}$

d) $\begin{bmatrix} 1 & 0 & 0 & \frac{3}{11} \\ 0 & 1 & 0 & \frac{7}{11} \\ 0 & 0 & 1 & -\frac{14}{11} \end{bmatrix}$

e) None of these

Answer: b Difficulty: 1

20.

Write the matrix in reduced row-echelon form: $\begin{bmatrix} 3 & 6 & -2 & 28 \\ -2 & -4 & 5 & -37 \\ 1 & 2 & 9 & -39 \end{bmatrix}$.

a) $\begin{bmatrix} 1 & 2 & 1 & 1 \\ 0 & 0 & 1 & -5 \\ 0 & 0 & 0 & 0 \end{bmatrix}$ b) $\begin{bmatrix} 0 & 0 & 0 & 0 \\ 1 & 2 & 0 & 6 \\ 0 & 0 & 1 & -5 \end{bmatrix}$ c) $\begin{bmatrix} 1 & 2 & 0 & 6 \\ 0 & 0 & 1 & -5 \\ 0 & 0 & 0 & 0 \end{bmatrix}$

d) $\begin{bmatrix} 1 & 2 & 1 & 1 \\ 0 & 0 & 1 & -5 \\ 0 & 0 & 0 & 3 \end{bmatrix}$ e) None of these

Answer: c Difficulty: 1

21.

Write the matrix in reduced row-echelon form: $\begin{bmatrix} 1 & 3 & -8 & 13 \\ 2 & -1 & 6 & -19 \\ -5 & 1 & 2 & 44 \end{bmatrix}$.

a) $\begin{bmatrix} 1 & 0 & 0 & -7 \\ 0 & 1 & 0 & 8 \\ 0 & 0 & 1 & \frac{1}{2} \end{bmatrix}$ b) $\begin{bmatrix} 1 & 0 & 6 & -4 \\ 0 & 1 & 2 & 9 \\ 0 & 0 & 2 & 1 \end{bmatrix}$ c) $\begin{bmatrix} 1 & 0 & 6 & -4 \\ 0 & 1 & -4 & 6 \\ 0 & 0 & 0 & 0 \end{bmatrix}$

d) $\begin{bmatrix} 1 & 1 & 8 & 5 \\ 0 & 1 & 2 & 9 \\ 0 & 0 & 2 & 1 \end{bmatrix}$ e) None of these

Answer: a Difficulty: 1

SHORT ANSWER

22.

Write the matrix in reduced row-echelon form: $\begin{bmatrix} 1 & 2 & -1 & 3 \\ 7 & -1 & 0 & 2 \\ 3 & 2 & 1 & -1 \end{bmatrix}$.

Answer:

$$\begin{bmatrix} 1 & 0 & 0 & \frac{5}{16} \\ 0 & 1 & 0 & \frac{3}{16} \\ 0 & 0 & 1 & -\frac{37}{16} \end{bmatrix}$$

Difficulty: 1

23. Write the matrix in reduced row-echelon form: $\begin{bmatrix} 21 & 14 & -7 & 10 \\ 7 & 7 & 7 & -1 \\ 3 & -14 & 28 & 23 \end{bmatrix}$.

Answer:

$$\begin{bmatrix} 1 & 0 & 0 & \frac{9}{7} \\ 0 & 1 & 0 & -\frac{9}{7} \\ 0 & 0 & 1 & -\frac{1}{7} \end{bmatrix}$$

Difficulty: 1

MULTIPLE CHOICE

24. Find the solution to the system of linear equations with the augmented matrix: $\begin{bmatrix} 2 & -1 & \vdots & 3 \\ 0 & 1 & \vdots & 2 \end{bmatrix}$

a) (3, 2) b) (2, 3) c) (-1, 3) d) $\left(\frac{5}{2}, 2\right)$ e) None of these

Answer: d Difficulty: 1

25. Find the solution to the system of linear equations with the augmented matrix: $\begin{bmatrix} 1 & 2 & -1 & \vdots & 4 \\ 0 & 2 & 1 & \vdots & -3 \\ 0 & 0 & 2 & \vdots & -4 \end{bmatrix}$.

a) $\left(3, -\frac{1}{2}, -2\right)$ b) (4, -3, -4) c) (1, 2, -1)
d) $\left(10, -\frac{5}{2}, -2\right)$ e) None of these

Answer: a Difficulty: 1

26. Find the solution to the system of linear equations with the augmented matrix: $\begin{bmatrix} 1 & 0 & 1 & \vdots & 0 \\ 0 & 1 & -2 & \vdots & 1 \end{bmatrix}$.

a) $(a, 1 + 2a, -a)$ b) $(-a, 2a + 1, a)$ c) $(a, 1 - 2a, a)$
d) $(-a, 1 - 2a, a)$ e) None of these

Answer: b Difficulty: 1

27. Find the solution to the system of linear equations with the augmented matrix: $\left[\begin{array}{cc:c} 2 & 1 & 7 \\ 5 & -3 & 1 \end{array}\right]$.

a) (3, 1) b) (1, 1) c) (4, -1)
d) (2, 3) e) None of these

Answer: d Difficulty: 1

28. Find the solution to the system of linear equations with the augmented matrix: $\left[\begin{array}{ccc:c} 1 & 0 & 1 & 1 \\ 2 & 1 & -1 & 2 \end{array}\right]$.

a) $(2a, -3a, a)$ b) $(1 - a, 3a, a)$ c) $(a + 2, 4a, -a)$
d) $(3a, 0, 2a)$ e) None of these

Answer: b Difficulty: 1

29. Find the solution to the system of linear equations with the augmented matrix: $\left[\begin{array}{ccc:c} 3 & 1 & 2 & 3 \\ 2 & -1 & 3 & 2 \end{array}\right]$.

a) $(a, 3a, -7a)$ b) $(3 + a, 2a, a)$ c) $(2a, 1 + a, a)$
d) $(1 - a, a, a)$ e) None of these

Answer: d Difficulty: 1

30. Use Gauss-Jordan elimination to solve the system of linear equations.

$$\begin{cases} x + 2y + z = 7 \\ 3x + z = 2 \\ x - y - z = 1 \end{cases}$$

a) $\left[\frac{2}{3}, \frac{20}{3}, -7\right]$ b) $\left[-\frac{7}{3}, \frac{1}{6}, 9\right]$ c) $\left[\frac{11}{6}, \frac{13}{3}, -\frac{7}{2}\right]$ d) $\left[-\frac{19}{3}, -\frac{2}{3}, \frac{44}{3}\right]$

Answer: c Difficulty: 1

SHORT ANSWER

31. Use Gauss-Jordan elimination to solve the system of linear equations.

$$\begin{cases} 4x - 3y + z = -8 \\ -2x + y - 3z = -4 \\ x - y + 2z = 3 \end{cases}$$

Answer: (-2, 1, 3) Difficulty: 1 Key 1: T

32. Use the matrix capabilities of a graphing utility to reduce the augmented matrix and solve the system of equations.

$$\begin{cases} 3x + 2y - 5z = -10 \\ 2x + 4y + z = 0 \\ x - 6y - 4z = -3 \end{cases}$$

Answer:
$\left(\frac{1}{2}, -\frac{3}{4}, 2\right)$

Difficulty: 1 Key 1: T

MULTIPLE CHOICE

33. Use Gaussian elimination with back-substitution or Gauss-Jordan elimination to solve the following system of linear equations.

$$\begin{cases} 3x + 2y + z = 7 \\ x - y + z = 6 \\ x + z = 5 \end{cases}$$

a) (2, -1, 3) b) $\left(1, -\frac{1}{2}, 5\right)$ c) (-1, 1, 2)
d) (0, 4, -1) e) None of these

Answer: a Difficulty: 1

34. Use Gaussian elimination with back-substitution or Gauss-Jordan elimination to solve the following system of linear equations.

$$\begin{cases} 2x + y - z = -3 \\ 4x - y + z = 6 \\ 2x + 3y + 2z = 9 \end{cases}$$

a) (1, -1, 4) b) $\left(\frac{1}{2}, 0, 4\right)$ c) $\left(\frac{1}{2}, 2, 0\right)$
d) $\left(\frac{3}{2}, -9, 0\right)$ e) None of these

Answer: b Difficulty: 1

35. Use Gaussian elimination with back-substitution or Gauss-Jordan elimination to solve the following system of linear equations.

$$\begin{cases} 2x + 3y - 4z = 4 \\ x - y - 5z = 0 \\ -2x + 4y + 5z = 9 \end{cases}$$

a) (-3, 2, -1) b) (3, -2, -1) c) (2, 1, 1)
d) (0, 4, 2) e) None of these

Answer: a Difficulty: 1

36. Find an equation of the parabola that passes through the points (1, 4), (2, 5), and (-1, -4).
a) $y = -3x^2 + 10x + 5$ b) $y = x^2 - x - 1$ c) $y = -2x^2 + 12x - 11$
d) $y = -x^2 + 4x + 1$ e) None of these

Answer: d Difficulty: 1

37. Find an equation of the parabola that passes through the points (1, -1), (2, 1), and (3, 7).
a) $y = x^2 + 5x - 5$ b) $y = x^2 - x - 1$ c) $y = -2x^2 + 12x - 11$
d) $y = 2x^2 - 4x + 1$ e) None of these

Answer: d Difficulty: 1

SHORT ANSWER

38. Find the equation of the parabola that passes through the given points. Use a graphing utility to verify your result.

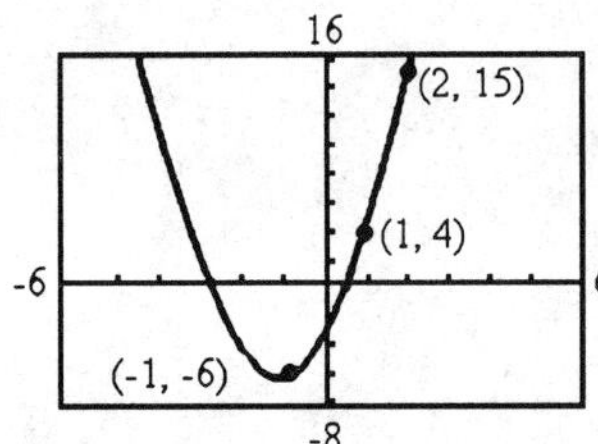

Answer:

$y = 2x^2 + 5x - 3$
Difficulty: 1 Key 1: T

39. Find the equation of the parabola that passes through the given points. Use a graphing utility to verify your result.

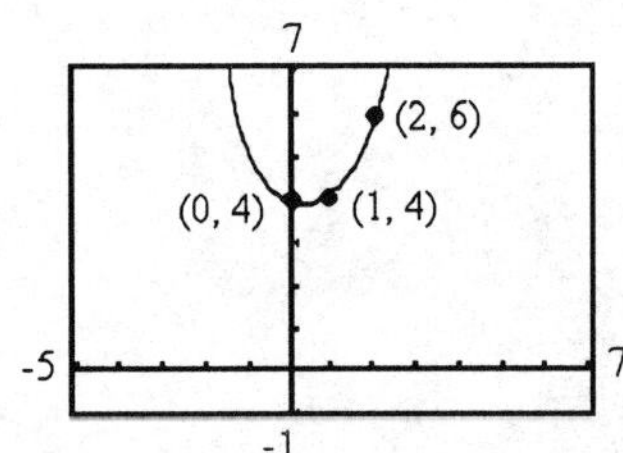

Answer:

$y = x^2 - x + 4$
Difficulty: 1 Key 1: T

MULTIPLE CHOICE

40. A small corporation borrowed $900,000; some at 7% interest, some at 8% interest, and some at 11% interest. How much was borrowed at 8% if the annual interest was $72,250 and the amount borrowed at 8% was $50,000 more than the amount borrowed at 11%?

a) $225,000 b) $175,000 c) $650,000
d) $450,000 e) None of these

Answer: a Difficulty: 2

41. A small corporation borrowed $900,000; some at 7% interest, some at 8% interest, and some at 11% interest. How much was borrowed at 11% if the annual interest was $71,500 and the amount borrowed at 7% was twice the amount borrowed at 8%?

a) $400,000 b) $800,000 c) $150,000
d) $300,000 e) None of these

Answer: c Difficulty: 2

Chapter 082: Operations with Matrices

MULTIPLE CHOICE

1.
Find x: $\begin{bmatrix} 3x+2 & 5 & 2 \\ 7 & 2y & x \\ 4 & -1 & y+1 \end{bmatrix} = \begin{bmatrix} x-4 & 5 & y/2 \\ 7 & 8 & -3 \\ 4 & -1 & 5 \end{bmatrix}$.

a) 4 b) -3 c) -1 d) 6 e) None of these

Answer: b Difficulty: 1

2.
Find x: $\begin{bmatrix} 9-2x & y & 0 \\ 4 & 2-y & 3 \\ 6 & \frac{2}{5}x & 5 \end{bmatrix} = \begin{bmatrix} -1 & 3 & 0 \\ 4 & -1 & x-2 \\ 6 & 2 & x \end{bmatrix}$.

a) -2 b) -3 c) 4 d) 5 e) None of these

Answer: d Difficulty: 1

3.
Find x: $\begin{bmatrix} x-1 & 4 & 5 \\ 2 & -1 & 5 \\ -6 & x & -9 \end{bmatrix} = \begin{bmatrix} -3 & 4 & 5 \\ 2 & -y/2 & y+3 \\ -6 & -2 & 4x-1 \end{bmatrix}$.

a) -2 b) -3 c) 4 d) 5 e) None of these

Answer: a Difficulty: 1

4.
Evaluate: $2\begin{bmatrix} 4 & 7 \\ 2 & 0 \end{bmatrix} - 3\begin{bmatrix} 1 & 2 \\ -1 & 5 \end{bmatrix}$.

a) $\begin{bmatrix} 5 & 8 \\ 7 & -15 \end{bmatrix}$

b) $\begin{bmatrix} 5 & 9 \\ 1 & -15 \end{bmatrix}$

c) $-1\begin{bmatrix} 3 & 5 \\ 3 & 5 \end{bmatrix}$

d) $-1\begin{bmatrix} 5 & 9 \\ 1 & 5 \end{bmatrix}$

e) None of these

Answer: a Difficulty: 1

SHORT ANSWER

5.
Evaluate: $3\begin{bmatrix} 2 & 7 \\ 9 & -1 \end{bmatrix} + 3\begin{bmatrix} 4 & 1 \\ 6 & 2 \end{bmatrix}$.

Answer:

$\begin{bmatrix} 18 & 24 \\ 45 & 3 \end{bmatrix}$

Difficulty: 1

6.

Evaluate: $3\begin{bmatrix} 7 & 5 & 2 \\ -1 & 1 & 0 \\ 0 & 3 & 6 \end{bmatrix} + 2\begin{bmatrix} 1 & 0 & 0 \\ 0 & 1 & 0 \\ 0 & 0 & 1 \end{bmatrix} - 4\begin{bmatrix} 1 & -1 & 2 \\ 7 & 1 & -1 \\ 2 & 5 & 1 \end{bmatrix}$.

Answer:

$$\begin{bmatrix} 19 & 19 & -2 \\ -31 & 1 & 4 \\ -8 & -11 & 16 \end{bmatrix}$$

Difficulty: 1

MULTIPLE CHOICE

7.

Given $A = \begin{bmatrix} 3 & 6 & -1 \\ 0 & 5 & 2 \end{bmatrix}$ and $B = \begin{bmatrix} 1 & 0 & 5 \\ -1 & 2 & 7 \end{bmatrix}$, find $3A - 2B$.

a) $\begin{bmatrix} 7 & 18 & -13 \\ 2 & 11 & -8 \end{bmatrix}$

b) $\begin{bmatrix} 7 & 18 & 2 \\ 0 & 11 & -8 \end{bmatrix}$

c) $\begin{bmatrix} 11 & 18 & 7 \\ -2 & 19 & 20 \end{bmatrix}$

d) $\begin{bmatrix} 7 & 18 & -13 \\ -2 & 9 & 20 \end{bmatrix}$

e) None of these

Answer: a Difficulty: 1

8.

Given $A = \begin{bmatrix} 1 & 2 & 3 \\ 4 & 7 & 1 \\ 0 & 3 & 2 \end{bmatrix}$ and $B = \begin{bmatrix} 0 & 0 & 1 \\ 1 & 4 & 0 \\ 2 & 3 & 7 \end{bmatrix}$, find $6A - 2B$.

a) $\begin{bmatrix} 30 & 72 & 52 \\ 32 & 10 & 6 \\ 1 & 6 & -8 \end{bmatrix}$

b) $\begin{bmatrix} 30 & 12 & 4 \\ 3 & 10 & 6 \\ 1 & 6 & -8 \end{bmatrix}$

c) $\begin{bmatrix} 6 & 12 & 16 \\ 22 & 34 & 6 \\ -4 & 12 & -2 \end{bmatrix}$

d) $\begin{bmatrix} 30 & 22 & 20 \\ 66 & 28 & 26 \\ 24 & 16 & 14 \end{bmatrix}$

e) None of these

Answer: c Difficulty: 1

9. Given $A = \begin{bmatrix} 2 & 4 & -1 \\ 1 & 0 & 4 \\ 8 & 1 & 2 \end{bmatrix}$ and $B = \begin{bmatrix} 1 & 1 & 1 \\ -1 & 0 & 0 \\ 4 & 10 & -2 \end{bmatrix}$, find $2A - 2B$.

a) $\begin{bmatrix} 2 & 6 & 4 \\ 4 & 0 & -8 \\ -8 & 18 & 1 \end{bmatrix}$ b) $\begin{bmatrix} 2 & 6 & -4 \\ 4 & 0 & 8 \\ 8 & -18 & 8 \end{bmatrix}$ c) $\begin{bmatrix} 0 & 6 & -4 \\ -4 & 0 & 4 \\ 4 & -9 & 0 \end{bmatrix}$

d) $\begin{bmatrix} 1 & 3 & -2 \\ 0 & 0 & 4 \\ 4 & -9 & 4 \end{bmatrix}$ e) None of these

Answer: b Difficulty: 1

10. Given $A = \begin{bmatrix} 3 & -2 & 4 \\ 0 & 0 & -1 \\ 3 & 2 & -1 \end{bmatrix}$ and $B = \begin{bmatrix} 3 & 1 & -1 \\ -1 & 0 & 0 \\ 2 & 4 & -2 \end{bmatrix}$, find $3A - 2B$.

a) $\begin{bmatrix} 3 & -8 & 14 \\ 2 & 0 & -3 \\ 5 & -2 & 1 \end{bmatrix}$ b) $\begin{bmatrix} 3 & -8 & 10 \\ 2 & 0 & -3 \\ 7 & -2 & -7 \end{bmatrix}$ c) $\begin{bmatrix} 6 & -1 & 3 \\ -1 & 0 & -1 \\ 5 & 6 & -3 \end{bmatrix}$

d) $\begin{bmatrix} 15 & -4 & 10 \\ -2 & 0 & -3 \\ 13 & 14 & 1 \end{bmatrix}$ e) None of these

Answer: a Difficulty: 1

11. Given $A = \begin{bmatrix} 3 & 2 & 2 \\ -1 & 0 & -1 \\ 0 & 1 & 0 \end{bmatrix}$ and $B = \begin{bmatrix} 1 & 1 & 0 \\ 0 & 1 & 1 \\ 2 & -1 & 2 \end{bmatrix}$, find $2A - 3B$.

a) $\begin{bmatrix} 8 & 7 & 4 \\ -2 & 3 & 1 \\ 6 & -1 & 6 \end{bmatrix}$ b) $\begin{bmatrix} 8 & 7 & 4 \\ -2 & -3 & -5 \\ -6 & -1 & -6 \end{bmatrix}$ c) $\begin{bmatrix} 3 & 1 & 4 \\ 2 & 3 & 5 \\ -6 & 5 & 6 \end{bmatrix}$

d) $\begin{bmatrix} 3 & 1 & 4 \\ -2 & -3 & -5 \\ -6 & 5 & -6 \end{bmatrix}$ e) None of these

Answer: d Difficulty: 1

12. Given $A = \begin{bmatrix} 1 & 0 & 3 \\ -1 & 2 & -2 \\ 1 & 1 & 2 \end{bmatrix}$ and $B = \begin{bmatrix} 1 & 1 & 0 \\ 3 & 1 & 2 \\ -1 & 1 & -1 \end{bmatrix}$, find $-2A + 5B$.

a) $\begin{bmatrix} 3 & 5 & -6 \\ 17 & 1 & 14 \\ -7 & 3 & -9 \end{bmatrix}$
b) $\begin{bmatrix} 3 & 5 & 6 \\ 13 & 9 & 6 \\ -3 & 8 & -1 \end{bmatrix}$
c) $\begin{bmatrix} 7 & 5 & 6 \\ 13 & 9 & 6 \\ -3 & 8 & -1 \end{bmatrix}$

d) $\begin{bmatrix} 3 & 5 & -6 \\ -17 & 0 & 14 \\ 7 & -3 & -9 \end{bmatrix}$
e) None of these

Answer: a Difficulty: 1

13. If $A = \begin{bmatrix} 2 & -1 \\ 3 & 1 \end{bmatrix}$ and $B = \begin{bmatrix} 4 & 0 \\ -1 & -1 \end{bmatrix}$, find $A - 2B$.

a) $\begin{bmatrix} -6 & -1 \\ 5 & -1 \end{bmatrix}$
b) 13
c) $\begin{bmatrix} -6 & -1 \\ 1 & 3 \end{bmatrix}$

d) $\begin{bmatrix} -2 & -1 \\ 5 & 3 \end{bmatrix}$
e) None of these

Answer: e Difficulty: 1

14. If $A = \begin{bmatrix} 2 & -1 \\ 3 & 1 \end{bmatrix}$ and $B = \begin{bmatrix} 4 & 0 \\ -1 & -1 \end{bmatrix}$, find $B - 2A$.

a) -14
b) $\begin{bmatrix} -6 & -1 \\ 5 & 3 \end{bmatrix}$
c) $\begin{bmatrix} 0 & -2 \\ -7 & -3 \end{bmatrix}$

d) $\begin{bmatrix} 0 & 2 \\ -7 & -3 \end{bmatrix}$
e) None of these

Answer: d Difficulty: 1

SHORT ANSWER

15. If $A = \begin{bmatrix} 2 & -1 \\ -3 & 4 \end{bmatrix}$ and $B = \begin{bmatrix} -2 & 0 \\ -1 & 3 \end{bmatrix}$, find C if $A + C = 2B$.

Answer:

$\begin{bmatrix} -6 & 1 \\ 1 & 2 \end{bmatrix}$

Difficulty: 1

16. Use a graphing utility to find *AB*, given

$$A = \begin{bmatrix} 1 & 3 & 6 \\ 4 & 1 & 3 \end{bmatrix} \text{ and } B = \begin{bmatrix} 0 & 1 & 6 \\ 3 & -1 & 1 \\ 5 & 2 & 3 \end{bmatrix}.$$

Answer:

$$\begin{bmatrix} 39 & 10 & 27 \\ 18 & 9 & 34 \end{bmatrix}$$

Difficulty: 1 Key 1: T

MULTIPLE CHOICE

17. Use a graphing utility to find *AB*, given

$$A = \begin{bmatrix} 2 & 1 \\ 3 & -2 \end{bmatrix} \text{ and } B = \begin{bmatrix} -1 & 5 \\ 6 & 2 \end{bmatrix}.$$

a) $\begin{bmatrix} 4 & 12 \\ -15 & 11 \end{bmatrix}$

b) $\begin{bmatrix} 13 & -11 \\ 18 & 2 \end{bmatrix}$

c) $\begin{bmatrix} 16 & 16 \\ -13 & 1 \end{bmatrix}$

d) $\begin{bmatrix} -2 & 5 \\ 18 & -4 \end{bmatrix}$

e) None of these

Answer: a Difficulty: 1 Key 1: T

18.

Use a graphing utility to multiply: $\begin{bmatrix} 2 & 3 & 4 \\ -1 & 0 & 2 \end{bmatrix} \begin{bmatrix} -1 & 4 \\ 0 & 1 \\ 5 & 2 \end{bmatrix}$.

a) $\begin{bmatrix} 18 & 19 \\ 11 & 0 \end{bmatrix}$

b) $\begin{bmatrix} -2 & 0 & 20 \\ -4 & 0 & 4 \end{bmatrix}$

c) $\begin{bmatrix} -6 & -3 & 4 \\ -2 & 0 & 6 \\ -1 & 2 & 4 \end{bmatrix}$

d) $\begin{bmatrix} -6 \\ 0 \\ 24 \end{bmatrix}$

e) None of these

Answer: a Difficulty: 1 Key 1: T

19. Use a graphing utility to find AB, given

$$A = \begin{bmatrix} 1 & -1 & 2 \\ 0 & 5 & 1 \\ -2 & 0 & -1 \end{bmatrix} \text{ and } B = \begin{bmatrix} -1 & 1 & 0 \\ 5 & -7 & 1 \\ 2 & 3 & -2 \end{bmatrix}.$$

a) $\begin{bmatrix} -1 & -2 & 0 \\ 0 & -35 & 1 \\ -4 & 0 & 2 \end{bmatrix}$

b) $\begin{bmatrix} -1 & 11 & 0 \\ 3 & -40 & 2 \\ 6 & 13 & 9 \end{bmatrix}$

c) $\begin{bmatrix} 6 & 3 & -2 \\ 0 & -10 & -1 \\ -12 & 0 & 1 \end{bmatrix}$

d) $\begin{bmatrix} -2 & 14 & -5 \\ 27 & -32 & 3 \\ 0 & -5 & 2 \end{bmatrix}$

e) None of these

Answer: d Difficulty: 1 Key 1: T

SHORT ANSWER

20. Use a graphing utility to find AB, given $A = \begin{bmatrix} 1 & 3 & 5 & 2 \\ -1 & 6 & 4 & 8 \end{bmatrix}$ and $B =$

$$\begin{bmatrix} 3 & 2 & 0 \\ 0 & 0 & 1 \\ 1 & 2 & -1 \\ 0 & 0 & 3 \end{bmatrix}$$

Answer:

$$AB = \begin{bmatrix} 8 & 12 & 4 \\ 1 & 6 & 26 \end{bmatrix}$$

Difficulty: 1 Key 1: T

MULTIPLE CHOICE

21. Given $A = \begin{bmatrix} 3 & -2 & 4 & 0 \\ 0 & 0 & -1 & 4 \\ 3 & 2 & -1 & -1 \end{bmatrix}$ and $B = \begin{bmatrix} 1 & 1 & 1 \\ -1 & 0 & 0 \\ 4 & 10 & -2 \end{bmatrix}$, find BA.

a) $\begin{bmatrix} 21 & 14 & 10 & -4 \\ -3 & -2 & 1 & -1 \\ 6 & 4 & 11 & 7 \end{bmatrix}$

b) $\begin{bmatrix} 21 & 43 & -5 \\ -4 & -10 & 2 \\ -3 & -7 & 5 \end{bmatrix}$

c) $\begin{bmatrix} 6 & 0 & 2 & 3 \\ -3 & 2 & -4 & 0 \\ 6 & -12 & 8 & 42 \end{bmatrix}$

d) Impossible

e) None of these

Answer: c Difficulty: 1

22. Given $A = \begin{bmatrix} 3 & -2 & 4 & 0 \\ 0 & 0 & -1 & 4 \\ 3 & 2 & -1 & -1 \end{bmatrix}$ and $B = \begin{bmatrix} 1 & 1 & 1 \\ -1 & 0 & 0 \\ 4 & 10 & -2 \end{bmatrix}$, find AB.

a) $\begin{bmatrix} 21 & 14 & 10 & -4 \\ -3 & -2 & 1 & -1 \\ 6 & 4 & 11 & 7 \end{bmatrix}$ b) $\begin{bmatrix} 21 & 43 & -5 \\ -4 & -10 & 2 \\ -3 & -7 & 5 \\ 0 & 0 & 0 \end{bmatrix}$ c) $\begin{bmatrix} 6 & 0 & 2 & 3 \\ -3 & 2 & -4 & 0 \\ 6 & -12 & 8 & 42 \end{bmatrix}$

d) Impossible e) None of these

Answer: d Difficulty: 1

23. Given $A = \begin{bmatrix} 2 & 4 & -1 \\ 1 & 0 & 4 \\ 8 & 1 & 2 \end{bmatrix}$ and $B = \begin{bmatrix} 1 & 1 & 1 \\ -1 & 0 & 0 \\ 4 & 10 & -2 \end{bmatrix}$, find AB.

a) $\begin{bmatrix} 11 & 5 & 5 \\ -2 & -4 & 1 \\ 2 & 14 & 32 \end{bmatrix}$ b) $\begin{bmatrix} -6 & -8 & 4 \\ 17 & 41 & -7 \\ 15 & 28 & 4 \end{bmatrix}$ c) $\begin{bmatrix} -5 & -8 & 4 \\ 17 & 41 & -7 \\ 15 & 28 & 4 \end{bmatrix}$

d) Impossible e) None of these

Answer: b Difficulty: 1

24. Given $A = \begin{bmatrix} 2 & 4 & -1 & 3 \\ 1 & 0 & 4 & 0 \\ 8 & 1 & 2 & 1 \end{bmatrix}$ and $B = \begin{bmatrix} 3 & 1 & -1 \\ -1 & 0 & 0 \\ 2 & 4 & -2 \end{bmatrix}$, find BA.

a) $\begin{bmatrix} -1 & 11 & -1 & 8 \\ -2 & -4 & 1 & -3 \\ -8 & 6 & 10 & 4 \end{bmatrix}$ b) $\begin{bmatrix} 0 & -2 & 0 \\ 11 & 17 & -9 \\ 27 & 16 & -12 \end{bmatrix}$ c) $\begin{bmatrix} -1 & -11 & 1 & 0 \\ -2 & 4 & -1 & -3 \\ 8 & -6 & 10 & -12 \end{bmatrix}$

d) Impossible e) None of these

Answer: a Difficulty: 1

25. Given $A = \begin{bmatrix} 2 & 4 & -1 & 3 \\ 1 & 0 & 4 & 0 \\ 8 & 1 & 2 & 1 \end{bmatrix}$ and $B = \begin{bmatrix} 3 & 1 & -1 \\ -1 & 0 & 0 \\ 2 & 4 & -2 \end{bmatrix}$, find AB.

a) $\begin{bmatrix} -1 & 11 & -1 & 8 \\ -2 & -4 & 1 & -3 \\ -8 & 6 & 10 & 4 \end{bmatrix}$ b) $\begin{bmatrix} 0 & -2 & 0 \\ 11 & 17 & -9 \\ 27 & 16 & -12 \end{bmatrix}$ c) $\begin{bmatrix} 6 & 4 & 1 & 3 \\ -1 & 0 & 0 & 0 \\ 16 & 4 & -4 & 0 \end{bmatrix}$

d) Impossible e) None of these

Answer: d Difficulty: 1

26. Use a graphing utility to find AB, given $A = \begin{bmatrix} 3 & -2 & 4 \\ 0 & 0 & -1 \\ 3 & 2 & -1 \end{bmatrix}$ and $B = \begin{bmatrix} 3 & 1 & -1 \\ -1 & 0 & 0 \\ 2 & 4 & -2 \end{bmatrix}$.

a) $\begin{bmatrix} 6 & -8 & 12 \\ -3 & 2 & -4 \\ 0 & -8 & 6 \end{bmatrix}$ b) $\begin{bmatrix} 19 & 19 & -11 \\ -2 & -4 & 2 \\ 5 & -1 & -1 \end{bmatrix}$ c) $\begin{bmatrix} 9 & -2 & -4 \\ 0 & 0 & 0 \\ 6 & 8 & 2 \end{bmatrix}$

d) Impossible e) None of these

Answer: b Difficulty: 1 Key 1: T

27. Use a graphing utility to find AB, given $A = \begin{bmatrix} 2 & 0 & 1 & 2 \\ 0 & 1 & 0 & 1 \\ -1 & -2 & 0 & 0 \end{bmatrix}$ and $B = \begin{bmatrix} 1 & 1 & 0 \\ 0 & 1 & 1 \\ 2 & -1 & 2 \end{bmatrix}$.

a) $\begin{bmatrix} 2 & 0 & 1 & 2 \\ 0 & 1 & 0 & 0 \\ -2 & 2 & 0 & 0 \end{bmatrix}$ b) $\begin{bmatrix} 4 & 2 & 3 \\ -1 & -2 & -1 \\ 6 & -5 & -1 \end{bmatrix}$ c) $\begin{bmatrix} 2 & 1 & 1 & 3 \\ -1 & -1 & 0 & 1 \\ 2 & -5 & 2 & 3 \end{bmatrix}$

d) Impossible e) None of these

Answer: d Difficulty: 1 Key 1: T

28. Use a graphing utility to find BA, given $A = \begin{bmatrix} 2 & 0 & 1 & 2 \\ 0 & 1 & 0 & 1 \\ -1 & -2 & 0 & 0 \end{bmatrix}$ and $B = \begin{bmatrix} 1 & 1 & 0 \\ 0 & 1 & 1 \\ 2 & -1 & 2 \end{bmatrix}$.

a) $\begin{bmatrix} 2 & 1 & 1 & 3 \\ -1 & -1 & 0 & 1 \\ 2 & -5 & 2 & 3 \end{bmatrix}$ b) $\begin{bmatrix} 4 & 1 & 2 \\ 0 & 1 & 1 \\ -1 & -3 & -2 \end{bmatrix}$ c) $\begin{bmatrix} 6 & -4 & 0 \\ 0 & 1 & 1 \\ -4 & -3 & -4 \end{bmatrix}$

d) Impossible e) None of these

Answer: a Difficulty: 1 Key 1: T

29.

Use a graphing utility to find BA, given $A = \begin{bmatrix} 3 & 2 & 2 \\ -1 & 0 & -1 \\ 0 & 1 & 0 \end{bmatrix}$ and $B = \begin{bmatrix} 1 & 1 & 0 \\ 0 & 1 & 1 \\ 2 & -1 & 2 \end{bmatrix}$.

a) $\begin{bmatrix} 3 & 2 & 0 \\ 0 & 0 & -1 \\ 0 & -1 & 0 \end{bmatrix}$ b) $\begin{bmatrix} 7 & 3 & 6 \\ -3 & 0 & -2 \\ 0 & 1 & 1 \end{bmatrix}$ c) $\begin{bmatrix} 2 & 2 & 1 \\ -1 & 1 & -1 \\ 7 & 6 & 5 \end{bmatrix}$

d) Impossible e) None of these

Answer: c Difficulty: 1 Key 1: T

30.

Use a graphing utility to find AB, given $A = \begin{bmatrix} 3 & 1 & 2 & 1 \\ 0 & 1 & 0 & 0 \\ 2 & 1 & 3 & -1 \end{bmatrix}$ and $B = \begin{bmatrix} 1 & 1 & 0 \\ 3 & 1 & 2 \\ -1 & 1 & -1 \end{bmatrix}$.

a) $\begin{bmatrix} 3 & 2 & 2 & 1 \\ 13 & 6 & 12 & 1 \\ -5 & -1 & -5 & 0 \end{bmatrix}$ b) $\begin{bmatrix} 4 & 6 & 0 \\ 3 & 1 & 2 \\ 2 & 6 & -1 \end{bmatrix}$ c) $\begin{bmatrix} 3 & 1 & 0 \\ 0 & 1 & 2 \\ -2 & 1 & -3 \end{bmatrix}$

d) Impossible e) None of these

Answer: d Difficulty: 1 Key 1: T

SHORT ANSWER

31.

Given $A = \begin{bmatrix} 3 & 2 & 2 & 1 \\ 13 & 6 & 12 & 1 \\ -5 & -1 & -5 & 0 \end{bmatrix}$ and $B = \begin{bmatrix} 1 & 1 & 0 \\ 3 & 1 & 2 \\ -1 & 1 & -1 \end{bmatrix}$, find BA.

Answer:

$$\begin{bmatrix} 16 & 8 & 14 & 2 \\ 12 & 10 & 8 & 4 \\ 15 & 5 & 15 & 0 \end{bmatrix}$$

Difficulty: 1

32. Given $A = \begin{bmatrix} 1 & 0 & 3 \\ -1 & 2 & -2 \\ 1 & 1 & 2 \end{bmatrix}$ and $B = \begin{bmatrix} 1 & 1 & 0 \\ 3 & 1 & 2 \\ -1 & 1 & -1 \end{bmatrix}$, find BA.

Answer:

$$\begin{bmatrix} 0 & 2 & 1 \\ 4 & 4 & 11 \\ -3 & 1 & -7 \end{bmatrix}$$

Difficulty: 1

MULTIPLE CHOICE

33. Find AB if $A = \begin{bmatrix} 2 & -1 & 0 \\ 3 & 4 & 1 \end{bmatrix}$ and $B = \begin{bmatrix} 0 & 1 \\ 4 & 3 \\ 5 & -1 \end{bmatrix}$.

a) $\begin{bmatrix} -4 & -1 \\ 21 & 14 \end{bmatrix}$

b) $\begin{bmatrix} 3 & 4 & 1 \\ 17 & 8 & 3 \\ 7 & -9 & -1 \end{bmatrix}$

c) $\begin{bmatrix} -2 & -1 \\ 21 & 14 \end{bmatrix}$

d) Cannot be done

e) None of these

Answer: a Difficulty: 1

SHORT ANSWER

34. Find BA if $A = \begin{bmatrix} 2 & -1 & 0 \\ 0 & 5 & 3 \\ 1 & -2 & -1 \end{bmatrix}$ and $B = \begin{bmatrix} 1 & 0 & -1 \\ 2 & 3 & 0 \end{bmatrix}$.

Answer:

$$\begin{bmatrix} 1 & 1 & 1 \\ 4 & 13 & 9 \end{bmatrix}$$

Difficulty: 1

MULTIPLE CHOICE

35.
Solve for X given $A = \begin{bmatrix} 3 & 1 \\ -2 & 5 \end{bmatrix}$ and $B = \begin{bmatrix} 1 & 1 \\ 1 & 9 \end{bmatrix}$: $2X - A = B$.

a) 17

b) $\begin{bmatrix} 5 & 1 \\ -5 & 1 \end{bmatrix}$

c) $\begin{bmatrix} 4 & 2 \\ -1 & 14 \end{bmatrix}$

d) $\begin{bmatrix} 2 & 1 \\ -\frac{1}{2} & 7 \end{bmatrix}$

e) None of these

Answer: d Difficulty: 1

36.
Solve for X given $A = \begin{bmatrix} 2 & 3 \\ 5 & -2 \end{bmatrix}$ and $B = \begin{bmatrix} 2 & 5 \\ -1 & 6 \end{bmatrix}$: $2X + A = B$.

a) $\begin{bmatrix} 2 & 4 \\ 2 & 2 \end{bmatrix}$

b) $\begin{bmatrix} 0 & 1 \\ -3 & 4 \end{bmatrix}$

c) $\begin{bmatrix} 4 & 8 \\ 4 & 4 \end{bmatrix}$

d) $\begin{bmatrix} 0 & 2 \\ -6 & 8 \end{bmatrix}$

e) None of these

Answer: b Difficulty: 1

37.
Solve for X given $A = \begin{bmatrix} -3 & 4 \\ 2 & 6 \end{bmatrix}$ and $B = \begin{bmatrix} 6 & 2 \\ 7 & 0 \end{bmatrix}$: $3X - A = B$.

a) $\frac{-44}{9}$

b) $\begin{bmatrix} -3 & \frac{2}{3} \\ -\frac{5}{3} & 2 \end{bmatrix}$

c) -4

d) $\begin{bmatrix} 1 & 2 \\ 3 & 2 \end{bmatrix}$

e) None of these

Answer: d Difficulty: 1

38. Write the matrix equation for the system of linear equations:

$$\begin{cases} 3x + 2y = 5 \\ 7x - 6y = 1 \end{cases}.$$

a) $[x \quad y] = \begin{bmatrix} 3 & 7 \\ 2 & -6 \end{bmatrix} \begin{bmatrix} 5 \\ 1 \end{bmatrix}$

b) $\begin{bmatrix} x \\ y \end{bmatrix} = \begin{bmatrix} 3 & 2 \\ 7 & -6 \end{bmatrix} \begin{bmatrix} 5 \\ 1 \end{bmatrix}$

c) $\begin{bmatrix} 3 & 2 \\ 7 & -6 \end{bmatrix} \begin{bmatrix} x \\ y \end{bmatrix} = \begin{bmatrix} 5 \\ 1 \end{bmatrix}$

d) $[x \quad y] \begin{bmatrix} 5 \\ 1 \end{bmatrix} = \begin{bmatrix} 3 & 7 \\ 2 & -6 \end{bmatrix}$

e) None of these

Answer: c Difficulty: 1

39. Write the matrix equation for the system of linear equations:

$$\begin{cases} 2x_1 + x_2 = 0 \\ 2x_1 + x_2 + x_3 = -1 \\ 2x_2 - x_3 + 3x_4 = 1 \\ 2x_3 - 3x_4 = 4 \end{cases}.$$

a) $\begin{bmatrix} 2 & 1 & 0 & 0 \\ 2 & 1 & 1 & 0 \\ 0 & 2 & -1 & 3 \\ 0 & 0 & 2 & -3 \end{bmatrix} \begin{bmatrix} x_1 \\ x_2 \\ x_3 \\ x_4 \end{bmatrix} = \begin{bmatrix} 0 \\ -1 \\ 1 \\ 4 \end{bmatrix}$

b) $\begin{bmatrix} 2 & 2 & 0 & 0 \\ 1 & 1 & 2 & 0 \\ 0 & 2 & -1 & 2 \\ 0 & 0 & 3 & -3 \end{bmatrix} \begin{bmatrix} x_1 \\ x_2 \\ x_3 \\ x_4 \end{bmatrix} = \begin{bmatrix} 0 \\ -1 \\ 1 \\ 4 \end{bmatrix}$

c) $\begin{bmatrix} 2 & 1 & 0 & 0 \\ 2 & 1 & 1 & 0 \\ 0 & 2 & -1 & 3 \\ 0 & 0 & 2 & -3 \end{bmatrix} \begin{bmatrix} 0 \\ -1 \\ 1 \\ 4 \end{bmatrix} = \begin{bmatrix} x_1 \\ x_2 \\ x_3 \\ x_4 \end{bmatrix}$

d) $\begin{bmatrix} 2 & 2 & 0 & 0 \\ 1 & 1 & 2 & 0 \\ 0 & 1 & -1 & 2 \\ 0 & 0 & 3 & -3 \end{bmatrix} \begin{bmatrix} 0 \\ -1 \\ 1 \\ 4 \end{bmatrix} = \begin{bmatrix} x_1 \\ x_2 \\ x_3 \\ x_4 \end{bmatrix}$

e) None of these

Answer: a Difficulty: 1

40. Write the matrix equation for the system of linear equations:

$$\begin{cases} 2x - 4y = 12 \\ x + 5y = 16 \end{cases}.$$

a) $[x \quad y] = \begin{bmatrix} 2 & -4 \\ 1 & 5 \end{bmatrix} \begin{bmatrix} 12 \\ 16 \end{bmatrix}$

b) $\begin{bmatrix} 2 & -4 \\ 1 & 5 \end{bmatrix} \begin{bmatrix} x \\ y \end{bmatrix} = \begin{bmatrix} 12 \\ 16 \end{bmatrix}$

c) $\begin{bmatrix} x \\ y \end{bmatrix} = \begin{bmatrix} 2 & -4 \\ 1 & 5 \end{bmatrix} \begin{bmatrix} 12 \\ 16 \end{bmatrix}$

d) $[x \quad y] \begin{bmatrix} 12 \\ 16 \end{bmatrix} = \begin{bmatrix} 3 & 7 \\ 2 & -6 \end{bmatrix}$

e) None of these

Answer: b Difficulty: 1

SHORT ANSWER

41. A farmer raises two crops, corn and wheat, which are shipped to three processors daily. The number of bushels of crop *i* that are shipped to processor *j* is represented by a_{ij} in the matrix

$$A = \begin{bmatrix} 125 & 75 & 100 \\ 100 & 150 & 125 \end{bmatrix}.$$

The profit per bushel is represented by the matrix

$$B = [\$1.25 \quad \$0.85].$$

Find the product *BA* and state what each entry of the product represents.

Answer:
$BA = [241.25 \quad 221.25 \quad 231.25]$

The farmer's total profit for the crops shipped to the first processor is $241.25, to the second processor is $221.25, and to the third processor is $231.25.

Difficulty: 2

42. A farmer raises two crops, corn and wheat, which are shipped to three processors daily. The number of bushels of crop *i* that are shipped to processor *j* is represented by a_{ij} in the matrix

$$A = \begin{bmatrix} 242 & 125 & 100 \\ 100 & 175 & 225 \end{bmatrix}.$$

The profit per bushel is represented by the matrix

$$B = [\$1.25 \quad \$0.85].$$

Find the product *BA* and state what each entry of the product represents.

Answer:
$BA = [387.50 \quad 305.00 \quad 316.25]$

The farmer's total profit for the crops shipped to the first processor is $387.50, to the second processor is $305.00, and to the third processor is $316.25.

Difficulty: 2

Chapter 083: The Inverse of a Square Matrix

MULTIPLE CHOICE

1. Determine which of the following matrices has an inverse.
   a) $\begin{bmatrix} 1 & -2 \\ -3 & 6 \end{bmatrix}$
   b) $\begin{bmatrix} 3 \\ 2 \end{bmatrix}$
   c) $\begin{bmatrix} 3 & 4 & -1 \\ 2 & 1 & 0 \end{bmatrix}$
   d) $\begin{bmatrix} 6 & 1 \\ -2 & 4 \end{bmatrix}$
   e) None of these

   Answer: d Difficulty: 1

2. Determine which of the following matrices has an inverse.
   a) $\begin{bmatrix} 2 & -5 \\ -4 & 10 \end{bmatrix}$
   b) $\begin{bmatrix} 2 & 6 \\ -4 & 12 \end{bmatrix}$
   c) $\begin{bmatrix} 0 \\ 2 \\ 5 \end{bmatrix}$
   d) $\begin{bmatrix} 4 & 2 \\ 1 & 7 \\ 0 & -1 \end{bmatrix}$
   e) None of these

   Answer: b Difficulty: 1

3. Determine which of the following matrices has an inverse.
   a) $\begin{bmatrix} -1 \\ 5 \\ 2 \end{bmatrix}$
   b) $\begin{bmatrix} 4 & -2 \\ -2 & 1 \end{bmatrix}$
   c) $\begin{bmatrix} -3 & 5 \\ 6 & -10 \end{bmatrix}$
   d) $\begin{bmatrix} -3 & 5 \\ -4 & 2 \end{bmatrix}$
   e) None of these

   Answer: d Difficulty: 1

4. Determine which of the following matrices has an inverse.
   a) $\begin{bmatrix} 1 & -7 \\ 2 & 14 \end{bmatrix}$
   b) $\begin{bmatrix} 2 & -7 \\ -4 & 14 \end{bmatrix}$
   c) $\begin{bmatrix} -6 & 9 \\ 4 & -6 \end{bmatrix}$
   d) $\begin{bmatrix} 4 \\ 1 \\ 3 \end{bmatrix}$
   e) None of these

   Answer: a Difficulty: 1

5. Determine which of the following matrices has an inverse.
   a) $\begin{bmatrix} -4 & -3 \\ 8 & 6 \end{bmatrix}$
   b) $\begin{bmatrix} 6 & 1 \\ -12 & -2 \end{bmatrix}$
   c) $\begin{bmatrix} -2 & -1 \\ 3 & 2 \end{bmatrix}$
   d) $[3 \quad 4 \quad 1]$
   e) None of these

   Answer: c Difficulty: 1

6. Determine which of the following matrices has an inverse.

a) $\begin{bmatrix} 3 & -6 \\ 2 & -4 \end{bmatrix}$

b) $\begin{bmatrix} 4 & 2 \\ 2 & 1 \end{bmatrix}$

c) $\begin{bmatrix} 2 & 3 \\ 5 & -1 \\ 1 & 0 \end{bmatrix}$

d) $\begin{bmatrix} 1 \\ 2 \\ 3 \end{bmatrix}$

e) None of these

Answer: e Difficulty: 1

7. Determine which of the following matrices has an inverse.

a) $\begin{bmatrix} \frac{1}{2} & 2 \\ \frac{3}{2} & 6 \end{bmatrix}$

b) $\begin{bmatrix} \frac{1}{3} & 15 \\ \frac{-1}{5} & -9 \end{bmatrix}$

c) $\begin{bmatrix} \frac{1}{2} & -3 \\ \frac{1}{8} & \frac{3}{4} \end{bmatrix}$

d) Both $\begin{bmatrix} \frac{1}{2} & 2 \\ \frac{3}{2} & 6 \end{bmatrix}$ and $\begin{bmatrix} \frac{1}{3} & 15 \\ \frac{-1}{5} & -9 \end{bmatrix}$

e) All of these

Answer: c Difficulty: 1

8. Given $A = \begin{bmatrix} 1 & 2 \\ -3 & 5 \end{bmatrix}$, find A^{-1}.

a) $\begin{bmatrix} -1 & -2 \\ 3 & -5 \end{bmatrix}$

b) $\begin{bmatrix} 1 & \frac{1}{2} \\ -\frac{1}{3} & \frac{1}{5} \end{bmatrix}$

c) $\begin{bmatrix} -\frac{4}{15} & \frac{1}{3} \\ -\frac{2}{3} & \frac{11}{15} \end{bmatrix}$

d) $\begin{bmatrix} \frac{5}{11} & -\frac{2}{11} \\ \frac{3}{11} & \frac{1}{11} \end{bmatrix}$

e) None of these

Answer: d Difficulty: 1

9. Given $A = \begin{bmatrix} 5 & 1 \\ -2 & 3 \end{bmatrix}$, find A^{-1}.

a) $\begin{bmatrix} \frac{5}{17} & \frac{1}{17} \\ -\frac{2}{17} & \frac{3}{17} \end{bmatrix}$ b) $\begin{bmatrix} \frac{3}{17} & -\frac{1}{17} \\ \frac{2}{17} & \frac{5}{17} \end{bmatrix}$ c) $\begin{bmatrix} 85 & 17 \\ 34 & 51 \end{bmatrix}$

d) $\begin{bmatrix} -\frac{2}{5} & \frac{1}{3} \\ \frac{3}{2} & -\frac{1}{2} \end{bmatrix}$ e) None of these

Answer: b Difficulty: 1

10. Given $A = \begin{bmatrix} 1 & 3 \\ 2 & 1 \end{bmatrix}$, find A^{-1}.

a) $\begin{bmatrix} 1 & \frac{1}{3} \\ \frac{1}{2} & 1 \end{bmatrix}$ b) $\begin{bmatrix} 1 & -3 \\ -2 & 1 \end{bmatrix}$ c) $\begin{bmatrix} \frac{1}{5} & \frac{3}{5} \\ \frac{2}{5} & \frac{1}{5} \end{bmatrix}$

d) $\begin{bmatrix} -\frac{1}{5} & \frac{3}{5} \\ \frac{2}{5} & -\frac{1}{5} \end{bmatrix}$ e) None of these

Answer: d Difficulty: 1

11. Given $A = \begin{bmatrix} 3 & 2 \\ 1 & 4 \end{bmatrix}$, find A^{-1}.

a) $\begin{bmatrix} \frac{2}{5} & -\frac{1}{5} \\ -\frac{1}{10} & \frac{3}{10} \end{bmatrix}$ b) $\begin{bmatrix} \frac{1}{3} & \frac{1}{2} \\ 1 & \frac{1}{4} \end{bmatrix}$ c) $\begin{bmatrix} 4 & -2 \\ -1 & 3 \end{bmatrix}$

d) $\begin{bmatrix} -3 & 1 \\ 2 & -4 \end{bmatrix}$ e) None of these

Answer: a Difficulty: 1

12. Given $A = \begin{bmatrix} 2 & 3 \\ 1 & 2 \end{bmatrix}$, find A^{-1}.

a) $\begin{bmatrix} \frac{1}{2} & \frac{1}{3} \\ 1 & \frac{1}{2} \end{bmatrix}$

b) $\begin{bmatrix} 2 & -3 \\ -1 & 2 \end{bmatrix}$

c) $\begin{bmatrix} -2 & 1 \\ 3 & -2 \end{bmatrix}$

d) $\begin{bmatrix} \frac{2}{7} & -\frac{3}{7} \\ -\frac{1}{7} & \frac{2}{7} \end{bmatrix}$

e) None of these.

Answer: b Difficulty: 1

13. Given $A = \begin{bmatrix} 2 & 3 \\ -3 & -3 \end{bmatrix}$, find A^{-1}

a) $\begin{bmatrix} -3 & -3 \\ 3 & 2 \end{bmatrix}$

b) $\begin{bmatrix} \frac{1}{2} & \frac{1}{3} \\ -\frac{1}{3} & -\frac{1}{3} \end{bmatrix}$

c) $\begin{bmatrix} \frac{1}{4} & \frac{1}{4} \\ -\frac{1}{4} & -\frac{1}{3} \end{bmatrix}$

d) $\begin{bmatrix} -1 & -1 \\ 1 & \frac{2}{3} \end{bmatrix}$

e) None of these

Answer: d Difficulty: 1

SHORT ANSWER

14. Given $A = \begin{bmatrix} \frac{3}{2} & -\frac{5}{2} \\ -1 & 2 \end{bmatrix}$, find A^{-1}.

Answer:

$\begin{bmatrix} 4 & 5 \\ 2 & 3 \end{bmatrix}$

Difficulty: 1

15\. Given $A = \begin{bmatrix} \frac{2}{5} & \frac{-6}{5} \\ \frac{3}{10} & \frac{3}{5} \end{bmatrix}$, find A^{-1}.

Answer:

$$\begin{bmatrix} 1 & 2 \\ -\frac{1}{2} & \frac{2}{3} \end{bmatrix}$$

Difficulty: 1

MULTIPLE CHOICE

16\. Given $A = \begin{bmatrix} 1 & 2 & 2 \\ 4 & 1 & 3 \\ -1 & 5 & 0 \end{bmatrix}$, find A^{-1}.

a) $\frac{1}{21}\begin{bmatrix} -15 & 10 & 4 \\ -3 & 2 & 5 \\ 21 & -7 & -7 \end{bmatrix}$

b) $\frac{1}{21}\begin{bmatrix} -15 & -22 & 28 \\ -3 & 27 & 25 \\ 21 & -7 & -7 \end{bmatrix}$

c) $\begin{bmatrix} 1 & 0 & 0 \\ 0 & 1 & 0 \\ 0 & 0 & 1 \end{bmatrix}$

d) $\begin{bmatrix} 1 & \frac{1}{2} & \frac{1}{2} \\ \frac{1}{4} & 1 & \frac{1}{3} \\ -1 & \frac{1}{5} & 0 \end{bmatrix}$

e) None of these

Answer: a Difficulty: 1

SHORT ANSWER

17\. Given $A = \begin{bmatrix} 1 & 3 & -1 \\ 0 & 2 & 1 \\ -1 & 1 & -2 \end{bmatrix}$, find A^{-1}.

Answer:

$$\begin{bmatrix} \frac{1}{2} & -\frac{1}{2} & -\frac{1}{2} \\ \frac{1}{10} & \frac{3}{10} & \frac{1}{10} \\ -\frac{1}{5} & \frac{2}{5} & -\frac{1}{5} \end{bmatrix}$$

Difficulty: 1

18. Given $A = \begin{bmatrix} 1 & 5 & -1 \\ 2 & 3 & -2 \\ -1 & -4 & 3 \end{bmatrix}$, find A^{-1}.

Answer:

$$\begin{bmatrix} -\frac{1}{14} & \frac{11}{14} & \frac{1}{2} \\ \frac{2}{7} & -\frac{1}{7} & 0 \\ \frac{5}{14} & \frac{1}{14} & \frac{1}{2} \end{bmatrix}$$

Difficulty: 1

19. Given $A = \begin{bmatrix} 1 & 1 & 1 \\ -1 & 0 & 0 \\ 4 & 10 & -2 \end{bmatrix}$, find A^{-1}.

Answer:

$$\begin{bmatrix} 0 & -1 & 0 \\ \frac{1}{6} & \frac{1}{2} & \frac{1}{12} \\ \frac{5}{6} & \frac{1}{2} & -\frac{1}{12} \end{bmatrix}$$

Difficulty: 1

MULTIPLE CHOICE

20. Given $C = \begin{bmatrix} 1 & 1 & 0 \\ 3 & 1 & 2 \\ -1 & 1 & -1 \end{bmatrix}$, find C^{-1}.

a) $\begin{bmatrix} 1 & 1 & 0 \\ \frac{1}{3} & 1 & \frac{1}{2} \\ -1 & 1 & -1 \end{bmatrix}$

b) $\begin{bmatrix} -1 & -1 & 0 \\ -3 & -1 & -2 \\ 1 & -1 & 1 \end{bmatrix}$

c) $\begin{bmatrix} \frac{3}{2} & -\frac{1}{2} & -1 \\ -\frac{1}{2} & \frac{1}{2} & 1 \\ -2 & 1 & 1 \end{bmatrix}$

d) $\begin{bmatrix} -\frac{3}{2} & 1 & -1 \\ \frac{1}{2} & 2 & 1 \\ -2 & 1 & 1 \end{bmatrix}$

e) None of these

Answer: c Difficulty: 1

21. Find A^{-1} if $A = \begin{bmatrix} 2 & 0 & 3 \\ -1 & 0 & 2 \\ 0 & 1 & 1 \end{bmatrix}$.

a) $\begin{bmatrix} 2 & -3 & 0 \\ -1 & -2 & 7 \\ 1 & 2 & 0 \end{bmatrix}$

b) $\frac{1}{7}\begin{bmatrix} 2 & -3 & 0 \\ -1 & -2 & 7 \\ 1 & 2 & 0 \end{bmatrix}$

c) $\begin{bmatrix} \frac{1}{2} & 0 & \frac{1}{3} \\ -1 & 0 & \frac{1}{2} \\ 0 & 1 & 1 \end{bmatrix}$

d) $\begin{bmatrix} 2 & -1 & 0 \\ 0 & 0 & 1 \\ 3 & 2 & 1 \end{bmatrix}$

e) None of these

Answer: b Difficulty: 1

SHORT ANSWER

22. Find A^{-1} if $A = \begin{bmatrix} 1 & -1 & -1 \\ 5 & 0 & 20 \\ 0 & 10 & -20 \end{bmatrix}$.

Answer:

$$\begin{bmatrix} \frac{4}{7} & \frac{3}{35} & \frac{2}{35} \\ -\frac{2}{7} & \frac{2}{35} & \frac{1}{14} \\ -\frac{1}{7} & \frac{1}{35} & -\frac{1}{70} \end{bmatrix}$$

Difficulty: 1

23. Use a graphing utility to find A^{-1} if it exists, given $A = \begin{vmatrix} 1 & 2 \\ 3 & 4 \end{vmatrix}$.

Answer:

$$\begin{bmatrix} -2 & 1 \\ 1.5 & -0.5 \end{bmatrix}$$

Difficulty: 1 Key 1: T

24. Use a graphing utility to find B^{-1} if it exists, given

$$B = \begin{bmatrix} 2 & -1 & 1 \\ 1 & 2 & -1 \\ 3 & -4 & 2 \end{bmatrix}.$$

Answer:

$$\begin{bmatrix} 0 & 0.4 & 0.2 \\ 1 & -0.2 & -0.6 \\ 2 & -1 & -1 \end{bmatrix}$$

Difficulty: 1 Key 1: T

25. Use a graphing utility to find C^{-1} if it exists, given

$$C = \begin{bmatrix} 1 & 0 & -2 & 3 \\ 1 & 1 & -3 & 2 \\ 2 & 1 & 0 & 3 \\ 0 & 1 & 0 & -3 \end{bmatrix}.$$

Answer:

$$\begin{bmatrix} 2.25 & -1.5 & 0.125 & 1.375 \\ -2.25 & 1.5 & 0.375 & -0.875 \\ -0.5 & 0 & 0.25 & -0.25 \\ -0.75 & 0.5 & 0.125 & -0.625 \end{bmatrix}$$

Difficulty: 1 Key 1: T

26. Use a graphing utility to find A^{-1} if it exists, given

$$A = \begin{bmatrix} 1 & 1 & 1 \\ 0 & 1 & 0 \\ 2 & -1 & 3 \end{bmatrix}.$$

Answer:

$$\begin{bmatrix} 3 & -4 & -1 \\ 0 & 1 & 0 \\ -2 & 3 & 1 \end{bmatrix}$$

Difficulty: 1 Key 1: T

27. Use a graphing utility to find A^{-1} if it exists, given

$$A = \begin{bmatrix} 1 & 4 & 3 \\ 2 & 6 & 1 \\ 1 & 0 & 3 \end{bmatrix}.$$

Answer:

$$\begin{bmatrix} -0.9 & 0.6 & 0.7 \\ 0.25 & 0 & -0.25 \\ 0.3 & -0.2 & 0.1 \end{bmatrix}$$

Difficulty: 1 Key 1: T

28. Use a graphing utility to find B^{-1} if it exists, given

$$B = \begin{bmatrix} 1 & 0 & 0 \\ 0 & -1 & 0 \\ 1 & 0 & 3 \end{bmatrix}.$$

Answer:

$$\begin{bmatrix} 1 & 0 & 0 \\ 0 & -1 & 0 \\ -1 & 0 & 1 \end{bmatrix}$$

Difficulty: 1 Key 1: T

29. Find A^{-1} if it exists given

$$A = \begin{bmatrix} \frac{1}{2} & -1 & \frac{1}{2} \\ \frac{1}{4} & 1 & -\frac{3}{4} \\ \frac{1}{4} & 0 & \frac{1}{4} \end{bmatrix}.$$

Answer:

$$\begin{bmatrix} 1 & 1 & 1 \\ -1 & 0 & 2 \\ -1 & -1 & 3 \end{bmatrix}$$

Difficulty: 2

MULTIPLE CHOICE

30. Given the system of linear equations with coefficient matrix A, use A^{-1} to find (x, y, z, w).

$$\begin{cases} x + y + z + w = 0 \\ 2x - y = -2 \\ 3z - 2w = 0 \\ y - 3z = 6 \end{cases} \qquad A^{-1} = \begin{bmatrix} \frac{3}{14} & \frac{11}{28} & \frac{3}{28} & \frac{5}{28} \\ \frac{3}{7} & -\frac{3}{14} & \frac{3}{14} & \frac{5}{14} \\ \frac{1}{7} & -\frac{1}{14} & \frac{1}{14} & -\frac{3}{14} \\ \frac{3}{14} & -\frac{3}{28} & -\frac{11}{28} & -\frac{9}{28} \end{bmatrix}$$

a) $(10, -15, -5, 0)$ b) $\left(\frac{2}{7}, \frac{18}{7}, -\frac{8}{7}, -\frac{12}{7}\right)$ c) $\left(\frac{3}{11}, \frac{18}{11}, -\frac{7}{11}, \frac{16}{11}\right)$

d) $(0, 1, -1, 0)$ e) None of these

Answer: b Difficulty: 1

31. Given the system of linear equations with coefficient matrix A, use A^{-1} to find (x, y, z, w).

$$\begin{cases} x + 2y = 1 \\ 3x + 8y + 5w = 0 \\ x + 4y + 3z + 10w = -1 \\ x - 3z = -1 \end{cases} \qquad A^{-1} = \begin{bmatrix} 3 & -1 & \frac{1}{2} & \frac{1}{2} \\ -1 & \frac{1}{2} & -\frac{1}{4} & -\frac{1}{4} \\ 1 & -\frac{1}{3} & \frac{1}{6} & -\frac{1}{6} \\ -\frac{1}{5} & 0 & \frac{1}{10} & \frac{1}{10} \end{bmatrix}$$

a) $\left(2, -\frac{1}{2}, 1, -\frac{2}{5}\right)$ b) $(3, -1, -1, 0)$ c) $\left(\frac{2}{3}, \frac{1}{6}, -\frac{5}{9}, \frac{2}{3}\right)$

d) $\left(1, 0, \frac{2}{3}, -\frac{5}{3}\right)$ e) None of these

Answer: a Difficulty: 1

32. Given the system of linear equations with coefficient matrix A, use A^{-1} to find (x, y, z).

$$\begin{cases} 3x + 2y + z = 5 \\ x - 4y = 6 \\ x - y + 3z = 6 \end{cases} \qquad A^{-1} = \frac{1}{39}\begin{bmatrix} 12 & 7 & -4 \\ 3 & -8 & -1 \\ -3 & -5 & 14 \end{bmatrix}$$

a) $(-2, -1, 1)$ b) $(-1, 6, -2)$ c) $(2, -1, 1)$

d) $(6, -1, 3)$ e) None of these

Answer: c Difficulty: 1

33. Given the system of linear equations with coefficient matrix A, use A^{-1} to find (x, y, z).

$$\begin{cases} 3x + y - z = -11 \\ x - y - z = -1 \\ x + 2y + 3z = 3 \end{cases} \qquad A^{-1} = \frac{1}{10}\begin{bmatrix} 1 & 5 & 2 \\ 4 & -10 & -2 \\ -3 & 5 & 4 \end{bmatrix}$$

a) (3, -2, 0) b) (2, -2, 3) c) (-1, 5, 1)
d) (-1, -4, 4) e) None of these

Answer: d Difficulty: 1

34. Given the system of linear equations with coefficient matrix A, use A^{-1} to find (x, y, z).

$$\begin{cases} 4x - y + z = 5 \\ x - 4y + z = 8 \\ 2x + 2y - 3z = -12 \end{cases} \qquad A^{-1} = \frac{1}{45}\begin{bmatrix} 10 & -1 & 3 \\ 5 & -14 & -3 \\ 10 & -10 & -15 \end{bmatrix}$$

a) (0, -1, 4) b) (0, 4, -2) c) (1, -1, 2)
d) (3, 0, 2) e) None of these

Answer: e Difficulty: 1

SHORT ANSWER

35. Use an inverse matrix to solve the system of linear equations.

$$\begin{cases} 2x + 2y = 12 \\ x + 3y = 16 \end{cases}$$

Answer: (1, 5) Difficulty: 1

MULTIPLE CHOICE

36. Use an inverse matrix to solve the system of linear equations.

$$\begin{cases} \frac{1}{4}x + \frac{1}{4}y + \frac{1}{4}z = \frac{5}{4} \\ x - \frac{1}{2}y + \frac{1}{2}z = \frac{1}{2} \\ -\frac{1}{4}x + \frac{1}{4}y + \frac{3}{4}z = \frac{1}{4} \end{cases}$$

a) (2, 3, 0) b) (-3, 0, 8) c) (2, 2, 1)
d) (-3, 6, 2) e) None of these

Answer: a Difficulty: 1

37. Use an inverse matrix to solve the system of linear equations.

$$\begin{cases} x + y + z = 0 \\ x + 2y + z = 1 \\ 2x + y + z = -1 \end{cases}$$

a) (2, -3, 1)
b) (-3, -5, 8)
c) (-1, 1, 0)
d) (-2, 1, 1)
e) None of these

Answer: c Difficulty: 1

SHORT ANSWER

38. Use an inverse matrix to solve the system of linear equations.

$$\begin{cases} 2x + 3y + 2z = 0 \\ x - 6z = 4 \\ x + y - 2z = 1 \end{cases}$$

Answer:
$\left(7, -5, \frac{1}{2}\right)$
Difficulty: 1

39. Use a graphing utility to solve the system of linear equations.

$$\begin{cases} 5x + y + 2z = 0 \\ x - 3z = -2 \\ 2x + y + z = 6 \end{cases}$$

Answer: (-2, 10, 0) Difficulty: 1 Key 1: T

MULTIPLE CHOICE

40. Use a graphing utility to solve the system of linear equations.

$$\begin{cases} x - y + z = 6 \\ 2x + z = 4 \\ -x - y - z = -4 \end{cases}$$

a) (4, 2, 4)
b) (3, -1, 2)
c) (1, -7, -2)
d) (2, -4, 0)
e) None of these

Answer: b Difficulty: 1 Key 1: T

41. Use a graphing utility to solve the system of linear equations.

$$\begin{cases} x + y + z = 4 \\ 2x + y + z = 6 \\ x + y + 2z = 9 \end{cases}$$

a) (2, 2, 0)
b) (-2, 3, 3)
c) (2, -3, 5)
d) (1, -1, 4)
e) None of these

Answer: c Difficulty: 1 Key 1: T

SHORT ANSWER

42. Use an inverse matrix to solve the system of linear equations.

$$\begin{cases} 3x + 2y + z = 1 \\ x - y = 10 \\ -x + 2z = 5 \end{cases}$$

Answer:
$\left(\frac{37}{11}, -\frac{73}{11}, \frac{46}{11}\right)$
Difficulty: 2

43. Use an inverse matrix to solve the system of linear equations.

$$\begin{cases} 6x + 6y - 5z = 11 \\ 3x + 6y - z = 6 \\ 9x - 3y + z = 0 \end{cases}$$

Answer:
$\left(\frac{1}{3}, \frac{2}{3}, -1\right)$
Difficulty: 2

MULTIPLE CHOICE

44. A small business borrows $90,000; some at 7%, some at 9%, and the rest at 10% simple interest. The annual interest is $7110, and twice as much is borrowed at 7% as at 9%. Set up a system where x, y, and z represent the amounts borrowed at 7%, 9% and 10%, respectively, then use the inverse of the coefficient matrix to find (x, y, z).
a) ($46,000, $23,000, $21,000) b) ($54,000, $27,000, $9000)
c) ($18,000, $36,000, $36,000) d) ($41,000, $20,500, $28,500)
e) None of these

Answer: b Difficulty: 2

45. A small business borrows $550,000; some at 7%, some at 8%, and the rest at 11% simple interest. The annual interest is $53,600, and one-third of the amount borrowed at 11% is borrowed at 7%. Set up a system where x, y, and z represent the amounts borrowed at 7%, 8% and 11%, respectively, then use the inverse of the coefficient matrix to find y.
a) $70,000 b) $90,000 c) $120,000
d) $130,000 e) None of these

Answer: a Difficulty: 2

46. A small business borrows $175,000; some at 7%, some at 10%, and the rest at 11% simple interest. The annual interest is $15,800, and the amount borrowed at 7% exceeds the amount borrowed at 10% by $20,000. Set up a system where x, y, and z represent the amounts borrowed at 7%, 10% and 11%, respectively, then use the inverse of the coefficient matrix to find x.

a) $90,000 b) $40,000 c) $75,000
d) $60,000 e) None of these

Answer: c Difficulty: 2

Chapter 084: The Determinant of a Square Matrix

MULTIPLE CHOICE

1. Find the determinant of the matrix: $\begin{bmatrix} 7 & -1 \\ 6 & -2 \end{bmatrix}$.

a) -20 b) -8 c) 8 d) 20 e) None of these

Answer: b Difficulty: 1

2. Find the determinant of the matrix: $\begin{bmatrix} 6 & 4 \\ 2 & -1 \end{bmatrix}$.

a) 2 b) -14 c) -2 d) 14 e) None of these

Answer: b Difficulty: 1

3. Find the determinant of the matrix: $\begin{bmatrix} 3 & -4 \\ 2 & 6 \end{bmatrix}$.

a) 10 b) 26 c) -26 d) -10 e) None of these

Answer: b Difficulty: 1

4. Find the determinant of the matrix: $\begin{bmatrix} 3 & -1 \\ 6 & 2 \end{bmatrix}$.

a) 12 b) -12 c) 0 d) 9 e) None of these

Answer: a Difficulty: 1

5. Find the determinant of the matrix: $\begin{bmatrix} 6 & -4 \\ 2 & -1 \end{bmatrix}$.

a) 2 b) -2 c) 14 d) -14 e) None of these

Answer: a Difficulty: 1

6. Find the determinant of the matrix: $\begin{bmatrix} 0 & 2 & 3 \\ 1 & -1 & 4 \\ 3 & 0 & 2 \end{bmatrix}$.

a) 9 b) 19 c) 29 d) 0 e) None of these

Answer: c Difficulty: 1

7. Find the determinant of the matrix: $\begin{bmatrix} 0 & -1 & 2 \\ 3 & 5 & 0 \\ 1 & -1 & 3 \end{bmatrix}$.

a) 25 b) -25 c) 7 d) -7 e) None of these

Answer: d Difficulty: 1

SHORT ANSWER

8.

Find the determinant of the matrix: $\begin{bmatrix} 2 & 3 & -1 \\ 0 & 5 & 0 \\ -1 & 1 & 2 \end{bmatrix}$.

Answer: 15 Difficulty: 1

9.

Find the determinant of the matrix: $\begin{bmatrix} 3 & 0 & 1 \\ -1 & 4 & -1 \\ 5 & -2 & 0 \end{bmatrix}$.

Answer: -24 Difficulty: 1

10.

Find the determinant of the matrix: $\begin{bmatrix} 3 & -1 & 6 \\ 2 & 0 & 4 \\ 1 & 6 & 2 \end{bmatrix}$.

Answer: 0 Difficulty: 1

11.

Find the determinant of the matrix $\begin{bmatrix} 0.1 & 0.4 & -0.2 \\ 0.3 & 0.2 & 0 \\ -0.1 & 0.4 & 0.3 \end{bmatrix}$ using a graphing calculator.

Answer: -0.058 Difficulty: 1 Key 1: T

MULTIPLE CHOICE

12.

Find the minor M_{23} for the matrix: $\begin{bmatrix} 3 & 1 & -2 \\ 0 & 2 & 3 \\ 1 & -2 & -2 \end{bmatrix}$.

a) 7 b) 9 c) -9 d) 13 e) None of these

Answer: e Difficulty: 1

13.

Find the minor M_{23} for the matrix: $\begin{bmatrix} 1 & 4 & -2 \\ 3 & -1 & 1 \\ 5 & 2 & 7 \end{bmatrix}$.

a) -95 b) -7 c) -18 d) 7 e) None of these

Answer: c Difficulty: 1

14.

Find the minor M_{13} for the matrix: $\begin{bmatrix} 2 & 1 & -2 \\ -6 & -1 & 3 \\ 1 & 4 & 5 \end{bmatrix}$.

a) 16 b) 1 c) -23 d) 5 e) None of these

Answer: c Difficulty: 1

15.

Find the minor M_{12} for the matrix: $\begin{bmatrix} 3 & 4 & 2 \\ -2 & -3 & 1 \\ 1 & 2 & -1 \end{bmatrix}$.

a) -8 b) 0 c) 3 d) 1 e) None of these

Answer: d Difficulty: 1

16.

Find the minor M_{32} for the matrix: $\begin{bmatrix} 5 & 1 & 2 \\ -1 & -4 & 1 \\ 2 & 5 & -3 \end{bmatrix}$.

a) 7 b) 3 c) 23 d) 27 e) None of these

Answer: a Difficulty: 1

17.

Find the cofactor C_{23} for the matrix: $\begin{bmatrix} 3 & 1 & -2 \\ 0 & 2 & 3 \\ 1 & -2 & -2 \end{bmatrix}$.

a) 7 b) 9 c) -9 d) -7 e) None of these

Answer: a Difficulty: 1

18.

Find the cofactor C_{21} for the matrix: $\begin{bmatrix} 3 & 1 & -2 \\ 0 & 2 & 3 \\ 1 & -2 & -2 \end{bmatrix}$.

a) 2 b) -6 c) 6 d) -2 e) None of these

Answer: c Difficulty: 1

19.

Find the cofactor C_{23} for the matrix: $\begin{bmatrix} 2 & 1 & 3 \\ -1 & 4 & 2 \\ 6 & -2 & -1 \end{bmatrix}$.

a) -10 b) -7 c) 2 d) -1 e) None of these

Answer: e Difficulty: 1

20.

Find the cofactor C_{32} for the matrix: $\begin{bmatrix} 1 & 4 & 1 \\ -6 & 7 & 1 \\ 2 & -5 & 2 \end{bmatrix}$.

a) -7 b) 5 c) -10 d) -6 e) None of these

Answer: a Difficulty: 1

21.

Find the cofactor C_{32} for the matrix: $\begin{bmatrix} 7 & 5 & 4 \\ 6 & -2 & 1 \\ 3 & 4 & 2 \end{bmatrix}$.

a) -43 b) -13 c) 17 d) 31 e) None of these

Answer: c Difficulty: 1

22.

Find the cofactor C_{13} for the matrix: $\begin{bmatrix} -1 & 5 & 1 \\ 2 & -6 & -1 \\ 4 & 3 & 5 \end{bmatrix}$.

a) 30 b) 18 c) 1 d) 11 e) None of these

Answer: a Difficulty: 1

SHORT ANSWER

23.

Find the determinant of the matrix: $\begin{bmatrix} 1 & -1 & 0 & 2 \\ 0 & 5 & 7 & 3 \\ 0 & 0 & 4 & 1 \\ 0 & 0 & 0 & 1 \end{bmatrix}$.

Answer: 20 Difficulty: 1

MULTIPLE CHOICE

24. Find the determinant of the matrix by the method of expansion by cofactors. $\begin{bmatrix} 0 & 5 & 2 & 0 \\ 1 & 0 & -1 & 0 \\ 3 & -2 & 0 & -1 \\ -1 & 1 & 0 & 0 \end{bmatrix}$

a) 0 b) 7 c) -16 d) -12 e) None of these

Answer: b Difficulty: 1

SHORT ANSWER

25. Find the determinant of the matrix:

$$\begin{bmatrix} 3 & 0 & 5 & 1 \\ 0 & -1 & 0 & -1 \\ -1 & 1 & 0 & 3 \\ 0 & 3 & 0 & 3 \end{bmatrix}.$$

Answer: 0 Difficulty: 1

MULTIPLE CHOICE

26. Find the determinant of the matrix. Use the method of expansion by cofactors. $\begin{bmatrix} 0 & 1 & -1 & 2 \\ 1 & -1 & 0 & 3 \\ 0 & 2 & 0 & 1 \\ -1 & 1 & 2 & -2 \end{bmatrix}$

a) -48 b) 12 c) -8 d) 2 e) None of these

Answer: c Difficulty: 1

27. Find the determinant of the matrix. Use the method of expansion by cofactors. $\begin{bmatrix} 0 & -2 & 0 & 4 \\ 1 & 1 & -2 & 3 \\ -1 & 3 & 5 & 1 \\ 3 & 0 & 1 & 0 \end{bmatrix}$

a) 276 b) -258 c) -102 d) 1125 e) None of these

Answer: b Difficulty: 1

28. Use the matrix capabilities of a graphing utility to find the determinant of the matrix: $\begin{bmatrix} 5 & -1 & 0 & 2 \\ 0 & 4 & 7 & 3 \\ 0 & 0 & 1 & 1 \\ 0 & 0 & 0 & 1 \end{bmatrix}$.

a) 11 b) -11 c) -20 d) 20 e) None of these

Answer: d Difficulty: 1 Key 1: T

29. Use the matrix capabilities of a graphing utility to find the determinant of the matrix: $\begin{bmatrix} 1 & 0 & 0 & 0 \\ 4 & 6 & 0 & 0 \\ -7 & 5 & -5 & 0 \\ 3 & 2 & 3 & -1 \end{bmatrix}$.

a) 11 b) -30 c) 30 d) -11 e) None of these

Answer: c Difficulty: 1 Key 1: T

30. Use the matrix capabilities of a graphing utility to find the determinant of the matrix: $\begin{bmatrix} 1 & 5 & 0 & 6 \\ 0 & -1 & 1 & 0 \\ -2 & 2 & 3 & 0 \\ 0 & 0 & 7 & 2 \end{bmatrix}$.

a) -54 b) 74 c) -74 d) 54 e) None of these

Answer: d Difficulty: 1 Key 1: T

31. Use the matrix capabilities of a graphing utility to find the determinant of the matrix: $\begin{bmatrix} 4 & 0 & 0 & 6 \\ 0 & 2 & 1 & 1 \\ -1 & 5 & -3 & 1 \\ 0 & 7 & 2 & 4 \end{bmatrix}$.

a) 250 b) -22 c) 118 d) 133 e) None of these

Answer: b Difficulty: 1 Key 1: T

32. Solve for x: $\begin{vmatrix} 5 + 2x & 3 \\ x - 1 & -6 \end{vmatrix} = 3$.

a) 34 b) -2 c) $-\frac{12}{5}$ d) -2, 34 e) None of these

Answer: b Difficulty: 2

33. Solve for x: $\begin{vmatrix} 7 - 2x & -1 \\ 5x + 2 & 4 \end{vmatrix} = 3$.

a) 9 b) -11 c) $\frac{23}{13}$ d) 9, -11 e) None of these

Answer: a Difficulty: 2

34. Solve for x: $\begin{vmatrix} 5 + 2x & -2 \\ 7 - x & 3 \end{vmatrix} = 5$.

a) 1 b) $\frac{1}{2}$ c) -6 d) -3 e) None of these

Answer: c Difficulty: 2

35. Solve for x: $\begin{vmatrix} 3x - 1 & -1 \\ 4 & x + 1 \end{vmatrix} = 4$.

a) 4 b) 0 c) $\frac{-1 \pm 2\sqrt{7}}{3}$ d) $-1, \frac{1}{3}$ e) None of these

Answer: d Difficulty: 2

36. Solve for x: $\begin{vmatrix} x - 1 & 3 \\ 3 & x + 1 \end{vmatrix} = 6$.

a) ± 1 b) ± 4 c) $\pm\sqrt{2}i$ d) 5 e) None of these

Answer: b Difficulty: 2

37. Solve for x: $\begin{vmatrix} x - 1 & x \\ 2 & x + 1 \end{vmatrix} = 7$.

a) -4, 2 b) 0 c) 5, 0 d) 1, -3 e) None of these

Answer: e Difficulty: 2

38. Evaluate: $\begin{vmatrix} 4u & 1 \\ 1 & 4v \end{vmatrix}$.

a) uv b) $4u + 4v - 1$ c) $16uv - 1$
d) $4uv - 2$ e) None of these

Answer: c Difficulty: 1

39. Evaluate: $\begin{vmatrix} e^{-x} & e^{2x} \\ -e^{-x} & 2e^{2x} \end{vmatrix}$.

a) $3e^{-2x^2}$ b) $3e^{x}$ c) $3e^{-2x}$
d) $2e^{2x}$ e) None of these

Answer: b Difficulty: 2

40. Evaluate: $\begin{vmatrix} x & \ln x \\ 1 & 1/x \end{vmatrix}$.

a) $\ln x - 1$ b) $1 - \ln x$ c) $-\ln x$
d) $\ln x$ e) None of these

Answer: b Difficulty: 1

SHORT ANSWER

41. Evaluate: $\begin{vmatrix} x \ln x & x \\ 1 + \ln x & 1 \end{vmatrix}$.

Answer: $-x$ Difficulty: 1

42. Evaluate: $\begin{vmatrix} e^{2x} & e^{x} \\ 2e^{2x} & e^{x} \end{vmatrix}$.

Answer:

$-e^{3x}$

Difficulty: 1

43. Use the matrix capabilities of a graphing utility to evaluate:
$$\begin{vmatrix} 3 & -2 & 4 & 3 \\ 2 & -1 & 0 & 4 \\ -2 & 0 & 1 & 5 \\ -2 & -3 & 0 & 2 \end{vmatrix}.$$

Answer: 270 Difficulty: 1 Key 1: T

44. Use the matrix capabilities of a graphing utility to evaluate:
$$\begin{vmatrix} 10 & -3 & 2 & 4 & 5 \\ -1 & 0 & -3 & 2 & 3 \\ 4 & -1 & -2 & 0 & 4 \\ 9 & 4 & -3 & 6 & 2 \\ -2 & 0 & -4 & 4 & 5 \end{vmatrix}.$$

Answer: 672 Difficulty: 1 Key 1: T

Chapter 085: Applications of Matrices and Determinants

MULTIPLE CHOICE

1. Use Cramer's Rule to solve for y in the system of linear equations:

$$\begin{cases} 3x + 2y + 4z = 12 \\ x - y + z = 3. \\ 2x + 7y - z = 9 \end{cases}$$

a) $y = \dfrac{\begin{vmatrix} 3 & 2 & 4 \\ 1 & -1 & 1 \\ 2 & 7 & -1 \end{vmatrix}}{\begin{vmatrix} 3 & 12 & 4 \\ 1 & 3 & 1 \\ 2 & 9 & -1 \end{vmatrix}}$ b) $y = \dfrac{\begin{vmatrix} 3 & 12 & 4 \\ 1 & 3 & 1 \\ 2 & 9 & -1 \end{vmatrix}}{\begin{vmatrix} 3 & 2 & 4 \\ 1 & -1 & 1 \\ 2 & 7 & -1 \end{vmatrix}}$ c) $y = \dfrac{\begin{vmatrix} 3 & 4 & 12 \\ 1 & -1 & 3 \\ 2 & 7 & 9 \end{vmatrix}}{\begin{vmatrix} 2 & 4 & 3 \\ -1 & 1 & 1 \\ 7 & -1 & 2 \end{vmatrix}}$

d) $y = \begin{vmatrix} 3 & 2 & 4 \\ 1 & -1 & 1 \\ 2 & 7 & -1 \end{vmatrix} \begin{vmatrix} 2 & 4 & 12 \\ -1 & 1 & 3 \\ 7 & -1 & 9 \end{vmatrix}$ e) None of these

Answer: b Difficulty: 1

2. Use Cramer's Rule to solve for x in the system of linear equations:

$$\begin{cases} 2x + 3y + 4z = 7 \\ x - 2y + 5z = 3. \\ \quad\quad 4x + 5z = 9 \end{cases}$$

a) $x = \dfrac{\begin{vmatrix} 7 & 3 & 4 \\ 3 & -2 & 5 \\ 9 & 0 & 5 \end{vmatrix}}{\begin{vmatrix} 2 & 3 & 4 \\ 1 & -2 & 5 \\ 4 & 0 & 5 \end{vmatrix}}$ b) $x = \dfrac{\begin{vmatrix} 2 & 3 & 4 \\ 1 & -2 & 5 \\ 4 & 0 & 5 \end{vmatrix}}{\begin{vmatrix} 7 & 3 & 4 \\ 3 & -2 & 5 \\ 9 & 0 & 5 \end{vmatrix}}$

c) $x = \begin{vmatrix} 2 & 3 & 4 \\ 1 & -2 & 5 \\ 4 & 0 & 5 \end{vmatrix} \begin{vmatrix} 7 & 3 & 4 \\ 3 & -2 & 5 \\ 9 & 0 & 5 \end{vmatrix}$ d) $x = \begin{vmatrix} 2 & 3 & 7 \\ 1 & -2 & 3 \\ 4 & 0 & 9 \end{vmatrix} \begin{vmatrix} 2 & 3 & 4 \\ 1 & -2 & 5 \\ 4 & 0 & 5 \end{vmatrix}$

e) None of these

Answer: a Difficulty: 1

3. Use Cramer's Rule to solve for y in the system of linear equations:

$$\begin{cases} 3x + 2y - 10z = 5 \\ x - y + z = 10. \\ -7x + 2z = 1 \end{cases}$$

a) $y = \dfrac{\begin{vmatrix} 3 & 5 & -10 \\ 1 & 10 & 1 \\ -7 & 1 & 2 \end{vmatrix}}{\begin{vmatrix} 3 & 2 & -10 \\ 1 & -1 & 1 \\ -7 & 0 & 2 \end{vmatrix}}$

b) $y = \dfrac{\begin{vmatrix} 3 & 2 & -10 \\ 1 & -1 & 1 \\ -7 & 0 & 2 \end{vmatrix}}{\begin{vmatrix} 3 & 2 & -10 \\ 1 & 10 & 1 \\ -7 & 1 & 2 \end{vmatrix}}$

c) $y = \dfrac{\begin{vmatrix} 2 & 5 \\ -1 & 10 \\ 0 & 1 \end{vmatrix}}{\begin{vmatrix} 3 & -10 \\ 1 & 1 \\ -7 & 2 \end{vmatrix}}$

d) $y = 5\begin{vmatrix} 3 & 2 & -10 \\ 1 & -1 & 1 \\ -7 & 0 & 2 \end{vmatrix} + 10\begin{vmatrix} 3 & 2 & -10 \\ 1 & -1 & 1 \\ -7 & 0 & 2 \end{vmatrix} + 1\begin{vmatrix} 3 & 2 & -10 \\ 1 & -1 & 1 \\ -7 & 0 & 2 \end{vmatrix}$

e) None of these

Answer: a Difficulty: 1

4. Use Cramer's Rule to solve for y:

$$\begin{cases} 3x - 2y + 2z = 3 \\ x + 4y - z = 2. \\ x + y + z = 6 \end{cases}$$

a) $y = \dfrac{\begin{vmatrix} 3 & -2 & 2 \\ 1 & 4 & -1 \\ 1 & 1 & 1 \end{vmatrix}}{\begin{vmatrix} 3 & 3 & 2 \\ 1 & 2 & -2 \\ 1 & 6 & 1 \end{vmatrix}}$

b) $y = \dfrac{\begin{vmatrix} 3 & 3 & 2 \\ 1 & 2 & -1 \\ 1 & 6 & 1 \end{vmatrix}}{\begin{vmatrix} 3 & -2 & 2 \\ 1 & 4 & -1 \\ 1 & 1 & 1 \end{vmatrix}}$

c) $y = \dfrac{\begin{vmatrix} 3 & 2 & 3 \\ 1 & -1 & 2 \\ 1 & 1 & 6 \end{vmatrix}}{\begin{vmatrix} 3 & -2 & 2 \\ 1 & 4 & -1 \\ 1 & 1 & 1 \end{vmatrix}}$

d) $y = \dfrac{\begin{vmatrix} 3 & 3 & -2 \\ 1 & 2 & 4 \\ 1 & 6 & 1 \end{vmatrix}}{\begin{vmatrix} 3 & 1 & 1 \\ -2 & 4 & 1 \\ 2 & -1 & 1 \end{vmatrix}}$

e) None of these

Answer: b Difficulty: 1

5. Use Cramer's Rule to solve for z:

$$\begin{cases} 2x - y + z = -3 \\ x + y + z = 4. \\ 3x - 2y + 5z = 1 \end{cases}$$

a) $z = \dfrac{\begin{vmatrix} 2 & -1 & 1 \\ 1 & 1 & 1 \\ 3 & -2 & 5 \end{vmatrix}}{\begin{vmatrix} 2 & -1 & -3 \\ 1 & 1 & 4 \\ 3 & -2 & 1 \end{vmatrix}}$

b) $z = \dfrac{\begin{vmatrix} 2 & -1 & 1 \\ 1 & 1 & 1 \\ 3 & -2 & 5 \end{vmatrix}}{\begin{vmatrix} -3 & 2 & -1 \\ 4 & 1 & 1 \\ 1 & 3 & -2 \end{vmatrix}}$

c) $z = \dfrac{\begin{vmatrix} 2 & -1 & -3 \\ 1 & 1 & 4 \\ 3 & -2 & 1 \end{vmatrix}}{\begin{vmatrix} 2 & -1 & 1 \\ 1 & 1 & 1 \\ 3 & -2 & 5 \end{vmatrix}}$

d) $z = \dfrac{\begin{vmatrix} -3 & -3 & 1 \\ 4 & 4 & 1 \\ 1 & 1 & 5 \end{vmatrix}}{\begin{vmatrix} 2 & -1 & -3 \\ 1 & 1 & 4 \\ 3 & -2 & 1 \end{vmatrix}}$

e) None of these

Answer: c Difficulty: 1

SHORT ANSWER

6. Use Cramer's Rule to solve the system of linear equations.

$$\begin{cases} 4x + 6y + 2z = 15 \\ x - y + 4z = -3 \\ 3x + 2y + 2z = 6 \end{cases}$$

Answer:

$\left(1,\ 2,\ -\frac{1}{2}\right)$

Difficulty: 2

7. Use Cramer's Rule to solve the system of linear equations.

$$\begin{cases} 5x + 5y + 4z = 4 \\ 10x - 5y + 2z = 11 \\ 5x - 5y + 2z = 7 \end{cases}$$

Answer:

$\left(\frac{4}{5},\ -\frac{2}{5},\ \frac{1}{2}\right)$

Difficulty: 2

MULTIPLE CHOICE

8. Use a determinant to find the area of the triangle with vertices (2, -1), (3, 2), and (5, 0).
   a) 4 b) 8 c) 6 d) 12 e) None of these

   Answer: a Difficulty: 2

9. Use a determinant to find the area of the triangle with vertices (-1, 4), (2, 6), and (1, 0).
   a) 0 b) 3 c) 4 d) 8 e) None of these

   Answer: d Difficulty: 2

SHORT ANSWER

10. Use a determinant to find the area of the triangle with vertices (-1, -3), (5, 6), and (0, 2).

    Answer:
    $\frac{21}{2}$

    Difficulty: 2

MULTIPLE CHOICE

11. Use a determinant to find the area of the triangle with vertices (1, 3), (7, 2), and (9, 5).
    a) 30 b) 25 c) 20 d) 10 e) None of these

    Answer: d Difficulty: 1

12. Use a determinant to find the area of the triangle with vertices (2, -4), (4, -1), and (7, -3).
    a) $\frac{13}{2}$ b) 13 c) 26 d) 17 e) None of these

    Answer: a Difficulty: 1

13. Use a determinant to find the area of the triangle with vertices (-5, 2), (0, 7), and (-4, 10).
    a) $\frac{39}{2}$ b) 70 c) $\frac{35}{2}$ d) 35 e) None of these

    Answer: c Difficulty: 1

14. Use a determinant to find the area of the triangle with vertices (-3, -10), (-5, -2), and (5, 1).
    a) 86 b) 43 c) 172 d) $\frac{43}{2}$ e) None of these

    Answer: b Difficulty: 1

SHORT ANSWER

15. Use a determinant to determine whether the points are collinear: (-7, 4), (-1, 2), and (2, 1).

    Answer: Yes Difficulty: 1

16. Use a determinant to determine whether the points are collinear: (2, 2), (0, 5), and (4, -4).

    Answer: No Difficulty: 1

17. Use a determinant to determine whether the points are collinear: (12, 6), (-1, -3), and (0, -1).

    Answer: No Difficulty: 1

18. Use a determinant to determine whether the points are collinear: (-3, -8), (6, 4), (12, 12).

    Answer: Yes Difficulty: 1

19. Use a determinant to determine whether the points are collinear: (-3, 6), (1, 2), (5, -2).

    Answer: Yes Difficulty: 1

20. Use a determinant to determine whether the points are collinear: (-2, -3), (1, -5), (3, -1).

    Answer: No Difficulty: 1

21. Use a determinant to determine whether the points are collinear: (-1, -1), (2, -3), (-2, 2).

    Answer: No Difficulty: 1

MULTIPLE CHOICE

22. Use a determinant to find an equation of the line passing through the points (-1, -3) and (0, -1).
    a) $2x + y = 1$ b) $x - y = 0$ c) $x - 2y = 1$
    d) $2x - y = 1$ e) None of these

    Answer: d Difficulty: 1

23. Use a determinant to find an equation of the line passing through the points (4, -2) and (-3, 1).
a) $3x - 7y + 2 = 0$ b) $7x + 3y + 2 = 0$ c) $3x + 7y + 2 = 0$
d) $3x + 7y - 2 = 0$ e) None of these

Answer: c Difficulty: 1

SHORT ANSWER

24. Use a determinant to find an equation of the line passing through the points (2, -5) and (-1, -1).

Answer: $4x + 3y = -7$ Difficulty: 1

MULTIPLE CHOICE

25. Use a determinant to find an equation of the line passing through the points (1, 2) and (-1, 6).
a) $x + 2y - 4 = 0$ b) $y = 2x$ c) $y = 3x^2 - 2x + 1$
d) $2x + y - 4 = 0$ e) None of these

Answer: d Difficulty: 1

26. Use a determinant to find an equation of the line that passes through the center of the circle $(x - 4)^2 + (y + 1)^2 = 5$ and the point (1, 3).
a) $2x - 5y + 13 = 0$ b) $3x + 4y - 13 = 0$ c) $4x + 3y - 13 = 0$
d) $5x - 2y + 13 = 0$ e) None of these

Answer: c Difficulty: 2

27. Use a determinant to find an equation of the line that passes through the center of the circle $(x + 3)^2 + (y - 2)^2 = 7$ and the point (1, 4).
a) $x - 2y + 7 = 0$ b) $2y - x + 7 = 0$ c) $x^2 + 3x - 2y + 4 = 0$
d) $3x + y - 7 = 0$ e) None of these

Answer: a Difficulty: 2

28. Use a determinant to find an equation of the line that passes through the vertices of the parabolas $y = (x - 2)^2 + 3$ and $y = (x - 5)^2 - 4$.
a) $x + y - 1 = 0$ b) $7x + 3y - 23 = 0$ c) $3y + 7x + 23 = 0$
d) $x - y + 1 = 0$ e) None of these

Answer: b Difficulty: 2

SHORT ANSWER

29. Use the matrix A to encode the message: HAPPY DAYS.

$$A = \begin{bmatrix} 1 & -2 & 2 \\ -1 & 1 & 3 \\ 1 & -1 & -4 \end{bmatrix}$$

Answer: 23 -31 -45 -9 -7 107 28 -32 -89 19 -38 38 Difficulty: 2

30. Use the inverse of the matrix $A = \begin{bmatrix} 1 & -2 & 2 \\ -1 & 1 & 3 \\ 1 & -1 & -4 \end{bmatrix}$ to decode the cryptogram.

21 -40 14 2 -11 32 16 -16 -66 15 -20 -31

Answer: SPRING BREAK Difficulty: 2

31. Find the uncoded row matrix of order 1×3 for the message SELL IT FAST, then encode the message using $A = \begin{bmatrix} 1 & -1 & 0 \\ 1 & 0 & 3 \\ -2 & 1 & -1 \end{bmatrix}$.

Answer: 0 -7 3 -6 -3 -9 8 -14 -6 -20 19 37 Difficulty: 1

32. Find the uncoded row matrix of order 1×3 for the message I LOVE MATH, then encode the message using $A = \begin{bmatrix} 1 & -1 & 0 \\ 1 & 0 & 3 \\ -2 & 1 & -1 \end{bmatrix}$.

Answer: -15 3 -12 27 -10 61 11 1 38 28 -20 24 Difficulty: 1

MULTIPLE CHOICE

33. Find the uncoded row matrix of order 1×3 for the message CALL ME LATER, then encode the message using $A = \begin{bmatrix} 1 & -1 & 0 \\ 1 & 0 & 3 \\ -2 & 1 & -1 \end{bmatrix}$.

a) 16 -12 4 4 3 -13 9 -13 3 1 9 -9 -20 -18 5
b) -20 9 -9 -14 1 -13 -19 7 -12 11 4 55 18 -18 0
c) -5 12 19 -3 6 6 2 13 -6 -6 3 -1 0 2 2
d) 3 1 12 12 0 13 5 0 12 1 20 5 18 0 0
e) None of these

Answer: b Difficulty: 1

34. Find the uncoded row matrix of order 1×3 for the message BE BACK SOON, then encode the message using $A = \begin{bmatrix} 1 & -1 & 0 \\ 1 & 0 & 3 \\ -2 & 1 & -1 \end{bmatrix}$.

a) -2 15 1 0 -3 -27 -2 8 19 15 -3 1
b) 7 -2 15 -3 1 0 -27 8 -19 2 -1 31
c) 2 5 0 2 1 3 11 0 19 15 15 14
d) 0 2 5 -3 1 0 0 -27 16 2 1 1
e) None of these

Answer: b Difficulty: 1

35. Decode the cryptogram:
129 -85 -38 -75 70 25 -9 18 3 188 -141 -58

using $A = \begin{bmatrix} 13 & -10 & -4 \\ -6 & 5 & 2 \\ 3 & -2 & -1 \end{bmatrix}$.

a) WELCOME HOME b) CLOSING OUT c) OUT TO LUNCH
d) PLEASE HURRY e) None of these

Answer: c Difficulty: 1

SHORT ANSWER

36. Use a graphing utility and Cramer's Rule to solve the system of equations.

$$\begin{cases} 2x + y + z = -2 \\ x + 2y + 3z = -3 \\ x - 3y - z = -5 \end{cases}$$

Answer: (-1, 2 -2) Difficulty: 2 Key 1: T

37. Use a graphing utility and Cramer's Rule to solve the system of equations.

$$\begin{cases} x - y - 2z = 3 \\ y + 3z = -2 \\ 3x + 4y - z = 11 \end{cases}$$

Answer: (2, 1, -1) Difficulty: 2 Key 1: T

38. Use a graphing utility and Cramer's Rule to solve the system of equations.

$$\begin{cases} x + 3y + z = 4 \\ 2x - y - 3z = 1 \\ 4x + y + z = 5 \end{cases}$$

Answer: (1, 1, 0) Difficulty: 2

39. Use a graphing utility and Cramer's Rule to solve the system of equations.

$$\begin{cases} 3x - y + 5z = 1 \\ 2x + y + z = 0 \\ -x + y - 2z = 0 \end{cases}$$

Answer: (-1, 1, 1) Difficulty: 2 Key 1: T

40. You are farming a triangular tract of land, as shown in the figure. From the northern most vertex A of the region, the distances to the other vertices are 2500 yards south and 1500 yards east to vertex B and 2000 yards south and 4000 yards east to vertex C. Use a graphing utility to approximate the number of square yards in the tract of land.

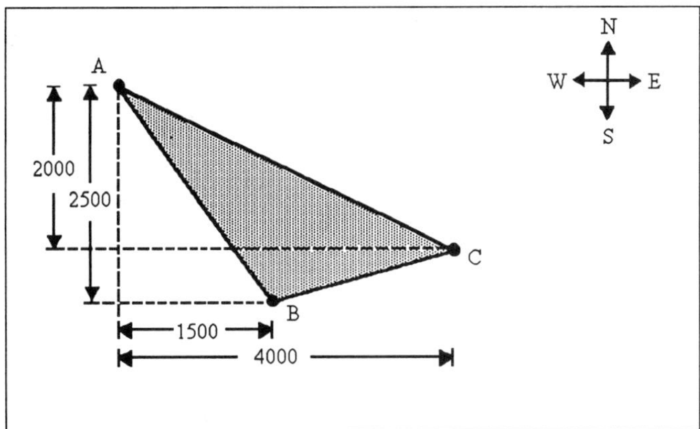

Answer: 1,750,000 square yards Difficulty: 2 Key 1: T

41. You are bidding on a triangular plot of land, as shown in the figure. To estimate the number of square feet, you start at one vertex, walk 75 feet west and 45 feet north to the second vertex, and then walk 60 feet east and 15 feet north to the third vertex. Use a graphing utility to determine how many square feet there are in the plot of land.

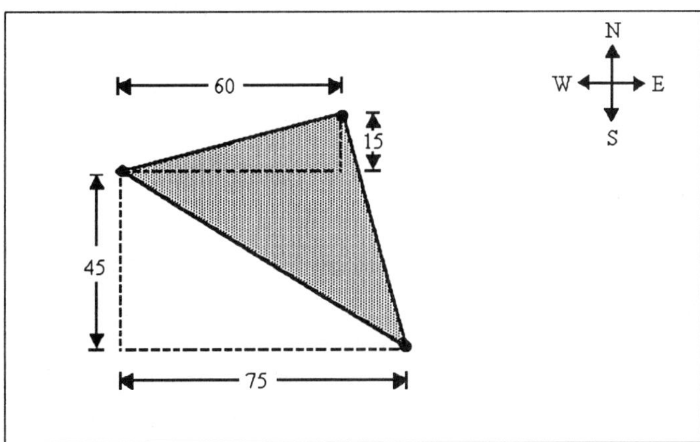

Answer: 1,912.5 square yards Difficulty: 2 Key 1: T

Chapter 091: Sequences and Series

MULTIPLE CHOICE

1. Write the first 5 terms of the sequence whose nth term is $a_n = (-1)^n(2n + 9)$. (Assume that n begins with 1.)
   a) -11, -13, -15, -17, -19,... b) -11, 13, -15, 17, -19,...
   c) -11, 2, -13, 4, -15,... d) -11, -24, -39, -56, -75,...
   e) None of these

   Answer: b Difficulty: 1

2. Write the first 5 terms of the sequence whose nth term is $a_n = n!$. (Assume that n begins with 0.)
   a) 0, 1, 2, 6, 24 b) 0, 1, 2, 6, 12 c) 1, 1, 2, 6, 12
   d) 1, 1, 2, 6, 24 e) None of these

   Answer: d Difficulty: 1

3. Write the first 5 terms of the sequence whose nth term is $a_n = 1 - \frac{1}{n}$.
   (Assume that n begins with 1.)
   a) $\frac{1}{2}, \frac{1}{4}, \frac{1}{8}, \frac{1}{16}, \frac{1}{32}$ b) $0, \frac{1}{2}, \frac{2}{3}, \frac{3}{4}, \frac{4}{5}$ c) $0, \frac{1}{2}, \frac{1}{3}, \frac{1}{4}, \frac{1}{5}$
   d) $1, \frac{1}{2}, \frac{2}{3}, \frac{3}{4}, \frac{4}{5}$ e) None of these

   Answer: b Difficulty: 1

SHORT ANSWER

4. Write the first 5 terms of the sequence whose nth term is
   $a_n = \frac{n!}{(n + 2)!}$. (Assume that n begins with 0.)

   Answer:
   $\frac{1}{2}, \frac{1}{6}, \frac{1}{12}, \frac{1}{20}, \frac{1}{30}$

   Difficulty: 1

5. Write the first five terms of the sequence whose nth term is
   $a_n = \frac{n}{n^2 + 1}$. (Assume that n begins with 1.)

   Answer:
   $\frac{1}{2}, \frac{2}{5}, \frac{3}{10}, \frac{4}{17}, \frac{5}{26}$

   Difficulty: 1

6. Write the first five terms of the sequence whose nth term is $a_n = \frac{n-2}{n^2+1}$. (Assume that n begins with 1.)

   Answer:
   $-\frac{1}{2}, 0, \frac{1}{10}, \frac{2}{17}, \frac{3}{26}$

   Difficulty: 1

7. Write the first five terms of the sequence whose nth term is $a_n = \frac{(-1)^n}{n!}$. (Assume that n begins with 1.)

   Answer:
   $-1, \frac{1}{2}, -\frac{1}{6}, \frac{1}{24}, -\frac{1}{120}$

   Difficulty: 1

8. Write the first five terms of the sequence whose nth term is $a_n = \frac{n!}{(n+2)!}$. (Assume that n begins with 0.)

   Answer:
   $\frac{1}{2}, \frac{1}{6}, \frac{1}{12}, \frac{1}{20}, \frac{1}{30}$

   Difficulty: 1

9. Write the first 5 terms of the sequence defined recursively. $a_1 = 3$, $a_{k+1} = 2(a_k - 2)$

   Answer: 3, 2, 0, -4, -12 Difficulty: 1

10. Write the first 5 terms of the sequence defined recursively. $a_1 = 20$, $a_{k+1} = \frac{a_k}{2}$

    Answer:
    $20, 10, 5, \frac{5}{2}, \frac{5}{4}$

    Difficulty: 1

MULTIPLE CHOICE

11. Find the 10th term of the sequence: $\frac{3^1}{2^0}, \frac{3^2}{2^1}, \frac{3^3}{2^2}, \frac{3^4}{2^3}, \frac{3^5}{2^4}, \ldots$

a) $\frac{3^{10}}{2^{10}}$ b) $\frac{3^{11}}{2^{10}}$ c) $\frac{3^{10}}{2^9}$ d) $\frac{3^{11}}{2^{11}}$ e) None of these

Answer: c Difficulty: 1

12. Find the 40th term of the sequence whose nth term is $a_n = 500\left[1 + \frac{0.095}{12}\right]^n$. (Assume that n begins with 1.)
a) 363.83 b) 752.19 c) 690.84 d) 685.42 e) None of these

Answer: d Difficulty: 1

13. Find the fifth term of the sequence whose nth term is $a_n = 2(3^{n-1})$. (Assume that n begins with 1.)
a) 486 b) -486 c) $\frac{1}{162}$ d) 162 e) None of these

Answer: d Difficulty: 1

14. Find the third term of the sequence whose nth term is $a_n = \frac{(-1)^{n+1}}{n}$.
(Assume that n begins with 1.)
a) $\frac{1}{3}$ b) $\frac{1}{81}$ c) $-\frac{1}{3}$ d) $\frac{1}{27}$ e) None of these

Answer: a Difficulty: 1

15. Find the tenth term of the sequence whose nth term is $a_n = \frac{2n + 1}{5 + 3(n - 1)}$. (Assume that n begins with 1.)
a) $\frac{21}{32}$ b) $\frac{21}{72}$ c) $\frac{22}{32}$ d) $\frac{19}{29}$ e) None of these

Answer: a Difficulty: 1

16. Find the fifth term of the sequence whose nth term is $a_n = \frac{(-1)^{n+1}}{(n + 1)^2}$. (Assumc that n begins with 1.)
a) $-\frac{1}{25}$ b) $\frac{1}{5}$ c) $\frac{1}{36}$ d) $\frac{1}{6}$ e) None of these

Answer: c Difficulty: 1

SHORT ANSWER

17. Use a graphing utility to graph the first ten terms of the sequence. (Assume n begins with 1.)

$$a_n = 2 + \frac{1}{n}$$

Answer: See graph below.

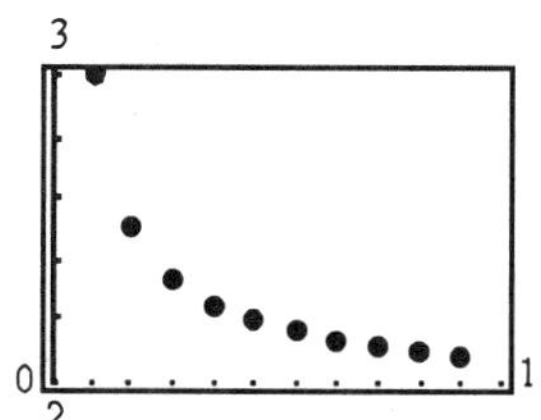

Difficulty: 1 Key 1: T

18. Use a graphing utility to graph the first ten terms of the sequence. (Assume n begins with 1.)

$$a_n = \frac{3n}{n + 1}$$

Answer: See graph below.

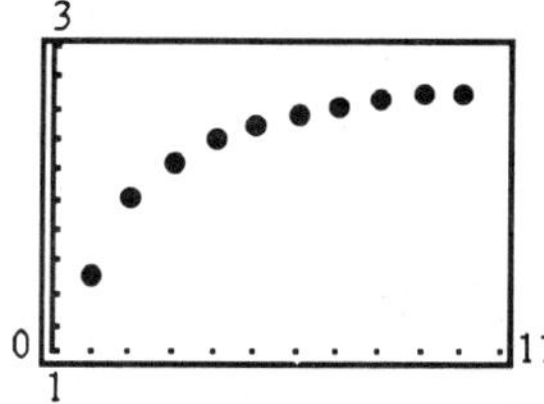

Difficulty: 1 Key 1: T

19. Use a graphing utility to graph the first ten terms of the sequence. (Assume n begins with 1.)

$$a_n = 4(1/2)^n$$

Answer: See graph below.

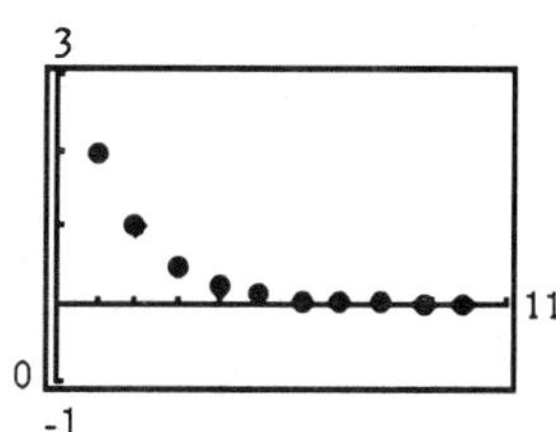

Difficulty: 1 Key 1: T

MULTIPLE CHOICE

20. Simplify: $\frac{8!}{5!}$.

a) $\frac{8}{5}$ b) 336 c) 56 d) 48 e) None of these

Answer: b Difficulty: 1

21. Simplify: $\frac{6!}{4!2!}$.

a) $\frac{3}{4}$ b) $\frac{1}{8}$ c) 15 d) 30 e) None of these

Answer: c Difficulty: 1

SHORT ANSWER

22. Simplify: $\frac{(2n)!}{(2n - 2)!}$.

Answer:

$4n^2 + 2n$

Difficulty: 2

MULTIPLE CHOICE

23. Simplify: $\frac{3(4!)}{7!}$.

a) 95,040 b) $\frac{15}{14}$ c) $\frac{1}{70}$ d) $\frac{1}{7}$ e) None of these

Answer: c Difficulty: 1

24. Simplify: $\frac{(2n)!}{(2n - 3)!}$.

a) $\frac{2n}{2n - 3}$ b) $2n(2n - 1)(2n - 2)$ c) $2n(n - 1)(n - 2)$
d) $\frac{2}{(n - 1)(n - 2)}$ e) None of these

Answer: b Difficulty: 1

25. Simplify: $\frac{(n + 1)!}{(n - 1)!}$.

a) $n + 1$ b) $n - 1$ c) $\frac{n + 1}{n - 1}$
d) $n^2 + n$ e) None of these

Answer: d Difficulty: 1

26. Find a formula for the *n*th term of the sequence. (Assume that *n* begins with 1.)

$$\frac{3}{2}, \frac{6}{4}, \frac{9}{12}, \frac{12}{48}, \frac{15}{240}, \ldots$$

a) $\dfrac{3n}{2n!}$ b) $\dfrac{3n}{n(n+1)}$ c) $\dfrac{3n}{n!(n+1)!}$

d) $\dfrac{3n}{2(n-1)!}$ e) None of these

Answer: a Difficulty: 1

27. Find a formula for the *n*th term of the sequence. (Assume that *n* begins with 1.)

$$\frac{1}{4}, \frac{2}{9}, \frac{3}{16}, \frac{4}{25}, \ldots$$

a) $a_n = 1 - \dfrac{3n}{n^2}$ b) $a_n = \dfrac{n}{(n+1)!}$ c) $a_n = \dfrac{1}{2} + \dfrac{n}{(n+1)^3}$

d) $a_n = \dfrac{n}{(n+1)^2}$ e) None of these

Answer: d Difficulty: 1

28. Find a formula for the *n*th term of the sequence. (Assume that *n* begins with 1.)

$$\frac{2}{1}, \frac{4}{1}, \frac{6}{2}, \frac{8}{6}, \frac{10}{24}, \ldots$$

a) $\dfrac{2^n}{(n+1)!}$ b) $\dfrac{3 - 2^n}{n(2^n)}$ c) $\dfrac{2n}{2n - 1}$

d) $\dfrac{2n}{(n-1)!}$ e) None of these

Answer: d Difficulty: 1

29. Find a formula for the *n*th term of the sequence. (Assume that *n* begins with 1.)

$$\frac{2}{1}, \frac{3}{2}, \frac{4}{3}, \frac{5}{4}, \frac{6}{5}, \ldots$$

a) $\dfrac{n+1}{n-1}$ b) $2 - \dfrac{1}{n}$ c) $1 + \dfrac{1}{n}$

d) $\dfrac{2n - 1}{n}$ e) None of these

Answer: c Difficulty: 1

30. Find a formula for the nth term of the sequence. (Assume that n begins with 1.)

$$1, 1, \frac{1}{2}, \frac{1}{6}, \frac{1}{24}, \ldots$$

a) $\frac{n+1}{n!}$ b) $\frac{n}{n!}$ c) $\frac{n}{2n!}$
d) $\frac{1}{2^n}$ e) None of these

Answer: b Difficulty: 1

31. Find the sum: $\sum_{n=3}^{6} \frac{3}{n-2}$.

a) $\frac{12}{9}$ b) $\frac{25}{4}$ c) $\frac{3}{16}$
d) $\frac{1}{2}$ e) None of these

Answer: b Difficulty: 1

32. Find the sum: $\sum_{n=1}^{4} \frac{n+1}{n+2}$.

a) $\frac{61}{20}$ b) $\frac{31}{20}$ c) $\frac{143}{60}$
d) $\frac{131}{60}$ e) None of these

Answer: a Difficulty: 1

33. Find the sum: $\sum_{i=1}^{4} (1-i)$.

a) -3 b) -6 c) 6 d) -5 e) None of these

Answer: b Difficulty: 1

34. Find the sum: $\sum_{k=2}^{6} (-1)^k(2k)$.

a) 40 b) -4 c) 6 d) 8 e) None of these

Answer: d Difficulty: 1

35. Find the sum: $\sum_{i=0}^{3} i!$.

a) 9 b) 6 c) 10 d) 7 c) None of these

Answer: c Difficulty: 1

SHORT ANSWER

36. Use a graphing utility to find the sum.

$$\sum_{i=1}^{5} (10 - 2i)$$

Answer: 20 Difficulty: 1 Key 1: T

37. Use a graphing utility to find the sum.

$$\sum_{k=0}^{5} \frac{k!}{2}$$

Answer: 77 Difficulty: 1 Key 1: T

38. Use a graphing utility to find the sum.

$$\sum_{j=1}^{4} \frac{3}{j + 2}$$

Answer: 2.85 Difficulty: 1 Key 1: T

39. Use a graphing utility to find the sum.

$$\sum_{i=0}^{4} \frac{(-1)^i}{i + 2}$$

Answer:

$0.38\overline{3}$

Difficulty: 1 Key 1: T

MULTIPLE CHOICE

40. Use sigma notation to write the sum: $\frac{2}{1} + \frac{3}{2} + \frac{4}{3} + \cdots + \frac{7}{6}$.

a) $\sum_{n=1}^{7} \frac{n}{n - 1}$

b) $\sum_{n=1}^{6} \frac{n + 1}{n}$

c) $\sum_{n=1}^{7} \frac{n}{n + 1}$

d) $\sum_{n=2}^{n} \frac{n}{n - 1}$

e) None of these

Answer: b Difficulty: 1

41. Use sigma notation to write the sum: $\frac{3}{1}+\frac{3}{4}+\frac{3}{9}+\frac{3}{16}+\frac{3}{25}$.

a) $\sum_{i=1}^{5} \frac{1}{i^2}$

b) $\sum_{i=1}^{5} \frac{3}{4i}$

c) $\sum_{i=1}^{6} \frac{3}{i^2}$

d) $\sum_{i=1}^{5} \frac{3}{i^2}$

e) None of these

Answer: d Difficulty: 1

42. Use sigma notation to write the sum: $\frac{2}{3}+\frac{4}{4}+\frac{6}{5}+\frac{8}{6}+\cdots+\frac{14}{9}$.

a) $\sum_{n=1}^{7} \frac{2n}{n+2}$

b) $\sum_{n=2}^{8} \frac{n+2}{n+1}$

c) $\sum_{n=0}^{6} \frac{n+2}{n+3}$

d) $\sum_{n=3}^{9} \frac{n-1}{n}$

e) None of these

Answer: a Difficulty: 1

SHORT ANSWER

43. Use sigma notation to write the sum: $\frac{1}{2}+\frac{2}{6}+\frac{3}{24}+\frac{4}{120}+\frac{5}{720}$.

Answer:

$$\sum_{n=1}^{5} \frac{n}{(n+1)!}$$

Difficulty: 1

MULTIPLE CHOICE

44. Use sigma notation to write the sum: $\frac{4}{2}+\frac{5}{4}+\frac{6}{6}+\frac{7}{8}$.

a) $\sum_{n=1}^{4} \frac{n+3}{2n}$

b) $\sum_{n=1}^{4} \frac{4n-1}{2n}$

c) $\sum_{n=1}^{4} \frac{2n+2}{2n}$

d) $\sum_{n=1}^{4} \frac{2^{n+1}+1}{n+2}$

e) None of these

Answer: a Difficulty: 1

SHORT ANSWER

45.
Find the fourth partial sum of $\sum_{i=1}^{\infty} 7\left(\frac{1}{2}\right)^i$.

Answer:
$S_4 = \frac{105}{16} = 6\frac{9}{16}$

Difficulty: 1

46.
Find the fourth partial sum of $\sum_{i=1}^{\infty} 8\left(\frac{1}{3}\right)^i$.

Answer:
$S_4 = \frac{320}{81} = 3\frac{77}{81}$

Difficulty: 1

MULTIPLE CHOICE

47. A deposit of $2000 is made in an account that earns 6% interest compounded monthly. The balance in the account after n months is given by

$$A_n = 2000\left(1 + \frac{0.06}{12}\right)^n, \quad n = 1, 2, 3, \ldots.$$

Find the balance in this account after 8 years ($n = 96$).

a) $3552.17 b) $2793.52 c) $2163.73
d) $3228.29 e) None of these

Answer: d Difficulty: 1

48. A deposit of $4000 is made in an account that earns 7% interest compounded quarterly. The balance in the account after n months is

$$A_n = 4000\left(1 + \frac{0.07}{4}\right)^n, \quad n = 1, 2, 3, \ldots .$$

Find the balance in this account after 8 years ($n = 32$).

a) $6968.85 b) $4595.53 c) $27,439.59
d) $9874.31 e) None of these

Answer: a Difficulty: 1

Chapter 092: Arithmetic Sequences and Partial Sums

MULTIPLE CHOICE

1. Which of the following is an arithmetic sequence?
   a) 1, 3, 9, 27, 81,...
   b) 1, 16, 36, 64, 100,...
   c) 2, 11, 20, 29, 38,...
   d) 3, -5, 7, -9, 11,...
   e) None of these

   Answer: c Difficulty: 1

2. Which of the following is an arithmetic sequence?
   a) 2, 4, 8, 16, 32,...
   b) -2, 4, -8, 16, -32,...
   c) 3, 6, 9, 12, 15,...
   d) All of these
   e) None of these

   Answer: c Difficulty: 1

3. Which of the following is an arithmetic sequence?
   a) 1, 3, 5, 7, 9,...
   b) 4, 7, 10, 13, 16,...
   c) -10, -6, -2, 2, 6,...
   d) All of these
   e) None of these

   Answer: d Difficulty: 1

4. Which of the following is an arithmetic sequence?
   a) 2, 3, 5, 7, 11,...
   b) $\frac{1}{2}, \frac{1}{3}, \frac{1}{4}, \frac{1}{5}, \frac{1}{6}, \ldots$
   c) $\frac{1}{2}, \frac{1}{4}, \frac{1}{6}, \frac{1}{8}, \frac{1}{10}, \ldots$
   d) All of these
   e) None of these

   Answer: e Difficulty: 1

5. Which of the following is an arithmetic sequence?
   a) $-\frac{1}{2}, -1, -\frac{3}{2}, -2, -\frac{5}{2}, \ldots$
   b) $\frac{2}{5}, \frac{2}{25}, \frac{2}{125}, \frac{2}{625}, \frac{2}{3125}, \ldots$
   c) -2, 2, -2, 2, -2,...
   d) All of these
   e) None of these

   Answer: a Difficulty: 1

6. Write the first 5 terms of the arithmetic sequence with $a_1 = 23$ and $d = -\frac{1}{2}$.
   a) $23, 22\frac{1}{2}, 22, 21\frac{1}{2}, 21$
   b) $23, 23\frac{1}{2}, 24, 24\frac{1}{2}, 25$
   c) $23, -\frac{23}{2}, \frac{23}{4}, -\frac{23}{8}, \frac{23}{16}$
   d) 23, -46, 92, -184, 368
   e) None of these

   Answer: a Difficulty: 1

7. Write the first 4 terms of the arithmetic sequence with $a_1 = 4$ and $d = -3$.
   a) $4, -\frac{4}{3}, \frac{4}{9}, -\frac{4}{27}, \ldots$ b) 4, 1, -2, -5,... c) 4, 7, 10, 13,...
   d) 4, -12, 36, -108,... e) None of these

   Answer: b Difficulty: 1

8. Write the first 4 terms of the arithmetic sequence with $a_1 = 4$ and $d = \frac{1}{2}$.
   a) $4, 2, 1, \frac{1}{2}, \ldots$ b) 4, 8, 16, 32,... c) $4, -2, 1, -\frac{1}{2}, \ldots$
   d) 4, 0, -4, -8 e) None of these

   Answer: e Difficulty: 1

9. Write the first 4 terms of the arithmetic sequence with $a_1 = 4$ and $d = -2$.
   a) 4, 2, 0, -2,... b) 4, 6, 8, 10,... c) $4, -2, 1, -\frac{1}{2}, \ldots$
   d) 4, -8, 16, -32,... e) None of these

   Answer: a Difficulty: 1

SHORT ANSWER

10. Write the first 4 terms of the arithmetic sequence with $a_1 = 3$ and $a_{14} = -36$.

    Answer: 3, 0, -3, -6 Difficulty: 1

11. Find the first 4 terms of the arithmetic sequence with $a_1 = 4$ and $a_{10} = 58$.

    Answer: 4, 10, 16, 22 Difficulty: 1

12. Find the first 4 terms of the arithmetic sequence with $a_7 = 23$ and $a_{16} = 50$.

    Answer: 5, 8, 11, 14 Difficulty: 1

MULTIPLE CHOICE

13. Find a_n for the arithmetic sequence with $a_1 = 5$, $d = -4$, and $n = 98$.
    a) -392 b) -387 c) -383 d) 393 e) None of these

    Answer: c Difficulty: 1

SHORT ANSWER

14. Find a_n for the arithmetic sequence with $a_1 = 12$, $d = \frac{1}{3}$, and $n = 52$.

    Answer: 29 Difficulty: 1

MULTIPLE CHOICE

15. Find the 99th term of the arithmetic sequence with $a_1 = 7$ and $d = -3$. (Assume that n begins with 1.)
   a) -287 b) -290 c) -293 d) -297 e) None of these

   Answer: a Difficulty: 1

SHORT ANSWER

16. Find the 30th term of the arithmetic sequence with $a_1 = -5$ and $d = \frac{1}{3}$. (Assume that n begins with 1.)

   Answer:
   $\frac{14}{3}$
   Difficulty: 1

MULTIPLE CHOICE

17. Find the ninth term of the arithmetic sequence with $a_1 = 4$ and $d = 10$. (Assume that n begins with 1.)
   a) 94 b) 84 c) 46 d) 49 e) None of these

   Answer: b Difficulty: 1

18. Find the eighth term of the arithmetic sequence with $a_1 = 5$ and $d = 8$. (Assume that n begins with 1.)
   a) 69 b) 48 c) 61 d) 104 e) None of these

   Answer: c Difficulty: 1

SHORT ANSWER

19. Find the seventeenth term of the arithmetic sequence with $a_1 = 2$ and $d = 7$. (Assume that n begins with 1.)

   Answer: 114 Difficulty: 1

MULTIPLE CHOICE

20. Find the sum of the first 50 terms of the arithmetic sequence: 25, 35, 45, 55, 65,....
   a) 27,000 b) 13,750 c) 12,875 d) 13,500 e) None of these

   Answer: d Difficulty: 1

21. Find the sum of the first 50 positive integers that are multiples of 3.
a) 7500 b) 3900 c) 3825 d) 7650 e) None of these

Answer: c Difficulty: 1

SHORT ANSWER

22. Find the sum of the first 40 positive integers that are multiples of 4.

Answer: 3280 Difficulty: 1

23. Find the sum of the first 30 terms of the sequence:
$\sqrt{2}, 2\sqrt{2}, 3\sqrt{2}, 4\sqrt{2}, 5\sqrt{2}, \ldots$

Answer:
$465\sqrt{2}$
Difficulty: 2

MULTIPLE CHOICE

24. Find the sum of the first n terms of the arithmetic sequence: -4, 5, 14, 23, 32, ...

a) $9n - 4$ b) $\dfrac{n(9n - 17)}{2}$ c) $\dfrac{1 - 9^n}{2}$

d) $\dfrac{n^2 - 9n}{2}$ e) None of these

Answer: b Difficulty: 1

25. Find the sum of the first 18 terms of the arithmetic sequence whose nth term is $a_n = 3n - 1$. (Assume that n begins with 1.)
a) 495 b) 53 c) 459 d) 445 e) None of these

Answer: a Difficulty: 1

SHORT ANSWER

26. Find the sum of the first 19 terms of the arithmetic sequence whose nth term is $a_n = n + 1$. (Assume that n begins with 1.)

Answer: 209 Difficulty: 1

MULTIPLE CHOICE

27. Find the sum: $\sum_{n=1}^{500} (3n + 5)$.

a) 756,500
b) 376,250
c) 752,500
d) 378,250
e) None of these

Answer: d Difficulty: 1

SHORT ANSWER

28. Find the sum: $\sum_{i=1}^{7} 2(i + 1)$.

Answer: 70 Difficulty: 1

MULTIPLE CHOICE

29. Find a formula for a_n for the arithmetic sequence with $a_1 = 5$ and $d = -4$. (Assume that n begins with 1.)

a) $a_n = -4n + 9$
b) $a_n = -4n + 5$
c) $a_n = 5n - 4$
d) $a_n = 9n - 4$
e) None of these

Answer: a Difficulty: 1

30. Find a formula for a_n for the arithmetic sequence with $a_3 = 15$ and $d = -2$. (Assume that n begins with 1.)

a) $a_n = -2n + 9$
b) $a_n = -2n + 19$
c) $a_n = -2n + 21$
d) $a_n = -2n + 15$
e) None of these

Answer: c Difficulty: 1

31. Find a formula for a_n for the arithmetic sequence with $a_2 = 12$ and $d = -3$. (Assume that n begins with 1.)

a) $a_n = 12n - 3$
b) $a_n = -3n + 15$
c) $a_n = -3n + 12$
d) $a_n = -3n + 18$
e) None of these

Answer: d Difficulty: 1

SHORT ANSWER

32. Find a formula for a_n for the arithmetic sequence with $a_2 = 15$ and $d = \frac{3}{2}$. (Assume that n begins with 1.)

Answer:

$a_n = -\frac{3}{2}n + 12$

Difficulty: 1

MULTIPLE CHOICE

33. Determine the seating capacity of an auditorium with 25 rows of seats if there are 20 seats in the first row, 24 seats in the second row, 28 seats in the third row, and so on.
    a) 1200 seats b) 1500 seats c) 1700 seats
    d) 1900 seats e) None of these

    Answer: c Difficulty: 2

34. Determine the seating capacity of an auditorium with 30 rows of seats if there are 25 seats in the first row, 28 seats in the second row, 31 seats in the third row, and so on.
    a) 1635 seats b) 1792 seats c) 2055 seats
    d) 3125 seats e) None of these

    Answer: c Difficulty: 2

35. Determine the seating capacity of an auditorium with 28 rows of seats if there are 24 seats in the first row, 28 seats in the second row, 32 seats in the third row, and so on.
    a) 2128 seats b) 2240 seats c) 2296 seats
    d) 2184 seats e) None of these

    Answer: d Difficulty: 2

SHORT ANSWER

36. A small business sells $8000 worth of products during its first year. The owner of the business has set a goal of increasing annual sales by $3500 each year for 11 years. Assuming that this goal is met, find the total sales during the first 12 years this business is in operation.

    Answer: $327,000 Difficulty: 2

37. A small business sells $6000 worth of products during its first year. The owner of the business has set a goal of increasing annual sales by $2500 each year for 7 years. Assuming that this goal is met, find the total sales during the first 8 years this business is in operation.

    Answer: $118,000 Difficulty: 2

Chapter 093: Geometric Sequences and Series

MULTIPLE CHOICE

1. Which of the following is a geometric sequence?
   a) 1, -3, 5, -7, 9,...
   b) 6, 3, 0, -3, -6,...
   c) 2, 4, 8, 16, 32,...
   d) -1, 0, -1, 0, -1,...
   e) None of these

   Answer: c Difficulty: 1

2. Which of the following is a geometric sequence?
   a) -2, 0, 2, 4, 6,...
   b) 2, 4, 8, 16, 32,...
   c) 2, 7, 3, 8, 4,...
   d) $2, \frac{1}{2}, \frac{1}{4}, \frac{1}{6}, \frac{1}{8}, \ldots$
   e) None of these

   Answer: b Difficulty: 1

3. Which of the following is a geometric sequence?
   a) -1, -3, -5, -7, -9,...
   b) 2, 3, 5, 7, 11,...
   c) 1, 2, 4, 7, 11, 16,...
   d) -2, 4, -8, 16, -32,...
   e) None of these

   Answer: d Difficulty: 1

SHORT ANSWER

4. Determine whether the sequence $3, -2, \frac{4}{3}, -\frac{8}{9}, \frac{16}{27}, \ldots$ is geometric. If it is, find its common ratio. If not, why not?

   Answer:

   Yes, $r = -\frac{2}{3}$

   Difficulty: 1

5. Determine whether the sequence $10, -8, \frac{32}{5}, \frac{-128}{25}, \ldots$ is geometric. If it is, find its common ratio. If not, why not?

   Answer:

   Yes, $r = \frac{-4}{5}$

   Difficulty: 1

MULTIPLE CHOICE

6. Find the common ratio of the geometric sequence $-4, 3, -\frac{9}{4}, \frac{27}{16}, -\frac{81}{16}, \ldots$

   a) $\frac{3}{4}$ b) $-\frac{3}{4}$ c) $\frac{4}{3}$ d) $-\frac{4}{3}$ e) None of these

   Answer: b Difficulty: 1

7. Write the first five terms of the geometric sequence with $a_1 = 2$ and $r = \frac{2}{3}$.

   a) $2, \frac{4}{3}, \frac{8}{9}, \frac{16}{27}, \frac{32}{81}$ b) $2, 3, \frac{9}{2}, \frac{27}{4}, \frac{81}{8}$ c) $2, \frac{8}{3}, \frac{10}{3}, 4, \frac{14}{3}$

   d) $2, \frac{4}{3}, \frac{2}{3}, -\frac{2}{3}$ e) None of these

   Answer: a Difficulty: 1

8. Write the first five terms of the geometric sequence with $a_1 = 3$ and $r = \frac{3}{2}$.

   a) $3, \frac{9}{2}, \frac{27}{4}, \frac{81}{8}, \frac{243}{16}$ b) $3, 2, \frac{4}{3}, \frac{8}{9}, \frac{16}{27}$ c) $3, \frac{9}{2}, 6, \frac{15}{2}, 9$

   d) $3, \frac{3}{2}, 0, -\frac{3}{2}, -3$ e) None of these

   Answer: a Difficulty: 1

9. Write the first five terms of the geometric sequence with $a_1 = 3$ and $r = \frac{1}{2}$.

   a) $3, 3\frac{1}{2}, 4, 4\frac{1}{2}, 5$ b) $3, 2\frac{1}{2}, 2, 1\frac{1}{2}, 1$ c) $3, \frac{3}{2}, \frac{3}{4}, \frac{3}{8}, \frac{3}{16}$

   d) $3, \frac{3}{2}, \frac{3}{4}, \frac{3}{6}, \frac{3}{8}$ e) None of these

   Answer: c Difficulty: 1

10. Write the first five terms of the geometric sequence with $a_1 = -3$ and $r = \frac{2}{3}$.

    a) $-3, -2\frac{1}{3}, -1\frac{2}{3}, -1, -\frac{1}{3}$ b) $-3, -3\frac{2}{3}, -4\frac{1}{3}, -5, -5\frac{2}{3}$

    c) $-3, -\frac{9}{2}, -\frac{27}{4}, -\frac{81}{8}, -\frac{243}{16}$ d) $-3, -2, -\frac{4}{3}, -\frac{8}{9}, -\frac{16}{27}$

    e) None of these

    Answer: d Difficulty: 1

11. Find the 20th term of the geometric sequence with $a_1 = 5$ and $r = 1.1$.
    a) 1.1665 b) 37.0012 c) 33.6375
    d) 30.5795 e) None of these

    Answer: d Difficulty: 1

12. Find the 23rd term of the geometric sequence with $a_1 = -23$ and $r = \sqrt{2}$.
    a) $-47104\sqrt{2}$ b) $-2048\sqrt{2}$ c) -2048
    d) -47104 e) None of these

    Answer: d Difficulty: 1

SHORT ANSWER

13. Find the 28th term of the geometric sequence: 2, 2.4, 2.88, 3.456, 4.1472,....

    Answer: 274.7411 Difficulty: 1

14. Find the 14th term of the geometric sequence with $a_1 = -11$ and $r = \sqrt{3}$.

    Answer:
    $-8019\sqrt{3}$
    Difficulty: 1

MULTIPLE CHOICE

15. Find the sum: $\sum_{n=0}^{10} 2(\frac{3}{5})^n$. Round your answer to four decimal places.
    a) 4.9698 b) 5.0000 c) 4.9819
    d) 55.0000 e) None of these

    Answer: c Difficulty: 1

16. Find the sum: $\sum_{j=0}^{40} 3(1.05)^j$. Round your answer to two decimal places.
    a) 383.52 b) 362.40 c) 984.00
    d) 22.18 e) None of these

    Answer: a Difficulty: 1

SHORT ANSWER

17. Find the sum: $\sum_{k=1}^{10} 4\left(\frac{3}{2}\right)^{k-1}$. Round your answer to three decimal places.

Answer: 453.320 Difficulty: 1

MULTIPLE CHOICE

18. Find the sum: $\sum_{n=1}^{15} 3\left(\frac{5}{4}\right)^{n}$. Round your answer to two decimal places.

a) 329.06
b) 260.85
c) 322.61
d) 271.15
e) None of these

Answer: a Difficulty: 1

19. Find the sum of the first 30 terms in the sequence. $2, \frac{5}{2}, \frac{25}{8}, \frac{125}{32}, \frac{625}{128}, \ldots$ Round your answer to two decimal places.

a) 791.25
b) 5161.88
c) 6454.35
d) 7116.42
e) None of these

Answer: c Difficulty: 1

SHORT ANSWER

20. Find the sum of the first 30 terms in the sequence.
$\sqrt{2}, 2\sqrt{2}, 3\sqrt{2}, 4\sqrt{2}, 5\sqrt{2}, \ldots$

Answer:

$465\sqrt{2}$

Difficulty: 1

MULTIPLE CHOICE

21. Find the sum of the first six terms of the geometric sequence with $a_1 = 2$ and $a_2 = -4$.

a) -42
b) $\frac{130}{3}$
c) 42
d) $-\frac{62}{3}$
e) None of these

Answer: a Difficulty: 1

22. Find the sum of the first 10 terms of the geometric sequence with $a_1 = 3$ and $a_2 = \frac{3}{2}$. Round to three decimal places.

a) 5.994 b) 7.286 c) 6.984
d) 9.117 e) None of these

Answer: a Difficulty: 2

23. Find a formula for the *n*th term of the geometric sequence with $a_1 = 2$ and $r = -\frac{1}{3}$. (Assume that *n* begins with 1.)

a) $a_n = \left(-\frac{2}{3}\right)^n$ b) $a_n = 2 - \frac{1}{3}n$ c) $a_n = 2\left(-\frac{1}{3}\right)^{n-1}$
d) $a_n = 2\left(-\frac{1}{3}\right)^n$ e) None of these

Answer: c Difficulty: 1

24. Find a formula for the *n*th term of the geometric sequence with $a_1 = 4$ and $r = \frac{1}{3}$. (Assume that *n* begins with 1.)

a) $a_n = \left(\frac{1}{3}\right)^n$ b) $a_n = 4\left(\frac{1}{3}\right)^{n-1}$ c) $a_n = 4\left(\frac{1}{3}\right)^n$
d) $a_n = 4 + \left(\frac{1}{3}\right)^n$ e) None of these

Answer: b Difficulty: 1

25. Find a formula for the *n*th term of the geometric sequence with $a_1 = \frac{1}{2}$ and $r = -\frac{1}{3}$. (Assume that *n* begins at 1.)

a) $a_n = \frac{1}{2}\left(-\frac{1}{3}\right)^{n-1}$ b) $a_n = \frac{1}{2}\left(-\frac{1}{3}\right)^n$ c) $a_n = \left(-\frac{1}{6}\right)^n$
d) $a_n = \frac{1}{2} - \frac{1}{3^n}$ e) None of these

Answer: a Difficulty: 1

26. Find a formula for the *n*th term of the geometric sequence with $a_1 = \frac{2}{3}$ and $r = -\frac{1}{5}$. (Assume that *n* begins at 1.)

a) $a_n = \frac{2}{3}\left(-\frac{1}{5}\right)^n$ b) $a_n = \left(-\frac{2}{15}\right)^n$ c) $a_n = -\frac{1}{5}\left(\frac{2}{3}\right)^n$
d) $a_n = \frac{2}{3}\left(-\frac{1}{5}\right)^{n-1}$ e) None of these

Answer: d Difficulty: 1

27. Find the sum of the infinite geometric series: $-7, -\frac{7}{3}, -\frac{7}{9}, -\frac{7}{27}, \ldots$

a) -5 b) $-\frac{21}{4}$ c) $-\frac{5}{2}$ d) $-\frac{21}{2}$ e) None of these

Answer: d Difficulty: 1

28. Find the sum of the infinite geometric series: 1, 0.9, 0.81, 0.729, ...

a) 23 b) 90 c) 10 d) 57 e) None of these

Answer: c Difficulty: 1

29. Find the sum of the infinite geometric series: $1, \frac{1}{3}, \frac{1}{9}, \frac{1}{27}, \ldots$

a) $\frac{3}{2}$ b) 3 c) $\frac{5}{3}$ d) $\frac{5}{2}$ e) None of these

Answer: a Difficulty: 1

SHORT ANSWER

30. Find the sum of the infinite geometric series with $a_1 = 9$ and $r = 0.7$.

Answer: 30 Difficulty: 1

MULTIPLE CHOICE

31. Evaluate: $\sum_{n=0}^{\infty} 2\left(\frac{1}{2}\right)^n = 2 + 1 + \frac{1}{2} + \frac{1}{4} + \frac{1}{8} + \ldots$

a) 4 b) 6 c) 8 d) 10 e) None of these

Answer: a Difficulty: 1

32. Evaluate: $\sum_{n=0}^{\infty} 4\left(\frac{2}{3}\right)^n = 4 + \frac{8}{3} + \frac{16}{9} + \frac{32}{27} + \ldots$

a) 8 b) 10 c) 12 d) 14 e) None of these

Answer: c Difficulty: 1

33. Evaluate: $\sum_{n=0}^{\infty} 3\left(-\frac{1}{2}\right)^n$.

a) 6 b) 4 c) 2 d) 0 e) None of these

Answer: c Difficulty: 1

34. Evaluate: $\sum_{n=0}^{\infty} 5\left(-\frac{2}{3}\right)^n$.

a) 6 b) 3 c) 1 d) 0 e) None of these

Answer: b Difficulty: 1

35. An individual buys a $100,000 term life insurance policy. During the next five years the value of the policy will depreciate at a rate of 4% per year. (That is, at the end of each year the depreciated value is 96% of the value at the beginning of the year.) Find the depreciated value of the policy at the end of five years.
a) $80,000 b) $84,934.66 c) $81,537.27
d) $78,275.78 e) None of these

Answer: c Difficulty: 2

36. Suppose in 1991 you accepted a job at $17,000. If you receive a 5% raise in salary each year, what will be your salary in 2001?
a) $25,116.74 b) $26,372.58 c) $27,691.21
d) $29,075.77 e) None of these

Answer: c Difficulty: 2

SHORT ANSWER

37. A city of 500,000 people is growing at a rate of 1% per year. Find a formula for the *n*th term of the geometric sequence that gives the population *n* years from now. Then estimate the population 20 years from now.

Answer: $a_n = 500{,}000(1.01)^n$; 610,095 Difficulty: 2

38. Suppose that you accept a job that pays a salary of $35,000 the first year. During the next 39 years, suppose you receive a 5% raise each year. Write a summation formula to represent your total salary after working *n* years. What would your total salary be over the 40-year period?

Answer:

$\sum_{i=1}^{n} 35{,}000(1.05)^{i-1}$; $S_{40} = \$4{,}227{,}992.10$

Difficulty: 2

39. Suppose that you accept a job that pays a salary of $35,000 the first year. During the next 39 years, suppose you receive a 6% raise each year. Write a summation formula to represent your total salary after working *n* years. What would your total salary be over the 40-year period?

Answer:

$\sum_{i=1}^{n} 35{,}000(1.06)^{i-1}$; $S_{40} = \$5{,}416{,}668.80$

Difficulty: 2

Chapter 094: Mathematical Induction

MULTIPLE CHOICE

1. Find the sum using the formulas for the sums of powers of integers: $\sum_{n=1}^{7} n^5$.

   a) 4219 b) 4676 c) 29,008 d) 61,776 e) None of these

   Answer: c Difficulty: 1

2. Find the sum using the formulas for the sums of powers of integers: $\sum_{n=1}^{8} (n^2 - n^3)$.

   a) -994 b) -1092 c) -1296 d) -1538 e) None of these

   Answer: b Difficulty: 1

3. Find the sum using the formulas for the sums of powers of integers: $\sum_{n=1}^{19} i^3$.

   a) 36,100 b) 3581 c) 44,100 d) 1,687,998 e) None of these

   Answer: a Difficulty: 1

4. Find the sum using the formulas for the sums of powers of integers: $\sum_{n=1}^{15} i^4$.

   a) 2,299,200 b) 1,337,340 c) 445,780
   d) 178,312 e) None of these

   Answer: d Difficulty: 1

5. Find the sum using the formulas for the sums of powers of integers: $\sum_{n=1}^{50} (n^2 - n)$.

   a) 42,925 b) 41,650 c) 44,100 d) 43,150 e) None of these

   Answer: b Difficulty: 1

6. Find the sum using the formulas for the sums of powers of integers: $\sum_{n=1}^{15} 4n^2$.

   a) 4960 b) 1240 c) 73,810 d) 74,400 e) None of these

   Answer: a Difficulty: 1

SHORT ANSWER

7. Find the sum using the formulas for the sums of powers of integers:

$$\sum_{n=1}^{20} 3n^2.$$

Answer: 8610 Difficulty: 1

8. Find the sum using the formulas for the sums of powers of integers:

$$\sum_{n=1}^{19} 2n^2.$$

Answer: 4940 Difficulty: 1

MULTIPLE CHOICE

9. Find the sum using the formulas for the sums of powers of integers:

$$\sum_{i=1}^{20} i^4.$$

a) 718,312　b) 4,933,320　c) 44,100
d) 722,666　e) None of these

Answer: d Difficulty: 1

10. Identify S_{k+1} given $S_k = \frac{2k - 1}{3k(k + 1)}$.

a) $\frac{2k + 1}{(3k + 1)(k + 1)}$　b) $\frac{2k + 1}{3(k + 1)(k + 2)}$　c) $\frac{2k}{3(k + 1)(k + 2)}$
d) $\frac{2k}{(3k + 1)(k + 2)}$　e) None of these

Answer: b Difficulty: 1

11. Identify S_{k+1} given $S_k = \frac{3}{k(k + 2)}$.

a) $\frac{3}{(k + 1)(k + 3)}$　b) $\frac{k^2 + 2k + 3}{k + 2}$　c) $\frac{3}{(k + 1)(k + 2)}$
d) $\frac{k^2 + 5}{k(k + 2)}$　e) None of these

Answer: a Difficulty: 1

12. Identify S_{k+1} given $S_k = \dfrac{(k+1)^2}{k(k-1)}$.

a) $\dfrac{2k^2 + 2k}{k(k+1)}$ b) $\dfrac{(k+2)^2}{k(k-1)}$ c) $\dfrac{(k+1)^2 + k(k-1)}{k(k-1)}$

d) $\dfrac{(k+2)^2}{k(k+1)}$ e) None of these

Answer: d Difficulty: 1

13. Identify S_{k+1} given $S_k = \dfrac{k(2k-1)}{3}$.

a) $\dfrac{2k(k+1)}{3}$ b) $\dfrac{2k^2 - k + 3}{3}$ c) $\dfrac{(k+1)(2k+1)}{3}$

d) $\dfrac{2k^2 - k + 1}{3}$ e) None of these

Answer: c Difficulty: 1

14. Identify S_{k+1} given $S_k = k(3k-1)$.

a) $(k+1)(3k+2)$ b) $3k(k+1)$ c) $k(3k-1)+1$
d) $3k^2 + 1$ e) None of these

Answer: a Difficulty: 1

15. Identify S_{k+1} given $S_k = k^2(k+1)^2$.

a) $(k^2+1)(k+2)^2$ b) $k^2(k+1)^2 + 1$ c) $(k+1)^2(k-1)^2$

d) $(k+1)^2(k+2)^2$ e) None of these

Answer: d Difficulty: 1

16. Identify S_{k+1} given $S_k = \dfrac{k}{2}(3k+2)$.

a) $\dfrac{3(k+1)^2}{2}$ b) $\dfrac{k+1}{2}(3k+2)$ c) $\dfrac{3k^2 + 2k + 2}{2}$

d) $\dfrac{k+1}{2}(3k+5)$ e) None of these

Answer: d Difficulty: 1

17. Identify S_{k+1} given $S_k = (k+1)(k-1)$.
a) $k(k+2)$ b) k^2 c) $k^2 - 2$
d) $(k+2)(k+1)$ e) None of these

Answer: a Difficulty: 1

18. Identify S_{k+1} given $S_k = \frac{k(k+1)}{2}$.

a) $\frac{k^2 + k + 2}{2}$　　b) $\frac{k^2 + 2}{2}$　　c) $\frac{(k+1)(k+2)}{2}$

d) $\frac{(k+1)(k+2)}{2k+1}$　　e) None of these

Answer: c　Difficulty: 1

SHORT ANSWER

19. Prove by mathematical induction: $1 + 2 + 2^2 + 2^3 + \cdots + 2^{n-1} = 2^n - 1$

Answer:

S_1:　$2^1 - 1 = 2 - 1 = 1$

S_k:　$1 + 2 + 2^2 + 2^3 + \cdots + 2^{k-1} = 2^k - 1$

S_{k+1}: $1 + 2 + 2^2 + 2^3 + \cdots + 2^k = 2^{k+1} - 1$

Assuming S_k, we have:

$$\begin{aligned}(1 + 2 + 2^2 + 2^3 + \cdots + 2^{k-1}) + 2^{(k+1)-1} &= (1 + 2 + \cdots + 2^{k-1}) + 2^k \\ &= (2^k - 1) + 2^k \\ &= 2^{k+1} - 1.\end{aligned}$$

So, the formula is valid for all $n \geq 1$.

Difficulty: 2

20. Prove by mathematical induction:

$$1^2 + 2^2 + 3^2 + \cdots + n^2 = \frac{n(n+1)(2n+1)}{6}$$

Answer:

Let $n = 1$, then $\frac{n(n + 1)(2n + 1)}{6} = \frac{(1)(2)(3)}{6} = 1 = 1^2$.

For $n = k$, $S_k = 1^2 + 2^2 + 3^2 + \cdots + k^2 = \frac{k(k + 1)(2k + 1)}{6}$.

For $n = k + 1$, $S_{k+1} = \frac{k(k + 1)(2k + 1)}{6} + (k + 1)^2$

$$= (k + 1)\left[\frac{k(2k + 1) + 6(k + 1)}{6}\right]$$

$$= \frac{(k + 1)(2k^2 + 7k + 6)}{6}$$

$$= \frac{(k + 1)(k + 2)(2k + 3)}{6}$$

$$= \frac{(k + 1)[(k + 1) + 1][2(k + 1) + 1]}{6}.$$

So, the formula is valid.

Difficulty: 2

21. Use mathematical induction to prove

$$\frac{1}{1 \cdot 3} + \frac{1}{3 \cdot 5} + \frac{1}{5 \cdot 7} + \cdots + \frac{1}{(2n - 1)(2n + 1)} = \frac{n}{2n + 1}.$$

Answer:

When $n = 1$, the formula is valid since $S_1 = \frac{1}{1 \cdot 3} = \frac{1}{3}$.

For $n = k$, assume S_k is true, $S_k = \frac{k}{2k + 1}$.

For $n = k + 1$, show $S_{k+1} = \frac{k + 1}{2k + 3}$

$$S_{k+1} = \left[\frac{1}{1 \cdot 3} + \frac{1}{3 \cdot 5} + \frac{1}{5 \cdot 7} + \cdots + \frac{1}{(2k - 1)(2k + 1)}\right] + \frac{1}{(2k + 1)(2k + 3)}$$

$$= S_k + \frac{1}{(2k + 1)(2k + 3)}$$

$$= \frac{k}{2k + 1} + \frac{1}{(2k + 1)(2k + 3)}$$

$$= \frac{k(2k + 3) + 1}{(2k + 1)(2k + 3)}$$

$$= \frac{2k^2 + 3k + 1}{(2k + 1)(2k + 3)}$$

$$= \frac{(2k + 1)(k + 1)}{(2k + 1)(2k + 3)}$$

$$= \frac{k + 1}{2k + 3}$$

So, the formula is valid.

Difficulty: 2

22. Use mathematical induction to prove

$$\frac{1}{1 \cdot 2} + \frac{1}{2 \cdot 3} + \frac{1}{3 \cdot 4} + \cdots + \frac{1}{n(n+1)} = \frac{n}{n+1}.$$

Answer:

Let $n = 1$, $S_1 = \frac{1}{1 \cdot 2} = \frac{1}{2}$.

For $n = k$, assume $S_k = \frac{k}{k+1}$ is true.

For $n = k + 1$ show $S_{k+1} = \frac{k+1}{k+2}$.

$$S_{k+1} = \left[\frac{1}{1 \cdot 2} + \frac{1}{2 \cdot 3} + \frac{1}{3 \cdot 4} + \cdots + \frac{1}{k(k+1)}\right] + \frac{1}{(k+1)(k+2)}$$

$$= S_k + \frac{1}{(k+1)(k+2)}$$

$$= \frac{k}{k+1} + \frac{1}{(k+1)(k+2)}$$

$$= \frac{k^2 + 2k + 1}{(k+1)(k+2)}$$

$$= \frac{(k+1)^2}{(k+1)(k+2)}$$

$$= \frac{k+1}{k+2}$$

So, the formula is valid.

Difficulty: 2

23. Use mathematical induction to prove

$$.6 + 11 + 16 + 21 + \cdots + (5n + 1) = \frac{n(7 + 5n)}{2}.$$

Answer:

For $n = 1$, $S_1 = \frac{1(7 + 5)}{2} = 6$.

For $n = k$, assume $S_k = \frac{k(7 + 5k)}{2}$ is true.

For $n = k + 1$ show $S_{k+1} = \frac{(k + 1)(5k + 12)}{2}$.

$$S_{k+1} = [6 + 11 + 16 + \cdots + (5k + 1) + [5(k + 1) + 1]$$

$$= S_k + (5k + 6)$$

$$= \frac{k(7 + 5k)}{2} + (5k + 6)$$

$$= \frac{7k + 5k^2}{2} + \frac{10k + 12}{2}$$

$$= \frac{5k^2 + 17k + 12}{2}$$

$$= \frac{(k + 1)(5k + 12)}{2}$$

So, the formula is valid.

Difficulty: 2

24. Use mathematical induction to prove

$$-3 + 1 + 5 + 9 + 13 + \cdots + (4n - 7) = n(2n - 5).$$

Answer:
For $n = 1$, $S_1 = -3 = 1(2 - 5) = -3$.

For $n = k$, assume $S_k = k(2k - 5)$.

For $n = k + 1$ show $S_{k+1} = (k + 1)(2k - 3)$.

$$S_{k+1} = -3 + 1 + 5 + 9 + 13 + \ldots + (4k - 7) + (4k - 3)$$

$$= S_k + (4k - 3)$$

$$= k(2k - 5) + (4k - 3)$$

$$= 2k^2 - k - 3$$

$$= (k + 1)(2k - 3)$$

So, the formula is valid.

Difficulty: 2

25. Use mathematical induction to prove $n < 3^n$ for all positive integers n.

Answer:
For $n = 1$, $1 < 3$.

For $n = k$, assume $k < 3^k$.

For $n = k + 1$, show $k + 1 < 3^{k+1}$.

$$k < 3^k$$

$$k + 1 < 3^k + 1 < 3^k + 3^k$$

$$k + 1 < 2(3^k) < 3(3^k)$$

$$k + 1 < 3^{k+1}$$

So, $n < 3^n$ for $n \geq 1$.

Difficulty: 2

26. Use mathematical induction to prove

$$\frac{1}{2} + \frac{1}{4} + \frac{1}{8} + \cdots + \frac{1}{2^n} < 1 \text{ for } n \geq 1.$$

Answer:

For $n = 1$, $\frac{1}{2} < 1$.

For $n = k$, assume $\frac{1}{2} + \frac{1}{4} + \frac{1}{8} + \cdots + \frac{1}{2^k} < 1$

For $n = k + 1$ show $\frac{1}{2} + \frac{1}{4} + \frac{1}{8} + \cdots + \frac{1}{2^k} + \frac{1}{2^{k+1}} < 1$ is true.

$$\frac{1}{2} + \frac{1}{4} + \frac{1}{8} + \cdots + \frac{1}{2^k} < 1$$

$$\frac{1}{2}\left[\frac{1}{2} + \frac{1}{4} + \frac{1}{8} + \cdots + \frac{1}{2^k}\right] < \frac{1}{2} \cdot 1$$

$$\frac{1}{4} + \frac{1}{8} + \frac{1}{16} + \cdots + \frac{1}{2^{k+1}} < \frac{1}{2}$$

$$\frac{1}{2} + \frac{1}{4} + \frac{1}{8} + \cdots + \frac{1}{2^{k+1}} < \frac{1}{2} + \frac{1}{2}$$

$$\frac{1}{2} + \frac{1}{2} + \frac{1}{8} + \cdots + \frac{1}{2^{k+1}} < 1$$

So, $\frac{1}{2} + \frac{1}{4} + \cdots + \frac{1}{2^n} < 1$ for $n \geq 1$.

Difficulty: 2

27. Use mathematical induction to prove

$$\frac{1}{3}+\frac{1}{9}+\frac{1}{27}+\cdots+\frac{1}{3^n}<1 \text{ for } n \ge 1.$$

Answer:

For $n = 1$, $\frac{1}{3} < 1$.

For $n = k$, assume $\frac{1}{3}+\frac{1}{9}+\frac{1}{27}+\cdots+\frac{1}{3^k}<1$ is true.

For $n = k + 1$ show $\frac{1}{3}+\frac{1}{9}+\frac{1}{27}+\cdots+\frac{1}{3^k}+\frac{1}{3^{k+1}}<1$.

$$\frac{1}{3}+\frac{1}{9}+\frac{1}{27}+\cdots+\frac{1}{3^k}<1$$

$$\frac{1}{3}\left[\frac{1}{3}+\frac{1}{9}+\frac{1}{27}+\cdots+\frac{1}{3^k}\right]<\frac{1}{3}\cdot 1$$

$$\frac{1}{9}+\frac{1}{27}+\frac{1}{81}+\cdots+\frac{1}{3^{k+1}}<\frac{1}{3}$$

$$\frac{1}{3}+\frac{1}{9}+\frac{1}{27}+\frac{1}{81}+\cdots+\frac{1}{3^{k+1}}<\frac{2}{3}<1$$

So, $\frac{1}{3}+\frac{1}{9}+\frac{1}{27}+\cdots+\frac{1}{3^n}<1$ for $n \ge 1$.

Difficulty: 2

28. Find a quadratic model for the sequence with the indicated terms.

$a_0 = 1$, $a_1 = 5$, $a_2 = 13$

Answer:

$a_n = 2n^2 + 2n + 1$

Difficulty: 1

29. Find a quadratic model for the sequence with the indicated terms.

$a_0 = -1$, $a_1 = \frac{3}{2}$, $a_2 = 8$

Answer:

$a_n = 2n^2 + \frac{1}{2}n - 1$

Difficulty: 1

30. Find a quadratic model for the sequence with the indicated terms.
$a_0 = -2,\ a_1 = 5,\ a = 22$

Answer:

$a_n = 5n^2 + 2n - 2$
Difficulty: 1

MULTIPLE CHOICE

31. Determine whether the sequence has a linear model, quadratic model or neither.
$a_1 = 2,\ a_n = a_{n-1} + n$
a) Linear b) Quadratic c) Neither

Answer: b Difficulty: 1

32. Determine whether the sequence has a linear model, quadratic model or neither.
$a_1 = 4,\ a_n = 2a_{n-1} + 3$
a) Linear b) Quadratic c) Neither

Answer: a Difficulty: 1

33. Determine whether the sequence has a linear model, quadratic model or neither.
$a_1 = 2,\ a_n = (a_{n-1})^3$
a) Linear b) Quadratic c) Neither

Answer: c Difficulty: 1

34. Determine whether the sequence has a linear model, quadratic model or neither.
$a_1 = 1,\ a_n = 2a_{n-1} + n$
a) Linear b) Quadratic c) Neither

Answer: c Difficulty: 1

35. Determine whether the sequence has a linear model, quadratic model or neither.
$a_1 = 4,\ a_n = a_{n-1} - n$
a) Linear b) Quadratic c) Neither

Answer: b Difficulty: 1

Chapter 095: The Binomial Theorem

MULTIPLE CHOICE

1. Evaluate: ${}_{12}C_{10}$.
   a) $\frac{1}{66}$ b) 66 c) 132 d) $\frac{1}{120}$ e) None of these

   Answer: b Difficulty: 1

2. Evaluate: ${}_{10}C_3$.
   a) 1000 b) 604,800 c) 720 d) 120 e) None of these

   Answer: d Difficulty: 1

3. Evaluate: ${}_{17}C_{14}$.
   a) 5.9×10^{13} b) 842,771 c) 4080 d) 680 e) None of these

   Answer: d Difficulty: 1

SHORT ANSWER

4. Evaluate: ${}_{12}C_9$.

   Answer: 220 Difficulty: 1

5. Evaluate: ${}_{45}C_2$.

   Answer: 990 Difficulty: 1

MULTIPLE CHOICE

6. Evaluate: ${}_6C_2$.
   a) 15 b) 30 c) 360 d) 12 e) None of these

   Answer: a Difficulty: 1

7. Evaluate: ${}_9C_7$.
   a) 181,440 b) 63 c) 72 d) 36 e) None of these

   Answer: d Difficulty: 1

8. Evaluate: ${}_8C_5$.
   a) 40 b) 336 c) 56 d) 6720 e) None of these

   Answer: c Difficulty: 1

9. Evaluate: ${}_9C_5$.
   a) 15,120 b) 126 c) 3024 d) 45 e) None of these

   Answer: b Difficulty: 1

10. Evaluate: ${}_6C_4$.

a) 24 b) 15 c) 30 d) 360 e) None of these

Answer: b Difficulty: 1

11. Evaluate: ${}_7C_4$.

a) 35 b) 28 c) 210 d) 840 e) None of these

Answer: a Difficulty: 1

12. Use the Binomial Theorem to expand then simplify: $(x - 3)^5$.
a) $x^5 - 15x^4 + 30x^3 - 30x^2 + 15x - 243$
b) $x^5 - 15x^4 + 900x^3 - 27{,}000x^2 + 50{,}625x - 243$
c) $x^5 - 15x^4 + 90x^3 - 270x^2 + 405x - 243$
d) $x^5 - 3x^4 + 9x^3 - 27x^2 + 81x - 243$
e) None of these

Answer: c Difficulty: 1

13. Use the Binomial Theorem to expand, then simplify: $(2x - 3)^3$.
a) $8x^3 - 324x^2 + 324x - 27$ b) $8x^3 - 36x^2 + 54x - 27$
c) $2x^3 - 18x^2 + 54x - 27$ d) $8x^3 - 12x^2 + 27x - 27$
e) None of these

Answer: b Difficulty: 1

14. Use the Binomial Theorem to expand, then simplify: $(3 - 2x)^3$.
a) $27 - 3x + 3x^2 - 8x^3$ b) $27 - 9x + 9x^2 - 8x^3$
c) $27 - 27x + 6x^2 - 8x^3$ d) $27 - 54x + 36x^2 - 8x^3$
e) None of these

Answer: d Difficulty: 1

15. Use Pascal's Triangle to evaluate the complex number $(2 - i)^4$.
a) 17 b) $-7 - 24i$ c) $13 + 6i$
d) 15 e) None of these

Answer: b Difficulty: 1

16. Use the Binomial Theorem to expand, then simplify: $(i - 1)^4$.
a) $4 - 8i$ b) $-4 - 8i$ c) -4
d) 6 e) None of these

Answer: c Difficulty: 1

17. Use the Binomial Theorem to expand, then simplify: $(i - 2)^4$.
a) $-24 + 9i$ b) $7 + 16i$ c) $31 - 40i$
d) $-7 - 24i$ e) None of these

Answer: d Difficulty: 1

SHORT ANSWER

18. Use Pascal's Triangle to expand $(x - 2y)^4$.

    Answer:

    $x^4 - 8x^3y + 24x^2y^2 - 32xy^3 + 16y^4$

    Difficulty: 1

MULTIPLE CHOICE

19. Use Pascal's Triangle to expand $(2x - y)^3$.
    a) $2x^3 - 6x^2y + 6xy^2 - y^3$
    b) $8x^3 - 4x^2y + 2xy^2 - y^3$
    c) $2x^3 + 3x^2y + 3xy^2 + y^3$
    d) $8x^3 - 12x^2y + 6xy^2 - y^3$
    e) None of these

    Answer: d Difficulty: 1

20. Use Pascal's Triangle to expand $(x + 3y)^3$.
    a) $x^3 + 6x^2y + 6xy^2 + 9y^3$
    b) $x^3 - 3x^2y + 6xy^2 - 27y^3$
    c) $x^3 + 9x^2y + 27xy^2 + 27y^3$
    d) $x^3 + 9x^2y + 9xy^2 + 3y^3$
    e) None of these

    Answer: c Difficulty: 1

21. Use Pascal's Triangle to expand $(3x + y)^4$.
    a) $81x^4 + 108x^3y + 54x^2y^2 + 12xy^3 + y^4$
    b) $3x^4 + 12x^3y + 18x^2y^2 + 12xy^3 + y^4$
    c) $81x^4 + 1728x^3y + 324x^2y^2 + 12xy^3 + y^4$
    d) $3x^4 - 12x^3y + 324x^2y^2 + 12xy^3 - y^4$
    e) None of these

    Answer: a Difficulty: 1

22. Use Pascal's Triangle to expand $(5x + 2y)^3$.
    a) $125x^3 + 450x^2y + 60xy^2 + 8y^3$
    b) $125x^3 + 150x^2y + 60xy^2 + 8y^3$
    c) $125x^3 + 50x^2y + 20xy^2 + 8y^3$
    d) $5x^3 + 60x^2y + 30xy^2 + 2y^2$
    e) None of these

    Answer: b Difficulty: 1

23. Use Pascal's Triangle to expand $(2x + y)^5$.
    a) $32x^5 + 16x^4y + 8x^3y^2 + 4x^2y^3 + 2xy^4 + y^5$
    b) $32x^5 + 80x^4y + 80x^3y^2 + 40x^2y^3 + 10xy^4 + y^5$
    c) $2x^5 + 10x^4y + 20x^3y^2 + 20x^2y^3 + 10xy^4 + y^5$
    d) $32x^5 + 10{,}000x^4y + 8{,}000x^3y^2 + 400x^2y^3 + 10xy^4 + y^5$
    e) None of these

    Answer: b Difficulty: 1

24. Use Pascal's Triangle to expand $(2a - b)^3$.
a) $8a^3 - 4a^2b + 2ab^2 - b^3$
b) $8a^3 + 12a^2b + 6ab^2 + b^3$
c) $8a^3 - 12a^2b + 6ab^2 - b^3$
d) $8a^3 - b^3$
e) None of these

Answer: c Difficulty: 1

25. Use Pascal's Triangle to expand $(3x + y)^3$.
a) $27x^3 + 27x^2y + 9xy^2 + y^3$
b) $27x^3 + 27x^2y + 9xy^2 - y^3$
c) $27x^3 + 9x^2y + 3xy^2 + y^3$
d) $27x^3 + y^3$
e) None of these

Answer: a Difficulty: 1

26. Find the coefficient of x^4y^3 in the expansion of $(x + 2y)^7$.
a) 35 b) 8 c) 1,680 d) 280 e) None of these

Answer: d Difficulty: 1

SHORT ANSWER

27. Find the coefficient of x^4y^3 in the expansion of $(2x + y)^7$.

Answer: 560 Difficulty: 1

MULTIPLE CHOICE

28. Find the coefficient of x^5y^7 in the expansion of $(5x + 2y)^{12}$.
a) 316,800,000
b) 400,000
c) 792
d) 7920
e) None of these

Answer: a Difficulty: 1

29. Find the coefficient of x^3y^5 in the expansion of $(3x + 2y)^8$.
a) 336
b) 48,384
c) 864
d) 52,488
e) None of these

Answer: b Difficulty: 1

30. Find the coefficient of x^2y^7 in the expansion of $(3x - 2y)^9$.
a) -1152
b) 1152
c) 41,472
d) -41,472
e) None of these

Answer: d Difficulty: 1

SHORT ANSWER

31. Find the coefficient of the x^2y^7 in the expansion of $(7x - 2y)^9$.

Answer: -225,792 Difficulty: 1

32. Find the 4th term in the expansion: $\left(\frac{1}{4} + \frac{3}{4}\right)^5$.

Answer:
$\frac{135}{512}$

Difficulty: 1

MULTIPLE CHOICE

33. Find the 5th term in the expansion: $\left(\frac{1}{3} + \frac{2}{3}\right)^5$.

a) $\frac{120}{243}$ b) $\frac{16}{243}$ c) $\frac{80}{243}$ d) $\frac{32}{243}$ e) None of these

Answer: c Difficulty: 1

34. Find the 4th term in the expansion: $(0.2 + 0.8)^5$.
a) 0.0064 b) 0.4096 c) 0.0512 d) 0.2048 e) None of these

Answer: d Difficulty: 1

35. Find the sum of the first 3 terms in the expansion of $(1 + 0.03)^7$.
a) 1.2289 b) 1.2299 c) 1.1935 d) 1.2415 e) None of these

Answer: a Difficulty: 1

36. Find the sum of the first 3 terms in the expansion of $(1 + 0.02)^7$.
a) 1.1260 b) 1.1487 c) 1.1484 d) 1.1540 e) None of these

Answer: c Difficulty: 1

37. Find the sum of the first 3 terms in the expansion of $(3 + 0.02)^7$.
a) 2291.1240 b) 2291.1012 c) 2275.9380
d) 2291.1141 e) None of these

Answer: b Difficulty: 1

SHORT ANSWER

38. Use a graphing utility to graph f and g on the same viewing window. What is the relationship between the two graphs? Use the Binomial Theorem to write g in standard form.

$$f(x) = x^3 - 2x \qquad g(x) = f(x + 3)$$

Answer:
g is a horizontal translation of f 3 units to the left;

$$g(x) = x^3 + 9x^2 + 27x + 27 - 2x - 6$$
$$= x^3 + 9x^2 + 25x + 21$$

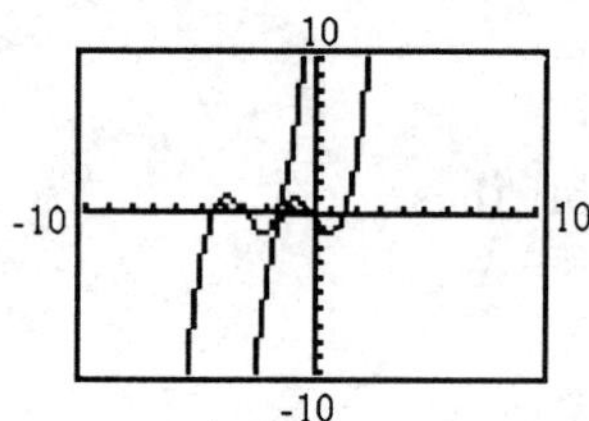

Difficulty: 2 Key 1: T

39. Use a graphing utility to graph f and g on the same viewing window. What is the relationship between the two graphs? Use the Binomial Theorem to write g in standard form.

$$f(x) = x^3 - 2x^2 \qquad g(x) = f(x - 1)$$

Answer:
g is a horizontal translation of f 1 unit to the right;

$$g(x) = x^3 - 3x^2 + 3x - 1 - 2(x^2 - 2x + 1)$$
$$= x^3 - 5x^2 + 7x - 3$$

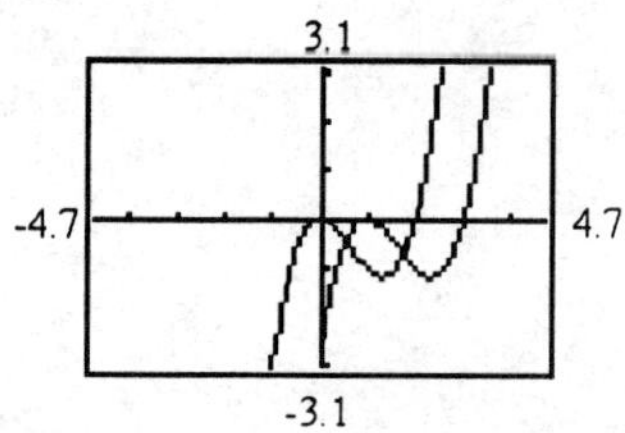

Difficulty: 2 Key 1: T

40. Use the Binomial Theorem to expand and simplify: $\left(\sqrt{x} + 2\right)^3$.

Answer:
$x^{3/2} + 6x + 12x^{1/2} + 8 = x\sqrt{x} + 6x + 12\sqrt{x} + 8$
Difficulty: 1

41. Use the Binomial Theorem to expand and simplify: $\left(\sqrt[3]{x} - 2\right)^3$.

Answer:
$x - 6x^{2/3} + 12x^{1/3} - 8 = x - 6\sqrt[3]{x^2} + 12\sqrt[3]{x} - 8$
Difficulty: 1

42. Use the Binomial Theorem to expand and simplify: $(2\sqrt{y} - 3)^4$.

Answer:
$16y^2 + 96y^{3/2} + 196y + 216y^{1/2} + 81$
$= 16y^2 + 96y\sqrt{y} + 196y + 216\sqrt{y} + 81$
Difficulty: 1

43. Use the Binomial Theorem to expand and simplify: $(2\sqrt{t} - \sqrt{x})^3$.

Answer:
$8t^{3/2} - 12tx^{1/2} + 6t^{1/2} - x^{3/2} = 8t\sqrt{t} - 12t\sqrt{x} + 6x\sqrt{t} - x\sqrt{x}$
Difficulty: 1

Chapter 096: Counting Principles

MULTIPLE CHOICE

1. Evaluate: ${}_{10}P_6$.
   a) 5040 b) 151,200 c) 210 d) 60 e) None of these

   Answer: b Difficulty: 1

2. Evaluate: ${}_{14}P_4$.
   a) 24,024 b) 8008 c) 5040 d) 720 e) None of these

   Answer: a Difficulty: 1

3. Evaluate: ${}_{7}P_4$.
   a) 840 b) 35 c) 10,920 d) 210 e) None of these

   Answer: a Difficulty: 1

4. Evaluate: ${}_{20}P_3$.
   a) 1140 b) 116,280 c) 6840 d) 4.05×10^{17} e) None of these

   Answer: c Difficulty: 1

5. Evaluate: ${}_{7}P_2$.
   a) 2520 b) 210 c) 21 d) 42 e) None of these

   Answer: d Difficulty: 1

6. Evaluate: ${}_{14}P_3$.
   a) 1.45×10^{10} b) 24,024 c) 2184 d) 364 e) None of these

   Answer: c Difficulty: 1

7. Find the number of distinguishable ways the letters LETTERFILE can be arranged.
   a) 3,628,800 b) 1024 c) 151,200 d) 5040 e) None of these

   Answer: c Difficulty: 1

SHORT ANSWER

8. Find the number of distinguishable ways the letters MISSISSIPPI can be arranged.

   Answer: 34,650 Difficulty: 1

MULTIPLE CHOICE

9. Find the number of distinguishable ways the letters OKEECHOBEE can be arranged.
   a) 75,600 b) 3,628,800 c) 151,200
   d) 1,814,400 e) None of these

   Answer: a Difficulty: 1

10. Find the number of distinguishable permutations using the letters in the word ARKANSAS.
    a) 40,320 b) 13,440 c) 6720 d) 3360 e) None of these

    Answer: d Difficulty: 1

11. Find the number of distinguishable permutations using the letters in the word CALCULATOR.
    a) 3,628,800 b) 43,360 c) 453,600
    d) 907,200 e) None of these

    Answer: c Difficulty: 1

SHORT ANSWER

12. Find the number of distinguishable permutations using the letters in the word MATHEMATICS.

    Answer: 4,989,600 Difficulty: 1

MULTIPLE CHOICE

13. Find the number of distinguishable permutations with the following letters:
    $\{A, A, A, B, B, C, C, C, C\}$.
    a) 2520 b) 1260 c) 362,880 d) 288 e) None of these

    Answer: b Difficulty: 1

14. How many different ways (subject orders) can three algebra books, two trigonometry books and two calculus books be arranged on a shelf?
    a) 5040 b) 210 c) 128 d) 823,543 e) None of these

    Answer: b Difficulty: 1

15. How many different ways (subject order) can seven algebra books, five trigonometry books, and four calculus books be arranged on a shelf?
    a) 140 b) 1,441,440 c) 65,536
    d) 2.1×10^{13} e) None of these

    Answer: b Difficulty: 1

16. An organization consisting of 54 members is going to elect four officers. No person may hold more than one office. How many different outcomes are possible?
    a) 354,294 b) 8,503,056 c) 316,251
    d) 7,590,024 e) None of these

    Answer: d Difficulty: 2

17. An organization consisting of 36 members is going to elect three officers. No person may hold more than one office. How many different outcomes are possible?
    a) 7140 b) 42,840 c) 6.2×10^{40}
    d) 3.7×10^{41} e) None of these

    Answer: b Difficulty: 1

18. How many ways can a ten-question multiple choice test be answered if each question has five possible answers?
a) 50 b) 120 c) 3,628,800 d) 9,765,625 e) None of these

Answer: d Difficulty: 1

19. How many ways can an eight-question multiple choice test be answered if each question has five possible answers?
a) 390,625 b) 4,838,400 c) 40,320 d) 120 e) None of these

Answer: a Difficulty: 1

20. A class of nine students line up single file for lunch. How many different ways can this occur if the six boys in the class must line up first?
a) 18 b) 60,480 c) 4320 d) 504 e) None of these

Answer: c Difficulty: 1

21. A group of nine students line up single file for lunch. How many different ways can this occur if the five boys must line up first?
a) 362,880 b) 2880 c) 15,120 d) 126 e) None of these

Answer: b Difficulty: 1

22. There are 20 girls in a beauty pageant. A queen, a first runner-up and a second runner-up are to be chosen. How many different outcomes are possible?
a) 1140 b) 6840 c) 2.4×10^{18}
d) 4.1×10^{17} e) None of these

Answer: b Difficulty: 1

SHORT ANSWER

23. A group of six students are seated in a single row at a football game. In how many different orders can they be seated?

Answer: 720 Difficulty: 1

MULTIPLE CHOICE

24. The flags of seven different countries are to be displayed in a row. In how many different orders can they be flown?
a) 5040 b) 1258 c) 128 d) 49 e) None of these

Answer: a Difficulty: 1

25. Seven members of a family line up to have their picture taken. In how many different ways can they be arranged?
a) 49 b) 128 c) 5040 d) 1258 e) None of these

Answer: c Difficulty: 1

26. If there are ten questions on a test, how many different versions of the same test can be made by rearranging the questions?
a) 1024 b) 100 c) 30,240 d) 3,628,800 e) None of these

Answer: d Difficulty: 1

27. Eight sailboats are entered in a race. In how many ways can they finish?
a) 6720 b) 256 c) 40,320 d) 1680 e) None of these

Answer: c Difficulty: 1

28. There are seven possible digits in a phone number. How many different phone numbers are possible if the first digit cannot be 0 and no digit can be used more than once?
a) 128 b) 181,440 c) 544,320 d) 5040 e) None of these

Answer: c Difficulty: 1

SHORT ANSWER

29. How many different ways can three chocolate, four strawberry and two butterscotch sundaes be served to nine people?

Answer: 1260 ways Difficulty: 1

MULTIPLE CHOICE

30. A license plate number consists of three letters followed by three digits. How many distinct license plate numbers can be formed?
a) 17,576,000 b) 30,844,800 c) 11,232,000
d) 12,812,904 e) None of these

Answer: a Difficulty: 1

31. If a license plate number consists of two letters followed by two digits, how many different license plate numbers are possible?
a) 58,500 b) 67,600 c) 256 d) 24 e) None of these

Answer: b Difficulty: 1

32. An auto license plate is made using two letters followed by three digits. How many license plates are possible?
a) 676,000 b) 468,000 c) 82 d) 1,757,600 e) None of these

Answer: a Difficulty: 1

SHORT ANSWER

33. A scrabble tray contains the tiles FERSXAI. How many different four-letter arrangements ("words") can be made?

Answer: 840 Difficulty: 1

Chapter 096: Counting Principles

MULTIPLE CHOICE

34. Determine the number of possible 5 digit ZIP codes.
    a) 120 b) 90,000 c) 3,628,800 d) 100,000 e) None of these

    Answer: d Difficulty: 1

SHORT ANSWER

35. A ship has six flags available for signaling. If a signal consists of hoisting three of the flags, how many different signals are possible?

    Answer: 120 Difficulty: 1

MULTIPLE CHOICE

36. A random number generator selects an integer from 1 to 20. Find the number of ways in which a number that is a multiple of three can be selected.
    a) 6 b) 720 c) 5 d) 120 e) None of these

    Answer: a Difficulty: 1

37. A random number generator selects two integers from 1 to 20. Find the number of ways that the sum of these two integers is 8.
    a) 4 b) 7 c) 9 d) 6 e) None of these

    Answer: b Difficulty: 1

SHORT ANSWER

38. Determine the number of seven digit telephone numbers that can be formed under the condition that each of the first three digits cannot be 0.

    Answer: 7,290,000 Difficulty: 1

MULTIPLE CHOICE

39. How many different three-letter arrangements ("words") can be made from the letters ABCDEFG?
    a) 24 b) 35 c) 840 d) 210 e) None of these

    Answer: d Difficulty: 1

40. A ship has eight flags available for signaling. If a signal consists of hoisting three of the flags, how many different signals are possible?
    a) 1680 b) 336 c) 56 d) 40,320 e) None of these

    Answer: b Difficulty: 1

41. If a special at a diner offers a choice of one each of two appetizers, four entrees and five desserts, how many distinct meals are possible under the special?
a) 20 b) 40 c) 60 d) 80 e) None of these

Answer: b Difficulty: 1

42. If a menu at a diner offers a choice of three appetizers, six entrees and four desserts, how many distinct meals are possible?
a) 72 b) 216 c) 24 d) 103,680 e) None of these

Answer: a Difficulty: 1

43. The chief designer for a large auto company is considering four different radiator grilles, two different headlight styles and five different front fender designs. How many front-end designs can be made using these three characteristics?
a) 80 b) 60 c) 40 d) 20 e) None of these

Answer: c Difficulty: 1

44. If a woman's wardrobe consists of two jackets, three skirts, and five blouses, how many different outfits consisting of a jacket, skirt, and blouse can be made?
a) 1440 b) 10 c) 90 d) 30 e) None of these

Answer: d Difficulty: 1

45. In how many ways can a subcommittee of five people be selected from a committee of ten people?
a) 252 b) 30,240 c) 6048 d) 1260 e) None of these

Answer: a Difficulty: 1

SHORT ANSWER

46. A record club offers new customers six free selections from a list of 130 different recordings. How many different introductory offers are possible?

Answer:
$$\frac{130!}{6!124!} = 5,963,412,000$$
Difficulty: 1

MULTIPLE CHOICE

47. In how many ways can a subcommittee of six people be selected from a committee of 12 people?
a) 665,280 b) 924 c) 720 d) 520 e) None of these

Answer: b Difficulty: 1

48. In how many ways can a subcommittee of nine people be selected from a group of 12 people?
a) 1320 b) 79,833,600 c) 362,880 d) 220 e) None of these

Answer: d Difficulty: 1

SHORT ANSWER

49. How many ways can four girls be picked from a group of 30 girls?

Answer: 27,405 Difficulty: 1

MULTIPLE CHOICE

50. A committee composed of three math majors and four science majors is to be selected from a group of 20 math majors and 16 science majors. How many different committees can be formed?
a) 2,074,800 b) 6840 c) 4.05×10^{17}
d) 320 e) None of these

Answer: a Difficulty: 2

51. A band director is taking auditions for a special pep band which requires three trumpets, one trombone, one saxophone, and two clarinets. There were five trumpet players, four trombone players, three saxophone players and 10 clarinet players who came to audition. How many possible combinations does the band director have?
a) 100 b) 600 c) 5400 d) 32,400 e) None of these

Answer: c Difficulty: 2

SHORT ANSWER

52. In how many ways can a committee consisting of two deacons and four regular church members be formed in a church that has five deacons and 120 regular members?

Answer: 82,145,700 Difficulty: 1

MULTIPLE CHOICE

53. A small college needs four additional faculty members: a mathematician, two chemists, and an engineer. In how many ways can these positions be filled if there are two applicants for mathematics, six applicants for chemistry and three applicants for engineering?
a) 180 b) 330 c) 90 d) 36 e) None of these

Answer: c Difficulty: 2

54. In how many ways can a committee of two boys and three girls be formed from a group of 10 boys and 12 girls?
a) 9900 b) 1320 c) 118,800 d) 265 e) None of these

Answer: a Difficulty: 1

55. In how many ways can a committee of three boys and three girls be formed from a group of 10 boys and 12 girls?
a) 340 b) 2040 c) 26,400 d) 960,400 e) None of these

Answer: c Difficulty: 1

56. In how many ways can a committee of two boys and four girls be formed from a group of six boys and nine girls?
a) 141 b) 90,720 c) 3054 d) 1890 e) None of these

Answer: d Difficulty: 1

57. Find the number of diagonals in a heptagon (7-sided polygon). A line segment connecting any two nonadjacent vertices is called a diagonal of the polygon.
a) 21 b) 14 c) 35 d) 28 e) None of these

Answer: b Difficulty: 2

58. Find the number of diagonals in a nonagon (9-sided polygon). A line segment connecting any two nonadjacent vertices is called a diagonal of the polygon.
a) 56 b) 36 c) 27 d) 18 e) None of these

Answer: c Difficulty: 2

Chapter 097: Probability

MULTIPLE CHOICE

1. Determine the sample space: "A number is chosen at random from the numbers one to five inclusive."
   a) {2, 3, 4} b) {1} c) $\left\{\frac{1}{5}\right\}$
   d) {1, 2, 3, 4, 5} e) None of these

   Answer: d Difficulty: 1

2. Determine the sample space: "A letter is selected from the word MATHEMATICS."
   a) {1} b) $\left\{\frac{1}{11}\right\}$ c) (M, A, T, H, E, M, A, T, I, C, S)
   d) {M, A, T, H, E, I, C, S} e) None of these

   Answer: d Difficulty: 1

3. Determine the sample space: "A letter is selected from the word FINITE."
   a) {F, I, N, T, E} b) {1} c) {F, I, N, I, T, E}
   d) $\left\{\frac{1}{6}\right\}$ e) None of these

   Answer: a Difficulty: 1

4. Determine the sample space: "A ball is selected from a bag containing seven balls, numbered from 1 to 7."
   a) The ball numbered 3 b) $\left\{\frac{1}{7}\right\}$ c) The set of 7 balls
   d) The balls numbered 3, 4 and 7 e) None of these

   Answer: c Difficulty: 1

5. A card is drawn at random from a standard deck of 52 playing cards. Find the probability that the card is a spade.
   a) $\frac{1}{13}$ b) $\frac{1}{4}$ c) $\frac{12}{13}$ d) $\frac{3}{4}$ e) None of these

   Answer: b Difficulty: 1

6. A card is drawn at random from a standard deck of 52 playing cards. Find the probability that the card is a 10 or an ace.
   a) $\frac{2}{13}$ b) $\frac{1}{169}$ c) $\frac{4}{13}$ d) $\frac{1}{4}$ e) None of these

   Answer: a Difficulty: 1

7. A card is drawn at random from a standard deck of 52 playing cards. Find the probability that the card is an ace or spade.
   a) $\frac{17}{52}$ b) $\frac{4}{13}$ c) $\frac{1}{52}$ d) $\frac{2}{13}$ e) None of these

   Answer: b Difficulty: 1

8. Two cards are randomly selected from a standard deck of 52 playing cards. Find the probability that one card will be an ace and the other will be a 10.
   a) $\frac{1}{52}$ b) $\frac{8}{663}$ c) $\frac{1}{169}$ d) $\frac{2}{13}$ e) None of these

   Answer: c Difficulty: 1

9. Find the probability of choosing an E when selecting a letter at random from those in the word COLLEGE.
   a) $\frac{2}{7}$ b) $\frac{1}{5}$ c) $\frac{2}{5}$ d) $\frac{1}{7}$ e) None of these

   Answer: a Difficulty: 1

10. Find the probability of choosing an A, B, or N when selecting a letter at random from those in the word BANANA.
    a) $\frac{1}{26}$ b) 0 c) 1 d) $\frac{1}{2}$ e) None of these

    Answer: c Difficulty: 1

SHORT ANSWER

11. In a group of 10 children, 3 have blond hair and 7 have brown hair. If a child is chosen at random, what is the probability that the child will have brown hair?

    Answer:
    $\frac{7}{10}$

    Difficulty: 1

MULTIPLE CHOICE

12. A bag contains four red balls and seven white balls. If a ball is drawn at random, what is the probability that it is a red ball?
    a) $\frac{1}{4}$ b) $\frac{4}{7}$ c) $\frac{1}{11}$ d) $\frac{4}{11}$ e) None of these

    Answer: d Difficulty: 1

13. A bag contains nine red balls and six white balls. If one ball is drawn at random from the bag, what is the probability that it is a red ball?
a) $\frac{1}{9}$ b) $\frac{3}{5}$ c) $\frac{2}{5}$ d) $\frac{3}{2}$ e) None of these

Answer: b Difficulty: 1

14. A bag contains nine red balls numbered 1 - 9 and six white balls numbered 10 - 15. If one ball is drawn at random, what is the probability that the number on it is even?
a) $\frac{3}{5}$ b) $\frac{7}{15}$ c) $\frac{4}{15}$ d) $\frac{1}{5}$ e) None of these

Answer: b Difficulty: 1

15. A bag contains nine red balls numbered 1 - 9 and six white balls numbered 10 - 15. If one ball is drawn at random, what is the probability that the number on it is divisible by three?
a) $\frac{1}{3}$ b) $\frac{1}{2}$ c) $\frac{2}{3}$ d) $\frac{2}{5}$ e) None of these

Answer: a Difficulty: 1

16. A bag contains nine red balls numbered 1 - 9 and six white balls numbered 10 - 15. If one ball is drawn at random, what is the probability that the number on it is divisible by five?
a) 3 b) $\frac{2}{3}$ c) $\frac{3}{5}$ d) $\frac{1}{5}$ e) None of these

Answer: d Difficulty: 1

17. A die is tossed 3 times. What is the probability that a two will come up all three times?
a) $\frac{1}{172}$ b) $\frac{1}{18}$ c) $\frac{1}{120}$ d) $\frac{1}{216}$ e) None of these

Answer: d Difficulty: 1

18. What is the probability of drawing a white marble from a box containing six white, three red and five black marbles?
a) $\frac{1}{6}$ b) $\frac{1}{14}$ c) $\frac{3}{7}$ d) $\frac{1}{15}$ e) None of these

Answer: c Difficulty: 1

SHORT ANSWER

19. A fair coin is tossed four times. What is the probability of getting heads on all four tosses?

Answer:
$\frac{1}{16}$

Difficulty: 1

MULTIPLE CHOICE

20. A fair coin is tossed four times. What is the probability of getting a head on the first toss and tails on the other three tosses?
a) $\frac{1}{8}$ b) $\frac{1}{16}$ c) $\frac{1}{12}$ d) $\frac{3}{16}$ e) None of these

Answer: b Difficulty: 1

21. A fair coin is tossed four times. What is the probability of getting exactly one head?
a) $\frac{1}{2}$ b) $\frac{1}{4}$ c) $\frac{1}{8}$ d) $\frac{1}{16}$ e) None of these

Answer: b Difficulty: 1

22. Two six-sided dice are tossed. What is the probability that the total is 11?
a) $\frac{1}{18}$ b) $\frac{1}{6}$ c) $\frac{1}{8}$ d) $\frac{2}{15}$ e) None of these

Answer: a Difficulty: 1

23. Two integers from 0 to 9 inclusive are chosen by a random number generator. What is the probability of choosing the number 2 both times?
a) $\frac{1}{10}$ b) $\frac{1}{100}$ c) $\frac{1}{50}$ d) $\frac{4}{5}$ e) None of these

Answer: b Difficulty: 1

SHORT ANSWER

24. Two integers between 1 and 40 inclusive are chosen by a random number generator. What is the probability that both numbers chosen are divisible by 4?

Answer:
$\frac{1}{16}$

Difficulty: 1

MULTIPLE CHOICE

25. What is the probability that in a group of 6 people at least 2 will have their birthdays within the same week?
a) 0.74 b) 0.50 c) 0.26 d) 0.47 e) None of these

Answer: c Difficulty: 2

SHORT ANSWER

26. What is the probability that 2 people chosen at random from a group of 8 married couples are married to each other?

Answer:
$\frac{1}{15}$

Difficulty: 1

27. There are 5 red and 4 black balls in a box. If 3 balls are picked without replacement, what is the probability that at least one of them is red?

Answer:
$\frac{20}{21}$

Difficulty: 1

MULTIPLE CHOICE

28. A box holds 12 white, 5 red, and 6 black marbles. If 2 marbles are picked at random, without replacement, what is the probability that they will both be black?
a) $\frac{36}{529}$ b) $\frac{247}{506}$ c) $\frac{15}{253}$ d) $\frac{6}{23}$ e) None of these

Answer: c Difficulty: 1

29. Five cards are drawn from an ordinary deck of 52 playing cards. What is the probability of getting exactly one ace? Round your answer to three decimal places.
a) 0.060 b) 0.299 c) 0.064 d) 0.341 e) None of these

Answer: b Difficulty: 1

30. Two six-sided dice are tossed. What is the probability that the total is seven?
a) $\frac{1}{2}$ b) $\frac{7}{12}$ c) $\frac{1}{6}$ d) $\frac{1}{3}$ e) None of these

Answer: c Difficulty: 1

31. Two six-sided dice are tossed. What is the probability that the total is nine?
a) $\frac{1}{6}$ b) $\frac{1}{9}$ c) $\frac{1}{8}$ d) $\frac{1}{3}$ e) None of these

Answer: b Difficulty: 1

32. Two six-sided dice are tossed. What is the probability that the total is 12?

a) $\frac{1}{12}$ b) $\frac{1}{18}$ c) $\frac{1}{36}$ d) $\frac{1}{30}$ e) None of these

Answer: c Difficulty: 1

33. Two six-sided dice are tossed. What is the probability that the total is ten?

a) $\frac{1}{12}$ b) $\frac{1}{4}$ c) $\frac{1}{18}$ d) $\frac{1}{8}$ e) None of these

Answer: a Difficulty: 1

34. Two cards are drawn with replacement from a box containing six blue cards numbered 1 - 6 and eleven white cards numbered 7 - 17. What is the probability that both cards are even-numbered?

a) $\frac{64}{289}$ b) $\frac{4}{17}$ c) $\frac{1}{34}$ d) $\frac{7}{34}$ e) None of these

Answer: a Difficulty: 1

35. Two cards are drawn with replacement from a box containing six blue cards numbered 1 - 6 and eleven white cards numbered 7 - 17. What is the probability that the first card is odd-numbered and the second card is white?

a) $\frac{99}{136}$ b) $\frac{99}{272}$ c) $\frac{99}{289}$ d) $\frac{20}{34}$ e) None of these

Answer: c Difficulty: 1

36. Drawing from a standard deck of 52 cards, what is the probability that the card is an eight or a face card?

a) $\frac{3}{169}$ b) $\frac{4}{13}$ c) $\frac{2}{13}$ d) $\frac{1}{48}$ e) None of these

Answer: b Difficulty: 1

37. Drawing from a standard deck of 52 cards, what is the probability that the card is an ace, king or queen?

a) $\frac{3}{13}$ b) $\frac{1}{13}$ c) $\frac{1}{2197}$ d) $\frac{1}{64}$ e) None of these

Answer: a Difficulty: 1

38. Drawing from a standard deck of 52 cards, what is the probability that the card is a five or a red jack?

a) $\frac{1}{13}$ b) $\frac{3}{26}$ c) $\frac{3}{13}$ d) $\frac{1}{238}$ e) None of these

Answer: b Difficulty: 1

39. A small business college has 800 seniors, 700 juniors, 900 sophomores and 1200 freshmen. If a student is randomly selected, what is the probability that the student is a junior or senior?
a) $\frac{13}{36}$ b) $\frac{1}{4}$ c) $\frac{5}{12}$ d) $\frac{5}{162}$ e) None of these

Answer: c Difficulty: 1

40. A small business college has 800 seniors, 700 juniors, 900 sophomores and 1200 freshmen. If a student is randomly selected, what is the probability that the student is a freshman or a senior?
a) $\frac{1}{4}$ b) $\frac{1}{54}$ c) $\frac{5}{12}$ d) $\frac{5}{9}$ e) None of these

Answer: d Difficulty: 1

41. A small business college has 400 seniors, 300 juniors, 500 sophomores and 600 freshmen. If a student is randomly selected, what is the probability that the student is a junior or a senior?
a) $\frac{1}{4}$ b) $\frac{2}{9}$ c) $\frac{7}{18}$ d) $\frac{1}{27}$ e) None of these

Answer: c Difficulty: 1

42. A small business college has 400 seniors, 300 juniors, 500 sophomores and 600 freshmen. If a student is randomly selected, what is the probability that the student is a freshman or a senior?
a) $\frac{2}{27}$ b) $\frac{5}{9}$ c) $\frac{1}{4}$ d) $\frac{5}{18}$ e) None of these

Answer: b Difficulty: 1

43. In drawing one card from a standard deck of 52 playing cards, what is the probability of obtaining a king or a club?
a) $\frac{1}{52}$ b) $\frac{17}{52}$ c) $\frac{4}{13}$ d) $\frac{2}{13}$ e) None of these

Answer: c Difficulty: 1

44. In drawing one card from a standard deck of 52 playing cards, what is the probability of obtaining an ace or a heart?
a) $\frac{4}{13}$ b) $\frac{1}{52}$ c) $\frac{17}{52}$ d) $\frac{2}{13}$ e) None of these

Answer: a Difficulty: 1

45. In drawing one card from a standard deck of 52 playing cards, what is the probability of obtaining a queen or a diamond?
a) $\frac{1}{52}$ b) $\frac{4}{13}$ c) $\frac{1}{26}$ d) $\frac{17}{52}$ e) None of these

Answer: b Difficulty: 1

46. In drawing one card from a standard deck of 52 playing cards, what is the probability that it is a jack or a spade?
a) $\frac{1}{52}$ b) $\frac{17}{52}$ c) $\frac{2}{13}$ d) $\frac{4}{13}$ e) None of these

Answer: d Difficulty: 1

47. In drawing one card from a standard deck of 52 playing cards, what is the probability that it is a diamond or a face card?
a) $\frac{11}{26}$ b) $\frac{17}{52}$ c) $\frac{3}{13}$ d) $\frac{1}{13}$ e) None of these

Answer: a Difficulty: 1

48. Before an election, a sample of 120,000 people throughout the county showed that 79,386 people would vote for Candidate A. If a person from the sample is chosen at random, what is the probability that the person is one of the people who said they would not vote for Candidate A?
a) 0.66 b) 0.34 c) 0.47 d) 0.53 e) None of these

Answer: b Difficulty: 1

49. If the probability of getting a rotten apple in a basket of apples is 12%, what is the probability of getting 3 good apples choosing one from each of three different baskets?
a) 0.9983 b) 0.0017 c) 0.8800 d) 0.6815 e) None of these

Answer: d Difficulty: 1

SHORT ANSWER

50. In an experiment in which 2 six-sided dice are tossed, what is the probability of *not* getting a sum of 10?

Answer:
$\frac{11}{12}$

Difficulty: 1

MULTIPLE CHOICE

51. If $P(A) = \frac{6}{11}$, find $P(A')$.
a) 0 b) 1 c) $\frac{5}{11}$ d) $\frac{5}{6}$ e) None of these

Answer: c Difficulty: 1

52. A "doctored" die is tossed 100,000 times and comes up six on 35,861 rolls. Find the probability of rolling a number other than 6 with this die.
a) 0.36 b) 0.64 c) 0.17 d) 0.83 e) None of these

Answer: b Difficulty: 1

SHORT ANSWER

53. A sample of nursing homes in a state reveals that 112,000 of 218,000 residents are female. If a nursing home resident is chosen at random from this state, what is the probability that the resident is male?

Answer:
$\frac{53}{109}$

Difficulty: 1

MULTIPLE CHOICE

54. There are 120 40-watt bulbs, 200 60-watt bulbs and 80 100-watt bulbs in an art gallery. All of the 60-watt bulbs and half of the 100-watt bulbs are transparent and the rest are not. While installing the bulbs, a worker dropped one of them. What is the probability that the broken bulb was not a transparent 100-watt bulb?
a) $\frac{1}{10}$ b) $\frac{1}{5}$ c) $\frac{9}{10}$ d) $\frac{2}{5}$ e) None of these

Answer: c Difficulty: 1

Chapter 101: Lines

MULTIPLE CHOICE

1. Find the slope of the line with the given inclination θ.
   a) $\frac{\sqrt{3}}{2}$ b) $\sqrt{3}$ c) $\frac{\sqrt{3}}{3}$ d) $\frac{1}{2}$ e) None of these

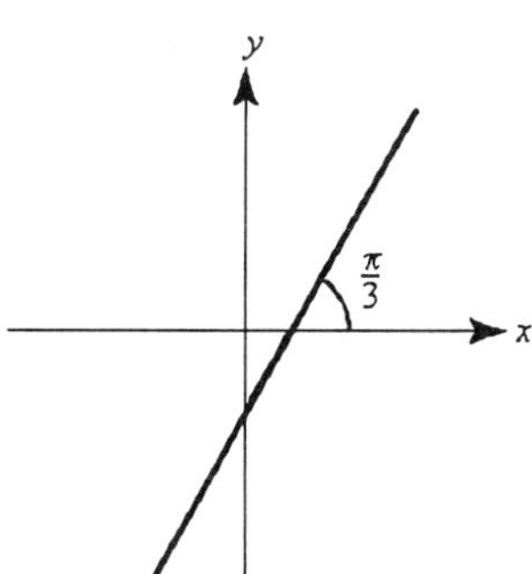

Answer: b Difficulty: 1

2. Find the slope of the line with the given inclination θ.
   a) $-\frac{\sqrt{3}}{2}$ b) $-\frac{1}{2}$ c) $-\sqrt{3}$ d) $-\frac{\sqrt{3}}{3}$ e) None of these

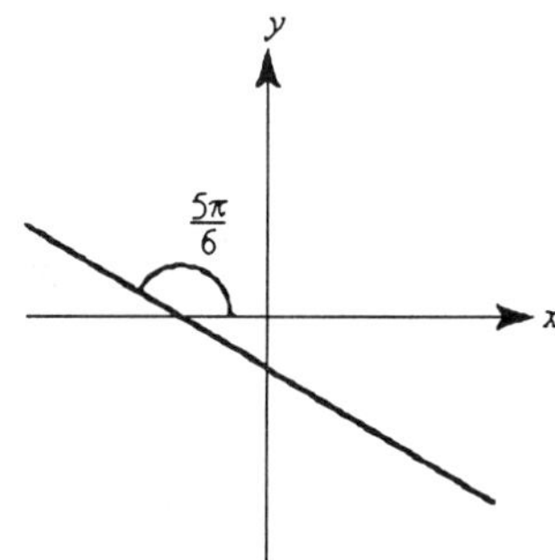

Answer: d Difficulty: 1

3. Find the slope of the line with the given inclination $\theta = 2.19$ radians
   a) -0.814 b) -1.403 c) -0.581 d) 1.403 e) None of these

Answer: b Difficulty: 1

4. Find the inclination, θ, of the line with the given slope $m = 1$.
   a) 135° b) 30° c) 45° d) 1.6° e) None of these

Answer: c Difficulty: 1

5. Find the inclination, θ, of the line with the given slope $m = -\frac{21}{5}$.
   a) 1.337 b) 1.805 c) .234 d) 3.119 e) None of these

Answer: b Difficulty: 1

6. Find the inclination, θ, of the line passing through the points (3, 4) and (-5, 7).
   a) 110.6° b) 20.6° c) 159.4° d) 85.2° e) None of these

   Answer: c Difficulty: 2

7. Find the inclination, θ, of the line passing through the points (2, -10) and (-5, -3).
   a) 2.356 b) 1.077 c) 0.166 d) 0.785 e) None of these

   Answer: a Difficulty: 1

8. Find the inclination, θ, of the line passing through the points (5, 0) and (-5, 5).
   a) 26.6° b) 153.6° c) 63.4° d) 116.6° e) None of these

   Answer: b Difficulty: 1

SHORT ANSWER

9. Find the inclination, θ, of the line: $3x + 2y - 7 = 0$.

   Answer: 2.159 Difficulty: 1

10. Find the inclination, θ, of the line: $7x - 2y - 6 = 0$.

    Answer: 1.293 Difficulty: 1

11. Find the inclination, θ, of the line: $2x - y = 0$.

    Answer: 1.107 Difficulty: 1

MULTIPLE CHOICE

12. Find the angle, θ, between the two lines:

    $3x + y + 6 = 0$

    $x - y - 3 = 0$

    a) 1.107 b) 0.785 c) 0.464 d) 0.927 e) None of these

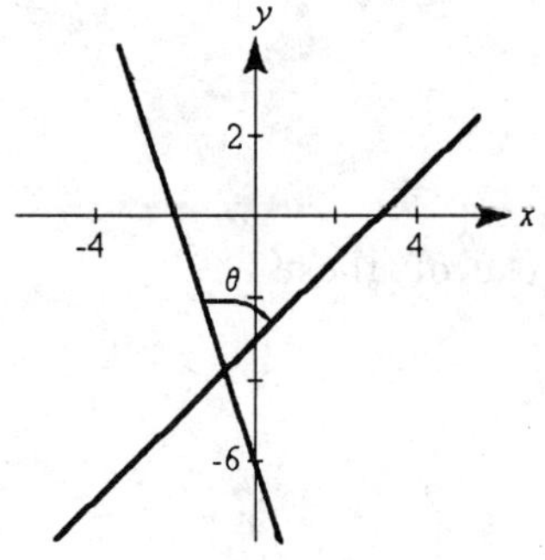

    Answer: a Difficulty: 2

13. Find the angle, θ, between the two lines:

$$x - 3y - 4 = 0$$

$$2x + 5y - 7 = 0$$

a) 0.464 b) 0.059 c) 0.869 d) 0.702 e) None of these

Answer: d Difficulty: 2

14. Find the angle, θ, between the two lines:

$$5x + 3y - 7 = 0$$

$$4x + y + 8 = 0$$

a) 1.361 b) 0.295 c) 0.637 d) 1.180 e) None of these

Answer: b Difficulty: 2

15. Find the angle, θ, between the two lines:

$$7x + 8y - 6 = 0$$

$$2x + 3y - 5 = 0$$

a) 7.5° b) 74.9° c) 26.6° d) 15.1° e) None of these

Answer: a Difficulty: 2

16. Find the angle, θ, between the two lines:

$$0.02x - 0.05y + 0.21 = 0$$

$$0.03x + 0.04y - 0.40 = 0$$

a) 15.1° b) 30.0° c) 58.7° d) 41.5° e) None of these

Answer: c Difficulty: 2

17. Find the distance between the point (0, 0) and the line $6x + 5y + 11 = 0$.

a) $\sqrt{11}$ b) $\dfrac{22\sqrt{61}}{61}$ c) $2\sqrt{11}$ d) $\dfrac{11\sqrt{61}}{61}$ e) None of these

Answer: d Difficulty: 1

18. Find the distance between the point (3, -5) and the line $x + y - 7 = 0$.

a) $\dfrac{9\sqrt{34}}{34}$ b) $\dfrac{5\sqrt{2}}{2}$ c) $\dfrac{9\sqrt{2}}{2}$ d) $\dfrac{-15\sqrt{2}}{2}$ e) None of these

Answer: c Difficulty: 1

19. Find the distance between the point (4, 8) and the line $x - 6 = 0$.

a) 2 b) 10 c) 14 d) 1 e) None of these

Answer: a Difficulty: 1

20. Find the distance between the point (6, -2) and the line $6x + 2y - 12 = 0$.
a) $\sqrt{10}$ b) $\frac{4\sqrt{10}}{5}$ c) 5 d) 10 e) None of these

Answer: a Difficulty: 1

21. Find the distance between the point (1, 6) and the line $5x - 2y = 0$.
a) $\frac{5\sqrt{29}}{29}$ b) $\sqrt{7}$ c) $\frac{7\sqrt{29}}{29}$ d) $\frac{7\sqrt{27}}{27}$ e) None of these

Answer: c Difficulty: 1

22. Find the distance between the parallel lines:

$2x + y - 7 = 0$

$2x + y + 5 = 0$

a) $\frac{19\sqrt{3}}{3}$ b) $\frac{12}{7}$ c) $\frac{14\sqrt{3}}{3}$ d) $\frac{12\sqrt{5}}{5}$ e) None of these

Answer: d Difficulty: 2

23. Find the distance between the parallel lines:

$3x + 2y - 6 = 0$

$3x + 2y + 10 = 0$

a) $\frac{19\sqrt{3}}{13}$ b) $\frac{16\sqrt{13}}{13}$ c) $\frac{16\sqrt{5}}{5}$ d) $\frac{16}{3}$ e) None of these

Answer: b Difficulty: 2

24. Given a triangle with vertices $A = (0, 5)$, $B = (2, 0)$, and $C = (-2, -4)$, find the altitude from vertex B to side AC.
a) $\frac{28\sqrt{85}}{85}$ b) $\frac{\sqrt{5}}{5}$ c) $\frac{6\sqrt{5}}{5}$ d) $3\sqrt{3}$ e) None of these

Answer: a Difficulty: 2

25. Given a triangle with vertices $A = (1, 5)$, $B = (-3, 4)$, and $C = (2, -6)$, find the altitude from vertex A to side BC.
a) $\frac{13\sqrt{5}}{5}$ b) $3\sqrt{3}$ c) 3 d) $\frac{9\sqrt{5}}{5}$ e) None of these

Answer: d Difficulty: 2

26. Given a triangle with vertices $A = (7, 2)$, $B = (0, 7)$, and $C = (-1, -10)$, find the altitude from vertex C to side AB.
a) $\frac{41\sqrt{3}}{2}$ b) $\frac{62\sqrt{74}}{37}$ c) $\frac{17\sqrt{74}}{74}$ d) $\frac{113\sqrt{74}}{74}$ e) None of these

Answer: b Difficulty: 2

27. Given a triangle with vertices $A = (5, 0)$, $B = (0, 10)$, and $C = (-5, 0)$, find the area of the triangle.
a) 50 sq. units b) 100 sq. units c) $10\sqrt{3}$ sq. units
d) $\frac{72}{2}$ sq. units e) None of these

Answer: a Difficulty: 2

28. Given a triangle with vertices $A = (10, 4)$, $B = (0, 0)$, and $C = (0, -4)$, find the area of the triangle.
a) 40 sq. units b) 8 sq. units c) 20 sq. units
d) 16 sq. units e) None of these

Answer: c Difficulty: 2

29. Given a triangle with vertices $A = (7, 2)$, $B = (-7, 4)$, and $C = (-3, -6)$, find the area of the triangle.
a) 246 sq. units b) $\frac{33\sqrt{2}}{5}$ sq. units c) 66 sq. units
d) $\frac{132\sqrt{5}}{5}$ sq. units e) None of these

Answer: c Difficulty: 2

30. Given a triangle with vertices $A = (3, 9)$, $B = (2, 5)$, and $C = (-1, 7)$, find the area of the triangle.
a) $\sqrt{17}$ sq. units b) 7 sq. units c) $\frac{14\sqrt{17}}{17}$ sq. units
d) 14 sq. units e) None of these

Answer: b Difficulty: 2

SHORT ANSWER

31. Find the magnitude of the interior angles.

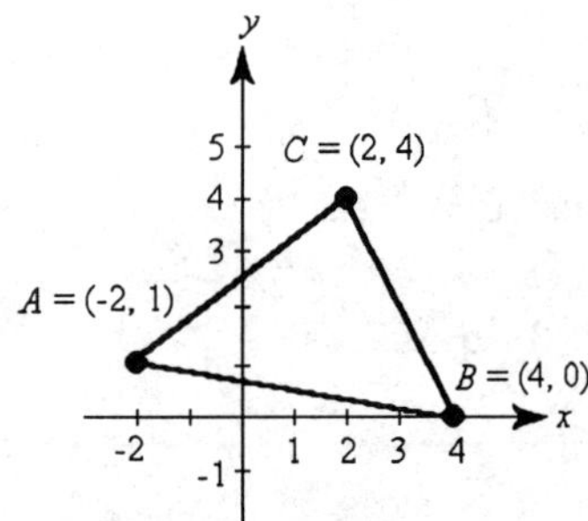

Answer:

$m_{BC} = -2$

$m_{AC} = \frac{3}{4}$

$m_{AB} = -\frac{1}{6}$

$\tan A° = \frac{22}{21} \Rightarrow A° = \arctan \frac{22}{21} = 46.3°$

$\tan B° = \frac{11}{8} \Rightarrow B° = \arctan \frac{11}{8} = 54.0°$

$\tan C° = \frac{11}{2} \Rightarrow C° = \arctan \frac{11}{2} = 79.7°$

Difficulty: 2

32. Find the magnitude of the interior angles.

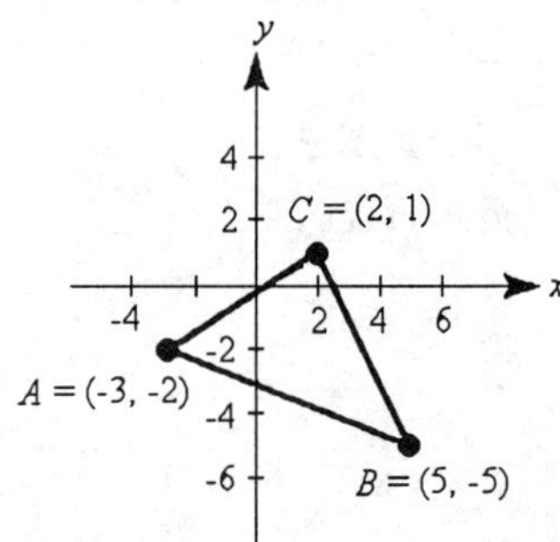

Answer:

$m_{AC} = \frac{3}{5}$

$m_{AB} = -\frac{3}{8}$

$m_{BC} = -2$

$\tan A° = \frac{39}{31} \Rightarrow A° = \arctan \frac{39}{31} = 51.5°$

$\tan B° = \frac{13}{14} \Rightarrow B° = \arctan \frac{13}{14} = 42.9°$

$\tan C° = 13 \Rightarrow C° = \arctan 13 = 85.6°$

Difficulty: 2

33. A straight road rises with an inclination of 7.0° from the horizontal. Find the slope of the road and the change in elevation after driving one quarter of a mile on the road.

Answer:

$$m = \tan 7.0° = 0.1228$$

$$\sin 7.0° = \frac{x}{\frac{1}{4}(5280)} \Rightarrow x \frac{5280}{4}(\sin 7.0°) \approx 161 \text{ ft}$$

Difficulty: 1

34. There is a rise of three feet for every horizontal change of two feet on a roof. Find the inclination of the roof.

Answer:

$m = \frac{3}{2} \Rightarrow \arctan \frac{3}{2} = 56.3°$

Difficulty: 1

35. A 175-foot radio tower is anchored on one side by a guy wire 55 feet from the base of the tower as shown. Find the inclination of the wire.

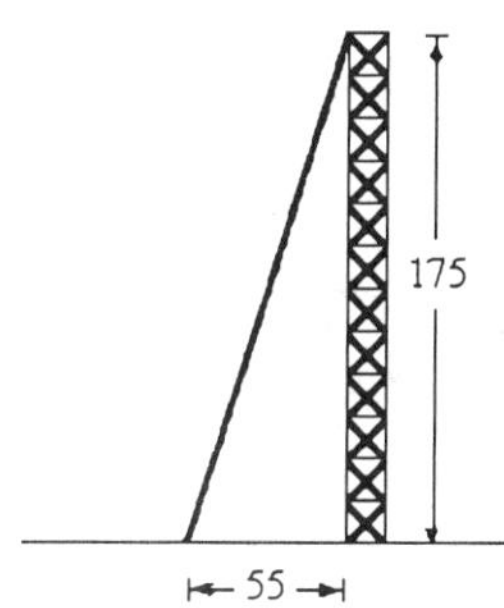

Answer:

$m = \frac{175}{55} \Rightarrow \arctan \frac{175}{55} = 72.6°$

Difficulty: 1

Chapter 102: Introduction to Conics: Parabolas

MULTIPLE CHOICE

1. Find the vertex of the parabola: $x^2 + 4x + 8y - 20 = 0$.
   a) (-2, -3) b) (-2, 16) c) (2, 2)
   d) (2, -3) e) None of these

   Answer: e Difficulty: 1

2. Find the vertex of the parabola: $(x + 3)^2 - 8(y + 6) = 0$.
   a) (3, 6) b) (-3, -6) c) (-3, -4)
   d) (-1, -6) e) None of these

   Answer: b Difficulty: 1

3. Find the vertex of the parabola: $x^2 - 4x - 4y + 16 = 0$.
   a) (2, 16) b) (3, 2) c) (2, 4)
   d) (2, 3) e) None of these

   Answer: d Difficulty: 1

4. Find the vertex of the parabola: $4y^2 + 4y - 16x + 13 = 0$.
   a) $\left(-\frac{1}{2}, \frac{3}{4}\right)$ b) (-1, 3) c) $\left(\frac{1}{2}, -\frac{3}{4}\right)$
   d) $\left(\frac{3}{4}, -\frac{1}{2}\right)$ e) None of these

   Answer: d Difficulty: 1

5. Find the vertex of the parabola: $y^2 + 10y - 20x + 37 = 0$.
   a) $\left(-5, \frac{3}{5}\right)$ b) $\left(\frac{3}{5}, -5\right)$ c) (12, -5)
   d) (-5, 12) e) None of these

   Answer: b Difficulty: 1

6. Find the focus of the parabola: $y^2 = -32x$.
   a) (8, 0) b) (-8, 0) c) (0, 8)
   d) (0, -8) e) None of these

   Answer: b Difficulty: 1

7. Find the focus of the parabola: $y^2 - 4y - 4x = 0$.
   a) (2, -1) b) (-1, 2) c) (2, 0)
   d) (3, 0) e) None of these

   Answer: e Difficulty: 1

8. Find the focus of the parabola: $y^2 - 6y - 12x - 15 = 0$.
   a) (6, -1) b) (-2, 6) c) (1, 3)
   d) (5, -3) e) None of these

   Answer: c Difficulty: 1

9. Find the focus of the parabola: $x^2 + 4x + 2y - 6 = 0$.
   a) $\left(-2, \frac{9}{2}\right)$ b) $\left(2, -\frac{11}{2}\right)$ c) $\left(-\frac{5}{2}, 5\right)$
   d) $\left(-2, \frac{11}{2}\right)$ e) None of these

   Answer: a Difficulty: 1

10. Find the focus of the parabola: $2y^2 + 8y + 2x + 7 = 0$.
   a) $\left(-\frac{5}{2}, \frac{1}{2}\right)$ b) $\left(\frac{1}{4}, -2\right)$ c) $\left(-\frac{5}{4}, \frac{1}{2}\right)$
   d) $\left(\frac{3}{4}, -2\right)$ e) None of these

   Answer: b Difficulty: 1

11. Find the directrix of the parabola: $y^2 = x$.
   a) $y = \frac{1}{4}$ b) $x = \frac{1}{4}$ c) $y = -\frac{1}{4}$
   d) $x = -\frac{1}{4}$ e) None of these

   Answer: d Difficulty: 1

12. Find the directrix of the parabola: $x^2 - 2x - y - 1 = 0$.
   a) $x = 1$ b) $y = \frac{1}{4}$ c) $4y + 9 = 0$
   d) $9x - 4 = 0$ e) None of these

   Answer: c Difficulty: 1

13. Find the directrix of the parabola: $x^2 - 6x - 8y + 25 = 0$.
   a) $y = 1$ b) $x = 5$ c) $y = 0$ d) $x = 1$ e) None of these

   Answer: c Difficulty: 1

14. Find the directrix of the parabola: $4y^2 + 12y + 8x - 5 = 0$.
   a) $x = 0$ b) $y = -1$ c) $x = \frac{9}{4}$ d) $y = -2$ e) None of these

   Answer: c Difficulty: 1

15. Find the directrix of the parabola: $y^2 - 12x + 12 = 0$.
   a) $y = -2$ b) $y = -3$ c) $y = 3$ d) $x = -2$ e) None of these

   Answer: d Difficulty: 1

SHORT ANSWER

16. Find the vertex, focus, and directrix of the parabola: $x^2 - 10x + 12y + 37 = 0$.

Answer:
Vertex: (5, -1)
Focus: (5, -4)
Directrix: $y = 2$

Difficulty: 1

17. Find the vertex, focus, and directrix of the parabola: $4y^2 - 4y + 4x + 5 = 0$.

Answer:
Vertex: $\left(1, \frac{1}{2}\right)$
Focus: $\left(\frac{5}{4}, \frac{1}{2}\right)$
Directrix: $x = \frac{3}{4}$

Difficulty: 1

18. Find the vertex, focus, and directrix of the parabola: $(x + 2)^2 - 16(y - 1) = 0$.

Answer:
Vertex: (-2, 1)
Focus: (-2, 5)
Directrix: $y = -3$

Difficulty: 1

19. Find the vertex, focus, and directrix of the parabola:
$x = \frac{1}{4}(y^2 - 20y + 100)$.

Answer:
Vertex: (0, 10)
Focus: (-1, 10)
Directrix: $x = 1$

Difficulty: 1

MULTIPLE CHOICE

20. Find the standard form of the equation of the parabola with vertex (0, 0) and focus (-3, 0).
a) $x^2 = -12y$ b) $y^2 = -12x$ c) $x^2 = 12y$
d) $y^2 = 12x$ e) None of these

Answer: b Difficulty: 1

21. Find an equation of the parabola with focus (3, 4) and directrix $x = 1$.
a) $y^2 - 4x - 8y + 24 = 0$
b) $y^2 - 8x - 6y + 41 = 0$
c) $x^2 - 6x - 6y + 33 = 0$
d) $x^2 - 6x - 4y + 25 = 0$
e) None of these

Answer: a Difficulty: 1

22. Find an equation of the parabola with vertex (3, 1) and focus (4, 1).
a) $y^2 - 4x - 2y + 13 = 0$
b) $4y^2 - x - 8y + 7 = 0$
c) $x^2 - 6x - 4y + 13 = 0$
d) $4x^2 - 24x - y + 37 = 0$
e) None of these

Answer: a Difficulty: 1

23. Find an equation of the parabola with vertex (2, -3) and focus (2, 0).
a) $y^2 + 6y - 12x + 33 = 0$
b) $x^2 - 4x + 12y + 40 = 0$
c) $x^2 - 4x - 12y - 32 = 0$
d) $y^2 + 6y + 12x - 15 = 0$
e) None of these

Answer: c Difficulty: 1

24. Find the standard form of the equation of the parabola with vertex (0, 0) and directrix $x = 12$.
a) $y^2 = -48x$
b) $y^2 = 48x$
c) $x^2 = -48y$
d) $x^2 = 48y$
e) None of these

Answer: a Difficulty: 1

25. Find an equation of the parabola with vertex (2, 1) and directrix $x = -1$.
a) $y^2 - 2y - 12x + 25 = 0$
b) $y^2 - 2y - 4x + 9 = 0$
c) $x^2 - 4x - 12y + 16 = 0$
d) $y^2 - 4y - 12x + 16 = 0$
e) None of these

Answer: a Difficulty: 1

26. Find an equation for the parabola shown below.
a) $x^2 + 6x - 8y + 25 = 0$
b) $x^2 + 6x + 4y + 1 = 0$
c) $y^2 - 4y + 4x + 16 = 0$
d) $y^2 - 4y - 4x - 8 = 0$
e) None of these

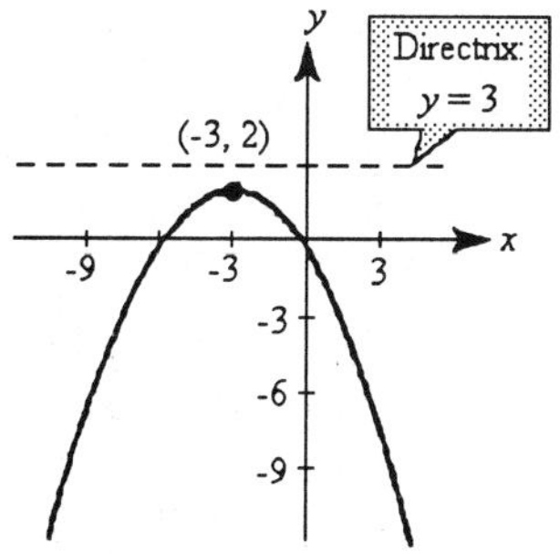

Answer: b Difficulty: 1

27. Find an equation for the parabola shown below.
   a) $y^2 - 4y - 12x + 28 = 0$
   b) $x^2 - 4x + 12y - 20 = 0$
   c) $x^2 - 4x - 12y + 28 = 0$
   d) $y^2 - 4y + 12x - 20 = 0$
   e) None of these

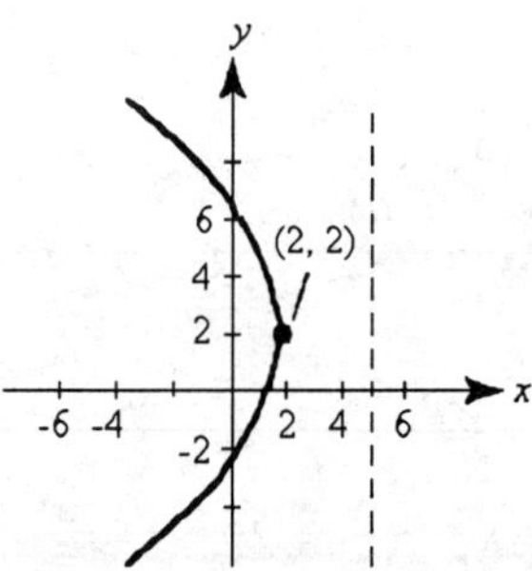

Answer: d Difficulty: 1

SHORT ANSWER

28. Find the standard form of the equation of the parabola with vertex (0, 0) and directrix $x = 7$.

Answer:

$y^2 = -28x$

Difficulty: 1

29. Find the standard form of the equation of the parabola with vertex (0, 0) and directrix $x = -5/2$.

Answer:

$y^2 = 10x$

Difficulty: 1

30. Find the standard form of the equation of the parabola with vertex (1, 4) and focus (1, 7).

Answer:

$(x - 1)^2 = 12(y - 4)$

Difficulty: 1

31. Write in standard form: $x^2 + 4x - 8y + 4 = 0$.

Answer:

$(x + 2)^2 = 4(2)y$

Difficulty: 1

32. Sketch the graph: $x^2 = 24(y - 2)$.

Answer: See graph below.

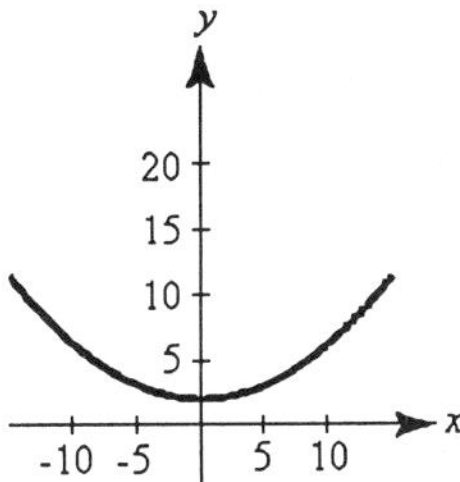

Difficulty: 1

33. Sketch the graph of the parabola $y^2 + 8x - 6y + 17 = 0$ and identify the vertex, focus, and directrix.

Answer:

$(y - 3)^2 = -8(x + 1)$
Vertex: $(-1, 3)$
Focus: $(-3, 3)$
Directrix: $x = 1$

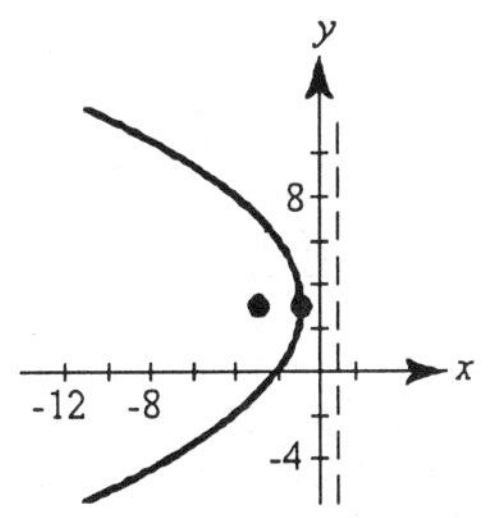

Difficulty: 1

34. Find an equation of the tangent line to the parabola $y = \frac{1}{4}x^2$ at the point $(4, 4)$.

Answer: $2x - y - 4 = 0$ Difficulty: 2

35. The course for a sailboat race includes a turn-around point marked by a stationary buoy. The sailboats must pass between the buoy and the straight shoreline. The boats follow a parabolic path past the buoy which is 40 yards from the shoreline. Find an equation to represent the parabolic path so that the boats remain equidistant from the buoy and the straight shoreline, using the buoy as the focus and the shoreline as the directrix.

Answer:

$x^2 = 4(20)y$
$x^2 = 80y$

Difficulty: 1

36. Determine the distance across the base of a parabolic arch that measures 30 feet at its highest point if the roadway through the center of the arch is 48 feet wide and must have a minimum clearance of 15 feet.

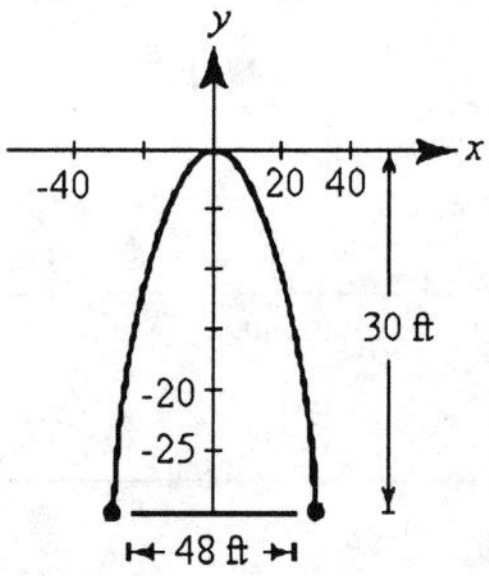

Answer:

$x^2 = 4py$

$24^2 = 4p(-15)$

$p = -\dfrac{144}{15}$

$x^2 = 4\left[-\dfrac{144}{5}\right](-30)$

$x^2 = 1152$

$x = 24\sqrt{2} \Rightarrow 2x = 48\sqrt{2} \approx 67.9$ ft.

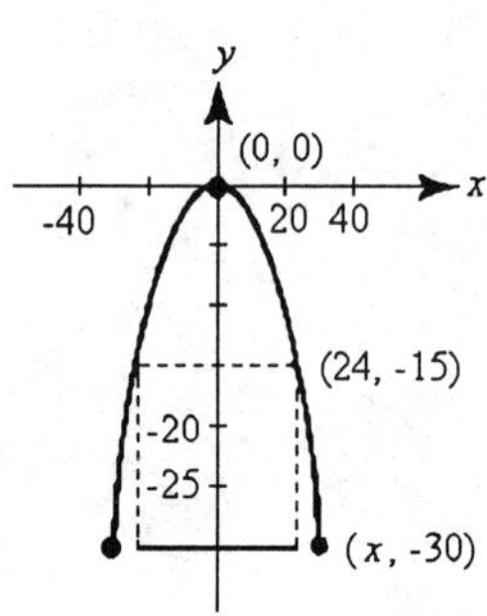

Difficulty: 1

Chapter 103: Ellipses

MULTIPLE CHOICE

1. Find the center of the ellipse: $4x^2 + 9y^2 - 32x + 18y + 37 = 0$.
   a) (16, -9) b) (-8, 2) c) (4, -1)
   d) (2, 3) e) None of these

   Answer: c Difficulty: 1

2. Find the center of the ellipse: $9x^2 + 4y^2 - 36x - 24y - 36 = 0$.
   a) (2, 3) b) (3, -2) c) $\left(2\sqrt{3}, 3\sqrt{3}\right)$
   d) (6, 48) e) None of these

   Answer: a Difficulty: 1

SHORT ANSWER

3. Find the center of the ellipse: $5x^2 + 2y^2 - 20x + 24y + 82 = 0$.

   Answer: (2, -6) Difficulty: 1

MULTIPLE CHOICE

4. Find the center of the ellipse: $x^2 + 2y^2 - 4x - 16y + 32 = 0$.
   a) (2, 4) b) (2, 8) c) (-2, -4)
   d) (4, 8) e) None of these

   Answer: a Difficulty: 1

SHORT ANSWER

5. Find the center of the ellipse: $36x^2 + 64y^2 - 36x - 96y - 531 = 0$.

   Answer:
   $\left(\frac{1}{2}, \frac{3}{4}\right)$
   Difficulty: 1

MULTIPLE CHOICE

6. Find one focus for the ellipse: $16x^2 + 9y^2 - 160x - 36y + 292 = 0$.
   a) $\left(5 - \sqrt{7}, 2\right)$ b) $\left(5, 2 + \sqrt{7}\right)$ c) (9, 2)
   d) (5, -2) e) None of these

   Answer: b Difficulty: 2

7. Find the foci of the ellipse: $\frac{x^2}{28} + \frac{y^2}{64} = 1$.
   a) (0, 8), (0, -8)   b) (6, 0), (-6, 0)   c) $\left(0, 2\sqrt{7}\right)$, $\left(0, -2\sqrt{7}\right)$
   d) (0, 6), (0, -6)   e) None of these

Answer: d Difficulty: 1

8. Find the foci of the ellipse: $16x^2 + 25y^2 - 96x + 200y + 144 = 0$.
   a) (-6, 4), (0, 4)   b) (3, -1), (3, -7)   c) (0, -4), (6, -4)
   d) (-3, 7), (-3, 1)   e) None of these

Answer: c Difficulty: 1

9. Find the foci of the ellipse: $16x^2 + 80y^2 - 16x - 40y - 71 = 0$.
   a) $\left(\frac{1}{2}, \frac{17}{4}\right)$, $\left(\frac{1}{2}, -\frac{15}{4}\right)$ b) $\left(\frac{1}{2}, \frac{9}{4}\right)$, $\left(\frac{1}{2}, -\frac{7}{4}\right)$ c) $\left(\frac{9}{2}, \frac{1}{4}\right)$, $\left(-\frac{7}{2}, \frac{1}{4}\right)$
   d) $\left(\frac{5}{2}, \frac{1}{4}\right)$, $\left(-\frac{3}{2}, \frac{1}{4}\right)$ e) None of these

Answer: d Difficulty: 1

10. Find the foci of the ellipse: $\frac{x^2}{81} + \frac{y^2}{225} = 1$.
   a) (0, 12), (0, -12)   b) (12, 0), (-12, 0)
   c) $\left(0, 3\sqrt{34}\right)$, $\left(0, -3\sqrt{34}\right)$ d) $\left(3\sqrt{34}, 0\right)$, $\left(-3\sqrt{34}, 0\right)$
   e) None of these

Answer: a Difficulty: 1

11. Find the vertices of the ellipse: $\frac{(x + 1)^2}{64} + \frac{(y - 4)^2}{36} = 1$.
   a) (5, 4), (-7, 4)   b) (-1, 12), (-1, -4)   c) (7, 4), (-9, 4)
   d) $\left(-1 \pm 2\sqrt{7}, 4\right)$ e) None of these

Answer: c Difficulty: 1

12. Find the vertices of the ellipse: $9x^2 + y^2 - 54x + 6y + 81 = 0$.
   a) (-3, 6), (-3, 0)   b) (0, 3), (-6, 3)   c) $\left(-3, 3 \pm 2\sqrt{2}\right)$
   d) (3, 0), (3, -6)   e) None of these

Answer: d Difficulty: 1

13. Find the vertices of the ellipse: $\frac{\left(x + \frac{1}{2}\right)^2}{8} + \frac{\left(y - \frac{1}{2}\right)^2}{4} = 1.$

a) $\left(\frac{-1 \pm 4\sqrt{2}}{2}, \frac{1}{2}\right)$ b) $\left(\frac{15}{2}, \frac{1}{2}\right), \left(-\frac{17}{2}, \frac{1}{2}\right)$ c) $\left(\frac{3}{2}, \frac{1}{2}\right), \left(-\frac{5}{2}, \frac{1}{2}\right)$
d) $\left(-\frac{1}{2}, \frac{1 \pm 4\sqrt{2}}{2}\right)$ e) None of these

Answer: a Difficulty: 1

14. Find the vertices of the ellipse: $2x^2 + y^2 + 20x + 48 = 0$.
a) $\left(-5 + \sqrt{2}, 0\right), \left(-5 - \sqrt{2}, 0\right)$ b) $\left(-5, \sqrt{2}\right), \left(-5, -\sqrt{2}\right)$
c) $(-4, 0), (-6, 0)$ d) $(-5, 1), (-5, -1)$
e) None of these

Answer: b Difficulty: 1

SHORT ANSWER

15. Find the vertices of the ellipse and sketch its graph: $x^2 + 5y^2 = 5$.

Answer:
Vertices: $\left(\pm\sqrt{5}, 0\right)$

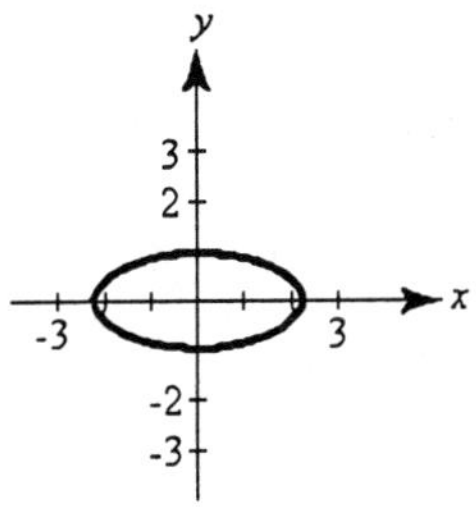

Difficulty: 1

16. Find the center, vertices, foci, and eccentricity of the ellipse, and sketch its graph:
$$\frac{(x - 2)^2}{1} + \frac{(y + 7)^2}{9} = 1.$$

Answer:

Center: (2, -7)
Vertices: (2, -4), (2, -10)
Foci: $\left(2, -7 + 2\sqrt{2}\right)$, $\left(2, -7 - 2\sqrt{2}\right)$

$e = \dfrac{2\sqrt{2}}{3}$

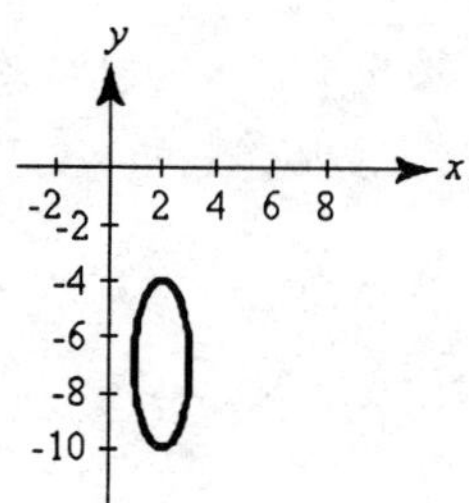

Difficulty: 1

MULTIPLE CHOICE

17. Find the eccentricity of the ellipse: $\dfrac{(x - 4)^2}{16} + \dfrac{(y + 5)^2}{25} = 1.$

a) $\frac{4}{5}$ b) $\frac{5}{4}$ c) $\frac{5}{3}$ d) $\frac{3}{5}$ e) None of these

Answer: d Difficulty: 1

18. Find the eccentricity of the ellipse: $14x^2 + 16y^2 = 224.$

a) $\frac{2\sqrt{14}}{7}$ b) $\frac{\sqrt{14}}{4}$ c) $2\sqrt{2}$ d) $\frac{\sqrt{2}}{4}$ e) None of these

Answer: d Difficulty: 1

19. Find the eccentricity of the ellipse: $\dfrac{(x\ \ 2)^2}{4} + \dfrac{(y + 1)^2}{9} = 1.$

a) $\frac{2}{3}$ b) $\frac{2}{\sqrt{5}}$ c) $\frac{\sqrt{5}}{3}$ d) $\frac{\sqrt{5}}{2}$ e) None of these

Answer: c Difficulty: 1

20. Find the eccentricity of the ellipse: $4x^2 + 9y^2 - 8x + 18y - 23 = 0$.
    a) $\frac{3}{4}$ b) $\frac{2}{3}$ c) $\frac{\sqrt{5}}{3}$ d) $\frac{2}{\sqrt{5}}$ e) None of these

    Answer: c Difficulty: 1

SHORT ANSWER

21. Find the standard form of the equation of the ellipse with center (0, 0), one focus (3, 0) and major axis of length 12.

    Answer:

    $\frac{x^2}{36} + \frac{y^2}{27} = 1$

    Difficulty: 1

MULTIPLE CHOICE

22. Find the standard form of the equation of the ellipse with vertices (±4, 0) and foci (±3, 0).
    a) $\frac{x^2}{7} + \frac{y^2}{9} = 1$ b) $\frac{x^2}{16} + \frac{y^2}{9} = 1$ c) $\frac{x^2}{16} + \frac{y^2}{7} = 1$
    d) $\frac{x^2}{16} - \frac{y^2}{9} = 1$ e) None of these

    Answer: c Difficulty: 1

23. Find the standard form of the equation of the ellipse with center (-1, 3), vertex (3, 3) and minor axis of length 2.
    a) $\frac{x^2}{16} + \frac{y^2}{4} = 1$ b) $\frac{x^2}{4} + \frac{y^2}{16} = 1$ c) $\frac{(x + 1)^2}{1} + \frac{(y - 3)^2}{16} = 1$
    d) $\frac{(x + 1)^2}{16} + \frac{(y - 3)^2}{1} = 1$ e) None of these

    Answer: d Difficulty: 1

SHORT ANSWER

24. Find an equation of the ellipse with foci (0, 2) and (0, 8) and vertices (0, 0) and (0, 10).

    Answer:

    $25x^2 + 16y^2 - 160y = 0$

    Difficulty: 1

MULTIPLE CHOICE

25. Find an equation of the ellipse with minor axis of length 8 and vertices (-9, 3) and (7, 3).
    a) $4x^2 + 8y^2 - 8x - 48y + 44 = 0$
    b) $16x^2 + 64y^2 + 32x - 384y - 432 = 0$
    c) $64x^2 + 128y^2 - 128x - 768y - 6976 = 0$
    d) $x^2 + y^2 + 8x + 8y + 64 = 0$
    e) None of these

    Answer: b Difficulty: 1

26. Find an equation of the ellipse with foci (-2, 3) and (2, 3), and major axis of length 8.
    a) $12x^2 + 16y^2 - 96y - 48 = 0$
    b) $16x^2 + 20y^2 - 120y - 140 = 0$
    c) $16x^2 + 12y^2 - 72y - 36 = 0$
    d) $20x^2 + 16y^2 - 96y - 176 = 0$
    e) None of these

    Answer: a Difficulty: 1

SHORT ANSWER

27. Find the standard form of the equation of the ellipse with major axis of length $2\sqrt{6}$ and foci $\left(-3,\ 1 + \sqrt{5}\right)$ and $\left(-3,\ 1 - \sqrt{5}\right)$.

    Answer:

    $$\frac{(x + 3)^2}{1} + \frac{(y - 1)^2}{6} = 1$$

    Difficulty: 2

MULTIPLE CHOICE

28. Write in standard form: $4x^2 + 9y^2 - 8x + 72y + 4 = 0$.
    a) $\frac{(x - 1)^2}{36} + \frac{(y + 4)^2}{16} = 1$
    b) $\frac{(x - 1)^2}{144} + \frac{(y + 8)^2}{64} = 1$
    c) $\frac{(x - 1)^2}{13/4} + \frac{(y + 4)^2}{13/9} = 1$
    d) $\frac{(x - 4)^2}{327} + \frac{(y + 36)^2}{436/3} = 1$
    e) None of these

    Answer: a Difficulty: 1

SHORT ANSWER

29. Write in standard form: $9x^2 + 4y^2 + 18x - 48y + 117 = 0$.

    Answer:

    $$\frac{(x + 1)^2}{4} + \frac{(y - 6)^2}{9} = 1$$

    Difficulty: 1

MULTIPLE CHOICE

30. Find the standard form of the equation of the ellipse with foci $\left(-\sqrt{11}, 5\right)$ and $\left(\sqrt{11}, 5\right)$ and a vertex $(6, 5)$.
 a) $\frac{x^2}{36} + \frac{(y-5)^2}{25} = 1$ b) $\frac{(x-5)^2}{36} + \frac{y^2}{25} = 1$ c) $\frac{y^2}{36} + \frac{(x-5)^2}{25} = 1$
 d) $\frac{x^2}{6} + \frac{(y-5)^2}{5} = 1$ e) None of these

 Answer: a Difficulty: 2

31. Find an equation of the ellipse with ends of minor axis $(5, -2)$ and $(1, -2)$, and a vertex $(3, 3)$.
 a) $25x^2 + 4y^2 - 150x + 16y + 141 = 0$
 b) $25x^2 + 4y^2 - 6x + 4y - 87 = 0$
 c) $5x^2 + 2y^2 - 30x + 8y - 47 = 0$
 d) $25x^2 + 4y^2 - 150x + 16y + 240 = 0$
 e) None of these

 Answer: a Difficulty: 2

32. Match the graph with the correct equation.
 a) $\frac{x^2}{1} + \frac{y^2}{3} = 1$ b) $\frac{x^2}{3} + \frac{y^2}{1} = 1$ c) $\frac{x^2}{9} + \frac{y^2}{1} = 1$
 d) $\frac{x^2}{2} + \frac{y^2}{9} = 1$ e) None of these

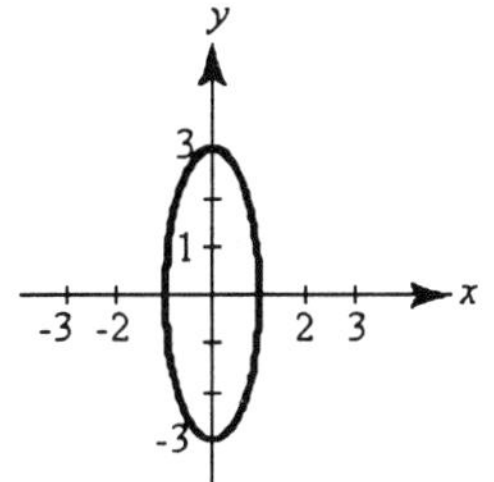

 Answer: e Difficulty: 1

33. Match the graph with the correct equation.
 a) $x^2 + 16y^2 - 4x - 4y - 8 = 0$ b) $x^2 + 16y^2 - 4x - 4y + 67 = 0$
 c) $x^2 + 16y^2 - 4x - 64y + 52 = 0$ d) $x^2 + 4y^2 - 4x - 16y + 4 = 0$
 e) None of these

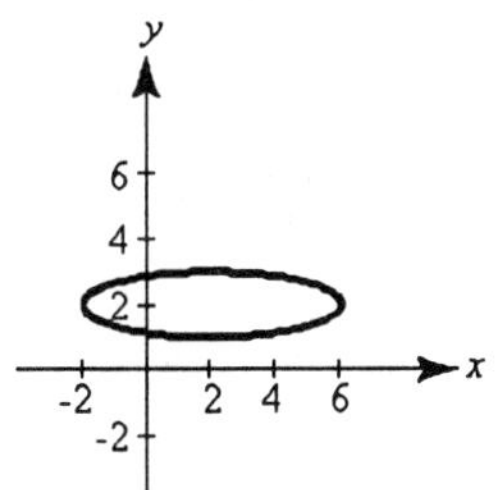

 Answer: c Difficulty: 1

SHORT ANSWER

34. A semi-elliptical archway is to be formed over the entrance to an estate. The arch is to be set on pillars that are 10 feet apart. The arch has a height of four feet above the pillars. Where should the foci be placed in order to sketch plans for the elliptical arch?

    Answer:

    $2a = 10 \Rightarrow a = 5,\ b = 4,\ c^2 = 25 - 16 = 9 \Rightarrow c = \pm 3$
    The foci should be placed 3 feet to the left and right of the center.

    Difficulty: 1

35. The ends of an oil tanker are elliptical. Warning signs are to be placed at the foci of the ellipse. The tanker is 15 feet wide at the widest point and 9 feet high at its highest point. Where should the signs be placed with respect to the center of the tanker?

    Answer:
    $2a = 15 \Rightarrow a = \frac{15}{2},\ 2b = 9 \Rightarrow b = \frac{9}{2},\ c^2 = \frac{225}{4} - \frac{81}{4} = \frac{144}{4} = 36 \Rightarrow c = \pm 6$
    The signs should be placed 6 feet to the left and right of the center.

    Difficulty: 1

Chapter 104: Hyperbolas

MULTIPLE CHOICE

1. Find the center of the hyperbola: $3x^2 - 4y^2 - 6x - 16y + 7 = 0$.
   a) (1, -2) b) (4, 3) c) (1, -8)
   d) (3, -8) e) None of these

   Answer: a Difficulty: 1

2. Find the center of the hyperbola: $9x^2 - y^2 + 54x + 2y + 71 = 0$.
   a) (9, -1) b) (-3, 1) c) (27, 1)
   d) (6, -1) e) None of these

   Answer: b Difficulty: 1

3. Find the center of the hyperbola: $25x^2 - 4y^2 + 50x + 8y + 121 = 0$.
   a) (2, 5) b) (1, -1) c) (-1, 1)
   d) (5, 2) e) None of these

   Answer: c Difficulty: 1

4. Find the center of the hyperbola: $25y^2 - 144x^2 + 150y - 576x - 3951 = 0$.
   a) (-2, -3) b) (2, 3) c) (-3, -2)
   d) (3, 2) e) None of these

   Answer: a Difficulty: 1

5. Find the center of the hyperbola: $16x^2 - 9y^2 + 160x - 54y + 175 = 0$.
   a) (3, -5) b) (5, -3) c) (-5, -3)
   d) (-3, 5) e) None of these

   Answer: c Difficulty: 1

6. Find the vertices of the hyperbola: $\frac{(x - 2)^2}{9} - \frac{(y + 7)^2}{12} = 1$.
   a) (5, -7), (-1, -7) b) (2, -4), (2, -10) c) (-2, 10), (-2, 4)
   d) (1, 7), (-5, 7) e) None of these

   Answer: a Difficulty: 1

7. Find the vertices of the hyperbola: $\frac{(x - 2)^2}{16} - \frac{(y + 1)^2}{9} = 1$.
   a) (2, 1), (2, -3) b) (0, 1), (-4, 1) c) (-2, 3), (-2, -1)
   d) (6, -1), (-2, -1) e) None of these

   Answer: d Difficulty: 1

8. Find the vertices of the hyperbola: $576y^2 - 49x^2 - 2304y - 98x - 25{,}969 = 0$.
   a) (23, 2), (-25, 2) b) (-1, 26), (-1, -22) c) (-1, 9), (-1, -5)
   d) (6, 2), (-8, 2) e) None of these

   Answer: c Difficulty: 1

9. Find the vertices of the hyperbola: $7x^2 - 4y^2 = 28$.
   a) $\left(0, \sqrt{3}\right), \left(0, -\sqrt{3}\right)$ b) $\left(0, \sqrt{7}\right), \left(0, -\sqrt{7}\right)$ c) (2, 0), (-2, 0)
   d) $\left(\sqrt{3}, 0\right), \left(-\sqrt{3}, 0\right)$ e) None of these

   Answer: c Difficulty: 1

10. Find the vertices of the hyperbola: $2y^2 - x^2 + 2x - 3 = 0$.
    a) (1, 1), (1, -1) b) (1, 2), (1, -2)
    c) $\left(0, 1 + \sqrt{2}\right), \left(0, 1 - \sqrt{2}\right)$ d) (0, 3), (0, -1)
    e) None of these

    Answer: a Difficulty: 1

11. Find the foci of the hyperbola: $2y^2 - 9x^2 - 18 = 0$.
    a) $\left(\pm\sqrt{11}, 3\right)$ b) $\left(0, \pm\sqrt{7}\right)$ c) $\left(0, \pm\sqrt{11}\right)$
    d) $\left(\pm\sqrt{7}, 0\right)$ e) None of these

    Answer: c Difficulty: 1

12. Find the foci of the hyperbola: $\frac{(x - 2)^2}{16} - \frac{(y + 1)^2}{9} = 1$.
    a) (2, 4), (2, -6) b) (3, -1), (1, -1) c) (7, -1), (-3, -1)
    d) (3, 1), (-7, 1) e) None of these

    Answer: c Difficulty: 1

13. Find the foci of the hyperbola: $25x^2 - 4y^2 + 50x + 8y + 121 = 0$.
    a) $\left(-1, 1 \pm \sqrt{29}\right)$ b) $\left(-1 \pm \sqrt{29}, 1\right)$ c) (-1, 4), (-1, -2)
    d) $\left(1 \pm \sqrt{29}, -1\right)$ e) None of these

    Answer: a Difficulty: 1

SHORT ANSWER

14. Find the foci of the hyperbola: $4y^2 - 5x^2 - 20 = 0$.

    Answer: (0, 3), (0, -3) Difficulty: 1

MULTIPLE CHOICE

15. Find the standard form of the equation of the hyperbola with center (0, 0), vertices (±3, 0), and foci $\left(\pm 3\sqrt{5}, 0\right)$.
    a) $\frac{x^2}{9} - \frac{y^2}{45} = 1$ b) $\frac{y^2}{9} - \frac{x^2}{45} = 1$ c) $\frac{x^2}{9} - \frac{y^2}{36} = 1$
    d) $\frac{x^2}{9} - \frac{y^2}{54} = 1$ e) None of these

    Answer: c Difficulty: 1

16. Find an equation of the hyperbola with center (-2, 4), one vertex (-2, 7), and one focus $\left(-2, 4 + \sqrt{15}\right)$.
a) $9y^2 - 6x^2 - 72y - 24x + 66 = 0$
b) $9x^2 - 6y^2 + 36x + 48y - 114 = 0$
c) $6x^2 - 9y^2 + 24x + 72y - 174 = 0$
d) $6y^2 - 9x^2 - 48y - 36x + 6 = 0$
e) None of these

Answer: d Difficulty: 2

17. Find the standard form of the equation of the hyperbola with center (0, -2), one vertex (0, -4), and one focus (0, 2).
a) $\frac{x^2}{12} - \frac{(y + 2)^2}{4} = 1$
b) $\frac{x^2}{4} - \frac{(y + 2)^2}{4} = 1$
c) $\frac{(y + 2)^2}{4} - \frac{x^2}{12} = 1$
d) $\frac{(y + 2)^2}{12} - \frac{x^2}{4} + = 1$
e) None of these

Answer: c Difficulty: 1

18. Find an equation of the hyperbola with vertices (2, 3) and (2, -1) and foci (2, 6) and (2, -4).
a) $21y^2 - 4x^2 - 84y + 8x - 4 = 0$
b) $4x^2 - 21y^2 - 16x + 42y - 89 = 0$
c) $21y^2 - 4x^2 - 42y + 16x - 79 = 0$
d) $21x^2 - 4y^2 - 84x + 8y - 4 = 0$
e) None of these

Answer: c Difficulty: 1

19. Find the standard form of the equation of the hyperbola with vertices (0, -1) and (4, -1), and foci (-2, -1) and (6, -1).
a) $\frac{(x - 2)^2}{16} - \frac{(y + 1)^2}{4} = 1$
b) $\frac{(x - 2)^2}{4} - \frac{(y + 1)^2}{12} = 1$
c) $\frac{(y + 1)^2}{12} - \frac{(x - 2)^2}{4} = 1$
d) $\frac{(x + 2)^2}{4} - \frac{(y - 1)^2}{12} = 1$
e) None of these

Answer: b Difficulty: 1

SHORT ANSWER

20. Find the standard form of the equation of the hyperbola with center (2, 5), one focus (2, 15), and transverse axis of length 12.

Answer:

$$\frac{(y - 5)^2}{36} - \frac{(x - 2)^2}{64} = 1$$

Difficulty: 2

MULTIPLE CHOICE

21. Find an equation of the hyperbola with vertices (9, 1) and (-1, 1), and one focus $\left(4 - \sqrt{29}, 1\right)$.
a) $4x^2 - 25y^2 - 32x + 50y - 61 = 0$ b) $4x^2 - 25y^2 - 8x - 2y - 115 = 0$
c) $4x^2 - 25y^2 - 32x - 50y + 38 = 0$ d) $x^2 - y^2 - 8x - 2y - 115 = 0$
e) None of these

Answer: a Difficulty: 2

22. Find the standard form of the equation of the hyperbola with ends of conjugate axis at (6, 3) and (-4, 3), and a vertex (1, 10).
a) $\frac{(y-3)^2}{49} - \frac{(x-1)^2}{25} = 1$ b) $\frac{(x-1)^2}{25} - \frac{(y-3)^2}{49} = 1$
c) $\frac{(y+3)^2}{49} - \frac{(x+1)^2}{25} = 1$ d) $\frac{(y-3)^2}{81} - \frac{(x-1)^2}{25} = 1$
e) None of these

Answer: a Difficulty: 1

23. Match the graph with the correct equation.
a) $\frac{x^2}{16} - \frac{y^2}{4} = 1$ b) $\frac{x^2}{4} - \frac{y^2}{16} = 1$ c) $\frac{y^2}{16} - \frac{x^2}{4} = 1$
d) $\frac{y^2}{4} - \frac{x^2}{16} = 1$ e) None of these

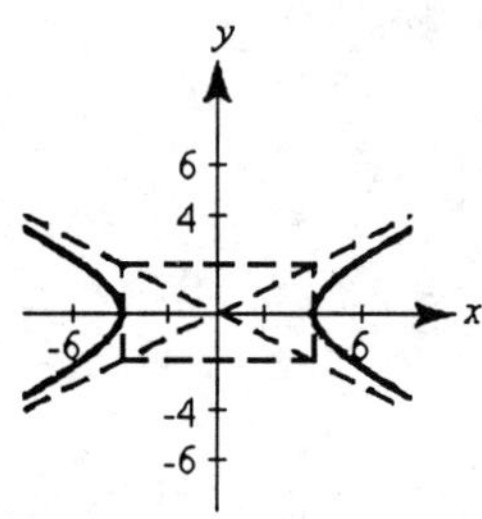

Answer: a Difficulty: 1

24. Identify the graph of $\frac{(x - 3)^2}{2} - \frac{(y + 1)^2}{9} = 1$.

a) I   b) II   c) III   d) IV   e) None of these

(I)

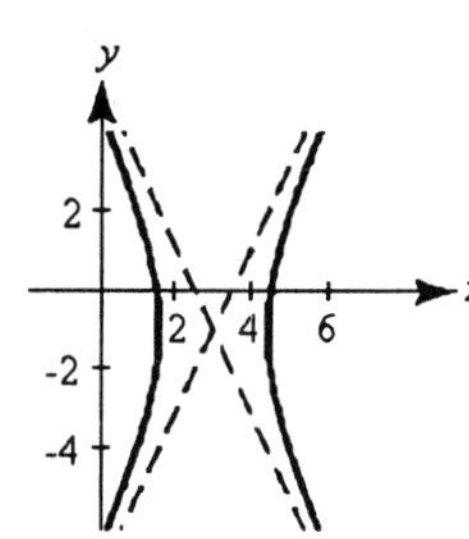

(II)

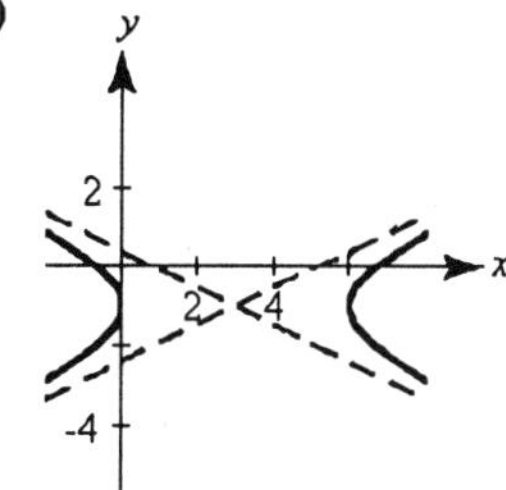

(III)

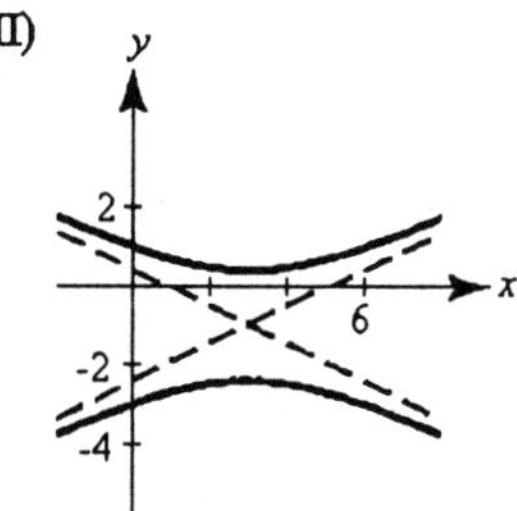

(IV)

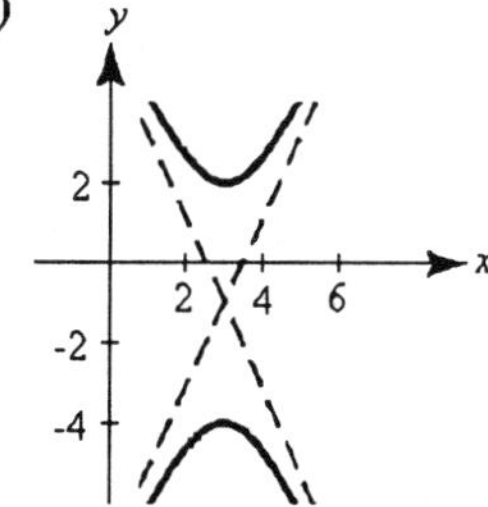

Answer: a   Difficulty: 1

SHORT ANSWER

25. Find the center, vertices, and foci of the hyperbola and sketch its graph: $\frac{x^2}{9} - \frac{y^2}{4} = 1$.

Answer:
Center: (0, 0)
Vertices: $(\pm 3, 0)$
Foci: $\left(\pm\sqrt{13}, 0\right)$

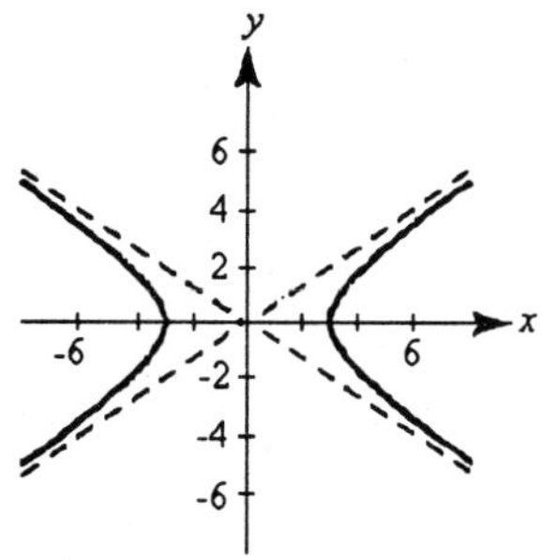

Difficulty: 1

26. Find the center, vertices, foci, and asymptotes of the hyperbola, and sketch its graph: $\dfrac{(x + 1)^2}{2} - \dfrac{(y + 3)^2}{3} = 1.$

Answer:
Center: (-1, -3)
Vertices: $\left(-1 - \sqrt{2}, -3\right), \left(-1 + \sqrt{2}, -3\right)$
Foci: $\left(-1 - \sqrt{5}, -3\right), \left(-1 + \sqrt{5}, -3\right)$
Asymptotes: $y = -3 + \frac{\sqrt{6}}{2}(x + 1)$, $y = -3 - \frac{\sqrt{6}}{2}(x + 1)$

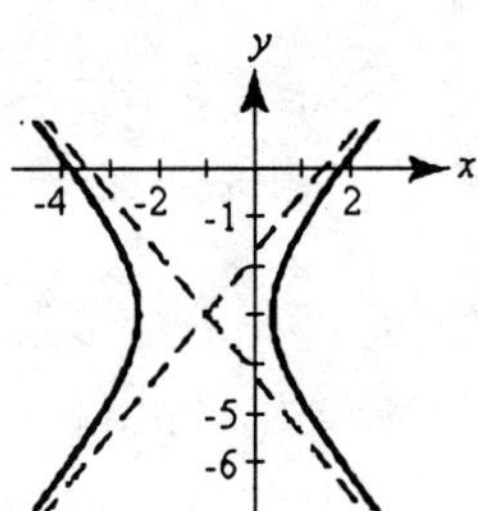

Difficulty: 2

27. Find the center, vertices, foci, and asymptotes of the hyperbola, and sketch its graph: $\dfrac{(y + 2)^2}{4} - \dfrac{(x + 1)^2}{16} = 1.$

Answer:
Center: (-1, -2)
Vertices: (-1, 0), (-1, -4)
Foci: $\left(-1, -2 + 2\sqrt{5}\right), \left(-1, -2 - 2\sqrt{5}\right)$
Asymptotes: $y = -2 + \frac{1}{2}(x + 1)$, $y = -2 - \frac{1}{2}(x + 1)$

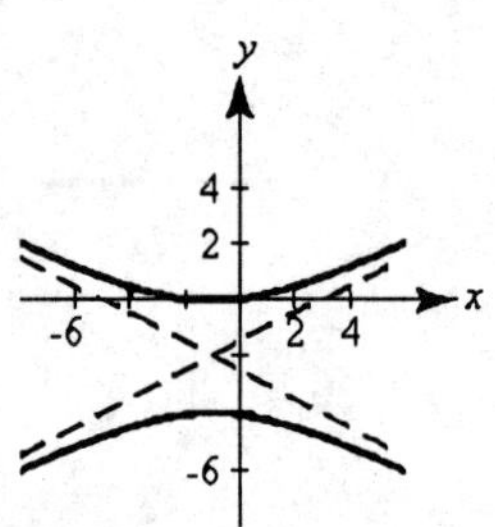

Difficulty: 2

MULTIPLE CHOICE

28. Which of the following is an asymptote of the hyperbola $5x^2 - 4y^2 - 20x - 16y - 16 = 0$?

a) $y = -2 + \frac{\sqrt{5}}{2}(x - 2)$

b) $y = 2 + \frac{\sqrt{5}}{2}(x + 2)$

c) $y = -2 + \frac{2}{\sqrt{5}}(x - 2)$

d) $y = 2 + \frac{2}{\sqrt{5}}(x + 2)$

e) None of these

Answer: a Difficulty: 2

SHORT ANSWER

29. Find the asymptotes of the hyperbola: $16y^2 - 4x^2 - 64 = 0$.

Answer:

$y = \pm\frac{x}{2}$

Difficulty: 1

30. Find the asymptotes of the hyperbola: $\frac{(y - 4)^2}{16} - \frac{(x + 2)^2}{4} = 1$.

Answer: $y = 2x + 8$, $y = -2x$ Difficulty: 1

31. Find the length of the conjugate axis of the hyperbola: $-2x^2 + 9y^2 - 20x - 108y + 256 = 0$.

Answer: 6 Difficulty: 1

MULTIPLE CHOICE

32. Find the length of the transverse axis of the hyperbola: $9x^2 - 16y^2 - 225 = 0$.

a) 10 b) 25 c) 5 d) 2 e) None of these

Answer: a Difficulty: 1

SHORT ANSWER

33. Find the standard form of the equation of the hyperbola with vertices (6, 3) and (-2, 3) and asymptotes $y = \frac{3}{4}x + \frac{3}{2}$ and $y = -\frac{3}{4}x + \frac{9}{2}$.

Answer:

$$\frac{(x - 2)^2}{16} - \frac{(y - 3)^2}{9} = 1$$

Difficulty: 2

MULTIPLE CHOICE

34. Find the eccentricity of the hyperbola: $2x^2 - 3y^2 = 24$.

a) $\frac{\sqrt{15}}{5}$ b) $\frac{\sqrt{3}}{3}$ c) $\frac{\sqrt{2}}{2}$ d) $\frac{\sqrt{15}}{3}$ e) None of these

Answer: d Difficulty: 1

SHORT ANSWER

35. A machine shop needs to make a small engine part by drilling two holes of radius, r, from a flat circular piece of radius, R. The area of the resulting machine part is 16 square inches. Write an equation that relates r and R.

Answer:

$$\pi R^2 - 2\pi r^2 = 16 \Rightarrow \frac{\pi R^2}{16} - \frac{\pi r^2}{8} = 1$$

Difficulty: 1

36. A small stained glass window is made by cutting out a circle of radius, R, from the center of a larger rectangular blue glass window and replacing it with a white colored piece of glass. The rectangular window has a length of four inches more than twice its width, w. The resulting area of blue stained glass is 1248 square inches. Show that the resulting equation relating w and R is that of a hyperbola.

Answer:

Area of original: $w(2w + 4) = 2w^2 + 4w$

Area of circle: πR^2

Area after circle removed:
$$\begin{aligned} 2w^2 + 4w - \pi R^2 &= 1248 \\ 2(w^2 + 2w) - \pi R^2 &= 1248 \\ 2(w^2 + 2w + 1) - \pi R^2 &= 1250 \\ w(w + 1)^2 - \pi R^2 &= 1250 \\ \frac{(w + 1)^2}{625} - \frac{\pi R^2}{1250} &= 1 \end{aligned}$$

Difficulty: 2

MULTIPLE CHOICE

37. Identify the graph of $3x^2 + 6x - 4y + 12 = 0$.

a) Circle b) Hyperbola c) Ellipse
d) Parabola e) None of these

Answer: d Difficulty: 1

SHORT ANSWER

38. Identify the conic corresponding to each of the following:
    (a) $3x^2 + 3y^2 - 6x + 18y + 10 = 0$
    (b) $3x^2 - 2y^2 + 6x - 8y + 1 = 0$
    (c) $x^2 + 2x + 4y^2 + 1 = 0$

    Answer: (a) Circle (b) Hyperbola (c) Ellipse Difficulty: 1

39. Identify the graph of $6x^2 - y^2 + 4x - 2y + 1 = 0$.

    Answer: Hyperbola Difficulty: 1

MULTIPLE CHOICE

40. Identify the graph of $4x^2 - 4y^2 - 6x + 16y - 11 = 0$.
    a) Circle b) Hyperbola c) Ellipse
    d) Parabola e) None of these

    Answer: b Difficulty: 1

41. Identify the graph of $6x^2 + 2y^2 - 12x + 4y - 7 = 0$.
    a) Circle b) Hyperbola c) Ellipse
    d) Parabola e) None of these

    Answer: c Difficulty: 1

42. Identify the graph of $3x^2 + 3y^2 - 6x + 9y - 10 = 0$.
    a) Circle b) Hyperbola c) Ellipse
    d) Parabola e) None of these

    Answer: a Difficulty: 1

SHORT ANSWER

43. Identify the graph of $3x^2 - y^2 - 6x + y - 7 = 0$.

    Answer: Hyperbola Difficulty: 1

44. Identify the graph of $4x^2 + y^2 - 6x + y - 7 = 0$.

    Answer: Ellipse Difficulty: 1

Chapter 105: Rotation of Conics

MULTIPLE CHOICE

1. Find the angle of rotation necessary to eliminate the xy-term: $x^2 + 4xy + y^2 - 1 = 0$.
a) 30° b) 45° c) 53.7° d) 60° e) None of these

Answer: b Difficulty: 1

2. Find the angle of rotation necessary to eliminate the xy-term: $7x^2 + 4xy + 4y^2 + 3 = 0$.
a) 26.6° b) 30° c) 45° d) 53.1° e) None of these

Answer: a Difficulty: 1

3. Find the angle of rotation necessary to eliminate the xy-term: $xy + 3x - 2y = 0$.
a) 30° b) 45° c) 53.1° d) 60° e) None of these

Answer: b Difficulty: 1

SHORT ANSWER

4. Find the angle of rotation necessary to eliminate the xy-term: $2x^2 + 2xy + y^2 + \sqrt{2}x - \sqrt{2}y = 0$.

Answer: 31.7° Difficulty: 1

5. Find the angle of rotation necessary to eliminate the xy-term: $8x^2 + 4xy + 3y^2 + 5 = 0$.

Answer: 19.3° Difficulty: 1

MULTIPLE CHOICE

6. Find the angle of rotation necessary to eliminate the xy-term: $9x^2 + 3xy + 3x + 4y = 0$.
a) 45° b) 9.2° c) 35.8° d) 18.4° e) None of these

Answer: b Difficulty: 1

7. Find the rotation formula for x of the equation: $x^2 + 2\sqrt{3}xy - y^2 = 2$.
a) $x = \frac{\sqrt{3}}{2}x' - \frac{1}{2}y'$
b) $x = \frac{\sqrt{3}}{2}x' + \frac{1}{2}y'$
c) $x = \frac{1}{2}x' - \frac{\sqrt{3}}{2}y'$
d) $x = \frac{1}{2}x' + \frac{\sqrt{3}}{2}y'$
e) None of these

Answer: a Difficulty: 1

8. Find the rotation formula for y of the equation: $xy - 2 = 0$.
a) $y = \frac{\sqrt{2}}{2}x' - \frac{\sqrt{2}}{2}y'$
b) $y = \frac{\sqrt{2}}{2}x' + \frac{\sqrt{2}}{2}y'$
c) $y = x'$
d) $y = y'$
e) None of these

Answer: b Difficulty: 1

9. Find the rotation formula for x of the equation: $9x^2 + 24xy + 2y^2 - 3 = 0$.
a) $x = \frac{24x' - 7y'}{25}$ b) $x = \frac{4x' + 3y'}{5}$ c) $x = \frac{24x' + 7y'}{25}$
d) $x = \frac{4x' - 3y'}{5}$ e) None of these

Answer: d Difficulty: 2

10. Find the rotation formula for y of the equation: $16x^2 + 24xy + 9y^2 = 3$.
a) $y = \frac{3x' - 4y'}{5}$ b) $y = \frac{4x' + 3y'}{5}$ c) $y = \frac{3x' + 4y'}{5}$
d) $y = \frac{7x' + 24y'}{25}$ e) None of these

Answer: c Difficulty: 2

11. Transform the xy-equation $y = \sqrt{3}x$ to an $x'y'$-equation by a rotation of 60°.
a) $y' = x'$ b) $y' = -\frac{\sqrt{3}}{2}x'$ c) $y' = \frac{\sqrt{3}}{2}x'$
d) $y' = 0$ e) None of these

Answer: d Difficulty: 2

12. Transform the xy-equation $x^2 - xy + y^2 = 4$ to an $x'y'$-equation by a rotation of $\pi/4$.
a) $3(y')^2 + (x')^2 = 8$ b) $2(y')^2 + (x')^2 = 8$ c) $(y')^2 + (x')^2 = 8$
d) $3(y')^2 + (x')^2 = 16$ e) None of these

Answer: a Difficulty: 2

SHORT ANSWER

13. Transform the xy-equation $6x^2 - 24xy - y^2 = 30$ to an $x'y'$-equation by a rotation of θ when $\arccos \theta = \frac{3}{5}$.

Answer:

$15(y')^2 - 10(x')^2 = 30$ or $\frac{(y')^2}{2} - \frac{(x')^2}{3} = 1$

Difficulty: 2

MULTIPLE CHOICE

14. Find the point (x', y') that corresponds to the point $(5, -3)$ in the xy-system after a rotation of $\pi/3$.

a) $\left(\frac{-5\sqrt{3} - 3}{2}, \frac{5 - 3\sqrt{3}}{2}\right)$
b) $\left(\frac{5 + 3\sqrt{3}}{2}, \frac{5\sqrt{3} - 3}{2}\right)$
c) $\left(\frac{5\sqrt{3} + 3}{2}, \frac{5 + 3\sqrt{3}}{2}\right)$
d) $\left(\frac{5 - 3\sqrt{3}}{2}, \frac{-5\sqrt{3} - 3}{2}\right)$
e) None of these

Answer: d Difficulty: 1

15. Find the point (x', y') that corresponds to the point $(2, 7)$ in the xy-system after a rotation of $\pi/6$.

a) $\left(\frac{7\sqrt{3} - 2}{2}, \frac{2\sqrt{3} + 7}{2}\right)$
b) $\left(\frac{2\sqrt{3} - 7}{2}, \frac{7\sqrt{3} + 2}{2}\right)$
c) $\left(\frac{2\sqrt{3} + 7}{2}, \frac{7\sqrt{3} - 2}{2}\right)$
d) $\left(\frac{7\sqrt{3} + 2}{2}, \frac{2\sqrt{3} - 7}{2}\right)$
e) None of these

Answer: c Difficulty: 1

16. Find the point (x', y') that corresponds to the point $\left(3\sqrt{2}, \sqrt{2}\right)$ in the xy-system after a rotation of $\pi/4$.

a) $(-2, 4)$ b) $(-4, 2)$ c) $(4, -2)$ d) $(4, 2)$ e) None of these

Answer: c Difficulty: 1

SHORT ANSWER

17. Find the xy-equation that simplifies to $(x')^2 = 4(y')$ when the axes are rotated through an angle of $\pi/3$.

Answer:

$x^2 + 3y^2 + 2\sqrt{3}xy + 8\sqrt{3}x - 8y = 0$

Difficulty: 2

18. Find the xy-equation that simplifies to $(x')^2 - 4(y')^2 = 4$ when the axes are rotated through an anglc of $\pi/6$.

Answer:

$-x^2 - 11y^2 + 10\sqrt{3}xy - 16 = 0$

Difficulty: 2

MULTIPLE CHOICE

19. Find the point (x, y) that corresponds to the point $\left(\sqrt{3}, 2\right)$ in the $x'y'$-system prior to a rotation of $\pi/6$.
a) $\left(\frac{5}{2}, \frac{3\sqrt{3}}{2}\right)$ b) $\left(\frac{1}{2}, \frac{3\sqrt{3}}{2}\right)$ c) $\left(\frac{1}{2}, -\frac{\sqrt{3}}{2}\right)$
d) $\left(\frac{3\sqrt{3}}{2}, \frac{1}{2}\right)$ e) None of these

Answer: b Difficulty: 1

20. Find the point (x, y) that corresponds to the point $(-1, 1)$ in the $x'y'$-system prior to a rotation of $\pi/3$.
a) $\left(\frac{-1 - \sqrt{3}}{2}, \frac{1 - \sqrt{3}}{2}\right)$ b) $\left(\frac{1 - \sqrt{3}}{2}, \frac{1 - \sqrt{3}}{2}\right)$ c) $\left(\frac{1 - \sqrt{3}}{2}, \frac{-1 - \sqrt{3}}{2}\right)$
d) $\left(\frac{1 + \sqrt{3}}{2}, \frac{1 + \sqrt{3}}{2}\right)$ e) None of these

Answer: a Difficulty: 1

21. Find the point (x, y) that corresponds to the point $\left(\sqrt{2}, -\sqrt{2}\right)$ in the $x'y'$-system prior to a rotation of $\pi/4$.
a) $(0, 0)$ b) $(2, 0)$ c) $(0, 2)$ d) $(2, 2)$ e) None of these

Answer: b Difficulty: 1

22. Write an equation $x^2 + 336xy + y^2 = 17$ in terms of the $x'y'$-system.
a) $\frac{337}{2}(x')^2 - \frac{335}{2}(y')^2 = 17$ b) $\frac{337}{2}(x')^2 + \frac{335}{2}(y')^2 = 17$
c) $169(x')^2 - 167(y')^2 = 17$ d) $169(x')^2 + 167(y')^2 = 17$
e) None of these

Answer: c Difficulty: 2

23. Write an equation $2x^2 + 24xy - 5y^2 = 9$ in terms of the $x'y'$-system.
a) $275(x')^2 - 350(y')^2 - 9 = 0$ b) $11(x')^2 + 14(y')^2 - 9 = 0$
c) $275(x')^2 + 350(y')^2 = 0$ d) $11(x')^2 - 14(y')^2 - 9 = 0$
e) None of these

Answer: d Difficulty: 2

24. Write an equation $x^2 + 24xy - 6y^2 = 5$ in terms of the $x'y'$-system.
a) $15(x')^2 - 10(y')^2 - 5 = 0$ b) $10(x')^2 - 15(y')^2 - 5 = 0$
c) $10(x')^2 + 15(y')^2 - 5 = 0$ d) $15(x')^2 + 10(y')^2 - 5 = 0$
e) None of these

Answer: b Difficulty: 2

25. Write the equation $x^2 - 4xy - 2y^2 = 3$ in terms of the $x'y'$-system. $\left[-\frac{\pi}{2} < 2\theta < \frac{\pi}{2}\right]$

a) $2(x')^2 - 3(y')^2 - 3 = 0$
b) $10(y')^2 - 15(x')^2 - 3 = 0$
c) $3(x')^2 + 2(y')^2 - 3 = 0$
d) $3(x')^2 - 2(y')^2 - 3 = 0$
e) None of these

Answer: a Difficulty: 2

SHORT ANSWER

26. Write the equation $x^2 + 2xy + y^2 - 8\sqrt{2}x + 8 = 0$ in terms of the $x'y'$-system.

Answer:

$2(x')^2 - 8(x') + 8(y') + 8 = 0$

Difficulty: 2

27. Write the equation $41x^2 + 24xy + 34y^2 + 25x + 50y - 25 = 0$ in terms of the $x'y'$-system.

Answer:

$50(x')^2 + 25(y')^2 + 50(x') - 25(y') + 25 = 0$

Difficulty: 2

28. Write the equation $3x^2 - 8xy - 3y^2 - 2\sqrt{5}x - 4\sqrt{5} = 0$ in terms of the $x'y'$-system. $\left[-\frac{\pi}{2} < 2\theta < \frac{\pi}{2}\right]$

Answer:

$5(x')^2 - 5(y')^2 - 4(x') - 2(y') - 4\sqrt{5} = 0$

Difficulty: 2

29. Write the equation $x^2 + 2xy + y^2 - 4\sqrt{2}x - 2\sqrt{2} + 2 = 0$ in terms of the $x'y'$-system.

Answer:

$2(x')^2 - 6(x') + 2(y') + 2 = 0$

Difficulty: 2

30. Write the equation $2x^2 + 24xy - 5y^2 + 3x - y - 9 = 0$ in terms of the $x'y'$-system.

Answer:

$11(x')^2 - 14(y')^2 + \frac{9}{5}(x') - \frac{13}{5}(y') - 9 = 0$

Difficulty: 2

31. Write the equation $3x^2 - 2xy + 3y^2 - 7 = 0$ in terms of the $x'y'$-system.

Answer:

$$2(x')^2 + 4(y')^2 - 7 = 0 \text{ or } \frac{(x')^2}{\frac{7}{2}} + \frac{(y')^2}{\frac{7}{4}} = 1$$

Difficulty: 2

MULTIPLE CHOICE

32. Identify the graph of $xy + 3 = 0$.
a) Circle
b) Ellipse
c) Parabola
d) Hyperbola
e) None of these

Answer: d Difficulty: 1

33. Identify the graph of $9x^2 - 36xy + 4y^2 - 6x + 16y - 10 = 0$.
a) Ellipse or Circle
b) Parabola
c) Hyperbola

Answer: b Difficulty: 1

34. Identify the graph of $9x^2 - 16xy + 4y^2 - 6x + 16y - 10 = 0$.
a) Ellipse or Circle
b) Parabola
c) Hyperbola

Answer: c Difficulty: 1

35. Identify the graph of $2x^2 - xy + y^2 + x + 2y - 1 = 0$.
a) Ellipse or Circle
b) Parabola
c) Hyperbola

Answer: a Difficulty: 1

SHORT ANSWER

36. Identify the graph of $x^2 - 2xy - y^2 + 5x - 6y - 10 = 0$.

Answer: Hyperbola Difficulty: 1

37. Identify the graph of $4x^2 + xy + 2y^2 - 2x - y - 1 = 0$.

Answer: Ellipse or Circle Difficulty: 1

MULTIPLE CHOICE

38. Identify the graph of $xy - 2y + 4x = 0$.
a) I b) II c) III d) IV e) None of these

(I)
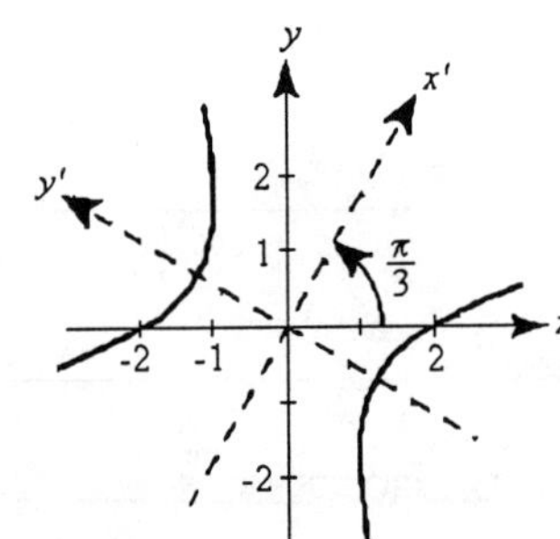

(II)
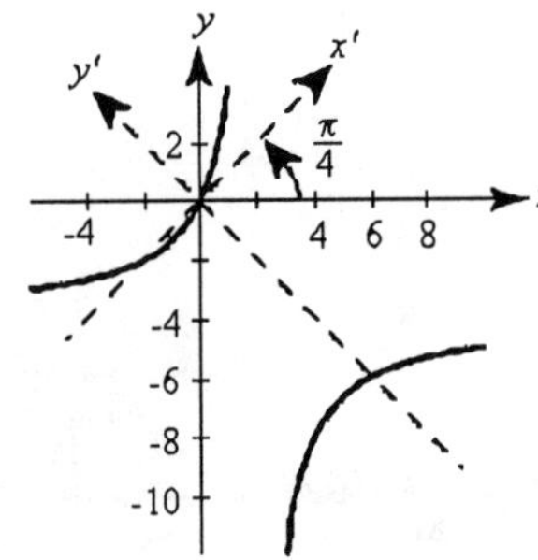

(III)
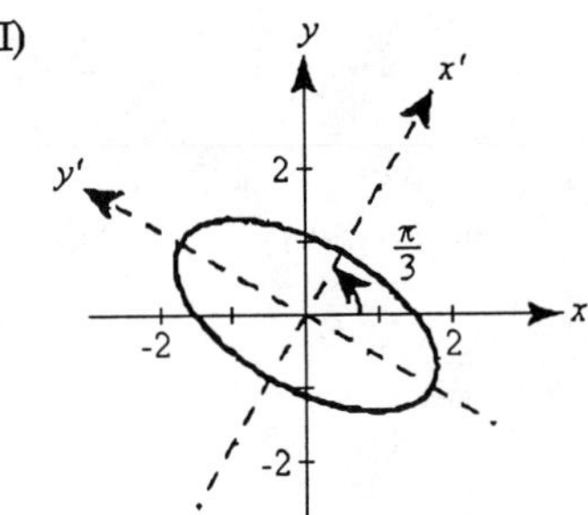

(IV)
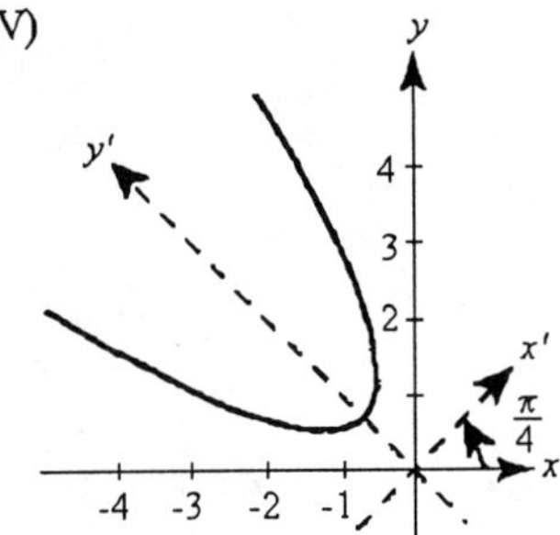

Answer: b Difficulty: 2

39. Identify the graph of $x^2 + xy + y^2 - 3 = 0$.
a) I b) II c) III d) IV e) None of these

(I)
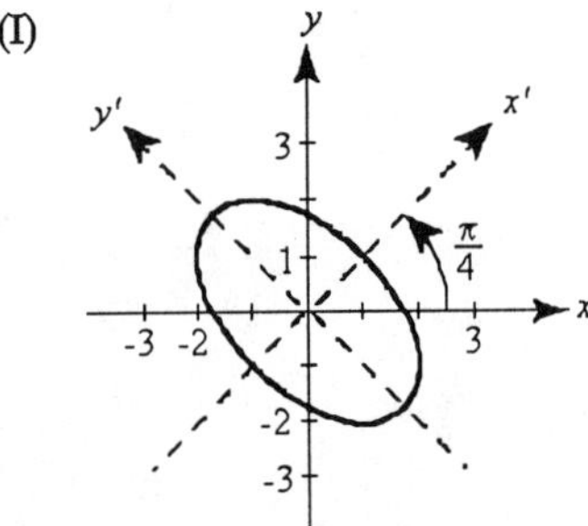

(II)
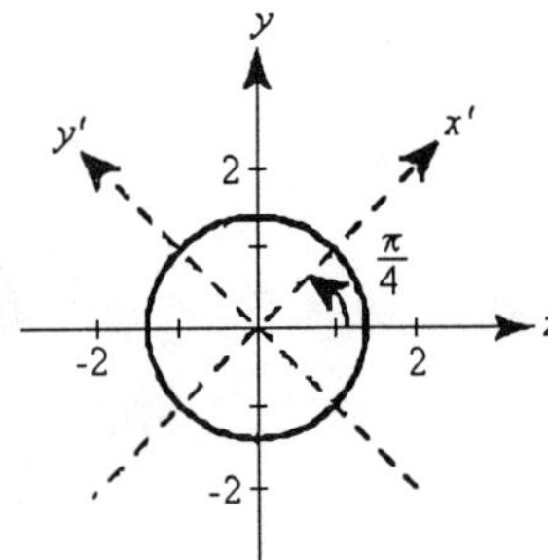

(III)
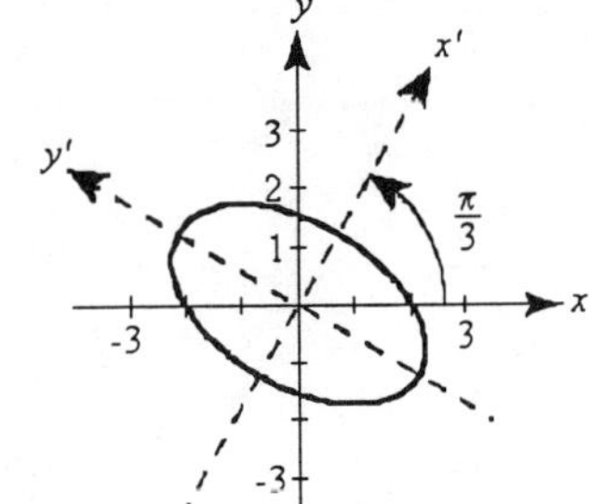

(IV)
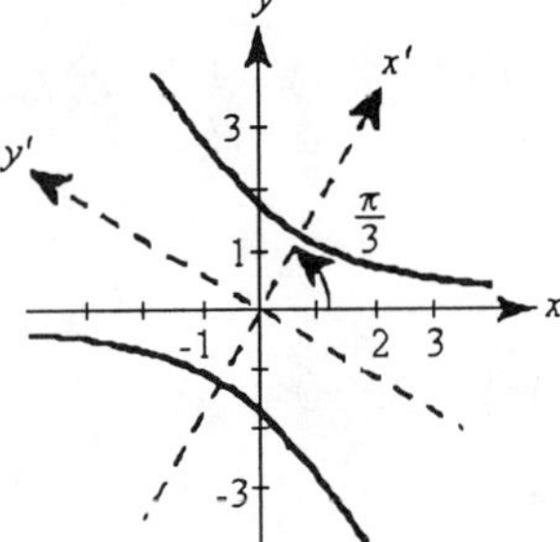

Answer: a Difficulty: 2

SHORT ANSWER

40. Rotate the axes to eliminate the xy-term from $2x^2 - 3xy + 2y^2 - 7 = 0$. Sketch the graph of the resulting equation showing both sets of axes.

Answer:

$\frac{1}{2}(x')^2 \ \frac{7}{2}(y')^2 - 7 = 0$ or $\frac{(x')^2}{14} + \frac{(y')^2}{2} = 1$

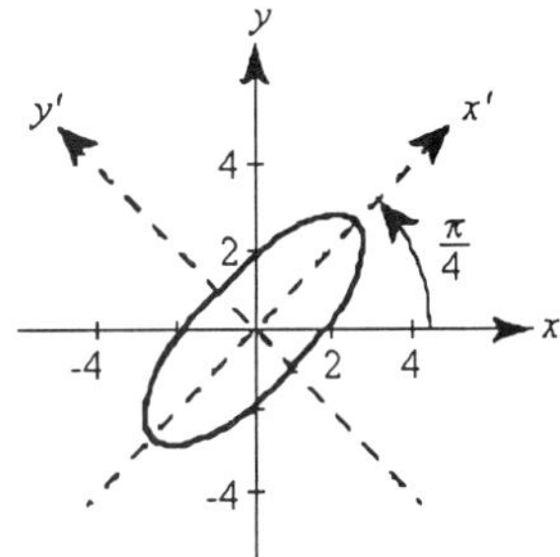

Difficulty: 2

41. Rotate the axes to eliminate the xy-term from $2x^2 + 4xy + 2y^2 = \sqrt{8}x - \sqrt{8}y = 0$. Sketch the graph of the resulting equation showing both sets of axes.

Answer:

$(x')^2 = y'$

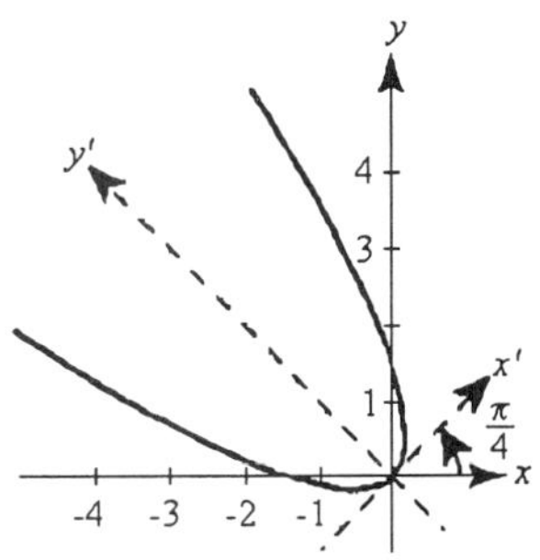

Difficulty: 2

42. Use a graphing utility to graph the equations and find any points of intersection of the graphs by the method of elimination.
$x^2 + y^2 - 2x - 4y + 4 = 0$
$-x^2 + y^2 + 2x - 4y + 2 = 0$

Answer: See graph below.

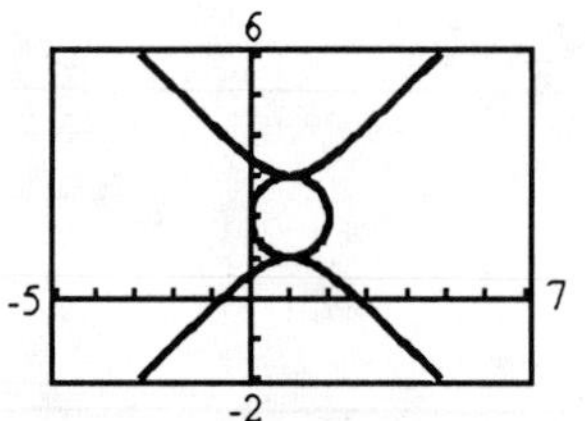

; (1, 3), (1, 1)

Difficulty: 2 Key 1: T

43. Use a graphing utility to graph the equations and find any points of intersection of the graphs by the method of elimination.
$4x^2 + y^2 + 8x - 2y - 3 = 0$
$x^2 + y^2 + 2x + 4y + 3 = 0$

Answer: See graph below.

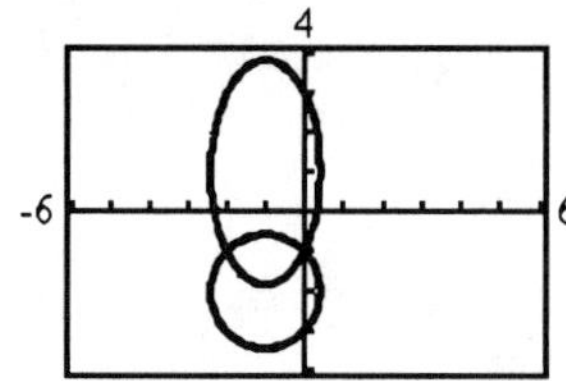

; (-2, -1), (0, -1)

Difficulty: 2 Key 1: T

44. Use a graphing utility to graph the equations and find any points of intersection of the graphs by the method of elimination.
$y^2 + x^2 - 4x + 8y - 16 = 0$
$y^2 - x^2 + 4x - 12y + 18 = 0$

Answer: See graph below.

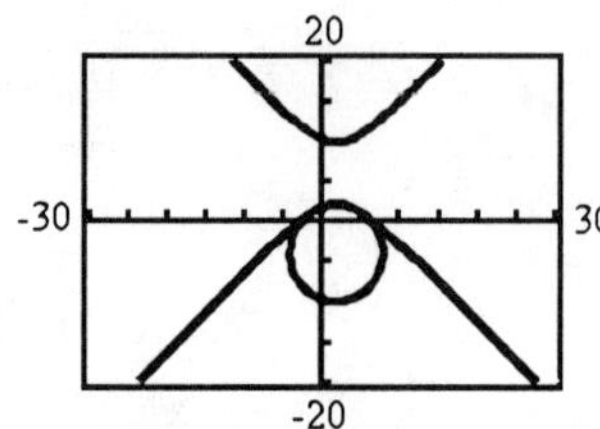

; $(2 + \sqrt{11}, 1), (2 - \sqrt{11}, 1)$

Difficulty: 2 Key 1: T

45. Use a graphing utility to graph the equations and find any points of intersection of the graphs by the method of substitution.
$x^2 + y^2 = 0$
$6x - y^2 = 0$

Answer: See graph below.

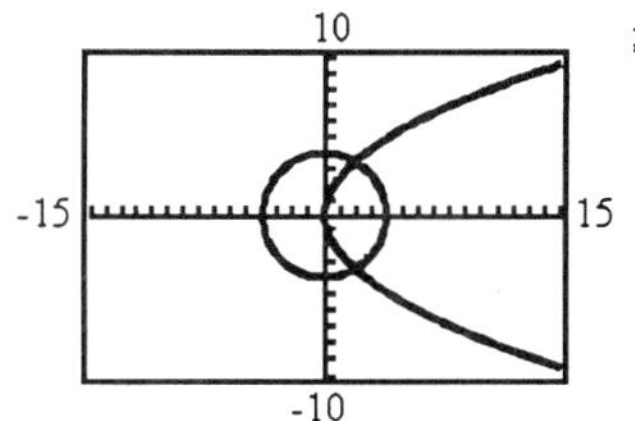

; $(2, 2\sqrt{3}), (2, -2\sqrt{3})$

Difficulty: 2 Key 1: T

46. Use a graphing utility to graph the equations and find any points of intersection of the graphs by the method of substitution.
$x^2 + y^2 = 17$
$x - y - 2 = 0$

Answer: See graph below.

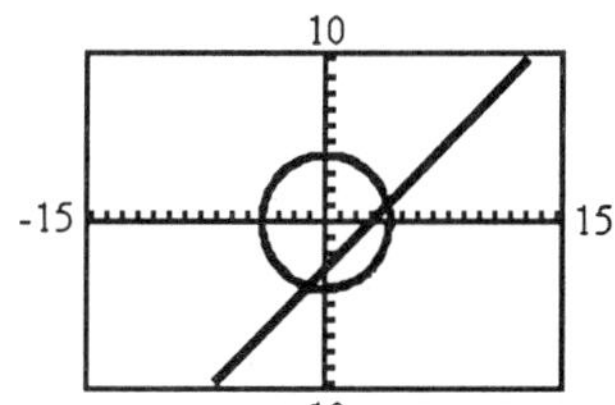

; $(4, 1), (-1, -4)$

Difficulty: 2 Key 1: T

47. Use a graphing utility to graph the equations and find any points of intersection of the graphs by the method of substitution.
$4x^2 + y^2 = 5$
$y - x + 2 = 0$

Answer: See graph below.

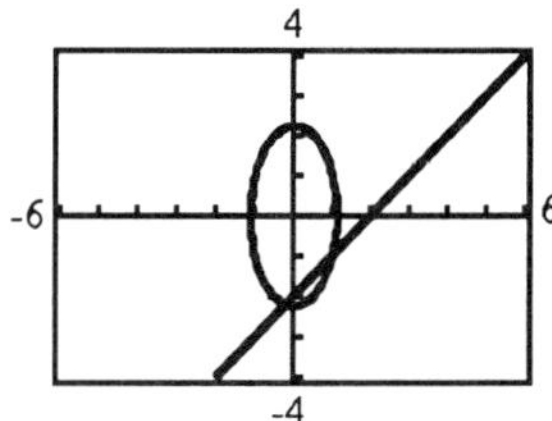

; $(-\frac{1}{5}, -\frac{11}{5}), (1, -1)$

Difficulty: 2 Key 1: T

Chapter 106: Parametric Equations

MULTIPLE CHOICE

1. Identify the curve for the parametric equations: $x = 3t - 6$ and $y = t - 4$.
 a) I b) II c) III d) IV e) None of these

(I)

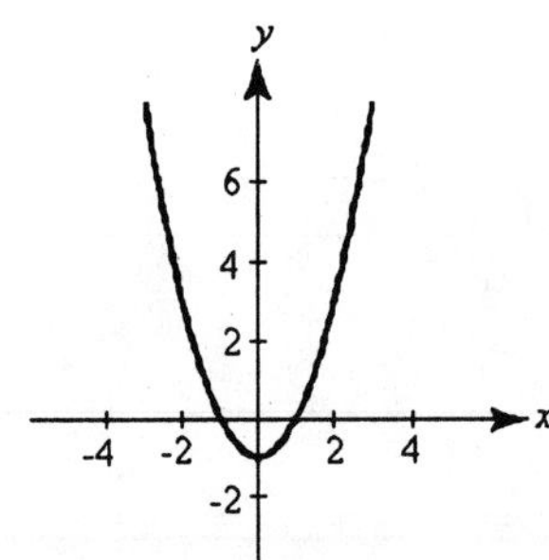

(II)

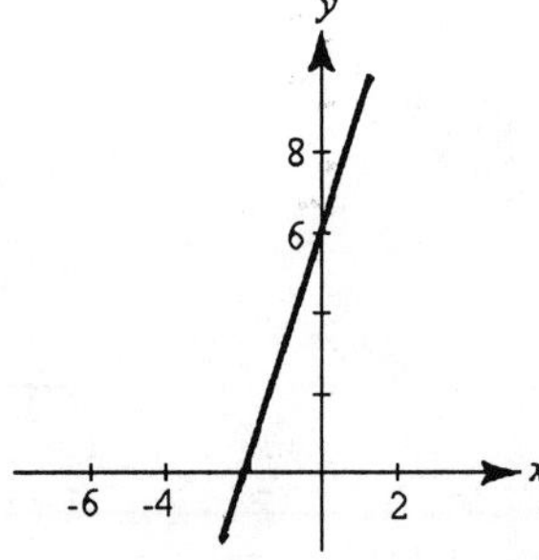

(III)

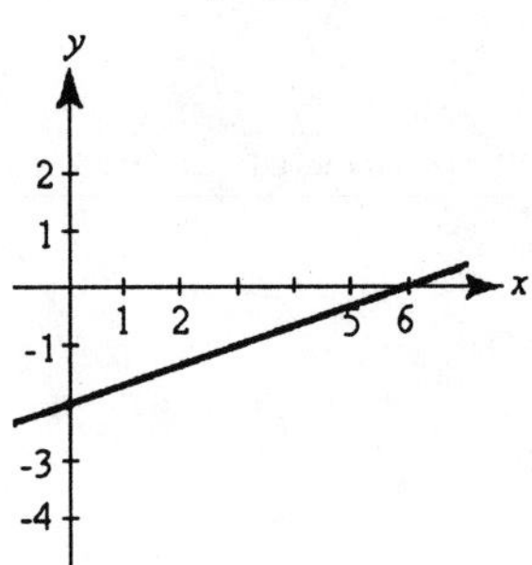

(IV)

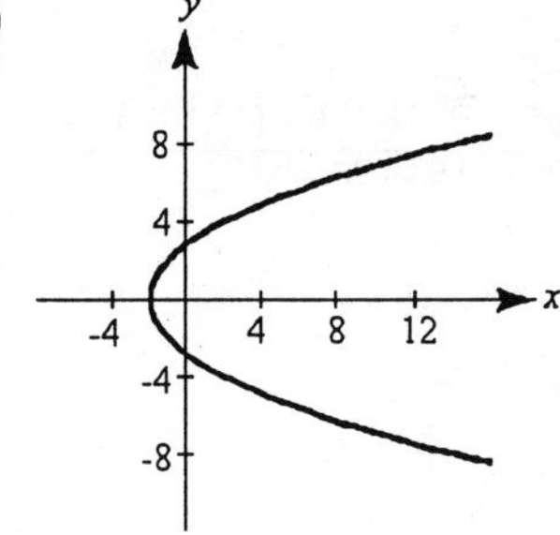

Answer: c Difficulty: 1

2. Identify the curve for the parametric equations: $x = 3t^2$ and $y = 1 - 2t^2$.
 a) I b) II c) III d) IV e) None of these

(I)

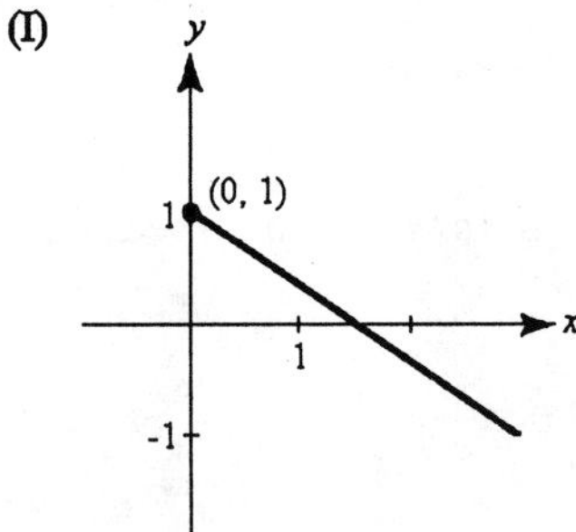

(II)

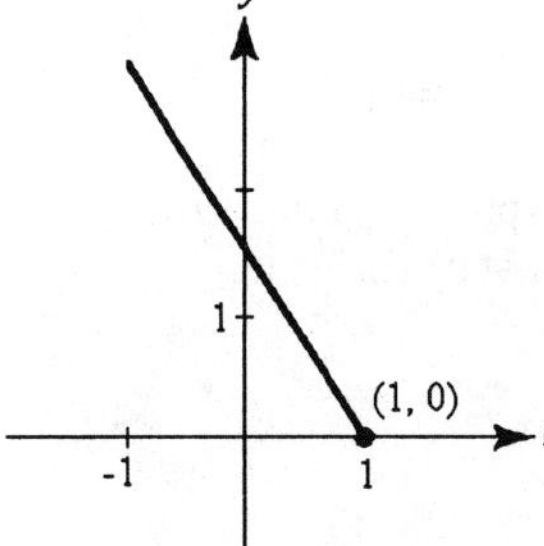

(III)

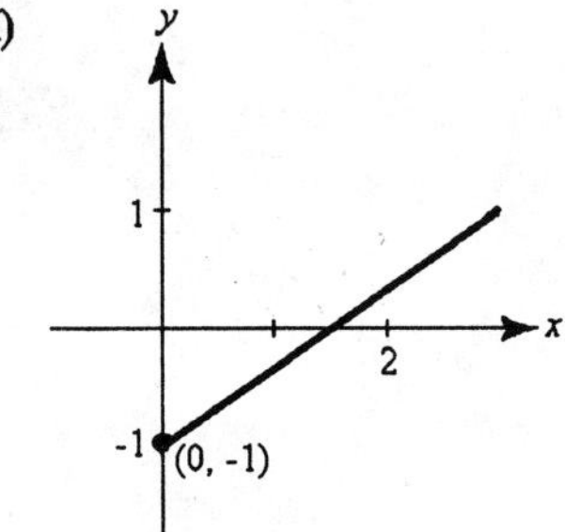

(IV)

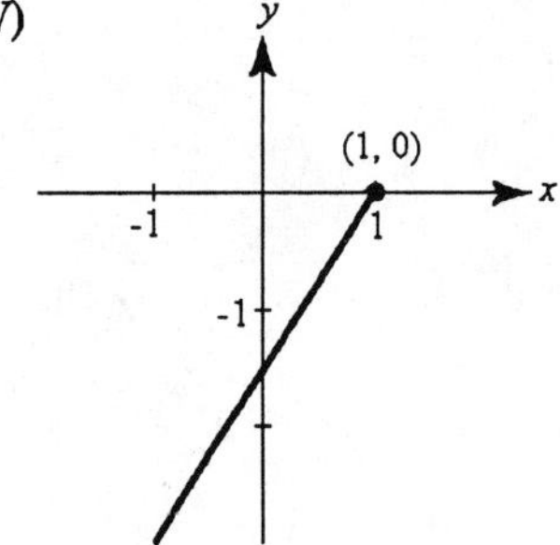

Answer: a Difficulty: 1

3. Identify the curve for the parametric equations: $x = 3t + 2$ and $y = t$.
   a) I b) II c) III d) IV e) None of these

(I)
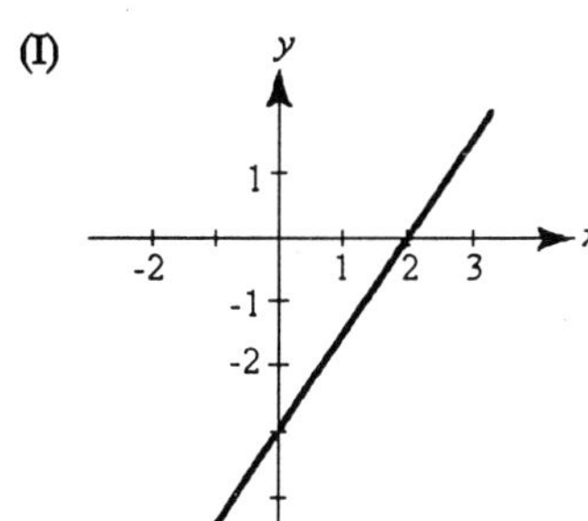

(II)
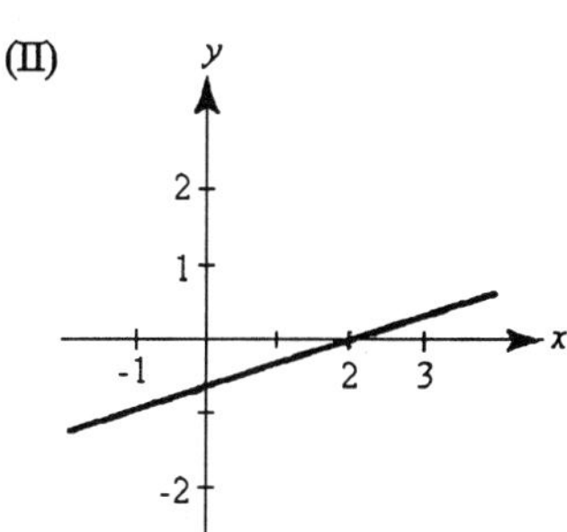

(III)
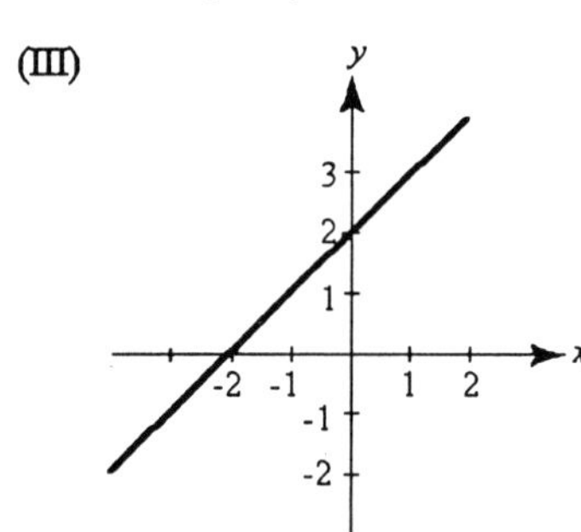

(IV)
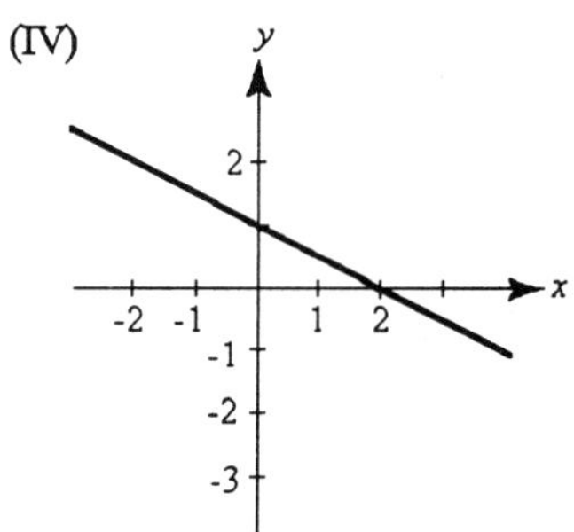

Answer: b Difficulty: 1

4. Identify the curve for the parametric equations: $x = t^2$ and $y = t - 1$.
   a) I b) II c) III d) IV e) None of these

(I)
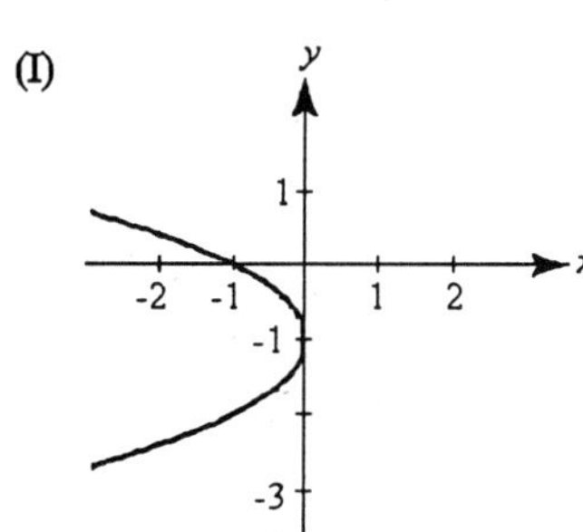

(II)
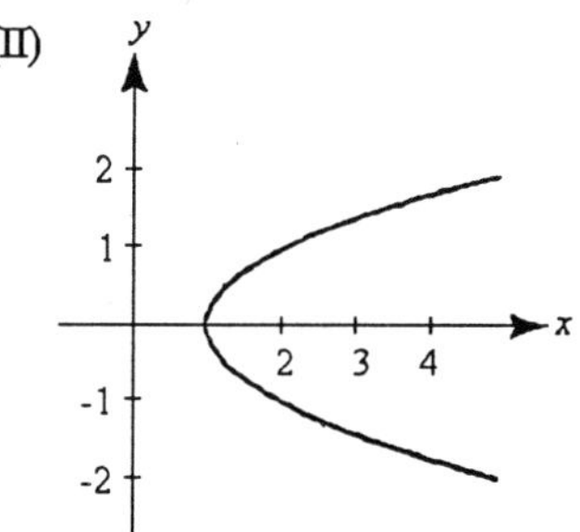

(III)
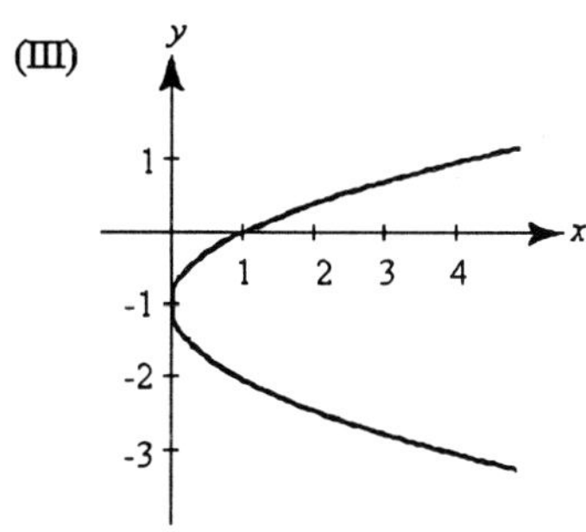

(IV)
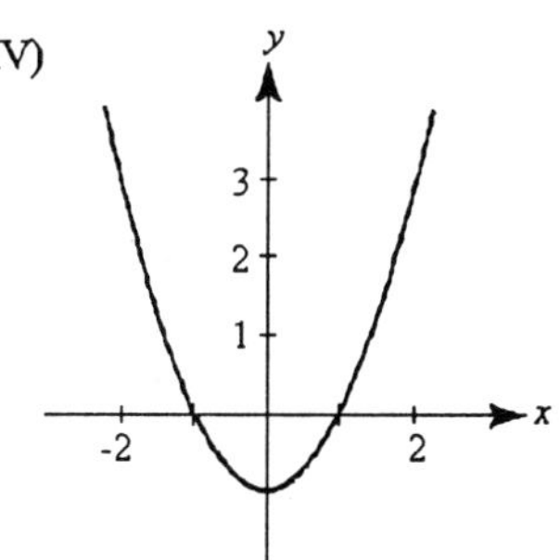

Answer: c Difficulty: 1

5. Identify the curve for the parametric equations: $x = 2t^2$ and $y = t + 1$.
a) I b) II c) III d) IV e) None of these

(I)

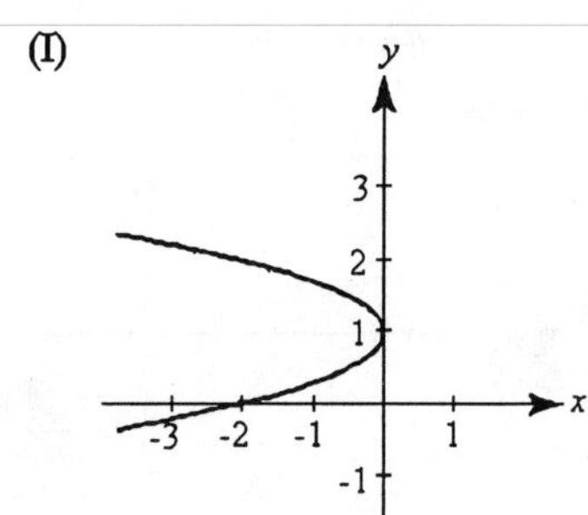

(II)

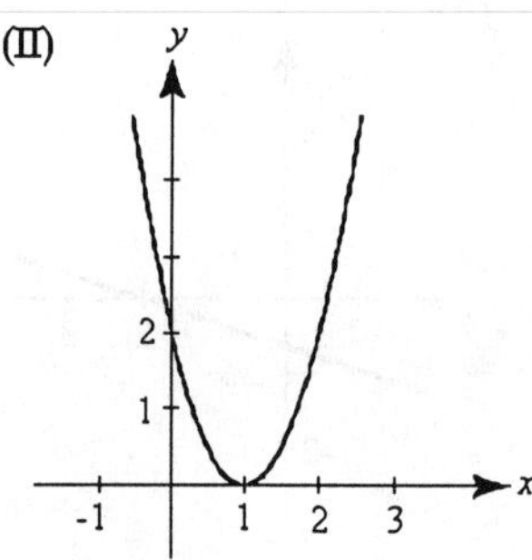

(III)

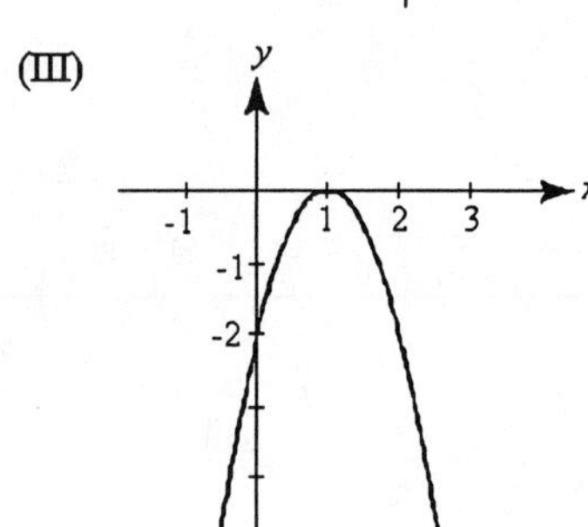

(IV)

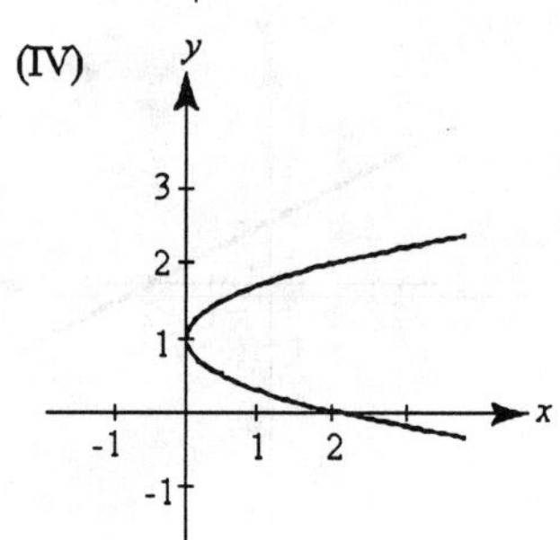

Answer: d Difficulty: 1

6. Identify the curve for the parametric equations: $x = \cos\theta$ and $y = 3\sin\theta$.
a) I b) II c) III d) IV e) None of these

(I)

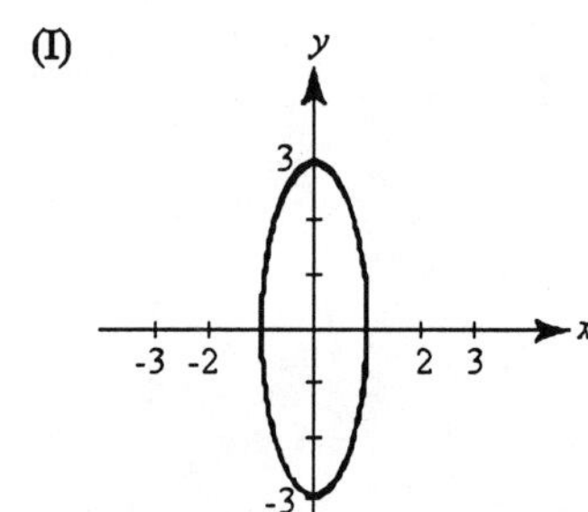

(II)

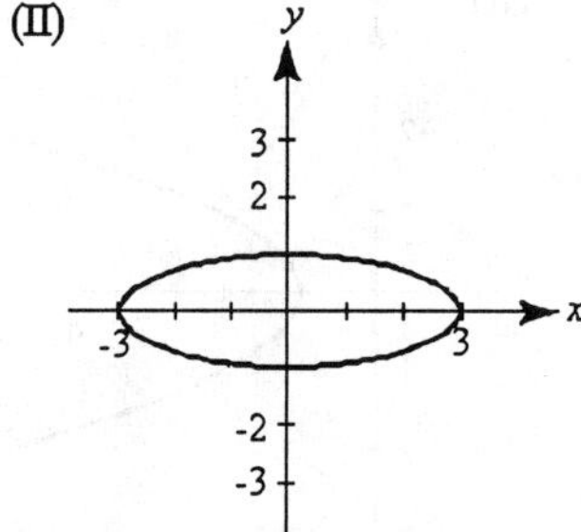

(III)

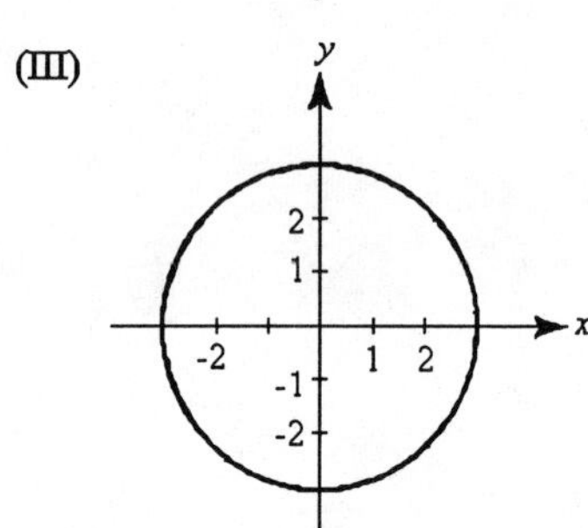

(IV)

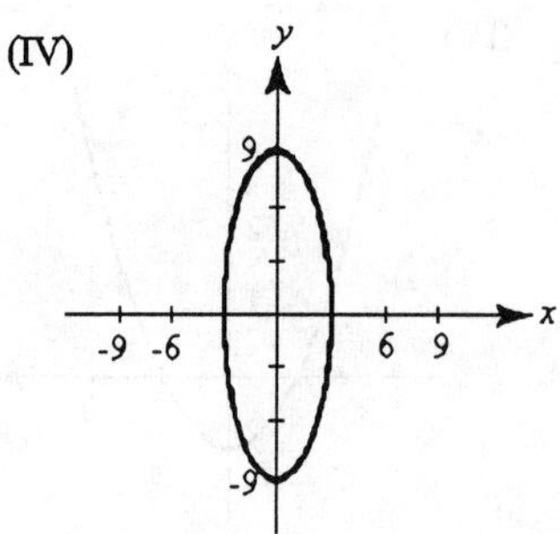

Answer: a Difficulty: 1

7. Identify the curve for the parametric equations: $x = 4 + \cos\theta$ and $y = -1 + \sin\theta$.
   a) I b) II c) III d) IV e) None of these

(I)

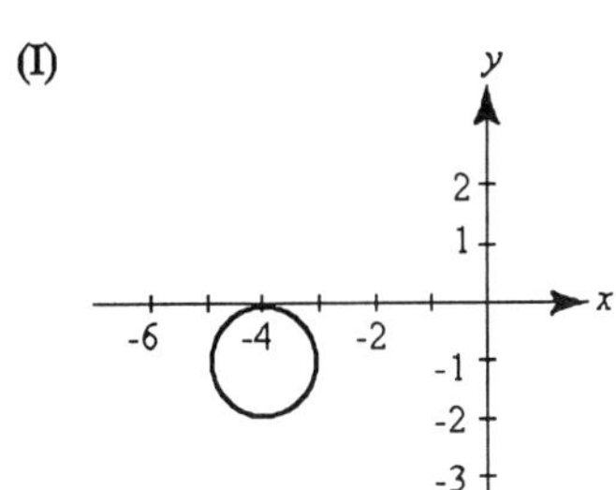

(II)

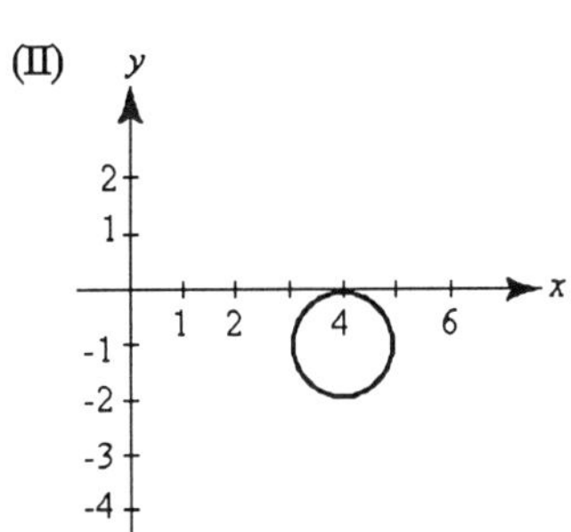

(III)

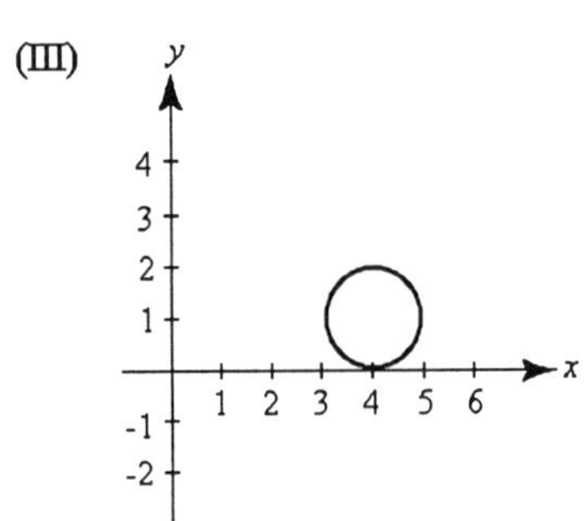

(IV)

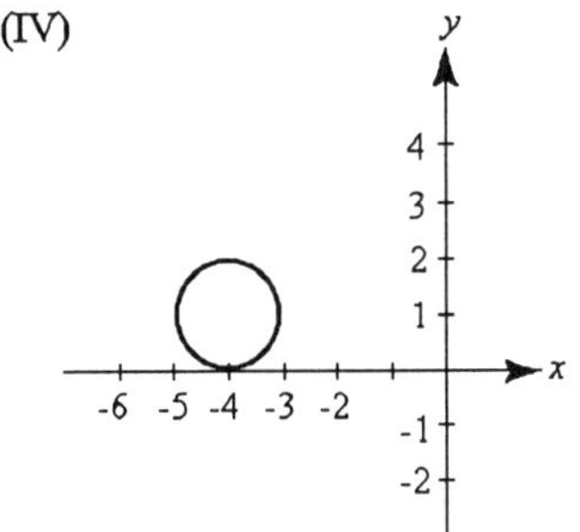

Answer: b Difficulty: 1

8. Identify the curve for the parametric equations: $x = 4\cos t$ and $y = 3\sin t$.
   a) I b) II c) III d) IV e) None of these

(I)

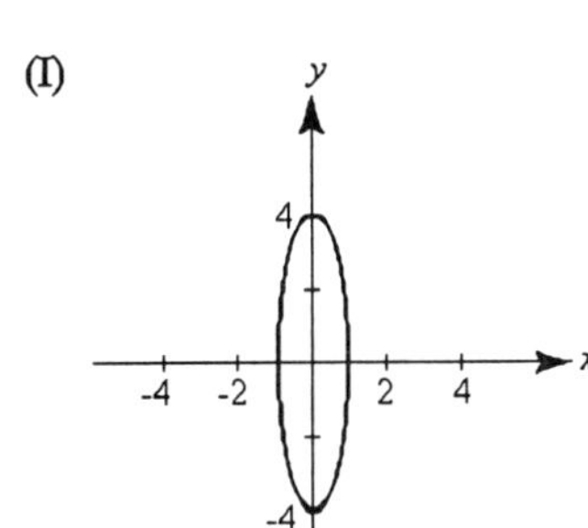

(II)

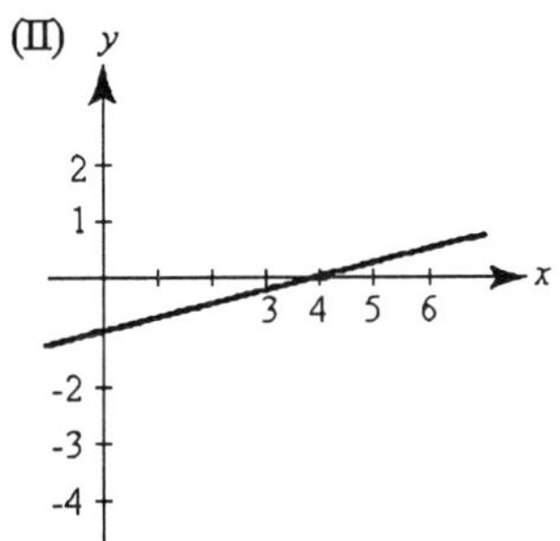

(III)

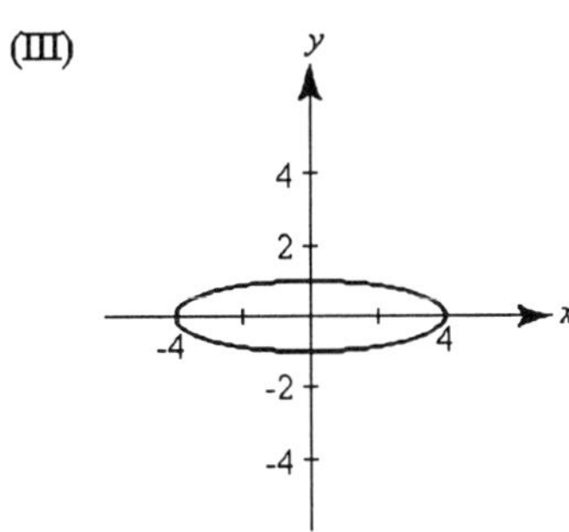

(IV)

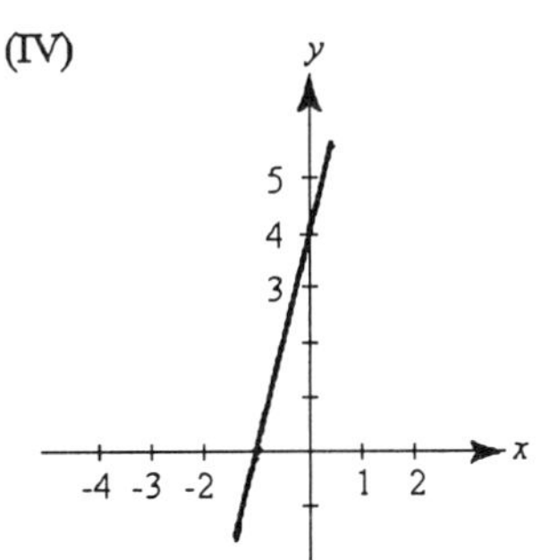

Answer: c Difficulty: 1

9. Identify the curve for the parametric equations: $x = -2 + \cos t$ and $y = \sin t$.
   a) I b) II c) III d) IV e) None of these

(I)

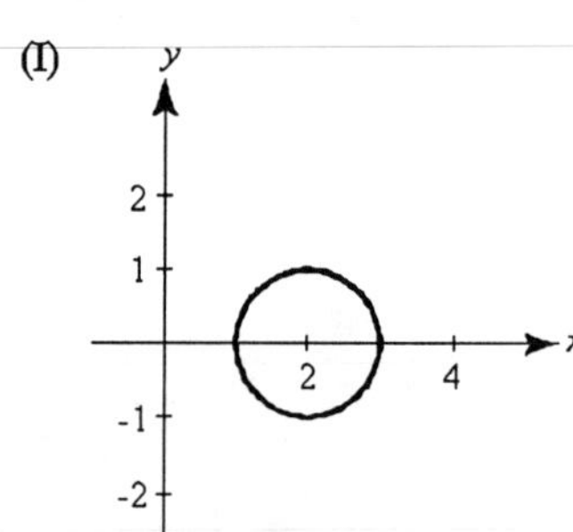

(II)

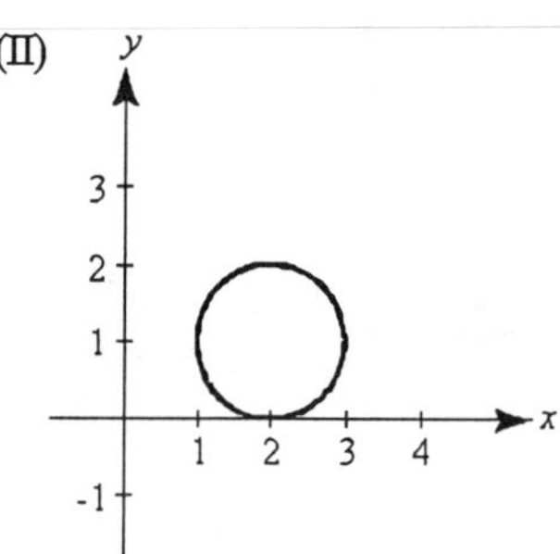

(III)

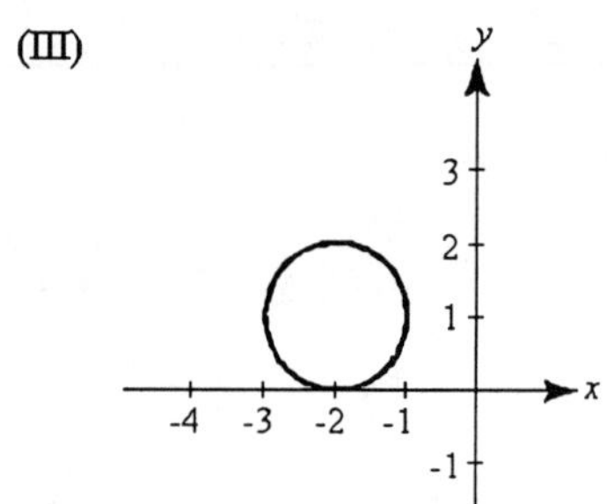

(IV)

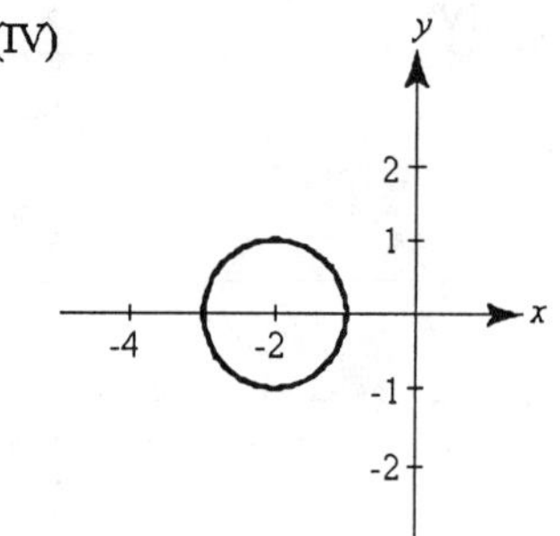

Answer: d Difficulty: 1

10. Identify the curve for the parametric equations: $x = 2t$ and $y = \sin t$.
   a) I b) II c) III d) IV e) None of these

(I)

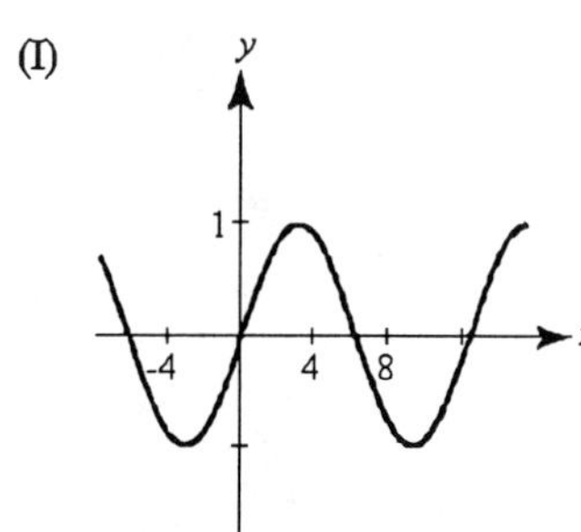

(II)

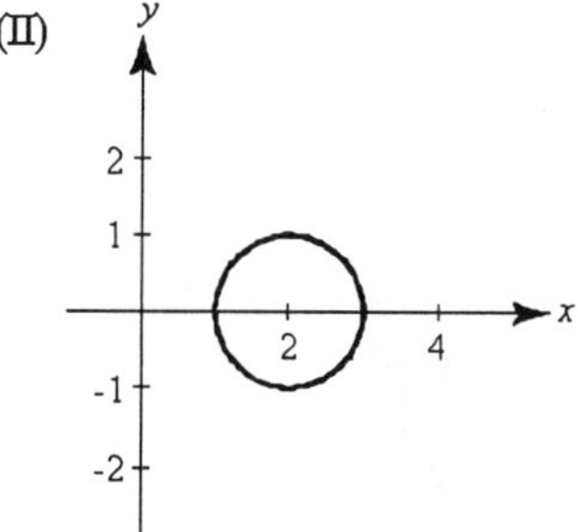

(III)

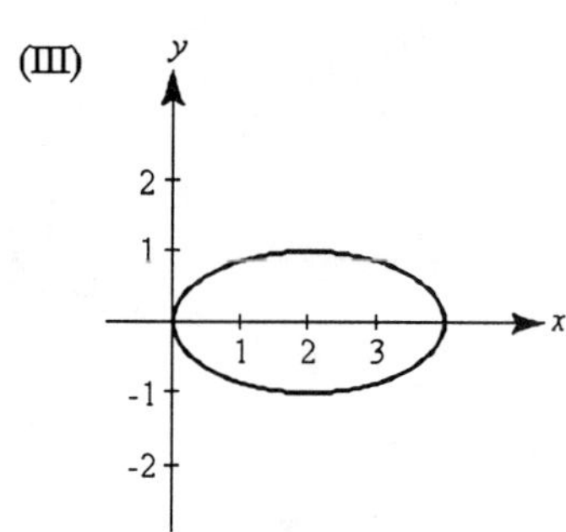

(IV)

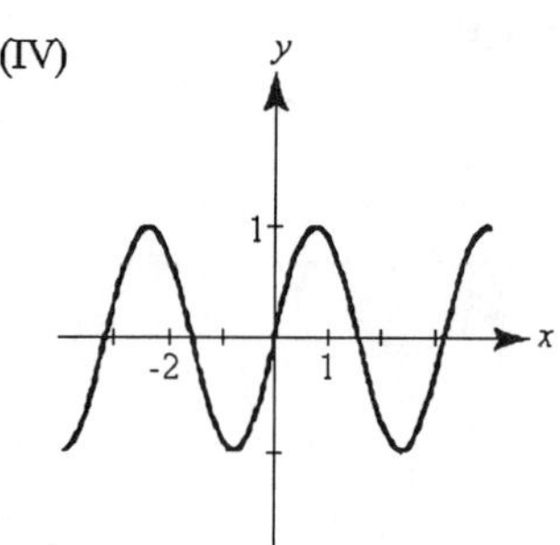

Answer: a Difficulty: 1

11. Eliminate the parameter and find a corresponding rectangular equation: $x = 3t^2$ and $y = 2t + 1$.
    a) $2x^2 + 3y^2 - 1 = 0$ b) $2x - 3y + 3 = 0$ c) $3y^2 - 4x + 1 = 0$
    d) $3y^2 - 4x - 6y + 3 = 0$ e) None of these

    Answer: d Difficulty: 1

12. Eliminate the parameter and find a corresponding rectangular equation: $x = 2\cos\theta$ and $y = \cos^2\theta$.
    a) $x + y = \cos\theta(2 + \cos\theta)$ b) $x - 2y = 0$ c) $y = \left(1 - \frac{x}{2}\right)^2$
    d) $x^2 = 4y$ e) None of these

    Answer: d Difficulty: 1

SHORT ANSWER

13. Eliminate the parameter and find a corresponding rectangular equation: $x = 1 + \cos\theta$ and $y = 2 - \sin\theta$.

    Answer:

    $x^2 + y^2 - 2x - 4y + 4 = 0$

    Difficulty: 2

14. Eliminate the parameter and find a corresponding rectangular equation: $x = 3 + \cos\theta$ and $y = \sin\theta - 1$.

    Answer:

    $x^2 + y^2 - 6x + 2y + 9 = 0$

    Difficulty: 2

15. Eliminate the parameter and find a corresponding rectangular equation: $x = t^3$ and $y = 1/t$.

    Answer:

    $xy^3 = 1$

    Difficulty: 1

16. Eliminate the parameter and find a corresponding rectangular equation: $x = e^t$ and $y = e^{2t}$.

    Answer:

    $y = x^2$

    Difficulty: 1

17. Eliminate the parameter and find a corresponding rectangular equation: $x = e^{-t}$ and $y = e^t$

Answer: $y = 1/x$ Difficulty: 1

MULTIPLE CHOICE

18. Eliminate the parameter and find a corresponding rectangular equation: $x = 3t + 1$ and $y = 2t$.
a) $2x - 3y - 2 = 0$ b) $2x - 3y - 3 = 0$ c) $x - 6y + 1 = 0$
d) $2x - 3y - 6 = 0$ e) None of these

Answer: a Difficulty: 1

19. Eliminate the parameter and find a corresponding rectangular equation: $x = t^2$ and $y = t + 1$.
a) $x - y^2 - 1 = 0$ b) $x - y^2 + 2y - 1 = 0$ c) $x - y + 1 = 0$
d) $x - y^2 - 2y - 1 = 0$ e) None of these

Answer: b Difficulty: 1

20. Eliminate the parameter and find a corresponding rectangular equation: $x = 2 \cos \theta$ and $y = 4 \sin \theta$.
a) $4x + 2y = 1$ b) $16x^2 - 4y^2 = 1$ c) $4x + 2y = 8$
d) $16x^2 + 4y^2 = 64$ e) None of these

Answer: d Difficulty: 1

SHORT ANSWER

21. Eliminate the parameter and find a corresponding rectangular equation: $x = -3 + 2 \cos \theta$ and $y = 1 + \sin \theta$.

Answer:

$$\frac{(x + 3)^2}{4} + (y - 1)^2 = 1 \text{ or } x^2 + 4y^2 + 6x - 8y + 9 = 0$$

Difficulty: 1

MULTIPLE CHOICE

22. Eliminate the parameter and find a corresponding rectangular equation: $x = t^3$ and $y = 1 - t$.
a) $y^3 - 3y^2 + 3y + x - 1 = 0$ b) $y^3 - 3y^2 + 3y - x - 1 = 0$
c) $y^3 + x - 1 = 0$ d) $y^3 - x - 1 = 0$
e) None of these

Answer: a Difficulty: 1

SHORT ANSWER

23. Given the line through (x_1, y_1) and (x_2, y_2) has parametric equations $x = x_1 + t(x_2 - x_1)$ and $y = y_1 + t(y_2 - y_1)$, find the parametric equations for the line passing through the points (4, 3) and (6, -10).

 Answer:
 $x = 4 + 2t$
 $y = 3 - 13t$
 Difficulty: 1

24. Given the line through (x_1, y_1) and (x_2, y_2) has parametric equations $x = x_1 + t(x_2 - x_1)$ and $y = y_1 + t(y_2 - y_1)$, find the parametric equations for the line passing through the points (5, -4) and (0, 5).

 Answer:
 $x = 5 - 5t$
 $y = -4 + 9t$
 Difficulty: 1

25. Given a circle with center (h, k) and radius r has parametric equations $x = h + r\cos\theta$ and $y = k + r\sin\theta$, find a set of parametric equations of a circle with center (-4, 5) and radius 4.

 Answer:
 $x = -4 + 4\cos\theta$
 $y = 5 + 4\sin\theta$
 Difficulty: 1

26. Given a circle with center (h, k) and radius r has parametric equations $x = h + r\cos\theta$ and $y = k + r\sin\theta$, find a set of parametric equations of a circle with center $\left(-10, \frac{1}{2}\right)$ and radius $\sqrt{7}$.

 Answer:
 $x = -10 + \sqrt{7}\cos\theta$
 $y = \frac{1}{2} + \sqrt{7}\sin\theta$
 Difficulty: 1

27. Given an ellipse in standard form with a horizontal major axis has parametric equations $x = h + a\cos\theta$ and $y = k + b\sin\theta$, find a set of parametric equations with vertices (4, 3), (-4, 3) and foci (2, 3), (-2, 3).

 Answer:
 $x = 4\cos\theta$
 $y = 3 + 2\sqrt{3}\sin\theta$
 Difficulty: 1

28. Given an ellipse in standard form with a horizontal major axis has parametric equations $x = h + a \cos \theta$ and $y = k + b \sin \theta$, find a set of parametric equations with vertices (10, 2), (-20, 2) and foci (8, 2), (-18, 2).

Answer:
$x = -5 + 15 \cos \theta$

$y = 2 + 2\sqrt{14} \sin \theta$

Difficulty: 1

29. Given a hyperbola in standard form with a horizontal transverse axis has parametric equations $x = h + a \sec \theta$ and $y = k + b \tan \theta$, find a set of parametric equations for the hyperbola with vertices $(\pm 10, 0)$ and foci $(\pm 12, 0)$.

Answer:
$x = 10 \sec \theta$

$y = 2\sqrt{11} \tan \theta$

Difficulty: 1

30. Given a hyperbola in standard form with a horizontal transverse axis has parametric equations $x = h + a \sec \theta$ and $y = k + b \tan \theta$, find a set of parametric equations for the hyperbola with vertices (12, 1), (22, 1) and foci (24, 1), (10, 1).

Answer:
$x = 17 + 5 \sec \theta$

$y = 1 + 4\sqrt{6} \tan \theta$

Difficulty: 1

MULTIPLE CHOICE

31. Find a set of parametric equations for the curve below.

a) $x = -1 + \sin t$, $y = -1 + 3 \sin t$
b) $x = 3 \cos t + 8$, $y = 2 + \cos t$
c) $x = \cos 2t$, $y = 2 \cos^2 t - 1$
d) $x = 1 + \cos t$, $y = 3 + \cos t$
e) None of these

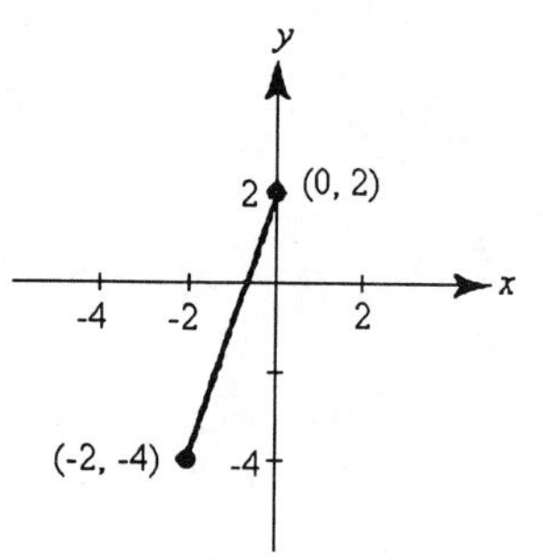

Answer: a Difficulty: 2

32. Find a set of parametric equations for the curve below.

a) $x = \frac{3}{2}t$
$y = t + 3$

b) $x = t$
$y = -\frac{2}{3}t + 3$

c) $x = -\frac{3}{2}t$
$y = t - 3$

d) $x = t$
$y = \frac{2}{3}t + 3$

e) None of these

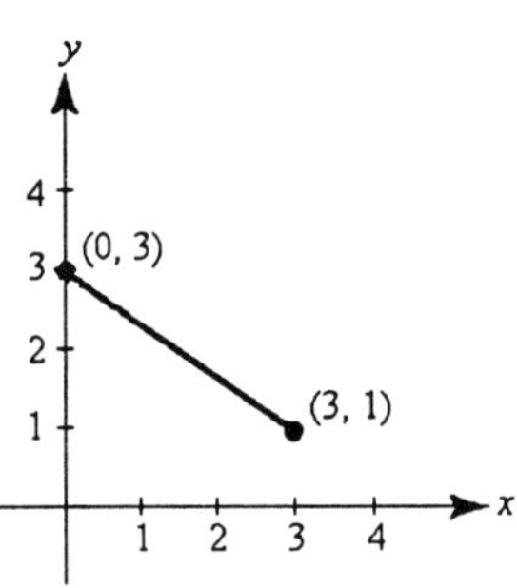

Answer: b Difficulty: 1

33. Find a set of parametric equations for the curve below.

a) $x = t$
$y = t$

b) $x = t$
$y = 3t + \frac{2}{3}$

c) $x = 3t$
$y = t + \frac{2}{3}$

d) $x = t$
$y = 3t + \frac{2}{3}$

e) None of these

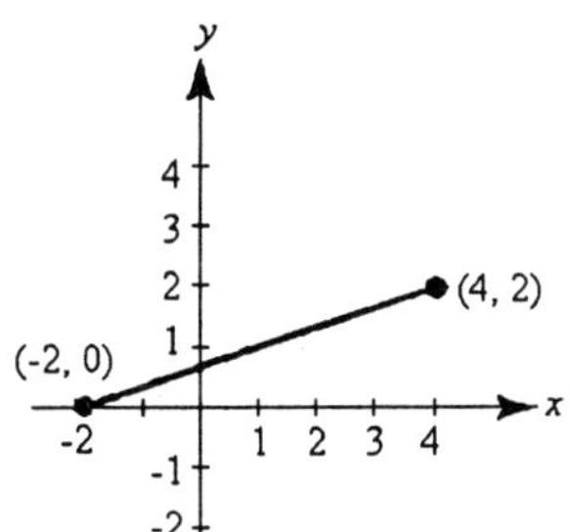

Answer: c Difficulty: 1

SHORT ANSWER

34. Find a set of parametric equations for the curve below.

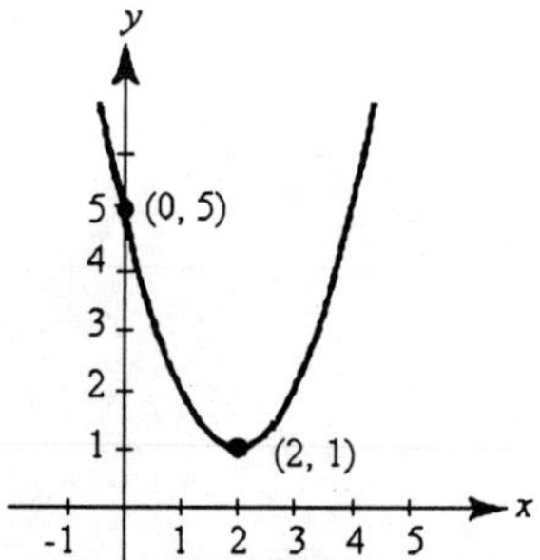

Answer:

$y = (x - 2)^2 + 1$
$t = x - 2 \Rightarrow x = t + 2$
$y = (t)^2 + 1 \Rightarrow y = t^2 + 1$

Difficulty: 2

35. Find a set of parametric equations for the curve below.

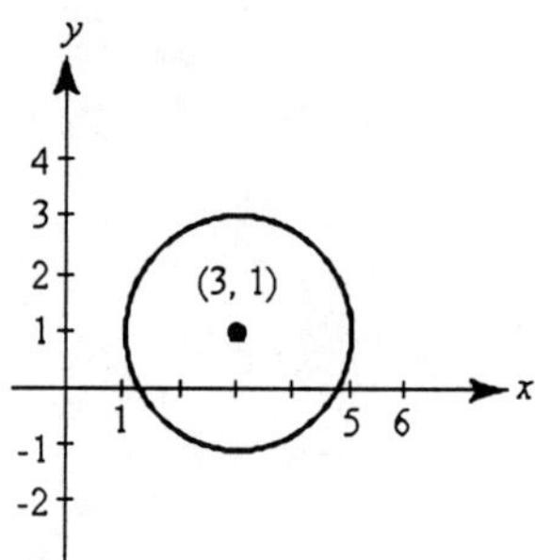

Answer:

Circle with center (3, 1), $r = 2$

$(x - 3)^2 + (y - 1)^2 = 4$

$$\frac{(x - 3)^2}{4} + \frac{(y - 1)^2}{4} = 1$$

$$\cos^2 t + \sin^2 t = 1$$

$$\cos t = \frac{x - 3}{2} \Rightarrow x = 3 + 2 \cos t$$

$$\sin t = \frac{y - 1}{2} \Rightarrow y = 1 + 2 \sin t$$

Difficulty: 2

36. Sketch the curve represented by the parametric equations $x = 1 + 3t$ and $y = t - 1$.

Answer: See graph below.

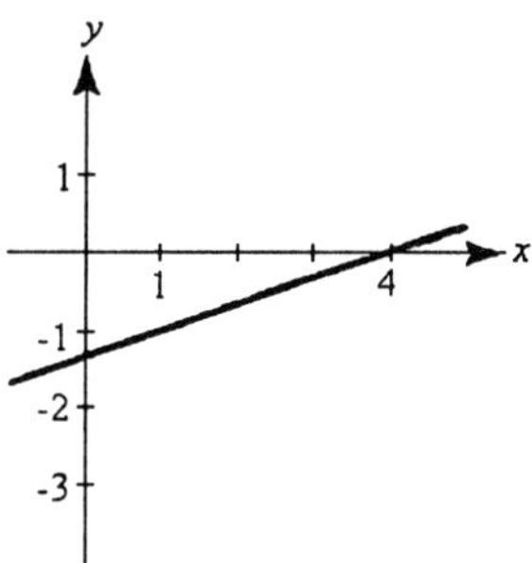

Difficulty: 1

37. If an object moves according to the parametric equations $x = 2t$ and $y = 3t^2$, sketch a graph of its motion for $0 \le t \le 3$.

Answer: See graph below.

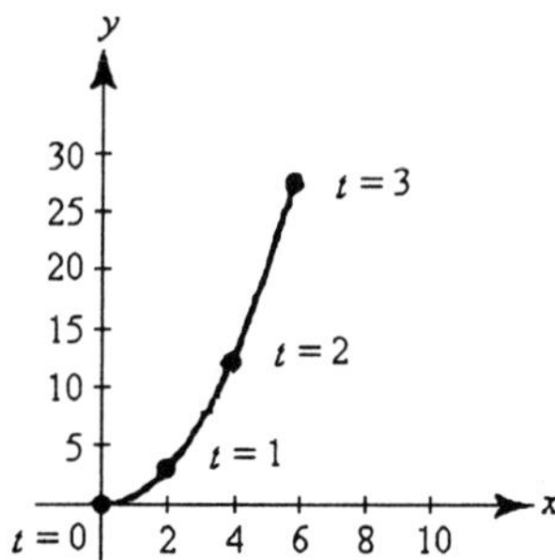

Difficulty: 1

38. A ball is thrown at an angle of θ and initial velocity V_0. The path of the ball has parametric equations $x = V_0 \cos \theta\, t$ and $y = V_0 \sin \theta\, t - 16t^2$. Sketch the curve of a ball if it is thrown at an angle of 45° and with an initial velocity of 60 feet per second.

Answer:

$\theta = 45°,\ V_0 = 60$

$x = 60 \cos 45°\, t \Rightarrow x = \dfrac{60}{\sqrt{2}}t$

$y = 60 \sin 45°\, t - 16t^2 \Rightarrow y = \dfrac{60}{\sqrt{2}}t - 16t^2$

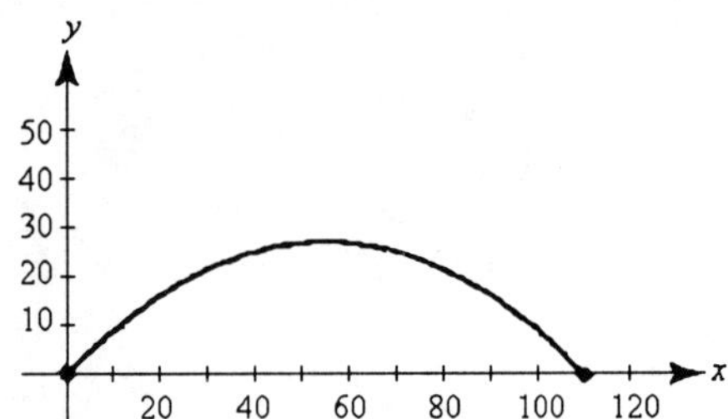

Difficulty: 2

39. Use a graphing utility to graph the curve represented by the parametric equations: $x = 3 \sin \theta$ and $y = 3 \cos \theta$.

Answer: See graph below.

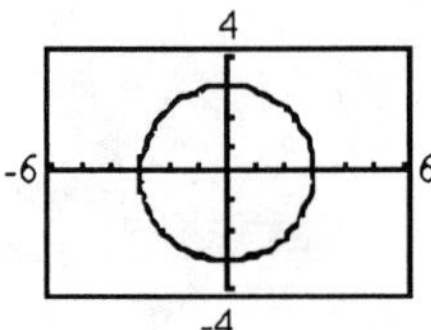

Difficulty: 1 Key 1: T

40. Use a graphing utility to graph the curve represented by the parametric equations: $x = \cos \theta$ and $y = \sin 2\theta$.

Answer: See graph below.

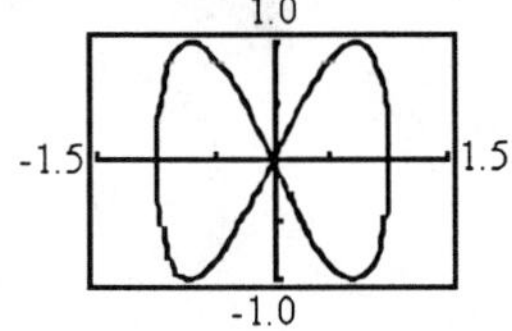

Difficulty: 1 Key 1: T

41. Use a graphing utility to graph the curve represented by the parametric equations: $x = 4 + \sin t$ and $y = 2 + \cos t$.

Answer: See graph below.

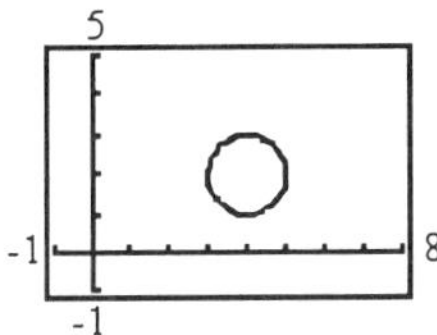

Difficulty: 1 Key 1: T

42. Use a graphing utility to graph the curve represented by the parametric equations: $x = t^2$ and $y = \ln t$.

Answer: See graph below.

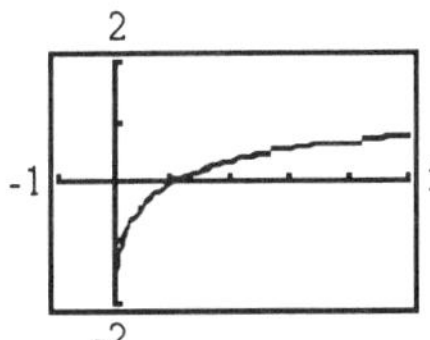

Difficulty: 1 Key 1: T

43. Use a graphing utility to graph the curve represented by the parametric equations: $x = |t - 1|$ and $y = 2 - t$.

Answer: See graph below.

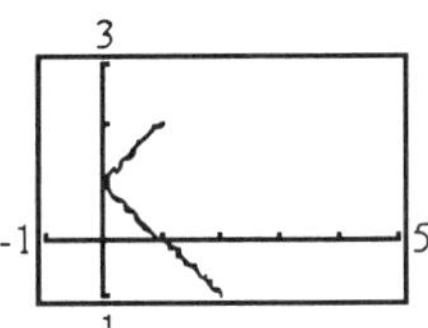

Difficulty: 1 Key 1: T

44. Use a graphing utility to graph the curve represented by the parametric equations: $x = |\sin 2t|$ and $y = t$.

Answer: See graph below.

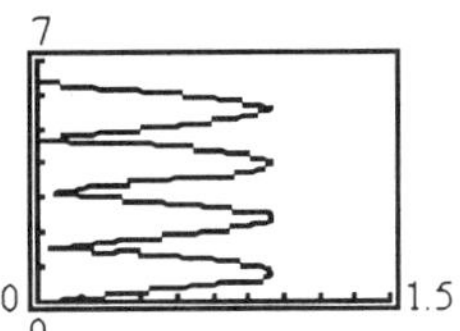

Difficulty: 1 Key 1: T

Chapter 107: Polar Coordinates

MULTIPLE CHOICE

1. Plot the point whose polar coordinates are $\left(3, \dfrac{\pi}{6}\right)$.

   a) I b) II c) III d) IV e) None of these

(I)

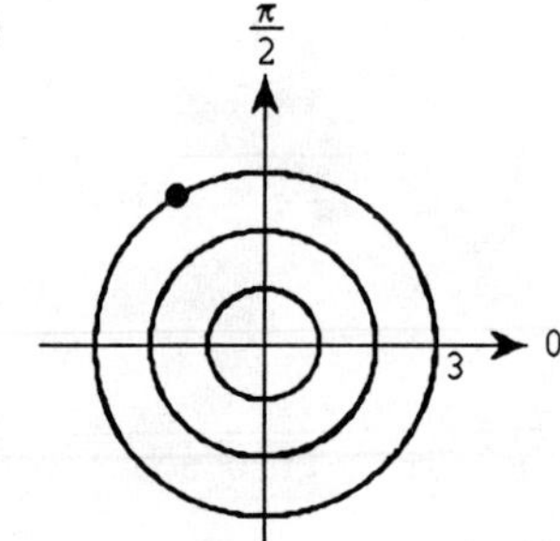

(II)

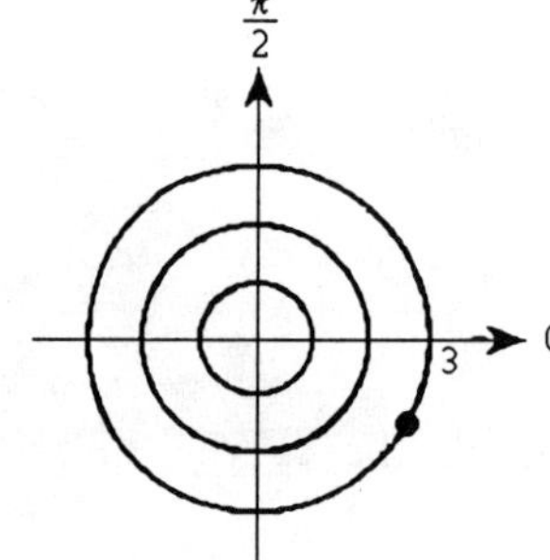

(III)

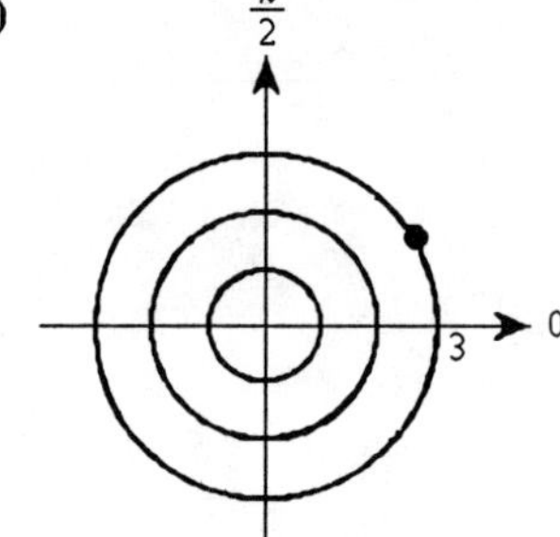

(IV)

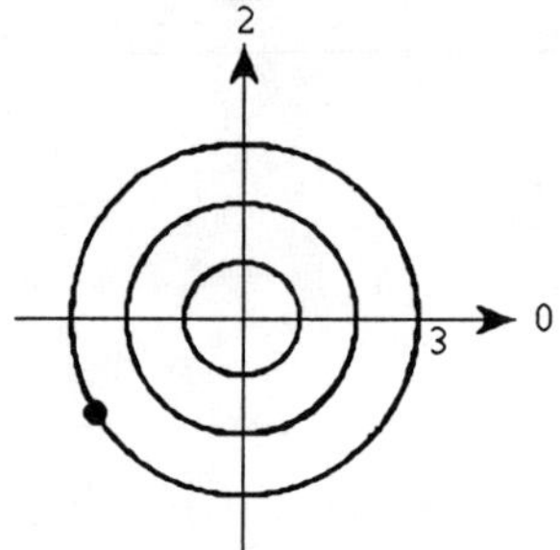

Answer: c Difficulty: 1

2. Plot the point whose polar coordinates are $\left(4, -\frac{\pi}{3}\right)$.

a) I b) II c) III d) IV e) None of these

(I)

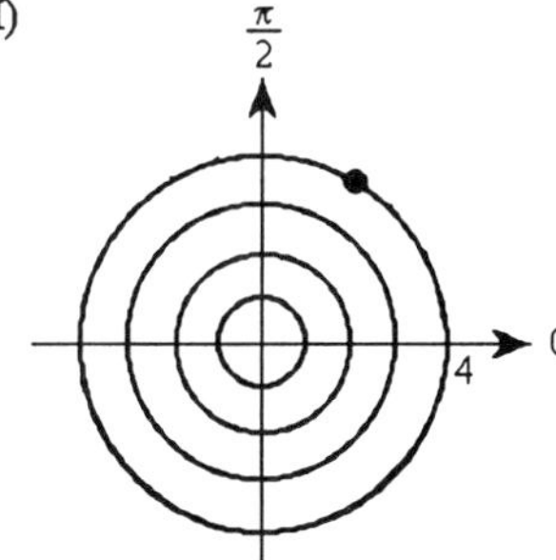

(II)

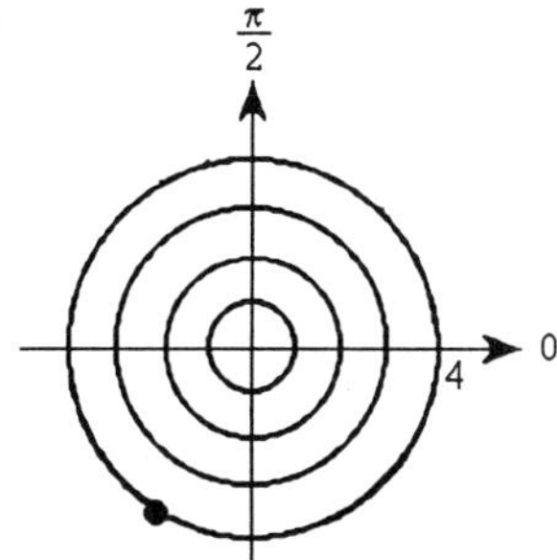

(III)

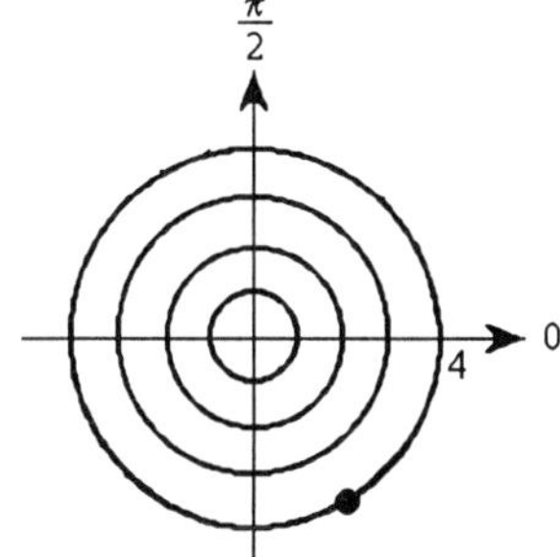

(IV)

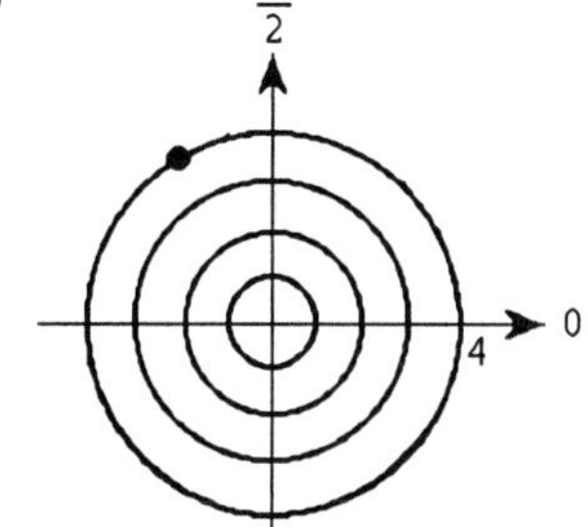

Answer: c Difficulty: 1

3. Plot the point whose polar coordinates are $\left(-2, -\frac{2\pi}{3}\right)$.

a) I b) II c) III d) IV e) None of these

(I)

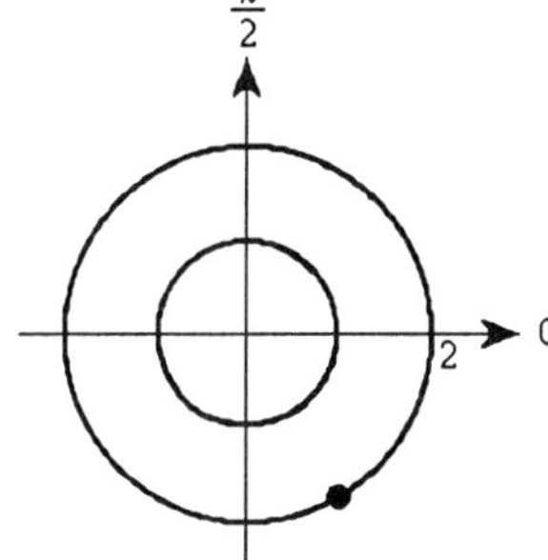

(II)

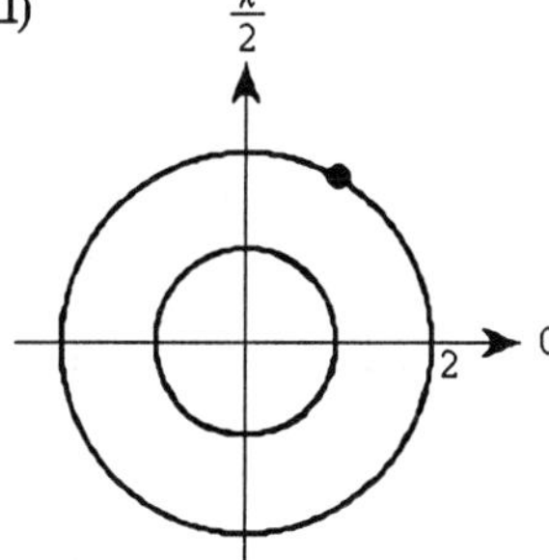

(III)

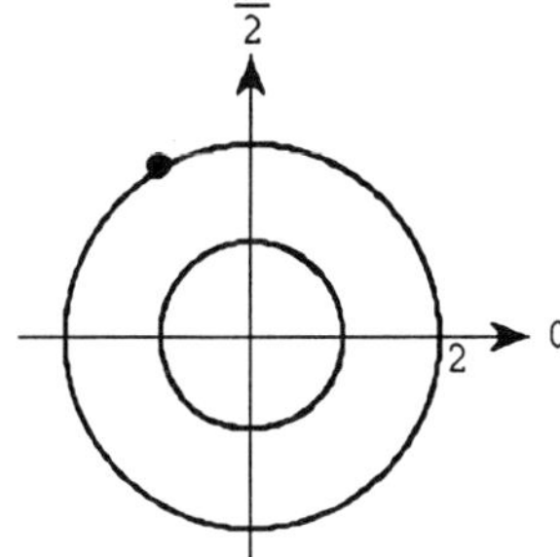

(IV)

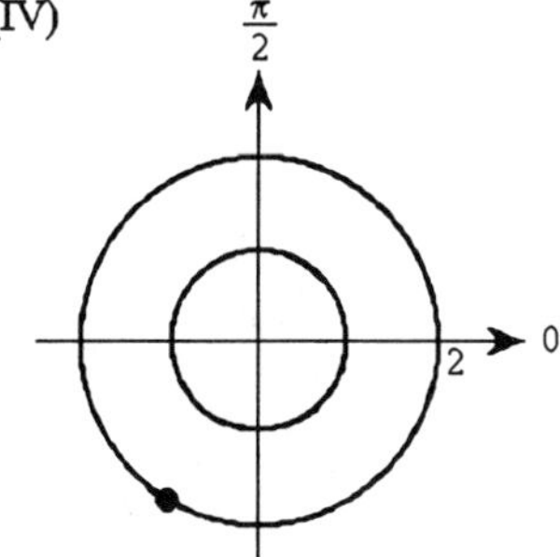

Answer: b Difficulty: 1

4. Plot the point whose polar coordinates are $\left(-2, \frac{15\pi}{4}\right)$.

a) I b) II c) III d) IV e) None of these

(I)

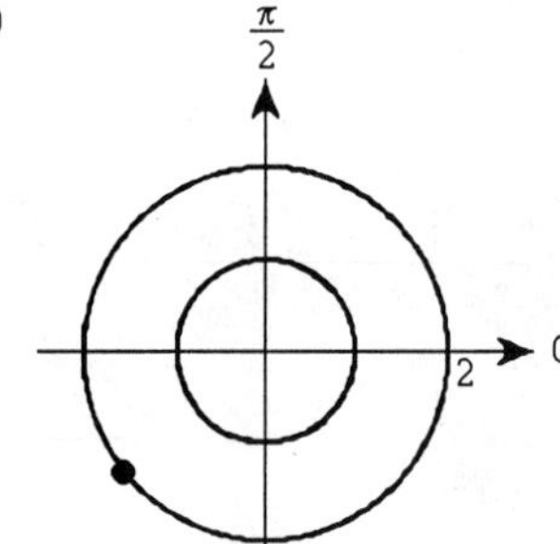

(II)

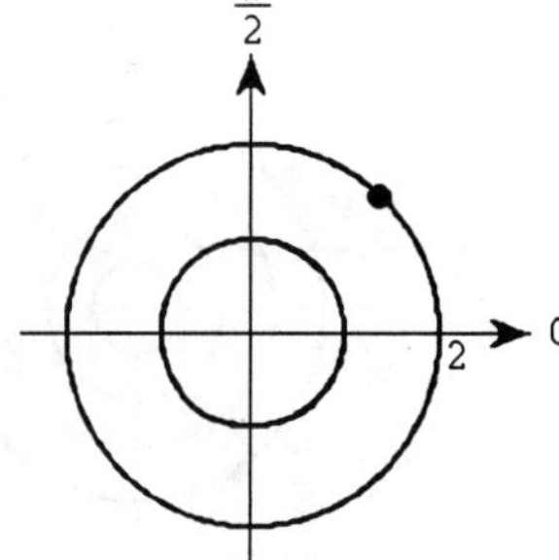

(III)

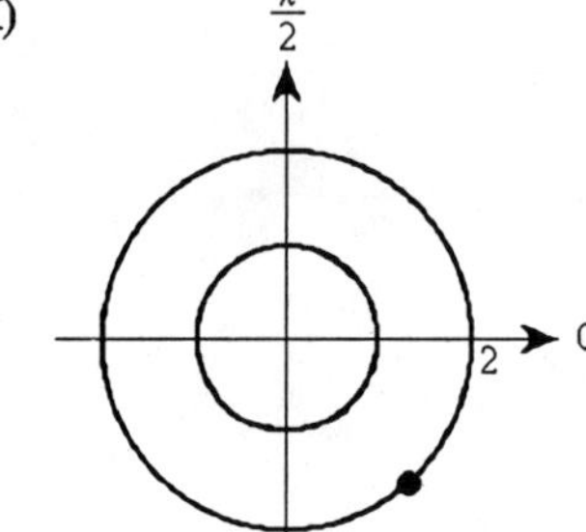

(IV)

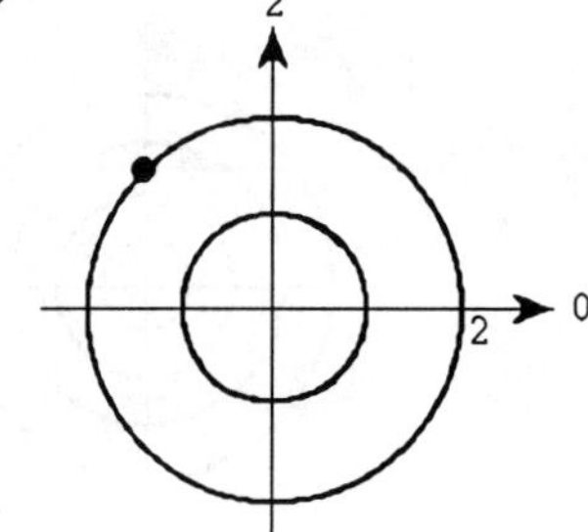

Answer: d Difficulty: 1

5. Plot the point whose polar coordinates are $\left(-3, \frac{\pi}{3}\right)$.

a) I b) II c) III d) IV e) None of these

(I)

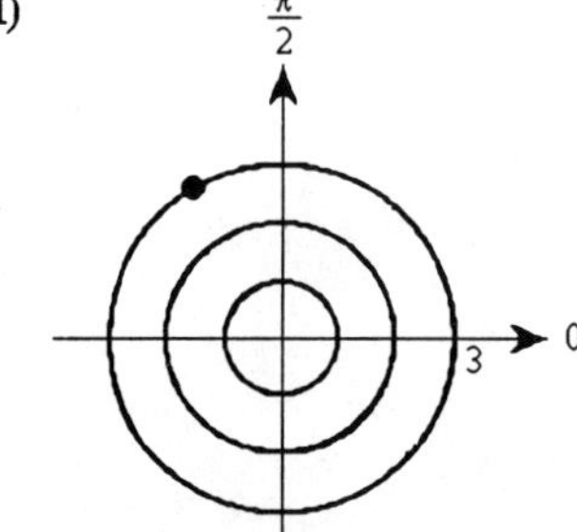

(II)

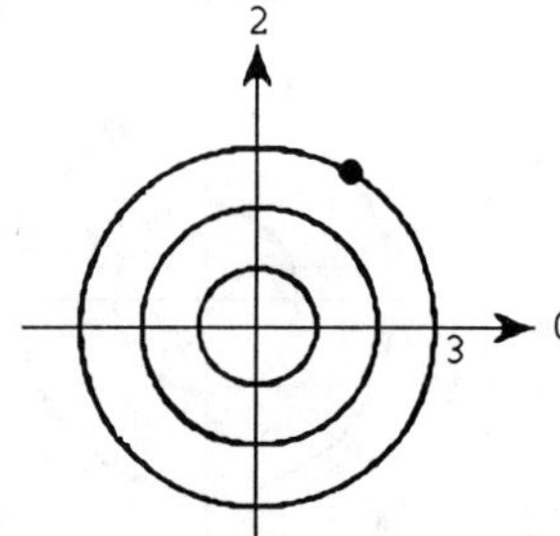

(III)

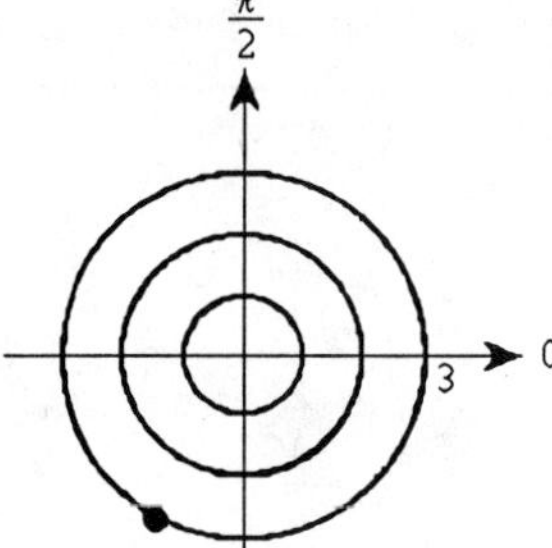

(IV)

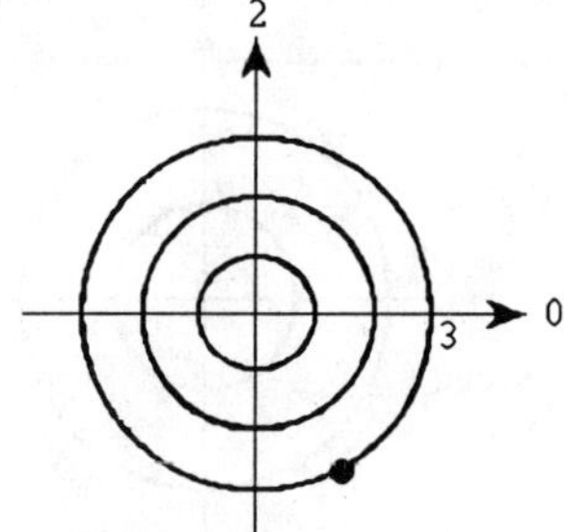

Answer: c Difficulty: 1

SHORT ANSWER

6. Plot the points whose polar coordinates are:
(a) $\left(3, \frac{\pi}{2}\right)$ (b) $\left(-2, \frac{\pi}{4}\right)$ (c) $\left(3, -\frac{\pi}{6}\right)$

Answer: See graph below.

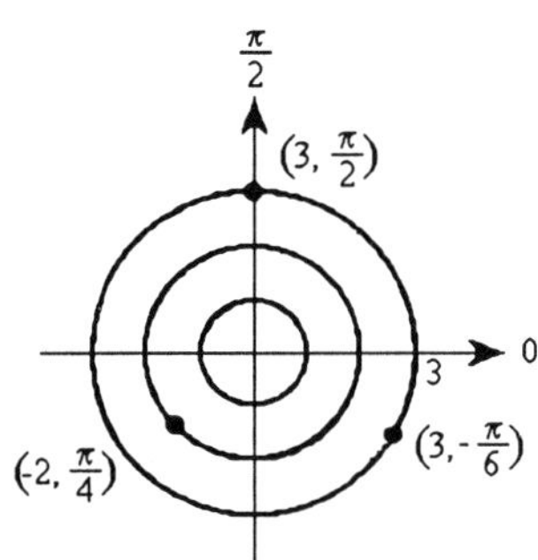

Difficulty: 1

MULTIPLE CHOICE

7. In polar coordinates, which of the following is *not* a correct representation for the point (3, π/4)?
a) $\left(-3, -\frac{3\pi}{4}\right)$ b) $\left(-3, -\frac{\pi}{4}\right)$ c) $\left(3, \frac{9\pi}{4}\right)$
d) $\left(-3, \frac{5\pi}{4}\right)$ e) None of these

Answer: b Difficulty: 1

8. In polar coordinates, which of the following is *not* a correct representation for the point (2, 5π/6)?
a) $\left(-2, -\frac{\pi}{6}\right)$ b) $\left(-2, \frac{11\pi}{6}\right)$ c) $\left(2, -\frac{11\pi}{6}\right)$
d) $\left(2, -\frac{7\pi}{6}\right)$ e) None of these

Answer: c Difficulty: 1

9. In polar coordinates, which of the following are correct representations for the point (-3, -π/3)?
a) $\left(3, -\frac{4\pi}{3}\right)$ b) $\left(3, \frac{2\pi}{3}\right)$ c) $\left(3, \frac{8\pi}{3}\right)$
d) $\left(-3, -\frac{8\pi}{3}\right)$ e) None of these

Answer: {a;b;c} Difficulty: 1

10. In polar coordinates, which of the following are correct representations for the point $(-1, 5\pi/4)$?

a) $\left(1, \frac{\pi}{4}\right)$ b) $\left(-1, -\frac{3\pi}{4}\right)$ c) $\left(-1, -\frac{7\pi}{4}\right)$

d) $\left(1, -\frac{15\pi}{4}\right)$ e) None of these

Answer: {a;b;d} Difficulty: 1

11. In polar coordinates, which of the following are correct representations for the point $(3, 6\pi/5)$?

a) $\left(-3, -\frac{4\pi}{5}\right)$ b) $\left(-3, -\frac{\pi}{5}\right)$ c) $\left(-3, \frac{4\pi}{5}\right)$

d) $\left(-3, -\frac{14\pi}{5}\right)$ e) None of these

Answer: e Difficulty: 1

SHORT ANSWER

12. Convert from polar to rectangular coordinates: $\left(3, \frac{5\pi}{3}\right)$.

Answer:

$\left(\frac{3}{2}, -\frac{3\sqrt{3}}{2}\right)$

Difficulty: 1

13. Convert from polar to rectangular coordinates: $\left(8, \frac{7\pi}{6}\right)$.

Answer:

$\left(-4\sqrt{3}, -4\right)$

Difficulty: 1

MULTIPLE CHOICE

14. Convert from polar to rectangular coordinates: $\left(-6, \frac{3\pi}{2}\right)$.

a) (-6, 0) b) (0, 6) c) (0, -6)

d) (6, 0) e) None of these

Answer: b Difficulty: 1

15. Convert from polar to rectangular coordinates: $\left(-1, -\frac{5\pi}{3}\right)$.

a) $\left(\frac{1}{2}, \frac{\sqrt{3}}{2}\right)$ b) $\left(-\frac{\sqrt{3}}{2}, -\frac{1}{2}\right)$ c) $\left(-\frac{1}{2}, -\frac{\sqrt{3}}{2}\right)$
d) $\left(\frac{\sqrt{3}}{2}, \frac{1}{2}\right)$ e) None of these

Answer: c Difficulty: 1

16. Convert from polar to rectangular coordinates: $(3, -\pi)$.

a) (3, 0)   b) (-3, 0)   c) (0, 3)
d) (0, -3)   e) None of these

Answer: b Difficulty: 1

17. Convert from rectangular to polar coordinates: (-4, 4).

a) $\left(4\sqrt{2}, \frac{\pi}{4}\right)$ b) $\left(4\sqrt{2}, \frac{3\pi}{4}\right)$ c) $\left(4\sqrt{2}, -\frac{\pi}{4}\right)$
d) $\left(-4\sqrt{2}, -\frac{7\pi}{4}\right)$ e) None of these

Answer: b Difficulty: 1

18. Convert from rectangular to polar coordinates: $\left(-1, -\sqrt{3}\right)$.

a) $\left(2, -\frac{4\pi}{4}\right)$ b) $\left(-2, \frac{\pi}{3}\right)$ c) $\left(-2, \frac{4\pi}{3}\right)$
d) $\left(-2, -\frac{\pi}{3}\right)$ e) None of these

Answer: b Difficulty: 1

19. Convert from rectangular to polar coordinates: $\left(5\sqrt{2}, -5\sqrt{2}\right)$.

a) $\left(-10, \frac{\pi}{4}\right)$ b) $\left(2\sqrt{5}, \frac{7\pi}{4}\right)$ c) $\left(10, \frac{7\pi}{4}\right)$
d) $\left(10\sqrt{2}, \frac{7\pi}{4}\right)$ e) None of these

Answer: c Difficulty: 1

20. Convert from rectangular to polar coordinates: (0, -4).

a) $\left(-4, \frac{\pi}{2}\right)$ b) $\left(-4, \frac{3\pi}{2}\right)$ c) $\left(-4, -\frac{\pi}{2}\right)$
d) $\left(4, -\frac{3\pi}{2}\right)$ e) None of these

Answer: a Difficulty: 1

21. Convert from rectangular to polar coordinates: $\left(-\sqrt{6}, \sqrt{2}\right)$.
a) $\left(8, \frac{5\pi}{6}\right)$
b) $\left(-2\sqrt{2}, \frac{\pi}{6}\right)$
c) $\left(2, -\frac{\pi}{6}\right)$
d) $\left(2\sqrt{2}, \frac{17\pi}{6}\right)$
e) None of these

Answer: d Difficulty: 1

SHORT ANSWER

22. Convert from polar to rectangular form: $r = 2 \cos \theta$.

Answer:

$x^2 + y^2 - 2x = 0$

Difficulty: 1

MULTIPLE CHOICE

23. Convert from polar to rectangular form: $r \sin \theta = -3$.
a) $x + 3 = 0$
b) $y + 3 = 0$
c) $y^2 + 3 = 0$
d) $y - 3 = 0$
e) None of these

Answer: b Difficulty: 1

24. Convert from polar to rectangular form: $r = 5$.
a) $x + y = 5$
b) $x^2 + y^2 = 5$
c) $x^2 + y^2 = 25$
d) $x + y = 25$
e) None of these

Answer: c Difficulty: 1

25. Convert from polar to rectangular form: $\theta = \frac{5\pi}{4}$.
a) $\sqrt{2}y - x = 0$
b) $y + x = 0$
c) $y - x = 0$
d) $\sqrt{2}y + x = 0$
e) None of these

Answer: c Difficulty: 1

26. Convert from polar to rectangular form: $r = 5 \cos \theta$.
a) $x^2 + y^2 - 25x = 0$
b) $x^2 + y^2 - 5x = 0$
c) $x - 5 = 0$
d) $x + 5 = 0$
e) None of these

Answer: b Difficulty: 1

27. Convert from polar to rectangular form: $r \sin^2 \theta = 3 \cos \theta$.
a) $y^2 - 3x = 0$
b) $xy - 3y = 0$
c) $x^2 + y^2 - 3x = 0$
d) $x^2 + y^2 - 9x = 0$
e) None of these

Answer: a Difficulty: 1

28. Convert from rectangular to polar form: $3x + 2y - 1 = 0$.
 a) $r = \dfrac{1}{3 \sin \theta + 2 \cos \theta}$
 b) $r = 3 \cos \theta + 2 \sin \theta - 1$
 c) $r = \dfrac{1}{3 \cos \theta + 2 \sin \theta}$
 d) $r = 3 \sin \theta - 2 \cos \theta - 1$
 e) None of these

 Answer: c Difficulty: 1

29. Convert from rectangular to polar form: $x^2 + y^2 - 4x + 2y = 0$.
 a) $r = 4 \cos \theta - 2 \sin \theta$
 b) $r = \sin \theta - 2 \cos \theta$
 c) $r = \cos^2 2\theta$
 d) $r = \dfrac{4}{1 - 2 \sin \theta}$
 e) None of these

 Answer: a Difficulty: 1

SHORT ANSWER

30. Convert from rectangular to polar coordinates: $\left(-\sqrt{3}, -1\right)$.

 Answer:
 $\left(2, \dfrac{7\pi}{6}\right), \left(-2, \dfrac{\pi}{6}\right)$
 Difficulty: 1

31. Convert from rectangular to polar form: $x^2 + y^2 - 4x + 6y = 0$.

 Answer: $r = 4 \cos \theta - 6 \sin \theta$ Difficulty: 1

MULTIPLE CHOICE

32. Convert from rectangular to polar form: $x^2 + y^2 + 2x + 5y = 0$.
 a) $r^2 + 2 \cos \theta + 5 \sin \theta = 0$
 b) $r + 2 \cos \theta + 5 \sin \theta = 0$
 c) $r^2 + 7 = 0$
 d) $2 \cos \theta + 5 \sin \theta + 1 = 0$
 e) None of these

 Answer: b Difficulty: 1

33. Convert from rectangular to polar form: $x^3 = 4y^2$.
 a) $r = 4 \cot^2 \theta \cos \theta$
 b) $r = 4 \cos \theta$
 c) $r = 4 \tan^2 \theta \cos \theta$
 d) $r = 4 \tan^2 \theta \sec \theta$
 e) None of these

 Answer: d Difficulty: 1

SHORT ANSWER

34. The town of Clinton is located 60 miles east and 90 miles south of the town of Clearfield. A small weather station in Clearfield detects on their radar screen a severe thunderstorm centered over Clinton. At what polar coordinates would the weather station report the storm to be centered?

Answer:

Rectangular coordinates: (60, -90)

Polar coordinates: $r = \sqrt{(60)^2 + (-90)^2} \approx 108.2$ miles

$$\theta = \tan\left[-\frac{90}{60}\right] \approx 303.7°$$

(108.2 miles, 303.7°)

Difficulty: 1

35. A polar bear discovers a source of food located 2.0 miles west and 5.0 miles south of the den. Find the polar coordinates of the food source from the den.

Answer:

Rectangular coordinates: (-2.0, -5.0)

Polar coordinates: $r = \sqrt{(-2.0)^2 + (-5.0)^2} \approx 5.4$ miles

$$\theta = \tan\left[\frac{-5.0}{-2.0}\right] \approx 248.2°$$

(5.4 miles, 248.2°)

Difficulty: 1

Chapter 108: Graphs of Polar Equations

MULTIPLE CHOICE

1. Determine the type of symmetry: $r = 2 \sin \theta$.
   a) Symmetric to the line $\theta = \frac{\pi}{2}$
   b) Symmetric to the polar axis
   c) Symmetric to the pole
   d) Symmetric to the line $\theta = \frac{\pi}{2}$, the polar axis, and the pole
   e) None of these

   Answer: a Difficulty: 1

2. Determine the type of symmetry: $r = 2$.
   a) Symmetric to the line $\theta = \frac{\pi}{2}$
   b) Symmetric to the polar axis
   c) Symmetric to the pole
   d) Symmetric to the line $\theta = \frac{\pi}{2}$, the polar axis, and the pole
   e) None of these

   Answer: d Difficulty: 1

3. Determine the type of symmetry: $r = 2 + \sin \theta$.
   a) Symmetric to the line $\theta = \frac{\pi}{2}$
   b) Symmetric to the polar axis
   c) Symmetric to the pole
   d) No symmetry
   e) None of these

   Answer: a Difficulty: 1

4. Determine the type of symmetry: $r = 2 \cos 3\theta$.
   a) Symmetric to the line $\theta = \frac{\pi}{2}$
   b) Symmetric to the polar axis
   c) Symmetric to the pole
   d) Symmetric to the line $\theta = \frac{\pi}{2}$ and the pole
   e) None of these

   Answer: b Difficulty: 1

5. Determine the type of symmetry: $r = \sin\left(\theta + \frac{\pi}{3}\right)$.
   a) Symmetric to the line $\theta = \frac{\pi}{2}$
   b) Symmetric to the polar axis
   c) Symmetric to the pole
   d) No symmetry
   e) None of these

   Answer: d Difficulty: 1

6. Determine the type of symmetry: $r = 7\cos 2\theta$.
a) Symmetric to the line $\theta = \frac{\pi}{2}$
b) Symmetric to the polar axis
c) Symmetric to the pole
d) Symmetric to the line $\theta = \frac{\pi}{2}$ and the pole
e) None of these

Answer: d Difficulty: 1

SHORT ANSWER

7. Determine the type(s) of symmetry of the graph of each of the following.
(a) $r = 3 + 4\cos\theta$ (b) $r = \sin 2\theta$

Answer:

(a) Symmetric to the polar axis

(b) Symmetric to the line $\theta = \frac{\pi}{2}$, the polar axis, and the pole

Difficulty: 1

MULTIPLE CHOICE

8. Find the values of θ for which $|r|$ is a maximum: $r = \sin 4\theta$.
a) $0, \pi$
b) $0, \frac{\pi}{4}, \frac{\pi}{2}, \frac{3\pi}{4}, \pi, \frac{5\pi}{4}, \frac{3\pi}{2}, \frac{7\pi}{4}$
c) $\frac{\pi}{2}, \frac{3\pi}{2}$
d) $\frac{\pi}{8}, \frac{3\pi}{8}, \frac{5\pi}{8}, \frac{7\pi}{8}, \frac{9\pi}{8}, \frac{11\pi}{8}, \frac{13\pi}{8}, \frac{15\pi}{8}$
e) None of these

Answer: d Difficulty: 1

9. Find the value(s) of θ for which $|r|$ is a maximum: $r = \cos\left(\theta - \frac{\pi}{2}\right)$.
a) $0, \pi$
b) $\frac{\pi}{2}, \frac{3\pi}{2}$
c) 0
d) $0, \frac{\pi}{2}, \pi, \frac{3\pi}{2}$
e) None of these

Answer: b Difficulty: 1

10. Find the value(s) of θ for which $|r|$ is a maximum: $r = 5 - 4\sin\theta$.
a) $0, \pi$
b) $\frac{\pi}{2}, \frac{3\pi}{2}$
c) $\frac{\pi}{2}$
d) $\frac{3\pi}{2}$
e) None of these

Answer: d Difficulty: 1

11. Find the value(s) of θ for which $|r|$ is a maximum: $r = 2 - 4\cos\theta$.
a) $0, \pi$ b) $\frac{\pi}{2}, \frac{3\pi}{2}$ c) π d) $\frac{3\pi}{2}$ e) None of these

Answer: c Difficulty: 1

SHORT ANSWER

12. Find the maximum value of $|r|$: $r = 1 + \sin 2\theta$.

Answer: 2 Difficulty: 1

13. Find the maximum value of $|r|$: $r = 15(1 - 2\cos\theta)$.

Answer: 45 Difficulty: 1

MULTIPLE CHOICE

14. Find the maximum value of $|r|$: $r = 3(1 + 2\sin\theta)$.
a) 3 b) $\frac{3}{2}$ c) 1 d) 9 e) None of these

Answer: d Difficulty: 1

15. Find the maximum value of $|r|$: $r = \frac{3}{5} - \frac{1}{2}\cos\theta$.
a) $\frac{1}{10}$ b) $\frac{3}{5}$ c) $\frac{11}{10}$ d) $\frac{7}{20}$ e) None of these

Answer: c Difficulty: 1

16. Find any zeros of r: $r = 8 + 16\sin\theta$.
a) $\frac{\pi}{6}$ b) $0, \pi$ c) $\frac{7\pi}{6}, \frac{11\pi}{6}$ d) $\frac{\pi}{2}, \frac{3\pi}{2}$ e) None of these

Answer: c Difficulty: 1

17. Find any zeros of r: $r = 6\left[\frac{1}{2} - \cos\theta\right]$.
a) $0, \pi$ b) $\frac{\pi}{3}, \frac{5\pi}{3}$ c) $\frac{2\pi}{3}, \frac{5\pi}{3}$ d) $\frac{\pi}{3}$ e) None of these

Answer: b Difficulty: 1

18. Find any zeros of r: $r = 1 + \cos 3\theta$.
a) π b) $\frac{\pi}{3}, \pi, \frac{5\pi}{3}$ c) $\frac{\pi}{6}, \frac{\pi}{2}, \frac{5\pi}{6}$ d) $\frac{\pi}{3}$ e) None of these

Answer: b Difficulty: 1

19. Find any zeros of r: $r = 2 - 4\sin 2\theta$.
a) $\frac{\pi}{6}, \frac{5\pi}{6}$ b) $0, \frac{\pi}{2}, \pi, \frac{3\pi}{2}$ c) $\frac{\pi}{4}, \frac{3\pi}{4}, \frac{5\pi}{4}, \frac{7\pi}{4}$.
d) $\frac{\pi}{12}, \frac{5\pi}{12}, \frac{13\pi}{12}, \frac{17\pi}{12}$ e) None of these

Answer: d Difficulty: 1

20. Find an equation for the graph below.
a) $r = 4 - 3\cos\theta$ b) $r^2 = 9\cos\theta$ c) $r = 2\cos 3\theta$
d) $r = 4 + 3\cos\theta$ e) None of these

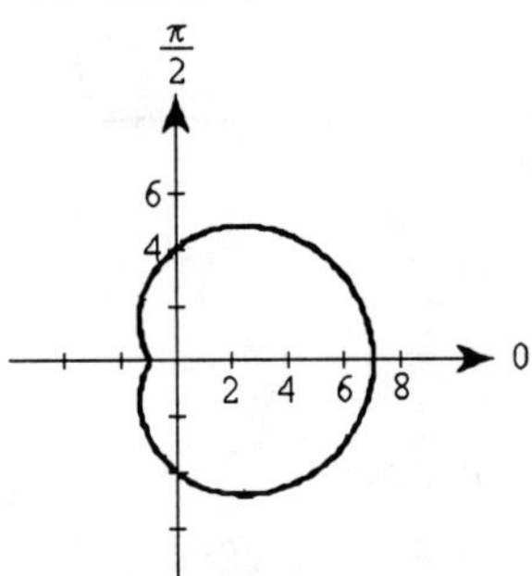

Answer: d Difficulty: 1

21. Find an equation for the graph below.
a) $r = 3\sin 4\theta$ b) $r^2 = 1 + 4\sin\theta$ c) $r = 3 - 4\cos\theta$
d) $r^2 = 4\cos 3\theta$ e) None of these

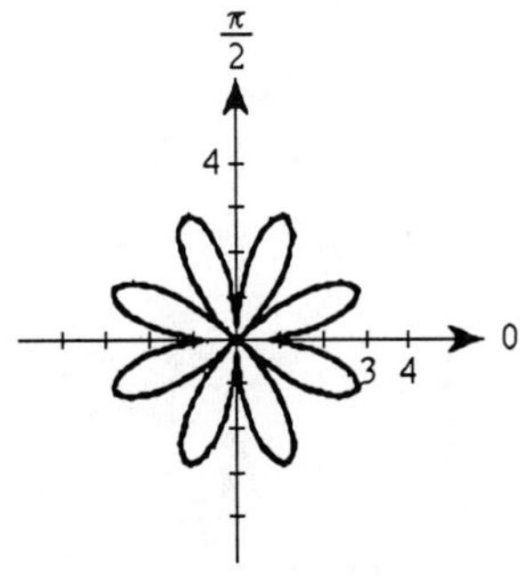

Answer: a Difficulty: 1

22. Find an equation for the graph below.
   a) $r^2 = 9 \cos 2\theta$ b) $r = 3 - 3 \sin \theta$ c) $r^2 = 3 \cos 2\theta$
   d) $r^2 = 9 \sin 2\theta$ e) None of these

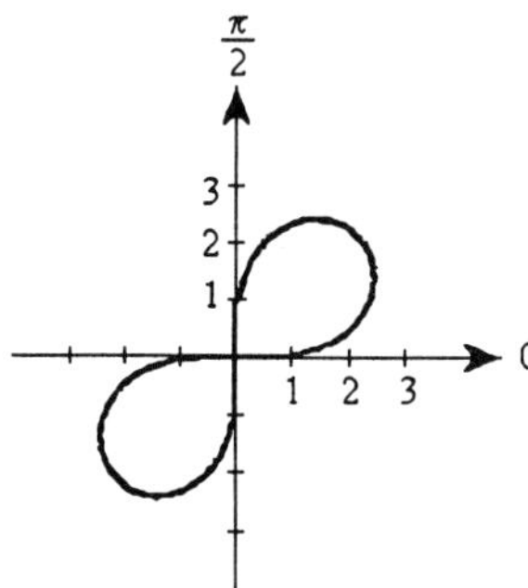

Answer: d Difficulty: 1

SHORT ANSWER

23. Sketch the graph of $r = 5 \sin 2\theta$.

Answer: See graph below.

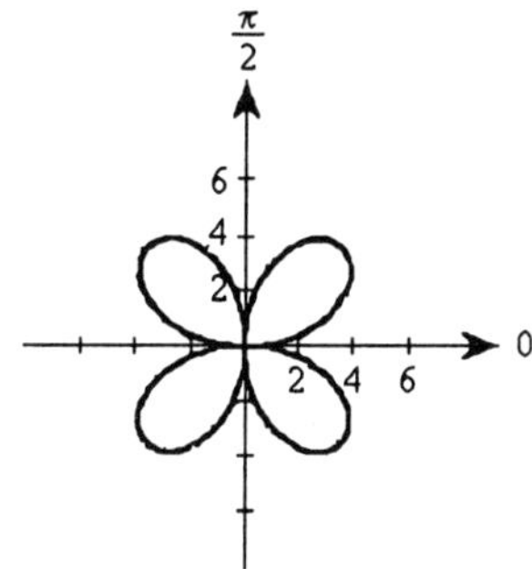

Difficulty: 1

24. Sketch the graph of $r = 1 - 2 \sin \theta$.

Answer: See graph below.

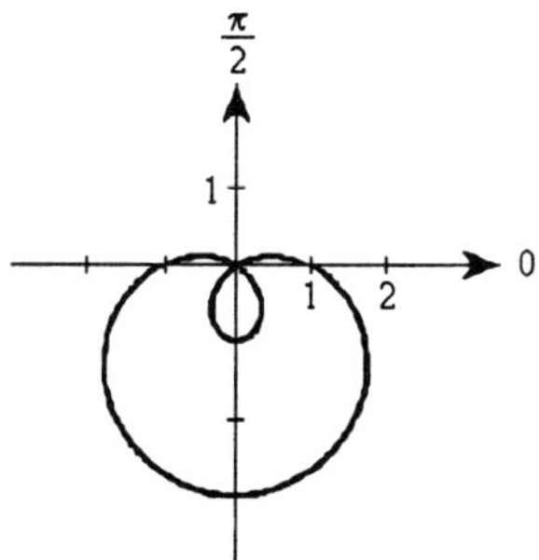

Difficulty: 1

MULTIPLE CHOICE

25. Find an equation for the graph below.
   a) $r = 5 + 4 \sin \theta$ b) $r = 4 - 5 \sin \theta$ c) $r = 4 + 5 \sin \theta$
   d) $r = 5 - 4 \sin \theta$ e) None of these

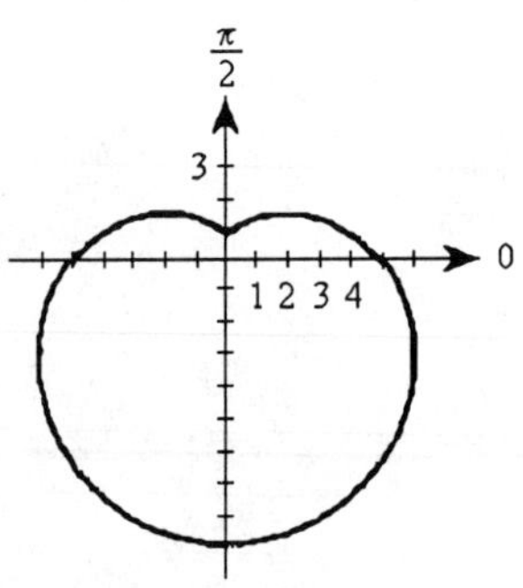

Answer: d Difficulty: 1

26. Find an equation for the graph below.
   a) $r = -5 \sin 5\theta$ b) $r = 5 \sin \theta$ c) $r = -5 \sin \theta$
   d) $r = \sin 5\theta$ e) None of these

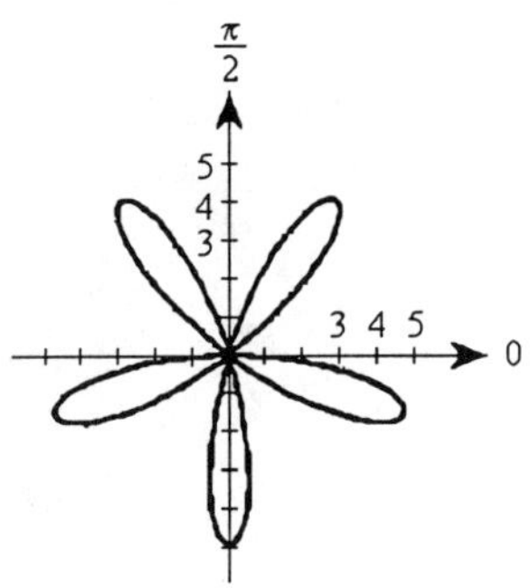

Answer: a Difficulty: 1

27. Find an equation of the graph below.

a) $r = \frac{1}{3} \csc \theta$ b) $r = 3 \sin \theta$ c) $r = 3 \csc \theta$

d) $r = \frac{1}{3} \sin \theta$ e) None of these

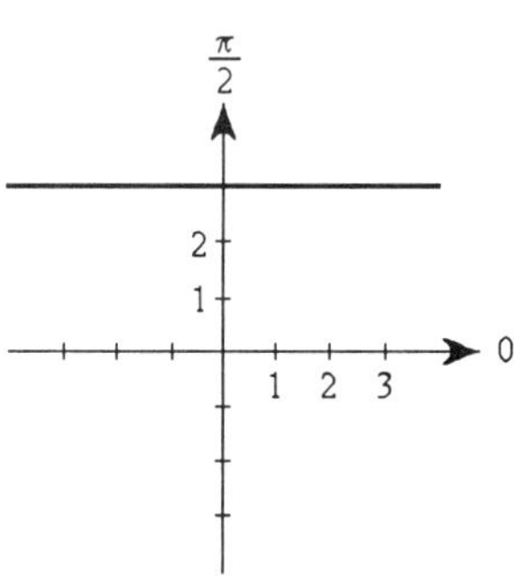

Answer: c Difficulty: 1

28. Find an equation for the graph below.

a) $r = 2 - 2 \sin \theta$ b) $r = 2(1 - 2 \sin \theta)$ c) $r = 2(1 + 2 \sin \theta)$

d) $r = 2 + 2 \sin \theta$ e) None of these

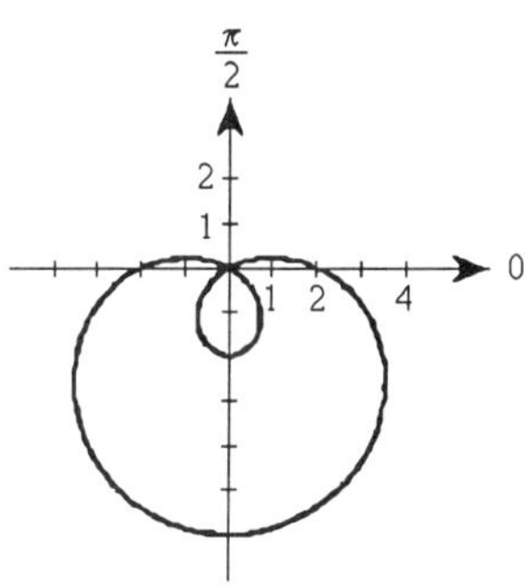

Answer: b Difficulty: 1

29. Find an equation for the graph below.

a) $r = 1 - \cos \theta$ b) $r = 1 - \sin \theta$ c) $r = 1 + \cos \theta$

d) $r = 1 + \sin \theta$ e) None of these

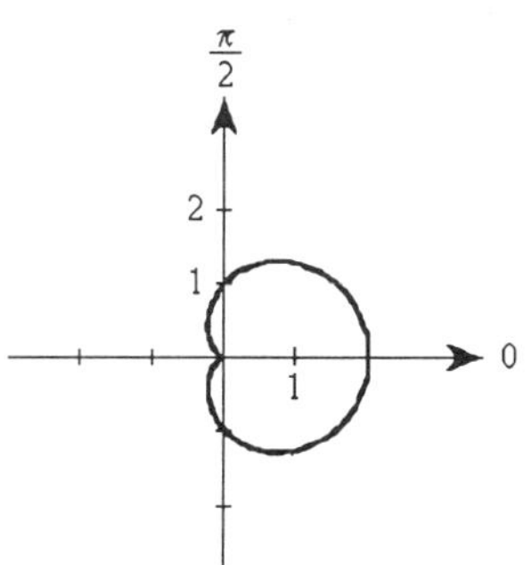

Answer: c Difficulty: 1

SHORT ANSWER

30. Sketch the graph of $r = \sin 8\theta$.

Answer: See graph below.

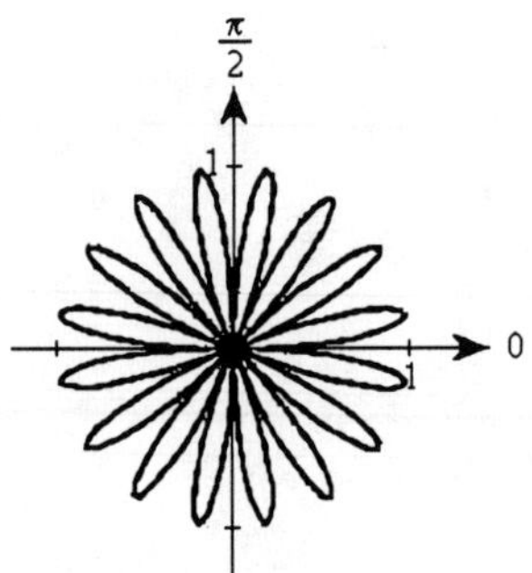

Difficulty: 1

31. Sketch the graph of $r^2 = 4 \sin 2\theta$.

Answer: See graph below.

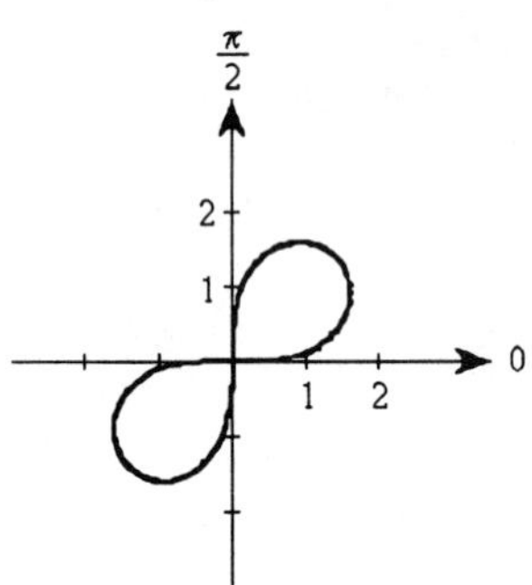

Difficulty: 1

MULTIPLE CHOICE

32. Identify the graph: $r = 2 + 3 \sin \theta$.
    a) Cardioid b) Limaçon with inner loop c) Dimpled limaçon
    d) Rose curve e) None of these

Answer: b Difficulty: 1

SHORT ANSWER

33. Classify each of the following as a cardioid, limaçon with inner loop, dimpled limaçon or rose curve. (State the number of petals.)

(a) $r = 8 \sin 3\theta$ (b) $r = 1 - 2 \cos \theta$
(c) $r = 5 + 3 \cos \theta$ (d) $r = 2(1 + \sin \theta)$

Answer:
(a) 3 petal rose curve **(b)** Limaçon with inner loop
(c) Dimpled limaçon **(d)** Cardioid

Difficulty: 1

34. Classify each of the following as a cardioid, limaçon with inner loop, dimpled limaçon or rose curve. (State the number of petals.)

(a) $r = 4 + 3 \cos \theta$ (b) $r = 2 \sin 3\theta$
(c) $r = 1 + \sin \theta$ (d) $r = 3 \cos 2\theta$

Answer:
(a) Dimpled limaçon **(b)** 3 petal rose curve
(c) Cardioid **(d)** 4 petal rose curve

Difficulty: 1

35. A speedway built in the shape of a lemniscate with an overpass at the point of intersection has an equation of $r^2 = 9.0 \times 10^6 \cos 2\theta$. Graph this equation.

Answer: See graph below.

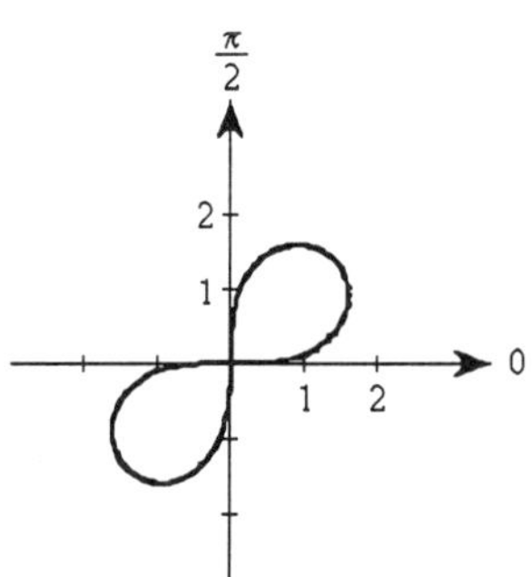

Difficulty: 1

36. Use a graphing utility to graph $r = 2 \cos 4\theta$.

Answer: See graph below.

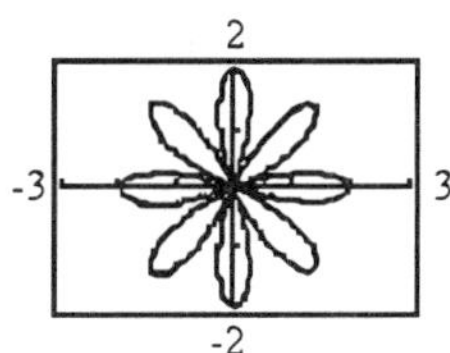

Difficulty: 1 Key 1: T

37. Use a graphing utility to graph $r = 2 - 4 \sin \theta$.

Answer: See graph below.

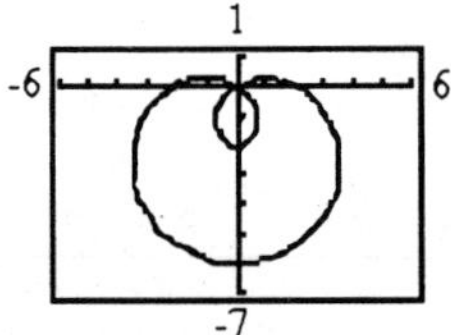

Difficulty: 1 Key 1: T

38. Use a graphing utility to graph $r = 1 + \cos \theta$.

Answer: See graph below.

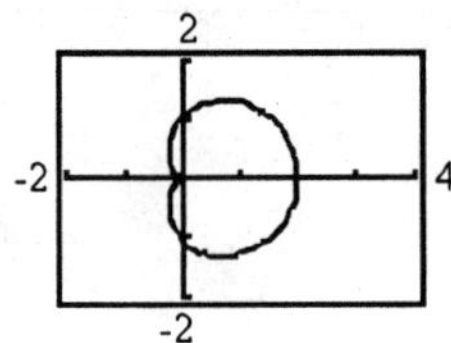

Difficulty: 1 Key 1: T

39. Use a graphing utility to graph $r^2 = 9 \sin 2\theta$.

Answer: See graph below.

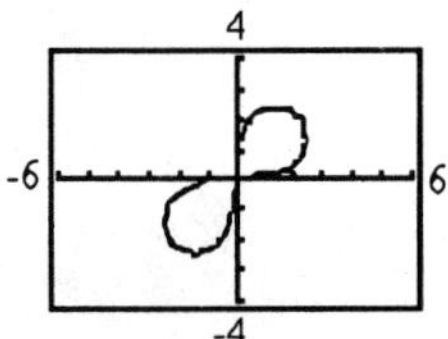

Difficulty: 2 Key 1: T

40. Use a graphing utility to graph $r^2 = 16 \cos 2\theta$.

Answer: See graph below.

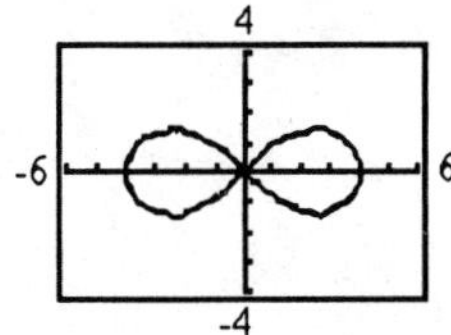

Difficulty: 2 Key 1: T

Chapter 109: Polar Equations of Conics

MULTIPLE CHOICE

1. Identify the graph: $r = \dfrac{3}{1 + 2\cos\theta}$.

a) Ellipse b) Hyperbola c) Parabola
d) Circle e) None of these

Answer: b Difficulty: 1

2. Identify the graph: $r = \dfrac{10}{3 - 3\cos\theta}$.

a) Parabola b) Ellipse c) Hyperbola
d) Cardioid e) None of these

Answer: a Difficulty: 1

3. Identify the graph: $r = \dfrac{4}{2 + \cos\theta}$.

a) Ellipse b) Parabola c) Hyperbola
d) Circle e) None of these

Answer: a Difficulty: 1

SHORT ANSWER

4. Identify the graph: $r = \dfrac{5}{5 + \frac{1}{5}\cos\theta}$.

Answer: Ellipse Difficulty: 1

5. Identify the graph: $r = \dfrac{1}{2 + 2\cos\theta}$.

Answer: Parabola Difficulty: 1

MULTIPLE CHOICE

6. Identify the graph: $r = \dfrac{1}{1 - 3\sin\theta}$.

a) Ellipse b) Parabola c) Hyperbola
d) Circle e) None of these

Answer: c Difficulty: 1

7. Identify the graph: $r = \dfrac{10}{3 + \cos\theta}$.

a) Ellipse b) Parabola c) Hyperbola
d) Circle e) None of these

Answer: a Difficulty: 1

8. Identify the graph: $r = \dfrac{\frac{1}{2}}{\frac{1}{2} + \sin\theta}$.

a) Ellipse　　b) Parabola　　c) Hyperbola
d) Circle　　e) None of these

Answer: c Difficulty: 1

9. Identify the graph: $r = \dfrac{6}{16 - 3\sin\theta}$.

a) Ellipse　　b) Parabola　　c) Hyperbola
d) Circle　　e) None of these

Answer: a Difficulty: 1

10. Identify the graph: $r = \dfrac{1}{4 - 4\cos\theta}$.

a) Ellipse　　b) Parabola　　c) Hyperbola
d) Circle　　e) None of these

Answer: b Difficulty: 1

11. Find a polar equation of the parabola with focus at the pole and directrix $x = 3$.

a) $r = \dfrac{3}{1 - \cos\theta}$　　b) $r = \dfrac{3}{1 + 3\cos\theta}$　　c) $r = \dfrac{3}{1 + \cos\theta}$
d) $r = \dfrac{3}{1 + \sin\theta}$　　e) None of these

Answer: c Difficulty: 1

12. Find a polar equation of the parabola with focus at the pole and directrix $y = -\frac{1}{2}$.

a) $r = \dfrac{2}{2 - \sin\theta}$　　b) $r = \dfrac{\frac{1}{2}}{1 - \sin\theta}$　　c) $r = \dfrac{2}{2 + \sin\theta}$
d) $r = \dfrac{\frac{1}{2}}{1 - \cos\theta}$　　e) None of these

Answer: b Difficulty: 1

13. Find a polar equation of the parabola with focus at the pole and directrix $x = -7$.

a) $r = \dfrac{7}{1 + 7\sin\theta}$　　b) $r = \dfrac{7}{1 + \cos\theta}$　　c) $r = \dfrac{7}{1 - \cos\theta}$
d) $r = \dfrac{7}{1 - 7\cos\theta}$　　e) None of these

Answer: c Difficulty: 1

14. Find a polar equation of the parabola with focus at the pole and directrix $y = \frac{3}{8}$.

a) $r = \dfrac{\frac{3}{8}}{1 + \cos\theta}$ b) $r = \dfrac{\frac{3}{8}}{1 - \sin\theta}$ c) $r = \dfrac{\frac{3}{8}}{1 - \cos\theta}$

d) $r = \dfrac{\frac{3}{8}}{1 + \sin\theta}$ e) None of these

Answer: d Difficulty: 1

15. Find a polar equation of the conic with eccentricity $e = \frac{1}{4}$, focus at the pole, and directrix $x = 2$.

a) $r = \dfrac{\frac{1}{2}}{1 + \frac{1}{4}\cos\theta}$ b) $r = \dfrac{\frac{1}{4}}{1 + \frac{1}{4}\cos\theta}$ c) $r = \dfrac{\frac{1}{2}}{1 - \frac{1}{4}\cos\theta}$

d) $r = \dfrac{\frac{1}{2}}{1 + \frac{1}{4}\sin\theta}$ e) None of these

Answer: a Difficulty: 1

16. Find a polar equation of the conic with eccentricity $e = 3$, focus at the pole, and directrix $y = -9$.

a) $r = \dfrac{27}{1 - 9\sin\theta}$ b) $r = \dfrac{27}{1 - 3\sin\theta}$ c) $r = \dfrac{27}{1 - 27\sin\theta}$

d) $r = \dfrac{27}{1 + 3\sin\theta}$ e) None of these

Answer: b Difficulty: 1

17. Find a polar equation of the conic with eccentricity $e = \frac{1}{8}$, focus at the pole, and directrix $x = -16$.

a) $r = \dfrac{2}{1 - \cos\theta}$ b) $r = \dfrac{16}{8 - \cos\theta}$ c) $r = \dfrac{16}{8 + \cos\theta}$

d) $r = \dfrac{2}{1 - \frac{1}{8}\sin\theta}$ e) None of these

Answer: b Difficulty: 1

18. Find a polar equation of the conic with eccentricity $e = 4$, focus at the pole, and directrix $y = \frac{1}{16}$.

a) $r = \dfrac{\frac{1}{4}}{1 + \frac{1}{4}\sin\theta}$ b) $r = \dfrac{\frac{1}{4}}{1 + 4\cos\theta}$ c) $r = \dfrac{4}{4 + \sin\theta}$

d) $r = \dfrac{1}{4 + 16\sin\theta}$ e) None of these

Answer: d Difficulty: 1

19. Find a polar equation of the parabola with vertex $(2, \pi/2)$ and focus at the pole.

a) $r = \dfrac{4}{1 + \sin\theta}$ b) $r = \dfrac{4}{1 - \sin\theta}$ c) $r = \dfrac{2}{1 + \sin\theta}$

d) $r = \dfrac{4}{1 + \cos\theta}$ e) None of these

Answer: a Difficulty: 1

20. Find a polar equation of the parabola with vertex $(3, \pi)$ and focus at the pole.

a) $r = \dfrac{3}{1 + \cos\theta}$ b) $r = \dfrac{6}{1 - \cos\theta}$ c) $r = \dfrac{3}{1 - \cos\theta}$

d) $r = \dfrac{6}{1 - \sin\theta}$ e) None of these

Answer: b Difficulty: 1

21. Find a polar equation of the parabola with vertex $(-5, 0)$ and focus at the pole.

a) $r = \dfrac{10}{1 - \cos\theta}$ b) $r = \dfrac{5}{1 + \cos\theta}$ c) $r = \dfrac{10}{1 + \cos\theta}$

d) $r = \dfrac{10}{1 - \sin\theta}$ e) None of these

Answer: a Difficulty: 1

22. Find a polar equation of the ellipse with focus at the pole and vertices $(3, \pi/2)$ and $(5, -\pi/2)$.

a) $r = \dfrac{15}{4 - \cos\theta}$ b) $r = \dfrac{15}{4 + \cos\theta}$ c) $r = \dfrac{15}{4 + \sin\theta}$

d) $r = \dfrac{15}{4 - \sin\theta}$ e) None of these

Answer: c Difficulty: 2

23. Find a polar equation of the ellipse with vertices (6, 0), (2, π) and focus at the pole.

a) $r = \dfrac{3}{1 - \cos\theta}$ b) $r = \dfrac{3}{1 - \frac{1}{2}\cos\theta}$ c) $r = \dfrac{6}{1 - \cos\theta}$

d) $r = \dfrac{6}{1 + \cos\theta}$ e) None of these

Answer: b Difficulty: 2

24. Find a polar equation of the ellipse with vertices (5, $\pi/2$), (15, $3\pi/2$) and focus at the pole.

a) $r = \dfrac{\frac{5}{6}}{1 + \frac{1}{2}\sin\theta}$ b) $r = \dfrac{5}{1 + \frac{1}{2}\sin\theta}$ c) $r = \dfrac{\frac{15}{2}}{1 + \frac{1}{2}\sin\theta}$

d) $r = \dfrac{\frac{15}{2}}{1 - \frac{1}{2}\sin\theta}$ e) None of these

Answer: c Difficulty: 2

25. Find a polar equation of the ellipse with vertices (1, 0), (5, π) and focus at the pole.

a) $r = \dfrac{\frac{10}{6}}{1 + \cos\theta}$ b) $r = \dfrac{10}{6 + 4\cos\theta}$ c) $r = \dfrac{10}{6 - 4\cos\theta}$

d) $r = \dfrac{10}{6 + 4\sin\theta}$ e) None of these

Answer: b Difficulty: 2

26. Find a polar equation of the ellipse with vertices $\left(10, \frac{\pi}{2}\right)$, $\left(2, \frac{3\pi}{2}\right)$ and focus at the pole.

a) $r = \dfrac{\frac{10}{3}}{1 + \frac{2}{3}\sin\theta}$ b) $r = \dfrac{5}{1 - \sin\theta}$ c) $r = \dfrac{5}{1 + \sin\theta}$

d) $r = \dfrac{\frac{10}{3}}{1 - \frac{2}{3}\sin\theta}$ e) None of these

Answer: d Difficulty: 2

27. Find a polar equation of the hyperbola with vertices (3, 0), (13, 0) and focus at the pole.

a) $r = \dfrac{\frac{39}{5}}{1 + \frac{8}{5}\cos\theta}$

b) $r = \dfrac{\frac{9}{8}}{1 - \frac{8}{5}\cos\theta}$

c) $r = \dfrac{\frac{9}{5}}{1 + \frac{8}{5}\cos\theta}$

d) $r = \dfrac{\frac{9}{8}}{1 - \frac{8}{5}\sin\theta}$

e) None of these

Answer: a Difficulty: 2

28. Find a polar equation of the hyperbola with vertices $(2, 3\pi/2)$, $(20, 3\pi/2)$ and focus at the pole.

a) $r = \dfrac{4}{9 - 11\sin\theta}$

b) $r = \dfrac{4}{9 + 11\sin\theta}$

c) $r = \dfrac{40}{9 + 11\sin\theta}$

d) $r = \dfrac{40}{9 - 11\sin\theta}$

e) None of these

Answer: d Difficulty: 2

29. Find a polar equation of the hyperbola with vertices $(4, \pi)$, $(6, \pi)$ and focus at the pole.

a) $r = \dfrac{16}{1 - 5\cos\theta}$

b) $r = \dfrac{24}{1 - 5\cos\theta}$

c) $r = \dfrac{24}{1 + 5\cos\theta}$

d) $r = \dfrac{16}{1 + 5\cos\theta}$

e) None of these

Answer: b Difficulty: 2

30. Find a polar equation of the hyperbola with vertices $(6, \pi/2)$, $(-20, 3\pi/2)$ and focus at the pole.

a) $r = \dfrac{\frac{36}{7}}{1 + \frac{13}{7}\sin\theta}$

b) $r = \dfrac{\frac{120}{7}}{1 - \frac{13}{7}\sin\theta}$

c) $r = \dfrac{\frac{36}{7}}{1 - \frac{13}{7}\sin\theta}$

d) $r = \dfrac{\frac{120}{7}}{1 + \frac{13}{7}\sin\theta}$

e) None of these

Answer: d Difficulty: 2

SHORT ANSWER

31. Find a polar equation of the ellipse with vertices $(1, 0)$, $(7, \pi)$ and focus $(0, 0)$.

Answer:

$$r = \frac{7}{4 + 3\cos\theta}$$

Difficulty: 2

32. Find a polar equation of the parabola with vertices $(3, \pi)$ and focus $(0, 0)$.

Answer:

$$r = \frac{6}{1 - \cos\theta}$$

Difficulty: 2

MULTIPLE CHOICE

33. Find a polar equation for the graph below.

a) $r = \dfrac{33}{4 - 7\sin\theta}$ b) $r = \dfrac{33}{4 + 7\sin\theta}$ c) $r = \dfrac{33}{7 - 4\sin\theta}$

d) $r = \dfrac{33}{7 + 4\cos\theta}$ e) None of these

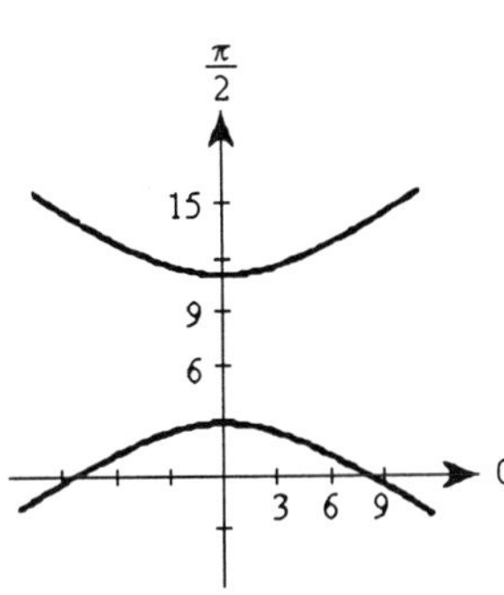

Answer: b Difficulty: 1

SHORT ANSWER

34. Identify the conic, then sketch the graph of the polar equation:

$$r = \frac{4}{1 + \sin\theta}.$$

Answer: Parabola;

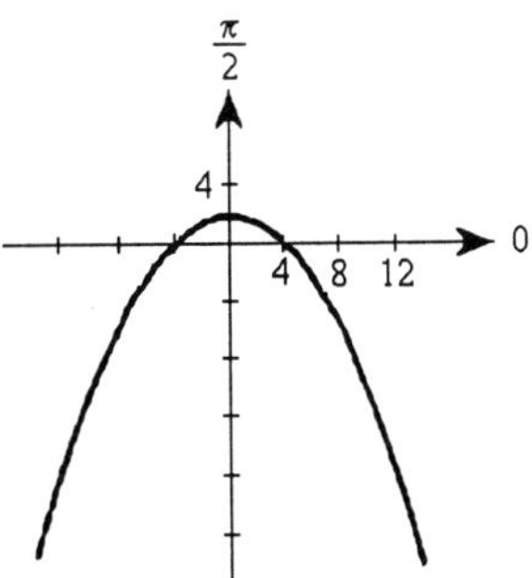

Difficulty: 1

35. Identify the conic, then use a graphing utility to graph the polar equation: $r = \frac{2}{1 + \sin\theta}$.

Answer: Parabola;

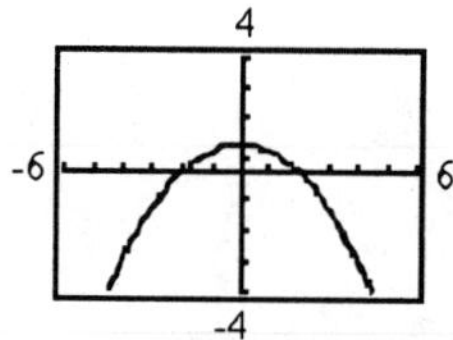

Difficulty: 2 Key 1: T

36. Identify the conic, then use a graphing utility to graph the polar equation: $r = \frac{4}{1 + 2\sin\theta}$.

Answer: Hyperbola;

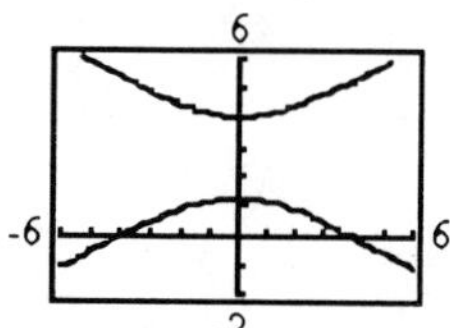

Difficulty: 2 Key 1: T

37. Identify the conic, then use a graphing utility to graph the polar equation: $r = \frac{4}{2 + \cos\theta}$.

Answer: Ellipse;

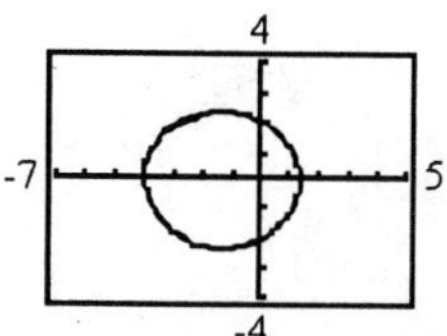

Difficulty: 2 Key 1: T

38. Identify the conic, then use a graphing utility to graph the polar equation: $r = \frac{4}{2 - \sin \theta}$.

Answer: Ellipse;

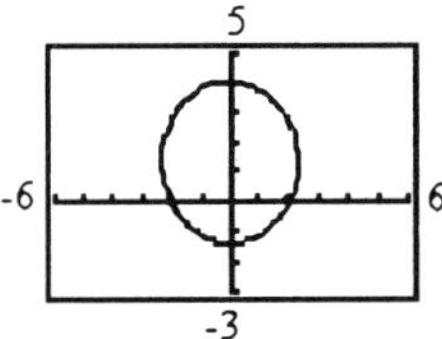

Difficulty: 2 Key 1: T

39. Identify the conic, then use a graphing utility to graph the polar equation: $r = \frac{4}{2 + 4 \cos \theta}$.

Answer: Hyperbola;

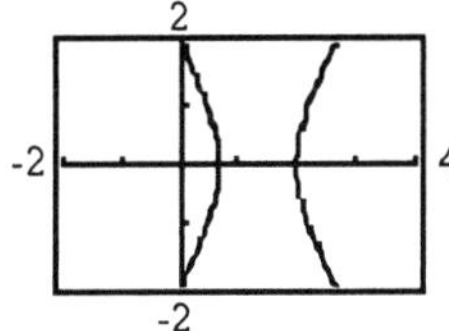

Difficulty: 2 Key 1: T

40. Identify the conic, then use a graphing utility to graph the polar equation: $r = \frac{2}{1 + \cos \theta}$.

Answer: Parabola;

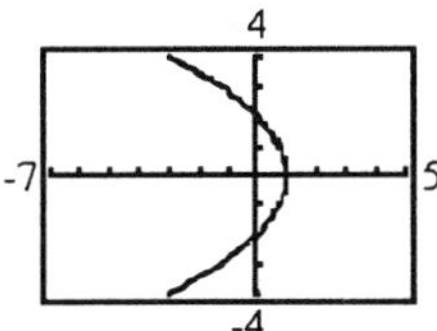

Difficulty: 2 Key 1: T

41. A racetrack is made in the shape of an ellipse. It is 1000 yards long at its longest point. A camera tower is 100 yards from the near end of the track. Find a polar equation of the track using the camera tower as a focus and the pole.

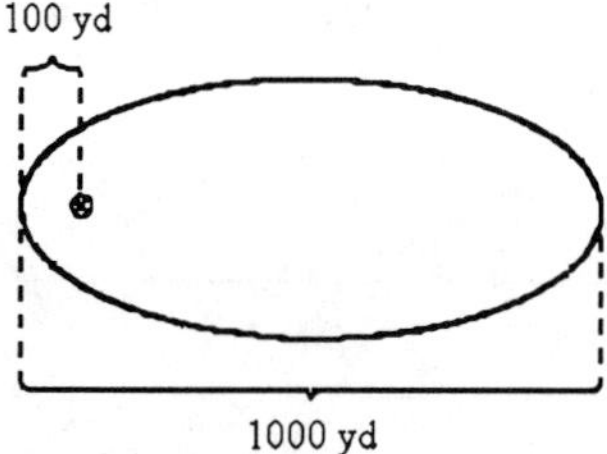

Answer:

Vertices: $(100, \pi)$, $(900, 0)$

$a = 500$

$c = 400$

$e = \frac{c}{a} = \frac{400}{500} = \frac{4}{5}$

$$r = \frac{ep}{1 - e\cos\theta} \Rightarrow 900 = \frac{\frac{4}{5}p}{1 - \frac{4}{5}\cos\theta} \Rightarrow 900 = \frac{\frac{4}{5}p}{\frac{1}{5}}$$

$$\Rightarrow 900 = 4p$$

$$\Rightarrow \frac{900}{4} = p$$

$$\Rightarrow \quad p = 225$$

$$\text{so } r = \frac{(225)\left[\frac{4}{5}\right]}{1 - \frac{4}{5}\cos\theta} \Rightarrow r = \frac{180}{1 - \frac{4}{5}\cos\theta} \Rightarrow r = \frac{900}{5 - 4\cos\theta}$$

Difficulty: 2

42. The swimming course for a triathlon includes a turnaround point marked by a stationary buoy. The swimmers must pass between the buoy and the straight shoreline. The swimmers follow a parabolic path past the buoy, which is 80 feet from the shoreline. Find a polar equation to represent the parabolic path so that the swimmers remain equidistant from the buoy and the straight shoreline, using the buoy as the focus.

Answer:

$p = 80$, $e = 1$

$$r = \frac{80}{1 - \sin\theta}$$

Difficulty: 1

PART 2 Chapter Tests and Final Exams

Test A **Name** ______________________ **Date** ______________

Chapter P **Class** ______________________ **Section** ____________

1. Identify the terms of the expression: $3x^2 - 6x + 1$.

(a) $3, -6, 1$ (b) x (c) $3x^2, -6x, 1$ (d) $3x^2, -6x$ (e) None of these

2. Simplify: $\left(\dfrac{x^{-3}y^2}{z}\right)^{-4}$.

(a) $\dfrac{z^4}{x^7y^6}$ (b) $\dfrac{y^2z^4}{x^7}$ (c) $\dfrac{x^{12}z^4}{y^8}$ (d) $\dfrac{z^4}{x^{12}y^8}$ (e) None of these

3. Simplify: $4\sqrt{9x} - 2\sqrt{4x} + 7$.

(a) $8x + 7$ (b) $8\sqrt{x} + 7$ (c) $2\sqrt{5x} + 7$

(d) Does not simplify (e) None of these

4. Simplify: $3x(7x - 6) - 4x(x - 2)$.

(a) $17x^2 - 10x$ (b) $-84x^4 + 240x^3 - 144x^2$ (c) $21x^2 - 14x$

(d) $72x^3 - 96x^2$ (e) None of these

5. Multiply: $[(x + 1) - y][(x + 1) + y]$.

(a) $x^2 + 2x + 1 - y^2$ (b) $x^2 + 1 - y^2$ (c) $x^2y^2 + y^2$

(d) $-x^2y^2 + 2xy^2 + y^2$ (e) None of these

6. Factor: $9x^2 - 42x + 49$.

(a) $(3x - 7)^2$ (b) $(9x - 7)^2$ (c) $(3x + 7)^2$

(d) $x(9x - 42 + 49)$ (e) None of these

7. Add, then simplify: $\dfrac{2}{x^2 - 9} + \dfrac{5}{x^2 - x - 12}$.

(a) $\dfrac{7}{(x^2 - 9)(x^2 - x - 12)}$ (b) $\dfrac{7x^2 - x - 21}{(x^2 - 9)(x^2 - x - 12)}$ (c) $\dfrac{7x - 7}{(x - 3)(x - 4)(x + 3)}$

(d) $\dfrac{7x - 23}{(x - 3)(x + 3)(x - 4)}$ (e) None of these

8. The solution to the linear equation $2 - 3[7 - 2(4 - x)] = 2x - 1$ is:

(a) $x = -\frac{3}{4}$. (b) $x = \frac{4}{3}$. (c) $x = \frac{3}{4}$. (d) $x = -\frac{4}{3}$. (e) None of these

9. Solve for x: $3x^2 - 6x + 2 = 0$.

(a) $\dfrac{3 \pm \sqrt{3}}{3}$ (b) $1 \pm \sqrt{3}$ (c) $\dfrac{3 \pm \sqrt{15}}{3}$

(d) $\dfrac{1}{3}, 2$ (e) None of these

10. Graph the solution: $2x - 4 < 8$.

(a) 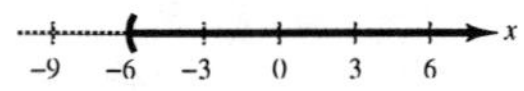 (b)

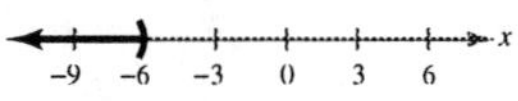

(c) 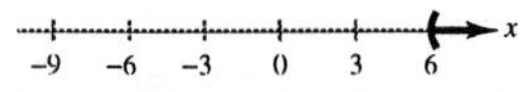 (d)

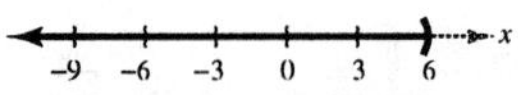

(e) None of these

11. Solve the inequality: $\dfrac{2}{x-1} \le \dfrac{3}{x+1}$.

(a) $(-1, 1) \cup [5, \infty)$ (b) $(-\infty, -1) \cup (1, 5]$ (c) $[5, \infty)$

(d) Empty set (e) None of these

12. Identify the type of triangle that has $(-5, -1)$, $(2, 2)$, and $(0, -3)$ as vertices.

(a) Scalene (b) Right isosceles (c) Equilateral

(d) Isosceles (e) None of these

Test B **Name** ______ **Date** ______

Chapter P **Class** ______ **Section** ______

1. Identify the terms of the expression: $6x^4 - 3x^2 + 16$.

(a) $6, -3, 16$ (b) x (c) $6x^4, -3x^2, 16$

(d) $6x^4, -3x^2$ (e) None of these

2. Simplify: $\left(\dfrac{3x^2y^3}{xw^{-2}}\right)^3$.

(a) $9w^6x^3y^9$ (b) $9w^{-8}x^8y^{27}$ (c) $27w^6x^3y^9$

(d) $3w^6x^3y^9$ (e) None of these

3. Simplify: $7\sqrt{25xy^2} - 4\sqrt{75xy^2} + 2\sqrt{12xy^2}$.

(a) $35|y|\sqrt{x} - 16|y|\sqrt{3x}$ (b) $19|y|\sqrt{2x}$ (c) $35|y|\sqrt{x} - 6|y|\sqrt{2x}$

(d) $5|y|\sqrt{38x}$ (e) None of these

4. Simplify: $(3x^4 - 7x^2) + 2x(x^2 - 1)(3x)$.

(a) $9x^4 - 13x^2$ (b) $9x^4 - 19x^3 - 2x$ (c) $3x^4 + 2x^3 - 7x^2 - 3x$

(d) $15x^7 - 50x^5 + 35x^3$ (e) None of these

5. Expand: $(3 + 2y)^3$.

(a) $9 + 6y^3$ (b) $27 + 8y^3$ (c) $27 + 54y + 36y^2 + 8y^3$

(d) $27 + 18y + 12y^2 + 8y^3$ (e) None of these

6. Factor: $3x^2 - 13x - 16$.

(a) $(3x - 16)(x - 1)$ (b) $(3x + 16)(x - 1)$ (c) $(x + 16)(3x - 1)$

(d) $(x - 16)(3x + 1)$ (e) None of these

7. Subtract, then simplify: $\dfrac{3}{x^2 + 2x + 1} - \dfrac{1}{x + 1}$.

(a) $\dfrac{4 - x}{x^2 + 2x + 1}$ (b) $\dfrac{-x^2 + 5x + 2}{(x + 1)(x^2 + 2x + 1)}$ (c) $\dfrac{-x^2 + x + 2}{(x + 2x + 1)(x + 1)}$

(d) $\dfrac{2 - x}{x^2 + 2x + 1}$ (e) None of these

8. The solution to the linear equation $3x - [x - 2(3 - 2x)] = -5$ is:

(a) $x = \frac{2}{11}$. (b) $x = \frac{11}{2}$. (c) $x = -\frac{2}{11}$. (d) $x = -\frac{11}{2}$. (e) None of these

9. Solve for x: $(x - 1)^2 = 3x + 5$.

(a) 1, 4 (b) $\dfrac{5 \pm \sqrt{39}}{2}$ (c) $\dfrac{5 \pm \sqrt{41}}{2}$

(d) $-1, 6$ (e) None of these

10. Graph the solution: $-3 \leq 2x + 1 \leq 5$.

(a) 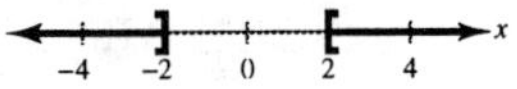 [number line graph]

(b) 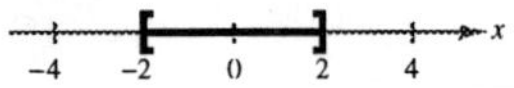 [number line graph]

(c) 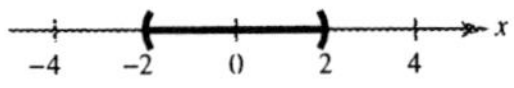 [number line graph]

(d) 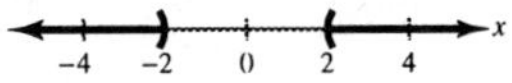 [number line graph]

(e) None of these

11. Solve the inequality: $\dfrac{3}{x-1} \leq \dfrac{2}{x+1}$.

(a) $(-\infty, -5]$

(b) $(-\infty, -5] \cup (-1, 1)$

(c) $[-5, -1) \cup (1, \infty)$

(d) $(-\infty, -2] \cup (1, \infty)$

(e) None of these

12. Identify the type of triangle that has $(0, 0)$, $(4, 0)$ and, $(2, 2\sqrt{3})$ as vertices.

(a) Scalene

(b) Right

(c) Isosceles

(d) Equilateral

(e) These points do not form a triangle.

Test C **Name** ________________ **Date** ________________

Chapter P **Class** ________________ **Section** ________________

1. Identify the terms of the expression: $12x^3 - 6x^2 + 2$.

(a) $12, -6, 2$ (b) x (c) $12x^3, -6x^2, 2$

(d) $12x^3, -6x^2$ (e) None of these

2. Simplify: $3x^2(2x)^3(5x^{-1})$.

(a) $30x^{-6}$ (b) $\frac{6}{5}x^6$ (c) $\frac{24}{5}x^4$ (d) $120x^4$ (e) None of these

3. Simplify: $2x^2y\sqrt[3]{2x} + 7x^2\sqrt[3]{2xy^3} - 4\sqrt[3]{16x^7y^3}$.

(a) $x^6y^3\sqrt[3]{2x}$ (b) $x^2y\sqrt[3]{2x}$ (c) $9x^2y\sqrt[3]{2x} - 8y\sqrt[3]{2x^7y}$

(d) $2x^3y$ (e) None of these

4. Simplify: $(5 - 2x)(3) - (3x + 2)(-2)$.

(a) $-6x^2 + 11x + 10$ (b) $-9x + 1$ (c) $-10x + 20$

(d) 19 (e) None of these

5. Multiply: $(2x - y)(x + y)$.

(a) $2x^2 - y^2$ (b) $2x^2 + xy - y^2$ (c) $-2x^2y^2$

(d) $x^2y^2 - xy$ (e) None of these

6. Factor: $3x^2 - 19x - 14$.

(a) $(3x + 2)(x - 7)$ (b) $(3x - 7)(x + 2)$ (c) $(3x - 2)(x + 7)$

(d) $(3x + 7)(x - 2)$ (e) None of these

7. Add, then simplify: $\dfrac{3}{x^2 + x - 2} + \dfrac{x}{x^2 - x - 6}$.

(a) $\dfrac{x^2 + 2x - 9}{(x - 3)(x + 2)(x - 1)}$ (b) $\dfrac{x^3 + 3x^2 - 5x - 6}{(x^2 + x - 2)(x^2 - x - 6)}$ (c) $\dfrac{4x - 10}{(x - 3)(x + 2)(x - 1)}$

(d) $\dfrac{3 + x}{2x^2 - 8}$ (e) None of these

8. The solution to the linear equation $3x - [2(3 - 2x) - x] = 4$ is:

(a) $x = \frac{5}{4}$. (b) $x = -\frac{4}{5}$. (c) $x = -\frac{5}{4}$. (d) $x = \frac{4}{5}$. (e) None of these

9. Solve for x: $4x^2 + 12x = 135$.

(a) $-\dfrac{9}{2}, \dfrac{15}{2}$ (b) $-\dfrac{5}{2}, \dfrac{3}{2}$ (c) $-\dfrac{15}{2}, \dfrac{9}{2}$

(d) $\dfrac{-3 \pm \sqrt{6}}{2}$ (e) None of these

10. Graph the solution: $-6 < 7x + 2 \le 5$.

(a) 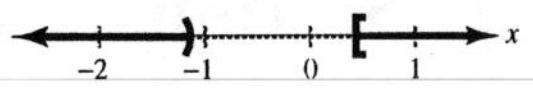 [number line graph]

(b) 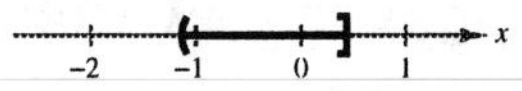 [number line graph]

(c) 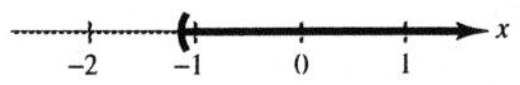 [number line graph]

(d) 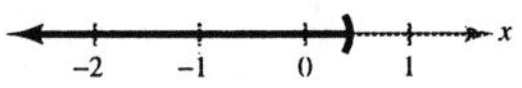 [number line graph]

(e) None of these

11. Solve the inequality: $\dfrac{2}{x+2} \ge \dfrac{3}{x-1}$.

(a) $[-8, \infty)$ (b) $[-8, -2) \cup (1, \infty)$ (c) $(-\infty, -8] \cup (-2, 1)$

(d) $(-\infty, -8]$ (e) None of these

12. Identify the type of triangle that has $(0, 0)$, $(4, 0)$, and $(2, 4\sqrt{2})$ as vertices.

(a) Scalene (b) Right (c) Isosceles

(d) Equilateral (e) These points do not form a triangle.

Test D **Name**__________ **Date**__________

Chapter P **Class**__________ **Section**__________

1. Identify the terms of the expression: $2x^4 - 3x^3 + 2x + 1$.

2. Simplify: $(3x^2y^3z)^{-2}(xy^4)$.

3. Simplify: $3\sqrt[3]{4x^5y^3} + 7x\sqrt[3]{32x^2y^6}$.

4. Write in standard form: $(3x^2 + 2x) + x(1 - 7x) + (2x + 5)$.

5. Expand: $(2x - 1)^3$.

6. Factor: $14x^2 - 19x - 3$.

7. A marble is tossed into a box whose base is shown. Find the probability that the marble will come to rest in the shaded portion of the box.

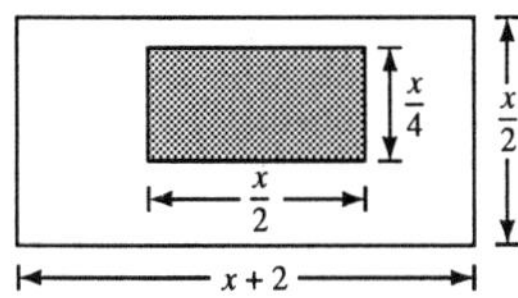

8. Solve the equation $3x - [5 - 2(1 - 2x)] = 7x - 5$.

9. Solve for x: $x^2 - 3x + \frac{3}{2} = 0$.

10. Graph the solution: $\frac{1}{2} < 3 - x < 5$.

11. Find the domain of $\sqrt{36 - x^2}$.

12. Find the length of the hypotenuse of the right triangle determined by the points $(1, 1)$, $(-2, 1)$, and $(-2, 4)$.

Test E **Name**____________ **Date**________

Chapter P **Class**____________ **Section**________

1. Identify the terms of the expression: $6x^3 - 2x^2 + 4x - 3$.

2. Simplify: $(-2x^2)^5(5x^3)^{-2}$.

3. Simplify: $(\sqrt[3]{81x^4y^9})(\sqrt[3]{2xy^2})$.

4. Write in standard form: $3x^2 - 2x(1 + 3x - x^2)$.

5. Expand: $[(x - 1) + y]^2$.

6. Factor: $35x^2 + 9x - 2$.

7. A marble is tossed into a triangular box whose base is shown. Find the probability that the marble will come to rest in the shaded portion of the triangle.

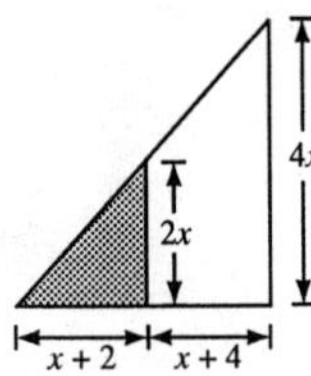

8. Solve the equation $3x + [2(1 - 2x) + 5] = 5 - 7x$.

9. Solve for x: $-3x^2 + 4x + 6 = 0$.

10. Graph the solution: $-16 \leq 7 - 2x < 5$.

11. Find the domain of $\sqrt{16 - 4x^2}$.

12. Find the length of the hypotenuse of the right triangle determined by the points $(-1, 1)$, $(3, 1)$, and $(3, -3)$.

Test A Name ______________ Date __________

Chapter 1 Class ______________ Section __________

1. Find the equation of the line passing through (6, 10) and (−1, 4).

(a) $7x - 6y + 18 = 0$ (b) $6x - 7y + 34 = 0$ (c) $6x - 5y + 14 = 0$

(d) $5x - 6y + 30 = 0$ (e) None of these

2. What is the slope of a line that is perpendicular to the line given by $2x + 3y + 9 = 0$?

(a) $\frac{2}{3}$ (b) $-\frac{2}{3}$ (c) $\frac{3}{2}$

(d) $-\frac{3}{2}$ (e) None of these

3. Find the equation of the line that passes through (1, 3) and is parallel to the line $2x + 3y + 5 = 0$.

(a) $3x - 2y + 3 = 0$ (b) $2x + 3y - 11 = 0$ (c) $2x + 3y - 9 = 0$

(d) $3x - 2y - 7 = 0$ (e) None of these

4. In which of the following equations is y a function of x?

(a) $3y + 2x - 9 = 17$ (b) $2x^2 + x = 4y$

(c) Both a and b (d) Neither a nor b

5. Given $f(x) = \begin{cases} 7x - 10, & x \le 2 \\ x^2 + 6, & x > 2 \end{cases}$, find $f(0)$.

(a) -10 (b) 0 (c) -4

(d) 6 (e) None of these

6. Which of the functions fits the data?

x	−2	0	1	3	5	10
y	−6	0	3	9	15	30

(a) $f(x) = x^3$ (b) $f(x) = \sqrt[3]{x}$ (c) $f(x) = |x|^3$

(d) $f(x) = 3x$ (e) None of these

7. Find the domain of the function $g(x) = \dfrac{5x}{x^2 - 7x + 12}$.

(a) All reals except $x = 0$ (b) All reals except $x = 3, 4$ (c) All reals except $x = -3, -4$

(d) All reals except $x = 12$ (e) None of these

8. Use the vertical line test to determine in which case y is a function of x.

(a)

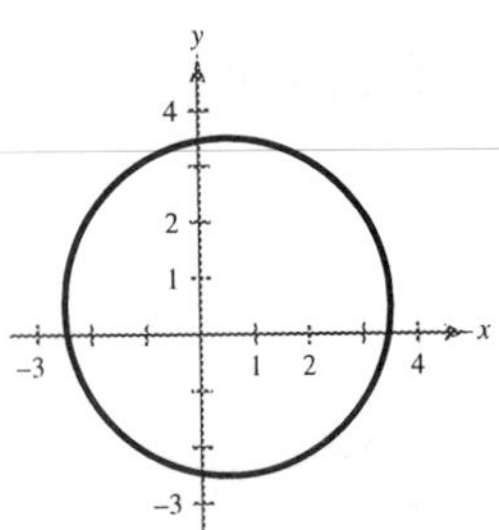

(b)

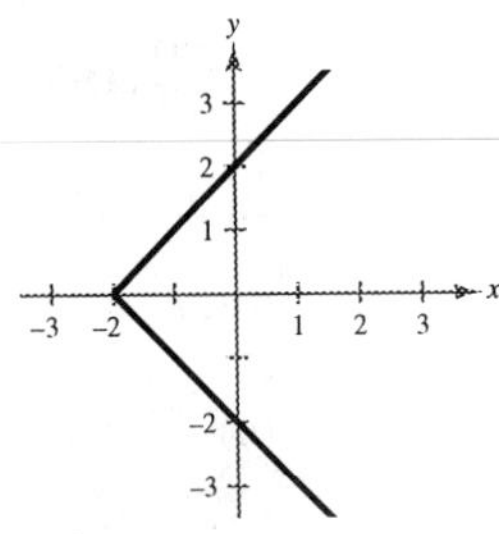

(c)

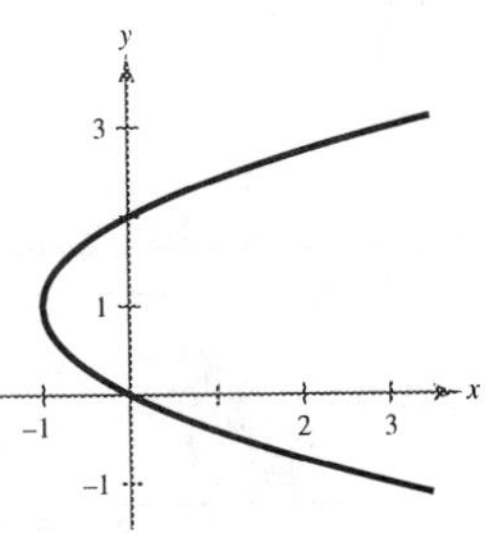

(d)

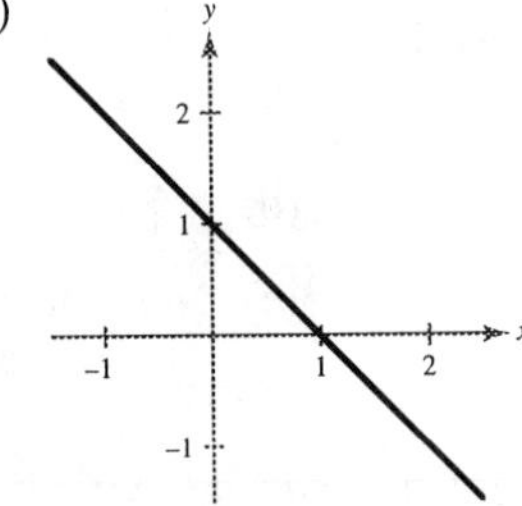

(e) None of these

9. The function $f(x) = 2x^3 + 4x$ is:

(a) odd (b) even (c) both (d) neither

10. Describe the transformation of the graph of $f(x) = x^2$ for the graph of $g(x) = (x + 9)^2$.

(a) Vertical shift 9 units up
(b) Vertical shift 9 units down
(c) Horizontal shift 9 units to the right
(d) Horizontal shift 9 units to the left
(e) None of these

11. The point $\left(0, -\frac{1}{2}\right)$ is on the graph of f. If g is a translation of f so that $g(x) = f\left(x + \frac{1}{2}\right) + 2$, then the coordinates of the translated point are:

(a) $\left(\frac{1}{2}, 2\right)$
(b) $\left(-\frac{1}{2}, -2\right)$
(c) $\left(\frac{1}{2}, \frac{3}{2}\right)$
(d) $\left(-\frac{1}{2}, \frac{3}{2}\right)$
(e) None of these

12. Given $f(x) = x - 2$ and $g(x) = 6 - 2x$, find $(f + g)(-2)$.

(a) 6
(b) 2
(c) -2
(d) -14
(e) None of these

13. Given $f(x) = x^2 - 2x$ and $g(x) = 2x + 3$, find $(f \circ g)(x)$.

(a) $4x^2 + 8x + 3$
(b) $2x^2 - 4x + 3$
(c) $2x^3 - x^2 - 6x$
(d) $3x^2 + x$
(e) None of these

14. Graphically, determine which sets of functions are not inverses of each other.

(a) $f(x) = 9 + x$
$g(x) = 9 - x$

(b) $f(x) = x^2$
$g(x) = -x^2$

(c) $f(x) = \dfrac{x + 3}{3}$
$g(x) = \dfrac{3}{x + 3}$

(d) All of these are inverses of each other.

(e) None of these are inverses of each other.

15. Find the inverse of the function: $f(x) = \dfrac{x + 3}{2}$.

(a) $2x - \dfrac{2}{3}$

(b) $\dfrac{2}{x + 3}$

(c) $2x - 6$

(d) $2x - 3$

(e) None of these

Test B **Name** ______________________ **Date** ____________

Chapter 1 **Class** ______________________ **Section** ____________

1. Find the equation of the line passing through $(-1, 16)$ and $(4, 2)$.

(a) $6x - y - 8 = 0$ (b) $14x + 5y - 66 = 0$ (c) $6x - y - 22 = 0$

(d) $14x + 5y - 48 = 0$ (e) None of these

2. What is the slope of the line perpendicular to the line $4x - 2y = 9$?

(a) $\frac{9}{2}$ (b) $\frac{9}{4}$ (c) $-\frac{1}{2}$

(d) 2 (e) None of these

3. Find the equation of the line that passes through $(2, -1)$ and is parallel to the line $2x + 7y = 5$.

(a) $2x - 7y - 11 = 0$ (b) $2x + 7y + 3 = 0$ (c) $2x + 7y - 12 = 0$

(d) $7x - 2y - 16 = 0$ (e) None of these

4. In which of the following equations is y a function of x?

(a) $2x + 3y - 1 = 0$ (b) $x^2 + 3y^2 = 7$ (c) $2x^2y = 7$

(d) Both a and b (e) Both a and c

5. Given $f(x) = \begin{cases} 3x + 4, & x \le 2 \\ x^2 + 1, & x > 2 \end{cases}$, find $f(3)$.

(a) 13 (b) 10 (c) 5

(d) 3 (e) None of these

6. For what values of x does $f(x) = g(x)$?

$f(x) = 3x + 1 \quad g(x) = x^2 - 3$

(a) 0 (b) 4, 1 (c) $-4, -1$

(d) $4, -1$ (e) None of these

7. Find the domain of the function $f(x) = \dfrac{2x - 1}{2x + 1}$.

(a) $(-\infty, 1) \cup (1, \infty)$ (b) $(-\infty, -1) \cup (-1, \infty)$ (c) $\left(-\infty, -\frac{1}{2}\right) \cup \left(-\frac{1}{2}, \infty\right)$

(d) $\left(-\infty, \frac{1}{2}\right) \cup \left(\frac{1}{2}, \infty\right)$ (e) None of these

8. Use the vertical line test to determine in which case y is a function of x.

(a)

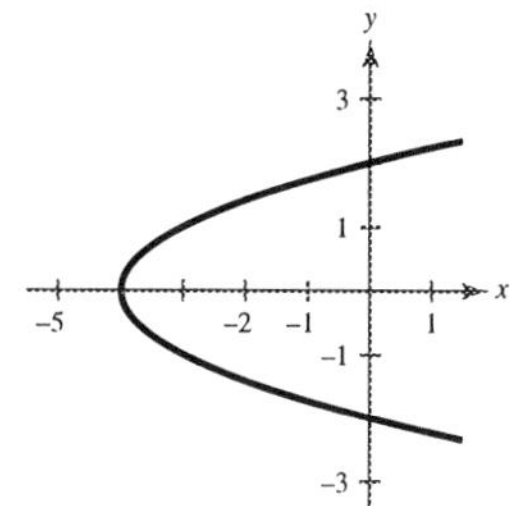

(b)

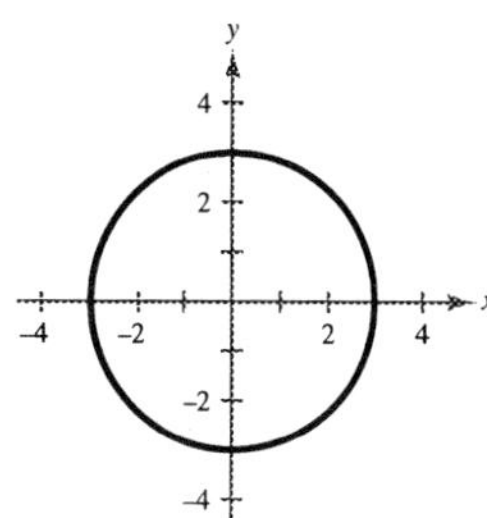

(c)

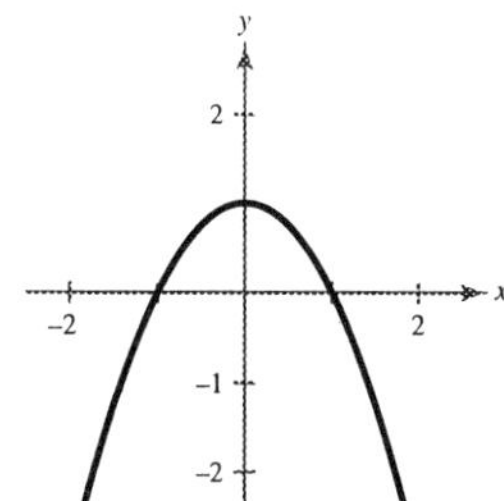

(d)

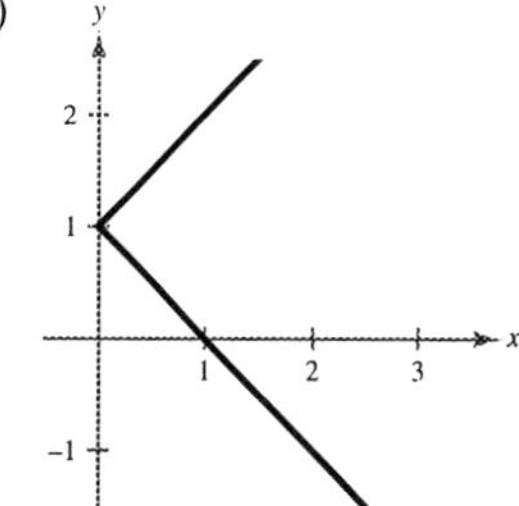

(e) None of these

9. The function $f(x) = 3x^2 - 5$ is:

(a) odd (b) even (c) both (d) neither

10. Describe the transformation of the graph of $f(x) = |x|$ for the graph of $g(x) = |x| - 20$.

(a) Vertical shift 20 units up
(b) Vertical shift 20 units down
(c) Horizontal shift 20 units to the right
(d) Horizontal shift 20 units to the left
(e) None of these

11. The point $\left(-\frac{3}{8}, 0\right)$ is on the graph of f. If g is a translation of f, so that $g(x) = f(x + 2) + \frac{1}{2}$, then the coordinates of the translated point are:

(a) $\left(2, \frac{1}{2}\right)$
(b) $\left(-2, -\frac{1}{2}\right)$
(c) $\left(\frac{13}{8}, \frac{1}{2}\right)$
(d) $\left(-\frac{19}{8}, \frac{1}{2}\right)$
(e) None of these

12. Given $f(x) = x$ and $g(x) = x^2 - 7$, find $(fg)(3)$.

(a) -13
(b) 29
(c) 5
(d) 6
(e) None of these

13. Given $f(x) = 4 - 2x^2$ and $g(x) = 2 - x$, find $(f \circ g)(x)$.

(a) $4x^2 - 16x + 20$
(b) $2x^2 - 4$
(c) $2x^2 - 2$
(d) $-2x^3 - 4x^2 - 4x + 8$
(e) None of these

14. Graphically determine which sets of functions are not inverses of each other.

(a) $f(x) = x + 5$ $g(x) = x - 5$

(b) $f(x) = x^3$ $g(x) = \sqrt[3]{x}$

(c) $f(x) = \dfrac{x+2}{4}$ $g(x) = 4x - 2$

(d) All of these are inverses of each other.

(e) None of these are inverses of each other.

15. Find the inverse of the function: $f(x) = \dfrac{4+5x}{7}$.

(a) $\dfrac{7}{5}(x - 4)$

(b) $\dfrac{1}{5}(7x - 4)$

(c) $-\dfrac{7}{4} - \dfrac{7}{5x}$

(d) $\dfrac{7}{4 + 5x}$

(e) None of these

Test C **Name** ____________________ **Date** ____________

Chapter 1 **Class** ____________________ **Section** __________

1. Find the equation of the line passing through $(3, -2)$ and $(5, 7)$.

(a) $2x - 9y + 53 = 0$ (b) $9x - 2y - 31 = 0$ (c) $5x - 2y - 11 = 0$

(d) $5x + 8y - 81 = 0$ (e) None of these

2. Find the slope of the line parallel to the line $3x - 4y = 12$.

(a) Undefined (b) 0 (c) $\frac{4}{3}$

(d) $-\frac{3}{4}$ (e) None of these

3. Find an equation of the line that passes through $(6, 2)$ and is perpendicular to the line $3x + 2y = 2$.

(a) $y = -\frac{3}{2}x + 11$ (b) $y = -\frac{2}{3}x + 6$ (c) $y = \frac{3}{2}x - 7$

(d) $y = \frac{2}{3}x - 2$ (e) None of these

4. In which of the following equations is y a function of x?

(a) $3y + 2x - 7 = 0$ (b) $5x^2y = 9 - 2x$ (c) $3x^2 - 4y^2 = 9$

(d) $x = 3y^2 - 1$ (e) Both a and b

5. Given $f(x) = \begin{cases} 2x - 1, & x \le -2 \\ x + 6, & x > -2 \end{cases}$, find $f(-6)$.

(a) -11 (b) -13 (c) 0

(d) 11 (e) None of these

6. For what values of x does $f(x) = g(x)$?

$f(x) = x^4 + 3x^2 \quad g(x) = 7x^2$

(a) $-4, 0, 4$ (b) $0, 2$ (c) 2

(d) $0, 2, -2$ (e) None of these

7. Find the domain of the function: $f(x) = \dfrac{1}{x + 2}$.

(a) $(-\infty, 2)$ (b) $(-\infty, -2) \cup (-2, \infty)$ (c) $(-\infty, -2)$

(d) $\left(-\infty, \dfrac{-1}{2}\right) \cup \left(\dfrac{-1}{2}, \infty\right)$ (e) None of these

8. Use the vertical line test to determine in which case y is a function of x.

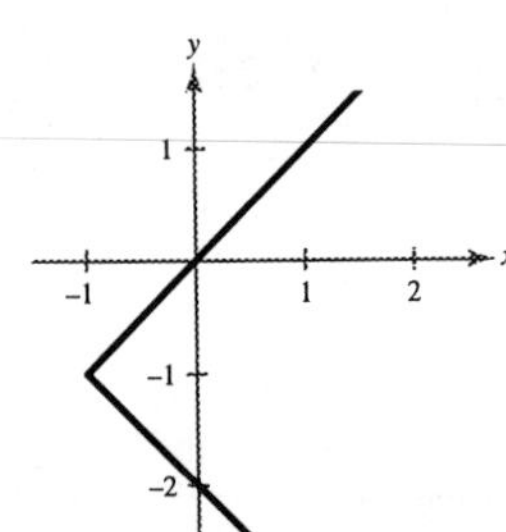

(b)

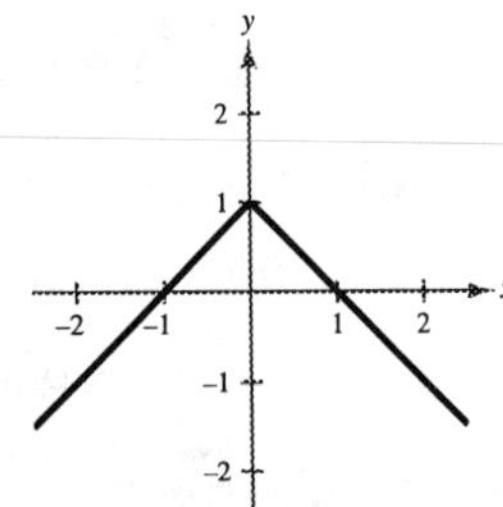

(c)

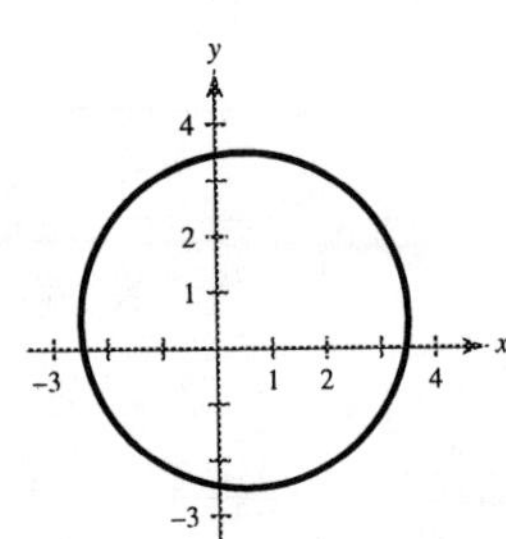

(d)

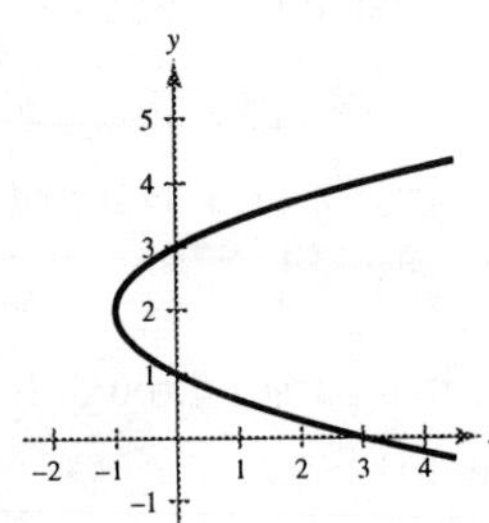

(e) None of these

9. The function $f(x) = 4x^2 - 8x + 6$ is:

(a) odd (b) even (c) both (d) neither

10. Describe the transformation of the graph of $f(x) = \sqrt{x}$ for the graph of $g(x) = \sqrt{x - 5}$.

(a) Vertical shift 5 units up
(b) Vertical shift 5 units down
(c) Horizontal shift 5 units to the right
(d) Horizontal shift 5 units to the left
(e) None of these

11. The point $\left(0, -\frac{3}{8}\right)$ is on the graph of f. If g is a translation of f so that $g(x) = f\left(x + \frac{3}{8}\right) - 1$, then the coordinates of the translated point are:

(a) $\left(-\frac{3}{8}, -\frac{11}{8}\right)$
(b) $(0, -1)$
(c) $\left(\frac{3}{8}, -\frac{4}{8}\right)$
(d) $\left(\frac{3}{8}, -1\right)$
(e) None of these

12. Given $f(x) = 9x + 1$ and $g(x) = 4 - x$, find $(f - g)(5)$.

(a) 37
(b) 47
(c) 55
(d) -46
(e) None of these

13. Given $f(x) = \frac{1}{x^2}$ and $g(x) = \sqrt{x^2 + 4}$, find $(f \circ g)(x)$.

(a) $\frac{1}{x^2 + 4}$ (b) $\frac{1}{\sqrt{x^2 + 4}}$ (c) $x^2 + 4$

(d) $\frac{1}{x^2\sqrt{x^2 + 4}}$ (e) None of these

14. Graphically determine which sets of functions are not inverses of each other.

(a) $f(x) = \frac{1}{2}x - 1$, $g(x) = 2x + 1$

(b) $f(x) = \sqrt[5]{x}$, $g(x) = \frac{1}{\sqrt[5]{x}}$

(c) $f(x) = \frac{x - 1}{5}$, $g(x) = x + \frac{1}{5}$

(d) All of these are inverses of each other. (e) None of these are inverses of each other.

15. Find the inverse of the function: $f(x) = \frac{2}{3x + 1}$.

(a) $\frac{3x - 1}{2}$ (b) $\frac{2 - x}{3x}$ (c) $\frac{3x + 1}{2}$ (d) $\frac{1 - x}{2}$ (e) None of these

Test D Name__________________ Date__________

Chapter 1 Class__________________ Section__________

1. Find the equation of the line passing through $(5, 9)$ and $(-1, -3)$.

2. Find an equation of the line that passes through $(8, 17)$ and is perpendicular to the line $x + 2y = 2$.

3. Morgan Sporting Goods had net sales of \$150,000 in January of this past year. In March, their net sales were \$300,000. Assuming that their sales are increasing linearly, write an equation of net sales, S, in terms of the month using $t = 1$ for January.

4. Select which of the two equations represents y as a function of x and specify why the other does not.

   (a) $x^2 + 5y - x = 7$ (b) $y^2 - 5x = 7$

5. $F(x) = -1 + 2x - x^2$. Find $F(k + 1)$ and simplify.

6. Find the domain of the function: $g(x) = \dfrac{x}{x^2 + 1}$.

7. Determine the domain and range of the function $f(x) = 3 - |x|$.

8. Determine the interval(s) over which the function is increasing: $y = \frac{2}{3}x^3 - x^2$.

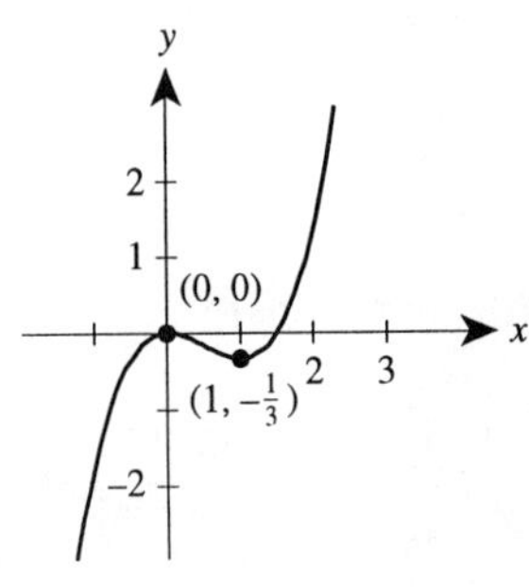

9. Find the zeros of the function $f(x) = \sqrt{12 - x^2}$.

10. Sketch the graph of $f(x) = |-x|$.

11. Given the graph of $y = x^4$ sketch the graph of $y = (x - 2)^4 + 6$.

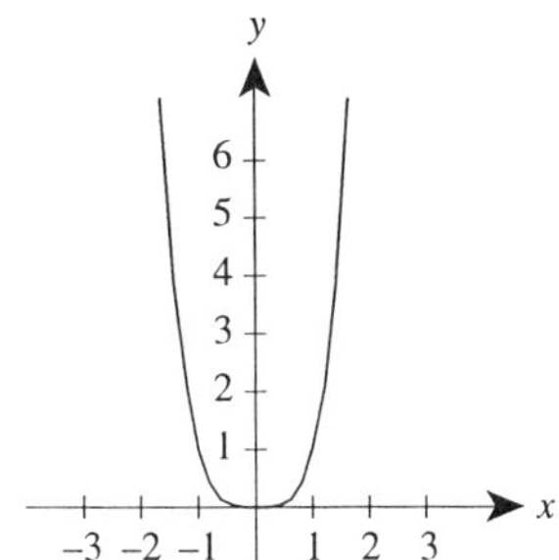

12. Use a graphing utility to graph $(f/g)(x)$ if $f(x) = 2x^2 - x$ and $g(x) = x$.

13. Given $f(x) = \dfrac{1}{x}$ and $g(x) = \dfrac{1}{x}$, find $(f \circ g)(9)$.

14. Graphically, determine whether the functions $f(x) = (x + 1)^3$ and $g(x) = \sqrt[3]{x} - 1$ are inverses of each other.

15. Given $f(x) = 2x^2 + 1$ for $x \geq 0$, find $f^{-1}(x)$.

Test E Name____________________ Date____________

Chapter 1 Class____________________ Section____________

1. Find the equation of the line passing through $(3, 7)$ and $(-1, -2)$.

2. Find an equation of the line that passes through $(3, 5)$ and is perpendicular to the line $x + 3y = 6$.

3. Curtis Area Schools had an enrollment of 2800 students in 1990 and 12,600 in 1998. Assuming the growth is linear, write an equation of the enrollment, E, in terms of the year using $t = 0$ for 1990.

4. Select which of the two equations represents y as a function of x and specify why the other does not.

   (a) $|x| + y = 4$ (b) $x + |y| = 4$

5. $F(x) = 5 + 2x - x^2$. Find $F(k + 1) - F(k)$ and simplify.

6. Find the domain of the function $h(x) = \dfrac{x + 4}{x(x - 5)}$.

7. Determine the domain and range of the function $f(x) = 3 - x^2$.

8. Determine the interval(s) over which the function is increasing: $y = \dfrac{1}{x^2 - 1}$.

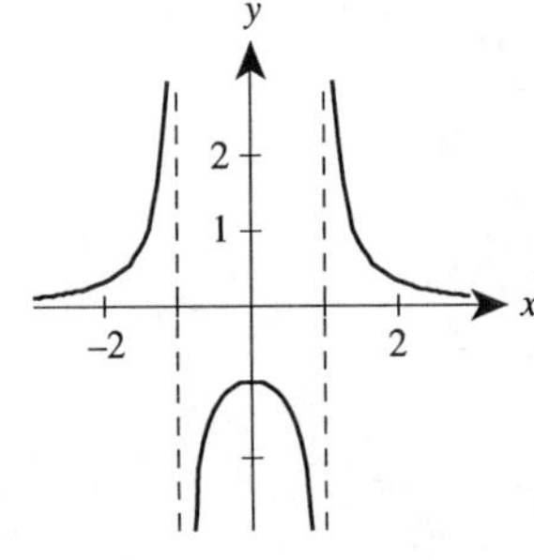

9. Find the zeros of the function $f(x) = \dfrac{x^2 - 4}{x^2 - 9}$.

10. Sketch the graph of $f(x) = -|x|$.

11. Given the graph of $y = x^2$ sketch the graph of $y = (x + 3)^2 - 1$.

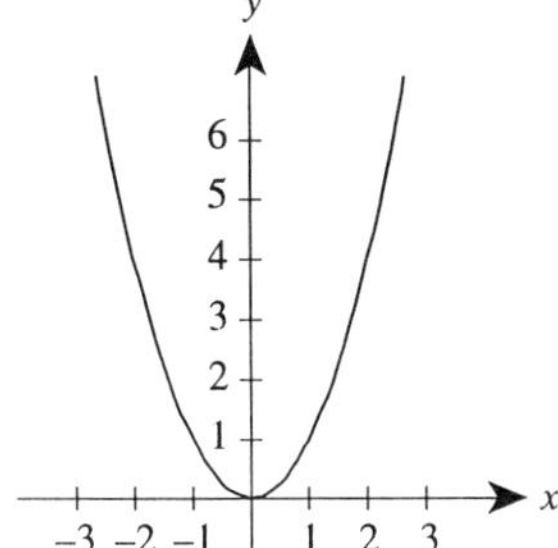

12. Use a graphing utility to graph $(fg)(x)$ if $f(x) = \dfrac{1}{x}$ and $g(x) = x + 2$.

13. Given $f(x) = x^3 + 4$ and $g(x) = \sqrt[3]{x}$, find $(f \circ g)(-3)$.

14. Graphically, determine whether the functions $f(x) = \sqrt{x^2 - 5}$ and $g(x) = x^2 + 5$ are inverses of each other.

15. Given $f(x) = \dfrac{2x + 1}{3}$, find $f^{-1}(x)$.

Test A **Name** ______ **Date** ______

Chapter 2 **Class** ______ **Section** ______

1. Write in the form $y = a(x - h)^2 + k$: $y = 2x^2 + 16x + 9$.

(a) $y = 2(x + 4)^2 - 7$ (b) $y = 2(x + 2)^2 + 5$ (c) $y = 2(x + 4)^2 - 23$

(d) $y = 2(x + 8)^2 + 73$ (e) None of these

2. Find the number of units that produce a maximum revenue, $R = 95x - 0.1x^2$, where R is the total revenue in dollars and x is the number of units sold.

(a) 716 (b) 475 (c) 371 (d) 550 (e) None of these

3. Determine the left-hand and right-hand behavior of the graph: $y = 4x^2 - 2x + 1$.

(a) Up to the left, down to the right (b) Down to the left, up to the right

(c) Up to the left, up to the right (d) Down to the left, down to the right

(e) None of these

4. Find a polynomial function with the given zeros: 0, -1, and 2.

(a) $f(x) = x(x - 1)(x + 2)$ (b) $f(x) = x(x + 1)(x - 2)$

(c) $f(x) = (x + 1)(x - 2)$ (d) $f(x) = (x + 1)^2(x - 2)$

(e) None of these

5. Divide: $(9x^3 - 6x^2 - 8x - 3) \div (3x + 2)$.

(a) $3x^2 - \frac{8}{3}x - \frac{7/3}{3x + 2}$ (b) $3x^2 - 4x - 2 + \frac{7}{3x + 2}$

(c) $3x^2 - 4x - \frac{3}{3x + 2}$ (d) $3x^2 - 4x - \frac{16}{3} + \frac{23/3}{3x + 2}$

(e) None of these

6. Find all of the real roots: $x^3 - 7x + 6 = 0$.

(a) $-3, 1, 2$ (b) $-2, -1, 3$ (c) $-6, -1, 1$

(d) $-1, 1, 6$ (e) None of these

7. Simplify, then write your result in standard form: $(6 + \sqrt{-9}) - 2i + 10 - \sqrt{16}$.

(a) $16 - 3i$ (b) $13 - 6i$ (c) $9 - 2i$

(d) $12 + i$ (e) None of these

8. Solve for x: $3x^2 = 4x - 2$.

(a) $\frac{2 \pm 2\sqrt{2}i}{3}$ (b) $\frac{2 \pm 2\sqrt{10}}{3}$ (c) $\frac{2 \pm \sqrt{2}i}{3}$

(d) $\frac{2 \pm \sqrt{10}}{3}$ (e) None of these

9. Write as a product of linear factors: $x^4 + 25x^2 + 144$.

(a) $(x^2 + 9)(x^2 + 16)$

(b) $(x + 3i)(x + 3i)(x + 4i)(x + 4i)$

(c) $(x + 3i)(x - 3i)(x + 4i)(x - 4i)$

(d) $(x - 3i)(x - 3i)(x - 4i)(x - 4i)$

(e) None of these

10. Find the vertical asymptote(s): $f(x) = \dfrac{1}{(x + 2)(x - 5)}$.

(a) $x = -2, x = 5$

(b) $y = 1$

(c) $y = 0$

(d) $y = 1, y = 0$

(e) None of these

11. Find the horizontal asymptote(s): $f(x) = \dfrac{x^2 - 1}{x^2 + 9}$.

(a) $y = 1$

(b) $y = 0$

(c) $x = 1$

(d) $x = \pm 1$

(e) None of these

12. Match the graph with the correct function.

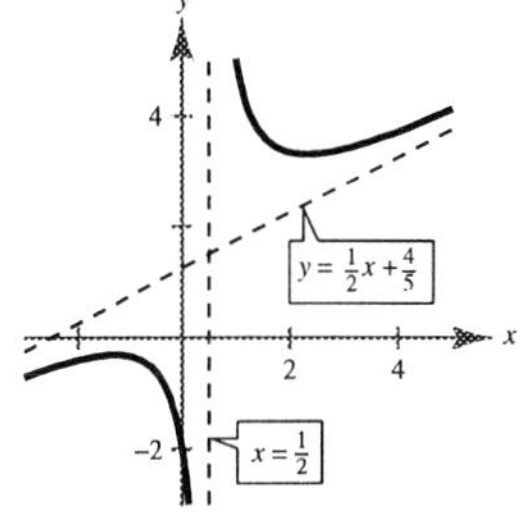

(a) $f(x) = \dfrac{1}{2x + 1}$

(b) $f(x) = \dfrac{x - 1}{2x + 1}$

(c) $f(x) = \dfrac{x^2 + 2x + 2}{2x - 1}$

(d) $f(x) = \dfrac{x^3 + 2x^2 + x - 2}{2x + 1}$

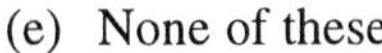
(e) None of these

13. Find the partial fraction decomposition: $\dfrac{4x + 23}{x^2 - x - 6}$.

(a) $\dfrac{4x}{x + 2} + \dfrac{23}{x - 3}$

(b) $\dfrac{2}{x + 2} - \dfrac{13}{x - 3}$

(c) $\dfrac{5}{x - 3} - \dfrac{2}{x + 2}$

(d) $\dfrac{7}{x - 3} - \dfrac{3}{x + 2}$

(e) None of these

Test B Name ______________ Date ______________

Chapter 2 Class ______________ Section ______________

1. Write in the form $y = a(x - h)^2 + k$: $y = x^2 - 8x + 2$.

(a) $y = (x - 4)^2 - 18$ (b) $y = (x - 4)^2 - 14$ (c) $y = (x - 8)^2 + 66$

(d) $y = (x - 4)^2 + 18$ (e) None of these

2. Find the number of units that produce a maximum revenue, $R = 400x - 0.01x^2$, where R is the total revenue in dollars and x is the number of units sold.

(a) 15,000 (b) 32,000 (c) 4500

(d) 20,000 (e) None of these

3. Determine the left-hand and right-hand behavior of the graph: $f(x) = -x^5 + 2x^2 - 1$.

(a) Up to the left, down to the right (b) Down to the left, up to the right

(c) Up to the left, up to the right (d) Down to the left, down to the right

(e) None of these

4. Find a polynomial function with the given zeros: $-2, -2, 1$, and 3.

(a) $f(x) = (x + 1)(x + 3)(x - 2)$ (b) $f(x) = (x - 2)^2(x - 1)(x - 3)$

(c) $f(x) = (x + 2)(x - 1)(x - 3)$ (d) $f(x) = (x + 2)^2(x - 1)(x - 3)$

(e) None of these

5. Divide: $(6x^3 + 7x^2 - 15x + 6) \div (2x - 1)$.

(a) $3x^2 + 2x - \dfrac{17}{2} - \dfrac{5}{2(2x - 1)}$ (b) $3x^2 + 5x - 5 + \dfrac{1}{2x - 1}$

(c) $3x^2 + 5x + 5 + \dfrac{11}{2x - 1}$ (d) $3x^2 + 4x - 17 + \dfrac{29/2}{2x - 1}$

(e) None of these

6. Find all of the real roots: $2x^3 + 5x^2 - x - 6 = 0$.

(a) $-3, -1, 1$ (b) $-1, \frac{3}{2}, 2$ (c) $-2, -\frac{3}{2}, 1$

(d) $-6, 2, 5$ (e) None of these

7. Simplify, then write your result in standard form: $(4 - \sqrt{-1}) - 2(3 + 2i)$.

(a) $-2 - 3i$ (b) $-2 + 5i$ (c) $-2 - 5i$

(d) $-2 + i$ (e) None of these

8. Solve for x: $3x^2 = x + 14$.

(a) $-7, \dfrac{2}{3}$ (b) $\dfrac{7}{3}, -2$ (c) $\dfrac{x + 14}{3x}$

(d) $-\dfrac{1}{6} \pm \dfrac{\sqrt{167}}{6}i$ (e) None of these

9. Write as a product of linear factors: $f(x) = x^4 - 3x^2 - 28$.

(a) $(x^2 + 4)(x^2 - 7)$
(b) $(x - 2i)(x + 2i)(x - \sqrt{7})(x + \sqrt{7})$
(c) $(x + 2i)(x + 2i)(x + \sqrt{7})(x - \sqrt{7})$
(d) $(x - 2i)(x - 2i)(x - \sqrt{7})(x + \sqrt{7})$
(e) None of these

10. Find the vertical asymptote(s): $f(x) = \dfrac{x + 3}{(x - 2)(x + 5)}$.

(a) $y = 2, y = -5, y = -3$
(b) $x = 2, x = -5, x = -3, x = 1$
(c) $x = 1$
(d) $x = 2, x = -5$
(e) None of these

11. Find the horizontal asymptote(s): $f(x) = \dfrac{3x - 2}{x + 2}$.

(a) $y = 0$
(b) $x = -2$
(c) $x = \frac{1}{3}$
(d) $y = 3$
(e) None of these

12. Match the graph with the correct function.

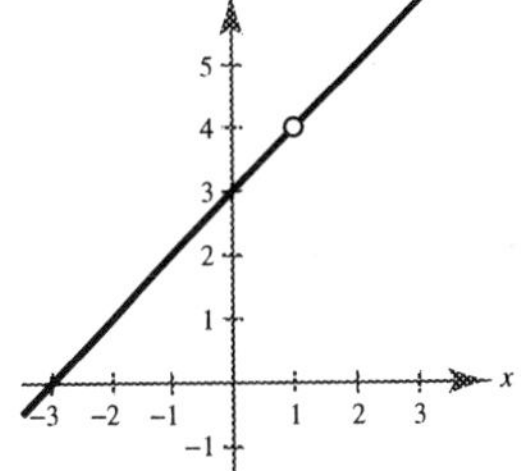

(a) $f(x) = \dfrac{x + 3}{x - 1}$
(b) $f(x) = x + 3$
(c) $f(x) = \dfrac{x - 1}{x^2 + 2x - 3}$
(d) $f(x) = \dfrac{x^2 + 2x - 3}{x - 1}$
(e) None of these

13. Find the partial fraction decomposition: $\dfrac{7}{3x^2 + 5x - 2}$.

(a) $\dfrac{6}{(3x - 2)} + \dfrac{1}{x - 1}$
(b) $\dfrac{3}{3x - 1} - \dfrac{1}{x + 2}$
(c) $\dfrac{6}{x + 2} - \dfrac{18}{3x - 1}$
(d) $\dfrac{4}{3x - 1} + \dfrac{2}{x + 2}$
(e) None of these

Test C
Chapter 2

Name ________________ Date ____________

Class ________________ Section ____________

1. Write in the form $y = a(x - h)^2 + k$: $y = -2x^2 - 4x - 5$.

(a) $y = -2(x - 1)^2 - 2$ (b) $y = (2x - 2)^2 - 1$ (c) $y = -2(x + 2)^2 - 1$

(d) $y = -2(x + 1)^2 - 3$ (e) None of these

2. The profit for a company is given by the equation

$$P = -0.0002x^2 + 140x - 250{,}000$$

where P is the profit in dollars and x is the number of units produced. What production level will yield a maximum profit?

(a) 700,000 (b) 350,000 (c) 893

(d) 350 (e) None of these

3. Determine the left-hand and right-hand behavior of the graph: $f(x) = 3x^5 - 7x^2 + 2$.

(a) Down to the left, up to the right (b) Down to the right, up to the left

(c) Up to the left, up to the right (d) Down to the left, down to the right

(e) None of these

4. Find a polynomial function with zeros: 1, 0, and -3.

(a) $f(x) = x(x - 3)^3(x + 1)^2$ (b) $f(x) = x^2(x - 1)(x + 3)$

(c) $f(x) = x(x - 3)(x - 1)$ (d) $f(x) = (x - 1)(x + 3)^2$

5. Divide: $(3x^4 + 2x^3 - 3x + 1) \div (x^2 + 1)$.

(a) $3x^2 + 2x + 3 - \dfrac{5x + 2}{x^2 + 1}$ (b) $3x^2 + 2x - 3 + \dfrac{-5x + 4}{x^2 + 1}$

(c) $3x^2 - x^2 - 4 + \dfrac{5}{x^2 + 1}$ (d) $3x^2 - x + 1 + \dfrac{-4x + 5}{x^2 + 1}$

(e) None of these

6. Find all of the real roots: $x^3 - 5x^2 + 5x - 1 = 0$.

(a) $1, 2, \pm 2\sqrt{3}$ (b) $1, 2 \pm \sqrt{3}$ (c) 1

(d) $-1, 2 \pm 2\sqrt{3}$ (e) None of these

7. Simplify, then write your result in standard form: $\left(4 - \sqrt{-25}\right) + 2\sqrt{-9} - 4i + 7$.

(a) $11 - 3i$ (b) $13 - 12i$ (c) $15 - 4i$

(d) $13 - 2i$ (e) None of these

8. Solve for x: $8x^2 = 2x - 3$.

(a) $\dfrac{2x - 3}{8}$ (b) $\dfrac{1}{16} + \dfrac{\sqrt{23}}{16}i$ (c) $2 \pm \dfrac{\sqrt{23}}{16}i$

(d) $\dfrac{1 \pm \sqrt{23}i}{8}$ (e) None of these

9. Write as a product of linear factors: $f(x) = x^4 - 5x^3 + 8x^2 - 20x + 16$.

(a) $(x + 2)(x - 2)(x - 4)(x - 1)$ (b) $(x + 4)(x + 1)(x - 2i)(x + 2i)$

(c) $(x - 4)(x - 1)(x + 2i)(x - 2i)$ (d) $(x + 4)(x + 1)(x + 2i)(x + 2i)$

(e) None of these

10. Find the vertical asymptote(s): $f(x) = \dfrac{x + 2}{x^2 - 9}$.

(a) $x = 3$ (b) $x = -2, x = -3, x = 3$ (c) $y = 0, x = -2$

(d) $x = -3, x = 3$ (e) None of these

11. Find the horizontal asymptote(s): $f(x) = \dfrac{x^2 - 4}{x^2 - 9}$.

(a) $y = \pm 3$ (b) $x = \pm 3$ (c) $y = 1$

(d) $y = 0$ (e) None of these

12. Match the graph with the correct function.

(a) $f(x) = \dfrac{x - 5}{x + 3}$ (b) $f(x) = \dfrac{5 - x}{x + 3}$

(c) $f(x) = -\dfrac{x + 5}{x + 3}$ (d) $f(x) = \dfrac{x + 5}{x + 3}$

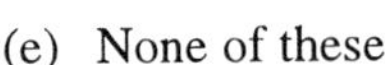

(e) None of these

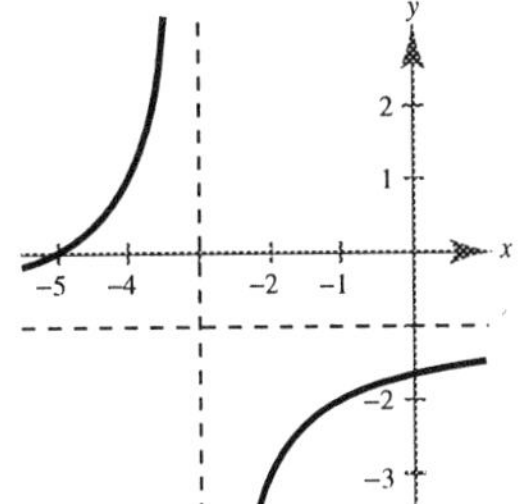

13. Find the partial fraction decomposition: $\dfrac{5x + 3}{x^2 - 3x - 10}$.

(a) $\dfrac{2}{x + 5} - \dfrac{7}{x - 2}$ (b) $\dfrac{7}{x - 5} - \dfrac{2}{x + 2}$ (c) $\dfrac{2}{x - 5} + \dfrac{3}{x + 2}$

(d) $\dfrac{4}{x - 5} + \dfrac{1}{x + 2}$ (e) None of these

Test D Name ______________ Date ______________

Chapter 2 Class ______________ Section ______________

1. Write in the form $y = a(x - h)^2 + k$: $y = -x^2 + 3x - 2$.

2. A rancher wishes to enclose a rectangular corral with 320 feet of fencing. The fencing is only required on three sides because of an existing stone wall. What are the dimensions of the corral of maximum area?

3. Determine the left-hand and right-hand behavior of the graph: $f(x) = -4x^3 + 3x^2 - 1$.

4. Use a graphing utility to graph the function: $f(x) = 2x^3 - 3x^2$.

5. Divide: $(6x^4 - 4x^3 + x^2 + 10x - 1) \div (3x + 1)$.

6. List the possible rational zeros of the function. Then use a graphing utility to graph the function to eliminate some of the possible zeros. Finally, determine all real zeros of the function: $f(x) = 3x^3 - x^2 - 12x + 4$.

7. Simplify, then write your result in standard form: $3(2 - \sqrt{-9}) + 2i(4i - 7)$.

8. Use the Quadratic Formula to solve for x: $5x^2 - 2x + 6 = 0$.

9. Write as a product of linear factors: $x^4 - 16$.

10. Find the horizontal asymptote(s): $f(x) = \dfrac{3x^2 + 2x - 16}{x^2 - 7}$.

11. Find the vertical asymptote(s): $f(x) = \dfrac{x^2 - 9}{x^2 - 6x + 8}$.

12. Use a graphing utility to graph $f(x) = \dfrac{2}{x - 1}$.

13. Find the partial fraction decomposition: $\dfrac{1 - x}{2x^2 + x}$.

Test E **Name**__________________ **Date**__________

Chapter 2 **Class**__________________ **Section**__________

1. Write the standard form of the equation of the parabola shown at the right.

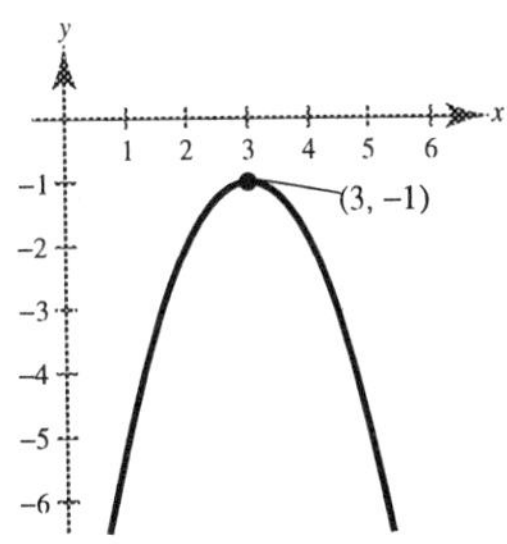

2. A rancher wishes to enclose a rectangular corral with 360 feet of fencing. The fencing is only required on three sides because of an existing stone wall. What are the dimensions of the corral of maximum area?

3. Determine the left-hand and right-hand behavior of the graph: $f(x) = 3x^4 + 2x^3 + 7x^2 + x - 1$.

4. Use a graphing utility to graph the function: $f(x) = -2x^4 + x$.

5. Divide: $(2x^4 + 7x - 2) \div (x^2 + 3)$.

6. List the possible rational zeros of the function. Then use a graphing utility to graph the function to eliminate some of the possible zeros. Finally determine all real zeros of the function: $f(x) = 2x^3 - x^2 - 18x + 9$.

7. Divide, then write the result in standard form: $\dfrac{3 + 7i}{3 - 7i}$.

8. Use the Quadratic Formula to solve for x: $3x^2 - 2x + 1 = 0$.

9. Write as a product of linear factors: $f(x) = x^4 - 100$.

10. Find the horizontal asymptote(s): $f(x) = \dfrac{x^2 - 3}{(x - 2)(x + 1)}$.

11. Find the vertical asymptote(s): $f(x) = \dfrac{x^2 - 4}{x^2 - 6x + 5}$.

12. Use a graphing utility to graph $f(x) = \dfrac{x}{x^2 - 1}$.

13. Find the partial fraction decomposition: $\dfrac{7x - 2}{3x^2 - x}$.

Test A **Name** ______________ **Date** ______________

Chapter 3 **Class** ______________ **Section** ______________

1. Match the graph with the correction function.

(a) $f(x) = 4^x - 5$ (b) $f(x) = 4^x + 5$

(c) $f(x) = 4^{-x} + 5$ (d) $f(x) = 4^{-x} - 5$

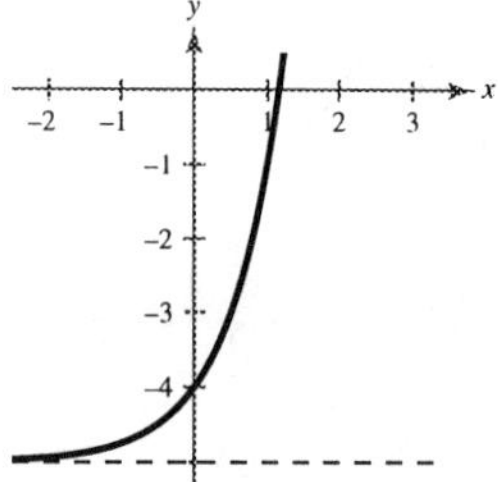

2. A certain population increases according to the model $P(t) = 250e^{0.47t}$ with $t = 0$ corresponding to 1995. Use the model to determine the population in the year 2000. Round your answer to the nearest integer.

(a) 40 (b) 1597 (c) 1998

(d) 2621 (e) None of these

3. \$1500 is invested at a rate of $6\frac{1}{4}\%$ compounded quarterly. What is the balance at the end of 2 years?

(a) \$4791.87 (b) \$1699.72 (c) \$1698.08

(d) \$1769.01 (e) None of these

4. Write the exponential form: $\log_b 37 = 2$.

(a) $37^2 = b$ (b) $2^b = 37$ (c) $b = 10$

(d) $b^2 = 37$ (e) None of these

5. Match the graph with the correct function.

(a) $f(x) = -3 + \ln x$ (b) $f(x) = 3 + \ln x$

(c) $f(x) = \ln(x - 3)$ (d) $f(x) = \ln(x + 3)$

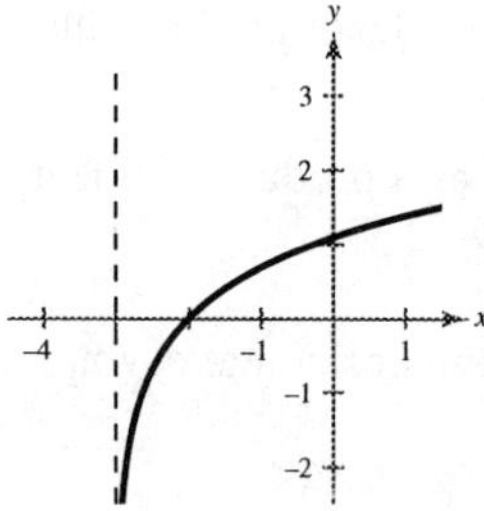

6. Write as the logarithm of a single quantity: $\frac{1}{4}\log_b 16 - 2\log_b 5 + \log_b 7$.

(a) $\frac{14}{25}$ (b) $\log_b \frac{2}{175}$ (c) 1

(d) $\log_b \frac{14}{25}$ (e) None of these

7. Evaluate $\log_a 16$, given that $\log_a 2 = 0.4307$.

(a) 0.0344 (b) 1.7228 (c) 4.4307

(d) 1.8168 (e) None of these

8. Identify the expression that is equivalent to $\log_4 2$.

(a) $\dfrac{\log 4}{\log 2}$ (b) $\dfrac{\ln 2}{\ln 4}$ (c) $4 \log 2$

(d) $2 \log 4$ (e) None of these

9. Write as a sum, difference or multiple of logarithms: $\log \sqrt[3]{\dfrac{xy^2}{z^4}}$.

(a) $\sqrt[3]{\dfrac{\log x + 2 \log y}{4 \log z}}$ (b) $\dfrac{\sqrt[3]{2 \log y^2 + \log x}}{-4 \log z}$ (c) $\dfrac{1}{3}(\log x + 2 \log y - 4 \log z)$

(d) $\dfrac{1}{3}\left(\dfrac{\log x + 2 \log y}{4 \log z}\right)$ (e) None of these

10. Solve for x: $\log(3x + 7) + \log(x - 2) = 1$.

(a) $\frac{8}{3}$ (b) $3, -\frac{8}{3}$ (c) 2

(d) $2, -\frac{5}{3}$ (e) None of these

11. The ice trays in a freezer are filled with water at 68° F. The freezer maintains a temperature of 20° F. According to Newton's Law of Cooling, the water temperature T is related to the time t (in hours) by the equation

$$kt = \ln \frac{T - 20}{68 - 20}.$$

After 1 hour, the water temperature in the ice trays is 49° F. Use the fact that $T = 49$ when $t = 1$ to find how long it takes the water to freeze (water freezes at 32° F).

(a) 3.27 hours (b) 2.75 hours (c) 5.10 hours

(d) 1.17 hours (e) None of these

12. The spread of a flu virus through a certain population is modeled by

$$y = \frac{1000}{1 + 990e^{-0.7t}}$$

where y is the total number infected after t days. In how many days will 820 people be infected with the virus?

(a) 10 days (b) 11 days (c) 12 days

(d) 13 days (e) None of these

Test B **Name** ____________ **Date** ____________

Chapter 3 **Class** ____________ **Section** ____________

1. Match the graph with the correct function.

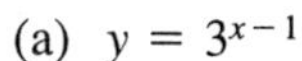

(a) $y = 3^{x-1}$ (b) $y = 3^x - 1$

(c) $y = 3^{1-x}$ (d) $y = 3^{-x} - 1$

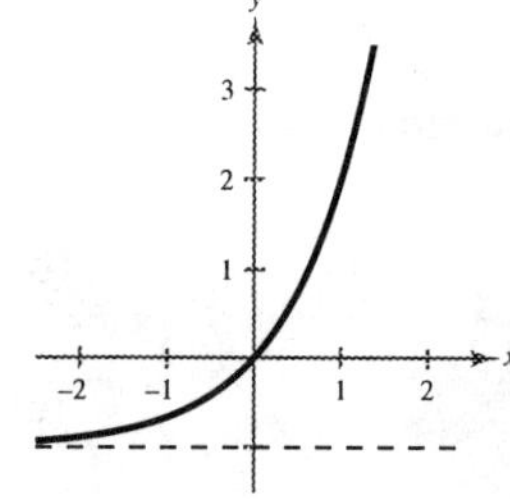

2. A certain population increases according to the model $P(t) = 250e^{0.47t}$ with $t = 0$ corresponding to 1990. Use the model to determine the population in the year 2000. Round your answer to the nearest integer.

(a) 400 (b) 4091 (c) 27,487

(d) 23,716 (e) None of these

3. \$1500 is invested at a rate of $6\frac{1}{4}$%compounded continuously. What is the balance at the end of 2 years?

(a) \$6816.87 (b) \$1699.72 (c) \$1698.08

(d) \$5235.51 (e) None of these

4. Write the exponential form: $\log_b 7 = 13$.

(a) $7^{13} = b$ (b) $b^{13} = 7$ (c) $b^7 = 13$

(d) $7^b = 13$ (e) None of these

5. Match the graph with the correct function.

(a) $f(x) = 3 + \log x$ (b) $f(x) = \log(x + 3)$

(c) $f(x) = \frac{1}{3} \log x$ (d) $f(x) = 3 \log x$

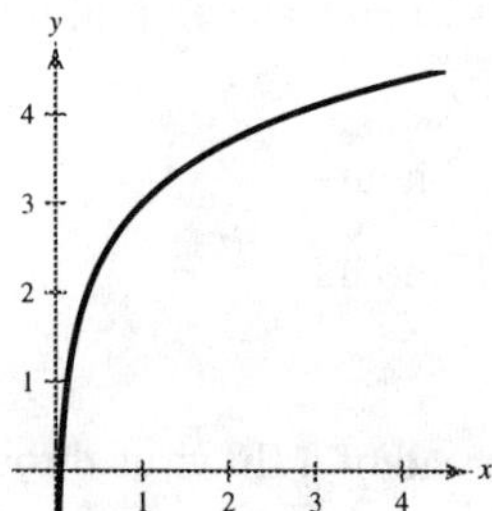

6. Write as the logarithm of a single quantity: $\frac{1}{2}[\ln(x + 1) + 2 \ln(x - 1)] + \frac{1}{3} \ln x$.

(a) $\ln \sqrt[3]{x}\,\sqrt{(x + 1)(x^2 - 1)}$ (b) $\ln \sqrt[3]{x}\,\sqrt{x^2 - 1}$ (c) $\ln \sqrt{x(x^2 - 1)}$

(d) $\ln \sqrt[3]{x(x + 1)(x - 1)^2}$ (e) None of these

7. Evaluate $\log_a 18$, given that $\log_a 2 = 0.2789$ and $\log_a 3 = 0.4421$.

(a) 1.1631 (b) 0.2466 (c) 0.0349

(d) 1.4420 (e) None of these

8. Identify the expression that is equivalent to $\log_5 3$.

(a) $\dfrac{\log 5}{\log 3}$ (b) $5 \log 3$ (c) $3 \log 5$

(d) $\dfrac{\ln 3}{\ln 5}$ (e) None of these

9. Write as a sum, difference or multiple of logarithms: $\log \sqrt[4]{\dfrac{x^2y}{z^3}}$.

(a) $\dfrac{1}{4}(2 \log x + \log y - 3 \log z)$ (b) $\dfrac{1}{4}\left(\dfrac{2 \log x + \log y}{3 \log z}\right)$ (c) $\sqrt[4]{\dfrac{2 \log x + \log y}{3 \log z}}$

(d) $\sqrt[4]{2 \log x + \log y - 3 \log z}$ (e) None of these

10. Solve for x: $\ln(7 - x) + \ln(3x + 5) = \ln(24x)$.

(a) $\frac{6}{11}$ (b) $\frac{7}{3}$ (c) $\frac{7}{3}, -5$

(d) $\frac{6}{11}, 5$ (e) None of these

11. The ice trays in a freezer are filled with water at 60° F. The freezer maintains a temperature of 20° F. According to Newton's Law of Cooling, the water temperature T is related to the time t (in hours) by the equation

$$kt = \ln \frac{T - 20}{60 - 20}.$$

After 1 hour, the water temperature in the ice trays is 44° F. Use the fact that $T = 44$ when $t = 1$ to find how long it takes the water to freeze (water freezes at 32° F).

(a) 2.4 hours (b) 3.2 hours (c) 1.7 hours

(d) 5.1 hours (e) None of these

12. The spread of a flu virus through a certain population is modeled by

$$y = \frac{1000}{1 + 990e^{-0.7t}}$$

where y is the total number infected after t days. In how many days will 690 people be infected with the virus?

(a) 10 days (b) 11 days (c) 12 days

(d) 13 days (e) None of these

Test C **Name** ________________ **Date** ________

Chapter 3 **Class** ________________ **Section** ________

1. Match the graph with the correction function.

(a) 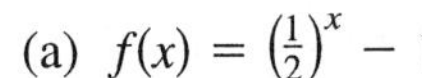 $f(x) = \left(\frac{1}{2}\right)^x - 1$ (b) $f(x) = 3^{-x^2} - 1$

(c) $f(x) = 3^{x+1}$ (d) $f(x) = 4^{-x}$

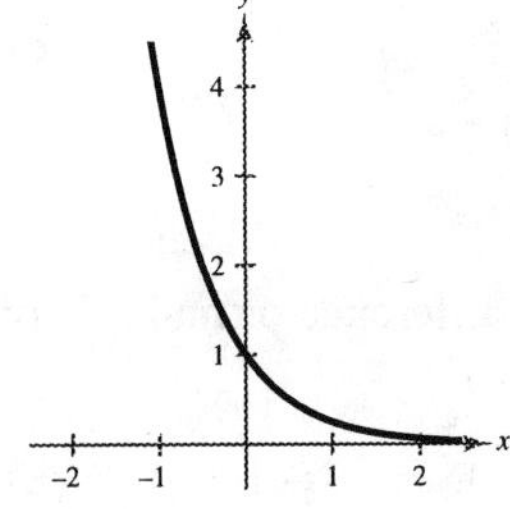

2. A certain population increases according to the model $P(t) = 250e^{0.47t}$ with $t = 0$ corresponding to 1992. Use the model to determine the population in the year 2000. Round your answer to the nearest integer.

(a) 400 (b) 2621 (c) 10,737

(d) 27,487 (e) None of these

3. \$1500 is invested at a rate of $7\frac{1}{4}\%$ compounded continuously. What is the balance at the end of 3 years?

(a) \$1864.45 (b) \$13,203.27 (c) \$1850.47

(d) \$4608.75 (e) None of these

4. Write the exponential form: $\log_7 b = 12$.

(a) $7^{12} = b$ (b) $b^7 = 12$ (c) $7^b = 12$

(d) $b^{12} = 7$ (e) None of these

5. Match the graph with the correct function.

(a) $f(x) = e^x$ (b) $f(x) = e^{x-1}$

(c) $f(x) = \ln x$ (d) $f(x) = \ln(x - 1)$

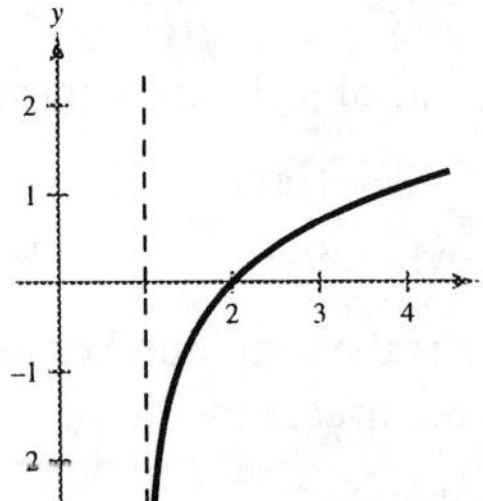

6. Write as the logarithm of a single quantity: $\log_2(x - 2) + \log_2(x + 2)$.

(a) $-2 + 2 \log_2 x$ (b) $\log_2(x^2 - 4)$ (c) $2 \log_2 x$

(d) $\log_2 2x$ (e) None of these

7. Evaluate $\log_a \frac{9}{2}$, given that $\log_a 2 = 0.2789$ and $\log_a 3 = 0.4421$.

(a) -0.0834 (b) 1.1631 (c) -0.3264

(d) 0.6053 (e) None of these

8. Identify the expression that is equivalent to $\log_6 3$.

(a) $\dfrac{\ln 3}{\ln 6}$ (b) $3 \log 6$ (c) $6 \log 3$

(d) $\dfrac{\log 6}{\log 3}$ (e) None of these

9. Write as a sum, difference or multiple of logarithms: $\sqrt{\dfrac{x^3y}{z^5}}$.

(a) $\sqrt{3 \log x + \log y - 5 \log z}$ (b) $\sqrt{\dfrac{3 \log x + \log y}{5 \log z}}$ (c) $\dfrac{1}{2}\left(\dfrac{3 \log x + \log y}{5 \log z}\right)$

(d) $\dfrac{1}{2}(3 \log x + \log y - 5 \log z)$ (e) None of these

10. Solve for x: $\log(7 - x) - \log(3x + 2) = 1$.

(a) $\frac{19}{31}$ (b) $-\frac{13}{31}$ (c) $-\frac{27}{29}$

(d) $\frac{9}{4}$ (e) None of these

11. The ice trays in a freezer are filled with water at 50° F. The freezer maintains a temperature of 0° F. According to Newton's Law of Cooling, the water temperature T is related to the time t (in hours) by the equation

$$kt = \ln \frac{T}{50}.$$

After 1 hour, the water temperature in the ice trays is 43° F. Use the fact that $T = 43$ when $t = 1$ to find how long it takes the water to freeze (water freezes at 32° F).

(a) 2.4 hours (b) 3.0 hours (c) 3.6 hours

(d) 2.1 hours (e) None of these

12. The spread of a flu virus through a certain population is modeled by

$$y = \frac{1000}{1 + 990e^{-0.7t}}$$

where y is the total number infected after t days. In how many days will 900 people be infected with the virus?

(a) 11 days (b) 13 days (c) 15 days

(d) 17 days (e) None of these

Test D **Name**________________ **Date**__________

Chapter 3 **Class**________________ **Section**__________

1. Without using a graphing utility sketch the graph of $f(x) = 3^x - 5$.

2. A certain population decreases according to the equation $y = 300 - 5e^{0.2t}$. Find the initial population and the population (to the nearest integer) when $t = 10$.

3. Find the balance in an account after 2 years if $2500 is deposited at an annual rate of 5% and interest is compounded continuously. When will the account double in value?

4. Write the logarithmic form: $5^2 = 25$.

5. Sketch the graph: $f(x) = 1 + \log_5 x$.

6. Write as a sum, difference, or multiple of logarithms: $\ln \dfrac{5x}{\sqrt[3]{x^2 + 1}}$.

7. Write as the logarithm of a single quantity: $\frac{1}{2}(\log_b 3 + \log_b x) - \log_b y$.

8. Evaluate $\log_b \left(\dfrac{14}{3b}\right)$, given that $\log_b 2 = 0.2789$, $\log_b 3 = 0.4421$, and

   $\log_b 7 = 0.7831$.

9. Solve for x: $\log x + \log(x + 3) = 1$.

10. Use a graphing utility to approximate the zero of $f(x) = 10e^{2x+1} - 5$ accurate to three decimal places.

11. Find the constant k so that the exponential function $y = 3e^{kt}$ passes through the points (0, 3) and (3, 5).

12. The demand equation for a certain product is given by $p = 450 - 0.4e^{0.007x}$. Find the demand x if the price charged is $300.

Test E **Name** ____________ **Date** ________

Chapter 3 **Class** ____________ **Section** ________

1. Without using a graphing utility sketch the graph of $f(x) = 3^x - 2$.

2. A certain population grows according to the equation $y = 40e^{0.025t}$. Find the initial population and the population (to the nearest integer) when $t = 50$.

3. Find the balance in an account after 2 years if \$3000 is deposited at an annual rate of 5% and interest is compounded continuously. When will the account double in value?

4. Write the logarithmic form: $3^5 = 243$.

5. Sketch the graph: $y = \ln(1 - x)$.

6. Write as a sum, difference, or multiple of logarithms: $\log \sqrt[5]{\dfrac{(x + 1)^3(x - 1)^2}{7}}$.

7. Write as the logarithm of a single quantity: $\frac{1}{2}(\log_b 6 + \log_b y) - \log_b x$.

8. Evaluate $\log_b \sqrt{10b}$, given that $\log_b 2 = 0.3562$ and $\log_b 5 = 0.8271$.

9. Solve for x: $x^2 - 4x = \log_2 32$.

10. Use a graphing utility to approximate the zero of $f(x) = 4e^{x-5/2} - 2$ accurate to three decimal places.

11. Find the constant k so that the exponential function $y = 2e^{kt}$ passes through the points (0, 2) and (2, 5).

12. The demand equation for a certain product is given by $p = 450 - 0.4e^{0.007x}$. Find the demand x if the price charged is \$250.

Test A **Name** ______________________ **Date** ____________

Chapter 4 **Class** ______________________ **Section** ____________

1. Determine which of the following angles is complementary to $\theta = \frac{\pi}{6}$.

(a) $\frac{5\pi}{6}$ (b) $\frac{13\pi}{6}$ (c) $\frac{\pi}{3}$ (d) $-\frac{11\pi}{6}$ (e) None of these

2. A central angle θ of a circle with radius 16 inches intercepts an arc of 19.36 inches. Find θ.

(a) 47.3519° (b) 1.21° (c) 69.3279° (d) 0.8264° (e) None of these

3. Find the point (x, y) on the unit circle that corresponds to the real number $t = -\frac{\pi}{4}$.

(a) $\left(\frac{\sqrt{2}}{2}, \frac{\sqrt{2}}{2}\right)$ (b) $\left(\frac{1}{2}, -\frac{1}{2}\right)$ (c) $(1, -1)$

(d) $\left(\frac{\sqrt{2}}{2}, -\frac{\sqrt{2}}{2}\right)$ (e) None of these

4. Give the exact value of $\tan \frac{4\pi}{3}$.

(a) $-\sqrt{3}$ (b) $\frac{1}{\sqrt{3}}$ (c) $-\frac{1}{\sqrt{2}}$ (d) $\sqrt{2}$ (e) None of these

5. A right triangle has an acute angle θ such that $\cot \theta = 15$. Find $\cos \theta$.

(a) $\sqrt{226}$ (b) $\frac{\sqrt{226}}{226}$ (c) $\frac{15\sqrt{226}}{226}$ (d) $\frac{\sqrt{226}}{15}$ (e) None of these

6. Find x for the right triangle shown at the right.

(a) $15\sqrt{2}$ (b) $15\sqrt{3}$

(c) 30 (d) $\frac{15}{2}$

(e) None of these

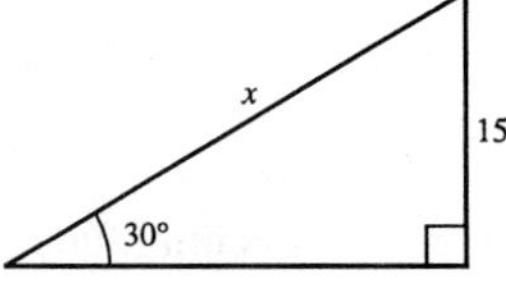

7. Given $\sin \theta = -\frac{1}{5}$ and $\tan \theta < 0$, find $\cos \theta$.

(a) $-\frac{\sqrt{26}}{5}$ (b) $\frac{\sqrt{26}}{5}$ (c) $-\frac{2\sqrt{6}}{5}$ (d) $\frac{2\sqrt{6}}{5}$ (e) None of these

8. Find two values of θ $(0 \le \theta < 2\pi)$ that satisfy $\sec \theta = 5.1258$. (Round your answer to 4 decimal places.)

(a) 1.7672 and 4.5160 (b) 1.3744 and 4.9087 (c) 1.1344 and 1.7672

(d) 1.7672 and 4.9088 (e) None of these

9. Determine the period: $f(x) = -\frac{2}{3}\cos\left(\frac{x}{3} - \frac{1}{2}\right)$.

(a) 6π (b) $\frac{2\pi}{3}$ (c) $\frac{2}{3}$ (d) $\frac{1}{2}$ (e) None of these

10. Match the graph with the correct function.

(a) $f(x) = 4\cos\left(3x - \frac{\pi}{2}\right)$ (b) $f(x) = 4\cos\left(x + \frac{\pi}{6}\right)$

(c) $f(x) = 4\sin\left(2x - \frac{\pi}{3}\right)$ (d) $f(x) = 4\cos\left(2x + \frac{\pi}{3}\right)$

(e) None of these

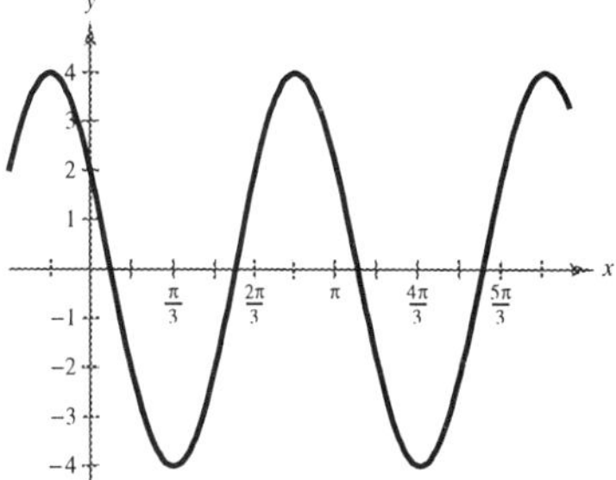

11. Match the graph with the correct function.

(a) $f(x) = \cot\left(x - \frac{\pi}{4}\right)$ (b) $f(x) = \tan\left(x - \frac{\pi}{4}\right)$

(c) $f(x) = -\cot(4x)$ (d) $f(x) = \tan 4x$

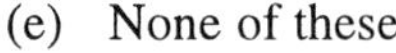
(e) None of these

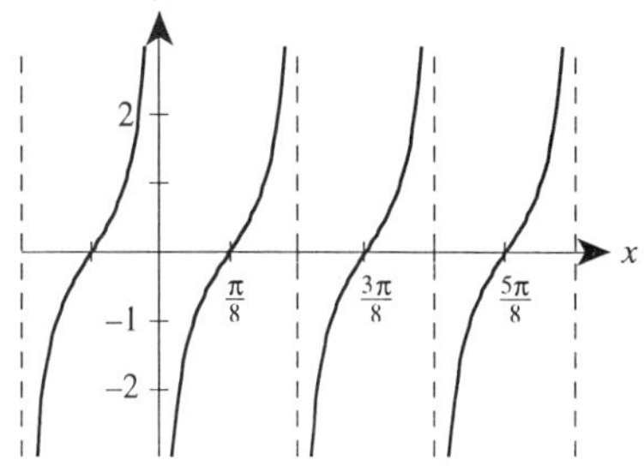

12. Which of the following is a vertical asymptote to the graph of $y = \csc 3x$?

(a) $x = \frac{\pi}{2}$ (b) $x = \frac{3\pi}{2}$ (c) $x = \frac{\pi}{3}$ (d) $x = \frac{\pi}{4}$ (e) None of these

13. Evaluate: $\arctan(-1)$.

(a) $\frac{\pi}{4}$ (b) $-\frac{\pi}{4}$ (c) $\frac{3\pi}{4}$ (d) $\frac{7\pi}{4}$ (e) None of these

14. Write an algebraic expression for $\sin\left(\arctan\frac{x}{5}\right)$.

(a) $\frac{x}{x+5}$ (b) $\frac{x}{\sqrt{x^2+25}}$ (c) $\frac{5}{\sqrt{x^2+25}}$ (d) $\frac{\sqrt{25-x^2}}{5}$ (e) None of these

15. A ship is 90 miles south and 20 miles east of port. If the captain wants to travel directly to port, what bearing should be taken?

(a) S 77.5° E (b) N 12.5° W (c) N 77.5° E (d) S 12.5° W (e) None of these

Test B **Name** ______________ **Date** ______________

Chapter 4 **Class** ______________ **Section** ______________

1. Determine which of the following angles is complementary to $\theta = \frac{\pi}{12}$.

(a) $\frac{5\pi}{12}$ (b) $\frac{11\pi}{12}$ (c) $\frac{13\pi}{12}$ (d) $\frac{25\pi}{12}$ (e) None of these

2. The central angle θ of a circle with radius 9 inches intercepts an arc of 20 inches. Find θ.

(a) 2.22° (b) 127.32° (c) 0.45° (d) 25.78° (e) None of these

3. Find the point (x, y) on the unit circle that corresponds to the real number $t = \frac{3\pi}{2}$.

(a) $(1, -1)$ (b) $(0, -1)$ (c) $(-1, 0)$ (d) $(-1, 1)$ (e) None of these

4. Give the exact value of $\cos\left(-\frac{3\pi}{4}\right)$.

(a) $-\frac{\sqrt{2}}{2}$ (b) $-\frac{1}{2}$ (c) $\frac{\sqrt{3}}{2}$ (d) $\frac{\sqrt{2}}{2}$ (e) None of these

5. A right triangle has an acute angle θ such that $\csc \theta = \frac{7}{3}$. Find $\tan \theta$.

(a) $\frac{2\sqrt{10}}{7}$ (b) $\frac{3\sqrt{10}}{20}$ (c) $\frac{2\sqrt{10}}{3}$ (d) $\frac{3}{7}$ (e) None of these

6. Find x for the triangle shown at the right.

(a) 0.1047 (b) 11.9638

(c) 5.4256 (d) 9.5547

(e) None of these

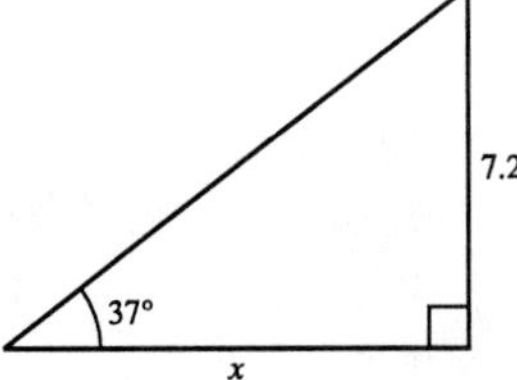

7. Given $\sin \theta = \frac{7}{13}$, and $\tan \theta < 0$, find $\tan \theta$.

(a) $\frac{7\sqrt{3}}{2}$ (b) $-\frac{2\sqrt{3}}{7}$ (c) $-\frac{2\sqrt{3}}{13}$ (d) $-\frac{7\sqrt{3}}{60}$ (e) None of these

8. Find two values of θ $(0 \le \theta < 360°)$ that satisfy $\csc \theta = 2.5593$.

(a) 23° and 157° (b) 67° and 293° (c) 157° and 293°

(d) 23° and 203° (e) None of these

9. Determine the period: $f(x) = -\frac{1}{2}\sin\left(\frac{3x}{2} - \frac{1}{2}\right)$.

(a) $\frac{1}{2}$ (b) $\frac{1}{2}\pi$ (c) $\frac{3\pi}{4}$ (d) $\frac{4\pi}{3}$ (e) None of these

10. Match the function with the correct graph: $f(x) = -4 \cos \frac{1}{2}x$.

(a)

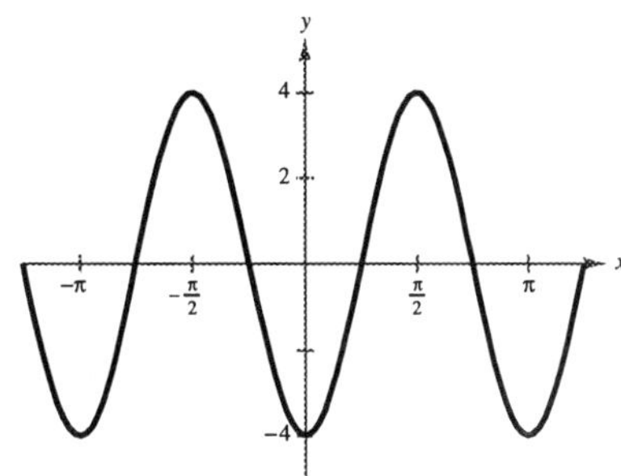

(b)

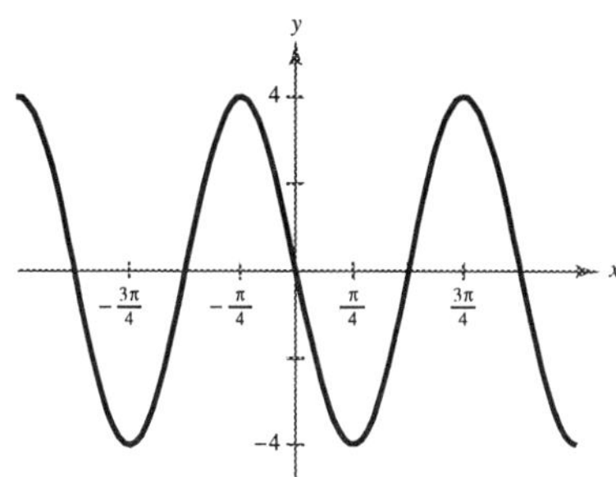

(c)

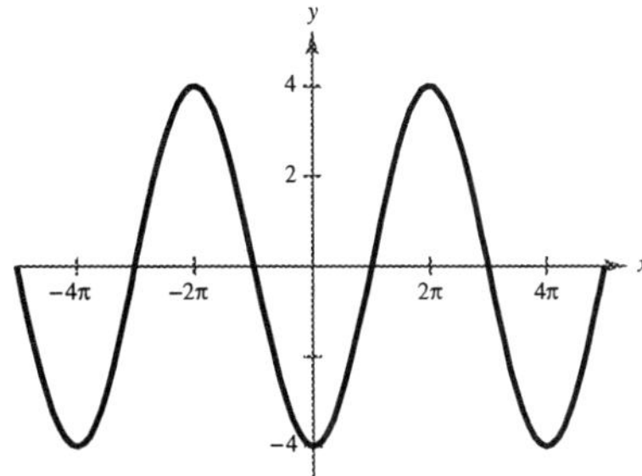

(d)

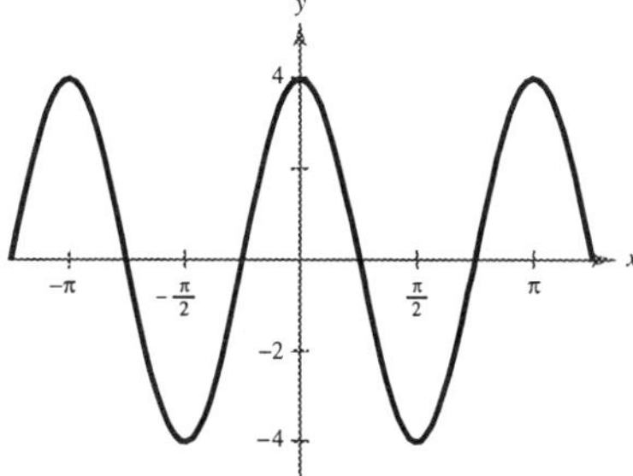

(e) None of these

11. Match the graph with the correct function.

(a) $f(x) = 3 \csc 2x$ (b) $f(x) = 3 \sec 2x$

(c) $f(x) = -3 \sec 2x$ (d) $f(x) = -3 \csc 2x$

(e) None of these

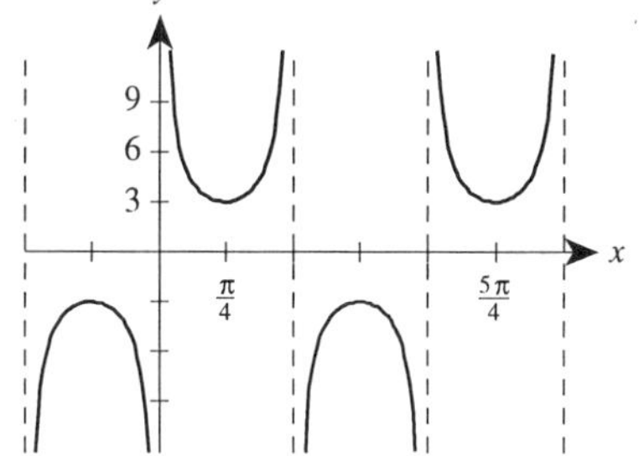

12. Which of the following is a vertical asymptote to the graph of $y = -\tan\left(x - \dfrac{\pi}{3}\right)$?

(a) $x = \dfrac{\pi}{3}$ (b) $x = \dfrac{\pi}{2}$ (c) $x = \dfrac{3\pi}{2}$ (d) $x = \dfrac{5\pi}{6}$ (e) None of these

13. Evaluate: $\arcsin\left(-\dfrac{1}{2}\right)$.

(a) $-\dfrac{\pi}{6}$ (b) $\dfrac{11\pi}{6}$ (c) $\dfrac{5\pi}{6}$ (d) $\dfrac{\pi}{6}$ (e) None of these

14. Write an algebraic expression for $\csc\left(\arccos \dfrac{x}{5}\right)$.

(a) $\dfrac{\sqrt{25 - x^2}}{5}$ (b) $\dfrac{\sqrt{25 + x^2}}{x}$ (c) $\dfrac{5}{\sqrt{25 - x^2}}$ (d) $\dfrac{x}{x + 5}$ (e) None of these

15. A ship leaves port and travels due west for 30 nautical miles, then changes course to S 30° W and travels 50 more nautical miles. Find the bearing to the port of departure.

(a) N 74° E (b) N 38.2° E (c) N 51.8° E (d) N 16° E (e) None of these

Test C **Name** ________________ **Date** ________________

Chapter 4 **Class** ________________ **Section** ________________

1. Determine which of the following angles is complementary to $\theta = \frac{2\pi}{7}$.

(a) $\frac{5\pi}{7}$ (b) $\frac{16\pi}{7}$ (c) $-\frac{10\pi}{7}$ (d) $\frac{3\pi}{14}$ (e) None of these

2. The central angle θ of a circle with radius 5 inches intercepts an arc of 15 inches. Find θ.

(a) 168.2° (b) 171.9° (c) 166.1° (d) 177.9° (e) None of these

3. Find the point (x, y) on the unit circle that corresponds to the real number $t = \frac{17\pi}{6}$.

(a) $\left(\frac{\sqrt{3}}{2}, \frac{1}{2}\right)$ (b) $\left(-\frac{1}{2}, \frac{\sqrt{3}}{2}\right)$ (c) $\left(-\frac{\sqrt{3}}{2}, \frac{1}{2}\right)$ (d) $\left(\frac{\sqrt{3}}{2}, -\frac{1}{2}\right)$ (e) None of these

4. Give the exact value of $\tan\left(-\frac{\pi}{3}\right)$.

(a) $-\frac{1}{\sqrt{2}}$ (b) $-\frac{1}{\sqrt{3}}$ (c) -2 (d) $-\sqrt{3}$ (e) None of these

5. A right triangle has an acute angle θ such that $\sin\theta = \frac{7}{9}$. Find $\tan\theta$.

(a) $\frac{7\sqrt{2}}{8}$ (b) $\frac{4\sqrt{2}}{7}$ (c) $\frac{\sqrt{130}}{7}$ (d) $\frac{9\sqrt{130}}{130}$ (e) None of these

6. Find x for the right triangle shown at the right.

(a) 9.7174 (b) 15.4411

(c) 14.8188 (d) 7.5518

(e) None of these

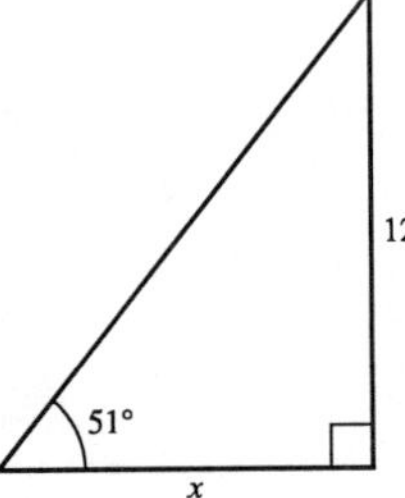

7. Find $\tan\theta$, for the angle θ shown at the right.

(a) $-\frac{9\sqrt{130}}{7}$ (b) $\frac{\sqrt{130}}{7}$

(c) $-\frac{7}{9}$ (d) $-\frac{9}{7}$

(e) None of these

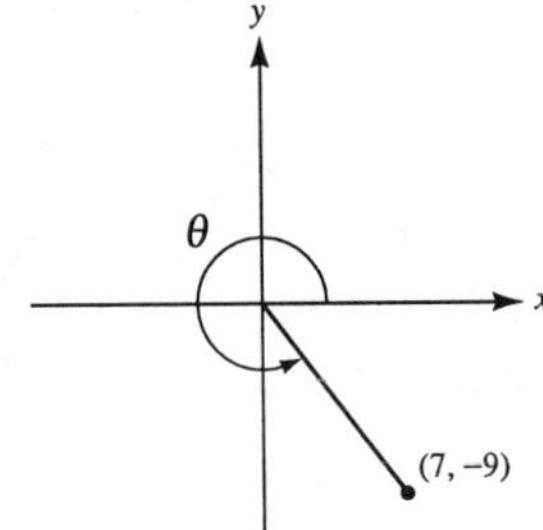

8. Find two values of θ $(0 \le \theta < 360°)$ that satisfy $\cot \theta = -0.2679$.

(a) 165° and 345° (b) 75° and 285° (c) 15° and 165°

(d) 105° and 285° (e) None of these

9. Determine the period of the function: $y = \frac{1}{2} \sin\left(\frac{x}{3} - \pi\right)$.

(a) $\frac{1}{2}$ (b) $\frac{2\pi}{3}$ (c) 6π (d) 3π (e) None of these

10. Match the function with the correct graph: $f(x) = \cos\left(2x - \frac{\pi}{3}\right)$.

(a)

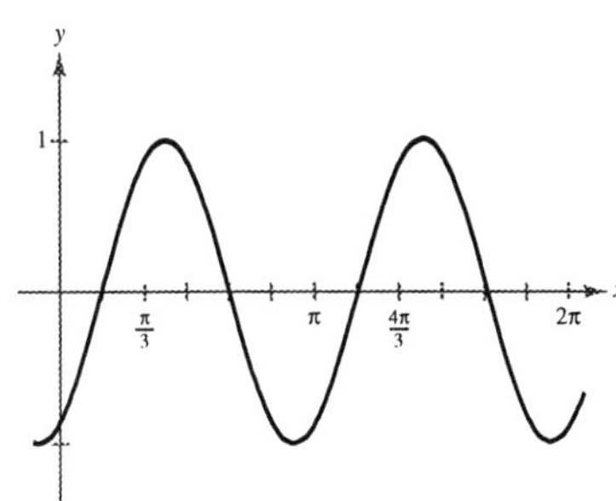

(b)

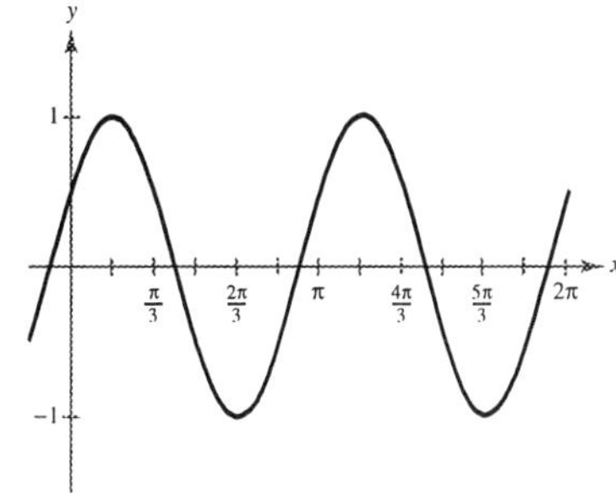

(c)

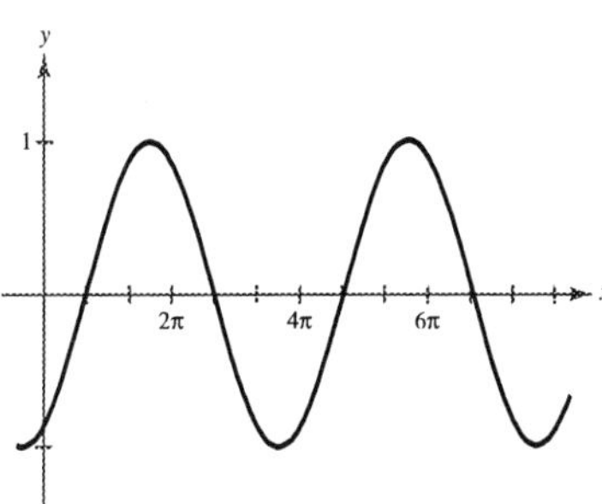

(d)

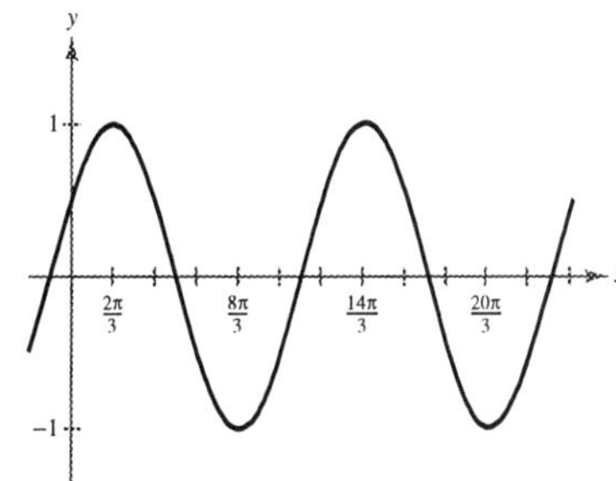

(e) None of these

11. Match the graph with the correct function.

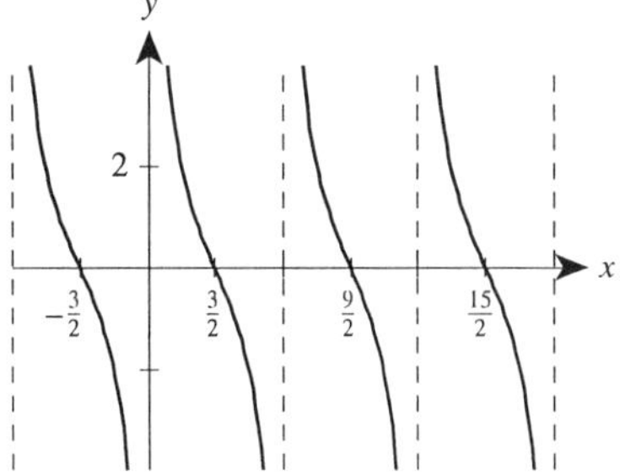

(a) $f(x) = 2 \cot 3\pi x$ (b) $f(x) = -2 \tan \frac{\pi x}{3}$

(c) $f(x) = 2 \cot \frac{\pi x}{3}$ (d) $f(x) = -2 \tan 3\pi x$

(e) None of these

12. Which of the following is a vertical asymptote to the graph of $y = \tan\left(2x - \frac{\pi}{3}\right)$?

(a) $x = \frac{5\pi}{6}$ (b) $x = \frac{5\pi}{12}$ (c) $x = \frac{6\pi}{5}$ (d) $x = \frac{\pi}{2}$ (e) None of these

13. Evaluate: $\arccos\left(-\frac{1}{2}\right)$.

(a) $-\frac{\pi}{6}$ (b) $\frac{11\pi}{6}$ (c) $\frac{5\pi}{6}$ (d) $\frac{\pi}{6}$ (e) None of these

14. Write an algebraic expression for $\tan(\arcsin x)$.

(a) $\frac{x\sqrt{1+x^2}}{1+x^2}$ (b) $\frac{1}{x}$ (c) $\frac{\sqrt{1-x^2}}{x}$ (d) $\frac{x\sqrt{1-x^2}}{1-x^2}$ (e) None of these

15. A ship leaves port and travels due east 15 nautical miles, then changes course to N 20° W and travels 40 more nautical miles. Find the bearing to the port of departure.

(a) S 21.8° W (b) S 43.7° W (c) N 15.2° E (d) S 68.3° W (e) None of these

Test D **Name**____________________ **Date**____________

Chapter 4 **Class**____________________ **Section**__________

1. Find an angle θ that is coterminal to $\frac{11\pi}{4}$ such that $0 \leq \theta < 2\pi$.

2. Find the arc length s shown in the figure.

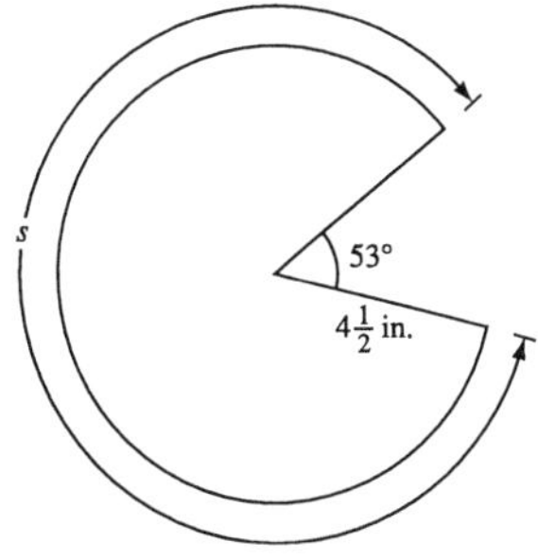

3. Find the point (x, y) on the unit circle that corresponds to the real number $t = \frac{4\pi}{3}$.

4. Give the exact value of $\cos\left(-\frac{\pi}{6}\right)$.

5. Use the triangle shown at the right to find $\tan \theta$.

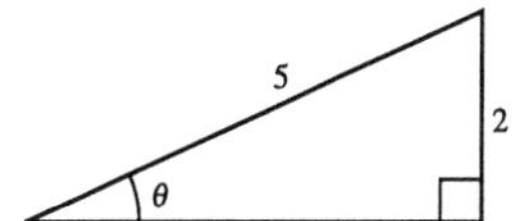

6. Find x for the triangle shown at the right.

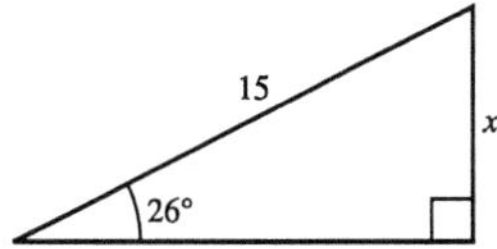

7. Determine the exact value of $\cos \theta$, if θ is in standard position and its terminal side passes through the point $(-3, 3)$.

8. Find two radian values of θ $(0 \leq \theta < 2\pi)$ that satisfy $\cos \theta = 0.7833$. (Round your answer to 4 decimal places.)

9. Determine the period and amplitude of the function: $f(x) = -7 \cos 3x$.

10. Use a graphing utility to graph the function: $f(x) = \cos\left(2x - \frac{\pi}{2}\right) + 1$.

11. Determine the period of the function: $y = 3 \tan 7x$.

12. Use a graphing utility to graph the function: $f(x) = x^2 \sin x$.

13. Evaluate: $\arcsin\left(-\frac{\sqrt{2}}{2}\right)$.

14. Use an inverse trigonometric function to write θ as a function of x (see figure).

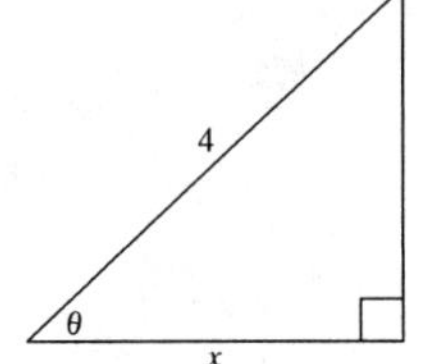

15. An airplane flying at 600 miles per hour has a bearing of S 34° E. After flying 3 hours, how far south has the plane traveled from its point of departure? (Round your answer to the nearest mile.)

Test E **Name**__________________ **Date**__________

Chapter 4 **Class**__________________ **Section**________

1. Find an angle θ that is coterminal to -495° such that $0 \leq \theta < 360^\circ$.

2. A bicycle wheel with an 18 inch diameter rotates 120°. What distance has the bicycle traveled?

3. Find the point (x, y) on the unit circle that corresponds to the real number $t = -\dfrac{7\pi}{4}$.

4. Give the exact value of $\sin \dfrac{7\pi}{6}$.

5. Use the triangle shown at the right to find $\cot \theta$.

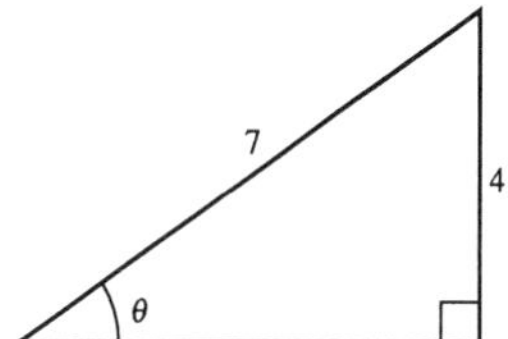

6. Find x for the triangle shown at the right.

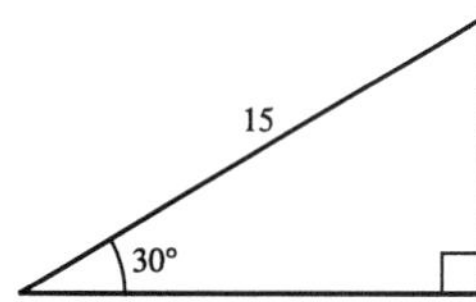

7. Find $\csc \theta$ for the angle θ shown at the right.

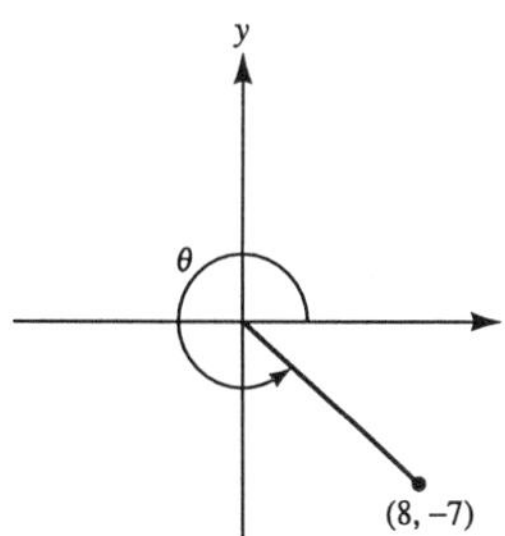

8. Find the reference angle for $\theta = -155^\circ$.

9. Determine the period and amplitude of the function: $f(x) = 5 \cos \dfrac{x}{2}$.

10. Use a graphing utility to graph the function: $f(x) = \sin\left(\dfrac{x}{2} + \dfrac{\pi}{8}\right)$.

11. Determine the period of the function: $f(x) = \frac{1}{5}\tan\left(3x + \frac{\pi}{2}\right)$.

12. Use a graphing utility to graph the function: $f(x) = x^2 \cos x$.

13. Evaluate: $\arcsin\left(-\frac{\sqrt{3}}{2}\right)$.

14. Use an inverse trigonometric function to write θ as a function of x (see figure).

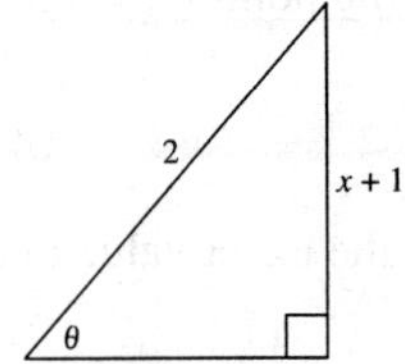

15. An airplane flying 550 miles per hour has a bearing of S 15° W. After flying 2 hours, how far south has the plane traveled from its point of departure? (Round your answer to the nearest mile.)

Test A
Chapter 5

Name____________________ **Date**____________

Class____________________ **Section**____________

1. Simplify: $\dfrac{\csc x}{\tan x + \cot x}$.

(a) $\cos x + \tan x$ (b) $\sin^2 + \cos x$ (c) $\csc^2 x \sec$

(d) $\cos x$ (e) None of these

2. Perform the addition and simplify: $\dfrac{\tan x}{\csc x} + \dfrac{\sin x}{\tan x}$.

(a) $\cos x$ (b) $\csc^2 x$ (c) $\sec^2 x$

(d) $\sec x$ (e) None of these

3. Verify the identity: $\dfrac{\sec^2 x}{\cot x} - \tan^3 x = \tan x$.

(a)
$$\begin{aligned}\frac{\sec^2 x}{\cot x} - \tan^3 x &= \sec^2 x \tan x - \tan^3 x\\ &= \tan x(\sec^2 x - \tan^2 x)\\ &= (\tan x)(1)\\ &= \tan x\end{aligned}$$

(b)
$$\begin{aligned}\frac{\sec^2 x}{\cot x} - \tan^3 x &= \frac{\sec^2 x - \tan^3 x(\cot x)}{\cot x}\\ &= \frac{\sec^2 x - \tan^3 x\left(\frac{1}{\tan x}\right)}{\cot x}\\ &= \frac{\sec^2 x - \tan^2 x}{\cot x}\\ &= \frac{1}{\cot x}\\ &= \tan x\end{aligned}$$

(c)
$$\begin{aligned}\frac{\sec^2 x}{\cot x} - \tan^3 x &= \frac{1 + \tan^2 x}{\cot x} - \tan^3 x\\ &= \frac{1}{\cot x} + \frac{\tan^2 x}{\cot x} - \tan^3 x\\ &= \tan x + \tan^3 x - \tan^3 x\\ &= \tan x\end{aligned}$$

(d) All of these are correct verifications.

(e) None of these

4. Verify the identity: $\dfrac{\sec x - \cos x}{\tan x} = \sin x.$

(a) $\dfrac{\sec x - \cos x}{\tan x} = \dfrac{\sec x - \cos x}{\dfrac{\sin x}{\cos x}}$

$= (\sec x - \cos x)\left(\dfrac{\cos x}{\sin x}\right)$

$= \sec x \sin x - \cos^2 x$

$= 1 - \cos^2 x$

$= \sin x$

(b) $\dfrac{\sec x - \cos x}{\tan x} = \dfrac{\sec x - \cos x}{\dfrac{1}{\cot x}}$

$= (\sec x - \cos x)(\cot x)$

$= \sec x \cot x - \cos x \cot x$

$= \dfrac{1}{\cos x}\left(\dfrac{\sin x}{\cos x}\right) - \cos x\left(\dfrac{\sin x}{\cos x}\right)$

$= \dfrac{\sin x}{\cos x} - \sin x$

$= \sin x - \sin x \cos x$

$= \sin x(1 - \cos x)$

$= (\sin x)(1) = \sin x$

(c) $\dfrac{\sec x - \cos x}{\tan x} = \dfrac{\sec x - \cos x}{\dfrac{1}{\cot x}}$

$= (\sec x - \cos x)(\cot x)$

$= \dfrac{1}{\cos x}\left(\dfrac{\cos x}{\sin x}\right) - \cos x\left(\dfrac{\cos x}{\sin x}\right)$

$= \dfrac{1}{\sin x} - \dfrac{\cos^2 x}{\sin x}$

$= \dfrac{1 - \cos^2 x}{\sin x}$

$= \dfrac{\sin^2 x}{\sin x} = \sin x$

(d) All of these are correct verifications.

(e) None of these

5. Find all solutions in the interval $[0, 2\pi)$: $2 \cos x - \sqrt{3} = 0.$

(a) $\dfrac{\pi}{6}, \dfrac{11\pi}{6}$ (b) $\dfrac{5\pi}{6}, \dfrac{7\pi}{6}$ (c) $\dfrac{\pi}{3}, \dfrac{5\pi}{3}$

(d) $\dfrac{2\pi}{3}, \dfrac{4\pi}{3}$ (e) None of these

6. Find all solutions in the interval $[0, 2\pi)$: $2 \cos^2(2\theta) - 1 = 0.$

(a) $\dfrac{\pi}{4}, \dfrac{3\pi}{4}, \dfrac{5\pi}{5}, \dfrac{7\pi}{4}$ (b) $\dfrac{\pi}{8}, \dfrac{3\pi}{8}, \dfrac{5\pi}{8}, \dfrac{7\pi}{8}, \dfrac{9\pi}{8}, \dfrac{11\pi}{8}, \dfrac{13\pi}{8}, \dfrac{15\pi}{8}$

(c) $\dfrac{\pi}{8}, \dfrac{\pi}{4}, \dfrac{3\pi}{8}, \dfrac{3\pi}{4}$ (d) $\dfrac{\pi}{2}, \dfrac{\pi}{4}, \dfrac{3\pi}{2}, \dfrac{3\pi}{4}, \dfrac{5\pi}{2}, \dfrac{5\pi}{4}, \dfrac{7\pi}{2}, \dfrac{7\pi}{4}$

(e) None of these

7. Evaluate: $\sin 105°$. (Use the fact that $105° = 60° + 45°$.)

(a) $\dfrac{\sqrt{6} + \sqrt{2}}{4}$ (b) $\dfrac{\sqrt{6} - \sqrt{2}}{4}$ (c) $\dfrac{\sqrt{2} + \sqrt{6}}{4}$

(d) $\dfrac{1 + \sqrt{3}}{2}$ (e) None of these

8. Simplify: $2 \sin(x + \theta) - \sin(x - \theta)$.

(a) $3 \cos x \sin \theta + \sin x \cos \theta$ (b) $\sin x \cos \theta + \cos x \sin \theta$ (c) $2 \cos x \sin \theta + \sin x \cos \theta$

(d) $\sin x + 3 \sin \theta$ (e) None of these

9. Find all solutions in the interval $[0, 2\pi)$: $\cos 2x + \sin x = 0$.

(a) $0, \dfrac{\pi}{4}, \dfrac{3\pi}{4}$ (b) $\dfrac{\pi}{2}, \dfrac{7\pi}{6}, \dfrac{11\pi}{6}$ (c) $\dfrac{\pi}{6}, \dfrac{5\pi}{6}, \dfrac{3\pi}{2}$

(d) $0, \dfrac{\pi}{4}, \dfrac{3\pi}{4}, \dfrac{5\pi}{4}, \dfrac{7\pi}{4}$ (e) None of these

10. Find the exact value of $\dfrac{7\pi}{12}$. $\left(\text{Use the fact that } \dfrac{1}{2}\left(\dfrac{7\pi}{6}\right) = \dfrac{7\pi}{12}.\right)$

(a) $\dfrac{\sqrt{2 - \sqrt{3}}}{2}$ (b) $\dfrac{\sqrt{2 + \sqrt{3}}}{2}$ (c) $-\dfrac{\sqrt{2 + \sqrt{3}}}{2}$

(d) $-\dfrac{\sqrt{2 - \sqrt{3}}}{2}$ (e) None of these

Test B **Name**__________ **Date**__________

Chapter 5 **Class**__________ **Section**__________

1. Simplify: $\dfrac{\cos^4 x - \sin^4 x}{\cos^2 x - \sin^2 x}$.

(a) $1 - 2\sin^2 x$ (b) $2\cos^2 x - 1$ (c) 1

(d) -1 (e) None of these

2. Perform the subtraction and simplify: $\dfrac{\sec x}{\sin x} - \dfrac{\sin x}{\cos x}$.

(a) $\csc x$ (b) $\tan x$ (c) $\cot x$

(d) $\cos^2 x$ (e) None of these

3. Verify the identity: $\dfrac{\cos x \csc x}{\cot^2 x} = \tan x$.

(a)
$$\frac{\cos x \csc x}{\cot^2 x} = \cos x\left(\frac{1}{\sin x}\right)\tan^2 x$$
$$= \frac{\cos x}{\sin x}\frac{\sin^2 x}{\cos^2 x}$$
$$= \frac{\sin x}{\cos x}$$
$$= \tan x$$

(b)
$$\frac{\cos x \csc x}{\cot^2 x} = \frac{\cos x \csc x}{1 - \csc^2 x}$$
$$= \frac{\cos x}{1} - \frac{\csc x}{\csc^2 x}$$
$$= \cos x - \frac{1}{\csc x}$$
$$= \frac{\cos x}{\sin x}$$
$$= \tan x$$

(c)
$$\frac{\cos x \csc x}{\cot^2 x} = \frac{\cos x \csc x}{1 - \tan^2 x}$$
$$= \cos x - \frac{\csc x}{\tan^2 x}$$
$$= \cos x - \frac{\left(\frac{1}{\sin x}\right)}{\left(\frac{\sin x}{\cos x}\right)}$$
$$= \cos x - \frac{1}{\sin x} \cdot \frac{\cos x}{\sin x}$$
$$= \frac{\cos x}{\sin x}$$
$$= \tan x$$

(d) All of these are correct verifications.

(e) None of these

4. Verify the identity: $\dfrac{\csc x}{\sin x} - \dfrac{\cot x}{\tan x} = 1.$

(a) $\dfrac{\csc x}{\sin x} - \dfrac{\cot x}{\tan x} = \csc x \tan x - \sin x \cot x$

$= \dfrac{1}{\sin x} \cdot \dfrac{\sin x}{\cos x} - \sin x \cdot \dfrac{\cos x}{\sin x}$

$= \dfrac{1 - \cos x}{\cos x}$

$= 1 - \dfrac{\cos x}{\cos x} = 1$

(b) $\dfrac{\csc x}{\sin x} - \dfrac{\cot x}{\tan x} = \dfrac{\csc x}{\left(\dfrac{1}{\csc x}\right)} - \dfrac{\cot x}{\left(\dfrac{1}{\cot x}\right)}$

$= \csc^2 x - \cot^2 x = 1$

(c) $\dfrac{\csc x}{\sin x} - \dfrac{\cot x}{\tan x} = \dfrac{\left(\dfrac{1}{\sin x}\right)}{\sin x} - \dfrac{\left(\dfrac{1}{\tan x}\right)}{\tan x}$

$= \dfrac{1}{\sin^2 x} - \dfrac{1}{\tan^2 x}$

$= \dfrac{\tan^2 x - \sin^2 x}{\sin^2 x \tan^2 x}$

$= \dfrac{\dfrac{\sin^2 x}{\cos^2 x} - \sin^2 x}{\sin^2 x\left(\dfrac{\sin^2 x}{\cos^2 x}\right)}$

$= \dfrac{\sin^2 x - \sin^2 x \cos^2 x}{\cos^2 x} \cdot \dfrac{\cos^2 x}{\sin^4 x}$

$= \dfrac{\sin^2 x(1 - \cos^2 x)}{\sin^4 x}$

$= \dfrac{\sin^2 x \cdot \sin^2 x}{\sin^4 x}$

$= \dfrac{\sin^4 x}{\sin^4 x} = 1$

(d) Both b and c are correct verifications.

(e) None of these

5. Find all solutions in the interval $[0, 2\pi)$: $\csc x + 2 = 0$.

(a) $\dfrac{\pi}{3}, \dfrac{2\pi}{3}$
(b) $\dfrac{\pi}{6}, \dfrac{5\pi}{6}$
(c) $\dfrac{4\pi}{3}, \dfrac{5\pi}{3}$
(d) $\dfrac{7\pi}{6}, \dfrac{11\pi}{6}$
(e) None of these

6. Find all solutions in the interval $[0, 2\pi)$: $2\sin^2\left(\dfrac{x}{4}\right) - 3\cos\left(\dfrac{x}{4}\right) = 0.$

(a) $\dfrac{\pi}{3}, \dfrac{5\pi}{3}$
(b) $\dfrac{4\pi}{3}$
(c) $\dfrac{4\pi}{3}, \dfrac{2\pi}{3}$
(d) $\dfrac{\pi}{6}, \dfrac{\pi}{3}$
(e) None of these

7. Evaluate: sin 255°. (Use the fact that 225° = 210° + 45°.)

(a) $\frac{\sqrt{6}-\sqrt{2}}{4}$ (b) $\frac{\sqrt{2}+\sqrt{6}}{4}$ (c) $-\frac{\sqrt{2}+\sqrt{6}}{4}$

(d) $\frac{\sqrt{2}+\sqrt{6}}{4}$ (e) None of these

8. Simplify: $\frac{\sin\left(\frac{\pi}{2}+h\right)-\sin\left(\frac{\pi}{2}\right)}{h}$.

(a) $\frac{\sin h}{h}$ (b) $\frac{\sin h - 1}{h}$ (c) 1

(d) $\frac{\cos h - 1}{h}$ (e) None of these

9. Find all solutions in the interval $[0, 2\pi)$: $\sin 2x + \sin x = 0$.

(a) $\frac{\pi}{2}, \frac{3\pi}{2}, \frac{2\pi}{3}, \frac{4\pi}{3}$ (b) $0, \frac{\pi}{3}, \pi, \frac{5\pi}{3}$ (c) $0, \frac{\pi}{3}$

(d) $0, \pi, \frac{2\pi}{3}, \frac{4\pi}{3}$ (e) None of these

10. Find the exact value of cos 157° 30′. $\left(\text{Use the fact that } \frac{1}{2}(315°) = 157° 30′.\right)$

(a) $\frac{\sqrt{2+\sqrt{2}}}{2}$ (b) $-\frac{\sqrt{1+\sqrt{2}}}{2}$ (c) $-\frac{\sqrt{2-\sqrt{2}}}{2}$

(d) $-\frac{\sqrt{2+\sqrt{2}}}{2}$ (e) None of these

Test C **Name** ____________ **Date** ____________

Chapter 5 **Class** ____________ **Section** ____________

1. Simplify: $\dfrac{\csc x \cos^2 x}{1 + \csc x}$.

(a) $\csc x + 1$ (b) $1 - \sin x$ (c) $\sin x - 1$

(d) $1 + \sin x$ (e) None of these

2. Perform the addition and simplify: $\dfrac{1}{1 + \sin x} + \dfrac{1}{1 - \sin x}$.

(a) 2 (b) $2 \sec^2 x$ (c) $2 \cos^2 x$

(d) 0 (e) None of these

3. Verify the identity: $\tan^2 x \cos^2 x + \cot^2 x \sin^2 x = 1$.

(a)
$$\begin{aligned} \tan^2 x \cos^2 + \cot^2 x \sin^2 x &= \frac{\cos^2 x}{\sin^2 x} \cdot \cos^2 x + \frac{\sin^2 x}{\cos^2 x} \cdot \sin^2 x \\ &= \frac{\cos^4 x + \sin^4 x}{\sin^2 x + \cos^2 x} \\ &= \frac{(\cos^2 x + \sin^2 x)^2}{(\sin^2 x + \cos^2 x)} \\ &= \frac{(1)^2}{(1)} = 1 \end{aligned}$$

(b)
$$\begin{aligned} \tan^2 x \cos^2 x + \cot^2 x \sin^2 x &= (1 - \sec^2 x) \cos^2 x + (1 - \csc^2 x) \sin^2 x \\ &= \cos^2 x - \cos^2 x \sec^2 + \sin^2 x - \sin^2 x \csc^2 x \\ &= \cos^2 x - \cos^2 x\left(\frac{1}{\cos^2 x}\right) + \sin^2 x - \sin^2 x\left(\frac{1}{\sin^2 x}\right) \\ &= \cos^2 x + \sin^2 x = 1 \end{aligned}$$

(c)
$$\begin{aligned} \tan^2 x \cos^2 x + \cot^2 x \sin^2 x &= \frac{\sin^2 x}{\cos^2 x} \cdot \cos^2 x + \frac{\cos^2 x}{\sin^2 x} \cdot \sin^2 x \\ &= \sin^2 x + \cos^2 x = 1 \end{aligned}$$

(d) All of these are correct verifications.

(e) None of these

4. Verify the identity: $\dfrac{1 + \tan x}{\sin x} - \sec x = \csc x.$

(a) $\dfrac{1 + \tan x}{\sin x} - \sec x = 1 + \tan x - \sin x \sec x$

$= 1 + \dfrac{\sin x}{\cos x} - \dfrac{\sin x}{\cos x}$

$= 1 \neq \csc x$

Therefore, this is not an identity.

(b) $\dfrac{1 + \tan x}{\sin x} - \sec x = \dfrac{1 + \tan x - \sin x \sec x}{\sin x}$

$= \dfrac{1 + \tan x - \sin x\left(\dfrac{1}{\cos x}\right)}{\sin x}$

$= \dfrac{1 + \tan x - \tan x}{\sin x}$

$= \dfrac{1}{\sin x} = \csc x$

(c) $\dfrac{1 + \tan x}{\sin x} - \sec x = 1 + \tan x - \sin x \sec x$

$= 1 + \tan x - \sin x\left(\dfrac{1}{\sin x}\right)$

$= 1 + \tan x$

$= \csc x$

(d) Both b and c are correct verifications.

(e) None of these

5. Find all solutions in the interval $[0, 2\pi)$: $\sin 2x = 0$.

(a) $0, \pi$ (b) $0, \dfrac{\pi}{2}, \pi, \dfrac{3\pi}{2}$ (c) $\dfrac{\pi}{2}, \dfrac{3\pi}{2}$

(d) $\dfrac{\pi}{4}, \dfrac{3\pi}{4}, \dfrac{5\pi}{4}, \dfrac{7\pi}{4}$ (e) None of these

6. Find all solutions in the interval $[0, 2\pi)$: $8 \sin\left(\dfrac{x}{2}\right) - 8 = 0$.

(a) $\dfrac{\pi}{2}, \dfrac{3\pi}{2}$ (b) $\dfrac{\pi}{4}, \dfrac{3\pi}{4}, \dfrac{5\pi}{4}, \dfrac{7\pi}{4}$ (c) π

(d) 0 (e) None of these

7. Evaluate: $\tan \dfrac{13\pi}{12}$. $\left(\text{Use the fact that } \dfrac{13\pi}{12} = \dfrac{4\pi}{3} - \dfrac{\pi}{4}.\right)$

(a) 1 (b) $1 + \sqrt{3}$ (c) $\sqrt{3} - 1$

(d) $2 - \sqrt{3}$ (e) None of these

8. Simplify: $\cos(2x - y)\cos y - \sin(2x - y)\sin y$.

(a) $\sin 2x$ (b) $\sin(2x - 2y)$ (c) $\cos(2x - 2y)$

(d) $\cos 2x$ (e) None of these

9. Find all solutions in the interval $[0, 2\pi)$: $\cos^2 x - \cos 2x = 0$.

(a) $0, \frac{\pi}{2}, \frac{3\pi}{2}$ (b) $0, \pi$ (c) ± 1

(d) $\frac{\pi}{6}, \frac{5\pi}{6}, \frac{7\pi}{6}, \frac{11\pi}{6}$ (e) None of these

10. Given $\sin u = -\frac{8}{13}$, find $\cos \frac{u}{2}$. $\left(\text{Assume } \frac{3\pi}{2} < u < 2\pi.\right)$

(a) $-\sqrt{\frac{13 - \sqrt{105}}{26}}$ (b) $-\sqrt{\frac{13 + \sqrt{105}}{26}}$ (c) $-\sqrt{\frac{13 - \sqrt{233}}{26}}$

(d) $\sqrt{\frac{13 + \sqrt{105}}{26}}$ (e) None of these

Test D **Name** ______________ **Date** ________

Chapter 5 **Class** ______________ **Section** ________

1. Given $\sin x = \frac{4}{7}$ and $\cos x = \frac{-\sqrt{33}}{7}$, find $\cot x$.

2. Rewrite the expression as a single logarithm and simplify.

   $\ln|\sin \theta| - \ln|\cos \theta|$

3. Verify the identity: $\dfrac{1 + \sin x}{\cos x \sin x} = \sec x(\csc x + 1)$.

4. Verify the identity: $\dfrac{\tan^2 x + 1}{\tan^2 x} = \csc^2 x$.

5. Find all solutions in the interval $[0, 2\pi)$: $3 \tan^2 2x - 1 = 0$.

6. Find all solutions in the interval $[0, 2\pi)$: $\tan^2 \theta \csc \theta = \tan^2 \theta$.

7. Find the exact value: $\dfrac{\tan 325° - \tan 25°}{1 + \tan 325° \tan 25°}$.

8. Simplify: $\sin\left(x + \dfrac{3\pi}{2}\right) \cos x$.

9. Rewrite the function and sketch its graph:

   $f(x) = 6 \cos^2 x - 3$.

10. Given $\cos x = -\frac{3}{7}$ and $\frac{\pi}{2} < x < \pi$, find $\cos \frac{x}{2}$.

Test E **Name** ______ **Date** ______

Chapter 5 **Class** ______ **Section** ______

1. Given $\cos(-x) = \frac{3}{4}$ and $\tan x = \frac{\sqrt{7}}{3}$, find $\sin(-x)$.

2. Rewrite the expression as a single logarithm and simplify.

$\ln|\sin\theta| - \ln|1 - \cos^2\theta|$

3. Verify the identity: $\sin x\left(\frac{\sin x}{1 - \cos x} + \frac{1 - \cos x}{\sin x}\right) = 2.$

4. Verify the identity: $\sec x \csc^2 x - \csc^2 x = \frac{\sec x}{1 + \cos x}.$

5. Find all solutions in the interval $[0, 2\pi)$: $2\sin^2 x = \sin x$.

6. Find all solutions in the interval $[0, 2\pi)$: $2\sin^2 2x + 5\sin 2x - 3 = 0$.

7. Simplify: $\frac{\tan 7x + \tan 5x}{1 - \tan 7x \tan 5x}.$

8. Simplify: $\cos\left(x + \frac{3\pi}{2}\right)\sin x.$

9. Rewrite the function and sketch its graph:

$g(x) = \left(1 - \sqrt{2}\sin x\right)\left(1 + \sqrt{2}\sin x\right).$

10. Given $\cos x = -\frac{2}{3}$ and $\frac{3\pi}{2} < x < 2\pi$, find $\cos\frac{x}{2}$.

Test A

Chapter 6

Name____________________ Date__________

Class____________________ Section__________

1. Given a triangle with $A = 41°$, $B = 72°$, and $a = 15$, find c.

(a) 19.6 (b) 10.7 (c) 21.0

(d) 7.8 (e) None of these

2. A television antenna sits on a roof. Two 78-foot guy wires are positioned on opposite sides of the antenna. The angle of elevation each makes with the ground is 23°. How far apart are the ends of the two guy wires?

(a) 71.8 feet (b) 76.3 feet (c) 143.6 feet

(d) 152.6 feet (e) None of these

3. Given a triangle with $a = 80$, $b = 51$, and $c = 113$, find C.

(a) 117.5° (b) 27.5° (c) 157.4°

(d) 62.5° (e) None of these

4. Ship A is 72 miles from a lighthouse on the shore. Its bearing from the lighthouse is N 15° E. Ship B is 81 miles from the same lighthouse. Its bearing from the lighthouse is N 52° E. Find the number of miles between the two ships.

(a) 84.57 (b) 44.44 (c) 49.29

(d) 90.75 (e) None of these

5. Find the direction of $\mathbf{v}$: $\mathbf{v} = 7\mathbf{i} - 2\mathbf{j}$.

(a) 344° (b) 16° (c) 164°

(d) 196° (e) None of these

6. Given $\mathbf{v}$ of magnitude 200 and direction 215°, and $\mathbf{w}$ of magnitude 150 and direction 162°, find $\mathbf{v} + \mathbf{w}$.

(a) $-21.2\mathbf{i} - 161.1\mathbf{j}$ (b) $350\mathbf{i} + 350\mathbf{j}$ (c) $50\mathbf{i} - 50\mathbf{j}$

(d) $-306.5\mathbf{i} - 68.4\mathbf{j}$ (e) None of these

7. Given $\mathbf{u} = 3\mathbf{i} + 2\mathbf{j}$ and $\mathbf{v} = \mathbf{i} - \mathbf{j}$, find $\mathbf{u} \cdot \mathbf{v}$.

(a) $3\mathbf{i}^2 - \mathbf{ij} - 2\mathbf{j}^2$ (b) $3\mathbf{i}^2 - 2\mathbf{j}^2$ (c) 5

(d) 1 (e) None of these

8. Find the angle between the vectors $\mathbf{v} = 3\mathbf{i} + 2\mathbf{j}$ and $\mathbf{w} = 7\mathbf{i} - 5\mathbf{j}$.

(a) 16.7° (b) 110.8° (c) 50.4°

(d) 69.2° (e) None of these

9. Rewrite in trigonometric form: $16 - 4i$.

(a) $4\sqrt{15}(\cos 14° + i \sin 14°)$ (b) $4\sqrt{15}(\cos 346° + i \sin 346°)$ (c) $4\sqrt{17}(\cos 346° + \text{i} \sin 346°)$

(d) $4\sqrt{17}(\cos 194° + i \sin 194°)$ (e) None of these

10. Find the cube roots: $-64i$.

(a) $-4i$, $4(\cos 330° + i \sin 330°)$, $4(\cos 330° - i \sin 330°)$

(b) $4i$, $4(\cos 90° + i \sin 90°)$, $4(\cos 270° - i \sin 270°)$

(c) $-4i$, $4(\cos 210° + i \sin 210°)$, $4(\cos 70° - i \sin 70°)$

(d) $4i$, $4(\cos 210° + i \sin 210°)$, $4(\cos 330° - i \sin 330°)$

(e) None of these

Test B **Name** ______________ **Date** ______________

Chapter 6 **Class** ______________ **Section** ______________

1. Given a triangle with $B = 87°$, $C = 24°$, and $a = 113$, find b.

   (a) 120.9 (b) 142.7 (c) 49.2
   (d) 94.4 (e) None of these

2. A television antenna sits on a roof. Two 76-foot guy wires are positioned on opposite sides of the antenna. The angle of elevation each makes with the ground is 24°. How far apart are the ends of the two guy wires?

   (a) 41.6 feet (b) 138.9 feet (c) 251.4 feet
   (d) 18.4 feet (e) None of these

3. Given a triangle with $a = 17$, $b = 39$, and $c = 50$, find A.

   (a) 16.88° (b) 73.12° (c) 163.12°
   (d) 106.88° (e) None of these

4. Determine the number of acres in a triangular parcel of land if the lengths of the sides measure 1507 feet, 1750 feet, and 970 feet. There are 43,560 square feet in 1 acre.

   (a) 15.9 acres (b) 21.7 acres (c) 19.2 acres
   (d) 16.8 acres (e) None of these

5. Find the direction of $\mathbf{v}$: $\mathbf{v} = \langle -1, -4 \rangle$.

   (a) 76° (b) 14° (c) 256°
   (d) 194° (e) None of these

6. Given $\mathbf{v}$ of magnitude 150 and direction 30°, and $\mathbf{w}$ of magnitude 75 and direction 206°, find $\mathbf{v} + \mathbf{w}$.

   (a) $97.0\mathbf{i} - 7.6\mathbf{j}$ (b) $62.5\mathbf{i} + 42.1\mathbf{j}$ (c) $225\mathbf{i} + 225\mathbf{j}$
   (d) $-7.4\mathbf{i} + 13.9\mathbf{j}$ (e) None of these

7. Given $\mathbf{v} = \mathbf{i}$ and $\mathbf{w} = 2\mathbf{i} - 3\mathbf{j}$, find $\mathbf{v} \cdot \mathbf{w}$.

   (a) -1 (b) $2\mathbf{i} - 3\mathbf{j}$ (c) 2
   (d) $\sqrt{13}$ (e) None of these

8. Find the angle between the vectors $\mathbf{u} = 2\mathbf{i} + 3\mathbf{j}$ and $\mathbf{v} = 7\mathbf{i} - \mathbf{j}$.

   (a) 0.43 radian (b) 1.12 radians (c) 6.44 radians
   (d) 0.22 radian (e) None of these

9. Rewrite in trigonometric form: $-2 + 3i$.

(a) $\sqrt{13}(\cos 56.3° + i \sin 56.3°)$

(b) $\sqrt{13}(\cos 123.7° + i \sin 123.7°)$

(c) $\sqrt{13}(\cos 236.3° + i \sin 236.3°)$

(d) $\sqrt{13}(\cos 303.7° + i \sin 303.7°)$

(e) None of these

10. Find the square roots: $-4i$.

(a) $2(\cos 135° - i \sin 135°), 2(-\cos 135° - i \sin 135°)$

(b) $2(\cos 135° + i \sin 135°), 2(\cos 67.5° + i \sin 67.5°)$

(c) $2(\cos 135° + i \sin 135°), 2(\cos 315° + i \sin 315°)$

(d) $2i, -2i$

(e) None of these

Test C **Name**____________________ **Date**____________

Chapter 6 **Class**____________________ **Section**____________

1. Given a triangle with $A = 20°$, $C = 110°$, and $a = 5$, find b.

(a) 2.2 (b) 50.0 (c) 11.2

(d) 13.7 (e) None of these

2. A television antenna sits on a roof. Two 72-foot guy wires are positioned on opposite sides of the antenna. The angle of elevation each makes with the ground is 26°. How far apart are the ends of the two guy wires?

(a) 24.9 feet (b) 21.5 feet (c) 112.1 feet

(d) 129.4 feet (e) None of these

3. Given a triangle with $a = 117$, $b = 230$, $c = 185$, find B.

(a) 96.6° (b) 6.6° (c) 53.0°

(d) 37.0° (e) None of these

4. Determine the number of acres in a triangular parcel of land if the lengths of the sides measure 1702 feet, 4021 feet, and 4000 feet. There are 43,560 square feet in 1 acre.

(a) 90.2 acres (b) 76.6 acres (c) 89.5 acres

(d) 46.2 acres (e) None of these

5. Find the direction of **v**: $\mathbf{v} = \langle -2, 5 \rangle$.

(a) 112° (b) 68° (c) 167°

(d) 193° (e) None of these

6. Given **v** of magnitude 50 and direction 315°, and **w** of magnitude 20 and direction 210°, find $\mathbf{v} + \mathbf{w}$.

(a) $18.0\mathbf{i} - 45.4\mathbf{j}$ (b) $52.7\mathbf{i} - 25.4\mathbf{j}$ (c) $18.0\mathbf{i} - 25.4\mathbf{j}$

(d) $52.7\mathbf{i} - 45.4\mathbf{j}$ (e) None of these

7. Given $\mathbf{u} = 3\mathbf{j}$ and $\mathbf{v} = 7\mathbf{i} + \mathbf{j}$, find $\mathbf{u} \cdot \mathbf{v}$.

(a) 10 (b) $7\mathbf{i} + 3\mathbf{j}$ (c) $3\mathbf{j}$

(d) 3 (e) None of these

8. Find the angle between the vectors $\mathbf{v} = 2\mathbf{i} - 3\mathbf{j}$ and $\mathbf{u} = \mathbf{i} + \mathbf{j}$.

(a) 1.8 radians (b) 0.2 radian (c) 1.4 radians

(d) 0.8 radian (e) None of these

9. Rewrite in trigonometric form: $7 - 2i$.

(a) $\sqrt{53}(\cos 344.1° + i \sin 344.1°)$ (b) $3\sqrt{5}(\cos 344.1° + i \sin 344.1°)$

(c) $3\sqrt{5}(\cos 15.9° + i \sin 15.9°)$ (d) $\sqrt{53}(\cos 15.9° + i \sin 15.9°)$

(e) None of these

10. Find the square roots: $81i$.

(a) $9(\cos 90° + i \sin 90°), 9(-\cos 90° - i \sin 90°)$

(b) $9(\cos 45° + i \sin 45°), 9(\cos 225° + i \sin 225°)$

(c) $9(\cos 45° - i \sin 45°), 9(-\cos 45° - i \sin 45°)$

(d) $9(\cos 90° + i \sin 90°), 9(\cos 45° + i \sin 45°)$

(e) None of these

Test D **Name** ______________________ **Date** ____________

Chapter 6 **Class** ______________________ **Section** ____________

1. Given a triangle with $A = 39°$, $B = 106°$, and $c = 78$, find a.

2. Two game wardens are known to be 1.5 miles apart and both observe a grizzly bear. The bear is N 22.5° E of Warden Wain and N 28.8° W of Warden Ryan. How far is each warden from the bear?

3. Given a triangle with $a = 78$, $b = 15$, and $c = 91$, find A, B, and C.

4. On a map the town of Morgan Run is due south of Davidson and is south east of Vicksburg. The distances from Morgan Run to Davidson and Vicksburg are 32 and 52 miles respectively. The distance between Davidson and Vicksburg is 42 miles. If a plane leaves Morgan Run to fly to Vicksburg, on what bearing should it travel? (See figure.)

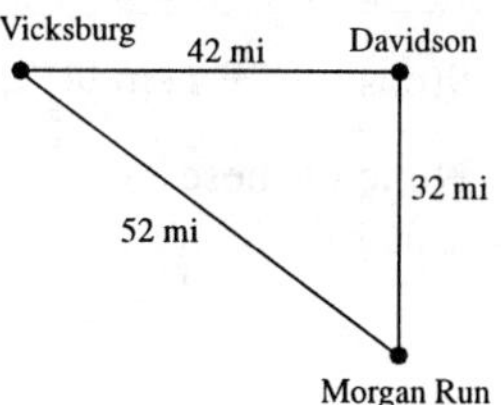

5. A vector $\mathbf{v}$ has initial point $(2, 5)$ and terminal point $(-1, 9)$. Find its magnitude and direction.

6. Given $\mathbf{v}$ of magnitude 100 and direction 172°, and $\mathbf{w}$ of magnitude 300 and direction 310°, find $\mathbf{v} + \mathbf{w}$.

7. Given $\mathbf{v} = 5\mathbf{i} - 2\mathbf{j}$ and $\mathbf{w} = -3\mathbf{i} + \mathbf{j}$, find $\mathbf{v} \cdot \mathbf{w}$.

8. Find the angle between the vectors $\mathbf{w} = 5\mathbf{i} + 2\mathbf{j}$ and $\mathbf{v} = -10 - 2\mathbf{j}$.

9. Rewrite in trigonometric form: $-2 + \sqrt{3}\,i$.

10. Find the cube roots: -64.

Test E **Name** ______________ **Date** ____________

Chapter 6 **Class** ______________ **Section** ____________

1. Given a triangle with $A = 102°$, $B = 23°$, and $c = 576.1$, find a.

2. A used car lot has a large balloon tied down to stakes 1500 feet apart. The angle of elevation from the stake at the west end of the lot to the balloon is 50°, and the angle of elevation from the stake at the east end of the lot to the balloon is 72°. What is the altitude of the balloon?

3. Given a triangle with $a = 135$, $b = 71.6$, and $c = 69$, find B.

4. A 120 foot tower is leaning. A 200 foot guy wire has been anchored 82 feet from the base of the tower. How far from vertical is the tower leaning?

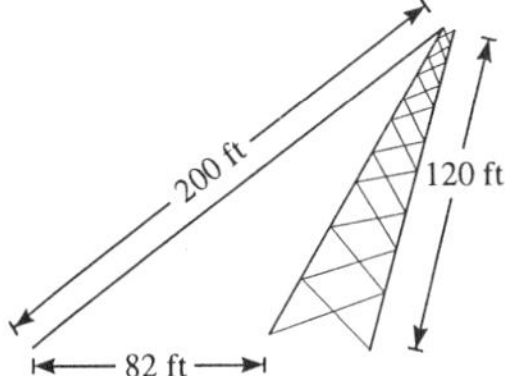

5. A vector $\mathbf{v}$ has magnitude 27 and direction $\theta = 216°$. Find its component form.

6. Given $\mathbf{v}$ of magnitude 300 and direction 90° and $\mathbf{w}$ of magnitude 250 and direction 253°, find $\mathbf{v} + \mathbf{w}$.

7. Given $\mathbf{v} = 3\mathbf{i} - 9\mathbf{j}$ and $\mathbf{w} = 2\mathbf{i} + \mathbf{j}$, find $\mathbf{v} \cdot \mathbf{w}$.

8. Find the angle between the vectors $\mathbf{w} = 3\mathbf{i} + 4\mathbf{j}$ and $\mathbf{v} = 10\mathbf{i} + 4\mathbf{j}$.

9. Rewrite in trigonometric form: $-17 + 32i$.

10. Find all solutions: $x^2 + 4i = 0$.

Test A **Name**____________ **Date**________

Chapter 7 **Class**____________ **Section**________

1. Solve the system by the method of substitution:

$$\begin{cases} x + y = 1 \\ x^2 + 3y^2 = 21 \end{cases}.$$

(a) $\left(\frac{3}{2}, -3\right)$ (b) $\left(3, -\frac{3}{2}\right)$ (c) $\left(-\frac{3}{2}, \frac{5}{2}\right), (3, -2)$

(d) $\left(\frac{3}{2}, -\frac{1}{2}\right), (-3, 4)$ (e) No solution

2. Find the number of points of intersection of the graphs:

$$\begin{cases} x^2 + y = 3 \\ x^2 + y^2 = 1 \end{cases}.$$

(a) 4 (b) 3 (c) 2

(d) 1 (e) 0

3. Solve the linear system by the method of elimination:

$$\begin{cases} 7x - 3y = 26 \\ 2x + 5y = 25 \end{cases}.$$

(a) $\left(-5, -\frac{61}{3}\right)$ (b) $(5, 3)$ (c) Infinitely many solutions

(d) No solution (e) None of these

4. Solve the following system of equations for x:

$$\begin{cases} \dfrac{3}{x} - \dfrac{2}{y} = 5 \\ \dfrac{1}{x} + \dfrac{4}{y} = 4 \end{cases}$$

(a) $\dfrac{1}{2}$ (b) 2 (c) 5

(d) $\dfrac{1}{5}$ (e) None of these

5. Use Gaussian elimination to solve the system of equations:

$$\begin{cases} x - 6y + z = 1 \\ -x + 2y - 4z = 3 \\ 7x - 10y + 3z = -25 \end{cases}.$$

(a) $(5, 1, 2)$ (b) $(-5, -1, 0)$ (c) $(-1, 3, 1)$

(d) No solution (e) None of these

6. Find an equation of the parabola, $y = ax^2 + bx + c$, that passes through $(0, 5)$, $(2, -5)$, and $(-3, -40)$.

(a) $y = 3x^2 - 2x - 7$ (b) $y = -4x^2 + 3x + 5$ (c) $y = 4x^2 + 3x + 5$

(d) $y = 9x^2 - 121$ (e) None of these

7. Match the graph with the correct inequality.

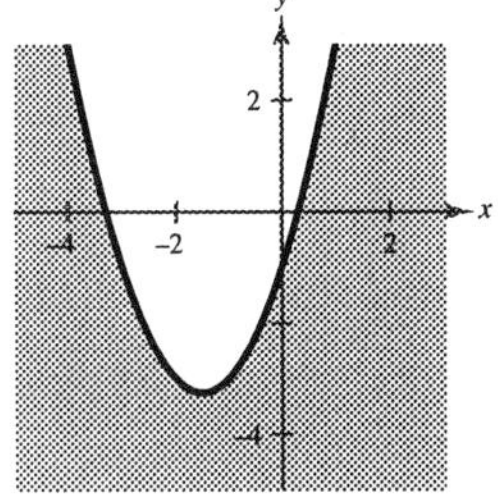

(a) $y < x^2 + 3x - 1$ (b) $y > x^2 + 3x - 1$

(c) $y \leq x^2 + 3x - 1$ (d) $y \geq x^2 + 3x - 1$

(e) None of these

8. Match the graph with the correct system of inequalities.

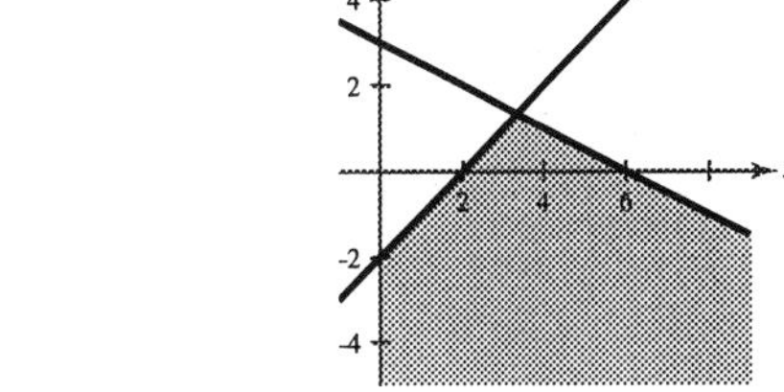

(a) $\begin{cases} x + 2y \leq 6 \\ x - y \leq 2 \\ y \geq 0 \end{cases}$ (b) $\begin{cases} x + 2y \geq 6 \\ x - y \geq 2 \\ x \geq 0 \end{cases}$

(c) $\begin{cases} x + 2y \leq 6 \\ x - y \geq 2 \\ x \geq 0 \end{cases}$ (d) $\begin{cases} x + 2y \geq 6 \\ x - y \geq 2 \\ y \geq 0 \end{cases}$

(e) None of these

9. Find the maximum value of the objective function $z = 5x + 6y$ subject to the following constraints.

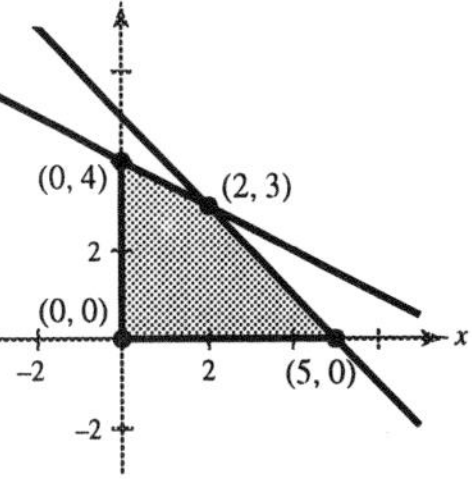

$$x \geq 0$$
$$y \geq 0$$
$$x + 2y \leq 8$$
$$3x + 3y \leq 15$$

(a) 30 (b) 28

(c) 25 (d) 24

(e) None of these

10. A company produces two models of calculators at two different plants. In one day Plant A can produce 140 of Model I and 35 of Model II. In one day Plant B can produce 60 of Model I and 90 of Model II. The company needs to produce at least 460 of Model I and 340 of Model II. Find the minimum cost. Assume it costs \$1200 per day to operate Plant A and \$900 per day for Plant B.

(a) $C = \$11,640$ (b) $C = \$8730$ (c) $C = \$5100$

(d) $C = \$3948$ (e) None of these

Test B **Name** ______________ **Date** ______________

Chapter 7 **Class** ______________ **Section** ______________

1. Solve the system by the method of substitution:

$$\begin{cases} 2x^2 + 2y^2 = 7 \\ x + y^2 = 7 \end{cases}.$$

(a) (2.8, 2.0), (−0.5, 7.3) (b) (4.6, 1.5), (−2.6, 3.1) (c) (2.8, −0.5)

(d) (4.6), (−2.6) (e) No solution

2. Find the number of points of intersection of the graphs:

$$\begin{cases} x^2 + y^2 = 2 \\ 2x + y = 10 \end{cases}.$$

(a) 4 (b) 3 (c) 2

(d) 1 (e) 0

3. Solve the linear system by the method of elimination:

$$\begin{cases} 2x + 4y = 7 \\ 3x + 6y = 5 \end{cases}.$$

(a) $\left(1, \frac{5}{4}\right)$ (b) (0, 0) (c) Infinitely many solutions

(d) No solution (e) None of these

4. Solve the following system of equations for y:

$$\begin{cases} \dfrac{2}{x} + \dfrac{3}{y} = 7 \\ \dfrac{3}{x} - \dfrac{1}{y} = 16 \end{cases}.$$

(a) 5 (b) −1 (c) $\frac{1}{5}$

(d) 2 (e) None of these

5. Use Gaussian elimination to solve the system of equations:

$$\begin{cases} x - y + z = 5 \\ 3x + 2y - z = -2 \\ 2x + y + 3z = 10 \end{cases}.$$

(a) (1, −1, 3) (b) (2, −5, −2) (c) (−1, 7, 13)

(d) (3, −9, −7) (e) No solution

6. Find the value of c in the quadratic equation, $y = ax^2 + bx + c$, if its graph passes through the points $(1, 0)$, $(-1, -6)$, and $(2, 9)$.

(a) -5 (b) -4 (c) 3

(d) 11 (e) None of these

7. Match the graph with the correct inequality.

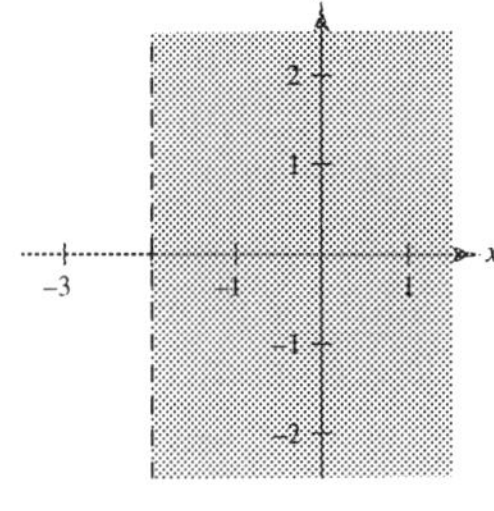

(a) $y > -2$ (b) $y < -2$

(c) $x > -2$ (d) $x \geq -2$

(e) None of these

8. Match the graph with the correct system of inequalities.

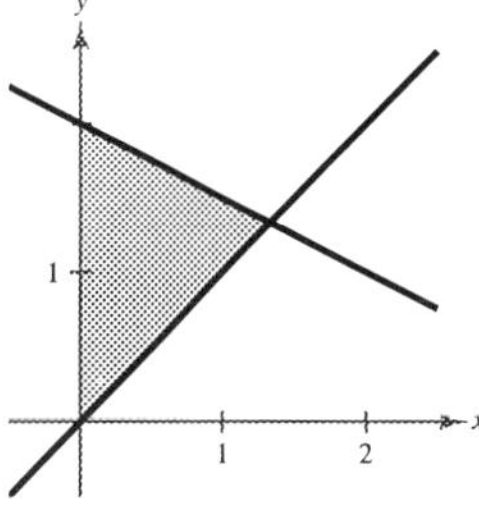

(a) $\begin{cases} x + 2y \leq 4 \\ x \leq y \\ x \geq 0 \end{cases}$

(b) $\begin{cases} x + 2y \geq 4 \\ x \leq y \\ y \geq 0 \end{cases}$

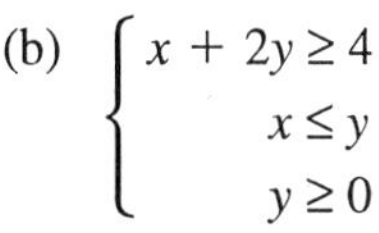

(c) $\begin{cases} x + 2y \leq 4 \\ x \leq y \\ y \geq 0 \end{cases}$

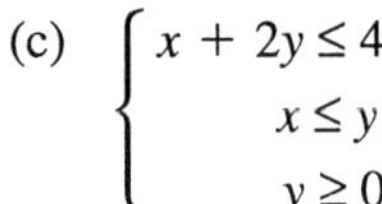

(d) $\begin{cases} x + 2y \leq 4 \\ y \leq x \\ y \geq 0 \end{cases}$

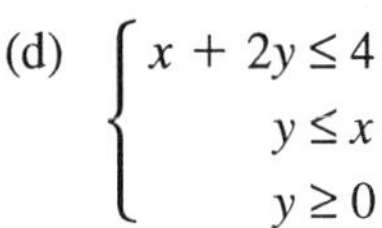

(e) None of these

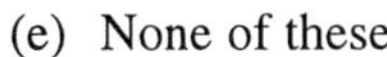

9. Find the maximum value of the objective function $z = 10x + 8y$ subject to the following constraints.

$$\begin{aligned} x &\geq 0 \\ y &\geq 0 \\ x + y &\leq 5 \\ 3x + y &\leq 12 \\ -2x + y &\leq 2 \end{aligned}$$

(a) 40 (b) 50

(c) 42 (d) 47

(e) None of these

10. A company produces two models of calculators at two different plants. In one day Plant A can produce 60 of Model I and 70 of Model II. In one day Plant B can produce 80 of Model I and 40 of Model II. The company needs to produce at least 460 of Model I and 340 of Model II. Find the minimum cost. Assume it costs \$1200 per day to operate Plant A and \$900 per day for Plant B.

(a) $C = \$7800$ (b) $C = \$9200$ (c) $C = \$7371$

(d) $C = \$5175$ (e) None of these

Test C **Name** ______ **Date** ______

Chapter 7 **Class** ______ **Section** ______

1. Solve the system by the method of substitution:

$$\begin{cases} x^2 + 2y = 6 \\ 2x + y = 3 \end{cases}.$$

(a) $(4, -5)$ (b) $(2, 1)$ (c) $(0, 3)$

(d) $(0, 3)$ and $(4, -5)$ (e) None of these

2. Find the number of points of intersection:

$$\begin{cases} x^2 + y^2 = 5 \\ x + 2y - 5 = 0 \end{cases}.$$

(a) 4 (b) 3 (c) 2

(d) 1 (e) 0

3. Solve the linear system by the method of elimination:

$$\begin{cases} 6x - 5y = 4 \\ 3x + 2y = 1 \end{cases}.$$

(a) $\left(\frac{13}{27}, -\frac{2}{9}\right)$ (b) $\left(-\frac{2}{9}, -\frac{8}{5}\right)$ (c) $\left(-\frac{8}{5}, -\frac{68}{25}\right)$

(d) $\left(2, \frac{8}{5}\right)$ (e) None of these

4. Solve the following system of equations for x:

$$\begin{cases} \dfrac{5}{x} - \dfrac{3}{y} = 2 \\ \dfrac{2}{x} + \dfrac{5}{y} = -24 \end{cases}.$$

(a) $-\dfrac{1}{2}$ (b) $-\dfrac{1}{4}$ (c) 5

(d) $-\dfrac{1}{3}$ (e) None of these

5. Use Gaussian elimination to solve the system of equations:

$$\begin{cases} 6x - 9y + 4z = -7 \\ 2x + 6y - z = 6 \\ 4x - 3y + 2z = -2 \end{cases}.$$

(a) $\left(\dfrac{1}{2}, \dfrac{2}{3}, -1\right)$ (b) $\left(\dfrac{11}{21}, 1, -\dfrac{2}{7}\right)$ (c) $\left(a, \dfrac{31a}{15}, \dfrac{44a}{5}\right)$

(d) No solution (e) None of these

6. Find the value of b in the quadratic equation, $y = ax^2 + bx + c$, if its graph passes through the points $(-1, 4)$, $(1, -2)$, and $(2, -2)$.

(a) -3 (b) 2 (c) -2

(d) -1 (e) None of these

7. Match the graph with the correct inequality.

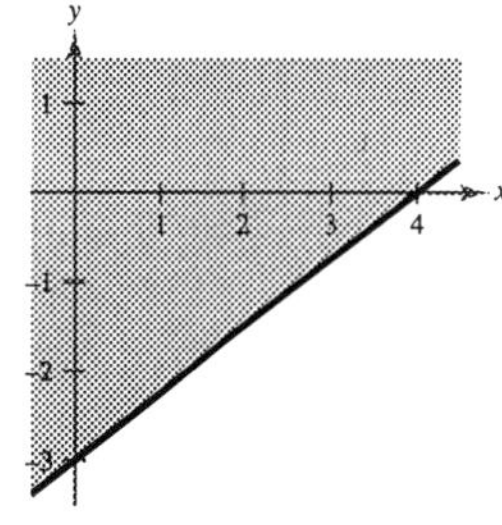

(a) $3x - 4y < 12$ (b) $3x - 4y \leq 12$

(c) $3x - 4y > 12$ (d) $3x - 4y \geq 12$

8. Match the graph with the correct system of inequalities.

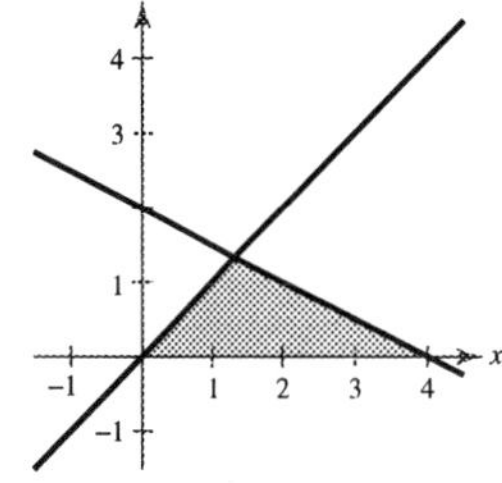

(a) $\begin{cases} x + 2y \leq 4 \\ x \leq y \\ x \geq 0 \end{cases}$ (b) $\begin{cases} x + 2y \leq 4 \\ y \leq x \\ y \geq 0 \end{cases}$

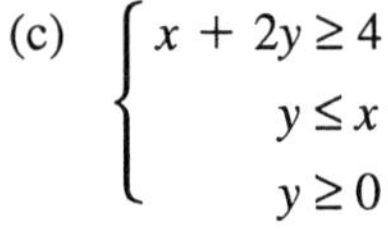

(c) $\begin{cases} x + 2y \geq 4 \\ y \leq x \\ y \geq 0 \end{cases}$

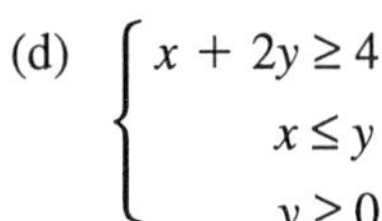

(d) $\begin{cases} x + 2y \geq 4 \\ x \leq y \\ y \geq 0 \end{cases}$

(e) None of these

9. Find the maximum value of the objective function $z = 3x + 2y$ subject to the following constraints.

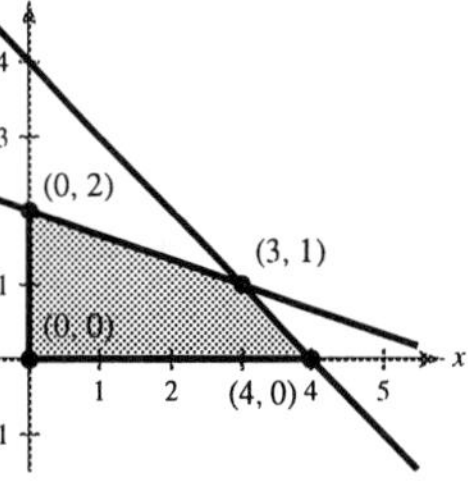

$$\begin{aligned} x &\geq 0 \\ y &\geq 0 \\ x + y &\leq 4 \\ x + 3y &\leq 6 \end{aligned}$$

(a) 12 (b) 11

(c) 10 (d) 9

(e) None of these

10. A company produces two models of calculators at two different plants. In one day Plant A can produce 70 of Model I and 40 of Model II. In one day Plant B can produce 80 of Model I and 90 of Model II. The company needs to produce at least 1370 of Model I and 1270 of Model II. Find the minimum cost. Assume it costs \$900 per day to operate Plant A and \$1200 per day for Plant B.

(a) $C = \$32{,}570$ (b) $C = \$28{,}575$ (c) $C = \$20{,}550$

(d) $C = \$19{,}500$ (e) None of these

Test D Name__________ Date__________

Chapter 7 Class__________ Section__________

1. Solve the system by the method of substitution:

$$\begin{cases} y = \dfrac{1}{x} \\ x + 5y = 6 \end{cases}.$$

2. Use a graphing utility to find all points of intersection of the graphs:

$$\begin{cases} (x-3)^2 + y^2 = 4 \\ -2x + y^2 = 0 \end{cases}.$$

3. Solve the system by method of elimination and verify the solution with a graphing utility:

$$\begin{cases} 2x - 5y = -4 \\ 4x + 3y = 5 \end{cases}.$$

4. How many liters of a 40% solution of acid must be combined with a 15% solution to obtain 30 liters of a 20% solution?

5. Use Gaussian elimination to solve the system of equations:

$$\begin{cases} x + 2y + z = 6 \\ 2x - y + 3z = -2 \\ x + y - 2z = 0 \end{cases}.$$

6. Find an equation of the parabola, $y = ax^2 + bx + c$, that passes through $(0, -5)$, $(2, 1)$, and $(-1, -14)$. Verify your result with a graphing utility.

7. Use a graphing utility to graph the inequality

$$x^2 + (y-1)^2 \le 25.$$

8. Sketch the graph of the system of inequalities.

$$\begin{cases} 2x + 3y \le 6 \\ x - 2y \ge -2 \end{cases}$$

9. Find the maximum value of the objective function $C = 3x + 2y$ subject to the following constraints.

$$\begin{aligned} x &\geq 0 \\ y &\geq 0 \\ 3x + 4y &\leq 25 \\ 3x - y &\leq 5 \end{aligned}$$

10. A merchant plans to sell two models of an item at costs of \$350 and \$400. The \$350 model yields a profit of \$85 and the \$400 model yields a profit of \$90. The total demand per month for the two models will not exceed 150. Find the number of units of each model that should be stocked each month in order to maximize the profit. Assume the merchant can invest no more than \$56,000 for inventory of these items.

Test E
Chapter 7

Name____________________ Date____________

Class____________________ Section____________

1. Solve the system by the method of substitution:

$$\begin{cases} 2x^2 - y = -2 \\ x - y = -2 \end{cases}.$$

2. Use a graphing utility to find all points of intersection of the graphs:

$$\begin{cases} x^2 - 4x + y = 0 \\ x - y = 0 \end{cases}.$$

3. Solve the system by method of elimination and verify the solution with a graphing utility:

$$\begin{cases} 6x + y = -2 \\ 4x - 3y = 17 \end{cases}.$$

4. The perimeter of a rectangle is 91 feet and the length is 8 feet more than twice the width. Find the dimensions of the rectangle.

5. Use Gaussian elimination to solve the system of linear equations:

$$\begin{cases} x + 3y + z = 0 \\ 5x - y + z + w = 0 \\ 2x + 2z + w = 2 \\ 3x + 2z - w = 10 \end{cases}.$$

6. Find an equation of the parabola, $y = ax^2 + bx + c$, that passes through $(1, 1)$, $(-1, 11)$, and $(3, 23)$. Verify your result with a graphing utility.

7. Use a graphing utility to graph the inequality

$$3x^2 + y \geq 6.$$

8. Sketch the graph of the system of inequalities.

$$\begin{cases} 2y - 3x \leq 10 \\ 2y \geq x^2 \end{cases}.$$

9. Find the maximum value of the objective function $z = 3x + 2y$ subject to the following constraints.

$$\begin{aligned} x &\geq 0 \\ y &\geq 0 \\ 3x + 4y &\leq 25 \\ 3x - y &\leq 5 \end{aligned}$$

10. A merchant plans to sell two models of an item at costs of \$350 and \$500. The \$350 model yields a profit of \$45 and the \$500 model yields a profit of \$60. The total demand per month for the two models will not exceed 145. Find the number of units of each model that should be stocked each month in order to maximize the profit. Assume the merchant can invest no more than \$56,000 for inventory of these items.

Test A **Name**________________ **Date**__________

Chapter 8 **Class**________________ **Section**__________

1. Write the matrix in reduced row-echelon form: $\begin{bmatrix} 3 & 1 & 1 & 7 \\ 1 & -2 & 0 & 5 \\ 1 & 1 & 2 & 6 \end{bmatrix}$.

(a) $\begin{bmatrix} 1 & 1 & 2 & 6 \\ 0 & 3 & 2 & 1 \\ 0 & 0 & 11 & 31 \end{bmatrix}$

(b) $\begin{bmatrix} 1 & 0 & 0 & \frac{21}{11} \\ 0 & 1 & 0 & -\frac{17}{11} \\ 0 & 0 & 1 & \frac{31}{11} \end{bmatrix}$

(c) $\begin{bmatrix} 1 & -2 & 0 & 5 \\ 0 & 1 & \frac{1}{7} & -\frac{8}{7} \\ 0 & 0 & 11 & 31 \end{bmatrix}$

(d) $\begin{bmatrix} 1 & 0 & 0 & \frac{3}{11} \\ 0 & 1 & 0 & \frac{7}{11} \\ 0 & 0 & 1 & -\frac{14}{11} \end{bmatrix}$

(e) None of these

2. Use Gaussian elimination with back-substitution or Gauss-Jordan elimination to solve the following system of linear equations.

$$\begin{cases} 3x + 2y + z = 7 \\ x - \ \ y + z = 6 \\ x \qquad\ + z = 5 \end{cases}$$

(a) $(2, -1, 3)$ (b) $\left(1, -\frac{1}{2}, 5\right)$ (c) $(-1, 1, 2)$

(d) $(0, 4, -1)$ (e) None of these

3. Given $A = \begin{bmatrix} 3 & 6 & -1 \\ 0 & 5 & 2 \end{bmatrix}$ and $B = \begin{bmatrix} 1 & 0 & 5 \\ -1 & 2 & 7 \end{bmatrix}$, find $3A - 2B$.

(a) $\begin{bmatrix} 7 & 18 & -13 \\ 2 & 11 & -8 \end{bmatrix}$ (b) $\begin{bmatrix} 7 & 18 & 2 \\ 0 & 11 & -8 \end{bmatrix}$ (c) $\begin{bmatrix} 11 & 18 & 7 \\ -2 & 19 & 20 \end{bmatrix}$

(d) $\begin{bmatrix} 7 & 18 & -13 \\ -2 & 9 & 20 \end{bmatrix}$ (e) None of these

4. Use a graphing utility to find AB, given $A = \begin{bmatrix} 3 & -2 & 4 \\ 0 & 0 & -1 \\ 3 & 2 & -1 \end{bmatrix}$ and $B = \begin{bmatrix} 3 & 1 & -1 \\ -1 & 0 & 0 \\ 2 & 4 & -2 \end{bmatrix}$.

(a) $\begin{bmatrix} 6 & -8 & 12 \\ -3 & 2 & -4 \\ 0 & -8 & 6 \end{bmatrix}$ (b) $\begin{bmatrix} 19 & 19 & -11 \\ -2 & -4 & 2 \\ 5 & -1 & -1 \end{bmatrix}$ (c) $\begin{bmatrix} 9 & -2 & -4 \\ 0 & 0 & 0 \\ 6 & 8 & 2 \end{bmatrix}$

(d) Impossible (e) None of these

5. Find the inverse of $A = \begin{bmatrix} 3 & 2 \\ 1 & 4 \end{bmatrix}$.

(a) $\begin{bmatrix} \frac{2}{5} & -\frac{1}{5} \\ -\frac{1}{10} & \frac{3}{10} \end{bmatrix}$

(b) $\begin{bmatrix} \frac{1}{3} & \frac{1}{2} \\ 1 & \frac{1}{4} \end{bmatrix}$

(c) $\begin{bmatrix} 4 & -2 \\ -1 & 3 \end{bmatrix}$

(d) $\begin{bmatrix} -3 & 1 \\ 2 & -4 \end{bmatrix}$

(e) None of these

6. Given a system of linear equations with coefficient matrix A, use A^{-1} to find (x, y, z).

$$\begin{aligned} 3x + 2y + z &= 5 \\ x - 4y &= 6 \\ x - y + 3z &= 6 \end{aligned} \qquad A^{-1} = \frac{1}{39}\begin{bmatrix} 12 & 7 & -4 \\ 3 & -8 & -1 \\ -3 & -5 & 14 \end{bmatrix}$$

(a) $(-2, -1, 1)$

(b) $(-1, 6, -2)$

(c) $(2, -1, 1)$

(d) $(6, -1, 3)$

(e) None of these

7. Find the determinant of the matrix: $\begin{bmatrix} 3 & -4 \\ 2 & 6 \end{bmatrix}$.

(a) 10

(b) 26

(c) -26

(d) -10

(e) None of these

8. Use the matrix capabilities of a graphing utility to find the determinant of the matrix:

$$\begin{bmatrix} 5 & -1 & 0 & 2 \\ 0 & 4 & 7 & 3 \\ 0 & 0 & 1 & 1 \\ 0 & 0 & 0 & 1 \end{bmatrix}.$$

(a) 11

(b) -11

(c) -20

(d) 20

(e) None of these

9. Use Cramer's Rule to solve for y in the system of linear equations:

$$\begin{cases} 3x + 2y + 4z = 12 \\ x - y + z = 3 \\ 2x + 7y - z = 9 \end{cases}.$$

(a) $y = \dfrac{\begin{vmatrix} 3 & 2 & 4 \\ 1 & -1 & 1 \\ 2 & 7 & -1 \end{vmatrix}}{\begin{vmatrix} 3 & 12 & 4 \\ 1 & 3 & 1 \\ 2 & 9 & -1 \end{vmatrix}}$ (b) $y = \dfrac{\begin{vmatrix} 3 & 12 & 4 \\ 1 & 3 & 1 \\ 2 & 9 & -1 \end{vmatrix}}{\begin{vmatrix} 3 & 2 & 4 \\ 1 & -1 & 1 \\ 2 & 7 & -1 \end{vmatrix}}$ (c) $y = \dfrac{\begin{vmatrix} 3 & 4 & 12 \\ 1 & -1 & 3 \\ 2 & 7 & 9 \end{vmatrix}}{\begin{vmatrix} 2 & 4 & 3 \\ -1 & 1 & 1 \\ 7 & -1 & 2 \end{vmatrix}}$

(d) $y = \begin{vmatrix} 3 & 2 & 4 \\ 1 & -1 & 1 \\ 2 & 7 & -1 \end{vmatrix} \begin{vmatrix} 2 & 4 & 12 \\ -1 & 1 & 3 \\ 7 & -1 & 9 \end{vmatrix}$

(e) None of these

10. Find the uncoded row matrix of order 1×3 for the message CALL ME LATER,

then encode the message using $A = \begin{bmatrix} 1 & -1 & 0 \\ 1 & 0 & 3 \\ -2 & 1 & -1 \end{bmatrix}$.

(a) 16 −12 4 4 3 −13 9 −13 3 1 9 −9 −20 −18 5

(b) −20 9 −9 −14 1 −13 −19 7 −12 11 4 55 18 −18 0

(c) −5 12 19 −3 6 6 2 13 −6 −6 3 −1 0 2 2

(d) 3 1 12 12 0 13 5 0 12 1 20 5 18 0 0

(e) None of these

Test B **Name**________________ **Date**__________

Chapter 8 **Class**________________ **Section**__________

1. Write the matrix in reduced row-echelon form: $\begin{bmatrix} 3 & 6 & -2 & 28 \\ -2 & -4 & 5 & -37 \\ 1 & 2 & 9 & -39 \end{bmatrix}$.

(a) $\begin{bmatrix} 1 & 2 & 1 & 1 \\ 0 & 0 & 1 & -5 \\ 0 & 0 & 0 & 0 \end{bmatrix}$ (b) $\begin{bmatrix} 0 & 0 & 0 & 0 \\ 1 & 2 & 0 & 6 \\ 0 & 0 & 1 & -5 \end{bmatrix}$ (c) $\begin{bmatrix} 1 & 2 & 0 & 6 \\ 0 & 0 & 1 & -5 \\ 0 & 0 & 0 & 0 \end{bmatrix}$

(d) $\begin{bmatrix} 1 & 2 & 1 & 1 \\ 0 & 0 & 1 & -5 \\ 0 & 0 & 0 & 3 \end{bmatrix}$ (e) None of these

2. Use Gaussian elimination with back-substitution or Gauss-Jordan elimination to solve the following system of linear equations.

$$\begin{cases} 2x + y - z = -3 \\ 4x - y + z = 6 \\ 2x + 3y + 2z = 9 \end{cases}$$

(a) $(1, -1, 4)$ (b) $\left(\frac{1}{2}, 0, 4\right)$ (c) $\left(\frac{1}{2}, 2, 0\right)$

(d) $\left(\frac{3}{2}, -9, 0\right)$ (e) None of these

3. Given $A = \begin{bmatrix} 1 & 2 & 3 \\ 4 & 7 & 1 \\ 0 & 3 & 2 \end{bmatrix}$ and $B = \begin{bmatrix} 0 & 0 & 1 \\ 1 & 4 & 0 \\ 2 & 3 & 7 \end{bmatrix}$, find $6A - 2B$.

(a) $\begin{bmatrix} 30 & 72 & 52 \\ 32 & 10 & 6 \\ 1 & 6 & -8 \end{bmatrix}$ (b) $\begin{bmatrix} 30 & 12 & 4 \\ 3 & 10 & 6 \\ 1 & 6 & -8 \end{bmatrix}$ (c) $\begin{bmatrix} 6 & 12 & 16 \\ 22 & 34 & 6 \\ -4 & 12 & -2 \end{bmatrix}$

(d) $\begin{bmatrix} 30 & 22 & 20 \\ 66 & 28 & 26 \\ 24 & 16 & 14 \end{bmatrix}$ (e) None of these

4. Use a graphing utility to find AB, given $A = \begin{bmatrix} 2 & 0 & 1 & 2 \\ 0 & 1 & 0 & 1 \\ -1 & -2 & 0 & 0 \end{bmatrix}$ and $B = \begin{bmatrix} 1 & 1 & 0 \\ 0 & 1 & 1 \\ 2 & -1 & 2 \end{bmatrix}$.

(a) $\begin{bmatrix} 2 & 0 & 1 & 2 \\ 0 & 1 & 0 & 0 \\ -2 & 2 & 0 & 0 \end{bmatrix}$ (b) $\begin{bmatrix} 4 & 2 & 3 \\ -1 & -2 & -1 \\ 6 & -5 & -1 \end{bmatrix}$ (c) $\begin{bmatrix} 2 & 1 & 1 & 3 \\ -1 & -1 & 0 & 1 \\ 2 & -5 & 2 & 3 \end{bmatrix}$

(d) Impossible (e) None of these

5. Find the inverse of $A = \begin{bmatrix} 2 & 3 \\ 1 & 2 \end{bmatrix}$.

(a) $\begin{bmatrix} \frac{1}{2} & \frac{1}{3} \\ 1 & \frac{1}{2} \end{bmatrix}$ (b) $\begin{bmatrix} 2 & -3 \\ -1 & 2 \end{bmatrix}$ (c) $\begin{bmatrix} -2 & 1 \\ 3 & -2 \end{bmatrix}$

(d) $\begin{bmatrix} \frac{2}{7} & -\frac{3}{7} \\ -\frac{1}{7} & \frac{2}{7} \end{bmatrix}$ (e) None of these

6. Given a system of linear equations with coefficient matrix A, use A^{-1} to find (x, y, z).

$$\begin{aligned} 3x + y - z &= -11 \\ x - y - z &= -1 \\ x + 2y + 3z &= 3 \end{aligned} \qquad A^{-1} = \frac{1}{10}\begin{bmatrix} 1 & 5 & 2 \\ 4 & -10 & -2 \\ -3 & 5 & 4 \end{bmatrix}$$

(a) $(3, -2, 0)$ (b) $(2, -2, 3)$ (c) $(-1, 5, 1)$

(d) $(-1, -4, 4)$ (e) None of these

7. Find the determinant of the matrix: $\begin{bmatrix} 3 & -1 \\ 6 & 2 \end{bmatrix}$.

(a) 12 (b) -12 (c) 0

(d) 9 (e) None of these

8. Use the matrix capabilities of a graphing utility to find the determinant of the matrix:

$$\begin{bmatrix} 1 & 0 & 0 & 0 \\ 4 & 6 & 0 & 0 \\ -7 & 5 & -5 & 0 \\ 3 & 2 & 3 & -1 \end{bmatrix}.$$

(a) 11 (b) -30 (c) 30

(d) -11 (e) None of these

9. Use Cramer's Rule to solve for y:

$$\begin{cases} 3x - 2y + 2z = 3 \\ x + 4y - z = 2. \\ x + y + z = 6 \end{cases}$$

(a) $y = \dfrac{\begin{vmatrix} 3 & -2 & 2 \\ 1 & 4 & -1 \\ 1 & 1 & 1 \end{vmatrix}}{\begin{vmatrix} 3 & 3 & 2 \\ 1 & 2 & -2 \\ 1 & 6 & 1 \end{vmatrix}}$

(b) $y = \dfrac{\begin{vmatrix} 3 & 3 & 2 \\ 1 & 2 & -1 \\ 1 & 6 & 1 \end{vmatrix}}{\begin{vmatrix} 3 & -2 & 2 \\ 1 & 4 & -1 \\ 1 & 1 & 1 \end{vmatrix}}$

(c) $y = \dfrac{\begin{vmatrix} 3 & 2 & 3 \\ 1 & -1 & 2 \\ 1 & 1 & 6 \end{vmatrix}}{\begin{vmatrix} 3 & -2 & 2 \\ 1 & 4 & -1 \\ 1 & 1 & 1 \end{vmatrix}}$

(d) $y = \dfrac{\begin{vmatrix} 3 & 3 & -2 \\ 1 & 2 & 4 \\ 1 & 6 & 1 \end{vmatrix}}{\begin{vmatrix} 3 & 1 & 1 \\ -2 & 4 & 1 \\ 2 & -1 & 1 \end{vmatrix}}$

(e) None of these

10. Find the uncoded row matrix of order 1×3 for the message BE BACK SOON,

then encode the message using $A = \begin{bmatrix} 1 & -1 & 0 \\ 1 & 0 & 3 \\ -2 & 1 & -1 \end{bmatrix}$.

(a) -2 15 1 0 -3 -27 -2 8 19 15 -3 1

(b) 7 -2 15 -3 1 0 -27 8 -19 2 -1 31

(c) 2 5 0 2 1 3 11 0 19 15 15 14

(d) 0 2 5 -3 1 0 0 -27 16 2 1 1

(e) None of these

Test C **Name** ______________ **Date** ______________

Chapter 8 **Class** ______________ **Section** ______________

1. Write the matrix in reduced row-echelon form: $\begin{bmatrix} 1 & 3 & -8 & 13 \\ 2 & -1 & 6 & -19 \\ -5 & 1 & 2 & 44 \end{bmatrix}$.

(a) $\begin{bmatrix} 1 & 0 & 0 & -7 \\ 0 & 1 & 0 & 8 \\ 0 & 0 & 1 & \frac{1}{2} \end{bmatrix}$ (b) $\begin{bmatrix} 1 & 0 & 6 & -4 \\ 0 & 1 & 2 & 9 \\ 0 & 0 & 2 & 1 \end{bmatrix}$ (c) $\begin{bmatrix} 1 & 0 & 6 & -4 \\ 0 & 1 & -4 & 6 \\ 0 & 0 & 0 & 0 \end{bmatrix}$

(d) $\begin{bmatrix} 1 & 1 & 8 & 5 \\ 0 & 1 & 2 & 9 \\ 0 & 0 & 2 & 1 \end{bmatrix}$ (e) None of these

2. Use Gaussian elimination with back-substitution or Gauss-Jordan elimination to solve the following system of linear equations.

$$\begin{cases} -2x + 3y - 4z = 4 \\ x - y - 5z = 0 \\ -2x + 4y + 5z = 9 \end{cases}$$

(a) $(-3, 2, -1)$ (b) $(3, -2, -1)$ (c) $(2, 1, 1)$

(d) $(0, 4, 2)$ (e) None of these

3. Given $A = \begin{bmatrix} 2 & 4 & -1 \\ 1 & 0 & 4 \\ 8 & 1 & 2 \end{bmatrix}$ and $B = \begin{bmatrix} 1 & 1 & 1 \\ -1 & 0 & 0 \\ 4 & 10 & -2 \end{bmatrix}$, find $2A - 2B$.

(a) $\begin{bmatrix} 2 & 6 & 4 \\ 4 & 0 & -8 \\ -8 & 18 & 1 \end{bmatrix}$ (b) $\begin{bmatrix} 2 & 6 & -4 \\ 4 & 0 & 8 \\ 8 & -18 & 8 \end{bmatrix}$ (c) $\begin{bmatrix} 0 & 6 & -4 \\ -4 & 0 & 4 \\ 4 & -9 & 0 \end{bmatrix}$

(d) $\begin{bmatrix} 1 & 3 & -2 \\ 0 & 0 & 4 \\ 4 & -9 & 4 \end{bmatrix}$ (e) None of these

4. Use a graphing utility to find BA, given $A = \begin{bmatrix} 2 & 0 & 1 & 2 \\ 0 & 1 & 0 & 1 \\ -1 & -2 & 0 & 0 \end{bmatrix}$ and $B = \begin{bmatrix} 1 & 1 & 0 \\ 0 & 1 & 1 \\ 2 & -1 & 2 \end{bmatrix}$.

(a) $\begin{bmatrix} 2 & 1 & 1 & 3 \\ -1 & -1 & 0 & 1 \\ 2 & -5 & 2 & 3 \end{bmatrix}$ (b) $\begin{bmatrix} 4 & 1 & 2 \\ 0 & 1 & 1 \\ -1 & -3 & -2 \end{bmatrix}$ (c) $\begin{bmatrix} 6 & -4 & 0 \\ 0 & 1 & 1 \\ -4 & -3 & -4 \end{bmatrix}$

(d) Impossible (e) None of these

5. Find the inverse of $A = \begin{bmatrix} 2 & 3 \\ -3 & -3 \end{bmatrix}$.

(a) $\begin{bmatrix} -3 & -3 \\ 3 & 2 \end{bmatrix}$ (b) $\begin{bmatrix} \frac{1}{2} & \frac{1}{3} \\ -\frac{1}{3} & -\frac{1}{3} \end{bmatrix}$ (c) $\begin{bmatrix} \frac{1}{4} & \frac{1}{4} \\ -\frac{1}{4} & -\frac{1}{3} \end{bmatrix}$

(d) $\begin{bmatrix} -1 & -1 \\ 1 & \frac{2}{3} \end{bmatrix}$ (e) None of these

6. Given the system of linear equations with coefficient matrix A, use A^{-1} to find (x, y, z).

$$\begin{cases} 4x - y + z = 5 \\ x - 4y + z = 8 \\ 2x + 2y - 3z = -12 \end{cases} \qquad A^{-1} = \frac{1}{45}\begin{bmatrix} 10 & -1 & 3 \\ 5 & -14 & -3 \\ 10 & -10 & -15 \end{bmatrix}$$

(a) $(0, -1, 4)$ (b) $(0, 4, -2)$ (c) $(1, -1, 2)$

(d) $(3, 0, 2)$ (e) None of these

7. Find the determinant of the matrix: $\begin{bmatrix} 6 & -4 \\ 2 & -1 \end{bmatrix}$.

(a) 2 (b) -2 (c) 14

(d) -14 (e) None of these

8. Use the matrix capabilities of a graphing utility to find the determinant of the matrix:

$$\begin{bmatrix} 1 & 5 & 0 & 6 \\ 0 & -1 & 1 & 0 \\ -2 & 2 & 3 & 0 \\ 0 & 0 & 7 & 2 \end{bmatrix}.$$

(a) -54 (b) 74 (c) -74

(d) 54 (e) None of these

9. Find the determinant of the matrix $\begin{bmatrix} 0 & -1 & 2 \\ 3 & 5 & 0 \\ 1 & -1 & 3 \end{bmatrix}$.

(a) 25 (b) -25 (c) 7

(d) -7 (e) None of these

10. Decode the cryptogram:
129 -85 -38 -75 70 25 -9 18 3 188 -141 -58 using

$A = \begin{bmatrix} 13 & -10 & -4 \\ -6 & 5 & 2 \\ 3 & -2 & -1 \end{bmatrix}$.

(a) WELCOME HOME (b) CLOSING OUT (c) OUT TO LUNCH

(d) PLEASE HURRY (e) None of these

Test D Name ________ Date ________

Chapter 8 Class ________ Section ________

1. Write the matrix in reduced row-echelon form: $\begin{bmatrix} 1 & 2 & -1 & 3 \\ 7 & -1 & 0 & 2 \\ 3 & 2 & 1 & -1 \end{bmatrix}$.

2. Find the equation of the parabola that passes through the given points. Use a graphing utility to verify your result.

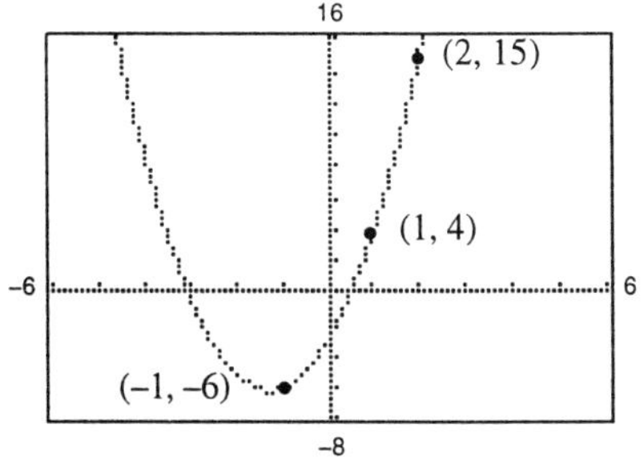

3. If $A = \begin{bmatrix} 2 & -1 \\ -3 & 4 \end{bmatrix}$ and $B = \begin{bmatrix} -2 & 0 \\ -1 & 3 \end{bmatrix}$. Find C if $A + C = 2B$.

4. Given $A = \begin{bmatrix} 3 & 2 & 2 & 1 \\ 13 & 6 & 12 & 1 \\ -5 & -1 & -5 & 0 \end{bmatrix}$ and $B = \begin{bmatrix} 1 & 1 & 0 \\ 3 & 1 & 2 \\ -1 & 1 & -1 \end{bmatrix}$, find BA.

5. Given $A = \begin{bmatrix} 1 & 3 & -1 \\ 0 & 2 & 1 \\ -1 & 1 & -2 \end{bmatrix}$, find A^{-1}.

6. Use an inverse matrix to solve the system of linear equations.

$$\begin{cases} 3x + 2y + z = 1 \\ x - y = 10 \\ -x + 2z = 5 \end{cases}$$

7. Evaluate the determinant: $\begin{vmatrix} x \ln x & x \\ 1 + \ln x & 1 \end{vmatrix}$.

8. Use the matrix capabilities of a graphing utility to evaluate:

$$\begin{vmatrix} 3 & -2 & 4 & 3 \\ 2 & -1 & 0 & 4 \\ -2 & 0 & 1 & 5 \\ -2 & -3 & 0 & 2 \end{vmatrix}.$$

9. Use Cramer's Rule to solve the system of linear equations.

$$\begin{cases} 4x + 6y + 2z = 15 \\ x - y + 4z = -3 \\ 3x + 2y + 2z = 6 \end{cases}$$

10. Use a graphing utility and Cramer's Rule to solve (if possible) the system of equations.

$$\begin{cases} x - y - 2z = 3 \\ y + 3z = -2 \\ 3x + 4y - z = 11 \end{cases}$$

Test E **Name** ______________________ **Date** ____________

Chapter 8 **Class** ______________________ **Section** ____________

1. Write the matrix in reduced row-echelon form: $\begin{bmatrix} 1 & 3 & -8 & 13 \\ 2 & -1 & 6 & -19 \\ -5 & 1 & 2 & 44 \end{bmatrix}$.

2. Find the equation of the parabola that passes through the given points. Use a graphing utility to verify your result.

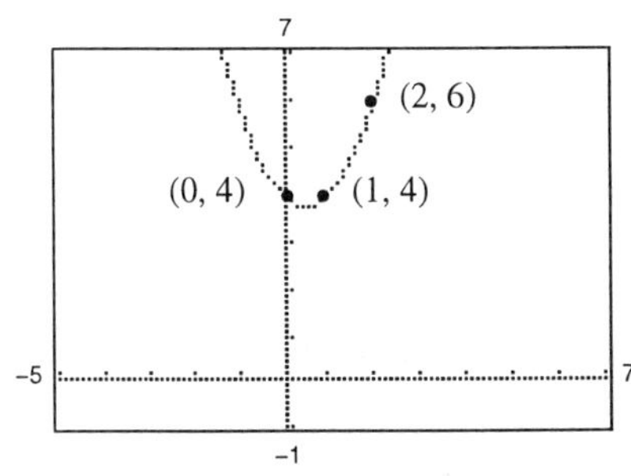

3. Use a graphing utility to find AB, given

$$A = \begin{bmatrix} 1 & 3 & 6 \\ 4 & 1 & 3 \end{bmatrix} \text{ and } B = \begin{bmatrix} 0 & 1 & 6 \\ 3 & -1 & 1 \\ 5 & 2 & 3 \end{bmatrix}.$$

4. Given $A = \begin{bmatrix} 1 & 0 & 3 \\ -1 & 2 & -2 \\ 1 & 1 & 2 \end{bmatrix}$ and $B = \begin{bmatrix} 1 & 1 & 0 \\ 3 & 1 & 2 \\ -1 & 1 & -1 \end{bmatrix}$, find BA.

5. Given $A = \begin{bmatrix} 1 & 5 & -1 \\ 2 & 3 & -2 \\ -1 & -4 & 3 \end{bmatrix}$, find A^{-1}.

6. Use an inverse matrix to solve the system of linear equations.

$$\begin{cases} 6x + 6y - 5z = 11 \\ 3x + 6y - z = 6 \\ 9x - 3y + z = 0 \end{cases}$$

7. Evaluate the determinant: $\begin{vmatrix} e^{2x} & e^{x} \\ 2e^{2x} & e^{x} \end{vmatrix}$.

8. Use the matrix capabilities of a graphing utility to evaluate:

$$\begin{vmatrix} 10 & -3 & 2 & 4 & 5 \\ -1 & 0 & -3 & 2 & 3 \\ 4 & -1 & -2 & 0 & 4 \\ 9 & 4 & -3 & 6 & 2 \\ -2 & 0 & -4 & 4 & 5 \end{vmatrix}.$$

9. Use Cramer's Rule to solve the system of linear equations.

$$\begin{cases} 5x + 5y + 4z = 4 \\ 10x - 5y + 2z = 11 \\ 5x - 5y + 2z = 7 \end{cases}$$

10. Use a graphing utility and Cramer's Rule to solve (if possible) the system of equations.

$$\begin{cases} x + 3y + z = 4 \\ 2x - y - 3z = 1 \\ 4x + y + z = 5 \end{cases}$$

Test A **Name**________________ **Date**__________

Chapter 9 **Class**________________ **Section**__________

1. Write the first 5 terms of the sequence whose nth term is $a_n = (-1)^n(2n + 9)$. (Assume that n begins with 1.)

(a) $-11, -13, -15, -17, -19 \ldots$ (b) $-11, 13, -15, 17, -19, \ldots$

(c) $-11, 2, -13, 4, -15, \ldots$ (d) $-11, -24, -39, -56, -75, \ldots$

(e) None of these

2. Find the sum: $\sum_{n=3}^{6} \frac{3}{n-2}$.

(a) $\frac{12}{9}$ (b) $\frac{25}{4}$ (c) $\frac{3}{16}$

(d) $\frac{1}{2}$ (e) None of these

3. Find a_n for the arithmetic sequence with $a_1 = 5, d = -4$, and $n = 98$. (Assume that n begins with 1).

(a) -392 (b) -387 (c) -383

(d) 393 (e) None of these

4. Find a formula for a_n for the arithmetic sequence with $a_1 = 5$ and $d = -4$. (Assume that n begins with 1.)

(a) $a_n = -4n + 9$ (b) $a_n = -4_n + 5$ (c) $a_n = 5n - 4$

(d) $a_n = 9n - 4$ (e) None of these

5. Write the first five terms of the geometric sequence with $a_1 = -3$ and $r = \frac{2}{3}$.

(a) $-3, -2\frac{1}{3}, -1\frac{2}{3}, -1, -\frac{1}{3}$ (b) $-3, -3\frac{2}{3}, -4\frac{1}{3}, -5, -5\frac{2}{3}$ (c) $-3, -\frac{9}{2}, -\frac{27}{4}, -\frac{81}{8}, -\frac{243}{16}$

(d) $-3, -2, -\frac{4}{3}, -\frac{8}{9}, -\frac{16}{27}$ (e) None of these

6. Find the sum of the infinite geometric sequence: $-7, -\frac{7}{3}, -\frac{7}{9}, -\frac{7}{27}, \ldots$.

(a) -5 (b) $-\frac{21}{4}$ (c) $-\frac{5}{2}$ (d) $-\frac{21}{2}$ (e) None of these

7. Find the sum using the formulas for the sums of powers of integers: $\sum_{n=1}^{8} (n^2 - n^3)$.

(a) -994 (b) -1092 (c) -1296

(d) -1538 (e) None of these

8. Identify S_{k+1} given $S_k = \dfrac{k(2k - 1)}{3}$.

(a) $\dfrac{2k(k + 1)}{3}$ (b) $\dfrac{2k^2 - k + 3}{3}$ (c) $\dfrac{(k + 1)(2k + 1)}{3}$

(d) $\dfrac{2k^2 - k + 1}{3}$ (e) None of these

9. Use the Binomial Theorem to expand, then simplify: $(x - 3)^5$.

(a) $x^5 - 15x^4 + 30x^3 - 30x^2 + 15x - 243$ (b) $x^5 - 15x^4 + 900x^3 - 27{,}000x^2 + 50{,}625x - 243$

(c) $x^5 - 15x^4 + 90x^3 - 270x^2 + 405x - 243$ (d) $x^5 - 3x^4 + 9x^3 - 27x^2 + 81x - 243$

(e) None of these

10. Determine the coefficient of x^5y^7 in the expansion of $(5x + 2y)^{12}$.

(a) 316,800,000 (b) 400,000 (c) 792

(d) 7920 (e) None of these

11. Evaluate: ${}_{10}P_6$.

(a) 5040 (b) 151,200 (c) 210

(d) 60 (e) None of these

12. Determine the number of ways the last four digits of a telephone number can be arranged if the first digit cannot be 0.

(a) 10,000 (b) 5040 (c) 9000 (d) 4536 (e) None of these

13. How many committees of three people can be made from a council of twelve people?

(a) 1320 (b) 220 (c) 1980 (d) 78 (e) None of these

14. A card is drawn at random from a standard deck of 52 playing cards. Find the probability that the card is a 10 or a heart.

(a) $\frac{17}{52}$ (b) $\frac{1}{169}$ (c) $\frac{4}{13}$ (d) $\frac{1}{26}$ (e) None of these

15. A small business college has 800 seniors, 700 juniors, 900 sophomores and 1200 freshmen. If a student is randomly selected, what is the probability that the student is a freshman or senior?

(a) $\frac{1}{4}$ (b) $\frac{1}{54}$ (c) $\frac{5}{12}$

(d) $\frac{5}{9}$ (e) None of these

Test B **Name** ______________________ **Date** ____________

Chapter 9 **Class** ______________________ **Section** ____________

1. Write the first 5 terms of the sequence whose nth terms is $a_n = n!$. (Assume that n begins with 0.)

   (a) 0, 1, 2, 6, 24 (b) 0, 1, 2, 6, 12 (c) 1, 1, 2, 6, 12

   (d) 1, 1, 2, 6, 24 (e) None of these

2. Find the sum: $\sum_{n=1}^{4} \frac{n+1}{n+2}$.

   (a) $\frac{61}{20}$ (b) $\frac{31}{20}$ (c) $\frac{143}{60}$

   (d) $\frac{131}{60}$ (e) None of these

3. Find the 99th term of the arithmetic sequence with $a_1 = 7$ and $d = -3$. (Assume that n begins with 1.)

   (a) -287 (b) -290 (c) -293

   (d) -297 (e) None of these

4. Find a formula for a_n for the arithmetic sequence with $a_3 = 15$ and $d = -2$. (Assume that n begins with 1.)

   (a) $a_n = -2n + 9$ (b) $a_n = -2n + 19$ (c) $a_n = -2n + 21$

   (d) $a_n = -2n + 15$ (e) None of these

5. Find the 20th term of the geometric sequence with $a_1 = 5$ and $r = 1.1$. (Assume that n begins with 1.)

   (a) 1.1665 (b) 37.0012 (c) 33.6375

   (d) 30.5795 (e) None of these

6. Find the sum of the infinite geometric sequence: 1, 0.9, 0.81, 0.729, ...

   (a) 23 (b) 90 (c) 10 (d) 57 (e) None of these

7. Find the sum using the formulas for the sums of powers of integers: $\sum_{n=1}^{50} (n^2 - n)$.

   (a) 42,925 (b) 41,650 (c) 44,100

   (d) 43,150 (e) None of these

8. Identify S_{k+1} given $S_k = k(3k - 1)$.

(a) $(k + 1)(3k + 2)$ (b) $3k(k + 1)$ (c) $k(3k - 1) + 1$

(d) $3k^2 + 1$ (e) None of these

9. Use the Binomial Theorem to expand, then simplify: $(2x - 3)^3$.

(a) $8x^3 - 324x^2 + 324x - 27$ (b) $8x^3 - 36x^2 + 54x - 27$

(c) $2x^3 - 18x^2 + 54x - 27$ (d) $8x^3 - 12x^2 + 27x - 27$

(e) None of these

10. Determine the coefficient of x^3y^5 in the expansion of $(3x + 2y)^8$.

(a) 336 (b) 48,384 (c) 864

(d) 52,488 (e) None of these

11. Evaluate: ${}_{14}P_4$.

(a) 24,024 (b) 8008 (c) 5040

(d) 720 (e) None of these

12. If a license plate number consists of two letters followed by two digits, how many different license plate numbers are possible?

(a) 58,500 (b) 67,600 (c) 256 (d) 24 (e) None of these

13. How many committees of four people can be formed from a council of twelve people?

(a) 11,880 (b) 8,950 (c) 48 (d) 495 (e) None of these

14. A card is drawn at random from a standard deck of 52 playing cards. Find the probability that the card is an ace or spade.

(a) $\frac{17}{52}$ (b) $\frac{4}{13}$ (c) $\frac{1}{52}$ (d) $\frac{2}{13}$ (e) None of these

15. A small business college has 400 seniors, 300 juniors, 500 sophomores and 600 freshmen. If a student is randomly selected, what is the probability that the student is a junior or a senior?

(a) $\frac{1}{4}$ (b) $\frac{2}{9}$ (c) $\frac{7}{18}$

(d) $\frac{1}{27}$ (e) None of these

Test C **Name** ______________ **Date** __________

Chapter 9 **Class** ______________ **Section** __________

1. Write the first 5 terms of the sequence whose nth term is $a_n = 1 - \frac{1}{n}$. (Assume that n begins with 1.)

(a) $\frac{1}{2}, \frac{1}{4}, \frac{1}{8}, \frac{1}{16}, \frac{1}{32}$ (b) $0, \frac{1}{2}, \frac{2}{3}, \frac{3}{4}, \frac{4}{5}$ (c) $0, \frac{1}{2}, \frac{1}{3}, \frac{1}{4}, \frac{1}{5}$

(d) $1, \frac{1}{2}, \frac{2}{3}, \frac{3}{4}, \frac{4}{5}$ (e) None of these

2. Find the sum: $\sum_{i=1}^{4} (1 - i)$.

(a) -3 (b) -6 (c) 6 (d) -5 (e) None of these

3. Find the ninth term of the arithmetic sequence with $a_1 = 4$ and $d = 10$. (Assume that n begins with 1.)

(a) 94 (b) 84 (c) 46 (d) 49 (e) None of these

4. Find a formula for a_n for the arithmetic sequence with $a_2 = 12$ and $d = -3$. (Assume that n begins with 1.)

(a) $a_n = 12n - 3$ (b) $a_n = -3n + 15$ (c) $a_n = -3n + 12$

(d) $a_n = -3n + 18$ (e) None of these

5. Find the 23rd term of the geometric sequence with $a_1 = -23$ and $r = \sqrt{2}$. (Assume that n begins with 1.)

(a) $-47{,}104\sqrt{2}$ (b) $-2048\sqrt{2}$ (c) -2048

(d) $-47{,}104$ (e) None of these

6. Find the sum of the infinite geometric sequence: $1, \frac{1}{3}, \frac{1}{9}, \frac{1}{27}, \ldots$.

(a) $\frac{3}{2}$ (b) 3 (c) $\frac{5}{3}$ (d) $\frac{5}{2}$ (e) None of these

7. Find the sum using the formulas for the sums of powers of integers: $\sum_{n=1}^{15} 4n^2$.

(a) 4960 (b) 1240 (c) 73,810

(d) 74,400 (e) None of these

8. Identify S_{k+1} given $S_k = k^2(k + 1)^2$.

(a) $(k^2 + 1)(k + 2)^2$ (b) $k^2(k + 1)^2 + 1$ (c) $(k + 1)^2(k - 1)^2$

(d) $(k + 1)^2(k + 2)^2$ (e) None of these

9. Use the Binomial Theorem to expand, then simplify: $(3 - 2x)^3$.

(a) $27 - 3x + 3x^2 - 8x^3$ (b) $27 - 9x + 9x^2 - 8x^3$ (c) $27 - 27x + 6x^2 - 8x^3$

(d) $27 - 54x + 36x^2 - 8x^3$ (e) None of these

10. Determine the coefficient of x^2y^7 in the expansion of $(3x - 2y)^9$.

(a) -1152 (b) 1152 (c) 41,472

(d) $-41{,}472$ (e) None of these

11. Evaluate: ${}_7P_4$.

(a) 840 (b) 35 (c) 10,920

(d) 210 (e) None of these

12. An auto license plate is made using two letters followed by three digits. How many license plates are possible?

(a) 676,000 (b) 468,000 (c) 82 (d) 1,757,600 (e) None of these

13. How many committees of three people can be formed from a council of 15 people?

(a) 1485 (b) 2730 (c) 455 (d) 45 (e) None of these

14. A card is chosen at random from a standard deck of 52 playing cards. Find the probability that the card is a heart or a face card.

(a) $\frac{25}{52}$ (b) $\frac{11}{26}$ (c) $\frac{9}{26}$ (d) $\frac{2}{52}$ (e) None of these

15. A small business college has 400 seniors, 300 juniors, 500 sophomores and 600 freshmen. If a student is randomly selected, what is the probability that the student is a freshmen or a senior?

(a) $\frac{2}{27}$ (b) $\frac{5}{9}$ (c) $\frac{1}{4}$

(d) $\frac{5}{18}$ (e) None of these

Test D **Name** ______ **Date** ______

Chapter 9 **Class** ______ **Section** ______

1. Write the first five terms of the sequence whose nth term is $a_n = \frac{n-2}{n^2+1}$. (Assume that n begins with 1.)

2. Use a calculator to find the sum.

$$\sum_{i=1}^{5} (10 - 2i)$$

3. Find a_n for the arithmetic sequence with $a_1 = 12$, $d = \frac{1}{3}$, and $n = 52$. (Assume that n begins with 1.)

4. Find the sum of the first 19 terms of the arithmetic sequence whose nth term is $a_n = n + 1$. (Assume that n begins with 1.)

5. Find the 28th term of the geometric sequence: 2, 2.4, 2.88, 3.456, 4.1472, . . .

6. Find the sum of the infinite geometric sequence with $a_1 = 9$ and $r = 0.7$. (Assume that n begins with 1.)

7. Find the sum using the formulas for the sums of powers of integers: $\sum_{n=1}^{20} 3n^2$.

8. Prove by mathematical induction: $1 + 2 + 2^2 + 2^3 + \cdots + 2^{n-1} = 2^n - 1$.

9. Use the Binomial Theorem to expand, then simplify: $(\sqrt{x} + 2)^3$.

10. Determine the coefficient of the x^2y^7 in the expansion of $(7x - 2y)^9$.

11. Evaluate: ${}_{13}P_6$.

12. In how many distinguishable ways can the letters MISSISSIPPI be arranged?

13. How many different ways can three chocolate, four strawberry, and two butterscotch sundaes be served to nine people?

14. In a group of 10 children, 3 have blond hair and 7 have brown hair. If a child is chosen at random, what is the probability that the child will have brown hair?

15. There are 5 red and 4 black balls in a box. If 3 balls are picked without replacement, what is the probability that at least one of them is red?

Test E
Chapter 9

Name____________________ **Date**____________

Class____________________ **Section**____________

1. Write the first five terms of the sequence whose nth term is $a_n = \dfrac{n!}{(n+2)!}$. (Assume that n begins with 0.)

2. Use a calculator to find the sum.
$$\sum_{k=0}^{5} \frac{k!}{2}$$

3. Find the 30th term of the arithmetic sequence with $a_1 = -5$ and $d = \frac{1}{3}$. (Assume that n begins with 1.)

4. Find a formula for a_n for the arithmetic sequence with $a_2 = 15$ and $d = \frac{3}{2}$. (Assume that n begins with 1.)

5. Find the 14th term of the geometric sequence with $a_1 = -11$ and $r = \sqrt{3}$. (Assume that n begins with 1.)

6. Find the sum of the first 30 terms in the sequence.
$\sqrt{2}, 2\sqrt{2}, 3\sqrt{2}, 4\sqrt{2}, 5\sqrt{2}, \ldots$

7. Find the sum using the formulas for the sums of powers of integers: $\displaystyle\sum_{n=1}^{19} 2n^2$.

8. Use mathematical induction to prove $n < 3^n$ for all positive integers n.

9. Evaluate: ${}_{13}C_6$.

10. Use the Binomial Theorem to expand, then simplify: $(2\sqrt{y} - 3)^4$.

11. Find the coefficient of x^4y^3 in the expansion of $(2x + y)^7$.

12. Find the number of distinguishable permutations using the letters in the word MATHEMATICS.

13. A group of six students are seated in a single row at a football game. In how many different orders can they be seated?

14. A fair coin is tossed four times. What is the probability of getting heads on all four tosses?

15. A sample of nursing homes in a state reveals that 112,000 of 218,000 residents are female. If a nursing home resident is chosen at random from this state, what is the probability that the resident is male?

Test A **Name**________________ **Date**________

Chapter 10 **Class**________________ **Section**________

1. Find the inclination, θ, of the line passing through the points (3, 4) and (−5, 7).

(a) 110.6° (b) 20.6° (c) 159.4° (d) 85.2° (e) None of these

2. Find the focus of the parabola: $y^2 - 4y - 4x = 0$.

(a) (2, −1) (b) (−1, 2) (c) (2, 0)

(d) (3, 0) (e) None of these

3. Find the center of the ellipse: $4x^2 + 9y^2 - 32x + 18y + 37 = 0$.

(a) (16, −9) (b) (−8, 2) (c) (4, −1)

(d) (2, 3) (e) None of these

4. Find the standard equation of the ellipse with vertices (±4, 0) and foci (±3, 0).

(a) $\frac{x^2}{7} + \frac{y^2}{9} = 1$ (b) $\frac{x^2}{16} + \frac{y^2}{9} = 1$ (c) $\frac{x^2}{16} + \frac{y^2}{7} = 1$

(d) $\frac{x^2}{16} - \frac{y^2}{9} = 1$ (e) None of these

5. Find the foci of the hyperbola: $2y^2 - 9x^2 - 18 = 0$.

(a) $(\pm\sqrt{11}, 3)$ (b) $(0, \pm\sqrt{7})$ (c) $(0, \pm\sqrt{11})$

(d) $(\pm\sqrt{7}, 0)$ (e) None of these

6. Identify the graph of $4x^2 - 4y^2 - 6x + 16y - 11 = 0$.

(a) Circle (b) Hyperbola (c) Ellipse

(d) Parabola (e) None of these

7. Find the angle of rotation necessary to eliminate the xy-term: $x^2 + 4xy + y^2 - 1 = 0$.

(a) 30° (b) 45° (c) 53.7° (d) 60° (e) None of these

8. Write the equation $x^2 + 336xy + y^2 = 17$ in terms of the $x'y'$-system.

(a) $\frac{337}{2}(x')^2 - \frac{335}{2}(y')^2 = 17$ (b) $\frac{337}{2}(x')^2 + \frac{335}{2}(y')^2 = 17$

(c) $169(x')^2 - 167(y')^2 = 17$ (d) $169(x')^2 + 167(y')^2 = 17$

(e) None of these

9. Eliminate the parameter and find a corresponding rectangular equation: $x = 3t^2$ and $y = 2t + 1$.

(a) $2x^2 + 3y^2 - 1 = 0$ (b) $2x - 3y + 3 = 0$ (c) $3y^2 - 4x + 1 = 0$

(d) $3y^2 - 4x - 6y + 3 = 0$ (e) None of these

10. Find a set of parametric equations for the curve at the right.

(a) $x = -1 + \sin t$ | (b) $x = 3\cos t + 8$
$y = -1 + 3\sin t$ | $y = 2 + \cos t$

(c) $x = \cos 2t$ | (d) $x = 1 + \cos t$
$y = 2\cos^2 t - 1$ | $y = 3 + \cos t$

(e) None of these

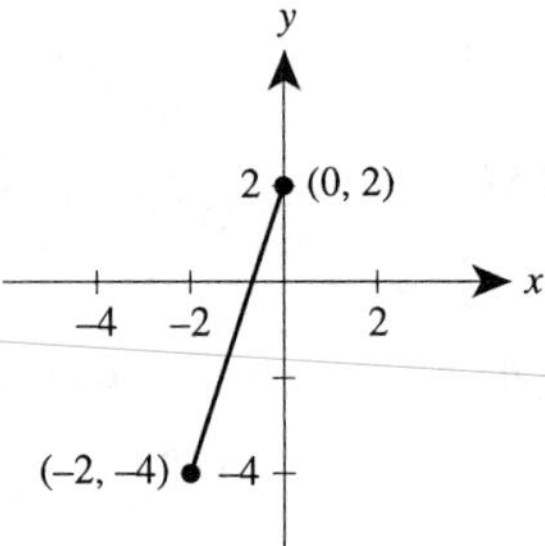

11. In polar coordinates, which of the following is *not* a correct representation for the point $(3, \pi/4)$?

(a) $\left(-3, -\dfrac{3\pi}{4}\right)$ (b) $\left(-3, -\dfrac{\pi}{4}\right)$ (c) $\left(3, \dfrac{9\pi}{4}\right)$

(d) $\left(-3, \dfrac{5\pi}{4}\right)$ (e) None of these

12. Convert from polar to rectangular form: $r \sin \theta = -3$.

(a) $x + 3 = 0$ (b) $y + 3 = 0$ (c) $y^2 + 3 = 0$

(d) $y - 3 = 0$ (e) None of these

13. Find the value(s) of θ for which $|r|$ is a maximum: $r = \cos\left(\theta - \dfrac{\pi}{2}\right)$.

(a) $0, \pi$ (b) $\dfrac{\pi}{2}, \dfrac{3\pi}{2}$ (c) 0

(d) $0, \dfrac{\pi}{2}, \pi, \dfrac{3\pi}{2}$ (e) None of these

14. Find an equation for the graph at the right.

(a) $r = 4 - 3\cos\theta$ (b) $r^2 = 9\cos\theta$

(c) $r = 2\cos 3\theta$ (d) $r = 4 + 3\cos\theta$

(e) None of these

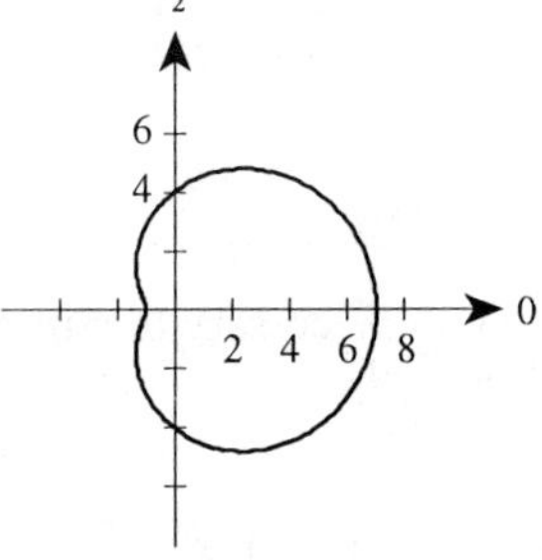

15. Identify the graph: $r = \dfrac{3}{1 + 2\cos\theta}$.

(a) Ellipse (b) Hyperbola (c) Parabola

(d) Circle (e) None of these

Test B **Name**____________________ **Date**____________

Chapter 10 **Class**____________________ **Section**____________

1. Find the inclination, θ, of the line passing through the points $(2, -10)$ and $(-5, -3)$.

(a) 135.0° (b) 61.7° (c) 9.5° (d) 45.0° (e) None of these

2. Find the focus of the parabola: $y^2 - 6y - 12x - 15 = 0$.

(a) $(6, -1)$ (b) $(-2, 6)$ (c) $(1, 3)$
(d) $(5, -3)$ (e) None of these

3. Find the center of the ellipse: $9x^2 + 4y^2 - 36x - 24y - 36 = 0$.

(a) $(2, 3)$ (b) $(3, -2)$ (c) $(2\sqrt{3}, 3\sqrt{3})$
(d) $(6, 48)$ (e) None of these

4. Find an equation of the ellipse with center $(-1, 3)$, vertex $(3, 3)$ and minor axis of length 2.

(a) $\frac{x^2}{16} + \frac{y^2}{4} = 1$ (b) $\frac{x^2}{4} + \frac{y^2}{16} = 1$ (c) $\frac{(x+1)^2}{1} + \frac{(y-3)^2}{16} = 1$
(d) $\frac{(x+1)^2}{16} + \frac{(y-3)^2}{1} = 1$ (e) None of these

5. Find the foci of the hyperbola: $\frac{(x-2)^2}{16} - \frac{(y+1)^2}{9} = 1$.

(a) $(2, 4), (2, -6)$ (b) $(3, -1), (1, -1)$ (c) $(7, -1), (-3, -1)$
(d) $(3, 1), (-7, 1)$ (e) None of these

6. Identify the graph of $6x^2 + 2y^2 - 12x + 4y - 7 = 0$.

(a) Circle (b) Hyperbola (c) Ellipse
(d) Parabola (e) None of these

7. Find the angle of rotation necessary to eliminate the xy-term: $7x^2 + 4xy + 4y^2 + 3 = 0$.

(a) 26.6° (b) 30° (c) 45° (d) 53.1° (e) None of these

8. Write the equation $2x^2 + 24xy - 5y^2 = 9$ in terms of the $x'y'$-system.

(a) $275(x')^2 - 350(y')^2 - 9 = 0$ (b) $11(x')^2 + 14(y')^2 - 9 = 0$
(c) $275(x')^2 + 350(y')^2 = 0$ (d) $11(x')^2 - 14(y')^2 - 9 = 0$
(e) None of these

9. Eliminate the parameter and find a corresponding rectangular equation: $x = 2\cos\theta$ and $y = \cos^2\theta$.

(a) $x + y = \cos\theta(2 + \cos\theta)$ (b) $x - 2y = 0$ (c) $y = \left(1 - \frac{x}{2}\right)^2$
(d) $x^2 = 4y$ (e) None of these

10. Find a set of parametric equations for the curve at the right.

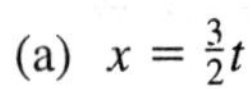

(a) $x = \frac{3}{2}t$ (b) $x = t$

$y = t + 3$ $y = -\frac{2}{3}t + 3$

(c) $x = -\frac{3}{2}t$ (d) $x = t$

$y = t - 3$ $y = \frac{2}{3}t + 3$

(e) None of these

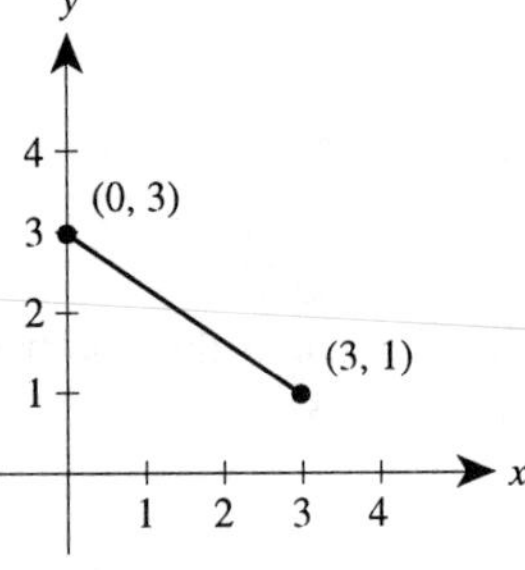

11. In polar coordinates, which of the following is *not* a correct representation for the point $(2, 5\pi/6)$?

(a) $\left(-2, -\frac{\pi}{6}\right)$ (b) $\left(-2, \frac{11\pi}{6}\right)$ (c) $\left(2, -\frac{11\pi}{6}\right)$

(d) $\left(-2, -\frac{7\pi}{6}\right)$ (e) None of these

12. In polar coordinates, which of the following is *not* a correct representation for the point $(2, 5\pi/6)$?

(a) $\left(-2, -\frac{\pi}{6}\right)$ (b) $\left(-2, \frac{11\pi}{6}\right)$ (c) $\left(2, -\frac{11\pi}{6}\right)$

(d) $\left(-2, -\frac{7\pi}{6}\right)$ (e) None of these

13. Find the values for θ for which $|r|$ is a maximum: $r = 5 - 4 \sin \theta$.

(a) $0, \pi$ (b) $\frac{\pi}{2}, \frac{3\pi}{2}$ (c) $\frac{\pi}{2}$

(d) $\frac{3\pi}{2}$ (e) None of these

14. Find an equation for the graph at the right.

(a) $r = 3 \sin 4\theta$ (b) $r^2 = 1 + 4 \sin \theta$

(c) $r = 3 - 4 \cos \theta$ (d) $r^2 = 4 \cos 3\theta$

(e) None of these

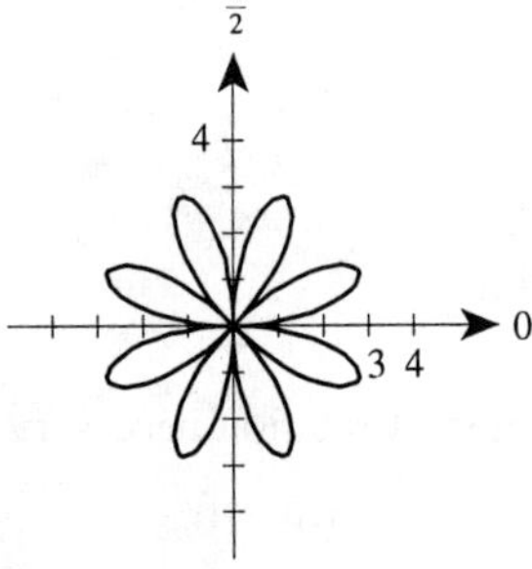

15. Identify the graph: $r = \dfrac{10}{3 - 3 \cos \theta}$.

(a) Parabola (b) Ellipse (c) Hyperbola

(d) Cardioid (e) None of these

Test C **Name** ______________ **Date** __________

Chapter 10 **Class** ______________ **Section** __________

1. Find the inclination, θ, of the line passing through the points $(5, 0)$ and $(-5, 5)$.

(a) 26.6° (b) 153.4° (c) 63.4° (d) 116.6° (e) None of these

2. Find the focus of the parabola: $x^2 + 4x + 2y - 6 = 0$.

(a) $\left(-2, \frac{9}{2}\right)$ (b) $\left(2, -\frac{11}{2}\right)$ (c) $\left(-\frac{5}{2}, 5\right)$

(d) $\left(-2, \frac{11}{2}\right)$ (e) None of these

3. Find the center of the ellipse: $x^2 + 2y^2 - 4x - 16y + 32 = 0$.

(a) $(2, 4)$ (b) $(2, 8)$ (c) $(-2, -4)$

(d) $(4, 8)$ (e) None of these

4. Find the equation of the ellipse with minor axis of length 8 and vertices $(-9, 3)$ and $(7, 3)$.

(a) $4x^2 + 8y^2 - 8x - 48y + 44 = 0$ (b) $16x^2 + 64y^2 + 32x - 384y - 432 = 0$

(c) $64x^2 + 128y^2 - 128x - 768y - 6976 = 0$ (d) $x^2 + y^2 + 8x + 8y + 64 = 0$

(e) None of these

5. Find the foci of the hyperbola: $25x^2 - 4y^2 + 50x + 8y + 121 = 0$.

(a) $\left(-1, 1 \pm \sqrt{29}\right)$ (b) $\left(-1 \pm \sqrt{29}, 1\right)$ (c) $(-1, 4), (-1, -2)$

(d) $\left(1 \pm \sqrt{29}, -1\right)$ (e) None of these

6. Identify the graph of $3x^2 + 3y^2 - 6x + 9y - 10 = 0$.

(a) Circle (b) Hyperbola (c) Ellipse

(d) Parabola (e) None of these

7. Find the angle of rotation necessary to eliminate the xy-term: $xy + 3x - 2y = 0$.

(a) 30° (b) 45° (c) 53.1° (d) 60° (e) None of these

8. Write the equation $x^2 + 24xy - 6y^2 = 5$ in terms of the $x'y'$-system.

(a) $15(x')^2 - 10(y')^2 - 5 = 0$ (b) $10(x')^2 - 15(y')^2 - 5 = 0$

(c) $10(x')^2 + 15(y')^2 - 5 = 0$ (d) $15(x')^2 + 10(y')^2 - 5 = 0$

(e) None of these

9. Eliminate the parameter and find a corresponding rectangular equation: $x = 2\cos\theta$ and $y = 4\sin\theta$.

(a) $4x + 2y = 1$ (b) $16x^2 + 4y^2 = 1$ (c) $4x + 2y = 8$

(d) $16x^2 + 4y^2 = 64$ (e) None of these

10. Find a set of parametric equations for the curve at the right.

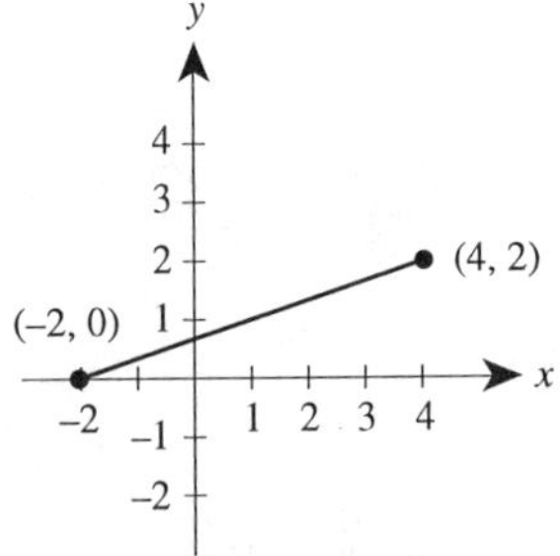

(a) $x = t$, $y = t$ (b) $x = t$, $y = 3t + \frac{2}{3}$

(c) $x = 3t$, $y = t + \frac{2}{3}$ (d) $x = 3t$, $y = 3t + \frac{2}{3}$

(e) None of these

11. In polar coordinates, which of the following are correct representations for the point $(-3, -\pi/3)$?

(a) $\left(3, -\frac{4\pi}{3}\right)$ (b) $\left(3, \frac{2\pi}{3}\right)$ (c) $\left(3, \frac{8\pi}{3}\right)$

(d) $\left(-3, -\frac{8\pi}{3}\right)$ (e) None of these

12. Convert from polar to rectangular form: $r\sin^2\theta = 3\cos\theta$.

(a) $y^2 - 3x = 0$ (b) $xy - 3y = 0$ (c) $x^2 + y^2 - 3x = 0$

(d) $x^2 + y^2 - 9x = 0$ (e) None of these

13. Find the values of θ for which $|r|$ is a maximum: $r = 2 - 4\cos\theta$.

(a) $0, \pi$ (b) $\frac{\pi}{2}, \frac{3\pi}{2}$ (c) π

(d) $\frac{3\pi}{2}$ (e) None of these

14. Find an equation for the graph at the right.

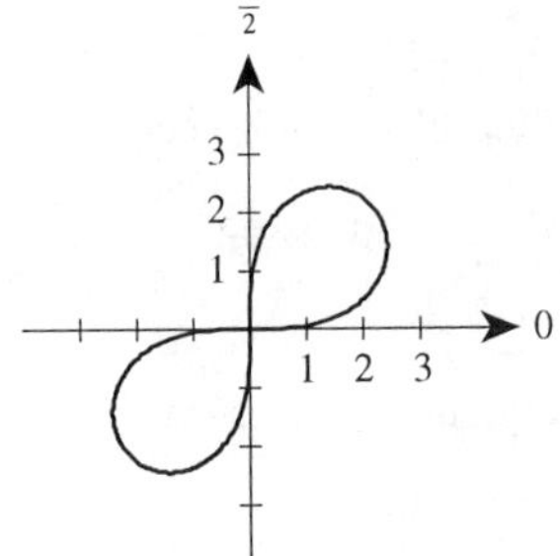

(a) $r^2 = 9\cos 2\theta$ (b) $r = 3 - 3\sin\theta$

(c) $r^2 = 3\cos 2\theta$ (d) $r^2 = 9\sin 2\theta$

(e) None of these

15. Identify the graph: $r = \dfrac{4}{2 + \cos\theta}$.

(a) Ellipse (b) Parabola (c) Hyperbola

(d) Circle (e) None of these

Test D **Name**____________________ **Date**____________

Chapter 10 **Class**____________________ **Section**__________

1. Find the inclination, θ, of the line: $3x + 2y - 7 = 0$.

2. Find the vertex, focus, and directrix of the parabola: $(x + 2)^2 - 16(y - 1) = 0$.

3. Find the center of the ellipse: $5x^2 + 2y^2 - 20x + 24y + 82 = 0$.

4. Find an equation of the ellipse with foci $(0, 2)$ and $(0, 8)$ and vertices $(0, 0)$ and $(0, 10)$.

5. Find the foci of the hyperbola: $4y^2 - 5x^2 - 20 = 0$.

6. Identify the graph of $3x^2 - y^2 - 6x + y - 7 = 0$.

7. Find the angle of rotation necessary to eliminate the xy-term: $2x^2 + 2xy + y^2 + \sqrt{2}x - \sqrt{2}y = 0$.

8. Write the equation $x^2 + 2xy + y^2 - 8\sqrt{2}x + 8 = 0$ in terms of the $x'y'$-system.

9. Eliminate the parameter and find a corresponding rectangular equation:
$x = 1 + \cos\theta$ and $y = 2 - \sin\theta$.

10. Find a set of parametric equations for the curve below.

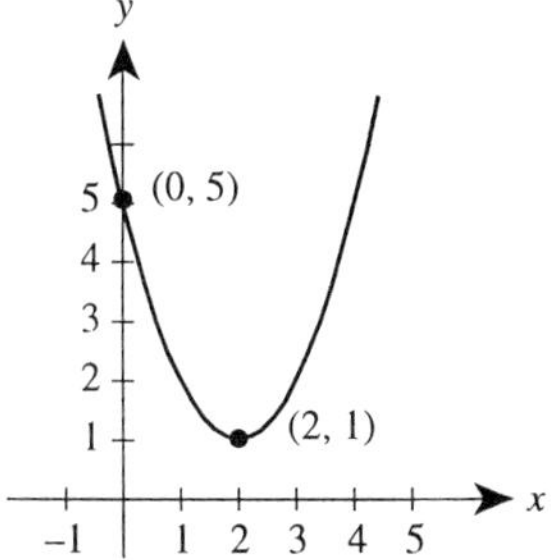

11. Convert from polar to rectangular coordinates: $\left(3, \dfrac{5\pi}{3}\right)$.

12. Convert from polar to rectangular form: $r = 2\cos\theta$.

13. Find the maximum value of $|r|$: $r = 1 + \sin 2\theta$.

14. Sketch the graph of $r = 5\sin 2\theta$.

15. Identify the graph: $r = \dfrac{10}{3 + \cos\theta}$.

Test E **Name** ________________ **Date** ________

Chapter 10 **Class** ________________ **Section** ________

1. Find the inclination, θ, of the line: $7x - 2y - 6 = 0$.

2. Find the vertex, focus, and directrix of the parabola: $x = -\frac{1}{4}(y^2 - 20y + 100)$.

3. Find the center of the ellipse: $36x^2 + 64y^2 - 36x - 96y - 531 = 0$.

4. Write the standard form of the equation of an ellipse with major axis of length $2\sqrt{6}$ and foci $(-3, 1+\sqrt{5})$ and $(-3, 1-\sqrt{5})$.

5. Find the asymptotes of the hyperbola: $16y^2 - 4x^2 - 64 = 0$.

6. Identify the graph of $4x^2 + y^2 - 6x + y - 7 = 0$.

7. Find the angle of rotation necessary to eliminate the xy-term: $8x^2 + 4xy + 3y^2 + 5 = 0$.

8. Write the equation $41x^2 + 24xy + 34y^2 + 25x + 50y - 25 = 0$ in terms of the $x'y'$-system.

9. Eliminate the parameter and find a corresponding rectangular equation: $x = 3 + \cos\theta$ and $y = \sin\theta - 1$.

10. Find a set of parametric equations for the curve below.

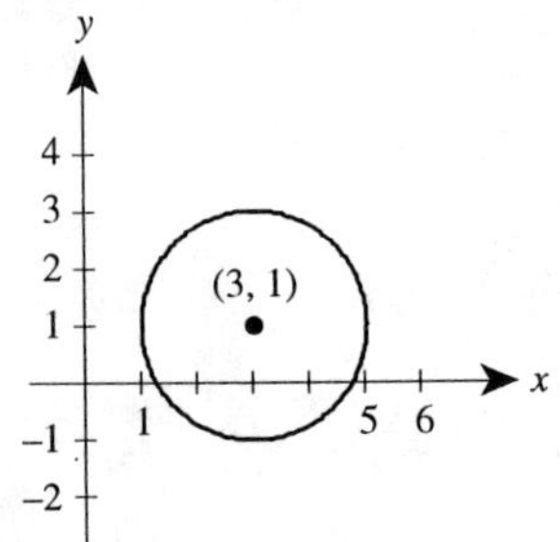

11. Convert from polar to rectangular coordinates: $\left(8, \frac{7\pi}{6}\right)$.

12. Convert from rectangular to polar form: $x^2 + y^2 - 4x + 6y = 0$.

13. Find the maximum value of $|r|$: $r = 15(1 - 2\cos\theta)$.

14. Sketch the graph of $r = 1 - 2\sin\theta$.

15. Identify the graph: $r = \dfrac{1}{2 + 2\cos\theta}$.

Precalculus **Name**____________________ **Date**____________

Multiple Choice **Class**____________________ **Section**__________

1. Simplify: $3x^2(2x)^3(5x^{-1})$.

(a) $30x^{-6}$ (b) $\frac{6}{5}x^6$ (c) $\frac{24}{5}x^4$

(d) $120x^4$ (e) None of these

2. Simplify: $2x^2y\sqrt[3]{2x} + 7x^2\sqrt[3]{2xy^3} - 4\sqrt[3]{16x^7y^3}$.

(a) $x^6y^3\sqrt[3]{2x}$ (b) $x^2y\sqrt[3]{2x}$ (c) $9x^2y\sqrt[3]{2x} - 8y\sqrt[3]{2x^7y}$

(d) $2x^3y$ (e) None of these

3. Factor completely: $3x^4 - 48$.

(a) $3(x - 2)^2(x + 2)^2$ (b) $3(x - 2)^4$ (c) $3x^2(x - 4)^2$

(d) $3(x^2 + 4)(x + 2)(x - 2)$ (e) None of these

4. The solution to the linear equation $2 - 3[7 - 2(4 - x)] = 2x - 1$ is:

(a) $x = -\frac{3}{4}$. (b) $x = \frac{4}{3}$. (c) $x = \frac{3}{4}$.

(d) $x = -\frac{4}{3}$. (e) None of these

5. Solve for x: $3x^2 - 6x + 2 = 0$.

(a) $\dfrac{3 \pm \sqrt{3}}{3}$ (b) $1 \pm \sqrt{3}$ (c) $\dfrac{3 \pm \sqrt{15}}{3}$

(d) $\dfrac{1}{3}, 2$ (e) None of these

6. Solve the inequality: $-16 \le 7 - 2x \le 5$.

(a) $x \le 1$ or $x \ge \frac{23}{2}$ (b) $-1 \le x \le \frac{23}{3}$ (c) $1 \le x \le \frac{23}{2}$

(d) $-\frac{23}{2} \le x \le 1$ (e) None of these

7. Find the equation of the line that passes through $(1, 3)$ and is perpendicular to the line $2x + 3y + 5 = 0$.

(a) $3x - 2y + 3 = 0$ (b) $2x + 3y - 11 = 0$ (c) $2x + 3y - 9 = 0$

(d) $3x - 2y - 7 = 0$ (e) None of these

8. Given $f(x) = x^2 - 3x + 4$, find $f(x + 2) - f(2)$.

(a) $x^2 - 3x + 4$ (b) $x^2 + x$ (c) $x^2 + x - 8$

(d) $x^2 - 3x - 4$ (e) None of these

9. Find the range of the function shown at the right.

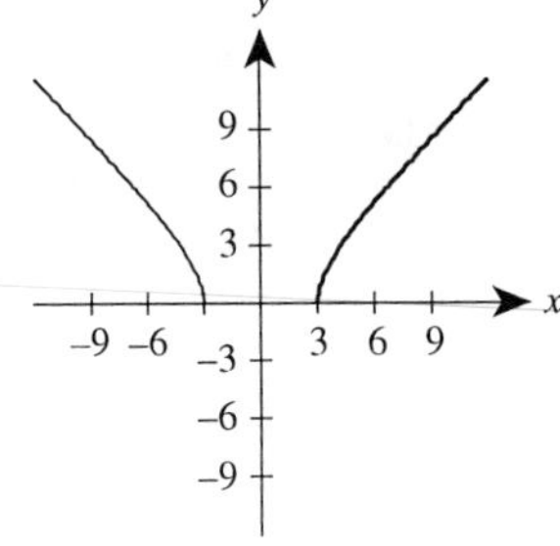

(a) $[-3, 3]$ (b) $(-\infty, -3], [3, \infty)$

(c) $[0, \infty)$ (d) $(-\infty, \infty)$

(e) None of these

10. Given $f(x) = \dfrac{1}{x^2}$ and $g(x) = \sqrt{x^2 + 4}$, find $(f \circ g)(x)$.

(a) $\dfrac{1}{x^2 + 4}$ (b) $\dfrac{1}{\sqrt{x^2 + 4}}$ (c) $x^2 + 4$

(d) $\dfrac{1}{x^2\sqrt{x^2 + 4}}$ (e) None of these

11. Find all the real zeros of the polynomial function: $f(x) = x^3 - 3x^2 - 4x$.

(a) $-1, 4$ (b) $-4, 1$ (c) $-1, 0, 4$ (d) $0, 4$ (e) None of these

12. An open box is made from a 10-inch square piece of material by cutting equal squares with sides of length, x, from all corners and turning up the sides. The volume of the box is $V(x) = 4x(5 - x)^2$. Estimate the value of x for which the volume is maximum.

(a) 2.0 inches (b) 1.7 inches (c) 3.4 inches (d) 2.5 inches (e) None of these

13. Find the vertical asymptote(s): $f(x) = \dfrac{x + 2}{x^2 - 9}$.

(a) $x = 3$ (b) $x = -2, x = -3, x = 3$ (c) $y = 0, x = -2$

(d) $x = -3, x = 3$ (e) None of these

14. Match the rational function with the correct graph: $f(x) = \dfrac{x^2}{x + 2}$.

(a)

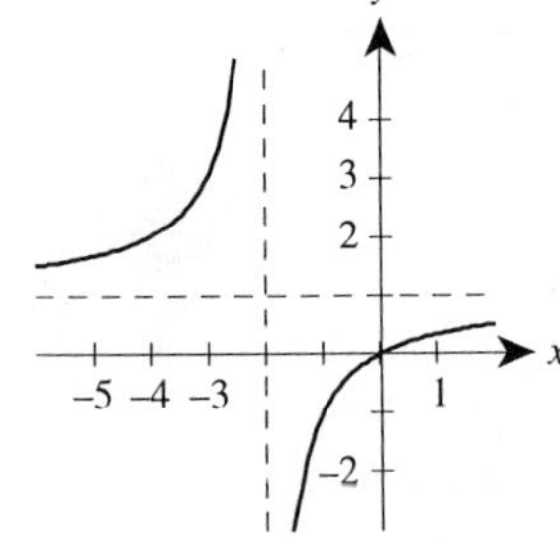

(b)

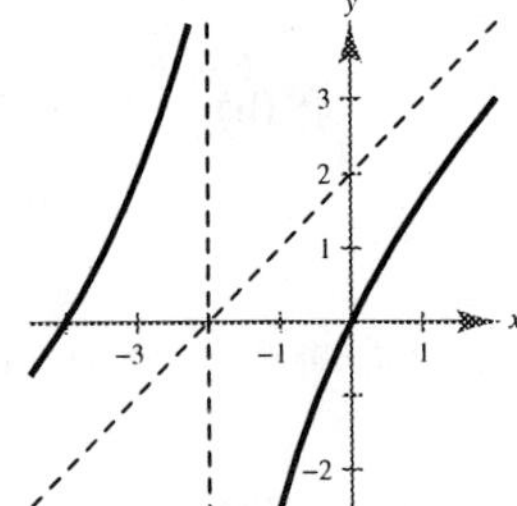

(c)

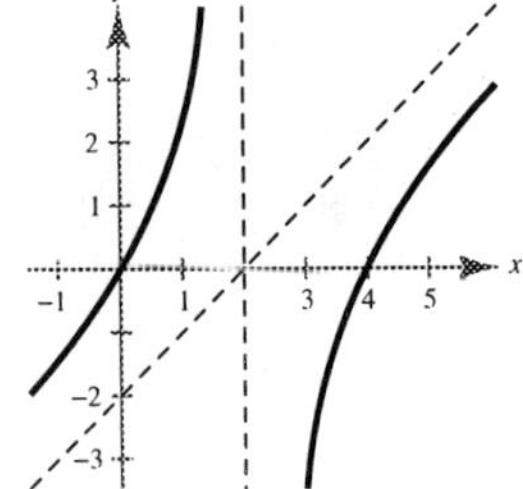

(d)

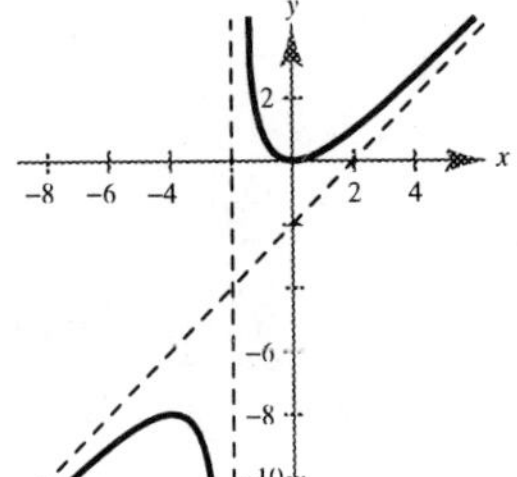

(e) None of these

15. Evaluate when $t = 3$: $y = \dfrac{300}{1 + e^{-2t}}$.

(a) 299.2582   (b) 213.3704   (c) 300.0025

(d) 107.4591   (e) None of these

16. Write as a sum, difference, or multiple of logarithms: $\log_b\left(\dfrac{x^3y^2}{\sqrt{w}}\right)$.

(a) $x^3 + y^3 - \sqrt{w}$ (b) $\dfrac{1}{3}\log_b x + \dfrac{1}{2}\log_b y - 2\log_b w$

(c) $3\log_b x + 2\log_b y - \dfrac{1}{2}\log_b w$ (d) $\dfrac{3\log x + 2\log y}{(1/2)\log w}$

(e) None of these

17. Solve for x: $\log(3x + 7) + \log(x - 2) = 1$.

(a) $\frac{8}{3}$ (b) $3, -\frac{8}{3}$ (c) 2   (d) $2, -\frac{5}{3}$ (e) None of these

18. The yield V (in millions of cubic feet per acre) for the forest at age t years is given by $V = 6.7e^{-48.1/t}$. Find the time necessary to have a yield of 2.1 million cubic feet per acre.

(a) 22.1 years   (b) 25.2 years   (c) 39.8 years   (d) 41.5 years   (e) None of these

19. A right triangle has an acute angle θ such that $\sin\theta = \frac{7}{9}$. Find $\tan\theta$.

(a) $\dfrac{7\sqrt{2}}{8}$ (b) $\dfrac{4\sqrt{2}}{7}$ (c) $\dfrac{\sqrt{130}}{7}$

(d) $\dfrac{9\sqrt{130}}{130}$ (e) None of these

20. Find $\tan\theta$, for the angle θ shown at the right.

(a) $-\dfrac{9\sqrt{130}}{7}$ (b) $\dfrac{\sqrt{130}}{7}$

(c) $-\dfrac{7}{9}$ (d) $-\dfrac{9}{7}$

(e) None of these

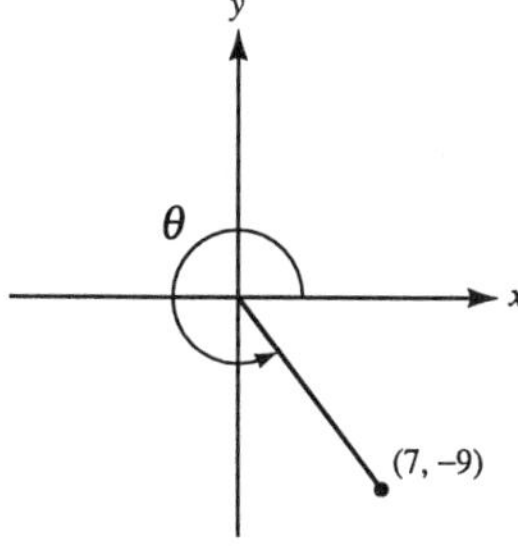

21. Match the graph with the correct function.

(a) $f(x) = 4\sin 2x$ (b) $f(x) = 2\sin 4x$

(c) $f(x) = 4\cos 4x$ (d) $f(x) = 2\cos 2x$

(e) None of these

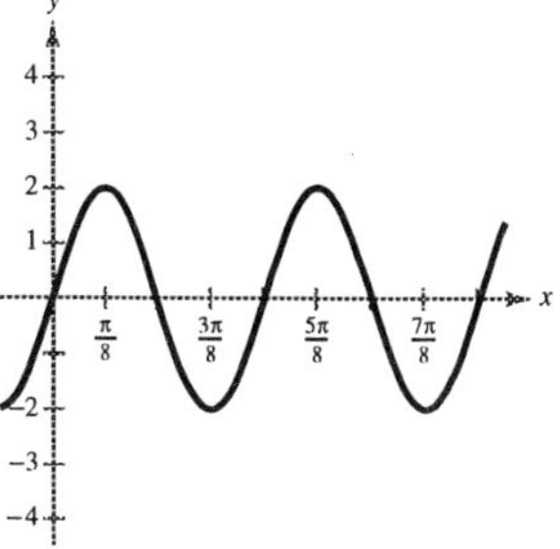

22. Determine the period of the function: $f(x) = \tan \dfrac{x}{2}$.

(a) π (b) 2π (c) $\dfrac{\pi}{2}$ (d) 4π (e) None of these

23. Write an algebraic expression for $\tan(\arcsin x)$.

(a) $\dfrac{x\sqrt{1+x^2}}{1+x^2}$ (b) $\dfrac{1}{x}$ (c) 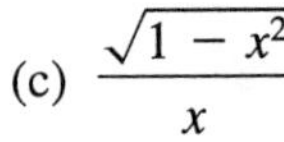 $\dfrac{\sqrt{1-x^2}}{x}$

(d) $\dfrac{x\sqrt{1-x^2}}{1-x^2}$ (e) None of these

24. From a point 300 feet from a building, the angle of elevation to the base of an antenna on the roof is 26.6° and the angle of elevation to the top of the antenna is 31.5°. Determine the height, h, of the antenna. (See figure.)

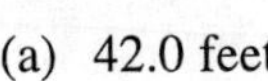
(a) 42.0 feet (b) 29.4 feet

(c) 33.6 feet (d) 45.1 feet

(e) None of these

25. Verify the identity: $\tan^2 x \cos^2 x + \cot^2 x \sin^2 x = 1$.

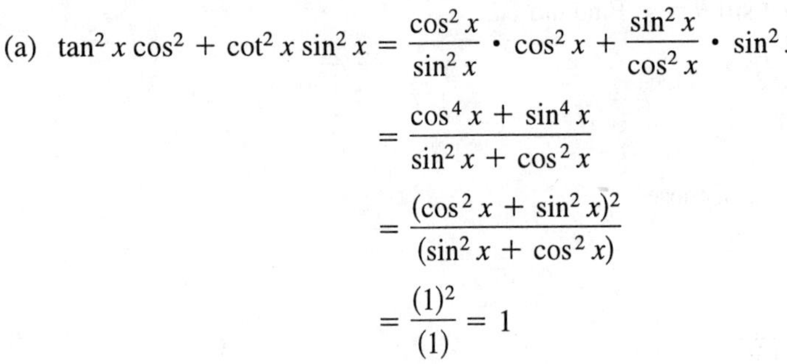

(a) $$\begin{aligned}\tan^2 x \cos^2 + \cot^2 x \sin^2 x &= \frac{\cos^2 x}{\sin^2 x} \cdot \cos^2 x + \frac{\sin^2 x}{\cos^2 x} \cdot \sin^2 x \\ &= \frac{\cos^4 x + \sin^4 x}{\sin^2 x + \cos^2 x} \\ &= \frac{(\cos^2 x + \sin^2 x)^2}{(\sin^2 x + \cos^2 x)} \\ &= \frac{(1)^2}{(1)} = 1\end{aligned}$$

(b) $$\begin{aligned}\tan^2 x \cos^2 x + \cot^2 x \sin^2 x &= (1 - \sec^2 x)\cos^2 x + (1 - \csc^2 x)\sin^2 x \\ &= \cos^2 x - \cos^2 x \sec^2 + \sin^2 x - \sin^2 x \csc^2 x \\ &= \cos^2 x - \cos^2 x\left(\frac{1}{\cos^2 x}\right) + \sin^2 x - \sin^2 x\left(\frac{1}{\sin^2 x}\right) \\ &= \cos^2 x + \sin^2 x = 1\end{aligned}$$

(c) $$\begin{aligned}\tan^2 x \cos^2 x + \cot^2 x \sin^2 x &= \frac{\sin^2 x}{\cos^2 x} \cdot \cos^2 x + \frac{\cos^2 x}{\sin^2 x} \cdot \sin^2 x \\ &= \sin^2 x + \cos^2 x = 1\end{aligned}$$

(d) All of these are correct verifications.

(e) None of these

26. Find all solutions in the interval $[0, 2\pi)$: $2\sin^3 x + \sin^2 x = 0$.

(a) $\frac{5\pi}{6}, \frac{11\pi}{6}$ (b) $\frac{4\pi}{3}, \frac{5\pi}{3}$ (c) $0, \frac{7\pi}{6}, \pi, \frac{11\pi}{6}$

(d) $0, \frac{\pi}{2}, \pi, \frac{4\pi}{3}, \frac{3\pi}{2}, \frac{5\pi}{3}$ (e) None of these

27. Simplify: $\sin\left(\frac{4\pi}{3} - x\right) + \cos\left(x + \frac{5\pi}{6}\right)$.

(a) $\cos x - \sin x$ (b) $-\sqrt{3}\cos x$ (c) $\sin x - \sqrt{3}\cos x$

(d) $\sin x$ (e) None of these

28. Find all solutions in the interval $[0, 2\pi)$: $\cos 2x + \sin x = 0$.

(a) $0, \frac{\pi}{4}, \frac{3\pi}{4}$ (b) $\frac{\pi}{2}, \frac{7\pi}{6}, \frac{11\pi}{6}$ (c) $\frac{\pi}{6}, \frac{5\pi}{6}, \frac{3\pi}{2}$

(d) $0, \frac{\pi}{4}, \frac{3\pi}{4}, \frac{5\pi}{4}, \frac{7\pi}{4}$ (e) None of these

29. Given a triangle with $C = 72°$, $A = 15°$, and $b = 342.6$, find a.

(a) 1258.92 (b) 88.79 (c) 6323.1

(d) 326.28 (e) None of these

30. Ship A is 72 miles from a lighthouse on the shore. Its bearing from the lighthouse is N 15° E. Ship B is 81 miles from the same lighthouse. Its bearing from the lighthouse is N 52° E. Find the number of miles between the two ships.

(a) 84.57 (b) 44.44 (c) 49.29 (d) 90.75 (e) None of these

31. Given **v** of magnitude 50 and direction 315°, and **w** of magnitude 20 and direction 210°, find **v** + **w**.

(a) 18.0**i** − 45.4**j** (b) 52.7**i** − 25.4**j** (c) 18.0**i** − 25.4**j**

(d) 52.7**i** − 45.4**j** (e) None of these

32. Find all points of intersection of the graphs:

$$\begin{cases} x^2 + y^2 = 3 \\ 2x^2 - y = 0 \end{cases}$$

(a) $\left(\frac{3}{2}, -2\right)$ (b) $\left(\pm\frac{\sqrt{3}}{2}, \frac{3}{2}\right)$ (c) $\left(\pm\frac{\sqrt{3}}{2}, \frac{3}{2}\right), (\pm 1, -2)$

(d) $(2, 14)$ (e) None of these

33. If $A = \begin{bmatrix} 2 & -1 \\ 3 & 1 \end{bmatrix}$ and $B = \begin{bmatrix} 4 & 0 \\ -1 & -1 \end{bmatrix}$, find $B - 2A$.

(a) -14

(b) $\begin{bmatrix} -6 & -1 \\ 5 & 3 \end{bmatrix}$

(c) $\begin{bmatrix} 0 & -2 \\ -7 & -3 \end{bmatrix}$

(d) $\begin{bmatrix} 0 & 2 \\ -7 & -3 \end{bmatrix}$

(e) None of these

34. Use Cramer's Rule to solve for y in the system of linear equations:

$$\begin{cases} 3x + 2y - 10z = 5 \\ x - y + z = 10. \\ -7x + 2z = 1 \end{cases}$$

(a) $y = \dfrac{\begin{vmatrix} 3 & 5 & -10 \\ 1 & 10 & 1 \\ -7 & 1 & 2 \end{vmatrix}}{\begin{vmatrix} 3 & 2 & -10 \\ 1 & -1 & 1 \\ -7 & 0 & 2 \end{vmatrix}}$

(b) $y = \dfrac{\begin{vmatrix} 3 & 2 & -10 \\ 1 & -1 & 1 \\ -7 & 0 & 2 \end{vmatrix}}{\begin{vmatrix} 3 & 2 & -10 \\ 1 & 10 & 1 \\ -7 & 1 & 2 \end{vmatrix}}$

(c) $y = \dfrac{\begin{vmatrix} 2 & 5 \\ -1 & 10 \\ 0 & 1 \end{vmatrix}}{\begin{vmatrix} 3 & -10 \\ 1 & 1 \\ -7 & 2 \end{vmatrix}}$

(d) $y = 5\begin{vmatrix} 3 & 2 & -10 \\ 1 & -1 & 1 \\ -7 & 0 & 2 \end{vmatrix} + 10\begin{vmatrix} 3 & 2 & -10 \\ 1 & -1 & 1 \\ -7 & 0 & 2 \end{vmatrix} + 1\begin{vmatrix} 3 & 2 & -10 \\ 1 & -1 & 1 \\ -7 & 0 & 2 \end{vmatrix}$

(e) None of these

35. Use sigma notation to write the sum: $\frac{2}{3} + \frac{4}{4} + \frac{6}{5} + \frac{8}{6} + \cdots + \frac{14}{9}$.

(a) $\displaystyle\sum_{n=1}^{7} \frac{2n}{n+2}$

(b) $\displaystyle\sum_{n=2}^{8} \frac{n+2}{n+1}$

(c) $\displaystyle\sum_{n=0}^{6} \frac{n+2}{n+3}$

(d) $\displaystyle\sum_{n=3}^{9} \frac{n-1}{n}$

(e) None of these

36. How many different ways (subject orders) can three algebra books, two trigonometry books and two calculus books be arranged on a shelf?

(a) 5040

(b) 210

(c) 128

(d) 823,543

(e) None of these

37. Two cards are randomly selected from a standard deck of 52 playing cards. Find the probability that one card will be an ace and the other will be a 10.

(a) $\frac{1}{52}$

(b) $\frac{8}{663}$

(c) $\frac{1}{169}$

(d) $\frac{2}{13}$

(e) None of these

38. Find the standard form of the equation of the ellipse with center $(-1, 3)$, vertex $(3, 3)$ and minor axis of length 2.

(a) $\frac{x^2}{16} + \frac{y^2}{4} = 1$ (b) $\frac{x^2}{4} + \frac{y^2}{16} = 1$ (c) $\frac{(x+1)^2}{1} + \frac{(y-3)^2}{16} = 1$

(d) $\frac{(x+1)^2}{16} + \frac{(y-3)^2}{1} = 1$ (e) None of these

39. Eliminate the parameter and find a corresponding rectangular equation: $x = 3t^2$ and $y = 2t + 1$.

(a) $2x^2 + 3y^2 - 1 = 0$ (b) $2x - 3y + 3 = 0$ (c) $3y^2 - 4x + 1 = 0$

(d) $3y^2 - 4x - 6y + 3 = 0$ (e) None of these

40. Find an equation for the graph at the right.

(a) $r = 5 + 4 \sin \theta$ (b) $r = 4 - 5 \sin \theta$

(c) $r = 4 + 5 \sin \theta$ (d) $r = 5 - 4 \sin \theta$

(e) None of these

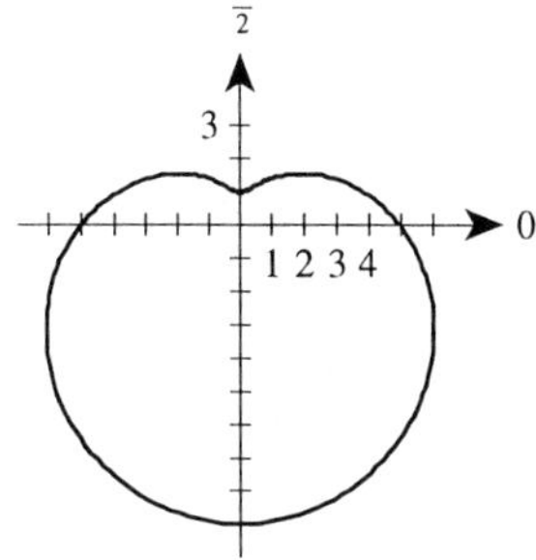

Precalculus Name ____________ Date ________

Open Ended Class ____________ Section ________

1. Simplify: $(-2x^2)^5(5x^3)^{-2}$.

2. Simplify: $3\sqrt[3]{4x^5y^3} + 7x\sqrt[3]{32x^2y^6}$.

3. Factor: $4x^3 + 6x^2 - 10x$.

4. Solve the equation: $3x - [5 - 2(1 - 2x)] = 7x - 5$.

5. Solve for x: $\dfrac{1}{x-1} + \dfrac{x}{x+2} = 2$.

6. Graph the solution: $-16 \le 7 - 2x < 5$.

7. Find the equation of the line that passes through $(-3, -2)$ and is parallel to the line $3x + 2y - 5 = 0$.

8. Given $f(x) = 3x - 7$, find $f(x + 1) + f(2)$.

9. Find the domain and range of the function shown at the right.

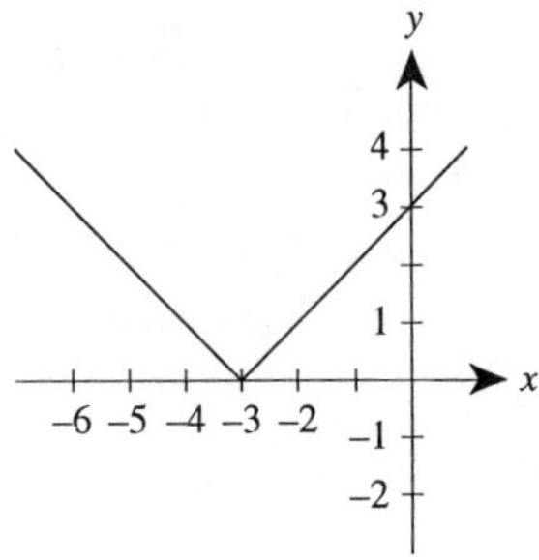

10. Given $f(x) = x^3 + 4$ and $g(x) = \sqrt[3]{x}$, find $(f \circ g)(-3)$.

11. Find all the real zeros of the polynomial function: $f(x) = 9x^4 - 37x^2 + 4$.

12. An open box is to be made from a 16-inch square piece of material by cutting equal squares from each corner and turning up the sides. Verify the volume of the box is $V(x) = 4x(8 - x)^2$. Graph the function using a graphing utility and use the graph to estimate the value of x for which $V(x)$ is maximum.

13. Find the vertical asymptote(s): $f(x) = \dfrac{x^2 - 9}{x^2 - 6x + 8}$.

14. Sketch the graph of $f(x) = \dfrac{x}{x^2 - 1}$. Label all intercepts and asymptotes.

15. Evaluate when $x = 65$: $200 - 5e^{0.002x}$.

16. Write as a sum, difference, or multiple of logarithms: $\ln \dfrac{5x}{\sqrt[3]{x^2 + 1}}$.

17. Solve for x: $\log x + \log(x + 3) = 1$.

18. The yield V (in millions of cubic feet per acre) for the forest at age t years is given by $V = 6.7e^{-48.1/t}$. Find the time necessary to have a yield of 1.7 million cubic feet per acre.

19. Use the triangle shown at the right to find $\tan \theta$.

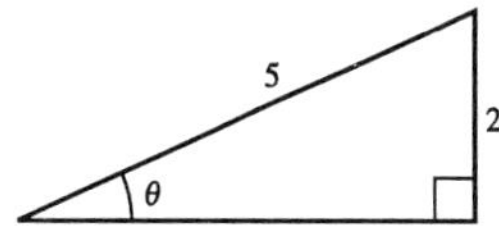

20. Find $\csc \theta$ for the angle θ shown at the right.

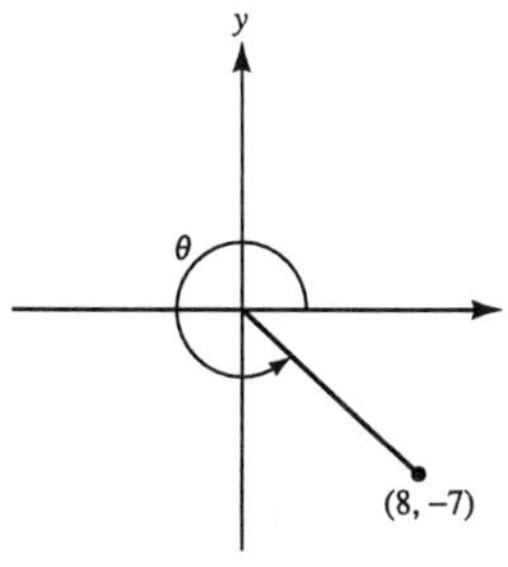

21. Sketch the graph of the function: $f(x) = 4 \sin(2x - \pi)$.

22. Determine the period of the function: $f(x) = 3 \tan 7x$.

23. Use an inverse trigonometric function to write θ as a function of x (see figure).

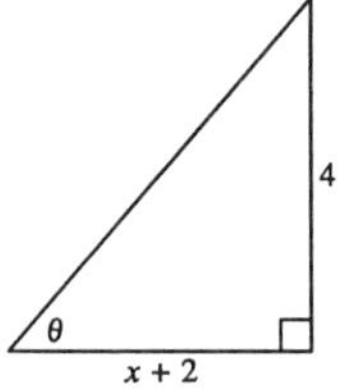

24. The angle of depression from the top of one building to the foot of a building across the street is 63°. The angle of depression to the top of the same building is 33°. The two buildings are 40 feet apart. What is the height of the shorter building? (See figure.)

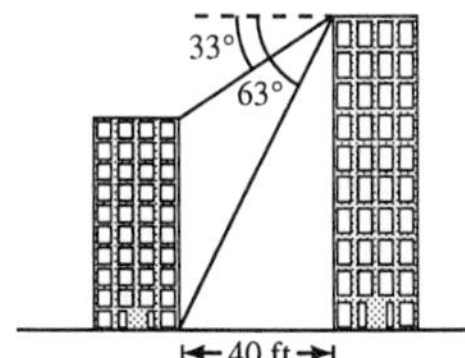

25. Verify the identity: $\sin x\left(\dfrac{\sin x}{1 - \cos x} + \dfrac{1 - \cos x}{\sin x}\right) = 2$.

26. Find all solutions in the interval $[0, 2\pi)$: $2 \sin^2 2x + 5 \sin 2x - 3 = 0$.

27. Simplify: $\sin\left(x + \frac{3\pi}{2}\right)\cos x$.

28. Find the exact zeros of the function in the interval $[0, 2\pi)$. Use a graphing utility to graph the function and verify the zeros.

$$f(x) = \sin 4x + \sin 2x.$$

29. Given a triangle with $A = 39°$, $B = 106°$, and $c = 78$, find a.

30. A boat leaves a port and sails 16 miles at a bearing of S 20° E. Another boat leaves the same port and sails 12 miles at a bearing of S 60° W. How far apart are the two boats at this point?

31. Given **v** of magnitude 100 and direction 172°, and **w** of magnitude 300 and direction 310°, find **v** + **w**.

32. Use a graphing utility to find all points of intersection of the graphs:

$$\begin{cases} x^2 - 4x + y = 0 \\ x - y = 0 \end{cases}.$$

33. If $A = \begin{bmatrix} 2 & -1 \\ -3 & 4 \end{bmatrix}$ and $B = \begin{bmatrix} -2 & 0 \\ -1 & 3 \end{bmatrix}$, find C if $A + C = 2B$.

34. Use Cramer's Rule to solve the system of linear equations.

$$\begin{cases} 4x + 6y + 2z = 15 \\ x - y + 4z = -3 \\ 3x + 2y + 2z = 6 \end{cases}$$

35. Use sigma notation to write the sum: $\frac{1}{2} + \frac{2}{6} + \frac{3}{24} + \frac{4}{120} + \frac{5}{720}$.

36. How many different ways can three chocolate, four strawberry, and two butterscotch sundaes be served to nine people?

37. In a group of 10 children, 3 have blond hair and 7 have brown hair. If a child is chosen at random, what is the probability that the child will have brown hair?

38. Write the standard form of the equation of the ellipse with major axis of length $2\sqrt{6}$ and foci $(-3, 1+\sqrt{5})$ and $(-3, 1-\sqrt{5})$.

39. Eliminate the parameter and find a corresponding rectangular equation: $x = 3 + \cos\theta$ and $y = \sin\theta - 1$.

40. Sketch the graph of $r = 1 - 2\sin\theta$.

PART 3 Answer Keys to Chapter Tests and Final Exams

Answers to CHAPTER P Tests

Test A

1. c **2.** c **3.** b **4.** a

5. a **6.** a **7.** d **8.** c

9. a **10.** d **11.** a **12.** b

Test B

1. c **2.** c **3.** a **4.** a

5. c **6.** e **7.** d **8.** b

9. c **10.** b **11.** b **12.** d

Test C

1. c **2.** d **3.** b **4.** d

5. b **6.** a **7.** a **8.** a

9. c **10.** b **11.** c **12.** c

Test D

1. $2x^4, -3x^2, 2x, 1$ **2.** $\dfrac{1}{9x^3y^2z^2}$ **3.** $(3 + 14y)xy\sqrt[3]{4x^2}$ **4.** $-4x^2 + 5x + 5$

5. $8x^3 - 12x^2 + 6x - 1$ **6.** $(2x - 3)(7x + 1)$ **7.** $\dfrac{x}{4(x + 2)}$

8. $x = \dfrac{1}{4}$ **9.** $\dfrac{3 \pm \sqrt{3}}{2}$ **10.**

$\frac{5}{2}$
−3 −2 −1 0 1 2 3 x

11. $[-6, 6]$ **12.** $3\sqrt{2}$

Test E

1. $6x^3, -2x^2, 4x, -3$ **2.** $-\dfrac{32x^4}{25}$ **3.** $3xy^3\ \sqrt[3]{6x^2y^2}$

4. $2x^3 - 3x^2 - 2x$ **5.** $x^2 - 2x + 1 + 2xy - 2y + y^2$ **6.** $(5x + 2)(7x - 1)$

7. $\dfrac{x + 2}{4(x + 3)}$ **8.** $x = -\dfrac{1}{3}$ **9.** $\dfrac{2 \pm \sqrt{22}}{3}$ **10.**

1 $\frac{23}{2}$
0 2 4 6 8 10 12 x

11. $[-2, 2]$ **12.** $4\sqrt{2}$

Answers to CHAPTER 1 Tests

Test A

1. b	**2.** c	**3.** b	**4.** c
5. a	**6.** d	**7.** b	**8.** d
9. a	**10.** d	**11.** d	**12.** a
13. a	**14.** e	**15.** d	

Test B

1. b	**2.** c	**3.** b	**4.** e
5. b	**6.** d	**7.** c	**8.** c
9. b	**10.** b	**11.** d	**12.** d
13. e	**14.** d	**15.** b	

Test C

1. b	**2.** e	**3.** d	**4.** e
5. b	**6.** d	**7.** b	**8.** b
9. d	**10.** c	**11.** a	**12.** b
13. a	**14.** e	**15.** b	

Test D

1. $2x - y - 1 = 0$

2. $y = 2x + 1$

3. $S = 75{,}000t + 75{,}000$

4. a; in b some values of x yield more than one y.

5. $-k^2$

6. All real x

7. Domain: all real x; Range: $f(x) \le 3$

8. $(-\infty, 0), (1, \infty)$

9. $2\sqrt{3}, -2\sqrt{3}$

10.

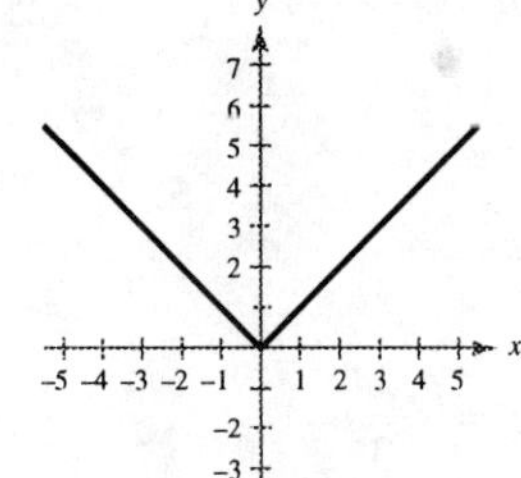

11.

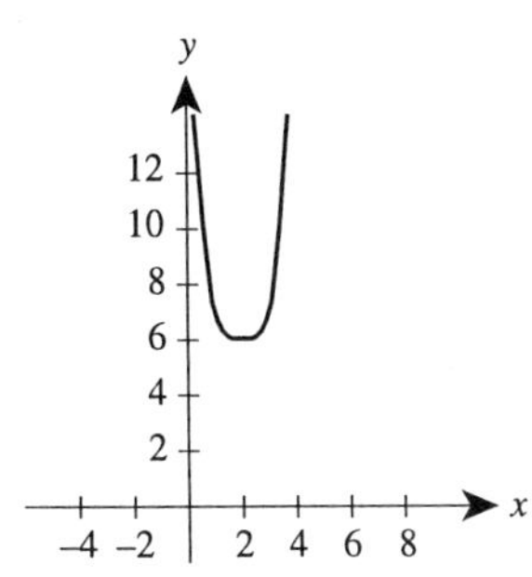

12.

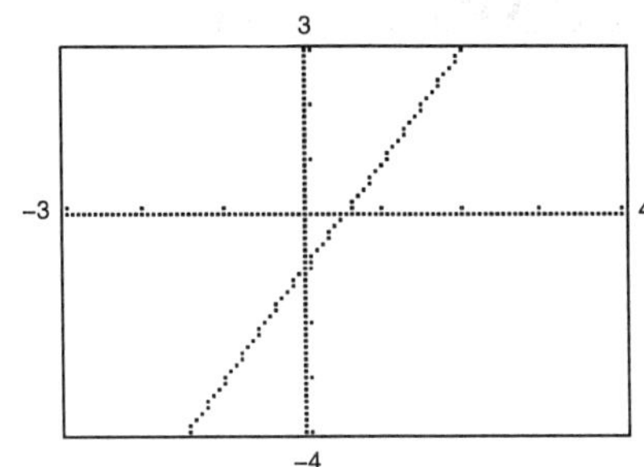

13. 9

14. Yes, they are inverses of each other.

15. $f^{-1}(x) = \sqrt{\dfrac{x-1}{2}}$

Test E

1. $9x - 4y + 1 = 0$

2. $y = 3x - 4$

3. $E = 1225t + 2800$

4. a; in b some values *of x* yield more than one *y*.

5. $1 - 2k$

6. All real, $x \neq 0, 5$

7. Domain: all real x; Range: $f(x) \leq 3$

8. $(-\infty, -1), (-1, 0)$

9. $2, -2$

10.

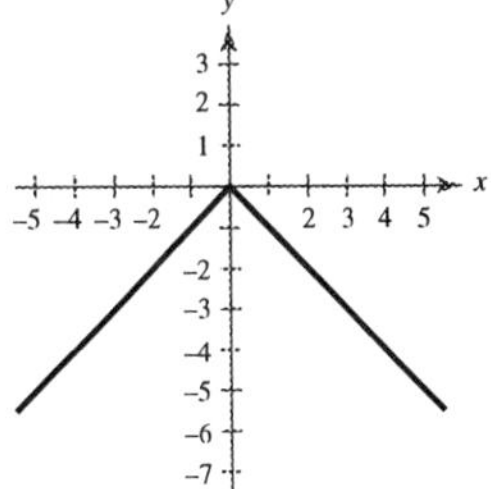

11.

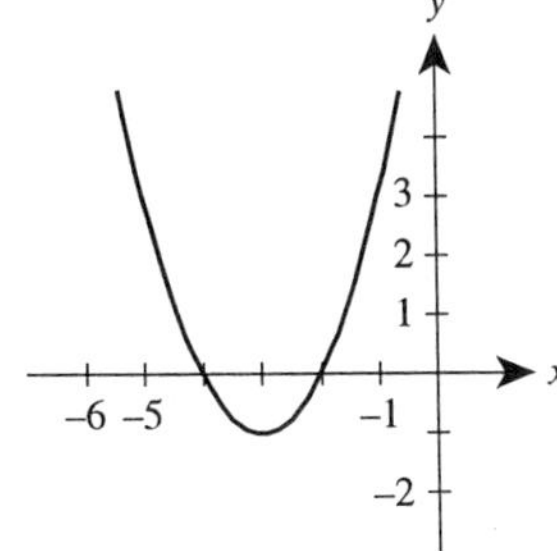

12.

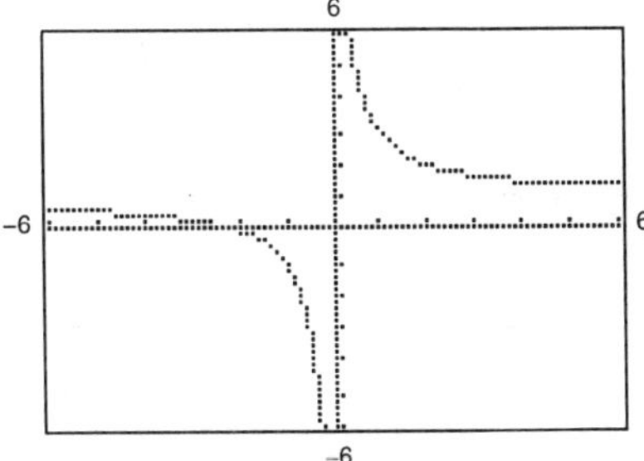

13. 1

14. No, they are not inverses of each other.

15. $f^{-1}(x) = \dfrac{3x - 1}{2}$

Answers to CHAPTER 2 Tests

Test A

1. c
2. b
3. c
4. b
5. c
6. a
7. d
8. c
9. c
10. a
11. a
12. c
13. d

Test B

1. b
2. d
3. a
4. d
5. b
6. c
7. c
8. b
9. b
10. d
11. d
12. d
13. b

Test C

1. d
2. b
3. a
4. b
5. b
6. b
7. a
8. d
9. c
10. d
11. c
12. c
13. d

Test D

1. $y = -\left(x - \frac{3}{2}\right)^2 + \frac{1}{4}$

2. 80 feet by 160 feet

3. Up to the left, down to the right

4. 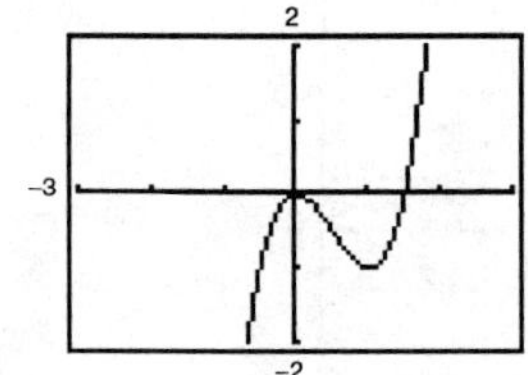

5. $2x^3 - 2x^2 + x + 3 - \dfrac{4}{3x + 1}$

6. $\pm\frac{1}{3}, \pm\frac{2}{3}, \pm1, \pm\frac{4}{3}, \pm2, \pm4;$

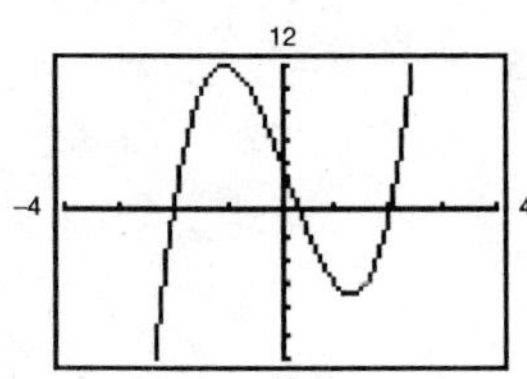

$x = 2, \frac{1}{3}, -2$

7. $-2 - 23i$

8. $\frac{1}{5}\left(1 \pm \sqrt{29}i\right)$

9. $(x + 2)(x - 2)(x + 2i)(x - 2i)$

10. $y = 3$

11. $x = 2, x = 4$

12.

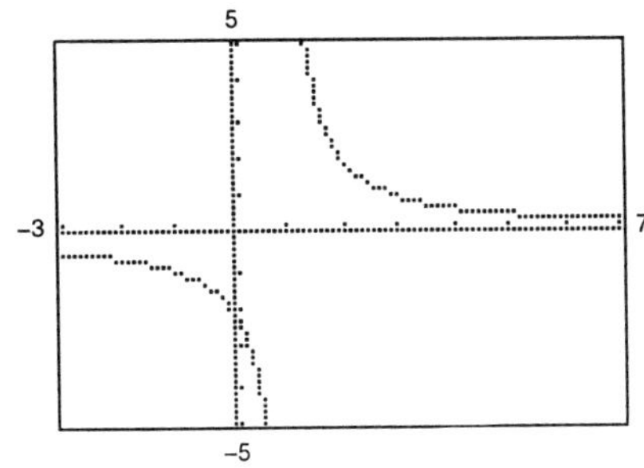

13. $\frac{1}{x} - \frac{3}{2x + 1}$

Test E

1. $f(x) = -(x - 3)^2 - 1$

2. 90 feet by 180 feet

3. Up to the left and right

4.

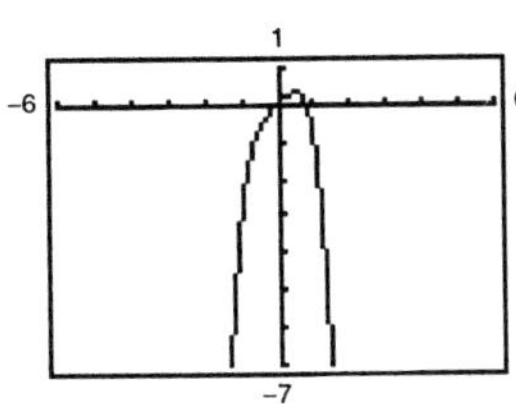

5. $2x^2 - 6 + \frac{7x + 16}{x^2 + 3}$

6. $\pm\frac{1}{2}, \pm 1, \pm\frac{3}{2}, \pm 3, \pm\frac{9}{2}, \pm 9$;

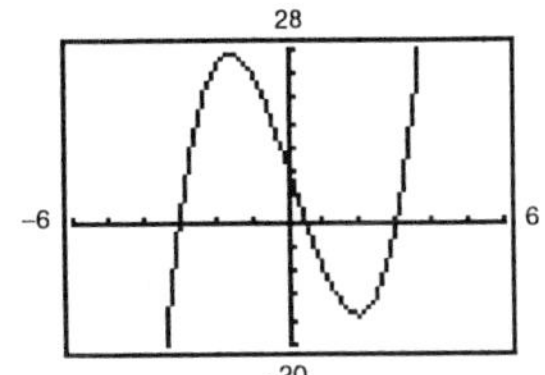

$x = -3, \frac{1}{2}, 3$

7. $-\frac{20}{29} + \frac{21}{29}i$

8. $\frac{1}{3}(1 \pm \sqrt{2}i)$

9. $(x + \sqrt{10})(x - \sqrt{10})(x + \sqrt{10}i)(x - \sqrt{10}i)$

10. $y = 1$

11. $x = 1, x = 5$

12.

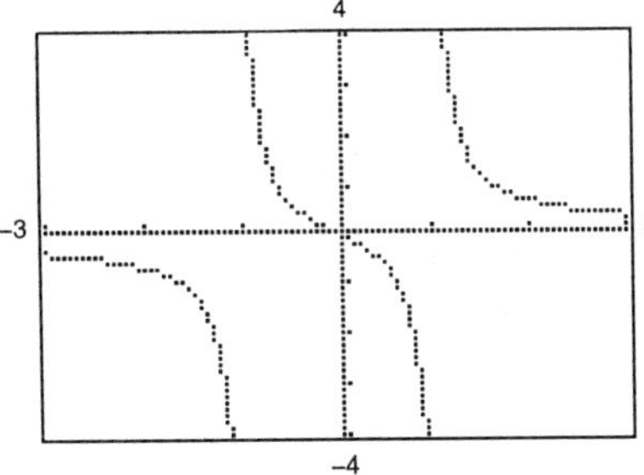

13. $\frac{2}{x} + \frac{1}{3x - 1}$

Answers to CHAPTER 3 Tests

Test A

1. a	**2.** d	**3.** c	**4.** d
5. d	**6.** d	**7.** b	**8.** b
9. c	**10.** a	**11.** b	**12.** c

Test B

1. b	**2.** c	**3.** b	**4.** b
5. a	**6.** e	**7.** a	**8.** d
9. a	**10.** b	**11.** a	**12.** b

Test C

1. d	**2.** c	**3.** a	**4.** a
5. d	**6.** b	**7.** d	**8.** a
9. d	**10.** b	**11.** b	**12.** b

Test D

1.

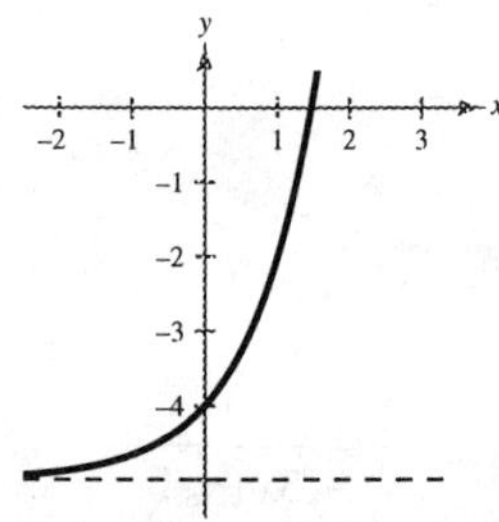

2. 295; 263

3. \$2762.93; about 14 years

4. $\log_5 25 = 2$

5.

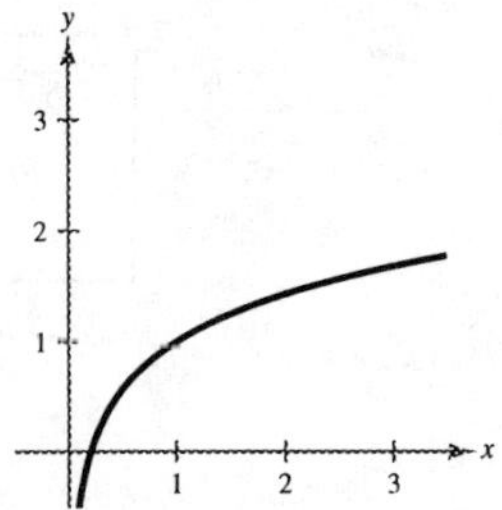

6. $\ln 5 + \ln x - \frac{1}{3}\ln(x^2 + 1)$

7. $\log_b\left(\frac{\sqrt{3x}}{y}\right)$

8. -0.3801

9. 2

10. -0.847

11. $k = \frac{1}{3}\ln\frac{5}{3}$

12. 847

Test E

1.

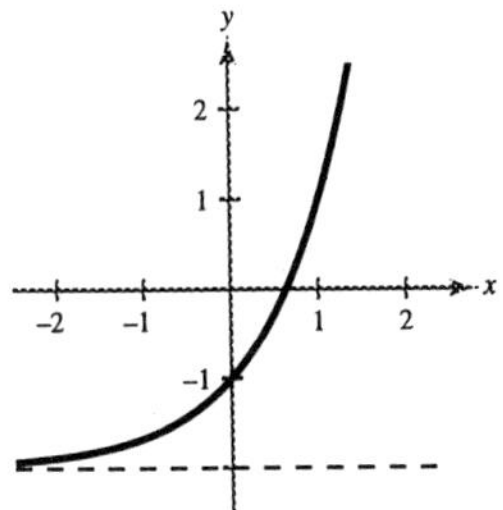

2. 40; 140

3. \$3315.51; about 14 years

4. $\log_3 243 = 5$

5.

6. $\frac{1}{5}[3 \log(x + 1) + 2 \log(x - 1) - \log 7]$

7. $\log_b\left(\frac{\sqrt{6y}}{x}\right)$

8. 1.09165

9. $-1, 5$

10. 1.807

11. $k = \frac{1}{2} \ln \frac{5}{2}$

12. 888

Answers to CHAPTER 4 Tests

Test A

1. c	**2.** c	**3.** d	**4.** e
5. c	**6.** c	**7.** d	**8.** b
9. a	**10.** d	**11.** c	**12.** c
13. b	**14.** b	**15.** b	

Test B

1. a	**2.** b	**3.** b	**4.** a
5. b	**6.** d	**7.** d	**8.** a
9. d	**10.** c	**11.** a	**12.** d
13. a	**14.** c	**15.** c	

Test C

1. d	**2.** b	**3.** c	**4.** d
5. a	**6.** a	**7.** d	**8.** d
9. c	**10.** b	**11.** c	**12.** b
13. e	**14.** d	**15.** a	

Test D

1. $\frac{3\pi}{4}$

2. 24.1 inches

3. $\left(-\frac{1}{2}, -\frac{\sqrt{3}}{2}\right)$

4. $\frac{\sqrt{3}}{2}$

5. $\frac{2\sqrt{21}}{21}$

6. 6.5756

7. $-\frac{\sqrt{2}}{2}$

8. 0.6708, 5.6123

9. Period: $\frac{2\pi}{3}$, Amplitude: 7

10.

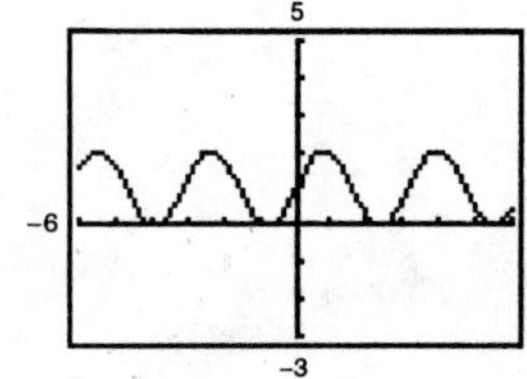

11. $\frac{\pi}{7}$

12. 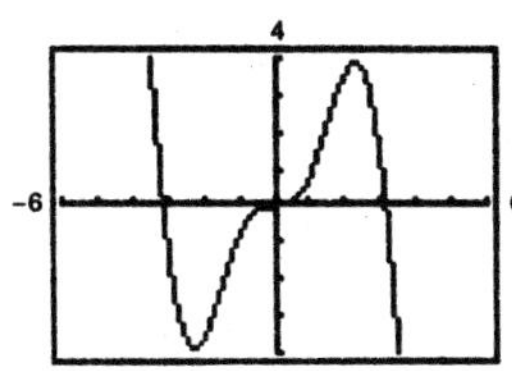

13. $-\frac{\pi}{4}$

14. $\theta = \arccos \frac{x}{4}$

15. 1492 miles

Test E

1. 225°

2. $6\pi \approx 18.85$ inches

3. $\left(\frac{\sqrt{2}}{2}, \frac{\sqrt{2}}{2}\right)$

4. $-\frac{1}{2}$

5. $\frac{\sqrt{33}}{4}$

6. $\frac{15\sqrt{3}}{2}$

7. $-\frac{\sqrt{113}}{7}$

8. 25°

9. Period: 4π, Amplitude: 5

10. 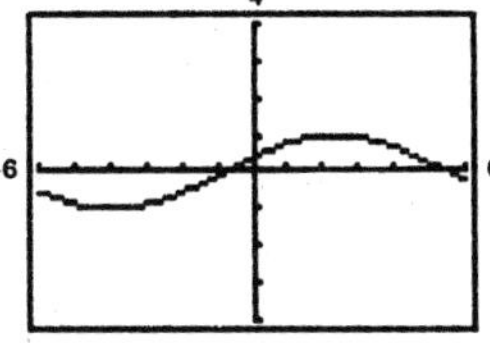

11. $\frac{\pi}{3}$

12. 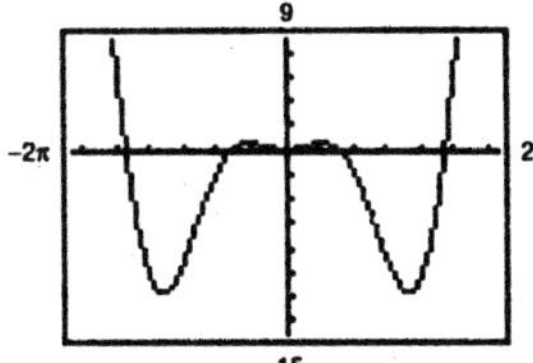

13. $-\frac{\pi}{3}$

14. $\theta = \arcsin\left(\frac{x+1}{2}\right)$

15. 1063 miles

Answers to CHAPTER 5 Tests

Test A

1. d 2. d 3. d 4. c
5. a 6. b 7. a 8. a
9. b 10. b

Test B

1. c 2. c 3. a 4. d
5. d 6. b 7. c 8. d
9. d 10. d

Test C

1. b 2. b 3. c 4. b
5. b 6. c 7. d 8. d
9. b 10. b

Test D

1. $-\frac{\sqrt{33}}{4}$

2. $\ln|\tan\theta|$

3. $$\frac{1+\sin x}{\cos x \sin x} = \frac{1}{\cos x \sin x} + \frac{\sin x}{\cos x \sin x}$$
$$= \sec x \csc x + \sec x$$
$$= \sec x(\csc x + 1)$$

4. $$\frac{\tan^2 x + 1}{\tan^3 x} = 1 + \frac{1}{\tan^2 x}$$
$$= 1 + \cot^2 x$$
$$= \csc^2 x$$

5. $\frac{\pi}{12}, \frac{5\pi}{12}, \frac{7\pi}{12}, \frac{11\pi}{12}, \frac{13\pi}{12}, \frac{17\pi}{12}, \frac{19\pi}{12}, \frac{23\pi}{12}$

6. $0, \frac{\pi}{2}, \pi$

7. $-\sqrt{3}$

8. $-\cos^2 x$

9. $f(x) = 3(2\cos^2 x - 1)$
$= 3\cos 2x$

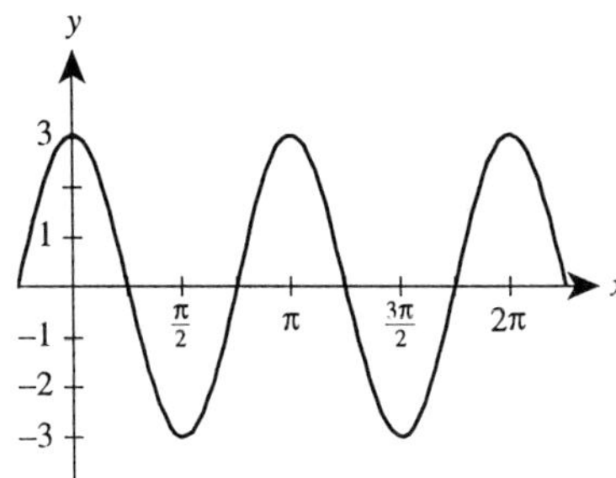

10. $\dfrac{\sqrt{14}}{7}$

Test E

1. $-\dfrac{\sqrt{7}}{4}$

2. $\ln|\csc\theta|$ or $-\ln|\sin\theta|$

3.
$$\begin{aligned}\sin x\left(\frac{\sin x}{1-\cos x}+\frac{1-\cos x}{\sin x}\right) &= \frac{\sin^2 x}{1-\cos x}+1-\cos x\\ &= \frac{1-\cos^2 x}{1-\cos x}+1-\cos x\\ &= \frac{(1+\cos x)(1-\cos x)}{1-\cos x}+1-\cos x\\ &= (1+\cos x)+1-\cos x\\ &= 2\end{aligned}$$

4.
$$\begin{aligned}\sec x\csc^2 x-\csc^2 x &= \csc^2 x(\sec x-1)\\ &= \frac{1}{\sin^2 x}\left(\frac{1}{\cos x}-1\right)\\ &= \frac{1}{1-\cos^2 x}\left(\frac{1-\cos x}{\cos x}\right)\\ &= \frac{1}{(1+\cos x)\cos x}\\ &= \frac{\sec x}{1+\cos x}\end{aligned}$$

5. $0, \dfrac{\pi}{6}, \dfrac{5\pi}{6}, \pi$

6. $\dfrac{\pi}{12}, \dfrac{5\pi}{12}, \dfrac{13\pi}{12}, \dfrac{17\pi}{12}$

7. $\tan 12x$

8. $\sin^2 x$

9. $g(x) = \left(1-\sqrt{2}\sin x\right)\left(1+\sqrt{2}\sin x\right)$
$= 1 - 2\sin^2 x$
$= \cos^2 x$

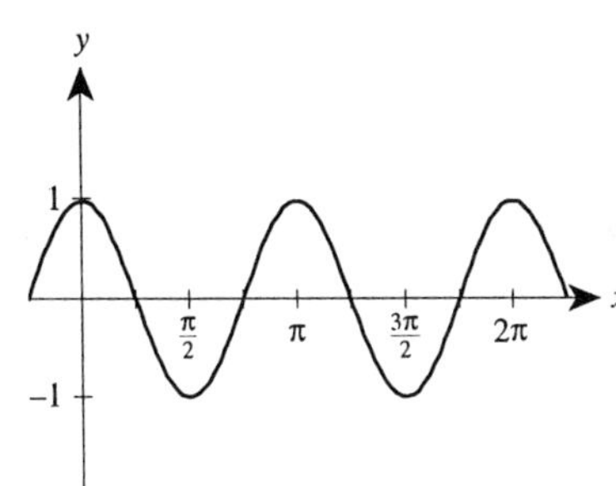

10. $-\dfrac{\sqrt{30}}{6}$

Answers to CHAPTER 6 Tests

Test A

1. c **2.** c **3.** a **4.** c

5. a **6.** d **7.** d **8.** d

9. c **10.** d

Test B

1. a **2.** b **3.** a **4.** d

5. c **6.** b **7.** c **8.** b

9. b **10.** c

Test C

1. c **2.** d **3.** a **4.** b

5. a **6.** a **7.** d **8.** a

9. a **10.** b

Test D

1. 85.6

2. 1.68 miles from Warden Ryan and 1.78 miles from Warden Wain

3. $A = 27.5°, B = 5.1°, C = 147.4°$

4. N 53.8° W

5. $\|\mathbf{v}\| = 5, \theta = 126.9°$

6. $93.8\mathbf{i} - 215.9\mathbf{j}$

7. -17

8. 169.5° or 2.96 radians

9. $\sqrt{7}(\cos 139.1° + i \sin 139.1°)$

10. $2 - 2\sqrt{3}i, -4, 2 + 2\sqrt{3}i$

Test E

1. 687.9

2. 1288.6 feet

3. 16.54°

4. 16.4°

5. $\langle -21.84, -15.87 \rangle$

6. $-73.1\mathbf{i} + 60.9\mathbf{j}$

7. -3

8. 31.3° or 0.55 radian

9. $36.235(\cos 117.98° + i \sin 117.98°)$

10. $-\sqrt{2} + \sqrt{2}i, \sqrt{2} - \sqrt{2}i$

Answers to CHAPTER 7 Tests

Test A

1. c **2.** e **3.** b **4.** a

5. b **6.** b **7.** c **8.** c

9. b **10.** c

Test B

1. e **2.** e **3.** d **4.** b

5. a **6.** a **7.** c **8.** a

9. d **10.** a

Test C

1. d **2.** d **3.** a **4.** a

5. a **6.** a **7.** b **8.** b

9. a **10.** d

Test D

1. $(1, 1); \left(5, \frac{1}{5}\right)$

2.

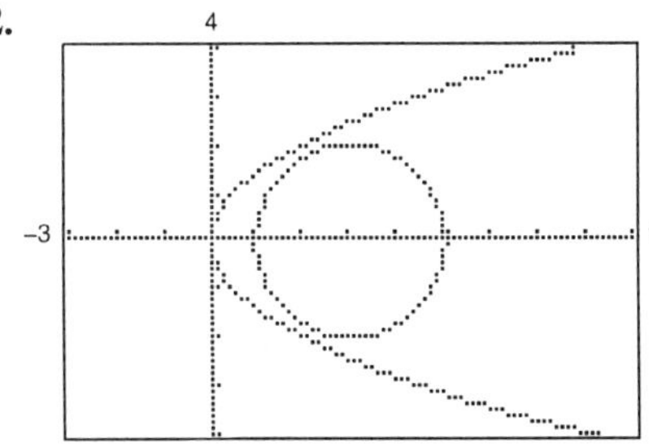

; No points of intersection

3. 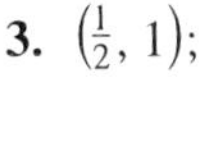 $\left(\frac{1}{2}, 1\right)$;

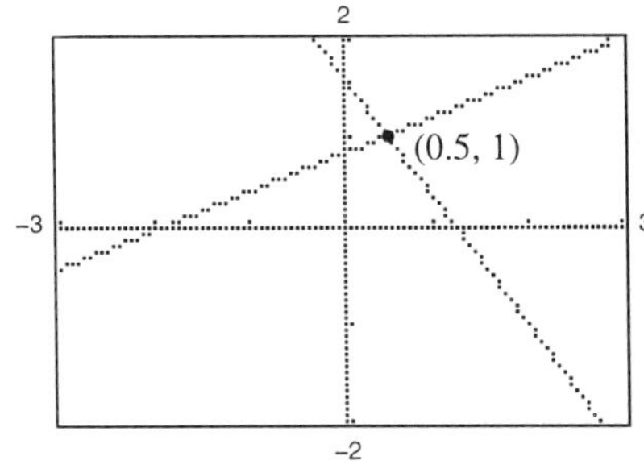

4. 6

5. $(-1, 3, 1)$

6. $y = -2x^2 + 7x - 5$;

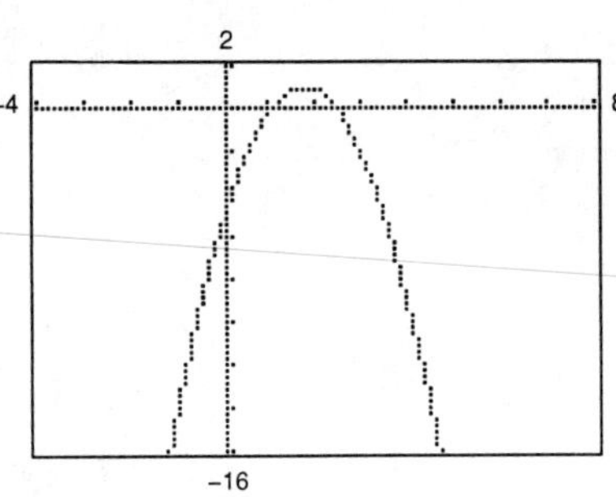

7.

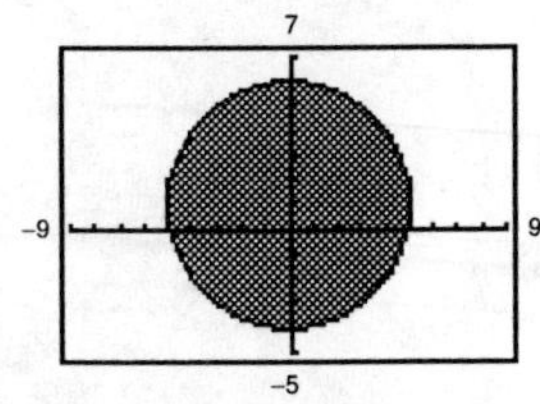

8.

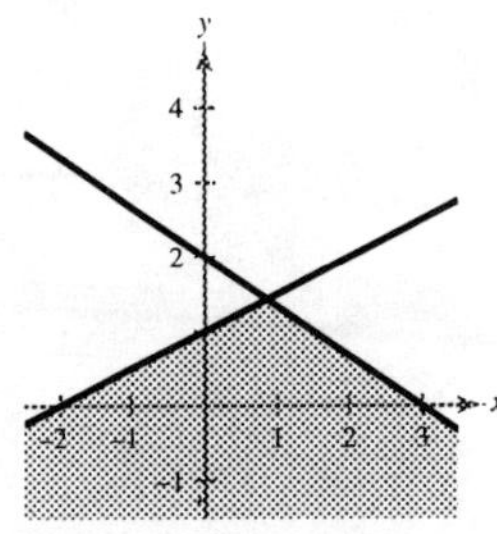

9. 17

10. 80 of the \$350 model; 70 of the \$400 model

Test E

1. $(0, 2), \left(\frac{1}{2}, \frac{5}{2}\right)$

2.

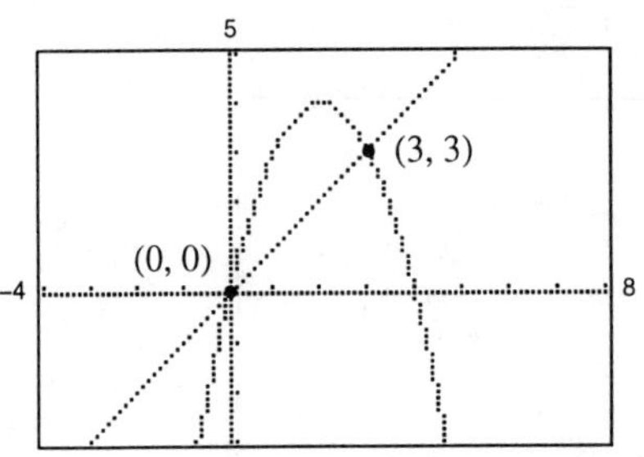

; (0, 0), (3, 3)

3. $\left(\frac{1}{2}, -5\right)$;

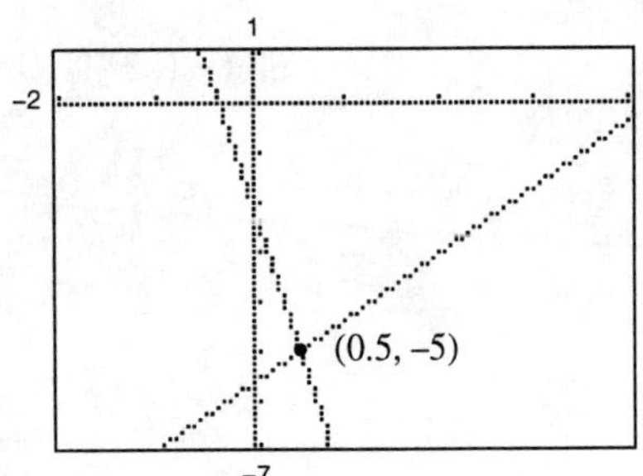

4. $L = 33$ feet, $W = 12.5$ feet

5. $x = 0, y = -1, z = 3, w = -4$

6. $y = 4x^2 - 5x + 2$;

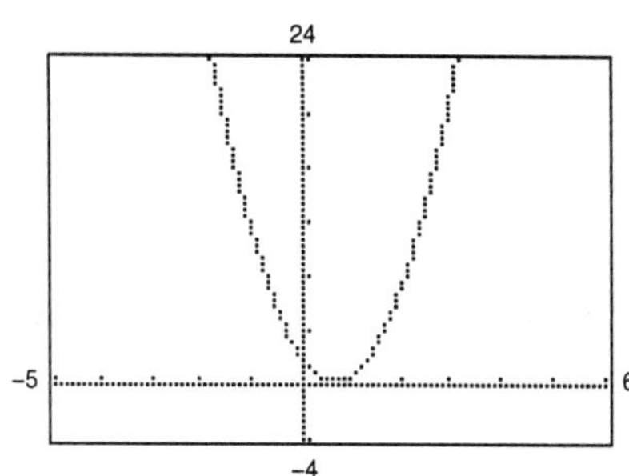

7.

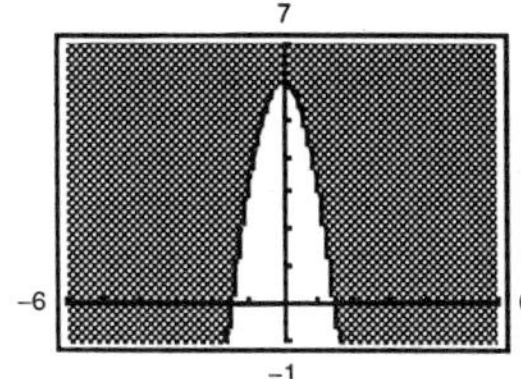

8.

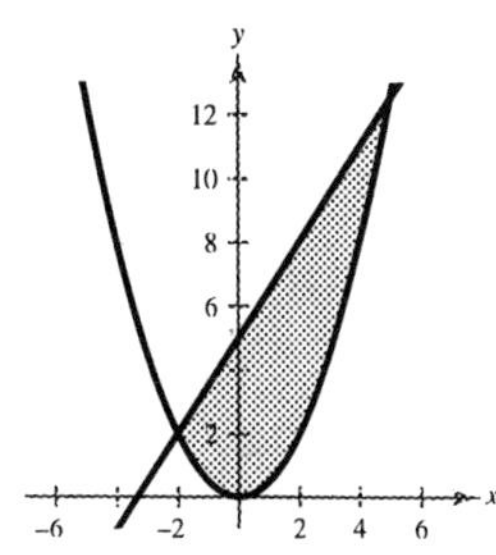

9. 17

10. 110 of the $350 model; 35 of the $500 model

Answers to CHAPTER 8 Tests

Test A

1. b	**2.** a	**3.** a	**4.** b
5. a	**6.** c	**7.** b	**8.** d
9. b	**10.** b		

Test B

1. c	**2.** b	**3.** c	**4.** d
5. b	**6.** d	**7.** a	**8.** c
9. b	**10.** b		

Test C

1. a	**2.** a	**3.** b	**4.** a
5. d	**6.** e	**7.** a	**8.** d
9. d	**10.** c		

Test D

1. $\begin{bmatrix} 1 & 0 & 0 & \frac{5}{16} \\ 0 & 1 & 0 & \frac{3}{16} \\ 0 & 0 & 1 & -\frac{37}{16} \end{bmatrix}$

2. $y = 2x^2 + 5x - 3$

3. $\begin{bmatrix} -6 & 1 \\ 1 & 2 \end{bmatrix}$

4. $\begin{bmatrix} 16 & 8 & 14 & 2 \\ 12 & 10 & 8 & 4 \\ 15 & 5 & 15 & 0 \end{bmatrix}$

5. $\begin{bmatrix} \frac{1}{2} & -\frac{1}{2} & -\frac{1}{2} \\ \frac{1}{10} & \frac{3}{10} & \frac{1}{10} \\ -\frac{1}{5} & \frac{2}{5} & -\frac{1}{5} \end{bmatrix}$

6. $\left(\frac{37}{11}, -\frac{73}{11}, \frac{46}{11}\right)$

7. $-x$

8. 270

9. $\left(1, 2, -\frac{1}{2}\right)$

10. $(2, 1, -1)$

Test E

1. $\begin{bmatrix} 1 & 0 & 0 & -7 \\ 0 & 1 & 0 & 8 \\ 0 & 0 & 1 & \frac{1}{2} \end{bmatrix}$

2. $y = x^2 - x + 4$

3. $\begin{bmatrix} 39 & 10 & 27 \\ 18 & 9 & 34 \end{bmatrix}$

4. $\begin{bmatrix} 0 & 2 & 1 \\ 4 & 4 & 11 \\ -3 & 1 & -7 \end{bmatrix}$

5. $\begin{bmatrix} -\frac{1}{14} & \frac{11}{14} & \frac{1}{2} \\ \frac{2}{7} & -\frac{1}{7} & 0 \\ \frac{5}{14} & \frac{1}{14} & \frac{1}{2} \end{bmatrix}$

6. $\left(\frac{1}{3}, \frac{2}{3}, -1\right)$

7. $-e^{3x}$

8. 672

9. $\left(\frac{4}{5}, -\frac{2}{5}, \frac{1}{2}\right)$

10. $(1, 1, 0)$

Answers to CHAPTER 9 Tests

Test A

1. b 2. b 3. c 4. a
5. d 6. d 7. b 8. c
9. c 10. a 11. b 12. c
13. b 14. c 15. d

Test B

1. d 2. a 3. a 4. c
5. d 6. c 7. b 8. a
9. b 10. b 11. a 12. b
13. d 14. b 15. c

Test C

1. b 2. b 3. b 4. d
5. d 6. a 7. a 8. d
9. d 10. d 11. a 12. a
13. c 14. b 15. b

Test D

1. $-\frac{1}{2}, 0, \frac{1}{10}, \frac{2}{17}, \frac{3}{26}$ 2. 20 3. 29 4. 209

5. 274.7411 6. 30 7. 8610

8. S_1: $2^1 - 1 = 2 - 1 = 1$

S_k: $1 + 2 + 2^2 + 2^3 + \ldots + 2^{k-1} = 2^k - 1$

S_{k+1}: $1 + 2 + 2^2 + 2^3 + \ldots + 2^k = 2^{k+1} - 1$

Assuming S_k, we have:

$$(1 + 2 + 2^2 + 2^3 + \ldots + 2^{k-1}) + 2^{(k+1)-1} = (1 + 2 + \ldots + 2^{k-1}) + 2^k$$
$$= (2^k - 1) + 2^k$$
$$= 2^{k+1} - 1$$

So, the formula is valid for all $n \geq 1$.

9. $x\sqrt{x} + 6x + 12\sqrt{x} + 8$ **10.** $-225{,}792$ **11.** 1,235,520

12. 34,650 **13.** 1260 **14.** $\frac{7}{10}$ **15.** $\frac{20}{21}$

Test E

1. $\frac{1}{2}, \frac{1}{6}, \frac{1}{12}, \frac{1}{20}, \frac{1}{30}$ **2.** 77 **3.** $\frac{14}{3}$ **4.** $a_n = -\frac{3}{2}n + 12$

5. $-8019\sqrt{3}$ **6.** $465\sqrt{2}$ **7.** 4940

8. For $n = 1$, $1 < 3$.

For $n = k$, assume $k < 3^k$.

For $n = k + 1$, show $k + 1 < 3^{k+1}$.

$$k < 3^k$$

$$k + 1 < 3^k + 1 < 3^k + 3^k$$

$$k + 1 < 2(3^k) < 3(3^k)$$

$$k + 1 < 3^{k+1}$$

So, $n < 3^n$ *for* $n \geq 1$.

9. 1716 **10.** $16y^2 + 96y\sqrt{y} + 196y + 216\sqrt{y} + 81$ **11.** 560

12. 4,989,600 **13.** 720 **14.** $\frac{1}{16}$ **15.** $\frac{53}{109}$

Answers to CHAPTER 10 Tests

Test A

1. c
2. e
3. c
4. c
5. c
6. b
7. b
8. c
9. d
10. a
11. b
12. b
13. b
14. d
15. b

Test B

1. a
2. c
3. a
4. d
5. c
6. c
7. a
8. d
9. d
10. b
11. c
12. b
13. d
14. a
15. a

Test C

1. b
2. a
3. a
4. b
5. a
6. a
7. b
8. b
9. d
10. c
11. a, b, c
12. a
13. c
14. d
15. a

Test D

1. $123.7°$
2. Vertex: $(-2, 1)$
Focus: $(-2, 5)$
Directrix: $y = -3$
3. $(2, -6)$
4. $25x^2 + 16y^2 - 160y = 0$
5. $(0, 3), (0, -3)$
6. hyperbola
7. $31.7°$
8. $2(x')^2 - 8(x') + 8(y') + 8 = 0$
9. $x^2 + y^2 - 2x - 4y + 4 = 0$
10. $x = t + 2$
$y = t^2 + 1$
11. $\left(\frac{3}{2}, \frac{-3\sqrt{3}}{2}\right)$
12. $x^2 + y^2 - 2x = 0$
13. 2
14. 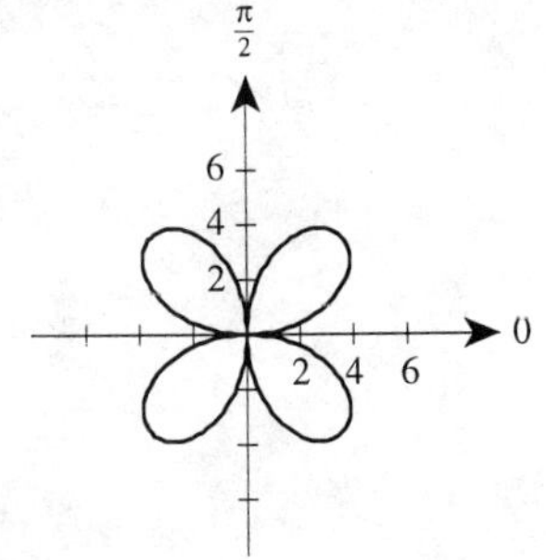

15. ellipse

Test E

1. 74.1°

2. Vertex: (0, 10)
Focus: (−1, 10)
Directrix: $x = 1$

3. $\left(\frac{1}{2}, \frac{3}{4}\right)$

4. $\frac{(x + 3)^2}{1} + \frac{(y - 1)^2}{6} = 1$

5. $y = \pm\frac{1}{2}x$

6. ellipse

7. 19.3°

8. $50(x')^2 + 25(y')^2 + 50(x') - 25(y') + 25 = 0$

9. $x^2 + y^2 - 6x + 2y + 9 = 0$

10. $x = 3 + 2 \cos t$
$y = 1 + 2 \sin t$

11. $\left(-4\sqrt{3}, -4\right)$

12. $r = 4 \cos \theta - 6 \sin \theta$

13. 45

14.

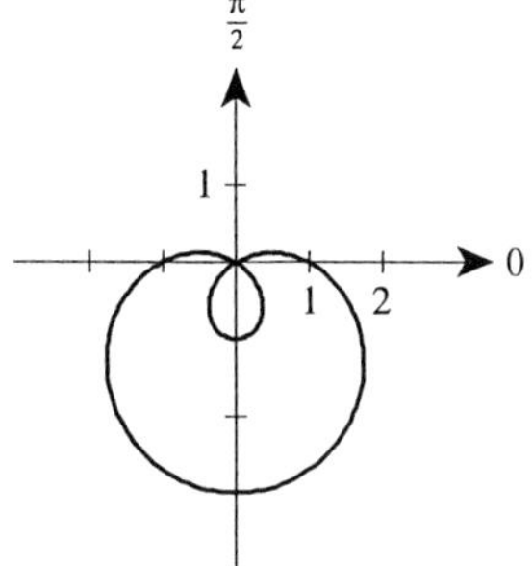

15. parabola

Precalculus FINAL EXAM Answers

Multiple Choice Test

1. d	**2.** b	**3.** d	**4.** c
5. a	**6.** c	**7.** a	**8.** b
9. c	**10.** a	**11.** c	**12.** b
13. d	**14.** d	**15.** a	**16.** c
17. a	**18.** d	**19.** a	**20.** d
21. e	**22.** b	**23.** d	**24.** c
25. c	**26.** c	**27.** b	**28.** b
29. b	**30.** c	**31.** a	**32.** b
33. a	**34.** a	**35.** a	**36.** b
37. c	**38.** d	**39.** d	**40.** d

Open Ended Test

1. $-\dfrac{32x^4}{25}$

2. $(3 + 14y)xy\sqrt[3]{4x^2}$

3. $2x(2x + 5)(x - 1)$

4. $x = \frac{1}{4}$

5. $-1 \pm \sqrt{7}$

6.

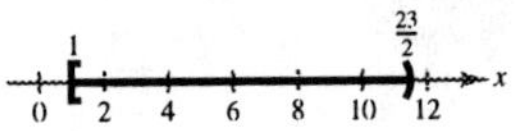

7. $3x + 2y + 13 = 0$

8. $3x - 5$

9. Domain: $(-\infty, \infty)$, Range: $[0, \infty)$

10. 1

11. $\pm 2, \pm\frac{1}{3}$

12.

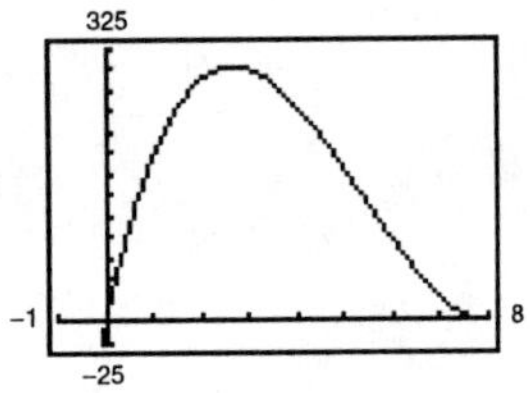

$x \approx 2.67$ inches

13. $x = 2, x = 4$

14.

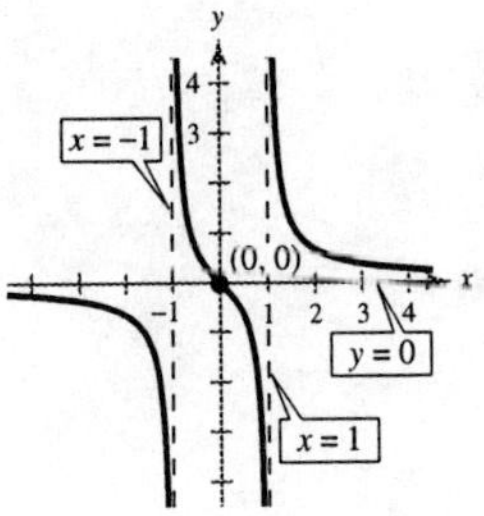

15. 194.3059

16. $\ln 5 + \ln x - \frac{1}{3}\ln(x^2 + 1)$

17. 2

18. 35 years

19. $\dfrac{2\sqrt{21}}{21}$

20. $-\dfrac{\sqrt{113}}{7}$

21

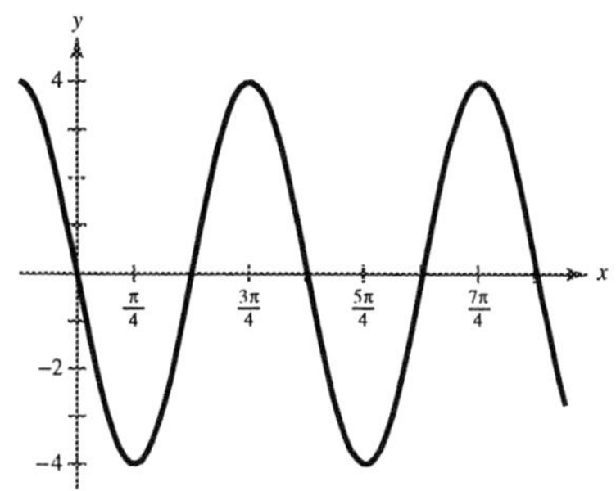

22. $\dfrac{\pi}{7}$

23. $\theta = \arctan\left(\dfrac{4}{x+2}\right)$

24. 52.5 feet

25. $\sin x\left(\dfrac{\sin x}{1-\cos x} + \dfrac{1-\cos x}{\sin x}\right) = \dfrac{\sin^2 x}{1-\cos x} + 1 - \cos x$

$$= \frac{1-\cos^2 x}{1-\cos x} + 1 - \cos x$$

$$= \frac{(1+\cos x)(1-\cos x)}{1-\cos x} + 1 - \cos x$$

$$= (1+\cos x) + 1 - \cos x = 2$$

26. $\dfrac{\pi}{12}, \dfrac{5\pi}{12}, \dfrac{13\pi}{12}, \dfrac{17\pi}{12}$

27. $-\cos^2 x$

28. $0, \dfrac{\pi}{3}, \dfrac{\pi}{2}, \dfrac{2\pi}{3}, \pi, \dfrac{4\pi}{3}, \dfrac{3\pi}{2}, \dfrac{5\pi}{3}$;

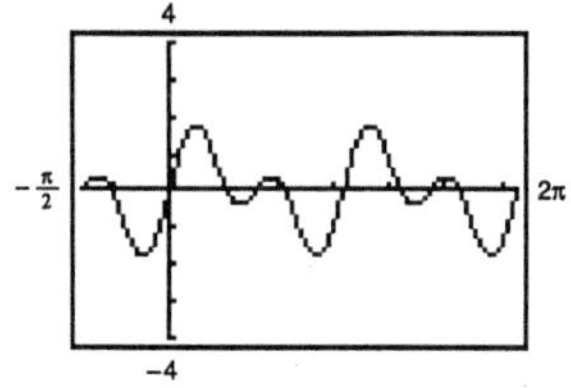

29. 85.6

30. 18.3 miles

31. $93.8\mathbf{i} - 215.9\mathbf{j}$

32.

5
(3, 3)
(0, 0)
−4
8
−3

33. $\begin{bmatrix} -6 & 1 \\ 1 & 2 \end{bmatrix}$

34. $\left(1, 2, -\frac{1}{2}\right)$

35. $\displaystyle\sum_{n=1}^{5} \frac{n}{(n+1)!}$

36. 1260 ways

37. $\frac{7}{10}$

38. $\dfrac{(x+3)^2}{1} + \dfrac{(y-1)^2}{6} = 1$

39. $x^2 + y^2 - 6x + 2y + 9 = 0$

40.

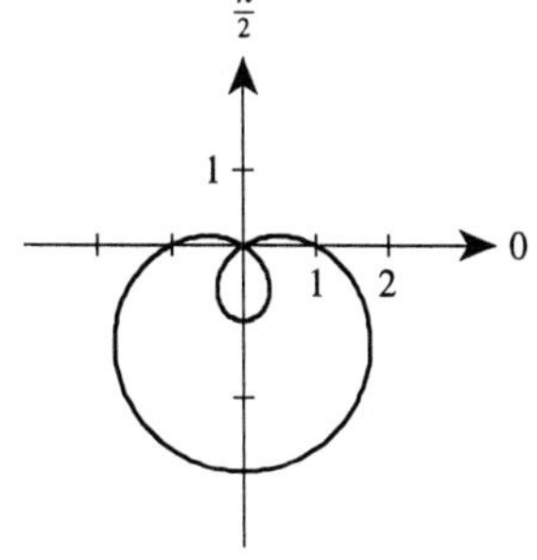